PENGUIN BOOKS

MEDIA LAW

Geoffrey Robertson Q.C. has argued many landmark media law cases in British and Commonwealth courts and in the European Court of Human Rights. He is Head of Doughty Street Chambers, a Recorder, Master of the Middle Temple and Visiting Professor at Birkbeck College, University of London. He has acted for many years as counsel to the *Wall Street Journal*, CNN, the *Far Eastern Economic Review* and other international publishers, and has represented many British newspapers and television companies. His books include *Freedom, The Individual and The Law*; *People Against The Press*; *Crimes Against Humanity: The Struggle for Global Justice*; *Geoffrey Robertson's Hypotheticals* and *Does Dracula Have AIDS*; a memoir, *The Justice Game*, was published in 1998. Mr Robertson has made many television and radio programmes, in Britain and Australia; his play *The Trials of Oz* received a BAFTA "Best Single Drama" nomination, and he was presented with the 1993 Freedom of Information Award. He is married to the author Kathy Lette: they live in London with their two young children.

Andrew Nicol Q.C. practises at Doughty Street Chambers. He has appeared in media cases in all levels of courts in the United Kingdom as well as advising clients in Hong Kong, Singapore, the United States and other jurisdictions. The Council of Europe has consulted him as an expert in media law and he has acted in Human Rights cases in Strasbourg. He is a Recorder of the Crown Court. He has worked and studied in the United States and Australia and taught law for 10 years at the London School of Economics. He has co-authored *Media Law and Human Rights* and *Subjects Citizens Aliens and Others* as well as an annual survey for the *Yearbook of Copyright and Media Law*. For three years he was the chair of the Immigration Law Practitioners' Association. He lives in London with his partner, Camilla Palmer, and their two sons.

Media Law

GEOFFREY ROBERTSON, Q.C.

AND

ANDREW NICOL, Q.C.

Fourth Edition

PENGUIN BOOKS

PENGUIN BOOKS

Published by the Penguin Group
Penguin Books Ltd, 80 Strand, London, WC2R 0RL, England
Penguin Putnam Inc., 375 Hudson Street, New York, New York 10014, USA
Penguin Books Australia Ltd, 250 Camberwell Road, Camberwell, Victoria 3124, Australia
Penguin Books Canada Ltd, 10 Alcorn Avenue, Toronto, Ontario, Canada M4V 3B2
Penguin Books India (P) Ltd, 11 Community Centre, Panchsheel Park, New Delhi – 110 017, India
Penguin Books (NZ) Ltd, Cnr Rosedale and Airborne Roads, Albany, Auckland, New Zealand
Penguin Books (South Africa) (Pty) Ltd, 24 Sturdee Avenue, Rosebank 2196, South Africa

Penguin Books Ltd, Registered Offices: 80 Strand, London, WC2R 0RL, England

www.penguin.com

First published by Longman's Group UK Ltd 1984
Second edition 1990
Third edition published by Penguin Books 1992
Fourth edition published by Sweet & Maxwell 2002
Published with additional changes by Penguin Books 2002
1

Printed in England by Clays Ltd, St Ives plc

CONTENTS

INTRODUCTION

The one and only proposition which is both absolute and undeniable in media law is that thought is free, and hence communicating with oneself via messages and images in the brain-pan cannot, however subversive or obscene, be interdicted. But communicate that message to anyone else, whether in a bottle cast onto the waves or in an e-mail silently sliding from a computer on the other side of the world, and the thought, thus emitted, becomes subject to interception by a network of laws designed to jam or distort it in the interests of States or corporations or other persons or entities whom the thought disquietens. This book examines the interference network, as it is liable to affect communications from and to and within the United Kingdom. The standpoint adopted, as in earlier editions, is not so much that of the message (which may be false, or horrible, or both) but that of the messenger, the human being with an absolute right to think and hence (we infer) a presumptive right to put the information or opinion contained in that message into the public domain.

Talk about "rights" is optimistic unless there can be identified a principle which has legal power, in the sense that courts and other official decision-makers recognise an obligation to uphold it. The Human Rights Act 1998, which came into force on October 2, 2000, provides what previous governments, and generations of judges, have never believed politic to entrench either in statute or common law, namely a guarantee of freedom of expression, a promise that "speech" will have a presumption made in its favour by any court invited to suppress it. This covenant—which enters British law by way of the incorporation of Article 10 of the European Convention on Human Rights—reflects the core belief of the eighteenth century republican revolutions in France and America, adopted as an article of faith in modern Human Rights instruments, that freedom of speech is a good in itself, an essential pillar of democratic order. This is the free speech principle, which assumes that liberty is best secured by a system that protects utterances irrespective of their merit, because in a free market of ideas and opinions the good will triumph over the bad. This approach has not hitherto appealed to British legislators, or to judges who act as custodians of the "common" (i.e. judge-made) law. They have never understood why a legal system should offer any protection to expression which is rude or defamatory or subversive of established authority, and they have insisted that publishers of news and views, like makers of cars and manufacturers of drugs, should be liable for any distress they might cause. In cases of contempt, blasphemy, libel, sedition, obscenity and official secrecy, they have designed the criminal law so that it bears more harshly on editors and journalists than on burglars and rapists: these media offences do not require proof of a guilty mind, or any "victim" damaged by the publication. In civil cases, judges have routinely suppressed the publication of newsworthy information on the ground that it is property which belongs in confidence to governments and corporations, and have constructed a vast libel industry on the illogical presumption that defamatory accusations are bound to be false (hence the publisher has the burden of proving them true). In Britain, it may be said that speech is free, but often very expensive.

The advent of a freedom of expression guarantee in the Human Rights Act has opened a new chapter in media law. It provides the opportunity to educate judges and regulators in the history and philosophy of freedom of speech, so they might understand how, in a democracy, infringements can only be justified in cases of overriding necessity to prevent demonstrable harm to other citizens. What the free speech guarantee in the Human Rights Act should do is to establish this as the new test for censorship, replacing the "balancing act" under which the "interest" of the media (often and cynically defined as making a profit) is weighed and often found wanting when compared with a State or corporate interest in suppressing confidential or "official" information. (This will take some time—British judges are wedded to a "balancing act" which appears to have Libran objectivity but which permits their own prejudices to tip the scales.) It is instructive to listen to the most effective legal argument ever presented on behalf of the media: Professor Hubert Wechsler's tape-recorded plea in *New York Times v. Sullivan*, which persuaded the Supreme Court that British libel law was incompatible with the free speech guarantee in the first amendment to the U.S. Constitution. He spoke of colonial history, of George III's use of criminal libel and sedition laws, of Madison and his address to the Virginia Congress—in short, of the free market-place of ideas that was an object of his country's struggle for independence and democracy. It is a measure of the conservatism of Britain's senior judges that they refuse to allow legal arguments even to be tape-recorded, but this advance and many others indicated in our text will only come about if media advocates are able to pepper their arguments with quotes from Voltaire and John Wilkes and Tom Paine and H.G. Wells, and with the spirit of those British editors and authors who have suffered imprisonment and even death in the struggle to establish the principle for which Article 10 stands. It is for this reason that the first chapter of *Media Law* offers a brief account of the history and philosophy behind the free speech guarantee, because this dimension should inform and imbue argument and decision-making whenever Article 10 is invoked—as it must be thanks to the Human Rights Act—in courts and tribunals and government departments and legislatures and local councils, whenever a decision threatens to impose a restraint on the media.

That media law should have a bedrock in Article 10, a common standard by which all restraints on publication may be judged, is a consummation devoutly wished in earlier editions of this work. *Media Law* first appeared in 1984, in the wake of attacks on investigative journalism both in the dying days of old Labour and the dawn of the new Thatcherism. The Labour Government had reneged on its promise of a Freedom of Information Act ("only 2 of your constituents would be interested" sneered its Home Secretary) and authorised outrageous prosecutions—against pacifists for inciting disaffection, against journalists on *Time Out* for revealing the existence of GCHQ, and against book publishers for offering such banal entertainments as *The Joys of Sex* and *Inside Linda Lovelace*. The Conservatives went easy on sex, but declared war on "video nasties" and played nanny to the nation by establishing a host of statutory regulators for television and video cassettes. An idealistic young clerk, Sarah Tisdall, was jailed for telling *The Guardian* that cruise missiles were coming to Greenham Common, and an entire generation of British judges proceeded to make fools of themselves by stopping the citizens of Britain from reading a book—*Spycatcher*—published in every other country of the world. We thought of calling the first edition *The Journalist's Toothbrush*, since journalists summoned to attend courts were generally advised to bring a toothbrush in the possible event of an order to spend a night in the cells. Defending journalists in this era was always difficult, because there were so few precedents which acknowledged the universality of the free speech principle. It was not part of the law of England.

Despite the exponential growth of case law and statutes affecting the media in the decade before the first edition, there was no academic or professional acknowledgment that "media law" might exist as a subject worthy of separate and coherent study. Defamation was part of the law of torts, breach of confidence was anchored in equity, official secrecy and contempt derived from specific statutes whilst blasphemy and sedition were crimes at common law. There were no textbooks on media law: a few elementary primers had appeared for trainee journalists, and for lawyers there was one weighty tome on libel and another on copyright, but no serious treatment of the subject in its entirety. The wood—or at least the overgrown jungle—of laws affecting the media could not be seen for the different trees of tort and property and crime. The object of earlier editions was to bring these disparate strands together, and tentatively to suggest that they might be approached by way of the organising principle in Article 10. This argument became more forceful as the European Convention on Human Rights became better known and understood. Although the first example of the potential impact of Article 10 came in 1979, when a suppression of *The Sunday Times* investigation of thalidomide was condemned by the European Court, it was perhaps not fully appreciated until the case of Bill Goodwin in 1995. He was a young journalist who had been ordered to disclose the name of the source of some confidential information: every judge at every level in Britain—the High Court, the Court of Appeal and the House of Lords—had held him guilty of contempt for standing on professional principle and declining to obey their order. The European Court ruled that the Article 10 guarantee required protection of journalistic sources (otherwise information available to the press would dry up) and the disclosure orders breached the journalist's Article 10 rights. That British judges should be so unanimously and fundamentally out of step with human rights principles—and have to stand corrected by jurists from Slovenia and Slovakia—came as a shock.

Such shocks, however often administered, could not change matters, so long as the Convention was not part of British law. "Freedom of the Press" remained a potent phrase, but the fact that it was protected by unwritten convention rather than by a constitution meant that there was no external brake to stop Parliament and the courts moving to restrict it in particular ways, as the mood and temper of the times seemed to require. Britain remained a country where "everything is permitted which is not specifically prohibited" but the specific prohibitions became much more numerous, because they never had to justify themselves against the standards set by Article 10. And secrecy, in Richard Crossman's phrase, remained "the British disease", however much the Official Secrets Act was amended, because of the ingrained reluctance of government, national and local, and the civil service, to share information with the public. Of course, as the 90s progressed, judges (with one ear cocked to Strasbourg) routinely paid lip service to the freedom of expression principle, without always understanding it. For example, the European Court has a rule (or at least a presumption) against "prior restraint"—imposing injunctions on news stories prior to their publication. Yet as late as 1999 one High Court judge injuncted a newspaper from publishing a report about the then Home Secretary's son selling cannabis, and another stopped the presses of *The Sunday Telegraph* when it carried a leaked section of the report of the Stephen Lawrence inquiry. Neither decision could be remotely justified under Article 10 as "necessary in a democratic society". The acid test of whether the Human Rights Act works will be whether it forecloses the possibility of decisions like these, because its presumption in favour of free speech will be incapable of overthrow unless the gag order answers to a "pressing social need".

Journalism is not just a profession. It is the exercise by occupation of the right to free expression available to every citizen. That right, being available to all, cannot in principle be withdrawn from a few by any system of licensing or professional registration, but it can be restricted and confined by rules of law that apply to all who take or are afforded the opportunity to exercise the right by speaking or writing in public. There are, as the length of this book attests, a myriad of rules that impinge upon the right to present facts and opinions and pictures to the public: we have made an attempt to state and to analyse them as a comprehensive and inter-related body of doctrine, underpinned by the free speech principle embodied in Article 10.

Free speech is, in practice, what remains of speech after the law has had its say: in newspapers, it is what is left of the copy by the "night lawyer". At first blush, the array of media laws and regulations appears formidable. There are criminal laws—of contempt, official secrecy, sedition, obscenity and the like—which can be enforced by fines and even by prison sentences. There are civil laws, relating to libel and breaches of copyright and confidence, which can be used to injunct public interest stories and programmes before publication, or to extract heavy damages afterwards. And there are laws that permit regulatory bodies to censor films and television programmes and video cassettes. These laws have emanated from different sources at different times: statutory laws, imposed by Parliament and interpreted by the courts; common law, built up by judges with reference to precedents from centuries of case law; decisions of regulatory bodies based on broad duties to ensure "good taste" and "due impartiality", not to mention informal "arrangements" like the lobby and the D-notice systems, which exert secret pressures and persuasions.

Newspapers and broadcasting organisations employ teams of lawyers to advise on stories that might otherwise court reprisals. Press lawyers are inevitably more repressive than press laws, because they will generally prefer to err on the safe side, where they cannot be proved wrong. The lawyer's advice provides a broad penumbra of restraint, confining the investigative journalist or broadcaster not merely to the letter of the law but to an outer rim bounded by the mere possibility of legal action. Since most laws pertaining to the media are of vague or elastic definition, the working test of "potential actionability" for critical comment is exceptionally wide. Journalists are often placed on the defensive: they are obliged to ask, not "what *should* I write" but "what *can* I write that will get past the lawyers?". The lawyers' caution is understandable if they are instructed by proprietors who want to avoid the high legal costs of defending, even successfully, actions brought by the Government or by wealthy private claimants.

For all these obstacles, however, media law is not as oppressive as it may at first appear. When there is a genuine public interest in publishing, legal snares can usually be side-stepped. We have been anxious, in writing this book, to emphasise ways in which legal problems can be avoided in practice. Many laws that are restrictive in their letter are enforced in a liberal spirit, or simply not enforced at all. Editors and broadcasters will be familiar with the solicitor's "letter before action", threatening proceedings in the event that investigations unflattering to clients are

published. Often such letters are bluff, and it is important to know how and
when that legal bluff can be called. In addition, it must be remembered
that the law can give as well as take away: quite apart from Freedom of
Information legislation, there are many little-known publicity provisions
that can be exploited by inquisitive reporters. Although the law creates
duties, it also provides rights that assist those who know what to look for
and where to find it. In the chapters on reporting significant areas of power
and influence—the courts, Whitehall, local government, Parliament and
business—we have endeavoured to highlight sections of the law that help,
rather than hinder, the investigative journalist. Our hope is that journalists
and broadcasters and their lawyers will regard the book not merely as a
manual for self-defence, but as a guide to a complicated armoury of legal
weapons for battering down doors unnecessarily shut in their faces.

This success will depend not only on the capacity of the judiciary to
absorb the free speech principle enshrined in Article 10. It will depend,
crucially, on the resolve of media executives and their lawyers to make
use of the new dispensation to challenge restrictions on their freedoms.
It is a sad reflection on those who work in the communications industry
that existing powers—of judicial review, for example—have been
invoked so infrequently as a means of challenging secrecy decisions.
Compared with the legal activism of their counterparts in America, who
have been astute to push First Amendment freedoms as far as they will
go, British editors and media executives have signally failed to use the
courts to extend their freedom to communicate—although that freedom is,
conversely, the right of their readers and viewers to receive information.
Most pathetic of all are the publicly funded BBC and the wealthy ITV
companies, which employ dozens of lawyers but which rarely challenge
decisions which keep radio microphones and television cameras out of the
courts (even the appeal courts) and out of tribunals investigating matters of
such acute public interest as the "Arms to Iraq" affair and the Stephen
Lawrence and "Bloody Sunday" inquiries. The absurd result is that "dramatic reconstructions" of these publicly important occasions play in
theatres and on television, inevitably in a partial and unrealistically edited
form, while the British public is denied the best evidence—the real thing—
on which to make up its mind. The Human Rights Act and the new
Freedom of Information law will only work to public advantage if there
is a determination on the part of the media to exploit them to the full.

The law is only one method of control over what is placed in the public
arena. Communicators are restrained by other forces: by shared ethical
assumptions, by non-legal rules that find favour with the Press Complaints
Commission and the Broadcasting Standards Commission, by pressure
from advertisers, by the political predilections of proprietors, and by the
host of subjective considerations that go to make up "editorial discretion". Press monopolies inhibit those with different views from launching out on their own. The law is often invoked by editors, executives, or

lawyers to support decisions to censor that are taken on other grounds, or instinctively: legal advice of this sort is usually convenient rather than correct. The decision to publish will involve a calculation of many risks—it is only when the apparition of a successful legal action tips the balance against publishing a story of genuine public interest that "freedom of expression" has been meaningfully curtailed by law. That happens often enough to be a matter for public concern. Whether it *should* happen as often as it does is open to doubt. If editors and programme makers and journalists were more aware of their legal rights, and more courageous in calling the lawyers' bluff, they might find that the law is not quite the ass it sometimes appears. Those journalists who have been prepared to fight for the principle that stories that advance the public interest should be published have usually been vindicated. At every stage, the media must insist upon their right to investigate and to publish such stories: if they are right in their identification of the public interest, they are unlikely to come to harm in the long run.

There are other forces working to reshape media law in the United Kingdom. The revolution in information technology has produced international newspapers, instantaneous satellite communication and contemporaneous book publishing. Commercial freedom in Europe requires some degree of uniformity, and the European Commission and Council of Ministers and the European Court of Justice are issuing directives and rulings that affect media law in Britain. The human rights dimension of media law, informed by decisions of the European Court of Human Rights in Strasbourg, has become increasingly important, highlighting the various ways in which the existing law fails to comply with the great principle expressed in Article 19 of the Universal Declaration of Human Rights:

> "Everyone has the right to freedom of opinion and expression; this right includes the freedom to hold opinions without interference and to seek, receive and impart information and ideas through any media and regardless of frontiers".

The organisation of media law upon human rights principles will be liberating, coming as it does at a time when technical advances have made censorship—of the internet, for example—increasingly difficult for the nanny state. But it will not prove a one-way street for freedom to publish: freedom of expression is one basic strand of a matrix which protects other basic values, such as privacy and fair trial. It is prudent to remember that the expression of facts and ideas and opinions, unlike the imagining of them in the individual thought process, never can be absolutely free. Words can do damage—by betraying a military position or by prejudicing a trial, or by inciting racial hatred. Even the Americans have come to agree that Congress can, despite the First Amendment, make laws stopping people from shouting "fire" in crowded theatres. It behoves all who wish journalists and broadcasters to enjoy "rights" to acknowledge that others have valid claims to legal protection as well— to lead a private life free from media harassment and embarrassment, to undergo a trial free from sensational prejudice, and to have false accusations corrected swiftly and with the same prominence as they are made. These "rights" have in some cases been too poorly protected, as the blind Goddess of British justice raises her sword against investigative journalism while her other hand fondles the Sunday muckraker. If those who work in the media wish to enjoy the freedom promised by the right to publish facts and opinions that are in the public interest, they may have to forgo some of the comparative freedom they enjoy to publish facts and opinions that are not.

Law does not exist in a social or political vacuum. Where rights to publish, such as are afforded by the open justice principle of the common law or by Article 10 of the European Convention, are presumptive rather than first-amendment absolute, there is always the danger that external pressures will expand or inflate the exceptions, so that freedom of expression will be overridden by the force of public opinion, however ignorant or prejudiced. Thus in July 2001, when Channel 4 broadcast an acute savage *Brass Eye* satire about tabloid treatment of paedophilia, showing how celebrities would lend their names to the most absurd campaigns, various Government ministers (who had not, of course, seen it) led the protest against the programme having been made at all, let alone shown in a late-night time slot. The tabloid press (against whom the satire was directed) naturally supported them and spineless regulators (both the ITC and the Broadcasting Standards Commission) in due course upheld the complaints. Channel 4 had every right to commission and broadcast a programme of this kind, which breached no law or regulation: the prospect that it will have the spirit to exercise that right by producing similar iconoclastic programmes was made less likely. The BBC found it necessary to apologise, under pressure from newspapers and the government, for a *Question Time* programme a few days after September 11 which asked too many hostile questions about American foreign policy and visibly upset one participant, the former American ambassador. "Free speech" (of which *Question Time* should be a prime example) is in such circumstances constrained not by law but by the sensitivity of broadcasting executives to public opinion—something more appropriately described, within the industry, as "fear of the fuss". In such cases, freedom of expression depends on the broadcasters themselves: whether they have the integrity and independence to distinguish between a fuss that is a genuine response to their breach of principle (*e.g.* programme bias or provocative pretence that extreme opinions are widely shared) or manufactured for partisan reasons by government spin-doctors and print media rivals.

The events of September 11 and their aftermath will have some impact on media law. Freedom of expression is a fundamental liberty, and although courts respect the famous (but dissenting) war-time dictum of Lord Atkin ("In the country, amid the clash of arms, the laws are not silent . . . they speak the same language in war as in peace"[1]) there is a more recent and realistic recognition by Lord Pearce that "in practice the flame of individual right and justice must burn more palely when it is ringed by the more dramatic light of bombed buildings".[2] The Government's only concrete proposal for legislation to limit media freedom, a sop to Muslim feelings by a new offence of "inciting religious hatred", was defeated in the House of Lords in December 2001. But it has become more likely that provisions in anti-terrorism legislation which *could* be interpreted as inhibiting reporting will be so interpreted, by the police and possibly by the courts. Broadcasters may need to invoke European Convention cases like *Jersild*[3] to justify decisions to disseminate offensive speech, and reporters in all media will have more difficulty in clinging to their *Goodwin*[4] right to protect sources who may be connected with terrorist organizations. Even without legislation, Lord Pearce's dictum will be in the mind-set of the judges, whose decisions on civil liberties issues became notably more principled after the peace process in Northern Ireland brought a virtual end to mainland bombings. One consequence of terror-consciousness is a judiciary more inclined to exercise its discretion (and much of media law is discretionary, or dependant on subjective "balancing" of the pros and cons of publication) in favour of police and governments and intelligence services, and against the right of free speech.

The media must fight to hold the gains achieved with the help of the HRA, and in some respects seek to extend them. The most alarming feature of September 11 lay in the fact that western intelligence totally failed to anticipate the attack, or to identify (let alone to apprehend) the worldwide terrorist network behind it. It is too readily overlooked that "intelligence" in its widest sense includes the public interest investigative capacity of the news media, which must share in the blame for failing to warn the public through its own investigations. Amongst the reasons for the failure, at least in the United Kingdom and Ireland, must be counted the laws of libel, which threaten heavy damages for any publication which suggests (other than by reference to official statements) that individuals or organisations have terrorist links. The most careful and important media investigations into the shadowy nether-world of terrorist crime will contain honest errors and lack evidence admissible in court, so any publication will be attended by very high risks. Claimants like the son of Colonel Gaddafi and the head of the Ghanaian secret service have been welcome to sue newspapers in the English courts (in the former case,

---

[1] *Liversidge v. Anderson* [1942] A.C. 206 at 244.
[2] *Conway v. Rimmer* [1968] A.C. 910 at 982.
[3] *Jersild v. Denmark* (1995) 19 E.H.R.R. 1.
[4] *Goodwin v. U.K.* (1996) 22 E.H.R.R. 123.

seeking to uncover western intelligence sources for unflattering stories) while courts in the Republic of Ireland have permitted defamation actions by IRA associates against English newspapers and books. The media can only play an original role in exposing terrorist networks and the politicians, bankers and lawyers who harbour them if Parliament is prepared to give them more effective public interest defences to defamation actions.

But Parliament—the MPs who comprise it and the governments that control it—has proved incapable of liberalising defamation law, for the simple reason that politicians are the principal beneficiaries of its unreformed, claimant-centric composition. This is a remarkable feature of defamation throughout the Commonwealth: MPs have a vested interest in a law that chills criticism and provides them with tax-free damages.[5] In the UK, the only "reform" in the past fifty years (the 1996 Defamation Act) made it easier for MPs to sue (the notorious Hamilton amendment) and more difficult for booksellers to plead an innocent dissemination defence. Because law-makers are mired in this conflict of interest, the judiciary bears a special responsibility to "develop" the common law of libel so as to protect speech that serves the public interest, by less inhibited examination of politicians and public figures. Awareness of the responsibility is dawning, under the impact of the First Amendment and its paler cousin, Article 10 of the ECHR: the creation of *Reynolds* privilege is an important first step. But two more changes in the common law are crucial. First, the burden of proof at defamation trials must be placed, as in other civil actions, on the claimant: the presumption of English law that defamatory statements are untrue is both absurd and conducive to miscarriages of justice.[6] Secondly, something must be done about the increasingly anachronistic "multiple publication rule", that every copy of a newspaper, and every hit on an internet site, amounts to a separate cause of action. It rests on jurisprudentially insecure foundations—*Duke of Brunswick*'s case, decided (wrongly) in 1849—but the House of Lords and the Court of Appeal have said it is too entrenched to be removed, other than by legislation. American judges fifty years ago had no difficulty adapting to the needs of new forms of communication by changing to a "single publication rule", and now the reality of internet communication demands that the UK follow suit. Otherwise, publishers will have little or no protection from statutes of limitation, web publishing will be put at risk, and foreign (especially US) publications may be withheld from the UK to avoid its over-stringent libel laws becoming a magnet for defamed forum-shoppers with international reputations.

There is no doubt that the legal rights of journalists and broadcasters

---

[5] *Theophanous v. The Herald and Weekly Times Ltd & Anor.* (1994) 182 CLR 104 at p. 174, per Deane J.

[6] This is the feature which prevents English libel judgements from being enforced in the US: *Telnikoff v. Matusevich* 347 Md. 561, 702 A.2d 230 (1997).

are in many other respects more secure now than they were when we last assessed them in 1992, for the third edition of this book. For that, we principally credit the impact of Article 10 of the European Convention, derived both from European Court decisions prior to the Human Rights Act and from the bold manner in which Article 10 jurisprudence was entrenched in that legislation. But credit is also owed to the liberal-mindedness of the current senior judiciary, more open than previous generations of Law Lords to first amendment learning vouchsafed by the US Supreme Court are more willing, when sitting in their somewhat arcane Privy Council capacity, as final appeal court for a dozen or so commonwealth nations, to strike down unconstitutional infringements of free speech. What is emerging, notwithstanding the nervousness and occasional truculence of judges in lesser courts, is a true appreciation of the constitutional role of the right to freedom of expression, as guarantor of the independence of a fourth estate. When this book was first published, judges invariably regarded the media with suspicion, and sometimes with contempt: this is being replaced by a grudging, and in some cases genuine, respect for the role of the media in a free and democratic society. Indeed, we have felt obliged in this edition to point out the many ways in which media executives fail to live up to the new judicial expectations: they fail to assert their rights by challenging film and television and video censorship rulings; they supinely accept decisions to exclude broadcasters from courts and (especially) tribunals; they meekly comply with ''D'' notices and actually belong to the committee which issues them; they accept decisions of the Broadcasting Standards Commission and they enthusiastically play along with the Press Complaints Commission, although it operates both as a shackle on the press and a fraud on the public. None of these compromises would be acceptable in the US, where editors are made of sterner stuff. The evidence in this book demonstrates that, for the first time in British history, freedom of speech may be safer in the hands of our senior judges than it is in the unprincipled and often hypocritical hands of our newspaper editors and film and television executives.

It is trite that every country gets the press it deserves, although the adage at least makes the point that the law cannot be held primarily responsible for media failures to give the public what it needs to know. The third Royal Commission on the Press suggested this balance:

> ''We define freedom of the press as that degree of freedom from restraint which is essential to enable proprietors, editors and journalists to advance the public interest by publishing the facts and opinions without which a democratic electorate cannot take responsible judgments.''[7]

---

[7] Royal Commission on the Press, Final Report, HMSO 1977, Cmnd 6810, Chap 2 para 3.

In the past, media apologists could blame the law for their failures—
to expose the likes of Robert Maxwell and Jeffrey Archer, to predict the
impending crash of Blue Arrow and Lloyds of London, or to reveal the
government's duplicity in selling arms secretly to Iraq. This excuse was
never fully justified, and henceforth will deserve a new and caustic
scrutiny: what effort did the media make to lift the constraint, or to make
use of its reporting rights? Unless the media organisations with the wealth
(and the duty) to challenge censorship decisions do so in the courts, the
cosy accommodations they prefer to make with politicians and power-
brokers will be perceived by those they represent—the viewing and
reading public—as selling out on the principle of freedom of expression
entrusted to their stewardship.

This is a book about the legal rights of journalists, broadcasters, authors,
internet providers, editors, dramatists, film makers, photographers, e-mai-
lers, website owners, producers and others who publish news or views
through the communications media. The introductory chapters describe
the common law safeguards of open justice, jury trial and the rule against
prior restraint, and go on to explain how Article 10 provides the procedural
pillar of freedom of expression in twenty-first century Britain. The next
section states the basic laws that apply to all publishing enterprises—
libel, contempt, confidence, copyright and obscenity. There follows an
examination of the laws applicable to particular areas of reporting: the
ground rules that open or close the doors of the courts, Whitehall,
Parliament, local government and commercial enterprises. Freedom of
information, the long-awaited "Open Sesame" of bureaucracy, is discussed by way of analysis of the new Act. Finally, there is an account of
the practices and procedures of our alphabet soup of regulatory bodies—
the British Broadcasting Corporation (BBC) and Independent Television
Commission (ITC), the British Board of Film and Video Classification
(BBFC), the Press Complaints Commission (PCC), the Broadcasting
Standards Commission (BSC), the Advertising Standards Authority
(ASA) and the British Advertising Clearance Centre (BACC), and finally
the proposed big brother of them all, OFCOM.

The views expressed in this book have been formed in the course of
defending individual writers, editors and artists, and it is to them that we
owe the greatest debt of thanks. We are grateful to Simone Hugo and
Kate Beattie for their work on the manuscript, our colleague Anthony
Hudson for research assistance, our editors at Penguin and Sweet and
Maxwell and to Susan Rickard and Robert Spicer for preparing the index
and list of cases. Kathy Lette and Camilla Palmer deserve the first
footnote, in this as in previous editions.

STOP PRESS

CHAPTER 1: FREEDOM OF EXPRESSION, UNDER "OPEN JUSTICE PRINCIPLE", p. 18.

The next step that the courts must take to develop the "open justice" principle in conformity with the realities of modern communication, is to permit their own proceedings to be televised. Research consistently demonstrates that the British public mainly receives news from television, not from newspapers. The essential justifications for "open justice"—that it protects against perjury, encourages witnesses to come forward and deters judicial misconduct—would be better served by television or radio coverage of courts. The evidence in any particular case does not merely comprise the words that are spoken, but the way in which they are spoken. (For this reason, appeal courts are reluctant to disturb the findings of trial judges who have "had the benefit of seeing the witnesses"—*i.e.* of observing their demeanor and body language.) If the public, too, is to "see justice done", its watchdog in the twenty-first century will be the broadcaster as well as the newspaper journalist. The rule which requires all courts and tribunals to admit the reporter clutching pen and notebook should logically be extended to admit the reporter with a digital video camera—subject to protocols which prohibit pictures of vulnerable witnesses and jurors.

It is a sad indictment of British broadcasters that so few have made serious applications to cover Tribunals of Enquiry, despite the fact that the Tribunals of Enquiry (Evidence) Act of 1921 contains no bar on photography—indeed, section 2(a) enjoins the widest publicity. In October 2001 the first full-blooded assertion of a broadcaster's right to televise proceedings (of the inquiry into mass-murdering doctor Harold Shipman) was made by CNN, drawing upon the terms of the 1921 Act, the open justice principle and Article 10. Janet Smith J was reluctant to acknowledge that broadcasters had a "right" to televise public inquiries, but she permitted cameras to capture and transmit the testimony of witnesses who did not object.[1] Television coverage of Shipman began in May 2002, under protocols which require a 60-minute delay between recording and broadcasting, in case there is a sudden need for a judicial edit. This is a real breakthrough: the next step is to create a presumption

---

[1] *The Shipman Enquiry: Application by Cable News Network (CNN)*, October 25, 2002, *per* Dame Janet Smith.

in favour of broadcasters by requiring reticent witnesses to show good reason why their testimony should not be televised.

The BBC application to broadcast evidence at the Lockerbie trial was turned down by the Scottish courts, for the good reason that some key non-compellable witnesses who lived abroad would not attend for fear of reprisals if visually identified.[2] In the absence of such reasons, there should be no objection. Scottish appeal courts, for example, generally permit their proceedings to be televised and thus allowed BBC coverage of the Lockerbie appeal, having ascertained that neither prosecution nor defence objected. In England, there is an inconvenient statutory bar erected in 1925—long before the advent of television—by section 41 of the Criminal Justice Act, passed to stop photography in courtrooms. It might be argued that "photograph" in this legislation refers to the flash photography which famously captured Dr Crippen in the Old Bailey dock, and not to unobtrusive and stationary digital cameras—an interpretation which section 3 of the Human Rights Act would assist, since this construction of the statute is more in keeping with the Article 10 right of the media freely to impart information. English judges were deeply antagonised by television coverage of the OJ Simpson trial, notwithstanding that it served the public interest by exposing an incompetent judge and a lying policeman. It was chiefly objectionable because of the accompanying "expert" commentaries and lawyers' press conferences, which would never be permitted under United Kingdom contempt laws and professional ethics rules. Courts and tribunals cannot indefinitely resist the logic of extending the open justice principle to the broadcaster as well as to the print journalist.

CHAPTER 2: THE HUMAN RIGHTS ACT, UNDER "ARTICLE 10: THE CORE PRINCIPLES", p. 41.

In 2002 the Court applied principle 6(c) to strike down several decisions by Austrian courts, which required newspapers to prove the truth of polemical attacks on right-wing politicians like Jorg Haider, whose rise to power has been greatly assisted by the country's unnecessarily repressive defamation laws. These decisions lend some support to the argument that the English libel law requirement that media defendants must prove the truth of their allegations may be a breach of the Convention, at least when it curbs discussion of politicians and public figures.[3]

[2] See *In the Petition of the British Broadcasting Corporation: High Court of Judiciary,* per Lord Macfadyen, March 7, 2000, CA, April 20, 2000.
[3] See *Dichand & Ors v. Austria,* Application No. 29271/95, February 26, 2002 (onus of proof on defence was an "excessive burden"); *Unabhangige Initiative v. Austria,* Application No. 28525/95, February 26, 2002 (burden of proof excessive in respect to a value judgement about Jorg Haider's racism).

CHAPTER 2: THE HUMAN RIGHTS ACT 1998, p. 57.

The Court of Appeal decided that *Guardian* editor Alan Rusbridger could challenge section 3 of the 1848 Treason Felony Act (which outlaws the peaceful advocacy of republicanism) by seeking a declaration that it is incompatible with the 1998 Human Rights Act (which imports the Article 10 "free speech" guarantee into English law). Although the courts will not normally occupy their time with hypothetical questions (there has been no prosecution for 150 years) they will grant such declarations in exceptional cases, and here the importance of free speech and the need for clarity in the criminal law justified an examination of the issue raised by *The Guardian*.[4]

CHAPTER 2: THE HUMAN RIGHTS ACT, UNDER "A NEW LEGAL LANDSCAPE", p. 65.

The case that demonstrates most clearly the true impact of the Human Rights Act in "constitutionalising" freedom of expression was decided by the Court of Appeal in March 2002. The ProLife Alliance, entitled to a free broadcast before the 2001 elections, wished to show picture of aborted foetuses. This was refused by television executives on the grounds of taste and decency, even for a late-night transmission time. The High Court, applying the judicial review test of whether the decision was rational, naturally decided that it was—the bureaucrats believed that some viewers would be shocked. But the Court of Appeal said that this approach was "profoundly mistaken".[5] Freedom of speech was now a "bedrock value" and any restriction had to be seen for what it was—an act of censorship—and justified as necessary in a democratic society. The Court had a special responsibility to the public to ensure that all political views were put before it in the most impactful way. Judges should not defer to the opinion of "experts": the Court had an overarching duty to ensure that political speech was not subject to censorship, at least in the absence of gratuitous sensationalism or dishonesty of presentation.

This head-on, full-blooded approach to freedom of speech is much to be welcomed. It was delivered in the context of protecting political speech at election time, although it should not be so confined—such speech is precious at all times, and must protection should extend to speech on economic, governmental and international matters as well. The *ProLife Alliance* case hopefully signals an end to the overdue deference that courts have shown to the decisions made by "expert" bodies like the

---

[4] *Rusbridger & Toynbee v. Attorney General* [2002] EWCA Civ 397 (March 20, 2002).
[5] *R (on the application of ProLife Alliance) v. BBC* [2002] 2 All E.R. 756.

PCC and BSC and ASA. Henceforth, the courts must ensure that these decisions are not merely rational, but that they are a necessary response to a "pressing social need".

CHAPTER 3: DEFAMATION, UNDER "WHO CAN BE SUED?", pp. 103–4.

The first "catch" in the 1996 Defamation Act requirement that any writ must follow within twelve months of publication—namely that judges might use their "equitable" discretion to extend time for tardy and undeserving claimants—has been discouraged by the Court of Appeal.[6] The judges emphasised that defamation is different to other torts, and free speech considerations should protect publishers from being vexed by delayed defamation actions. Since damage to reputation must be repaired promptly if it is to be repaired at all, claimants who delay longer than 12 months cannot expect to be indulged.

However, the second "catch" identified in the 1996 reform—the *Duke of Brunswick* "multiple publication" rule that every publication constitutes a new and separate cause of action—will operate to deny any relief to publishers whose works remain in circulation for more than a year or are accessible through the worldwide web. American judges extirpated the rule from their common law after World War Two, adopting the more realistic "single publication rule", which treats the primary communication—the original circulation of a book or newspaper, or broadcast of a television programme or uploading on to a website—as one global tort, from the time of which the limitation period begins to run in respect of every subsequent communication of the offending words. English judges, made of less stern stuff, have despaired of change, because of "how firmly entrenched the principle in the *Duke of Brunswick*'s case is in our law".[7] This horse-and-buggy rule survives to shackle the internet, although the Court of Appeal helpfully suggested that a timely hyperlink might protect a web publisher from libel action: "Where it is known that archive material is or may be defamatory, the attachment of an appropriate notice warning against treating it as the truth will normally remove any sting from the material".[8]

---

[6] *Steedman v. BBC* [2001] EWCA Civ 1534.
[7] *Loutchansky v. Times Newspapers (No. 2)* [2002] 1 All E.R. 652 at 673.
[8] *Ibid.* at 676e, per Lord Phillips MR.

CHAPTER 3: DEFAMATION, UNDER "FAIR COMMENT", p. 120.

The Court of Appeal decision in *Skrine v. Euromoney Publications Plc* makes it easier to characterise a long investigative article as comment, rather than as statements of fact, if "the author of the article does not each a conclusion, he poses questions and records the concerns of others".[9] The publisher of an article which accurately records a series of suspicious facts, quotes authoritative sources who make defamatory deductions, but maintains an overall authorial skepticism by hanging a question mark over allegations of blame and responsibility, may thus be relieved of the difficult task of proving the truth of all the defamatory imputations of fact, and bear instead the much lighter burden of showing that the author honestly believed that further investigation was needed into the suspicious circumstances.

CHAPTER 3: DEFAMATION, UNDER "QUALIFIED PRIVILEGE", p. 133.

The Court of Appeal decision in *Loutchansky v. Times Newspapers Ltd (No. 1)*,[10] which held that the media's entitlement to a qualified privilege defence had to be judged at the time of publication, turning a blind eye to all that might emerge through subsequent investigation, is artificial: it ignores the reality of reporting on a rolling news story, where facts for and against the plaintiff may emerge over a period of coverage, and it prevents the court from making an informed judgment on editorial responsibility which in the real world continues long after the original defamation is published. For example, responsible editors who promptly publish corrections and apologies should, under a qualified privilege plea, have this conduct taken into account in their favour. But *Loutchansky (No. 1)* forecloses such an approach.

In *Loutchansky (No. 2)*,[11] however, another Court of Appeal turned *Reynolds* privilege into a full-blown defence of responsible journalism in pursuit of the public interest. It rejected as "too stringent" the approach of the trial judge (criticised at p. 153, footnote 43) which required that the editorial decision to publish be beyond professional reproach: instead, the decision had only to be one that a reasonable editor might have taken, notwithstanding that other editors would have pulled the story. The Court was realistic: *Reynolds* privilege really attached to the publication itself and not (like other privileges) to the occasion of publication: it was a

---

[9] [2001] EWCA Civ 1479.
[10] *Loutchansky v. Times Newspapers Ltd* [2001] 4 All E.R. 115.
[11] *Loutchansky v. Times Newspapers Ltd (No. 2)* [2002] 1 All E.R. 652.

recognition by the Court that the article was in the public interest because it served the public's right to know. If the article served that purpose, the privilege could hardly be lost because the editor happened to be motivated either by spite or by recklessness. (The Court of Appeal accepted, in effect, the point made in this text (at p. 133) that the factors which determine the existence of the privilege (Lord Nicholl's "top 10" test) include the self-same factors which will determine whether the publisher is actuated by malice.) "Reynolds privilege" was in a class of its own, "a different jurisprudential creature" which required the editor to prove that the decision to publish was professionally responsible: that finding, in passing the "top 10" test, subsumed and surmounted the issue of malice.

The Court of Appeal has permitted "neutral reportage" to claim *Reynolds* privilege without the need to verify defamatory allegations.[12] The newspaper defendant had reported a vicious spat between leaders of the Saudi dissident community in London, which included allegations ("your mother is a whore") that were doubtless of interest to the readership but that the paper, in publishing, had (understandably) in no way attempted to verify. The trial judge had denied them *Reynolds* privilege on account of this failure, but the Court of Appeal pointed out that their arm's length position was the very reason why they should have it. "It is the fact that the allegation of a particular nature has been made which is in this context important, and not necessarily its truth or falsity." Qualified privilege may henceforth be bestowed upon the neutral reporting of attributed allegations which the newspaper has made no effort to verify; so long as it does not "adopt" the allegation by suggesting that it is true. Although the *Al-Fagih* imputations were made in the context of a political dispute, the principle should cover accurate reportage of all outbursts that are "newsworthy" because of the fact that they are made rather than the fact that they are true. Thus *Reynolds* privilege mitigates the straitjacket of the "repetition rule" which ordinarily requires newspapers that report another's accusation to be in a position to prove it (see p. 114, footnote 12): so long as the report is careful to give an accusation no extra credence, the fact that it has been made will, if newsworthy, obtain protection (although the paper would be well advised to seek out, and to publish, the reply of the party under attack). The papers which paid massive damages to the former Ugandan Foreign Minister, Princess Elizabeth of Toro, as a result of reporting *verbatim* Idi Amin's crazed allegations about her sexual behaviour in an airport toilet (see p. 138) would today be protected by *Reynolds* privilege: her right to reputation would now be trumped by the need for the British public to know, of a dictator its government had helped to power, that he was mad, bad, and dangerous to know.

---

[12] *Al-Fagih v. H H Saudi Research Marketing UK Ltd* [2002] E.M.L.R. 215.

CHAPTER 4: OBSCENITY, BLASPHEMY AND RACE HATRED, UNDER "RACE HATRED", p. 218.

The United Kingdom is obliged under Article 20(2) of the International Covenant of Civil and Political Rights to prohibit advocacy of racial or religious hatred that constitutes incitement to violence or discrimination—an obligation adequately fulfilled by existing public order law.[13] In December 2001 the Home Secretary's attempt to introduce a new criminal offence of incitement to religious hatred was rejected by Parliament.

CHAPTER 5: CONFIDENCE AND PRIVACY, UNDER "THE OBLIGATION OF CONFIDENCE", p. 225.

Correction: in the quotation from Megarry J. in *Coco v. Clark* the last sentence should read: ". . . Thirdly, there must have been an *unauthorised* use of the information to the detriment of the person communicating it."

CHAPTER 5: CONFIDENCE AND PRIVACY, UNDER "PROTECTION OF SOURCES", p. 265.

In *Interbrew SA v. Financial Times Ltd*[14] the Court of Appeal ruled that five media organisations should hand over leaked documents that might identify a source who had maliciously attempted to manipulate the market in Interbrew shares. Journalists cannot complain (although they did) about orders to disclose sources who have exploited their credulity and their publishing power to cause damage or profit to others. Journalists had more cause to complain about the behaviour of the Saville Enquiry, which has clearly breached the ECHR and the rule in *Goodwin* by ordering several journalists to disclose their sources of information about "Bloody Sunday" and its aftermath. The Enquiry said it was acting "in the interests of justice", but no justice is possible for the victims of "Bloody Sunday" thirty years ago: in reality, the Tribunal acts in the interests of history, which does not feature among the section 10 excuses for breaching professional confidences. The journalists have refused to comply, and the courts should in due course uphold their refusal.

---

[13] See Bob Hepple, "Freedom of Expression and the Problem of Harassment", *Freedom of Expression, Freedom of Information* (Beatson and Cripps ed., OUP, 2000), p. 177.
[14] [2002] E.M.L.R. 446 CA.

CHAPTER 5: CONFIDENCE AND PRIVACY, UNDER "DATA PROTECTION", p. 279.

The potential of the Data Protection Act to provide a cause of action for infringement of privacy was shown by the case of *Naomi Campbell v. Mirror Group Newspapers Ltd.*[15] Her claim under section 13 of the Act was successful, because details of her drug therapy treatment were "sensitive personal data" relating to her physical or mental health. Section 32 (which provides exemption to journalists in their processing of personal data) had no application after publication, and *The Mirror* failed in its defence that exposing details of her treatment was in the substantial public interest.

CHAPTER 5: CONFIDENCE AND PRIVACY, UNDER "PRIVACY", pp. 284–7.

The Sun reported that three police officers had been disciplined for making a racist remark about an asylum seeker, after they had been exposed by a "black clerk". Ensuing readers' letters waxed furious at the clerk's "treachery" and a subsequent article oozed with indignation at her behaviour. The clerk in question, Ms Thomas, received hate mail at work and suffered distress and anxiety, so she sued for compensation under the Harassment Act. The Court of Appeal stressed that it was not enough that articles contained unreasonable opinions or even that they would foreseeably cause distress—"harassment" described conduct targeted at an individual which is calculated to cause alarm or distress and which is oppressive and unreasonable. *The Sun*'s articles, calculated to incite racial hatred of an individual, were capable of amounting to harassment.[16]

CHAPTER 5: UNDER "PRIVACY", p. 287.

Early signs are that the courts will resist privacy claims unless they are grounded upon breaches of confidentiality or harassment. Heather Mills, the partner of Sir Paul McCartney, was unable to obtain an injunction to prevent publication of the address of her new house. Her fear of stalkers was not sufficient to persuade the judge that this information, which in any case would have been known to many in her locality, should be suppressed by court order. In *Beckham v. MGN Ltd.*[17] there was evidence

---

[15] [2002] EWHC 499 QB March 27, 2002.
[16] *Thomas v. News Group Newspapers Ltd* [2002] E.M.L.R. 4 CA.
[17] *Beckham v. MGN Ltd.*, unreported, June 28, 2001, *per* Eady J.

of specific threats, so an injunction was granted to prevent publication of photographs of the interior of the Beckhams' new house.[18]

In *A v. B (a company) and another*[19] the Court of Appeal set new guidelines for privacy injunctions against the press. The case concerned Blackburn Rovers' captain Gary Flitcroft, married with children, who had affairs with two women who then sold their stories to the *Sunday People*. He obtained a pre-trial injunction to stop publication, but this was lifted by the Court of Appeal. It considered that the requirement in section 12(3) of the HRA (that any injunction to curb freedom of expression should only be granted pre-trial if success at the eventual trial was likely) demanded a slightly higher standard of probability than had the "real prospect of success" test in *American Cyanamid*. The fact that the injunction would interfere with freedom of the press was of particular importance, creating a presumption against granting it, irrespective of whether the particular publication would be in the public interest (although a clear public interest in publication strengthens the presumption). Any applicant for an injunction must show a confidential relationship (but that can arise whenever there is a reasonable expectation of privacy) and the fact that the information has been obtained by unlawful means may be a powerful (but not decisive) factor in favour of granting it. Public figures have a right to privacy, but the media is entitled to scrutinise them closely, either because they are "role models" from whom the public expects higher standards or because they have themselves courted publicity. The Court of Appeal approved the decision of Ousley J in *Theakston v. MGN Ltd*[20] in which a *Top of the Pops* presenter had been refused an injunction to prevent publication of an account, bought from prostitutes, of his night in a brothel. (The judge did, however, restrain publication of the photographs which they had taken with the intention of blackmailing Theakston.)

The *A v. B* guidelines were set to resolve the uncertainty in the lower courts about whether a separate tort of invasion of privacy could or should develop. The Court of Appeal's answer (which may not be that eventually given by the House of Lords) is that no new tort is necessary: the Article 8 right to privacy, along with the countervailing Article 10 right to free speech, are both "absorbed" into the long-established action for breach of confidence, which is thereby given "new strength and breadth". This is all very metaphysical, and intellectually unsatisfactory since the obligation of confidence traditionally arises from a solemn relationship between two human parties: the Court of Appeal gives it a "new breadth" by applying it to any "intrusion in a situation where a person can reason-

---

[18] For further discussion of the privacy issue see pp. 63–64, 687–694, 790–791 and 810–811.
[19] [2002] 2 All E.R. 545.
[20] [2002] E.M.L.R. 22.

ably expect his privacy to be protected''. But having widened the net of prospective claimants, it then removes most prospects of success from public figures and ''role models'' by making them a ''legitimate subject of attention'' whether or not the story is genuinely in the public interest. As the Court remarks, with unaccustomed cynicism (and factual inaccuracy), ''the Courts must not ignore the fact that if newspapers do not publish information which the public are interested in, there will be fewer newspapers published, which will not be in the public interest''. On this reasoning, the upshot of *A v. B* has been to boost the market in ''kiss and sell'' stories.

These guidelines do establish, however unsatisfactorily, a basis for asserting (and rejecting) privacy claims as breaches of confidence. The law is moving towards a more definite identification of the subject matter which deserves its protection, borrowing a judicial definition from the High Court of Australia:

> ''Certain kinds of information about a person, such as information relating to health, personal relationships or finances, may be easy to identify as private; as may certain kinds of activity, which a reasonable person, applying contemporary standards of morals and behaviour, would understand to be meant to be unobserved. The requirement that disclosure or observation of information or conduct would be highly offensive to a reasonable person of ordinary sensibilities is in many circumstances a useful practical test of what is private.''[21]

In *Naomi Campbell v. Mirror Group Newspapers Ltd*[22] the supermodel recovered compensatory damages of £2,500 and aggravated damages of £1,000 for the publication of details of her attendance at meetings of Narcotics Anonymous. Although she had lied in the past about her use of drugs and so could not complain about publication of the fact that she was having addiction therapy, she nonetheless had a legitimate expectation that her use of the counselling services of NA and the details of her attendance there would remain private. The information had come from either a fellow sufferer or a member of her staff, and so was impressed with confidentiality: Campbell had suffered detriment in the form of shock and distress and inability to return for more ''anonymous'' treatment; this was aggravated by vicious and unfair attacks on her by *Mirror* columnists for bringing the action. Despite her lies and self-promotion, she was entitled to a ''residual area of privacy'' which included the right to keep her medical and psychiatric treatment a secret. In another case, Naomi Campbell succeeded in a breach of confidence claim against a

---

[21] *ABC v. Lenah Game Meats* [2001] HCA 63 at para 42, per Glesson CJ.
[22] [2002] EWHC 499 QB March 27, 2002.

former assistant who had sold details of her personal life to *The News of the World*. The assistant had been entitled to bring her contract with Ms Campbell to an end because of the latter's bad behaviour, but this did not terminate the duty of confidence and on the facts there was no public interest defence.[23] Bodyguards and personal assistants will usually be injuncted if their celebrity employer gets wind of their impending leaks to the tabloids, although the court orders should be limited to revelation of intimate personal details. Lady Archer obtained an injunction after details of her expensive face-lift were revealed: although all could see the result, it was nonetheless a medical procedure to which confidentiality attached.

CHAPTER 6: COPYRIGHT, UNDER "DEFENCES", p. 322.

In *Ashdown v. Telegraph Group Ltd* the Court of Appeal rejected the argument that the Human Rights Act had no effect on copyright defences: while it would normally be necessary in a democratic society to protect the rights of a copyright owner, that was not invariably so and circumstances could arise in which freedom of expression would only be fully effective if an individual is permitted to reproduce copyright material.[24] The Copyright Act would have to accommodate Article 10 in these exceptional cases, either by the courts refusing an injunction (thus leaving the claimant with only a monetary remedy); or else by providing a public interest defence.[25] Nonetheless, it found that the *Sunday Telegraph* could claim no public interest in pirating Paddy Ashdown's memoirs, which had been

> "deliberately filleted in order to extract colourful passages that were most likely to add flavour to the article thus to appeal to the readership of the newspaper . . . We do not consider it arguable that Article 10 requires that the Telegraph Group should be able to profit from this use of Mr. Ashdown's copyright without paying compensation".[26]

---

[23] *Naomi Campbell v. Frisbee* [2002] EWHC 328 Ch March 14, 2002.
[24] [2001] 4 All E.R. 666.
[25] Public interest as a defence to a copyright action had been narrowly construed in *Hyde Park Residence Ltd v. Yelland* (see p. 321) by Aldous L.J. but in *Ashdown* the Court of Appeal preferred the less restrictive approach of Mance L.J. in *Yelland*, which refused to tie the public interest down to precise categories.
[26] *Ashdown*, p. 686.

CHAPTER 6: COPYRIGHT, UNDER "MORAL RIGHTS", p. 334.

Passing off was used successfully to complain of "false endorsement" in *Irvine v. Talksport Ltd.*[27] Damages were fixed at £2,000 on basis that this was the reasonable royalty fee which the claimant could have charged for the use of his name.[28]

CHAPTER 6: COPYRIGHT, UNDER "REMEDIES", p. 341.

Northamptonshire Health Care NHS Trust v. News Group Newspapers Ltd[29] is an example of the circumstances in which additional damages will be awarded against newspapers. *The Sun* had published a photograph of a convicted killer which had been stolen from his medical files at Rampton. Rampton's health authority owned copyright in the photograph and were entitled to damages for its infringement. The compensatory damages were only £450, but were bumped up to £10,000 because *The Sun* must have realised that the photo was stolen. The newspaper had also delayed in giving a full explanation and had never apologised for the considerable upset it had caused at Rampton.

CHAPTER 7: CONTEMPT OF COURT, UNDER "WITNESSES", p. 366.

In March 2002 the government once again announced its intention to make newspaper payments to witnesses in criminal cases a criminal offence, and the Lord Chancellor's Department issued another consultation paper on the subject. This move, after exposure of press payments to the teenage witnesses at the trial of teacher Amy Gehrig, was a slap in the face of the PCC, since it was accompanied by ministerial statements that self-regulation was inadequate. Foolishly, the Department recommends that the offence carry two years in prison: a heavy financial penalty would be perfectly adequate to deter this very occasional form of media misbehaviour.

---

[27] [2002] 2 All E.R. 414 Ch.D.
[28] [2002] EWHC 539 Ch March 25, 2002.
[29] [2002] EWHC 409 Ch.

CHAPTER 7: CONTEMPT OF COURT, UNDER "TELEVISION COVERAGE OF CRIMINAL TRIALS", p. 368.

A web publisher uploaded material which would be prejudicial to a trial, but before the case became "active" or "sub judice". However, it remained there after the case had become active. The Court decided, on the basis of the *Duke of Brunswick* "multiple publication rule" that an internet archive was "published" for the purposes of the Contempt of Court Act for as long as it was accessible to the public. But, the longer it remained on line, the less the chance that a juror might either stumble across it or choose to access it, so in the particular circumstances of the case there was not a substantial risk of serious prejudice.[30]

CHAPTER 8: REPORTING THE COURTS, UNDER "PUBLIC ACCESS TO THE COURTS", pp. 415 AND 422, AND "GATHERING INFORMATION", p. 479.

In *Clibbery v. Allan*[31] the Court of Appeal reviewed the 1991 Family Procedure Rules in the unusual context of a case where a long-term mistress, abandoned by a prominent businessman, had shown his heartless affidavits to the media after failing in her Family Court claims upon him. Since they had no children, and the proceedings did not involve an acquisition into his finances, the Court saw no reason for prohibiting the disclosure. But although paying lip service to the importance of the "open justice" principle, it made sure that family proceedings would normally be heard in secret unless the Court directs otherwise. This creates an anomalous distinction with other civil gases, governed by CPR 39.2, where "private hearings" are for administrative convenience: members of press and public can ask to be admitted, and what goes on can be reported if the case does not fall within the categories listed in the 1920 Administration of Justice Act. The unsatisfactory aspect of *Clibbery* is its refusal to treat *Scott v. Scott* as a constitutional decision which should override rules of court made by committees of administrators and judges. These rules have no democratic legitimacy: they are often made for convenience and without proper attention to free speech principles. There is need for much more transparency in family courts, and the Court's reason for resistance—that parties (mainly husbands) are put under some compulsion to disclose all their assets—does not justify a cloak of secrecy over the entire proceedings.

---

[30] *H.M. Advocate v. Beggs (No. 2)* 2002 SLT 139 HCJ. For other decisions on the meaning of publication, see pp. 450–51.
[31] [2002] 1 All E.R. 865, CA.

CHAPTER 8: REPORTING THE COURTS: "REPORTING RESTRICTIONS", p. 432.

In *Briffet and Bradshaw v. DPP*,[32] a section-39 order had been made by a High Court judge in proceedings for judicial review of a school expulsion decision. The judge had simply said "order under section 39 Children and Young Persons Act. Reporting restrictions apply in respect of the Applicant and this matter be listed as 'ex parte K'". The Administrative Court said that this order was too vague and general. "Section 39 orders constituted a significant curtailment of press freedom and courts had to be vigilant to see that they were justified and made in clear and unambiguous terms."

CHAPTER 8: REPORTING THE COURTS, UNDER "SECRECY ORDERS", p. 456.

In *H v. Associated Newspapers Ltd* the Court of Appeal said that courts should only order that parties be referred to by initials if their identification would defeat the very purpose of the proceedings.[33]

CHAPTER 8: REPORTING THE COURTS, UNDER "SECRECY ORDERS", p. 466.

The Court of Appeal has said that a defendant does not have a right of appeal under Criminal Justice Act 1988, section 159, against the *refusal* of a crown court judge to make an order restricting publicity. The defendant's rights were adequately protected by a right to appeal against conviction at the end of the trial.[34]

CHAPTER 8: REPORTING THE COURTS, UNDER "GATHERING INFORMATION", p. 478.

In *Lily Icos Ltd v. Pfizer Ltd*[35] the Court of Appeal reviewed the principles to be applied when one or both of the parties asked for an order that the confidentiality attaching to discovered documents should continue notwithstanding that they had been referred to in open court. The Court said that very good reasons would be required for departing from the

[32] [2002] E.M.L.R. 12 Admin Ct.
[33] [2002] E.M.L.R. 425 CA.
[34] *R v. L* CA Criminal Division February 22, 2002.
[35] [2002] 1 All E.R., CA.

normal rule of publicity which had been reinforced by Articles 6 and 10 of the ECHR. The court would require specific proof that a party would be damaged by publication.

CHAPTER 8: REPORTING THE COURTS: PROTECTION FROM LIBEL, p. 489.

The defence of qualified privilege for reporting court proceedings extends to reports of material whose publication is prohibited by the Judicial Proceedings (Regulation of Reports) Act 1926. No civil action for damages may be maintained for its breach.[36]

CHAPTER 9: REPORTING LESSER COURTS AND TRIBUNALS, UNDER "COURTS MARTIAL", p. 496.

This Act will permit one or two NCOs to join the panel of judges trying other ranks. The military (and thus far the English judiciary) strenuously deny that officer-class justice can be perceived as injustice, even in a case where a jury of officers had to decide between the word of a squaddie defendant and that of their fellow officer, who accused him of rape.[37] The Court Martial system has now been found to be in breach of Article 6 of the ECHR,[38] and will require more thoroughgoing reform—preferably abolition—so that soldiers accused of serious offences can have the right to jury trial.

CHAPTER 9: REPORTING LESSER COURTS AND TRIBUNALS, UNDER "PUBLIC INQUIRIES", p. 511.

The Administrative Court has held that Article 10 creates no presumption that inquiries set up by the government must sit in public.[39] There is, however, a suggestion that it would be imperative to hold inquiries in public where the subject matter was government misconduct or alleged want of integrity.

---

[36] *Nicol v. Calendonian Newspapers Ltd*, April 15, 2002, Court of Session, Outer House.
[37] *R v. Schofield*, July 30, 2001, Courts Martial Appeal Court.
[38] *Morris v. U.K.* [2002] ECHR 38784/97, February 26, 2002.
[39] *Persey v. Secretary of State for Health* [2002] EWHC 371 Admin March 15, 2002; *Howard v. Secretary of State for Health* [2002] EWHC 396 Admin March 15, 2002.

CHAPTER 9: UNDER "PUBLIC INQUIRIES", p. 512.

CNN applied to televise the Shipman Inquiry, asserting a right based on section 2 of the 1921 Act, which provides that the Inquiry must not "refuse to allow the public or any portion of the public to be present at any of the proceedings", unless the subject matter or nature of the evidence makes this inexpedient. CNN argued that this 1921 statute, passed when broadcasting was in its infancy and when cameras were still allowed in court, must be given a modern interpretation consistent with Article 10 and section 3 of the HRA: it now gives access to the journalist with the digital camera as much as the journalist with the pen and notebook. Smith J. exercised her discretion in favour of permitting cameras to cover the most important part of the Inquiry, when police and health officials would be questioned about their failure to detect Shipman's multiple murders. Although prepared to exempt distressed witnesses (such as relatives of murder victims and Shipman's employees) the Judge ruled that:

"... witnesses who are professionally qualified or are public servants or have clearly defined duties, for which they have received training, should in my view be prepared to accept [the process of broadcasting] whether or not they might face challenging cross examination and possible criticism in the Report" (paragraph 98).[40]

This is an important precedent and may pave the way for future television coverage of inquiries under the 1912 Act and, hopefully, of other tribunals.

CHAPTER 10: REPORTING PARLIAMENTS, ASSEMBLIES AND ELECTIONS, UNDER "CONTEMPT OF PARLIAMENT", p. 535.

As a result of The Guardian's stand over the "cash for questions" report in 1997, however, it is highly unlikely that any editor or journalist need fear proceedings for contempt of Parliament by publishing leaked documents, if the leak serves the public interest:

Prime Minister John Major promised that Sir Gordon Downey's Privileges' Committee Report into allegations that Tory MPs had been bribed to advance the interests of Mohammed Al Fayed would be published before the General Election. In breach of this promise,

---

[40] The Shipman Inquiry: Application by Cable News Network (CNN), October 25, 2002, per Dame Janet Smith.

he prorogued Parliament before the report could be completed. But because *The Guardian* had been the complainant, Downey had sent it transcripts of his secret hearings, at which half a dozen Tory MPs standing for re-election had confessed to acceptance of cash and favours and other improper conduct. *The Guardian*'s editor, Alan Rusbridger, decided that the public interest in learning of this misbehaviour overrode his duty of confidentiality and justified committing contempt of Parliament by publishing the truth about the MPs a few weeks before the election. Publication made "Tory sleaze" a dominant issue, and the misbehaving MPs as well as their party were swept from office. The Privileges Committee took no action against the editor.[41]

CHAPTER 10: REPORTING PARLIAMENTS, ASSEMBLIES AND ELECTIONS, UNDER "CONFLICTS OF INTEREST", p. 537.

Since 2002 a register has also been kept of the interests of the members of the House of Lords. A code of conduct for members of the House of Lords provides a list of interests which must be registered. Though detailed, this is less onerous than the equivalent requirements for MPs. The register is open for public inspection and can be viewed on the House of Lords website at http://www.parliament.the-stationery-office.co.uk/pa/ld/ldreg/reg01.htm.

CHAPTER 10: REPORTING PARLIAMENTS, ASSEMBLIES AND ELECTIONS, UNDER "ELECTION REPORTING", p. 546.

In the 2001 general election the ProLife Alliance's party election broadcast was banned, as it was in the 1997 elections, by BBC controllers on grounds of "taste" and "decency" because it showed an aborted foetus. The Court of Appeal declared that the decision had been unlawful in view of the overriding importance of freedom of political expression at election time.[42] The first sentence in the judgment of Laws LJ declared that 'this case is about the censorship of political speech", a refreshing change from the weasel words that usually accompany judicial deference to ministers, mandarins and media regulators. The Court in 1997 had been excessively deferential to the judgment of the broadcasters: in 2001, after the HRA, a far more intensive review was required in the particularly

---

[41] Geoffrey Robertson, *The Justice Game* (Vintage, 1997), pp. 355–6.
[42] *ProLife Alliance v. BBC* [2002] EWCA Civ 297, March 14, 2002.

sensitive context of political speech at election times. Henceforth, the courts will uphold bans imposed on election broadcasts for gratuitous sensationalism or dishonesty, but not for genuine messages that would upset some viewers.

CHAPTER 10: REPORTING PARLIAMENTS, ASSEMBLIES AND ELECTIONS, UNDER
"ELECTION REPORTING", p. 549.

The requirement to provide information for election registers which could then be bought by commercial organisations was found to conflict with the Data Protection Directive, Article 8 of the ECHR and Article 3 of the 1st Protocol to the ECHR.[43]

CHAPTER 11: REPORTING WHITEHALL, UNDER CHAPTER TITLE, p. 553.

Action against intelligence officers and journalists for publishing their memoirs will seem inconsistent and hypocritical now that former MI5 Director Dame Stella Rimmington has insisted upon publishing her autobiography. Although she submitted the book for vetting, juries may feel that if an ex-Director can get away with it (and receive large royalties), so too should less highly placed spies, soldiers and SAS men with a story to tell. The Law Lords in *Shayler* have installed judicial review as the procedure by which security service insiders can now free their memoirs from the shackles of the Official Secrets Act, which makes it an absolute offence to leak intelligence information (although the Court of Appeal in *Shayler* conceded that the defences of duress and necessity could in principle be invoked by defendants to charges under the Official Secrets Acts).[44]

When the Court of Appeal and later the House of Lords considered the trial judge's ruling in *Shayler* that the prosecution did not have to show harm and that public interest in disclosure was no defence, the court heard from counsel representing most national newspapers, concerned about their potential liability for complicity in or incitement of section 1(1) offences by security or intelligence officers. Helpfully, the Court of Appeal said, "It would have to be an extreme case on the facts for a prosecution for incitement to be justified having regard to the structure of the Official Secrets Act which attaches such importance to the status of the individual

---

[43] *R (on the application of Robertson) v. City of Wakefield Metropolitan Council* [2002] 2 W.L.R. 889 Admin. Ct.
[44] *R v. Shayler* [2002] 2 W.L.R. 754.

charged.''[45] The *Daily Mail* had paid £40,000 to Shayler for his information, but there was no hint that the Court thought this would be sufficient to make out an ''extreme case''.

CHAPTER 11: REPORTING WHITEHALL, UNDER THE OFFICIAL SECRETS ACT, p. 565.

The House of Lords in *R v. Shayler* has confirmed that section 1(1) of the Official Secrets Act, which forbids disclosure at any time by intelligence officers of any aspect of their work, contains no trace of any ''public interest'' defence.[46] However, in order to justify their ruling that this absolute offence complies with Article 10, the Law Lords had to create some rules and procedures which would allow an MI5 officer to publish public interest concerns or even memoirs. So they acknowledged the ''right'' of serving or retired SIS personnel to apply for permission to publish, any refusal being subject to full judicial review, in which the court would consider the reasonableness rather than merely the rationality of the ban. The judges were adamant that the officer should be entitled to legal representation (notwithstanding the sensitivity of his prospective disclosures) and that the courts should give full credit to free speech arguments for releasing the information. Journalists are entitled to be sceptical about the prospect of English judges ordering the release of SIS information to the media, but the very fact that officials and former officials are now entitled to submit manuscripts and to legal assistance and to an appeal to the courts is an important development brought about not by Parliament but by the advent of the Human Rights Act. The Thatcher Government passed the 1989 Official Secrets Act with the declared and vindictive purpose of ensuring that Peter Wright and his ilk would henceforth take their secrets with them to their graves. *Shayler* now provides a means for exposing them prior to the funeral, even if publication will do some damage to security interests. It remains to be seen, however, whether intelligence officials have the courage or self-confidence to insist that their anxieties or reminiscences be shared with the public.

---

[45] *R v. Shayler* [2001] 1 W.L.R. 2206 CA at p. 2237.
[46] *R. v. Shayler* [2002] 2 W.L.R. 754.

CHAPTER 11: UNDER "SPECIFIC SECRECY LEGISLATION", p. 574.

These promises were successfully invoked by the editor of *The Mail on Sunday* to obtain permission to publish stories critical of MI5 which derived from David Shayler, even though they were covered by an injunction. Home Secretary Jack Straw agreed that publication could not cause real damage to the service as long as he was quoted in the articles denying that they had any truth.

CHAPTER 11: UNDER "DA-NOTICES", p. 579.

Shortly after the World Trade Center atrocity on September 11, 2001, the D-Notice Secretary, Rear Admiral "Nick" Wilkinson, wrote to all newspaper and broadcasting editors asking that they "minimise speculation" about any coming military action in Afghanistan.[47] This was a ridiculous suggestion, since speculation was being fuelled by government ministers and CNN and the American press (which would never comply with a D-Notice system) were full of it. Although the Secretary describes D-Notices as a "voluntary and informal system of advice"[48] it remains a form of censorship by wink and nudge, by threat and through the complicity of media executives. It is ironic that they continue to co-operate with this secret pressure (*Private Eye* honourably excepted) just at a time when the military and government itself is acknowledging the need for openness in its dealing with the media. Nothing was heard of D-Notices in respect of Kosovo in 1998 and NATO's media briefings by Jamie Shea and Alistair Campbell were notable for their detail compared with the tight-lipped MOD during the Falklands conflict.

CHAPTER 11: UNDER "MINISTERIAL AND CIVIL SERVANT MEMOIRS", p. 580.

In reality, ministerial memoirs are now so commonplace that the "Radcliffe Guidelines" serve little purpose. Ministers of the Thatcher and Major governments, including the Prime Ministers, have published memoirs without any trouble from the Cabinet Secretary and in 2002 Mo Mowlam became first minister of the Blair era to decline to submit to cabinet office censorship.

---

[47] Jessica Hodgson, "A Gentleman's Agreement", *The Guardian*, October 1, 2001.
[48] Rear Admiral Wilkinson, to letters page of *The Guardian*, October 3, 2001.

CHAPTER 11: UNDER "EUROPEAN UNION", p. 585.

A new regulation[49] came into force on 3 December 2001, which was made under the Amsterdam Treaty and which replaces Council decision 93/731 on access to Council documents and decision 94/90 on public access to Commission documents. As before, the new regulation starts with a general right of access to the documents of the EU institutions to any citizen of the Union and any natural or legal person residing or having its registered office in a Member State. Access must, however, be refused if disclosure would undermine the public interest in public security, defence and military matters, international relations or the financial, monetary or economic policy of the Community or a Member State or the privacy and the integrity of the individual, particularly in accordance with Community legislation regarding the protection of personal data. The institutions must also refuse access to internal documents if this would undermine the institution's decision-making process. All these later categories of case, though, are subject to a proviso that there is not an overriding public interest in disclosure. To make the rights of access more meaningful each of the Community's institutions are required to maintain a publicly accessible register of its documents.

CHAPTER 11: UNDER "FREEDOM OF INFORMATION ACT 2000", p. 607.

In *Norman Baker MP v. Secretary of State for the Home Department*, the Information Tribunal (National Security Appeals) quashed a certificate by the Home Secretary which had been issued under very similar provisions in the Data Protection Act 1998, section 28. The certificate excused MI5 from virtually all of the obligations of a data controller under the DPA and allowed it to "neither confirm nor deny" whether it held any data. The Tribunal said that the certificate was unreasonable because it did not require MI5 to make an individualised assessment of whether complying with the request would endanger national security.[50]

---

[49] Regulation (EC) No. 1049/2001.
[50] Decision of October 1, 2001.

Richard Desmond's pornographic publications did not feature in the advice from the Office of Fair Trading to the Government: it recommended approval of his purchase of Express Newspapers on competition grounds but disclaimed any expertise in assessing his moral fitness. This was left to ministerial judgement, and Trade Secretary Stephen Byers saw no cause for concern in the fact that Desmond had made his money by selling pictures of women masturbating: he had been deemed morally fit to donate £100,000 to the Labour Party shortly before the takeover.[51] This ethically neutral approach to Desmond by regulators and ministries contrasts with their chorus of disapproval in 1990 about *Daily Sport* publisher David Sullivan's attempt to gain a foothold in real newspapers. Their argument, that the influence of porn proprietors would "harm both the accurate presentation of news and the free expression of opinion", was not logical then and now appears to have been abandoned.

The Financial Services and Markets Tribunal's rules of procedure create a presumption that the Tribunal's hearings will be in public.[52] However, it can sit in private on the joint application of both parties or else if satisfied that a private hearing would be in the interests of morals, public order, national security or the protection of the private lives of the parties or that unfairness to the public of the interests of consumers might result from a public hearing. There are, though, two important qualifications: the Tribunal must not sit in private if this would be prejudicial to the interests of justice and it must also consider whether only part of the proceedings needs to be in private. Its decisions must be given publicly or published in writing. If all or part of the proceedings were in private, the Tribunal can restrict publicity to all or part of its decision but, consistently with the principle of proportionality, must minimise any such restriction.

Judicial deference to decisions made by regulators of taste and ethics such as the PCC and the ASA, exemplified by the refusal to review the

[51] "Advice over Express Takeover Revealed", *The Times*, May 28, 2002.
[52] The Financial Services and Markets Tribunal Rules 2001, S.I. 2001 No. 2476, rr.17–20.

PCC's *Anna Ford* ruling (see p. 691) is inconsistent with the Court of Appeal's new approach under the Human Rights Act. In the *ProLife Alliance* case,[53] it said that the Courts have an overarching constitutional duty to protect freedom of expression, as a bedrock principle, *a fortiori* against nervous regulators acting in the interests of the press or advertising industries.

The PCC's authority was undermined in 2002 when the cabalistic nature of its relationships with the Palace and the *News of the World* came to light (Guy Black, the executive head of the PCC, lives with his predecessor in that position, Mark Boland, now Princes Charles's private secretary: both men holiday with Rebekah Wade, editor of *News of the World*). These incestuous links were alleged to have played some undefined but undignified role in the coverage of Prince Harry's drink and drug problems. PCC Chairman Lord Wakeham became engulfed in the Enron scandal; and will be replaced by Sir Christopher Meyer. Meanwhile PCC adjudicators continued as inconsistently as ever. *Harry Potter* author J.K. Rowling fared better on her holiday beach than Anna Ford: her complaint against *OK* magazine was upheld, the difference apparently being that the photograph showed her with an 8-year-old daughter rather than a 68-year-old lover.[54] Vanessa Feltz was said to have no reason to complain about a false account of several trysts with a bouncer for no better reason than that she had publicly discussed other aspects of her private life; the Prime Minister's complaint about the revelation that his son had applied to an Oxbridge college was upheld, despite the obvious public and political interest in this choice. The Court of Appeal in *A v. B* directed that henceforth, in privacy or confidence cases where the PCC role was relevant, advocates should avoid reliance on individual decisions of the PCC.[55]

The ASA affects to regulate internet advertising and commercial e-mails, although its only deterrent power is to publish adverse adjudications on its website—www.asa.org.uk. Its battle with the puerile French Connection group continues to make news, as it regularly condemns their "fcuk" advertising, and most recently the promotion of their website www.fcukingbugger.com, giving priceless publicity to the group's clothing chain every time it advertises its condemnations.[56] In 2002 it referred three companies to the Director General of Fair Trading for continuing to falsely advertise health products and it ruled against several dishonest direct mailing and direct faxing promotions. Such conduct would be

---

[53] *R (on the application of ProLife Alliance) v. BBC* [2002] 2 All E.R. 756.
[54] "Think Before You Snoop", *The Times*, October 5, 2001, p. 19. The PCC urges editors to obtain parental consent before invading children's privacy, although other editors who used these pictures simply cropped J.K. Rowling's daughter out of the photograph.
[55] *A v. B & C* [2002] EWCA Civ. 337 (March 11, 2002) para 11 guideline xv.
[56] *A Year in Review, ASA Annual Report* 2001.

better deterred by criminal prosecutions for deception, rather than by a slap on the wrist from an industry-friendly regulator.

CHAPTER 14: MEDIA SELF REGULATION, UNDER "THE PRESS COMPLAINTS COMMISSION", p. 691.

Editors who rely on the *Anna Ford* decision to stalk celebrities on the beaches of the world should take care to crop their children out of the picture: J.K. Rowling (*Harry Potter* author) could not complain about being followed to a lonely beach in Mauritius and tele-photoed from offshore, but *OK!* magazine was condemned for putting her daughter in the frame as well.[57]

CHAPTER 15: CENSORSHIP OF FILMS AND VIDEO, p. 766.

The point (No. 6) that the mandatory BBFC classification system denies to parents one of the rights of family life (namely, to take your children to films you know are suitable for them) was brought home to fathers and mothers throughout the land in the summer of 2002, when the Board classified *Spider-Man* as a "12", thereby denying cinema access to its natural audience of 7–9-year-old boys, even with parental accompaniment.[58] The BBFC used the same excuse as it had with *Rambo III* (p. 757), namely, that Peter Parker's aggressive punishment of villains carries the dangerous message "that violence is a way of solving problems" (never mind that this is a message that George W. Bush sends every time he opens his mouth). At least the Board is aware that imposition of "12" certificates on films that parents might wish to take their younger children to see is unacceptable, and out of line with the voluntary systems which operate in America and Europe: Andreas Whittam Smith, in his first and last report as President, accepts that the "12" certificate should operate as a "PG-12" warning to parents about the presence of violence and bad language, rather than as an outright prohibition.[59] Children would be permitted to enter cinemas to watch films with this rating, if accompanied by an adult. This new system was tested in a pilot project in cinemas in

---

[57] "Think Before You Snoop", *The Times*, October 5, 2001, p. 19. The PCC urges editors to obtain parental consent before invading children's privacy, although other editors who used these pictures simply cropped J.K. Rowling's daughter out of the photograph.

[58] "Young Spider-Man fans caught in censor's web" Helen Rumbelow, *The Times*, June 8, 2002.

[59] *BBFC Annual Report* 2001, p. 4.

November 2002, and worked to general satisfaction:[60] any decision to adopt it, however, will require Home Office approval.

Chapter 16: broadcasting law, p. 769.

In May 2002 the Government published a draft Communications Bill, which provides for a merger of the ITC, the Radio Authority and the BSC (but not the BBFC), together with the Director-General of Communications, into one regulatory authority, OFCOM, which will have supervisory functions over the contents of anything that is broadcast or transmitted by means of an electronic communications network. There are some ''big brother'' aspects of the draft bill which may impinge on freedom of expression, such as the power to require notification from electronic publishers, to set conditions and to punish by way of fine. These deserve close attention during the bill's Parliamentary passage.

Chapter 16: broadcasting law, under ''the broadcasting standards commission'', p. 800.

The BSC was challenged to uphold the classic Article 10 free speech right to impart in the public interest ideas which can shock or disturb, when it adjudicated complaints by senior Government ministers (and several hundred viewers) about a savage *Brass Eye* satire on the hysterical treatment of paedophilia in the tabloid press, broadcast in July 2001. The Commission, predictably, failed to support the freedom of expression principle, ruling that the programme generated a level of shock and distress which outweighed its public interest purpose. It was condemned, in the BSC judgement, not because of its quality but by reference to the volume of complaints. The decision disregards not only the right of Channel 4 to screen provocative and unsettling programmes to mature audiences late at night, but the rights of millions of viewers who watched and did not complain.[61] It is pleasing to record that in 2002 Channel 4 defied the regulators by showing, late at night, a repeat of the programme.

---

[60] *Ibid.*, p. 11 and 25.
[61] See Mark Lawson, ''Babying the Public is Just Offensive'', *The Guardian*, September 8, 2001.

CHAPTER 16: BROADCASTING LAW, UNDER "ENFORCING THE CODES", p. 821.

The UK is obliged, by the Television without Frontiers Directive, to ensure that British-based broadcasters do not "buy up" an event listed by another government, so as to deprive its public of watching that event free-to-air. The House of Lords upheld an ITC decision to refuse consent to TVD (a pay-to-view company broadcasting to Denmark) purchasing exclusive rights to World Cup qualifiers which Denmark were playing, which were listed events under Danish law.[62]

---

[62] *R. v. Independent Television Commission ex p. TVDanmark I Ltd* [2001] 1 W.L.R. 1604.

ACKNOWLEDGEMENTS

The authors and publishers would like to thank the following for granting permission to reproduce material from the following works:

All Parliamentary material (extracts from Royal Commission and Select Committee Reports, Hansard, House of Commons Papers and White Papers) are reproduced by kind permission of Her Majesty's Stationery Office.

Betjeman, J. "In Westminster Abbey", *Collected Poems of John Betjeman* (John Murray)

Blom-Cooper, Louis, *Guns for Antigua* (Duckworth, 1990)

Dicey, A.V., *An Introduction to the Study of Law on the Constitution*, (10th ed, Macmillan, 1985)

Editorial, "Cinematography and the Child", *The Times*, April 12, 1913

Media Lawyer newsletter (Nov.–Dec. 1997)

Press Complaints Commission Annual Review (2000)

Press Complaints Commission Report No. 48, *Taylor v. News of the World*, January 26, 2001, Case 1

Press Complaints Commission Report No. 52, *Stewart-Brady v. Liverpool Echo and The Mirror*, January 24, 2001, Decision No. 3

Press Council, *The Press and the People*

Wells, H.G., *The Rights of Man*, (Penguin, 1940)

While every care has been taken to establish and acknowledge copyright, and contact the copyright owners, the publishers tender their apologies for any accidental infringement. They would be pleased to come to a suitable arrangement with the rightful owners in each case.

CHAPTER 1

FREEDOM OF EXPRESSION

"Think of what our nation stands for—
Books from Boots and country lanes,
Free speech, free passes, class distinction,
Democracy and proper drains".

1. COMMON LAW BEGINNINGS

In John Betjeman's England, "free speech" washes like fluoride
through the suburban water supply, but as a cultural assumption rather
than a constitutional right. When liberty exists as a state of mind, unprotected by enforceable legal rights, it gets limited in ways congenial to
those in power. That is why Britain has the most friendly libel law in
the Western world for claimants wealthy enough to exploit it, a law so
adverse to media defendants that American courts refuse to recognise
it. That is why section 1 of the Official Secrets Act 1989 makes it a
crime, to which there can be virtually no defence, for intelligence service personnel to reveal any detail of their employment, no matter how
trivial or how long ago—an offence so Draconian and so politically
manipulable that when MI5 renegade David Shayler was arrested in
Paris, the French courts refused to send him back to the Old Bailey for
trial. The European Court of Human Rights condemned the use of
breach of confidence injunctions to stop the British public reading *Spycatcher* after it had been published everywhere else in the world, and
criticised the contempt power which threatens journalists with jail for
refusing to identify the sources of their information. Britain has the
most paternalistic cinema censorship of any advanced nation, which
deprives parents of the right to accompany their children to movies
classified beyond their age group. When the Thatcher Government
deemed members of a particular political party—Sinn Fein—too subversive to be broadcast on radio or television the courts were powerless
to intervene: they could not protect a "right" to free speech because no
such "right" existed.

The legal position of free speech in a country without a constitutional guarantee (indeed, without a written Constitution) has been explained by the Law Lords:

> "Free" in itself is vague and indeterminate. It must take its colour from the context. Compare, for instance, its use in free speech, free love, free dinner and free trade. Free speech does not mean free speech: it means speech hedged in by all the laws against defamation, blasphemy, sedition and so forth. It means freedom governed by law . . .".[1]

Although the European Convention, incorporated into British law on October 2, 2000 by the Human Rights Act (HRA), had been promoted by the spin-doctor's slogan "rights brought home", Article 10 (which guarantees freedom of expression) never has been at home in Britain. Although many other sections of the Convention, guaranteeing free trial and habeas corpus and due process, owe their providence to English law, and (as we shall see) the "open justice" principle and rule against prior restraint were first formulated here, no generalised right of free expression, however common in rhetoric, entrenched itself in law. Magna Carta was silent on the subject, as might be expected in 1215, an age in which kings and barons reacted to an insult by lopping off the offending tongue—or head. The first statutory prohibition on speech came in 1275, and it set an unpropitious tone for British law ever since: the crime of "*scandalum magnatum*" expressly protected "the great men of the realm" from any statements which might arouse the people against them. Since true statements were especially prone to arouse public unrest, Lord Coke's famous maxim "the greater the truth the greater the libel" accurately reflected a criminal libel law invented to deter critics of the establishment. To this end it soon developed some irrational presumptions which survive today—*e.g.* that defamatory statements are false unless proved true, and cause damage without any need for the claimant to prove loss.

In 1476 Caxton's printing press rolled at Westminster, and it was not long before the King's judges in the Star Chamber devised ways to outlaw subversive exponents of this new technology. Sedition and blasphemy (in the age when the King ruled by divine right) were punished ferociously by cutting off the ears: a second offence meant the stumps of the ears were cut off as well, and the brand "SL" for "seditious libeller" burned into the author's forehead. In order the better to censor subversive or heretical literature, a licensing system was established giving a printing monopoly to members of the Stationers' Company, empowered by Royal Charter in 1557 to imprison unlicensed printers

---

[1] *James v. Commonwealth of Australia* [1936] A.C. 578 at p. 627.

and destroy their presses. The first *civil* law restriction on free speech came as a result of the Star Chamber's efforts to stop duelling (the traditional method of redressing damage to reputation): it encouraged protagonists to sue each other for libel instead, with the loser paying damages. Henry VIII proclaimed that no play could be performed without a licence from "the Master of the Revels", an officer of the Lord Chamberlain, whose control over British theatre in the interest of good politics and (later) good taste was to last until 1968.

These licensing systems admitted of no appeal, and were deployed to stamp out the work of dissidents (especially pro-Catholic propagandists) who were, when caught, sometimes hung, drawn and quartered for treason. Cromwell's republican revolution abolished the Star Chamber, but the Puritans introduced a licensing system which comprised 27 censors selected from "the good and the wise"—lawyers, doctors, schoolmasters and ministers of religion—who solemnly ordered seditious and irreligious books to be burned by the public hangman. The reintroduction of licensing at least provoked the poet Milton to utter his immortal cry for freedom of expression, the *Aeropagitica*:

> "Promiscuous reading is necessary to the constituting of human nature. The attempt to keep out evil doctrine by licensing is like the exploit of that gallant man who thought to keep out the crows by shutting his park gate ... Lords and Commons of England, consider what nation it is whereof ye are: a nation not slow and dull, but of a quick, ingenious and piercing spirit. It must not be shackled or restricted. Give me the liberty to know, to utter and to argue freely according to conscience, above all liberties".

Republican and then royalist governments alike turned a deaf ear: licensing was given statutory force after the restoration in 1660, and Milton's *Paradise Lost* was sent to the hangman for burning because it suggested that an eclipse of the sun "with sudden fear of change perplexes monarchs". But where the *Aeropagitica* failed, bureaucracy and corruption succeeded: the licensing system was abolished for the printed word in 1695 after incompetence, fraud and extortion destroyed the Stationers' Company. The "glorious revolution" was not at all glorious for Catholics, but it produced the Bill of Rights of 1689, Article 9 of which declares:

> "That the freedom of speech and debates or proceedings in Parliament ought not to be impeached or questioned in any court or place out of Parliament".

This is the one free speech right to be found in English constitutional law, but it belongs only to M.P.s and to peers, giving them absolute privilege against libel actions over allegations they make in the course of Parliamentary proceedings. It has proved a useful democratic right, when extended in the nineteenth century to the press and then to the broadcast media when they carry reports of Parliamentary debates. But it means little more than free speech for elected politicians and elevated party hacks who are reluctant to use it in the confines of Westminster other than in their party's interest. It is a right with which the people and the press have never been trusted.

The demise of licensing as a means of suppressing attacks on church or State did not much matter, since the criminal courts began to punish libels, whether critical of the church (blasphemy) the Government (sedition) or the great men of the realm (criminal libel). In the course of the eighteenth century a fourth crime was added, namely obscene libel, an offence against good manners and decency. From the outset the targets were more political than pornographic: the radical pamphleteer John Wilkes outwitted the Government over his popular polemics excoriating George III and his ministers, but when in 1763 he privately circulated a parody on Pope, on the theme that:

> ". . . life can little more supply
> than just a few good fucks, and then we die".

The new law of obscenity provided the excuse for silencing him. This "Essay on Women" was solemnly read to the House of Lords by Lord Sandwich, one of his political enemies, and when one peer protested as the first four-letter word was uttered under Parliamentary privilege, the others shouted "go on, go on". The Draconian use of sedition laws against aggrieved colonists in America provided one of the cues for revolution, ignited in January 1776 by Tom Paine, the former English customs official, whose incendiary pamphlet *Common Sense* explained, when all the talk was of appeasement with the Crown, why it would be necessary to fight for liberty. It was Paine who, in this hour of universal ferment, lent his drafting skills to Jefferson for the Declaration of Independence and then to Lafayette for the French constitution; he returned to London for six months in 1790 to write *The Rights of Man* at the Angel Inn, Islington. It became one of the most influential books ever written, and Paine's work was hailed throughout Europe and America. But in Britain, the Englishman who can claim to be the founding father of free speech was persecuted for sedition: he fled back to France, so the trials continued of booksellers who dared to stock his work. (His later book, *The Age of Reason*, would send dozens of free thinkers to prison for selling a blasphemous libel.) It was, however, in the chant of the mob outside the Old Bailey at the end of these late-eighteenth century sedition trials that the free speech principle was first heard in the land: the shout was "Paine and the Freedom of the Press".

By this time, of course, the principle had been embedded in the First

Amendment to the U.S. Constitution by way of a reaction to oppressive use of the common law of sedition. Free speech entered the U.S. Constitution because it was perceived as a defining quality of Republican government. As Madison argued in his Report to the General Assembly of Virginia in 1798, the former British Sedition Acts should now be made unconstitutional because the revolutionary new American Constitution would create a form of government under which "the people, not the government, possess the absolute sovereignty". This form of government was "altogether different" from the British model, under which the Crown was sovereign and the people were subjects. "Is it not natural and necessary, under such different circumstances", Madison asked, "that a different degree of freedom in the use of the press should be contemplated?" It was, in the following words of the First Amendment:

> "Congress shall make no law respecting an establishment of religion, or prohibiting the free exercise thereof; or abridging the freedom of speech or of the press; or the right of the people peacefully to assemble and to petition the government for a redress of grievances".

The French, too, had canonised free speech in Articles 9 and 10 of the 1789 Declaration on the Rights of Man and the Citizen:

> "No-one is to be disquieted because of his opinions . . . Free communication of ideas and opinions is one of the most precious of the rights of man".

This was a tribute to the influence of Voltaire ("I don't like what you say but will defend to my death your right to say it"; "I know many books which fatigue, but none which have done real evil") and to the iniquitous system of *lettres de cachet* (imprisonment without trial on royal command) visited upon critics of the *ancien régime*. The sudden removal of censorship in France had a most striking effect, releasing a "polemical incontinence that washed over the whole country" within two years.[2]

It was free speech as the precursor to revolution which Pitt feared most, and the decade before and after the turn of the nineteenth century was marked in Britain by the Government's increased use of the sedition laws. At first, convictions were assured by virtue of the rule that the jury could only decide whether the defendant had published the libel: it was for the judge to decide whether the words were seditious or not. Lord Erskine, the barrister who defended Paine, famously pre-

---

[2] Simon Schama, *Citizens* (Penguin, 1989), p. 521.

vailed upon a jury to defy the rule and acquit the Dean of St Asaph of seditious libel for urging universal suffrage. The judge, however, over-ruled the jury and entered a conviction, which was upheld by the appeal court. Public anger at judicial defiance of the jury procured the passage in 1792 of Fox's Libel Act, which reserved the decision on whether words were libellous to the jury alone. From this point, media defend-ants had a fighting chance: there were famous scenes where the mob carried Erskine in triumph from the Old Bailey after he secured acquit-tals for publishers of *The Rights of Man*. The Government responded by packing juries with men of property and "guinea men" (this was the sum they received if they convicted). Nonetheless, it was the chant of the mob outside the Old Bailey and the struggle for Fox's Libel Act that produced the impression—subsequently hardening into an unwrit-ten article of constitutional faith—that the jury is a true guarantor of free speech. The common law never adopted a free speech principle, although by the nineteenth century it had fashioned three procedural devices which still offer some practical support to the liberty of the press. Britain had trial by jury, an "open justice" principle, and a rule against prior restraint. It is instructive at this point to examine the pre-sent operation of the three safeguards devised by the common law, so as to understand why it was necessary to supplement them with a free speech principle drawn from the evolving international law of human rights.

2. TRIAL BY JURY

No citizen can lose his or her liberty for longer than a year (the max-imum sentence magistrates may impose) without at least the opportunity of trial by a jury of 12 good men and women and true. Legal history has many examples of "jury nullification" of bad laws or the directions of bad judges, beginning in 1670 when an Old Bailey jury, (despite being locked up for several days without food or water or even a chamber pot) refused to convict the Quakers Penn and Mead for sedi-tion. The jury system has served ever since to temper mercy with justice to defendants in the criminal courts,[3] but in the course of the nineteenth century it came to be accorded a special role in the protection of free speech: the jury's constitutional right to acquit, irrespective of the law or of the evidence, was touted as a better practical protection for free speech than any number of constitutional guarantees. This argument was formulated by Professor A. V. Dicey, writing in 1885:

---

[3] Lord Devlin, *Trial by Jury*, the Hamlyn Lectures, (1956, revised ed., Stevens 1966).

"Freedom of discussion, is, then, in England little else than the right to write or say anything which a jury, consisting of 12 shopkeepers, think it expedient should be said or written . . . Yet nothing has in reality contributed so much to free the press from any control. If a man may publish anything which 12 of his countrymen think is not blameable, it is impossible that the Crown or the Ministry should exert any stringent control over writings in the press . . . The times when persons in power wish to check the excesses of public writers are times at which a large body of opinion or sentiment is hostile to the executive. But under these circumstances it must, from the nature of things, be at least an even chance that the jury called upon to find a publisher guilty may sympathise with his language . . . as fair and laudable criticism of official errors. What is certain is that the practical freedom of the English press arose in great measure from the trial of "press offences" by a jury".[4]

Dicey's argument was dubious even at the time when it was made. True it was that Fox's Libel Act had given juries a power to decide the merits of defamation cases, and so some sedition prosecutions brought by George III's unpopular ministers had been thrown out in the 1790s. But other cases had succeeded, including hundreds brought for blasphemous libel in the nineteenth century when booksellers were regularly jailed for stocking *The Age of Reason* and one exceedingly pious panel even convicted the publisher of Shelley's *Queen Mab*. Indeed, only one of the hundreds of blasphemy prosecutions in the nineteenth century failed, and that was because the Lord Chief Justice summed up for an acquittal. There was a similarly high success rate for obscenity prosecutions, especially in respect of the works of foreign writers like Zola and Flaubert. Jury verdicts for much of the twentieth century serve further to undermine Dicey's theory: the propertied classes privileged to sit on juries disapproved of radicals, and generally convicted in trials involving libel or official secrecy.

What did give Dicey's theory a new lease of life was the abolition of property and age qualifications for jurors in 1972: the modern jury now has more shoplifters than shopkeepers amongst its numbers. The first beneficiaries of the change were pornographers, who had always been convicted before 1972. Now, they were increasingly acquitted by a younger and more broadminded generation of jurors (after a run of obscenity acquittals at the Old Bailey, Rupert Murdoch felt safe to introduce "Page 3" nudes to *The Sun*). After the acquittal of *Inside Linda Lovelace* in 1977, the DPP decided to mount no further obscenity prosecutions in relation to the written word. In 1985 an Old Bailey jury

---

[4] A. V. Dicey, *An Introduction to the Study of Law of the Constitution*, (10th ed., Macmillan), pp. 246–251.

gave the final push to the discredited section 2 of the Official Secrets Act by acquitting Clive Ponting, despite the fact that he was obviously guilty of breaching it by supplying a Labour M.P. with secret information which falsified government statements about the sinking of the *Belgrano*. There have been other recent examples of juries showing a bias in favour of the freedom to publish, irrespective of the letter of the law or the weight of evidence: in 1992 the pacifists Randle and Pottle were acquitted of helping atom bomb spy George Blake to escape, despite (or because of) the fact that they had written a book confessing their guilt, entitled *The Blake Escape, How we Freed George Blake— and Why*.[5] In the year 2000, juries were still tender to honest radicals, acquitting demonstrators who destroyed genetically modified crops and attacked nuclear submarines. So government law officers are reluctant today to put journalists and publishers in the dock of a criminal court, for fear that "the gang of twelve" will live up to its historic reputation and acquit. For all their determination to pursue David Shayler, an MI5 official who sold his work secrets to *The Mail on Sunday*, the law officers refused to contemplate a prosecution of that newspaper or its journalists who had interviewed him.

The role of trial by jury as a guarantor of free speech is limited in practice to protecting the speech of defendants who are likeable. Unpopular artists, essaying themes which shock or disgust, remain targets for jury prejudice, like *Gay News* in 1977 (convicted for publishing a "blasphemous" poem imagining Christ as a homosexual) and artists convicted for exhibiting "foetal earrings". Moreover, any sympathy towards the press displayed by jurors at the Old Bailey is replaced by hostility as they walk up Fleet Street to the High Court, where they bring back libel verdicts against newspapers. Jurors who would never send a journalist to jail are happy to award heavy damages against his proprietor, even on behalf of the likes of Jeffrey Archer. His award of £500,000 in 1986 (for an editor's logical assumption that since he had paid £2,000 to a prostitute he must have had sex with her) was followed by £1 million to Elton John and a £1.5 million award against the historian Nicolai Tolstoy. Damages of this order severely chilled investigative journalism in Britain during that Conservative era of the '80s and early '90s. Eventually the European Court declared that such massive and unprecedented awards infringed the right to freedom of expression.[6] Now libel damages are unlikely to exceed £200,000, and are invariably outstripped by legal costs.

The practical refutation of Dicey's complacent proposition that trial by jury is the guarantor of free speech is the fact that juries are being

[5] Randle and Pottle, *The Blake Escape, How we Freed George Blake—and Why?* (Harrap).
[6] *Tolstoy Miloslavsky v. United Kingdom* (1995) 20 E.H.R.R. 442.

progressively eliminated. They remain the tribunal for common law crimes that are rarely charged (seditious, blasphemous and criminal libel), for obscenity and official secrecy offences and certain terrorist and "incitement to disaffection' crimes. This is not a long list, because successive British governments have tried to avoid the embarrassment and inconvenience of jury trial where media freedom is involved. They have returned to the "licensing" approach of the Star Chamber by appointing censorship bodies for film, television, video and even computer games and by relying increasingly on civil rather than criminal law to injunct and restrain media publication on grounds of copyright or confidence or official secrecy. Three unattractive expedients used to bypass the jury are—

Obtaining interim injunctions

Claimants—especially the Government—prevail on judges to ban publication for the "interim" period before trial on grounds of confidence or copyright. Suppressed information soon becomes stale, and the case is not worth the cost to the media defendant of fighting a trial a year or so later.

Creating media offences triable only in magistrates courts

Breaches of restrictions on court reporting, for example, which carry fines of up to £5,000, are not triable by jury. In such cases, magistrates are much more likely to convict.

Prosecuting for contempt of court

Contempt carries a maximum penalty of two years and is the only serious crime in English law which is not triable by a jury. Judges in contempt cases are judges in their own cause, and have convicted in many cases where juries would probably have acquitted—*e.g.* Granada Television for refusing to name its "mole" within British Steel; Harriet Harman for giving a journalist access to documents read out in open court; *The Independent* for publishing excerpts from *Spycatcher* at a time when the Government was trying to stop the British public from reading a book on open sale in other countries.

The increasing tendency of governments to avoid the right of jury trial by running to High Court judges or by creating "media offences" punishable only by judges or magistrates is disturbing. A blatant example came in 1981 when it was made a criminal contempt punishable with two years' imprisonment for journalists, after a trial was over, to interview jurors about their deliberations. The crime was necessary, said the lawyer-M.P.s who supported the legislation, to preserve the integrity of the jury system. This integrity was hardly preserved by stripping jurors of their right to free speech by a new criminal offence that itself carried no right to trial by jury.

Where a right to trial by jury exists, the Attorney-General should not side-step it by approaching the High Court for an injunction to stop the publication or for a declaration that the publication is unlawful:

> The Voluntary Euthanasia Society published a booklet entitled *A Guide to Self-Deliverance*, which discussed the pros and cons of committing suicide and described in detail a number of efficacious methods for so doing. After evidence came to light that some members of the Society had committed suicide by following methods described in the booklet, the Attorney-General sought to dissuade the Society from further dissemination of the *Guide* by applying to the High Court for a declaration that its publication amounted to the crime of aiding and abetting suicide. But this offence carries the right to jury trial, and the judge declined to usurp the jury's role by declaring that future conduct by the Society would necessarily amount to an offence.[7]

The principle that judges in civil courts must not usurp the jury's role of deciding a publisher's guilt or innocence is of some constitutional importance, although today it is limited to occasional trials of publishers of material alleged to be obscene or officially secret or provocative of racial hatred. The jury functions as a regular media law tribunal only in civil defamation actions, where either party has a right to demand jury trial "unless the court is of the opinion that the trial requires any prolonged examination of documents" and the involvement of a jury would be "inconvenient" when compared to the savings in time and costs if the trial were heard by a judge sitting alone.[8] Although the court even then retains a discretion to order jury trial, the modern reluctance to do so is demonstrated by the case of *Aitken v. Preston*:

> Jonathan Aitken was a cabinet minister when *The Guardian* and *World in Action* accused him of procuring women for Arab clients, illegal arms-dealing and lying about a junket to the Ritz in Paris. Some of the allegations involved extensive documentary evidence, but *The Guardian* demanded that the claimant's integrity—or lack of it—should be decided by a jury, given the public perception that a jury verdict was more credible than that of a judge. The Court of Appeal, however, reached a contrary conclusion: the claimant's political standing meant that the public interest would be better served by a reasoned judgment, which by setting out the basis for its conclusions, would settle the allegations more authoritatively

---

[7] *Att.-Gen. v. Able* [1984] 1 All E.R. 277; and see *Gouriet v. Union of Post Office Workers* [1978] A.C. 435.

[8] Supreme Court Act 1981, s. 69, and see *Safeways Stores v. Albert Tate*, December 19, 2000, when the Court of Appeal held that s. 69 at least guaranteed an option for jury trial which could not be overborne by Civil Procedure Rules which allowed summary judgment in defamation cases.

than a jury's verdict encapsulated in an answer "yes" or "no" to the question of whether he had been defamed.[9]

The reasoning in *Aitken* must apply whether there are documents to examine or not: a detailed judgment is preferred—by judges—to a monosyllabic jury verdict. Judges naturally think that they afford quicker, cheaper and cleverer justice than the pooled wisdom of twelve citizens selected at random, but editors (especially of newspapers like *The Guardian*, regularly sued by unprepossessing politicians) feel that a jury would give them a fairer hearing and be more robust about inferring corrupt conduct. (Some evidence for this is provided by the "cash for questions" case in 1999, when the jury preferred to credit the earthy accusations of Harrods boss Al Fayed over the slick dissemblings of ex-MP Neil Hamilton.) However, tabloid editors sued by celebrities worry that jurors are dazzled by actors and soap-stars, whose complaints would underwhelm judges who do not watch them on television. So on the one hand, the media which bear the burden of proving truth can have that unfair burden lightened by the fact that "a jury can do justice, whereas the judge, who has to follow the law, may not".[10] On the other, jury sympathy is readily attracted to claimants who sit with tear-jerking family members carefully positioned directly in front of the jury box throughout the trial. Juries gave ludicrously high awards in the days before defamation damages were capped, culminating in a £600,000 award to the wife of serial killer Peter Sutcliffe which famously provoked *Private Eye* editor Ian Hislop to exclaim "If that's justice, I'm a banana". This case prompted the Court of Appeal to abandon its non-interventionist approach to jury verdicts, which have now, with help from the European Convention, been brought under control, but the punitive behaviour of civil juries towards newspapers has helped to persuade many that "it may now be over-romantic to conceive of juries as champions of freedom of speech as in the days of Penn and Mead".[11] In 2001 the Court of Appeal, for the first time, overturned a star-struck jury verdict on the ground that it was irrational in failing to comprehend all the evidence of corruption against the claimant, Bruce Grobbelaar.[12]

The *Aitken* principle that public interest is better served by a reasoned verdict is a logical development if society looks to the courtroom as a mechanism for extracting and declaring truth. In criminal cases juries are not truth-finders, but rather decide whether guilt has been proven "beyond reasonable doubt". Most of those they acquit are in fact guilty, but have not been proven guilty to that high standard. But if society

---

[9] *Aitken v. Preston & Ors* [1997] E.M.L.R. 415.
[10] Lord Devlin, *Trial by Jury: the Hamlyn Lecture*, (1956, rev. ed. Stevens, 1966).
[11] Lord Cooke, *Reynolds v. Times Newspapers Ltd* [2001] 2 A.C. 127 at 226.
[12] *Grobbelaar v. News Group Newspapers Ltd* [2001] 2 All E.R. 437.

requires a symbolic public endorsement then "the verdict of the jury" carries the most popular imprimatur. Judges, anyway, can be lacking in street-wisdom and "common sense" and are always constrained by the rules of evidence. The Court of Appeal became quite starry-eyed in *Aitken* about the virtues of a reasoned judgment, ignoring the many reasoned judgments which history has shown to be based on tainted evidence or poor logic or social bias or simple ignorance of the way of the world. A libel action, it must be remembered, is not a Royal Commission, or any sort of inquisitive proceeding in which the judge acts as investigator of truth: he or she remains an adjudicator between adversary parties, confined to the limited evidence they are capable of calling. The trial is less appropriate as a vehicle for discovering truth than as a process for declaring and enforcing "rights", with the judge's main task to strike an overall compromise between (in libel) the right of free speech and the right of reputation, with the latter accorded respect to the extent that it does no serious damage to the former. The case of *Reynolds v. Times Newspapers* in 1999 created a "public interest privilege" in libel actions, the occasions for which are to be decided by the judge. The result will be a partnership role in which the judge will decide whether the press has qualified for a free speech defence and the jury will decide whether it has been made out.

THE OPEN JUSTICE PRINCIPLE

One of the few examples of a free speech "right" embedded in the British common law is the principle that justice must not only be done but must be seen to be done and hence "Every court in the land is open to every subject of the King." This was given the force of a constitutional principle by the House of Lords in the case of *Scott v. Scott* in 1913, which adopted Jeremy Bentham's rationale:

> "Publicity is the very soul of justice. It is the keenest spur to exertion and the surest of all guards against improbity. It keeps the judge himself, while trying, under trial. . . .".[13]

What Bentham was rationalising and applauding in this passage was not so much a public right as a tradition: the English court hearing emerged from the Middle Ages looking (and sounding) like an ill-conducted public meeting. Publicity was needed in order to attract witnesses to the trial and to promote the deterrent effect of the punishment, as well as serving to keep judges up to the mark and improving the

---

[13] *Scott v. Scott* [1913] A.C. 417, approving Bentham at 447.

behaviour of lawyers. But the "open justice" principle can also be characterised as an aspect of free speech:

> "Whether or not judicial virtue needs such a spur, there is also another important interest involved in justice done openly, namely that the evidence and argument should be publicly known, so that society may judge for itself the quality of justice administered in its name, and whether the law requires modification ... the common law by its recognition of the principle of open justice ensures that the public administration of justice will be subject to public scrutiny. Such scrutiny serves no purpose unless it is accompanied by the rights of free speech, *i.e.* the right publicly to report, to discuss, to comment, to criticise, to impart and to receive ideas and information on the matters subjected to scrutiny. Justice is done in public so it may be discussed and criticised in public".[14]

Open justice has other important virtues. The prospect of publicity deters perjury: witnesses are more likely to tell the truth if they know that any lie they tell might be reported and provoke others to come forward to discredit them. Media reporting of court cases enhances public knowledge and appreciation of the workings of the law, and it assists the deterrent effect of heavy jail sentences in criminal cases. Above all, fidelity to the open justice principle keeps Britain free from the reproach that it permits "secret courts" of the kind that have been instruments of repression in so many other countries.

The case that comes closest to accepting the principle as a rule of law enforceable by journalists is *R. v. Felixstowe Justices, ex p. Leigh*:[15]

> David Leigh, an experienced reporter on *The Observer*, was writing an article about a controversial case that had been heard in Felixstowe Magistrates' Court. The clerk of the court refused to supply him with the names of the lay justices who had decided it, pursuant to a policy that was being adopted by an increasing number of magistrates' courts of declining to identify justices to the public or the press. Leigh, with the backing of his newspaper and the NUJ, brought an action against the justices in the High Court, which granted him a declaration that the policy of anonymity was "inimical to the proper administration of justice and an unwarranted and unlawful obstruction to the right to know who sits in judgment". The judgment endorsed the importance of the court reporter as "the watchdog of justice", and the vital significance of press comment and criticism of the behaviour of judges and magistrates. Although there was no specific statutory requirement that justices should be named, the court deduced

---

[14] *Home Office v. Harman* [1982] 1 All E.R. 532 at 546–7 *per* Lord Scarman.
[15] *R v. Felixstowe Justices, ex p. Leigh* [1987] 1 All E.R. 551.

such a requirement from the fundamental nature of the open justice principle.

The importance of *Leigh* is that the court was prepared to treat the
open justice principle as a "right", namely as an enforceable rule of
law that could be asserted by a journalist to strike down a discretionary
policy, rather than merely as a desirable state of affairs that could none
the less give way to judicial convenience. This is, in effect, the distinction between a "right" enforceable by a citizen-journalist against the
State, and a paternalistic system which promises free speech but when
it comes to the crunch, always "balances" that value against private
rights that judges think are important, like reputation and State claims
to national security. Just how little value may be placed in the balance
on the side of press freedom is demonstrated by the majority of law
lords in *Home Office v. Harman*, which held solicitor Harriet Harman
in contempt for showing documents to David Leigh, though they had
been read out in open court. This decision (overtly influenced by the
fact that the documents were used to criticise the Government's prisons
policy) is a typical pre-Convention balancing act, where free speech—
in this case, informed criticism of government—is given little or no
weight against property rights, government policy, and a procedural rule
that documents disclosed by a party in a civil action should only be
used for the purposes of that action. The majority judges were unable
to recognise a wider purpose of informing the public about the issues
in the action. Harriet Harman M.P. took her case to Strasbourg, where
the British Government was forced to concede that the decision against
her was a breach of Article 10 of the Convention. The Rules of the
Supreme Court were in consequence changed to allow general use of
documents once they had been read in open court—an ironic example
of how the European Convention can still be necessary to enforce a
principle that derives from, and should be fundamental to, British
domestic law.
    Article 6 guarantees the right of everyone on trial, whether for a
criminal offence or as party to a civil action, to "a fair and *public*
hearing". However, it goes on in Euro-weasel mode:

> "Judgment shall be pronounced publicly but the press and public
> may be excluded from all or part of the trial in the interests of
> morals, public order, or national security in a democratic society,
> where the interests of juveniles or the protection of the private life
> of the parties so require, or to the extent strictly necessary in the
> opinion of the Court in special circumstances where publicity
> would prejudice the interests of justice".

These exceptions are actually *wider* than United Kingdom domestic law allows under the "open justice" principle of *Scott v. Scott*, which confines the common law and limits exceptions to those contained in statutes passed by Parliament (which in recent years, unfortunately, have become legion). British courts have refused, for example, to permit "secret trials" on grounds of morals or public order, or to uphold gagging orders imposed to protect the private lives of witnesses or parties. The press has not needed the Convention to challenge successfully such diverse rulings as an order not to name a witness from a famous family lest publicity might interfere with her cure for heroin addiction[16]; an order not to publish the address of a former MP defendant lest his estranged wife should discover his whereabouts and harass him[17]; and an order that reporters should leave the court so that a distressed defendant could explain in privacy the matrimonial problems that drove her to drink before she drove her car.[18] In all these cases trial courts had been moved by personal plight to overlook the fundamental principle that trials must be open in every respect. That this great principle is firmer in British domestic law than in the European Convention gives rise to an important question, namely whether the incorporation of the Convention could operate to cut down any of the basic rights that are already enjoyed—in this case, a basic English right which was watered down by the Convention draftsmen to accommodate the less vigorous practice in other European jurisdictions. The answer is found in section 11 of the Human Rights Act, headed "safeguard for existing human rights" which provides:

"11. A person's reliance on a Convention right does not restrict –

   (a) any other right or freedom conferred on him by or under any law having effect in any part of the United Kingdom. . . .".

This means that whenever the media or its lawyers wish to oppose applications for secret hearings or gag orders, it would be a grave mistake to rely on Article 6 of the Convention alone, because this is more restrictive than the historic principle which emerges from the common law as declared in *Scott v. Scott*. Section 11 will in many cases have to be invoked to *prevent* judges from knee-jerk applications of an Article 6 exception, on the basis that a much more generous right of court reporting had crystallised in English law by 1998 and cannot be cut back by the mealy-mouthed exceptions in Article 6. It is even open to question whether Article 6 can be invoked at all by the press—the right to a public hearing is vouchsafed to the defendant, usually the very party who wants secrecy in order to avoid embarrassment.

---

[16] *R v. Central Criminal Court, ex p. Crook, The Times*, November 8, 1984.
[17] *R. v. Evesham Justices, ex p. McDonagh* [1988] 1 All E.R. 371.
[18] *R. v. Malvern Justices, ex p. Evans* [1988] 1 All E.R. 371.

There are nonetheless an increasing number of statutory exceptions to the open justice principle, settled in the United Kingdom by Parliament often with little or no debate, and no objection from Britain's unaware and unorganised media interests. Some of these are reasonable. For example, rape victims are entitled to anonymity in order to mitigate their humiliation and to encourage other victims to come forward. In youth courts, juvenile offenders may not be identified; the public and press may be excluded from Official Secrets Act trials where publication of the evidence might endanger national security, and the testimony given at pre-trial criminal proceedings usually cannot be published until the trial is over, to avoid prejudicing the jury. But other restrictions are less justifiable; the least being the law which enables judges to prevent publication of derogatory allegations in mitigation speeches and the practice of permitting injunctions against Sunday newspapers to be granted by judges on the telephone on Saturday, without any recording of the call let alone any provision that transcripts of it should be publicly available. Other secretive practices have been discouraged by the recent civil procedure reforms, such as the routine exclusion of the media from in-chambers hearings relating to property in divorce cases, to bail applications in Crown Courts, and to some applications for injunctions in the Queen's Bench Division of the High Court. These breaches of the open justice principle are incompatible with the rule in *Scott v. Scott* and must now face a presumption in favour of public hearings.[19] That it remains important to remind courts—and especially tribunals—of the constitutional necessity of complying with this rule is exemplified by the recent case of *R v. London (North) Industrial Tribunal, ex p. Associated Newspapers*[20];

> Council tax payers and ratepayers in North London were interested in, and doubtless appalled by the expense of, claims of sex discrimination and victimisation brought against Camden Council and its chief executive by his deputy, the Council solicitor. After the case received embarrassing coverage in the local press, Camden's Q.C. persuaded the employment tribunal that it would be better for everyone if the public hearings were not reported at all, at least until after the judgment. Local newspapers (the *Camden New Journal* and the *Ham and High*) protested in vain by letter, but lacked the funds to challenge this improper gag. *The Mail on Sunday* did so by judicial review, whereupon the High Court, applying *Scott v. Scott* and *Leigh v. Felixstowe*, held that the Tribunal should not have

---

[19] See CPR, r. 39.2 and the Practice Direction under CPR, Part 39, para. 1, which followed a decision favouring open justice in civil cases by Lord Woolf: *Hodgson v. Imperial Tobacco* [1998] 1 W.L.R. 1056.

[20] *R. v. London (North) Industrial Tribunal, ex p. Associated Newspapers* [1998] I.C.R. 1212.

made the order. Although it had a statutory power to restrict reporting of evidence which identified persons affected by allegations of sexual misconduct, the open justice principle required that this power should only apply to those involved in the incident. It could not possibly be used to hide the name of the Council or the Chief Executive. Public reporting of judicial proceedings was a "fundamental constitutional principle" said Mr Justice Keane: it was so firmly embedded in English law that only statutory inroads were permissible, and they must be interpreted as narrowly as possible.

The judge in this case accepted that the European Convention added nothing to the common law principle of open justice: indeed, Articles 10 and 6, even when read together, only pallidly reflect the force of the rule in *Scott v. Scott.* So these English case precedents remain more helpful than the Convention in the continual battle against magistrates and judges and members of tribunals who will always believe in their hearts that the press should report only their judgment at the end of a case, and not confuse the public by prior reporting of the evidence.

One interesting application of the open justice principle is that reporters are accorded special status as "representatives" or "watchdogs" of the public. They should be invited to come into court in circumstances where it is inconvenient for the public to be admitted. In *R v. Waterfield* the trial judge had cleared the court while the jury was shown allegedly obscene films, fearing that "gasps, giggling and comment" from the press bench and the public gallery might distract the jurors from their solemn duty. The Court of Appeal said that the press should have been allowed to remain:

". . . the public generally are interested in cases of this kind, and for not unworthy reasons. Concepts of sexual morality are changing. Whenever a jury in this class of case returns a verdict, whether of guilty or not guilty, intelligent readers of newspapers and weekly journals may want to know what kind of film was under consideration. Experience during the past decades has shown that every acquittal tends to lead to the greater exposure to public gaze of what previous generations thought seemly only in private, if seemly anywhere. Members of the public have to depend on the press for information on which to base their opinions; but if allegedly indecent films are always shown in closed courtrooms the press cannot give the public the information which it may want and which is necessary for the formation of public opinion . . . . It follows, so it seems to us, that normally, when a film is being shown to a jury and the judge, in the exercise of his discretion, decides that it should be done in a closed courtroom or in a cinema,

he should allow representatives of the press to be present. No harm
can be done by doing so: some good may result".[21]

Parliament has given journalists the right to be present, even though
the rest of the public is excluded, in the case of youth courts[22] and
family proceedings in magistrates' courts.[23] Similarly, the public but not
the press can be kept out of an adult court while a child or young person
gives evidence in relation to a sex offence.[24]

The principle that the press may remain to represent the public should
be applied in every case where a judge decides to clear the public gallery, except where national security is demonstrably at stake. Judges
have power to order any reporting to be postponed until the end of the
trial, and should do so rather than take the more Draconian course of
excluding the press. Secret hearings are wrong in principle and (with
the alternative of postponement orders under the Contempt of Court Act
1981) are unnecessary in practice. Journalists should be fully conversant
with their rights to appeal against any exclusion from the courtroom or
any secrecy order made under the Contempt of Court Act. These rights
are contained in section 159 of the Criminal Justice Act 1988 and the
rules made thereunder, and are set out in detail in Chapter 8.

The principle of open justice has its physical symbol—the press
bench—in almost every courtroom. This piece of furniture has become
something of a shibboleth: both the Magistrates' Association and the
NUJ have said that it should be regarded as sacrosanct. This attitude
may have the effect of blunting the critical edge of press coverage, by
encouraging court reporters to perceive themselves as part and parcel
of the court process, rather than as objective critics of its workings.
However, the press should jealously protect its right to sit centre-stage
in the interests of audibility and accuracy. As the United States Supreme
Court has put it, while media representatives enjoy the same right of
access as the public, they are often provided with special seating and
priority of entry so that they may report what people in attendance have
seen and heard. This contributes to the public understanding of the rule
of law and to comprehension of the functioning of the entire criminal
justice system.[25] See "Stop Press" section for further details.

---

[21] [1975] 2 All E.R. 40.
[22] Children and Young Persons Act 1933, s. 47(2).
[23] Magistrates' Courts Act 1980, s. 69(2).
[24] Children and Young Persons Act 1933, s. 37(1).
[25] *Richmond Newspapers Inc. v. Commonwealth of Virginia*, 448 U.S. 555 (1980) at
    587, and see *Re Andrew Dunn and the Morning Bulletin Ltd* (1932) St. R. Qd. 1 at
    p. 15 where the existence of a press bench was said to be a crown command sanc-
    tioned by custom and common sense: on this basis, any decision to remove or
    requisition it for an overflow of lawyers might be challengeable.

THE RULE AGAINST PRIOR RESTRAINT

The British contribution to the philosophy of free speech might be summed up in the Duke of Wellington's phrase "publish and be damned". The media is free to publish and be damned, so long as damnation comes after, and not before, the word gets out. Journalists cannot claim to be above the law, but what they can claim, in every country that takes free speech seriously, is a right to publish first, and take the risk of conviction afterwards. Cromwell destroyed that liberty by appointing 27 fit and proper persons—schoolmasters, lawyers, ministers of religion, doctors (the sort of people found nowadays in the regulatory bodies for broadcasting and video)—to censor public reading. They were obliged to reject any book that was "contrary to good life or good manners". (Their modern counterparts are obliged to reject any television programme that is offensive to public feeling, good taste or decency.) The public grew to hate the licensors, and after their abolition the rule against prior restraint was given definitive shape by the venerated legal writer Blackstone:

> "The liberty of the press is indeed essential to the nature of a free state; but this consists in laying no previous restraints on publications, and not in freedom from censure for criminal matter when published. Every free man has an undoubted right to lay what sentiments he pleases before the public; to forbid this is to destroy the freedom of the press; but if he publishes what is improper, mischievous or illegal, he must take the consequences of his own temerity."[26]

It was this message that went out in the eighteenth century, and became enshrined in the First Amendment to the American Constitution. It was endorsed by the Supreme Court, in its historic *Pentagon Papers* decision. The United States Government learnt of the *New York Times'* plan to publish a set of confidential army research papers on the history of American involvement in Vietnam. It tried to injunct the newspaper, on the ground that the papers contained military and diplomatic secrets, the disclosure of which would substantially damage the national interest. The Supreme Court refused:

> "Any system of prior restraint on expression comes to this court bearing a heavy presumption against its constitutional validity. The only effective restraint upon executive policy and power in the areas of national defence and international affairs may be an

---

[26] William Blackstone, *Commentaries on the laws of England*, 1765, Book IV, pp. 151–2.

enlightened citizenry—informed and critical public opinion which alone can here protect the values of democratic government. For without an informed and free press there cannot be an enlightened people."[27]

The justices accepted that publication of those documents would harm the national interest and might even make the newspaper guilty of a criminal offence. But it was entitled to publish and be damned. Only when the Government could prove that disclosure would cause "grave and irreparable injury to the public interest"—details, for example, of troop deployment in wartime or information that might trigger a nuclear war—was a court entitled to stop the presses.

The rule against prior restraint thus became, for the U.S., a constitutional consequence of the First Amendment. In England it was no more than an application of the general common law maxim that everything is permitted except that which is expressly forbidden—or retrospectively forbidden by a verdict of guilt or award of damages. In libel actions the principle has held up well, and there is a plethora of precedents for the proposition that no injunction will be granted to stop the circulation of defamatory statements prior to trial if the media defendant declares on affidavit that it intends to justify the defamation as true or else to plead fair comment or privilege.[28] However, the lack of any constitutional provision in the United Kingdom has meant that before the Human Rights Act came into force the rule against prior restraint became badly eroded in other areas of media law. Applications for injunctions, which impose prior restraint by stopping presses from rolling and film from running, are most commonly based on a complaint that the information about to be revealed has been obtained in breach of confidence. Where that information relates to national security, all that the Government has to show is that publication might cause *some* injury to the national interest—a test that would ensure that the British equivalent of the *Pentagon Papers* would never see the light of day.

This main exception to the rule against prior restraint, namely the interim injunction granted for an alleged breach of confidence, was (until the Human Rights Act) generally decided upon the "balance of convenience" test (called the *American Cynamid* test after the case in which it was first enunciated—a case which had nothing to do with media freedom). All that the claimant needed do to obtain a restraining order was to show a prima facie (*i.e.* arguable) case, and that the public interest in protecting the confidence was not, on the "balance of con-

---

[27] *New York Times v. U.S.*, 403 U.S. 713 (1971) at 729.
[28] *Bonnard v. Perryman* (1891) 2 Ch. 269 (justification); *Quartz Hill Consolidated Mining v. Beal* (1882) 20 Ch. D. 501 (privilege); *Fraser v. Evans* (1969) 1 Q.B. 349 (fair comment).

venience", outweighed by some urgent public interest in publication. In cases involving alleged military secrets, the courts have virtually applied a presumption in favour of granting the injunction until trial on the basis that if the information is allowed into the public domain the Government will be unable to repair the damage. Although in every case the judge must balance the commercial or property rights of the claimant in controlling the information against the value of the defendant's right of free speech, for many judges brought up in a world that accords pre-eminent value to rights of property, this seemed like balancing hard cash against hot air.

One of the worst examples of prior restraint was the injunction that stopped the scheduled screening of a Thames Television documentary on the pregnancy drug Primodos, because its director, David Elstein, had picked up the idea for the story while privately training the directors of the claimant—the company which manufactured the drug. Lord Denning thought the programme should be shown:

> " . . . the *public* interest in receiving information about the drug Primodos and its effects far outweighs the *private* interest of the makers in preventing discussion of it."[29]

He was outvoted by his brethren. One said:

> "The law of England is indeed, as Blackstone declared, a law of liberty; but the freedoms it recognises do not include a licence for the mercenary betrayal of business confidences."[30]

This misses Blackstone's point. The rule against prior restraint is designed to allow publishers to publish even if this means betraying a confidence—a betrayal that, as Lord Denning points out, may be very much in the public interest—so long as they pay any damages that may be appropriate. Nonetheless, this decision—in the early '80s—reflected a typical tendency among judges to give property values more weight than media freedom. This tendency reached extraordinary heights during the *Spycatcher* litigation, when a majority of Law Lords at one point narrowly upheld an interim injunction on newspapers publishing details from a book that was on open sale throughout the rest of the world, numerous copies of which were circulating in Britain.[31] This decision was ludicrous: all confidentiality in the information had evaporated with overseas publication, and no additional damage to the national interest could possibly have been done by re-publication of the

---

[29] *Schering Chemicals Ltd v. Falkman Ltd* [1981] 2 All E.R. 321, at 334.
[30] *ibid.* at 338.
[31] *Att.-Gen. v. Guardian Newspapers Ltd* [1987] 3 All E.R. 316.

contents of the book in the British press. The majority judges evinced patriotic hostility to an MI5 turncoat and his publishers, whose profits they said they were entitled to curtail (although it was their own newsworthy action in banning the book which continued to increase the world-wide sales). The House of Lords in two subsequent cases has retreated from the position it adopted in the original *Spycatcher* litigation, by making plain that the Government must prove some damage to the national interest and that no such damage can be established where the information has already been placed in the public domain by being published abroad.

The European Court of Human Rights in 1991 held that the continuing injunction on publishing *Spycatcher* in Britain long after it had become a best-seller in other countries was an infringement of the Article 10 guarantee of freedom of expression. A narrow majority of the judges was not persuaded, however, that Article 10 prohibited prior restraint in all circumstances, at least when governments were concerned to protect security information that had not yet seen the light of day. But it did acknowledge that:

> ". . . the dangers inherent in prior restraints are such that they call for the most careful scrutiny on the part of the Court. This is especially so as far as the press is concerned, for news is a perishable commodity and to delay its publication, even for a short period, may well deprive it of its value and interest." [32-33]

It follows that courts in Britain, in order to comply with the Convention, must accept "newsworthiness" as a public interest value that weighs heavily against the grant of an interim injunction sought against newspapers and broadcast organisations. Although the majority of Euro-judges did not strike down the "balance of convenience" *American Cynamid* test, five dissenting judges would have done so, on the ground that punishment should come after publication and not before, except in circumstances defined in the Convention as:

> "a time of war or other public emergency threatening the life of the nation" and even then only "to the extent strictly required by the exigencies of the situation".

This approach now accords with section 12 of the Human Rights Act, which requires courts to give special consideration to free speech claims in deciding whether to grant interim injunctions. Thus Posh Spice and husband David Beckham were unable to stop author Andrew Morton

---

[32-33] *The Observer and Guardian v. United Kingdom* (1991) 14 E.H.R.R. 153, para. 60.

from publishing, after the Human Rights Act came into operation, a biography of them which drew on confidential revelations from their bodyguard.

The most enduring damage done by the *Spycatcher* litigation to the rule against prior restraint was the emergence of a legal doctrine that once a secrecy injunction has been granted against one newspaper, every other section of the media becomes effectively bound by its terms, on pain of punishment for contempt:

> *The Guardian* ran a news story that briefly referred to certain allegations made by Peter Wright in *Spycatcher*. The Government sued for breach of confidence and obtained an "interim injunction" against it repeating the story prior to the trial. Before Wright's trial in Australia took place, *The Independent* came into possession of the manuscript of *Spycatcher* and published a much more detailed account of the book's contents. Instead of proceeding against *The Independent* for breach of confidence, the Government prosecuted it for contempt of court, committed by flouting the spirit of the injunction imposed on *The Guardian. The Independent* argued that it could not in natural justice be bound by order made against another newspaper, on different facts, and which it had been given no opportunity to oppose. The Court of Appeal, however, ruled that every newspaper that had notice of the original injunction against *The Guardian* was under an obligation to comply with its terms until it was discharged.[34] The House of Lords subsequently confirmed that a third party, although not bound by an injunction restraining another newspaper from publishing confidential information, was guilty of contempt if it nullified the purpose of the original proceedings by destroying the confidentiality of the information, *i.e.* by publishing it.[35]

The doctrine that an injunction against one publication can effectively bind all who know of it seriously undermines the rule against prior restraint. It means that a claimant (often, the Government) with no more than an arguable case for suppressing a story on breach of confidence grounds can obtain, at a secret High Court hearing, an injunction against one defendant (perhaps a journal whose financial position does not permit a legal contest) and thereafter try to enforce it against every media outlet in the country. Although the doctrine was created in the course of a panicked reaction by the courts to bogus claims of a national security peril asserted by the Thatcher Government, it has subsequently been exploited by private corporations wishing to keep their secrets under wraps. It requires newspapers which wish to publish stories about a matter some aspect of which is affected by an injunction against another publication, to apply to the court for guidance on whether their

---

[34] *Att.-Gen. v. Newspaper Publishing plc* [1987] 3 All E.R. 276, CA.
[35] *Att.-Gen. v. Times Newspapers Ltd* [1992] 1 A.C. 191, HL.

story trespasses upon the order already in existence—a procedure calculated in national security cases to give the Government the whip hand. This is because the Treasury Solicitor, acting for the security services, must be notified, and he can make life very expensive for publishers by opposing and appealing any relaxation. "We have a bottomless purse" was the very first threat made by the Treasury Solicitor's office to the managing director of Heinemann, to dissuade him from publishing *Spycatcher*. (When this failed, MI5 sent an emissary to Heinemann's owner, Paul Hamlyn, threatening that he would never get a peerage if he published—a threat that made him even keener to do so. His peerage was amongst the first announced by the new Labour Government.)

The erosion of the rule against prior restraint by judges granting "interim injunctions" to restrain alleged breaches of confidence and copyright has been the most noticeable example of the law's failure to develop a coherent and principled approach to media freedom. Since the passage of the Human Rights Act the courts have been inclined to allow newspaper editors more freedom to determine for themselves whether publication will breach an existing injunction, and have notably rejected the Government's contention that they must first submit their article to the Attorney-General for clearance.[36] The absurdity of the *Spycatcher* ban was the result of a dogged judicial insistence on viewing the memoirs of a former MI5 employee as the "property" of the Government, and conducting the litigation as if he had stolen the office furniture. The "balance of convenience" approach is now questionable in light of the Human Rights Act (section 12 and Article 10) and does not apply in libel actions, where the rule against prior restraint still operates. No injunction will be granted to restrain the repetition of an allegedly libellous statement if the publishers indicate an intention to call evidence at the trial to prove the truth of their statement, or to defend it as honest comment. This *is* a firm rule, and it means that the courts will not force publishers to withdraw or recall books and magazines from distribution if they are prepared to swear an affidavit verifying their intention to justify the allegation that is the subject-matter of the libel. Another example of the rule against prior restraint is the *Voluntary Euthanasia Society* case, where the Attorney-General was refused an injunction against a publication the authors of which were entitled to have the legality of their actions decided at a trial before a jury. On this principle it has been authoritatively stated that no injunction should be granted by the civil courts to restrain the dissemination of allegedly obscene books, as such a step would pre-empt the ultimate decision of a jury.[37]

The rule against prior restraint will not always prevail over the sanc-

---

[36] *Att.-Gen. v. Punch*, [2001] E.M.L.R. 24.
[37] Viscount Dilhorne in *Gouriet v. Union of Post Office Workers*, note 7 above.

tity of contract, however, and individuals who voluntarily agree to give up freedom of speech in return for employment or payment can be held to their bargain, if necessary by the court granting injunctive relief against publication, unless their revelations are trivial or have been published elsewhere or are important to the public interest. In 1990 the Court of Appeal had no hesitation in injuncting a former royal servant from publishing anywhere in the world his memoirs of life with the Royal Family. It dismissed the notion that a defence to the breach might be mounted on the basis that the secrecy clause in his employment contract was void as contrary to public policy, because it would deny to foreigners their rights to receive information.[38] The British courts are traditionally over-protective of royal privacy, and in other cases, where the public interest in the information is genuine, claimants may be refused an injunction and left to their remedy (if any) in damages.[39] Decided cases suggest that in practice judges are predisposed to permit Royals and the security service to gag disloyal employees, but are sceptical of the rights of other employers like Mohammed Al Fayed, whose attempts to enforce confidentiality clauses against disloyal employees have always been rejected.

In deciding whether to grant an injunction, the court must at least overcome the presumption that free speech will not be restrained before trial of any action which seeks to suppress it. Exactly how much weight it is given will depend on the personal values of the judge and the interest value of the story. But however damaging to individuals may be the consequences of a publication, the right to free speech must prevail unless the individuals possess an established legal right that the publication would infringe:

> In the case of *Re X (A Minor)* the mother and stepfather of a sensitive 14-year-old girl sought to stop publication of a book that ascribed depraved and immoral behaviour to her deceased father. There was evidence that the book, if published, would almost certainly come to her attention, and would cause her serious psychological damage. The judge at first instance invoked the wardship powers of the court to protect the girl: he weighed her interests against that of the publishers, and concluded that the balance came down in favour of restraining publication, since the book could be rendered harmless by excising a few paragraphs. The Court of Appeal held that this was an incorrect approach. Even if there were no public interest in publication, the right to free speech could not in principle be subordinated to the welfare of an individual whose established legal

---

[38] *Att.-Gen. v. Barker* [1990] 3 All E.R. 257.
[39] See, for example, the decision of Kerr L.J. in *Cambridge Nutrition Ltd v. BBC* [1990] 3 All E.R. 523, CA, where a company marketing a controversial diet was refused an injunction to stop a BBC programme notwithstanding a claim that the makers were in breach of contract.

rights were not infringed. The court had a duty to protect the liberty to publish, by ensuring that the existing ambit of restraints was not extended.[40]

The *Spycatcher* principle that prior restraint is impermissible in respect of information which has already been placed in the public domain (even if it is the international and not the domestic domain) must apply despite the fact that the activity of the defendant has placed it there. That was the conclusion of the European Court in *Vereniging Weekblad BLUF! v. The Netherlands*, where that Government had seized the print-run of a left-wing newspaper (BLUF!), which had reproduced an internal report from its secret service. The editors immediately reprinted and defiantly distributed several thousand copies to crowds on the streets of Amsterdam. Applying *Spycatcher*, the Court held that this action destroyed the confidentiality of the material, so the order to withdraw the edition could no longer be maintained as necessary in a democratic society. The Dutch Government's argument that this was tantamount to accepting that "crime pays" was rejected by pointing out that the editors could have been prosecuted for distributing State secrets: what was impermissible was to restrain such material at a point when it was no longer secret.[41] This approach is something of a cop-out: a technical way for the court to invalidate an act of censorship without deriding a Government which has behaved oppressively (the report obtained by *BLUF!* proved the Dutch secret service had targeted the anti-nuclear movement so there was a public interest justification for reproducing it). The Court always adopts a restrained approach in these politically delicate cases. A good example is Ireland's abortion obsessions, when clinics were banned from telling women about the availability of abortions in other countries. Instead of condemning the Irish judges for their bigotry, the Court decided that since the information could be found by opening a telephone book, the ban on clinics providing it was "disproportionate".[42] Where injunctions serve no religious or security purpose, the Court may venture to be more outspoken. When the Swiss courts, at the behest of the manufacturers of microwave ovens, misused an unfair competition law to stop a "nutty professor" from expounding his views about the dangers to human health from irradiated food, this violation was vigorously condemned as censorship of an opinion which was fully entitled to be heard in public debate.[43]

The rule against prior restraint, so comprehensively ignored by

---

[40] *Re X (A Minor)* [1975] 1 All E.R. 697, CA.
[41] *Vereniging Weekblad BLUF! v. The Netherlands* (1995) 20 E.H.R.R. 189.
[42] *Open Door Counselling and Dublin Well Women Clinic v. Ireland* (1993) 15 E.H.R.R. 244.
[43] *Hertel v. Switzerland* (1998) 28 E.H.R.R. 534.

English courts during the *Spycatcher* debacle, is now making a come-back, at least in cases which do not concern royalty, national security or children. In refusing to stop the Advertising Standards Association from publishing an adjudication which was subject to judicial review, Mr Justice Laws spoke (albeit unhistorically) of freedom of expression as a "sinew" of the common law, with a "traditional" principle that "the courts will not prevent the publication of opinion or the dissemination of opinion save on pressing grounds".[44] In an important development of prisoners' rights, the Court of Appeal refused the Home Secretary an injunction to stop transmission of a television documentary which included an unapproved prison interview with serial killer Dennis Neilson. The Government's claim that this would distress his victims' relations cut no ice (they could always switch off) and there was a public interest in the programme, if only in showing why the remorseless Neilson should never be released. Although the way in which the programme-makers had obtained the video of the interview was murky and probably unlawful, the Court declined to grant an injunction by applying the "balance of convenience" test, which would of course have suppressed the film until after a trial a year or so in the future.[45] However, the Courts have been much more anxious about media impact on children, and the paternalistic judges in the family division often injunct programmes about juveniles, however great the public interest. The most extreme example, *Re Z*, (these cases are all reported under the acronym of "X" "Y" or "Z") related to an inspirational television programme about a child who overcame learning difficulties with the help of a revolutionary learning technique developed in Israel. The Court of Appeal stopped the programme from being made, deciding for itself, contrary to the view of the girl's conscientious and caring mother, that publicity deriving from the fact that her estranged father was a prominent politician would not be in her best interests. Such is the paternalism built into the English common law (as into English common life) that courts may one day decide they have the power to stop Mrs Worthington from putting her daughter on the stage.

The fourth pillar of freedom of speech in Britain is the principle that the Government has no direct control over the press. If ministers wish to stop a news story, they must like any other litigant ask the court to

---

[44] *R v. Advertising Standards Authority Ltd, ex p. Vernons Organisation Ltd* [1992] 1 W.L.R. 1289 at 1293.

[45] *Secretary of State for the Home Department v. Central Broadcasting Limited, The Times,* January 28, 1993.

grant an injunction. The Government does have advantages over other litigants, namely a bottomless purse to pay for litigation and a judiciary disposed to believe, at first blush, that its claims about danger to national security are true. This is a far cry from controlling the press, which has never been attempted in practice since the collapse of licensing at the close of the seventeenth century. The Government may exert pressure behind the scenes through the operation of the D-notice committee, but a D-notice has no legal force: it is merely "advice" to the media, drawn up by a joint committee of representatives of the press and the armed forces. It is not a crime to break a D-notice—many newspapers have done so without prosecution, and it is difficult to understand why they bother to collaborate with a system which relies on nudges and winks rather than legal rules.

In extreme circumstances the Government does acquire certain direct legal powers over radio and television. In the case of the BBC, these are contained in the Licence Agreement that forms part of the Corporation's charter. Clause 19 enables the Home Secretary, when in his opinion there is an emergency and it is "expedient" so to act, to send troops in to "take possession of the BBC in the name and on behalf of Her Majesty". This clause was framed during the General Strike, when Winston Churchill and other members of the Government wanted to commandeer the Corporation. It has never been used for that purpose, although Sir Anthony Eden contemplated invoking it for government propaganda during the Suez crisis, and during the Falklands recapture it provided the legal basis for the Government's use of BBC transmitters on Ascension Island to beam propaganda broadcasts at Argentina.

A more dangerous power is contained in section 13(4) of the Licence Agreement, which gives the Home Secretary the right to prohibit the BBC from transmitting any item or programme, at any time. The power is not limited, like clause 19, to periods of emergency. The only safeguard against political censorship is that the BBC "may" (not "must") tell the public that it has received a section 13(4) order from the Home Secretary. This clause was invoked in 1972 by the Director-General, Lord Hill, when the Home Secretary Reginald Maudling threatened a section 13(4) order to stop transmission of a debate about Government actions in Ulster. Lord Hill called his bluff by threatening to make public the reason why the programme could not be shown. Of course, a less courageous Director-General could simply cancel the programme without revealing the existence of a Government order. A parallel power in section 10 of the 1990 Broadcasting Act entitles the Home Secretary to order the Independent Television Commission (ITC) to "refrain from broadcasting any matter or classes of matter" on commercial television. These powers were last invoked for the purpose of direct political censorship in 1988 when the BBC and the IBA (the predecessor of ITC) were ordered not to transmit any interviews with representatives of Sinn

Fein, the Ulster Defence Association, the IRA or certain other extremist groups, or to broadcast any statement that incited support for such groups. The ban was a plain infringement on the right to receive and impart information: it prevented representatives of lawful political organisations (several M.P.s and dozens of local councillors) from stating their case on matters that had no connection with terrorism, and it denied to the public the opportunity to hear supporters of violent action being questioned and exposed (the Thatcher Government believed that terrorists survive by the "oxygen of publicity", but television confrontations generally demonstrate the moral unattractiveness of those who believe that the end justifies the means). The ban prohibited only the actual voices of IRA and UDA members and supporters, so broadcasters minimised its impact by the simple expedient of using actors with Irish accents whose voices were dubbed. In 1991 the House of Lords, in refusing to strike down the ban as "unreasonable", drew attention to its limited effect, which, in view of the dubbing option, they regarded more as an irritant than an infringement.[46]

The 1988 broadcasting bans are the only examples of direct political censorship. A more subtle form of political influence on the content of television programmes is provided by the Government's power of appointment to controlling bodies (the BBC Board of Governors and the ITC). All recent governments have appointed some BBC and IBA members for political reasons, and the Chairmanship of the BBC in particular will go to a government loyalist. The make-up of these bodies can be particularly important when governments exert pressure over a particular programme, as happened to the BBC in the case of *Real Lives* (an examination of the IRA sympathiser in Belfast) and to the IBA in the case of *Death on the Rock* (a *This Week* programme about the SAS shooting of the three IRA members in Gibraltar). The *Real Lives* episode in 1985 severely damaged the BBC's reputation for independence when its Board of Governors cravenly banned the scheduled programme after Mrs Thatcher had condemned it, unseen, as likely to encourage support for terrorists. BBC journalists took strike action in protest, and the programme was eventually screened with a few face-saving deletions, but the episode called into question the Board of Governors' commitment to freedom of expression. The IBA was made of sterner stuff when the Foreign Secretary called for the banning of *Death on the Rock*. It supported Thames Television's decision to screen the programme, which gave viewers a much fuller appreciation of the shootings than had been possible from Government statements and Ministry of Defence briefings. An independent inquiry chaired by Lord Windlesham conclusively refuted the Government's allegations that the programme had

---

[46] *R v. Secretary of State for Home Dept, ex p. Brind* [1991] 1 A.C. 696.

been deliberately biased and had prejudiced the inquest in Gibraltar.[47] The importance of the programme was later demonstrated by the European Court ruling against the United Kingdom that the shootings of the suspects had violated their right to life.[48]

The best antidote to censorship is publicity. Reporters and producers have a public duty to speak out if their vision of truth is suppressed by Government appointees. When the IBA banned a programme about RUC brutality, the producers protested by making a copy available to the BBC, which had no hesitation in showing it as part of a news feature about the IBA decision. Most censorship decisions appear faintly ridiculous in the light of day. None more than the BBC's heavy-handed interference with *Willie—the Legion Hall Bombing*, a play by Caryl Churchill. The prologue criticised Ulster non-jury courts in a manner that BBC executives found unacceptable. So they rewrote and re-recorded the text. In protest, both Ms Churchill and her director succeeded in having their names removed from the credits by threatening legal action. Then they held a press conference to release their original text, which most newspapers juxtaposed with the sanitised version prepared by the Corporation in major news stories on the day of transmission. This ensured the play—and its intended message—a very much wider audience than it would otherwise have obtained.

The theatre has been free from political censorship since 1967, when the Lord Chamberlain's power to license stage plays was abolished. The cinema, however, is subject to the British Board of Film and Video Classification (BBFC), a private body, which nonetheless exercises considerable influence over the way the law is enforced. It is financed by the film and video industries, and will grant certificates only to movies that it considers are within the limits of public acceptability. In practice, the Director of Public Prosecutions does not prosecute films with BBFC certificates for cinema showing, so distributors prepared to pay the certification fee and to carry out the "cuts" insisted upon by the Board are in effect guaranteed freedom from police harassment. This arrangement secures a quiet legal life for the film industry in general, although it is resented by some film makers who are obliged to tailor their product to BBFC standards in order to secure distribution outlets. The Video Recording Act gives the BBFC statutory recognition as the body charged with licensing films for sale or rent on video cassettes and DVDs. In relation to videos, the BBFC has become a fully-fledged State censorship board, charged by law with determining whether material on video is "suitable for viewing in the home" and with determining whether particular cassettes can be sold or hired to children. Its decisions are enforced by police and by trading standards officers, and

---

[47] *The Windlesham Rampton Report on Death on the Rock* (Faber, 1989).
[48] *McCann v. U.K.* (1995) 21 E.H.R.R. 97.

heavy fines and even prison sentences can be imposed for non-compliance with its directives.

Many of the criminal laws that affect the media—official secrets and prevention of terrorism, and most of the laws relating to contempt, reporting restrictions and obscenity—cannot be invoked in the criminal courts by anyone except the Attorney-General or the Director of Public Prosecutions (who works under the Attorney's superintendence). Likewise, the Attorney alone may enforce the ITC's statutory duties in cases where no individual can show that a breach will involve a personal injury. In all these cases the Attorney-General is not *bound* to take legal action, even if the law has clearly been broken. He has a *discretion*—to prosecute or not to prosecute—depending on his view of the public interest. In exercising his discretion he is entitled to take into account any consideration of public policy that bears on the issue—and the public policy in favour of free speech is important in deciding whether to launch official secrets or contempt or obscenity prosecutions. Actions that appear to compromise free speech are likely to be criticised in Parliament, where the Attorney must answer for both his and the DPP's prosecution policy.

There have been cases where the Attorney has refused to act even after judges have called for prosecution. Sometimes his decisions are made on grounds of convenience: after most newspapers in Britain committed contempt of court over the arrest of "Yorkshire Ripper" Peter Sutcliffe, the Attorney decided against prosecuting on the ground that he would have to put dozens of editors in the dock.[49] On other occasions the public interest of an "illegal" revelation has tipped the balance against invoking legal discipline against the journalist who revealed it. For example, it is usually contempt to publish a story that causes the discharge of a jury mid-trial. This consequence was caused by London Weekend Television when commentator Christopher Hitchens revealed that a juror in an official secrets case was a former member of the SAS, and by *The Guardian* when it published details of information discovered by police when they "vetted" a jury that was trying some anarchists.[50] In both cases the trial judges complained to the Attorney-General, who decided that prosecution would not be in the public interest. No doubt the decision was heavily influenced by the fact that both stories were correct and had revealed controversial practices in the administration of justice.

There is a danger in placing over-much reliance on the Attorney's discretion. He is, after all, a member of the Government, as well as the leader of the legal profession. In deciding "public policy", he will obviously be influenced by the outlook of the political party of which

[49] *Press Conduct in the Sutcliffe Case*, Press Council Booklet No. 7, 1983, pp. 50–2.
[50] David Leigh, *The Frontiers of Secrecy*, Junction Books, 1980, chap. 4.

he is a member and by the values of the profession that he leads. These influences will not always incline him to the view that revelation of particular legal or political material is necessarily in the public interest. There is another danger. The decision to publish often hinges on the question: "Will the Attorney prosecute if we do?". There is a natural temptation to seek an answer from the horse's mouth, so to speak, by submitting the controversial material to the Attorney for an indication of his attitude. This has been done by the BBC (which is notoriously craven in legal matters) and by several newspapers. It comes perilously close to making the Attorney, in effect, a political censor, an official to whom the media can go, cap in hand, with the question "please sir, may we publish this?" The danger, of course, is that if his answer is "no", the material will then not be published. This would be a pity if the Attorney were bluffing, and the prospect of scaring off awkward media revelations will always provide a great temptation for attorneys-general to bluff.

Trial by jury, the openness of courts, the rule against prior restraint and the absence of laws permitting direct government interference have ensured that the British media enjoy a relative freedom from censorship, by comparison with many other countries. But the fact that media freedom was until October 2000 protected by unwritten convention rather than by a bill of rights meant that there was no external brake upon Parliament or the courts moving to restrict it in particular ways, as the mood of times or the exigencies of the cold war or the scale of IRA activities might permit. Britain was famously a country where "everything is permitted, which is not specifically prohibited", but the specific prohibitions became more numerous, without having to justify themselves against the overriding principle of public interest required by Article 10. Strasbourg court decisions became of increasing importance in the two decades following the *Sunday Times v. United Kingdom* thalidomide case in 1979 and judges sometimes pronounced their satisfaction that the media law of England was compatible with Article 10 of the Convention, but in this they were frequently mistaken—as European Court decisions were prone to point out. In Chapter 2 we describe how international human rights standards should come in time to revolutionise and to organise British media law.

CHAPTER 2

THE HUMAN RIGHTS ACT

Safeguards for free speech offered by common law were inadequate to protect public-interest journalism from attack for discomfiting the government or the judiciary or wealthy private litigants. It lacked any organising principle, of the kind which had come to shield the American media through the First Amendment. This gap was eventually filled by a free speech formulation taken from human rights treaties to which English writers and lawyers had made a significant contribution.

The law of international human rights did not take any meaningful shape until the Nuremberg trial after the Second World War. Previously, it had been assumed that international law could only affect states and not individuals, and since it did not permit intervention in the *internal* affairs of states, governments could gag and oppress their citizens as they pleased. In Britain, the government became more relaxed about the press as the nineteenth century progressed and the danger of republican revolution passed. But in the colonies—the far-flung British Empire—there remained every need of laws to prevent the natives becoming restless. This was bluntly admitted in 1899 by the English Law Lords who sat, as the court of final appeal for the colonies, in the judicial committee of the Privy Council. Oppressive press laws like "scandalising the court" served imperialistic (indeed, racist) purposes:

> "Committals for contempt of court by scandalising the court itself have become obsolete in this country. Courts are satisfied to leave to public opinion attacks or comments derogatory or scandalous to them. But it must be considered that in small colonies, consisting principally of coloured populations, the enforcement in proper cases of committal for contempt of court for attacks on the court may be absolutely necessary to preserve in such a community the dignity and respect for the court."[1]

---

[1] *McLeod v. St Aubyn* [1889] A.C. 549, at 561.

The imperial ambitions of major powers like Britain and France, and what seemed to be an endemic racism in America (manifested in its "Jim Crow" laws) stifled any political support for international human rights between the wars: the subject was never mentioned at the League of Nations and was never seriously advanced by any major thinker or statesman of the period.[2] Its revival began at the instigation and inspiration of British writer H. G. Wells, who led a campaign urging the adoption by "Parliamentary peoples" of a Declaration of Rights, which he prepared with the help of Viscount Sankey, a former Labour Lord Chancellor, and writers like J. B. Priestly and A. A. Milne (who would motor up from Pooh corner to help with the draft). In 1940 Penguin books published *H. G. Wells on the Rights of Man*. It was translated into 30 languages and syndicated in newspapers throughout the world, and inspired U.S. President Franklin D. Roosevelt to make his "four freedoms" speech in 1941: an appeal for a post-war world based on four elemental freedoms, the first of which was freedom of speech. In the work of H. G. Wells and his colleagues we can locate the seeds of Article 19 of the Universal Declaration and Article 10 of the European Convention. In a modest English way he eschewed the messianic preambles of the revolutionary French and American declarations and declared that "man" (including woman) was entitled to:

> ". . . easy access to information upon all matters of common knowledge throughout his life, in the course of which he would enjoy the utmost freedom of discussion . . . A man is subject to the free criticism of his fellows, although he shall have adequate protection from any lying or misrepresentation that may injure him. All administrative records about a man shall be open to his personal and private inspection. There shall be no secret dossiers in any administrative department. All dossiers shall be accessible to the man concerned and subject to verification and correction".[3]

Here, for the first time since the eighteenth century revolutions, was an attempt by English writers to re-invent the human rights idea, in a homely and literate way. Their spirit—the spirit in which judges should now apply Article 10 and the Freedom of Information Act—is tolerant and fundamentally anti-bureaucratic. Government must have no secrets from its citizens, and courts must never restrain matters appropriate for discussion. There must be privacy for family homes, but no 30-year rules, covering up advice to Ministers, no secret dossiers except for ongoing police investigations. The vision which is central to the *right*

---

[2] See G. Robertson, *Crimes Against Humanity—the Struggle for Global Justice* (Penguin, 2002), Chap. 1.
[3] *H. G. Wells on the Rights of Man* (Penguin, 1940).

to receive and to impart information is that we will get along better if access is easy and unrestricted, and that any attempt by government or by powerful groups to restrain that access must be viewed with the greatest suspicion.

This was the modern intellectual authority for Article 19 of the Universal Declaration of Human Rights, adopted by the UN in 1948. By this time, there was no doubt about the fundamental importance of free speech: Nazi ideology had gone without serious challenge in Germany in the thirties because of Hitler's crack-down on dissenting publishers and journalists after the Reichstag fire. So Article 19 of the Universal Declaration provided that:

> "Everyone has the right to freedom of opinion and expression; this right includes freedom to hold opinions without interference and to seek, receive and impart information and ideas through any media and regardless of frontiers."

Article 19 is not absolute: Article 12 gives everyone the right to legal protection against "arbitrary interference with privacy" and against "attacks upon his honour and reputation", and reconciliation of the two Articles pivots upon the Article 29(2) rule that any freedom may be limited by laws if they are passed solely for the purposes of securing respect for the rights of others according to the just requirements of "the general welfare in a democratic society". (H. G. Wells had put it more pithily: "citizens should have adequate protection from lying, or misrepresentation which injures").

The Soviet Union and its puppets abstained from the vote in favour of the Universal Declaration in 1948, and the Berlin airlift and the millions confined in Stalin's gulag emphasised how much of a threat communism might become to the advancement of human rights. One response made by the nations of Western Europe was to draw up a European Convention on Human Rights, as a regional equivalent of the Universal Declaration, to provide a roll call of those rights under threat in the East. It borrowed almost word for word from Article 19 to construct Article 10(1):

> "Everyone has the right to freedom of expression. This right shall include freedom to hold opinions and to receive and impart information and ideas without interference by public authority and regardless of frontiers."

Instead of leaving exceptions to a vague sweeping-up provision at the end, the Convention sets them out in Article 10(2):

> "The exercise of these freedoms, since it carries with it duties and responsibilities, may be subject to such formalities, conditions,

restrictions or penalties as are prescribed by law and are necessary in a democratic society, in the interests of national security, territorial integrity or public safety, for the prevention of disorder or crime, for the protection of health or morals, for the protection of the reputation or the rights of others, for preventing the disclosure of information received in confidence, or for maintaining the authority and impartiality of the judiciary''.

The European Convention on Human Rights has now been ratified by all 41 Member States of the Council of Europe. It was produced to establish a legal (alongside a military) bulwark against both the resurgence of fascism and the encroachment of communism—the latter prospect, when drafting began in 1949, serving as a special spur to entrench free speech and privacy rights of the very kind that Stalin was extinguishing in the east. The draftsman of the final text was a retired lawyer from the Home Office. Britain was the first country to ratify the Convention, which came into force in 1953—although for the next 20 years hardly anyone noticed. This was because it was not until 1966 that Britain permitted its individuals to petition the Court in Strasbourg: until then, the only complainants could be states, and they rarely took each other to court. The first successful individual complaint against the United Kingdom was not until 1975: it was brought by a prisoner whose correspondence was routinely read and censored by the prison governor.[4] In 1979 the European Court found the United Kingdom guilty of the first Article 10 violation of the rights of the media, committed by the House of Lords decision that *The Sunday Times* could not publish an account of the thalidomide tragedy, lest it affect civil damages claims which had long been stalled in the courts.[5] Thereafter, rulings against Britain were frequently delivered, although they had no direct impact on domestic law because the Convention was only a treaty, signed by Government, which could not become "law" unless and until its provisions were adopted by Parliament. This was finally done by the Human Rights Act 1998, which came into force on October 2, 2000.

From that date onwards, the Convention has operated as part of the United Kingdom's domestic law, introduced by a statute (the Human Rights Act 1998) which by section 12 gives Article 10 especial prominence. So Article 10 is now a constitutional right to the extent that freedom of expression can be asserted in all courts against all public authorities (although it cannot prevail over the clear words of a statute, which can only be changed by Parliament). No constitutional right can have meaning without some sense of the historical anvil on which it was forged. Article 10 may have entered United Kingdom law with the

---

[4] *Golder v. U.K.* (1975) 1 E.H.R.R. 524.
[5] *Sunday Times v. U.K.* (1979) 2 E.H.R.R. 245.

deceptive slogan of a "right brought home"; the plain historical truth is that free speech as a right never has had a home in Britain. It must be recognised as Tom Paine's right, for which dozens of his booksellers and his fellow free-thinkers, Williams and Carlisle and Bradlaugh, fought and were sentenced to hard labour by brutal judges, in prisons pervaded by filth and disease. It will be the sincerest tribute our courts can pay their memory if the common law under which they were persecuted—criminal libel, blasphemy and sedition—are declared incompatible with the new right to freedom of expression.[6]

ARTICLE 10: THE CORE PRINCIPLES

The European Court of Human Rights has delivered many judgments declaring national laws or court decisions to be infringements of Article 10. Over the years it has crystallised its freedom of expression case law into a number of basic principles, the first formulated in a 1976 complaint from Great Britain over the suppression of *The Little Red Schoolbook* on the pretext of obscenity. The book gave robust advice to teenagers about sex and suggested that they might consider going on strike against poor teaching: a London judge ordered copies to be destroyed because it was "subversive of authority". This decision appears even more ridiculous today than it did at the time, and although the Eurocourt wrongly declined to uphold the complaint by Richard Handyside (the book's publisher), at least it articulated the first core principle of Article 10:

> 1. Freedom of expression constitutes one of the essential foundations of a democratic society and one of the basic conditions for its progress and for each individual's self-fulfilment. It is applicable not only to "information" or "ideas" that are favourably received or regarded as inoffensive or as a matter of indifference, but also to those that offend, shock or disturb. Such are the demands of pluralism, tolerance and broadmindedness without which there is no "democratic society".[7]

This principle echoes Voltaire: we may not like what you say, but liberal society defends to its death your right to say it. This embodies an assumption that free speech is necessary to the personality of the citizen, to the continuing health of democracy and to social progress:

---

[6] Ironically, such declarations may come only if the Government tries to revive these arcane laws, otherwise there will be no "victim" to bring an action under the HRA: see *Rusbridger v. Att.-Gen.*, June 22, 2001 (Administrative Court).

[7] *Handyside v. U.K.* (1976) E.H.R.R. 737, paras 48–49. For a recent formulation of the core principles see *Bladet Tromso v. Norway* (1999) 29 E.H.R.R. 125.

these are the important goals which demand tolerance from governments.

The sentiments behind Article 10(1) are nonetheless subject to the many exceptions contained in Article 10(2), which avowedly protects:

(a) the public interest (national security, territorial integrity, public safety, prevention of disorder or crime, protection of health and morals)

(b) competing individual rights (such as a citizen's right to reputation and to keep private information confidential)

(c) the authority and impartiality of judges.

When do these exceptions override freedom of speech? Only when they can rebut the presumption Article 10(1) erects in its favour:

> 2. This freedom is subject to exceptions, however these must be strictly construed and the need for any restrictions must be established convincingly.[8]

The first core principle would be meaningless if exceptions as broad as those in Article 10(2) could automatically defeat it. For that reason core principle 2 is all-important: the State defending the restriction bears the burden of proving its necessity in democratic society, *i.e.* not only that an Article 10(2) ground convincingly exists, but that it generates a "pressing social need" for the restriction in question. Article 10 should not be seen as requiring an equal "balance" between, on the one hand, the value of freedom of expression and on the other, the value of national security, crime prevention, etc. It does not decide a competition between free speech and the values listed in Article 10(2); the latter are simply "a number of exceptions which must be strictly interpreted".[9]

> 3. Any infringement of free speech must be "prescribed by law". That means that the restriction must be clear, certain and predictable. Law, to be "prescribed", must be adequately accessible and formulated with sufficient precision to enable citizens to regulate their conduct.

A judge who exercised some common-law power in an entirely novel way would be in breach of the Convention, even if he claimed to act "in the interests" of one of the excepted values. It has to be said, however, that the Court has been loathe to apply this rule, even in such obvious cases as the vague United Kingdom law of blasphemy. How-

---

[8] *Observer and Guardian v. U.K.* (1992) 14 E.H.R.R. 153 at para. 55 (The "*Spy-catcher*" case).

[9] *Sunday Times v. U.K.* (1979) 2 E.H.R.R. 245 at 271.

ever, in a decision which will have important consequences for dragnet English crimes penalising conduct deemed contrary to public morals, the Court declared that the free-speech rights of fox-hunt protesters were wrongly infringed when they were bound over to keep the peace by not in future behaving "*contra bonos mores*"—a Latin phrase translated as "engaging in conduct which is wrong rather than right in the judgment of the majority of fellow citizens". This was insufficiently precise to amount to a legal rule at all: it did not define or describe the proscribed conduct, but merely referred to majority opinion which might characterise it as "wrong".[10] Thanks to Article 10 the will of the people is not, as such, the supreme law, or any law at all. A particular restriction will fail the test if it is not referable to any identifiable law: a patient detained in an Austrian psychiatric hospital whose request for access to radio and television was rejected out of hand succeeded at Strasbourg because the State had passed no law permitting or imposing such restrictions.[11] Although a proviso to Article 10 permits States to licence television and radio stations, they must do so by enacting a law which prescribes reasonable guidelines for applications. The Privy Council used European Court authorities on core principle 3 to invalidate the radio licensing system in Antigua, which gave unfettered discretion to the Government which it had used to grant licences only to the Prime Minister's family.[12]

> 4. Any infringement must be "necessary in a democratic society", and "necessary", although not synonymous with "indispensable", means more than "useful", "reasonable" or "desirable". It implies the existence of a "pressing social need".

This is the rule upon which most Article 10 cases eventually turn. Social needs found "pressing" usually relate to ensuring fair trial or defeat of terrorism or protecting the public from racial violence, but even these important needs are not overriding: they must be urgent, and the restriction must rationally serve to advance them. The Spycatcher decision, for example, rejected the United Kingdom Government's argument that it was "necessary" to punish MI5 turncoat Peter Wright by banning his book in Britain: given its massive sales throughout the world the ban was ineffective and "a futile measure cannot be a necessary one". This is an important ruling for cases where confidential

---

[10] *Hashman and Harrup v. U.K.* (2000) 30 E.H.R.R. 241, paras 31–39. See also *Silver v. U.K.* (1983) 5 E.H.R.R. 347 which emphasises that Government circulars purporting to restrict free speech cannot be "law" unless authorised by or under statute, or common law or European Union legislation.

[11] *Herczegfalvy v. Austria* (1993) 15 E.H.R.R. 437; *Silver v. U.K.* (1983) 5 E.H.R.R. 347.

[12] *Observer Publications Ltd v. Matthews and Att.-Gen. of Antigua* (2001) 10 B.H.R.C. 252.

information gets posted on the internet: the law cannot be asked to put genies back into bottles.

> 5. Even when the social need is pressing, the particular infringement, looking at the context and content of the banned communication, must be "proportionate to the legitimate aims pursued" and the Government bears the burden of passing the proportionality test by adducing sufficient reasons".[13]

The "proportionality test" is important, and novel in English law. It means that even when media restrictions have been imposed by a Government acting in good faith, in pursuance of a legitimate aim to advance a value contained in an Article 10(2) exception, the European Court will strike it down if, in all the circumstances of the case, the restriction was ineffectual to advance the aim, or irrelevant to it, or insufficiently justified (such as the ban on *Spycatcher* in the United Kingdom, which could not rationally support the interests of national security once the book was published elsewhere). The Convention cannot be used to complain of laws in the abstract, however Draconian their effect. There must be a "victim" who has suffered a real "violation" (see Article 34): if the law in question has a legitimate aim and responds to a pressing social need, a particular application or aspect of it may nonetheless be so disproportionate as to breach the convention. Thus in *Tolstoy v. United Kingdom* the Court held that although the law of civil libel might in general terms respond to a social need to protect reputation from untruths, the lack at that time of proper judicial control over damages (leading, in that case, to a £1.5 million award) lacked all proportion and constituted a breach of the Convention.

> 6. It follows from principle 1 that the news media plays an essential watchdog role in a democratic society, and (subject to rights of confidence and reputation) it has a duty to impart information and ideas on matters of public interest. From this duty it follows that:
>
> (a) reporters have a correlative right to protect sources of information;
> (b) since news is a perishable commodity and its publication urgent
>
>> (i) there must be latitude allowed to journalists in their method of presentation—for error or exaggeration or even provocation
>> (ii) even a short enforced delay in news dissemination engages Article 10 protection;
>
> (c) the scope for criticism of politicians and power-wielders and persons whose conduct is of public importance is wider than that for private individuals: the need for open discussion of politics may prevail over the protection of reputation.

---

[13] *Handyside*, paras 48—49; *Sunday Times*, paras 62 and 67; *Lingens* para. 40.

Under this principle the Court has begun to develop a jurisprudence tailored to the particular needs of the news media. The right to protect sources, established by the *Goodwin* case, is the most notable example, but there are others which show how the Court is becoming educated in the way that the press actually has to function in order to get the news out.

> 7. States enjoy a certain margin of appreciation in assessing the need for an interference with freedom of expression, but the extent of the margin will be strictly supervised by the Court which must decide whether the State has discharged the burden of proving the necessity principle (3 above). The national "margin of appreciation" is circumscribed by the interest of democratic society in ensuring and maintaining a free press.[14]

This principle only applies to decisions of the European Court of Human Rights, and has no relevance to national courts which are tasked with applying the Convention. The "margin of appreciation" is the latitude which an international court allows to nation states to bend human rights rules in the supposed interests of its own cultural values and traditions. Decisions that turn on the "margin of appreciation" are to that extent cop-outs, and the Strasbourg court has been particularly prone to cop-out on questions of morality. A pronounced Catholic bias in the appointed judges has led to several poorly reasoned rulings that censorship of anti-Catholic plays and films are within State margins. *Handyside* itself is an example of using the "margin of appreciation" doctrine to avoid a principled but potentially unpopular decision to condemn the ban on *The Little Red Schoolbook*, and the Court has similarly fudged decisions on blasphemy laws in Austria and in the United Kingdom by holding that they are within these States' "margin of appreciation". The important point to remember, however, is that these decisions do not mean that the blasphemy law is consistent with the Convention, but merely that any inconsistency is tolerable at an international level. The British courts, newly empowered by the Human Rights Act, could and should declare the law to be incompatible with Convention rights.

APPLYING THE CORE PRINCIPLES

The core principles of Article 10 have been supplemented by consistent applications of them in familiar contexts or to familiar subjects. The free speech infringements most commonly struck down have been pun-

---

[14] *Worm v. Austria* (1997) 25 E.H.R.R. 454.

ishments for criticising governments and politicians. Here the principle is that democracy requires two kinds of latitude in communications relating to those who wield political power:

(a) comparatively greater freedom to publish information about them, and

(b) a very extensive freedom to comment upon their performances.

The leading case involved the Austrian journalist Peter Lingens, who had been convicted and fined under a criminal libel law for accusing the Chancellor, Bruno Kriesky, of "the basest opportunism" and "immorality" for seeking a political alliance with a party led by a former Nazi. This was plainly disproportionate: the Court declared that

> "Freedom of political debate is at the very core of the concept of a democratic society which prevails throughout the Convention. The limits of acceptable criticism are accordingly wider as regards a politician as such than as regards a private individual. Unlike the latter, the former inevitably and knowingly lays himself open to close scrutiny of his every word and deed by both journalists and the public at large, and he must consequently display a greater degree of tolerance." [15]

While Article 10(2) allows politicians some privacy, when acting in an official capacity their reputations may be sullied in the interests of open discussion of political issues. This will certainly be the case in respect of value-judgments and opinions, offered in good faith, and not susceptible of proof or disproof. The lesson of *Lingens* is that comment on politicians must be free, even if factual statements about them can be made subject to defamation laws. In a subsequent case, a provocative attack on the neo-Nazi politician, Jorg Haider, was protected from a private prosecution brought by this hypocrite (who repeatedly complains to the court when his own freedom to criticise opponents is curbed). The Court emphasised that the "greater degree of tolerance" which *Lingens* enjoined politicians to display was the case "especially when he himself makes public statements that are susceptible of criticism".[16] By requiring the journalist to prove his opinion (as distinct from the facts on which it was based) the Austrian criminal libel law was a clear infringement of free speech.

Factual statements (as opposed to comments) were considered in *Castells v. Spain*, where an opposition politician had been convicted of

---

[15] *Lingens v. Austria* (1986) 8 E.H.R.R. 407 at para. 42.
[16] *Oberschlick v. Austria* (1991) 19 E.H.R.R. 389 at para. 59.

"insulting the Government" by accusing it in some detail of supporting right-wing death squads in its Basque region. Castells had sought to prove the truth of his allegations, but his evidence was rejected as irrelevant: the crime was committed simply by insulting the authorities in a manner which would contribute to public disorder. The European Court emphasised the importance of free speech for politicians, and the duty of the press to impart information and ideas, and ruled that "the limits of permissible criticism are wider with regard to the Government than in relation to a private citizen or even a politician".[17] The failure of Spanish law to admit truth as a defence meant that this application of its sedition law was beyond the needs of a democracy, even one torn by civil strife.

The European Court may articulate fine principles, but its application of them can, as in all courts, be influenced by political pressures and prejudices. *Castells* was decided at a time when Basque terrorism had receded, and after evidence had emerged that supported Castells' allegations of Government complicity. For an example of judicial cowardice in the face of the *Castells* principle, compare the decision in *Zana v. Turkey*, when 12 of the court's 20 judges upheld the conviction of a local politician who, whilst held in a military prison, told journalists that he supported the PKK (but was "not in favour of massacres"). For this statement, the prisoner received an extra 12 months' imprisonment. In an unprincipled judgment, the Eurocourt majority mouthed the core principles yet found that the publication (for which Zana, as a prisoner, was not responsible) might "exacerbate an explosive situation" and the punishment was therefore "necessary in a democratic society". The eight-judge minority correctly pointed out that since Article 10 applies to ideas that offend or shock, "the mere fact that in his statement the applicant indicated support for a political organisation whose aims and means the Government rejects and combats cannot, therefore, be a sufficient reason for prosecuting and sentencing him".[18] In less stressful times and countries, the Court has insisted that "a person opposed to official ideas and positions must be able to find a place in the political arena", and has followed *Castells* in according special protection to the views of the people's representatives, even if they only represent peoples at the European Parliament.[19] It condemned France for expelling from Polynesia a "green" German MEP for holding anti-nuclear demonstrations: free speech is permitted if it merely makes the natives restless, but not if it will persuade them to revolt.

The importance of European Court decisions for English courts applying the Human Rights Act lies in the principles extrapolated from

---

[17] *Castells v. Spain* (1992) 14 E.H.R.R. 445 at 477, para. 46.
[18] *Zana v. Turkey* (1999) 27 E.H.R.R. 667 at 701 (partly dissenting opinion).
[19] *Piermont v. France* (1995) 20 E.H.R.R. 301.

Article 10, rather than in the application of those principles to specific cases, which often turns on the "margin of appreciation" and can be internally inconsistent, especially when the decision is taken by an ordinary chamber of nine judges (rather than in a "grand chamber" of 20 or so). Inconsistency is particularly apparent in respect of rulings about the right of journalists to criticise the courts, which is subject to an Article 10(2) exception "for maintaining the authority and impartiality of the judiciary". The correct approach is to limit the free speech right by reference to the Article 6 right to a fair trial, so that attacks on defendants or on judges that are calculated to prejudice a particular trial are impermissible while the trial continues but not otherwise, subject of course to the redress offered by the law of civil libel (and judges, like anyone else, must be entitled to sue in order to redress false statements about themselves). This was the Court's approach in *De Haes v. Belgium*, where it condemned the Belgian courts for awarding compensation to judges who had been severely (and to some extent unfairly) criticised in a series of magazine articles for having extreme right-wing sympathies and for extending them to favour a litigant with similar views. "Journalistic freedom" the Court said memorably "also covers possible recourse to a degree of exaggeration, or even provocation".[20] While not approving the polemical and aggressive tone of the articles, the Court was mindful of the fact that Article 10 protects not only information but the form in which it is conveyed.

This marked a welcome refusal to follow a previous case, *Prager and Oberschlick v. Austria*, where a narrow majority (the vote was five to four) contrived to find that a criminal libel conviction for a justifiable critique of the Austrian judiciary ("Danger! Harsh Judges! ") did not violate the Convention. The majority held that the article "undermined public confidence in the integrity of the judiciary as a whole"—ignoring the media's right in a democracy to question the integrity of judges as well as politicians.[21] It also made use of the *canard* that judges "are subject to a duty of discretion that precludes them from replying"—which is nonsense, since they can reply from their privileged position on the bench, or by suing for civil libel, or (in the United Kingdom) by having the Lord Chancellor's department put out a corrective statement. As the minority judgment points out, it was the deployment of criminal sanctions (the private prosecution was launched by one of the criticised judges) that is disproportionate—judges are public figures who enjoy public privileges, and "must in return accept exposure to unrestricted criticism where it is made in good faith".[22]

---

[20] *De Haes and Gijsels v. Belgium* (1998) 25 E.H.R.R. 1 at 55, para. 46.
[21] *Prager and Oberschlick v. Austria* (1996) 21 E.H.R.R. 1 at 20, para. 36.
[22] *ibid.* at 22, dissenting opinion of Judge Pettiti.

Restrictions on free speech are acceptable if they merely postpone publication of opinions on guilt or innocence until after a criminal trial conducted before jurors or lay judges: this is the premise of United Kingdom contempt law, which satisfies the Convention now that it only bites on publications that create a substantial risk that a trial will be seriously prejudiced.[23] But whenever judges deal with critics of the courts they sit as judges in their own cause and European judges are no less biased than national judges when it comes to approving punishment of those who criticise fellow judges. A blatant example is the Eurocourt decision in *Barfod v. Denmark*, where a prosecution and fine for some perfectly temperate and substantially true remarks about the unfitness of local government employees to decide cases involving their own employer was upheld by the European Court, which said that the Danish court would be lowered in public esteem.[24] What lowered it in public esteem, of course, was not the article, but a fact to which the article drew attention, namely that the judges had put themselves in a position where bias was reasonably perceived.

These cases arise from continental laws derived from the *Code Napoleon*, which penalised "insults" to public servants and officials. There are a number of unsatisfactory cases where European judges have shown a lingering attachment to the obnoxious idea that criminal law should protect public servants and policemen from verbal abuse. This is another area where the English tradition is more robust, and where English judges should use Article 10 in a more creative and liberal fashion than their Strasbourg colleagues, most of whom think that "civil servants must enjoy public confidence in conditions free of undue perturbation"—sentiments with which Sir Humphrey Appleby would entirely agree.[25] English law, fortunately, has few parallels, other than in disciplinary rules for the armed services and prison inmates. There is a valuable ruling in *Grigoriades v. Greece* where the Court judged that a conscript sentenced to three months in prison for writing a letter to senior officers condemning the Greek army as "a criminal and terrorist apparatus" had been wrongly prosecuted:

"Article 10 does not stop at the gates of army barracks. It applies

---

[23] This is the real justification for the decision in *Worm v. Austria* (1998) 25 E.H.R.R. 454, which related to an article which argued that the defendant was guilty whilst he was being tried. Some of the language used by the Court majority on that occasion (its reference to "the spectacle of pseudo-trials in the media" having "nefarious consequences" for acceptance of courts as places of trial) was over the top.

[24] *Barfod v. Denmark* (1989) 13 E.H.R.R. 478.

[25] *Janowski v. Poland* (1999) 29 E.H.R.R. 705, para. 33. Compare these pathetic comments by a grand chamber with the vigorous dissent of the English judge, Sir Nicholas Bratza, and with the different view of an earlier and better court in *Thorgeirson v. Iceland* (note 29 below).

to military personnel as to all other persons and permits soldiers to express opinions, even directed against the army as an institution, so long as the manner and scope of their expression does not amount to a serious threat to discipline".[26]

Since soldiers have a correlative right to receive information, the ruling in *Grigoriades* may sound the death knell of the English offence of incitement to disaffection, or at least to the way it was used in the 1970s against pacifists who leafleted army bases urging conscientious objection to service in Northern Ireland.

There are a number of European Court judgments which are having a beneficial effect on the way English courts approach problems of media law, because they accept as a starting-point that the dissemination of news and opinion is a value to be protected so far as possible, and they teach that some protection must be extended to methods of news-gathering which get results, however unattractive or unfair or corner-cutting they may seem in the cold light of the courtroom. *Goodwin v. United Kingdom* is a prime example of the Court endorsing a journalistic ethic—source protection—at odds with English judicial sensibilities. Another such case is *Jersild v. Denmark*, which actually warns:

> "It is not for this Court, *nor for the national courts for that matter*, to substitute their own views for those of the press as to what technique of reporting should be adopted by journalists . . . Article 10 protects not only the substance of the ideas and information expressed, but also the form in which they are conveyed."[27]

This approach enabled the Court to condemn the conviction under Denmark's draconian race-hate laws of a television journalist and editor for producing a news programme which looked at the rise of racism amongst young unemployed in Copenhagen. Not surprisingly, the professional judgment of the broadcasters was that the programme would have little impact unless racists were featured under their Ku Klux Klan banners and in their own neanderthal voices ("Niggers are not human beings, man, they are animals . . . so are foreign workers . . . we jump on their cars and throw white paint in their faces . . . people should be allowed to keep slaves, man"). These extremists were convicted for insulting a racial group (no Article 10 protection for *them* in Europe)[28]

---

[26] *Grigoriades v. Greece* (1997) 27 E.H.R.R. 464 at 482, para. 45.
[27] *Jersild v. Denmark* (1995) 19 E.H.R.R. 1, at 26, para. 31.
[28] The European Commission (which until 1998 would "filter" cases for the Court) always rejected complaints by racists about their hate-speech convictions on the ground that their Article 10 rights were trumped by Article 17 (which provides that nothing in the Convention implies "any right to engage in any activity . . . aimed at

and the broadcasters were fined for abetting them. The Court ruled this a violation, since the broadcasters had no racist purpose themselves and had relied on their professional judgment that the item as transmitted had genuine news value. The Court pointed out that news reporting based on interviews, even with criminals, was an important technique used by journalists to serve their "public watchdog" role, and to convict them of criminal offences (even with small fines) would seriously hamper the media in producing public interest stories. *Jersild* is valuable, both to dissuade courts from imposing criminal convictions on journalists acting professionally and in drawing attention to the importance of protecting the methods of investigative journalism as well as its fruits.

Another seminal decision is *Thorgeir Thorgeirson v. Iceland* where the applicant, an author, was convicted of "insulting civil servants" (in this case, policemen) by accusing them of brutality, the insults being contained in an "open letter" to the Minister of Justice urging a public inquiry. The Iceland Government argued that Article 10's latitude towards criticism of politicians, established by *Lingens* and *Castells*, did not apply to employed public servants, but on this occasion the Court observed that "there is no warrant for distinguishing between political discussion and discussion of other matters of public concern."[29] The airing of allegations of brutal policing, although second-hand and unprovable, were nonetheless matters of public concern appropriately mentioned in the course of a call for an independent inquiry to verify or refute them. It was therefore unreasonable to require the allegations to be proved true as a condition of avoiding a criminal conviction and a fine which even if small would still deter serious investigative journalism. This approach influenced the House of Lords when in 1998 it decided to extend a public interest privilege to articles which report serious allegations as part of a call for an inquiry, so long as journalists act reasonably and without malice.

In these cases, the Eurocourt is trying to deter the use of Napoleonic "insult" crimes against journalists and broadcasters who act according to professional conscience. Notwithstanding the fact that the usual punishment is a small fine, the court has repeatedly stressed the "seriousness of a criminal conviction . . . having regard to the existence of other means of intervention and rebuttal, particularly through civil remedies".[30] With the Human Rights Act in force, this should deter

---

the destruction of any of the rights and freedoms set forth herein . . ."). See *Glimmerveen v. Netherlands* (1979) 18 D.R. 187, and comments in Chap. 4.

[29] *Thorgeirson v. Iceland* (1992) 14 E.H.R.R. 843 at 865, para. 64.

[30] *Lehideux and Isorni v. France* (1998) 5 B.H.R.C. 540 at para. 53. Even a token fine (for attempting to rehabilitate the Nazi collaborator, Marshal Pétáin) was held to be disproportionate, because of the stigma of criminal conviction.

English prosecutors from charging journalists with crimes like official secrecy, sedition and contempt or even deploying criminal charges of an inconsequential nature which may have been committed incidentally in pursuing the story. Such as tactic will be more difficult after the *Fressoz and Roire* case:

> The applicants were the editor and a journalist from *Le Canard enchaîné*, the French equivalent of *Private Eye*. During a bitter strike over workers' wages at a major French car factory, the applicants got hold of its chairman's income tax return, showing how he had received massive pay increases at a time when he was denying any extra pay to his workers. It was an offence to publish tax assessments, and the applicants were convicted after doing so to illustrate and confirm their story about the chairman's pay rises. This information could lawfully have been obtained from other public sources, and in these circumstances the Court decided the conviction could not be justified: "Article 10 protects journalists' rights to divulge information on issues of general interest provided they are acting in good faith and on an accurate factual basis and provide 'reliable and precise' information in accordance with the ethics of journalism". Since the purpose of the unlawful publication was not to damage the chairman but to contribute to a debate of public moment about remuneration in the car industry, the conviction was unreasonable and disproportionate. France was ordered to pay the applicants' legal costs and to reimburse them the sum of compensation (10,000 francs) they had been ordered to pay to the greedy executive.[31]

Fressoz and Roire is a significant case where the Eurocourt in grand chamber has (as in *Goodwin*, below) invalidated an application of otherwise unobjectionable domestic law because it is deployed against journalists who have acted in accordance with professional ethics. There was nothing objectionable about the French statute prohibiting publication of tax assessments—it was an elemental privacy protection for taxpayers, justifying prosecution of any tax officials who might leak such documents. The journalists had plainly broken the law, although they had done so not with malice towards the taxpayer, but in order to verify for readers a story of public importance. The implication from the European Court judgment is that journalists who commit minor offences incidentally and in the course of developing or confirming important information should always be able to invoke a "public interest" defence. In other words, British statutory or common law crimes which do not have such defences (they are termed "strict

---

[31] *Fressoz and Roire v. France* 5 B.H.R.C. 654, para. 54.

liability offences") should not be levelled against journalists who have acted in conformity with their own professional codes.

The decision in *Fressoz and Roire* turned on a new core principle (our eighth) first developed in 1996 in *Goodwin v. United Kingdom* (below), namely:

8. "the safeguard offered by Article 10 to journalists in relation to reporting on articles of general interest is subject to the proviso that they are acting in good faith in order to provide accurate and reliable information in accordance with the ethics of journalism".

If this proviso is satisfied, then the journalist is entitled to defeat a claim under Article 10(2), no matter how clearly made out. Thus the French journalists were able to resist application of a criminal law they had undoubtedly broken, and Mr Goodwin was entitled to commit contempt by disobeying a court order to name his source. Another application of core principle 8, which has significance for English libel practice, is *Bergens Tidende v. Norway*:

The applicant, a Norwegian daily newspaper, had been ordered to pay very heavy damages to a cosmetic surgeon whose professional career and business were ruined by articles in which several of his clients detailed their unsuccessful operations. They spoke out after the surgeon had been favourably profiled in the same newspaper, and their accounts recited failures that had happened and their honest, if emotional, feelings. Although in reality the surgeon was not incompetent, as the article implied, because he had conducted thousands of successful cosmetic operations. The bad publicity had clearly damaged the surgeon's right to professional reputation, but this was not sufficient to override the freedom of the press to impart information on matters of legitimate public concern, where the newspaper had reported accurately and ethically on an important controversy relating to public health.[32]

The importance of this case is that the Court made a broad-brush public interest judgment, namely that newspapers should not be penalised in damages for reporting the ordeals of women with leaky implants who had suffered damage while under the care of otherwise competent plastic surgeons. British libel courts would have treated this case on a much more artificial footing, as turning on whether the "ordinary reader" would take the allegations to mean that the surgeon was incompetent. If so (and this was an impression which many readers would have gathered) then the newspaper would have lost, since it could not "justify" (*i.e.* prove true) this meaning. If the Human Rights Act is to have effect on libel pleadings, this narrow concentration on the mean-

[32] *Bergens Tidende v. Norway* (2001) 31 E.H.R.R. 430.

ing of words should be replaced by a broader test of whether the publication of them genuinely served the public interest, irrespective of damage to individual reputation. This was the approach taken by the Strasbourg court in another case involving a Norwegian newspaper held to have defamed seal-hunters by accusing them of unlawfully "flaying alive" their quarry. They had not been offered a right of reply, but since the allegations were based on an official report and the newspaper had given voice to all sides in its long-running balanced coverage of a controversial issue, the damage to reputation was a relevant but insufficient reason "to outweigh the vital public interest in ensuring an informed public debate over a matter of local and national as well as international interest".[33] This is a valuable example of the proportionality test protecting public interest journalism conducted in good faith, despite a failure to check facts and the presence of some error and exaggeration.

ARTICLE 10: SOME UNITED KINGDOM DECISIONS

A number of cases from Britain have proved seminal in developing the core principles of Article 10, and they deserve special study because of the impact they have had on extending press freedom. The potential of the Convention was first demonstrated by the *Sunday Times* case:

> *The Sunday Times* proposed to publish an article about the marketing of thalidomide, a pregnancy drug that had caused birth deformities, despite the existence of long-running legal actions for negligence between parents and the drug manufacturers which might eventually come to trial. English courts ruled that the article could not be published, because it "prejudged" issues in litigation, and was therefore a contempt of court. The newspaper and its journalists applied to the European Court, claiming that the ban was an infringement of their right to freedom of expression. The British Government argued that the contempt law, as applied in this case, was necessary to uphold both "the authority of the judiciary" and the legal rights of the drug manufacturers. The Court held for *The Sunday Times*. It said that the thalidomide disaster was a matter of public concern, and the mere fact that litigation was in progress did not alter the right and, indeed, responsibility of the mass media to impart information of public interest. The public had a right to be properly informed, which could be denied them only if the article unarguably presented a threat to judicial authority. In the circumstances, the article was moderate in tone and presented both sides of the case; it would not have prejudiced a trial (before a judge sitting without a jury) or added much to the growing moral pressure on the manufacturers to settle the claim. It followed that the interference by the English courts did not correspond to a social need sufficiently pressing to outweigh the public interest in freedom of expression. It was

---

[33] *Bladet Tromsø v. Norway* (1999) 29 E.H.R.R. 125 at para. 73.

both out of proportion to any social need to protect the impartiality of the courts and the rights of litigants, and it was not a restriction necessary in a democratic society to uphold these values.[34]

The Sunday Times decision meant that because of its treaty obligations, the British Government was obliged to change the law on contempt of court. This it did by the 1981 Contempt of Court Act: no longer would investigative stories be stopped merely because they might "prejudice" litigation at some future time. This historic case marked the first impact of the Convention on English common law. There were more to come, although not all of them went to the Court for judgment. There was a filter—a European Commission of Human Rights—which excluded hopeless cases. If it decided that a case was likely to succeed however, it would offer "friendly settlement" so that the Government might put its law in order to avoid a court hearing. An historic case where the United Kingdom agreed to legislate to give the media specific legal rights is *Hodgson and Channel 4 v. United Kingdom*[35]:

> Until 1989 newspapers and television stations had no right to challenge a gag order imposed by a judge at a criminal trial. Journalists had no standing to apply to the trial judge to lift the order, and there was no avenue open for them to appeal to any other court. This situation was in blatant breach of Article 13 of the European Convention, which requires that anyone whose rights (*e.g.* to freedom of expression) are violated should have an "effective remedy". Channel 4 had no remedy at all when the judge at the controversial Official Secrets trial of Clive Ponting issued an order banning the television station from using actors to read each evening from the day's transcripts. So both Channel 4 and Godfrey Hodgson (the programme's presenter) filed a complaint with the European Commission at Strasbourg, which upheld the complaint under Article 13. The United Kingdom Government accepted this ruling, and negotiated a "friendly settlement" with the complainants, which took the form of drafting a new law (now section 159 of the Criminal Justice Act 1988), giving the media a special right to appeal to the Court of Appeal against gag orders or decisions to exclude the press and public from any part of a trial.

The *Hodgson* case shows how individual journalists can use the Convention to enhance the rights of the media generally. The initiative originally came from an Old Bailey reporter, Tim Crook, who challenged a secrecy order in the Divisional Court, in a case that established that the media had no effective remedy under English law. (It is a strict prerequisite of a complaint to Strasbourg that any possible domestic remedy should first be exhausted.) He then filed his application with

---

[34] *The Sunday Times v. U.K.* (1979) 2 E.H.R.R. 245.
[35] *Hodgson and Others v. U.K. and Channel 4 v. U.K.*, Decision on admissibility, March 9, 1987, 51 D.R. 136.

the European Commission, which was favourably settled by the British Government after the ruling in *Hodgson*. Both Crook and NUJ officials, along with Hodgson and Channel 4's lawyers, participated in the settlement negotiations which led to the drafting of section 159.

The European Court next struck a blow against national security, ruling that the use of pre-publication injunctions to stop *Spycatcher* from being published in England was an infringement of Article 10.[36] This decision hardly came as a surprise, although in this case the Court emphasised that the media had a duty to impart information (principle 6, above) and that the public had a correlative right to receive it. "Were it otherwise, the press would be unable to play its vital role of *public watchdog*". The Court uttered the warning about prior restraint discussed in Chapter 1. After *Spycatcher* had been published outside Britain, the Government could only justify the ban on the basis that this would reduce sales and thus "punish" the author by loss of royalties thereby perhaps deterring other spies motivated to write memoirs for money. This, the Court decided, was a "relevant" but not "sufficient" reason for the ban: it could not prevail against the duty of the press to purvey information (already available overseas) on a matter of legitimate public concern.[37]

Prime Minister Margaret Thatcher had been determined to punish Peter Wright and his publishers, no matter what damage she did to free speech or to the security service itself. Regrettably, many British judges of that time upheld the Government's bogus claim of national security. Their behaviour might be explained by the absence of any presumption in favour of free speech in the common law, in which they had been brought up, and which always gave precedence to rights of property. In similar vein, England's highest judiciary, *en masse*, could not understand how a journalist's promise to protect his source could prevail over a corporation's right to protect its profits: what came as a shock to the judges and as a boon to working journalists was the 1996 decision in *Goodwin v. United Kingdom*, which extended Article 10 protection to journalistic sources:

> Trainee journalist Bill Goodwin had been fined (he could have been imprisoned) for contempt by refusing to disclose the identity of the source who leaked to him confidential information which showed that an aggressive private company's financial position was not as sound as it publicly pretended. Goodwin worked for *The Engineer* magazine, and had been tipped off with details from the company's still-secret business plan: when he rang the company to confirm them, it responded by rushing to court to obtain an injunction against any publication and an order for him to name

---

[36] *Observer and Guardian v. U.K.*, 14 E.H.R.R. 153 at 191, para. 59–60.
[37] *ibid.* at para. 68–69.

his source. The company complained that public exposure of its refinancing problems might cost hundreds of jobs. The defendant denied that the source, who had provided him with reliable information before, was criminal or malicious, but this did not stop the British courts from inferring (wrongly) that the source had been involved in stealing a copy of the business plan or else must have been a high executive deserving exposure and punishment for corporate disloyalty. All judges at all stages in Britain held the journalist in contempt, but the European Court overruled them:

> "Protection of journalistic sources is one of the basic conditions for press freedom . . . Without such protection, sources may be deterred from assisting the press in informing the public on matters of public interest. As a result the vital public watchdog role of the press may be undermined and the ability of the press to provide accurate and reliable information may be adversely affected . . . such a measure cannot be compatible with Article 10 of the Convention unless it is justified by an overriding requirement in the public interest."[38]

That the contempt finding was "necessary in a democratic society" had to be proved ("convincingly established") by the United Kingdom in terms of a "pressing social need": criminalisation of the journalist had to be a proportionate response to the aim of protecting corporate confidentiality. The Court decided that since the company was protected by the injunction against publication, it could not go further and demand the unmasking of the source in order to retrieve its document or sue for compensation or dismiss for disloyalty. Its obvious private interest in such reprisals was insufficient to displace the *public* interest in source protection. The punishment of the journalist was disproportionate to the aim of protecting corporate privacy, because this would have the consequence of "drying up" news sources.

In 1998 the United Kingdom suffered another unexpected defeat, when Article 10 was used to challenge an election statute—section 75 of the Representation of the People Act (1983)—which then prohibited pressure groups from spending more than £5 during the election period in promoting or opposing the election of a particular candidate. The £5 limit was a disproportionate restriction, unnecessarily severe in light of the legitimate aim of the legislation, namely of securing an equal playing field for all candidates. Decided in 1998, *Bowman v. United Kingdom* was the first human rights claim opposed (and lost) by the new Labour Government.

> Mrs Bowman was secretary of an anti-abortion group which leafleted voters in various constituencies with a factual account of the views and voting records on abortion of all local candidates. She was prosecuted under section 75 for incurring more than £5 expenditure, in one particular

---

[38] *Goodwin v. U.K.* (1996) 22 E.H.R.R. 123 at 143, para. 39.

constituency, after a complaint on behalf of Alice Mahon M.P., the pro-choice Labour candidate. Other pressure groups had been threatened with prosecution at these elections for promoting discussion of candidate positions on controversial issues (Charter 88 was warned that it could not spend more than £5 to hire a hall in which local candidates would be quizzed about their support for a bill of rights). The Eurocourt held that a ban on the distribution of factual information about particular candidates at election time was disproportionate to the section 75 object of securing an equal playing field for individual candidates, because it had the effect of precluding third party campaigns in local constituencies. It derided the United Kingdom argument that Mrs Bowman could disseminate the information by standing for Parliament herself or by owning newspapers (which are exempted from section 75): she had no effective channel to communicate the facts other than by leaflets. A law which limited her expenditure to a futile £5 was unnecessary and disproportionate.[39]

Bowman, like *Goodwin* is an impressive example of the Court spelling out of Article 10 a free speech implication that had never previously been noticed. In both cases the test of "proportionality" is applied, to emphasise an implication drawn from the free speech guarantee—that it entails source protection, or that it becomes especially precious during elections. In Bowman, the Court could give Article 10 particular force because it served to further another Convention objective, in this case the right to free elections "under conditions which will ensure the free expression of the opinion of the people in the choice of the legislature".[40] Where a complainant can demonstrate that an act of censorship had damaged, in its course, not only freedom of expression but another Convention right, the case for striking it down is particularly strong.

THE HUMAN RIGHTS ACT 1998

The European Convention was cemented into English constitutional law by the new Labour Government in 1998. There was very little opposition to the measure: the slogan "rights brought home" emphasised that it would no longer be necessary to go off on a seven-year trek to Strasbourg to obtain relief which would now be available instantly in the High Court. A handful of Tory cynics complained about the extra powers it would give to an untrustworthy judiciary (this had previously

---

[39] *Bowman v. U.K.* (1998) 26 E.H.R.R. 1 at paras 41–47. The law was in consequence amended by the Political Parties Elections and Referendums Act 2000, but only to permit expenditure of £500.
[40] See First Protocol to the ECHR, Art. 3.

been a concern of Labour's left wing, which fell silent in the early flush of enthusiasm for Blairite manifesto reforms). Since previous governments had rejected demands for a Bill of Rights on the basis that it would undermine "Parliamentary sovereignty"—the right of a Government backed by a parliamentary majority to pass any law it liked, however absurd or inhumane, and to require the judiciary loyally to implement it—most interest in the Human Rights Act focused not on the Convention (which is imported into law as a Schedule to the Act) but on the new powers and procedures to implement it.

"This Bill will increase individual rights in the United Kingdom" announced the Prime Minister in his introduction to the 1997 White Paper (*Rights Brought Home*) which preceded the Human Rights Act. Its preamble declares it:

> "An Act to give *further* effect to rights and freedoms guaranteed under the European Convention . . .". [our italics]

"Further" is an important word, signalling that this is not legislation which preserves the status quo: rights like free speech are to be enhanced as a result of the legislation. The point is made again in section 11: the Convention cannot be used so as to *restrict* a freedom enjoyed before its enactment (for example, the bold British "open justice" principle cannot be read down by reference to its more cautious European counterpart in Article 6). The really significant aspect of the Human Rights Act, however, is that it provides legal power for the media to go on the attack.

Section 6 makes it unlawful for a "public authority" (that phrase includes courts and tribunals) to act in a way which is incompatible with Article 10, unless such action is required by a statute passed by Parliament (*i.e.* by "primary legislation"). Where "secondary legislation"—rules made by government under powers given by primary legislation—is concerned, this must be construed so far as possible in conformity with the Convention, or else declared *ultra vires* unless the incompatibility is expressly required by primary legislation. In all other cases—*i.e.* where common not statute law is concerned ("common law" like libel and breach of confidence is law made by judges over the centuries), or where a judge is exercising a discretion (including cases where a statute gives that discretion) Article 10 is in the driving seat: the court must give it full force and credit. It is not sufficient for public authorities merely to "take account" of Article 10 or to "have regard" to it: they must not act in any way incompatibly with it.

"Public authorities" which are bound to act in accordance with the freedom of expression guarantee include not only courts and tribunals, but government departments, local authorities, police and prison officials and "any person certain of whose functions are functions of a public nature". This clearly includes statutory media regulators like the ITC, the Radio Authority, the Broadcasting Standards Commission and certain private bodies which have acquired statutory functions, like the Advertising Standards Authority and the British Board of Film and Video Classification together with its Video Appeals Committee. It probably includes the Press Complaints Commission, which although it has no statutory underpinning serves a public function and was established as an alternative to government regulation. [41] The PCC should welcome this duty to uphold free speech in its adjudications: it has not yet been called upon to answer a judicial review challenge. It has thus far not objected to attempts to judicially review its decisions. Newspapers of course are themselves private bodies. So are Channel 5 and the various cable and satellite broadcasters, although the ITC which regulates them is a public authority for the purposes of the Act. The BBC is set up under a Royal Charter and has undertaken regulatory duties parallel to those of the ITC: there is no reason why it should not be similarly bound. It has been challenged on judicial review—notably over its allocation of election broadcasts[42]—and in this and other respects it will probably be obliged by law to uphold Article 10 (and Article 8, which guarantees the right to privacy). Channel 4, as a statutory corporation with statutory duties, is likely to be similarly affected.

By section 7 of the Human Rights Act any victim whose free speech might have been infringed or is threatened with infringement may, within a year, bring a specific action against the infringing authority in the High Court, or else rely on Article 10 in legal proceedings brought on other grounds. There is only one catch: the claimant must be a "victim", *i.e.* a person directly affected by a violation, real or prospective. The Human Rights Act on this "victim test" incorporates Article 34 of the European Convention, under which journalists, publishers and printers have all been held "victims" of criminal and civil laws which affect publications. Since Article 10 protects the right to *receive* as well as to impart information and ideas, it may be possible for readers and viewers with a genuine interest in access to suppressed material to bring legal proceedings to quash a ban. On this basis, the European Court permitted Irish women of childbearing age to complain about a ban on the publication of information about overseas abortion

---

[41] The PCC, although a voluntary body, performs public duties and hence is arguably capable of being judicially reviewed: *R v. Press Complaints Commission, ex p. Stewart Brady* [1997] E.M.L.R. 185 and see Lewis, *Judicial Remedies in Public Law*, 2nd ed. para 2–069. The Government indicated its view that the PCC was a "public authority" for the purposes of the HRA: *Hansard* 314 H.C. Debs (6th series) col. 414.

[42] *R. v. BBC, ex p. Referendum Party* [1997] C.O.D. 459. The Divisional Court declined to make a ruling on the BBC's liability to judicial review.

facilities.[43] There is some uncertainty in Convention jurisprudence about when victimhood is "potential" enough to permit action: Mrs Bowman was permitted to challenge the ban on election campaigning by her pressure group even though she had been acquitted—the fact that she had been prosecuted several times before made a future prosecution a real possibility.[44] The editor of *The Guardian* was held not to be a "potential victim" when he sought to challenge the ban on advocacy of republicanism in the 1848 Treason Felony Act—the last time the Act had been used to jail a republican editor was 1848.[45] Journalists should be able to seek a "declaration of incompatibility" in respect of archaic common laws and repressive statutes under which their writings might be censored, notwithstanding the fact that these laws are not enforced: the policy might change, and their very existence exerts a chilling effect.[46] However, in 2001 the "victimhood" test is an unnecessary and irritating technicality which will serve to protect some offensive laws and practices: many judges, led by Lord Woolf, protested about its adoption but to no avail—the Government wanted to avoid test cases brought by interest groups.[47] It is, however, unacceptable that rules and decisions which infringe human rights should persist because interest groups which could fund the litigation to strike them down are denied the standing to do so. Newspapers are handicapped in bringing test cases against obnoxious legislation: *The Guardian* also wanted to challenge the Act of Settlement 1701, which provides that the Crown should descend only to Protestants and to men ahead of women, but its editor, a male and a commoner, could not claim to be a victim. (The Princess Royal declined the newspaper's offer to fund her challenge to the line of succession.)

In the case of statutes which on their face require an unacceptable infringement of free speech, the court has two options. First and foremost, it is given a brand new power of statutory interpretation—really, of statutory re-interpretation. Under section 3(1):

> "So far as it is possible to do so, primary legislation and subordinate legislation must be read and given effect in a way which is compatible with the Convention rights".

---

[43] *Open Door and Dublin Well Women Clinic v. Ireland* (1992) 15 E.H.R.R. 244.

[44] *Bowman v. U.K.* (1998) 26 E.H.R.R. 1.

[45] *Rusbridger v. Att.-Gen.*, June 22, 2001 (Administrative Court) and see *Times Newspapers Ltd v. U.K.* [1990] 65 D.R. 307, where the European Commission disallowed an application by *The Times* protesting against the size of libel damages because it had not (unlike other newspapers) suffered through an actual case.

[46] See *Norris v. Ireland* (1988) 13 E.H.R.R., paras 32–34, where an Irish homosexual was held a "victim", although "the risk of prosecution was minimal".

[47] See Lester and Pannick, *Human Rights Law and Practice* p. 38.

This is an imaginative way of reconciling the new judicial power to protect basic rights with the age-old constitutional principle that Parliament must retain sovereignty. If it is *possible* to give statutory language an interpretation which accords with the Convention, that interpretation must prevail. This is not a power to be underrated. When a barrister says that your case is "arguable", that decodes as meaning he will be happy to accept a fee for the pleasure of making an argument which is likely to fail. But section 3 turns that which is merely arguable into an argument which should succeed, if it is the only plausible argument which can make a statute conform to the Convention. In so far as language permits, the court must choose a construction of statutory words which most effectuates free speech—there will be a presumption in favour of the meaning which least restricts the media, even if it is a strained interpretation of the legislative language compared with other meanings which more honestly reflect Parliament's intention to ignore or limit human rights. Section 3 has a radical impact which means that "well-entrenched ideas may have to be put aside, sacred cows culled".[48]

If it is simply not possible to fashion the statutory language into a meaning consistent with Article 10, then the High Court may issue a "declaration of incompatibility". This will, in cases which the Government deems "compelling", provide the Minister with the power immediately to amend the law by an Order in Council. But "compelling" is a difficult test to satisfy, and this emergency power is unlikely to be used. Nonetheless, a "declaration of incompatibility" provides a real impetus to amend the law in due course, if only because it will be a clear signal for the European Court of Human Rights (which retains its supervisory role) to find Britain in breach of the Convention if no remedial action is taken.

As to the meaning of Article 10, there are three basic guides:

   (i) the language of the Article itself, with its structure long established in Convention law;

   (ii) section 2 of the Human Rights Act, which says that British courts *must* take into account Strasbourg case-law;

   (iii) section 12 of the Human Rights Act, which gives "particular importance" to Article 10 in certain circumstances.

(i) *Article 10 itself*

We all have the right to freedom of expression, to hold opinions and to receive and impart information and ideas without interference, subject to such restrictions as are prescribed by law and are necessary in a

---

[48] *R v. Lambert* [2001] 3 All E.R. 577, HL *per* Lord Slynn at para 6. See also *R v. A* [2001] 3 All E.R. 1, HL, especially Lord Steyn at paras 32–46.

democratic society in the interests of national security, prevention of crime, protection of morals, protection of the reputation and rights of others, preventing disclosure of confidential information or maintaining the authority of the judiciary.

The first trap for unwary judges is to think this is no more than a statement of the good old British balancing act, the "free speech does not mean free speech" approach in *James v. Commonwealth*. But what the European Court has said, in its *Sunday Times v. United Kingdom* judgment of 1979, is that Article 10 is *not* a balance between free speech and other values of equal weight. Article 10(2) should be looked upon as containing "a number of exceptions which must be strictly construed and narrowly interpreted and convincingly established". Once the Court is satisfied that there has been an infringement, the burden shifts to the Government or to the party seeking to justify the breach to prove that the infringing law is a clearly defined restriction which legitimately serves an Article 10(2) value and its application is necessary—not expedient—to serve a pressing social need in a democratic society, and is a reasonably proportionate response to that need. In short, the Act writes into British law, for the first time, a presumption in favour of free speech, putting the burden on the censor to justify, as a matter both of necessity and of logic, the restriction imposed.

(ii) *European case law: the "core principles"*

Section 2 of the Act says that the court must take into account any opinions of the European Court and even of the now defunct European Commission. This section is valuable, up to a point, because it gives authority to the "core principles" which Strasbourg has developed for Article 10. Equally, section 2 will provide precedent in English law for decisions like *Goodwin*, spelling out a right to protect journalistic sources from the general Article 10 guarantee, and *Bowman* with its insistence that the free marketplace of ideas is more, not less, important at election time.

But there are dangers in applying Strasbourg decisions, because many of them turn not on an application of principle but on what is called the "margin of appreciation"—a doctrine which accords some latitude to Member States in adapting the principles to their own culture and conditions. It is really no more than a self-denying ordinance developed by international courts for situations (especially in respect of laws relating to morals) where they are nervous about imposing their judgment over that of the domestic authorities. What English courts must appreciate is that they have *no* margin of appreciation: they sit *on* the margin, and Strasbourg decisions which apply this doctrine provide no precedent. The case of *Wingrove v. United Kingdom*, for example, which rejected the complaint of a film-maker refused a certificate for *Visions of Ecstasy* because of blasphemy, provides no authority at all for an English court to reject a Human Rights Act challenge to the blasphemy law, because *Wingrove* was a decision taken by reference to the United Kingdom's "margin of appreciation", and the European Court said—in terms—that our domestic courts are in touch with "vital forces" in this country, and it is for them to decide how or whether to protect religion.[49] So *Wingrove* should not inhibit British judges from giving Tom Paine at last his due by abolishing this oppressive and discriminatory relic of the common law.

It is important to note that section 2 says that Strasbourg cases must be "taken into account" (not followed slavishly and used as a precedent) and only "so far as it is relevant to the proceedings". This is just as well, because although the "core principles" of Article 10 are reasonably stated, some Eurocourt decisions—especially those emanating from nine-judge chambers—are unimpressive and a few have actually been retrogressive. It was a mistake for Section 2 to require that attention be paid to all decisions of the now-defunct European Commission (originally, a filter for the Court) because some of them are short and poorly argued, especially decisions in the 1990s wrongly declaring inadmissible a flood of cases with which the court could not cope, and some in the 1970s before Article 10 principles were fully developed.

The application of Convention rights entails a measuring of what has been done to an alleged victim against the relevant rule in the Convention, as elaborated in the "core principles" stated in Strasbourg case law. Sometimes, of course, the violation will be blatant, *e.g.* when an act of censorship directly infringes Article 10 and has no excuse (or "legitimate aim") that can relate to the exceptions in Article 10(2). More often, however, the decision is reached by applying what is termed the doctrine of *proportionality*—a legal approach that is new to English courts, but which has been introduced into their decision-making by the Human Rights Act. Firstly, the act which is subject of the complaint must be recognised as an infringement of the freedom of expression guarantee. Then, the Court must inquire whether the rule authorising the infringement was sufficiently clear to be "prescribed by law" and had a "legitimate aim", *i.e.* an objective which corresponds to one of the exceptions set out in Article 10(2). (If it has no "legitimate aim" then the Court need go no further—it is a violation, pure and simple.) Then comes the final question of whether the restriction is "necessary in a democratic society", *i.e.* whether it answers to a pressing social need.

This can often be resolved by applying the proportionality test—is the infringement "proportionate" to the legitimate aim it pursues, or

---

[49] *Wingrove v. U.K.* (1996) 24 E.H.R.R. 1.

does it go further than is necessary in a democratic society to achieve that purpose—*e.g.* a "blanket" ban where a narrower ban would suffice, or a restriction which discriminates between rich and poor, or a punishment which is over-severe or not necessary at all because a civil remedy would serve the same purpose. In judicial review proceedings, English courts will declare unlawful an administrative decision which is irrational, in that it bears little logical relationship to the purpose it is meant to serve, but the proportionality test permits a much broader review. The purpose must be "legitimate" (in the sense that it genuinely reflects an Article 10(2) exception) and the measures in pursuance of it must be fair and calculated sensibly to achieve that purpose, and go no further than is necessary in a democracy to protect the excepted value. Proportionality, in other words, is a test of reasonableness which goes beyond the English test of rationality (English judges refer to their rationality test, confusingly, as *Wednesbury* reasonableness"[50])—and it is a "reasonableness" constituted by avoiding any infringement of a bedrock democratic right deemed basic to social progress and individual self-fulfilment.[51] The "proportionality" test for reviewing administrative decisions, imported into English law by the HRA, is transforming the *"Wednesbury* unreasonableness" standard into a test of "reasonableness" *simpliciter.*[52]

(iii) *Section 12—Freedom of expression*

The passage of the Human Rights Act through Parliament was marked by a display of a very English hypocrisy: the two institutions which preach loudest about human rights—the church of England and the press of England—both wanted to be exempted from it. The church because it wanted to keep on discriminating and the press because it wanted to continue to invade privacy. Although God was given only a minor dispensation, Rupert Murdoch and his local vicar, Lord Wakeham (Chairman of the Press Complaints Commission), managed to persuade the Government to insert a novel provision to entrench "freedom of expression". Section 12 of the Human Rights Act provides that a court must have particular regard to the importance of the right to freedom of expression in actions against the media. It applies only to civil proceedings—although it is difficult to accept that freedom of expression can be particularly important in the High Court and important, but not

---

[50] This phrase stems from the name of the case in which the irrationality test was first adopted—*Associated Provincial Picture Houses v. Wednesbury Corp.* [1948] K.B. 223.

[51] See *Lingens v. Austria* (1986) 8 E.H.R.R. 407 at 418–9, paras 41–2.

[52] This is the logical result of the House of Lords decision in *R. v. Secretary of State for Home Department, ex p. Daly* [2001] U.K.H.L. 26.

particularly important, down at the Old Bailey. It applies not only when legal proceedings relate to "material which appears to the court to be journalistic" (which is fair enough) but to material "which the respondent *claims* to be journalistic" (where the *Sunday Sport* is concerned, the difference may be crucial). In such cases the court is enjoined by section 12(4)(b) to have particular regard to the public interest in publication or alternatively to "any relevant privacy code" which includes the PCC Code of Conduct). The section reads as follows:

"1. This Section applies if a court (which includes a tribunal) is considering whether to grant any relief which, if granted, might affect the exercise of the Convention right to freedom of expression . . .

3. No such relief is to be granted so as to restrain publication before trial unless the court is satisfied that the applicant is likely to establish that publication should not be allowed.

4. The Court must have particular regard to the Convention right to freedom of expression and, where the proceedings relate to material which the respondent claims, or which appears to the Court, to be journalistic, literary or artistic material (or to conduct connected with such material), to—

(a) the extent to which—

(i) the material has, or is about to, become available to the public; or
(ii) it is, or would be, in the public interest for the material to be published;

(b) any relevant privacy code. . . ."

The object of the media proprietors who lobbied for section 12 was to discourage the courts from using Article 8 to develop a privacy law. It is doubtful whether section 12 does this effectively, and some commentators have suggested that it serves no useful purpose.[53] But section 12 has a capacity to rise above its unprepossessing origins and to put Article 10 in lights by giving its presumption in favour of free speech a special force. It serves to divorce the free speech principle in Article 10(1) from the exemptions in 10(2), and states in terms that the public interest in publication is to be brought into particular consideration. It places a lot of obstacles in the path of that bane of Sunday newspaper life, the Saturday afternoon interim injunction. This can no longer be granted on the "balance of convenience" principle: the court must henceforth be satisfied that the claimant is likely to win—a test which

[53] *e.g.* Lester and Pannick, *Human Rights Law and Practice*, p. 47 where it is suggested that s.12 adds "nothing of substance".

is closer to that for libel injunctions (which are rarely granted). Moreover, the judge must pay particular regard not only to the freedom of expression right *and* to the public interest, but also "to the extent to which the material has, or is about to, become available to the public". So that's goodbye to *Spycatcher*, where the book was already on sale to every public except the British, and to *Schering v. Falkman*, where the information suppressed as "confidential" could have been gathered from press clippings. It means that henceforth, courts should rarely if ever grant injunctions to suppress material which has "escaped" on the internet.

This requirement that the Court must take into account "the extent to which the material is about to become available" reflects the impossibility of containing newsworthy information, once it has escaped its gatekeeper, and signals the end of injunctions like that granted in 1999 against the *Sunday Telegraph* to stop premature publication of the Stephen Lawrence Report. This has been the consequence of the new Bill of Rights in South Africa, which has had a markedly liberalising effect on media law. In *Government of South Africa v. Sunday Times* the facts were almost identical to the Lawrence Report case: the South African Government tried to injunct premature publication of a report into corruption by invoking a statutory regulation that prohibited publication of such reports until presented to the President. The court struck down the regulation as contrary to the freedom of expression guarantee, and held that no injunction could be granted in the absence of the clearest proof of serious harm.[54]

Section 12(3) makes new provision for pre-trial injunctions, by providing that no such relief (*i.e.* that might affect the right to freedom of expression) is to be granted "unless the court is satisfied that the applicant is likely to establish that publication should not be allowed". This makes clear that courts cannot simply apply the test in *American Cyanamid* of determining whether or not to grant an injunction on the balance of convenience. That will no longer be a proper approach. Difficult as it may be in the rushed circumstances in which applications are often heard and with the evidence then only in an incomplete state, the court will have to determine the likelihood of the claimant succeeding at trial. The onus is on the claimant who will have to demolish any realistic defences which might be advanced at trial.

Section 12 serves to entrench the right of free speech in newsworthy cases. But what about cases where the news is unworthy—of no public interest, obtained by outrageous invasion of privacy? The original point of section 12 was to give the media a special privilege so it could ward off privacy claims and injunctions. But this may backfire, because section 12 (4) (b) requires the court to "pay particular regard to any relev-

---

[54] *Government of the Republic of South Africa v. Sunday Times Newspaper* (1995) 1 L.R.C. 168.

ant privacy code". It does not say "pay particular regard to the existence of an alternative remedy offered by the Press Complaints Commission (PCC) or the Broadcasting Standards Commission (BSC)". It says "pay particular regard to the relevant *code*". So: the very first thing the judge must ask in any civil action is "bring me the code". And, as the Home Secretary pointed out:

> "The fact that a newspaper complied with the terms of the code operated by the PCC—or conversely that it has breached the code—is one of the factors the courts should take into account in considering whether to grant relief".[55]

This means that judges will have the duty, in press/privacy cases, of calling for the PCC code (or the BSC code, when the case concerns television) and deciding whether it has been breached. This will be a hostage to fortune, for as we shall see the PCC code is designed as a public relations exercise, rather than as a principled statement of media freedom. For example, it purports to prohibit publication of photographs of people taken "on *public* or private property where there is a reasonable expectation of privacy". The law, by definition, denies privacy to those in public places, but if section 12 incorporates the PCC code, the result will be to extend the law of privacy, in some cases contrary to the interests of investigative television. Similarly, the PCC rule that "Journalists and photographers must neither obtain nor seek to obtain information or pictures through harassment or persistent pursuit" may be invoked by crooks and con men to obtain injunctions against door-stepping programmes of the kind popularised by Roger Cook. So the tabloid press may rue the day it prevailed on the Government to put the PCC code—in some respects an unrealistic and over-interfering code— in the hands of the judiciary, to interpret and to adjudicate breaches. It may conduce to the rapid development of privacy law, not along the narrow lines of Article 8, but glossed with broad judicial interpretations of a vague PCC code.

The news media, contrary to their own beliefs, may well gain from Article 8. It requires respect for private and family life, home and correspondence, and erects the barrier test of "necessity" to limit intrusions by State and public authorities. Strasbourg jurisprudence establishes that it protects a person's office or other place of work,[56] so it will in consequence benefit journalists who are faced with police searches or other intrusions by State agents. Although United Kingdom law requires police to go through a special procedure before they can seize journalistic material, in practice they encounter little difficulty from judges

---

[55] *Hansard*, July 2, 1998, 315 H.C. (6th Series) col. 538–9.
[56] *Niemetz v. Germany* (1992) 16 E.H.R.R. 97.

who are generally anxious to let them have, for example, unpublished photographs or untransmitted video footage of violent demonstrations. The Convention criteria of "proportionality" should inject a new rigour into judicial scrutiny of police applications.

A NEW LEGAL LANDSCAPE

The advent of the Human Rights Act has important implications for every area of media law and it will be some years before its impact can be finally assessed. British judges acquired some experience in giving force to constitutional protections for freedom of expression by dint of their service on the Privy Council, which still hears final appeals from a number of Commonwealth countries whose constitutions embody human rights guarantees. As early as 1967, for example, they struck down a Maltese law prohibiting civil servants from bringing into their place of work any newspaper that had been condemned by the Catholic Church.[57] In 1990 they stopped the prosecution of the Antiguan journalist, Tim Hector, who faced imprisonment for publishing "a false statement . . . likely to undermine public confidence in the conduct of public affairs". This law could not be justified as a necessary interference with free speech in a democratic society: since the very purpose of criticising officials was to undermine public confidence in their stewardship, the law was by its own definition a cloak for political censorship. The law was not saved by the requirement that the statement should be false: freedom of speech, the Privy Council correctly held, would be gravely impeded if would-be critics had to verify all their facts before they could speak without fear of criminal charges.[58]

A Convention-based approach to the free speech right is exemplified by another case from Antigua, *de Freitas v. Permanent Secretary of Ministry of Agriculture*[59]:

> A Royal Commission in Antigua exposed the corruption which riddled that country's Government and tainted in particular the Minister of Agriculture, who declined to resign or pay back the bribes he had accepted. A civil servant in his department was observed at a peaceful demonstration against Government corruption: he was suspended and disciplined under a law which prevented public servants from expressing opinions on matters of political controversy. The Privy Council ruled that this blanket restraint was disproportionate to the legitimate objective of securing neutrality in the bureaucracy and could not reasonably be justified in a demo-

[57] *Olivier v. Buttigieg* [1967] 1 A.C. 115.
[58] *Hector v. Att.-Gen. of Antigua and Barbuda* [1990] 2 A.C. 312.
[59] *Ellroy de Freitas v. Permanent Secretary of Ministry of Agriculture, Fisheries Lands and Housing* [1999] A.C. 69.

cratic society: it followed that his rights under the Constitutional guarantee of free speech had been infringed. The question was whether the challenged provision arbitrarily or excessively violated the enjoyment of a guaranteed right, to be decided by application of a tripartite test for proportionality, namely whether:

(1) the legislative object is sufficiently important to justify limiting a fundamental right;
(2) the measures designed to meet the legislative objective are rationally connected to it; and
(3) the means used to impair the right or freedom are no more than is necessary to accomplish the objective.

It is a measure of the international reach of human rights jurisprudence that this tripartite test for disproportionality comes into English law via an Antiguan appeal to the Privy Council which adopted it from a decision of the Chief Justice of Zimbabwe who picked it up from decisions of South African and Canadian judges who had in turn drawn on the "proportionality" jurisprudence of the European Court of Human Rights. Despite (in fact, because of) this pedigree, the formula is unsatisfactory, with its plodding language and lawyerly "on the one hand but then on the other" qualifications. The Privy Council decision only came alive when it moved into the top gear of the First Amendment, citing with approval Justice Brennan's full-blooded condemnation of blanket bans on the expression of opinion:

"The objectionable quality of vagueness and overbreadth (depends) upon the danger of tolerating, in the area of First Amendment freedoms, the existence of a penal statute susceptible of sweeping and improper application . . . These freedoms are delicate and vulnerable, as well as supremely precious in our society. The threat of sanctions may deter their exercise almost as potently as the actual application of sanctions . . . Because First Amendment freedoms need breathing space to survive, government may regulate in the area only with narrow specificity."[60]

Even in the "phoney war" period before the Human Rights Act took full effect, it had a major impact. The first recorded beneficiary was an Algerian refugee, Fateh Rechachi, who had been charged under section 16B of the Prevention of Terrorism Act with possessing information "likely to be of use to terrorists"—including guerrilla warfare books available from major bookstores. In 1999 he challenged the DPP's decision to prosecute him as irrational, on the basis that the DPP had

---

[60] *National Association for the Advancement of Colored People v. Button* (1963) 371 U.S. 415, 432–33.

an obligation to respect the Act and not prosecute in contravention of it, even though it was not yet in force. The Chief Justice, ruling on the Human Rights Act for the very first time, declared section 16B a "blatant contravention" of the Convention because it reversed the presumption of innocence (the defendant had to prove "reasonable excuse" for his possession of freely available literature once police suspected him of helping terrorists). This breached Article 6 (right to a fair trial) and violated Article 10 as well. The case against Rechachi was dropped.[61] This was an astonishing result, given the penchant of British judges to uphold anti-terrorist legislation, but there were more shocks in store, especially the opinion of the Law Lords in the case of *R v. Home Secretary, ex p. Simms*[62]:

> A prison rule prohibited prisoners from being interviewed by journalists. It was upheld by the Court of Appeal on the basis that conviction deprived persons of free speech rights, and that the rule served a legitimate aim in preventing publications which might distress victims or their relatives. The House of Lords, however, held that free speech rights could only be infringed so far as was necessary for prison discipline, not to prevent media investigations of miscarriages of justice. The Court accepted that the media had been of crucial importance in spotlighting wrongful convictions, and had a legitimate role in correcting errors in the functioning of the criminal justice system. Applying the proportionality approach of the European Convention, the Court struck down the rule in its blanket form as *ultra vires*, in that it unnecessarily curtailed both the prisoners' right to free expression and damaged "the safety valve of effective investigative journalism".

The force of Article 10 as entrenched by section 12 of the Human Rights Act was demonstrated in the landmark libel case of *Reynolds v. Times Newspapers*.[63] The House of Lords was called upon to decide whether the common law of libel possessed a "public interest privilege" protecting journalists who published statements on important subjects which they believed to be true, but which turned out to be either incorrect or unprovable. Most previous decisions had rejected any such principle: privilege had been accorded only to private communications or reports from official bodies, and it had been doubted whether newspapers, no matter how carefully or reasonably they acted, could avoid strict liability for defamations published to the world at large except perhaps in the gravest of emergencies. The Human Rights Act helped

---

[61] Unlike the associated case against *Kebilene & Ors* which proceeded to the House of Lords, where it was held that the Divisional Court should not have reviewed the DPP's decision until the HRA came into force. See [2000] 2 A.C. 326.

[62] [2000] 2 A.C. 115.

[63] [1999] 3 W.L.R. 1010.

the *Reynolds* court to fashion a new public interest privilege for news reporting and investigative journalism, so long as it is published without malice after reasonable checks for accuracy and with elemental fairness to the victim (*e.g.* by publishing his explanation or at least inviting his comments). In *Reynolds*, Lord Steyn describes the Human Rights Act as a "new legal landscape"—freedom of expression has become a constitutional right, a rule which exists in the highest legal order. Exceptions must be justified as necessary in a democracy. "In other words, freedom of expression is the rule and regulation of speech is the exception requiring justification . . . if it is underpinned by a pressing social need". In redressing the traditional English imbalance which has historically favoured reputation over free speech, the judges produced in 1999 a solution which had been specifically rejected by an official committee in 1975 (the Faulks Committee on Defamation) when human rights law was unappreciated and (for most lawyers) non-existent. They did so by applying the "core principles" of Article 10, as explained in cases like *Goodwin* and *Lingens* and *Castells*, with assistance from decisions in other Commonwealth jurisdictions, whilst bearing in mind the imminent operation of the Human Rights Act with its section 12 requirement "to have particular regard to the importance of the right to freedom of expression".

The sea change wrought in media law by the Human Rights Act was apparent in the first House of Lords decision after it came into operation on October 2, 2000. In *McCartan Turkington Breen v. Times Newspapers*,[64] a firm of Irish solicitors who had acted for a soldier (Mr Clegg) convicted of murder was defamed in a press release issued by a support group, extracts from which were published in *The Times*. Whether the newspaper could claim qualified privilege for a report of a "public meeting" depended on how that phrase—originating in a nineteenth century statute—should be construed. The lower courts had no doubt that it did not cover either a small gathering to which reporters were invited, or a press release which had not been read at the gathering. The House of Lords, however, insisted that the Victorian-era statutory language should be given a meaning consistent with modern society and "the crucial importance of press freedom" as the means by which public debates are now conducted. In order to permit informed participation by citizens in public life, the press served as "the eyes and ears of the public to whom they report"—not only by reporting protest meetings, but by attending press conferences (unknown in Victorian days) and reproducing press statements. The old legislation according a privilege in aid of reporting could therefore be extended to modern

---

[64] [2001] 2 A.C. 277.

conditions, on the principle that "the path of safety lies in the opportunity to discuss freely supposed grievances and proposed remedies".[65]

That the Law Lords turned for guidance in their first post-Human Rights Act media law decision to a principle formulated by the notable American jurist Louis Brandeis (whose free speech utterances includes the classic "sunlight is said to be the best of disinfectants") is a hopeful sign that the developed law of the First Amendment will be used to enhance British media freedom, as well as the more cautious (and more Europrosaic) core principles of the European Court of Human Rights. This underlines the failure of the English common law, lacking any constitutional basis, to offer satisfactory intellectual principles by which free speech clashes with other values can be resolved. It also affords a pleasing irony, in that the philosophy behind U.S. decisions has been heavily influenced by English writers like Tom Paine and John Stuart Mill, prophets who may now at last be honoured in their own country. The "free market place of ideas" which underpins U.S. media law thinking derives from Mill's argument in *On Liberty* that any censorship of opinion is counterproductive, because it is only by "collision of adverse opinion" that truth will out. This was harnessed to the all-powerful American belief in competition to produce the theory, famously articulated by Justice Holmes in 1919, that "the best test of truth is the power of thought to get itself accepted in the competition of the market". Market distortions being what they later became in the U.S., this was not altogether satisfactory and European jurisprudence reverts to a more classic Millian formulation, referring to "the demands of pluralism, tolerance and broadmindedness without which there is no democratic society". Courts in both countries have additionally recognised that free speech is a necessary condition of the individual soul— as Justice Thurgood Marshal put it in the self-exploring sixties, "Freedom of expression serves not only the needs of the polity but also those of the human spirit—a spirit that demands self-expression." The poet Milton put it rather better in the *Aeropagitica*, three centuries previously.

At any event, these portentous propositions are now a part of English law, thanks to section 12 of the Human Rights Act and Article 10. Lord Steyn promulgated them in his speech in *Simms*, striking down a prison rule that prohibited a convict from complaining to journalists that he had suffered a miscarriage of justice:

> "Freedom of expression is, of course, intrinsically important: it is valued for its own sake. But it is well recognised that it is also instrumentally important. It serves a number of broad objectives.

---

[65] Brandeis J., *Whitney v. California* (1927) 274 U.S. 357 at 375–6.

First, it promotes the self-fulfilment of individuals in society. Secondly, in the famous words of Holmes, J. (echoing John Stuart Mill) "the best test of truth is the power of the thought to get itself accepted in the competition of the market": *Abrams v. U.S.* (1919) 250 U.S. 616 at 630 *per* Holmes J., dissenting. Thirdly, freedom of speech is the lifeblood of democracy. The free flow of information and ideas informs political debate. It is a safety valve: people are more ready to accept decisions that go against them if they can in principle seek to influence them. It acts as a brake on the abuse of power by public officials. It facilitates the exposure of errors in the governance and administration of justice of the country."

These, then, are the human rights rationales for freedom of expression, finally incorporated into English law at the turn of the twenty-first century. When line-drawing exercises are called for in the courts, it will henceforth be necessary for the would-be censor to prove that public harm is real rather than speculative. In a reversal of a long-standing common law approach to street demonstrations (which permitted them to be banned if hypothetical bystanders would be outraged) the High Court in 1999 ruled that a tiresome bible-basher should not have been moved on by police from her makeshift pulpit on the steps of Wakefield cathedral. Justice Stephen Sedley remarked:

"free speech includes not only the inoffensive but the irritating, the contentious, the eccentric, the heretical, the unwelcome and the provocative provided it does not tend to provoke violence. Freedom only to speak inoffensively is not worth having. What Speakers Corner (where the law applies as fully as anywhere else) demonstrates is the tolerance which is both extended by the law to opinion of every kind and expected by the law in the conduct of those who disagree, even strongly, with what they hear. From the condemnation of Socrates to the persecution of modern writers and journalists, our world has seen too many examples of state control of unofficial ideas. A central purpose of the European Convention on Human Rights has been to set close limits to any such assumed power . . .".[66]

---

[66] *Redmond-Bate v. DPP* (1997) 7 B.H.R.C. 375.

CHAPTER 3

DEFAMATION

London is the libel capital of the world. American journalists dub it "a town named Sue" since its claimant-friendly environment attracts litigants unable or unwilling to take their chances under American or European defamation laws which afford better protection for media defendants.[1] The Russian oligarch Boris Berezovsky, defamed by *Forbes* (an American business magazine), chose to sue in London rather than America (where his prospect of success, thanks to the First Amendment, would have been minimal) although the dispute was between foreigners and had no connection with Britain.[2] English law is the preferred option of international public figures because it has traditionally tilted the balance against freedom of speech, with the practical consequence that foreign publishers fearful of attracting an English libel action cut passages critical of wealthy and powerful public figures, or else do not publish here at all (the fate of Kitty Kelley's U.S. best-seller alleging scandals in the monarchy, *The Royals*). Even Daniel Moynihan's celebrated aphorism about his friend Henry Kissinger ("Henry doesn't lie because it's in his interests. He lies because it's in his nature.") was solemnly edited out of books on American politics before they were published here. That Britain should have become a no-go area for information freely published elsewhere in the world poses a serious question: in the global village created by instantaneous electronic communication, does it make any sense for people to have different reputations in different parts of town?

Law must reconcile the right to free speech with the right to reputation. Since American law gives a great deal of protection to defamatory words published in good faith about public figures, and English law

---

[1] The classic study is *Gatley on Libel and Slander*, (9th ed., Milmo & Rogers, 1998). A helpful and streetwise text is David Price, *Defamation: Law Procedure and Practice* (2nd ed., Sweet & Maxwell, 2000). The definitive account of increasingly important American law is by Judge Robert Sack, *Sack on Defamation* (3rd ed., Practising Law Institute, 1999). An enjoyable and insightful romp through recent libel trials is provided by David Hooper, *Reputations Under Fire*, Little, Brown and Co., 2000.

[2] *Berezovsky v. Michaels* [2000] 1 W.L.R. 1004, HL.

gives little, it would seem to follow that speech is accorded more respect in the U.S. Ironically, the contrary is true: in Britain we have an almost supernatural belief in the power of words to wound and destroy. Any mildly critical reference to a prominent person brings forth a pompously threatening solicitor's letter, but in America defamatory words scattered on the raging sea of communication are usually ignored. (For all the apparent permissiveness of the First Amendment, those who write for American publication suffer the schoolmarmish omnipresence of the "fact checker"—a spur to professionalism unknown to the British journalist). Those who believe the English law of libel is an exquisite flower to be preserved in full bloom fail to notice that it has produced a society where it is hard to keep a bad man down (see the crooked career of Robert Maxwell, never exposed by the British press, partly because he owned 30 per cent of it but mainly because the other 70 per cent was intimidated by his libel writs). But the sad fact is that mainstream media interests do not much care about improving the right to report what powerful people do in their business, so long as they can tell readers what they do in bed.

There is nothing objectionable in the principle that a person's reputation should be protected from falsehoods: problems arise because the practices and procedures of the libel law can also work to prevent the exposure of wrongdoing. Cases that come to trial are merely the tip of an iceberg that deep-freezes large chunks of interesting news and comment. In news rooms, libel is the greatest inhibition upon freedom of speech. The task for the journalist and broadcaster is to understand it sufficiently to call the bluff of those who seek to suppress important truths. That the bluff succeeds more often that it should may be the fault of the unconscionably heavy legal costs that can attend even a successful defence, or the business caution of libel insurers who increasingly influence how, or whether, libel writs should be resisted. But journalists who are well versed in legal defences have more latitude than is commonly thought. When the destination is important, the writer's craft can often be steered around the libel minefield. As Lord Devlin pointed out,

> "A man who wants to talk at large about smoke may have to pick his words very carefully if he wants to exclude the suggestion that there is also a fire: but it can be done."[3]

The presence of smoke can be reported much more readily now, thanks to the incorporation of Article 10 of the European Convention on Human Rights, provided some careful checks are made to ensure that it is not bellowing from a smoke machine. That much was estab-

---

[3] *Lewis v. Daily Telegraph* [1964] A.C. 234 at 285.

lished by the landmark case of *Reynolds v. Times Newspapers*, in which the judiciary, despairing of legislative reform by self-interested politicians, cautiously created a public interest defence, the first feature on the "new legal landscape" vouchsafed by the 1998 Human Rights Act. To appreciate the way in which libel law will undergo further transformation, the past—that other country—must briefly be revisited.

THE CHANGING LANDSCAPE

Defamation began in the eleventh century, before the invention of printing, as a creation of the ecclesiastical courts, which would set the village Murdoch in the stocks for disobeying the injunction of Leviticus: "Thou shalt not go up and down as a tale-bearer among the people". Slander initially was a criminal offence: the first statute came in 1275, creating the offence of "*scandalum magnatum*" expressly to protect "the great men of the realm" against discomfiture from stories which might arouse the people against them. It was the threat to civil order which was the gravamen of the criminal offence, hence Lord Chief Justice Coke's famous maxim "The greater the truth the greater the libel"—the populace would be more likely to revolt if allegations against the aristocracy were real rather than imagined. As Coke himself explained, with homely seventeenth century sexism, "a woman would not grieve to have been told of her red nose if she had not one indeed." The Star Chamber enforced the libel laws with monumental ferocity—William Prynne had his ears cut off for criticising the immorality of courtiers; when he repeated his accusations in a *News of the World* style polemic entitled "Women Actresses—Notorious Whores" they cut off the stumps of his ears, and branded his forehead with the letters "SL" for "seditious libeller". But this penal jurisdiction was always exercised on the basis of an apprehended threat to peace.

The Star Chamber permitted civil action for libel when it banned duelling, the traditional method of redressing damage to reputation. As a result the courts became inundated with libel actions brought by insulted nobles. There was plenty of raw material in early common law to fashion a rule supportive of free speech over reputation, although it was never expressed in broad principle, always in pettifogging points of pleading. By the end of the eighteenth century Erskine's stand against judicial control of the jury had produced Fox's Libel Act (establishing the right of juries rather than judges to decide whether words were defamatory) and the claimant bore the burden of proving that the words were false, had been published or spoken maliciously, and had caused real damage. But in the nineteenth and twentieth century, the common law was re-fashioned to serve the British class system from the perspective of that extraordinary institution, the Victorian club. The idea that large sums of money must be awarded to compensate people for words which "tend to lower them in the estimation of right-thinking members of society" directly derives from an age when social, political and legal life was lived in gentlemen's clubs in Pall Mall, an age when escutcheons could be blotted and society scandals resolved by writs for slander. Libel damages came in this period to call for a metaphysical evaluation of dignity, the idea being that they should show the world a person's real value, rather than being used to punish the publisher for error. Libel was a method for deciding whether the claimant really was a gentleman (one leading case involved allegations of cheating at cards, another of shooting foxes—just not done, old chap, to *shoot* a fox: a gentleman hunts it down with dogs). Public men had a social obligation to clear their names from calumny (an obligation that did for Oscar Wilde): the judges helped these upper-class claimants by creating "presumptions" that any slur on their character must be false, published maliciously and would do their reputations serious damage in "right-minded society". These presumptions had the effect of reversing the burden of proof, so that accusers (notably the emerging popular press) made accusations at their peril.

Thus developed a law heavily weighted towards reputation over free speech. Assertions of fact had to be proved by those who made them, with no public interest defence, unless made on an occasion of *privilege*, such as a debate in Parliament or by sworn evidence in court. There were a limited number of occasions where social intercourse amongst the upper classes demanded at least a qualified privilege for defamation—notably to write critical references about servants and tradesmen—but judges were always reluctant to extend this indulgence to the media in respect of reporting to the public at large. As recently as 1983, the Court of Appeal in *Blackshaw v. Lord* said that the only defamatory allegation the media might be privileged to report (and then only if it was believed true) would concern an emergency such as the planting of bombs or the poisoning of supermarket food.[4] Damages in this period were often awarded for statements subsequently proved true. Thus John Profumo, when Minister for War, collected libel damages for the suggestion that he was dallying with prostitute Christine Keeler, a few weeks before he admitted the truth in Parliament. Liberace won a fortune when *The Daily Mirror* insinuated he might be homosexual, which indeed he was. There were a large number of cases, and an untold number of settlements, where justifiable journalism was punished by heavy damages—hence the chill factor that inhibited the British press from proper reporting of enveloping scandals such as the sale of arms to Iraq and the collapse of Lloyd's of London. The common law of

---

[4] *Blackshaw v. Lord* [1983] 2 All E.R. 311 at 327.

libel was condemned by the European Court of Human Rights because of the uncontrolled jury discretion to award massive damages,[5] and American courts refused (for the first time since the Boston Tea Party), to enforce British judgments—on the grounds that English libel law was "antipathetic to the First Amendment".[6] In America, defamation actions cannot succeed unless the media are proved at fault: the claimant must show that the allegations were false and published with a reckless or negligent disregard for the truth. What U.S. courts found repugnant about United Kingdom law was how it placed the burden of proving truth on the defendant, and held him liable to pay damages for statements he honestly believed to be true and had published without negligence.

The judges have recently found some way out of this impasse by developing the doctrine of qualified privilege—that mid-nineteenth century creation to allow masters to slander their servants. It was, Baron Parke had ruled in *Toogood v. Spyring*,[7] for "the common convenience of society" that masters should communicate honestly with each other about the shortcomings of their workers, and this "common convenience" was later extended to allow newspapers to publish the results of professional disciplinary hearings, foreign court actions and the like. But the Appeal judges in *Blackshaw* pointed out that the media only enjoyed the privilege if they could prove they had a *duty* to publish, and it could not envisage the media having a *duty*, except in an emergency, to publish defamatory allegations which turned out to be untrue. But this narrow, formalistic concept of "duty" was rejected by the High Court of Australia and the Court of Appeal of New Zealand in cases brought in both countries by a former Prime Minister of New Zealand, David Lange.[8] It was, they ruled, for the common convenience of citizens of modern society that reasonably researched allegations should be published about powerful public figures, which would be "privileged" from libel actions even if they subsequently turned out to be untrue. This antipodean breakthrough was gratefully accepted by the English courts (looking over their shoulder at the imminent arrival of the European Convention) in the cases of *Reynolds*[9] and *Gaddafi*,[10] to fashion a new public interest defence for investigative journalism. If the research is careful, the treatment fair, and the defamatory statements of fact honestly believed to be true, the media have a new public interest

---

[5] *Tolstoy Miloslavsky v. U.K.* (1995) 20 E.H.R.R. 442.
[6] *Bachchan v. India Abroad Publications*, 585 N.Y.S 2d 661 (1992); *Telnikoff v. Matusevitch* 702A 2d 230 (Md. 1997).
[7] *Toogood v. Spyring* (1834) 1 C.M.&R. 181.
[8] See *Lange v. Atkinson No. 1* [1998] 3 N.Z.L.R. 424 and *No. 2* [2000] N.Z.L.R. 385 and *Lange v. ABC* (1997) 189 C.L.R. 520.
[9] *Reynolds v. Times Newspapers Ltd* [2001] 2 A.C. 127.
[10] *Gaddafi v. Telegraph Group Ltd* [2000] E.M.L.R. 431.

defence, although it comes with a catch—a heavy duty on the publisher to prove that its editor and journalists acted fairly and reasonably and in reliance on apparently authoritative sources. Defamation is not yet a civil wrong constituted, like other torts, by the fault of the defendant, although the decision in *Reynolds* at least moves it in that direction. Article 10, given special force by section 12 of the Human Rights Act will require further changes and clarifications. But no challenge to the judiciary is greater than to cut through the technicalities of libel pleading and procedure, and the daunting cost of defamation proceedings.

COSTS AND COMPLEXITIES

In the year 2001, a contested fortnight's defamation trial—including all the applications which would proceed it—could easily cost each side £750,000, and the loser would have to pay 75 per cent of the winner's costs, on top of damages which might amount to six figures. This level of legal fees deters all but wealthy claimants (or those, like police officers, who are backed by unions or associations). The media may in consequence libel the poor with impunity: legal aid will rarely be granted[11] and although lawyers are now permitted to act on a conditional fee basis, the high cost and uncertain outcome of most libel actions mean that contingency arrangements will only be made in strong cases. The main alternative to legal action is an approach to the Press Complaints Commission (PCC) which takes on the role of a poor person's libel court. But a ruling from this press-funded, toothless body cannot compare with a verdict after a trial by judge and jury: it comes with no award of damages, or even compensation for job loss or medical bills occasioned by the publication of falsehoods. (For the inadequacies of the PCC, see Chapter 14). The lack of legal aid for libel defendants amounts to a serious failure in the practical protection of free speech: individuals may be bankrupted, and small magazines sent into liquidation as the result of libel defeats. In 1999 *Living Marxism* was forced to close after an unnecessarily high libel award of £350,000 plus costs, while in an oppressive (but ridiculous) trial McDonalds sued two unemployed protestors for casting slurs on their burgers, in leaflets which would have lain abandoned in gutters had the legal action not put them

---

[11] The prohibition on State funding of libel and malicious falsehood cases is found in the Access to Justice Act 1999, Sched. 2, para. 1(f). It is not absolute, because the Lord Chancellor may authorise funding of particular cases or classes of case: see the Legal Services Commission Funding Code, Pt 3C. There have been no examples thus far of decisions to fund libel cases.

on websites throughout the world. There is a sense that this area of law really is the preserve of the rich: one official committee reported that any extension of legal aid would bring "over the fence" disputes to court (the poor being assumed to quarrel in crowded tenements rather more often that the rich accuse one another of cheating at cards).[12] The legal aid position is difficult to reconcile with Article 6 of the Convention, which requires the state to provide access to the courts and to guarantee "equality of arms" at trial.[13] Libel may be a wholly unsatisfactory law, but the answer is to reform it and not to deny its benefits to disadvantaged sections of society.

Libel should be straightforward, but the law and court procedures have grown extremely complex. As long ago as 1966 the Court of Appeal said that "lawyers should be ashamed that they have allowed the law of defamation to have become bogged down in such a mass of technicalities".[14] But the mass continued to expand. In 1989 the same court described libel proceedings as "an archaic saraband"—lawyers reached for their dictionaries to find this meant "a slow and stately Spanish dance in triple time".[15] The fault was not solely that of libel solicitors—those "Sue Grabbit & Runne" practitioners whose overblown phraseology is a running joke in *Private Eye*. Lawyers are trained to take every available point, and judges have left them too many available points to take by pettifogging rules requiring each side to plead the "meaning" it claims the words are capable of bearing. Instead of each trial focusing on whether the jury accepts the claimant's case for overriding the defendant's right of free expression—an approach the European Convention would seem to require—the court engages in textual exegesis to determine which "meanings" the judge thinks the words are reasonably capable of bearing, before the jury hear evidence limited to those meanings to decide whether the true "meaning" (they may derive their own) has been justified. These pre-trial skirmishings add enormously to the costs: senior solicitors and some Q.C.s charge about £400 an hour, so a major contested case can easily run up £1 million in costs. Libel verdicts are notoriously unpredictable and sometimes irrational. Defences that should serve to protect the media, such as fair comment and qualified privilege, are contingent upon findings of fact, sometimes by star-struck juries: if claimants have more lovable characters and more celebrity witnesses than media defendants, these fine defences may not work as well as textbooks suggest they should. When

---

[12] The Faulks Committee on Defamation, Cmnd, 5909 (1975).
[13] This argument was rejected by the European Commission in *Steel and Morris v. U.K.* (1993) 18 E.H.R.R. CD 172, although in 2001 the Court decided to re-examine it: *McVicar v. U.K.* unreported, May 10, 2001.
[14] *Boston v. Bagshaw & Sons* [1966] 1W.L.R. 1126.
[15] *Morrell v. International Thompson Publishing Ltd* [1989] 3 All E.R. 733.

media defendants face costs of up to £1 million to defend an action,
(including a risk of paying 75 per cent of the claimant's similar costs
in the event that they lose), then free speech becomes too expensive:
there is overwhelming pressure to sacrifice it by apologising and paying
substantial damages, or by not publishing the criticism in the first place.

There was hope in 1999 that the procedural reforms devised by Lord
Woolf would provide for more efficient "case management" of libel
actions, but so far judges have been reluctant to use their new powers
to strike out claims that are delayed or brought as "gagging writs" or
with the real object of harassment or uncovering journalistic sources.
Since the only legitimate object of a defamation action is to restore a
damaged reputation, the courts should throw out any claim brought for
ulterior purposes, but this is always difficult to prove.[16] Tactics that can
be characterised as an "affront to the courts" or "in wholesale disregard
of the norms of conducting serious litigation" will extinguish a claim,
but this is strong language[17] and judges prefer to deploy less drastic
deterrents, such as cost orders which provide no deterrent to wealthy
complainants who harass the media to discourage investigations.

The Law Society has produced a pre-action "protocol" for defamation which it claims will save expense and ensure that cases are dealt
with quickly and fairly.[18] A letter of claim must be "sent out at the
earliest reasonable opportunity" to the offending media, identifying the
facts which are inaccurate or the comment alleged to be insupportable,
preferably explaining the defamatory meaning which the claimant
alleges the words to bear. The media defendant should give reasons for
rejecting the claim and indicate the meaning that it attributes to its
offending words. Since "meaning" is now a highly technical pleading
matter on which cases can be won or lost, barristers will often be
brought in to settle the "Letter of Claim" and "Response", thus increasing legal costs from the outset. The protocol recommends an alternative
means of dispute resolution, namely arbitration by "a lawyer experienced in the field of defamation". It does not occur to the Law Society
that many disputes are best resolved for free—i.e. without any lawyers,
by the victim telephoning the editor and obtaining a retraction.

Each case that goes to trial is an elaborate gamble. How much should
be paid into court, and when? If the defendant makes a payment into
court, the claimant may seize it and call it quits. If the claimant presses

---

[16] A rare example is afforded by the case of *Grovit v. Doctor* [1997] 1 W.L.R. 640.
[17] *Habib Bank v. Jaffer* (2000) C.P.L.R. 438. The Court of Appeal has been particularly weak-willed towards dilatory and hopeless claimants: see *Khahili v. Bennett*
   [2000] E.M.L.R. 996, CA.
[18] Pre-Action Protocol for Defamation (August, 2000), submitted under the Civil Procedure Rules. The Protocol has no legal status, but breaches of it could induce an
   adverse award of costs.

on and wins, but is awarded no more in damages than the amount of
the "payment in", the claimant must foot the entire legal bill incurred
by both the sides since the day of the payment.[19] In one celebrated case,
a colonel with a penchant for spanking unsuspecting women sued the
Sunday People for exposing his activities: because it exaggerated the
truth, but not much, he was awarded a derisory halfpenny. But the
newspaper was saddled with the legal costs of the trial, which it could
have avoided by "paying in" the lowest denomination coin of the realm
before the trial began. The publishers of *Exodus* had greater foresight.
When sued for libel by Dr Dering, an Auschwitz prison doctor criticised
in the book, they "paid in" the derisory sum of £2 before the trial. Dr
Dering declined this contemptible compensation, and risked crippling
legal costs on a trial that he hoped would win him heavy damages. The
jury awarded him the libel raspberry—a halfpenny—so he was forced
to pay for the whole action. When *Coronation Street* actor Bill Roache
sued the *Sun* for suggesting that everybody thought he was as boring in
real life as the character he played, the newspaper had the foresight to
"pay in" £50,000, which Roache thought too small a sum to compensate him for the libel. The case went to trial, and the jury (who are kept
in the dark, in true game-show tradition, about "payments in") awarded
him precisely £50,000, leaving him to pay his own legal costs, estimated
at over £100,000.[20] In circumstances like these, the temple of law
becomes a casino.

DEFAMATION DEFINED

The test

Whether a statement is *capable* of bearing a defamatory meaning is a
question of law, to be decided by the judge. A defamatory meaning is
one that, in the circumstances of publication, would be likely to make
reasonable and respectable people think less of the claimant. The test
is variously described as "lowering the claimant in the estimation of
right-thinking people generally"; "injuring the claimant's reputation by

---

[19] The claimant has 21 days to accept the "payment in", CPR, r. 36.11. After that
time the claimant may still accept the offer, but only with leave of the court, which
should not be granted if the risks have changed (*e.g.* by a new plea of justification):
Proetta v. Times Newspaper [1991] 4 All E.R. 46. A claimant can make a "Part 36
offer" of the remedies he is prepared to accept. If the defendant rejects this offer
and the claimant does better than it at trial, the court can award (a) indemnity costs
and (b) interest on costs (CPR, r. 36.21). For a defendant, losing in these circumstances can be very expensive.
[20] *Roache v. News Group Newspapers Ltd* [1998] E.M.L.R. 161, CA.

exposing him to hatred, contempt or ridicule" and "tending to make the
claimant be shunned and avoided". It is all a question of respect and
reputation—not just of the claimant as a human being, but as a
worker—a public official, business executive, professional or performer.
To allege incompetence at playing the tuba would not lower most
people in the eyes of their fellow citizens—unless they happened to be
professional tubists. To say that someone votes Conservative is not a
libel—unless it be said of a Labour M.P., and, in consequence, would
be defamatory in its implication of personal and political hypocrisy.

False statements not necessarily libellous

The law of libel will not correct all, or even most, false statements. It
can be activated only when a false statement actually damages a reputation. An assertion is not defamatory simply because it is untrue—it must
lower the victim in the eyes of right-thinking citizens. However irksome
it may be to have inaccuracies published about one's life or behaviour—
dates misstated, non-existent meetings described, and qualifications
misattributed—there must be a "sting" in the falsehood that reflects
discredit in the eyes of society. To publish falsely of an Irish priest that
he informed on members of the IRA is not defamatory: it may cause
him to be executed by terrorists, but "the very circumstances which will
make a person be regarded with disfavour by the criminal classes will
raise his character in the estimation of right-thinking men. We can only
regard the estimation in which a man is held by society generally."[21]

Context and contemporary standards

Whether statements are capable in law of being defamatory depends on
the content and context of the whole article or programme, and the
impression it would convey to the average reader or viewer. It is not
helpful to lay down hard and fast rules: judges and juries place themselves (without very much difficulty) in the position of "right-thinking
members of society", and ask themselves whether they think the statement would injure the claimant's reputation. A statement that the claimant has supplied information to the police about a crime would not, as
we have seen, be defamatory. Nor would a suggestion that claimants
are poor—unless they are in business and the implication is that they
are unable to pay their debts. The court must bear contemporary social
standards in mind. The values of judges in the deep south of the United
States of America, who once held it defamatory to suggest that a white
person has "coloured" blood, would not be shared in Britain. Not, one

---

[21] *Mawe v. Pigott* (1869) I.R. 4 CL 54. And see *Byrne v. Deane* [1937] 1 K.B. 818.

hopes, for the reason given in 1848 by the Chief Justice, who held that being black was "a great misfortune, but no crime".[22]

Clearly these decisions call for value judgments: in 1921 a judge held that reasonable citizens would not think less of a trade unionist if it were claimed that he had worked during a strike[23]: some juries might reach a different decision today. Ideas about immorality and what constitutes dishonourable conduct change over time, but the views of judges change more slowly than most. Would it still be defamatory to describe a heterosexual as "gay"? Damages of £18,000 (a massive sum in 1959) were awarded against the *Daily Mirror* for that very imputation about Liberace, but by today's standards an imputation of homosexuality would not of itself be defamatory, unless made of a married person (in 1999 Tom Cruise and Nicole Kidman collected damages from the *Sunday Express* for suggesting that their marriage was a sham). In 1934 the Court of Appeal somewhat emotionally rejected the argument that it did not lower Princess Yousoupoff in reputation to suggest that she had been raped by Rasputin[24]; by today's standards it could hardly be said that the innocent victim of a sex (or any other) crime would be diminished in the eyes of "right-thinking" members of the community. However, libel juries are not noted for progressive thinking. The *New York Times* mistakenly said that superstar chef Marco Pierre White had "bouts with drink and drugs" in his past, and argued that its error was not defamatory—it meant he had successfully rehabilitated himself and so could not lower him in the eyes of right- (*i.e.* liberal) minded gastronomes.[25] The jury, however, awarded him damages of £75,000 to assuage his feelings.

Appellate judges are frequently at odds over what is capable of amounting to a defamation. In one case they expended thousands of words of legal learning over Julie Burchill's suggestion that actor Stephen Berkoff was particularly ugly. Lord Justice Millett, dissenting from the majority finding that this imputation could indeed defame the thespian, concluded

> "However difficult it may be, we must assume that Miss Julie Burchill might be taken seriously. The question then is: is it defamatory to say of a man that he is "hideously ugly'? It is a common experience that ugly people have satisfactory social lives—Boris Karloff is not known to have been a recluse—and it is a popular belief for the truth of which I am unable to vouch that ugly men are particularly attractive to women".[26]

[22] *Hoare v. Silverlock* (1848) 12 Q.B. 630 at 632, *per* Lord Denman C.J.
[23] *Mycroft v. Sleight* (1921) 90 L.J.K.B. 883, *per* Mr Justice McCardie.
[24] *Yousoupoff v. MGM Pictures Ltd* (1934) 50 T.L.R. 581.
[25] *Marco Pierre White v. New York Times*, April 7, 2000 (unreported).
[26] *Berkoff v. Burchill* [1996] 4 All E.R. 1008.

Article 10 should now protect Burchillian speech which is offensive, shocking and distasteful, because readers must be credited with the ability to discern when it is the writer, rather than her target, who deserves these adjectives.

The "ordinary reader" test

In deciding what words mean for the purpose of defamation, the intention of the writer or speaker is largely irrelevant. The test is the effect on the ordinary reader, who is endowed for this purpose with considerable wisdom and knowledge of the way of the world. The literal meaning is not conclusive: the ordinary reader knows all about irony. To say of John Smith "His name is certainly not George Washington" is capable of being a statement defamatory of Smith: the ordinary reader knows that George Washington could never tell a lie, and is likely to infer that Smith is therefore untruthful.[27] The ordinary reader is impressed by the tone and the manner of publication, and the words chosen to headline a story. In a popular paper the headline "False profit return charge against Investment Society" suggests fraud and not an arguable error by accountants in attributing profit to capital rather than income.[28]

The courts accept that ordinary readers are not literal-minded simpletons. They are capable of divining the real thrust of a comment, and able to respond to a joke, even a joke in bad taste, in the spirit intended by the commentator. In this sense, the author's intention does play an indirect part in determining the meaning of the words in question, because that meaning should be decided by the ordinary reader's response to the question "What on earth is the author getting at?".[29]

However, this sensible approach has been overlaid by a more complicated set of instructions from the Court of Appeal, as a result of a rule change that gave trial judges the power to strike out pleaded meanings they think the offending words are not reasonably capable of bearing. This change[30] was intended to reduce the length and expense of jury trials by excluding unreasonable meanings and the evidence called to support the truth of such meanings, but ironically it has worked, instead, to encourage more expensive interlocutory skirmishes about "meaning" and to deprive some defendants of the right to defend the

---

[27] *Grubb v. Bristol United Press Ltd* [1963] 1 Q.B. 309, *per* Holroyd Pearce L.J.
[28] *English & Scottish Co-operative Properties Mortgage & Investment Society Ltd v. Odhams Press Ltd* [1940] 1 K.B. 440 at 452 *per* Slesser LJ.
[29] *Schild v. Express Newspapers Ltd The Times*, October 5, 1982, CA.
[30] First effected in 1994 and now contained in CPR, Pt 53, PD 4.1.

meaning they really intended. The principles, which seek to exclude meanings that are "strained of forced or utterly unreasonable" are[31]:

(1) The material bears the natural and ordinary meaning it would convey to the ordinary reasonable reader or viewer absorbing it on one occasion.

(2) Ordinary and reasonable readers and viewers are neither naïve nor unduly suspicious; although they can read between the lines in the light of their general knowledge they are nevertheless fair minded and not "avid for scandal".[32]

(3) The court should be wary of conducting an over-elaborate analysis of the words complained of, and equally of taking an over-literal approach to its task: the ordinary reader does not analyse an article like a lawyer poring over a contract.

(4) The court should test the meaning by reference to the standard of comprehension of the likely readers or viewers.

However serious a prime-time television programme like *World in Action*, it will be watched for entertainment by some viewers whose first impressions must be brought into account. On the other hand, an article in a legal or accounting magazine will be tested by its impact on lawyers or accountants. Thus the meaning of an article about Russian tycoon Boris Berezovsky in *Forbes*—an American business magazine—might be tested by its impact not on the law's traditional construct of reasonableness, "the man on the Clapham omnibus", but by the man or woman in business class on the transatlantic jumbo.[33]

How the minds of ordinary readers receive and interpret newspaper stories is an interesting question of psychology, but evidence from ordinary readers as to how they understood the article is never admitted. In law, the answer depends on assumptions by lawyers. What do ordinary readers think when their eyes catch the fact that someone is being investigated by the police?

In *Lewis v. Daily Telegraph* the newspaper announced:

"INQUIRY ON FIRM BY CITY POLICE. Officers of the City of London Fraud Squad are inquiring into the affairs of Rubber Improvement Ltd. The investigation was requested after criticisms of the chair-

---

[31] These tests are extrapolated from a number of recent cases, beginning with *Mapp v. News Group* [1997] E.M.L.R. 397; *Gillick v. BBC* [1996] E.M.L.R. 267; *Skuse v. Granada TV* [1996] E.M.L.R. 278.

[32] *Lewis v. Daily Telegraph*, n. 3 above, *per* Lord Reid.

[33] *Berezovsky v. Forbes Inc.*, Eady J., November 10, 2000 (unreported).

man's statement and the accounts by a shareholder at a recent company meeting. The chairman is Mr John Lewis, former Socialist M.P."

The inquiry subsequently exonerated Lewis and his company. They
sued, claiming that the news story implied, to the ordinary reader, that
they were involved in fraud. The newspaper argued that the ordinary
reader, possessed of a fairer and less suspicious mind, would presume
innocence. The House of Lords held that the statement was not capable
of meaning that the claimants were guilty of fraud. "The ordinary man,
not avid for scandal", would not infer guilt merely because an inquiry
was under way.[34]

So suspects, innocent until proven guilty, may be described as
"assisting police with their inquiries" and have no remedy in libel.
Unless, of course, the story is written in a way that suggests that police
have reason to suspect them. Much—very much, in financial terms—
depends upon the care with which the story is written, as the same
newspaper once again discovered in *Hayward v. Thompson*.[35]

During police investigations into Norman Scott's allegations that he had
been the target of a conspiracy to murder in order to protect a former
lover (Liberal leader Jeremy Thorpe M.P.), the *Daily Telegraph* obtained
a scoop from a police source. It published:

"TWO MORE IN SCOTT AFFAIR
The names of two more people connected with the Norman Scott affair
have been given to the police. One is a wealthy benefactor of the
Liberal Party . . . Both men, police have been told, arranged for a lead-
ing Liberal supporter to be 'reimbursed' £5,000, the same amount Mr
Andrew Newton alleges he was paid to murder Scott."

Mr Jack Hayward, the wealthy benefactor, claimed that the article
meant that he was guilty of participating in or condoning a murder plot.
The newspaper, relying on the *Lewis* case, said that the words would
mean to the ordinary reader no more than that an inquiry was under way,
and that Hayward would be able to assist it. The jury awarded Hayward
£50,000, and the Court of Appeal upheld the verdict because the article
was capable of implying guilt. Its headline put the wealthy benefactor
"in" the Scott affair, and the copy never got him out of it. "In" means
"in", and that implication of involvement with a conspiracy was reinforced by the phrase "connected with" and the inverted commas around
"reimbursed". These stylistic features of the story as published would
give the ordinary reader the impression that Hayward was an accomplice
in the plot.

---

[34] [1964] A.C. 234.
[35] *Hayward v. Thompson* [1981] 3 All E.R. 450.

The *Hayward* case underlines the importance of the way in which the story is presented to the public. The art is to put across the important information without using a language or style that carries a defamatory implication. That art was demonstrated with conspicuously different talents by British editors and journalists in the aftermath of the revelation that Jeffrey Archer, best-selling novelist and deputy chairman of the Conservative party, had paid a prostitute £2,000 to leave the country. Newspapers that jumped to the conclusion that he had engaged in sex with the woman were sued for libel, but were unable to discharge the burden of proving a case that hinged upon the word of a prostitute against the word of the claimant and his "fragrant" wife (in his case helped by evidence which many years later turned out to have been fabricated). The *Star* was ordered to pay £500,000 damages after a trial that amassed an estimated £750,000 in legal costs. Newspapers that had confined themselves to reporting the facts, and left readers to draw their own conclusions, were not sued.

However, any such invitation to readers should not load the odds in favour of a particular conclusion by inflaming their suspicions. The author who is anxious to wound but fearful to strike too obviously will not escape. If the reader is invited to be suspicious and is nudged towards a defamatory explanation that the writer "did not care or did not dare to express in direct terms", the publication will be capable of carrying a defamatory imputation and a lesser meaning based on mere (or even reasonable) suspicion may be withdrawn from the jury.[36]

Bane and antidote

Libel is for the most part common law, *i.e.* created and developed by judges. For many generations they regarded journalists as akin to waspish insects whose "sting" (*i.e.* the defamatory meaning) might be "drawn" if the allegation was watered down or dismissed in subsequent passages. Other judges regarded journalists more as vipers, hence the "bane and antidote" rule that defamatory words (the poison) could be "cured" by applying an "antidote"—*i.e.* emollient expressions later in the text. This rule (although not its pejorative language) remains valuable because it underlines the importance of context: a complainant cannot single out a passage which taken in isolation is defamatory if the context makes clear it is not. The rule offers some protection to tabloids which sell on sensational headlines, because of the (often false) assumption that "ordinary readers" read the entire article:

---

[36] See *Jones v. Skelton* [1963] 1 W.L.R. 1362 and now *Forbes v. Berezorsky (No. 2)*, July 31, 2001, where the Court of Appeal found that the "entire thrust" of the publication pointed to actual guilt rather than reasonable suspicion of guilt.

"STREWTH! WHAT'S HAROLD UP TO WITH OUR MADGE?"
This *News of the World* banner headline was accompanied by a photograph which appeared to show the actors who played Harold and
Madge Bishop, a respectable married couple from *Neighbours*, naked
and engaging in perverse sexual antics. Only by reading the small text
of the article did it become clear that the actors' faces had been
superimposed on pornographic pictures without their consent, so as to
become "unwitting stars of a sordid computer game" whose makers
were castigated in what Lord Bridge noted was "a tone of self-
righteous indignation which contrasts oddly with the prominence given
to the main photograph". But for all the newspaper's humbuggery, it
was saved by the "bane and antidote" rule which required the whole
publication to be taken together, on the assumption that a fair-minded
reader of the complete text would not think less of the actors since
they were clearly described as the victims of a hoax.[37]

The *Neighbours* case was an example of the antidote in the article
curing completely the bane of the defamatory headline and picture, at
least for "readers" of *News of the World* who bothered to read every
line. Most "bane and antidote" cases are more finely balanced, and will
be decided by a jury which may take a dim view of exaggerated headlines and similar tabloid ploys. The *Express on Sunday* failed to persuade the Court of Appeal that a hagiographic article about the then
wedded bliss of Tom Cruise and Nicole Kidman completely cured
another article on the next page which retailed defamatory rumours
about them. Rather than face the wrath of a star-struck jury with arguments about "bane and antidote" the newspaper apologised and paid a
large sum in damages—a year before the happy couple announced their
divorce.[38]

Defamatory innuendo

The test of the ordinary reader is subject to qualification in the case of
statements that are not defamatory on their face, but that carry discreditable implications to those with special knowledge. To say that a man
frequents a particular address has no defamatory meaning to ordinary
readers—except to those who know that the address is a brothel. Here,
libel is by *innuendo*, *i.e.* the statement is defamatory to those with
knowledge of facts not stated in the article. If it is said of a barrister
that he has refused to appear for an unsavoury criminal, the ordinary
reader may applaud, but his professional reputation is lowered amongst
colleagues who understand the story to mean that he has betrayed his

---

[37] *Charleston v. News Group Newspapers Ltd* [1995] 2 A.C. 65 applying *Chalmers v. Payne* (1835) 2 Cr. M. & R. 156.
[38] *Cruise v. Express Newspapers* (1998) E.M.L.R. 780.

ethical duty to appear "on the taxi rank" for all who seek his services. Where the sting is not a matter of general knowledge, its defamatory capacity is judged by its impact upon ordinary readers who have such knowledge—if the claimant can first prove that such persons were amongst the actual readership.

LIBEL AND SLANDER DISTINGUISHED

There are irritating, complicated and unnecessary distinctions in law between two types of defamation—libel and slander. Libel is a defamatory statement made in writing or—in the case of films and videotapes—at least in some permanent form. Slander is a defamatory statement made by word of mouth or by gesture. Claimants may sue for libel even though they have suffered no financial loss, but for slander (with certain exceptions) they must be able to prove actual damage and not mere injury to feelings. Historically, the distinction is explained by the view that writing was a premeditated and calculated act, which affected reputation much more drastically and permanently than off-the-cuff comments. With the advent of radio, television and satellite broadcasting, this reasoning is anachronistic, and Parliament has enacted that words spoken in theatres, and in broadcasts for general reception, shall be deemed libels and not slanders.[39] The same provision is made for words spoken on television programmes.[40] However, the distinction still remains in certain areas, notably criminal libel, extempore statements at public meetings and noises of disapproval. Dramatists or actors whose work is maliciously booed or hissed off the stage must sue their tormentors for slander rather than libel.

The importance of the distinction is that there can be no action for slander unless the claimant has suffered damage that can be calculated in monetary terms. Victims of verbal assaults who suffer hurt feelings, sleepless nights, physical illness, or ostracism by friends and neighbours cannot bring an action.[41] There are only five exceptions: accusations of a crime punishable by imprisonment, suggestions that the claimant carries a contagious disease; adverse reflections on a person's ability to carry out an office, business or profession; slanders on the reputation or credit of tradespeople; and words imputing unchastity or adultery to a woman or a girl.[42] Only in these five cases may the claimant sue for slander without having to prove financial loss.

---

[39] See Theatres Act 1968, s. 4(1) and Defamation Act 1952, ss. 1,16(3).
[40] Broadcasting Act 1990, s. 166.
[41] *Argent v. Donigan* (1892) 8 T.L.R. 432; *Lynch v. Knight* (1861) 9 H.L. Cas. 592.
[42] Slander of Women Act 1891.

Malicious falsehood

A statement may be entirely false and deeply upsetting to the person about whom it is made. But unless it tends to lessen respect for that person, then as we have seen it will not be defamatory. The victim may have an action for *malicious falsehood*, however, if it can be proved that the untrue statement was made spitefully, dishonestly or recklessly, and that it has in fact caused financial loss.

> Stephane Grappelli, the renowned jazz violinist, employed English agents who booked him for certain concerts. Grappelli claimed they acted without reference to him, and the concerts had to be cancelled. The reason given by the agents was: "Stephane Grappelli is very seriously ill in Paris and is unlikely ever to tour again". This was an entirely false statement, obviously damaging to a thriving professional musician. However, the statement was not defamatory: to say that someone is seriously ill might excite pity, but not ridicule or disrespect. Grappelli had to be content with an action for malicious falsehood.[43]

The action for malicious falsehood is less favourable to claimants than defamation. They have no right to jury trial, and they have to prove that the words were false (in libel, the burden of proving the words are true is on the defendant), that the words were published maliciously and that they were likely to cause financial loss. Their damages, however, if they surmount these hurdles, may well be on a similar scale to those in defamation, since the Court of Appeal has held they can recover aggravated damages for injury to feelings caused by publication of the untruth.[44] If there is real doubt over whether a falsehood is defamatory, complainants may be well advised to shoulder this extra burden by suing for malicious falsehood rather than have their "meanings" struck out as non-defamatory. But there is nothing to stop a claimant choosing to bring a defamation claim as a malicious falsehood. The leading case on the subject is *Joyce v. Sengupta*[45]:

> Love letters written to Princess Anne by Captain Lawrence were stolen from her rooms in Buckingham Palace and delivered to *The Sun* newspaper. The police were unable to finger the culprit, but they boasted to the *Daily Mail* that they could prove it was Linda Joyce, Anne's maid. When this nonsense was published, the poor but innocent Ms Joyce could not afford to sue for libel—instead, she obtained legal aid which was then available to bring an action for malicious falsehood (malicious falsehood claims, like libel claims, cannot now generally be funded on legal aid). The newspaper, outraged that a poor person should have found a means

---

[43] *Grappelli v. Derek Block Holdings Ltd* [1981] 2 All E.R. 272.
[44] *Khodaparast v. Shad* [2000] E.M.L.R. 265.
[45] *Joyce v. Sengupta* [1993] 1 All E.R. 897, CA.

of fighting its calumnies, argued that her action was an "abuse of process", but the Court of Appeal had no sympathy: the necessary quality of "malice" could be inferred from the grossness of the falsehood and the cavalier way it was published. The newspaper settled the action by paying damages to Ms Joyce.

Complainants may wish to proceed against defamers in malicious falsehood or for some obscure common law tort like "conspiracy to injure" in order more easily to obtain an interim injunction. This "prior restraint" is virtually impossible to obtain in libel, but may be more readily available on the "balance of convenience" test which applies to the grant of injunctions in other cases. However, section 12 of the Human Rights Act 1998 largely corrects the anomaly, and courts should not, on principle, be prepared to give injunctions in malicious falsehood cases against publishers who wish to defend the truth of their statement or the privilege of the occasion on which it was made. Even before the Human Rights Act, courts indicated that freedom of speech would be a crucial factor in any balancing exercise involved in granting pre-trial injunctions. In a conspiracy to injure case, "the important questions are questions of public interest, not of private rights". The public interest of free speech, in allowing allegations of financial misconduct to come to the attention of investors and regulatory authorities, defeated the claimant's claim for an injunction before trial.[46]

WHO CAN SUE?

Any living individual, if made the identifiable subject of defamatory attack, may take legal action. This includes infants (who sue "by their litigation friend"), lunatics, bankrupts and foreigners. Animals however, are fair game.

The question of who *can* sue is less important than the question of who *will* sue. The enormous cost of contested libel actions means that many claimants will need financial support from unions or employers. Some organisations find that supporting libel actions on behalf of their members is politically convenient because it assures them a better or more polite press; the Police Federation is one example. There is nothing to stop such organisations offering to pay the costs of libel actions, and editors deciding to settle will bear in mind the strength of the organisation behind the claimant. In recent years the use of *public* funds for individual libel actions has been heavily criticised, and it may well be an unlawful use of ratepayers' or taxpayers' money to fund libel actions brought by ministers or civil officials over attacks on their political or moral integrity. John Major when Prime Minister sued *The New States-*

---

[46] *Femis-Bank (Anguilla) v. Lazar* [1991] 2 All E.R. 865.

man and *Scallywag* for publishing rumours that he was having an affair with a Downing Street caterer: he was careful to pay his own legal expenses. There is nothing to stop a private benefactor from bankrolling libel victims and Sir James Goldsmith for many years sponsored a fund to assist right wing litigants. However, under section 51 of the Supreme Court Act 1981 the benefactor may have to pay the newspaper's costs if the latter is successful.[47] The wealthy but gullible backers of Neil Hamilton's unsuccessful libel action against Mohammed Al Fayed found to their discomfort that the court had power to unmask them, and then to order a contribution to the defendant's costs (although the judge eventually forebore to do so on the grounds that they had acted out of charitable motives to help a poor man assert a claim against a rich opponent).

The dead

The dead cannot sue or be sued for libel. Indeed, if a claimant dies on the day before the trial, the action dies as well. Neither the trustees of the estate nor the outraged relatives have any form of legal redress. This right to speak ill of the dead is justified in the interests of historians and biographers, and by the practical difficulties of subjecting deceased persons to cross-examination. In 1975 the Faulks Committee on libel expressed great concern about stories that added to the grief of a widow, and recommended that relatives should be allow to sue within five years of death (a cynical estimate, critics suggested, of the length of a widow's solicitude). There may be some unseemliness about assassinating characters still warm in their graves, but at least they cannot feel the slings and arrows of outrageous libels.

Companies

A company may sue for defamation, but only in respect of statements that damage its business reputation. In legal theory a company has no feelings capable of injury, although adverse reports may lower the value of its "goodwill" asset. Normally, individual officers or employees identified from the criticism will additionally have an action.

Local authorities

In 1993 the House of Lords held that a local authority could not bring an action in defamation because there was a danger of elected bodies using such a power to stifle legitimate public criticism of their activities.

---

[47] *Singh v. The Observer Ltd* [1989] 1 All E.R. 751; [1989] 3 All E.R. 777, CA; *Hamilton v. Al Fayed The Times*, July 23, 2001.

This case—*Derbyshire County Council v. Times Newspapers*—was an early landmark in fashioning English law to favour free speech. The House of Lords warned of the "chilling effect" of defamation on free speech if public bodies could sue their critics. It was of "the highest public importance" that "any governmental body should be open to public criticism". The Law Lords approved a vigorous pronouncement that it "would be a serious interference . . . if the wealth of the State, derived from the State's subjects, could be used to launch against those subjects actions for defamation because they have, falsely and unfairly it may be, criticised or condemned the management of the country".[48]

State corporations

The decision in *Derbyshire* means that nationalised industries and government-run corporations lack standing to sue for libel. In *British Coal Corporation v. NUM* it was held that BCC, which was established by the Government and very much subject to ministerial control, was a "governmental" body and hence disabled from using defamation law to sue a miner's newspaper which had accused it of impropriety in managing pension funds.[49]

Political parties

A further extension of the rule in *Derbyshire* disentitles political parties to sue for libel. Even if they exercise no "governmental" power, the "free market-place of ideas" in a democracy requires all parties—even newcomers like the Referendum Party—to be subject to uninhibited public criticism, especially when contesting elections.[50]

Trade unions

Trade unions and most unincorporated associations cannot sue for libel. This was decided in 1979 by *EETPU v. Times Newspapers*, which held that the capacity of trade unions to sue had been removed by section 2(1) of the Trade Union and Labour Relations Act 1974.[51] The practical

---

[48] *Derbyshire County Council v. Times Newspapers* [1993] A.C. 534 at 557–9, *per* Lord Keith.

[49] *British Coal Corporation v. National Union of Mineworkers*, French J., June 28, 1996 (unreported).

[50] *Goldsmith v. Bhoyrul* [1997] 4 All E.R. 268, *per* Buckley J.

[51] *EETPU v. Times Newspapers* [1980] Q.B. 585. Although note that this decision, by a single judge, has not been tested and its reasoning has been questioned: Gatley, 9th ed., para. 8.23. Even so, the rule in *Derbyshire* should apply by analogy, since there must be an important public interest in permitting uninhibited criticism of powerful representative bodies like trade unions.

significance of this change is mainly to reduce the damages by removing one possible claimant, rather than by removing the prospect of an action. Most criticisms of trade unions will reflect upon individual officers, who will usually be financially supported by their union in efforts to vindicate their own reputations.

Groups

There is, in defamation law, a certain safety in numbers. Defamatory comment may not be actionable if it refers to people by class rather than by name. Whether an individual member of the class can sue depends upon the size of the class and the nature of the comment: there must be something in the circumstances to make the ordinary reader feel that the claimant personally is the target of the criticism. To say "All barristers are thieves" does not entitle any one of 9,000 barristers to sue—the class is too large for the comment to single out individuals. But to say "All barristers in chambers at 10 Doughty Street are thieves" might be sufficiently specific to allow the individual barristers in those chambers to take action, at least if the context showed the allegation was a serious reference to each person and not an example of "the habit of making unfounded generalisations . . . ingrained in ill-educated or vulgar minds, . . . or intended to be facetious exaggeration".[52] In 1971, the small group of regular journalists at the Old Bailey received £150 damages each for the intolerable insult of being collectively described in the *Spectator* as "beer-sodden hacks". The question always is whether the defamation is of the class itself (in which case no action arises) or whether ordinary readers would believe that it reflected directly on the individual claimant. When the *News of the World* alleged that unnamed CID officers from Banbury police station had committed rape, that allegation reflected on each officer at Banbury because that CID office had only twelve members.[53] Had the allegation been less specific—had it referred only to "certain police officers in Oxfordshire", for example—the Banbury officers would not have been able to prove that what was published related to them.

Identification

The test, in every case, is whether reasonable people would understand the words to point to the claimant personally, and the journalist cannot escape simply by widening the net of suspects. The statement "Either A or B is the murderer" entitles *both* A and B to sue over a statement that carries the defamatory meaning that there is a substantial prospect

---

[52] *Knupffer v. London Express Newspapers* [1944] A.C. 116, *per* Lord Atkin.
[53] See *Riches v. Newsgroup* [1986] 1 Q.B. 265.

that each is guilty. The distinction is not always easy to keep in mind:

> Lord Denning, once Britain's most experienced judge in defamation cases, published a book in which he criticised a jury in Bristol for acquitting black defendants who had been charged with rioting. Two members of the jury threatened to sue, because the comments (which were based upon gossip at Temple dinners) suggested they had been false to their oaths by acquitting black defendants because they (the jurors) were black. The publishers withdrew and pulped all 10,000 copies of the book.

A writer will not necessarily escape by criticising "some" members of a class if other evidence serves to identify the claimant as a member of the criticised section. An article stating that "some Irish factory-owners" were cruel to employees enabled one particular owner to obtain damages, because other references in the article pointed to his factory. "If those who look on know well who is aimed at", the target may sue.[54] Where the knowledge depends upon special circumstances of which not everyone is aware, the claimant has to prove that the article was published to persons who were able to make the identifying connection.

> In the Jack Hayward case, the *Daily Telegraph* argued that the claimant could not be identified from the description "a wealthy benefactor of the Liberal party". Unfortunately for the newspaper that party had very few wealthy benefactors and evidence was admitted to show that others imme-diately made the connection. His friends put two and two together, and so did the media, which besieged his home by telephone and helicopter. In a national newspaper with a wide circulation the inference was that some readers would know the special facts which identified him.[55]

The moral of these cases is that journalists cannot avoid liability for defamation merely by avoiding the naming of names. Any story that carries the imputation of discreditable conduct by somebody will be actionable by a claimant who can show that at least some readers would recognise him as the person being criticised, or that the facts in the story necessarily imply such an allegation against him. An allegation that drugs are being supplied as a "liquid cosh" to modify behaviour at a particular prison may point a sufficient finger at the medical officers working at that prison, even though they are not referred to by name. When a newspaper falsely alleged that Kerry Packer had "fixed" the result of a cricket match involving the West Indian team, its captain (Clive Lloyd) was entitled to damages even though he was not named in the article and had not been playing in the particular match. The

---

[54] *Le Fanu v. Malcomson* (1848) 1 H.L. Cas. 637.
[55] See *Hayward v. Thompson*, n. 34 above.

"ordinary reader" would infer that "fixing" had involved the team as well as Packer, and that the captain of the team would have been party to the plot even though he had not played in the match.[56]

Those unintentionally defamed

Where a journalist *intends* to refer to an unnamed individual, it is reasonable that the individual should have an action for libel if others have correctly identified him or her as the target, whatever literary device has been used as camouflage. Asterisks, blanks, initials and general descriptions will not avail if evidence proves that readers have solved the puzzle correctly. Much less satisfactory, however, is the harsh rule that holds a writer responsible for *unintentional* defamation, where readers have jumped to a conclusion that never was in the author's mind. This rule is the bane of fiction writers, who must take special care to ensure that the more villainous characters in their plots cannot be mistaken for living persons. The leading case is *Hulton v. Jones*.[57]

> In 1909 the *Sunday Chronicle* published a light-hearted sketch about a festival in Dieppe, dwelling upon the tendency of sober Englishmen to lead a "gay" life (in the 1909 sense of the word) when safely across the Channel. "Whist! There is Artemus Jones with a woman who is not his wife, who must be, you know—the other thing . . .". Whist! There were very heavy libel damages awarded to one Artemus Jones, a dour barrister practising on the Welsh circuit. Five of his friends thought the article referred to him—an identification made all the more far-fetched by the fact that the fictitious character was described as a Peckham Church Warden. The House of Lords upheld the award, ruling that the writers' intention was immaterial; what mattered was whether reasonable readers would think that the words used applied to the claimant.

Authors who employ fictional characters with realistic status or occupations should check available sources to ensure their characters could not be confused with persons of the same name and position. The entire print-run of one major novel had to be pulped because the author had chosen the actual name of a noble family to describe a fictional unsavoury aristocrat. A check with *Debretts* or *Who's Who* would have revealed the danger.

The rule that imposes liability for unintentional defamation has absurd results, such as the case where the wife of a race-horse owner pictured with a woman he had described to the photographer as his fiancée was allowed to recover damages on the basis that her neighbours

---

[56] *Lloyd v. David Syme & Co. Ltd* [1986] A.C. 350.
[57] *Hulton v. Jones* [1910] A.C. 20.

would think that she was living in sin.[58] Equally unsatisfactory is the decision that Harold Newstead, a bachelor hairdresser living in Camberwell, was libelled by a perfectly accurate report that another Harold Newstead, also a Camberwell resident, had been gaoled for bigamy ("I kept them both till the police interferred").[59] The *Newstead* case is used to warn young journalists of the importance, in court reporting, of giving occupations and addresses of defendants and witnesses, so that confusion can be avoided. Journalists should insist on receiving these details from the court clerk by citing the case of *R. v. Evesham Justices ex p. McDonagh*[60]:

> A former Tory M.P. was charged with driving without a tax disc. He begged the court not to disclose his home address lest his ex-wife discovered it and harassed him. The court allowed him to write the address on a piece of paper rather than state it publicly. The Divisional Court held that defendants' addresses must be given publicly in court. The well-established practice, which helped to avoid wrongful identification and risks of libel action, should not be departed from for the comfort of defendants.

The problems of "unintentional defamation" underline the general unsuitability of libel law as a method of correcting innocent mistakes. The wife and the bachelor in the above cases should have been entitled to insist that the confusion be cleared up by a published clarification, but they should not have been able to obtain an award of damages against a newspaper that was not at fault. This is a problem that a "legal right of reply"—requiring a correction without compensation—could resolve more effectively than the cumbersome "offer to make amends" procedure which still requires damages and costs. Cases like *Hulton v. Jones*, should they recur, are clear candidates for the "proportionality" axe under the 1998 Human Rights Act, and the days of "unintentional defamation" may be numbered since both the House of Lords (in *Reynolds*) and the European Court are requiring proof of the defendant's *fault* as a precondition for damages. The first blow against unintentional defamation was struck in 2001 when an actress was denied the right to sue the *Sunday Mirror* over a squalid advertisement for an internet porn site which featured a model who was her "spitting image'. Although her friends and relatives had been horrified by the belief that she had taken to pornography, Morland J. refused to follow the *Newstead* and *Artemus Jones* cases on the basis that Article 10 now excluded strict

---

[58] *Cassidy v. Daily Mirror* [1929] 2 K.B. 331.
[59] *Newstead v. London Express* [1940] 1 K.B. 377.
[60] [1988] 1 All E.R. 371. In criminal cases, witnesses need not be asked for their address unless this is material to the case: *Archbold* 2001, para. 8–71(a).

liability for "look-alike" defamation.[61] At a charity auction in 2000 large amounts were bid by people clamouring to have their name immortalised by any character in the works of leading fiction writers: humourless prigs like Artemus Jones should only be allowed to sue where their names are used maliciously or negligently.

WHO CAN BE SUED?

As a general rule, everyone who can sue for libel can also be sued for libel if responsible for a defamatory publication. There seems to be an exception in the case of trade unions, which cannot sue for libel (see above) but can nevertheless be made defendants as a result of the abolition of their immunity in tort by section 15 of the 1982 Employment Act. Unincorporated associations are not entities which can be sued, but their officials and employees may be liable. Editors and journalists employed on journals published by these organisations are therefore at great financial risk, and should ensure that their contracts of employment indemnify them against costs and damages that may accrue from libel actions, which are often brought by opponents of their employers' policies.

Every person who is responsible for a defamatory publication is a candidate for a claim: author, editor, informant, printer, proprietor and distributor. Complainants invariably sue the corporate body which publishes or broadcasts the libel, and usually join the editor and the journalist. It is clear that a larger-than-life proprietor who personally owns the publishing business is liable, even if the defamatory article is published without his knowledge, because he selects and controls his editors,[62] but equally clear that the directors of publishing companies can only be sued if they knew about or were personally involved in the defamatory publication.[63] Where does a figure like Rupert Murdoch stand, the moving spirit in a corporate publishing empire?

> In 1995 the *Sunday Times* devoted its front page to a ridiculous story about former Labour leader Michael Foot, under the banner heading "KGB: FOOT WAS OUR AGENT". The false insinuation was extracted from a book by a former KGB agent which the newspaper, to Murdoch's knowledge, had bought for serialisation. Foot sued in the most spectacular way, by taking out a writ for exemplary damages against Murdoch personally, described as the "moving spirit" of *Times Newspapers* who had "caused to be published" the offending words. Murdoch moved to strike

---

[61] *Kerry O'Shea v. MGN Ltd*, May 4, 2001.
[62] *R v. Gutch* (1829) M.&M. 432, (Tenterden C.J.).
[63] *Evans v. Spritebrand Ltd* [1985] 1 W.L.R. 317.

out the action, on the basis that the editor had authorised the publication, while Foot maintained that he was liable because he had chosen a compliant editor schooled in sensationalist journalism. The issue of proprietorial responsibility went unresolved: the *Sunday Times* settled the case with a public apology and payment to Foot of damages and costs.

Normally the corporate defendant will pay all the damages and costs, and claimants will not bother to sue proprietors personally. However, a media mogul whose publications attack his political enemies might well be made liable for exemplary damages, on the theory pioneered in the *Foot v. Murdoch* litigation. British newspapers have been dominated by larger than life chief executives: their power over policy and news values means they influence the "news" which the newspaper itself makes by front page "splash" stories.[64] There may be cases where the jury considers it necessary that a chief proprietor who has encouraged and profited from publication of reckless and circulation-seeking defamations should be "taught that tort does not pay" by an award of exemplary damages because "one man should not be allowed to sell another man's reputation for profit".[65]

Avoiding responsibility

Journalists whose bylines are on defamatory stories can exculpate themselves by proving that the defamation was added to their copy without their consent (a common occurrence where the "sting" emanates from clumsy sub-editing). They should think carefully before allowing their reputation to be sacrificed by a "tactical apology" prepared by lawyers acting in the interests of their employers. An important case that casts helpful light on a journalist's rights in this situation is *UCATT v. Brain*.[66]

> A trade union employed a journalist to edit its newspaper. He was subject to the direction of the General Secretary, who sometimes insisted on the publication of articles seen as politically important for the union. One such article, written by the General Secretary, was ordered to be printed and the editor had no option other than to deliver it to the printers. It libelled the claimant, who issued a writ against the editor. The union's lawyers decided to apologise, and the editor was directed to approve the

---

[64] It has long been accepted that notwithstanding the fact that a national newspaper is published by a company, "chief proprietors" exert a determinative influence on its character and contents: see *Royal Commission on the Press* 1947–49, Chapter V. The argument for fixing a mogul with liability irrespective of knowledge draws support from the assumptions of s.57 of the Fair Trading Act 1973 and the Broadcasting Act's restrictions on media ownership.

[65] *Rookes v. Barnard* [1964] A.C. 1129 at 1226, *per* Lord Devlin.

[66] *UCATT v. Brain* [1981] I.C.R. 542.

apology, which was to be made in open court. The editor, fearing that this would reflect on his credit as a journalist, declined. He was sacked. The Court of Appeal upheld his claim for damages for wrongful dismissal. It pointed out that he had a good defence to the action, namely that he was not responsible for publication. The solicitors had a conflict of interests, and should have arranged for him to receive independent legal advice. The union acted wrongfully in dismissing him for insisting on his legal rights.

Employers have no right to bargain away journalists' reputations without their consent merely because some sacrifice of those reputations would be in the interests of management. Journalists should take independent advice before they agree to fall on their pens.

Writers and speakers cannot be held responsible unless they authorise, or at least foresee, the publication that causes complaint. Participants in a television programme, for example, who are told that there is a "pilot" that will not be transmitted, cannot be held responsible for defamatory statements they have made if it is subsequently screened at prime time. If the defamatory material has been supplied "off the record" by a third party, a difficult question arises. The informant is responsible in law but the journalist, having promised confidentiality, will be under an ethical duty not to reveal the name of the informant. The claimant may want, even more than damages, to discover the identity of the source. In defamation cases journalists can usually keep the identity of informants a secret although they may find that their refusal to answer such questions is a ground for increasing the sum total of damages.[67] It may also, of course, be the reason why the action is lost in the first place, because evidence for the truth of the statement is unavailable from the person who originally made it.

Book publishers usually insist on contracts in which the author indemnifies them against defamation liability or warrants that the manuscript is libel-free. This practice reflects the superior bargaining power of the publisher in negotiating the agreement rather than a custom appropriate to the book trade, so where an indemnity clause is overlooked, the courts will not imply one into the contract by reference to custom and usage.[68] Freelancers who submit articles to newspapers and magazines cannot in consequence be made automatically liable for all the publisher's legal costs of defending a libel action, in the absence of express agreement. However, even in the absence of a contractual agreement the courts can apportion liability between defendants responsible for the same publications.[69] In practice most publishers will be insured against libel and may pay for the defence of the author

---

[67] *Hayward v. Thompson*, n. 34 above, *per* Lord Denning at 459.

[68] *Eastwood v. Ryder*, *The Times*, July 31, 1990.

[69] Civil Liability (Contribution) Act 1978, s. 1.

under their policy, until such point as interests in the litigation begin to diverge—usually by the insurers wishing to settle and the author wishing to fight. Legal aid is in practice unavailable for libel defendants and some authors in this position confront the agonising choice between denouncing their own story or mortgaging their home to pay for the legal costs of defending it.

Statements in open court

A public apology defames the author of the article apologised for by suggesting that the author has written carelessly. An author who has not approved the apology is entitled to sue the person who has issued it.[70] Unapologetic authors cannot sue if the retraction is made through the procedure known as "a statement in open court". These statements are privileged and so too are any press reports of them. Authors may nevertheless disassociate themselves from the apology, or even approach the judge before whom the statement is to be made and ask him to refuse to sanction it because of the reflection that it would cast upon their reputations. However, courts are predisposed in favour of settlements, and are reluctant to prevent statements being made that dispose of libel actions, even when such statements imply criticisms of others:

> The historian Richard Barnet sued both Brian Crozier and the *Spectator* over the allegation that he was associated with KGB-influenced institutions. The magazine found that it could not justify the Crozier allegations and agreed to apologise, pay damages and make a statement in open court publicly retracting the libel. Crozier sought to delay the making of the statement on the ground that it defamed him and might prejudice the jury in Barnet's action against him, which would come on for trial some six months later. The Court of Appeal held that although "the court should be vigilant to see that the benefit of the procedure of making a statement in open court is not used to the unfair disadvantage of a third party", the public interest in allowing libel actions to be settled outweighed the damage that Crozier apprehended. Had the statement been plainly defamatory of Crozier, the court would have ordered the settlement to be postponed until after his trial, and may not have allowed it to be made at all under the cloak of absolute privilege.[71]

The statement in open court is a procedural device used in many libel settlements, often after the claimant has "taken out" money that has been paid into court by the defendant. It is valuable as a means of helping the claimant to restore his reputation (at least when the statement is reported) but it can be exploited to present a false picture under

---

[70] *Tracy v. Kemsley Newspapers, The Times*, April 9, 1954.
[71] *Barnet v. Crozier* [1987] 1 All E.R. 1041.

the pressure to avoid trial. Although judges must approve the statement
before it is made, they normally make no inquiries and allow the parties
to say whatever they have agreed. Under pressure to compromise a
legal action which will cost hundreds of thousands of pounds to fight,
defendants often "agree" to statements by which claimants whitewash
their conduct or praise themselves in hagiographic terms. It follows that
"statements in open court" are sometimes more akin to public relations
announcements than to records of truth.

A nice point arises when defendants, for commercial reasons, make
a payment into court which is less than can be properly described as
"substantial" (in 2001, that adjective was applied to damages exceeding
£10,000). Is a claimant, on taking that money, entitled to make a privileged statement in open court declaring himself vindicated? The Court
of Appeal has held that "it is wrong for complainants to assume that if
they do take money out of court they are entitled as of right to be
whitewashed by defendants . . .". The judge "should look at the relationship between the gravity of the allegations in the alleged libel and
the amount of money which is paid into court".[72] This guidance was
applied in 1992 to prevent an Italian prince from declaring himself vindicated by a payment of £1,000 lodged by the *Daily Mail* which it
claimed to have made to avoid the costs of the trial rather than in
acknowledgment of the falsity of its gossip.[73] When the *Wall Street
Journal* "paid in" a fraction of the cost of a long trial it objected to the
claimant's draft statement unless it was permitted to read a counter-
statement emphasising that its allegations had not been fully withdrawn.[74] Popplewell J. overruled the objection, but jurisprudence on
Article 6 of the European Convention ("each party must be afforded a
reasonable opportunity to present his case . . . under conditions which
do not place him at a substantial disadvantage *vis-à-vis* his opponent"[75])
supports the case for such a counter-statement in rare cases when the
parties have agreed to a settlement, but disagree over what to say about
it. The preferable alternative of course, is to say nothing. However keen
judges are to facilitate settlements, they should not lend the courts
imprimatur to one-sided statements unless the claimant has obtained
substantial damages or else the wording is agreed by the defendant.

---

[72] *Church of Scientology of California v. North News Ltd* (1973) 117 S.J. 566.
[73] *Ruspoli v. Dempster*, December 14, 1992, Alliot J., (unreported).
[74] *Keen v. Dow Jones Publishing Co. (Europe) Inc.* Dow Jones was given leave to
appeal by the Court of Appeal, but the point was not pursued.
[75] *Dondo Beheer BV v. The Netherlands* (1993) 18 E.H.R.R. 213, at 229–30. Australian courts adopt a similar approach, and insist that judges ensure the accuracy
and fairness of statements in open court: *Eyre v. Nationwide News Pty Ltd* (1968)
13 F.L.R. 180.

Foreign publications

Many journalists resident in Britain write for overseas publications. American law provides a special "public figure" defence: however inaccurate a speculation about the conduct of a person in the public eye, the journalists who make it will not be liable unless they have acted maliciously. The better view is that no action can be brought in Britain against the author of an article circulated only in America unless the article is also actionable under the law of the country where the publication took place.[76] It would follow that journalists writing for American publications have considerably more latitude in criticising public figures so long as their articles are not reprinted in Britain.

The claimant-friendliness of English libel law, most notoriously its requirement that the media bears the burden of proving truth, attracts many wealthy foreign forum-shoppers in search of favourable verdicts that they would not obtain at home, or in the home countries of publishers whose newspapers and magazines have an international circulation. The rule which gives them the opportunity to sue a foreign publication with a minute circulation in the United Kingdom dates from 1849, when the Duke of Brunswick dispatched his manservant to a newspaper office to obtain a back issue of the paper in order to sue for a libel he had overlooked for 17 years.[77] This single publication was deemed sufficient to constitute the tort of libel, and from this anachronistic case springs the absurd but venerated rule that in this country a single publication—even if only in a library—will be an actionable tort. The rigour of this rule is mitigated by the requirement that foreign publishers may only be served out of the jurisdiction by leave of the court, which should only be granted in the case of torts which are appropriate for trial in London. Thus when a European "gentleman of no occupation" came to England in the hope of collecting libel winnings from continental newspapers, a few copies of which had been circulated here, carrying articles accusing him of fraud, he failed to establish that his case was "a proper one for service out of the jurisdiction" (*i.e.* for dragging the foreign publishers into English courts) because he had no real and substantial grievance connected with England: the claimant, the publishers and the alleged fraud were all located abroad.[78] This was an early

---

[76] This "double actionability rule" is preserved for defamation claims by the Private International Law (Miscellaneous Provisions) Act 1995, s. 13. But if the author is domiciled in the U.K., he can be sued in respect of publications in other European countries which are parties to the Brussels and Lugano Conventions, incorporated into U.K. law by the Civil Jurisdiction and Judgments Acts 1982 and 1991.

[77] *Duke of Brunswick v. Harmer* (1849) 14 Q.B. 185.

[78] *Kroch v. Rossell* [1937] 1 All E.R. 725.

application of the *forum non conveniens* doctrine, whereby an English court can refuse to accept a case that would be more suitably tried, for the interests of the parties and the ends of justice, by the courts of another country.[79]

This doctrine has prevented American public figures from suing American magazines in England to protect reputations earned in America. A Californian company and its chief executive were sent packing because they had only a minor operation in Britain and the U.S. magazine they wished to sue sold only 1,200 copies here: it would have been obviously unfair to force the publishers to defend themselves under a law foreign to both parties and in respect of an article mainly about U.S. operations.[80] A similar fate befell Texan oil man Oscar Wyatt (on whom the *Dallas* character J.R. Ewing was based): his plea that he was connected with England directly through the presence of corporate offices and carnally because his son was the first to commit adultery with the Duchess of York was insufficient to maintain an action against *Forbes* magazine.[81] These claimants had made their reputations in America, which was the appropriate place for them to sue U.S. magazines. It is different, however, when the claimant is English or has worked here for many years, and will (all things being equal) be permitted to proceed against a foreign publication with a small circulation in the United Kingdom, especially if it has damaged him in a local or ethnic community.[82]

The global reach of the mass media, not only through satellite broadcasting and internationally distributed papers but most significantly by the internet, invites the courts of every advanced country to treat defamation as one global tort (rather than a multiple wrong committed by every single publication and every internet hit) and to yield jurisdiction to the country whose courts are best placed to decide the truth of the allegation. Any such development will have to come by international treaty: the Brussels Convention, an exercise of rigid pan-Europeanism, permits actions to be brought *either* in the European Union State where the publisher is based (with damages for the Europe-wide distribution) *or* in any and every EEC state where publication occurs (with damages in each action limited to reputational injury within the particular location).[83] This permits forum-shopping within Europe, although with one exception, all these European countries have incorporated the Euro-

---

[79] *Spiliada Maritime Corp. v. Cansulex Ltd* [1987] A.C. 460.

[80] *Chadha & Osicom v. Dow Jones & Co. Inc.* [1999] E.M.L.R. 724, CA.

[81] *Wyatt v. Forbes*, December 2, 1997, Morland J., (unreported).

[82] *Schapira v. Ahronson* [1999] E.M.L.R. 735, although note that the defendant Israeli newspaper had made the tactical mistake of accepting service in England (thus assuming the burden of proving that England was inappropriate) and a good deal of the evidence was located within this jurisdiction.

[83] *Shevill v. Presse Alliance* [1995] 2 A.C. 18.

pean Convention on Human Rights. The lone exception is the Republic of Ireland, where defamation law is antediluvian. The Republic is a fly-trap for English publishers: IRA figures who would not dare to venture into English courts sue over books and newspapers distributed in Ireland, without having to surmount the public interest defence vouchsafed to English law by *Reynolds*. The Law Lords have resisted any global theory of defamation liability, on the ground that it is incompatible with the primitive *Duke of Brunswick* rule that every publication is a separate tort[84]:

> Boris Berezovsky, the controversial Russian oligarch, sued *Forbes* magazine for the damage done to his "English" reputation by allegations that he had made his billions through corruption, gangsterism and murder. *Forbes* sold only 1,900 copies in England but 800,000 in the U.S. The trial judge ruled that Russia and the U.S. were both more appropriate places for trying the action, because Berezovsky had an entirely Russian reputation and the defendant magazine was based in the U.S. The Court of Appeal was more struck by Beresovsky's connections in England (he had property and ex-wives in Chelsea and children at Oxbridge and commercial connections here) and by the fact that United Kingdom-based banks and businesses would look at him askance. The Law Lords divided three-two over the correctness of the trial judges' decision, the majority ruling that he had paid insufficient attention to publication in Britain as a factor in favour of jurisdiction, the minority saying that he was "entitled to decide that the English court should not be an international libel tribunal for a dispute between foreigners which had no connection with this country".[85]

Time limits

Justice requires libel actions to be brought as soon as possible following publication to provide speedy and effective redress for wronged claimants and for the sake of media defendants who wish to justify, since "memories fade ... sources become untraceable ... records are retained only for short periods". This was the rationale for a reduction in the standard three-year period in which personal injury claims must be brought, a reform achieved by the 1996 Defamation Act, which requires claimants to sue in libel and in malicious falsehood within one year of "the date on which the cause of action accrued", *i.e.* the date of the defendant's last publication of the defamatory matter.[86] This salutary provision, which gives complainants a deadline by which to put up or

---

[84] *Berezovsky v. Forbes* [2000] E.M.L.R. 643.
[85] *Berezovsky v. Forbes* [2000] E.M.L.R. 643 at 666, *per* Lord Hoffman.
[86] Defamation Act 1996, s.5(2) and 5(4) amending s.4A and s.32A of the Limitation Act 1980.

shut up, is undermined in two respects. The 1996 Act gives the court a broad discretion to permit proceedings after the time-limit expires, if this is "equitable". There is a danger that judges will interpret "equitably" as turning on whether the action can still be fairly tried, rather than on the need to penalise tardy claimants whose usual excuse is that the libel did not come to their attention for over a year (which usually means it could not have done them much damage).[87] The second catch, which makes the provision useless for publishers of books remaining in circulation or even newspapers which sell "back issues", is that the reform does not affect the *Duke of Brunswick* rule that every sale is a separate cause of action. By making the deadline run from the last sale of a single copy (by which a cause of action accrues) rather than from the first appearance of the work, authors and publishers remain at risk for as long as the book remains in circulation or an article remains available on a newspaper's website.

Innocent dissemination

Distributors or wholesalers of newspapers, books and magazines have a special defence of "innocent dissemination". Obviously they cannot be expected to vet all the publications they sell, and it would be grossly unfair to hold them responsible for libels of which they could have no knowledge. In such cases they will escape, unless they have been negligent and ought to have known that the publication was likely to contain libellous matter. The strictness of the defence has unfortunate consequences for some controversial publications: distributors are prone to equate political radicalism with a propensity to libel, and are thus provided with a ready-made legal excuse for a decision not to stock them.

A claimant determined to damage a journal that torments him can, at least if that journal has a poor track record in libel actions, sue the distributors and settle on terms that they will not stock the publication in the future. For most small newsagents the prospect of defending a major libel case is frightening, and when Sir James Goldsmith threatened *Private Eye*'s distributors in this fashion, many of them caved in. The magazine's loss of circulation was dramatic and Lord Denning held that Goldsmith's flurry of "frightening writs" was an abuse of legal process. His fellow judges, however, pointed out that Goldsmith had merely *used* the legal process according to his rights. Any threats to press freedom came, not from Goldsmith, but from the law that allowed him to sue distributors of libel-prone magazines. If the

---

[87] The court is, however, required to examine the reasons for the delay: it was unimpressed by one solicitor's excuse that he missed the deadline because he had consulted an out-of-date textbook: *Hinks v. Channel 4*, March 3, 2000, Morland J.

law threatened press freedom, it was for Parliament, not the courts, to change it.[88]

Two decades later, Parliament got around to making some minor amendments to the innocent dissemination defence—most significantly by extending its protection to printers and to broadcasters of "live" programmes such as radio talk-backs and television chat shows, where the station has no control over off-the-cuff defamations uttered by studio guests. These two steps forward in the 1996 Defamation Act are accompanied by one step backwards: the distributor must prove not only that he took reasonable care but that "he did not know, and had no reason to believe what he did caused or contributed to the publication of a defamatory statement".[89] The old common law defence of "innocent dissemination" exculpated a disseminator who knew the statement was prima facie defamatory but reasonably believed it would not be held libellous because it was true or privileged or honest comment. Under the Act (which by implication supersedes the common law defence) the disseminator is not "innocent" if he has some reason to think merely that a statement in a publication he distributes is defamatory (*i.e.* lowering the repute) of somebody. The statute requires "reasonable care" and potential knowledge of defamations to be tested by reference to "the nature of the publication" and "the previous conduct or character of the author, editor or publisher". This means that large distributors like Smiths and Menzies will still insist on indemnities before they stock *Private Eye* or any new publication with a name like *Scallywag*.

THE RULE AGAINST PRIOR RESTRAINT

The courts will not stop publication of defamatory statements where the person who wants to make them is prepared to defend them. Threats by angry complainants and their solicitors to stop the presses with eleventh-hour libel injunctions are largely bluff:

> "The court will not restrain the publication of an article, even though it is defamatory, when the defendant says he intends to justify it or to make it fair comment on a matter of public interest. The reason sometimes given is that the defences of justification and fair comment are for the jury, which is the constitutional tribunal, and not for the judge. But a better reason is the importance in the public interest that the truth should out ... The right of free

---

[88] *Goldsmith v. Sperrings* [1977] 1 W.L.R. 478.
[89] Defamation Act 1996, s.1(1)(c).

speech is one which it is for the public interest that individuals should possess, and, indeed, that they should exercise without impediment, so long as no wrongful act is done. There is no wrong done if it is true, or if it is fair comment on a matter of public interest. The court will not prejudice the issue by granting an injunction in advance of publication."[90]

If the claimant can prove immediately and convincingly that the defendant is intending to publish palpable untruths, an injunction might be granted in advance of the publication, so long as the precise terms of the libel can be identified.[91] Otherwise, the rule against prior restraint must prevail in libel actions. When an injunction was granted to stop the circulation of information by a shipping exchange accusing the claimant of fraud the Court of Appeal lifted it as a matter of principle, even though a hearing on the merits was set for the following day. "The only safe and correct approach is not to allow an injunction to remain, even for a single day, if it was clearly wrong for it to have been granted."[92]

The rule against prior restraint is secure in libel cases "because of the value the court has placed on freedom of speech and freedom of the press when balancing it against the reputation of a single individual who, if wronged, can be compensated in damages".[93] It applies whenever the defendant raises the defences of justification and fair comment, and will apply if the defence is to be qualified privilege unless the evidence of malice is so overwhelming that no reasonable jury would sustain the privilege. The Court of Appeal has even refused to injunct a magazine that had published an allegation it could not justify, where it might succeed at trial for other reasons:

> Soraya Kashoggi sought an injunction to withdraw *Woman's Own* from circulation when it published a statement that she was having an extra-marital affair with a Head of State. The magazine could not prove the truth of this statement, which it had sourced to an MI5 report, but claimed to be able to justify the "sting" of the libel, namely that the claimant was a person given to extra-marital affairs, a number of which had been referred to in the article without attracting complaint. The Court of Appeal held that the rule against prior restraint would still operate, given that this

---

[90] *Fraser v. Evans* [1969] Q.B. 349, *per* Lord Denning at 360. The rule derives from the case of *Bonnard v. Perryman* [1891] 2 Ch. 269.

[91] *British Data Management v. Boxer Commercial Removals plc* [1996] 3 All E.R. 707, CA.

[92] *Harakas v. Baltic Mercantile and Shipping Exchange* [1982] 2 All E.R. 701 at 703, *per* Kerr L.J.

[93] *Herbage v. Pressdram Ltd* [1984] 2 All E.R. 769, *per* Griffiths L.J.

defence might succeed at the trial. If it did not, the claimant would be adequately compensated by damages.[94]

One important practical benefit of this rule is that journalists can (as they *must* to obtain qualified privilege) approach the subject of their investigation for a response to an article in draft without fear that they will receive a pre-publication injunction instead of a quote. However, one trap for unwary players can be sprung by a determined litigant who seeks an interim injunction at the outset of his action. In order to invoke the rule against prior restraint the defendant must state on affidavit his intention to justify the allegation. If, contrary to this sworn determination, the defence of justification is not proceeded with when the matter comes to trial, or it fails dismally at trial, his conduct in recklessly signalling a defence that does not materialise can inflate the damages. *Private Eye* fell into this trap when it beat off an interim injunction from Robert Maxwell by promising to prove at trial that he had financed Neil Kinnock's foreign travel in the hope of being awarded a peerage. Its defence of justification was withdrawn at the trial when its "highly placed sources" went to ground. It escaped being required to identify them, but its conduct in promising a plea of justification and persisting in such a plea until the last moment was punished by damages of £50,000. The jury found the libel itself to be worth only £5,000.[95]

The stringency of the rule against prior restraint in defamation led some claimants to frame their actions as claims for breach of confidence, where injunctions were granted more readily on the "balance of convenience" test.[96] This tactic has been rendered less effective by section 12 of the Human Rights Act, with its requirement that particular attention be paid in such cases to freedom of expression and to the extent to which the material has already been published and/or is in the public interest. Under section 12, the "balance of convenience" test is replaced by the burden on the applicant to prove that he is likely to succeed at trial—a higher hurdle. There can be no *ex parte* injunctions (the tactic of a claimant going privately to a judge and obtaining an injunction to stop publication for a few days until the case can be argued by both parties) because now an applicant must take all practical steps to notify the publisher of the hearing (s. 12(2)).

When the principle of free speech collides with the principle of fair trial, however, the former must give way. Courts may grant injunctions to stop defamatory publications that would prejudice pending criminal trials. This jurisdiction is not often used—the normal procedure is for

---

[94] *Kashoggi v. IPC Magazines Ltd* [1986] 3 All E.R. 577.

[95] See *Maxwell v. Pressdram* [1987] 1 All E.R. 656.

[96] Although the courts were willing to look at the real grievance—see *Service Corporation International PCC v. Channel 4* [1999] E.M.L.R. 83, Lightman J.

the Attorney-General to bring proceedings for contempt once the trial
has concluded. But in 1979 the Court of Appeal, at the behest of Mr
Jeremy Thorpe, stopped the *Spectator* from publishing an election
address by Auberon Waugh, "Dog-Lovers Candidate" from North
Devon, on the grounds that it contained defamatory matter that would
prejudice Thorpe's impending trial for conspiracy to murder his former
lover, whose dog had been shot instead by a soft-hearted hit-man.[97] The
Attorney General subsequently stopped the staging of a musical comedy
about the fraudulent life of Robert Maxwell, lest it prejudice the fraud
trial of his sons. Election law has a special provision (section 106 of
the Representation of the People Act) which permits injunctions to stop
a "false statement of fact in relation to the candidate's personal character or conduct" although the burden of proving falsity falls on the candidate. The courts will require proof to a high standard, because elections are the very time democracy demands the utmost freedom of
speech.[98]

DEFENCES GENERALLY

Burden of proof

Claimants must prove that the words of which they complain have a
defamatory meaning, that the words refer to them, and that the defendant was responsible for publishing them. Once these matters are established the burden shifts to the defendants. They must convince the jury
that the words were true, or the comment was honest, or that publication
of the report was "privileged". The burden of proving these defences
rests squarely on the media, although proof does not have to be "beyond
reasonable doubt" but rather "on the balance of probabilities": 51 per
cent proof will suffice, unless the accusation is of a criminal offence,
when juries are told "the more serious the allegation, the more cogent
the evidence required to prove it". A simple but far-reaching reform in
libel law, which would enhance freedom of expression, would be to
reverse this burden: to oblige the claimant to prove, on balance, the
falsity or unfairness of the criticism. This modest proposal was rejected
in 1975 by the Faulks Committee; "It tends to inculcate a spirit of
caution in publishers of potentially actionable statements which we

---

[97] *Thorpe v. Waugh* (unreported). See (1979) Court of Appeal Transcript No. 282.
[98] *Bowman v. U.K.* (1998) 26 E.H.R.R. 1.

regard as salutary" [99] was its pompous response to a reform now clearly seen to be necessary to effectuate free speech as well as to bring libel law into line with other civil actions. A reversal of the burden of proof is essential if the purpose of Article 10 is to be achieved, namely to inculcate a salutary spirit of caution in wealthy public figures who wish to use the law to silence their critics.

There is mounting evidence that this unfair and anomalous rule causes jury confusion and can produce injustice. The rule stems, of course, from the absurd presumption that every defamation is false. Libel trials commence with this (often false) assumption that the claimant has a spotless character and then the media defendant bears the burden of disproving it, and by admissible evidence. This is impossible where witnesses have died or have been promised confidentiality, and difficult when the evidence comes (as in sleaze cases it often does) from criminals or low-life characters or even from investigative journalists (who can look fairly grubby in the witness box). Juries instinctively hesitate to find they have proved their allegations against glamorous film stars or experienced policemen or popular sportsmen. In 2001 the Court of Appeal for the first time took the extreme step of quashing a libel jury verdict on the grounds of perversity. It had awarded £85,000 to an obviously corrupt Bruce Grobbelaar after having been "skilfully deflected from the path of logic" by forensic tactics and then "left undecided about Grobbelaar's story"—a result fatal to the defendants on whom the burden of proof lay.[1] Had Grobbelaar borne the legal onus of disproving the *Sun*'s allegations, he would not have won the unjust verdict and would in all probability not have had the effrontery to come to court in the first place. In every other civil action claimants must prove their case in order to win damages: why should libel be any different? The "affront to justice" by the Grobbelaar verdict was not caused by the irrationality of the jury, but by the irrationality of a legal rule that assumes all defamations are false and which forces media defendants to prove them true.

The meaning of "malice"

A number of important defences available to the media in libel cases can be defeated if the claimant proves that the publication was actuated

---

[99] Committee on Defamation, HMSO, 1975, Cmnd. 5909, para. 141. Compare American libel law, where both public figure and private claimants bear the burden of proving that allegedly libellous statements are false: *Philadelphia Newspapers v. Hepps* 475 U.S. 797 (1986). The public figure must further prove express malice, although a private claimant may recover against a negligent publisher: *Curtis Publishing Co. v. Butts* 388 U.S. 130 (1967). The reversal of the burden of proof is the main reason why American courts refuse to enforce English libel awards.

[1] *Grobbelaar v. Newsgroup Newspapers Ltd* [2001] 2 All E.R. 437.

by "malice". In ordinary language "malice" means "spite" or "ill-will". But in libel law it generally refers to dishonest or reckless writing or reporting—the publication of facts that are known or suspected to be false, or opinions that are not genuinely held. These qualities may exist without feelings of spite or revenge, so that malice in law has a wider meaning than colloquial usage suggests. On the other hand, the mere existence of personal antagonism between writer and claimant will not defeat a legitimate defence if the published criticism, however intemperate, is an honest opinion. For the careful and conscientious journalist or broadcaster, the legal meaning of "malice" provides vital protection for honest comment, the more so because the burden of proving that malice was the dominant motive shifts to the claimant. Such proof is necessary before a claimant can succeed against unfair and exaggerated criticism (the "fair comment" defence) or against false statements made on certain public occasions (which are protected by the defence of "qualified privilege").

The importance of the legal meaning of "malice" in the defence of free speech is emphasised by the House of Lords" decision in the case of *Horrocks v. Lowe*[2]:

> Lowe was a Labour councillor who launched an intemperate attack on Horrocks, a Tory councillor whose companies had engaged in land dealings with the Tory-controlled local authority. "His attitude was either brinkmanship, megalomania or childish petulance . . . he has misled the Committee, the leader of his party, and his political and club colleagues" said Lowe of Horrocks at a council meeting. Speeches on such occasions, and reports of them, are protected by "qualified privilege"—a defence that will fail only if the claimant can show that the defendant was actuated by malice. In the ordinary sense of the word Lowe *was* malicious—his political antagonism had, the trial judge found, inflamed his mind into a state of "gross and unreasoning prejudice". Nonetheless, he genuinely believed that everything he said was true. On that basis the House of Lords held that he was not "malicious" in law.

A passage in Lord Diplock's speech is generally regarded as the classic exposition of the meaning of legal malice:

> "What is required on the part of the defamer to entitle him to the protection of the privilege is positive belief in the truth of what he published . . . If he publishes untrue defamatory matter recklessly, without considering or caring whether it be true or not, he is in this, as in other branches of the law, treated as if he knew it to be false. But indifference to the truth of what he publishes is not to be equated with carelessness, impulsiveness or irrationality in

---

[2] [1975] A.C. 135 at 149.

arriving at a positive belief that it was true. The freedom of speech protected by the law of qualified privilege may be availed of by all sorts and conditions of men. In affording to them immunity from suit if they have acted in good faith in compliance with a legal or moral duty or in protection of a legitimate interest the law must take them as it finds them . . . In greater or less degree according to their temperaments, their training, their intelligence, they are swayed by prejudice, rely on intuition instead of reasoning, leap to conclusions on inadequate evidence and fail to recognise the cogency of material which might cast doubt on the validity of the conclusions they reach. But despite the imperfection of the mental process by which the belief is arrived at it may still be "honest', that is, a positive belief that the conclusions they have reached are true. The law demands no more."[3]

"Malice" is an imprecise term, and bears a different nuance in the defence of fair comment than in qualified privilege. To defeat a fair comment plea the claimant must prove dishonesty or at least a reckless disregard for the truth—the defendant's *actual* malice (his spite or hatred of the claimant) will not negative the defence so long as he honestly believed in the opinions he expressed.[4] Qualified privilege, however, may be lost if the defendant misused the occasion of publication for an ulterior and vicious purpose, even though he believed at the time in the truth of allegations which have turned out to be false. This will rarely be the case with mainstream media reporting, although actual malice may sometimes poison the motives of informants. Newspapers will not normally be aware of improper motives lying behind otherwise defensible statements they report from spiteful informants: in such cases the better view is that they are not "infected" by the improper motivation of the accusers, unless either they ought to have known of it or the accuser was in their employ.[5]

Recklessness as to the truth or falsity of accusations may amount to malice, but carelessness does not, nor do impulsiveness or irrationality. Lack of care for the consequences of exuberant reporting is not malice and nor is mere inaccuracy or a failure to make inquiries or accidental or negligent misquotation.[6] The claimant must show that the defendant has turned a blind eye to truth in order to advance an ulterior object. An example is provided by one Parkinson, a Victorian clean-up cam-

[3] *ibid.*
[4] *Albert Cheng v. Tse Wai Chun Paul*, Court of Final Appeal, Hong Kong, November 13, 2000, judgment by Lord Nicholls.
[5] *Egger v. Viscount Chelmsford* [1965] 1 Q.B. 248.
[6] *Pinniger v. John Fairfax* (1979) 53 A.L.J.R. 691, *per* Barwick C.J.; *Brooks v. Muldoon* [1973] N.Z.L.R. 1.

paigner, whose moral objection to "public dancing" led him to allege that a ballet at the Royal Aquarium had involved a Japanese female catching a butterfly "in the most indecent place you could possibly imagine". Confronted with evidence that the performer in question was neither Japanese nor female, and in any event was dressed in pantaloons, Parkinson confessed that he had difficulty observing the performance and that his object in making the allegation was to have the Aquarium's dancing licence revoked. His pursuit of moral ends did not justify his reckless disregard for truth, and his malice destroyed the privilege to which he would otherwise have been entitled.[7] "The law protects the freedom to express opinions, not vituperative make-believe".[8]

It is sometimes said that criticism of the claimant after the claim form has been issued, and a failure to apologise prior to trial, is evidence of malice. This approach is wrong in principle. Other critical statements made about a claimant are irrelevant unless they shed light on the defendant's state of mind at the time he or she wrote the article that gave rise to the action. It is not necessarily a sign of "malice" to refuse an apology, or to repeat the allegations prior to trial or to persist in them at trial;[9] this may be no more than steadfastness in the cause (although if the allegations turn out to be false, such conduct will increase the damages).

TRUTH AS A DEFENCE

The defence of justification

Truth is a complete defence to any defamatory statement of fact, whatever the motives for its publication and however much its revelation is unjustified or contrary to the public interest. The legal title of the defence is "justification", and it operates whenever the defendants can show, by admissible evidence, that their allegation is, on balance, substantially correct. The question of "substance" may be significant—it is not necessary to prove that every single fact stated in the criticism is accurate, so long as its "sting" (its defamatory impact) is substantially true. Minor errors, such as dates or times or places, will not be held against the journalist if the gist of the allegation is justified. Even mistakes that diminish reputation will not count if they pale into minor significance beside the truth of major charges. Section 5 of the 1952

---

[7] *Royal Aquarium v. Parkinson* [1892] 1 Q.B. 431.
[8] *Albert Cheng v. Tse Wai Chun Paul*, Court of Final Appeal, Hong Kong, November 13, 2000, *per* Lord Nicholls.
[9] See *Broadway Approvals Ltd v. Odhams Press Ltd* [1965] 2 All E.R. 523.

Defamation Act provides that the defence of justification shall not founder by failure to prove every charge, "if the words not proved to be true do not materially injure the claimant's reputation, having regard to the truth of the remaining charges". So even where baseless charges do "materially injure" a claimant's reputation, accurate criticisms in the same article may amount to a "partial justification", which reduces the damages by reducing the value of the reputation. To say that a man is guilty of terrorism and drunken driving will be justifiable if he is a teetotal terrorist. It will, however, be gravely libellous if he is a drunken driver but not a terrorist. There are limits, of course, to the distance that truth will stretch. A generalised criticism cannot be justified if it is based on one isolated incident. A statement that a reporter is a "libellous journalist" implies some proven propensity to defame: it is not justified by the fact that the journalist was once in his or her career obliged to apologise.[10]

Facts should normally be allowed to speak for themselves: to spell out a conclusion may spell danger. For example, it may be a fact that a writer has used the work of others without permission. But to describe the writer as a "deliberate plagiarist" may overlook another, but unknown fact: that he or she was assured at the time of using the material that the originator's consent had been forthcoming. It follows that although the writer is a plagiarist, he is not a *deliberate* plagiarist. Libel lawyers are nervous of the word "lie" because it implies that a person said something that he or she *knew* was untrue. Since this is usually difficult to prove, they will often suggest changing it to "misled", "misrepresented" or some other phrase that does not necessarily connote a dishonest state of mind.

The fact that a defamatory statement has been made or the fact that a defamatory rumour exists is no "justification" for publishing it. The law requires the "truth" in such cases to be the truth of the rumour, not the truth of the fact that it is circulating. As Lord Devlin has explained:

> ". . . you cannot escape liability for defamation by putting the libel behind a prefix such as 'I have been told that . . .' or 'it is rumoured that . . ', and then asserting that it was true that you had been told or that it was in fact being rumoured . . . For the purpose of the law of libel a hearsay statement is the same as a direct statement, and that is all there is to it."[11]

However, the context of the article may remove or reduce the rumour's impact on the claimant's reputation. Much will depend on the reaction of the reasonable reader. In most cases the publication of a

---

[10] *Wakeley v. Cooke* (1849) 4 Exch. 511.
[11] *Lewis v. Daily Telegraph Ltd*, [1964] A.C. 234 at 283.

rumour will give it currency and credit. But if the gist of the article is genuinely to demolish the rumour, or to demolish the credibility of its mongers rather than its victim, the article as a whole may not bear a defamatory meaning. There was a week in 1986 when Fleet Street and Westminster were convulsed with a rumour that Home Secretary Leon Brittan had been caught interfering sexually with a small boy; no newspaper dared to print what all "in the know" were discussing until *Private Eye* published the story with the explanation that it was utterly false and circulated to damage the Home Secretary by an anti-Semitic faction in MI5. This form of publication reproduced the rumour in order to kill it, and a relieved Home Secretary announced that he would be taking no proceedings against *Private Eye*.

A rumour may be reported (with great care) if its existence (irrespective of its truth) has public significance. Its victim should be allowed to reply and renounce the allegation and the publisher must be scrupulous not to indicate expressly or impliedly that the allegation is true. In many spheres of public life justice should be seen to be done, and officials should be seen to be above reproach. So a paper might report that a community believed that certain police officers had been unnecessarily violent in arresting suspects. The report would need to include any denial by the police, but it might go on to comment that irrespective of whether the allegations were true or not, their existence undermined the confidence of the community in the officers, who for this reason should be transferred. Justification may fail if the newspaper cannot prove that the police officers had behaved in a way which brought reasonable suspicion upon them,[12] but the defendant would in this situation have the comfort of falling back on the new *Reynolds* defence of qualified privilege.

Practical problems

Further problems with the defence of justification arise from the law's procedures. Although truth is a defence, proving it in court may be impossible. There is the burden of proof—squarely on the defendant. There is the crippling legal cost of preparing a full-blooded counter-attack. There is the difficulty of calling witnesses who may have died

---

[12] Because the so-called "repetition rule" that publication of rumour and suspicion can only be justified if there are reasonable grounds (objectively judged) which stem from some conduct on the part of the claimant. See *Shah v. Standard Bank* [1998] 4 All E.R. 155, CA, and *Stern v. Piper* [1997] Q.B. 123, CA. The rigidity of this rule is difficult to square with recent European Court decisions, notably *Bladet Tromsø v. Norway* (1999) 29 E.H.R.R. 125 and *Thoma v. Luxembourg*, March 29, 2001 (Application No. 38432/97) although the Court of Appeal has declined an invitation to find the rule incompatible with the Convention: see *Forbes v. Berezovsky (No. 2)*. July 31, 2001.

or gone abroad, or who may have been promised confidentiality. And then there is the risk of failure, which inflates the damages on the basis that the defendant is not merely a defamer, but a defamer who has persisted in the injury to the last. There is no doubt that difficulties of this sort mean that many true statements are not published, or if they are, soon become the subject of apologies rather than defences.

Other problems stem from the ambiguities of language and the complex rules of pleading. Claimants will plead the most exaggerated meanings that their counsel consider the words will conceivably bear in order to maximise the insult and humiliation (and hence the damages). The defence may well be able to prove the words true in some less defamatory meaning, but will fail unless that is the meaning the jury chooses to adopt as the "true" meaning. There will be legal pressure to settle the case: successful defendants do not recover all of their costs, and the simplest of libel actions will run up a six-figure sum in costs for each party prior to trial. Damages, at the end of the forensic day, never exceed the cost of the lawyers who have obtained them.

No one defamation action is the same as any other: general rules about pleading and meaning require adaptation to an infinite variety of contexts and linguistic usage. What has to be justified as "true" is not a set of words in their literal meaning, but the imputation they convey—and they may convey several. English law's approach insists on one defamatory "sting", but a long article or broadcast programme may carry a number of defamatory meanings, some true and others false. This invites a great deal of pre-trial tactical skirmishing: the claimant will only sue on the false imputations, but the defendant will seek to call evidence of other "stings" that can be proved. This will not be allowed if the meaning is separate or distinct from the meaning of which complaint is made,[13] but in most cases there will be an overlap, if not a hopeless entanglement, and the judge will have to resort to case management techniques and proportionality doctrine to limit the issues and the evidence. The parties are not entitled to turn the proceedings into a wide-ranging investigation akin to a public inquiry, but in principle "the action should be so structured that the defendant is not prevented from deploying his full essential defence and so that the claimant, if he wins, will obtain proper vindication upon a proper basis".[14] Recent provisions for (a) exchange of witness statements, (b) disclosure of documents which might be relevant to advancing or undermining either party's case[15] and (c) threats of adverse costs orders unless the parties make "timely admissions of fact" to reduce the need for live evidence,[16] all

---

[13] *Polly Peck v. Trelford* [1986] Q.B. 1000 at p1002.
[14] *McPhilemy v. Times Newspapers Ltd* [1999] E.M.L.R. 751 at 771.
[15] See *Evans v. Granada TV* [1996] E.M.L.R. 413.
[16] See *U.S. Tobacco v. BBC* [1998] E.M.L.R. 816.

follow the "cards on the table" philosophy of the Woolf reforms, although last minute evidence which tends to prove truth is usually admitted to avoid the reproach that a verdict for the claimant was a "false vindication". This is as it should be: the very publicity attending libel proceedings sometimes produces evidence that claimants hoped had disappeared forever. Recent claimants like ex-minister Jonathan Aitken, the soap actress Gillian Taylforth and South African journalist Jani Allen were fatally tarnished by evidence which only turned up in the hands of their nemesis, the late George Carman Q.C., in the course of their cross-examinations at the trial.

Placing a defence of justification on the record is a serious step: the media defendant takes upon itself the task of proving that its allegations are true, thereby adding insult to the original injury. A failed plea will mean heavier damages and much heavier costs. Before the pleading is entered a defendant must not only believe the truth of his words but also have some evidence to support them, or reasonable grounds for thinking that the evidence will be available at the trial. "Reasonable grounds" must be more than a Micawberish hope that something will turn up, but defendants who have reason to believe that the truth will out—*e.g.* from documents which must be in the possession of the claimant—are entitled to put down a plea of justification so as to oblige their opponent to disclose them.[17]

On the other hand, the difficulties of proving justification should not be exaggerated. The adage that "truth will out" is assisted by the law. The defendant may rely on facts that emerge after publication—and in such cases the length of time before trial may be a positive boon. Most importantly, the defence may be helped by court rules relating to "discovery of documents". Claimants must make available to the defence all documents in their possession that are relevant to the matters in dispute—and sometimes there will be found, amongst office memoranda and other internal documents, material that goes to justify the original allegation. The order for discovery is often the point of no return for the claimant in a libel action: it is the stage at which some prefer to discontinue rather than to open their files. The most sensational collapse of a libel case in recent British history was that brought by Neil Hamilton M.P. and lobbyist Ian Greer against *The Guardian* for publishing Al Fayed's claim that they accepted his bribes. A few days before the trial began, documents that they and the cabinet office (on *subpoena*) were forced to disclose indicated that both men had skeletons in their cupboards. Their last-minute withdrawal triggered the "Tory sleaze" allegations which, a few months later, swept that party from power in the 1997 elections.[18]

---

[17] *McDonalds Corp. v. Steel* [1995] 3 All E.R. 615.
[18] See David Leigh and Ed Vulliamy, *Sleaze—The Corruption of Parliament* (Fourth Estate, 1997).

Finally there is always the prospect of cross-examining the claimant. Libel claimants are virtually obliged to go in the witness box. One claimant who failed to take the stand was David Bookbinder, leader of Derbyshire County Council, who in 1991 sued Norman Tebbitt over the latter's criticisms of his political policies. The tactic proved disastrous: Bookbinder was savagely derided for his cowardice by defence counsel, and the jury found Tebbitt's criticisms to be fair comment. Once in the witness box, claimants may be cross-examined in detail about matters relevant to their claim and may have their reputation traduced.[19] Their answers may support the defence of justification—although rarely as dramatically as football manager Tommy Docherty, a libel claimant who collapsed so utterly under cross-examination that he was subsequently prosecuted for perjury. A sympathetic jury acquitted him after his counsel had luridly described the terrors and confusions for claimants of undergoing cross-examination in libel actions. Jonathan Aitken, an M.P. and former cabinet minister, was destroyed not by cross-examination but by last minute discovery of hotel and airline records which proved him not only a liar but a scoundrel who had expected his wife and 16-year-old daughter to tell lies in support of his claim. He was jailed for 18 months—a sentence which could have been heavier, so as to deter anyone else prepared to suppress the truth by perverting the course of justice. It may be that the four year sentence imposed on Jeffrey Archer, for fabricating evidence in support of his libel action, will have this effect.

Reporting old criminal convictions

There are special rules relating to publication of past criminal convictions. A conviction—or, for that matter, an acquittal—by a jury is no more than an expression of opinion by at least 10 out of 12 people about the defendant's guilt. One ingenious convict, Alfie Hinds, sued a police officer for stating in the *News of the World* that he had been guilty as charged. Hinds convinced the libel jury that he had been wrongfully convicted, so the newspaper's defence of justification failed.[20] Parliament, recognising the danger—perhaps more to respect for the law than to press freedom—changed the law, so that now the very fact of a conviction is deemed to be conclusive evidence of its correctness. The prosecution's evidence does not have to be presented to the court all over again.[21]

---

[19] But not, regrettably, by reference to specific acts of misconduct that fall outside the pleaded meanings: see the rule in *Scott v. Sampson* (1881–82) L.R. 8 Q.B.D. 491.

[20] *Hinds v. Sparks (No. 2), The Times*, October 20, 1964; see similarly *Goody v. Odhams Press Ltd, Daily Telegraph*, June 22, 1967.

[21] Civil Evidence Act 1968, s. 13(1).

However, this rule—and indeed the basic rule that truth is a complete defence—is subject to one exception in relation to past convictions. It is socially desirable that offenders should be able to "live down" a criminal past, and the Rehabilitation of Offenders Act 1974 is designed to assist this process. The Act applies only to convictions that have resulted in a sentence of no more than 30 months' imprisonment, and which have been "spent"—*i.e.* a certain period of time has elapsed since the passing of sentence. The length of that period depends on the seriousness of the punishment: where there has been any period of imprisonment between six months and 30 months, the conviction becomes "spent" after 10 years have elapsed. Seven years is the rehabilitation period for prison sentences of six months or under; five years for all other sentences that fall short of imprisonment, save for an absolute discharge, which is "spent" (not that it should carry a blameworthy connotation in any event) after a bare six months. There are short rehabilitation periods for juvenile offenders and persons subject to court orders or disqualifications.

The provisions of the Act are complex, but they have little effect on media freedom. The press may publish details of "spent" convictions and, if sued, may successfully plead justification or fair comment, unless the claimant can show that the publication of this particular truth has been actuated by malice.[22] Since there can be no dishonesty involved in stating the truth, an overwhelming desire to injure the claimant rather than to inform the public must, and it rarely can, be proved (newspapers have routinely reported the "spent" convictions of National Front leaders for example). But journalists minded to look at court or police records should bear in mind that an official persuaded to show them a "spent" conviction is liable to a fine, and if they make their persuasion more persuasive by a bribe or obtain access to the record dishonestly, they themselves are liable to imprisonment for up to six months.[23]

There is no inhibition on digging up an old acquittal. Nor does the fact of an acquittal debar the media from alleging that the defendant was really guilty at all. The jury's verdict is "final" only so far as punishment by the criminal court is concerned. Naturally, such allegations will rarely be made, although the defence of "justification" does not require them to be proved to the high criminal standard, "beyond reasonable doubt". Where there is a strong evidence of guilt, defendants given the benefit of the doubt by a jury in a criminal trial will normally be reluctant to chance their luck a second time by bringing a libel action, although the rule that the media must prove guilt by cogent evidence encouraged the acquitted Bruce Grobbelaar to sue the newspaper which had provided the prosecution evidence. It is noticeable that *Rough Just-*

[22] Rehabilitation of Offenders Act 1974, s. 8.
[23] *ibid.* s. 9

ice programmes and books invariably deal with wrongful convictions and never wrongful acquittals (which are much more common). In this respect libel law clearly exercises a "chilling effect" on the media, which are forced to cover up the extent to which dangerous criminals sometimes walk free as a result of police or prosecution mistakes. A notable exception was made in the case of the men acquitted of the murder of black teenager Stephen Lawrence: the *Daily Mail*, which trumpeted their guilt, presumably calculated that they had neither the money nor the courage to sue.

FAIR COMMENT

The defence of "fair comment" protects the honest expression of opinion, no matter how unfair or exaggerated, on any matter of public interest. The question for the court is, whether the views could honestly have been held on facts known at the time. Whether the jury agree with it or not is irrelevant. "A critic is entitled to dip his pen in gall for the purpose of legitimate criticism: and no one need be mealy-mouthed in denouncing what he regards as twaddle, daub or discord."[24] The defence is called "fair comment"—a misnomer, because it in fact defends unfair comment, so long as that comment amounts to an opinion that an honest (but not necessarily fair-minded) person might express on a matter of public interest, and that has in fact been expressed by a defendant who was not actuated by malice.

> "Every latitude must be given to opinion and to prejudice, and then an ordinary set of men with ordinary judgment must say [not whether they agree with it, but] whether any fair man would have made such a comment . . . Mere exaggeration, or even gross exaggeration, would not make the comment unfair. However wrong the opinion expressed may be in point of truth, or however prejudiced the writer, it may still be within the prescribed limit. The question which the jury must consider is this—would any fair man, however prejudiced he may be, however exaggerated or obstinate his views, have said that which this criticism has said."[25]

---

[24] *Gardiner v. John Fairfax & Sons* (1942) 42 S.R. (NSW) 171, at 174 *per* Jordan C. J..

[25] *Merivale v. Carson* (1887) 20 Q.B.D. 275, at 280 *per* Lord Esher. "Fairness" plays no part in the "fair comment" defence, which is open to the obstinate and prejudiced commentator, and whose views must be honest but not necessarily reasonable or fair: *Branson v. Bower* [2001] E.H.L.R. 33.

Distinction between fact and opinion

The fair comment defence relates only to *comment*—to statements of opinion and not to statements of fact. This is the most important, and most difficult, distinction in the entire law of libel. A defamatory statement of fact must be *justified* (*i.e.* proved true)—which is a much more onerous task than defending a defamatory comment on the basis that it was made honestly. The difficulty arises when facts and opinions are jumbled together in the same article or programme. A form of words may, in one context, be opinion (and therefore defensible as "fair comment") while in another context appear as a factual statement, consequently requiring proof of correctness. There is no hard-and-fast rule: once again, the test is that of ordinary readers. Would they, on reading or hearing the words complained of in context, say to themselves "that is an opinion" or "so that is the fact of the matter"? Unattributed assertions in news stories and headlines are likely to be received as factual, while criticism expressed in personalised columns is more likely to be regarded as opinion, especially when it appears to be an inference drawn by the columnist from facts to which reference has been made. Writers can help to characterise their criticisms as comment with phrases like "it seems to me", "in my judgment", "in other words", etc., although such devices will not always be conclusive. To say, without any supporting argument, "In my opinion Smith is a disgrace to human nature" is an assertion of fact. To say "Smith murdered his father and therefore is a disgrace to human nature" makes the characterisation a comment upon a stated fact. Where a defamatory remark is made baldly, without reference to any fact from which the remark could be inferred, it is not likely to be defensible as comment, especially if it imputes dishonesty or dishonourable conduct. In deciding the scope of a fair comment plea and the degree of interpretative sophistication to bring to bear on the question of whether a passage is "comment" or "fact", the court should have regard to the constitutional importance of the fair comment defence as a protection for freedom of expression.[26]

The cause of freedom of expression was damaged, however, by the House of Lords in 1991 in *Telnikoff v. Matusevitch*, a decision that ignores the realities of newspaper reading and places a burden on editors to identify fully the subjects commented upon in their "letters" page.[27]

> The claimant wrote an article for the *Daily Telegraph* attacking the BBC World Service for recruiting mainly members of the USSR's national minorities for its Russia service. The defendant wrote, and the *Telegraph*

---

[26] See *London Artists Ltd v. Littler* [1969] 2 Q.B. 375; *Slim v. The Daily Telegraph* [1968] 2 Q.B. 157; *Silkin v. Beaverbrook Newspapers Ltd* [1985] 2 All E.R. 516.
[27] *Telnikoff v. Matusevitch* [1991] 4 All E.R. 817.

published, a "letter to the editor" in response, characterising the claimant's views, as expressed in this article, as racist and anti-Semitic. The claimant sued and the outcome hinged on whether the words used in the letter could be construed as *comment* (in which case the defendant succeeded) or *fact* (in which case the defendant lost, because they were untrue). This in turn hinged on whether the jury could construe the letter in isolation (when it was read literally, it appeared to be making statements of fact) or in the wider context of the original article (on which the letter was plainly intended as a comment). The House of Lords, reversing the Court of Appeal, held that the jury should be permitted to look at the letter only as published. This decision is wrong, because letters to the editor are generally written—and sensibly read—as comments upon articles and opinions previously expressed in the newspaper.

The law should encourage readers to exercise free speech by writing letters to newspapers, and encourage editors to publish, in the public interest, as many of these letters as possible. The rule in *Telnikoff* requires editors either to reject or censor a letter if its critical statements cannot be proved in court, or else to republish the criticised article again so that its naïvest readers will realise that the letter is stating its author's *opinion*. As the latter course will normally prove impractical, the *Telnikoff* decision shrinks the area of robust criticism permitted to "letters to the editor" pages by the fair comment defence and provides some legal excuse for oversensitive editors who censor or reject letters critical of the newspaper's own correspondents. In any event the *Telnikoff* rule is incompatible with European Court decisions which stress that allegedly defamatory words in a newspaper should be considered in light of previous articles on the same subject.[28]

Some assistance in deciding whether offending words are fact or comment may be derived from the policy behind the distinction, that defamatory statements which clearly reflect the writer's subjective value judgment (*e.g.* as an inference from or comment upon other facts) should be easier to defend because they do less harm: readers will not take them as gospel truth, but will be more likely to think about the facts for themselves and make up their own minds. This assumes, of course, that the facts upon which the comment is made are true, or (as provided by section 6 of the Defamation Act) stated truly enough to sustain the fairness of the comment. The burden of establishing that words are comment rather than fact, and express an opinion which a geniune commentator may honestly hold, falls on the defendant. If these conditions are objectively established the defendant must succeed, unless the claimant can prove that he was actuated by legal malice, *i.e.* that he did not genuinely hold the view to be expressed. Although proof

---

[28] See *Bladet Tromso v. Norway* (1999) 29 E.H.R.R. 125 and *Bergens Tidende v. Norway* (2001) 31 E.H.R.R. 430.

of actual malice (improper motives such as spite or a private grudge) will defeat a claim of qualified privilege, it should not be permitted to undermine the protection the law affords to honest comment. This right to express opinions cannot be denied to commentators who wish to injure their political or personal enemies or are motivated by unworthy desires for publicity or revenge. As Lord Nicholls has pointed out,

> "The presence of these motives . . . is not a reason for excluding the defence of fair comment . . . liberty to make such comments, genuinely held, on matters of public interest lies at the heart of the defence of fair comment . . . commentators of all shades of opinion are entitled to 'have their own agenda'. Politicians, social reformers, busybodies, those with political or other ambitions and those with none, all can grind their axes. The defence of fair comment envisages that everyone is at liberty to conduct social and political campaigns by expressing his own views . . .".[29]

The opinion must have some factual basis

The defence of fair comment will not succeed if the comment is made without any factual basis. An opinion cannot be conjured out of thin air—it must be based on *something*. And that something should either be accurately stated in the article or at least referred to with sufficient clarity to enable to reader to identify it. It is not necessary to set out all the evidence for the writer's opinion: a summary of it or a reference to where it can be found is sufficient. Even a passing reference is sufficient if readers will understand what is meant. The leading case is *Kemsley v. Foot*.[30]

> Michael Foot once launched an attack in *Tribune* on what he termed "the foulest piece of journalism ever perpetrated in this country in many a long year", indicating a particular article in the *Evening Standard*. The editor of that paper and the writer could not sue for this honest, if exaggerated, appraisal of their work. However, Foot's article was titled "Lower than Kemsley"—a proprietor whose stable of newspapers did not include the *Evening Standard*. Did the headline amount to a statement of fact—*i.e.* that Lord Kemsley was a byword for publishing dishonest journalism— or an opinion about the quality of journalism in Kemsley newspapers? The House of Lords held that the readers of *Tribune* in the context of the copy would regard the headline as a comment on the quality of the

---

[29] *Albert Cheng v. Tse Wai Chun Paul*, Hong Kong Court of Final Appeal, November 13, 2000, p. 10 of transcript.
[30] *Kemsley v. Foot* [1952] A.C. 345 at 356, and see *Hunt v. Star Newspapers* (1908) 2 K.B. 309.

Kemsley press, rather than as a factual statement about the character of the proprietor. There was sufficient reference to the factual basis of the comment—namely the mass-circulation Kemsley newspapers—to enable readers to judge for themselves whether the comment was reasonable.

Given the rule that a fair comment must state or refer to the facts upon which it is based, to what extent might the falsity of those facts destroy the defence? Clearly, the comment that "Smith is a disgrace to human nature" could not be defended if the stated fact, *e.g.* that Smith was a patricide, was false. Often comments will be inferences from a number of facts—some true, some partly true, and some not true at all. These difficulties have resolved themselves into the question: is the comment fair in the sense of being one that the commentator could honestly express on the strength of such of his facts as can be proved to be true? Take the case of the prudish Mr Parkinson, who attended the butterfly ballet. His opinion that it was grossly indecent was genuine to the extent that his inclination was to think every form of dance inde-cent. However, his stated grounds for that opinion were a figment of his imagination: his misdescriptions of the performance were so funda-mental as to vitiate any factual basis for his criticism. The defence of honest comment would not have availed him. The defence protects the honest views of the crank and the eccentric, but not when they are based on dishonest statements of fact.

The rule will not apply to defeat comments that are based on facts that, although untrue, have been stated on occasions protected by privil-ege. Trenchant editorials are sometimes written on the strength of state-ments made in court or Parliament. These will be protected as fair com-ment, even if the "facts" subsequently prove unfounded.[31] However, a publisher has this additional latitude only if, at the same time, it carries a fair and accurate report of the court or parliamentary proceedings (or other privileged occasion) on which the comment is based. Thus *Time Out* was not entitled to rely, in factual support of a fair comment defence of an attack on boxer-turned-businessman George Walker, on a statement made by a police officer at his Old Bailey trial 35 years previously linking him to membership of a criminal gang. Privilege attached to such a statement only in the context of a fair and accurate report of the case itself—a hearing in 1956 when the future chairman of Brent Walker was gaoled for two years for stealing a consignment of women's underwear.[32]

---

[31] *Mangena v. Wright* [1909] 2 K.B. 958; *Grech v. Odhams Press Ltd* [1958] 2 Q.B. 276; *London Artists Ltd v. Littler*, n.27 above.

[32] *Brent Walker Group plc and George Walker v. Time Out Ltd* [1991] 2 All E.R. 753.

Absence of malice

The fair comment defence is defeated by proof that the writer or publisher was actuated by malice. Defendants are entitled to give evidence
of their honest state of mind, and to explain why their dominant motive,
irrespective of any dislike they may feel for the claimant, was to comment on a matter of public interest. The courts have repeatedly insisted
that "irrationality, stupidity or obstinacy do not constitute malice though
in an extreme case they may be some evidence of it."[33] A failure to
apologise or to publish a retraction will not normally be evidence of
malice, but rather of consistency in holding sincere views. But editors
who refuse to retract damaging comments after clear proof that they are
wildly exaggerated may lay themselves open to the inference from this
conduct that they were similarly reckless at the time of the original
publication.

Hard-hitting criticism and savage satire can generally be successfully
defended as honest comment. *News of the World* editor Derek Jameson
notably failed to prove that the writers of the BBC satirical programme
Week Ending were dishonest in portraying him as stupid and lubricious:
his record as editor of down-market newspapers allowed them to
describe his editorial policy as being "all the nudes fit to print and all
the news printed to fit". It would have been a sad day for British satire
had Jameson won this presumptuous action. To prove that virulent criticisms are "malicious" it must be shown that they do not reflect the
honest belief of their writer. Charlotte Cornwall was described as "a
middle-aged star [who] can't sing, her bum is too big and she has the
sort of stage presence that jams lavatories . . . looks just as ugly *with*
make-up." The defendants knew that the actress was aged 34 and was
of normal weight and appearance: the article was written with malice
because it had heaped upon her insults that could not have reflected
anyone's honest opinion.

Public interest

The defence of fair comment may be sustained only if the comment is
on a matter of public interest. This is an easy test to satisfy: the only
cases where it has failed have been criticisms of the private lives of
persons who are not public figures. The courts have held that the public
is legitimately interested, not merely in the conduct of public officials
and institutions, but of private companies whose activities affect individual members of the public. The conduct of a professional person
towards a client or an employer towards a worker are also matters that
may attract legitimate public interest. Anyone who throws a hat into a

---

[33] *Turner v. MGM* [1950] 1 All E.R. 449 *per* Lord Porter at 463.

public arena must be prepared to have it mercilessly, though not maliciously, trampled upon.

Whose comment is it?

There is an important question about the application of the fair comment defence to comment by a third party that is published in a newspaper. The editor may not agree with sentiments in a "letter to the editor"; if sued for libel, does the editor lose the defence of fair comment because it cannot be said that the opinion is honestly his? It is clear that publishers may rely upon the defence of fair comment to the same extent as the person whose comment it was, so if the author of the letter is also sued, or is prepared to testify, the honesty of his or her views will support the newspaper's defence. If the author does not come forward, however, the expression of opinion may still be defended as fair comment if it can be shown to satisfy the test of whether a hypothetical commentator person could honestly express the opinion on the proven facts.[34] This was the second—and more satisfactory—decision of the House of Lords in *Telnikoff v. Matusevitch*, which rejected the claimant's contention that the defendant, to succeed on a fair comment defence, has to prove that the comment was the honest expression of his views. On the contrary, the burden is on the claimant to prove that a comment is objectively unfair in the sense that no man, however prejudiced and obstinate, could have held the views expressed by the defendant.[35]

ABSOLUTE PRIVILEGE

Accurate reports of certain public occasions are "privileged"—which is to say that any defamatory statements arising from them cannot be made the subject of a successful libel action. Privilege is either "absolute"—a complete defence—or "qualified", *i.e.* lost only if the speaker or reporter is actuated by malice. Although it is unseemly that the law should protect the publication of malicious falsehoods, absolute privilege is justified on the practical ground that without it, persons with a public duty to speak out might be threatened with vexatious actions for slander and libel. The existence of "absolute privilege" for the profes-

---

[34] The minority view in the Canadian case of *Cherneskey v. Armadale Publishers* (1978) 90 D.LR. (3d) 371 is to be preferred to the majority opinion: see *Telnikoff* [1991] 4 All E.R. 817, HL above, and *Lyon v. Daily Telegraph* [1943] 2 All E.R. 316.

[35] *Telnikoff v. Matusevitch* [1991] 4 All E.R. 817, HL.

sional utterances of M.P.s and judges and lawyers is a recognition (by M.P.s and judges and lawyers) of the law's potential for suppressing truth and silencing justifiable criticism. Protection is given to the malicious and the reckless as the price of protecting from the threat of vexatious litigation all who are under a powerful duty to state facts and opinions frankly.

Thus politicians may say whatever they choose in Parliament or at the proceedings of select committees (see Chapter 10). Judges, lawyers and witnesses may not be held responsible for any statement uttered in court. The Ombudsman's reports are absolutely privileged, as are ministers of the Crown, officers of the armed forces and high-level government officials in their reports and conversations about matter of State. Reports of the Lord Chancellor, the Legal Services Ombudsman, Director General of Fair Trading, the Monopolies Commission and other quasi-judicial authorities attract similar protection.[36] In these cases the absolute privilege attaches only to the maker of the statement: when it is reported or broadcast, the organisation that does so is protected by a privilege that is qualified and not absolute.

The one occasion when written and broadcast reports of statements made by persons who possess absolute privilege are themselves absolutely privileged is when they concern proceedings in the courts. This important media privilege is now consolidated in section 14 of the 1996 Defamation Act, which ordains absolute protection for contemporaneous reports of proceedings heard in public in any court in the United Kingdom, or in regional or international courts such as the European Court of Human Rights in Strasbourg, the European Court of Justice in Luxembourg and the Hague Tribunal dealing with war crimes in former Yugoslavia and Rwanda. The reports must be fair and accurate and the requirement of contemporaneity means that absolute privilege is only attracted when they are published as "news"—whether on television or the internet or in the papers—as soon as the practicalities of the medium permits. When published later, *e.g.* in a book or other retrospective on the case, the privilege will be qualified rather than absolute.

QUALIFIED PRIVILEGE

The law recognises the importance of encouraging statements made from a social or moral duty. It accords them a privilege from action for defamation, on the condition that they are made honestly. However unfounded the allegations made on a protected occasion may subsequently prove, they are privileged unless made with malice. Communications made out of social or moral duty—references between

---

[36] For a complete list see *Galtey*, Chap. 13, para. 13.46.

employers, for example, or allegations about criminal conduct made to the police—are made on privileged occasions. So, too, are communications made to further a common interest—a circular published to shareholders in a company, or to fellow members of a trade union, or an inter-office memorandum. A communication is protected if it is made to a person who has a duty to receive and act upon it: thus complaints to "higher authority" are privileged whenever the authority complained to is in a position to investigate or discipline or supervise. Journalists who observe what they regard as improper behaviour by judges or lawyers could provide information to the Lord Chancellor's Department without running any risk of a libel action.[37]

The defence of qualified privilege has been developed in accordance with social needs. The early cases were overly concerned to protect the gentry's right to communicate gossip about disloyal or dishonest servants. The growth of commerce saw protection extended to references given by bankers and employers, and to information shared among traders. Parliament then intervened to give special protection to press reports of statements made on significant public occasions. The most recent development has been at the hands of the judiciary, extending qualified privilege to protect media investigations of public scandals. This important development had been emphatically resisted by English judges throughout the twentieth century. "Privilege" arose from an occasion, or a relationship, which necessarily required the freedom to pass on rumours or suspicions. Passing on suspicions to the police was commendable: publishing them to all the world was deplorable, to be punished by heavy damages if they could not be proved correct. This was the judicial mindset in the Court of Appeal in *Blackshaw v Lord* decided in 1983—the last major free-speech case in which nobody bothered to mention the European Convention.[38] "No privilege attaches yet to a statement on a matter of public interest believed by the publisher to be true and in relation to which he has exercised reasonable care" said this court, fifteen years before it was decided that such a privilege did exist. What, apart from a new generation of judges, can explain the sea-change?

Academic criticism of defamation—the only "tort" (civil wrong) in which recovery of damages did not hinge on proving 'fault'—played some part, as did the decision of the US Courts to refuse to enforce English libel awards partly because the law lacked any 'public interest' defence. More importantly, by the time the Human Rights Act was passed, it had become apparent from cases such as *Lingens v Austria* that Article 10 of the European Convention required some such defence, at least for criticisms of politicians and powerful government figures.

---

[37] *Beach v. Freeson* [1972] 1 Q.B. 14.
[38] *Blackshaw v. Lord* [1983] 2 All E.R. 311.

Lingens, a seasoned political commentator, published attacks on Bruno Kreisky, the President of the Austrian Socialist Party, accusing him of "immorality" and "the basest opportunism" for contemplating a political alliance with ex-Nazis. Lingens was privately prosecuted by Kreisky, and convicted and fined for defamation. The court held that this was a breach of the Convention guarantee of free speech, because it would deter journalists from contributing to public discussions of issues affecting the life of the community:

> "The limits of acceptable criticism are wider as regards a politician as such than as regards a private individual . . . the former inevitably and knowingly lays himself open to close scrutiny of his every word and deed by both journalists and the public at large, and he must consequently display a greater degree of tolerance."[39]

Under the Convention, libel claims count as a restriction on press freedom and must therefore respond to a "pressing social need" and be no wider in operation than is "necessary in a democratic society". Some better protection for free speech had been forged by judges in the highest courts of Australia and New Zealand, fashioning a public interest defence out of the common law clay of qualified privilege, permitting it to cling to any occasion on which the media took all reasonable care in publishing information believed to be true about government or political matters.[40] This did not offer as much protection as the First Amendment, under which all public figures (whether politicians or not) were fair game "absent of malice", but it marked a cautious development of the common law in that direction. "Development" of law is a euphemism: judges in this situation effectively act as legislators and lack the precision tools (not to mention the democratic legitimacy) which fashion an Act of Parliament. However, it was obvious that M.P.s had no interest or inclination to reform the libel laws (from which they draw considerable financial and political benefit): an attempt to include a public interest defence in the 1996 Defamation Act was overwhelmingly rejected. There was nothing for it but for the courts to drag the law of libel into line with Article 10, and an extension of "qualified privilege" to protect publication to the world of important information was the only avenue the common law offered.

Reynolds: a public interest privilege?

The Court of Appeal extended qualified privilege as a defence for investigative journalism by two decisions in 1998, Reynolds v. Times Newspapers and Gaddafi v. Sunday Telegraph. The case law was more

---

[39] Lingens v. Austria (1986) 8 E.H.R.R. 407 at 425.
[40] See Lange v. Australian Broadcasting Corp. (1997) 189 C.L.R. 520.

authoritatively framed by the House of Lords following the *Reynolds* appeal, in 1999. These cases establish that the publication to a general audience of information which the public has a "right to know" may, notwithstanding that it later turns out to be false, be made on an occasion of privilege—a status lost only if the publisher is actuated by malice, legal (*i.e.* dishonesty or recklessness towards truth) or actual (*e.g.* spite or desire for personal profit). So long as it is not acting maliciously, a newspaper is entitled to put into the public domain information which has been reasonably checked and sourced, as part of a discussion of matters of serious public concern. Journalists will not lose the protection of the defence if they refuse to disclose their sources, or if they have acted in the heat of the news moment to put out what seems at the time to be an important and newsworthy story. The twin preconditions for the existence of the privilege are (1) that the newspaper has a "duty" to publish because the information appears important and credible and its subject (the claimant) has been treated fairly, whilst (2) its readers (in most cases, the general public) have a legitimate (rather than a prurient or passing) interest in receiving it. If these conditions are fulfilled, statements which defendants cannot "justify" (because they can not be proved true) may nonetheless be *"Reynolds*-privileged".

Ironically, the case which created the defence did not extend it to the newspaper defendant, because the claimant had been unfairly treated:

> Albert Reynolds, the Irish ex-premier, sued the *Sunday Times* for accusing him (in its English edition), of lying to Parliament and deceiving his coalition partner, but made no mention of the explanation he had given to the House for his conduct. Its Irish edition carried a longer and more balanced article making no such allegations. The House of Lords rejected the newspaper's argument that because Reynolds was a powerful political figure the occasion of publication was necessarily privileged, but its ground-breaking judgment held that privilege *could* attach to any communication, whether or not about politics, so long as it related to a matter of serious public interest, was credible and had been published with reasonable care and fairness in all the circumstances. *The Sunday Times* lost because it had behaved unreasonably, omitting Reynold's explanation and unfairly sensationalising allegations never made in its Irish edition.[41]

As a harbinger of the uncertainty that attends this judge-made defence, the Law Lords divided three–two on the question of whether unfairness necessarily precluded *The Sunday Times* from reliance upon the privilege. It would have been more rational and practical to bestow privilege prima facie on every communication of public importance, but allow it to be lost if the claimant could prove that the media defendant

[41] *Reynolds v. Times Newspapers Ltd* [2001] 2 A.C. 127.

behaved unreasonably or recklessly, before or after publication. Instead, the judges devised a 10-point code of journalistic conduct, by which the existence of privilege is to be assessed. Although stressing that this laundry-list is not exhaustive, subsequent judges (and even the Court of Appeal in *Grobbelaar*) have regarded it as written on stone. The 10 "factors" which must be considered and balanced to decide whether the circumstances of a publication conduce to its protection by qualified privilege were formulated by Lord Nicholls as follows:

1. The seriousness of the allegation. The more serious the charge, the more the public is misinformed and the individual harassed. This (like most of the 10 factors) cuts both ways. An allegation which is not serious will not have the genuine public interest which is a pre-condition of the privilege.

2. The nature of the information, and the extent to which the subject-matter is a matter of public concern. The more serious the allegation, the more it will be a matter of legitimate *public* concern.

3. The source of the information. Some informants have no direct knowledge of events. Some have their own axes to grind, or are being paid for their stories. Journalists will be expected to have checked out their sources, and to satisfy the court (especially where they choose to keep them anonymous) that their information was not tainted by malice. Since many sources of perfectly accurate but confidential information do divulge it out of spite or ambition or personal animosity this fact will not of itself defeat the privilege, but will place a greater obligation on the journalist to verify the story by making other inquiries. Similarly, purchased information is not for that reason unreliable, although it does place the journalist on notice that sensations in the story may be related to the source's sensation of receiving a large sum of money for revealing it. In these circumstances of "cheque-book journalism" the courts will expect the newspaper to have some corroboration. Judges have also taken into account the existence of well-placed sources who have refuted or failed to corroborate the defamatory information. Such "dogs that did not bark in the night time" will damage the claim to qualified privilege.

4. The status of the information. The allegation may have already been the subject of an investigation which commands respect. The "status" of the information refers here to the authority that can be attributed to its source: an allegation given credit by an internal inquiry, audit or police investigation clearly has an impact which would assist the argument that the public ought to know of it. Similarly, defamatory remarks made (to use examples given by the Court of Appeal in

Reynolds) in a "government press release, or the report of a public company chairman or the speech of a university vice-chancellor" would derive "status" from the respect due to their source, although (as Lord Steyn pointed out in his speech in *Reynolds*) this ought not to depend upon the leak coming from within the "establishment". But if a powerful figure "in the know" believes and privately disseminates a defamatory rumour, there is a public interest argument for putting it into the public domain so that it can be refuted as false or acted upon if true.

5. *The steps taken to verify the information.* This factor assumes that *some steps* will be taken, and journalists must demonstrate that these were reasonable enough in the circumstances. The implication is that editors who publish without making any effort to corroborate will lose the privilege.

6. *The urgency of the matter. News is often a perishable commodity.* This dimension, taken from European Court judgments, calls for a recognition that information which can be characterised as "news" or "newsworthy" should be put into circulation as soon as possible. Of course this does not excuse a failure to make basic checks or (when fairness requires) to attempt to contact the victim. However, Lord Nicholls urged judges to remember that "journalists act without the benefit of the clear light of hindsight. Matters which are obvious in retrospect may have been far from clear in the heat of the moment". The English courts post-*Reynolds* have tended to devalue this factor: judges cannot understand why a news story cannot wait a few days.[42]

7. *Whether comment was sought from the claimant. He may have information others do not possess or have not disclosed. An approach to the claimant will not always be necessary.* This is a feature of fairness, which is a precondition of asserting the privilege. The claimant cannot complain if he had made himself unavailable for comment or was genuinely uncontactable at the time (a fact which should feature in the story). An approach is unnecessary if an explanation is unlikely to be forthcoming or is already on the record or if prior contact is reasonably feared to put sources at risk or provoke an application to injunct publication. The weight of this factor in favour of privilege will be much reduced if the opportunity provided for comment does not give the victim a reasonable chance to make a considered response—if, for example, he is "ambushed" or "door-stepped".

8. *Whether the article contained the gist of the claimant's side of the story.* This is a further factor determining fairness. Privilege will

---

[42] See *James Gilbert Ltd v. MGN Ltd* [2000] E.M.L.R. 680.

not of course be lost if the claimant goes to ground or declines to vouch-
safe any explanation, and it will be enhanced if the claimant's explanation has been published without adverse comment or obvious cynicism.
The House of Lords attached over-much importance to this factor in its
actual decision in *Reynolds* (see above).

*9. The tone of the article. A newspaper can raise queries or call
for an investigation. It need not adopt allegations as statements of fact.*
This factor marks an important advance in the protection of investigative journalism, to the extent that it will permit the publication of rumour
and suspicion if the writer does not adopt them as true, but rather examines them fair-mindedly and explains why the public interest demands
further inquiry. Conversely, a tone of sensationalism or exaggeration in
presentation will remove the privilege—as where rumour is luridly par-
aded as fact, guilt is pre-judged, and the claimant is subjected to a
campaign of vilification. It was for deploying these techniques that *The
Sun* lost its public interest privilege in exposing the corrupt behaviour
of Bruce Grobbelaar.

10. The circumstances of the publication including the timing. This
is a "sweep up" heading that permits other considerations to come into
play. The question of timing will rarely be definitive, since "news is a
perishable commodity" but media defendants which rush headlong into
"scoops" will derive some comfort if readers include those citizens who
need to be warned quickly in order to protect themselves—*e.g.* against
purchasing toxic food or falling prey to ongoing confidence tricks.

One factor which should be of great importance but which is necessarily omitted from this "top 10" is whether subsequently the media
defendant has promptly and prominently acknowledged falsehoods and
errors in the original story, and has proffered a suitable apology. Any
sensible law of defamation should encourage defendants to "set the
record straight", and there is no conceptual difficulty in speaking of a
privilege being "lost" or "enhanced" by the publisher's subsequent
conduct. Regrettably, *Reynolds* privilege will be held to exist (or not)
once and for all, at the time of first publication. There is scope here
for further development, because European human rights jurisprudence
recognises that the balance between free speech and the right to reputation should be viewed realistically over a period of time rather than
artificially confined to the moment of publication. (See "Stop Press").

The proliferation of "factors", and the notion that they will have
to be "balanced" means that subjectivity comes into play: judges will
second-guess editors, and tend to display disdain for tabloids and ignorance of the realities of news editing. Thus *Reynolds* is by no means an
unmixed blessing for the media. The 10-point test pivots upon "reasonableness" and honourable behaviour and will often prove too onerous

for a profession which recognises itself in Nick Tomalin's definition of a good reporter (one "possessed of rat-like cunning, a plausible manner and a little literary ability"). Juristically, *Reynolds* moves defamation cautiously towards a fault-based tort, but does so by concentrating on the possible "faults" of editors and journalists. The original decision in *Loutchansky v Times Newspapers Ltd*[43] took the form of a litany of criticisms of the journalist and his news editor based on their failure to satisfy some of the "top 10" points, most notably in failing to be sceptical of sources and in making inadequate efforts to contact the claimant so as to give him an opportunity to reply.

One conceptual problem with *Reynolds* is that the 10 factors which determine the existence of the privilege are mostly the self-same factors which bear on whether the publisher has been actuated by malice, either by recklessness towards truth by having some improper personal motive, (proof of "actual malice" can defeat the defence of privilege, although not the defence of fair comment). Since *Reynolds*, there have been several libel actions aborted by judges on finding the occasion of publication covered by privilege, and by finding (for much the same reasons) no exigent evidence of malice. This procedure was approved as "fair, sensible and economic" by the Court of Appeal in *GKR Karate v. Yorkshire Post*.[44]

> A karate club sued a local newspaper over a story accusing it of "ripping off" members. The defence of justification would take six weeks to try, but the qualified privilege defence could be decided at a three-day hearing. The trial judge directed that the issues of privilege and malice should be tried first, and the Court of Appeal agreed—since these largely depended upon the defendant's state of mind, which had to be determined at the time of publication, they could logically be separated from the complicated factual dispute over the truth of the allegations. In due course, the trial judge found that the "balancing exercise" mandated by *Reynolds* came down in favour of the existence of the privilege: the journalist had acted honestly and reported allegations made by an authoritative source; the local public needed to be warned quickly for its own protection against dishonest door-to-door canvassing, and the article was unsensational in tone. Although there were some admitted inaccuracies and "over-egging", these did not outweigh the public interest in the free flow of information or amount to malice.[45]

The *GKR* decision on privilege was distinguished by the Court of Appeal in *Grobbelaar v. News Group*.[46]

---

[43] *Loutchansky v. Times Newspapers*, April 27, 2001 (Gray J.).

[44] *GKR Karate Ltd v. Yorkshire Post Newspaper Ltd* [2000] 2 All E.R. 931.

[45] Reported as *GKR Karate (U.K.) Ltd v. Yorkshire Post (No. 2)* [2000] E.M.L.R. 410 (Sir Oliver Popplewell).

[46] [2001] 2 All E.R. 437.

The Sun's claim to privilege for its exposure of goalkeeper Grobbelaar's acceptance of bribes to lose matches was rejected because of the sensational and unfair way in which the story—of admitted public importance—was investigated and presented. The paper, which had used an *agent provocateur*, trumpeted Grobbelaar's guilt in emotive terms on its front pages in a sustained character assassination . It door-stepped his wife ("shameful secret has Deb in tears") and delighted in the prospect of his young children being taunted at school. It was as if the paper "had placed Mr Grobbelaar in the stocks, to be publicly mocked, abused and derided for the amusement of the populace". If the media choose to present their exposés in this way, they cannot claim any privilege: they must prove them true—a task which *The Sun* in fact achieved, but only on this appeal.

Qualified privilege is a developing defence for cautious and responsible investigative journalism, and not for tabloid sensationalism. Judges will decide if a particular story "merits" privilege, assisted by jury findings (if necessary), on any facts in dispute. The most difficult issue, which *Reynolds* does not resolve, is how the defence will operate when defamatory allegations in the story are based on confidential sources, whose "status" and reliability may be asserted but cannot by definition be proved. The Court of Appeal considered this problem in *Gaddafi v. Telegraph Group*.[47]

The eldest son of Colonel Gaddafi, dictator of Libya, sued over a story alleging his involvement in attempts to breach economic sanctions imposed as a result of the Lockerbie bombing. *The Sunday Telegraph* was permitted to enter a defence of qualified privilege, and to plead that its sources included members of a "western government security agency", whose lives could be at risk if their identities were disclosed. The court upheld the right of journalists to protect the confidentiality of their source whilst maintaining a qualified privilege defence, so long as sufficient disclosure was provided to enable some evaluation of the status and reliability of their information.

Gadaffi is a valuable ruling for investigative journalists, whose process of deduction is often assisted by sources who would be exposed to danger or embarrassment if named, and to whom confidentiality must be promised as a condition of assistance. It enables defendants to claim the privilege, on condition that they provide enough detail to have claims for source reliability tested under cross-examination. It may be difficult for the claimant to prove that unidentified sources are tainted with malice, but equally the journalist will be handicapped in the courtroom by his refusal to prove just how well-placed and authoritative

---

[47] *Gaddafi v. Telegraph Group Ltd* [2000] E.M.L.R. 431.

a source may have been. As Lord Steyn commented in *Reynolds*: "If a
newspaper stands on the rule protecting its sources, it may run the risk
of what the judge and jury will make of the gap in the evidence".[48]

Reply to an attack

The "right of reply" privilege is often overlooked, but its constitutional
significance for the protection of freedom of expression deserves to be
recognised. It is based on the simple proposition of self-defence: if you
are verbally attacked, you are entitled to strike back with some vehe-
mence to defend your reputation. The media that carry your response
share your privilege, so long as the publicity given to your condemnation of your attacker is reasonably commensurate with the publicity
given to the original attack. The right of reply privilege was established
by the House of Lords in the case of *Adam v. Ward*[49]:

> The claimant, an officer but not a gentleman, used his position as an M.P.
> to make a vindictive attack upon a general in his former regiment. The
> defendant, Secretary to the Army Council, issued a statement in support
> of the general, which defamed the M.P. and was published in newspapers
> throughout the Empire. The Law Lords held that this publication was
> protected by qualified privilege: the Council had a duty to leap to the
> general's defence, and the privilege was not lost by the fact of world-wide
> publication, because "a man who makes a statement on the floor of the
> House of Commons makes it to all the world . . . it was only plain justice
> to the General that the ambit of contradiction should be spread so wide
> as, if possible, to meet the false accusation wherever it went."

The rule in *Adam v. Ward* offers consolation to victims of attacks
made under the "coward's cloak" of parliamentary privilege: they may
reply in kind through newspapers, which will be liable for the defamatory content of their reply only if it is irrelevant to the subject-matter of
the attack, or if it defames other persons who bear no responsibility for
the attack. The right of reply privilege does not merely protect responses
to criticisms made in Parliament, of course; it is a privilege of general
application, arising from the legitimate interest of individuals in protecting their reputations, and it is shared by the media when it facilitates
that interest.

Parliamentary and court reports

At common law, all fair and accurate reports of Parliament and the
courts are protected by qualified privilege. This is a safety net for press

---

[48] *Reynolds* above, at 214.
[49] *Adam v. Ward* [1917] A.C. 309.

coverage that falls outside statutory protection for absolute privilege—because, for example, it is not published as soon as practicable after the event. The application of this qualified privilege is considered in detail in Chapter 8 and Chapter 10.

Other public occasions

Section 15 of and Schedule 1 to the Defamation Act 1996 bestow qualified privilege on reports of a range of "official" public occasions and events which have taken place anywhere in the world. The Schedule is in two parts. The first accords qualified privilege unconditionally; the second grants it subject to the condition that a reasonable right of reply must have been afforded to victims of its privileged defamations.

Part I privilege extends to fair and accurate reports of public proceedings in parliaments, courts, public inquiries, international organisations and conferences, and to publication of extracts from public registers, statements by judges or court officers, or material produced by governments or international organisations or conferences.

Part II privilege extends, subject to affording the victim a reasonable right of reply, to fair and accurate reports of, *inter alia*,

- findings or decisions of any organisation formed in the United Kingdom or in Member States of the European Union, and empowered by its constitution to exercise control over, or adjudicate on, matters relating to:

    (a) art, science, religion or learning;
    (b) any trade, business, industry or profession;
    (c) persons connected with games, sports or pastimes and who are contractually subject to the association;
    (d) the promotion of charity;

- proceedings at any lawful public meeting, (whether or not admission is restricted) that is called to discuss any matter of public concern;

- proceedings at a general meeting of a United Kingdom company, and any document circulated to members;

- proceedings of any meeting open to the public within the United Kingdom of

    (a) a local authority or its committees;
    (b) justices of the peace acting in non-judicial capacities;
    (c) committees of inquiry appointed by Act of Parliament or by the Government;
    (d) local authority inquiries;
    (e) bodies constituted under Acts of Parliament;

- "any notice or other matter" issued for the information of the public by or on behalf of any government or legislature within the European Union, or by any international organisation or conference. This includes notices issued by any agency performing "governmental functions", which include police functions. This does not, however, cover information that has been leaked from such sources, nor does it include unauthorised and off-the-cuff comments made by junior officials. To be protected, the information must be issued or approved by some person in departmental authority. Journalistic speculation and inference about official statements are not protected by statutory privilege, although may qualify in some circumstances for *Reynolds* privilege at common law.[50]

These Part II privileges are "subject to explanation and contradiction", which means that they will not apply where an editor or programme controller has refused the claimant's request to publish a reasonable statement in reply, or has done so in an inadequate manner. Claimants must supply their own set of words—a bare demand for retraction is insufficient to defeat the privilege.[51] So long as it is reasonable in "tone and length", it must be published with a prominence appropriate to the original report.

These privileges attach to reports of public statements and public documents. They do not extend to the contents of confidential or internal documents or to reports of evidence given in closed court. However, the current tendency—under the impetus of the 1998 Human Rights Act—is to give these statutory definitions of privilege (many of which date from nineteenth-century statutes) a wide and contemporary meaning. The approach is exemplified by the first case to be decided after the Human Rights Act came into force, *McCartan Turkington Breen v. Times Newspapers*.[52]

> The claimants were a firm of Northern Ireland solicitors who had represented Private Lee Clegg at the trial in which he had been convicted of murdering a terrorist suspect. A support group held a press conference at which defamatory allegations were made about his lawyers' competence both in statements and in a press release handed out to journalists. Part II of the Schedule grants statutory privilege to fair and accurate reports of "public meetings", and the House of Lords held that this phrase was apt to cover both a press conference and a press release. The object of the statutory privilege was to encourage the media to serve as a channel for public debate, and these days press conferences and press releases have

---

[50] *Blackshaw v. Lord* above at n.38.
[51] *Khan v. Ahmed* [1957] 2 Q.B. 149.
[52] [2001] 2 A.C. 277.

largely superseded the "public meeting" as a means of communicating political ideas and protests about injustice. The court went out of its way to recognise "the cardinal importance of press freedom" and the reporter's role as a medium of communication: the public interest supported a wide reading of the statutory privilege.

Most of the reports protected by Schedule I statutory privilege would also attract qualified privilege at common law under *Reynolds*: the advantage of bringing them within statutory protection is that the uncertainties of applying the 10-point test are avoided.

Statutory qualified privilege has been available since the late nineteenth century, but limited to newspaper reports of courts and meetings and organisations within the United Kingdom. The 1996 reforms amplified the privilege to cover reports of courts and governments worldwide, and not merely in newspapers. This will mean, of course, that reports of libellous and lying statements made by or on behalf of barbaric dictators and oppressive regimes will be protected, although as the Neill committee pointed out, "What renders such Governments unattractive may very well from time to time lead to their being of particular legitimate interest to the British public".[53] The reform will prevent any repetition of the cases in 1980 when Princess Elizabeth of Toro, accomplice of the mass-murdering Idi Amin, collected large libel damages from all English national newspapers. They had reported, accurately, Amin's crazed accusation, when he fired her as his foreign minister, that she had been found having oral sex in a toilet at Orly airport. The fact that he was capable of making such a statement was important evidence of the nature of the beast (first backed by Britain and then President of the OAU) and it was for that reason important that newspapers report it. Such reports should now attract Part II privilege under Schedule 1, para. 9(1)(b) (as a statement by a head of government): Princess Elizabeth would be legally entitled to have published a reasonable letter contradicting it, but not to damages. A fair report quoting her denial would be protected by common law *Reynolds* privilege as well.

The 1996 Defamation Act provides that Schedule 1 qualified privilege will be lost if reports are not fair and accurate, and that the privilege will not protect "matter which is not of public concern and the publication of which is not for the public benefit" (section 15(3)). This should be easy to satisfy, since the public meetings and events listed in Schedule 1 are, almost by definition, of public concern. The leading case on the approach to these questions is *Tsikata v. Newspaper Publishing plc*.[54]

---

[53] Supreme Court Procedure Committee Report on Practice and Procedure in Defamation (1991) Chapter XII. 6.
[54] [1997] 1 All E.R. 655.

The Independent published in 1992 an article about politics in Ghana, which made a passing reference to the fact that a judicial inquiry 10 years before had accused the claimant (head of the country's secret service) of masterminding the murder of three judges. The newspaper's report was true as far as it went, although it did not add that the evidence against the claimant had been insufficient to support a prosecution and some of it had been retracted. Tsikata argued that the passing reference was not a "report" of the judicial inquiry that had condemned him 10 years before, and the lapse of time meant that in any event the reference was not "fair and accurate". The Court of Appeal said that the Schedule should be construed so as to give effect to the clear intention of Parliament and not by the adoption of a narrow linguistic approach. Thus the short statement of the inquiry finding was protected, irrespective of its timing (the Schedule does not require reports to be contemporaneous) and notwithstanding the subsequent developments to which the paper had made no reference. This failure to present the full picture did not mean that the report, as presented, lacked public benefit. The privilege to report matters of record overseas relieves the media of the expense of having to conduct its own foreign inquiries: investigative journalism may be a virtue, but the law should not make it a necessity.

It is curious that the archaic "public benefit" requirement survives: the whole point of providing qualified privilege for the records and events listed in Schedule 1 is that they relate to matters of public concern, and the public benefit question only serves to confuse the jury. Nonetheless, the Court of Appeal has held that this issue, like the issue of fairness and accuracy, is a question of fact that must be left to the jury rather than be decided by the judge, even in cases where there are "strong grounds" in favour of a factual finding (of fairness or public benefit) that would conclude the issue in the media's favour at the outset.[55]

OTHER DEFENCES

Consent

People can—and often do for large sums of money—agree to be defamed. Should they then turn around to bite the hand that takes down

---

[55] *Kingshott v. Associated Kent Newspapers Ltd* [1991] 2 All E.R. 99. The Court of Appeal insisted that the question of whether allegations about corruption of local councillors, made by a mayor at a planning inquiry, was a "matter of public concern" and had to be left to the jury: it was not so obvious that it could be decided by a judge! *Kingshott* may be overruled if the issue returns to the House of Lords: see the discussion in *Reynolds* (above) at 636–7; 646 and in *McCartan Turkington* (above) at 933.

their volunteered confessions, they will fail. Consent to publication is a complete defence.[56] The consent must, however, relate to the actual libel published, and not merely to the grant of an interview in which the libellous subject was not specifically canvassed. The narrowness of the consent defence—turning upon consent to the actual libel, or to publication of the words substantially as they were used—can no longer be justified under freedom of expression principles. If libel turns into a fault-based tort, claimants whose own conduct is responsible for scurrilous rumours should be denied recovery. Anyone who is the author of their own misfortune—by failing to check their own publicity, or failing to nail a lie at the earliest opportunity—should be open to a defence of "voluntary assumption of risk" or at least a reduction in damages on grounds of contributory negligence. This is the case in American law, where it is a complete defence to show that the defamation would not have been published at all had the claimant not acted so as to induce a belief in its truth.[57] But in London the *New York Times* was not permitted to argue that claimant Marco Pierre White was responsible for its correspondent's error in misreading an ambiguous passage in his "autobiography" (because White had not written it himself and had failed to check it prior to publication under his name). Morland J. held that defamation remained a tort of strict liability, offering no scope for "contributory negligence" or for a "consent" defence which alleged the claimant was at fault.[58] But watch this space.

Offer of amends

Most libel actions are settled, before or after service of the claim, by negotiations between solicitors which can result in published corrections and apologies (sometimes in open court) and payment of an agreed sum in damages. The Neill Committee was anxious, however, to discourage unreasonable claimants who had defendants "over a barrel" as the result of an indefensible defamation, but who refused all settlement offers in order to harass the defendants or to insist they be dragged to trial. The 1996 Defamation Act gives media defendants an opportunity to bail out by making an "offer of amends", *i.e.* a written offer to publish a suitable

---

[56] *Monson v. Tussaud's Ltd* (1894) 1 Q.B. 671 (note the characterisation of the defence as "acquiescence" by Davey L.J.; *Maire v. News of the World* [1972] 1 Q.B. 441 at 448 A–B *per* Lord Denning.

[57] "It would be ironical and certainly inequitable for the plaintiff to profit here from his own misstatements. Further, it would be no less unfair to treat the publisher as even partially culpable for a false publication where he has reasonably relied upon the plaintiff's own sworn representations". *Friedman v. Boston Broadcasters Inc.* 13 Media Law Reporter 1742 at 1744, and see *Sack on Defamation* (2nd ed.) Chap. 2, para. 2.

[58] *White v. New York Times*, April 2000 (unreported).

correction and sufficient apology in a reasonable manner, together with such compensation and legal costs as may be agreed (or fixed by the court). If the claimant refuses the offer, the defendant may raise it as a statutory defence so long as he has made a proper offer and runs no other defence: to rebut it, the claimant must justify his refusal by proving the original defamation was published maliciously (in the sense that it was false and the defendant knew he had reason to believe it was false). A failure to rebut this defence will mean the claimant gets nothing—he cannot at that point take the offer and run. Unfortunately, Parliament managed to turn a good idea into a complicated and uncertain statutory provision.[59]

A prompt correction and apology for an indefensible defamation serves two purposes besides setting the record straight. In many cases it satisfies the complainant—and, where it is accompanied by payment of costs, it will satisfy his lawyer as well. If the complainant is still determined to become a claimant, the fact that a prompt apology has been made can be relied upon by the defendant to reduce the amount of damages. It is obviously prudent, however, for the potential media defendant to seek a disclaimer of further legal action as a condition of publishing the apology. Once an apology is given, the defendant will be hard put to contest liability later.

DAMAGES

Those who throw sticks and stones that break bones can be better off in law than those who project hurtful words that leave no permanent mark. In 1987 libel damages of £500,000 were awarded to Jeffrey Archer against a newspaper that alleged he had sex with a prostitute, and Elton John set a short-lived record with his £1 million settlement against the *Sun*. In 1989, the wife of the "Yorkshire Ripper" was awarded £600,000 by a jury to compensate her for a trifling story in *Private Eye*. This last award was described by the Court of Appeal as a sum "so unreasonable as to be divorced from reality"[60] and it urged judges in future to give some help to juries about the real value of money. In the first case in which such guidance was received, the jury returned with a new British and Commonwealth record of £1.5 million, against an author who had attacked Lord Aldington as a "war criminal" over his role in the forcible repatriation of Cossacks. The judge had

---

[59] See Defamation Act 1996, ss. 2–5. Even if the defendant relies on some other defence to contest liability, he can still plead the offer to mitigate damages: (s. 5(5)).

[60] *Sutcliffe v. Pressdram Ltd* [1990] 1 All E.R. 269, CA.

warned the jury not to award "Mickey Mouse money", by which he apparently intended to refer to a sum so large as to be unrealistic (such as £1.5 million). The jury may have understood the phrase to refer to small or trifling amounts, and followed his direction by awarding the sort of sum they imagined in the coffers of Scrooge McDuck. The prospect of massive awards of damages served as a real threat to freedom of expression in the Thatcher era—which may be why some of her unprepossessing associates escaped exposure. In any event the award was so disproportionate that the European Court had no difficulty declaring it a breach of Article 10.[61]

In 1991 the Court of Appeal was empowered (by section 8 of the Courts and Legal Services Act) to substitute its own award in place of excessive damages, without having to put the parties to the inconvenience of a new trial. This power has been used (with impetus from Article 10) to effect a wholesale reform in the way libel damages are calculated. The break with the past began in 1993, when a jury award of £250,000 to television presenter Esther Rantzen was declared disproportionate to any damage she had suffered (her successful television career had continued) and was cut by more than half.[62] The freedom of expression guarantee meant, said the Court of Appeal, that henceforth libel awards should not be so large as to deter investigative journalism, and juries should be given judicial guidance on how to keep them in proportion. This guidance had to be provided in a more concrete shape after Elton John persuaded a star-struck jury to compensate him over-lavishly for an invented story about his bizarre eating habits. In future, juries would be told about the level of damages which judges currently award for the pain and suffering resulting from negligently caused personal injuries (ranging from £25,000 for loss of an eye to £130,000 for serious brain damage) because "it is in our view offensive to public opinion, and rightly so, that a defamation plaintiff should recover damages for injury to reputation greater, perhaps by a significant factor, than if that same plaintiff had been rendered a helpless cripple or a insensate vegetable".[63]

With these words, the court ushered to a close an era in which celebrity claimants regularly won damages far in excess of £200,000, a sum which must now be seen as the outside limit for the worst defamations. Trial judges cannot trample on the constitutional right of a jury to set

---

[61] *Tolstoy Miloslavsky v. U.K.* (1996) E.M.L.R. 152.
[62] *Rantzen v. Mirror Group Newspapers* [1993] 4 All E.R. 975.
[63] *John v. MGM Ltd* [1996] 2 All E.R. 35 at 54, CA. Damages for negligently caused personal injuries have since increased – the top of the range is about £200,000 (*Heil v. Rankin* [2000] 3 All E.R. 138, CA) and this may now be taken as the cap on libel damages in the absence of proved financial loss.

whatever figure it chooses, but the certainty of Court of Appeal intervention if it aims too high permits them to direct a jury more robustly. Juries are given an appropriate "bracket" or range: an award below it would be "niggardly" and above it "extravagant". By this means, jury damages in defamation are now kept within reasonable limits.

Compensatory and aggravated damages

The basic award will comprise "compensatory damages" *i.e.* a sum that will sufficiently redress the wrong by nullifying the pain caused by the false accusation and at the same time emphasising the value of the good name that has been temporarily besmirched. This basic sum (influenced by the gravity of the libel—especially whether it has challenged the claimant's "core attributes of personality" such as integrity, honesty and loyalty) may be "aggravated" by the injury which the defendant has added to the insult by refusing to publish a timely correction or apology, or by defending the action in a spirit of enmity.

Damage to reputation is a concept that has no equivalent in money or money's worth. It is inflated by the feeling that it should be large enough to "vindicate" claimants by showing the world that their names deserve respect and to "console" them for being exploited to boost the circulation of tabloid newspapers. A refusal to correct or apologise for an obvious mistake will enlarge the damages, as will the seriousness of the libel and the degree to which it is repeated. By the same token, the promptness of the apology, the honesty of the mistake, and pre-existing flaws in the claimant's reputation are matters that will go to reduce the final sum. The extent of circulation and the prominence given to defamatory remarks are factors that should influence the award, and the claimant may also recover damages for the repetition of the libel in other publications that the defendant might reasonably have foreseen would follow as a natural and probable consequence of his own publication.[64] The claimant's feelings may be wounded if he or she is subjected to aggressive cross-examination, especially if it is designed to support what transpires to be an unsuccessful plea of justification, so this forensic factor may be brought into account. On the other hand, the jury can be asked to take the claimant's own conduct into account in reducing the damages. If the claimant has been cleared of the allegations after a publicised inquiry, or has obtained retractions and damages from

---

[64] Thus the BBC could be compelled to compensate a claimant defamed in a drama-documentary not merely in relation to the damage done to his or her reputation amongst those viewers who watched the programme, but also in relation to newspaper readers who had read the "sting" of the defamation in reviews of the programme. See *Slipper v. BBC* [1991] 1 All E.R. 165.

other publications, his or her wounds may be considered to have partially healed.[65]

One aspect of the law of libel damages that is particularly irksome for the defendant is the rule in *Scott v. Sampson* which limits evidence to proving the claimant's "general bad reputation" but does not permit proof of specific acts of misconduct unless the jury has heard about these pursuant to a defence of justification which has failed to prove the truth of the real defamatory imputation.[66] This is a ridiculous rule that can put the jury in blinkers when it makes a damages award. Defamation committees have recommended its abolition, but on the two occasions when reform has been introduced in Parliament (as part of the 1952 and 1996 Defamation Bills) it has been resisted by M.P.s concerned lest their libel damages be reduced once juries are reminded of discreditable incidents in their past. In 2000 the Court of Appeal decided that the rule could be side-stepped in relation to a trial in which the amount of damages was the only issue, but it continues to apply, illogically, in cases where the defendant contests liability.[67]

Exemplary damages

Damages in libel cases are not meant to punish the press, but when a publisher deliberately or recklessly sets out to defame another, with the object of making a profit out of that defamation by increasing circulation, the law permits "punitive" damages to be awarded. In *Cassell & Co v. Broome*[68]:

> The young David Irving (who 30 years later failed to clear his name of holocaust-denial) wrote a book about the fate of a wartime convoy, blaming it upon the negligence of a particular captain, Broome. Cassell & Co. published the book. The jury awarded punitive damages of £40,000 against Irving, and a further £40,000 against Cassell. The House of Lords upheld the award as punishment for author and publisher, as there was evidence that both were reckless about the truth of the defamatory statements in the book, and indeed hoped that they would cause a sensation so that the book's sales would increase.

Punitive damages in libel cases are a legal anomaly. They amount to a fine for misbehaviour, but have no upper limit. They are generally

---

[65] s. 12 of the Defamation Act 1952 permits evidence to be given of other damages recovered for the same or similar libels, so as to ensure the claimant is not in effect compensated twice over.

[66] See *Scott v. Sampson* (1882) 8 Q.B.D. 491; *Plato Films v. Speidel* [1961] A.C. 1090 and *Pamplin v. Express Newspapers* [1988] 1 W.L.R. 116.

[67] *Burstein v. Times Newspapers Ltd* December 20, 2000, CA.

[68] *Cassell & Co. v. Broome* [1972] A.C. 1027.

awarded by juries, who have neither the power nor the proficiency to impose a sentence in any other area of law. They do not, like other fines, go into the public purse, but into the pocket of victims who have already been compensated by the same jury for damage to their reputation. They are, indeed, difficult to distinguish from the "aggravated damages" to which a claimant is entitled by virtue of the suffering caused by the newspaper's high-handed or insulting conduct. They are not awarded in Scotland, and the Faulks Committee (and the Court of Appeal in 1985) recommended their abolition.[69] However, in the *Elton John* case, the Court of Appeal preferred to set stricter limits to the circumstances in which punitive damages could be awarded, and to their amount. Critically, what must be proved by the claimant is that the defendant cynically published for profit an allegation in the truth of which he had no honest or genuine belief. Carelessness is not enough, nor is the routine fact of commercial publication: the court must be sure of reprehensible behaviour, constituted by a deliberate calculation that more money would be made by putting out a story that could well be false than by waiting to check out its veracity. Only when these conditions are satisfied, and it is further plain that compensatory or aggravated damages are insufficient to teach the defendant that tort does not pay, will an additional punitive award be justified. An irresponsible front page "splash" story about Elton John's behaviour at a party (which a simple check would have established he did not attend) was calculated to increase circulation and so qualified for exemplary damages, but the jury went over the top by awarding £275,000. The tabloid would be taught its lesson, the Court of Appeal somewhat optimistically concluded, by a reduced fine of £50,000.[70]

Trial by jury

Section 69 of the Supreme Court Act 1981 entitles any party to a defamation action to require a trial by jury, "unless the court is of the opinion that the trial requires any prolonged examination of documents or accounts or any scientific or local investigations which cannot conveniently be made by a jury." Even in these cases the court has a discretion to order jury trial, although it will apply a presumption in favour of trial by judge alone if satisfied that otherwise the trial would be so complicated, costly and lengthy that the administration of justice would be likely to suffer.[71] The Court of Appeal has in such cases refused a jury even though the allegation accuses the claimant of committing criminal offences, although where the trial affects national interests or the honour

---

[69] See *Riches v. News Group Newspapers Ltd* [1986] Q.B. 256.
[70] *John v. MGN Ltd* above, n. 63 at 59–64.
[71] *De L'Isle v. Times Newspapers Ltd* [1988] 1 W.L.R. 49.

and integrity of national personalities it may decide otherwise.[72] This was the case in *Lord Rothermere v. Bernard Levin & Times Newspapers*, where the defendants had published an attack ("Profit and dishonour in Fleet Street") on Rothermere's integrity in closing down a newspaper. Although the trial would involve a prolonged examination of financial documents, the Court of Appeal was moved by the personal plea of the editor of *The Times* that free speech issues should be decided by a jury.[73] That was in 1973: in 1997 the Court of Appeal took a very different view:

> Jonathan Aitken M.P. resigned as a cabinet minister to sue *The Guardian* over claims that he was unfit for public office. The case would involve prolonged examination of documents and as such was inconvenient for jurors, but the newspaper argued that discretion ought nonetheless to be exercised in favour of trial by jury because that was the most acceptable tribunal for deciding whether the conduct of an elected official had fallen below proper standards. The court rejected "public perception" as a lodestar, in favour of the interests of justice which would be better served "by a painstaking, dispassionate, impartial, orderly approach to deciding where truth lies". A general jury verdict was no substitute for a reasoned judicial decision on whether the claimant had misconducted himself.[74]

Aitken reflects a more general judicial disenchantment with the jury as a sensible tribunal for settling libel actions, echoed by the first Court of Appeal decision (in *Grobbelaar*) to reverse jury finding as "perverse". Claimants are less inclined to opt for jury trial in the hope of obtaining outsize damages now that awards have been brought under tighter judicial control, although the value and attendant publicity of vindication by a jury rather than a judge alone still exerts attraction for celebrities. Media defendants prefer juries for tactical reasons in cases where claimants are unpopular or unpleasant or politically controversial: their hope is that jurors will take a more instinctive, broad-brush approach to allegations in respect to which nit-picking judges might require a stricter standard of proof. Where a case involves a choice as to which party is the lesser of the two evils—Mr Neil Hamilton or Mr Mohammed Al Fayed, for example—judges would be well advised to leave the decision in the inscrutable lap of 12 good men and women and true.

The Defamation Act provides an alternative to expensive jury trial by way of summary disposal of claims by a judge alone.[75] But this

---

[72] *Goldsmith v. Pressdram Ltd* [1988] 1 W.L.R. 64; *Beta Construction Ltd v. Channel 4* [1990] 1 W.L.R. 1042.

[73] *Rothermere v. Bernard Levin & Times Newspapers* (1973) (unreported).

[74] *Aitken v. Preston* [1997] E.M.L.R. 15.

[75] Defamation Act 1996, ss. 8–10.

procedural benefit carries the downside for claimants that their maximum in damages is £10,000. The courts are still (if reluctantly) prepared to recognise that defendants have a qualified right to trial by jury, sufficient to exclude libel actions from the general rule permitting summary judgment,[76] so long as there is a material issue of fact in dispute between the parties.

CRIMINAL LIBEL

If a libel is extremely serious, to the extent that a court is prepared to hold that it cannot be compensated by money and deserves to be punished as a crime, its publisher may be made the target of a prosecution. Criminal libel is an ancient offence that is now unlikely to be invoked against the media by prosecuting authorities: the Law Commission has recommended its abolition,[77] and one Law Lord has further pointed out that its scope conflicts with the European Convention on Human Rights.[78] There have been a few modern instances in which it has been invoked by private individuals as part of a vendetta against their journalist-tormentors. In 1977 Sir James Goldsmith was granted leave to prosecute the editor of *Private Eye*.[79] The following year a London magistrate, struck by the notion that there should not be one law for the rich unavailable to the poor, permitted a man named Gleaves to bring proceedings against the authors and publishers of a book entitled *Johnny Go Home*, based on a Yorkshire television documentary that had exposed his insalubrious hospitality to feckless youths. Neither case was an edifying example of law enforcement. Goldsmith was allowed to withdraw his prosecution after a settlement with *Private Eye*, and an Old Bailey jury took little time to acquit the authors of *Johnny Go Home* after a two-week trial. These precedents do not hold out great hope for private prosecutors determined to teach their critics a lesson in the criminal courts.

The arcane offence of *scandalum magnatum* was created by a statute of 1275 designed to protect "the great men of the realm" against discomfiture from stories that might arouse the people against them.[80] The

---

[76] CPR, Pt 24 was held *ultra vires* for libel actions: *Safeway v. Tate* [2001] 2 W.L.R. 1377 as explained by *Alexander v. Arts Council of Wales* [2001] 4 All E.R. 205 at 217.

[77] The Law Commission, *Working Paper No. 84*, HMSO, 1982. The U.S. Supreme Court has declared laws that punish falsehoods unconstitutional, unless that require proof of express malice: *Garrison v. Louisiana* 379 U.S. 64 (1964).

[78] *Gleaves v. Deakin* [1980] A.C. 477 at 493 *per* Lord Diplock.

[79] See Richard Ingrams, *Goldenballs* (Deutsch, 1979).

[80] *ibid.* p. 10, and see generally J. R. Spencer, "*Criminal Libel—Skeleton in the Cupboard*" [1977] Crim. L.R. 383.

purpose of criminal libel was to prevent loss of confidence in government. It was, essentially, a public order offence, and since true stories were more likely to result in breaches of the peace, it spawned the aphorism "The greater the truth, the greater the libel."[81] Overtly political prosecutions were brought in its name, against the likes of John Wilkes, Tom Paine and the Dean of St Asaph. Most of its historical anomalies survive in the present offence. Truth is not a defence, unless the defendant can convince a jury that publication is for the public benefit.[82] The burden of proof lies on the defendant, who may be convicted even though he or she honestly believed, on reasonable grounds, that what was published was true and a matter of public interest. In certain circumstances the offence extends to defamation of the dead,[83] and may even be brought where the attack has been published about a class of persons rather than an individual.[84]

For all its theoretical scope, there are several safeguards. Leave must be obtained from a High Court judge before any prosecution can be brought in, at least against proprietors and editors, in relation to an article in a newspaper or periodical.[85]

This safeguard of leave from a High Court judge may be side-stepped by prosecuting only the journalist who supplied the copy, and the incorrigible Mr Gleaves has made repeated use of this loop-hole in the statutory language of section 8. Although the Divisional Court in *Gleaves v. Insall* approved a literal reading of this archaic section (which omits to mention reporters and journalists) it did so without the benefit of section 3 of the Human Rights Act, which should now allow the section to be construed so as to include them, since this would be the only possible reading which could conform with Article 10. (There being no necessity nor any public benefit in prosecuting journalists rather than editors for a criminal offence which in its terms infringes freedom of expression).[86] The judge must be satisfied that there is an exceptionally strong prima facie case, that the libel is extremely serious and that the public interest requires the institu-

---

[81] *De Libellis Famosis* (1606) 5 Co. Rep. 125 (a) and (b).

[82] In *R. v. Perrymann, The Times*, 19 January–9 February 1892, a jury actually found that an editor's allegation that a solicitor was party to a serious corporate fraud was true, but it was not in the public interest that this truth should be published!

[83] See *Hilliard v. Penfield Enterprises* [1990] I.R. 38, where the deceased's wife sought to prosecute the publishers of a magazine for alleging that her husband had been a member of the IRA. Justice Gannon refused leave, on the grounds that criminal defamation of the dead required a malevolent intention to injure surviving members of his family by the vilification of his memory.

[84] See G. Zellick, *Libelling the Dead* (1969), 119 N.L.J. 769, and (in relation to class libels) *R. v. Williams* (1822) 5 B. and Ald. 595.

[85] Law of Libel Amendment Act 1888, s. 8.

[86] The Divisional Court decision in *Gleaves v. Insall* (1999) E.M.L.R. 779 was given before the Human Rights Act came into operation, and did not consider the argument for giving the 1888 Act a construction consistent with it.

tion of criminal proceedings. In deciding whether these tests are satisfied the judge must look not just at the prosecution's case, but must take into account the likelihood of the newspaper successfully raising a defence.[87] In one 1982 case Mr Justice Taylor refused to allow a man who had been described by the *Sunday People* as a violent and drunken bully to bring a prosecution for criminal libel. He heard evidence from the newspaper that undermined the applicant's evidence, and decided that there was not "a case so clear as to be beyond argument a case to answer". He further held that in any event the public interest did not require the institution of criminal proceedings.[88] These same tests should be satisfied before a magistrate commits anyone for trial in relation to a libel that has not appeared in a newspaper or periodical. There is no offence of "criminal slander", with the result that public speakers appear immune, at least in relation to off-the-cuff remarks.[89]

Criminal libel corresponds to no "pressing social need" of the sort that the European Court insists should justify restraints on free expression, and its continuing existence is difficult to reconcile with the decision in *Lingens v. Austria*.

The law of criminal libel is an unnecessary relic of the past that has no place in modern jurisprudence. There have been suggestions that it should be replaced by a new law of criminal defamation, which would make it an offence deliberately to publish a serious falsehood. The difficulties of definition and of trial procedure, however, make such suggestions impracticable.[90] Moreover, as the Privy Council pointed out in *Hector v. Att.-Gen. of Antigua and Barbuda*:

> "it would in my view by a grave impediment to the freedom of the press if those who print or distribute matter reflecting critically on the conduct of public authorities could only do so with impunity if they could first verify the accuracy of all statements of fact on which the criticism was based."[91]

The absurdity of taking the law of criminal defamation seriously was well illustrated in 1990, when the British Board of Film Classification sought to ban the Pakistani feature video *International Guerrillas* on the grounds that it amounted to a criminal libel on Mr Salman Rushdie, whom it depicted, in James Bond-style fantasy, as a sadistic terrorist.

---

[87] *Goldsmith v. Pressdram Ltd* [1977] Q.B. 83.

[88] *Desmond v. Thorne* [1982] 3 All E.R. 268.

[89] Defamation Act 1952, s. 17(2) and see *Gatley on Libel*, para. 1600. Words broadcast on television or radio, however, are deemed to be published in permanent form: Broadcasting Act 1990, s. 16(1).

[90] See G. Robertson, "The Law Commission on Criminal Libel" [1983] Public Law 208.

[91] [1990] 2 All E.R. 103 at 106.

Mr Rushdie announced that if criminal libel proceedings were brought on his behalf, he would give evidence for the defence. The Video Appeals Committee decided that the prospect of a prosecution, let alone a conviction, was too far-fetched to justify the ban.[92]

CONCLUSION

A claimant once brought a defamation action over the allegation that he was a highwayman. The evidence at the trial proved that he *was* in fact a highwayman. The claimant was arrested in the courtroom, committed to prison and then executed. Few defamation actions end so satisfactorily for the defence.

The media constantly complain about defamation law, with some justice in respect of the burden of proof, the escalation of legal costs and other defects pointed out in this chapter. The recent development of a public interest privilege in *Reynolds* has improved protection for professionally-conducted investigative journalism, but the media as a body and newspapers as an industry have shown scant interest in improving ethical standards. No civilised society can permit a privately owned press to run vendettas against individuals powerless to arrest the spread of falsehoods and innuendoes. In the United States the Supreme Court held in the great case of *The New York Times v. Sullivan* that no libel action could succeed if the claimant was a public figure and the allegation was honestly and diligently made.[93] This ruling has freed the American media to probe Watergate and Irangate in a depth and a detail that could not be attempted in equivalent circumstances in Britain, where the merest hint of impropriety in public life calls forth a libel writ. But the public figure doctrine denies virtually any protection to persons who are prominent in public affairs, simply because of that fact. True, public figures voluntarily step into a fish-tank that entails close public scrutiny of their every move, and they ordinarily enjoy greater access to channels of communication that provide an opportunity to counter false statements. But that opportunity is circumscribed, none the less, and in a country where proprietors with powerful partisan views control 80 per cent of national newspapers, there is an understandable reluctance to give them a blank cheque to attack political enemies.

Two essential freedoms—the right to communicate and the right to reputation—must in some way be reconciled by law. British libel law errs by inhibiting free speech and failing to provide a system for cor-

---

[92] Video Appeals Committee, Appeal No. 0007, September 3, 1990.
[93] *The New York Times Co v. Sullivan*, 401 U.S. 265 (1964).

recting factual errors that is speedy and available to all victims of press distortion. American libel law gives no protection at all to the reputation of people in the public eye. Some European countries have opted for a more acceptable solution in the form of right-to-reply legislation, which allows an "ombudsman" to direct newspapers to publish corrections and counter-statements from those who claim to have been misrepresented. What is required is a speedy and effective legal procedure that secures corrections and counter-statements while reserving damages for cases where claimants have suffered financial loss or been the victims of malice. There is no indication that government or Parliament will bring forth legislation to provide such far-reaching reforms, and the ability of judges to do so by common law development is limited, save for their ability to "cull sacred cows" by virtue of the Human Rights Act.[94]

When journalists receive libel writs, they will generally be well advised to seek expert assistance, although there are times where a robust extra-legal response will be more effective:

> The much celebrated correspondence in the matter of *Arkell v. Pressdram* involved only two letters: the first, from the solicitors Goodman Derrick & Co, to the editor of *Private Eye*, ended with the familiar legal demand: "Mr Arkell's first concern is that there should be a full retraction at the earliest possible date in *Private Eye* and he will also want his costs paid. His attitude to damages will be governed by the nature of your reply." To this the magazine responded: "We note that Mr Arkell's attitude to damages will be governed by the nature of our reply and would therefore be grateful if you could inform us what his attitude to damages would be, were he to learn that the nature of our reply is as follows: fuck off."

---

[94] See Lord Slynn in *R v. Lambert* [2001] 3 All E.R. 577, HL. Although the power of re-interpretation in s. 3 of the HRA applies only to statutes, courts themselves are public authorities and must apply the common law compatibly with the Convention, a duty which permits them to abrogate long-standing doctrines. See *Aston Cantlow v. Wallbank* [2001] 3 All E.R. 393.

CHAPTER 4

OBSCENITY, BLASPHEMY AND RACE HATRED

"The constitutional protection accorded to the freedom of speech and of the press is not based on the naïve belief that speech can do no harm but on the confidence that the benefits society reaps from the free flow and exchange of ideas outweigh the costs society endures by receiving reprehensible or dangerous ideas."[1]

Censorship of writing, drama and film on grounds of morality is achieved by laws that apply two sets of standards. One prohibits "obscene" articles likely to deprave and corrupt readers and viewers, while the other allows authorities to act, in certain circumstances, against "indecent" material that merely embarrasses the sexual modesty of ordinary people. Obscenity, the more serious crime, is punished by the Obscene Publications Act 1959, either after a trial by judge or jury or by "forfeiture proceedings" under a law that authorises local justices to destroy obscene books and films discovered within their jurisdiction. Disseminators of "indecent" material that lacks the potency to corrupt are generally within the law so long as they do not dispatch it by post, or seek to import it from overseas, or flaunt it openly in public places. Both "obscenity" and "indecency" are defined by reference to vague and elastic formulae, permitting forensic debates over morality that fit uneasily into the format of a criminal trial. These periodic moral flash-points provide scant control over the booming business of sexual delectation. Occasional forfeiture orders, based upon the same loose definitions, are subject to the inconsistent priorities and prejudices of constabularies in different parts of the country, and offer no effective deterrent.

The deep division in society over the proper limits of sexual permissiveness is mirrored by an inconsistent and ineffective censorship of

---

[1] *Hercey v. Hustler Magazine* (1988) 485 U.S. 959.

publications that may offend or entertain, corrupt or enlighten, according to the taste and character of individual readers. The problem of
drawing a legal line between moral outrage and personal freedom
has become intractable at a time when one person's obscenity is
another person's bedtime reading.

Bedtime viewing, however, is subject to more stringent controls.
Reliance is placed upon the statutory duty of the Independent Television Commission to ensure that nothing is transmitted on the commercial airwaves that is in bad taste or is likely to prove offensive to
public feeling. Although no similar legal duty has been imposed
upon the BBC, the Corporation has undertaken to ensure that its
broadcasters also bow to identical dictates of public decency. Television was subjected to the Obscene Publications Act in 1990, although
it is difficult to imagine how obscene material could slip through
these controls and no prosecution has yet been brought against broadcasters. Films screened in public cinema are subject to the test of
obscenity, although the film industry, in order to obtain additional
insurance against prosecution, has voluntarily bound itself to comply
with the censorship requirements of the British Board of Film Classification, a private body established and funded by the industry itself.
The importance of the BBFC is enhanced by local licensing requirements which generally require that all films screened shall have been
approved by the BBFC and by the law that video shops shall carry
only films that have been granted an appropriate BBFC certificate.
Licensed sex shops are also obliged to sell only videos that have
been certified by the Board. In this way a form of pre-censorship is
imposed on feature films and videos that is not inflicted upon books
or magazines or theatres.

The obscenity and indecency laws, and the arrangements for film
censorship, are generally directed against sexual explicitness. However, the tests applied are sufficiently broad to catch material that
encourages the use of dangerous drugs or that advocates criminal
violence. Distributors of horror movies on video cassettes have been
convicted on the basis that explicitly violent scenes are likely to
corrupt a significant proportion of home viewers. In this chapter the
scope and general principles of laws relating to obscenity, indecency,
blasphemy, conspiracy and incitement to racial hatred are examined
in some detail. In Chapters 15 and 16 the extent to which their
principles are applied to television, film and video will be considered
separately along with the statutory duties and censorship systems
that work in these media to regulate the treatment of controversial
subjects.

OBSCENITY

History

The history of obscenity provides a rich and comic tapestry on the futility of legal attempts to control sexual imagination.[2] The subject-matter of pornography was settled by 1650; writers in subsequent centuries added new words and novel settings, but discovered no fundamental variation on the finite methods of coupling. The scarlet woman, pornography's picaresque and picturesque prop, gained one dimension with the development of photography and another with the abolition of stage censorship, but the modern exploits of Linda Lovelace were old hat to Fanny Hill.

The central irony of the courtroom crusade—what might be termed 'the *Spycatcher* effect"—is always present: seek to suppress a book by legal action because it tends to corrupt, and the publicity attendant upon its trial will spread that assumed corruption far more effectively than its quiet distribution. *Lady Chatterley's Lover* sold three million copies in the three months following its prosecution in 1961. The last work of literature to be prosecuted for obscenity in a full-blooded Old Bailey trial was an undistinguished paperback entitled *Inside Linda Lovelace*. It has sold a few thousand copies in the years before the 1976 court case: within three weeks of its acquittal 600,000 copies were purchased by an avid public. That trial seems finally to have convinced the Director of Public Prosecutions (DPP) of the unwisdom of using obscenity laws against books with any claim to literary or sociological merit.[3]

The courts first began to take obscenity seriously as a result of private prosecutions brought in the early nineteenth century by the Society for the Suppression of Vice, dubbed by Sydney Smith "a society for suppressing the vices of those whose incomes do not exceed £500 per annum".[4] A law against obscene libel was created by the judges, although Parliament gave some assistance in 1857 with an Obscene Publications Act, which permitted magistrates to destroy immoral books found within their jurisdiction. The Act did not, however, define obscenity. Lord Chief Justice Cockburn, in the 1868 case of *R. v. Hicklin*, obliged with a formula that has influenced the subject ever since:

> "I think the test of obscenity is this, whether the tendency of the

---

[2] See generally Geoffrey Robertson, *Obscenity* (Weidenfeld & Nicholson, 1979) and Alan Tarvis, *Bound and Gagged—A Secret History of Obscenity in Britain* (Profile Books, 2000).

[3] *Committee on Obscenity and Film Censorship* (The Williams Committee), HMSO, 1979, Cmnd 7772, Chap. 4, para. 2.

[4] *Edinburgh Review*, XXVI, January 1809.

matter charged as obscenity is to deprave and corrupt those whose minds are open to such immoral influences, and into whose hands a publication of this sort may fall."[5]

Armed at last with a definition of obscenity, Victorian prosecutors proceeded to destroy many examples of fine literature and scientific speculation.[6]

Under the law of obscene libel, almost any work dealing with sexual passion could be successfully prosecuted. The *Hicklin* test focused upon the effect of the book on the most vulnerable members of society, whether or not they were likely to read it. One "purple passage" could consign a novel to condemnation, and there was no defence of literary merit. D. H. Lawrence's *The Rainbow* was destroyed in 1915, and *The Well of Loneliness* suffered the same fate in 1928 at the hands of a magistrate who felt that a passage that implied that two women had been to bed ("And that night they were not divided") would induce "thought of a most impure character" and "glorify a horrible tendency".[7] The operation of the obscenity law depended to some extent upon the crusading zeal of current law officers. There was a brief respite in the 1930s, after a banned copy of *Ulysses* was found among the papers of a deceased Lord Chancellor. But in 1953 the authorities solemnly sought to destroy copies of *The Kinsey Report*, and in 1956 a number of respectable publishers—Secker & Warburg, Heinemann, and Hutchinson—were all tried at the Old Bailey for "horrible tendencies" discovered in their current fiction lists. The Society of Authors set up a powerful lobby, which convinced a Parliamentary Committee that the common law of obscene libel should be replaced by a modern statute that afforded some protection to meritorious literature.[8] The Obscene Publications Act of 1959 was the result. The measure was described in its preamble as "an Act to amend the law relating to the publication of obscene matter; to provide for the protection of literature; and to strengthen the law concerning pornography".

The 1959 Obscene Publications Act emerged from a simplistic notion that sexual material could be divided into two classes, "literature" and "pornography", and the function of the new statutory definition of obscenity was to enable juries and magistrates to make the distinction between them. The tendency of a work to deprave or corrupt its readers

---

[5] (1868) L.R. 3 Q.B. 360 at 371.
[6] See *R. v. Thomas* (1906) 67 J.P. 456: "In the Middle Ages there were things discussed which if put forward now for the reading of the general public would never be tolerated."
[7] See Vera Brittain, *Radclyffe Hall—A Case of Obscenity* (Femina, 1968) pp. 91–92.
[8] See Norman St John Stevas, *Obscenity and the Law* (Secker & Warburg, 1956).

was henceforth to be judged in the light of its total impact, rather than by the arousing potential of "purple passages". The readership to be considered was the actual or at least predictable reading public rather than the precocious 14-year-old schoolgirl into whose hands it might perchance fall—unless it were in fact aimed at or distributed to 14-year-old schoolgirls, by whose vulnerability to corruption it should then be judged. It was recognised that a work of literature might employ, to advance its serious purpose, a style that resembled, or had the same effect as, the pornographer's: here the jury was to be assisted to draw the line by experts who would offer judgments as to the degree of importance the article represented in its particular discipline. Works of art or literature might be obscene (*i.e.* depraving or corrupting) but their great significance might outweigh the harm they could do, and take them out of the prima facie criminal category established by section 1 of the Act.

In fact, the 1959 Act has worked to secure a very large measure of freedom in Britain for the written word. It took two decades and a number of celebrated trials for the revolutionary implications of the legislation to be fully appreciated and applied. The credit for securing this freedom belongs not so much to the legislators (many of whom later professed themselves appalled at developments) but to a few courageous publishers who risked jail by inviting juries to take a stand against censorship, and to the ineptitude and corruption of police enforcement. The first major test case—over D.H. Lawrence's *Lady Chatterley's Lover*—enabled the full force of the reformed law to be exploited on behalf of recognised literature. The book fell to be judged, not on the strength of its four-letter words or purple passages, but on its overall impact, as described by leading authorities on English literature. In 1968 the appeal proceedings over *Last Exit to Brooklyn* established the right of authors to explore depravity and corruption without encouraging it: writers were entitled to turn their readers' stomachs for the purpose of arousing concern or condemning the corruption explicitly described. The trials of the underground press in the early '70s discredited obscenity law in the eyes of a new generation of jurors, and acquittals of hard-core pornography soon followed. These came in the wake of apparently scientific evidence that pornography had a therapeutic rather than a harmful effect. Popular permissiveness was reflected in jury verdicts, and the repeal of obscenity laws in several European countries made it impossible for the authorities to police the incoming tide of eroticism. And if pornography did not corrupt its readers, it certainly corrupted many of those charged with enforcing the law against it. Public cynicism about obscenity control was confirmed when 12 members of Scotland Yard's "dirty squad" were jailed after conviction for involvement in what their judge described as "an evil conspiracy which turned the Obscene Publications Act into a vast protection racket".[9] After the acquittal of *Inside Linda Lovelace* in 1976, the authorities largely abandoned the attempt to prosecute books for which any claim of literary merit could be made. The Williams Committee, which reported on the obscenity laws in 1979, recommended that all restraints on the written word should be lifted—a position that they thought had already been achieved *de facto*.[10]

Since the Williams Report, the only books that have been prosecuted have either glorified illegal activities, such as the taking of dangerous drugs, or have been hard-core pornography lacking any literary pretension or sociological interest. In the late 1980s the need for education about the dangers of transmitting the AIDS virus justified a degree of public explicitness that would have been unthinkable in previous decades. By the end of the twentieth century, the BBFC had been obliged to license video pornography for adult purchase (see Chap. 15) and adult "top shelf" magazines followed this lead. However, the forces of feminism have done more than the cohorts of Mrs Whitehouse to challenge public acceptance of erotica, and there can be no guarantee that some future legal onslaught against sexually explicit art and literature would not succeed. In 1988 a complaint from a Hampshire clergyman had the DPP rereading the works of Henry Miller, and seriously contemplating a test-case prosecution. In 1991 the DPP resisted trenchant demands that he should prosecute Century-Hutchinson for re-issuing the works of de Sade, and Picador for publishing *American Psycho*, a novel by Brett Easton Ellis of some kind of literary merit, which included highly explicit descriptions of serial killings of women. In 1998, provincial policemen descended on Random House, threatening prosecution for publishing a lavish book of Robert Mapplethorpe photographs (priced at £75), a copy of which they had discovered in a university library. A Q.C.'s opinion, obtained by Random House, persuaded the DPP to drop the proceedings. The latitude he allowed to respectable white publishers did not extend to black "rap" artists from the American urban ghetto, and the Island Records group Niggaz With Attitude suffered the first obscenity case brought in relation to a compact disc. It was solemnly played to elderly lay justices at Redbridge Magistrates' Court, who found it impossible to conclude that whatever it was that they were hearing could excite sexually.

The test of obscenity

The complete statutory definition of obscenity is contained in section 1 of the Obscene Publications Act:

---

[9] Barry Cox, John Shirley and Martin Short, *The Fall of Scotland Yard* (Penguin, 1977) p. 158.

[10] Williams Committee, *Obscenity and Film Censorship*, n. 3 above.

"For the purposes of this Act an article shall be deemed to be obscene if its effect or (where the article comprises two or more distinct items) the effect of any one of its items is, if taken as a whole, such as to tend to deprave and corrupt persons who are likely, in all the circumstances, to read, see or hear the matter contained or embodied in it."

In any trial the prosecution must prove beyond reasonable doubt that the material is obscene. Its task is complicated by the following interpretations of the statutory definition.

The tendency to deprave and corrupt

"Deprave" means "to make morally bad, to pervert, to debase or corrupt morally" and corrupt means "to render morally unsound or rotten, or destroy the moral purity or chastity of, to pervert or ruin a good quality, to debase, to defile".[11] The definition implies that the tendency must go much further than merely shocking or disgusting readers.[12] Thus "obscene", in law, has a very different, and very much stronger, meaning than it possesses in colloquial usage. The convictions of the editors of *Oz* magazine were quashed because their trial judge had suggested that "obscene" might include what is "repulsive, filthy, loathsome, indecent or lewd." To widen its legal meaning in this way was "a very substantial and serious misdirection."[13]

In *Knuller v. DPP* the Law Lords considered that the word "corrupt" implied a powerful and corrosive effect, which went further than one suggested definition, "to lead morally astray". Lord Simon warned:

"Corrupt is a strong word. The Book of Common Prayer, following the Gospel, has 'where rust and moth doth corrupt'. The words 'corrupt public morals' suggest conduct which a jury might find to be destructive of the very fabric of society."[14]

Lord Reid agreed:

"... corrupt is a strong word and the jury ought to be reminded of that ... The Obscene Publications Act appears to use the words 'deprave' and 'corrupt' as synonymous, as I think they are. We may regret we live in a permissive society but I doubt whether

---

[11] See C. H. Rolph, *The Trial of Lady Chatterley* (commem. ed., Penguin, 1990) pp. 227–8. The present law is stated in detail in Robertson, n. 2 above, Chap. 3.

[12] See *R. v. Martin Secker & Warburg Ltd* [1954] 2 All E.R. 683.

[13] *R. v. Anderson* [1971] 3 All E.R. 1152.

[14] [1973] A.C. 435 at 491.

even the most staunch defender of a better age would maintain that all or even most of those who have at one time or in one way or another been led astray morally have thereby become depraved or corrupt."[15]

These dicta in *Knuller* emphasise that the effect of publication must go beyond immoral suggestion or persuasion and constitute a serious menace.

"Obscenity" is a much narrower concept that "sexual explicitness". This important distinction was emphasised by the Divisional Court in the 1991 case of *Darbo v. CPS* when it held that an Obscene Publications Act warrant authorising police to search for "material of a sexually explicit nature" was invalid, because material in this category was by no means necessarily "obscene" in the sense that it might be likely to deprave and corrupt consumers.[16] This is recognised by the BBFC guidelines on 18R certificates issued in 2000 after the *Makin' Whoopee* decision. Indeed, there is much to be said for the view of the Chief Justice of South Australia in respect of most ideologically rapid pornographic publications: "I do not think that the arousal of erotic feelings in an adult male is itself an offence—there is, to my mind, something ludicrous about the application of such portentous words as 'deprave' and 'corrupt' to these trivial and insipid productions."[17]

The aversion defence

One important corollary of the decision that obscene material must have more serious effects than arousing feelings of revulsion is the doctrine that material that in fact shocks and disgusts may *not* be obscene, because its effect is to discourage readers from indulgence in the immorality so unseductively portrayed. Readers whose stomachs are turned will not partake of any food for thought. The argument, however paradoxical it sounds, has frequently found favour as a means of exculpating literature of merit:

> *Last Exit to Brooklyn* presented horrific pictures of homosexuality and drug-taking in New York. Defence counsel contended that its only effect on any but a minute lunatic fringe of readers would be horror, revulsion and pity. It made the readers share in the horror it described and thereby so disgusted, shocked and outraged them that instead of tending to encourage anyone to homosexuality, drug-taking or brutal violence, it would have precisely the reverse effect. The failure of the trial judge to put this

---

[15] [1973] A.C. 435 at 456–7.
[16] *David John Darbo v. DPP*, *The Times*, July 11, 1991, Divisional Court (Mann L.J. and Hidden I.) June 28, 1991.
[17] *Popow v. Samuels* [1973] 4 S.A.S.R. 594 *per* Bray C.J.

defence before the jury in his summing up was the major ground for
upsetting the conviction.[18]

The aversion argument was extracted from its literary context and
elevated into a full-blown defence of crudity in the *Oz* case:

> "One of the arguments was that many of the illustrations in *Oz*
> were so grossly lewd and unpleasant that they would shock in the
> first instance and then would tend to repel. In other words, it was
> said that they had an aversive effect and that, far from tempting
> those who had not experienced the acts to take part in them, they
> would put off those who might be tempted so to conduct
> themselves . . .".[19]

The most valuable aspect of the aversion defence is its emphasis on
the context and purpose of publication. Writing that sets out to seduce,
to exhort and pressurise the reader to indulge in immorality, is to be
distinguished from that which presents a balanced picture and does not
overlook the pains that may attend new pleasures. For over a century
prosecutors thought it sufficient to point to explicitness in the treatment
of sex, on the assumption that exposure to such material would automatically arouse the libidinous desires associated with a state of depravity.
Now they must consider the overall impact and the truthfulness of the
total picture. Books that present a fair account of corruption have a
defence denied to glossy propaganda. In deciding whether material
depraves and corrupts, the jury must lift its eyes from mere details and
consider the tone and overall presentation. Does the material glamorise
sex or does it "tell it like it is?".

In 1991 the aversion defence assisted Island Records to argue successfully that a record by rap musicians Niggaz With Attitude was not
obscene. Despite the profusion of four-letter words and aggressively
unpleasant imagery, it was inconceivable that anyone in their right
mind—or even their wrong mind—would be sexually aroused by songs
like "One Less Bitch" or "To Kill a Hooker". These songs were said
to be "street journalism", reflecting the degradation and depravity of
life among the drug gangs in the ghetto suburbs of Los Angeles. The
magistrates agreed that the record was more likely to arouse distaste
and fear than lust, and directed that the 30,000 records, cassettes and
compact discs seized by Scotland Yard's Obscene Publications Squad
should be released.[20]

---

[18] *R. v. Calder & Boyars Ltd* [1969] 1 Q.B. 151.
[19] *R. v. Anderson* [1971] 3 All E.R. 1152 at 1160.
[20] See "Niggaz Court Win Marks Changing Attitude", *The Guardian*, November 8,
1991; and "NWA Cleared of Obscenity Charges", *Melody Maker*, November 16,
1991.

The target audience

An article is only obscene if it is likely to corrupt "persons who are likely, having regard to all relevant circumstances, to read, see or hear the matter contained or embodied in it." Thus the Act adopts a relative definition of obscenity—relative, that is, to the "likely" rather than the "conceivably possible" readership. This is further emphasised by section 2(6) of the Act, which provides that in any prosecution for publishing an obscene article "the question whether an article is obscene shall be determined without regard to any publication by another person, unless it could reasonably have been expected that the publication by the other person would follow from the publication by the person charged." Where the charge is possession for gain, the question whether the article is obscene is similar (although stated in different and confusing words by section 1(3)(b) of the 1964 Act): it

> "shall be determined by reference to such publication for gain of
> the article as in the circumstances it may reasonably be inferred
> he had in contemplation and to any further publication that could
> reasonably be expected to follow from it, but not to any other
> publication".

In other words, the jury must consider the impact not only on intended customers but on those to whom the customers could reasonably be expected to show or pass on the material, but not its impact on other persons who might (but could not reasonably be expected or be likely to) gain access to it as a result of the defendant's original act of publication.[21]

These statutory provisions ensure that the publication in question is judged by its impact on its primary audience—those people who, the evidence suggests, would be likely to seek it out and to pay the asking-price to read it, or else be sufficiently interested to borrow it or attend a viewing. They reject the "most vulnerable person" standard of *Hicklin*, with its preoccupation with those members of society of the lowest level of intellectual or moral discernment. They also reject another standard employed frequently in the law, that of the "average" or "reasonable" man, and focus on "likely" readers and proven circumstances of publication. A work of literature is to be judged by its effect on serious-minded purchasers, a comic book by its effect on children, a sexually explicit magazine sold in an "adults only" bookstore by its effect on adult patrons of that particular shop. The House of Lords has confirmed that "in every case, the magistrates or the jury are called on

---

[21] *R. v. O'Sullivan* [1995] Cr. App. R. 455.

to ascertain who are the likely readers and then to consider whether the article is likely to deprave and corrupt them."[22]

> In *R. v. Clayton & Halsey* the proprietors of a Soho bookshop were charged with selling obscene material to two experienced members of Scotland Yard's Obscene Publications Squad. These officers conceded that pornography had ceased to arouse any feelings in them whatsoever. The prosecution argument that the pictures were "inherently obscene" and tended of their very nature to corrupt all viewers was rejected.[23]

Although judges sometimes loosely talk of material that is "inherently obscene" or "obscene *per se*", it is clear that this concept is irreconcilable with the legislative definition of obscenity.[24] The quality of obscenity inheres whenever the article would tend to corrupt its actual or potential audience; the degree of that corruption becomes relevant when it is necessary to balance it against the public interest, if a "public good defence" has been raised under section 4 of the Act.

The significant proportion test

The 1959 Act requires a tendency to deprave and corrupt "persons" likely in the circumstances to read or hear the offensive material. But how many persons must have their morals affected before the test is made out? The answer was given by the Court of Appeal in the *Last Exit to Brooklyn* case. The jury must be satisfied that a *significant proportion* of the likely readership would be guided along the path of corruption:

> "Clearly section 2 cannot mean all persons; nor can it mean any one person, for there are individuals who may be corrupted by almost anything. On the other hand, it is difficult to construe 'persons' as meaning the majority of persons or the average reader. This court is of the opinion that the jury should have been directed to consider whether the effect of the book was to tend to deprave and corrupt a significant proportion of those persons likely to read it. What is a significant proportion is a matter entirely for the jury to decide.[25]

---

[22] *DPP v. Whyte* [1972] 3 All E.R. 12 at 17. The U.S. Supreme Court has ruled that children must be excluded from the relevant "community" whose standards are at issue, unless there is evidence that they were intended recipients of the material: *Pinkus v. U.S.* 434 U.S. 919.

[23] *R. v. Clayton & Halsey* [1962] 1 Q.B. 163.

[24] *Att.-Gen.'s Reference No. 2 of 1975* [1976] 2 All E.R. 753.

[25] *R. v. Calder & Boyars Ltd*, n. 18 above.

The significant proportion test has been applied at obscenity trials ever since. It protects the defendant in that it prevents the jury from speculating on the possible effect of adult literature on a young person who may just happen to see it, although it does not put the prosecution to proof that a majority, or even a *substantial* number of readers would be adversely affected. This was emphasised by the House of Lords in *Whyte*'s case, where local justices had mistakenly interpreted "significant proportion" to mean "the great majority". Lord Cross accepted that the significant proportion test was the standard that the justices were required to apply, but stressed that "a significant proportion of a class means a part which is not numerically negligible but which may be much less than half."[26]

The dominant effect principle

In obscenity trials before the 1959 legislation it was unnecessary for juries to consider the overall impact of the subject-matter on its likely readers. Prosecuting counsel could secure a conviction merely by drawing attention to isolated "purple passages" taken out of context. The Select Committee on the Obscene Publications Act had stressed the importance of considering the "dominant effect" of the whole work:

> "The contrary view, under which a work could be judged obscene by reference to isolated passages without considering the total effect, would, if taken to its logical conclusion, deprive the reading public of the works of Shakespeare, Chaucer, Fielding and Smollett, except in expurgated editions. We therefore recommend that regard should be paid in any legislation to the effect of a work as a whole."[27]

This recommendation was duly embodied in the 1959 statute, which provided that "an article shall be deemed to be obscene if its effect or (where the article comprises two or more distinct items) the effect of any one of its items is, if taken as a whole, such as to tend to deprave and corrupt ...". In the *Lady Chatterley* case Mr Justice Byrne instructed his jury to consider the total effect of the work after reading it from cover to cover. "You will read this book just as though you had bought it at a bookstall and you were reading it in the ordinary way as a whole."[28]

The effect of the dominant impact test is to enable the courts to take account of the psychological realities of reading and film viewing, in so

---

[26] *DPP v. Whyte* [1972] 3 All E.R. 12 at 24, 25.
[27] *Report of the Select Committee on Obscene Publications*, 1958, para. 18.
[28] Rolph, *Lady Chatterley*, p. 39.

far as the audience is affected by theme and style and message, so that isolated incidents of an offensive nature are placed in context. The injunction that an article must be "taken as a whole" will apply to books and plays: in the case of magazines, however, which are made up of separate articles, advertisements and photographs, the dominant effect principle has less force. In such cases the publication is considered on an "item-by-item" basis: the prosecution may argue that obscenity attaches only to one article or photograph, and that the other contents are irrelevant.[29] A suggestion by the Court of Appeal in 1999 that the "item-by-item" test could apply to films is misguided, unless (possibly) the film were to comprise separate segments shot by different directors on different themes.[30] The intention of Parliament was to ensure that the jury considered the "dominant effect" of any artistic work, and the question is whether the experience of watching it through from beginning to end will have a corrupting effect on likely viewers, the impact of a single scene being considered in the context of the whole film, and not in isolation.

The publisher's intentions

The Obscene Publications Act is an exception to the general rule that criminal offences require an intention to offend. It does not matter whether the purpose is to educate or edify, to corrupt or simply to make money. The *effect* of the work on a significant proportion of the likely audience is all that matters in deciding whether it is obscene under section 1. However, the publisher's intentions may be very important when a public good defence is raised under section 4 of the Act, namely that although the work is obscene, its publication is nonetheless justified in the public interest. In the *Lady Chatterley* case Mr Justice Byrne directed that "as far as literary merit or other matters which can be considered under section 4 are concerned, I think one has to have regard to what the author was trying to do, what his message may have been, and what his general scope was."[31]

A limited defence is provided by the Obscene Publications Act for those defendants who act merely as innocent disseminators of obscene material. Section 2(5) of the 1959 Act reads:

"A person shall not be convicted of an offence against this section (*i.e.* the offence of publishing obscene material) if he proves that he had not examined the article in respect of which he is charged

---

[29] *R. v. Anderson* [1971] 3 All E.R. 1152 at 1158.
[30] See *Criminal Law Review*, October 1999, p. 670 commenting on the decision in *R. v. Goring*, January 14, 1999, CA.
[31] Rolph, *Lady Chatterley*, pp. 121–122.

and had no reasonable cause to suspect that it was such that his publication of it would make him liable to be convicted of an offence against this section."

The onus of proof is placed on the defendant under this section. The defendant must show, on the balance of probabilities, both that he did not examine the article and that he entertained no suspicions about the nature of its contents. It is often possible to judge pornographic books by their covers and a bookseller would probably fail if he admitted to catching sight of a provocative cover picture or suggestive title. In *R. v. Love* the Court of Appeal quashed the conviction of a director of a print company who had been absent at the time a printer order for obscene books was accepted, and who had no personal knowledge of the contents of those books.[32] Even though he had accepted general responsibility for his company's operations, and would probably have agreed to print the books had the decision been referred to him, he could not be convicted unless he had been given specific notice of the offensive material. The defendant who had not "examined", in the sense of personally inspected, the offending items might have nonetheless been given reasonable cause to suspect obscenity by clandestine or unorthodox behaviour on the part of the supplier. Any evidence that, for example, a printer has specially increased his profit margin to cover a risk factor would be fatal to a section 2(5) claim. Conversely, if the accused can show that the material came to him in the normal course of business from a reputable supplier, he may have a defence. Cases on the liability of distributors for libels in newspapers emphasise the importance for this defence of establishing that the business—of printing, distributing or retailing—was carried on carefully and properly. The test is whether the unwitting distributor *ought* to have known that the material would offend.[33]

The contemporary standards test

Although the Act does not make reference to the current climate of opinion about sexual explicitness, juries in obscenity trials are enjoined to keep in mind the current standards of ordinary decent people. They "must set the standards of what is acceptable, of what is for the public good in the age in which we live."[34] Logically, of course, they do no such thing: however much the material offends the standards of decent people, the entirely distinct and key issue is whether it causes harm by

---

[32] *R. v. Love* (1955) 39 Cr. App. R. 30.
[33] See *Emmens v. Pottle* (1885) 16 Q.B.D. 354; *Sun Life Assurance Co. of Canada. v. W. H. Smith Ltd* (1934) 150 L.T. 211.
[34] *R. v. Calder & Boyars*, n. 18 above, at 172 *per* Salmon L.J.

tending to corrupt some of its readers or viewers. Contemporary stand-ards should only be relevant to the obscenity decision as a yardstick to judge the behaviour of consumers after exposure, and perhaps to support the familiar defence arguments that the items prosecuted "pale into insignificance" or are "a drop in the ocean" besides lurid sexuality oozing from the top shelf of newsagents, Channel 5, women's maga-zines and satellite television.[35] The collective experience of twelve arbit-rarily chosen people is assumed to provide a degree of familiarity with popular reading trends, with what is deemed acceptable on television and at cinemas and on the internet and with the degree of explicitness that can be found in publications on sale at local newsagents. A pub-lisher is not, however, permitted to argue that he should be acquitted because his publication is less obscene than others that are freely circu-lated.[36]

The 1959 Act does, however, provide for two situations in which comparisons are both permissible and highly relevant. Under section 2(5), it may be that a defendant has "no reasonable cause to suspect" the obscenity of a book that he has not personally examined because he knows that similar books have been acquitted, or are freely circulated. And under the public good defence it may be relevant to the jury's task of evaluating the merit of a particular book to compare it with other books of the same kind, and to hear expert evidence about the current climate of permissiveness in relation to this kind of literature. This exception was recognised by Mr Justice Byrne in the *Lady Chatterley* case when he permitted expert witnesses to compare the novel with other works by Lawrence and various twentieth-century writers, and to discuss the standards for describing sexual matters reflected in modern literature. At one point in the trial he agreed that:

> "other books may be considered, for two reasons, firstly, upon the question of the literary merit of a book which is the subject-matter of the indictment . . . [where] it is necessary to compare that book with other books upon the question of literary merit. Secondly . . . other books are relevant to the climate of literature."[37]

Where a public good defence is raised, juries may be asked to make comparisons in order to evaluate the real worth of the publication at

---

[35] A robust example of the Court of Appeal applying liberal contemporary standards—albeit to reject a hypothetical attempt by a sex line operator to avoid payment of its advertising bill by arguing that its own explicit adverts were obscene (and hence the contract was unlawful), is found in Simon Brown L.J.'s judgment in *Armhouse Lee Ltd v. Chappell, The Times*, August 7, 1996.

[36] *R. v. Reiter* [1954] 2 Q.B. 16; *R. v. Elliott* [1996] 1 Cr. App. R. 432, CA.

[37] Rolph, *Lady Chatterley*, p. 127.

stake, and they may be told by experts about the state of informed contemporary opinion on subjects dealt with in those publications.

Prohibited acts

There are two separate charges that may be brought in respect of obscene publications. It is an offence to *publish* an obscene article contrary to the Obscene Publications Act of 1959, and it is an offence to *have an obscene article for publication for gain*, contrary to the Obscene Publications Act of 1964. A charge under the 1959 Act requires some *act* of publication, such as sale to a customer or giving an obscene book to a friend. There must be some evidence connecting the defendant with movement of the article into another's hands.[38] Mere possession of an obscene book will not satisfy the definition of publication in section 1(3)(b), which governs both Acts:

> "For the purposes of this Act a person publishes an article who (a) distributes, circulates, sells, lets on hire, gives, or lends it, or who offers it for sale or for letting on hire; or (b) in the case of an article containing or embodying matter to be looked at or a record, shows, plays or projects it, or where the matter is data stored electronically, transmits that data."[39]

The Act relates to an "article" which is widely defined by s1(2) to mean,

> "any description of article containing or embodying matter to be read or looked at or both, any sound record, and any film or other record of a picture or pictures".

Obscene negatives were included in the definition in 1964, and prints processed from them which are found in the defendant's possession for gain can be the subject of prosecution, irrespective of who may own the copyright.[40] The 1959 Obscene Publications Act definition catches forms of communication which were unheard of in 1959: the Court of Appeal made this clear in 1980 when deciding that video cassettes were within it because they were articles which produced pictures and sounds.[41] This decision was relied upon in the 1997 case of *R. v. Fellows* which held that a computer hard disk was an "article" and that data

---

[38] *Att.-Gen.'s Reference No. 2 of 1975*, n. 24 above.
[39] The references to data were added by Sched. 9 to the Criminal Justice and Public Order Act 1994 to cover electronic transmission of obscene material.
[40] *R. v. Taylor* (1995) Cr. App. R. 131.
[41] *Att.-Gen.'s Reference No. 5 of 1980* [1980] 3 All E.R. 816.

stored in the disk was "published" for the purpose of the Act (*i.e.* was "shown played or projected") to those who gained access to a "child porn" internet archive by means of a password.[42] Anything that "ordinary literate persons" in 1959 would understand as communicating words or pictures was capable of being the subject of prosecution, however new the technology. This means that anything which titillates through ocular or aural reception is covered: the only "articles" excluded would be those which provide erotic experiences by smell or taste or movement (a chair which offered a sensual electronic massage would not be an "article" for the purposes of the Act).

An article is "published" when matter recorded on it is included in a television or sound programme, and there is a defence for producers and participants who are unaware that a programme they are involved with might include obscene material, or that their material might be published in a way that would attract liability. Any seizure of recordings by police, or any prosecution, requires the consent of the Director of Public Prosecutions.[43]

Those who participate in or promote obscene publications are entitled to acquittal if they intend their work to be "published" in a manner that falls outside the Act, *e.g.* because they genuinely believe that distribution will be confined to a select group immune from corruption or to those countries that do not have laws against obscene publications. A film producer, for example, who makes a "blue movie" in England and then takes the negative to Denmark for development and ensuing commercial distribution is unlikely to be held to have committed an offence under English law, unless he is aware of plans to re-import copies for sale in Britain. Major English studios sometimes make two versions of feature films, a "hard" edition for continental distribution and a "soft" version suitable for home consumption. But the prosecution is not put to specific proof that obscene material is intended for publication in a manner that will infringe the Act, if such publication is a common-sense inference from the circumstances of production. In *R. v. Salter and Barton* two actors were charged with aiding and abetting by performing in an obscene movie, but they denied any knowledge of the producer's purpose or his distribution plans. The Court of Appeal held that ignorance could not avail them, although positive belief in a limited publication would have provided a defence. They could also have avoided liability if, more than two years before the prosecution was brought, they had taken some step to disassociate themselves from the continuing distribution of the film.[44]

The question of whether production or possession of magazines or

---

[42] *R. v. Fellows* [1997] 1 Cr. App. R. 244, CA.
[43] Broadcasting Act 1990, s. 162 and Sched. 15.
[44] *R. v. Salter & Barton* [1976] Crim. L.R. 514.

films that might be considered obscene if published on the home market is in breach of the law if they are destined for export abroad will depend upon their likely effect on readers and viewers in the country of distribution. The courts cannot apply British standards of morality in such cases: they must consider the standards prevailing in the country of export, and the class of persons in that country who are likely to obtain them. The House of Lords has accepted that in some cases of this kind the court will not have sufficient evidence to form an opinion: since the burden of proof rests upon the prosecution, there should be an acquittal. The same result should be achieved if evidence is received that the material is acceptable under the laws of the country for which it is destined.[45]

It is an offence in England to design, advertise or sell passwords to an obscene internet website, even if it is located abroad: the offending scenes are "published" under section 1(3)(b) when downloaded to the desk-top computers of password holders.[46] On the *Salter & Barton* principle it should not be an offence to store images on a website abroad, honestly believing that they would not be transmitted back to Britain.

The public good defence

Section 4 of the Act provides that the defendant to an obscenity charge "shall not be convicted"—despite the fact that he has been found to have published an obscene article—if "publication of the article in question is justified as being for the public good . . ." The ground upon which the defence may be made out is that publication, in the case of books and magazines, is "in the interests of science, literature, art or learning, or of other objects of general concern". The ground for exculpating plays and films is somewhat narrower: they must be "in the interests of drama, opera, ballet or any other art, or of literature or learning".[47] Section 3(1) of the Theatres Act 1968, the counterpart of section 4, was drafted in more restricted terms because the inclusion of "science" and of "other objects of general concern" was thought irrelevant to the protection of quality theatre: plays that could not be justified by reference to dramatic "art" or to "learning" were unlikely to be redeemed by any other feature. Television and radio programmes have the widest possible defences: the Broadcasting Act of 1990 combines the grounds of public good available for both books and films (Sched. 15, para. 5(2)).

---

[45] *Gold Star Publications Ltd v. DPP* [1981] 2 All E.R. 257.
[46] *R. v. Waddon*, April 6, 2000, CA.
[47] Law Commission, *Report on Conspiracy and Criminal Law Reform, No. 76*, HMSO, 1976, Chap. 3, paras 69–76.

"In the interests of"

The exculpatory grounds set out in section 4(1) might have been expressed in terms of "merit", but public good is not served by merit alone. An article may be "in the interests of" literature and learning without being either literary or learned. Section 4(1) looks to the advancement of cultural and intellectual values, and the expert opinion as to the "merits of an article" must be able to relate to the broader question of "the interests of" art and science. A publication of obscene primitive art may lack objective merit, but nonetheless may be defended on the grounds of its contribution to art history. (The DPP once considered a complaint about the ancient drainage ditch at Cerne Abbas, which forms the outline of a giant with a truly giant-size erection. In the interests of history, and the interests of the local tourist trade, he declined the request to allow grass to grow strategically over the offending area.)

The *Oz* editors contended that although their "Schoolkids Issue" had no particular literary or artistic brilliance, its publication was "in the interests of" literature and art because it gave creative youngsters the opportunity to display their potential talents in a national magazine. The end product was in the interests of sociology, not because of any profundity in its contents, but because sociologists were interested in the results of the experiment of giving schoolchildren an uncensored forum to air their grievances.

"Science, literature, art or learning"

The jury must decide as an issue of fact whether and to what extent obscene material serves the interests of any of these "intellectual or aesthetic values". The Court of Appeal has construed "learning" to mean "the product of scholarship . . . something whose inherent excellence is gained by the work of a scholar".[48] It follows that a publication cannot be defended under section 4 because of its value as a teaching aid, since this would require assessment of its effect upon readers' minds. A sex education booklet is not defensible because it provides good sex education, but if research has gone into its compilation, then no matter how ineffectual or misguided as an instructional aid, it possesses some inherent worth as "a product of scholarship". This result is hardly rational, but it represents a logical extension of the quest for intrinsic merit.

"Learning" overlaps with "science", which is defined in most dictionaries as "knowledge acquired by study". A publication may possess scientific interest if it adds to the existing body of knowledge or if it presents known facts in a systematic way. Recent legislation defines

---

[48] *Att.-Gen.'s Reference No. 3 of 1977* [1978] 1 W.L.R. 1123.

"science" to include the social sciences and medical research, and works with serious psychiatric, psychological or sociological interest would qualify for a public good defence. Studies of human sexual behaviour might contribute to scientific knowledge, and even pornographic fantasies, if genuine and collected for a serious sociological purpose, could legitimately be defended.

"Literature" is widely defined as "any printed matter", and the courts have been prepared to give copyright protection to the most pedestrian writing.[49] In the context of section 4, however, experts would be required to find some excellence of style or presentation to redeem the assumed tendency to corrupt. Excellence of prose style is not the only criterion for literary judgments, however, and books may be defended on the strength of wit, suspense, clarity, bombast or research if these qualities distinguish them in a particular genre of literature or in a particular period of literary history. Similarly, "art" comprehends the application of skill to any aesthetic subject, and is not conventionally confined to the production of beautiful images.[50]

In both the *Oz* and *Nasty Tales* cases underground comics were accepted as "art" for the purpose of a section 4 defence. One expert, the painter Felix Topolski, reminded the court that "unexpected elements, when brought together, produce an act of creation . . . I think one should accept that any visual performance if executed in earnest, is a branch of artistic creation."[51] In 1975 the New Zealand courts held that drawings of toilet fittings were artistic works—a conclusion that the surrealist school would never have doubted.[52]

"Other objects of general concern"

In *DPP v. Jordan* the House of Lords ruled that the psychiatric health of the community allegedly served by "therapeutic" pornography was not an "object of general concern" for the purposes of section 4. Their Lordships declined to elucidate the phrase, beyond affirming that it had a "mobile" meaning, which changed in content as society changes, and that:

- it referred to objects of general concern similar to those aesthetic and intellectual values specifically enumerated in section 4;

---

[49] See cases referred to in Chap. 6.
[50] *Hensher (George) Ltd v. Restawhile Upholstery (Lancs.) Ltd* [1976] A.C. 64. See generally P. H. Karlen, "What is Art? A Sketch for a Legal Definition", 94 L.Q.R. 383.
[51] Tony Palmer, *The Trials of Oz* (Blond & Briggs, 1971), pp. 170–171.
[52] *P. S. Johnson and Associates Ltd v. Bucko Enterprises* [1975] 1 N.Z.L.R. 311.

- it could not comprehend any object that was served by direct impact of publication on the mind of likely readers;

- it related to "inherent personal values of a less transient character assumed, optimistically perhaps, to be of general concern".[53]

There are many objects that survive these three tests. Among the "objects of general concern" advanced on behalf of *Lady Chatterley's Lover* were its ethical and Christian merits: "I suppose the section is sufficiently elastic to say that such evidence is admissible" remarked the judge, as he permitted the Bishop of Woolwich to testify to the book's contribution to human relations and to Christian judgments and values.[54] Other witnesses testified to its educational and sociological merits, and the editor of *Harper's Bazaar* was called as an expert on "popular literature". In the *Last Exit to Brooklyn* case the Court of Appeal conceded that "sociological or ethical merit" might be canvassed.[55] Other objects of general concern that have been relied upon at obscenity trials include journalism, humour, politics, philosophy, history, education and entertainment.

Expert evidence

Where a section 4 defence is available, experts can be called to give evidence, and indeed it is difficult to imagine the defence carrying any credibility without them. Strictly speaking, the Act requires the jury to conclude that the article is obscene before they consider the public good evidence, although in reality the impression made by the experts is likely to influence the decision on the obscenity issue. Expert opinion on the *effect* of the article is strictly inadmissible, but the Jesuitical distinction drawn by the courts between the "effect" of literature (which must not be canvassed) and its merits is wholly artificial. Literature and art have merit precisely *because* of their impact on the mind and their capacity to arouse emotions. Experts called under section 4 will inevitably give evidence about the theme and moral purpose of the work, and this evidence will be relevant, as a matter of common sense if not of law, to the question of whether it depraves or corrupts.

In certain cases the courts have permitted experts to be called by the prosecution and the defence to assist the jury in relation to the obscenity question if the subject-matter of the work or its impact upon a restricted class of consumer is not likely to be within the experience of the ordin-

---

[53] *DPP v. Jordan* [1977] A.C. 699 at 719 *per* Lord Wilberforce.
[54] Rolph, *Lady Chatterley*, p. 73.
[55] *R. v. Calder & Boyars*, n. 18 above, at 171.

ary person. When a book about the pleasures of cocaine was prosecuted for obscenity, scientific evidence was called to acquaint the jury with the property of the drug and its likely effects, so that they could decide (it being assumed they would not themselves have experienced cocaine) whether, if the book did encourage experimentation, the behaviour of the experimenters could be characterised as depraved and corrupt.[56] Similarly, when a company that had manufactured chewing gum cards for distribution to very young children was alleged to have depraved their minds with scenes of violence, child psychiatrists were called to give expert opinion as to the likely impact of the cards on the mind and behaviour of children in that age group.[57]

These precedents were taken further in the *Niggaz With Attitude* case. Dr Guy Culmberbatch, a former Home Office expert on the effects of pornography, had been commissioned by Island Records to carry out field research on the effects of listening to NWA albums, which he did, with the co-operation of large numbers of disc jockeys, school and university students and members of rap clubs. His study was helpful in identifying that they understood the lyrics in the context of American black experience, and not as any encouragement to antisocial behaviour in England. There is no reason in principle why this sort of evidence by social scientists should not be called by parties who are "showing cause" under section 3 as to why an article should not be destroyed, and are consequently not bound by the rules of evidence in criminal cases.

Prosecution practice

The enforcement of the obscenity laws is now directed largely at "hard core pornography". This has no legal definition, although juries are often told that "pornography is like an elephant. You cannot define it, but you know it when you see it."[58]

Despite the uncertainty of the law, there is some consistency in prosecution targets.[59] Descriptions of sexual deviations are much more likely to be attacked than accounts of "normal" heterosexual behaviour. In practice, prosecution authorities ignore the message of an article and concern themselves instead with the physical incidents photographed or described. Stories may degrade women by depicting them as objects to be manipulated for fun and profit, without attracting a prosecution. DPP officials have their lines to draw, and for many years they drew them

---

[56] *R. v. Skirving* [1985] 2 All E.R. 705.
[57] *DPP v. A. & BC Chewing Gum Ltd* [1968] 1 Q.B. 159.
[58] Judicial likening of obscenity to the definition of an elephant appears to have begun in 1964 with Justice Potter Stewart in *Jacobellis v. Ohio*, 378 U.S. 184 at 197.
[59] See Robertson, *Obscenity*, Chap. 10.

at the male groin: nudity was acceptable and even artistic, but to erect a penis was to provoke a prosecution. After the BBFC changed its guidelines in 2000 so as to permit 18R videos to show actual sexual intercourse, the DPP became more relaxed about erections on the inside pages of "top shelf" magazines, so long as nothing much happens. (For modern censors, it is now a case of Emission Impossible). The decision which caused the 18R revolution, and thus had a direct effect on liberalising "top shelf" erotica, was that of Hooper J. in *R. v. Video Appeals committee, ex p. BBFC.*[60]

The House of Lords has held that the arousing of libidinous thoughts falls squarely within the mischief aimed at by the Act,[61] but common-or-garden pornography is usually made the subject of forfeiture proceedings in which no conviction is recorded and no punishment (other than the destruction of the goods) can be imposed. These "section 3" proceedings (so called because the forfeiture code is contained in section 3 of the Obscene Publications Act 1959) serve little purpose other than to waste the time of the police and the local magistrates' courts. An order for forfeiture made by justices in one district is of no use as a precedent in others. The publishers of "top shelf" magazines cheerfully accept occasional stock losses, usually without even bothering to intervene (which section 3 entitles them to do) to argue that their goods should not be destroyed.

The essential quality of pornography is its breach of social taboos, hence its frequent references to behaviour that most consumers would never wish to emulate in real life—incest, bestiality, necrophilia, coprophilia and so on. The real obscenity of bestiality pictures lies not in their effects on readers' minds, but in the circumstances surrounding their production. Procuring women for intercourse with animals would seem to be an indefensible case of human exploitation, which could be prosecuted and punished under the Sexual Offences Act. The Cinematograph Films (Animals) Act of 1937 may also be relevant: it prohibits the exhibition of films the making of which involves cruelty to animals. This obscure piece of legislation is faithfully applied by the BBFC, which has ordered cuts in a number of Walt Disney films and videos with scenes that may have involved infliction of cruelty on animals. It should not, however, suppress films that are commentaries on cruel sports. The distributors of bizarre strains of pictorial pornography depicting extreme sexual violence, simulated necrophilia and human excretory functions are almost invariably convicted. Juries, inclined to support freedom for voyeurs, are less keen to promote freedom for ghouls.

---

[60] [2000] E.M.L.R. 850.
[61] *DPP v. Whyte* [1972] 3 All E.R. 12.

Drugs

There is no indication in the debates that surrounded the Obscene Publications Act that "obscenity" pertained to anything but matters of sex. United States legislation and practice is so confined, but in Britain the courts have interpreted the statutory definition of "obscene" to encompass encouragements to take dangerous drugs and to engage in violence.

The first case to push the notion of "obscenity" beyond the bounds of sex arose from forfeiture proceedings in 1965 against *Cain's Book*, a novel by Alex Trocchi that dealt with the life of a New York heroin addict. In the ensuing Divisional Court case, it was held that:

> "there was a real danger that those into whose hands the book came might be tempted at any rate to experiment with drugs and get the favourable sensations highlighted by the book."[62]

Cain's Book contained seductive descriptions of heroin consumption, but cannabis smoking cannot be classed as a "depraved and corrupt" activity:

> The publishers of some 20 books about prohibited drugs—*Cooking with Cannabis, The Pleasures of Cocaine, How to Grow Marijuana Indoors under Lights* and the like—were acquitted after a four-week trial at the Old Bailey. The prosecution failed to convince the jury that taking or cultivating cannabis was a depraved activity, given the widespread use of the drug, or that books that provided factual information about both the pains and the pleasures of harder drugs would be likely to encourage readers to experiment. Subsequently, however, the publishers of a pamphlet entitled *Attention Coke Lovers* were convicted because it exuded enthusiasm for "freebasing"—a highly dangerous method of inhaling a chemically-enhanced concentration. The Court of Appeal upheld the trial judge's decision to permit scientific experts to be called to explain the effects of cocaine to enable the jury to come to a proper conclusion as to the effect of the drug.[63]

The distinction between, on the one hand, providing factual information about drugs and, on the other, encouraging their use can be difficult to draw. Any publication that deals with drug-taking would be well advised to emphasise repeatedly both the physical dangers and the criminal penalties that attach to drug usage. The rule against "highlighting favourable sensations" has never been applied to novelists: the favourable descriptions of opium-taking in the *Count of Monte Cristo* and the

---

[62] *Calder v. Powell* [1965] 1 Q.B. 509 at p. 515.
[63] *R. v. Skirving* [1985] Q.B. 819.

apparently productive use of cocaine by Sherlock Holmes have not led
to obscenity prosecutions.

Violence

Any material that combines violence with sexual explicitness is a candidate for prosecution. Yet there are many gradations between a friendly
slap and a stake through the heart, and most "spanking" magazines
escape indictment. "Video-nasties", however, that combine pornography with powerful scenes of rape and terror have been successfully
prosecuted. More difficulty is experienced with the depiction of violence in non-sexual contexts. The Divisional Court in one case approved
the prosecution of a manufacturer of childrens' swap cards depicting
scenes of battle, on the theory that they were capable of depraving
young minds by provoking emulation of the violence portrayed.[64] In the
Last Exit case the Court of Appeal confirmed that the test of obscenity
could encompass written advocacy of brutal violence.[65] The difficulty
with these decisions is that they permit the conviction of publications
that are not normally regarded as "obscene", and that require expert
evidence to establish the existence of their corrupting potential. The
prevalence of violence in the mass media must raise serious doubts as
to whether any one publication should be singled out for prosecution
under an Act designed to suppress pornography.

Horror publications

In one respect the obscenity formula has been specifically adapted to
outlaw depictions of non-sexual violence that might prove harmful to
children. In 1955 Parliament sought to prohibit the importation and sale
of American "horror comics", which had been blamed by psychiatrists
for causing an upsurge in juvenile delinquency. The Children and
Young Persons (Harmful Publications) Act 1955 was designed, in the
words of the Solicitor-General, to prevent "the state of mind that might
be induced in certain types of children by provoking a kind of morbid
brooding or ghoulishness or mental ill-health".[66] It prohibits the printing, publication or sale of:

> "any book, magazine or other like work which is of a kind likely
> to fall into the hands of children or young persons and consists

---

[64] *DPP v. A & BC Chewing Gum Ltd* [1968] 1 Q.B. 159.
[65] *R. v. Calder & Boyars Ltd* [1969] 1 Q.B. 151.
[66] *Hansard*, H.C. Debs [1955] Vol. 539, Col. 6063. And see Martin Barker, *A Haunt
of Fears: The History of the British Horror Comics Campaign* (Pluto, 1984).

wholly or mainly of stories told in pictures (with or without the addition of written matter), being stories portraying

(a) the commission of crimes; or
(b) acts of violence or cruelty; or
(c) incidents of a repulsive or horrible nature;

in such a way that the work as a whole would tend to corrupt a child or young person into whose hands it might fall."

Although the measure was perceived as urgent and important at the time it was passed, there have been no prosecutions. Criminal proceedings require the consent of the Attorney-General, although this safeguard does not apply to imported comics, which may be seized and forfeited at the instance of customs officials. In 1976 customs officers prevailed upon Southampton magistrates to destroy the illustrated tales of Edgar Allan Poe, although the same bench ordered the release of *The Adventures of Conan the Barbarian* after evidence from a child psychiatrist that the Conan legend would be perceived as moral and even romantic by children inured to the adventures of *Starsky and Hutch*.

Child involvement

Undoubtedly the greatest concern over sexually explicit publications is the prospect of the involvement of young people, either as consumers or as models. This concern is reflected in the 1959 Act by its reference to the circumstances of the publication and the likely readership. The test of obscenity varies with the class of persons likely to read or see the publication. Instead of imposing censorship at the point of distribution, by making the actual sale of erotic material to children a crime, it must be established that the material on trial is *aimed* at impressionable young people. The case of the chewing gum cards illustrates how material that could be considered harmless if sold to adults by inclusion in cigarette cartons may be made the subject of obscenity proceedings if it is marketed in children's chewing gum packets.

No mercy can be expected in the courts for those who involve young persons, even with their consent, in modelling sessions for sexually explicit photographs. Section 1(1) of the Indecency with Children Act 1960 provides that:

"any person who commits an act of gross indecency with or towards a child under the age of fourteen, or who incites a child under that age to commit such an act with him or another, shall be liable on conviction on indictment to imprisonment . . ."

This provision would cover most cases in which children were encouraged to pose for erotic pictures, although the requirement of some indecent action "with or towards" the child may arguably exclude photographic sessions in which an indivdual child poses provocatively without any physical contact with, or direction from, the photographer or procurer.[67] The prosecution must prove that the defendant did not believe the child to be 14 or over.[68]

The Protection of Children Act 1978

The gap in statutory protection for children of 14 and 15 was closed in 1978 by the Protection of Children Act. Section 1 of the Act makes it an offence, punishable by up to 10 years in prison[69]:

> "(a) to take, or permit to be taken, or to make any indecent photograph or pseudo-photographs of a child (meaning in this Act under the age of 16); or
> (b) to distribute or show such indecent photographs or pseudo-photographs; or
> (c) to have in his possession such indecent photographs, with a view to their being distributed or shown by himself or others; or
> (d) to publish or cause to be published any advertisement likely to be understood as conveying that the advertiser distributes or shows such indecent photographs, or intends to do so."

A defendant "distributes" photographs within the meaning of this section if he merely shows them to another, without any desire for gain. "Indecent photographs" include films, film negatives and any form of video recording and "data which is stored on a computer disc or by other electronic means which is capable of conversion into a photograph". The advent of the internet is signalled by the awkward concept of the "pseudo-photograph" clumsily defined as "an image, whether made by computer graphics or otherwise howsoever, which appears to be a photograph". This phraseology forced the Court of Appeal to decide that a collage—a photograph of the head of a young girl sellotaped onto a photograph of a woman's body—was not within the section since it appeared to be (and was) two photos rather than one, although had it been photocopied then the image may have been within the Act.[70]

---

[67] *R. v. Sutton* [1977] 1 W.L.R. 1086, at 1089.

[68] *B. v. DPP* [2000] 2 W.L.R. 452.

[69] Increased from an original maximum of three years by s. 41 of the Criminal Justice and Court Services Act 2000.

[70] *Atkins v. DPP* [2000] 1 W.L.R. 1427.

Computer-generated images of different body parts may fall within section 7(8):

> "If the impression conveyed by a pseudo-photograph is that the person shown is a child, the pseudo-photograph shall be treated for all purposes of this Act as showing a child and so shall a pseudo-photograph where the predominant impression conveyed is that the person shown is a child notwithstanding that some of the physical characteristics are those of an adult".

The offences must be construed to relate to real and human children: obscene images of Rupert Bear (hero of the *Oz* trial) or of Bart Simpson, Rugrats and other cartoon juveniles are not prohibited, other than by the law of copyright.

The 1978 Act is effectively deployed against those who use computers to deliver child pornography. Anyone who consciously downloads such an image from the internet "makes" a photograph for the purposes of section 1(1)(a) and will be guilty if he deliberately prints them out, even if the internet site where they were uplinked is abroad.[71] (Ageing popstar Gary Glitter pleaded guilty to this offence in 2000, and received a four-month sentence for material kept for personal use.) Providing a "password" to access such data is a form of "showing" it.[72] The cases demonstrate that the courts will ignore technical or legislative distinctions in order to effectuate Parliament's intent to punish every new way in which sexual images of children may be exploited. These decisions prima facie breach Article 8 of the European Convention, which guarantees respect for privacy, but the interference will probably be justified "for the protection of health or morals, or for the protection of the rights and freedoms of others".

There is no defence to section 1(a) other than that the photographs are not indecent; or, if indecent, do not depict persons under 16; or that the accused in any event played no part in their production. The prosecution does not even have to prove that the defendant knew the child was under 16, and so paediatric evidence as to the age of the child is neither required nor admissible.[73] Section 1(d) does not even require the photographs on offer to be themselves indecent—an advertiser is guilty if his wording is "likely to be understood as conveying" a willingness to sell or show nude pictures of children within the prohibited age group. If the charge is laid under section 1(b) or (c), however, the distributor or exhibitor is entitled to an acquittal if he can establish on the balance of probabilities.

---

[71] *R. v. Bowden* [2000] 2 W.L.R. 1083.
[72] *R. v. Fellows* (1997) Cr. App. R. 244.
[73] *R. v. Land* [1998] 1 Cr. App. R. 301.

- that he had a legitimate reason for distributing or showing the photographs or (as the case may be) having them in his possession; or

- that he had not himself seen the photographs and did not know nor had any cause to suspect them to be indecent.[74] The defendant must show that he had no reason to suspect the photographs were indecent, *not* that he had no cause to expect they were indecent photographs of children.[75]

The test of indecency

The courts have been unable to provide a meaningful definition of "indecent", short of "offending against recognised standards of propriety" or "shocking, disgusting and revolting ordinary people". The leading authority in cases concerning photographs of children involved the decision that *Boys are Boys Again*, a book comprising 122 photographs of naked boys, was an indecent import. Mr Justice Bridge accepted that the publication was not obscene, and would not infringe the current standards of decency if it depicted naked children without sexual overtones. But he held that this publication, although borderline, lacked innocence:

" . . . the conclusion that I reach is that if the book is looked at as a whole . . . the very essence of the publication, the reason for publishing it, is to focus attention on the male genital organs. It is a series of photographs in the great majority of which the male genitals, sometimes in close-up, are the focal point of the picture . . . they aim to be interesting pictures of boys' penises . . . '."[76]

This precedent, although unreported, has been of crucial importance in limiting the Protection of Children Act offence to pictures with some element of lewdness or sexual provocation. It was read to the House of Commons by the Minister of State for the Home Office to underscore a promise that "indecency" would not be interpreted loosely: "that is exactly how I would expect the issue under the Bill to be decided" he said of Bridge J.'s approach "I think, frankly, that there is no danger that ordinary family snapshots, or legitimate sex education material,

---

[74] The Protection of Children Act 1978, s. 1(4).

[75] *R. v. Matrix* [1997] Crim. L.R. 901, CA.

[76] *Commissioners of Customs and Excise v. Sun & Health Ltd*, March 29, 1973 (unreported) Royal Courts of Justice, transcript, pp. 5 and 6.

would be caught by the terms of the Bill".[77] So when newsreader Julia Somerville's "ordinary family snapshots" of her children in the bath were processed by Boots and delivered, in an unpleasant breach of her family privacy, to the local police, no action (apart from leaking the story to the press) was taken. The *Sun & Health* case ruling was revived in 2001:

> The Saatchi gallery opened a photographic exhibition "I am a Camera", which was attended (at the instigation of *News of the World*) by Scotland Yard's paedophile squad. They threatened that unless the gallery removed certain photographs, they would seize them and prosecute the gallery. One picture showed a five-year-old boy urinating in the snow by the side of an alpine road, and the other showed him (with his sister) naked on a Caribbean beach. The latter was on the cover of an expensive book which had been published to coincide with the exhibition: its publisher was threatened with prosecution unless it was withdrawn from sale. The police claimed the pictures would be of interest to paedophiles, as undoubtedly they would. However, the DPP decided that no action could or should be taken: applying the *Sun and Health* test, they were not "indecent" because they had not been posed provocatively (the photographer, in fact, was the children's mother) and there was no element of lewdness or erotic detail in these "ordinary family snapshots". The DPP's decision was justified, shortly after it was made, by the Chief Justice's comments in *Smethurst* (see below). Other reasons given for not prosecuting included a concern that the exhibitor and the book publisher could raise a "legitimate reason" defence.[78]

The "legitimate reason" defence

In deciding whether the photograph is indecent the jury is not permitted to hear evidence about the defendant's motive for taking it. The only intention that is relevant is the deliberate intention to take a photograph: whether it is indecent depends solely upon whether the jury is satisfied that the resultant picture is a breach of recognised standards of propriety.[79] That decision, however, must at least be informed by the age of the child: this may play a part in the question of whether the picture is a breach of recognised standards of propriety. Thus a photograph of a topless female model in a provocative pose that may not be accounted

---

[77] *R. v. Graham-Kerr* (1989) 88 Cr. App. R. 302; *R. v. Smethurst, The Times*, April 13, 2001, CA.

[78] Lord Harris of Greenwich, May 18, 1978, *Hansard* Vol. 392, No. 81, col. 563 and see the Minister's speech during the third reading debate: "the test of indecency already exists to separate photographs which are offensive from those which are innocent or which have been taken with a clinical rather than a prurient approach". *Hansard*, H.L., Vol. 394, No. 103, col. 334.

[79] See *The Guardian*, March 10, 2001, pp. 3 and 16 and March 16, 2001, p. 1.

indecent if the model is above the age of consent may be held to infringe the Act once the jury realises that the model is 14—much younger than she looks.[80] It is doubtful whether expert evidence would be admitted as to the artistic merit of the photograph, unless this were advanced as a "legitimate reason" for showing or distributing it. There could be no objection in principle to such a defence being raised to justify an exhibition of photographs of historical interest, or pictures included in a documentary about the evils of child pornography. Photographic evidence of the torture or maltreatment of children may be highly indecent, but should not be the subject matter of a prosecution under this section where the purpose of the exhibition is legitimately to arouse anger or compassion.

The legitimate reason defence is new to the criminal law, but it has a potentially wide application. It should protect investigative journalists who acquire indecent photographs of children in order to expose a corruption racket, so long as they do not pay money to procure the taking of the photographs that would not have otherwise come into existence. What constitutes a "legitimate reason" is in every case a question of fact: the Court of Appeal conceded in 2000 that it would protect a genuine researcher, although "a measure of scepticism" would be appropriate towards academics who stock-pile such material.[81] The "legitimate reason" defence received an important acknowledgment by the CPS in 2001 when giving reasons for the refusal to prosecute the Saatchi gallery over its "I am a Camera" exhibition. The DPP accepted submissions made on behalf of the gallery that the artistic merit of the pictures provided a "legitimate reason" to exhibit them in a reputable art gallery and to publish them in an expensive (£42) art book recording the show. Expert evidence of artistic merit would clearly be relevant if a defendant wished to raise such a defence in court.

There is no logic at all in allowing a legitimate reason defence to a distributor or exhibitor, but not a taker, of photographs that are found to be indecent. The decision in *Graham-Kerr* that the circumstances of the photography and the motivation of the photographer are irrelevant means that a paediatrician who photographs children's genitalia for legitimate medical purposes has no defence to a prosecution. The "safeguard" is that a prosecution can be brought only by the DPP, but a bad law is never justified by the hope that it will be sensibly enforced. Doctors will not be prosecuted, but "artists" who pose children provocatively are at risk. Photographers have no defence if the jury finds their pictures indecent, unless they can establish that they took the picture by accident or that the child just happened to run in front of the camera. When the *Graham-Kerr* rule excluding *mens rea* was challenged as

[80] *R. v. Owen* (1988) 86 Cr. App. R. 291.
[81] *Atkins v. DPP* [2000] 1 W.L.R. 1427.

inconsistent with Articles 8 and 10 of the ECHR, the Court of Appeal agreed that "No one could possibly suggest that a family taking photographs of their own children (naked) in the ordinary way would be a situation where it would be appropriate to prosecute" but declined to reinterpret the legislation or declare it incompatible.[82] A strict liability offence was the only way to protect children from exploitation, although an "inappropriate prosecution" (such as was threatened by Scotland Yard against the Saatchi gallery) might well be held to infringe Article 10 and/or be stayed as an abuse of process.

Films

Section 7(2) of the Act defines "indecent photograph" to include "an indecent photograph comprised in a film", while section 7(3) provides:

> "Photographs (including those comprised in film) shall, if they show children and are indecent, be treated for all purposes of this Act as indecent photographs of children."

This section has complicated the task of the British Board of Film Classification when faced with feature films that include child actors in immodest or disgusting scenes. Such scenes are deemed, by section 7(3), to constitute "indecent photographs of a child" even if the child is not participating in, or even aware of, the indecency. A plot that calls for a child to discover parents making love may be difficult to film or to distribute without contravention of the Act, and the artistic merit or overall purpose will not redeem an offending scene. One orgy scene from the film *Caligula* was cut by the BBFC because among the onlookers were women suckling babies. The newborn infants were sleeping in blissful ignorance of the catamite revels, but technically the scene contravened the Act, because it was indecent and it depicted persons under 16. The Hollywood vogue for casting child actors and actresses in major "adult" movies means such films may require cuts before distribution in the United Kingdom, although much will depend on the cinematic merit of the film. In 1999 the BBFC courageously gave *Lolita* an "18" certificate: its scenes of pubescent sexuality were played by an actress over 16 and were not indecent in any exploitative sense, being redeemed by the integrity of the film (and the acting of Jeremy Irons). In the same year the BBFC finally agreed to classify *The Exorcist* as fit for video release despite some bad language from the "possessed" child: films which became classics (*The Exorcist* was released in 1973) cannot forever be denied the seal of BBFC approval.

---

[82] *R. v. Smethurst, The Times*, April 13, 2001.

Advertisements

Section 1(d) affects film and magazine titles, and requires careful vetting of advertising copy. Even if the product itself does not infringe the Act, "any advertisement likely to be understood as conveying that the advertiser distributes or shows such indecent photographs" may be prosecuted, without the benefit of a "legitimate reason" defence. Films with titles that evoke the thought of under-age sex will be difficult to publicise. In the week that the Act came into force, one West End cinema pointedly changed the name of its current offering from *Schoolgirls* to *18-Year-Old Schoolgirls*.

Possession

In 1988 Parliament created a new offence of *possessing* an indecent picture of a child (Criminal Justice Act, s, 160). This is another example of the law relating to obscenity extending to material confined to the privacy of the home, without publication or possession for gain. Another unattractive feature of the offence was added in 2000: the maximum penalty was increased to five years' imprisonment and/or an unlimited fine.[83] The defendant at least is permitted to raise the legitimate reason defence or to maintain that although the photograph was in his possession he had not viewed it and had no reason to suspect its indecency. He is also entitled to an acquittal if he can prove that the photograph was sent to him unsolicited "and that he did not keep it for an unreasonable time". This places a duty upon unwary recipients of child pornography in the post either to destroy it or to hand it in at their local police station. This offence is a candidate for attack under the Human Rights Act, although it may be doubted whether British and European judges would follow the lead of the Constitutional Court of South Africa, which struck down a prohibition on merely possessing indecent matter as being incompatible with constitutional guarantees of free speech and personal privacy.[84]

Procedures and penalties

The offence of obscenity on a conviction by a jury, carries a maximum term of three years imprisonment and an unlimited fine.

Defendants may elect to be tried in magistrates' courts, where the penalty is reduced to a maximum of six months and/or a fine of £5,000. Such an election is rarely made, because magistrates are prone to convict for this offence with little hesitation or regard for legal niceties.

---

[83] s. 41, Criminal Justice and Courts Service Act 2000.
[84] *Case v. Minister of Security* (1997) 1 B.H.R.C. 541.

Juries, on the other hand, can be reluctant to convict in cases that do not involve children, violence or animals. Prosecuting authorities, mindful of the difficulties of jury trial, prefer to use the forfeiture procedure laid down by section 3 of the Obscene Publications Act, which entitles them to seize under warrant a stock of obscene material and have it destroyed at the nearest magistrates' court. Any person claiming an interest in the material may contest its forfeiture, but the procedure has little deterrent effect: the case is brought against the material, rather than its publishers, and has no criminal consequence whatsoever. Section 3 is often used by police and prosecuting authorities as a device for avoiding jury trial. If a publisher wished to contest a section 3 seizure before a jury (at the risk of a jail sentence if convicted) he can invoke a parliamentary assurance that this wish will be granted.[85]

This is open to question whether section 3 forfeiture orders conform with the European Convention on Human Rights. Although States are entitled to use obscenity laws to protect the morals of their citizens, penalties must be proportionate to the aim of restricting freedom of expression only to the extent that is strictly necessary in a democratic society. In *Handyside v. U.K.* the European Court of Human Rights declined to find that section 3 was a breach of the Convention when it was used (with Handyside's consent) to test the lawfulness of circulating *The Little Red Schoolbook*, which gave controversial advice to schoolchildren about sex and drugs.[86] The decision might be otherwise if the forfeiture procedures were used to destroy original artwork. In 1988 the European Court upheld a Swiss decision that paintings held to be obscene when publicly exhibited should be deposited in a National Museum for safekeeping and limited viewing: the artist had been entitled to apply for their return, which he successfully did some years later. However, the court recognised a "special problem" in the confiscation of original artworks, and the implication from its decision is that a forfeiture order under section 3 requiring the destruction of such items would be an infringement of Article 10.[87]

The only two significant countries that still routinely jail first offenders for obscenity offences are Great Britain and the People's Republic of China. The Court of Appeal bound itself to send all pornographers to prison, irrespective of their circumstances, with a good deal of huffing, puffing and bluffing in 1982. ("When news of this judgment reaches Soho, we think it is likely that there will be a considerable amount of stocktaking within the next seventy-two hours, because if there is not, there is likely to be a depletion of the population of that

---

[85] Given by Sir Peter Rawlinson, the Solicitor-General, on July 7, 1964. See *Hansard*, col. 302, and Robertson, *Obscenity*, p. 106.

[86] *Handyside v. U.K.* [1976] E.H.R.R. 737.

[87] *Müller v. Switzerland* (1988) 13 E.H.R.R. 212.

area in the next few months"[88]). This overblown rhetoric is still followed, even by humane judges,[89] although the principle that the court should pass the shortest possible sentence consistent with its public duty means that pornographers spend less time in prison.[90] Severe fines might be a more sensible alternative. Those involved in making or distributing child pornography can always expect a substantial prison sentence. In addition, anyone convicted of possessing or distributing or smuggling indecent pictures of children is automatically placed on the sex offenders' register, and required to notify police of any changes of name or address. This is a punishment—registration will exclude them from jobs and include them in lists of potential suspects for other crimes—but it is one mandated by Parliament: the court has no discretion to make or to cancel such an order.[91]

The cinema and film censorship

Film censorship today operates on three different levels. The distributors of feature films may be prosecuted under the Obscene Publications Act if the Director of Public Prosecutions deems that audiences are likely to be "depraved and corrupted" by their offerings. Irrespective of the DPP's decision, district councils may refuse to license particular films for screening within their jurisdiction. Most councils rely upon the advice of the BBFC, which may insist upon cuts before certifying the films' fitness for the public screen or for certain age groups, or may refuse to issue any certificate at all. Councils may also limit the number of sex cinemas in their locality, or prohibit such cinemas altogether. Finally, customs authorities are empowered to refuse entry to any foreign film they choose to classify as "obscene". Neither theatre producers nor book publishers suffer institutional restrictions laid down by trade censors or local councillors, and the standards of acceptability imposed by these bodies are such that cinema censorship is more pervasive and more arbitrary than the limitations imposed upon many other forms of artistic expression. These standards are examined in Chapter 15. The present discussion is concerned only with the application of the obscenity law to films and video-cassettes. It was not until 1977, after ingenious private prosecutors had belaboured film distributors with the old common-law offence of holding indecent exhibitions, that the Obscene Publications Act was extended to cover the public screening

---

[88] *Holloway* [1982] 4 Cr. App. R. (S) 128.
[89] See the six month prison sentence for a first offence approved by the Chief Justice in *R. v. Ibrahim* [1998] 1 Cr. App. R. (S) 157.
[90] A more realistic approach is evident from *Tunnicliffe & Greenwood* [1999] 2 Cr. App. R. (S) 88. See also *Lloyd & Ristic* February 3, 1992, CA.
[91] Sex Offenders Act 1997, s. 1 and Sched. 1.

of feature movies.[92] In 1979 the Court of Appeal extended the Act to video cassettes by interpreting its wide language to include a form of entertainment that had not been foreseen when the Act was passed.[93]

Limitations on prosecution

The Criminal Law Act 1977 abolishes the common law offences, including the conspiracies to corrupt public morals and to outrage public decency, in relation to cinemas.[94] The consent of the DPP is required for any prosecution of a feature film, defined as "a moving picture film of a width of not less than sixteen millimetres", and no order may be made to forfeit such a film unless it was seized pursuant to a warrant applied for by the DPP.[95] The Law Commission recommended these restrictions on proceedings to ensure that uniform standards applied throughout the country, and to discourage vexatious or frivolous prosecutions.[96]

Public good defence

The public good defence provided for films by section 53(6) of the Criminal Law Act is narrower than that which applies to books and magazines, omitting the grounds of "science" and "other objects of general concern" in favour of those objects enumerated in the Theatres Act, namely the interests of "drama, opera, ballet or any other art, or of literature or learning". The Law Commission noted that "films have themselves an archival and historical value as social records, as well as being used for industrial, educational, scientific and anthropological purposes", and assumed that these merits would be canvassed under the head of "learning".[97] Cameramen who film contemporary horrors are providing evidence that will be "in the interests of" present and future scholarship. Expert evidence is admissible, and if a certified film were prosecuted, representatives of the BBFC could expatiate on the merits of the work. Such testimony might, in any event, be acceptable as evidence of fact: the BBFC certificate, screened at the commencement, would comprise part of the "article" on trial, and the jury would be entitled to an explanation of what it meant. In cases brought against horror movies, film critics have been permitted to testify to the merits

---

[92] Criminal Law Act 1977, s. 53.
[93] *Att.-Gen.'s Reference No. 5 of 1980* [1980] 3 All E.R. 816.
[94] See Criminal Law Act 1977, s. 53(3).
[95] *ibid.*, s. 53(2) and (5). The DPP's consent should be obtained before application for a summons: See *R. v. Angel* (1968) 52 Cr. App. Rep. 280; *Price v. Humphries* [1958] 2 Q.B. 353.
[96] Law Commission, *Report No. 76*, Part III, para. 78.
[97] *ibid.* at paras 69–76.

of the film as cinematic art, its technical qualities, its dramatic effects, its message or moral, and its value as popular entertainment. Not always successfully: when *Guardian* film critic Derek Malcolm was called to explain the merits of a video nasty entitled *Nightmares in a Damaged Brain* he claimed that it was "very well executed". "So was the German invasion of Belgium" snapped the judge.

Television and radio

The 1990 Broadcasting Act applies the Obscene Publications Act to television and radio in much the same way as it has been applied to feature films. The section 4 defence is available (in a wider formulation than that which applies to plays and films) and no prosecution may be brought or forfeiture ordered except by or with the consent of the DPP. The censorship constraints on broadcasting are dealt with in detail in Chapter 16.

THEATRE CENSORSHIP

In 1737 Sir Robert Walpole, goaded beyond endurance by caricatures of himself in plays of Henry Fielding, introduced legislation empowering the Lord Chamberlain to close down theatres and imprison actors as "rogues or vagabonds" for uttering any unlicensed speech or gesture. Thereafter political satire was banned or heavily censored for "immorality", and as late as 1965 the Lord Chamberlain would not allow a stage version of Fielding's *Tom Jones* to be performed with bedroom scenes.[98] In 1843 a new Theatres Act was passed to consolidate the Lord Chamberlain's power to prohibit the performance of any stage play "whenever he shall be of opinion that it is fitting for the preservation of good manners, decorum or the public peace to do so".

The Lord Chamberlain's office remained eager to impose political, as well as moral, censorship, until its powers were abolished in 1968. Commercial managements accepted political discipline without demur but State-subsidised companies had no profits at stake, and the RSC launched an all-out attack after the Lord Chamberlain objected to one of its plays on the grounds that it was "beastly, anti-American, and left-wing". In 1966 the Joint Committee on Theatre Censorship commenced its deliberations. Dramatists, State theatre companies and drama critics overwhelmingly demanded the abolition of the Lord Chamber-

---

[98] Richard Findlater, *Banned!—A Review of Theatrical Censorship in Britain.* (MacGibbon & Kee, 1967) p. 175. See Nicholas de Jongh, *Politics Privacy and Perversions—The Censoring of the English Stage 1901–1968* (2000).

lain's powers, and convinced the Joint Committee that pre-censorship provided a service neither to playgoers nor to dramatic art.[99] Its recommendations were embodied in the 1968 Theatres Act. The 1843 Act was repealed and the test of obscenity installed as the sole basis for theatre censorship.

> ". . . a performance of a play shall be deemed to be obscene if, taken as a whole, its effect is such as to tend to deprave and corrupt persons who are likely, having regard to all relevant circumstances, to attend it."

Decisions on the interpretation of section 1 of the Obscene Publications Act now apply with equal force to stage plays, with the exception of the "item-by-item" test: all performances, even of revues comprising separate sketches, will not infringe the law by reason only of one salacious scene, unless it is sufficiently dominant or memorable to colour the entire presentation. Obscenity is defined by reference to the circumstances of the staging and to its impact upon an audience more readily ascertainable than readership for books on general sale. A more stringent test would apply to West End theatres, trading from tourists and coach parties, than to "fringe" theatres or clubs with self-selecting patronage.

Plays defined

The Theatres Act applies to "plays", defined as:

> "(a) any dramatic piece, whether involving improvisation or not, which is given wholly or in party by one or more persons actually present and performing and in which the whole or a major proportion of what is done by the person or persons performing, whether by way of speech, singing or acting, involves the playing of a role; and
>
> (b) any ballet given wholly or in part by one or more persons actually present or performing, whether or not it falls within paragraph (a) of this definition."

Reference to "improvisation" includes ad libbing and extempore performances, although the requirement of role play excludes the stand-up comedian, unless the routine consists of playing different characters in a series of sketches. It would exclude some variety performances, although music-hall numbers usually require melodramatic characterisations that, arguably, involve the "playing of a role". "Ballet" is broadly

---

[99] *Report of the Joint Committee on Censorship of the Theatre* (HMSO, 1967) H.C. 255; H.C. 503.

defined in the *Oxford English Dictionary* as the "combined performance of professional dancers on the stage" and subsection (b) expressly excludes the requirement of role play. It may therefore be more embracing than the 1843 Act, which applied only to dancing that was set within some dramatic framework.

In *Wigan v. Strange*, a case under the 1843 Act, the High Court held that whether a "ballet divertissement constituted an entertainment of the stage" was a finely balanced question of fact:

> "A great number of females, it seems, dressed in theatrical costume, descend upon a stage and perform a sort of warlike dance: then comes a *danseuse* of a superior order, who performs a *pas seul*. If this had been all nobody would have called the performance a stage play. But the magistrate adds that the entrance of the *première danseuse* was preceded by something approaching to pantomimic action. The thing so described certainly approaches very nearly to a dramatic performance: and it is extremely difficult to tell where the line is to be drawn."[1]

The Law Commission has doubted whether displays of tribal dancing could be classed as "ballet", and ballroom or discotheque performances, even by professional troupes of dancers, would fall outside the definition.[2]

The Act applies to every "public performance", defined to include any performance "which the public or any section thereof are permitted to attend, whether for payment or otherwise", and any performance held in a "public place" within the meaning of the Public Order Act 1936, namely:

> ". . . any highway, public park or garden, any seat bench, and any public bridge, road, lane, footway, square, court, alley or passage, whether a throughfare or not; and includes any open space to which, for the time being, the public are permitted to have access, whether on payment or otherwise."[3]

This would cover street theatre, open-air drama and "end of the pier" shows. It would also include performances in restaurants,[4] public houses,[5] buses and railway carriages,[6] and possibly boats on public

---

[1] *Wigan v. Strange* (1865) L.R. 1 C.P. 175, *per* Erle C.J.

[2] Law Commission, *Report No. 76*, Part III, para. 93.

[3] Theatres Act 1968, s. 18 and Public Order Act 1936, s. 9.

[4] *R. v. Hochlauser* (1964) 47 W.W.R. 350; *R. v. Benson* (1928) 3 W.W.R. 605.

[5] *R. v. Mayling* [1963] 1 All E.R. 687.

[6] *R. v. Holmes* (1853) Dears. C.C. 207 at 209. *Langrish v. Archer* (1882) 10 Q.B.D. 44.

hire.[7] But the Act does not apply to any performance "given on a domestic occasion in a private dwelling" or to a performance "given solely or primarily" for the purposes of rehearsal, or for the making of a film, a television or radio broadcast, or a performance to be included in a programme service.[8] Whether the occasion was "domestic" or whether the performance was "primarily" for rehearsal or recording purposes are questions of fact for the jury. Public "previews" of a play prior to its opening night would not be characterised as exempted rehearsals if tickets were issued to the general public, albeit at a reduced rate. Similarly, out of town "try outs" could not be classed as "rehearsals", although they are designed to test audience reaction and frequently occasion script changes prior to the West End run. A performance staged primarily for the purposes of recording or filming or broadcasting is exempt from the operation of the Act, even where a large audience is invited to supply appropriate applause. Outrages to public decency that take place at rehearsals and filmed performances could still be prosecuted at common law.[9]

Local councils retain control over the front of house displays, which they require to remain within the realms of public decency, and they are entitled to withhold licences from theatres that do not comply with fire regulations or other health and safety requirements. They are not, however, permitted to impose any licence conditions relating to the content of plays performed in the theatre. In 1987 Westminster Council contemplated action against the Institute of Contemporary Arts for staging a theatrical performance that featured a "female Lenny Bruce", but had to accept that it could not use its licensing powers as a back door method of censorship. Enforcement of the ban in the 1899 Indecent Advertisements Act on "any written matter which is of an indecent or obscene nature" may depend on the place of exhibition. The Royal Court theatre in Sloane Square bill-boarded Mark Ravenhill's *Shopping and Fucking*, but the play transferred to Shaftesbury Avenue in a blaze of neon asterisks, as *Shopping and F******g*.

Public good defence

The Joint Committee recommended that "every effort should be made to see the trial takes place in circumstances that are likely to secure a proper evaluation of all the issues at stage including the artistic and

---

[7] *DPP v. Verrier* [1991] 4 All E.R. 18 sets out the test to be applied to determine whether an area is a public place.

[8] Theatres Act 1968, s. 7.

[9] Section 7(2), which exempts rehearsals, etc., from the provision of the Theatres Act, also removes from these occasions the protection of s. 2(4), namely the restriction on proceedings at common law.

literary questions involved."[10] A public good defence contained in section 3 admits expert evidence to justify stage performances that are "in the interests of drama, opera, ballet or any other art, or of literature or learning". The "merit" to which experts must testify is not of the play itself, but of "the giving of the performance in question", so that pedestrian writing may be redeemed by the excellence of acting, direction or choreography. Experts who have not witnessed the performance may nonetheless testify to its dramatic, literary or educative value by reference to the script, which under section 9 "shall be admissible as evidence of what was performed and of the manner in which the performance . . . was given."

Limits on police powers

Police have no power to close down the performance, or to seize programmes, scripts or items of stage property unless they feature writing or representations that contravene the Obscene Publications Act. Their power is limited solely to attendance, and is enforceable by warrant issued under section 15 by a justice who is given reasonable grounds to expect that the performance will infringe the Act.

Liability for prosecution

The Theatres Act applies to any person who, whether for gain or not, "presented or directed" an obscene performance. In *R. v. Brownson*, the defendants "presented" and "directed" by their actions in commissioning the script, engaging the cast, directing rehearsals, organising the performances, managing the premises and promoting the production.[11] Although rehearsals themselves fall outside the scope of the Act, a director will be liable for scenes prepared under his instruction after opening night, even though his association with the production may have ended. Section 18(2) provides that a person shall be taken to have directed a performance of a play given under his direction notwithstanding that he was not present during the performance. A director is not responsible, however, for obscenity introduced after his departure: the Act applies to "an obscene performance", and imposes liability only on those who have presented or directed *that* performance. Promoters, on the other hand, may be vicariously liable for obscenity inserted without their knowledge if the play is presented under their auspices. The wording of section 2(2) suggests strict liability, and in *Grade v. DPP*, a case under the 1843 Act, it was held that a promoter "presented" a play with unlicensed dialogue, although the offending words had been inserted

---

[10] *Report on Censorship*, para. 50.
[11] *R. v. Brownson* [1971] Crim. L.R. 551.

without his knowledge and without any negligence on his part.[12] Producers who act in a personal capacity are more vulnerable than those who operate through a corporate structure, in which case section 16 imposes liability only on those who act knowingly or negligently.

Actors will not be liable for any offence arising from participation in an obscene performance unless the obscenity arises from their own deviation from the script, whereupon they become the "director" of their own unrehearsed obscenity. Section 18(2) provides:

(a) a person shall not be treated as presenting a performance of a play by reason only of his taking part therein as a performer

(b) a person taking part as a performer in a performance of a play directed by another person shall be treated as a person who directed the performance if without reasonable excuse he performs otherwise than in accordance with that person's direction . . .".

What constitutes "reasonable excuse" is a question of fact, and actors unable to control themselves in shows requiring simulated sex acts might perhaps plead automatism or provocation. The actors' union, Equity, insists that theatre managements give written notice of any scenes of nudity or sexual simulation prior to the contract of engagement.

The Theatres Act makes no reference to the liability of dramatists. The Solicitor-General advised the Joint Committee that an obscene playscript would constitute an "article" within the meaning of section 1(2) of the Obscene Publications Act.[13] A dramatist "publishes" a playscript by giving it to a producer, but it does not become an "obscene article" unless it is likely to deprave the people who read it—*i.e.* members of the theatre company, and not the theatre audience, who do not see "the article" (*i.e.* the script itself) but the play, which is not an "article" and is not "published" to them by the dramatist. Prosecution under the Obscene Publications Act would therefore be unlikely to succeed, and an author cannot normally be said to "present or direct" a performance that is contrary to the Theatres Act. It follows that dramatists are liable only if their script calls for blatant obscenity or if they assist in some other way to mount a performance that is likely to deprave and corrupt.

Evidence

Section 10 empowers senior police officers to order the presenter or director of a play to produce a copy of the script on which the perform-

[12] *Grade v. Director of Public Prosecutions* [1942] 2 All E.R. 118.
[13] *Report on Censorship*, p. 54.

ance is based. "Script" is defined in section 9(2) as the text of any play, together with stage directions for its performance. This script becomes admissible as evidence both of what was performed and of the manner in which the performance was given, thereby ensuring that courts are not obliged to rely upon police recollections of dialogue and action. Neither the effect nor the merit of drama can be fully appreciated from textual study, but there is an evidential obstacle to restaging the performance for court proceedings. In *R. v. Quinn and Bloom* the Court of Appeal rejected the film of a striptease performance taken three months after the date of the offence, because there was no guarantee that the reconstruction exactly mirrored the performance on the date charged in the indictment.[14] *Quinn*'s case was a disorderly-house charge, which carried no public good defence, and it may be that the rule would be relaxed in a Theatres Act prosecution if the defence of dramatic merit were invoked. Comparative evidence has been admitted under section 14 of the Obscene Publications Act,[15] and reconstructions of accidents for the benefit of the court are common in civil cases.[16] A restaged performance might be inadmissible on the question of obscenity on the occasion charged, but it would be highly relevant to a jury's assessment of theatrical merit.

The *Romans in Britain* prosecution

In 1981 a private prosecution was brought against Michael Bogdanov, a National Theatre director, charging that he had procured an act of gross indecency between two actors on the stage of the Olivier Theatre as part of a scene in the play *The Romans in Britain*, contrary to section 13 of the Sexual Offences Act 1956. This was a bold attempt to sidestep provisions of the Theatres Act that require the Attorney-General's consent to any prosecution of a stage play, and to avoid the defences that would otherwise be available under that legislation, notably the strict test of obscenity and the public good defence. The prosecution, in the event, collapsed in mid-trial for technical reasons (a not uncommon risk in private prosecutions) and reportedly left the prosecutrix with a large bill in legal costs. It did, however, occasion some concern in theatrical circles. The Theatres Act does not protect persons connected with a play from prosecution for actual criminal offences simply because they happen to be committed on stage. What it was intended to protect them against, with the possible and very narrow exception relating to section

---

[14] *R. v. Quinn & Bloom* [1962] 2 Q.B. 245.

[15] *R. v. Penguin Books* [1961] Crim. L.R. 176; see Rolph, *Lady Chatterley*, p. 127.

[16] See *Gould v. Evans & Co.* [1951] 2 T.L.R. 1189 and *Buckingham v. Daily News* [1956] 2 Q.B. 534.

13 of the Sexual Offences Act, is subjection to any form of legal censorship other than that provided for by the Theatres Act itself.

The *Report of the Joint Committee on Censorship of the Theatre* specifically recommended "that no criminal prosecution (whether under statute or common law) arising out of the performance of a play should take place without the order of the Attorney-General having been first obtained."[17] This was to secure "the prevention of frivolous prosecutions" and to ensure the "most important" principle that "there should be an absolutely uniform application of the law throughout the country". When the Bill received its second reading in the House of Commons, its proposer assured the House that 'No prosecution may take place without the consent of the Attorney-General. We considered this necessary to prevent vexatious or frivolous prosecutions by outraged individuals or societies and to ensure uniformity of enforcement."[18] In the course of the debate this passage was approved and adopted by the Government spokesman (the Secretary of State for Home Affairs), who noted that "It would be particularly oppressive if a prosecution were otherwise launched . . . Those concerned with the presentation of plays are entitled to the protection which the Attorney-General's consent gives."[19] This position was maintained during the Bill's passage in the Lords, where the Government spokesman noted that the Attorney was obliged to read a play of which complaint had been made and to ask himself the question "Is it in the public interest that there should be a prosecution here?".[20] Section 8 of the Theatres Act duly provides that proceedings shall not be instituted "except by or with the consent of the Attorney-General."

When *The Romans in Britain* was first performed at the National Theatre there was considerable criticism and comment about a scene that called for a simulated homosexual rape, perpetrated by three Roman soldiers upon a young Druid priest. Mrs Mary Whitehouse, the "clean up" campaigner, asked the Attorney-General to prosecute under the Theatres Act: the DPP investigated, and reported that no prosecution would be likely to succeed. The Attorney refused his consent to allow a private prosecution to go forward, whereupon Mrs Whitehouse sent her solicitor to view the play, and he convinced a magistrate to issue a summons against Bogdanov under section 13 of the Sexual Offences Act. This section is directed at male persons who masturbate themselves or others in public toilets and parks. It punishes men who procure the commission of acts of gross indecency in public. The allegation against Michael Bogdanov was that he, being a male, "procured" a male actor

[17] H.C. 355, H.C. 503, para. 48.
[18] Mr C. R. Strauss, February 23, 1968. *Hansard*, Vol. 759, col. 830.
[19] *ibid.* at col. 866.
[20] Lord Stow Hill, House of Lords, June 20, 1968. *Hansard*, col. 964.

playing the part of a Roman soldier to commit an act of gross indecency with another male, namely the actor playing the young Druid. The artificiality of the proceedings is demonstrated by the fact that had any of the participants been female, section 13 could not have been applicable.

The prosecutrix had discovered a loophole in the law, applicable in a very limited way to plays directed by males that contain scenes calling for simulation of homosexual activity that a jury might find to be "grossly indecent". Although the intention of Parliament was to abolish all residual offences in relation to the staging of plays, the section of the Theatres Act designed to achieve this was not comprehensively drafted. It abolished common law conspiracy offences, obscene and blasphemous libel and the like, but it overlooked the existence of s. 13.[21] It could be argued that the prosecution was so obviously artificial that it would be oppressive to allow it to proceed, or that the Theatres Act by implication excluded a prosecution under section 13 where the purpose of the proceedings was to effect an act of censorship of drama.[22] This interpretation now had added force by application of section 3 of the 1998 Human Rights Act, which requires statutes to be interpreted "so far as possible" to conform with free speech guarantees. These issues have yet to be resolved, and the collapse of *The Romans in Britain* prosecution makes that case an unsatisfactory precedent. The judge held that the prosecution had presented prima facie evidence of an section 13 offence. Had the case continued, the defence would have argued that even if section 13 were applicable, no offence had been committed by staging the play, because there was no act of "procuration" by the director. The acts and dialogue that formed the basis of the charge took place by agreement between the author, the director, the actors and others. A person who does something from his or her own free will "and without any force or persuasion on the part of any other person cannot be said to have been procured . . . ."[23] At the committal proceedings Sir Peter Hall described how the scene was the result of a consensus between the parties involved and refuted the suggestion that the director had exerted any pressure or persuasion upon the actors.[24]

Section 13 offences are committed for purposes of sexual gratification in circumstances that admit of no argument or ambiguity. The sex scene in *The Romans in Britain* was simulated in circumstances, and with a

---

[21] See Theatres Act 1968, s. 2(4).

[22] It is apparent from a review of the Joint Report and the debates that Parliament intended the Theatres Act to "cover the field" of possible criminal offences committed in respect of the performance of plays. Neither the Law Officers (at p. 54 of the Joint Report) nor the Home Office (p. 106) suggested that s. 13 of the Sexual Offences Act could be an appropriate charge.

[23] *R. v. Christian* (1913) 78 J.P. 112.

[24] For an account of this case, see Geoffrey Robertson, *The Justice Game* (1998, Vintage), Chap. 7.

purpose, that negated the allegation of indecency.[25] The prosecution evidence was that the act of gross indecency consisted in one male actor holding his penis in an erect position, advancing across the stage and placing the tip of the organ against the buttocks of the other actor. This was the testimony of Mrs Whitehouse's solicitor, who had been seated, appropriately enough, in the gods—some 70 yards from the stage. He admitted, under cross-examination, that he may have mistaken the tip of the penis for the actor's thumb adroitly rising from a fist clenched over his groin. Shortly afterwards the prosecution collapsed, relieving the jury from further consideration of a "thumbs up" defence, which might have provided a complete answer to the charge.

INDECENCY LAWS

The obscenity laws are designed to ban material that is likely to cause social harm. Indecency, on the other hand, is not concerned with "harm" in any demonstrable sense, but rather with the outrage to public susceptibilities occasioned by unlooked-for confrontations with unseemly displays.

Obscenity is punished because it promotes corruption, "indecency" because it is a public nuisance, an unnecessary affront to people's sense of propriety. For the most part, the indecency laws will not affect freedom of expression or art. They are generally confined to maintaining decorum in public places. However, the prohibitions on sending indecent material through the post may affect the distribution of books and magazines, and the ban on importation of indecent articles was continually used to stop controversial feature films from entering the country until the European Court intervened in 1986 (see p. 160). The most important aspect of "indecency" as a test for censorship does not derive from the criminal law at all, but from the statutory duty imposed on broadcasting bodies to ensure that anything offensive to decency is not broadcast on commercial radio or television. The legal definition can become relevant for the purpose of contesting their rulings.

The test of indecency

"Indecency" has been defined by the courts as "something that offends the ordinary modesty of the average man . . . offending against reco-

---

[25] Even if the motive of sexual gratification is proven, the assault must be "accompanied with circumstances of indecency on the part of the defendant". *Beal v. Kelley* [1951] 2 All E.R. 763. No act can be divorced from the circumstances in which it takes place. See *R. v. George* [1956] Crim. L.R. 52; *Wiggins v. Field* [1968] Crim. L.R. 503; 112 S.J. 656; *Abrahams v. Cavey* [1968] 1 Q.B. 479, and *R. v. Armstrong* (1885) 49 J.P. 745.

gnised standards of propriety at the lower end of the scale".[26] In *Knuller v. DPP*, Lord Reid added: "Indecency is not confined to sexual indecency; indeed it is difficult to find any limit short of saying that it includes anything which an ordinary decent man or woman would find to be shocking, disgusting or revolting."[27] However, the courts recognise that minimum standards of decency change over time, and that "public decency must be viewed as a whole"; and the jury should be "invited, where appropriate, to remember that they live in a plural society, with a tradition of tolerance towards minorities."[28] This consideration assumes importance in those cases where the allegedly offensive article is destined for a restricted group whose right to receive material of minority interest may overcome the adverse reaction of jurors who do not share the same proclivities.

"Indecency" is not an objective quality, discoverable by examination as if it were a metal or a drug. In some cases courts have been prepared to accept that the context of publication may blunt the offensiveness of particular words or phrases:

> *Wiggins v. Field* arose from a public reading of Allan Ginsberg's poem "America", which included the line "Go fuck yourself with your atom bomb". The reader was charged with using "indecent language" in contravention of a local byelaw, but the Divisional Court said that the case ought never to have been brought. "Whether a word or phrase was capable of being treated as indecent language depended on all the circumstances of the case, the occasion, when, how and in the course of what it was spoken and perhaps to a certain extent what the intention was." It decided that in the work of a recognised poet, read without any intention of causing offence, the word "fuck" could not be characterised as "indecent".[29]

That this question may assume crucial importance is illustrated by *Attorney-General, ex rel. McWhirter v. IBA*. The Independent Broadcasting Authority, required by statute to ensure so far as possible that television programmes do not include anything that "offends against good taste or decency", defended its decision to screen tasteless scenes in a programme about avant-garde film-maker Andy Warhol on the ground that the dominant effect of the film was not offensive. The Court of Appeal agreed that the film "taken as a whole" was not offensive: it depicted "indecent incidents", but "whether an incident is indecent

---

[26] *R. v. Stanley* [1965] 1 All E.R. 1035 at 1038.

[27] *Knuller v. DPP* [1973] A.C. 435 at 458.

[28] *ibid.*, at 495, *per* Lord Simon of Glaisdale.

[29] *Wiggins v. Field* (1968) 112 S.J. 656; [1968] Crim. L.R. 503. For a similar approach in relation to pictures displayed in an avant-garde gallery, see *In The Appeal of Marsh* (1973) 3 D.C.R. (N.S.W.) 115.

must depend upon all the circumstances, including the context in which the alleged indecent matter occurs."[30]

The question is whether "ordinary decent people" would be horrified, not at the publication itself, but by all the circumstances of its exposure.[31] This approach is consonant with the purpose of indecency offences: "the mischief resides not so much in the book or picture *per se* as in the use to which it is put . . . what is in a real case a local public nuisance."[32]

There is no measure of agreement about the extent to which the notion of indecency in law pertains to matters other than sex. It is usually used to denote sexual immodesty, which would exclude some publications that fall within the narrower statutory definition of "obscene". On the other hand, descriptions of drug-taking or brutal violence might be perceived as breaches of recognised standards of propriety, along with the expression of extreme social, political or religious viewpoints. Violence coupled with eroticism, such as sado-masochism and flagellation, is clearly within the definitions. In 1992 Customs and Excise obtained a jury conviction in relation to importation of a video film of pit bull terriers fighting brutally to the death. The indecency, and indeed obscenity, of the film was doubtless found in its tendency to encourage the keeping and organisation of fights involving these dogs, which had been made illegal in the United Kingdom after recent tragic incidents.

The indecent article must infringe current community standards. A "community standard" is something that emerges from the consensus reached in a jury deliberation: it is neither a fact capable of proof nor an idea that can be canvassed by experts. Where the question of indecency turns on the circumstances or meaning of a publication, however, some assistance may be provided. In some cases expert opinion has been introduced as testimony of fact, to explain the reputation of authors and artists and to provide general information about the work at issue. In 1977 customs officers seized a number of books about classic art edited by international experts, despite the fact that many of the original pictures had been displayed at public galleries in England. Art critics testified to the standing of the editors and the artists, and gave details of a recent exhibition of some of the offending works at the Victoria and Albert Museum. In the same year a professor of English literature traced for a court the etymology of the allegedly indecent word "bollocks", from the literal meaning of "testicles", which appeared in early editions of the Bible (the King James edition replaced it by "stones"), to its modern colloquial meaning of "rubbish" or "nonsense". The promoters of the record album *Never Mind the Bollocks,*

---

[30] [1973] Q.B. 629, especially at 659.
[31] *Crowe v. Graham* (1968) 41 A.J.L.R. 402 *per* Windeyer J.
[32] *Galletly v. Laird* (1953) S.C. (J.) 16 *per* Cooper L.J. at 26.

Here's the Sex Pistols were cleared of displaying an indecent advertise-ment, thereby relieving them from changing the title to *Never Mind the Stones, Here's the Sex Pistols.*

Indecency offences

It is an offence to deal with indecent articles in the following circum-stances.

Using the post

Section 11 of the Post Office Act 1953 (now section 85 of the Postal Services Act 2000) prohibits the enclosure in a postal packet of "any indecent or obscene print, painting, photograph, lithograph, engraving, cinematograph film, book, and written communication, or any indecent or obscene article whether similar to the above or not." The penalty is a fine of up to £5,000 in the magistrates' court, or up to 12 months' imprisonment as well as a fine if prosecuted at a Crown Court. The prohibition applies whether or not the posting is solicited, and there is no public good defence available. In practice, prosecutions are generally confined to cases where complaints are made about unsolicited mail-ings, or where packages containing erotic magazines have broken open in the course of mailing. The possibility of prosecution is an irritant to publishers with mail order business: some, to be on the safe side, deliver their goods by rail, where there is no equivalent prohibition, although a much higher theft rate.

Section 4 of the 1971 Unsolicited Goods and Services Act provides:

> "A person shall be guilty of an offence if he sends or causes to be sent to another person any book, magazine or leaflet (or advertising material for any such publication) which he knows or ought reas-onably to know is unsolicited and which describes or illustrates human sexual techniques."

There is some ambiguity in the meaning of "human sexual tech-niques". The clause originally proscribed "sexual techniques", the word "human" being added at the insistence of the Ministry of Agriculture to protect its flow of breeding information to farmers. There was another ambiguity—was it essential for the "book magazine or leaflet" *itself* to describe human sexual techniques, or did the words in parentheses make it an offence for a leaflet merely to advertise a book about such tech-niques? The Divisional Court opted for the latter interpretation in a case where the unsolicited letter announced the firm's catalogue of books dealing with human sexuality without actually describing or illustrating either the catalogue or the books listed in it. The court ruled:

"It is clearly within the mischief of this legislation that there should be a prohibition of advertising material of that kind, even though the advertising material does not of itself contain illustrations or descriptions of human sexual techniques."[33]

Public display

The Indecent Displays (Control) Act of 1981 makes it an offence to display indecent matter in, or so as to be visible from, any public place. A place is "public", for the purposes of the Act, if members of the public have access to it, although it loses this quality if persons under 18 are refused admission. It also loses its character as a public place if access is by payment in order to see the indecent display, or the place is a shop with a prominent exterior display of a notice in the following terms:

> "WARNING. Persons passing beyond this notice will find material on display which they may consider indecent. No admittance to persons under 18 years of age."

The prohibition on the public display of indecency contained in this legislation does not apply to:

- television broadcasting or programme services;
- exhibitions inside art galleries and museums;
- exhibitions arranged by, or in premises occupied by, the Crown or local authorities;
- performances of a play;
- films screened in licensed cinemas.

The Act provides severe penalties for infringement, but its provisions have been much less dramatic in controlling indecent displays than the licensing powers given to local councils in the Local Government (Miscellaneous Provisions) Act 1982. These powers enable local councils to prescribe conditions to regulate displays and advertising of licensed sex shops and sex cinemas, and to withdraw licences if the conditions (which invariably prohibit public display of indecent matter) are breached. The prospect that the shop will be closed down is a more effective deterrent than the possibility of prosecution.

There are some surviving local bylaws and nineteenth-century police "town clauses" Acts that entitle magistrates to fine persons involved with indecent acts and articles in public places. They are usually

---

[33] *DPP v. Beate Uhse (U.K.) Ltd* [1974] Q.B. 158.

invoked by vice squad officers who frequent public lavatories in the hope of catching masturbators, but may have a wider application. The courts have been inclined to interpret these offences narrowly, confining them to situations where the public at large is caused genuine offence, as distinct from prying and provocative policemen.[34]

Telephone messages

Section 43 of the Telecommunications Act 1984 makes it an offence to "send any message by telephone which is grossly offensive or of an indecent obscene or menacing character". This offence appeared in the earlier Post Office Acts, doubtless to deter unpleasant and unsolicited calls. (Although whether it is apt to catch one breed of telephone nuisance, the "heavy breather", depends upon whether exhalation of breath amounts to a "message"). This section acquired a new importance when the privatisation of British Telecom led to the introduction of telephone services that provided allegedly erotic recorded messages at an expensive dialling rate. In 1986, in response to public criticism, British Telecom required its "telephone information and entertainment providers" to abide by a special Code of Practice, monitored by an independent committee (ICSTIS) empowered to receive complaints and to discontinue any service that breaches the Code (see Chapter 14). Section 43 applies only to telephone messages originating in the United Kingdom, so there is nothing to stop those who wish to experience international dirty-talk from dialling verbally explicit services in the United States or Europe, which are available to credit card holders.

Customs offences

Section 42 of the 1876 Customs Consolidation Act prohibits the importation into the United Kingdom of "indecent or obscene prints, paintings, photographs, books, cards, lithographic or other engravings, or any other indecent or obscene articles".

The test of "indecency" imposed a different standard for imported books and magazines to that which governs home-produced literature, and the result, if not the intention, was for many years to protect the British indecent publications industry from overseas competition. Imported publications that did not tend to deprave or corrupt and could not therefore be suppressed by internal controls, were destroyed at ports of entry if they shocked or disgusted customs officials—people who have more experience in financial than in moral evaluation. The prohibition was even applied to film transparencies and negatives, inoffensive enough on casual inspection until processing and projection made their

---

[34] See *Cheeseman v. DPP* [1991] 3 All E.R. 54.

indecency apparent.[35] The phrase "any other indecent . . . article" was
not interpreted *ejusdem generis* with the preceding references to printed
matter: it covered sex toys, statutes, chessmen, dildos, inflatable rubber
women, penis-shaped plastic mouth-organs and any other objects that
the wit or perversity of the human imagination could make for indecent
use.

It was a life-size rubber German sex-doll that finally broke the customs barrier and secured the right to import from the EEC films and
books that were "indecent" but not obscene. It became the unlikely
subject-matter of the important decision of the Court of Justice of the
European Communities in *Conegate Ltd v. Customs and Excise Commissioners* in 1986[36]:

> A sex-shop chain was ordered to forfeit a consignment of rubber dolls
> imported from Germany that British courts regarded as "indecent" within
> the 1876 prohibition. On reference to the European Court, it was held that
> the prohibitions on "indecent" imports breached Article 30 of the Treaty
> of Rome, which prevents restrictions on trade between Member States.
> The restriction could not be justified on public morality grounds under
> Article 36, because the British Government had not legislated to prevent
> the manufacture or the marketing other than by post or public display of
> indecent material within Britain. Since the item could be lawfully made
> and sold in Britain, because it was not obscene, Britain could not discrim-
> inate against Common Market suppliers by applying import restrictions.

The consequence of the decision in *Conegate* has, for practical purposes, been to amend the 1876 law by removing the prohibition on
indecent articles. Although in strict law this applies only to importations
from Common Market countries, the Commissioners of Customs and
Excise have accepted that it is impossible in practice to make distinctions between the same goods on the basis of the country of origin of
their shipment. As a result, it abandoned the prosecution of Gay's the
Word, a bookshop catering to homosexuals, which had imported a wide
range of "indecent" literature from the United States. (The customs'
evaluation of "indecency" may be gathered form the fact that the books
included works by Oscar Wilde, Jean Genet, Gore Vidal and Christopher Isherwood.) It follows that prosecutions of literature under customs regulations will henceforth be confined to consignments of hard-
core pornography, a ban on which the Court of Justice of the European
Communities has held to be justifiable under Article 36 on public morality grounds.[37] There may also be forfeiture proceedings brought in rela-

---

[35] *Derrick v. Commissioners of Customs and Excise* [1972] 1 All E.R. 993.
[36] [1987] Q.B. 254.
[37] *R. v. Henn & Darby* [1980] A.C. 850 and see *Wright v. Customs and Excise* [1999]
1 Cr. App. R. 69.

tion to "borderline" books, in respect of which the decision will hinge
on whether the court regards them as likely to be the subject of conviction if prosecuted in Britain under section 1 of the Obscene Publications
Act. The Court of Appeal has held that in considering a customs forfeiture claim the court need decide only whether the books "tend to deprave
and corrupt" likely readers so as to fall foul of the obscenity definition
in section 1 of the 1959 Act: if so, it may order forfeiture without
considering whether they might be exculpated by a section 4 "public
good" defence.[38] This decision is difficult to reconcile with the
reasoning in *Conegate* and may now be incompatible with incorporated
Article 10 of the ECHR. If an obscene book may be manufactured and
marketed within Britain because of its literary merit, there can be no
logical reason or pressing local need for preventing its importation from
other countries on moral grounds.

Customs officers who intercept articles considered obscene may proceed either by seeking forfeiture without criminal consequence to the
importer, or by charging the importer with one of a variety of "smuggling" offences in the Customs and Excise Management Act 1979. A
criminal charge will be preferred only where there is evidence of a
positive and dishonest intention to evade the prohibition, so that cases
other than commercial importation of hard-core pornography will normally proceed to a civil forfeiture hearing, either before local justices or
before a High Court judge.[39] Whenever goods are seized, the importer
must be notified and has one month to apprise the Commissioners of
his intention to dispute their claim for forfeiture, otherwise the goods
will be destroyed. In disputed cases the Commissioners must institute
proceedings, unless they decide on reflection that the seizure was overzealous, in which case they are empowered to release the goods subject
to "such conditions, if any, as they think proper".[40] Conditions can be
imposed only if the article has been seized at point of entry: an importer
whose goods have cleared customs and who has paid the appropriate
duty cannot, in the absence of dishonesty, be subject to any restriction
if customs officers think with hindsight that it was an obscene import.
One rule that should not survive ECHR challenge is that the customs
can seize and the courts can condemn anything "mixed, packed or
found with" material liable to forfeiture. It has been held that the court
is entitled to forfeit all books seized from a person's flat, even though
only some were found indecent or obscene. Customs interceptions are
mainly confined to hard-core pornography. The last attempt to prohibit
a work of artistic merit—*My Trouble with Women* by celebrated American underground cartoonist Robert Crumb (creator of "Felix the Cat"

[38] *R. v. Bow Street Magistrates, ex p. Noncyp Ltd* [1990] 1 Q.B. 123, CA.
[39] Customs and Excise Management Act 1979, s. 139 and Sched. 3.
[40] *ibid.*, s. 152.

and "Mr Natural")—ended ignominiously at Uxbridge 1996. The magistrates, after hearing evidence of Crumb's genius, ordered customs to release the stock and pay £6,000 costs to the importer.

THE COMMON LAW

Corrupting public morals

There are several arcane common law offences that can be revived "to guard the moral welfare of the State against attacks which may be more insidious because they are novel and unprepared for."[41] The charge of "conspiracy to corrupt public morals", for example, could be used against any writing or broadcasting (unlike the Obscene Publications Act, it can apply to television) that a jury might hold to be destructive of the moral fabric of society. In practice it is now rarely used, and confined to publications that carry advertisements seeking to procure illegal sexual liaisons. It was thus employed in 1981 against organisers of the Paedophile Information Exchange (whose publications had carried advertisements from members that the defendants would facilitate the distribution of child pornography).

The crime has had a colourful history. Its roots lie in the power exercised by Star Chamber judges to punish offences against conventional manners and morals. It was revived in 1961 to prosecute the publisher of *The Ladies Directory*, a "who's who" of London prostitutes.[42] Its scope was reduced by the House of Lords in 1971:

> *IT* (*International Times*) was convicted for publishing a "Gentleman's Directory" among its classified advertisements. The prosecution evidence established that these advertisements were answered by homosexuals through a box-number service provided by the magazine. The advertisements were worded in a way that could, and apparently did, attract schoolchildren. The House of Lords affirmed the newspaper's conviction, on the ground that these box-numbered advertisements set up an "apparatus of liaison" that would facilitate homosexual contact with under-age youths.[43]

The Law Lords restricted the future ambit of the offence in the following ways:

- the defendant must *intend* to corrupt public morals in the manner alleged in the indictment. The prosecution had to prove

---

[41] *Shaw v. DPP* [1962] A.C. 220 at 28.
[42] *ibid*.
[43] *Knuller*, n. 27 above.

that the editors of *IT* inserted the advertisements with shared intention to debauch and corrupt the morals of their readers by encouraging them to indulge in homosexual conduct.[44] In this respect, at least, the conspiracy charge is more onerous for the prosecution than an obscenity offence, in which the defendant's intention is irrelevant.[45]

- The jury must be told that "corrupt" is a strong word. It implies a much more potent influence than merely "leading astray morally". The jury must keep current standards in mind,[46] and not be given "too gentle a paraphrase or explanation of the formula".[47] The words "corrupt public morals" suggest conduct which a jury might find to be destructive of the very fabric of society."[48]

- The essence of the offence was not the publication of a magazine, but the use of that publication to procure the advancement of conduct that the jury considered corrupt. The corruption in the *IT* case did not arise from obscenity, but from "the whole apparatus of liaison organised by the appellants".[49] The jury may have decided that the only objectionable advertisements were those that might attract under-age youths, as distinct from practising adult homosexuals, when published in a magazine bought by thousands of young persons.

- The charge does not invite "a general tangling with codes of morality".[50] The courts possess no residual power to create new offences. The conspiracy charge should be applied only to "reasonably analogous" new circumstances.[51]

- Homosexual contact advertising, or any other sort of encouragement to homosexuality, does not necessarily amount to a corruption of public morality. In every case it is for the jury to decide, on current moral standards, whether the conduct alleged amounts to public corruption.[52]

- Prosecutions for conspiracy should not be brought against publishers who would, if charged under the Obscene Publications

---

[44] *Knuller*, n. 27 above, at 460.
[45] See *Shaw v. DPP* [1962] A.C. 220 at 228, CA.
[46] *Knuller*, n. 27 above, at 457, *per* Lord Reid.
[47] *ibid.* 460, *per* Lord Morris.
[48] *ibid.* 491, *per* Lord Simon.
[49] *ibid.* 446 (*arguendo*, at 497, *per* Lord Kilbrandon.
[50] *ibid.* at 490, *per* Lord Simon.
[51] *ibid.* at 455, *per* Lord Reid.
[52] *ibid.* at 490, *per* Lord Simon.

Act, be entitled to raise a public good defence. An undertaking to this effect was given to Parliament by the Law Officers in 1964, and it should be honoured by the legal profession.[53]

Outraging public decency: art galleries

A similarly restrictive approach was placed on the allied offence of conspiracy to outrage public decency in the *IT* case. That applied only to circumstances in which an exhibition would outrage those who were invited to see it, and the court stressed that prosecution would be subject to the Law Officers' undertaking that conspiracy would not be charged in any way that might circumvent the public good defence in the Obscene Publications Act.[54] But the common law offence of outraging public decency was revised in 1989 to punish an artist and the proprietor of an art gallery who exhibited a surrealist work featuring earrings that had been fashioned from human foetuses. This prosecution, *R. v. Gibson*, was a breach at least of the spirit of the Law Officers' undertaking, since there were a number of distinguished artists and critics prepared to testify that the work had artistic merit but this evidence was inadmissible on the common law charge, which has no public good or artistic merit defence.

> The defendants were charged with creating a public nuisance and outraging public decency by exhibiting the foetal earrings as part of a sculpture displayed within an art gallery open to the public. As the work of alleged art was not plainly visible from the public footpath outside the gallery, the public nuisance charge was dismissed. The Court of Appeal upheld the public indecency conviction, because the requirement of "publicity" for that offence had been satisfied by the general invitation to the public to enter the gallery and view the exhibits. The Crown did not have to prove that the artist and proprietor had intended to outrage decency: although the prosecution must prove intention when it charges common law conspiracies, this fundamental requirement of criminal law can be avoided simply by charging the substantive offence.[55]

Although the facts of this case were highly exceptional, it showed how the protections for art and literature solemnly enacted by Parliament in 1959 could be circumvented by the device of charging an offence at common law. The test of "outrage" is vague and subjective, calling for a value judgment verdict, which will depend not on any provable public standard or any deliberate intention to outrage, but on

---

[53] June 3, 1964, *Hansard*, Vol. 695, col. 1212. See *Knuller*, n. 27 above, at 459 *per* Lord Reid, at 466 *per* Lord Morris, at 480 *per* Lord Diplock, 494 *per* Lord Simon.
[54] *Knuller*, above, at 468, *per* Lord Morris and at 494, *per* Lord Simon.
[55] *R. v. Gibson* [1990] 2 G.B. 619.

the "gut reactions" of the jurors who happen to be empanelled to try the case. The majority verdict procedure, which allows a conviction despite two dissenters, further undermines the protection for minority tastes and views—it is not surprising that in the "foetal earrings" case, the *Oz* trial and the *Gay News* blasphemy prosecution, conviction was by 10–2 majority. The dissenters represented a substantial minority of citizens who presumably wished either to have access to the material or not to interfere with the rights of those who did.

The drafters of the 1959 Obscene Publications Act sought to exclude the Philistine presumptions of common law by providing in section 2(4), that "a person publishing an article shall not be proceeded against for an offence at common law consisting of the publication of any matter contained or embodied in the article *where it is of the essence of the offence that the matter is obscene*" [our italics]. But in *Gibson* the Court of Appeal decided that "obscene" in section 2(4) had its special statutory meaning ("tending to deprave and corrupt") and hence did not ban prosecution for a common law offence the essence of which was the lesser charge of "indecency" (i.e. arousing feelings of shock and disgust). There is an alternative construction which would give effect to Parliament's obvious intent, namely to give "obscene" in section 2(4) its natural and ordinary meaning, the essence of which includes indecency and the arousing of feelings of disgust. The Chief Justice accepted that this was a "possible" construction,[56] and since it is the *only* construction consistent with freedom of expression it may be required by application of section 3 of the Human Rights Act 1998.

The offence of "outraging public decency" is so vague that any novel prosecution may not be "prescribed by law" for purposes of Article 10. The Court of Appeal has persistently refused to define it, other than as conduct which fills the jury with extreme distaste, such as (in 1999) secretly video-taping women in a public lavatory.[57] Prosecutors only reach for this charge when they have no other shot in their locker. It was noteworthy that it was not the basis for the conviction of sculptor Anthony-Noel Kelly, who had used the body parts of mummified corpses, purloined from a teaching hospital, to add a death-like dimension to his exhibits (he was caught after a gallery patron recognised a late relative). Although there is no property in a corpse, Kelly was convicted as accomplice to the theft of body parts which had been worked on for preservation and teaching purposes.[58]

Art galleries were regular targets for overzealous policemen, until the much-publicised collapse in 1970 of the case against John Lennon and Yoko Ono's lithographic account of their honeymoon. In 1987 the Bank

---

[56] [1990] 2 G.B. 619.
[57] *R. v. Choi* May 7, 1999, CA.
[59] *R. v. Kelly* [1999] Q.B. 621.

of England brought a misguided but hilarious prosecution against an artist, Boggs, who had dared to "reproduce" the currency of the realm on large canvases: his triumphant acquittal (in record time) by an Old Bailey jury offers practical assurance that laws against counterfeiting will never again vex mischievous artists.[59] In 1997 the DPP declined all demands to prosecute the Royal Academy of Arts over its controversial *Sensations* exhibition. A pot of paint, but not a summons, was thrown at its picture of Myra Hindley, iconess of evil. The Academy was sensibly sensitive about suggestive sculptures of children by Jake and Dinos Chapman: these it confined to a guarded room to which only over-18s were allowed entrance.

The most serious attack on art came in 2001, when Scotland Yard's paedophile squad threatened the Saatchi gallery in North London with prosecution unless they removed some photographs of nude children from the "I am a Camera" exhibition. This was a thuggish attempt at censorship by threat rather than by law: the pictures lacked the element of lewdness or repulsion necessary for "indecency", and Saatchi had the courage (and connections) to call the police's bluff by arranging for the photographs to be published, in colour, in *The Guardian*. (The BBC had promised it would show them at 11.30 p.m. as part of a late-night debate on the case, but the Corporation is always cowardly in such matters and—like the *News of the World*—scrambled the children's genitals, achieving a genuinely perverse effect). One week after the police threat the DPP announced that since no jury would be likely to convict and the gallery might in any event have a "legitimate reason" for the exhibition, no further action was taken.

This problem of excluding the infinitely elastic common law is not suffered by producers of feature films or television and radio programmes. By 1977 the inadequacy of section 2(4) had been recognised, and the law was amended by adding a new subsection, 4(A), which excluded, in relation to films, any prosecutions at common law where the essence of the offence was indecency or conspiracy or offensiveness or disgust or injury to morality. The same blanket formula was used in paragraph 6 of Schedule 15 to the 1990 Broadcasting Act to remove the threat of common law prosecution from the electronic media.

Living theatre, happenings, performance art, strip-tease, discotheque programmes, variety shows and the like may fall outside the definition of a "play" for the purpose of the Theatres Act, but organisers and managers of premises where the performance takes place may be prosecuted for the common law offence of "keeping a disorderly house". This offence, created by eighteenth-century judges to curb cock-fighting and bear-baiting, is now primarily used against over-excitable hen par-

---

[59] *R. v. Boggs* (November 1987, Central Criminal Court). See G. Robertson, *The Justice Game*, Chap. 12 ("Come Up and See my Boggs").

ties and stag nights. A disorderly house is simply a place of common resort that features performances that are obscene, grossly indecent or "calculated to injure the public interest so as to call for condemnation and punishment".[60] The programme should be considered as a whole and not condemned because of an isolated incident of indecency, and the jury should bear in mind the place and circumstances of the performance, and the nature of the audience, in deciding whether there has been an outrage to public decency. ("A film shown in one place—for example a church fête—might outrage public decency, whereas shown in another place it might not.")[61] The prosecution has to prove that the premises were "habitually" used for indecent performances, which probably means, in practice, more than twice. In 1991 the landlord of the Wagon and Horses in Rochdale had his conviction quashed because the "exotic male dancers" who had excited beyond endurance a party of 70 women had done so only on one isolated occasion.[62]

BLASPHEMY

Indecent descriptions applied to sacred subjects may amount to the crime of blasphemy. The offence relates to outrageous comments about God, holy personages, or articles of the Anglican faith, and is constituted by vilification, ridicule or indecency. The intention of the publisher is irrelevant and the words must speak for themselves. Once publication has been proved, the only question remaining for the jury is "whether the dividing line . . . between moderate and reasoned criticism on the one hand and immoderate or offensive treatment of Christianity or sacred objects on the other, has been crossed".[63]

There has only been one prosecution for blasphemy since 1922, the controversial case of *Whitehouse v. Lemon*[64]:

> *Gay News* published a poem about a homosexual's conversion to Christianity, which metaphorically attributed homosexual acts to Jesus Christ. Professor James Kirkup intended to celebrate the universality of God's love; in so doing he referred explicitly to acts of sodomy and fellatio. Leave was obtained for a private prosecution against both editor and publishing company for the offence of blasphemous libel, in that they "unlaw-

---

[60] *R. v. Quinn & Bloom* [1962] 2 Q.B. 245.
[61] *R. v. Cinecentre Ltd* (Bush J.) Birmingham Crown Court, March 15, 1976. See generally Robertson, *Obscenity*, pp. 223–9.
[62] *Moores v. DPP* [1991] 4 All E.R. 521.
[63] *R. v. Lemon and Gay News Ltd* (1978) 67 Cr. App. R. 70 at 82.
[64] *Whitehouse v. Lemon* (1978) 68 Cr. App. R. 381. For an account of the *Gay News* Trial, see Geoffrey Robertson, *The Justice Game* (Vintage), Chap. 6.

fully and wickedly published or caused to be published a blasphemous libel concerning the Christian religion, namely an obscene poem and illustration vilifying Christ in his life and in his crucifixion". The jury convicted, by 10 votes to 2, and the House of Lords confirmed by 3–2 the trial judge's ruling that the publisher's intentions were irrelevant, and that there was no need for the prosecution to prove any risk of a breach of the peace.

This decision confirms that blasphemy is no longer a crime of disbelief or irreverence. Attacks upon Christianity, no matter how devastating, will not be blasphemous unless they are expressed in an outrageously indecent or scurrilous manner. Although no evidence may be called about literary merit, the jury may be invited to consider the dominant effect of the work. Moreover, evidence of the place and circumstances of publication would be relevant to the likelihood of public outrage,[65] and evidence as to the character of the readership would be admissible on the issue of whether resentment was likely to be aroused.[66]

The prosecution must lead prima facie evidence that the accused was responsible for the blasphemous publication. The defendants may exculpate themselves by proving that the decision to publish was made without their knowledge and without negligence. This defence is provided by section 7 of the Libel Act 1843, which places the onus on the defendant "to prove that such publication was made without his authority, consent or knowledge, and that the said publication did not arise from want of due care and caution on his part". Section 7 will normally protect newspaper proprietors who entrust questions of taste to editorial discretion, although it would also avail an editor who was absent at the time of publication or had delegated responsibility for content to the editors of particular sections or pages.[67] Newspaper prosecutions must be commenced by leave of a High Court judge under section 8 of the Law of Libel Amendment Act 1888.

In a report on the law of blasphemy in 1986 the Law Commission recognised three fundamental defects[68]:

- Its ambit is so wide that it is impossible to predict in advance whether a particular publication would constitute an offence.

- The sincerity of the publisher is irrelevant.

---

[65] *R. v. Boulter* (1908) 72 J.P. 188.
[66] Transcript of summing up in *R. v. Lemon*, Central Criminal Court, July 11, 1977, p. 15.
[67] *R. v. Holbrook (No. 1)* (1877) 3 Q.B.D. 60; *R. v. Holbrook (No. 2)* (1878) 4 Q.B.D. 42.
[68] Law Commission, *Working Paper No. 79: Offences Against Religion and Public Worship*, 1981.

- Blasphemy protects only Anglican beliefs,[69] and the criminal law is not an appropriate vehicle for upholding sectional religious tenets.

Although some have suggested that the law should be extended to protect all religions, the Law Commission despaired of any definition that could draw workable distinctions between Baptists, Scientologists, Rastafarians, Anglicans and Moonies and distinctions would, in any event, now amount to discrimination contrary to Article 14 of the ECHR.[70] The majority of the Commission concluded that a reformed law of blasphemy would serve no purpose necessary to modern society. The claims of public order, morality and the rights of individuals provide insufficient justification. Its conclusion is reinforced by the absence of prosecutions for blasphemy in England between 1922 and 1977 and ever since 1977; the withering away of the crime in Scotland (there are no recorded cases since the 1840s, and it is doubtful whether the offence any longer exists); and the demise of prosecutions in Northern Ireland, despite the sectarianism of that most tragic "plural society". Apparently, the scope of the offence in Wales is uncertain, as a consequence of the disestablishment of the Welsh Church in 1920.[71]

It is unlikely that the DPP would take action against publications with any literary or artistic value. *Whitehouse v. Lemon* was a private prosecution brought without official support: its wisdom was much doubted by many Anglicans. No action was taken against the feature film *Monty Python's Life of Brian*, which held sacred subjects up to considerable, if clever, ridicule. However, the very existence of a blasphemy law is calculated to encourage some Christians to believe they can enforce a conventional presentation of sacred themes in the arts. Martin Scorsese's film *The Last Temptation of Christ* led to demands (most notably from the retired *Gay News* trial judge) that its distributors should be prosecuted. While its presentation of Christ's humanity was challenging and unorthodox, the film lacked any element of vilification or scurrility, and on this basis the BBFC classified it as appropriate for screening to adults and the DPP declined to prosecute. The episode reinforces the view that a criminal law that holds a publisher strictly liable for an artistic work liable to shock the Christian on the Clapham omnibus is inappropriate to an age in which the creeds of passengers to Clapham, if they have any, are many and various.

The fate of blasphemy under the Human Rights Act 1998 has yet to

---

[69] The difficulties in defining "religion" are exemplified in the Australian High Court decision that scientology qualifies: *Church of the New Faith v. Commissioner for Pay-Roll Tax* (1983) 57 A.J.L.R. 785.
[70] Geoffrey Robertson, *The Justice Game* (Vintage), Chap. 6.
[71] Law Commission, *Working Paper No. 79*, p. 32.

be decided: the English courts may declare it incompatible with Article 10 of the Convention. This issue was raised in Strasbourg after the BBFC used the possibility of a blasphemy prosecution as an excuse for refusing to certify *Visions of Ecstasy*—a 20-minute experimental video about the erotic trances of St Theresa of Avila. The judges of the European Commission on Human Rights decided overwhelmingly (by 14–2) that this ban was a breach of Article 10: although it might be necessary for States to curb *gratuitous* offence to religious sensibilities, the BBFC ban was a disproportionate act of prior restraint because there was no danger, if the video were given an 18 certificate, of adults being unwillingly confronted with it:

> "The fact that certain Christians, who had heard of the existence of the video, might be outraged by the thought that such a film was on public sale and available to those who wished to see it, cannot amount to a sufficiently compelling reason to prohibit its lawful supply".[72]

This simple—and correct—approach was muddied, however, when the case came before a chamber of the Court less impressively constituted than the Commission. It decided, by 7–2, that the BBFC ban was within a state's "margin of appreciation" (always elastic in matters of religion and morality). Because there was no European consensus about blasphemy laws, the question of their compatibility with free speech should be decided by national courts: "State authorities are in principle in a better position than the international judge" to decide whether or to what extent their laws protecting religious feelings are "necessary in a democratic society".[73] *Wingrove* is not a Euro-precedent in favour of blasphemy law, but rather a direction that every country must decide for itself. The Court majority drew attention to "the high level of profanation" required in English law to constitute the crime, suggesting that this might justify it as means to protect "the rights of others" under Article 10(2). The Commission's answer, that Christians cannot claim a "right" to stop others privately viewing profanation at a level which does not breach obscenity law, is more persuasive.[74]

---

[72] *Wingrove v. U.K.* (1996) 24 E.H.R.R. 1, para. 60 (Commission).

[73] *ibid.* para. 58 (Court). Latest evidence about British democracy is that although 26 million of the 59 million population have been baptised in the Church of England, only 13.9% of citizens are members of any church and a mere 2.34% attend Anglican services.

[74] The Court, over-influenced by its Catholic judges, has been particularly irresolute on the issue, permitting Austria to ban a film of the controversial play *Council of Love: Otto-Preminger Institute v. Austria* (1995) 19 E.H.R.R. 34. This decision could be interpreted as having a public order rationale, since the film was to be screened in a Catholic town where breaches of the peace were reasonably apprehended. Paragraph 55 of the Court decision—suggesting a "balancing act" between

The unfairness of a law that protects only Christian sensibilities was highlighted in 1989 by the outrage felt amongst the Muslim community by the publication of Salman Rushdie's celebrated novel *The Satanic Verses*. This grievance was legitimate only to the extent that Muslims could correctly claim that the blasphemy law in Britain discriminated against their religion. But had it been extended to cover all faiths, Rushdie could have been prosecuted without the right to a literary merit defence, and without even being given an opportunity to argue that he had no intention to blaspheme. He would have been at risk of conviction merely by proof that the book was likely to outrage and insult believers—which it most certainly did, although much of the "outrage" seems to have been orchestrated by Muslim activists rather than to have arisen as a spontaneous reaction to reading the work. To punish Rushdie in these circumstances would have been offensive to justice, but no more so than the punishment of the editor of *Gay News*. The Secretary of State for the Home Department responded to Muslim demands for the extension of the blasphemy laws in a considered statement of the Government's position. He stressed "how inappropriate our legal mechanisms are for dealing with matters of faith and individual belief", remarked that a prosecution of *The Satanic Verses* would be "damaging and divisive", and noted that "the Christian faith no longer relies on the law of blasphemy, preferring to recognise that the strength of their own belief is the best armour against mockers and blasphemers".[75] Atlhough the Government showed no desire to follow through the logic of this position by abolishing the blasphemy law, it is difficult to imagine, in the light of this statement, that it would sanction a public prosecution for blasphemy.

The Rushdie affair demonstrated the absurdity of blasphemy law, either as a protection for Christianity or (in an extended and reformed version) as a protection for all religious sensibilities. In 1990 the Archbishop of Canterbury declared in favour of abolishing the law altogether, and the Divisional Court seemed of much the same view after examining it for five days at the behest of Muslims who sought to commit Rushdie and his publishers for trial at the Old Bailey.

> The Bow Street magistrate had refused to issue a summons in respect of *The Satanic Verses* on the grounds that the offence of blasphemy protected only the Christian religion. The High Court held that this decision was

Article 10 and Article 9 (the right to peaceful worship)—is plainly wrong. The Commission took a more principled view of the rights of minorities to entertain themselves in private in without interference by moral busybodies: *see Scherer v. Switzerland* (1994) 18 E.H.R.R. 276, a case which regrettably did not come before the Court because of the applicant's death.

[75] Statement by John Patten, November 1989.

correct: the early precedents established that the crime was confined to attacks upon the Established Church, so that it appears that other Christian denominations are protected only in so far as their fundamental tenets coincide with those of the Church of England. The court accepted that this was a "gross anomaly", but the anomaly arose from the "chains of history", which could be unlocked only by Parliament. Even if the court had power to extend the law to other religions, however, it would refrain from doing so because of the "insuperable" problems in defining religion, in expecting juries to understand obscure theologies, and because of the danger of divisive and obscurantist prosecutions. The court accepted that "the existence of an extended law of blasphemy would encourage intolerance, divisiveness and unreasonable interference with freedom of expression", and "would be likely to do more harm than good."[76]

The European Commission rejected an application by the Muslims who had brought *The Satanic Verses* case, on the ground that the Convention gave no right to bring a private prosecution and hence they could not show that any Convention right was infringed when it was rejected.[77] This approach, which is correct, is difficult to reconcile with the Commission's earlier rejection of an application by *Gay News* against their private prosecution. The Commission accepted that the conviction would not be justified as preventing disorder or protecting morals, but rather in protecting Mrs Whitehouse's right not to have her religious feelings offended[78]—the very basis upon which the Muslims had sought to prosecute Salman Rushdie. The Divisional Court's approach—that the Article 9 guarantee of freedom to manifest religious beliefs does not entitle believers to prosecute those who criticise or even ridicule those beliefs, is to be preferred.

Sex shops

The Indecent Displays (Control) Act, 1981 and sections of the Local Government (Miscellaneous Provisions) Act of 1982 apply to these "adult only" centres. Section 2 of the latter legislation gives local authorities power to insist that sex shops and cinemas within their jurisdiction be licensed. Although the grant of a licence does not confer an immunity from prosecution for obscenity in relation to material stocked in the shop, it has meant in practice that authorities proceed more cautiously by way of inspection, rather than by seizure. The new licensing system has reduced the outlets for sex magazines and videos, as local councils may decide how many (if any) licences to grant on the basis of

---

[76] *R. v. Bow Street Magistrates' Court, ex p. Chaudhury* [1991] 1 All E.R. 306.
[77] *Chaudhury v. U.K.* Application No. 17439/90, March 5, 1991.
[78] *Gay News v. U.K.* (1993) 5 E.H.R.R. 123.

the needs and character of the locality in question. A shop will require a licence if it occupies premises:

> "used for a business which consists to a significant degree of selling, hiring, exchanging, lending, displaying or demonstrating:
> (a) sex articles; or
> (b) other things intended for use in connection with, or for the purpose of stimulating or encouraging—
> (i) sexual activity; or
> (ii) acts of force or restraint which are associated with sexual activity."

This section applies only to sex shops: it does not cover the premises used by publishers to prepare and edit magazines or videos that deal with sexual activity. Nor would it cover general newsagencies or bookshops that stock small amounts of "adult" material—although the concept of "sex articles" is widely defined to encompass books, magazines, videos, records and films dealing with sexual subjects. The Divisional Court has ruled that the "significant degree of business" test exempts ordinary newsagents and corner stores whose sales of such items form a part of their turnover.[79] There is no requirement that these items should be "indecent": if they deal with sexual behaviour and their sale is a significant part of the business of the establishment, the shopkeeper will require a local authority licence. It is an offence to operate a sex shop without a licence or to breach a licence condition.[80]

RACE HATRED

Freedom of expression entails the right to entertain ideas of any kind, and to express them publicly. The mode or the manner of the expression, however, may properly be regulated in the interests of the freedom of others to go about their business in public without being gratuitously assaulted or defamed, and may properly be curtailed in order to avoid public disorder which may follow provocative dissemination of racist ideas. This was the basis of the first anti-incitement laws, passed in Britain in 1965, after several years of racial violence of the most serious kind, by a Labour Government whose commitment to freedom of speech was weakened after the infamous Smethwick by-election in which a Labour majority evaporated in the face of the slogan, "If you

---

[79] *Lambeth Borough Council v. Grewal* (1995) 82 Cr. App. R. 301, QBD.
[80] The prosecution must first prove the defendant's intention to do so: *Westminster City Council v. Croyolgrange Ltd* [1986] 2 All E.R. 353.

want a nigger for a neighbour, vote Labour". This law has been amended on several occasions—the 1986 Public Order Act being the last—in an effort to make convictions easier to obtain. Nevertheless, prosecutions, which can be brought only with the Attorney-General's consent, are comparatively infrequent.

Section 18 of the 1986 Act makes it an offence to use threatening, abusive or insulting words or behaviour with the intent of stirring up racial hatred or in circumstances where racial hatred is likely to be stirred up. Section 19 makes it an offence to publish threatening or abusive or insulting material either with an intention to provoke racial hatred or in circumstances where such hatred is likely to be stirred up by the publication, "Racial hatred" means hatred against a group defined by colour, race or national origin, thereby including Jews, Sikhs[81] and Romany gypsies, but excluding Zionists, Rastafarians[82] and "gypsies" or travellers in general.[83] The term "racial group" is not defined by reference to religion, which means that Muslims in general (whose mosques are targets of much of the race-hate in the United Kingdom) are unprotected. The better view is that ethnic or country-based Muslim sects (such as the Ahmadis from Pakistan) are entitled to protection, but the DPP does not agree and the courts have so far refused to put him right[84-85] (see "Stop Press" section for further details).

Section 22 of the Public Order Act has been amended by section 164 f the 1990 Broadcasting Act so that the offence of inciting racial hatred may now be committed by the transmission of television or radio pro-grammes. Those vulnerable to prosecution are the television company (including the BBC), the programme producer and the person who is recorded making the incitement. This undesirable change in the law makes it more hazardous to produce programmes about racism, because the offence may be committed irrespective of the producer's intention, if "having regard to all the circumstances racial hatred is likely to be stirred up". Must current affairs programme makers henceforth ensure that racists say nothing that might attract the audience, and are editori-ally depicted in an unflattering light? The fact that this is generally the case when racists are allowed to speak for themselves will be sufficient if the programme is professionally produced and examines a subject of public interest: a prosecution in these circumstances would breach Art-icle 10. This was the decision of the European Court in the important case of *Jersild v. Denmark*:

[81] *Mandla v. Dowell Lee* [1983] 1 All E.R. 1062.
[82] *Crown Suppliers v. Dawkins* [1993] I.C.R. 517.
[83] *Commission for Racial Equality v. Dutton* [1989] 1 All E.R. 306.
[84-85] See *R. v. DPP, ex p. Merton B.C.* [1999] C.O.D. 161, HC, and [1999] C.O.D. 358, DC.

Broadcasters were convicted of racial insult by producing a documentary on the growing phenomenon of ethnic hatred amongst young people in Copenhagen. The purpose of transmitting interviews with racists was not to promote their xenophobia but to expose and analyse a matter of great public concern. The Court rejected the Government's argument that the producers should have "counterbalanced" or refuted these racist views: Article 10 did not permit the State to impose an editorial line or to tell journalists how to perform their professional duty. Although the racist statements that were broadcast did not of themselves enjoy protection under Article 10 (the interviewees themselves were convicted) this protection was attracted when they were repeated in the context of a serious media investigation. "The punishment of a journalist for assisting in the dissemination of statements made by another person in an interview would seriously hamper the contribution of the press to discussion of matters of public interest" and was in these circumstances an indefensible violation of Article 10.[86]

The offence can be committed by the public performance of a play (section 20) although a drama's propensity to stir up racial hatred is to be judged with regard to all the circumstances and "taking the performance as a whole". Racist abuse heaped on Shylock and Othello by Shakespearean characters is therefore defensible, and there have been no prosecutions of stage plays since the offence first appeared in the Theatres Act of 1968. However, the Royal Court Theatre's cancellation of the play *Perdition* in 1987 after pressure from Jewish interests shows that the question may not be of entirely academic interest.

Further potential for inhibiting free speech is contained in the offence of possessing racially inflammatory material or recordings with a view to publication in circumstances where racial hatred is likely to be stirred up (section 23). Authors and television researchers who collect such material in order to condemn it will not be at risk, but it might be argued that uncritical displays of Nazi memorabilia or unvarnished publications of "Hitler diaries" and the like could revive old hatreds. The protection of books of genuine historic interest is provided, not by the words of the Act, but by the need to obtain the Attorney-General's consent to prosecution. It is unfortunate that Parliament did not make section 23 subject to a defence that the play or the publication or collection was in the interests of drama, literature, history or other subjects of general concern.

There are various defences to these charges, generally pivoting upon lack of awareness of the real nature of the speech or writing or lack of any reason to suspect that they would be delivered or disseminated in circumstances where racial hatred would be provoked. If an offence is committed on a television or radio broadcast, the programme contractor

---

[86] *Jersild v. Denmark* (1995) 19 E.H.R.R. 1.

and the programme producer and director may be prosecuted as well as the person who has uttered the offensive words. In the case of plays, liability is limited to producers and directors, unless an actor commits the offence by an unscheduled departure from the script—in which case he is deemed to be the "director" of his own impromptu performance. Section 25 of the Public Order Act permits a court to order the forfeiture of any written material or recording that has been used to commit an offence. Section 26 precludes reports of parliamentary proceedings and court reports from becoming the subject-matter of a prosecution under the Act.

There is no doubt that the race hate laws have a potential for punishing the expression of genuine political statements, albeit couched in crude or insulting terminology. This can apply particularly to activists from oppressed minorities, whose rhetoric is designed to jolt what they perceive as white complacency. In Britain the law was used, at least in its first decade of operation, more effectively against Black Power leaders than against white racists. The first person to be gaoled for a race hatred offence was Michael X, convicted by a white jury in 1967 for some fairly routine black-consciousness rhetoric of the period.[87] Ironically, Michael X was standing in for Stokely Carmichael, an American black activist banned from entering Britain, who 30 years later was applauded by the Macpherson Report into the Stephen Lawrence murder for identifying the phenomenon of "institutional racism" which had become rife in the Metropolitan Police. Enforcement history of the offence demonstrates the danger of prosecuting racist ideas (because it gives them more publicity). When in 1991 the Dowager Lady Birdwood, an old and rabid racist, was convicted for distributing anti-Semitic propaganda, Judge Brian Capstick Q.C. wisely frustrated her desire to be made a martyr: he imposed a conditional discharge and ordered her to pay prosecution costs. Systematic racist vilification— such as crude cartoons in National Front newspapers—has been punished by prison sentences.[88] The Stephen Lawrence inquiry recommended an extension of the law to punish racist utterances in private homes and meetings, but this would almost certainly breach Article 8 of the ECHR.[89] The U.S. Supreme Court has struck down hate speech laws which pivot on causation of anger or resentment rather than the incitement of violence.[90]

The common law offence of seditious libel can be committed by "promoting ill-will and hostility between different classes of Her Maj-

---

[87] R. v. Malik [1968] 1 All E.R. 582.
[88] See R. v. Edwards (1983) 5 Cr. App. R. (S.) 145; R. v. Morse & Tyndall (1986) 8 Cr. App. R. (S.) 369.
[89] Report of an Inquiry by Sir William Macpherson (1999), Recommendation 39.
[90] RAV v. City of St Paul, 563 U.S. 377 (1992).

esty's subjects". In *R. v. Caunt*[91] the editor of *The Morecambe and Heysham Visitor* faced this charge for suggesting that violence against British Jews might be the only way of stemming Zionists' terrorists' activities against British forces in Palestine. He was acquitted. The statutory offences have effectively superseded this aspect of sedition.

In 1990 the Divisional Court held that an attempt to prosecute the author and publisher of *The Satanic Verses* for sedition was misconceived. The allegation that publication of the book was calculated to create hostility between Muslims and other classes of citizens was, even if true, insufficient to constitute the offence: there had to be proof of incitement to violence against the State.[92]

The court also rejected an attempt to prosecute the publisher, Penguin Books, under section 14 of the Public Order Act, for provoking unlawful violence by distributing the books to shops that later suffered bomb attacks. Even if the book's contents could be described as "threatening, abusive or insulting" for the purposes of section 4, that section required that the unlawful violence should be the direct and immediate result of the publication of the insulting words. The act of distributing a book to retail outlets cannot sensibly be regarded as the immediate and direct cause of unlawful violence to which the bookseller may later be subjected by terrorists or fanatics.[93]

---

[91] Wade (1948) 64 L.Q.R. 203. See also Caunt, *An Editor on Trial*, privately published, 1947.

[92] *R. v. Bow Street Magistrates' Court ex p. Chaudhury*, n. 76 above.

[93] *R. v. Horseferry Road Justices, ex p. Sadatan* [1991] 1 All E.R. 342.

CHAPTER 5

CONFIDENCE AND PRIVACY

The claimant in an action to stop a publication on grounds of confidence is claiming a right to protect privacy, or at least private property. The court must be persuaded that the public interest requires the confidence to be preserved. This is not difficult for individuals and private organisations, whose expectation of privacy is itself a public interest prima facie meriting protection. It is not sufficient, though, for the Government or public bodies to plead embarrassment: they must positively demonstrate the public harm that would follow disclosure. Whoever the claimant, the law recognises that the claim to confidence cannot be absolute and that there will be cases where it is outweighed by the public interest in disclosure. The courts are fond of reminding media defendants that not everything of interest to the public is in the public interest: there is a distinction between stories that appeal merely to prurient or morbid curiosity and those that contribute new and useful information to public debate.

There is also in this area a greater willingness to grant an interim injunction, suppressing publication until trial. This means that claimants will, whenever possible, choose to rely on these doctrines as a pretext for stopping articles and broadcasts that they fear because of criticism contained in them. It is anomalous that Blackstone's rule against prior restraint, soundly embedded in libel law, should be more precarious when the case comes within a different legal category. The courts argue that damages can compensate an unjustified libel, whereas a secret once published cannot be made confidential again.[1] But the danger of injunctions covering up iniquitous behaviour is demonstrated by the fact that six months before Robert Maxwell's corporate villainy came to light upon his death, he was able to obtain injunctions preventing the press from publishing any suggestion that his companies had indulged in "dubious accounting devices" or had "sought to mislead . . . as to the value of the assets of the company". The media were even banned from reporting the fact that this order had been made.

The impact of an "interim injunction" is in practice "permanent"

---

[1] See *Lion Laboratories Ltd v. Evans* [1984] 2 All E.R. 477 at 433.

rather than "interim". It amounts to an order suppressing any publication of the information until trial of the action, which may not take place for a year or so. By that time the information may be stale news or have been overtaken by events. Thus media organisations that lose the argument at the interim stage rarely bother to renew it at a trial—and in such cases "prior restraint" means permanent restraint.

Breach of confidence is a civil remedy affording protection against the disclosure or use of information that is not publicly known, and that has been entrusted in circumstances imposing an obligation not to disclose that information without the authority of the person who has imparted it. Whenever a journalist acquires information that is "secret", in the sense that the source from which it is generated has taken steps to restrict its circulation, the first question to be asked is whether an obligation of confidence exists in relation to its use. If it does, the further question arises as to whether, notwithstanding that it is the subject of confidence, it may be published because of its public importance. There will usually be a third question of overriding practical importance: can it be published without the danger of an injunction? These will be considered in turn.

"Privacy is not yet a right that the law recognises as such. There are periodic attempts by M.P.s to introduce a statutory right to privacy when Fleet Street's excesses plumb new depths. Their problem is to find a satisfactory test for defining unwarranted intrusions into private lives which allows the investigation of stories of real public interest. Despite the absence of any comprehensive right, privacy can sometimes be indirectly protected by actions for trespass, copyright and data protection. But there is growing judicial support for developing the law of breach of confidence to provide a remedy for invasion of privacy by the press. The public hostility to "chequebook journalism" and "kiss and tell" stories is reflected in the increasing confidence with which judges slap injunctions on "exclusives" about celebrities and members of the Royal Family. Many of the recent cases discussed in this chapter can be explained as decisions in support of the right to be left alone, or at least the right not to be embarrassed by the publication of details about private life sold to the media by disloyal or disenchanted friends or retainers. Where such information is of genuine public importance, the media will be well advised to keep details of publication secret until the very last moment. The device used by the *Sunday Times* to avoid a Government injunction on its *Spycatcher* serialisation by publishing its first edition as a "dummy" without any reference to the story may be an expedient that will be deployed again.

THE OBLIGATION OF CONFIDENCE

Information cannot be embargoed simply because it is confidential or private. As the House of Lords said in the *Spycatcher* case, it must have been communicated to a confidant in circumstances where he has notice, or is held to have agreed, that the information is confidential, so that it would be "just" in all the circumstances that he should be stopped from disclosing the information to others.[2] The Lords drew on the principles expounded by Megarry J. in *Coco v. A. N. Clark (Engineers) Ltd*[3] who described them as follows:

> "First, the information must be of a confidential nature ... The second requirement is that the information must have been communicated in circumstances importing an obligation in confidence ... Thirdly, there must have been an authorised use of the information to the detriment of the person communicating it."

Megarry J. later stated that he wished to keep open the question whether detriment was really required, and the view of the House of Lords in *Spycatcher* was that it will not always be necessary to show it. An anonymous benefactor may sue to restrain the revelation of his identity, even though the breach of confidentiality will give him favourable (but unwanted) publicity.

The spring from which the common law of breach of confidence still flows is the case of *Prince Albert v. Strange*[4] decided in 1848. It is, in one sense, a familiar example of English judges bending over backwards to please the Royal Family, but in so doing they found a way of restraining the modern celebrity rip-off:

> Queen Victoria and her consort, Prince Albert, amused themselves and their close friends by making private etchings and drawings, which were kept under lock and key at Windsor Castle. Prince Albert sent the etchings to a shop for impressions to be made of them; a workman took surreptitious copies which the defendant reproduced in a catalogue and sought to exhibit. The judges, in order to give Prince Albert the utmost redress, did not decide in his favour on the basis of copyright, or even of property, but rather upon a principle of protecting privacy and providing relief against "a sordid spying into the privacy of domestic life" (the court was much moved by evidence that the Queen—so unamused in public— obtained pleasure from making the etchings in private and giving them to close friends: her happy pastime would be sullied if they were put on public display). The court injuncted both the catalogue and the exhibition,

---

[2] *Att.-Gen. v. Guardian Newspapers Ltd (No. 2)* [1990] 1 A.C. 109 at 281.
[3] [1969] R.P.C. 41 at 47–48.
[4] (1848) 2 De G. & Sm. 652.

on the grounds that they invaded the right to privacy, in the sense of a right to control one's possessions and enjoy them precisely because they are not seen by or available to others.

Prince Albert is the basis upon which confidentiality has been asserted in marital communications, unpublished manuscripts and personal diaries. It has generally been treated as an authority for impressing property of personal or sentimental value with confidentiality and thus extending the protection afforded by breach of confidence to some aspects of personal privacy.

The Lords in *Spycatcher* recognised three limiting principles—where information was already in the public domain and where the public interest justified disclosure (these two will be considered in more detail) or where the information was trivial. As to the later, Megarry J. in *Coco*'s case had said magisterially, "equity ought not to be invoked merely to protect trivial tittle-tattle, however confidential".[5]

The most common relationships that are impressed with a duty of confidence are contractual, domestic, governmental and legal. These will be examined in turn, but it is important to remember that obligations to preserve confidence are not confined to the original confidant. Others (such as journalists) to whom the secrets are leaked will owe a similar duty of confidence as long as they knew or should have known that the information was originally intended to have a restricted circulation.

However, in a busy newsroom, where tip-offs come orally, at second and third hand, claimants may be hard put to prove that their private information reached the journalist in a form which was still impressed with confidentiality.

> A company which published a private newsletter to a handful of clients providing confidential information about the cocoa market sued Dow Jones for breaking its confidence (as well as its copyright) by reporting the substance of the newsletter. Its journalist had obtained this information by telephone from several newsletter subscribers, who volunteered the information in breach of their own agreement with the claimant to keep it secret. The journalist did not know of this confidentiality arrangement, so neither she nor her employer could be affected by it (*PCR Ltd v. Dow Jones Telerate Ltd* [1998] F.S.R. 170).

Breach of confidence is an area of law whose boundaries the courts have expanded. In 1978 the criminal courts held that information could

---

[5] *Coco v. A.N. Clark (Engineers) Ltd*, n.3. above. The trouble is that, today, the more trivial the tittle-tattle, the more valuable it is to tabloid newspapers and glossy magazines.

not be stolen[6] and hence computer hacking was not a crime until Parliament then passed the Computer Misuse Act 1990.[7] A Crown Court recorder was refused an injunction in 1988 to stop *The Sun* publishing letters that had been stolen from his homosexual lover. This was consistent with the Law Commission's views in 1981 that publication of stolen information could not be restrained.[8] Yet in 1990 the House of Lords had no hesitation in ordering a journalist to disclose the name of a source who was assumed (wrongly) to have provided him with confidential information from a stolen document[9] and in a series of cases the courts have held that if lawyers receive their opponents' papers through obvious muddle or oversight, they are under an obligation to return them and can be restrained from making use of any confidential information which the papers contain.[10] Future potential extension of breach of confidence has been signalled by Lord Goff in *Spycatcher* who said a duty of confidence would arise:

"where an obviously confidential document is wafted by an electric fan out of a window into a crowded street, or where an obviously confidential document, such as a private diary, is dropped in a public place and then picked up by a passer by";[11]

and by Mr Justice Laws in 1995:

"If someone with a telephoto lens were to take from a distance and with no authority a picture of another engaged in some private act, his subsequent disclosure of the photograph would, in my judgment, as surely amount to a breach of confidence as if he had found or stolen a letter or diary in which the act was recounted and proceeded to publish it. In such a case, the law would protect what might reasonably be called a right of privacy, although the name accorded to the cause of action would be breach of confidence. It is, of course, elementary that, in all such cases, a defence based on the public interest would be available."[12]

---

[6] *Oxford v. Moss* (1968) 68 Cr. App. R. 183.
[7] See *R. v. Gold and Schifreen* [1988] A.C. 1063, and see below at p. 280 for the 1990 Act.
[8] *Breach of Confidence* Report No. 100 (HMSO 8388, 1981), para. 4.9.
[9] *X. v. Morgan Grampian Publishers Ltd* [1990] 1 A.C. 109, at 281.
[10] See, *e.g. English and American Insurance Co. Ltd v. Herbert Smith* [1988] F.S.R. 232; *Derby and Co. Ltd v. Weldon (No. 8)* [1991] 1 W.L.R. 73.
[11] *Att.-Gen. v. Guardian Newspapers Ltd (No. 2)* [1990] 1 A.C. 109 at 281.
[12] *Hellewell v. Chief Constable of Derbyshire* [1995] 1 W.L.R. 804 at 807. These remarks were not part of the binding reasoning of the decision and it will be necessary for a future court to consider whether they should prevail over the opposite conclusion in the *Our Dogs* case (see below at p. 276) which was not cited in *Hellewell*.

It was this capacity of the law of breach of confidence to develop which persuaded the European Commission on Human Rights to dismiss the claim of Earl Spencer and his wife that their right to privacy had been violated by press articles and photographs of the Countess taken while she was at a private clinic suffering from an eating disorder. The Commission held that because the Earl and his wife had not tried to sue the papers for breach of confidence over their purchase of the story from the sources (who were suspected to be friends of the Spencers), they had not given the British courts a proper opportunity to provide them with redress.[13]

A similar expansive trend can be seen in the attitude to information obtained from telephone tapping. Those who use the telephone system have to take the risk that their conversations may be overheard as a result of a warrant issued by the Home Secretary.[14] Private tapping of a message in the course of transmission by means of a public telecommunications system is an offence.[15] Until 2000, the legislation only prohibited the tapping of messages as they passed through the *public* system, and thus it did not criminalise (for instance) the interception of the signal between a cordless telephone and its base unit.[16] Nor did it prevent an employer covertly listening in to an employee's extension. This lack of regulation was condemned by the European Court of Human Rights as a violation of employees' rights of privacy under Article 8[17] and the new legislation has now widened the prohibition so that it covers intentional and unlawful interception of a message in the course of transmission in a private telecommunication system.[18] In *Francome v. Mirror Group Newspapers Ltd*[19] the Court of Appeal held that there was an arguable case that a telephone user could sue an illegal interceptor either for breach of confidence or for breach of statutory duty. The 2000 Act now expressly makes such interception actionable.[20]

---

[13] *Spencer v. U.K.*, Application Nos 28851/95 & 28852/95 (1998) 92 D.R. 56; (1998) 25 E.H.R.R. CD 105.

[14] *Malone v. Metropolitan Police Commissioner (No. 2)* [1979] Ch. 344.

[15] Regulation of Investigatory Powers Act 2000, s. 1(1). The same provision bans interception of mail in the course of transmission in a public postal service.

[16] *R. v. Effik* [1995] 1 A.C. 309.

[17] *Halford v. U.K.* (1997) 24 E.H.R.R. 523.

[18] Regulation of Investigatory Powers Act 2000, s. 1(2). The private system must be linked up to a public system, but it is *not* necessary that the particular intercepted message made use of this connection. At least part of the apparatus for the system must be in the U.K. and this part must be used for making the connection to the public service: *ibid.*, s. 2(1).

[19] [1984] 2 All E.R. 408, CA.

[20] Regulation of Investigatory Powers Act 2000, s. 1(3).

Contractual relationship

The first matter to be considered by a media organisation when information is offered or obtained from an employee is not the civil law of confidence but the criminal provisions of the Prevention of Corruption Act 1906. It is an offence to offer an incentive or reward to any employee for doing any act in relation to his principal's business. These laws against bribery and corruption may in some circumstances "catch" (*i.e.* apply to) payments to informers. The media are protected by the requirement that any payment must be proved to have been made "corruptly"—a jury would doubtless acquit if the payment was necessary to extract information that revealed a public scandal. Payments to ex-employees are not caught so long as they were not promised prior to resignation, and a genuine consultancy fee would not be legally objectionable.

> In 1987 *The Observer* was prosecuted at the Old Bailey for an offence under the Prevention of Corruption Act. It had paid £10,000 to an employee of the Ministry of Defence for documents and information revealing that millions of pounds of public money had been lost through mismanagement and failure to supervise defence contractors. The employee had been gaoled at an earlier trial for corruptly accepting a bribe from *The Observer*, but the newspaper was acquitted of offering the money corruptly. The newspaper's editor and senior journalists explained that they had been led to believe that the employee had resigned his office before they paid him for acting as a consultant. This case demonstrates the importance of bearing the Prevention of Corruption Act in mind before any payment is made to a source.

Employment and consultancy contracts generally have "secrecy" clauses in which employers and advisers undertake to keep to themselves information acquired in the course of the relationship. Even without a specific clause, the courts will imply an undertaking that information given in confidence to the employee will not be used to the employer's detriment.[21] This does not cover everything that employees learn in the course of their business. "Trivial tittle-tattle",[22] embarrassing *faux pas* or personal mannerisms of colleagues and superiors[23] are not usually within this duty of confidence.

---

[21] *Facenda Chicken v. Fowler* [1987] Ch. 117, CA. The need for "detriment" is controversial. The prevailing view in *Att.-Gen. v. Guardian Newspapers Ltd (No. 2)* [1988] 3 All E.R. 545 was that if detriment were needed, there might be sufficient detriment for private litigants in the unwanted disclosure of confidential information; but where the Government was the claimant, it would have to show harm to the public interest as the "detriment" before disclosure would be restrained.

[22] *Coco v. A.N. Clark Engineers Ltd* [1968] E.S.R. 415.

[23] *G.D. Searle & Co. v. Celltech* [1982] F.S.R. 92, CA.

Where there is a clear contractual promise to keep matters confidential—*e.g.* not to publish or broadcast anything learnt or witnessed during employment—the courts are prepared to grant injunctions to enforce the promise. Thus when a former royal servant breached the secrecy clause in his employment contract by writing a book, aptly titled *Courting Disaster*, the Court of Appeal issued an injunction to stop him from publishing it anywhere in the world. The clause was not limited in territory or time, and the court saw no reason of a public policy nature not to force the defendant to honour an agreement he had voluntarily made in return for employment. The court did accept that an unlimited covenant might, in some cases, be attacked for obscurity or illegality or on public policy grounds, such as being in restraint of trade.[24] The author of *Courting Disaster* made no claim that the publication of his book would serve any public interest, either in Britain or abroad. Had there been a significant public interest in the publication of the book, this would serve as a defence to a breach of contract action based on a confidentiality covenant, just as it would if the action had been directly for breach of confidence.

The duty to respect the confidence is impressed as well on a newspaper that knows or must suspect that its source acquired the information in confidence. When Granada Television obtained secret documents from a mole at British Steel, it knew that the papers were not intended to go beyond senior officials of the company. Since the documents were labelled "confidential" and "restricted", the position would have been the same if they had been sent anonymously through the post.[25] But there is no magic in a "confidential" label and if there is some other sign that despite this heading, they had been given wider publicity, a newspaper can make use of them.[26] Conversely, even without such a

---

[24] *Att.-Gen. v. Barker* [1990] 3 All E.R. 257. The United States Supreme Court would not permit an injunction to be granted in such a situation, on prior restraint principles, but it might impose a "constructive trust" so that royalties from the book went to the employer: *Snepp v. U.S.* 444 508 (1980). The House of Lords reached the same result by a different route when it ordered the spy George Blake to account for the royalties due from the publishers of his book *No Other Choice*, published in breach of his undertaking to M16 not to disclose any official information gained by him as a result of his employment. Damages for breach of undertakings (*i.e.* contracts) are normally intended to put the aggrieved party in the position they would have been in if the contact had been performed, but exceptionally the court considered that they should be assessed by reference to Blake's profit: *Att.-Gen. v. Blake* [2000] 3 W.L.R. 625. If Barker's book had been published in the United States, it would seem (from the European Court decision in *Spycatcher*) that prior restraint on its publication in Britain would be an infringement of Article 10. The publishers could, however, be sued for heavy damages for inducing a breach of contract.

[25] *British Steel Corp. v. Granada Television Ltd* [1981] 1 All E.R. 417.

[26] *Dunsford and Elliott Ltd v. Johnson & Firth Brown Ltd* [1977] 1 Lloyd's Rep. 505.

warning, a paper must take care over documents whose contents are manifestly for a restricted audience.

For the most part, the rush to court for an order to "deliver up" confidential documents is simply closing the gate after the horse has bolted. the media organisation that has obtained the confidential documents will already have published the most interesting aspects of them, and often an approach to the court will do no more than verify their authenticity in the public mind. However, journalists should be aware of the danger that an order for "delivery up" may pose to their source— if, for example, the documents are a numbered copy, if a name has been underlined in a distribution list, if the source has added handwritten comments or if they are likely to carry the source's fingerprints. Copies produced by a word processor may have deliberate minor differences to identify them. This is, apparently, a favourite technique for keeping track of high-level government documents. The *Guardian* newspaper signally failed to protect its source when it handed over secret documents about the arrival of Cruise missiles at Greenham Common. The documents had been sent to the paper anonymously by an MOD clerk, Sarah Tisdall, who was identified in this way and later jailed for six months. Granada Television, more sensibly, took care to excise tell-tale signs from its copies of British Steel documents before returning them. Protecting sources by destroying or mutilating documents they have provided can make the media organisation liable for contempt charges if an order for delivery up of these documents has already been made. This problem should not arise if destruction takes place before a court order, but in such a case a public interest defence might be harder to prove.[27] Since the only physical damage suffered is the replacement cost of the paper, it will add little to the claimant's claim. (See further "Protection of Sources", pp. 253–276). Journalists should be aware that it is a criminal offence dishonestly to destroy the original of a government document.[28]

Authors and programme makers should be cautious about entering into service contracts with organisations that they may alter wish to criticise:

> Television-programme maker David Elstein was hired by Schering Chemicals to tutor its executives in how to cope with media interviews on the subject of Primodos, a pregnancy drug that had turned out to have dangerous side-effects. Elstein was paid £200 a day for conducting the three-day course. It gave him the idea of making a programme about the drug, which he subsequently produced for Thames Television. He took care to avoid using any of the confidential information he had acquired during

---

[27] *BSC v. Granada Television Ltd*, n.25 above.
[28] Theft Act 1968, s. 20.

his consultancy. However, the majority in the Court of Appeal injuncted *The Primodos Affair* on the grounds that Elstein had entered upon a personal confidential obligation to Scherings, which he had betrayed by making the programme. Although he did not use confidential information, he had unfairly exploited his confidential relationship with Scherings by accepting further payment from Thames to make a programme about them.[29]

The decision in *Schering Chemicals* is incompatible with the European Convention, and has been criticised on other grounds by the Law Commission.[30] Thames Television, lamentably, did not appeal it. However, the authority of the case can be narrowed so that it applies only to persons in Elstein's special position of divided loyalty. The court was heavily influenced by what it termed the "treachery" of a man who had been hired to help foster the company's image and accepted payment for producing a programme that was critical of the same company's record. Had he instead passed the idea and information to another producer without taking any payment, the position would have been different.

Domestic relationships

Although there is no fully developed or coherent substantive law protecting personal privacy in Britain, some veil of secrecy may be drawn over domestic intimacy by the doctrine of breach of confidence, which can stop the betrayal by one party of the secrets of a marriage. In 1967 a newspaper was stopped from publishing the Duke of Argyll's account of his stormy marriage with the Duchess.[31] The decision was expressed to cover *communications* between husband and wife pursuant to "the normal confidence and trust" that is judicially assumed to exist in marriage. The *Argyll* decision has been cited with approval in several subsequent cases. However, the courts would be unlikely to stop an autobiography by one partner published some years after the relationship had ended. (The Duke of Argyll's revelations were touted for publication in the immediate aftermath of a bitter divorce, and the court's decision was influenced by the fact that they contained items of evidence that could not have been reported.) The Prince of Wales obtained an *ex parte* injunction against the publication of purported tape recordings of his conversations with his bride-to-be, Lady Diana. This accords with *Francome*'s case in which a well-known jockey was able to restrain publication of information obtained from illegal taps on his telephone. The relationship need not be marital or even heterosexual:

---

[29] *Schering Chemicals Ltd v. Falkman Ltd* [1981] 2 All E.R. 321.
[30] Law Commission, *Breach of Confidence*, at paras 6.67–9.
[31] *Argyll v. Argyll* [1967] Ch. 302.

Ms Stephens had a lesbian affair with a woman who was subsequently killed by her husband. She talked about it to Ms Avery, another close friend, who passed on the confidences to *The Mail on Sunday*, which published a story. The newspaper attempted to strike out Ms Stephens' claim for damages for breach of confidence on the grounds that the lesbian relationship was immoral and information relating to it should not be protected. It also argued that since Ms Stephens and Ms Avery were merely friends, there was nothing in their relationship to attract a duty of confidence. The judge did not have to decide which party would finally succeed, but he rejected the newspaper's claim that there was no case to be tried. He accepted the principle that the court would not protect a confidence relating to matters with a grossly immoral tendency, but said that in the late 1980s there was no consensus over what, if any, kind of consensual sexual conduct between adults was grossly immoral. The courts would enforce confidences even between friends.[32]

The case was followed in 1997 when Michael Barrymore was granted an injunction to prevent *The Sun* publishing further articles based on interviews with Barrymore's former lover. As Mr Justice Jacob said:

> "The fact is that when people kiss and later one of them tells, that second person is almost certainly breaking a confidential arrangement. It all depends on precisely what they do. If they merely indicate that there has been a relationship, that may not amount to a breach of confidence and that may well be the case here, because Mr Barrymore had already disclosed that he was homosexual, and merely to disclose that he had had a particular partner would be to add nothing new. However, when one goes into detail (as in *The Sun* article), about what Mr Barrymore said about his relationship with his wife and so on, one has crossed the line into breach of confidence."[33]

In *Spycatcher (No. 2)* Lord Keith said "The right to personal privacy is clearly one which the law should in this field seek to protect." He gave the example of an anonymous donor of a very large sum to a worthy cause. Such a person ought to be able to restrain a breach of confidence in his identity in connection with the donation.[34]

A limitation on *Argyll* was imposed when the late John Lennon was denied an injunction to stop publication of his ex-wife's memoirs about their marriage. Both had already written and talked in public about the relationship, so the singer was unable to show that the information was still confidential.[35] In *Stephens v. Avery* and *Barrymore* the judges used the test of whether the information was known to a "substantial number

---

[32] *Stephens v. Avery* [1988] 2 All E.R. 477.
[33] *Barrymore v. Newsgroup Newspapers Ltd* [1997] F.S.R. 600.
[34] *Att.-Gen. v. Guardian Newspapers (No. 2)*, n.11 above, at pp. 639–40.
[35] *Lennon v. News Group Newspapers and Twist* [1978] F.S.R. 573.

of people", so that injunctions to preserve confidence can still be granted even though the secrets are known to a few close friends or relations.

Government confidences

The Official Secrets Acts place restrictions on civil servants leaking information to the press, although Cabinet Ministers will almost always be able to authorise themselves to discuss matters with the media. However, in 1975 the Attorney-General invoked the civil law of confidence to try to stop publication of Richard Crossman's memoirs. The Lord Chief Justice agreed that public secrets could be restrained by the court, but it had to be satisfied that any restriction was in the public interest. Cabinet discussions come within this category and could be protected, but not forever. It is not the case that "once a confidence, always a confidence". Stale secrets will not be protected and the Crossman memoirs were not injuncted because they related to confidential meetings that had taken place at least 10 years prior to publication.[36] Outside the context of the Cabinet room, it will be hard for the Government to show the necessary public interest in suppression, unless national security is involved. The Australian High Court has refused to accept that its Foreign Minister could stop the publication of diplomatic cables between the Australian Embassy in Djakarta and Canberra on grounds of breach of confidence when no security secrets were revealed and their potential for embarrassment was insufficient to warrant an injunction:

> "It is unacceptable in our democratic society that there should be a restraint on the publication of information relating to government when the only vice of that information is that it enables the public to discuss, review and criticize government action. Accordingly, the court will determine the Government's claim to confidentiality by reference to the public interest. Unless disclosure is likely to injure the public interest, it will not be protected. The court will not prevent the publication of information which merely throws light on the past workings of government, even if it be not public property, so long as it does not prejudice the community in other respects. Then disclosure will itself serve the public interest in keeping the community informed and in promoting discussion of public affairs. If, however, it appears that disclosure will be inimical to the public interest because national security, relations with

---

[36] *Att.-Gen. v. Jonathan Cape Ltd* [1976] Q.B. 752. See Hugo Young, *The Crossman Affair* (Hamish Hamilton and Jonathan Cape, 1976).

foreign countries or the ordinary business of government will be prejudiced, disclosure will be restrained."[37]

This principle was the key to the media's ultimate success in the English litigation over *Spycatcher*:

The *Guardian* and *Observer* published the main allegations in Peter Wright's book *Spycatcher* at the time when the book was the subject of confidentiality proceedings in Australia. On the eve of publication of the book in the Untied States, *The Sunday Times* began to serialise it. All were injuncted in England from publishing any further matter from the book until a trial could take place in this country. This injunction was upheld by the House of Lords. In the meantime the book, having been published in the United States, became an international best-seller. The newspapers continued to defend their right to publish at the trial and in the subsequent appeals. They successfully opposed the grant of a permanent injunction. The House of Lords accepted that Peter Wright, like other members and former members of the security services, was under a life-long duty to keep confidential any information he learnt in the course of his work. However, the Lords endorsed the views of the Australian High Court (which are quoted above). The Government, unlike private individuals and organisations, had to show that the public interest would be harmed by publication. Because of the widespread dissemination of the book's contents, the Attorney-General could not do that and the injunction against all the newspapers came to an end. The *Observer* and *Guardian* articles had contained nothing damaging to the public interest and so they did not have to compensate the Government for the stories they had already published. But *The Sunday Times* had jumped the gun and its instalment had included material from *Spycatcher* that had not been published elsewhere previously. It did not help the paper that publication of the whole book in the United States followed days later: it had deliberately engineered a profitable scoop and had to account to the Government for the profits it made by the increase in its circulation.[38]

In 1991 the European Court of Human Rights unanimously ruled that the injunctions upheld by the English courts after *Spycatcher* had been published abroad were an infringement of Article 10. Widespread foreign publication had destroyed all claim to confidentiality, and the Government's case had undergone a "curious metamorphosis". It had used the same language ("the interests of national security") to disguise its real objective, in the post-publication period, of protecting the security service from embarrassment in Britain and deterring its past and present members who might be minded to follow in Wright's footsteps. This

---

[37] *Commonwealth of Australia v. John Fairfax Ltd* (1981) 32 A.L.R. 485. For similar sentiments of U.S. courts, see *New York Times v. U.S.* 403 U.S. 713 (1971).
[38] *Att.-Gen. v. Guardian Newspapers Ltd (No. 2)*, see n.11 above.

was not a sufficient reason to bring into play the national security exception to Article 10's freedom of expression guarantee. The Court narrowly held (by 14 votes to 10) that the Government had been entitled to seek an injunction on national security grounds *prior* to publication abroad, because of the risk that the book might contain material damaging to the intelligence services.[39]

The extra burden which public bodies must carry of showing positively that disclosure would harm the public interest may apply as well to private bodies to whom public functions have been contracted out:

> The accountants KPMG Peat Marwick had prepared a report for Liverpool City Council on a cable-laying contract which the Council had entered into and which had caused extensive losses. The accountants failed in their attempt to restrain the *Liverpool Echo* from publishing material from the report. Because the review could as well have been done by the chief executive or councillors there was no reason for the accountants to have a lesser onus to discharge. The judge held that in any case the newspaper would have satisfied the public interest defence.[40]

Documents subject to discovery

The process of discovery, whereby one party to litigation is obliged to disclose private documents relevant to the case, is protected by the laws both of contempt of court and of breach of confidence. A barrister, solicitor or litigant who discloses such documents to the media may be punished for contempt and the media may be restrained from publishing their contents by an injunction for breach of confidence (see p. 477). The *Sunday Times* obtained some of its information about the process of thalidomide manufacture by purchasing documents disclosed by Distillers to an expert witness. Despite the obvious public interest in the matter, the court granted the junction on the basis that a greater public interest in the proper administration of justice required it to protect the confidentiality of the process of document discovery.[41]

Similarly, statements given to prosecution authorities by suspects are confidential in the sense that they cannot be used other than for the authorities' statutory functions.

> The SFO co-operated with the makers of a BBC documentary about the agency's rather mixed performance. It disclosed a statement by Robert Bunn, one of the defendants in the Maxwell trial. The court held that this

---

[39] *Observer and Guardian v. U.K.* (1991) 14 E.H.R.R. 153.

[40] *KPMG Peat Marwick v. Liverpool Daily Post & Echo* March 29, 1994, Pill J., unreported, but see Courtney, Newell and Rasaiah, *The Laws of Journalism* (Butterworths, 1995), para. 12.22.

[41] *Distillers Co. (Biochemicals) Ltd v. Times Newspapers Ltd* [1975] Q.B. 613.

would ordinarily amount to a breach of confidence which could not be justified by the SFO seeking to defend its record (if it were, the court said, the confidentiality in all cases would be precarious and the accused would be likely to be deterred from making such statements). However, in the present case the judge in the criminal trial had read the statement to himself while in open court. This put the contents of the statement into the public domain and there was no confidence left to protect.[42]

Other duties of confidence

The categories of confidential relationships are not closed, and courts have found them to exist (or, rather, because the issue usually arises on an interlocutory injunction, have held it is *arguable* that they exist) in many other contexts. For instance, in *Hellewell v. Chief Constable of Derbyshire*,[43] Mr Justice Laws held that a duty of confidence could arise when the police took a "mugshot" of a suspect at a police station. The photograph will not only show the suspect's face (which is not confidential) but its setting will invite an inference that he is suspected of an offence (which may well not be a public fact). Hellewell could not prove that the police had gone beyond a reasonable use of the photograph for the prevention or detection of crime, so he could not show a *breach* of confidence. By contrast, when Myra Hyndley's confessions to the Moors' murders 20 years afterwards were incorporated into a book written by the investigating police officer, he was sued by his employers (the police authority) for breach of confidence. This was a clear case of use of confidential police material for non-policing purposes.

A duty of confidence was also imposed on a press photographer who booked into a hotel in whose grounds the band "Oasis" was preparing a photographic shoot for the cover of their new album. Because of the security arrangements it was seriously arguable that the photographer ought to have realised that the assembly of props and people for the cover picture was confidential.[44] Similarly the makers of the film *Frankenstein* starring Kenneth Branagh and Robert de Niro obtained an injunction to restrain the publication of photographs of the set, costumes or prosthesis used in the film. The photographs had probably been taken on the set despite security arrangements and notices prohibiting photography.[45]

---

[42] *Bunn v. BBC* [1998] 3 All E.R. 552, Lightman J.
[43] [1995] 1 W.L.R. 804.
[44] *Creation Records Ltd v. News Group Newspapers* [1997] E.M.L.R. 444.
[45] *Shelley Films Ltd v. Rex Features Ltd* [1994] E.M.L.R. 134, Ch.D. In this case, unlike the Oasis case, the injunction was additionally granted to prevent infringement of copyright. The defendant photographic agency did, however successfully resist an order to name its source for the photographs.

Both of these cases involved secrets which were time-limited. Once the album and the film were released, anyone could see what had previously been embargoed. This did not prevent the courts granting injunctions. However, the temporary character of the confidential material did trouble the Court of Appeal in a case concerning Lady Thatcher's memoirs:

> Harper Collins, the publishers of *The Downing Street Years* had sold first and exclusive serialisation rights to Times Newspapers. In unexplained circumstances, the Daily Mirror obtained a copy of the book and stole a march on *The Times* by beginning to publish extracts first. An injunction was refused. The Court appreciated the commercial importance of preserving confidentiality until *The Times* had the opportunity to exploit the rights which it had purchased, but thought that this novel extension of the law of confidence should not be created on an application for an interlocutory injunction. A second (and possibly more influential) consideration was that the claimants were forced to concede a public interest in publication of Lady Thatcher's views on John Major and other members of the present Cabinet so far as they were inconsistent with her previously published opinions. Drafting an injunction in sufficiently clear and precise terms to permit the *Mirror* to disclose this news proved impossible and for this reason as well the injunction was refused.[46]

One case in 2000 came tantalisingly close to forging a right to privacy from a breach of confidence claim.

> The main reason for security arrangements at the wedding of Michael Douglas and Catherine Zeta-Jones was that the happy couple had sold exclusive photographic rights to the magazine *OK!* Somehow unauthorised photographs were obtained by *OK!*'s rival *Hello!* The Douglases and *OK!* discovered this very shortly before *Hello!*'s publication and obtained an injunction in the High Court. The next day, *Hello!* appealed and the Court of Appeal set the injunction aside. It accepted that it was certainly arguable that the arrangements made to tell guests that photography was not allowed were sufficient to impress a duty of confidence on the guests. They could, of course, see what was happening and probably could not have been prevented from describing it in their own words, but, in the old newspaper phrase, a picture was worth a thousand words. The difficulty which the judges foresaw was that at trial it might emerge that the photographer was an intruder on whom no duty of confidentiality could have been imposed. The judges (to varying degrees) thought that an English law of privacy was on its way, but this particular case did not need to resolve the issue. The Douglases' claim to privacy was consider-

---

[46] *Times Newspapers Ltd v. MGN Ltd* [1993] E.M.L.R. 443, CA. It was subsequently reported that MGN paid £35,000 plus interest to settle the case: *Media Lawyer*, September/October, 1999, p. 11.

ably diluted because they were seeking to protect not a small private wedding, but a grand occasion to which 250 guests had been invited and which, by their arrangement with *OK!* was due to be publicised throughout the world. The injunction was discharged in the end because of the application of familiar common law principles concerning the relative difficulties of assessing loss. If the injunction was refused and the claimants won at trial, their losses would be large but not so difficult to compute. If the injunction was granted but the defendants won at trial, they would have been entitled to compensation, but calculating their losses from an injunction which would effectively have prevented them from publishing that issue of *Hello!* at all would have been extremely difficult. The *Hello!* case fizzes with ideas about privacy but it provides no firm answers.[47]

PUBLIC INTEREST DEFENCE

The media are justified in publishing information in breach of confidence if the public interest in doing so outweighs the public interest in preserving the confidence. This defence originated from the more narrow rule that the courts would not restrain the disclosure of iniquity[48]:

John McVicar agreed to write a book with one Cork, a former policeman, about corruption in the Metropolitan Police. Cork was to have the right to approve the manuscript before publication. In some of his conversations with McVicar he asked the writer to turn off his tape-recorder so as to speak in confidence. Unknown to Cork, McVicar had a second machine taped to his leg, which continued to record after the open machine had been switched off. Cork never approved the manuscript, but the *Daily Express* wished to publish his allegations of corruption. The publication was undoubtedly in breach of confidence and in breach of contract, but Mr Justice Scott accepted that evidence of the corruption thus revealed was properly a matter of public interest, the publication of which could not be restrained. He said that: "newspapers had many functions and practices, some more attractive than others, but one function was to provide a means whereby corruption might be exposed. That could rarely be done without informers and often breaches of confidence."[49]

In other cases the courts held that the wrongdoing alleged did not have to amount to a crime to justify publication. They began to formulate the defence more widely than "iniquity" and developed a general

[47] *Douglas v. Hello! Ltd* [2001] 2 All E.R. 289, CA.
[48] *Gartside v. Outram* (1856) 26 L.J. Ch. 113, at 130.
[49] *Cork v. McVicar, The Times*, October 31, 1995.

principle of balancing the public interest in disclosure against the public
interest in preserving confidence.

> The sales manager of a large laundry firm resigned and took some of the
> firm's documents to a newspaper, which used them to allege that the firm
> was engaging in monopolistic practices and evading tax. The Court of
> Appeal held that this was misconduct of a kind that disentitled the firm
> to injunct the newspaper article. The defence extended beyond proof of
> crime or fraud to "any misconduct of such a nature that it ought in the
> public interest to be disclosed to others".[50]

> An author of a book about scientology described courses offered by
> that organisation, and certain of its practices, based upon information he
> had obtained in breach of confidence. The Court of Appeal refused an
> injunction: "There is good ground for thinking that these courses contain
> such dangerous material that it is in the public interest that it should be
> made known.[51]

> The public relations officer employed by singer Tom Jones sold his
> memoirs to a newspaper, which began to publish them under the rubric
> "Tom Jones Superstud. More Startling Secrets of the Family". The court
> refused an injunction, because the article revealed hypocrisy:

>> "If a group of this kind seek publicity which is to their advantage . . .
>> they cannot complain if a servant or employee of theirs afterwards
>> discloses the truth about them. If the image which they fostered was
>> not a true image, it is in the public interest that it should be
>> corrected . . . it is a question of balancing the public interest in main-
>> taining the confidence against the public interest in knowing the
>> truth . . . The public should not be misled".[52]

In the important case of *Lion Laboratories v. Evans and Express
Newspapers*[53] the Court of Appeal unequivocally ruled that the public
interest defence to an action for breach of confidence was not limited
to situations where there had been serious wrongdoing by the claimant.
If the media could produce evidence to show that the public had a
serious and legitimate interest in the revelation, then publication was
excusable even if the claimant's behaviour could not be criticised. Thus
the *Daily Express* was permitted to publish internal documents extracted
from the manufacturer of the intoximeter that revealed doubts about the
efficacy of a machine being used by police to obtain convictions to
convict for drink-driving offences. Although no "iniquity" attached to
the claimant, the possibility of wrongful convictions raised a matter of
vital public interest." Similarly, no iniquity was involved in the story

---

[50] *Initial Services Ltd v. Putterill* [1968] 1 Q.B. 396.
[51] *Hubbard v. Vosper* [1972] 1 All E.R. 1023.
[52] *Woodward v. Hutchins* [1977] 2 All E.R. 751.
[53] *Lion Laboratories v. Evans and Express Newspapers* [1985] Q.B. 526.

published by the *Daily Mirror* on the basis of leaked information that the Maastricht Referendum Campaign had received a donation of £250,000 via a Swiss Bank account. The judge nonetheless held after a critical appraisal that the defendants had a strong potential defence of public interest.[54]

The House of Lords in the second *Spycatcher* appeal has authoritatively confirmed that this is the correct approach.[55] Peter Wright did indeed make allegations of serious wrongdoing by the security services, including an assassination attempt on Colonel Nasser and an MI5 plot to destabilise the Labour Government of Harold Wilson. However, these occupied a relatively small part of the book and if *Spycatcher* had not been published abroad, the media may not have been able to show a public interest sufficiently compelling to justify publication in Britain of Wright's descriptions of his life in MI5 and his suspicions about fellow members of the service.

This approach is also now reflected in section 12(4) of the Human Rights Act which says:

> "The Court must have particular regard to the importance of the Convention right of freedom of expression and, where the proceedings relate to material which the respondent claims, or which appears to the court, to be journalistic, literary or artistic material (or to conduct connected with such material), to—(a) the extent of which (i) the material has, or is about to become available to the public; or (ii) it is, or would be, in the public interest for the material to be published."

What the courts have decided in the cases culminating with *Spycatcher* and the *Cavendish Memoirs* in the House of Lords (see below p. 245) is that in every case where public interest is raised as a defence, the court (both at the "interim injunction" stage and more fully at the trial) must perform a balancing exercise by deciding whether the beneficial effects of publication outweigh the damage that may be caused both to the claimant and to the public. It is public interests rather than private interests that must be considered, although the private interest of the claimant is dressed up as a public interest by the judicial assumption that there is a general public interest that confidences should be

---

[54] *Maastricht Referendum Campaign v. Hounan* May 28, 1993 (unreported), Jonathan Parker J. *London Regional Transport v. London Underground Ltd and the Mayor of London*, August, 24, 2001, CA, confirmed that a public interest in disclosure can sometimes take precedence over an express undertaking of confidence.

[55] [1988] 3 All E.R. at 649 (Lord Griffiths), at 659 (Lord Goff). See also *BSC v. Granada*, n. 25 above, where the point was not argued but Lords Fraser and Salmon (the latter in a dissenting judgment) approved the "balance of public interests" approach: see at 468 and 472.

respected. This formula operates in practice to allow the court (*i.e.* the judges) to produce an outcome influenced by subjective appreciation of the evidence. The decision will be based on the value judgment of the judge rather than any precise legal rule. In many cases such value judgments will reflect popular attitudes—especially where the media are stopped from publishing details extracted by chequebook journalism about the private lives of popular claimants such as television presenters and members of the Royal Family. The judge's sense of fair play, however, will protect the privacy of some whom the majority might wish to oppress, such as Myra Hindley (the *Sun* was injuncted from publishing her parole request) and persons suffering from AIDS. The unsatisfactory cases are those where judicial attitudes reflect the conditioning of class or professional life, leading to an appreciation of public interest that cannot be objectively supported. Only a lawyer, for example, could so highly value the process of discovery as to accord its confidentiality a status that outweighed the revelation of reasons for the thalidomide tragedy or the benefits of supplying journalists with documents that have been read in open court.[56] One perennial problem is to convince judges that a corporate claimant's right to privacy in respect to documents that reveal secret operations should not prevail over the public benefit of knowing about the questionable activities of powerful corporations. The problem is to find acceptance for the principle that the right to impart and receive important information outweighs any rights of property in that information.

The Court of Appeal in *Lion Laboratories* made important comments on the public interest defence. It repeated the distinction between matters that were in the public interest and those that were merely interesting to the public (like many epigrams, its superficial simplicity conceals great difficulties in application). It warned the press of the danger of confusing the public interest with its own interests in increasing sales from sensational exposures. It also indicated that the *degree* of disclosure has to be justified in the public interest. The Court of Appeal made the same point in the *Francome* case. Assuming that the telephone taps did indicate breaches of Jockey Club regulations, this might justify disclosure to the Jockey Club or the police, but not to the world at large. Lord Griffiths in *Spycatcher (No. 2)* similarly said that a person who came across confidential information of misdeeds by the security services might be entitled to tell the proper authorities, but not necessarily to publish it to the world.[57] Again, these propositions defy rational explanation in a world where police are corrupt or lazy and incompetent, where professional institutions over protect their own member and

---

[56] *Distillers (Biochemicals) Ltd v. Times Newspapers Ltd* [1975] Q.B. 613 and *Home Office v. Harman* [1983] A.C. 280.
[57] [1988] 3 All E.R. at 657.

where no "proper authority" is capable of tough action against the security services. The court accepted that the *Express* was entitled to take the view that publication would put more pressure on the department than a "discreet behind-the-doors approach". A campaign of public pressure on authority was "an essential function of a free press, and we would all be the worse off if the press was unduly inhibited in this field".[58] Except, it would seem, if the campaign concerns the security services.

Essentially the balance has to be struck in the light of the circumstances of each individual case. *Spycatcher* was a rare occasion when the press persevered and, having been injuncted before trial, carried on to a full hearing, by which time the balance (tipped by publication abroad) came down in its favour. One case where the balance clearly tipped the other way concerned the revelation of medical records:

> A newspaper paid £100 to employees of a health authority for details of two doctors who had been identified as having AIDS. The paper published one story saying that there were doctors continuing to practise although they had AIDS and that the Department of Health and Social Security wished to conceal the fact. A second article intended to name the doctors. The health authority obtained an interim injunction. At the trial the judge found that the public interest in protecting confidentiality of patients generally and AIDS patients in particular (because they might not otherwise identify themselves) outweighed the public interest in publication. The health authority had done no wrong and the injunction did not stop the debate about AIDS or whether doctors with the disease should continue to practise.[59]

The prevalence of references to public interest may be confusing. The wider and now accepted formulation of the defence is available to the media to justify publication once the claimant has made out a case for an injunction. However, in order to make out that case when the claimant is the Government or a public body, it has to be shown that an injunction would positively be in the public interest. This preliminary hurdle was too high for the Attorney-General in *Spycatcher* (because the book had been widely published overseas), as it had been for his predecessor in the *Crossman Diaries* case (because the Cabinet "secrets" were old hat).[60]

PUBLIC DOMAIN

Information cannot be protected from disclosure if it can be gleaned from public sources or if its originator has already circulated it to a

---

[58] [1984] 2 All E.R. 434–5.

[59] *X. v. Y.* [1988] 2 All E.R. 648.

[60] *Att.-Gen. v. Jonathan Cape Ltd* [1975] 3 All E.R. 484; see also *Commonwealth of Australia v. John Fairfax Ltd*, n. 37 above.

number of outsiders. These general principles are based upon consider-able authority.[61] The majority decision in *Schering Chemicals*,[62] so far as it conflicts with these principles, has been doubted by the Law Commission.[63] The case can in any event be distinguished on the basis that Elstein had the idea for the programme while working for Scherings, and sold that idea, in breach of confidence, to Thames Television.

In the second *Spycatcher* case the House of Lords accepted that the Government could not prevent further publication of the Wright book even though, far from being responsible for its initial dissemination, it had done everything possible to stop it. The reality was that the material was no longer confidential. Lord Keith observed that publication abroad might not always prevent an injunction in Britain. Personal confidences (such as medical conditions) about a British resident might, for instance, cause extra embarrassment if published in Britain despite their prior foreign publication.[64] The majority of the Lords thought that Wright himself would not be free to publish his book despite the fact that anyone else could, because he should not be allowed to profit from his own wrong. Their conclusion was prompted by Wright's betrayal of trust and by resentment at the profits he was making from the book, and it compares unfavourably with the view taken by Lord Goff, who pointed out that neither Wright nor his publishers had been represented on the appeals, and it was difficult to see why they of all the world should be restrained from repeating what had become public know-ledge.[65] The majority decision means that profits from sales in Britain cannot enter the calculations of retired spies who publish their reminis-cences abroad. Once published, they can be "pirated" by the British press without any concern about copyright. Any royalties paid to the spy by his authorised publisher can be recovered by the Government as damages for breach of the spy's continuing contractual obligation to keep quiet.[66]

Spycatcher showed the importance of a foreign publication. The Government made well-publicised attempts to stop publication in other courts but generally without success. The High Court of Australia, for instance, refused an injunction, holding that there was no Australian public interest at risk and that the English Attorney-General could not

---

[61] *Saltman Engineering Co. Ltd v. Campbell Engineering Ltd (1948)* [1963] 3 All E.R. 413; *O. Mustad and Sons v. S. Allcock Co. Ltd (1928)* [1963] 3 All E.R. 416; *Att.-Gen. v. Guardian Newspapers Ltd (No. 2)*, above. See also Andrew Nicol *Breach of Confidence and the Media* (1981) 12 E.I.P.R. 348; the Law Commission, *Breach of Confidence*, paras 4.16–17; and Alan Boyle [1982] Public Law 574.

[62] See n. 29 above.

[63] *Att.-Gen. v. Guardian Newspapers Ltd (No. 2)*, n. 21 above, at 643.

[64] See n. 21 above.

[65] *Att.-Gen. v. Guardian Newspapers Ltd* [1988] 3 All E.R. 545 at 662–4.

[66] See *Att.-Gen. v. Blake* [2001] 1 A.C. 268.

use the Australian courts to enforce British governmental interests.[67] The Attorney-General had no better success in the Irish courts in relation to the book *One Girl's War* by Joan Millar.

> The book concerned the wartime experiences of a woman working for MI5, notably the shock she received on discovering that her boss (who had promised to marry her) was happier in the arms of men. None of the events described was later than 1945, and none was germane to current operations. Somewhat reluctantly the English courts granted an injunction because it was arguably a breach of Ms Millar's lifetime duty of confidence and because the Attorney-General had an arguable case that national security would be harmed by any publication by a member of the security services. It reached this conclusion even though the Irish courts had refused to enjoin the book. The latter had held that no Irish public interest was affected.[68]

The rationale for *One Girl's War* injunction has been effectively overruled by a decision of the House of Lords (hearing an appeal from the Scottish courts) in 1989:

> Anthony Cavendish, a former member of MI6, was refused authorisation to publish his memoirs, *Inside Intelligence*. He nonetheless had copies printed and distributed them as "Christmas cards" in 1987 to 279 friends. The English courts granted an interlocutory injunction to prevent Times Newspapers publishing the Cavendish material. *The Scotsman* refused to undertake not to publish. The House of Lords held that although members of the security service were under a life-long duty of confidence, the Crown would be granted an injunction to prevent publication only if the public interest would be harmed. Prior publication was the other most relevant circumstance. An interlocutory injunction was refused. Lord Templeman referred to the standard in Article 10 of the European Convention that restraints on free speech should be imposed only where necessary in a democratic society. He said that the courts should be guided by legislation as to what was necessary and not impose restraints different from or more severe than Parliament had thought appropriate. The Official Secrets Act 1989 had not come into force at the time of this decision, but Lord Templeman was guided by its requirement that publication of matters relating to the security services by an "outsider" would only be punishable if harm resulted.[69]

---

[67] *Att.-Gen. for England and Wales v. Heinemann Publishers Ltd* (1988) 78 A.L.R. 449, HCA.

[68] *Att.-Gen. v. Turnaround Distribution Ltd* [1989] F.S.R. 169, QBD; *Att.-Gen. for England and Wales v. Brandon Book Publishers Ltd* [1989] F.S.R. 37. The injunction against *One Girl's War* was lifted by consent after the European Court of Human Rights' decision on *Spycatcher*.

[69] *Lord Advocate v. Scotsman Publications Ltd* [1989] 2 All E.R. 852, HL. After this decision, the English court accepted that its injunction should not continue.

Criminal convictions are invariably announced in open court so are in the public domain and cannot be considered confidential information. Consequently a police officer who disclosed a journalist's previous convictions to his editor could not be liable for breach of confidence even though the officer had allegedly used the Police National Computer to obtain the details.[70] This case was followed in 1997 when the High Court held that convictions for paedophile offences could not be confidential information so that their disclosure to the owner of a caravan site could not give a remedy for breach of confidence.[71]

The European Court of Human Rights has criticised penalties or restrictions on the publication of information which is already in the public domain.[72] It seems to make no difference (at least so far as restraining further publication is concerned) that the material was put into the public domain by the defendant.[73] As we have seen, the Human Rights Act 1998, s. 12(4) requires the court to take account of the extent to which information has, or is about to, become available to the public.

PROCEDURE

Who can sue?

Actions for breach of confidence can be brought only by the "person or organisation to whom the confidence is owed".

> *The Sunday Times* obtained, from a source in the Greek military junta, a report commissioned by that Government from a British public relations firm advising how the junta could improve its fascistic image. The public relations consultants were refused an injunction: they were owed no duty of confidence by the Greek Government, whence the leak had come, and only that Government would have the standing to sue. "The party complaining must be the person who is entitled to the confidence and to have it respected".[74]

---

[70] *Elliott v. Chief Constable of Wiltshire, The Times*, December 5, 1996, CA. The journalist was not necessarily without a remedy. If he could prove that the disclosure was malicious, made with intent to harm him for an improper purpose and that he had suffered damage as a result, the officer could be sued for misfeasance in public office. Unauthorised disclosure by the Criminal Records Agency or by an authorised recipient of its certificates is an offence under the Police Act 1997, s. 124.

[71] *R v. Chief Constable of the North Wales Police, ex p. AB* [1997] 4 All E.R. 691 affd [1998] 3 All E.R. 310, CA.

[72] See, *e.g. Fressoz and Roire v. France* (1999) 5 B.H.R.C. 654.

[73] *Weber v. Switzerland* (1990) 12 E.H.R.R. 508; *Vereinigung Weekblad Bluf! v. Netherlands* (1995) 20 E.H.R.R. 189.

[74] *Fraser v. Evans* [1969] 1 All E.R. 8.

This has the consequence, for instance, that a prison or special hospital would not have standing to seek an injunction to protect any duty of confidence owed only to a prisoner or patient.[75] However, there might be circumstances when a duty of confidence owed to the authority (*e.g.* by members of staff) was also under threat in which case it would have standing to sue. The courts have jurisdiction in appropriate cases to grant an injunction to prevent interferences with the discharge of an authority's public responsibilities. These interferences could, conceivably, take the form of a publication, but in that case the Article 10 rights of the publisher would be an important consideration.[76]

Interim injunctions

The Human Rights Act introduces two new restrictions on the grant of injunctions which restrict freedom of expression. These will be particularly important for the media in the context of breach of confidence injunctions.

In the first place, injunctions are not to be made in the defendant's absence unless the court is satisfied that all reasonable steps were taken to notify the defendant of the hearing or that there are compelling reasons why notice should not be given.[77] This brings the practice that was previously supposed to have been followed more forcefully to the attention of judges who are often asked to act on very short notice.

In the second place, pre-trial injunctions are not to be granted unless the court is satisfied that the applicant is likely to establish at trial that publication should not be allowed.[78] This ought to turn the courts away from their predominant concern with preserving the status quo and focus attention instead on whether the claimant's case is sufficiently strong to stand a good chance of success at trial. In the *Douglas* case (which concerned just such an application for a pre-trial injunction) the Court of Appeal accepted that section 12 required the court to "look at the merits of the case and not merely to apply the *American Cyanamid* test." Of course, in viewing what was the likely outcome at trial the court would consider any Convention rights of the claimant and some rights (such as a right to life) would have considerable importance.[79]

The section acknowledges the pre-eminent importance of the free

---

[75] *Broadmoor Special Hospital Authority v. Robinson* [2000] Q.B. 775, CA.
[76] *ibid.*
[77] Human Rights Act 1998, s. 12(2).
[78] *ibid.*, s. 12(3).
[79] *Douglas v. Hello!* [2001] 2 All E.R. 289, CA, at paras 149–153.

flow of information and opinion, as a human right which cannot be
infringed by the court on the basis that the publisher may subsequently
be compensated—because this cannot compensate the public for being
deprived of the information. What claimants must henceforth establish
is that they are likely to succeed in obtaining a permanent injunction at
the eventual trial, such burden being made the heavier by the fact that
at that trial the court will (a) be required to have particular regard to
the defendants' right to freedom of expression, and (b) to the prospect
that the material will enter the public domain, and (c) to the public
interest.[80]

The first to benefit from section 12 when the Human Rights Act
came into force was Andrew Morton, biographer of Princess Diana and
Monica Lewinsky, who had turned his talents to Posh 'n' Becks:

> Morton's publisher paid a former bodyguard to divulge details of his work
> for Victoria and David Beckham. The bodyguard was injuncted, but the
> court permitted Morton to complete his "unauthorised biography" of the
> pair, and to argue that such information as he received from the bodyguard
> was not subject to an enforceable duty of confidentiality because it was
> already in the public domain (the claimants had talked interminably to the
> media about their private lives, and Beckham was about to publish his
> own autobiography) or was trivial or else related to a matter of public
> interest (described by Morton as "the Faustian bargain which those who
> profit from iconic status must make with the tabloid press"). Morton's
> book was published, with a few deletions: the claimants accepted they
> could not at trial obtain an injunction in respect to these three classes of
> material, and so were debarred by section 12 from injuncting the whole
> book temporarily.

In breach of confidence lawsuits the critical stage is usually the
application for an injunction pending the trial. If the publisher beats off
that challenge and is able to print or broadcast the story, the action will
often evaporate, because it would be either pointless or too embarrassing to continue with a claim merely for financial compensation. If the
story is injuncted, the publisher will often lose interest, because by the
time the case comes to trial, years later, it will no longer be topical.

The risk of an injunction depends on the owner knowing that copies
have escaped. Normally, the media would wish to contact the owner to
confirm the authenticity of the documents prior to publishing them, and
to give the owner an opportunity to answer any allegations made on the
basis of the documents. Such contact would put the owner on notice,
and be sufficient evidence for an application for an injunction. The
dilemma is real and at times agonising. When the *Daily Mail* was sup-

---

[80] Human Rights Act, 1998, s. 12(4).

plied with apparently genuine documents implicating executives of British Leyland in an overseas pay-off scandal, it chose to publish without notifying British Leyland. The result was enormous libel damages when the documents were revealed as forgeries—a fact that British Leyland would have been able to establish convincingly had it been asked. Had the documents been genuine, of course, British Leyland might have obtained an injunction against their publication. The case shows how the present law of breach of confidence encourages bad press practice: had it been clear law that the public interest in the story would have defeated the confidence claim, the newspaper would have had no hesitation in putting its allegations to British Leyland prior to publication.[81]

Applications for these interim injunctions can be made at very short notice and must be speedily resolved. The evidence is frequently incomplete and almost always given on affidavit rather than orally. The courts are conscious of these problems, and most judges are aware of the presumption against prior restraint.[82] In libel cases the courts are extremely reluctant to injunct a publication that the defendant asserts is the truth or fair comment, and similar criteria are used in application for injunctions on the grounds of injurious falsehood or contempt of court.[83] Lord Denning has expressed the view that in breach of confidence cases the courts should accept the defendant's assertion of public interest in the story as enough to defeat the injunction application.[84] Alternatively, the court might base its decision on a preliminary view of the two sides' arguments.[85]

Lord Denning's view attracted support from other judges only when (as in the *Tom Jones* case) the allegation of breach of confidence was interwoven with an action for libel.[86] Otherwise, before the Human Rights Act, the claimant had to show only an arguable case. Now section 12 requires proof that the claimant is likely to succeed at trial. If the claimant can cross this higher hurdle, he must still show that his loss (in the event of publication) could not be adequately compensated in damages. Claimants rarely have difficulty in persuading a court that breach of confidence had no easy money equivalent. It was then for the defendant to show that delay in publication until trial would similarly

---

[81] See *The Times*, May 20, 1997, May 5, 1979, March 28, 1980.

[82] See now Human Rights Act 1998, s. 12.

[83] *Bonnard v. Perryman* [1891] 2 Ch. 269; *Clement & Johnson v. Associated Newspapers Ltd, The Times*, July 30, 1924; *Trevor & Sons v. Solomon* (1978) 248 E.G. 797; *Herbage v. Times Newspapers Ltd, The Times*, May 1, 1981 (all libel cases); *Bestobell Paints Ltd v. Bigg* [1975] F.S.R. 421 (injurious falsehood); *Att.-Gen. v. BBC* [1980] 3 All E.R. 161 at 172, 183 (contempt of court; see also Chap. 7).

[84] As in *Fraser v. Evans*, n. 74 above, at 12 and *Hubbard v. Vosper* [1972] 2 Q.B. 84; [1972] 1 All E.R. 1023.

[85] *Commonwealth of Australia v. John Fairfax*, n. 37 above, at 491.

[86] *Woodward v. Hutchins* [1972] 2 All E.R. 751, 755 *per* Lawton. L.J.

be difficult to compensate in money terms. This is because a claimant, as the price of an interlocutory injunction, will usually have to give an undertaking to pay such compensation if at the trial it cannot make out a case for a permanent injunction. An important exception to this rule is that the Crown, when acting to enforce the law, is not required to give an undertaking of this type.[87] If either party would suffer uncompensatable loss, the court has to consider the "balance of convenience" between the two; what lawyers describe as the *American Cyanamid* test, after the case in which it was first applied.[88]

In breach-of-confidence cases this approach favours suppression, simply because allowing publication of the secret is an irreversible step and preservation of the secret is what such actions are usually all about. The claimant is not interested in compensation years later, which will be fairly minimal even if in the event the information is true.

In cases involving the security services the courts have been particularly sympathetic to Government applications for interlocutory injunctions. The BBC was injuncted from broadcasting a rather scholarly series of discussions on the moral dilemmas of security work called *My Country Right or Wrong* because it included interviews with former members of the security services.[89] The injunction was lifted only after the Attorney-General had obtained transcripts on discovery and confirmed that the programmes were harmless. The most notorious example of judicial obeisance to Government claims of national security was *Spycatcher (No. 1)*, where by a majority of 3–2 the House of Lords held that the Attorney-General could still maintain an injunction despite its publication and massive sales in the United States and elsewhere.[90]

CONFIDENTIAL IDEAS

In the cases discussed above, breach of confidence has been deployed to suppress the revelation of embarrassing information that may have no commercial value. However, it is also relevant to the media in terms of its prime purpose, namely in preventing, or compensating for, the unfair exploitation of programme ideas and treatments. Normally, this

---

[87] *F. Hoffman La Roche AG v. Secretary of State for Trade and Industry* [1975] A.C. 295. A second exception is that a legally-aided claimant will not be denied an injunction because his or her cross-undertaking is valueless: *Allan v. Jambo Holdings Ltd* [1980] 1 W.L.R. 1252, CA.

[88] *American Cyanamid Co. v. Ethicon Ltd* [1975] AC 396.

[89] *Att.-Gen. v. BBC, The Times*, December 18, 1987.

[90] *Att.-Gen. v. Guardian Newspapers* [1987] 3 All E.R. 316.

form of piracy is combated by an action for breach of copyright. However, as we shall see, there can be no copyright in an idea, or even in
an elaborated idea that is not reduced to material form and substantially
copied. The planning stage for television programmes and plays will
frequently involve luncheons and meetings at which ideas are discussed,
and the law will in some circumstances impose obligations to honour
the confidence of those who impart original ideas that have commercial
value. In order for the claimant to succeed:

- the concept must be clearly identifiable, and have some significant element of originality not already in the realm of public
  knowledge. The originality may consist in a significant "twist"
  or "slant" to a well-known story;

- the concept must have been developed to the stage at which it
  has commercial potential and is capable of being realised as an
  actuality. A full synopsis is not necessary in cases in which a
  short statement, or oral elaboration, fulfil these criteria;

- the concept must have been given or expressed to the defendant
  in circumstances in which all parties recognise a moral obligation not to make further use of it without the consent of the
  communicator.

These principles were laid down in the case of *Fraser v. Thames
Television*.[91]

Thames screened a fictional series called *Rock Follies*, about the experiences of a three-girl rock group. The idea had originated with the manager
of an actual group called Rock Bottom, who proposed to Thames that
they should produce a series based on the formation of the group and the
subsequent experiences of its members. The concept was discussed at a
series of meetings with Thames executives, producer and writer, at a time
when the latter were seriously considering production using the Rock
Bottom group. This arrangement fell through, but Thames, using the other
performers, developed the concept into a successful series. *Rock Follies*
was substantially based on the characters and actual experiences of the
Rock Bottom girls and their manager, and a number of "twists" and
"slants" in the final treatment were based on information imparted by
them in the course of negotiations in which all parties were jointly concerned commercially in the possible use of the idea. These negotiations
would be recognised, in the television profession, as covered by an ethical
obligation of confidence. The concept was clearly original: although the
mere idea of an all-female rock group may be hackneyed, the "slant" of
focussing on the members as characters and professional actresses in their

---

[91] *Fraser v. Thames Television Ltd* [1984] Q.B. 44.

own right, and using the actual experiences of Rock Bottom, put sufficient flesh on the idea to justify its protection. The very fact that it was eventually turned into a much-acclaimed series was evidence of its commercial attractiveness and its ability to be realised in actuality. The claimants were awarded damages in the order of half a million pounds.

In deciding whether an idea was imparted in circumstances which imposed a duty of confidence, the court will take account of trade practice and the subjective perception of the parties, but neither can be conclusive of this essentially objective question, *i.e.* were the circumstances such that a duty of confidence was imposed?[92]

For all the difficulties that confidence and copyright may pose to exposure journalism, there is another side to these laws, which protect the creator of original work from having it copied and exploited without authorisation. The wire service, the video copier, the vast array of technology now available for mass reproduction and dissemination has made creative talent exceptionally vulnerable to piracy, and media interests have had to devote a great deal of their resources to protective measures against copyright theft. At the most serious level, this involves well-organised piracy, which can be combated only by severe application of the criminal law. But as an everyday problem for media organisations, the question of giving credit where credit is due can involve the most complicated and delicate considerations. Plots and themes and ideas can be lost over luncheons, borrowed subconsciously, and pass through the minds of a daisy-chain of progenitors. Unless questions of plagiarism are amicably resolved, they can involve authors and programme-makers in bitter and costly legal disputes. A BBC department was plunged into an unedifying quarrel over Desmond Wilcox and his book of *The Explorers* series. The rights of journalists became hopelessly entangled in the dispute over "The Ballsoff Memorandum"—a confidential note, mentioning sources by name, passed between a journalist and the editor of the *Observer*, leaked to and published by *Private Eye*.[93] The claimant, supported by the *Observer*'s editor, claimed that the magazine's action was a breach of copyright, which damaged the public interest by revealing journalistic sources; *Private Eye* argued that the public interest was served by revealing these sources and by showing the machinations behind the editorial policies of a major newspaper. The case was eventually decided upon a technicality, but it demonstrated, in the course of a long trial and a complicated judgment, how the "rights" claimed for journalists can be mutually confusing and contradictory when one part of the press seeks to investigate the confidential arrangements of another.

---

[92] *De Maudsley v. Palumbo* [1996] E.M.L.R. 460.
[93] *Beloff v. Pressdram Ltd* [1973] 1 All E.R. 241.

Protection of sources

It is a basic tenet of journalistic ethics that, in the words of the NUJ code of conduct, "A journalist shall protect confidential sources of information". But English judges have such an ingrained hostility to those who breach confidence—particularly corporate confidence—that they have developed the common law to provide themselves with power to order the unmasking of anyone involved in tortious wrongdoing. This is reasonable enough when it identifies corrupt employees who sell trade secrets to competitors; it is unreasonable when it threatens journalists with prison unless they breach their code of conduct and betray their news sources. Legislation (namely section 10 of the Contempt of Court Act 1981) invites judges to balance the interests of free speech against four interests which may favour revelation of sources, but this "balancing act" is highly subjective. Judges, mostly ignorant of the way the media works, may not understand the value of news as such (irrespective of whether it reveals iniquity) and the vital need to protect the sources for it, however unprepossessing or traitorous. This need was recognised by the European Court in *Goodwin v. United Kingdom* in a famous statement of principle[94]:

> "Protection of journalistic sources is one of the basic conditions for press freedom, as is reflected in the laws and professional codes of conduct in a number of Contracting States and is affirmed in several international instruments on journalistic freedoms. Without such protection, sources may be deterred from assisting the press in informing the public on matters of public interest. As a result the vital public watchdog role of the press may be undermined and the ability of the press to provide accurate and reliable information may be adversely affected. Having regard to the importance of the protection of journalistic sources for press freedom in a democratic society and the potentially chilling effect an order of source disclosure has on the exercise of that freedom, such a measure cannot be compatible with Article 10 of the Convention unless it is justified by an overriding requirement in the public interest."

Under section 2 of the Human Rights Act English courts must treat *Goodwin* as a precedent. Since it goes against the judicial grain, it is worth explaining why the European Court's statement of principle is correct.

Journalists are persons who exercise by profession the right to freedom of expression guaranteed to all by Article 10 of the Convention. They can claim no special privilege by virtue of this profession: journal-

---

[94] *Goodwin v. U.K.* (1996) 22 E.H.R.R. 123, para. 39.

ists are not above the law of their land. But it is through their professional commitment that in real life most information and many ideas—the "expression" to which Article 10 refers—gets imparted to the public. For that reason, the journalist is described as a "watchdog" for the public: a creature trained to react at unusual or suspicious movements, or when from instinct it gathers that things are not entirely what they seem. The watchdog is suffered and indeed protected by Article 10, because of the public importance of what it *may* do, notwithstanding that it often acts precipitously or mistakenly, by barking at shadows or frightening law-abiding citizens.

Although the case law relating to Article 10 predominantly concerns the expression of offensive or unfashionable political opinions or ideas, most of the information which is received and imparted in democracies falls under the generic description of "news"—the facts that are read in newspapers or heard on radio or television or internet news bulletins. It is the work of journalists to gather that raw factual material, to call up further research, to check and compare and conduct interviews, and ultimately to present the factual material as information for the public. This involves a combination of skills—of research and analysis, comprehension of complicated subjects, and of writing and presentation. But that is not all. One essential skill of investigative journalism is the cultivation of sources of information. Unless the law affords real protection to the confidential relationship between the journalist and his cultivated source, both the quantity and quality of "news" will be diminished.

Some news simply happens: the plane crash and the ferry disaster are public events, reported at first, then analysed with the help of sources inside the airline or ferry company, or the airline or ferry manufacturer, or inside the regulatory agency whose failure contributed to the disaster. A good deal of news, in modern society, is announced: by the press release, the publicity brochure, the press conference or the public relations department. There are in Britain 25,000 persons employed in public relations offices in Government departments, *feeding* news to journalists. There are many more—hundreds of thousands—employed in the same capacity by public and private companies. All these professional propagandists are concerned not only to announce news, but to put a "spin" upon it—a version most favourable to their employer. Sometimes, journalists can read between the lines of press handouts, and divine the real news which may not be so favourable to the employer. But mainly they are reliant upon the sources that they cultivate for information which does, or may have, news value.

The cultivation of sources is thus professionally essential for journalists. It is a basic tool of their trade, the means by which newsworthy information is extracted, other than from those paid to give it a particular spin. Were it not for "unofficial sources" obligingly talking "off the record" to journalists, there would simply be much less news in newspapers. There would be fewer facts and less information for discussion, for dispute and sometimes for retraction, in democratic society. That is the first reason why Article 10 protects, not just the right to impart information to the public, but the preceding right to cultivate and protect the news sources which provide much of that information in the first place. If sources, frightened of exposure and reprisal, decide not to talk, there will not only be less news, but the news which is published will be less reliable. It will not be checked for spin.

Sources, however carefully cultivated, are delicate blooms. They come in many varieties. Invariably, they have some reason for seeking anonymity. Sometimes, the position they hold makes it unseemly that they should be identified speaking to the press. Mostly, they have come by the knowledge that they think it right to impart because they are in some relationship which can be termed confidential—an employee, or a professional adviser, or a friend or relative. They apprehend that they will in some way suffer if their identity is discovered: maybe just hostility, more often reprisals in the form of loss of job or loss of trust. Almost always, they could be sued for breach of confidence by those on whom they inform. So most journalistic sources would decide not to impart information at all if there was any appreciable risk that their identity would subsequently be disclosed. That is why it is so vital to the values protected by Article 10 that the initial channel of communication, between source and journalist, should not be closed by the source's fear of being found out.

So the way the free press works—and it is an institution that has developed its working practices over centuries—is that journalists cultivate sources by promising them confidentiality. That is a solemn promise, made in the service of greater public interest, and it binds the conscience of the individual journalist. He should be prepared to go to prison, or suffer any financial penalty, rather than have the name dragged from him. The promise is not, however, absolute, because no promise of confidentiality *can* be absolute. Grounded in morality, it may have to give way when morality dictates that it must. Such occasions will be rare, but can readily be hypothesized: when the promise has been elicited by a trick, or it turns out that the source has tried to involve the journalist in a serious criminal conspiracy, or when breach of the promise is necessary to save an innocent life or to enable the recovery of a snatched child, and so on. No future source would distrust a journalist who breached his promise in such a case.

The law is entitled to provide for these situations, precisely because they are situations where source revelation is not inimical to the value of freedom of expression. Since source protection is an essential element in securing that value, then domestic law is only entitled to withdraw that protection to serve a value so imperative that it is more important than freedom of expression. The journalist whose source genuinely imperils national security, or threatens innocent life or continues to commit serious crime, can be obliged by law to break a confidence he should never expect to keep. Orders made in such rare cases would not frighten off sources who are the mainstay of news and information: they would recognise the moral imperative of disclosure, and would realise it could never happen to them.

Regrettably, despite the decision in *Goodwin*, English courts may and sometimes do order disclosure outside these exceptional circumstances. Their power to do so depends on who is asking the question and why.

The police and other investigators

If the inquiries are being made by the police (for instance, in connection with leaked information), journalists are in the same position as anyone else: they are, in general, under no duty to provide answers. Although this may make the police investigation more difficult, the obdurate interviewee is *not* committing the offence of obstructing the police in the course of their duties.[95]

However, the police have an exceptional power to insist on answers to their questions concerning suspected breaches of section 1 of the Official Secrets Act 1911.[96] The Home Secretary is politically responsible for these powers and must normally give his prior approval. The police cannot use them if they only suspect an offence under the Official Secrets Act 1989: Parliament made clear by the Official Secrets Act 1939 that compulsory inquisitions can be used only for detecting grave breaches of national security. The limited duty to tell the police of information relating to terrorist activities is considered in Chapter 11.

There is a growing parliamentary trend to give investigators the power to compel answers from their interviewees. Under the Financial Services Act 1986 the Department of Trade and Industry can appoint inspectors to investigate alleged insider dealing. The inspectors can require *any person* to produce documents and/or attend to answer the inspector's questions on oath.[97] The inspector can refer a failure to comply to the court. If the court finds that the interviewee has no reasonable excuse for refusing to answer, it can punish the refusal as if it were a contempt of court.[98] A specific provision prevents inspectors asking about legal advice or other matters covered by legal privilege.

As Jeremy Warner of *The Independent* discovered, "any person" can include journalists. The inspectors who summoned him were investigating

---

[95] Police Act 1996, s. 89(2); *cf. Rice v. Connolly* [1966] 2 Q.B. 414.
[96] The Official Secrets Act 1920, s. 6.
[97] Financial Services Act 1986, s. 177.
[98] *ibid.*, s. 178(1) and (2).

suspected leaks of price-sensitive information from the Department of Trade and the Monopolies and Mergers Commission (the predecessor of the Competition Commission). Two stories by Warner indicated that he had a source in these departments. Warner refused to identify him or her. There is no specific defence for journalists in the Financial Services Act, but the House of Lords, ruled that section 10 of the Contempt of Court Act 1981 (see p. 203) should be applied by analogy. In Warner's case they found that the disclosure of his source was necessary for the "prevention of crime" and he could be required to answer. Warner persisted in his refusal and was fined £20,000.[99]

Similar powers to compel attendance and answers to questions are given to inspectors appointed to look into a company's affairs[1] and to the Director of the Serious Fraud Office.[2]

When the Financial Services and Markets Act 2000 is brought fully into force the range of subjects into which there can be compulsory inquisition will be extended yet further. Inspectors can be appointed either by the Secretary of State or by the Financial Services Authority to investigate specific allegations of infringements of a broad variety of offences or regulatory requirements with which providers of financial services are supposed to comply.[3] In addition to questioning those immediately involved, inspectors can require third parties to attend before them, answer questions, otherwise provide such information as the investigators may require and/or produce relevant documents.[4] As with the 1985 and 1986 Acts, if a person fails to comply with an inspector's requirement, the inspector can certify the default to the court which, if satisfied that the person concerned failed without reasonable cause to comply with the requirement, may deal with him as if he were in contempt.[5] The phrase "without reasonable cause" would allow a journalist who was asked to reveal a source to invoke section 10 of the Contempt of Court Act and Article 10 of the Convention. It would then be for the inspector in the first place and the court in the second to

---

[99] In *Re An Inquiry under the Company Securities (Insider Dealing) Act 1985* [1988] A.C. 660 and (1998) *The Independent*, January 27, Ch. D. *N.B.*: the 1985 Act has been repealed and replaced by the Financial Services Act 1986, which will in turn be repealed by the 2000 Act (see below).

[1] Companies Act 1985, ss. 434 and 436. This does not expressly give a "reasonable excuse" defence, but the court's power to punish silence as contempt is discretionary and ought not to be exercised where Contempt of Court Act 1981, s. 10 or Article 10 would apply.

[2] Criminal Justice Act 1987, s. 2. A magistrates' court can punish non-compliance with a fine on level 5 (currently £5,000) or a sentence of six months' imprisonment, but, as with the Financial Services Act, only if there is no reasonable excuse for failure to answer the Director's questions.

[3] Financial Services and Markets Act 2000, s. 168.

[4] *ibid.*, at ss. 172 and 173.

[5] *ibid.*, at s. 177(1).

consider whether the conditions under which a journalist can be required to reveal a source were fulfilled.

If a person knows that an investigation is, or is likely to be conducted, he commits an offence if he destroys, falsifies, conceals or otherwise disposes of a document which he knows or suspects is or would be relevant to the investigation. The offence is punishable with six months' imprisonment and/or a fine up to the statutory maximum (currently £5,000) in the magistrates' court and up to two years' imprisonment in the Crown Court.[6]

Claimants in libel actions

There is a well-settled rule of practice that a defendant in a defamation action will not be required to name the writer or informant of the words complained of *at the pre-trial stage*.[7] This means that a publisher cannot be required to name its source in answer to a request for further information unless (exceptionally) the court orders otherwise. Although this protection lasts only until trial, it remains important because so many libel actions are settled before then. At trial, publishers now have the protection of section 10 of the Contempt of Court Act 1981 and Article 10 of the Convention and are unlikely to be ordered to disclose a source unless the identity is essential to enable the court to rule on a defence that has been raised. Even then, the problem can be resolved albeit expensively by withdrawing or modifying the defence. The rule has been applied in contempt proceedings so that the courts will not insist that the editor or publisher disclose the name of its source or writer.[8]

Claimants do not normally have difficulty in identifying someone to sue for an alleged libel in a newspaper. Every newspaper should carry the name and address of its printer (who is currently liable for any libel it contains; see p. 96).[9] If this obligation is broken, the claimant cannot compel people who had no connection with the libel to reveal the printer's name simply because they are aware of his identity.[10]

The courts

In what circumstances will a court compel journalists to disclose their sources? Journalists may attend court voluntarily to defend or assert

---

[6] Financial Services and Markets Act 2000, at s. 17(4) and (5).

[7] *Hennessy v. Wright* (1888) 21 Q.B.D. 509; *BSC v. Granada Television*, n.25 above; C.P.R. r. 533.

[8] *Re Bahama Islands Reference* [1893] A.C. 138.

[9] Newspapers, Printers and Reading Rooms Repeal Act 1869, Sched. 2.

[10] *Ricci v. Chow* [1987] 3 All E.R. 534, CA.

their rights, or to give evidence on behalf of others, or they may be forced by a witness order (in criminal trials) or *subpoena* (in civil cases) to attend to give evidence.

Witness summonses: admissible evidence and materiality

No witness can be made to answer a question or produce documents unless they are relevant to an issue in dispute between the parties.

> ITN successfully resisted a *subpoena* from a claimant in a civil action to produce all its untransmitted film of a rock festival at Windsor which had lasted several days. The Court of Appeal held that this was too wide and oppressive since the court was concerned only with one small incident.[11] A television company will be ordered to produce its "off-cuts" only if they are clearly important to help the court determine an issue.

The common law imposes wide-ranging duties on prosecutors to disclose material which might possibly have a bearing on the case. These duties have been refined by legislation,[12] but they still place a heavy onus of discovery on prosecutors and on governmental agencies that are part of "the apparatus of prosecution" such as the police and forensic science services. This is fundamentally different from the obligations which can be imposed on a third party witness, who can only be required to produce documents or things likely to be material evidence. The documents must be admissible in evidence and witness summonses cannot be used for fishing expeditions to obtain documents or evidence which might or might not prove on examination to be admissible.[13] Consequently a journalist who wrote about a conversation between a colleague and a police source in connection with the arrest of Kevin Maxwell successfully applied to have his witness order set aside: the only evidence which the journalist could give was inadmissible hearsay (*i.e.* what his colleague told him) and the identity of the colleague, who might have been able to give first hand evidence, was not itself material to any issue in the case.

Witness orders can be made by both magistrates' and crown courts and in both cases there is a procedure for setting aside the order.[14] Where the documentary material is voluminous or particularly sensitive

---

[11] *Senior v. Holdsworth, ex p. Independent Television News Ltd* [1976] Q.B. 23, CA.

[12] Criminal Procedure and Investigations Act 1996, Pt I.

[13] *R. v. Derby Magistrates' Court, ex p. B* [1996] A.C. 487.

[14] Magistrates' Courts Act 1980 s. 97(1) and Criminal Procedure (Attendance of Witnesses) Act 1965 ss. 2–2E. In the magistrates' court the applicant for the summons must demonstrate that the witness is likely to be able to give material evidence, although this burden is reversed in the Crown Court: *R. v. Reading J.J. ex p. Berkshire County Council* [1996] 1 Cr App. R. 239 DC.

the trial judge may, in his discretion, permit the witness to appoint an independent competent counsel to review the documents for their materiality to the issues in the trial.[15] This device was used at an Old Bailey trial in 1996 when an investigative journalist objected to production of his research documents and records of interviews.

Changes to the procedure for witness' summonses in the Crown Court made in 1996[16] mean that applications for summonses will normally be on notice to the prospective witness and objections can be taken at that stage. If the order is made despite the objection, it can require production of documents in advance of the trial, which is a result that can already be achieved in the civil courts.[17] Disobedience to a witness summons can result in the issue of an arrest warrant and up to 3 months imprisonment.[18]

Journalists' privilege: Contempt of Court Act s. 10

The common law did not give journalists an absolute right to preserve the confidentiality of their sources, but it did recognise that the judge had a discretion as to whether to force journalists to name their sources even where their identity was relevant to an issue in dispute.[19]

> Journalist Jack Lundin succeeded in showing that a trial of a police sergeant for corruptly providing information to a gambling casino about its rival customers would not be assisted by his disclosing the name of his source for an exposé of the whole affair that he had written for *Private Eye*. The prosecution case was already in a shambles and his evidence could not repair the damage. He was not guilty of contempt in refusing to answer because this was not necessary in the interests of justice.[20]

The common law position has now been strengthened by section 10 of the Contempt of Court Act 1981:

> "No court may require a person to disclose, nor is any person guilty of contempt of court for refusing to disclose, the source of information contained in a publication for which he is responsible unless it is established to the satisfaction of the court that it is necessary in the interests of justice or national security or for the prevention of disorder or crime."

---

[15] *R. v. W(G); R. v. (W)(E)* [1996] Crim. L.R. 904, CA, Crim. Div.
[16] Criminal Procedure and Investigations Act 1996, s. 66.
[17] Civil Procedure Rules, r.34.2.
[18] Criminal Procedure (Attendance of Witnesses) Act 1965, ss. 3 and 4.
[19] *BSC v. Granada Television*, n.25 above.
[20] *Att.-Gen. v. Lundin* (1982) 75 Cr. App. R. 90.

The pre-conditions for the protection in section 10 have been inter-preted broadly. Thus they apply even if the court's order is not in terms to require the source to be identified but rather the doing of an act (typically the return of a leaked document) which may have that result.[21] The section also applies even though it is not certain that the effect of the order will be identification of the source: it is enough if there is a reasonable chance that this will happen.[22] The phrase "contained in a publication for which he is responsible" requires further analysis.

> The claimant, an internet service provider, was the target of a sustained attack by a contributor to the defendants' internet discussion groups. When it complained about the defamatory postings, they were removed and eventually the defendants barred the contributor from access to their sites. However, the claimant wanted to sue the contributor for libel and brought proceedings against the defendants to force them to identify him. The defendants argued that they promised their contributors anonymity. Disclosure would also infringe the Data Protection Act and be contrary to the Contempt of Court Act, s. 10. Robert Owen J. ruled (uncontroversially) that the Data Protection Act 1998, section 35 allowed disclosure in obedience to a court order and/or the purpose of legal proceedings. But he also held that a section 10 only applied where a person was "responsible" in a legal sense for a publication. This is doubtful since section 10 can be invoked where there has been no actual publication and where no question of the defendant's legal responsibility arises. However, the judge went on, in a decision which was incompatible with *Goodwin*, to find a disclosure order necessary in the interests of justice because of the seriousness of the defamatory postings, their persistence and the potentially vast audience which they could reach.[23]

Section 10 establishes a presumption in favour of journalists who wish to protect their sources, but that presumption will be rebutted if the court concludes that revelation is necessary on one or more of the four stated grounds. "Necessary" is the key word in the section—it is not satisfied by proof that revelation is merely "convenient" or "expedient". The source's name must be "really needed" in the following situations.

---

[21] *Secretary of State for Defence v. Guardian Newspapers Ltd* [1985] A.C. 339, see below.

[22] *ibid.*

[23] *Totalise plc v. Motley Fool Ltd, The Times*, March 15, 2001.

In the interests of justice

This is the widest and most dangerous of the exceptions to the general principle enshrined in section 10. Regrettably, the House of Lords has chosen to interpret it in a way that inevitably permits subjective judicial value judgments on a journalist's conduct and the importance of his information, rather than by reference to principle. The question the court must ask in any case when an application is made for an order that a journalist name his source is whether the interests of justice in providing the name to the applicant "are of such preponderating importance in the indivdual case that the ban on disclosure imposed by the opening words of the section really needs to be overridden".[24]

This means that a journalist's ethical duty to protect his source will be overridden whenever the court, conducting a "balancing exercise", decides that the public interest in the applicant's right (generally) to take legal action against the source to protect property in information) outweighs the journalist's qualified right to maintain the pledge of confidence to his source. Some of the factors to be placed in the balance have been described by Lord Bridge:

> "One important factor will be the nature of the information obtained from the source. The greater the legitimate public interest in the information which the source has given to the publisher or intended publisher, the greater will be the importance of protecting the source. But another and perhaps more significant factor which will very much affect the importance of protecting the source will be the manner in which the information was itself obtained by the source. If it appears to the court that the information was obtained legitimately, this will enhance the importance of protecting the source. Conversely, if it appears that the information was obtained illegally, this will diminish the importance of protecting the source unless, of course, this factor is counterbalanced by a clear public interest in publication of the information, as in the classic case where the source has acted for the purpose of exposing iniquity".[25]

This approach emerged from a case in 1990 where a young journalist narrowly escaped prison after defying the courts by refusing to name his source.

---

[24] *X. v. Morgan Grampian Publishers Ltd & Others* [1991] 1 A.C. 1, *per* Lord Oliver at 44.

[25] *ibid*. This approach would endorse the decision in *Handmade Films v. Express Newspapers plc* [1986] F.S.R. 463, where a newspaper was held to be protected by s. 10 from disclosing to a film company the source from whom it obtained photographs of pop-star Madonna on a film set: no serious damage was threatening the claimant, and its loss could be compensated in monetary terms.

Bill Goodwin, a journalist on *The Engineer* magazine, received information from a source that a leading private company in a much-publicised
field was, contrary to its publicity, experiencing financial difficulties and
urgently seeking to raise a large loan. When Goodwin telephoned the
company to seek information and comment, the company responded by
obtaining a breach-of-confidence injunction and by seeking disclosure of
the name of his source. It produced evidence that convinced the courts
that the information leaked to the journalist must have come from a stolen
copy of a confidential corporate plan, and that the source may well have
been in contact with the thief. It needed the source's name in order to
obtain further injunctions and perhaps to trace the thief. The Court of
Appeal ordered the journalist to place the name of his source in a sealed
envelope and to hand it to the court to abide the outcome of final appeal
to the House of Lords. The journalist refused to put his source in peril
by this device and was found guilty of contempt. The House of Lords
subsequently confirmed that "the interests of justice" outweighed the
prima facie protection of section 10, because the source had been complicit in a grave breach of confidentiality, the information did not reveal
"iniquity" and had no great public interest value, and the company might
suffer severe damage unless it was able to identify the employee or consultant who was prepared to pass its secrets on to the press. The journalist
was ultimately fined £5,000 for refusing to obey the court's order against
which he lodged a complaint to Strasburg.

The House of Lords' decision illustrates how the judicial value
accorded to property rights tends to prevail over ethical claims by the
journalists in balancing exercises that require a subjective appreciation
of competing public interests. The case arose from a routine situation
where a journalist received unpaid and unsolicited confidential information of a newsworthy nature, and behaved very properly in checking it
with the company prior to publication. The English courts were not
prepared, however, to recognise any public interest in news-gathering
that fell short of revelation of "iniquity", and were overimpressed by
allegations of potential damage made by company officials in affidavits
that had not been tested under cross-examination. The importance of
the Strasbourg decision in *Goodwin v. United Kingdom*,[26] which held
that the approach of the English courts (exemplified by Lord Bridge's
"balancing act") had led to a breach of the Convention, is that it recognises the crucial importance of news-gathering as such to freedom of
expression, and so casts that mantle of Article 10 protection over
sources—whether high-minded or malicious and whether revealing
front page iniquity or run-of-the-mill facts worth only a passing mention
on the inside page. The European Court was unimpressed by Lord
Bridge's balancing act: it pointed out[27] that Article 10 jurisprudence

[26] (1996) 22 E.H.R.R. 123.
[27] para. 45.

would generally "tip the balance of competing interests in favour of the interest of democratic society in securing a free press". Thus the claimant's various interests, in eliminating the threat in its midst, in staunching the leak, in unmasking a disloyal aid or obtaining damages did not, even cumulatively, "outweigh the vital public interest in the protection of the applicant's source". That would need "an overriding requirement in the public interest" which could not be found in *Goodwin*'s case: the employee was substantially protected against further disclosure of his business plan by the injunction.

The Government did nothing to alter the Contempt Act after the decision in *Goodwin* came down in 1996, and, until it acquired additional force by section 2 of the Human Rights Act in October 2000, its reception was mixed.

In one important case, *Gaddafi v. Daily Telegraph*[28] the Court of Appeal applied it directly to permit journalists to protect their sources even when asserting that they were so reliable there was a "qualified privilege" in communicating their information (See Chapter 3, p. 134). However, a different Court of Appeal in *Camelot Group plc v. Centaur Communications Ltd*,[29] while purporting to follow *Goodwin*, in fact travestied it by ordering the return of financial accounts which exposed the greed and hypocrisy of national lottery directors and which had been leaked to *Marketing Week*. The Court of Appeal reasoned that the public interest was not engaged because the accounts would have published in due course. This ignores the importance of news, and its perishability (recognised in *Reynolds*) and is irreconcilable with other European Court decisions.[30]

Camelot is a pre-Human Rights Act authority which should not be followed: as the Court of Appeal said in the first case *after* the Act came into force, "the decisions of the European Court demonstrate that the freedom of the press has in the past carried greater weight in Strasbourg than it has in the courts of this country"[31] *Ashworth* itself marks a valuable recognition, as a result of *Goodwin v. United Kingdom*, that the "chilling effect" of court orders requiring source disclosure is not affected by the importance of the information or the mercenary motives of the source. As Laws L.J. put it, "the true position is that it is always prima facie contrary to the public interest that press sources should be disclosed; and in any given case the debate which follows will be conducted upon the question whether there is an overriding public interest, amounting to a pressing social need, to which the need to keep press sources confidential should give way".[32]

---

[28] [2000] E.M.L.R. 431.
[29] [1998] 1 All E.R. 251, CA.
[30] Notably *Freesoz and Roire v. France* (1999) 5 B.H.R.C. 654.
[31] *Ashworth Hospital Authority v. MGN Ltd* [2001] 1 All E.R. 991, 1012, CA.
[32] *ibid.* at 1012.

No such overriding interest could be discovered in the facts of *Camelot*. In *Ashworth* itself, it was found in the need to protect the privacy of patients of a mental hospital from having their intimate and detailed records, held on the hospital's database, sold to the tabloids by a disloyal employee they could not identify. The case involved the corrupt behaviour of an employee, who in breach of the Prevention of Corruption Acts as well as in breach of contract, was supplying documents impressed with utmost confidentiality—medical and psychiatric records—about inmates whose crimes made them of interest to the tabloids. In such circumstances it is hardly surprising that the court made an order to unmask the source: the "interests of justice" were in effect the overlapping interest of detecting and punishing serious criminal conduct. That is how section 10 should be read, as confined to "the interests of criminal justice", and as applying to journalists and editors who incite employees to act corruptly, especially where that conduct is designed to damage another's Convention right.

But even this righteous-sounding principle has its limits: losers of confidences, even through the agency of venal sources and cheque book journalists, cannot complain if their own negligence or lack of security has provided the opportunity of the loss. When Elton John's barrister tore up the draft of his confidential advice to the singer and left it in his Chambers' waste-paper bin, it quickly found its way—pieced back together—to the *Daily Express*. Morland J., over-impressed by the legal professional privilege attaching to the document, ordered the newspaper to identify its source, but the Court of Appeal pointed out that the fault lay with the Chambers in failing to have a proper security system or to institute any internal inquiry. Lord Woolf said that no journalist should be ordered to breach a solemn professional obligation unless all other ways of ascertaining the source had been exhausted.[33] This explains why Broadmoor Hospital failed to obtain an order for source disclosure against a local newspaper to which had been leaked a report on the escape of two convicted murderers. The Hospital had not conducted a leak inquiry before applying to the court and had not produced evidence that such inquiries would have been fruitless.[34] The judge also held that because the newspaper's story had concerned security at Broadmoor in which there was a lively public interest, he would not in any case have ordered disclosure.[35]

---

[33] *Sir Elton John v. Express Newspapers plc* [2000] 3 All E.R. 257, CA.
[34] *Specialist Hospital Service Authority v. Hyde* (1994) 20 B.M.L.R. 75.
[35] For other examples of cases where source discourse has been refused, see *Sanders v. Punch Ltd* [1998] 1 W.L.R. 986; *Essex C.C. v. Mirror Group Newspapers Ltd* [1996] 1 F.L.R. 585; *Maastricht Referendum Campaign v. Hounam*, May 28, 1993, unreported, Ch D; *Chief Constable of Leicestershire Constabulary v. Garavelli*, July 30, 1996, unreported, QBD.

In the interests of national security

Journalists who withhold disclosure on this ground can expect to go to prison for their contumely. The precedent was created when three were gaoled at the Vassall spy tribunal, and in 1985 the editor of *The Guardian* declined similar martyrdom by handing over the documents from which the identity of his unknown source—Sarah Tisdall—was deduced. Journalists who have a direct relationship with their source, to whom they have personally promised confidentiality, may feel they have no alternative but to take punishment, even if the name is demanded on grounds of national security. It was some belated consolation to *The Guardian* that when its appeal reached the House of Lords, the final ruling at least applied a more stringent test to the evidence that the Government must produce to overcome the presumption in favour of protecting sources:

> *The Guardian* published extracts from papers that concerned the deployment of Cruise missiles at Greenham Common and that had been sent to it anonymously. The Secretary of State for Defence demanded their return but the newspaper refused, saying that this might reveal their source. The House of Lords held that the value of the documents was negligible and since the purpose of the exercise was to enable the Ministry to deduce the source, the paper could invoke section 10. The section applied even though there was only a reasonable chance (rather than a certainty) that the paper's source would be revealed. The burden of proof lay with the Government to demonstrate that one of the exceptions applied. Although three of the five Law Lords were persuaded that national security required the leaker to be identified, all of them stressed that this conclusion could not be reached merely upon the Government's say-so. There had to be realistic evidence that national security was imperilled.[36]

The prevention of disorder

The higher courts have not as yet been asked to consider the meaning of this exception. It is difficult to see how it could be relevant to evidence given at civil trials, although journalists summonsed to criminal courts as witnesses in cases arising from continuing and violent industrial action might be called upon to answer. This exception is probably unnecessary, since the serious "disorder" required to overcome the presumption would inevitably entail the commission of criminal offences.

The prevention of crime

This is a significant exception for all journalists who publish investigations into crime and corruption. The very impact of their work may

---

[36] *Secretary of State for Defence v. Guardian Newspapers Ltd* [1985] A.C. 339.

result in police inquiries or official investigations, and their sources will be sought after to provide the leads. Jeremy Warner suffered in exactly this way (see p. 256). The House of Lords ruled that the phrase "prevention of crime" in section 10 does not require the investigator to show that disclosure is necessary to forestall a particular crime: it was sufficient if disclosure would enable prosecution for an offence already committed, or would assist in the prevention of crime in the future. The court will, however, be less inclined to order disclosure under this head at the instance of a private claimant or a body that has suffered crime but has no public duty to investigate or prevent it. The Health Authority that successfully suppressed the story about doctors with AIDS failed on this basis to obtain an order for the newspaper to disclose the name of its employee who had corruptly and criminally sold its records: it had no public duty to prosecute claims, and the purpose of its action was predominantly to stop publication rather than to stop crime.[37]

Practical considerations

Even when disclosure would be necessary in the interests of justice or for one of the other purposes set out in section 10, the judge still has a discretion not to press journalists to disclose their source. As Lord Justice Donovan has put it:

> "over and above [the requirements that the answer is necessary and admissible] there may be other considerations, impossible to define in advance, but arising out of the infinite variety of fact and circumstances which a court encounters which may lead a judge to conclude that more harm than good would result from compelling a disclosure or punishing a refusal to answer."[38]

One such consideration is the undesirability of ordering disclosure prior to trial. So far as the purpose of interlocutory orders is to preserve the status quo, in most cases this can be adequately protected by orders prohibiting or limiting the use of the leaked material. Ordering the disclosure of a source or the return of documents to the claimant at the pre-trial stage does more than this. Once the source's identity is made known, the situation cannot be reversed if at trial it transpires that the claimants are not entitled to the order or documents they seek.[39]

---

[37] *X v. Y* [1988] 2 All E.R. 648.

[38] *Att.-Gen. v. Mulholland* [1963] 1 All E.R. 767, 773 and see Lord Denning at 771. Since the qualifying conditions of the 1981 Act are stringent, it will be rare that this discretion is exercised in favour of the journalist.

[39] *Francome v. Mirror Group Newspapers Ltd* [1984] 2 All E.R. 413, 415, 416; *Handmade Films (Productions) Ltd v. Express Newspapers Plc*, [1986] F.S.R. 463.

Leaked documents

A media defendant sued for the recovery of leaked documents may be tempted to resist the claim on the principle that it cannot be obliged to provide information that might implicate itself in a crime. This would be an arguable defence if, for instance, the circumstances of its obtaining the document could make it an accessory to theft or the handling of stolen goods. Such a defence was raised by Granada when British Steel sued to discover the identity of the television company's informant, but the courts ruled that the risk of prosecution was remote. The defence is a two-edged sword, because to admit to participating in possible criminal behaviour undermines any public interest claim that might be made in the same proceedings. A further problem is section 72 of the Supreme Court Act 1981, which removes the privilege against self-incrimination in civil proceedings that concern "commercial information or other intellectual property", although it is doubtful whether Government policy documents, for example, would fall into this category. The privilege against self-incrimination may therefore be of value to journalists who refused to co-operate with Scotland Yard inquiries into breaches of the Official Secrets Act 1989 after leaks to them of Government documents. Section 72 of the Supreme Court Act, designed to facilitate civil proceedings against video pirates, should not be available as a devious method for probing journalistic sources.

In practice, of course, a newspaper would now be advised to destroy any documents that might incriminate a source as soon as it is aware that the owner is likely to demand their return. If this step is taken before legal proceedings have been formally initiated, it will not amount to contempt of court and the owner would be left with only a civil claim of minimal damages for lost property. Granada Television adopted the expedient of mutilating the British Steel documents to remove all identifying marks before returning them. *The Guardian*, however, made the mistake of both admitting to possession of the document and acknowledging the presence on it of identifying marks in correspondence with Government solicitors before legal action was taken. It preserved the document, in over-optimistic reliance on section 10 of the Contempt of Court Act. If "leaked" documents are destroyed before the initial of legal proceedings for their recovery no offence is committed by the media, unless the document is an "*original* document of or belonging to any Government department" [our italics]. Section 20 of the Theft Act 1968 makes it an offence dishonestly to destroy or deface such documents.

Public Interest Disclosure Act 1998

Some protection for sources who are "whistleblowers" is given by the Public Interest Disclosure Act 1998. The scheme is bolted on to employment legislation[40] so that dismissal where an employee has made a "protected disclosure" is unfair and gives a right to all the remedies for unfair dismissal[41] although the usual maximum limits on compensation for unfair dismissal do not apply in these circumstances.[42] A worker who suffers other detriment because of a protected disclosure is also entitled to compensation.[43]

All of these remedies depend on the employee having made a "protected disclosure". So what kinds of disclosures are protected?

In the first place the disclosure must be a "qualifying disclosure", that is the worker must reasonably believe that it tends to show the commission of a criminal offence, failure to comply with a legal obligation, a miscarriage of justice, the health or safety of an individual is endangered, damage to the environment or concealment of any of the above. The matters can be in the past, present or future; in or outside the United Kingdom. However, it does not apply if the worker commits a criminal offence by making the disclosure.[44]

In the second place, the Act does not necessarily protect even qualifying disclosures to the press. The worker must make the disclosure in good faith, reasonably believe the information to be true and not make the disclosure for purposes of personal gain. In addition, he must reasonably believe that he would be subjected to a detriment if he made the disclosure to his employer, or he has disclosed substantially the same information previously to his employer or to a prescribed regulator[45] or there is no regulator and the worker reasonably believes that evidence would be destroyed if he made disclosure to his employer. A yet further condition is that the disclosure must be reasonable in all the circumstances. The statute sets out some of the matters to be examined in deciding whether disclosure is reasonable. They include the identity of the person to whom the disclosure is made, the seriousness of the employer's actions and whether they are continuing or likely to occur in the future.[46]

These requirements can be curtailed and a disclosure will still be protected if the relevant failure is of an exceptionally serious nature and the worker is in good faith, reasonably believes it to be true, does not act for personal gain and the disclosure is reasonable in the circumstances.[47]

---

[40] The 1998 Act inserted a number of new ss. into the Employment Rights Act 1996.
[41] Employment Rights Act 1996, s. 103A.
[42] *ibid.*, at s. 127B and Public Interest Disclosure (Compensation) Regulations 1999, S.I. 1999 No. 1548.
[43] *ibid.*, at ss. 47B, 48(1A) and 49(6).
[44] Employment Rights Act, s. 43B.
[45] The regulators are defined by The Public Interest Disclosure (Prescribed Persons) Order 1999, S.I. 1999 No. 1549.
[46] Employment Rights Act 1996, s. 43G.
[47] Employment Rights Act 1996, s. 43H.

Any attempt by employers to make employees contract out of their rights under these provisions is void.[48]

Although the Act does generally apply to Crown employees, it does not apply to police officers[49] nor does it apply to employment for the purposes of MI5, MI6 or GCHQ.[50]

POLICE POWERS OF SEARCH AND SEIZURE

Prior to 1984 the right of the police to search premises and seize evidence was a confusing jumble of common law powers and statutes passed to cater for specific situations. The Police and Criminal Evidence Act 1984 both rationalised and broadened these powers.[51] It created a threefold division.

Excluded material

This includes "journalistic material", defined as "material acquired or created for the purposes of journalism". The holder need not be a professional journalist if the material was acquired or created for journalistic purposes. The term would cover an anonymous package of leaked material sent to a journalist since it includes material that is sent to a recipient for the purposes of journalism.[52] Importantly, journalistic material is only "excluded" if it is held in confidence. This means that most film whether taken by broadcasting crews or still photographers is not "excluded material". Generally, the police are not entitled a search warrant for excluded material. Exceptionally, they may do so if some other statute authorises the grant of a warrant. They must then obtain an order from a circuit judge.[53] The Official Secrets Acts are examples of statutes that may allow such an order to be made (see p. 572).

---

[48] *ibid.*, at s. 43J.

[49] *ibid.*, at s. 200.

[50] Employment Relations Act 1999, Sched. 8, para. 1.

[51] However, the 1984 Act only applies to England Wales. Thus it does not protect media organisations in Scotland: 1984 Act, s. 120(1). Nor does it protect media organisations in England or Wales for whose premises a Scottish court has issued a search warrant: *R. v. Manchester Stipendiary Magistrate, ex p. Granada Television Ltd* [2000] 1 All E.R. 135, HL. This differentiation is unlikely to withstand the Human Rights Act.

[52] Police and Criminal Evidence Act 1984, s. 13. If the material is not in the possession of someone who acquired or created it for journalistic purposes, it loses its status as "journalistic material".

[53] *ibid.*, Sched. 1, para. 3.

Special procedure material

This includes journalistic material that is not "excluded material".[54] The police must again apply to a circuit judge, but the conditions on which an order will be made are more relaxed than for excluded material. They must show that there are reasonable grounds for believing[55] that a serious arrestable offence has been committed, that the material is likely to be of substantial value (whether by itself or together with other material) to the investigation, and that the material is likely to be relevant evidence. Finally and most importantly, the police must show that the public interest requires an order to be made, taking into account the benefit to the investigation of the material and the circumstances in which the material is held.[56] Several courts (including the House of Lords) have echoed the comment:

> "The special procedure . . . is a serious inroad upon the liberty of the subject. The responsibility for ensuring that the procedure is not abused lies with circuit judges. It is of cardinal importance that circuit judges should be scrupulous in discharging that responsibility."[57]

Applications are made, after notice to the holder of the material, to a circuit judge. Either in the notice or at the hearing the police must describe in broad terms the offences being investigated.[58] Initially, the application is made to a judge in chambers, but in hearing applications against the press, judges have shown themselves willing to adjourn the case into open court so that the public can attend and the case can be reported (see p. 419).

On many occasions the police have used these powers to obtain orders requiring the press to hand over film and photographs of demonstrations. The first concerned disorders in Bristol[59]; the second an investigation by the Police Complaints Authority into complaints about the police violence at a major demonstration at Wapping during the

---

[54] Police and Criminal Evidence Act 1984, s. 14.

[55] "Reasonable grounds for *believing*" is a tougher test than the usual requirement for a search warrant that there are "reasonable grounds for *suspecting*"—see *R. v. Crown Court at Southwark, ex p. Bowles* [1998] 2 All E.R. 193, 200.

[56] Sched. 1, para. 2.

[57] *R. v. Maidstone Crown Court, ex p. Waitt* [1988] Crim. L.R. 384 cited with approval in *R. v. Crown Court at Southwark, ex p. Bowles* [1998] 2 All E.R. 193, 200, HL.

[58] *R. v. Crown Court at Manchester, ex p. Taylor* [1988] 2 All E.R. 769.

[59] *Chief Constable of Avon and Somerset v. Bristol United Press, The Independent,* November 4, 1986, application for leave to apply for judicial review refused; *R. v. Crown Court at Bristol, ex p. Bristol Press Agency Ltd* [1987] Crim. L.R. 329.

Times Newspapers dispute.[60] In every case the photographers argued that their job would be made more dangerous if the crowds they were photographing knew that their pictures could become prosecution evidence. One press photographer had already been killed in the Brixton disorders after capturing a looter on film and a leaflet distributed at a demonstration in autumn 1994 against the Criminal Justice Act condemned "the pigs and their friends in the media". If the danger increased, so too would the likelihood that violent confrontations would not be covered by photographers. In consequence, the public would be less well informed and the police investigators would not even have the benefit of photographs that would otherwise have been taken and published. No court has accepted these arguments. Courts have been reluctant to accept these arguments as a reason for refusing to order disclosure although occasionally they have refused because the police have not tried other methods before seeking a production order, or have failed to demonstrate that the photographs will be of evidential value.

The Divisional Court in 2000 gave a powerful endorsement to protecting the media by the Special Procedure.[61]

> *The Guardian* published the text of a letter from David Shayler, an ex-MI5 employee who was at that stage living in Paris and resisting extradition to the U.K. on charges under the Official Secrets Act (Shayler had made various allegations of misdeeds by MI5 including hatching a plot to assassinate Colonel Gadaffi. *The Observer* published an article commenting on a letter which Shayler had previously sent to the Home Secretary again in connection with the alleged plot). An Old Bailey judge ordered the newspapers to produce all files, documents and records relating to the articles. The Divisional Court largely set aside the orders. It stressed:
>
> - even in national security cases applicants for orders must produce evidence. If the evidence was too sensitive to be disclosed, it should be heard by the judge in chambers without the respondent being present.
>
> - The judge had to reach his own decision on whether the access conditions were fulfilled. It was not sufficient for the judge to decide that the police officer's view that they were, was reasonable.
>
> - The factors mentioned in the access conditions—the benefit of the material to the investigation and the conditions under

---

[60] *Wyrko v. Newspaper Publishing Plc, The Independent*, May 27, 1988.
[61] *R. (Bright) v. Central Criminal Court* [2001] 1 W.L.R. 662.

which the person held the material—set the parameters for the public interest test. However, a broader range of factors could be taken into account when the judge exercised the residual discretion. These might include the impact of the order on third parties, the police delay, and any disproportion between the potential benefit to the investigation and harm to the respondent or the impact of an order on freedom of expression or the effect which it might have of implicating the journalist in a criminal offence.

Bright's case is a welcome reminder to circuit judges that they must not automatically accede to police applications for production orders against newspapers. Nonetheless, it is unlikely to deter them from ordering disclosure of untransmitted footage or unpublished photographs of riots and demonstrations. Judges have regularly paid tribute to the courage of photographers and camera crews who cover such events, but they have also regularly been sceptical as to whether production orders would appreciably increase the risk that they face. The European Commission which rejected a complaint from the BBC that a court order to produce untransmitted film from the Broadwater Farm disorders infringed Article 10.[62]

Once a person has been served with a notice of application for an order under these provisions, concealment, destruction or alteration of the material can be treated as contempt of court.[63] Nothing limits what can be done with the material before a notice is served. Four freelance photographers who were at a violent anti-Murdoch demonstration transferred their negatives to the International Federation of Journalists in Brussels and gave up all further rights to them before they were served with notices. Mr Justice Alliott subsequently ruled that this was not a contempt of court.

Other material

This may be seized subject only to the normal safeguards for search warrants. These may be granted by a magistrate without any right on the part of the media to object and without the need to apply the public interest test for "special procedure" material. Once police are lawfully present on premises (whether under a magistrates' warrant or because of some other power) they are entitled to seize (but not to search for) any material that they have reason to believe has either been obtained in consequence of the commission of an offence or is evidence of an offence, and which it is necessary to seize in order to prevent it being

---

[62] *BBC v. U.K.* (1996) 21 E.H.R.R. CD 93.
[63] Police and Criminal Evidence Act 1984, Sched. 1, para. 11.

concealed, lost, damaged, altered or destroyed. If the material is held on a computer that can be accessed from the premises, the police can demand a print-out. Under these powers the police cannot demand material that is covered by legal privilege, but they can seize "special procedure" or "excluded" material.[64] Further (complex) provisions are made by the Criminal Justice and Police Act to give the police additional powers of seizure including situations where material which is otherwise seizable is mixed with special procedure or excluded material. Broadly, judicial consideration of whether to allow the police to examine and use the material then takes place after the seizure.[65]

The debates over the Police and Criminal Evidence Act raised the issue of principle as to whether journalists should claim special protection from the normal process of the law. Although such protection was initially sought by media organisations, many of their members subsequently changed their minds when it became apparent that the special treatment awarded them in the Act would necessarily involve the courts in defining "journalism" and in operating a special regime that would accord to practitioners favoured treatment by comparison with ordinary citizens. The special status offered by the Act infringes the principle that journalism is not a profession, but the exercise by occupation of the citizen's right to freedom of expression. In retrospect, the media organisations (such as the Guild of British Newspaper Editors) who supported the Government's offer of "special protection" for journalists fell into an obvious trap, and damaged their members' interests. Prior to the 1984 statute, police had not been granted access to untransmitted material at common law. But once a statutory route for obtaining that material came into existence, albeit with "special protections", the police naturally exploited it and courts naturally decided that the protection was not very special after all. Judges generally believe that investigation of crime must have a higher priority than journalistic principles, and the decisions in the Bristol, Wapping and Poll Tax demonstration cases were all decided by this judicial preference. Police applications for untransmitted material have become routine after every violent demonstration, and the media objections to production are routinely dismissed.

AUTHORISED BURGLARY AND BUGGING

Dramatic new powers to enter and interfere with property and radio signals were provided by the Police Act 1997. The powers can be exer-

---

[64] Police and Criminal Evidence Act 1984, s. 19.
[65] Criminal Justice and Police Act 2001, ss. 50–70.

cised if the action would be of substantial value in the prevention or detection of serious crime and its objective could not reasonably be achieved by other means.[66] "Serious crime" for this purpose means that it involves the use of violence, results in substantial financial gain or is conduct by a large number of people in pursuit of a common purpose, or if it is an offence for which a person over 21 with no previous convictions could reasonably be expected to be sentenced to a term of 3 years imprisonment or more.[67] If these conditions are fulfilled authorisation can be given by senior police officers but if they are unavailable specified deputies can act in their place. The Act creates a series of Commissioners (headed by a Chief Commissioner) who will all be judges of the High Court or above. A Commissioner must be given notice of the authorisation. Usually this will be after the event, but in certain cases, a Commissioner must give prior approval. These special cases include situations where the action is likely to result in any person acquiring knowledge of "confidential journalistic material"[68] which is defined[69] in essentially the same terms as confidential journalistic material which is "excluded" for the purposes of the Police and Criminal Evidence Act 1984 (see p. 276). Other special cases include authorisation for intrusions onto property used as a dwelling or an office.[70] This protection can be dispensed with where the authorising police officer believes that the case is urgent.[71] A complaints system has been set up under the Regulation of Investigatory Powers Act 2000 by way of an appeal to the RIPA Tribunal.[72] This is modelled on the complaints systems under the Security Services legislation which has not upheld a single complaint in its first decade of operation.

The end of the Cold War and the peace process in Northern Ireland has released the Security Service for an expanded role in combating serious crime within the United Kingdom.[73] The definition of serious crime is the same as for the Police Act 1997 and despite the government's repeated statements that it was directed at organised crime, the statutory definition is far wider. The greater reach of the security services means a potentially wider domestic target for their substantial powers.

The Regulation of Investigatory Powers Act 2000 greatly increased the powers of the police and the security and intelligence services to intercept communications, and to carry out "intrusive surveillance." In

---

[66] Police Act 1997, s. 93(2).
[67] *ibid*, s. 93(4).
[68] *ibid*., s. 97(2)(b).
[69] *ibid*., s. 100.
[70] *ibid*., s. 97(2)(a).
[71] *ibid*., s. 97(3).
[72] Regulation of Investigatory Powers Act 2000, s. 65.
[73] Security Services Act 1996, s. 1 adding s. 1(4) to the Security Service Act 1989.

the case of the police and customs, authorisation for such activities has to be approved in advance by a "Surveillance Commissioner" (one of the Commissioners appointed for similar purposes under the Police Act). The security and intelligence services need only the Secretary of State's approval. There is no special procedure for intrusions which will interfere with journalistic material. Complaints (in the unlikely event that a potential complainant learns of the surveillance) can again be made to the RIPA Tribunal.

The vague terms in which these powers are cast, the lack of adequate safeguards and the unsatisfactory character of the means of redress means that there will inevitably be a challenge to their compatibility with Article 8 of the European Convention on Human Rights.

PRIVATE PHOTOGRAPHS

The Copyright Act 1988 took a small step to preserve privacy in domestic photographs. Before the 1988 Act a person who commissioned a photograph was the first owner of copyright in it. That rule has been changed and copyright now first belongs to the photographer. However, if the photograph has been commissioned for private and domestic purposes, the person commissioning it has the right not to have the photograph issued to the public, displayed in public, broadcast or included in a cable programme. This right is included in the generic description of "moral rights" in the Copyright Act (see p. 332).[74] The right is not infringed if the photograph is incidentally included in an artistic work, film, broadcast or cable programme.[75] More importantly, the right is not infringed if the commissioner has consented to its use.[76] The consent does not have to be in writing, but it would be prudent to obtain a written consent in order to avoid later argument about whether it was given or not. The practical result of these changes is that, for example, a photograph, commissioned by a family of a daughter who is later murdered, will not be able to be used without the family's consent. Courts are more than willing to award punitive damages against photographers for the "flagrancy" of a breach of copyright in circumstances

---

[74] Copyright, Designs and Patents Act 1988, s. 85. For discussion fo the meaning of "commission" in the Copyright Act 1956, see *Apple Corp. v. Cooper* [1993] F.S.R. 286 although for some obscure reason the definition of "commission" in the 1998 Act (see s. 263) does not expressly apply to the moral rights part of the 1988 Act. This moral right lasts as long as the copyright in the photograph (see s. 86).

[75] *ibid.*, s. 85(2).

[76] *ibid.*, s. 87.

where they supply private photographs of suddenly newsworthy people to the press.[77]

The case of *Sports & General Press Agency v. Our Dogs Publishing Co.* deserves to be engraved on every press photographer's lens: it establishes their right to snap and to publish anyone in a public place or, in the absence of trespass, in a private place without their consent. ("No person possesses a right of preventing another person photographing him any more than he has a right of preventing another person giving a description of him.")[78] To the distress of the Ladies Kennel Club, the magazine to which they had sold "exclusive rights" to photograph their dog show was unable to stop a rival paper publishing pictures taken by a freelance who had paid for an admission ticket, which had no condition excluding photographs. Where, however, the private pictures have been stolen from the photographer, the latter will be entitled to restrain their publication in the press. Pictures of Princess Margaret dressed as Mae West at a private party were denied to readers of the *Daily Mail* at the suit of the woman who took them, and whose son later stole and sold them to the newspaper without his mother's consent.[79]

Of course, photographs may also be protected by a duty of confidence and, perhaps (depending on how the ideas in *Douglas v. Hello!* are developed)[80] by a right of privacy.

DATA PROTECTION

Data protection legislation was overhauled by the Data Protection Act 1998 under pressure from a European Directive.[81] A major innovation is that the new regime applies not only to data held on computers but also to manual filing systems if they are structured by reference to individuals or by reference to criteria relating to individuals in such a way that particular information relating to a particular individual is readily accessible. A second important difference is that data held for journalistic purposes (whether in manual systems or computers) will be exempt from many of the major requirements of the new scheme. However, because the exemption is dependent on conditions which will not always be fulfilled, it remains necessary for journalists to have a working understanding of the new system.

---

[77] *Williams v. Settle* [1960] 1 W.L.R. 1072.
[78] [1916] 2 K.B. 880.
[79] *Lady Anne Tennant v. Associated Newspapers Group* [1979] F.S.R. 298.
[80] See p. 238.
[81] Directive 95/46/EC.

"Data controllers" (people who determine the purposes for which personal data[82] are processed) must be registered with, or give formal notification to, the Information Commissioner (who replaces the Data Protection Registrar) if they use automated systems or if given special notice by the Commissioner.[83] Journalists are *not* exempt from the requirement to register or give notification.

Data subjects are ordinarily entitled to be informed that data about them is being processed, to be given a description of the data, the purposes for which it is being processed and the people to whom the data may be disclosed. They are also entitled to a copy of the data (unless this would involve disproportionate effort) and to be told its source (unless the source is an individual who does not consent to disclosure and it is not reasonable to require disclosure in any case).[84] In many cases data subjects can insist that personal data in respect of them is not processed[85] and a court may order that data which is inaccurate (*i.e.* incorrect or misleading as to any matter of fact) is rectified, blocked, erased or destroyed.[86]

Data controllers must also abide by the data protection principles. These are, in brief:

- the data must be processed fairly and lawfully and only for one of the prescribed purposes. For data concerning "sensitive" matters[87] there is a narrower group of permitted purposes.[88].

- it must be adequate, relevant and not excessive for the purpose;

- it must be accurate and where necessary, kept up-to-date;

- it must not be kept for longer than is necessary;

- it must be processed in accordance with the rights of data subjects;

- appropriate technical and organisational measures must be

---

[82] "Personal data" is widely defined as "data which relate to a living individual who can be identified from those data or from those data and other information which is in the possession of, or is likely to come into the possession of, the data controller" s. 1(1).

[83] Data Protection Act 1988, s. 16.

[84] *ibid.* ss. 7 and 8. For the national security exceptions see s. 28 and *Baker v. Secretary of State for Home Department*, October 1, 2001 (below, p. 606).

[85] *ibid.* s. 10

[86] *ibid.*, s. 14

[87] Defined as meaning racial or ethnic origin, political opinions, religious or other beliefs, trade union membership, physical or mental health or condition, sexual life, commission or alleged commission of any offence, or criminal proceedings in relation to the data subject, *ibid.*, s. 2.

[88] *ibid.*, Scheds 2 and 3.

taken against unauthorised or unlawful processing and against accidental loss or destruction of or damage to the data;

● it must not be transferred out of the EEA unless the country to which it is taken or sent gives adequate protection for the rights of data subjects.[89]

The Commissioner (currently Elizabeth France) can serve an enforcement notice if she is satisfied that a data controller has contravened any of the these principles. An individual who suffers damage because a data controller has contravened any requirement of the Act is entitled to claim compensation.[90]

The special provisions for journalistic material give exemption from: the data protection principles (except those concerning security of data); data subject access rights; the rights of data subjects to prevent data processing; the rights of data subjects to correct inaccuracies; and rights concerning automated decision-making.[91] However, these important exemptions are dependent on satisfying three conditions:

● the processing is undertaken with a view to the publication by any person of any journalistic, literary or artistic material; and

● the data controller reasonably believes that, having regard in particular to the special importance of freedom of expression, publication would be in the public interest; and

● the data controller reasonably believes that, in all the circumstances, compliance with the provision in question is incompatible with the purposes of journalism.

The Court can take into account a relevant and designated Code of Practice for the purpose of deciding whether a belief that the publication would be in the public interest is a reasonable one. By this means the Codes of the Press Complaints Commission, the Broadcasting Standards Commission, the Independent Television Commission, the Radio Authority and the Producers Guidelines of the BBC (all of which have been designated[92]) may be given more significance.

The Commissioner is given powers to investigate whether data is being held for journalistic purposes or whether it is being processed with a view to the publication of any journalistic, literary or artistic material which has not previously been published by the data control-

---

[89] Data Protection Act 1988, Sched. 1.
[90] *ibid.*, s. 13.
[91] *ibid.*, s. 32.
[92] The Data Protection (Designated Codes of Practice) Order 2000, S.I. 2000 No. 418—see further Chap. 14 for these Codes.

ler.[93] To assist her to reach such a decision, she can demand access to relevant information by serving a special information notice.[94] These powers in principle permit a government official, albeit in an independent office, to investigate journalists' files although as of 2001 no such attempt has been made. It is also troubling that the exceptions for legal professional privilege and the privilege against self-incrimination are far from adequate. Appeals lie to the Information Tribunal against the Commissioner's demands for information and also against her determinations or enforcement notices.[95] There is some further protection in that an enforcement notice in relation to data processed for journalistic purposes can only be served with the leave of the court, which must be satisfied that the contravention of the data protection principles is of substantial public importance.[96]

There are further dangers for the media in the new offences of unlawfully obtaining, disclosing or procuring the disclosure of personal data or information contained in it without the consent of the data controller. However, there is a defence that in the particular circumstances the act was justified as being in the public interest.[97] These offences can only be prosecuted by the Commissioner or the DPP. They are not imprisonable. Magistrates are limited to a £5,000 fine. Defendants who elect or are sent for jury trial face an unlimited fine if convicted.[98]

Computer Misuse

Imprisonment for up to six months (as well as a fine) can be imposed for the separate offence of gaining unauthorised access to computer material.[99] This offence was aimed at computer hackers[1] and it is an essential ingredient for the offence that the access to data which was secured was unauthorised. Access is of four types: altering or erasing the program of data; copying or moving the data; using it; or outputting it,[2] but if the defendant was authorised to have the type of access in question, no offence is committed merely because access of that type was secured for an unauthorised purpose.[3]

In 1995 journalist John Arlidge was charged with computer misuse.

---

[93] Data Protection Act 1988, s. 45.

[94] *ibid.*, s. 44.

[95] Data Protection Act 1988, at ss. 48 and 49.

[96] *ibid.*, s. 46.

[97] *ibid.*, s. 55

[98] *ibid.*, s. 60.

[99] Computer Misuse Act 1990, s. 1.

[1] See The Law Commission Report No. 186, *Computer Misuse*, (HMSO 819, 1989).

[2] Computer Misuse Act 1990, s. 17(2).

[3] *DPP v. Bignall* [1998] 1 Cr.App.R. 1, DC, but see comments in *R. v. Bow Street Met. Stip. Magistrate, ex p. Govt of USA* [1999] 4 All E.R. 1 HL.

The Independent had run a story about the insecurity of British Telecom computers, which BT hotly denied. One of its employees, a computer operator, contacted the newspaper and offered to prove that BT's denial were false, which he did by demonstrating to its reporter how easily he could obtain sensitive information through access on his computer at BT's premises. Both operator and journalist were prosecuted, but the case against the operator collapsed since he had been given a password and general authorisation to secure the access, albeit he did so for a purpose (showing BT to be liars) of which BT would not have approved. The case against Arlidge was in consequence dropped, but had the operator's authority been restricted the prosecution would have had to prove that the reporter knew of that restriction. In addition, it may be doubted whether a reporter who stands by and watches while an operator voluntarily obtains unauthorised access can be said to "cause a computer to perform any function"—an ingredient of the offence. The Law Commission intended the section 1 offence to "exclude mere physical access, and mere scrutiny of data, without interaction with the operation of the computer". It emphasised that 'electronic eavesdropping' is not an offence.[4]

PRIVACY

English law is far more attuned to property rights than to human rights; privacy has traditionally been protected, if at all, through a collection of quasi-proprietary actions. Breach of confidence remedies have been built on the notion that confidential information is akin to property whose owner ought to be able to control its use.

Similarly, actions for trespass have been brought against intrusive snappers. Damages were awarded in one case against a defendant who secretly installed a microphone above the claimant's bed.[5] But this remedy is of limited use. Apart from the time that it takes to obtain even an injunction without notice, it can only restrain entry on the claimant's own land.[6] Where a defendant stands on public ground or in a place where he is permitted to be and spies through binoculars or telephoto lenses, no trespass takes place. In *Bernstein v. Skyways Ltd*[7] Lord Bernstein failed to obtain an injunction to stop aerial photography of his house and grounds. A flight several hundred feet up from his land

---

[4] Law Commission, *Computer Misuse* above, para. 3.26 and for *R. v. Arlidge*, see Paul Davies, "Computer Misuse", *New Law Journal*, December 1, 1995, p. 1776.
[5] *Sheen v. Clegg Daily Telegraph*, June 22, 1967.
[6] *Victoria Park Racing Co. v. Taylor* (1937) 58 C.L.R. 479.
[7] [1978] Q.B. 479.

did not interfere with his right to enjoy it and there was no general right
to stop the taking of photographs. The court warned that it might be
different if there was constant surveillance amounting to nuisance.

Of course, there is no trespass in doing what a landowner permits:

> A cinema owner agreed to pay a percentage of each day's takings to the
> owners of the films that he rented. The film owners employed inspectors
> to visit cinemas and check attendances. The cinema owner alleged that
> the inspectors were trespassing, because they came with a secret purpose
> for which they had no permission. The court held there was no trespass.
> The inspectors did nothing they were not invited to do and their motives
> for being present were irrelevant.[8]

The case is important for journalists whose observations and reports
are often unwelcome to those they visit. However, its limits are also
important. A journalist would not normally exceed his or her licence by
observing, remembering and reporting, but the operation of a television
camera might well be beyond a general invitation to the public to enter
the land. This is why film crews have to submit to the sometimes irksome business of obtaining consent to film from landowners. Unless
paid for, licences to come on to land can also be revoked. The landowner must allow a reasonable time for invited journalists to depart,
but after this lapses, the former invitees become trespassers.

Even where the behaviour of media employees plainly amounts to a
trespass, the courts are most reluctant to deprive the media of the fruits
of the civil wrong by granting injunctions against publication of photographs or films obtained in the course of the trespass. The common
example is "footage in the door" television journalism, whereby alleged
conpersons, shysters and religious hucksters are confronted at their
place of business by victims accompanied by television cameramen and
reporters. Although the cameras may continue to roll long after any
licence to enter has been withdrawn, the courts, while not excluding the
possibility of an injunction if the media has behaved abusively, will
generally take the view that damages will be an adequate remedy and
will decline to injunct a broadcast of the film.[9] However, the High Court
has condemned a police force for inviting the media to be present on
operations to film or photograph suspects and has urged the Home
Office to issue new guidelines which balance the creditable wish of the

---

[8] *Byrne v. Kinematograph Renters Association* [1958] 2 All E.R. 579, 593.
[9] See *Church of Scientology v. Transmedia Productions Pty Ltd* (1987) Aust. Torts
Reports 80–101; *Lincoln Hunt (Aust) Pty Ltd v. Willesee* (1986) 4 N.S.W.L.R. 457.
Emcorp Pty Ltd v. Australian Broadcasting Corp. [1988] Qd R. 169; *Bradley v.
Wingnut Films Ltd* [1993] 1 N.Z.L.R. 415.

police to show that they have nothing to hide and the privacy right of suspects to avoid having their humiliation recorded by the media.[10]

The case that seemed to block any development of a common law right to privacy was *Kaye v. Andrew Robertson & Sport Newspapers*[11]:

> The *Sunday Sport* obtained what its editor described as a "good old fashioned scoop" when its reporters walked into actor Gordon Kaye's hospital room while he was recovering from brain surgery, photographed him and recorded his ramblings for publications as a "world exclusive". Kaye's family was unable to obtain an injunction for libel (as the *Sunday Sport* indicated its intention of defending the claim) or on the basis of trespass (there was no unlawful entry, and no evidence that the photography caused physical distress or damage). All that the court could do was to grant a limited injunction preventing the newspaper from pretending that Gordon Kaye had voluntarily consented to the interview, this being a "malicious falsehood" in that it represented that he had abandoned a valuable property right (*i.e.* the right to tell the exclusive story of his accident). All three judges in the Court of Appeal lamented their inability to give a satisfactory remedy for this "monstrous invasion of privacy".

Such a remedy is available under American law, where ordinary people have a right to protect themselves against unreasonable intrusion on their physical solitude,[12] and celebrities have an exclusive legal right to control and profit from the commercial use of their names and personalities. (Johnny Carson was able to stop the manufacture of the "Here's Johnny" portable toilet.)[13] English courts may in the future have to apply foreign privacy laws where publication has taken place abroad. The common law rule that a person who complained of a wrong done abroad had to show that the act was contrary to the laws of England and the place where the wrongful act (*e.g.* publication) was done have generally been scrapped in favour of a presumption that the English courts will apply the law of the place where the harm was suffered.[14]

---

[10] *R. v. Maylebone Magistrates Court, ex p. "Get Stuffed", New Law Journal*, August 14, 1998, DC.

[11] [1991] F.S.R. 62, CA.

[12] *e.g. Barber v. Time Inc.* (1942) 159 S.W. 2nd 291, where a woman with an insatiable appetite won damages against *Time* for publishing a photograph of her taken without her consent in hospital, captioned "starving glutton". See also *Contrell v. Forest City Publishing*, 419 U.S. 245 (1974), where a newspaper was held to have invaded privacy by inventing facts of a personal and sensitive nature about the plaintiff.

[13] *Carson v. Here's Johnny Portable Toilets Inc.* (1983) 698 F. 2d 831. Compare *Byron v. Johnston* (1816) 2 Mer 29, where Lord Byron stopped a bad poem being falsely attributed to him.

[14] See Private International Law (Miscellaneous Provisions) Act 1995, ss. 9–15. *N.B.* there is an important exception for defamation actions where the common law "double actionability" requirement still applies, *ibid.* at s. 13.

Harassment

Prior to 1997 there was only minimal protection against harassment[15] in the criminal law. However, the Protection from Harassment Act 1997 has introduced broad new powers. Intended to give relief against "stalking", its ambit is much wider. It prohibits a course of conduct[16] which amount to "harassment".[17] "Harassment" includes alarming a person or causing distress.[18] The attentions or investigations of unwelcome reporters often cause distress. There is a defence if the alleged harasser shows that the course of conduct was pursued for the purpose of preventing or detecting crime.[19–20] Although the Secretary of State can issue a conclusive certificate that conduct was done on behalf of the Crown in relation to the prevention or detection of crime—see s. 12—there is no reason why an investigative reporter in appropriate circumstances should not also be able to prove that he had the same purpose and is therefore entitled to the defence. It is also a defence—see s.10(c)—for the alleged harasser to show that pursuit of the course of conduct was reasonable, so if a charge was brought against a journalist, the fact that he was acting in accordance with his professional code would be relevant to show reasonableness.

Harassment in breach of the Act is a summary criminal offence with a maximum penalty of six months' imprisonment. It is an arrestable offence so that the police can apprehend a person whom they have reasonable grounds to believe has committed it.[21] In addition, the victim can take civil proceedings (see "Stop Press" section for further details).

As well as damages (including damages for anxiety) the court can grant an injunction. If the victim believes that the harasser has engaged in conduct which is prohibited by the injunction, a court may attach a power of arrest to the injunction. If breach of the injunction is made out without reasonable excuse the maximum penalty is increased to five years imprisonment.[22] A novel feature of the Act is that on conviction of a harassment offence, the criminal court can make an order restraining the defendant from specified conduct for the purpose of pro-

---

[15] Conspiracy and Protection of Property Act 1875.

[16] "Conduct" includes speech. To be a "course of conduct" there must be at least two occasions: Protection from Harassment Act 1997, s. 7(2) and (3).

[17] Protection from Harassment Act 1997, s. 1.

[18] *ibid.*, s. 7(2).

[19–20] *ibid.*, s. 1(3)(a). Although the Secretary of State can issue a conclusive certificate that conduct was done on behalf of the Crown in relation to the prevention or detection of crime—see s. 12—there is no reason why an investigative reporter in appropriate circumstances should not also be able to prove that he had the same purpose and is therefore entitled to the defence.

[21] *ibid.*, s. 2.

[22] *ibid.*, s. 3.

tecting the victim from further harassment.[23] This might, for instance, include a prohibition on going within a specified distance of the victim's house. Breach of the restraining order without reasonable excuse is a separate offence with a maximum penalty of six months.

The Calcutt Committee recommended new crimes of uninvited entry on private property to obtain information for publication, using surveillance devices surreptitiously for the same end, and photographing individuals without their consent while they are standing on private land.[24] The criminal offences, although subject to a public interest defence where exposure of "seriously anti-social conduct" is intended, were misconceived, and have given police unparalleled powers to arrest reporters and television camera crews as they went about their ordinary business. Law should not be used actively to suppress publication of the truth. It can, however, usefully work to *deter* publication of unimportant private truths if it provides an effective remedy for victims of invasion of privacy. An effective remedy—the right to bring a civil action, legally aided where appropriate, and to obtain compensation and damages—is precisely what English law does not, at present, offer and self-regulation through the Press Complaints Commission is a hollow pretence (see Chapter 14).

PRIVACY AND THE HUMAN RIGHTS CONVENTION

The Human Rights Act has provided fresh impetus for judges to develop privacy protection. Article 8 of the Convention provides that:

> "Everyone has the right to respect for his private and family life, his home and his correspondence".

Like the rest of the Convention, Article 8 is concerned with providing guarantees against the activities of the government or other public bodies. But the European Court has developed an idea that in some respects the Convention puts a "positive obligation" on the Member States to make provision in their laws for other rights as against the government or as against other private bodies or individuals. This idea of "positive obligation" has been used particularly in the context of Article 8. Thus the Court has said that there is a positive obligation on the government to provide penal sanctions for those who sexually abuse

---

[23] Protection from Harassment Act 1997, s. 5.
[24] *Report of the Committee on Privacy and Related Matters* (Calcutt Report), HMSO, 1990, Cmnd 1102, para. 6.33–5.

women suffering from mental disorders[25] to take positive measures to allow for the integration of illegitimate children into their families[26]; to provide legal aid to give protection to women against an alcoholic and violent husband and to give her access to the divorce courts[27]; and to provide information on environmental pollution.[28]

None of these cases directly answer the question whether there is a positive obligation on Member States to create a law against the protection of privacy intrusions by the media. The issue has been raised on several occasions on applications from the U.K., but none has yet gone beyond the admissibility stage and on each occasion the Commission found that other remedies did or could have satisfied any requirement under the Convention.[29] Most recently, the Commission held that the developing law of breach of confidence could well satisfy whatever positive obligations existed in this area.[30]

When the Human Rights Bill was debated, the media were vociferous in their concern that the U.K. courts would develop a fully-fledged right of privacy in our law. The result was the inclusion of s. 12 in the Human Rights Act. which gave some protection against interim injunctions and underlined the importance of the extent to which material the claimant sought to suppress was already in the public domain or was of public interest. However, it also obliged the court to have regard to "any relevant privacy code". The courts will read this as a further stimulus to develop a U.K. law of privacy.

We have already seen that (except obliquely through measures such as the Data Protection Act and the Protection from Harassment Act), Parliament has refused to legislate to protect privacy from media intrusion. The European Convention and the Human Rights Act may spur the judiciary to act instead. The law of breach of confidence has shown capacity for growth and in *Spencer v. United Kingdom*[31] the Government persuaded the European Commission of Human Rights that it could go yet further. The argument was not lost on the Court of Appeal in *Douglas v. Hello!*[32] which considered that *Kaye v. Robertson* might well be decided differently today.

---

[25] *X and Y v. The Netherlands* (1985) 8 E.H.R.R. 235 at para. 23.

[26] *Marckx v. Belgium* (1979) 2 E.H.R.R. 305.

[27] *Airey v. Ireland* (1979) 2 E.H.R.R. 305.

[28] *Guerra v. Italy* (1998) 26 E.H.R.R. 357.

[29] *Winer v. U.K.*, Application No. 10871/84 (1986) 48 D.R. 154; *N. v. Sweden*, Application No. 11366/85 (1986) 50 D.R. 173; *Stewart-Brady v. U.K.*, Application No. 27436/95, July 2, 1997 (1997) 90 D.R. 45; *Stewart-Brady v. U.K.*, Application No. 36908/97, October 21, 1998.

[30] *Spencer v. U.K.*, Application Nos 28851/95 & 28852/95 (1998) 92 D.R. 56; (1998) 25 E.H.R.R. CD 105.

[31] See above n. 30.

[32] See above p. 238.

Another example of the capacity for growth of the law of breach of confidence under the stimulus of the Human Rights Act was the injunction granted by the High Court to protect the new identities of the killers of Jamie Bulger after their release from custody.[33] The judge recognised that the statutory powers which had afforded them some protection during their minority could not be invoked once they reached 18. However, their new identities and appearances were confidential and she considered the need to protect them was paramount in view of the risk of revenge attacks. The real risk of such attacks permitted the applicants to invoke Article 2 of the Convention—the right to life. She granted the injunction against the world so that it would apply directly against all newspapers (even those not party to the proceedings) rather than rely on the indirect effect of the law of contempt.[34] She ordered that the restrictions would continue in force even if information as to the new identities was published abroad or on the internet, although it is difficult to see how this restriction could be sustained if the information became widely available (see "Stop Press" for further details).

---

[33] *Venables v. News Group Newspapers Ltd* [2001] 1 All E.R. 908.
[34] See p. 383.

CHAPTER 6

COPYRIGHT

"The sweat of a man's brows, and the exudations of a man's brains, are as much a man's own property as the breeches upon his backside."

Laurence Sterne, *Tristram Shandy*.

The law against breach of copyright protects creative work that has been reduced to material form from being used by others without permission. It is the most technical branch of the law dealt with in this book. Its essential purpose, shared with the law against breach of confidence, is to prevent the plagiarism or unfair exploitation of creative work. As such, it affords vital protection to writers, and is the basis of the measures taken by publishing and broadcasting organisations to combat piracy. But as a corollary to this purpose, it may inhibit the media's freedom to report and expose matters of public interest, where such reportage necessarily involves publication of documents written by or belonging to persons or organisations who wish to keep them private.

Most occasions on which the media will wish to use copyright material do not pose problems, either because the originator is only too happy for his or her exudations to be publicised, or because arrangements have been made to pay a suitable royalty or licensing fee. Difficulties are encountered, however, when use of copyright material is made without formal acknowledgment, or in the context of an article or broadcast that makes use of private documents for the purpose of criticising those to whom copyright belongs. Even with the best will in the world, the egos of artists involved in the different stages of putting together a feature may provoke irreconcilable differences of opinion as to the due credit to be given in the final product. Untangling such disagreements is hard for several reasons. The law of copyright was revised in the Copyright, Designs and Patents Act 1988, but its reforms generally apply only to works created after the statute came into effect. The Copyright Act 1956 (which it replaced) will therefore be important for years to come. In some cases it will be necessary to consult even earlier (and now repealed) legislation. To add to the confusion the 1988

Act has itself been amended often (under the impetus of requirements from the European Union) by regulations. Yet further changes are in prospect as a result of the Copyright Directive (2001/29/EC) which must be implemented into U.K. law by December 22, 2002. The structure of the law is still highly complex and a book of this type can only be a guide to its most important aspects for those writing, producing or editing new material. This book concentrates on the present generation of rules. Readers who need to consider works which were not created in previous centuries ought to consult specialist textbooks.[1]

There are five basic questions in copyright law.

● *Does copyright exist in the source material?* The 1988 Act establishes the following categories of copyright:

   (a) original literary, dramatic or musical works;
   (b) original artistic works;
   (c) sound recordings;
   (d) films;
   (e) broadcasts;
   (f) cable programmes;
   (g) published editions.

The legal meanings of these categories are broader than their everyday use. Moreover, multiple copyrights can exist in a particular work. In the case, for instance, of a television documentary, there will be literary copyright in the script, dramatic copyright in the screenplay and musical copyright in any background music. The totality will be entitled to copyright as a film, and once aired will have a further copyright as a television broadcast.

Copyright begins from the time the work is made. There is no longer any need to register the work, and even the copyright symbol © is not necessary in the United Kingdom, although it is if the work is to be published in a country that is a member of only the Universal Copyright Convention (see p. 304). Until the 1988 Act it was common for this effective monopoly to last a very long time, particularly in the case of unpublished literary, dramatic and musical works, which could, in theory, enjoy perpetual copyright. The scope for rights to be perpetual has been virtually abolished. A rare exception is *Peter Pan,* for whose exploitation the Great Ormond Street Hospital is still entitled to collect royalties, thanks to the will of J. M. Barrie and a special amendment to the 1988 bill. All other works (such as those that were published under the 1956 Act) have finite

---

[1] *e.g.* Laddie, Prescott, Vitoria, *The Modern Law of Copyright and Designs* (Butterworths, London, 3rd ed., 2000); *Copinger and Skone James on Copyright* (Sweet and Maxwell, London, 1999).

protection, and once this is over, the work can be reproduced in any fashion. For example, the emergence of the Gilbert and Sullivan operas from the copyright cocoon ended the D'Oyly Carte monopoly on their staging, and outraged Savoyard purists with *The Rock Mikado*, *The Jazz Mikado* and *The Black Mikado*. Although the standard period of copyright used to be 50 years after the end of the year in which the author died, this was extended in 1996 to 70 years (see p. 304).

- *Who owns the copyright?* Ownership will decide who has the right to license use of the copyright and who has the power to take legal action against infringement. The Act lays down rules for determining who is the first owner: usually this is the author or maker of the work. It also envisages the transfer of rights to others and specifies certain formalities if these are to be effective. "Moral rights" created by the Act cannot be transferred except to the estate of the author or maker on their death. They can, however, be waived.

- *Does the proposed use of copyright material infringe the law?* Copyright gives the owner an exclusive right to use the work in specific ways. Infringement is the use of the work in one of these ways without the owner's consent. The possible means of infringement may differ according to the type of work, but each involves some element of copying, reproduction or performance. Ignorance of the owner's rights is no excuse, but it may diminish the amount of compensation that has to be paid. A secondary type of infringement is committed by those in the chain of distribution of infringing copies who know that the merchandise is pirated.

- *Is there a defence?* There is no infringement if the reproduction was permitted or licensed by the copyright owner. In addition, there is an important statutory defence of "fair dealing" with the work for the purpose of criticism, review or reporting current events. There are other defences, protecting court reports, old films and preparations made for broadcasting. In some cases enforcement of copyright may be contrary to the policy of the law. This public interest defence may have been strengthened by the Human Rights Act.

- *Will the publication infringe some other right similar to copyright?* Although a publication has successfully steered clear of the shoals of copyright, it may still run into legal difficulties because of other similar rights. Manufacturing quotes may not infringe copyright, but it can lead to a claim to damages for false attribution of authorship. Malicious falsehoods about a rival's goods can be costly. Performers have rights that are akin to copyright. The 1988 Act also brought English law into line with the Berne Convention on Copyright and introduced the concept of "moral rights" for authors and directors: (a) to be identified as such; and (b) not to have their work subjected to "derogatory treatment". Regulations in 1996 introduced a new "publication right" for those who publish previously unpublished works in which copyright has expired.[2]

The civil claim of "passing off" will sometimes provide a remedy for claimants whose name or work or goodwill is misappropriated by others for commercial gain. Thus Dow Jones Inc was able to force Ladbrokes to disband "The Ladbrokes/Dow Jones Index", a gambling operation related to the rise and fall of the Dow Jones Index, which wrongly implied that Dow Jones had consented to or benefited from the operation. *The Mail on Sunday* was able to obtain an injunction, on grounds of passing-off, to stop an advertiser from arranging with distributors and newsagents to insert printed advertising leaflets in its colour supplement. The newspaper successfully argued that the public would assume that the advertisements had its approval and were under its control, and that the connection might damage its goodwill.[3]

EXISTENCE OF COPYRIGHT

Original literary, dramatic or musical works

This is the first classification of material that is subject to protection.[4] "Literary" work does not imply any particular quality of language.[5] The most turgid prose can be a literary work, as can programme schedules, letters, football fixture lists, opinion polls and even railway timetables if reproduced in detail. However, the work must be "recorded in writing or otherwise".[6] There can be no copyright in a literary idea, or suggestion for a story, though it may be imparted in circumstances that would be protected by the law of confidence (see p. 250). Copyright can exist in a literary work only if it is recorded, but it need not be recorded in writing. Memoirs dictated on to a tape are protected even before the tape is transcribed. Similarly, a speaker delivering a lecture from prepared notes will have copyright in the speech. Conversely a spontaneous or extempore speaker will not have copyright, unless, that is, the speech is recorded with or without the permission of the speaker.[7]

---

[2] Copyright and Related Rights Regulations 1996, S.I. 1996 No. 2967, regs 16–17.
[3] *Associated Newspapers plc v. Insert Media Ltd.* [1991] 1 W.L.R. 571, CA.
[4] Copyright, Designs and Patents Act 1988, s. 3.
[5] *University of London Press Ltd v. University Tutorial Press Ltd* [1916] 2 Ch. 601 at 608.
[6] Copyright, Designs and Patents Act 1988, s. 3(2). "Writing" includes "any form of notation or code. Whether by hand or otherwise and regardless of the method by which or medium in or on which it is recorded": *ibid.*, s. 178.
[7] Copyright, Designs and Patents Act 1988, s. 3(3).

This will mean that people interviewed by reporters have copyright in the words they utter if the journalist has taken an accurate note or recorded them. However, there is a defence to prevent this extension of literary copyright acting as a form of censorship (see p. 330).

An "original" work for the purposes of the Act has been variously described as a work the creation of which has involved the expenditure of "skill, labour and judgment"; "selection, judgment and experience"; or "labour, skill and capital". These tests operate to exclude protection only where compilations are basic and commonplace. In consequence, protection has been afforded to mathematical tables that the compiler had worked out for himself, hire-purchase forms, broadcast programme schedules and even street directories. The 1988 Act unambiguously provides that a computer program can be a literary work with its own copyright protection.[8]

Special provision is also made for copyright in databases.[9] In addition to copyright protection, there is now a "database right" which prevents the extraction or reutilisation of the whole or substantial part of the contents of the database.[10] The right lasts for only 15 years from the making of the database, but if during that time it is made available to the public the 15 years runs from that release. However, it is a common feature of databases that they are updated periodically. If any substantial change is made to the contents of the database which would result in the database being considered to be a substantial new investment a new term of protection will begin to run.[11]

Copyright can also be acquired in compilations, translations, abridgments and anthologies. So, for instance, a list of Stock Exchange prices and a football pools coupon have copyright. The requirement is the same: the author's own contribution must have required a degree of skill and labour that led to the new work having some recognisably different quality to its source or sources. A person who translates a speech into a different language clearly transforms it sufficiently to satisfy this test. Copying the translation would then infringe the rights of both the original author and the translator. A slavish copy, that adds nothing, rearranges nothing or selects nothing would have no claim to be a literary work unless, possibly, the text of the original were inaccessible.

The skill and labour expended by a reporter or stenographer in taking

---

[8] Copyright, Designs and Patents Act 1988, s. 3(1)(b).

[9] See CDPA, s. 3(1)(d), s. 3A and other amendments to the Act made by Copyright and Rights in Databases Regulations, S.I. 1997 No. 3032. The Regulations were prompted by the EU Directive on the Legal Protection of Databases Council Dir. 96/9/E.C.

[10] Database Regulations reg. 16.

[11] *ibid.*, reg. 17.

down a speech in shorthand may be sufficient to attract copyright protection against other newspapers who "lift" a substantial part of the report. Thus in *Walter v. Lane*,[12] a *Times* reporter was entitled to damages when his version of a politician's public speech was copied word for word by a rival newspaper. This would not mean, of course, that no other paper could report the speech: another reporter present would have an equal right to file a separate account of it. Though both accounts might be identical, neither would be derived from the other and both would enjoy copyright. As each of these reporters would have copyright, both papers could prevent their less diligent rivals from copying their reports. (The politician in *Walter v. Lane* would, since the 1988 Act, have copyright in his speech because of the act of the reporter in recording it, but the reporter's defence (see p. 330) would mean that the politician could not prevent its appearance in the paper.) The term "originality" is also misleading. The work must require some skill and labour, but it need not also be novel. It is enough if the creator of the work can truthfully say "this is all my own work".[13]

False attribution of authorship

Copyright apart, journalists must exercise care in attributing quotations or in ghosting articles for others. False attribution of remarks to which exception is taken can lead to a claim for damages.

> Dorothy Squires obtained £100 damages for false attribution of authorship in 1972 from the *News of the World,* whose reporter had inaccurately written up an interview concerning her marriage to Roger Moore. This sum was in addition to libel damages that were awarded in the same case. The paper was not excused because it was following an apparent Fleet Street custom of making up quotes for willing interviewees. The paper was liable if the "author" disliked "her" lines.[14]

Parody is an unreliable defence:

> The *Evening Standard* published a weekly spoof, "Alan Clark's Diaries", satirising the opinions of the former cabinet minister. Clark's name and photograph appeared at the head of column. So too did the name of the real author, Peter Bradshaw, but its impact was not enough, so the judge ruled, to disabuse the reader who skimmed the newspaper of the impres-

---

[12] [1900] A.C. 539.
[13] Whitford Committee, *Copyright Law 1977* HMSO, Cmnd. 6732, para. 33.
[14] *Moore v. News of the World* [1972] 1 All E.R. 915. *Cf. Jenkins v. Socialist Worker The Times,* February 28, 1977, Similar care must be taken with quotes attributed to the dead. Their estates can claim damages for false attributions made up to twenty years after death: Copyright, Designs and Patents Act 1988, s. 86(2).

sion that the Diaries really had been written by Mr Clark. Much was obvious fantasy, incredible and wild exaggeration, but the judge thought that a substantial body of readers would be fooled into thinking that Clark was truly the author. Although a false attribution of authorship could be neutralised, the corrective had to be as bold, precise and compelling as the false statement so that it would prevent a substantial body of readers from being misled. This decision correctly stated the test as whether a substantial (or large) number of the paper's ordinary readers would be misled more than momentarily. The application of the test to the facts, however, was highly questionable. The judge treated the *Evening Standard* as a publication which is skim-read by morons in a hurry to get home after a tiring day at the office. He seemed over-impressed by Clark (who had a Toad-like quality of inspiring affection) and lacked understanding of the art of parody: his ruling that the *Evening Standard* should have put Bradshaw's authorship in lights would have made the whole exercise heavy-handed and unfunny. The decision can only be justified on the grounds that the *Evening Standard* is the kind of paper in which readers would not expect to find a parody (or believe it was a parody when they saw it). The judgment should not therefore discomfit *Private Eye* or other magazines which readers do expect to contain parodies.[15]

False attribution can provide a useful remedy for freelance writers whose copy is misused.

> Geoffrey Cannon, a respected authority on nutritional values of different foods, was commissioned to write an article for *Today* newspaper. He did so, but the article was never published. Instead, his name was appended to another article on the same subject, expressing opinions with which he profoundly disagreed. He was awarded substantial damages in 1988 for the false attribution.

The 1988 Act substantially enlarged the scope of false attribution, which it categorises as a matter of moral rights. It prohibits the false attribution of authorship of a literary, dramatic, musical or artistic work and falsely describing someone as the director of a film. It prohibits falsely representing a literary, dramatic or musical work as an adaptation of a person's work or a copy of an artistic work as having been copied by the artist. An altered artistic work must not knowingly be passed off as the original. The section now spells out in detail who is to be liable for these wrongs: in some (but not all) cases they are confined to those who knew or had reason to believe that the attribution

---

[15] *Clark v. Associated Newspapers Ltd* [1998] R.P.C. 261, Lightman J. The judge also held that the spoof had been "passed off" as the real thing. The *Standard* was injuncted from repeating anything similar and an inquiry as to damages was ordered.

was false; in certain cases the liability is limited to those who deal with the falsely described article in the course of business.[16]

News stories and programme formats

There is "no copyright in news itself, although there is copyright in the form in which it is conveyed".[17] This means merely that a newspaper cannot obtain exclusive rights to cover an event by being first on the scene, or stop rivals from repeating facts of public importance that it is first to report.

The *Daily Express* sued *Today* newspaper for breach of copyright because, in time-honoured press tradition, *Today* had "copied", in its second edition, an "exclusive" *Express* story on prostitute-about-town Pamela Bordes. *Today* responded by suing Express Newspapers for breach of copyright when its own exclusive story — from a Royal relative it had paid to criticise the Royal Family — was pirated. The Vice-Chancellor, Sir Nicolas Browne Wilkinson, refused to find that there could be copyright in the substance of a news story, although there would have been a breach if a substantial part of the original reporter's words had been copied verbatim:

> "I would hesitate a long time before deciding that there is copyright in a news story which would be infringed by another newspaper picking up that story and reproducing the same story in different words. Such a conclusion would strike at the root of what I think is the practice of the national press, namely to search the columns of other papers to find stories which they have missed and then using the story so found in their own newspaper by rewriting it in their own words. If it were the law that such practice constituted breach of copyright, the consequences, as it seems to me, would be that a paper that obtained a scoop from a confidential source would obtain a monopoly on that piece of news. That would not be in the public interest as it would prevent the wider dissemination of the news to the public at large."[18]

What *is* protected by copyright, under the rubric of "form" or "mode of expression", is not merely language and paragraph arrangement, but *original work*, which in the case of a news article would include the skill, labour and judgment that had been expended upon research, "put-

---

[16] Copyright, Designs and Patents Act 1988, s. 84. The prohibitions apply to *any* part of a protected work, not just substantial parts: see 1988 Act, s. 89(2).

[17] *Springfield v. Thame* (1903) 89 L.T. 242. Note that this case was decided before Parliament gave the press a "fair dealing" defence for reporting current events.

[18] *Express Newspapers plc v. News (U.K.) Ltd* [1990] 1 W.L.R. 1320.

ting together" and presentation. The principle is that "the plaintiff has a right to say that no one is to be permitted ... to take a material and substantial part of his work, his argument, his illustrations, his authorities, for the purpose of making or improving a rival publication."

Journalists who find their stories "borrowed" in detail by other publications, without an agency agreement and without an appropriate attribution, may have a good cause of action. If what is pirated is merely the facts, retold in different words, then the courts will find that this is a custom engaged in by newspapers over a very long time, and impliedly consented to by all who work on them. But where the borrowing is substantial and verbatim, and reproduces quotations from third parties (who have a separate copyright), then the principle in *Walter v. Steinkopf* is likely to be applied:

> Rudyard Kipling's news dispatches, printed in *The Times*, were regularly and substantially reproduced without that newspaper's consent in the *St James Evening Gazette*. Mr Justice North held that its copyright had been infringed:
>
>> "In the present case what the defendants have had recourse to is not a mental operation involving thought and labour and producing some original results, but a mechanical operation with scissors and paste, without the slightest pretension to an original result of any kind; it is a mere production of "copy" without trouble or cost ... it is not immaterial to look at the number and character of the passages taken, in the whole; and also to bear in mind that it is not a mere casual trespass on the plaintiff's right, occurring now and again at long intervals, and not likely to be repeated; but deliberate, persistent abstraction of matter from the plaintiff's paper, which the defendants justify and insist on their right to continue. For the purposes of their own profit they desire to reap where they have not sown, and to take advantage of the labour and expenditure of the plaintiffs in procuring news for the purpose of saving labour and expense to themselves.
>>
>> It is said there is no copyright in news. But there is or may be copyright in the particular forms of language or modes of expression by which information is conveyed, and not the less so because the information may be with respect to the current events of the day ...".[19]

The problem of deliberate borrowing in journalism will be considered further in relation to the requirement of "substantiality" and the defence of "fair dealing".

Literary copyright will obviously exist in the scripts of television and radio programmes. In some cases they will also have protection as dramatic works. However, the badge or characteristic of other programmes

---

[19] *Walter v. Steinkopf* [1892] 3 Ch. 489.

may be less easy to define. Hughie Green discovered how difficult it was to prevent others using the same idea.

> Hughie Green had compered *Opportunity Knocks* in the United Kingdom for many years. He had devised the use of a "clapometer" to measure the audience's reaction to the different acts that appeared in his talent contest. Certain stock phrases, such as "For X . . . opportunity knocks", were used in most programmes, but the content of each programme changed each week and Hughie Green's own words were usually ad lib. New Zealand Television took the same idea and used similar techniques in a television programme with the same name. Hughie Green failed in his attempt to injunct them. The title was too trite to attract copyright. The clapometer and the other features of the programme's format were too nebulous to be described as a "dramatic work" and too imprecise to be protected as "literary copyright".[20]

There is a lively current debate over the fairness of the *Opportunity Knocks* decision, and a lobby (enthusiastically joined by lawyers in the entertainment industry) for its reversal by legislation and for the creation of "format rights" that would entitle creators of ideas for game shows to stop others from copying these ideas. The makers of *Have I Got News for You*, popular for its rehearsed spontaneity, sued in Australia a local show, *Good News Week,* which was obviously based on their format. They lost — both were comedy programmes relying upon similar routines, but the jokes which were the essence of both programmes were completely different. Freedom of expression is better advanced by retaining the present copyright rule, which protects the way in which ideas are expressed, but not the ideas themselves.

Published editions

In addition to protecting the content of a literary, musical or dramatic work, the 1988 Act also gives copyright to its typographical arrangement (assuming that it has been published[21]). Originality is not required, but a straightforward reproduction of a previous published edition is not given a new copyright.[22] What is protected is the whole of the "edition". An edition is the product, generally between covers, which the publisher offers to the public. The idea of this copyright is to give protection to the skill and labour in the overall design of the edition. Applying this test the House of Lords decided that a practice by Marks and Spencer of circulating photocopies of interesting clippings from newspapers to its senior executives did not infringe the copyright of

[20] *Green v. Broadcasting Corp. of New Zealand* [1990] R.P.C. 700, PC.
[21] Copyright, Designs and Patents Act 1988, ss. 8 and 15.
[22] 1988 Act, s. 8(2).

the newspapers in their published editions. Although the photocopies obviously copied the typeface and arrangement of the individual articles, they did not take all or even a substantial part of the overall design of the newspaper as a whole.[23]

Published edition copyright is a more restricted right than other copyrights in that it lasts for only 25 years from the end of the year of publication (by comparison with 70 years after the death of the author(s) for published literary works) but for that period, facsimile copies can be made only with the consent of the owner of this copyright as well as the owner of the literary or other work itself.

Artistic works

Copyright can subsist in the following original artistic works.[24]

(a) irrespective of artistic quality: paintings, drawings, diagrams, maps, charts, plans, engravings, etchings, lithographs, woodcuts or similar works (collectively referred to as "graphic works"), photographs, sculptures or collages;

(b) works of architecture, being either buildings or models for buildings;

(c) work of artistic craftsmanship not falling within (a) or (b).

The first of these categories is likely to be most important for journalists—in particular, paintings, drawings and photographs. These words are given a wide definition. In one case a picture of a hand holding a pencil that was marking a cross next to the name of a favoured election candidate was said to be a sufficient drawing to have copyright.[25] Cartoon comic strips also have copyright under this head.[26]

"Photograph" means "a recording of light or other radiation on any medium on which an image is produced or from which an image may be any means be produced and which is not part of a film.[27] Films are excluded because they are separately protected. This apart, the definition

---

[23] *Newspaper Licensing Agency Ltd v. Marks and Spencer plc* [2001] U.K.H.L. 38, July 12, 2001. The Court of Appeal [2000] 4 All E.R. 239 had decided that when a newspaper came in several ss. or supplements, the "edition" was the composite whole. The House of Lords thought that separate and distinct parts might have their own copyright of this kind.

[24] 1988 Act, s. 4.

[25] *Kenrick & Co v. Lawrence & Co* (1890) 25 Q.B.D. 99, decided under the Copyright (Works of Art) Act 1862.

[26] *King Features Syndicate Inc. v. O. & M. Kleeman Ltd* [1941] A.C. 417, HL.

[27] Copyright, Designs and Patents Act 1988, s. 4(2)

is broad and would include, for instance, holograms and also the photographic "plates" that are used in photolithographic printing.

As with literary works, artistic works in the first category are protected whatever their aesthetic value. Similarly, all "artistic works" are only protected if they are "original", in the sense that some skill and labour must have been involved in producing them. Buckingham Palace is a hackneyed subject for tourists' photographs but each picture enjoys copyright, as in each case the photographer will have chosen the distance and angle from which to take it. Similarly, a photocopy montage of clippings or headlines may have sufficient originality to have photographic copyright, but a photocopy of a page of someone else's work falls on the other side of the line: as an exact copy it lacks originality and no particular skill or labour has been required to produce it.[28]

> The band Oasis, organised a photographic shoot at a country club hotel for the cover of their new album. A Rolls Royce was arranged so as to appear to be rising out of the swimming pool. Members of the group were placed around the pool in different poses. A photographer from *the Sun* managed to book a room in the hotel, gained access to the shoot and took photographs of his own which were then published in the paper. Oasis' licensee failed to establish copyright in the scenes which had been photographed: the assembly was too ephemeral to qualify as a "collage" and had nothing in common with "sculpture". It was not an "artistic work". The claimants did, however, succeed in obtaining an interim injunction on breach of confidence grounds.[29]

Sound recordings

This expression is widely defined as:

(a) a recording of sounds from which the sounds may be reproduced, or

(b) a recording of the whole or any part of a literary, dramatic or musical work from which sounds reproducing the work or any part may be reproduced.

(c) regardless of the medium on which the recording is made or the method by which the sounds are reproduced or produced.[30]

---

[28] *Reject Shop plc v. Manners* [1995] F.S.R. 870.
[29] *Creation Records Ltd v. News Group Newspapers* [1997] E.M.L.R. 444, Lloyd J.
[30] Copyright, Designs and Patents Act 1988, s. 5A(1).

Consequently while this type of copyright is commonly used to protect recordings of music, it would include, for example, a tape recording of a conversation. There is no test of originality, but a copy of a previous sound recording does not acquire its own copyright.[31]

The sound track accompanying a film is to be treated as part of the film[32] but this does not affect any copyright subsisting in the film sound track as sound recording copyright.[33] Thus if an infringer copies the film plus the sound track only the owner of the film copyright can take action but if the infringer instead (or as well) copies the sound track on its own it is the owner of the sound recording copyright who is able to complain.

Films

"Films"[34] are again broadly defined as "a recording on any medium from which a moving image may by any means be produced". It is therefore irrelevant whether the film is shot on an ordinary camera or by using a magnetic videotape or is generated by a computer. As with sound recordings, there is no requirement of originality, but again as with sound recordings, a mere copy of a previous film does not attract a fresh film copyright.[35] The recording of a computer program that produces abstract patterns when fed through a machine would also qualify as a "film". Dramatic works or sound recordings that are only embodied in a film can now enjoy a separate copyright, but a photograph that is part of a film does not have its own copyright.[36] This limitation is less appropriate to cartoon films. Each drawing made for the animation has a separate artistic copyright. This was clearly the case when animators like Walt Disney commissioned separate paintings for each frame. The huge costs of that method of production can now be cut by using a single drawing and washable inks. The picture can then be re-photographed for the following frame, by altering only the part that needs to "move". The picture in each state lasts only a few minutes and this impermanence creates a doubt as to whether each enjoys artistic copyright. Of course, each picture is captured on the film, but a photograph can be an artistic work only if it is *not* part of a film.

No court has yet had to decide on whether a series of still photographs taken by motordrive cameras are protected as artistic works or

---

[31] *ibid.*, s. 5A(2).

[32] 1988 Act, s. 5B(2) as inserted by The Duration of Copyright and Rights in Performances Regulations 1995, S.I. 1995 No. 3297.

[33] 1988 Act, s. 5B(5).

[34] *ibid.*, s. 5B.

[35] *ibid.*, s. 5A(4).

[36] *ibid.*, s. 4(2).

as a film. Clearly they are intended to be developed singly, but if (as is sometimes the case) they are "capable of being shown as a moving picture" then the spool would be protected only as a film.

Broadcasts and cable programmes

"Broadcast" is defined as "a transmission by wireless telegraphy of visual images, sounds or other information which is capable of being lawfully received by members of the public or is transmitted for presentation to members of the public".[37] Thus, television and radio have their own copyright in addition to that which pre-recorded programmes enjoy as sound recordings or films. "Wireless telegraphy" is defined[38] as "the sending of electromagnetic energy over pathways not provided by a material substance or arranged for that purpose" and therefore excludes cable (which has its own form of copyright — see below), or the services that rely on telephone lines.[39] It is no longer the BBC and the ITC which exclusively enjoy the broadcasters' copyright: the 1988 Act removed this limitation, no doubt with an eye to deregulation. Satellite broadcasts are protected if decoding equipment for their encrypted signals has been made available to the public by or with the broadcasters' permission.[40]

Cable programmes in a service "which consists wholly or mainly in sending visual images, sounds or other information by means of a telecommunications system, otherwise than by wireless telegraphy, for reception (a) at two or more places [whether simultaneously or not], or (b) for presentation to members of the public"[41] have their own copyright. This wide definition not only catches what would colloquially be called cable programmes, but a variety of other telephonic means of communication. The scope is cut back by some complex exceptions. Broadly, the Act excludes from cable copyright those services that are solely for the internal benefit of a business, for a single individual or for use in premises that have a single occupier. The "catalogue" of interactive services, e.g. home banking or home shopping, is protected by cable copyright (as well as, of course, by any literary copyright that it might also have) but the consumer's response is not.

The internet may be the vehicle for another form of cable programme.

---

[37] Copyright, Designs and Patents Act 1988, ss. 6 and 7.

[38] ibid., s. 178.

[39] But not if microwave energy is used, thus ensuring that cable programmes which use this form of transmission are not treated as broadcasts.

[40] Under s. 298 the broadcasters are given remedies against unlicensed producers and sellers of equipment that decodes their signals, whether in the U.K. or abroad. See BBC Enterprises Ltd v. Hi Tech Xtravision Ltd [1991] 2 A.C. 327.

[41] Copyright, Designs and Patents Act 1988, s. 7(1).

The pursuers[42] were publishers of *The Shetland Times* which reproduced its articles on a website. The front page of the site gave headlines on to which an inquirer could click to retrieve the text. At the bottom of the text was a note inviting comments or suggestions to be sent to an e-mail address. Once the site became established the publishers hoped to sell advertising on the front page. The defenders set up another website called *The Shetland News*. Their home page included a list of headlines, some of which were taken from *The Shetland Times*. These also used hypertext links to provide access to the articles but by-passing *The Shetland Times* front page and its (prospective) advertising. In *The Shetland Times Ltd v. Wills*[43] the Court of Session held that it was arguable that the pursuers were providing a "cable programme service" which involved the publisher "sending" data from the website to the inquirer's computer. (This is not in fact an accurate description of how the web works. Searchers send "get messages" from their computers which "pull" the information from the server and take back it in electronic bursts to be reassembled on screen. The broadcaster "pushes" information out; the web server has it "pulled" out by the searcher and the technologies are entirely different.) However, it was plainly arguable that the service did not become "interactive" because comments and suggestions were solicited — these were not an essential element of the service the primary function of which was to distribute news. The pursuers were granted an interim interdict (the Scottish equivalent of an interim injunction). The litigation was later settled on terms that *The Shetland News* acknowledge each story as emanating from *The Shetland Times* and include a legible image of the *Times'* masthead.[44]

As with sound recordings and films, there is no requirement that a broadcast or a cable programme be original. However, as with sound recordings and films, a simple copy of a previous broadcast or cable programme would not be entitled to a fresh copyright.

Territorial connection

Copyright can be claimed only if there is a connection between the work and either the United Kingdom or a country that is a party to an international copyright convention giving reciprocal rights. In general terms, *unpublished* works are protected if the author or maker was a national of, or resident or domiciled in, Britain or one of the other countries that have subscribed to the Berne Copyright Convention or the Universal Copyright Convention. Where a company may own copyright, it is sufficient if it is incorporated in one of these countries.[45] Most

---

[42] The equivalent Scottish term for claimants.
[43] [1997] F.S.R. 604, OH.
[44] See *Media Lawyer*, Nov–Dec 1997. p. 17.
[45] 1988 Act, ss. 1(3) and 153–155.

of the developed countries are parties to one or both of these conventions, although some have joined relatively recently.[46] The personal connection between the author and Britain is also sufficient to give copyright in *published* works. Alternatively, they will be protected if the work's first publication took place in Britain or one of the Convention countries.

Television, radio broadcasts and cable programmes are protected if made or sent from a place in the United Kingdom or from a Convention country.

PERIOD OF COPYRIGHT

Our previous edition commented that this subject had been generally simplified by the 1988 Act. The Act has since been amended by regulations[47] which the United Kingdom was required to adopt to conform with a European Directive[48] and as a result the position is much more complex. The previous standard copyright period of 50 years was thought to be too short and has been extended in many (but not all) contexts to 70 years. The literary estates of D.H. Lawrence and Rudyard Kipling were among those to benefit from this extension. The European Directive is intended to harmonise the copyright laws of the Member States and the price of this objective was a tortuous compromise.

For works created after January 1, 1996 or works which then had copyright protection in the United Kingdom, the normal position is:

- literary, dramatic, musical or artistic works: 70 years from the author's death. If authorship is unknown copyright lasts 70 years from the making of the work or, if during that period it is made available to the public, 70 years from when that occurs.[49]

- Computer-generated literary, etc., works still have 50 years from the making of the work.[50]

- Crown and Parliamentary copyrights remain as before the 1995 regulations. In literary, musical or artistic works Parliamentary copyright last for 50 years from the making of the work. Crown

---

[46] See The Copyright (Application to Other Countries) Order 1993, S.I. 1993 No. 942 as amended.

[47] The Duration of Copyright and Rights in Performances Regulations 1995, S.I. 1995 No. 3297.

[48] Council Directive No. 93/98/ EEC OJ No. L290, 24.11.93, p. 9.

[49] 1988 Act, s. 12 as amended by the 1995 Regulations.

[50] *ibid.*, s. 12(7).

copyright in these types of work lasts for 125 years, or, if shorter, 50 years from commercial publication. In other types of work the period of Crown and Parliamentary copyright generally follows the standard rules.[51]

- Sound recording copyright lasts for 50 years from the making of the work, or, if during that period it is released, 50 years from release.[52]

- Film copyright lasts for 70 years from the last to die of: the principal director, the author of the screenplay, the author of the dialogue or the composer of music specially created for and used in the film. If the identity of one or more of these participants is unknown, the 70 years runs from the death of the last known. If they are all unknown it runs for 70 years from the making of the film or, if during that period the film is released, for 70 years from release.[53]

- Broadcast and cable copyright extends for 50 years from the year in which the broadcast was made or included in a cable programme.[54]

- Copyright in a published edition lasts 25 years from first publication.[55]

In all cases copyright runs until December 31 of the last year of the period. Generally speaking works which originate outside the EEA[56] and which are not made by an EEA national will have only the period of protection of the national law of their country of origin (if this is less than the period which the Act gives to an EEA national).[57]

It is not possible here to examine the intricacies of works with joint authors or the complications which arise when works have been made many years ago and so lived (or slumbered) through several different legislative regimes or where the work although out of copyright in the United Kingdom in 1995 continued to enjoy protection in another EEA State. For all these situations the specialist textbooks should be consulted. However, one important rule to note is that unpublished works remained in copyright indefinitely until the 1988 Act. They then became subject to a further 50-year maximum which the Duration Regulations

---

[51] 1988 Act, ss. 12(9), 163(3) and 165(3).
[52] *ibid.*, s. 13A.
[53] *ibid.*, s. 13B.
[54] *ibid.*, s. 14.
[55] 1988 Act, s. 15.
[56] The EEA presently includes the countries of the E.U. plus Norway, Liechtenstein and Iceland.
[57] See ss. 12(6), 13A(4), 13B(7) and 14(3). "Country of origin" is defined in s. 15A.

have now extended to 70 years (*i.e.* until 2059). This method of calculating the period of copyright prevails if it produces a longer period
than the normal guidelines described above.[58]

INFRINGEMENT OF COPYRIGHT

Copying

Literary, dramatic, musical or artistic works

The most common method of infringing copyright in these types of
works is by copying them — that is, by reproducing all or a substantial
part of them — in any material form.[59] The reproduction need not be
exact. Obviously, copyright would be of no value if it could be avoided
by a sham alteration of a word or two. It is a more difficult question as
to whether drastic alterations of language or form exonerate a story
whose substance is taken from an earlier work. The question is particularly important for the media. Can a story from a rival newspaper or
broadcaster be reproduced if it is rewritten first? In the United States
the answer would clearly be no, as the Hearst newspaper chain discovered. Its war reporters in World War I were not as effective as those
of Associated Press. Hearst therefore lifted its war news from AP's East
Coast editions and telegraphed the copied stories to California in time
to compete with AP's West Coast editions. The United States Supreme
Court held that this misappropriation of AP's skill and labour was
wrongful competition and could be stopped.[60]

Under United Kingdom copyright legislation the question would turn
upon whether the borrowing was "substantial". This test would be satisfied if a story in newspaper A, based on original research and interviews, was repeated in newspaper B. Thus, each paper in the *Today/
Express* litigation (see p. 296) was found to have infringed the other's
copyright in the quotations that had appeared in the original articles and
that were copied by the rival paper.[61]

Parliament has accepted and catered for the peculiar position of news.
It has given the media a limited licence to plagiarise literary, dramatic
and musical works for the purpose of reporting current events, if they
provide a sufficient acknowledgment of their source (see "Fair
Dealing", p. 314). Consequently, it is only if a newspaper has failed to

---

[58] Duration Regulations, reg. 15(1).
[59] *ibid.,* regs. 16(1) (a), (3) and 17(2).
[60] *International News Service v. Associated Press* 248 U.S. 215 (1918)
[61] *Express Newspapers plc v. News (U.K.) Ltd* [1990], n. 18 above.

acknowledge its indebtedness to a rival that it would need to argue that it had not infringed the other's copyright. It is not at all clear that a court would be sympathetic in such a circumstance. A clue to the likely attitude is the response to the *St James Gazette*'s argument that in copying Rudyard Kipling's dispatches in *The Times* the paper was only following a hallowed Fleet Street custom. A highwayman, the judge caustically remarked, might as well plead the frequency of robbery on Hounslow Heath.[62]

In 1980 the High Court of Australia held that journalists who had obtained secret Government cables could, without breaking the Government's copyright, relay the content and essence of the documents if they chose their own language.[63] They could summarise the effects of the cables and pick out the highlights, but verbatim reproduction would be an infringement. The courts can grant injunctions where the reproduction (although quite different in form) draws on the skill and labour that the claimant had invested in making the original:

> The script of an historical event (the Charge of the Light Brigade) had been drawn from facts recounted in a history book without further original research. An injunction was granted even though the language of the book had not been reproduced, the order of events was different and fresh material had been added.[64]

As the court stated in a similar case:

> "No man is entitled to avail himself of the previous labours of another for the purpose of conveying to the public the same information, although he may append additional information to that already published."[65]

Substantial part

The test is whether, irrespective of language, a "substantial part" of the original work has been reproduced. For this reason, the courts would not prevent others from using a commentator's apt epithet or a dramat-

---

[62] *Walter v. Steinkopf* [1892] 3 Ch. 489, 499. The *Daily Express* tried a similar argument in its litigation with *Today* but was precluded from blowing hot and cold: the existence of the action would have fatally undermined its own claim that the copyright in its quotations had been enjoyed. See also *Banier v. News Group Newspaper Ltd*, p. 320 below.

[63] *Commonwealth of Australia v. John Fairfax and Sons Ltd* (1981) 32 A.L.R. 485, High Court of Aust.

[64] *Harman Pictures NV v. Osborne* [1967] 1 W.L.R. 723.

[65] *Elanco Products Ltd v. Mandops (Agrochemicals) Specialists Ltd* [1980] R.P.C. 213, CA. See also *Independent Television Publications Ltd v. Time Out Ltd* [1984] F.S.R. 64.

ist's smart pun. Whether a taking is "substantial" is a matter of the judge's impression. Quality is more important that quantity in determining substantiality — a Dow Jones reporter who took all the significant information from a private report on the cocoa market (including figures of the actual cocoa-pod count in various countries) had not copied much in terms of length, but everything in terms of significance. Consequently, her articles were held to infringe copyright in the private report.[66]

On the same principle, while a cartoon can be artistic copyright, the joke behind it cannot: it is too ephemeral. Other cartoonists can raise the same laugh so long as their drawings are different.[67]

In these cases, where the defendant has altered the original work, a useful test is whether the defendant has incorporated a substantial part of the independent skill, labour, etc., contributed by the original author in creating the copyright work.[68] Thus, the degree of change that a defendant must make may vary according to the degree of skill that has gone into producing the original. Although a picture of a hand holding a pencil and making a cross might be entitled to copyright, the fact that it had taken no great skill to produce is recognised by protecting it only against close imitations: a picture of a hand in a slightly different position was not an infringement.[69] In the same way, copyright in an anthology of quotations is not infringed by a later work that uses some of the same material but in combination with other sources and in a different arrangement.[70]

The main purpose of copyright is to allow the inventors of original works to exploit them commercially. Where the claimant's and the defendant's works do compete and more than minimal effort has gone into producing the original work, it is not easy to persuade a court that the copying is insubstantial. It will not use a crude quantitative criterion, but rather a qualitative one. The most frequently cited judicial test looks to the commercial reality: "what is worth copying prima facie is worth protecting."[71]

Copyright is not just a battleground between commercial rivals. Satire and parody may involve the repetition of a large part of the work that

---

[66] *PCR Ltd v. Dow Jones Telerate Ltd* [1998] F.S.R. 170.
[67] *McCrum v. Eisner* (1917) 117 I.T. 536; (1917–23) M.C.C. 14.
[68] *Designers Guild Ltd v. Russell Williams (Textiles) Ltd* [2000] 1 W.L.R. 2416, HL
[69] *Kenrick v. Lawrence,* see n.25 above.
[70] *Warwick Film Productions Ltd v. Eisinger* [1969] Ch. 508.
[71] *University of London Press Ltd v. University Tutorial Press Ltd* [1916] 2 Ch. 601, 610. This attitude is strikingly manifest where the compiler of a directory has made use of a rival publication rather than carry out the original research itself. There may be an infringement of copyright in the competing work even if it is only used to compile a mailing list for a questionnaire for the new work; *Waterlow Directories Ltd v. Reed Information Services Ltd* [1992] F.S.R. 409.

is being lampooned. It, too, will be judged by the "substantial part" test in deciding whether there has been an infringement.[72] However, the satirist and the parodist may have a fair-dealing defence (see pp. 314–320). In any case, the targets of their barbs may risk making greater fools of themselves by taking legal action.

If they should, there are two other (albeit vaguer) principles that the courts can invoke either in assessing whether there has been an infringement or in deciding whether to grant a discretionary remedy such as an injunction. The first is a recognition that copyright law must not be used as a means of oppression:

> *Red Star Weekly* used the four lines of a popular song called "Her Name is Mary" as the opening paragraph of a serial story. The court said this was not a breach of copyright. Care had to be taken not to allow the Copyright Acts to be used as a means of oppression. Here the defendant was using part of the claimant's work for a totally different purpose: a purpose that would have no adverse effect on the defendant's sales.[73]

The second principle is that the courts are unlikely to interfere (especially at the interlocutory stage) where the alleged infringer adapts the owner's work to make a political point:

> The Campaign for Nuclear Disarmament printed a pamphlet *30 Questions and Answers About CND*. On its cover the CND symbol was interwoven with a map of Britain. The Coalition for Peace Through Security, a group opposed to CND, produced a counter-publication, *30 Questions and Honest Answers About CND*. The design of the cover was very similar except that the CND symbol had been adapted to resemble a hammer and sickle. CND was refused an interlocutory injunction because it had suffered no financial loss and the judge was reluctant to restrain political controversy.[74]

Programme schedules

An example of how copyright law can operate to prevent one part of the media announcing what another part is doing was for many years provided by the monopoly that the BBC and the ITV companies, respectively, gave to the *Radio Times* and *TV Times* for publishing their weekly programme schedules: an indulgence that made these the largest-selling journals in Britain. The courts consistently held that the

---

[72] See *Schweppes v. Wellingtons* [1984] E.S.R. 210, *Williamson Music Ltd v. The Pearson Partnership* [1987] F.S.R. 97; contrast *Joy Music Ltd v. Sunday Pictorial Newspapers* [1960] 1 All E.R. 703.

[73] *Chappell & Co. Ltd v. D.C. Thompson & Co. Ltd* (1928–35) M.C.C. 467. See also *British Leyland Motor Corp. v. Armstrong Patents Co. Ltd* [1986] A.C. 577.

[74] *Kennard v. Lewis* [1983] F.S.R. 346.

schedules were literary works like other intellectual property which the broadcasters were entitled to protect.[75]

In 1990 the Government finally legislated to end the broadcasters' copyright monopoly in programme schedules. An early attempt to challenge such monopolies under the European Convention of Human Rights had failed, on the grounds that Article 10 guaranteed freedom to exploit information only to those who produced it.[76] However, subsequently the E.U. Commission held that the programme monopoly schedule infringed Article 86 of the Treaty of Rome, and directed broadcasters to provide weekly advance listings of their programmes to all who requested them.[77] In order to conform with this ruling, the British Government introduced section 176 of the Broadcasting Act 1990, which requires the BBC, Channel 4 and all services regulated by the ITC or the Radio Authority to provide a list of a full week's programmes at least 14 days in advance to all those wishing to publish this information. The information may be limited to programme titles and must be paid for by those wishing to publish it, at rates that, if they cannot be agreed, should be decided by the Copyright Tribunal in terms of what it considers "reasonable in the circumstances".[78] The BBC and independent television companies reacted churlishly to the loss of their monopoly, and demanded an astronomical £8 million per year for allowing national and local newspapers and magazines to publish their programme listings. Two hundred publishers appealed to the Copyright Tribunal, which proceeded to adjudicate on the charges after a five-week public hearing and brought them down substantially.[79] An appeal against its decision was settled.[80]

Derivation

From the examples given so far it should be apparent that a copy will be an infringement only if it is derived from the claimant's work. A picture of a winning goal cannot be lifted from one newspaper by its rivals without committing a breach of copyright, but if two photographers took identical pictures from the same spot, both pictures could be published without impinging on each other's copyright. If a newspaper were to copy a table of fixtures from a football pools coupon, it

---

[75] *BBC v. Wireless League Gazette Publishing Co.* [1926] Ch. 433; *Independent Television Publications Ltd v. Time Out Ltd* [1984] E.S.R. 64.

[76] *De Geillustreede v. The Netherlands* [1979] F.S.R. 173.

[77] *Magill TV Guide v. Independent Television Publications* [1990] F.S.R. 71, E.C. Comm. Followed by the ruling of European Court of First Instance to similar effect: *BBC v. E.C. Commission, T–70/89* [1991] 4 C.M.L.R. 669.

[78] Broadcasting Act 1990, Sched. 17.

[79] *News Group Ltd v. Independent Television Publications Ltd* [1993] R.P.C. 173.

[80] See [1993] EMLR 133.

would breach the pools organiser's copyright, but it could publish an identical table if it obtained the information by its own researches.

This causal connection need not be direct. The owners of the *Popeye* cartoon copyright were able to stop an infringer from producing Popeye dolls. The dolls had been copied, not from the cartoon, but from other dolls that had been produced under the claimant's licence.[81] This case, incidentally, also illustrates the possibility of infringing a two-dimensional artistic work by a three-dimensional copy.[82]

A photographer or painter can also indirectly copy an earlier work by using the photograph or painting to recreate the model or scene from which the first artist worked. The copying can then be in the similarity of composition, angle, lighting and general effect,[83] although, as with other examples of infringement, the less skill that was invested in the first work, the closer must be the resemblance to the second before the courts will accept there has been infringement.

Once the link between the original and the copy is proved, it is unnecessary for the copyright owner to show that the defendant intended to plagiarise.[84] Unconscious imitation is still an infringement, though, as will be shown, the defendant's innocence may affect the remedies available to the claimant.

Other types of infringement

Copying other works

Copying a published edition means making a facsimile copy of it.[85] Copying a substantial part will suffice, but the copy must have appropriated the presentation and lay out of the original work.

> When Marks and Spencer circulated photocopies of articles which concerned its business to its employees they were sued for infringement of copyright in the typographical arrangements in the source newspapers. However, the House of Lords said that the relevant work was not the individual articles, but the newspaper as a whole. Taking that as the original work Marks and Spencer had not copied a substantial part of any one paper.[86]

---

[81] *King Features Syndicate Inc. v. O. & M. Kleeman Ltd*, [1941] A.C. 417, HL; see also Copyright, Designs and Patents Act 1988, s. 16(3)(b).

[82] Copyright, Designs and Patents Act 1988, s. 17(3)(b).

[83] *Gross v. Seligman* (1914) 212f 930 (1911–16) M.C.C. 219; *Turner v. Robinson* (1860) 10 I. Ch. R. 121, s. 10.

[84] *e.g. Byrne v. Statist Co.* [1914] 1 K.B. 622.

[85] Copyright, Designs and Patents Act 1988, s. 17(5).

[86] *Newspaper Licensing Agency Ltd v. Marks and Spencer plc* [2001] 3 W.L.R. 290, HL.

Copyright in a film, television broadcast or cable programme can be infringed by taking a photograph of any image forming part of the work.[87]

There can be copying of any type of work even if the copy is transient or incidental to some other use.[88] This can be important for the protection of copyright in computer programs or material stored on computer discs. Calling up a file to be read on a computer would be to make an infringing copy (assuming, of course, it was without the permission of the copyright owner), even if the copy disappears without trace when the machine is switched off. Although incidental copying is prima facie an infringement, there are important defences (see p. 329).

Broadcast and cable

Any type of copyright (apart from a published edition) will be infringed if the work is included in a broadcast or cable programme.[89] Responsibility is shared between the broadcaster who actually transmits the programme (*e.g.* the BBC, the ITC) and the company contracting to provide the programme (*e.g.* Carlton, Capital Radio).[90]

Adaptation

Literary, dramatic and musical (but not artistic) works are also protected against adaptations. This includes turning a non-dramatic work into a dramatic one and vice versa; translating the work into a different language, and turning the work into a strip cartoon. An arrangement or transcription of a musical work is an adaptation. A computer program can be "translated" by converting it into or out of a computer language or code or into another language or code but this is not an infringement if it is done only incidentally in the course of running the program.[91]

Publication, rental, lending and public performance

Sometimes the owner of the copyright will make or authorise copies to be made, but wish to keep them for his own use. The unauthorised issuing of such copies (as well as infringing copies) to the public is an infringement.[92] Liability is here limited to the person who puts the copies into public circulation (the newspaper publisher, for instance)

---

[87] Copyright, Designs and Patents Act 1988, s. 17(4).

[88] *ibid.*, s. 17(6).

[89] *ibid.*, s. 20.

[90] *ibid.*, s. 6(3).

[91] *ibid.*, s. 21.

[92] *ibid.*, s. 18 as amended by the Copyright and Related Rights Regulations, S.I. 1996 No. 2967, reg. 9.

and does not apply to others in the chain of distribution. Thus, whole-salers or retailers would not be liable for "issuing to the public". They will be liable, if at all, for secondary infringement (see below), which depends on knowledge that the merchandise is an infringement. Copy-right in a literary, dramatic or musical work, an artistic work (other than buildings or their models or works of applied art) and in a film or sound recording carries the additional right to control the rental or lending of the work. There are exceptions for certain libraries and the Government has the power to establish a statutory licensing scheme with the Copy-right Tribunal setting royalties in the absence of agreement.[93]

The public performance of a literary, dramatic or musical work is another matter in which the copyright owner is entitled to control. "Performance" includes lectures, addresses, speeches and (parsons beware!) sermons. It will also include a presentation by means of sound or visual aids. Owners of the copyright in sound recordings, films, broadcasts and cable programmes can similarly restrict the public play-ing of their works.[94]

A new right, "publication right" was introduced in 1996.[95] This is a right akin to copyright for the first publisher of a previously unpublished work in which copyright has expired. It is confined to literary, dramatic, musical and artistic works[96] and films and it is dependent on the work being published by a national of the European Economic Area and in the territory of the EEA. The right is more limited than copyright. Of particular importance is the fact that publication right only lasts for 25 years and no moral rights are engaged.

Authorising infringement

In addition to suing the person who actually does these prohibited acts, the copyright owner can also pursue those who "authorise" them.[97] "Authorising" includes sanctioning, approving or countenancing the infringement. So contributors who supply articles or photographs to magazines would be liable for authorising the infringement if they did not own the copyright. Attempts have been made to hold newspapers liable for "authorising" infringement of musical copyright when they have carried advertisements for, or stories about, home-taping. These

---

[93] For the details see the Copyright and Related Rights Regulations S.I. 1996 No. 2967 regs 10–15 which add or amend the following ss. of the 1988 Act: ss. 18A, 36A, 40A, 66, 93A, 133, 142, 93B, 93C, 117 and 124.

[94] Copyright, Designs and Patents Act, 1988, s. 19.

[95] Copyright and Related Rights Regulations 1996 S.I. 1996 No. 2967 regs 16. & 17.

[96] Because unpublished works had perpetual copyright before 1989 and were then given protection until 2039 there will be little immediate practical effect of the new publication right on these types of work.

[97] *ibid.*, s. 16(2).

have generally failed because the claimants were unable to prove that the publication had any influence on the readers' actions.[98] A similar action against the maker of twin-deck tape recorders also failed.[99]

Secondary infringement

All the methods of infringement considered so far are regarded as "primary infringement" by some form of copying, performing or broadcasting. The Copyright Act goes further and allows the copyright owner to take action against others in the chain of distribution and exploitation of infringing copies. Thus importing, possessing in the course of a business, selling, letting for hire, offering or exposing for sale or hire, exhibiting in public for trade or other purposes, and certain types of distributing in each case of infringing copies makes the person concerned liable to the copyright owner.[1] Secondary liability is also imposed on a range of other people who might be commercially involved in primary infringement by, for instance, dealing in articles specifically designed or adapted for making infringing copies or taking steps to enable an infringing performance to take place.[2]

Whereas primary infringement does not depend on guilty knowledge, these secondary infringements do require knowledge or reason to believe that the copies are illegitimate. For this reason, claimants who assert that their rights have been abused will sometimes write to major wholesalers putting them on notice of their claims. This step should not be taken lightly, for the claimants may be liable in damages for lost sales if their claims are not later substantiated.

However, printers are under no separate duty to inquire into the purpose to which their copies will be used and so will not be liable for general damages in the tort of negligence if they print infringing copies.[3]

DEFENCES

Fair dealing

The use of reasonable extracts from the work of others is not an infringement of copyright if it is for the purpose of:

---

[98] *RCA Corp v. John Fairfax & Sons* [1982] R.P.C. 91 Sup. Co of NSW; *A. & M. Records Inc. v. Audio Magnetics Inc. (U.K.)* [1979] F.S.R. 1 (where the advertiser was the defendant).

[99] *CBS Songs Ltd v. Amstrad Consumer Electronics plc* [1988] A.C. 1013.

[1] Copyright, Designs and Patents Act 1988, s. 23.

[2] *ibid.*, ss. 24–6.

[3] *Paterson Zochonis and Co Ltd v. Merfaken Packaging Ltd* [1986] 3 All E.R. 522, CA.

- research or private study, where a literary, dramatic, musical or artistic work is used, or

- criticism or review, or

- reporting current events.[4]

The fair dealing defences require that an acknowledgment be given to the originator if the work is used in any medium for criticism or review or, in the case of the print media, if it is used for the purpose of reporting current events. News stories on television, radio, film or cable television or in a sound recording are not required to carry an acknowledgment. Where an acknowledgment is required, it must identify the work by its title rather than by general description. It must also identify the author unless he or she is anonymous.[5] A logo may be sufficient to identify the author.[6] As long as the source and author are identified as such in the text, neither the word "acknowledgment" nor expressions of gratitude are required.

The dealing must be fair. A publisher or broadcaster will not need to resort to the defence unless a substantial part of the work has been taken, for only then will there be a prima facie infringement to which a defence is necessary. However, the defence will be lost if the taking is "unfair" in the sense of being out of all proportion to the permitted purpose. Critics can illustrate their points by quotations, and where the original work is short, it can be reproduced in its entirety, but the quotation must be a basis for criticism or review; if the purpose is only to convey the same information as the original, and so compete with it, the use will be unfair.[7] So, too, with the use of a work for the purpose of reporting current events. The court will consider whether the copying was reasonable and appropriate for the purpose and the defence may be lost if the court determines that the newspaper or broadcaster took an excessive amount of the source material.[8] Fairness depends on individual circumstances. The question of fairness is judged by the amount taken in order to achieve the permitted purpose: the justice or otherwise of the comments upon the extract is irrelevant.

Thus Carlton Television was able to justify using 30 seconds from a nine-minute feature about Mandy Allwood, the woman fertilised with eight

[4] Copyright, Designs and Patents Act 1988, ss. 29–30.
[5] *ibid.*, s. 178.
[6] *Pro Sieben Media AG v. Carlton U.K. Television Ltd* [1999] 1 W.L.R. 605. CA.
[7] *Hubbard v. Vosper* [1972] 2 Q.B. 84, *per* Lord Denning; *Johnstone v. Bernard Jones Publications Ltd* [1938] 1 Ch. 599; *Associated Newspapers Group plc v. News Group Newspapers* Ltd [1986] R.P.C. 515.
[8] *PCR Ltd v. Dow Jones Telerate Ltd* [1998] F.S.R. 170, Lloyd J.; *Ashdown v. Telegraph Group Ltd, The Times*, August 1, 2001, CA (see below p. 319).

embryos, who had sold (via Max Clifford) her story to a German television company. The court was impressed by the fact that the extract was
quite short and was used to illustrate a "Big Story" attack on cheque-book
journalism.[9]

Copyright protects the form of literary, dramatic or musical works,
but the criticism need not be limited to the language or means of expression that the author has chosen. It is legitimate to copy substantial parts
of the original in order to criticise its substance, content and values.

The Mind Benders was a book written by a former member of the Church
of Scientology. It included extracts from manuals by and directives of L.
Ron Hubbard, the cult's founder, in order to expose and criticise its practices and beliefs. Although the documents had not previously been published, the court refused an interim injunction. Lord Denning said:

"We never restrain a defendant in a libel action who says he is going
to justify. So in a copyright action, we ought not to restrain a defendant
who has a reasonable defence of fair dealing ... the law will not
intervene to suppress freedom of speech except where it is abused".[10]

In that case, the defendant was commenting on the claimant's own
works. This is not essential. Extracts of a reasonable length can be used
as part of a review of some third party's work (for instance, if used for
the purpose of comparison).[11]

In 1993 Channel 4 commissioned a critique of Stanley Kubrick's film
A Clockwork Orange. This had been withdrawn from United Kingdom
distribution since 1974 because of fears that it had spawned copycat violence. However, it was shown elsewhere in Europe and the programme
makers purchased a laser disc copy of the film in Paris. The programme
contained a proper acknowledgment, but the copyright owners claimed
that the fair dealing defence was not available because: (1) of the under-
hand way in which the disc was bought, (2) the unrepresentative selection
of clips used in the programme, (3) the clips totalled 8 per cent of the
film and 40 per cent of the programme and (4) the purpose of the programme was to further a campaign for the film to be shown in the United
Kingdom. The Court of Appeal: (1) rejected the criticism of the method
by which the laser disc had been obtained: criticism of a work in the
public domain would seldom if ever be unfair because of the manner in
which the copy had been obtained; (2) It was not for the court to judge
whether the chosen clips were unrepresentative: even if they were the
defence would not be destroyed if the programme maker's purpose was

---

[9] Pro Sieben AG v. Carlton U.K. Television Ltd [1999] 1 W.L.R. 605, CA.
[10] Hubbard v. Vosper, [1972] 2 Q.B. 84.
[11] Copyright, Designs and Patents Act 1988, s. 30(1).

genuine criticism or review; (3) the amount of the extracts did not exceed fair dealing and (4) any campaign for the film to be shown in the United Kingdom was inextricably entwined with the nature of the film itself. This was a rare example of the court holding on an interlocutory application that a defence was so impregnable that the claimant had not even raised a serious issue to be tried.[12]

In order to benefit from the fair dealing defence, the original work must be used "for the purpose of" criticism or review, reporting current events or research or private study. The court does not need to investigate the defendant's state of mind. The words "in the context of" or "as part of an exercise in" can be substituted for the phrase "for the purpose of" without any alteration in meaning.[13]

Yet while the context in which the original work was used is assessed objectively, the intentions and motives of the defendant may be material in deciding whether the use was "fair"[14]

The scientology case also shows that, at least in some circumstances, the fair dealing defence is available in connection with unpublished works. Some of the extracts were taken from bulletins and letters that had been sent only to scientology initiates. Lord Denning said that this was a sufficiently wide circle to make them subject to public criticism.[15] A company circular sent only to shareholders or a management study report distributed to top executives and union officials[16] may come within the same category. Even where the document has been seen by only a very few people, the fair dealing defence is not automatically excluded.

In 1968 a secret report written for the Greek military junta was leaked to *The Sunday Times*, which proposed to publish extracts from it along with a commentary. The Court of Appeal agreed that the newspaper had an arguable defence of fair dealing because it was only going to use extracts from the report in the course of a story commenting upon it and criticising it.

"Copyright does not subsist in the information contained in the report. It exists only in the literary form in which the information is dressed.

---

[12] *Time Warner Entertainments Company LP v. Channel Four Television Corp. plc* [1994] E.M.L.R. 1, CA.
[13] *Pro Sieben AG v. Carlton U.K. Television Ltd* [1999] 1 W.L.R. 605, CA at 614; *Hyde Park Residence Ltd v. Yelland* [2000] R.P.C. 604, CA at 612.
[14] *ibid.*
[15] *Hubbard v. Vosper*, n. 10 above, at 1028.
[16] *Sun Printers Ltd v. Westminster Press Ltd* [1982] 1 I.R.L.R. 292.

If *The Sunday Times* were going to print this report in full, thus taking the entire literary form, it might well be a case for an injunction."[17]

However, the restricted circulation of the original document and the absence of consent to publication are certainly factors that the courts have taken into account in deciding whether a dealing is fair. The court in *Fraser v. Evans* may have been influenced by the fact that the document was a government (albeit foreign government) document and a matter of public concern. In an Australian case the judge hinted that the fair dealing defence might be wider for criticism or review of government papers.[18]

Fair dealing for the purpose of reporting current events is obviously of importance to the media. Before this statutory defence was introduced, a newsreel film was held to have infringed the musical copyright in *Colonel Bogey*. The film had included a 20-second shot of a high school band playing that tune as the Prince of Wales opened a new hospital.[19] Today such a newsreel would be protected as a report of a current event and, since it was part of a film, no acknowledgment would be necessary.

The meaning of *current* event has yet to be fully explored. The court thought it at least arguable in 1974 that the details of the effect of thalidomide were not then "current" because the drug had been withdrawn 12 years previously.[20] This is a doubtful interpretation, given that the consequences of thalidomide last a lifetime. In any event, had the case gone further, *The Sunday Times* (which wanted to publish substantial extracts from Distillers' private documents) could well have argued that there was a contemporary debate over the morality of Distillers' delay in reaching a settlement and that its proposed story was highly relevant to this "current event." However the *Sun* was unable to argue that it was reporting a current event when it copied letters from the Duke and Duchess of Windsor to which the *Daily Mail* had obtained exclusive rights for a limited period.[21] A broader view was taken in 1999 when the Court of Appeal said: "'criticism or review' and 'reporting current events' are expressions of wide and indefinite scope. Any attempt to plot their precise boundaries is doomed to failure. They are expressions which should be construed liberally".[22]

In accordance with this approach, the Court of Appeal was prepared

---

[17] *Fraser v. Evans,* [1969] 1 All F.R. 8. These cases qualify an earlier decision saying that an unpublished work could never be reproduced for criticism and review: *British Oxygen Co Ltd v. Liquid Air Ltd* [1925] Ch. 383 at 393.

[18] *Commonwealth of Australia v. John Fairfax,* (1981) 32 A.L.R. 485 at 495.

[19] *Hawkes and Son (London) Ltd v. Paramount Film Service Ltd* [1934] Ch. 593.

[20] *Distillers Co. (Biochemicals) Ltd v. Times Newspapers Ltd* [1975] Q.B. 613 at 626.

[21] *Associated Newspapers Group v. News Group Newspapers* [1986] R.P.C. 515.

[22] *Pro Sieben Media AG v. Carlton U.K. Television Ltd* [1999] 1 W.L.R. 605 at 614.

to find that a *News of the World* story about the relationship between
Dodi Fayed and Princess Diana arguably still concerned a current event
one year after their deaths in a Paris car crash. There had been a regular
stream of media stories in the intervening time and Dodi's father,
Mohammed Al-Fayed, had given statements to the press on the subject
shortly before the publication in question.[23] Similarly, the Court of
Appeal agreed that the *Sunday Telegraph* had an arguable case that its
articles concerning a meeting between Tony Blair and Paddy Ashdown
to discuss coalition government and which centred on a leaked note of
the meeting written by the latter, were for the purpose of reporting
current events even though they were published two years after the
meeting. The court said that the defence was clearly intended to protect
the media in informing the public about "matters of current concern to
the public" despite the fact that the events themselves might not be
recent in time. However, the Court of Appeal found that the newspaper
had no arguable defence that it had acted "fairly". It had quoted too
extensively from the note. It competed with other newspapers to whom
the claimant wanted to sell serialisation rights of his memoirs (of which
the note would have been part) and the note was unpublished at the
time of the newspaper articles.[24]

The 1988 Act significantly broadened the fair dealing defence. Under
the earlier law, none of the aspects of fair dealing applied to the use of
film, sound recording, broadcast or cable copyright. This restriction still
applies to the research and private study aspect of the defence, but these
works can, as a result of the 1988 Act be used for criticism, review or
news reporting. There is no longer, therefore, any copyright obstacle
to the BBC presenting a critical and illustrated review of television
programmes on ITV, or vice versa. The ramifications of the extended
fair dealing defence were considered by Mr Justice Scott in 1991 in
BBC v. British Satellite Broadcasting Ltd.[25]

> BSB, shortly before its absorption into Sky, successfully defended as fair
> dealing its use of short excerpts from BBC live broadcasts of World Cup
> matches in its sports-news programmes. Mr Justice Scott held that fairness
> was ultimately a matter of impression, and what impressed him was the
> fact that the excerpts were short (between 14 and 37 seconds) and were
> replayed no more than four times in genuinely informational sports-news
> bulletins. They were also acknowledged as having been shot by the BBC.
> This was not a statutory requirement, but an indication of overall fairness.
> There was no oblique motive rendering the use unfair, and although the
> BBC complained that the satellite channel was using only the best bits
> (*i.e.* the scoring of the goals), it was these clips that had obvious relevance

---

[23] *Hyde Park Residence Ltd. v. Yelland* [2000] R.P.C. 604.
[24] *Ashdown v. Telegraph Group Ltd*, *The Times*, August 1, 2001, CA.
[25] [1992] 1 Ch. 141.

to the news updates. The judge refused to limit the fair dealing defence to general news programmes, and confirmed that sporting clashes were as much current events as any other newsworthy incidents.

The 1988 Act also allows artistic works to be used for reporting current events. Significantly, this liberalisation was not extended to photographs. This means that a newspaper still cannot reproduce a rival's "scoop" photograph, even with acknowledgment, in order to report a news story. The law of copyright thus gives special force to the newsroom adage that a picture is worth a thousand words. One rather unsavoury kind of chequebook journalism involves the purchase by newspapers or news agencies of an exclusive right to exploit family snapshots of notorious criminals. If relatives are paid large sums by a particular news group for the exclusive copyright in a photograph, the law will prevent rival papers from publishing the same picture, however much a matter of public interest it has become.

The Sun had been covering the fight of Princess Caroline of Monaco against the hair-loss illness alopecia. Other papers had obtained a licence to publish photographs of her by the international photographer, Francois-Marie Banier. *The Sun* had published unauthorised copies and the "fair dealing for current events" defence did not apply to photographs. *The Sun* argued that it was a common practice for a newspaper which could not obtain a licence to reprint a photograph already published in the media to copy the picture anyway and negotiate a suitable royalty after the event. The judge described the practice as plainly unjustified and unlawful and granted an injunction and damages. An incensed judge might also award additional damages[26].

There are, however, problems with this strictly legal approach. The market in the memorabilia of mass murder and the like would collapse if the law were changed to permit all media to publish such photographs for the purpose of reporting current events. News should not be the subject of copyright, and photographs that are specially newsworthy should not be confined to one newspaper merely because it happened to be the highest bidder.

Public interest

In a number of cases the courts have developed a defence of "public interest" to claims for copyright infringement. The 1988 Act does not spell out this defence, but it does recognize its existence.[27] Thus in

---

[26] *Banier v. News Group Newspapers Ltd* [1997] F.S.R. 812.
[27] Copyright, Designs and Patents Act 1988, s. 171(3).

Beloff v. Pressdram[28] the court agreed that *Private Eye* would have been entitled to publish a copied memorandum, if the magazine had been able to show that it disclosed an "iniquity". It is not now necessary to point to any such misconduct on the part of the claimant for a public interest defence to succeed. The ruling to this effect in *Lion Laboratories v. Daily Express* (the intoximeter case) was made in relation to a claim for breach of copyright as well as for breach of confidence. The Court of Appeal indicated that the public interest defence applied to both civil actions. Documents supplied by "moles" will generally be subject to copyright: in order to contest the grant of an interim injunction the media must raise a serious public interest defence that might succeed at the trial.

In the important 1990 case of *Express Newspapers v. News Ltd* the Vice-Chancellor accepted unhesitatingly that there was a defence to breach of copyright, as to breach of confidence, "if the information was such that it was in the public interest to know it". In that case, however, the whining of a minor member of the Royal Family amounted to "sensational journalism, not a serious discussion of matters of public interest". In any case the whole basis of the defence was the public's need to know which could hardly be relied upon when the same story had already appeared in the claimant's paper.[29]

However, in 2000 the Court of Appeal re-examined all of these authorities and decided that while there was a "public interest" defence to a copyright claim, it was much narrower than in the context of a breach of confidence action. The copyright defence was confined to situations where it would be contrary to the policy of the law for copyright to be enforced. Without attempting a comprehensive definition of what was meant by this phrase, the Court of Appeal suggested that the law would refuse to enforce copyright if the work was (i) immoral, scandalous or contrary to family life; (ii) injurious to public life, public health and safety or the administration of justice; or (iii) incited or encouraged others to act in a way which injured the public good as exemplified in (ii) above.[30]

Human Rights Act

In *Ashdown v. Telegraph Group Ltd*[31] the newspaper argued that the fair dealing and public interest defences needed to be re-evaluated in the light of the Convention right of freedom of expression. It claimed that its story was on a matter of significant public and political interest

---

[28] [1973] 1 All E.R. 241.
[29] *Express Newspapers plc v. News (U.K.) Ltd* [1990] 3 All E.R. 376 at 382.
[30] *Hyde Park Residence Ltd v. Yelland* [2000] R.P.C. 604, CA at 625.
[31] *The Times*, August, 1, 2001, CA.

(detailed plans between the leader of the Liberal Democrats and the Prime Minister for coalition government and the consequential co-operation between two parties which were supposed to be in opposition) and that it needed to quote extensively from the copy of the claimant's work which had been leaked to it in order to give the story credibility (Downing Street had already tried to play down the significance of the discussions). It argued that these were the sort of circumstances in which the Strasbourg court would critically scrutinise an interference with freedom of expression. The Convention case law also emphasised that the necessity for an interference had to be demonstrated on the facts of the specific case (see "Stop Press" section for further details).

Government publications

Most governmental publications are covered by copyright, which is vested in either the Crown or Parliament.[32] Copyright gives the Government a valuable asset which it exploits to the tune of about £200 million per year. Licences are only given free of charge for brief extracts from a Crown copyright work and for legislation and statutory instruments if there is value added to the publication (such as a commentary). The whole subject of Crown Copyright was reviewed in a Green Paper in 1998[33] and a White Paper in 1999.[34] The Government proposes to retain Crown copyright but there are an increasing number of categories where it has agreed to waive it.[35] In the same spirit, Ordnance Survey in 1998 announced that for a trial period it would not object to the use of limited extracts from its maps on the editorial pages of newspapers and magazines.[36] However, it continues to charge for other commercially produced maps. In 2000, the Court rejected an argument that it was abusing a dominant market position by charging a licence fee for O.S. maps and road categorisation information and road development information.[37] The AA reportedly settled the litigation for £20 million.[38]

Immorality

Public policy may *restrict* the claimant's ability to make out a cause of action. In 1916, one judge held that Elinor Glyn's novel *Three Weeks* was incapable of enjoying copyright protection because of its shocking

---

[32] 1988 Act, ss. 163–167.
[33] See *Crown Copyright in the Information Age,* (HMSO, 1998) Cm. 3819
[34] *The Future Management of Crown Copyright* (HMSO) Cmnd. 3819.
[35] See Chap. 5 of the White Paper and the Guidance Notes from HMSO at www.hmso.gov.uk/guides/htm.
[36] See *Media Lawyer* January 1998, p. 25.
[37] *HMSO v. Automobile Association* September 25, 2000, Ch D.
[38] The *Times* March 6, 2001.

moral values — it advocated free love and justified adultery.[39] In the early nineteenth century Lord Chancellor Eldon enthusiastically exercised this power and ruled that on grounds of public policy there was no copyright in Southey's subversive poem "Wat Tyler" nor in Byron's blasphemous poem "Cain". Other works were denied copyright protection because they were blasphemous, defamatory or likely to deceive the public.[40] Public policy moves (albeit slowly) with the times. While the courts will still refuse their assistance to material that has a grossly immoral tendency, there is no common view as to what kind of sexual conduct between consenting adults is grossly immoral. The Vice-Chancellor remarked in 1988 that "works of Elinor Glyn if published today would be widely regarded as, at the very highest, very soft pornography",[41] although in fact they would not be regarded as anything other than Mills and Boon-style romances. In the second *Spycatcher* appeal the House of Lords thought that Peter Wright would be unable to assert copyright in his book because it represented a gross breach of trust.[42]

There can be an element of hypocrisy in raising a "gross immorality" defence to excuse a publication made in breach of confidence. In the case that prompted the Vice-Chancellor's comment (*Stephen v. Avery* — see p. 233) the *Mail on Sunday* had argued that a lesbian affair was so grossly immoral as to produce a tendency in others to immoral conduct. Not, as the Vice-Chancellor observed, an easy argument for a paper that had just given nationwide publicity to the material. The consequence of accepting the argument that a work is too outrageous to be protected by copyright is that others may copy it at will and (since no licence fees can be charged) a good deal more cheaply than works that are copyright protected.

There is currently a refreshing unstuffiness about moral issues amongst judges in the Chancery Division of the High Court, which deals with copyright and patents. Their brethren in the criminal courts are likely to find most things indecent, and in this tradition a dour Comptroller General of Patents Designs and Trademarks refused to register a design for a model of a Scotsman doll with "mimic male genitalia" under his kilt. This design was, in his opinion, "contrary to law or morality" and hence unsuitable for registration under the Registered Designs Act 1949. The court noted that the design was to commemorate a wedding at which at least one guest had apparently worn nothing beneath his kilt, and that while some would find the doll distasteful, its registration could hardly be injurious to morality. The Registry had been wrong to apply a rigid taboo against the design of the

---

[39] *Glyn v. Weston Feature Film Co.* [1916] 1 Ch. 261.
[40] Phillips (1977) 6 Anglo-Am. I. R. 138.
[41] *Stephens v. Avery* [1988] Ch. 449.
[42] *Att.-Gen. v. Guardian Newspapers Ltd (No. 2)* [1990] 1 A.C. 109.

penis, and to imagine that registration would give the design "an official stamp of approval".[43]

Licences

Who owns the copyright?

Owners of copyright cannot complain of infringement if they have licensed or granted permission for the use in question. This begs the important question: who is the owner? Analysing this issue is a two-stage process: determining who was the first owner of the work and then assessing whether ownership has subsequently been transferred.

The first owner of a literary, dramatic, musical or artistic work is the author, *i.e.* its creator.[44] Under the earlier law, copyright in photographs normally belonged first to the owner of the film or other material on which the picture was taken. Now the rule for photographs is the same as for other artistic works. Computer-generated works belong to the person who made the arrangements for their creation.[45] The author of a sound recording is similarly defined as the person who makes the arrangements necessary for the recording. An amendment to the Copyright Act in 1996 made special provision for the authorship of films. As previously, the person who made the arrangements necessary for the making of the film is one of the authors, but the principal director (if a different person) is also treated as a joint author.[46]

Determining the person or persons who made the arrangements necessary for the making of a film or sound recording can be a vexed matter. The courts will examine who initiated the project and undertook responsibility for seeing it through. Responsibility for obtaining the finance is likely to be part of the necessary arrangements, although the Act pointedly does not confer first copyright on the commissioner of the film. Allowing access to an event which would happen independently of the film makers may not constitute the type of arrangement which the Act contemplated, but an active role in arranging film locations may be different. The parties' intentions may show that they were undertaking arrangements on their own behalf or to assist and for the benefit of someone else.[47] The elusiveness of the statutory definition, the possibil-

---

[43] In *Re Masterman's Design* [1991] R.P.C. 89.

[44] Copyright, Designs and Patents Act 1988, s. 9(1).

[45] *ibid.*, s. 9(3).

[46] See Copyright and Related Rights Regulations 1996, S.I. 1996 No. 2967, reg. 18 amending ss. 9(2), 10, 11 and 178 of the 1988 Act. *N.B.* these changes apply to films made on or after July 1, 1994.

[47] See *Adventure Film Productions SA v. Tully* [1993] E.M.L.R. 376, Ch D, a case under the 1956 Act but which used the same expression; *Beggars Banquet Records*

ity of several people fulfilling the criteria and so becoming joint owners and the serious expense and disruption from disputes as to ownership of copyright mean that there can be a heavy price for not clarifying in advance of filming who is to be the first copyright owner.

The author of a broadcast is the person who makes it.[48] This will include the owner of the transmitter (*e.g.* the ITC and BBC), but only if that person has responsibility for the broadcast's content. British Telecom may facilitate direct broadcasting by satellite but has no involvement in its content and therefore does not share in the copyright. The 1988 Act enlarged the first owners in a broadcast to include the persons providing the programmes and who contract for their transmission. Therefore, commercial TV and radio stations share copyright in their broadcasts with the ITC.

Copyright in a cable programme is first owned by the programme provider, and copyright in a published edition (*i.e.* typographical arrangement) is first owned by the publisher.[49] A work (such as this book) may have joint authors, in which case they will jointly be the first owners of the copyright. However, if their contributions are distinct (*e.g.* if the chapters of a book were divided between them), then each would have a separate copyright in his or her own part.[50]

Literary, dramatic, musical or artistic works made by employees in the course of their employment are first owned by their employers.[51]

Employers can agree to allow their employees to have first copyright,[52] but there is no other statutory provision for altering the first allocation of the right. Nonetheless, the courts have shown a dangerous willingness to introduce ideas of equity and trusts. In one case an advertising agency that was undoubtedly the first legal owner of the copyright was found to hold the copyright on trust for the commissioner of its drawings.[53] In the *Spycatcher* case the House of Lords suggested that if copyright could subsist in such a scandalous book, it belonged in equity to the Crown.[54] This is a mistake brought on by judicial apoplexy at Wright's unpunished treachery. An ex-employee of a secret Government agency who writes his memoirs may breach his employer's confidence but not his copyright. Nonetheless, the Treasury Solicitor

---

Ltd v. Carlton Television Ltd [1993] E.M.L.R. 349, Ch D; *Century Communications Ltd v. Mayfair Entertainments U.K. Ltd* [1993] E.M.L.R. 335, Ch D.

[48] *ibid.*, ss. 9(1)(*b*) and 6(3).
[49] *ibid.*, s. 9(1) (c) and (d).
[50] *ibid.*, s. 10.
[51] *ibid.*, s. 11(2)
[52] Copyright, Designs and Patents Act 1988, s. 11(2).
[53] *Warner v. Gestetner* [1988] E.I.P.R. D–89 see also *Antocks Lairn v. Bloohn* [1971] F.S.R. 490.
[54] *Att.-Gen. v. Guardian Newspapers Ltd (No. 2)* [1990] 1 A.C. 109.

often threatens proceedings for copyright over books which breach the notices of the DA Notice Committee, especially Andy McNab's accounts of life in the SAS.[55]

Once the first owner of the copyright is settled, the possibility of transfer must be considered. Copyright can be assigned, but to be fully effective the transfer needs to be in writing and signed by the assignor.[56] An assignment can be made in advance of the creation of the work, in which case it takes effect as soon as the work is made and the first owner's rights are immediately passed on.[57] An oral or unsigned transfer is not wholly ineffective: it allows the transferee to call for a proper assignment and will bind third parties who have notice of it, but it can be disregarded by a bona fide third party who purchases the copyright without notice of the informal assignment.

Implied licences

No special formality is required for a licence to be granted. It need not be express, but can be implied from the circumstances or by custom. A reader who sends a letter to the editor of a newspaper impliedly consents to its publication, and impliedly agrees as well to any editing that is necessary for reasons of space.[58] Submission of a feature article connotes a similar implied licence, albeit subject to payment of an appropriate fee.[59] Press releases clearly carry an implied licence to copy, at least if publication is made after any embargo.

Exclusive licences

Although an informal licence is effective to protect the media, it is less satisfactory if there is a danger that the publication will be pirated by others. A publisher who is merely a licensee can take action only against the pirates indirectly by calling on the owner of the copyright to sue them. This is inconvenient: authors, even if protected by an indemnity against costs, are sometimes shy of litigation. The problem can be avoided if the publisher takes an assignment. If the author is unwilling to part completely with the copyright, an almost identical advantage can be obtained by taking an exclusive licence: again the licence must be in writing and signed by the licensor.[60]

---

[55] David Hooper, *On Her Majesty's Copyright, The Guardian* October 10, 1995.
[56] Copyright, Designs and Patents Act 1988, s. 90(3).
[57] *ibid.*, s. 91.
[58] *Springfield v. Thame* (1903) 89 I.T. 242; *Roberts v. Candiware Ltd* [1980] F.S.R. 352.
[59] *Hall-Brown v. Iliffe and Sons Ltd* (1928–35) M.C.C. 88.
[60] Copyright, Designs and Patents Act 1988, s. 92.

Adequate licences

Publishers and broadcasters must take care to obtain a licence from owners of all the copyrights in the item that they wish to use. If a copyright is owned by two or more people, each of them must give consent. Copyright can be infringed by a publisher who acted in good faith, and a number of reported cases concern licences that were inadequate because they were incomplete or obtained from the wrong person.[61] It is also important for the media to obtain a licence adequate for all intended purposes. For example, a broadcaster dealing with a playwright must obtain permission to film (if the play is to be pre-recorded) as well as to broadcast. The broadcaster need not, however, expressly provide for the right immediately to retransmit the material via cable television; a licence to broadcast a work carries with it the right to include it in a cable programme.[62]

Copyright Tribunal

Collective licensing, the Copyright Tribunal and competition

It is obviously impractical for individual copyright owners to police all possible infringements. The music industry first recognised the advantage of collective enforcement of copyrights. Now the Performing Rights Society (PRS) and Phonographic Performance Ltd respectively control practically all performing and sound-recording rights in music in the United Kingdom. Similar societies represent the interests of publishers and authors.[63] Equally, there is the potential for these monopolies to act against the public interest. The 1956 Act established the Performing Rights Tribunal to adjudicate on disputes between rights owners and those who needed licences. The 1988 Act renamed the Tribunal the Copyright Tribunal and extended its jurisdiction.

The Tribunal's principal role is to hear disputes about either licensing schemes (standard terms, conditions and tariffs) or one-off licences in three areas.[64]

- the schemes of societies in relation to literary, dramatic, musical or artistic works or films that cover the work of more than one author;

- schemes or licences (whether by societies or individual

---

[61] *e.g. Byrne v. Statist Co*, [1914] 1 K.B. 622.
[62] Copyright, Designs and Patents Act 1988, s. 73.
[63] See Laddie Prescott and Vitoria *The Modern Law of Copyright and Designs* (3rd ed. Butterworths, London, 2000) Chap. 25.
[64] The 1988 Act, ss. 116–135.

owners) in relation to sound recordings (other than the sound
tracks of films), broadcasts, cable programmes and published
editions;

- schemes or licences (whether by societies or individual
  owners) in relation to the rental of sound recordings, films or
  computer programs.

In these areas the Tribunal can determine whether the offered terms are
reasonable and whether an excluded category or use under a scheme
ought to be licensed. The Tribunal must particularly try to prevent
unreasonable discrimination by the copyright owners.[65] "Discrimination" does not mean just unequal treatment on grounds of race or sex
(though that would no doubt be unreasonable) but any discrimination
between licensees or potential licensees. Thus, under the 1956 Act the
Tribunal held that it was unreasonable for the PRS to offer a discount
to the Cinema Exhibitors Association but not to the smaller Association
of Independent Cinemas.

The 1988 Act introduced two new statutory licences.[66] The first concerns rental of sound recordings, films or computer programs. The Secretary of State is empowered to introduce statutory licences for these.[67]
The second concerns the Competition Commission, formerly the Monopolies and Mergers Commission (MMC) and requires some explanation.

Under the Competition Act 1980 anyone could refer to the Office of
Fair Trading an "anti-competitive practice". A good example was the
practice of the BBC and ITV companies refusing to allow anyone other
than the *Radio Times* and *TV Times* to print radio and television listings
a week in advance. The London magazine *Time Out* referred this practice to the Director-General of Fair Trading. He found that the practice
was anti-competitive and referred the matter to the MMC. The Commission was obliged to reconsider the issue of anti-competitiveness and, in
this case, upheld the Director-General's view. It then had to consider
the critical question of whether the practice worked against the public
interest. In *Time Out*'s case the Commission was evenly divided and the
challenge failed; it was left to Parliament finally to end the broadcasters'
monopoly by section 176 of the 1990 Broadcasting Act (see above, p.
309). More generally, if the Competition Commission finds a refusal to
grant a licence to be anti-competitive and against the public interest it
can grant a statutory licence and fix its conditions.[68]

The 1956 Act introduced a statutory licence to replay musical works
once a record of the work had been issued to the public. The 1988

---

[65] *ibid.*, s. 129.
[66] A third concerns photocopying by educational establishments, *ibid.*, s. 141.
[67] *ibid.*, s. 66.
[68] The 1988 Act, s. 144.

Act abolished this. The Broadcasting Act 1990 brought back something similar. It allows the broadcasting of sound recordings in the absence of agreement from the copyright owner and in advance of the Copyright Tribunal fixing the terms. There are complex and stringent conditions for the exercise of this right. In outline, the broadcaster must have been refused a licence by the appropriate licensing body, have given notice of his intention to exercise the right, be ready to pay the charge agreed or set by the Tribunal, be prepared to include in the broadcast a statement reasonably required by the licensing body and provide reasonably required information about the programmes that incorporate the recording. A similar scheme is established to prevent licensing bodies prescribing maximum "needletime" — the proportion of any period of broadcasting that can be given over to records.[69]

Other defences

Incidental inclusion

Copyright in any work is not infringed by its incidental inclusion in an artistic work, sound recording, film, broadcast or cable programme.[70] "Incidental" has been said to mean casual, inessential, subordinate, merely background.[71] The use of music or lyrics will not be treated as incidental if they are deliberately included.

Reports of judicial and parliamentary proceedings

Reports of judicial or parliamentary proceedings will not be a breach of any copyright as long as the report is first-hand.[72] Plagiarising the published report of a rival is not protected. Interestingly, the proceedings do not, apparently, have to be in public. Copyright is not therefore among the restrictions that curtail the reporting of private court hearings (see Chapter 8). "Judicial" is widely interpreted to mean any court, tribunal or person having authority to decide any matter affecting a person's legal rights or liabilities.[73]

---

[69] *ibid.*, sections. 135A—G added by the Broadcasting Act 1990, s. 175. And see the decision of the Tribunal in *AIRC y. PPL and BBC (intervenor)* [1993] E.M.L.R. 181 and, in relation to "narrowcasting" by satellite broadcasters, *AEI Rediffusion Music Ltd v. PPL* [1998] R.P.C. 335.

[70] Copyright, Designs and Patents Act 1988, s. 31.

[71] *IPC Magazine Ltd v. MGN Ltd* [1998] F.S.R. 431.

[72] Copyright, Designs and Patents Act 1988, s. 45.

[73] *ibid.*, s. 178.

Other aspects of public administration

There is no copyright objection to reporting the proceedings of a Royal Commission or statutory inquiry.[74] There is more limited right to copy material from public registers, but this is hedged with restrictions, notably the need to obtain the permission of the keeper of the record.[75] Material in the Public Record Office can be copied.[76] If any other statute specifically authorises an act, then that act will not involve infringement of copyright.[77]

Contemporaneous notes of a speaker

Since the 1988 Act, copyright can be claimed by a speaker in his extempore pronouncements if the words are recorded, whether or not the recording is done for the speaker's benefit. Prima facie it would restrict a journalist who took a note or made a tape-recording in order to report the event. This development would have been a major handicap for the media were there not also a new defence that limits its extent. This defence applies if the speaker's words have been recorded directly (and not, for instance, copied from someone else's record) and not taken from a broadcast or cable programme. The person in lawful possession of the record must sanction its use. If these conditions are satisfied, the record can be used for reporting a current event or in a broadcast or cable programme without infringing the speaker's copyright.[78]

Public reading

A reasonable extract from a literary or dramatic work can be read or recited in public without infringing copyright. A sound recording, broadcast or cable programme can be made of the reading, but only if the record or programme consists mainly of material that does not have to rely on this defence.[79]

Abstracts of scientific or technical articles

Technical articles are often accompanied by an abstract or summary of their contents. Unless a licensing scheme has been certified by the

---

[74] *ibid.*, s. 46.

[75] *ibid.*, s. 47; only plans and drawings marked in a specified manner can be copied without infringing copyright under s. 47(2): Copyright (Material Open to Public Inspection) (Marking of Copies) Order 1990, S.I. 1990 No. 1427.

[76] Copyright, Designs and Patents Act 1988, s. 49.

[77] *ibid.*, s. 50.

[78] *ibid.*, s. 58.

[79] Copyright, Designs and Patents Act 1988, s. 50.

Government, these abstracts can be copied and issued to the public without infringing copyright.[80]

Special use of artistic work

Buildings, sculptures, models for buildings and works of artistic crafts-manship on permanent public display can be photographed, graphically represented, included in a film, broadcast or included in a cable pro-gramme without infringing copyright.[81]

An artistic work that is put on sale can be included in a catalogue or otherwise copied for the purpose of advertising the sale.[82] Although an artist may dispose of copyright in a work, he or she will not infringe the copyright by copying the work in the course of making another, provided the main design of the first is not repeated.[83]

Broadcasts and cable

Radio and television broadcasts and cable programmes can now be legitimately recorded for private and domestic use, but only for the purposes of time-shifting.[84] This limitation is, in practice, unenforce-able.

A photograph of a television screen that is taken for private and domestic purposes will not infringe copyright in the broadcast or cable programme.[85] A copyright owner who has licensed its use in a broadcast or cable programme gives an implied right to make ephemeral record-ings and film of it for the purpose of preparing the broadcast.[86]

The BBC, ITC and Radio Authority can make use of copyright works for their regulatory functions without being guilty of infringe-ment.[87]

Television, radio and cable can be relayed in pubs and other places to which the public are admitted without being charged for admission.[88] There will be no infringement in the broadcast, cable, film or sound recordings, but copyright permission is still needed in relation to any musical, literary, dramatic or artistic works that are included in the broadcast or cable programme. In practice, use of these copyrights is licensed by collectives of copyright owners (see p. 327).

---

[80] *ibid.*, s. 60.
[81] *ibid.*, s. 62.
[82] *ibid.*, s. 63.
[83] *ibid.*, s. 64.
[84] *ibid.*, s. 70.
[85] *ibid.*, s. 71.
[86] *ibid.*, s. 68.
[87] Copyright, Designs and Patents Act 1988, s. 69.
[88] *ibid.*, s. 72.

Four "moral rights" were created by the 1988 Act:

- the right to be identified as author or director (the right to be identified);

- the right not to have the work subjected to derogatory treatment (the right of integrity);

- the right not to be falsely described as author or director;

- the right to privacy in certain types of photographs.

The latter two are dealt with elsewhere (see p. 293 for false attribution of authorship; p. 276 for privacy in photographs).

These first two rights were introduced to bring English law into line with the Berne Copyright Convention. They depend on there being a copyright work and they last as long as copyright in the work,[89] but the owner of the copyright may be quite different from the owner of these moral rights. Copyright can be assigned and, to assist in its exploitation, it frequently is. Moral rights are intended to protect the integrity of the author or director. They cannot be assigned, except on death, when they pass to the author's or director's estate.[90]

The significance of moral rights depends on commercial practice, for while the rights cannot be sold, they can be waived,[91] and the right to be identified as author or director depends on a positive act of assertion. In many European countries the law does not allow waiver of moral rights. But in Britain where it does powerful television and publishing companies set their lawyers in motion immediately the Act came into force to devise standard clauses to waive or exclude moral rights. It will take many years before the right not to have one's original work distorted is accepted as immutably belonging to all creative artists.

Right to be identified as author or director

The right belongs to the author of a literary, dramatic, musical or artistic work or the director of a film.[92] It does not apply to a computer-generated work, a computer programmer, the designer of a typeface, an employee (whose employer is the first owner of the copyright) or a director when someone else has made the arrangements for the film

---

[89] *ibid.*, s. 86.

[90] *ibid.*, ss. 94 and 95.

[91] To be fully effective a waiver must be in writing, but an oral or informal waiver may estop the author or director from asserting the right against those the waiver was intended to benefit, *ibid.*, s. 87.

[92] Copyright, Designs and Patents Act 1988, s. 77(1).

(and so that other person is the first owner of the copyright in it).[93] The right is not infringed if any one of the defences to an infringement action apply (notably if there is a fair dealing with the work for the purpose of reporting current events on a sound recording, film broadcast or cable).[94] The right does not apply at all to the author or director of a work made for the purpose of reporting current events.[95] Nor does it apply in relation to the publication in a newspaper, magazine or similar periodical or in an encyclopedia, dictionary, yearbook or other collective reference work where the work was made for that purpose or used for it with the author's consent.[96]

The right must be asserted. This is a formal act that must be done in writing: the Act specifies precise forms of assertion for different types of work.[97]

If all of these conditions have been fulfilled and the right has not been waived or given up by consent, then the author or director must be identified as such in connection with various public promotions of the work or any substantial part of it.[98]

Derogatory treatment

The right not to have a work subjected to derogatory treatment applies also to authors of literary, dramatic, musical or artistic works and to film directors.[99] As with the right to be identified, it applies to specified public dealings with the altered work.[1] It goes further, though, in applying to the public use of *any* part of the work (whether substantial or not).[2]

The exceptions to this right are a more limited version of those to the "identity" right.[3] Employees may not have copyright or the right to be identified, but they do (subject to their waiver or consent) have the right not to have their work subjected to derogatory treatment if they are or have been publicly identified in the work.[4] Most of the defences that apply to both infringement of copyright and the right to be identified do not permit derogatory treatment. Fair dealing, which is sufficient to

---

[93] *ibid.*, s. 79(2) and (3).
[94] *ibid.*, see s. 79(4) for details.
[95] *ibid.*, s. 79(5).
[96] *ibid.*, s. 79(6).
[97] *ibid.*, s. 78.
[98] *ibid.*, ss. 77 and 89(1).
[99] *ibid.*, s. 80(1).
[1] Copyright, Designs and Patents Act 1988, s. 80.
[2] *ibid.*, s. 89(2).
[3] *ibid.*, s. 81.
[4] *ibid.*, s. 82.

excuse an infringement of copyright, will not necessarily be a defence to breach of a moral right.[5].

So what is "derogatory treatment"? The Act explains that treatment is derogatory "if it amounts to distortion or multilation of the work or is otherwise prejudicial to the honour or reputation of the author or director".[6]

The first person to assert his new "integrity right" in British courts was pop singer George Michael, who alleged that five compositions he had originally recorded with Wham had been subject to derogatory treatment by being remixed to alter some of the lyrics and to introduce "fill-in music" provided by others between his compositions, on an album entitled *Bad Boys Megamix*. The court found that the distortion of his original and creative spirit arguably amounted to derogatory treatment, and granted an interim injunction until the action could be tried.[7]

Not all derogatory dealings will offend the right of integrity. There must be derogatory "treatment" and this means that something must be done to alter the work or add to it. The juxtaposition of the work and a context that is objectionable to the author is not a breach: a feminist photographer could not complain under this head if her pictures were displayed amongst an exhibition of pornography.

There is an echo here of the law's reluctance to allow famous (or, indeed, any) people a monopoly over the use of their names and faces. Two of the Beatles were refused an injunction to prevent the sale of a record of interviews with them. The L.P. was called *The Beatles Tapes* and had pictures of the group inside the sleeve. The maker had a licence from the photographer but not from the Beatles. However, the musicians had no copyright to assert, and the L.P. was not passed off as their work.[8]

The new moral right not to have work derogatorily treated is also infringed by those who deal in articles that infringe it. Like secondary infringement of copyright, however, there is only liability if the dealer knows or has reason to believe that it is an infringing article.[9]

---

[5] *ibid.*, s. 81.
[6] *ibid.*, s. 80(2)(b).
[7] *Morrison Leahy Music Ltd v. Lightbond Ltd* [1993] E.M.L.R. 144.
[8] *Harrison and Starkey v. Polydor Ltd* [1977] 1 F.S.R. 1. Other celebrities have failed because their names or likenesses were borrowed for use in a quite different area of business (see the Uncle Mac case *McCulloch v. May* (1947) 65 P.R.C. 58 and the Abba case, *Lyngstad v. Anabas* [1977] F.S.R. 62. Australian courts have been more sympathetic: *Henderson v. Radio Corp. Pty Ltd* [1969] R.P.C. 218.
[9] Copyright, Designs and Patents Act 1988, s. 83.

TITLES

Most titles—of plays, books, magazines, films and newspapers—are not copyright because by themselves they are not sufficiently substantial to qualify as a "literary work" or because they consist of only a few common words and lack the "originality" which is a key element to qualify for literary copyright.[10] Even an invented word (*e.g.* "Exxon") would not be protected by copyright if it has meaning only when used with other words.[11] Like much of copyright law, this is all a question of degree. Consequently, the longer type of newspaper headline may qualify as a literary work.[12]

The cover of a magazine or newspaper may be protected by artistic copyright. This is likely to be particularly important in the case of a periodical where the words and pictures on the cover will be different from one issue to another but which will conform to a common template. The copyright in this artistic work would be infringed by a rival who copied the same features.[13]

Copyright apart, the choice of a title and getup for a new product will be constrained by the laws of passing off and trademarks. "Passing off" prevents one trader from misrepresenting his goods as the goods of, or associated with, another trader who has an established reputation likely to be harmed. Thus the University of Oxford obtained an injunction to prevent Pergamon Press from publishing *The Pergamon Oxford Dictionary of Perfect Spelling*.[14] However, the courts have been very wary of allowing even an established trader to obtain an effective monopoly in ordinary English words so that quite minor differences will be enough to prevent an injunction[15] and, in some cases, even the very same title will not create a sufficient risk of confusion or amount to a misrepresentation.[16]

---

[10] *Dick v. Yates* (1881) 18 Ch. D 76.

[11] *Exxon Corp. v. Exxon Insurance Consultants Ltd* [1992] Ch. 119.

[12] See *Shetland Times Ltd v. Dr Jonathan Wills* [1997] F.S.R. 604, OH, where the defenders conceded the possibility.

[13] *EMAP National Publications Ltd v. Security Publications Ltd* [1997] F.S.R. 891; *IPC Magazine Ltd v. MGN Ltd* [1998] F.S.R. 431.

[14] *University of Oxford v. Pergamon Press Ltd, The Times,* October 19, 1977 CA.

[15] *Baylis and Co. (The Maidenhead Advertiser) v. Derlenko* [1974] F.S.R. 284 where the *Maidenhead Advertiser* was unable to stop a free sheet from using the name *The New Advertiser*. In the *EMAP National Publications* case (above) both parties produced magazines for classic car owners. The defendants' title *"Classics"* would not, by itself, have been enough to establish passing off in the claimants' magazine *"Practical Classics"*.

[16] *Box Television Ltd v. Haymarket Magazines Ltd, The Times,* March 3, 1997, where the claimants operated a cable television music channel called "The Box" but could not prevent the defendants from publishing a magazine with the same slang expression for television as its title.

Registration of a trademark gives stronger protection. Because the trader will have had to establish the reputation, distinctiveness and originality of the mark in order to have it registered, these matters do not have to be proved again in infringement proceedings. Consequently the publishers of a new magazine or newspaper should always check the proposed title against the Register of Trademarks to see if their idea will trespass on a registered mark in that type of goods or services. The existence of a registered mark does not necessarily mean that a title which incorporates the mark will be an infringement:

> The defendants published a book called *A Sweet Little Mystery — Wet Wet Wet — The Inside Story*. The band, Wet Wet Wet, had registered their name as a trade mark. However, the registration of a trade mark could not be used to prevent publishers using the protected name in the title of a book about the owner: the defendants could rely on Trade Marks Act 1994, section 11(2)(b) because they used the mark to indicate the contents of the book not its origin. The judge said, "It would be a bizarre result of the trade mark legislation, the primary purpose of which is to 'guarantee the trade mark as indication of origin', if it could be used to prevent publishers from using the protected name in the title of a book about the company or product." but note that the defence in section 11(2) is dependent on the proviso (not disputed in this case) that "the use is in accordance with honest practices in industrial or commercial matters."[17]

The advent of the internet seemed for a time to offer new scope for public confusion as trademarks and other well-known brand names were registered as the names of websites or other domains by companies which had nothing to do with the original products. However, the courts are ready to grant injunctions to prevent actual or threatened infringement of trade marks or passing off in this manner.[18]

RIGHTS IN PERFORMANCES

"Bootlegging", or the making and selling of illicit recordings of a live performance, has been another unwanted side-effect of the growth in recording technology. It can harm the commercial interests of both the

---

[17] *Bravado Merchandising Services Ltd v Mainstream Publishing (Edinburgh) Ltd* [1996] FSR 205, OH. Doubts about the case were expressed by the Court of Appeal in *Philips Electronics BV v. Remington Consumer Products* [1998] R.P.C. 283, but see the discussion in Laddie, Prescott and Vitoria at para. 37.11. See also *The European Ltd v. The Economist Newspapers Ltd* [1998] F.S.R. 283, CA for the need to prove confusing similarity between two marks.

[18] *British Telecommunications plc v. One in A Million Ltd* [1999] 1 W.L.R. 903, CA. See the similar decision concerning registration of companies with the same names as well-known trade marks: *Direct Line Group Ltd v. Direct Line Estate Agency* [1997] F.S.R. 374.

performer and anyone to whom the (lawful) recording rights have been awarded. A related issue is the extent to which the performer (or recording company) can control the subsequent use of legitimate recordings under the 1988 Act. The rights are independent of copyright,[19] although the provisions frequently run parallel to each other and an infringement of the performance rights will often also involve a breach of copyright. However, because they are independent, the people who enjoy the rights may be different to the persons who hold the copyright.

Rights are given to performers themselves and to those who have exclusive recording rights. All the rights are conditional on there being a "performance", which can be dramatic, musical, a reading or recitation or a performance of a variety act or similar presentation.[20] As with copyright law, the performer qualifies for protection only if he or she has some connection with the United Kingdom or another country that is party to the relevant international convention[21] or another member of the EEA.[22]

The Act then controls "recordings" of a performance. This term is not synonymous with "sound recording" in copyright law. It can mean a film or a sound recording made either directly from the live performance or indirectly from a broadcast, cable programme or another recording.[23]

The performer's rights are infringed by a person who makes a recording (otherwise than for private and domestic use) or broadcasts the performance live or includes it in a cable programme without the performer's consent, or who makes a recording of the performance directly from a broadcast or cable programme including the live performance.[24] A performer's rights are also infringed by copying (other than for private and domestic use) a recording of the performance. This is now described as the performer's "reproduction right".[25]

Further sub-divisions of performers' rights include "distribution right" (in essence is the right to control the issuing of copies of a recording of a performance to the public[26]), lending and rental rights in recordings of the performance[27] and the right to receive equitable remuneration when a commercially published sound recording of the

---

[19] Copyright, Designs and Patents Act 1988, s. 180(4)(a).
[20] ibid., s. 180(2).
[21] The 1961 Rome Convention for the Protection of Performers, Producers of Phonograms and Broadcasting Organisations.
[22] Copyright, Designs and Patents Act 1988, s. 206.
[23] ibid., s. 180(2).
[24] The 1988 Act, s. 182(1) as substituted by the Related Rights Regulations 1996, reg. 20.
[25] ibid., s. 182A.
[26] ibid., s. 182B.
[27] ibid., s. 182C.

performance is played in public or included in a broadcast or cable programme service.[28] Other infringements of the performers' rights are committed by showing, playing in public, broadcasting or including in a cable programme an unauthorised recording.[29] In all cases the prohibition extends to a substantial part of the performance. As with copyright, there are "secondary infringements" of commercial dealing with infringing recordings.[30] Some of the performers' rights (reproduction, distribution, rental and lending) can be assigned, disposed of on death or insolvency like other property.[31] Others cannot be transmitted except to a limited extent on the owner's death.[32]

Exclusive recording contractors have similar, though slightly narrower, rights to control the use of unauthorised recordings.[33] "Authorised" here means permitted either by the contractor or the performer.

All the rights in performances have exceptions broadly comparable to the defences to copyright actions.[34] Performers rights generally run for 50 years from the performance, or, if during that period it is released, 50 years from the release.[35] The period may be different if the performer is a non-EEA national and his or her home State provides for a shorter period.[36] The civil and criminal remedies for the infringement of the rights also resemble the copyright remedies.[37] If performers cannot be traced or if they unreasonably refuse their consent, the Copyright Tribunal can give a licence in their place and fix appropriate terms.[38]

REMEDIES

Injunctions

Injunctions are normally granted if the claimant succeeds at the trial of a copyright action, though they have been refused because the infringement was trivial, the chance of repetition was slight or claimant had

---

[28] *ibid.*, s. 182D.

[29] *ibid.*, s. 183.

[30] *ibid.*, s. 184.

[31] *ibid.*, ss. 191A and 191B.

[32] *ibid.*, s. 192A.

[33] *ibid.*, s. 185–8.

[34] *ibid.*, Sched. 2.

[35] *ibid.*, s. 191 (as amended by the Duration Regulations 1995. A comparable regime is established for revived performance rights to revived copyright: see Duration Regulations, regs 34 and 35, exceptions Sched. 2.

[36] 1988 Act, s. 191(3) and (4).

[37] *ibid.*, ss. 194–200 and see below.

[38] 1988 Act, s. 190.

acquiesced or delayed unconscionably.[39] In the case of moral rights the court is given a discretion to order that the act be prohibited unless it is accompanied by a sufficient disclaimer dissociating the author or director from the work.[40] More significant for the media is the prospect of a pre-trial injunction against the use of copyright documents in a book or as part of a news story. The principles upon which such "prior restraint" may be resisted are discussed earlier (see p. 19).

Private search warrants and compulsory disclosure

The growth of video and other copyright piracy has led the courts to grant powerful orders for obtaining and preserving evidence of infringement. If there is strong evidence to show that copyright has been or will be infringed in a way that would cause serious harm to the owner of the copyright, and if the owner can prove that vital evidence might be destroyed as soon as word of the institution of proceedings reaches the suspected pirates, then the court can in effect issue a private search warrant. It is prepared to do so in the absence of the proposed defendant, and before notice of the proceedings has been served on the defendant. Applications are usually heard in private. These orders were previously known as *Anton Piller* orders[41] after the case that established the court's jurisdiction to make them. They are now called "search orders".[42] They require the defendants to allow the owners to inspect their premises, usually in the company of the owner's solicitor, and to copy or photograph relevant articles and documents or to detain them until the action is heard. These orders will almost certainly constitute an interference with the right to respect for private life under Article 8 of the European Convention (Article 8 being capable of protecting business as well as domestic premises against State intrusion) and/or with the peaceful enjoyment of possessions under Protocol 1, Art. 1.[43] If the orders are "necessary in a democratic society" to protect the rights of others they will not breach Article 8, nor will Article 1 of Protocol 1 be violated if they are justified in the public interest. However, the court must be satisfied that the orders are proportionate and strike a fair balance between the interests of society and the individual.

The courts can also order the defendants to disclose on oath information that the claimants need to enforce their rights, such as the names

---

[39] Laddie, Prescott and Vitoria, *The Modern Law of Copyright and Designs* (3rd ed., Butterworths, 2000), para. 39.35.

[40] Copyright, Designs and Patents Act 1988, s. 103(2), and see s. 178 for the meaning of "sufficient disclaimer".

[41] *Anton Piller KG v. Manufacturing Processes* [1976] Ch. 55.

[42] See Civil Procedure Act 1997, s. 7 and Civil Procedure Rules, Pt 25, r.25.1(1)(h).

[43] *Niemetz v. Germany* (1993) 16 E.H.R.R. 97.

of their suppliers and customers.[44] These *Norwich Pharmacal* orders can also be made to discover the source of leaked confidential information (see p. 262). Some infringements of copyright are criminal offences (see below) but defendants cannot refuse to answer questions on the grounds that the answers may incriminate them: their privilege against self-incrimination has been taken away by statute.[45] Instead, there is a bar on the answers being used in any subsequent prosecution for a related offence.[46]

Defendants can apply to have these orders set aside. They are rarely successful, but if they are, or if the claimants fail in their action at the trial, the defendants would normally be entitled to compensation.

In 1985, in the first contested case involving an *Anton Piller* order, the High Court awarded £10,000 damages in trespass against a firm of solicitors that had overzealously executed an order which had been obtained upon unsatisfactory evidence. Mr Justice Scott emphasised the need for applicants to produce overwhelming evidence of piracy causing considerable damage, and of the imminence of the danger of destruction of evidence, before *Anton Piller* orders should be made:

> "What is to be said of the *Anton Piller* procedure which, on a regular and institutionalised basis, is depriving citizens of their property and closing down their businesses by orders made *ex parte*, on applications of which they know nothing and at which they cannot be heard, by orders which they are bound, on pain of committal, to obey, even if wrongly made? . . . even villains ought not to be deprived of their property by proceedings at which they cannot be heard."[47]

Damages

Successful claimants can claim compensation for damage to the value of their copyright, which will either be the amount of profits lost as a result of the competitor's action or the fee that they could properly have charged the defendant for using their copyright material.[48] Until the 1988 Act a copyright owner had the further right to the value of the infringing article (*i.e.* damages in conversion).[49] This could far exceed the harm to the copyright and was accurately described as draconian.

---

[44] *Norwich Pharmacal v. Commissioners of Customs and Excise* [1974] A.C. 133.
[45] Supreme Court Act 1981, s. 72.
[46] Defined in Supreme Court Act 1981, s. 72(6); see *Universal City Studies Inc. v. Hubbard* [1983] 2 All F.R. 596.
[47] *Columbia Picture Industries v. Robinson* [1987] Ch. 38. See further guidelines in *Universal Thermosensors Ltd v. Hibben* [1992] 1 W.L.R. 840.
[48] Copyright, Designs and Patents Act 1988, s. 96(2).
[49] Copyright Act 1956, s. 18.

The present Act has abolished the conversion damages remedy. The court has also a power to award additional damages where the infringement has been particularly flagrant, or where the defendant's profit was so large that compensatory damages would not be adequate.[50] There must have been some "scandalous conduct, deceit and such like which includes deliberate and calculated copyright infringement". In one case a photographer sold to the press a wedding photograph of a man who had subsequently been murdered. The photographer had neither the copyright nor permission from the family, and he was made to pay extra damages.[51]

Breach of copyright does not require guilty knowledge. However, if defendants do not know that copyright subsists in the work that is infringed, they are excused from paying damages.[52] They may be subjected, though, to other remedies, such as an injunction or an account of any profit that they have made out of the infringement.[53]

Breach of all four moral rights is actionable as breach of a statutory duty.[54] This means that the claimant can claim compensation to be put in as good a position as if the wrong had not been committed. In considering remedies for breach of the right to be identified the court must specifically take account of any delay in asserting the right.[55]

Account of profits

Damages compensate claimants for what they have lost, but an enterprising defendant may have used the plagiarised work in a way that yielded a profit in excess of what the claimant could have obtained for it. The courts can order the defendant to "account" for this excess profit to the claimant.[56]

---

[50] Copyright, Designs and Patents Act 1988, s. 97(2).
[51] *Williams v. Settle* [1960] 1 W.L.R. 1072. The court described its award differently, but in a comparable situation today additional damages would be likely.
[52] Copyright, Designs and Patents Act 1988, s. 97(1). This is a narrow exception. It does not help those who make a mistake as to who is the copyright owner. Nor can a publisher plead ignorance of the copyright — everyone is presumed to know the law. All reasonable care must have been taken, including any appropriate inquiries. After making these, the defendant must still have no grounds for believing that copyright exists. Because of all these restrictions, the defence is really only of benefit where the copied work is old or originates from a country where it is not reasonably possible to discover whether the necessary conditions for copyright are fulfilled. However, if the defence is available, neither ordinary nor additional damages can be awarded: *Redrow Homes Ltd v. Bett Brothers plc* [1999] 1 A.C. 197.
[53] Copyright, Designs and Patents Act 1988, s. 97(1).
[54] *ibid.*, s. 103(1).
[55] 1988 Act, s. 78(5).
[56] Laddie, *et al.*, *The Modern Law of Copyright and Designs*, para. 39.47.

An account is a discretionary remedy. It will be refused if the breach was trivial or if the claimant delayed unreasonably before starting proceedings. If the court is prepared to order an account of profits, the claimant will have to elect between this remedy and damages. If an account is chosen, the claimant will not be entitled to claim the statutory additional damages as well.[57] In order to allow the claimant to make an informed choice, the defendant will often first be ordered to disclose financial information to the claimant as to the net profit which was made by the infringement.

Delivery up of copies

The court can order the defendant to hand over to the claimant any infringing copy and articles specifically designed for making copies of a particular copyright that the owner of the article knows or has reason to believe has been or is to be used for making infringing copies.[58] The application must be brought within six years of the infringing article being made.[59] Like an account of profits, delivery up is a discretionary remedy, and the court must consider whether the rights of the owner can be adequately protected in some other way. Anyone with an interest in the article is entitled to make representations as to why delivery up should not be ordered and to appeal against the order.[60]

Criminal offences

The Copyright Act 1956 criminalised certain types of infringement, but the penalties were low and the scope of the offences was haphazard. The criminal sanctions were progressively toughened, particularly in response to the growth of the trade in pirated videos and music cassettes. The 1988 Act continued that trend.[61]

A wide range of offences has now been created for those who are both commercially and knowingly involved in copyright infringement. On summary conviction magistrates can sentence to prison for six months and fine the statutory maximum (currently £5,000). Conviction on indictment can lead to a fine (for which there is no upper limit) and

---

[57] *Redrow Homes Ltd v. Bett Brothers plc* (above).
[58] Copyright, Designs and Patents Act 1988, s. 99.
[59] *ibid.*, s. 113: the period is extended if the copyright owner is under a legal disability, *e.g.* is still a minor, or if the owner was prevented by fraud or concealment from knowing the facts of the case.
[60] *ibid.*, s. 144.
[61] 1988 Act, s. 107.

a two-year prison sentence.[62] The criminal court can make forfeiture orders similar to the civil courts' powers to order delivery up.[63] Magistrates can issue search warrants where there are grounds for believing that an offence of manufacturing, importing or distributing infringing copies is or is about to be committed.[64] This power now relates to infringement of any type of copyright work (no longer just sound recordings or films, as under the previous law). In executing the warrant the police may seize any evidence of dealing in infringing copies, but cannot take items subject to legal privilege, excluded material or special procedure material[65] (see also p. 270).

An interesting precedent was established in 1991 when a freelance photographer, David Hoffman, brought a private prosecution against a local liberal councillor in Tower Hamlets, who had used one of his photographs in a leaflet attacking the Labour Party. The councillor was convicted of criminal infringement of copyright, fined £200 and ordered to pay the photographer's legal costs. Victims of copyright infringement may find this an extreme remedy, and one that brings them no financial compensation, although it would undoubtedly prove effective against persistent violators and those who use copyright material for purposes that the copyright holder finds particularly deplorable. In *Thames and Hudson v. DACS*[66] Evans-Lombe J. held that criminal proceedings were not confined to pirates and could, in principle, be invoked by the Artists Collection Society against the well-known publishers of art histories and studies. (The prosecution later failed on its facts.)

Copyright owners can also enlist the aid of customs officers in their fight against pirated works. The owner of copyright in a published literary, dramatic or musical work can give notice in writing asking that infringing copies of the work be treated as prohibited goods for a period not exceeding five years. Owners of copyright in sound recordings and films can make a similar request if the time and place of the arrival of the expected infringing copies can be specified. Classifying the infringing copies as "prohibited goods" does not make their importation a criminal offence, but it does mean that they are liable to be seized and forfeited unless the importer has them only for his private and domestic use.[67]

---

[62] *ibid.*, s. 107. In *R. v. Lewis (Christopher)* [1997] 1 Cr.App.R. (S) 208, CA the defendant was sentenced to 12 months' immediate imprisonment for distributing infringing articles. He had operated a computer bulletin board for passing around computer games. Over a three month period, 934 games had been downloaded and 592 had been uploaded. Each was worth about £40.

[63] Copyright, Designs and Patents Act 1988, s. 108.

[64] *ibid.*, s. 109.

[65] *ibid.*, s. 109(2); Police and Criminal Evidence Act, s. 9(2).

[66] [1995] F.S.R. 153.

[67] Copyright, Designs and Patents Act 1988, s. 111.

The Bank of England is given a monopoly over all representations of legal tender, and it is a criminal offence against section 18 of the Forgery and Counterfeiting Act 1981 to "reproduce on any substance whatsoever, and whether or not on the correct scale, any part of a British currency note" without the Bank's consent. The Bank's singular lack of any sense of humour (or indeed common sense) led to the Old Bailey prosecution in 1987 of an artist named Boggs over paintings of banknotes, which were worth considerably more than the notes themselves and were much increased in value by the publicity that attended his trial. The paintings had been clumsily seized from an art gallery exhibition, and witnesses from the Bank asserted the astonishing proposition that any artist who wished to depict a banknote in a painting had first to submit a sketch in triplicate for approval. The legal argument turned on the meaning of the word "reproduction" as applied to art (is the *Mona Lisa* no more than the reproduction of a sixteenth-century Italian woman?) and experts solemnly placed Boggs in the tradition of *trompel'oeil* painters. The jury, doubtless surprised to be summonsed to Court No. 1 of the Old Bailey to judge an art exhibition, acquitted after a 10-minute retirement.[68]

---

[68] See Geoffrey Robertson, *The Justice Game* (Vintage, 1999), Chap. 12; Laurence Weschler, *Boggs—A Comedy of Values* (Chicago, 1999).

CHAPTER 7

CONTEMPT OF COURT

The power to punish for contempt of court is the means by which the legal system protects itself from publications that might unduly influence the result of litigation. The dilemmas caused by conflict between the demands of a fair trial and a free press are real enough. We pin a certain faith on the ability of juries, judges and tribunals to resolve disputes, so we are justified in being concerned about the effect of outside influence on their deliberations, especially the sort of pressure generated by circulation-seeking sensationalism. The smooth working of the legal system is a very important, but not always overriding, consideration in holding the delicate balance of public interest between the rights of defendants and litigants to a fair trial and the need for society to know about the issues involved in their cases and about the effectiveness of the system that resolves those issues. Too many contempt decisions, especially before the 1981 Contempt Act, treated "the public interest" as synonymous with "the interests of those involved in the legal process", imposing secrecy and censorship without regard for the countervailing benefits of a free flow of information about what happens in the courts.

The rationale behind the contempt law is an abiding British fear of "trial by media" of the sort that often disfigures major trials in America, where the First Amendment permits press TV and radio to comment on a court case. The principle is firmly ensconced in the value-system of lawyers and legislators, and the media ignore it at their peril, even in relation to the trial of the most obviously guilty or most unpopular defendants. When the *Daily Mirror* published sensationalised suggestions that a man arrested for one particularly foul murder was not only guilty, but guilty of other murders as well, its editor was gaoled for

---

There are three principal textbooks on contempt: *Arlidge, Eady and Smith on Contempt* (2nd ed., Sweet & Maxwell, 1999); Miller, *Contempt of Court*, (3rd ed. OUP, 2000); Borrie and Lowe, *The Law of Contempt of Court* (3rd ed., Butterworths, 1996). Recommendations for reform following the thalidomide story injunction were made by the Phillimore Committee's *Report on Contempt of Court*, HMSO, 1974, Cmnd 5794. Sir John Fox's book *The History of Contempt of Court* (1927) explains lucidly the history of contempt, with an appropriate sense of the absurd.

three months.[1] The *Sun* was fined £75,000 for publishing prejudicial material about a man whose private prosecution the newspaper had agreed to fund. The penalty for the massively prejudicial publicity surrounding the arrest of "Yorkshire Ripper" Peter Sutcliffe came in a more permanent form: Parliament refused to amend the Contempt Bill, then under consideration, to make it easier for the press to report newsworthy developments in criminal investigations between the time of arrest and the time of charge.

The power to punish for contempt may be justified by reference to the European Convention on Human Rights: Article 6 provides that:

> "In the determination of his civil rights and obligations or of any criminal charge against him, everyone is entitled to a *fair and public hearing* within a reasonable time by an independent and *impartial* tribunal established by law." [our italics]

A fair hearing is one of "the rights of others" that can justify a restriction on freedom of speech guaranteed by Article 10 if the restriction is "prescribed by law" and not disproportionate to the aim of securing a fair trial before a tribunal unswayed by media prejudice.

The purpose of the law of contempt in relation to the media is to prevent publications that might realistically bias the tribunal or tilt the balance of its procedures unfairly against one side. It is normally a criminal offence, carrying a maximum penalty of two years' imprisonment and an unlimited fine, although the High Court may injunct a potentially contemptuous article or broadcast if action is taken prior to publication. Contempt is the only serious criminal offence that is punishable without trial by jury: cases are decided by High Court judges, who are, inevitably, judges in their own cause in relation to material that reflects adversely upon the administration of justice. The vagueness of the concept, and its intimate relationship with the operation of the legal process, force the media to rely upon professional legal advisers rather more heavily than in other areas of media law. Reliance on professional advice will not preclude a finding of guilt, but it will always mitigate the penalty and exclude any prospect of imprisonment.

The law of contempt serves a valuable purpose in so far as its operation is confined to placing a temporary embargo on publication of information that would make a jury more likely to convict a person who is on trial, or shortly to face trial. Without such a law, the legal system would be forced to adopt the expensive, and not entirely successful, expedients used in notorious trials in America, where jurors are quizzed at length as to what they have seen in the press or on television and are then sequestered under guard in hotels, denied access to family,

---

[1] *R. v. Bolam, ex p. Haigh* (1949) 93 S.J. 220.

newspapers and television programmes for the duration of the case. For all the fuss that is made about "trial by media", it is very rare for convictions to be quashed because of adverse publicity. An exceptional case occurred when Government minister Tom King chose to announce the abolition of the right to silence, on the grounds that it was being exploited by Irish terrorists, on the very day that three Irish defendants had claimed their right to silence on charges of plotting to murder Tom King. There was massive publicity and the subsequent convictions were overturned on appeal.[2] The Taylor sisters (convicted of murder) were freed on appeal in part because of unfair publicity which meant that they could not be re-tried.[3]

Judges occasionally decide that a fair trial is impossible because of earlier press reporting: one notable example was the trial of West Midlands police officers charged with conspiracy to pervert the course of justice because of their role in the Birmingham six affair.[4] Another example was the trial of Geoffrey Knights who was charged with injuring the driver of his partner, the *EastEnders* star, Gillian Taylforth.[5] But the Court of Appeal usually takes a robust attitude towards publicity. Rosemary West's convictions of multiple murders at her Cromwell Road "House of Horrors" were upheld despite the most sensational reporting. The Court of Appeal said that it would be ludicrous if heinous crimes could not be tried because of the extensive publicity they inevitably engendered: all that is required is that the trial judge takes particular care to warn the jury to try the case only on the evidence.[6] The Privy Council in dismissing an order for a retrial by a Scottish court said:

> "The principal safeguard of the objective impartiality of the tribunal is the trial process itself and the conduct of the trial by the trial judge. On the one hand there is the discipline to which the jury will be subjected of listening to and thinking about the evidence. The actions of seeing and hearing the witnesses may be expected to have a far greater impact on their minds than such residual recollections as may exist about reports in the media. This impact can be expected to be reinforced on the other hand by such warn-

---

[2] *R. v. McCann* (1990) 92 Cr. App. R. 239.

[3] *R. v. Taylor (Michelle Ann and Lisa Jane)* (1993) 98 Cr. App. R. 361 and see *R. v. Wood The Times,* July 11, 1995, CA.

[4] *R. v. Reade, Morris and Woodwiss,* Central Criminal Court, October 15, 1993, Garland J.

[5] *R. v. Knights,* Harrow Crown Court, October 3, 1995, Sanders—for further details of these and other examples see Nicol and Rogers: "Annual Review of Media Reporting Restrictions" in *The Yearbook of Media and Entertainment Law 1996,* OUP, edited by Barendt, Bate, Dickens and Gibbons.

[6] *R. v. West* [1996] 2 Cr. App. R. 374 and see *R. v. Michael Stone* [2001] Crim.L.R. 465, CA.

ings and directions as the trial judge may think it appropriate to give them as the trial proceeds in particular when he delivers his charge before they retire to consider their verdict."[7]

This theme—that the trial process makes jurors focus on the evidence to the exclusion of earlier press reporting which can be neutralised by effective judicial directions are regularly repeated.[8] It has been borne out by some spectacular acquittals after sensationally prejudicial publicity. Kevin and Ian Maxwell were acquitted despite years in the press pillory and so was the "Grope Doc" accused of rape, whose prosecution was both sponsored and prejudiced by the *Sun* (see p. 377). Jeremy Thorpe, the former leader of the Liberal Party, was acquitted after years of media speculation that he was guilty of conspiracy to murder and the Kray twins were actually acquitted of a second murder charge only weeks after their convictions at their first trial had received a blaze of publicity.[9]

More systematic studies into the effect of publicity on juries is precluded in England by the Contempt of Court Act which makes it an offence to investigate what went on in the jury room even if juror anonymity is preserved.[10] However, in New Zealand a study by the Law Commission concluded that the impact of pre-trial publicity and prejudicial media coverage was minimal.[11] An Australian study reached similar conclusions.[12] Furthermore, as Lord Hope said in *Montgomery v. HMA:* "the entire system of trial by jury is based upon the assumption that the jury will follow the instructions which they receive from the trial judge and that they will return a true verdict in accordance with the evidence."[13]

The reality is that defence lawyers delight in using the fact of prejudicial publicity to win sympathy for their clients from juries which distrust newspapers and who have their distrust reinforced by media-hostile judges. Often defence lawyers will begin their campaign against press coverage with an abuse of process application at which they urge the court to dismiss the case because it cannot be fairly tried. They may try to summon journalists to give evidence on such applications, but the court should be vigilant to ensure that their questioning is confined to

---

[7] Lord Hope in *Montgomery v. HMA*, [2001] 2 W.L.R. 779.

[8] See *Att.-Gen. v. News Group Newspapers Ltd* [1987] Q.B.1; *Ex parte Telegraph plc* [1993] 1 W.L.R. 980, 987; *Gee v. BBC* (1986) 136 N.L.J. 515, CA.

[9] *R. v. Kray* (1969) 53 Cr. App. Rep. 412.

[10] Contempt of Court Act 1981, s. 8—see below p. 392.

[11] Warren Young, Neil Cameron and Yvette Tinsley, *Juries in Criminal Trials: Part 2* Chap. 9, para. 287, N.Z.L.C. preliminary paper No. 37, Nov. 1999.

[12] New South Wales Law and Justice Foundation, *Managing Prejudicial Publicity* 2001.

[13] [2001] 2 W.L.R. 77 at 810.

relevant matters. If allegations of contempt are to be put against journalists, they should be told of their right to object on grounds of self-incrimination and must be given the opportunity to seek legal advice.[14]

The critical issue that arises in deciding whether a newspaper is guilty of contempt is whether its effect on the date of its publication caused a *risk* of prejudice. The safety of a conviction, on the other hand, will depend on the cumulative impact of publicity in all the media over the trial period and before. Thus newspapers have been found guilty of contempt, although the conviction of the defendant whose trial they were alleged to have prejudiced was upheld[15] and conversely, trials aborted because of press publicity have not necessarily led to findings of contempt against the relevant newspapers.[16] Following the successful appeal of the Taylor sisters, the Law Officers refused to take proceedings for contempt against the press. The sisters tried to challenge this decision, but the Divisional Court ruled that the historical immunity of the Attorney General from judicial review prevented his decision from being challenged. It was difficult to reconcile with the remarks of the Court of Appeal in quashing the Taylors sisters' convictions but it was not so irrational that (had the immunity not existed) it would have been quashed.[17]

Nonetheless, as Simon Brown L.J. said in 1997[18]:

"It seems to me important in these cases that the courts do not speak with two voices, one used to dismiss criminal appeals with the court roundly rejecting any suggestion that prejudice resulted from media publications, the other holding comparable publications to be in contempt, the courts on these occasions expressing grave doubts as to the jury's ability to forget or put aside what they have heard or read.

... unless a publication materially affects the course of trial [by requiring the place of trial to be moved or its start delayed], or requires directions from the court well beyond those ordinarily required and routinely given to juries to focus their attention on evidence called before them rather than whatever they may have heard or read outside court, or creates at the very least a seriously arguable ground for an appeal on the basis of prejudice, it is unlikely to be vulnerable to contempt proceedings under the strict liability rule."

---

[14] *Att.-Gen. v. Morgan* [1998] E.M.L.R. 294, 307. See p. 253 *et. seq.* for the position when journalists are questioned about their sources.

[15] See *Thomson Newspapers Ltd v. Att.-Gen.* [1968] 1 All E.R. 268, *R. v. Malik* [1968] 1 All E.R. 582, 585.

[16] *Att.-Gen. v. MGN Ltd* [1997] 1 All E.R. 456.

[17] *R. v. Solicitor-General, ex p. Taylor* (1996) 8 Admin. L. R. 206.

[18] *Att.-Gen. v. Unger* [1998] E.M.L.R. 280, 291.

The same judge has said that if the publication creates a seriously arguable ground of appeal, this would be sufficient to establish strict-liability contempt.[19] The concern that the Court did not speak with two voices was echoed in *Att.-Gen. v. Guardian Newspapers Ltd*[20] but while Collins J. in that case broadly endorsed the approach of Simon Brown L.J., Sedley L.J. thought that to ask whether the publicity would have been sufficient to justify the grant of permission to appeal against con-viction set the test too low. He thought that it was better to postulate (a) that the jurors had read the publication, (b) an application to dis-charge the jury had been made and refused, (c) the judge had given proper directions, (d) conviction was not inevitable, (e) the jury con-victed, and then to consider whether the prejudicial publicity would have led to a successful appeal against conviction.

The fear of "trial by media" was taken to extremes when British courts stopped publication of editorial criticism by *The Sunday Times* of the moral position of Distillers, the giant corporation that had mar-keted the deforming drug thalidomide, in relation to its offer of financial settlement to parents of the drug's victims. The newspaper was cam-paigning to increase that offer, against a background of protracted and complicated High Court litigation which might never have come to trial. In 1973 the House of Lords held that contempt law prohibited the pub-lication of material that pre-judged the issue of whether Distillers had been negligent in marketing the drug. Two of the judges also said that editorial comment designed to put moral pressure on Distillers to aban-don its legal defence and to negotiate a higher settlement was con-tempt.[21] This decision was widely condemned by Parliament and the press, and an official committee, headed by Lord Justice Phillimore, was established to recommend reforms in the law of contempt.[22] In due course the European Court of Human Rights confirmed that the British contempt law, as declared by the House of Lords in the *Sunday Times* case, was in breach of the Convention guarantee of freedom of expres-sion[23] (see p. 50). In order to bring British law into conformity with the European Convention, the Government was obliged to legislate. This was one of the purposes of the Contempt of Court Act 1981, which now governs most (but not all) aspects of what was previously judge-made law.

---

[19] *Att.-Gen. v. Birmingham Post* [1998] 4 All E.R. 49, QBD.
[20] [1999] E.M.L.R. 904.
[21] *Att.-Gen. Times Newspapers Ltd* [1974] A.C. 273.
[22] Phillimore Committee, *Contempt of Court*, see above.
[23] *Sunday Times v. U.K.* (1979) 2 E.H.R.R. 245.

TYPES OF CONTEMPT

For media purposes, contempt may be divided into five categories.

- *Strict liability contempt.* So called because it may be committed by journalists and editors without the slightest intention of prejudicing legal proceedings. This class of contempt is perpetrated by publication of material that creates a substantial risk that justice, in relation to a case presently before the courts, will be seriously impeded or prejudiced. It can be committed only when a particular case is "active". In a criminal matter this is generally after an individual has been arrested, and in civil litigation this stage is reached when the date for the trial or hearing is set. This form of contempt is often committed accidentally (*e.g.* when newspapers publish details of an individual's previous convictions without realising that he or she is facing fresh criminal charges). Its harshness is mitigated by special defences that apply when the publisher has taken particular care to avoid the danger, or when the prejudicial matter has been published as part of a discussion of matters of public importance. The media are protected from frivolous cases at the hands of disappointed litigants by the rule that any prosecution must be sanctioned by the court or by the Attorney-General.

- *Deliberate contempt.* This occurs on the rare occasions when a publisher deliberately sets out to influence legal proceedings. Greater use has been made of this category of contempt to sidestep the protections for the media in the 1981 Act. Deliberate contempt may also be committed by placing unfair pressure on a witness or a party to proceedings.

- *Scandalous attacks on the judiciary.* This is an anachronistic relic of eighteenth-century struggles between partisan judges and their vitriolic critics. It survives only as a threat to publications that make false and "scurrilous" attacks on the judiciary. The little recent authority shows that honest and temperate criticism of the administration of justice can be published without risk of prosecution.

- *Jury deliberations.* The Contempt of Court Act 1981 introduced an offence of publishing accounts of how jurors reached their verdict.

- *Disobedience to an order of the court.* This chapter deals with rules that apply generally to the enforcement of court orders, but orders which control access to courts or which restrict reporting are considered in Chapter 8, "Reporting the Courts".

STRICT LIABILITY CONTEMPT

Contempt is committed if a publication "creates a substantial risk that the course of justice in the proceedings in question will be seriously impeded or prejudiced."[24] Liability is "strict" in the sense that the prosecution does not have to prove that the publisher intended to prejudice legal proceedings. However, it still bears the burden of showing, beyond reasonable doubt, that the publication created a substantial risk of serious prejudice. The prejudice need not have materialised but the degree of its risk must be "substantial", as distinct from merely possible or remote. Thus a BBC programme that was broadcast only in the southwest region was not in contempt of a trial that was about to take place in London.[25] Of course, a local story might be picked up by the press agencies or by the national media, but if this endangered the trial, it would be the responsibility of those who had given it the broader coverage. The original broadcaster could be liable only if it had sold the story or otherwise been instrumental in giving it a wider audience. When a jury trial is alleged to have been put at risk, it is always worth reviewing how widely the publication was distributed in the area from which the jury was to be drawn. Distributors should have accurate circulation figures and the local Crown Court's Administrator should help in identifying the geographical area from which its jurors are drawn. In 1998 *Sunday Business* was acquitted of contempt of the trial of John Fashanu, Bruce Grobbelaar and others. The likelihood of a copy being sold to a juror in the court's catchment area was about 2,000:1 against and this small chance of any potential juror seeing the articles in question was influential in the finding that there was no substantial risk of serious prejudice[26]

The impediment or prejudice created by the publication must itself be of a serious kind. This means, at least in criminal cases, that it must be of a nature that could tip the final verdict one way or the other.[27] A useful test of whether the prejudice is "serious" is to consider whether it can readily be cured by the court itself, rather than by a prosecution or an injunction against publication. The simplest device is for the trial judge to ask jurors who may have seen the prejudicial material to stand down from the panel: this was done in the Jeremy Thorpe case when two books containing evidence from the committal (at which reporting restrictions had been lifted) had been published before the trial.[28] Where

---

[24] Contempt of Court Act 1981, s. 2(2).

[25] *Blackburn v. BBC, The Times,* December 15, 1976.

[26] *Att.-Gen. v. Sunday Newspapers Ltd* [1999] C.O.D. 11, QBD.

[27] *Att.-Gen v. English* [1982] 2 All E.R. 903 at 919.

[28] David Leigh, *The Frontiers of Secrecy,* (Junction Books, 1980) p. 74. To the authors' chagrin, none of the jurors had read either book.

publicity has been more diffuse, this device may be impracticable. To ask jurors "Have you seen anything published about the defendant's previous convictions?" would obviously draw attention to the very material of which they should be kept ignorant. However, a variation of the device can be effective as the trial progresses. Jurors in one police corruption prosecution were ordered by the judge not to see a play at the Royal Court theatre about the same subject. This was a far more sensible course than banning the play.

Another example of a situation where a reasonable alternative course of action was available to reduce the seriousness of apprehended prejudice is the 1991 case of *Re Central Television*.[29]

> A trial judge feared that the jury in a much-publicised fraud case might be affected by radio and television reports of the case on the night they were to be sent to a hotel while considering their verdict. He therefore used Contempt Act powers to "postpone" all radio and television reports about the trial until the verdict had been delivered, and told the jurors that they could relax and watch television without the danger of prejudice. The Court of Appeal criticised the judge's priorities: the public right to have trials reported overrode the comfort of jurors. If the judge had any real reason to fear prejudicial media comment, he should simply have directed that the jurors were to have no access to radio and television during their overnight stay at the hotel.

A 1992 case has emphasised that the "substantial risk" of prejudice must be a *practical* risk, in the sense that it must carry a prospect that the outcome of the trial would be different without the offending publication, or that it would necessitate the discharge of the jury:

> An article in *The Guardian* criticised the over-sensitivity to the press of judges in big fraud trials. It referred to a current Manchester trial where a judge had imposed reporting restrictions for no better reason than that some of the defendants were facing further committal proceedings. The Attorney-General argued that any revelation that a defendant was facing other charges would amount to contempt if it created "more than a remote risk" of prejudice. The High Court held that this proposition was too wide. For example, revelation of the fact that a defendant was also facing minor charges would not bias a jury against him.[30]

---

[29] *Re Central Television plc* [1991] 1 All E.R. 347.

[30] *Att.-Gen. v. Guardian Newspapers Ltd (No. 3)* [1992] 1 W.L.R. 874. Another media-friendly application of this principle is found in *Schering Chemicals v. Falkman* [1982] Q.B. 1, where the Court of Appeal thought that no civil judge would be influenced by a television programme about a case that had to be tried, and the appearance on it of experts who would give evidence was perfectly proper: they could be cross-examined in court.

The twin burdens on the prosecution, under the Contempt Act, to prove both "*substantial* risk" and "*serious* prejudice" give considerable latitude to the news media in reporting the background to a sensational case. This was confirmed by an early test of the legislation in respect of national newspaper reporting of the arrest of Michael Fagan, a trespasser who had found his way into the Queen's bedchamber in Buckingham Palace[31]:

> Fagan had been charged with burglary (by stealing part of a bottle of wine he had found in the Palace). He faced other unconnected charges of taking a car without permission and of assaulting his stepson. *The Sun* described Fagan as a "junkie", a glib liar and a thief of Palace cigars. None of these descriptions were held to be likely to cause a substantial risk of prejudice. The *Daily Star* referred to an alleged confession by Fagan to theft of the wine. This went to the heart of the case against him and was found to be contempt. *The Mail on Sunday* alleged that Fagan had had a homosexual affair with Commander Trestrail (the Queen's bodyguard) and called Fagan "a rootless neurotic with no visible means of support". This was found to pose a sufficiently serious risk of prejudice to be prima facie contempt, but the paper successfully relied upon the public interest defence in section 5 (see p. 371) because the story was part of a report on a matter of general public interest, namely the Queen's safety. Finally, *The Sunday Times* was found guilty of contempt because it exaggerated the charge against Fagan in relation to his stepson: the paper implied he was accused of wounding when in fact he was charged with the less serious crime of assault occasioning actual bodily harm.

The period of time between publication and trial is a major factor in determining whether the article poses a substantial risk of prejudice. There cannot be strict liability contempt at all if publication took place before the case became "active".[32] Yet even if the proceedings are active, the courts have become much more attentive to the significance of the time which is likely to elapse between publication and the hearing.[33]

In rejecting the Attorney-General's application to commit several newspapers for contempt of the Geoff Knights' case (see p. 347), the court set out a helpful list of the applicable principles[34]:

- each case must be decided on its own facts so that while previous examples may be helpful they are only guides;

---

[31] *Att.-Gen. v. Times Newspapers Ltd, The Times*, February 12, 1983.

[32] Contempt of Court Act 1981, s. 2(3)—see p. 368 below for the "active" or *sub judice* periods.

[33] See, *e.g. Att.-Gen. v. MGN Ltd* [1997] 1 All E.R. 456, 461; *Att.-Gen. v. Independent News Ltd* [1995] 2 All E.R. 370; *Att.-Gen. v. News Group Newspapers Ltd* [1987] Q.B. 1 and *Att.-Gen. v. Unger* [1998] E.M.L.R. 280.]

[34] *Att.-Gen. v. MGN Ltd* [1997] 1 All E.R. 456.

- the court will look at each publication separately[35] and test liability at the time of publication. However a later publication can exacerbate a risk of prejudice which has already been created by earlier publications;

- in the exercise of risk assessment, a small risk multiplied by a small risk results in an even smaller risk;

- in deciding whether there has been a substantial risk of "serious" prejudice the court will examine: (a) the likelihood of the publication coming to the attention of a potential juror (the number of copies circulating in the area from which the jury will be drawn is of obvious importance), (b) the likely impact of the publication on the ordinary reader (prominence of the article and the novelty of its content matter for this purpose), (c) the residual impact at the time of trial.

- The residual impact is of crucial importance and will be affected by the length of time between publication and trial, the focusing effect of listening over a prolonged period to evidence a case and the likely curative effect of the judge's directions to a jury.

Which court?

The seriousness of the risk and the degree of the prejudice will hinge in the first place on the nature of the tribunal that is to try the issue which is the subject of media treatment. The first question for a journalist writing about a pending case is, therefore, "who will judge it?".

Trial by jury

Jurors, drawn at random from the general public, are assumed to be most susceptible to media influence. The publication of prejudicial information about any person awaiting jury trial is consequently dangerous. But jurors are not expected to remember, let alone to believe, everything they happen to read in newspapers. As the judge at the much-publicised Kray trials commented, "I have enough confidence in my fellow-countrymen to think that they have got newspapers sized up and they are capable in normal circumstances of looking at the matter

---

[35] This was of critical importance in the *Knights'* case and the *Taylor* sisters' case. Subsequently the Lord Chancellor announced that s. 2 would be amended so that newspapers could not avoid their responsibility for their contribution to cumulative prejudicial effect but several years later no change to the law has been introduced.

fairly and without prejudice even though they may have to disregard what they read in a newspaper".[36]

Trial by magistrates

Most criminal cases are tried in magistrates' courts, either by district judges (Magistrates' Courts), formerly known as stipendiary magistrates . . . or by a bench of lay justices. The district judge is a full-time professional lawyer and unlikely to be influenced by media reports. More care must be taken in cases that are to be decided by lay justices, who have minimal legal training, although their experience as regular members of the tribunal and the guidance they receive from their clerk would make them more difficult to influence than jurors sitting on a case for the first time. Arguments on these lines were accepted by the Divisional Court in dismissing a defendant's challenge to his conviction by magistrates because of widespread publicity which had been given to his previous conviction.[37]

Trial by judge

Almost all civil actions (other than libel and claims against the police) are heard by judges sitting alone. The Court of Appeal in *Schering Chemicals v. Falkman* found it impossible to accept that a television programme could affect the views of a High Court judge.[38] Indeed, Lord Salmon has said "I am and have always been satisfied that no judge would be influenced in his judgment by what may be said by the media. If he were, he would not be fit to be a judge."[39] Publicity in relation to a case to be heard by a single judge would need to be both false and intemperate, before contempt proceedings would be likely to succeed. As a former Chief Justice has explained:

> "A judge is in a very different position to a juryman. Though in no sense a superhuman, he has by his training no difficulty in putting out of his mind matters which are not evidence in the case. This indeed happens daily to judges on Assize. This is all the more so in the case of a member of the Court of Appeal, who in regard to an appeal against conviction is dealing almost entirely with

---

[36] (1969) 53 Cr. App. R. 412. *Gee v. BBC* (1986) 136 N.L.J. 515, CA was an example of a civil case to be heard by a jury that the court did not think would be seriously prejudiced by another programme on a similar subject shortly after the case had been set down but months before the likely trial date.

[37] *R. v. Croydon Magistrates' Court, ex p. Simmons* [1996] C.L.Y., para. 1662.

[38] See above and also *Re Lonrho plc and Observer Ltd* [1990] 2 A.C. 154.

[39] Quoted by Robin Day in his note of dissent to the Phillimore Report, para. 4.

points of law and who in the case of an appeal against sentence is considering whether or not the sentence is correct in principle."[40]

The courts will be rather more protective of civil cases where a judge sits with non-lawyer assessors, *e.g.* a Crown Court judge hearing appeals from a magistrates' court, or a county court judge hearing complaints of sex or race discrimination. But even so, it will be unusual for there to be a real risk of prejudice.[41]

Appeal hearings

No publisher or broadcaster has been punished for contempt of an appeal court in the last 60 years. This record reflects Lord Reid's comment in the *Sunday Times* case:

> "It is scarcely possible to imagine a case when comment could influence judges in the Court of Appeal or noble and learned Lords in this House. And it would be wrong and contrary to existing practice to limit proper criticism of judgments already given but under appeal."[42]

The Court of Appeal was unduly sensitive when it stopped Channel 4 from broadcasting a dramatic re-enactment of the appeal of the "Birmingham Six" until after its decision had been given.[43] This was essentially a public relations management exercise because none of the judges would have been influenced by the programme, but it "might affect the public view of the judgment of the court". The court misused its contempt powers by postponing the programme in order to prevent the public from pre-judging the judges. The ban was wrong in law and is unlikely to be repeated: the Court of Appeal's confident assessment in 1987 that the "Birmingham Six" were guilty was reversed three years later, when the credibility of police and scientific evidence was finally demolished. In 1999 the High Court of Justiciary in Scotland strongly doubted whether the Channel 4 decision was compatible with the 1981 Act.[44]

---

[40] *R.v. Duffy, ex p. Nash* [1960] 2 O.B. 188 at 198.

[41] *R.v. Bulgin, ex p. BBC, The Times,* July 14, 1977.

[42] *Att.-Gen. v. Times Newspapers* (above n.21) at 301, and see Lord Simon at 321. The unsuccessful attempts were *R.v. The People, The Times,* April 5, 1925; *R. v. Davies, ex p. Delbert-Evans* [1945] 1 K.B. 435; *R. v. Duffy, ex p. Nash,* n.40 above; *Re Lonhro,* n.38 above.

[43] *Att.-Gen. v. Channel Four Television Co, The Independent,* December 3, 1987; *The Times,* December 18, 1987, CA.

[44] *Al Meghrahi v. Times Newspapers Ltd,* August 10, 1999, HCJ—Scots Courts website.

The most recent and authoritative case on contempt of appellate courts is the most permissive so far as media comment is concerned. It arose, in quite extraordinary circumstances, in the course of "Tiny" Rowland's crusade to damnify the Al Fayed brothers and the Government decision that had allowed them to defeat him in the battle to take over the House of Fraser, which owns Harrods:

> Rowland brought legal proceedings against the Secretary of State for Trade and Industry to compel him to disclose an unpublished report of an investigation into the takeover, which was critical of the Al Fayeds and their supporters. Lonhro (Rowland's company) lost the case in the High Court and in the Court of Appeal, but shortly before it was due to be heard in the House of Lords the company was sent, anonymously, a copy of the report. This it managed to publish in a special Thursday edition of the Sunday newspaper *The Observer,* which was also owned by Lonhro. Many copies were distributed before the Government managed to obtain the inevitable injunction, and amongst the list of distinguished personages who were sent copies of the newspaper were four of the five Law Lords listed to hear the appeal. The members of this panel were scandalised that Lonhro should apparently have attempted to influence their decision, and ordered that the company (together with *The Observer*) should stand trial before the House of Lords Appellate Committee on charges of contempt. Lonhro succeeded in removing from the Committee those Law Lords who had determined that the prosecution should be brought, on the grounds that they would otherwise be seen as "judges in their own cause." The Law Lords who eventually ruled that Lonhro had not been guilty of contempt did so on the basis that:
>
> ● the possibility that a professional judge would be influenced by anything he might read about a case he has to decide is remote;
> ● "it is difficult to visualise circumstances in which any court in the United Kingdom exercising appellate jurisdiction would be in the least likely to be influenced by public discussion of the merits of a decision appealed against or of the parties' conduct in the proceedings";
> ● Lonhro's action had pre-empted the very remedy it was seeking from the court, namely publication of the report. But it was not a contempt for it to have taken the law into its own hands and to have achieved its purpose extrajudicially, at least in the absence of any injunction against publication having been granted in aid of the party resisting disclosure in the legal proceedings that were pre-empted.[45]

These rulings make it highly unlikely that public discussion of any case that is subject to appeal will be treated as a contempt on the basis that it is likely to prejudice the course of justice in appeal proceedings.

---

[45] *Re Lonhro plc and Observer Ltd* [1990] 2 A.C. 154.

Contempt risks

The risk of contempt may arise in numerous situations, and it is impossible to lay down hard and fast rules. The following areas, however, present clear dangers.

Criticising the decision to prosecute

The decision to prosecute is not mechanical. It involves the exercise of a discretion and consideration of the public interest, and as such can legitimately be the object of comment and criticism at the time when it is taken; objectors need not wait until the case is over. Consequently, much greater latitude is given to comments hostile to the prosecution than to those critical of the defendant, especially if they deal with issues of principle and do not purport to settle facts in dispute.[46] The use by prosecuting authorities of unusual or discredited laws can always be a subject of debate even at the time of trial. In 1974 the Attorney-General refused to halt a television documentary critical of incitement to disaffection laws at a time when pacifists were standing trial under this legislation, despite a request from the trial judge.

The Director of Public Prosecution and the police must tolerate a greater degree of criticism, because of their public role. Anti-prosecution commentaries are on much more dangerous ground if they attack prosecution witnesses or are likely to influence their evidence.

Anticipating the course of the trial

Predicting the outcome of a trial, or even giving odds on a particular jury verdict, would in most cases amount to contempt because they create a "climate of expectation" which jurors may find difficult to resist. However, considerable freedom is given to the media in publishing informed speculation as to the issues that are likely to be raised, so long as no opinion is expressed as to the way they should be resolved:

> Shortly before the trial of a company fraud, a newspaper published details of the case that would be of interest to investors in the company concerned, and added that "mourners over the fiasco are likely to hear a little inside history of the business". The Court of Appeal said that the con-

---

[46] Old examples of criticism of a prosecution, e.g. *R. v. Mason, The Times,* December 7, 1932; *R. v. Nield, The Times,* January 27, 1909 would now be unlikely to be contempt under the strict liability rule because the risk of prejudice would not be substantial.

tempt proceedings should not have been brought, because the speculation
would cause no substantial prejudice to parties to the action.[47]

It is commonly—and wrongly—believed that a defendant must stay
silent throughout the long period between arrest and trial. In cases
where the arrest has been attended with publicity (invariably prejudicial
to the defendant) there can be no objection to his repeated public assertion of innocence (which is, after all, echoing the law's most sacred
presumption). Nor is it necessarily contempt to publish a book by or
about him. John Stonehouse, M.P. published an account of his disappearance before his trial on insurance fraud charges, and Ernest Saunders and his son gave an account of his stewardship of Guinness in a
book that received considerable publicity a few months before his trial
on matters arising from the Guinness takeover of Distillers. Such literary effusions carry the danger for the author that they will be used in
evidence against him or as fodder for his cross-examiner but this is not
relevant to contempt. Where caution is required is in any references to
prosecution witnesses, and any comment on specific charges or issues
that the jury will have to decide. Mere repetition of matters already
published should not be a problem, but overt attempts to elicit support
for a defendant must be avoided (the title of Saunders' book was
changed, on legal advice, from *Scapegoat* to *Nightmare*).

Contempt creates a difficult problem for individuals who are not witnesses, but who receive adverse publicity as a result of references to
them at the trial or in pre-trial proceedings. Can they rebut false allegations while the trial is in motion? Not, it seems, when the result would
be to suggest that a party to it is a liar. When a man on trial at the Old
Bailey for serious offences made the fantastic claim that Edward Heath
(in company with an Inspector of Police) had raped his wife, Heath
instructed counsel to attend the court to put his denial on public record.
This was not permitted until after the verdict. When Greville Janner
M.P. was falsely and irrelevantly accused of buggery by a witness at
the trial of Frank Beck in 1991, he maintained a stoic silence "on legal
advice" until the jury convicted, and then launched a parliamentary
campaign to remove the absolute privilege attached to press reports of
court proceedings where allegations are made against third parties.
(Janner and his supporters showed no enthusiasm for removing the
absolute privilege attaching to reports of M.P.s' speeches in Parliament,
a source of much greater unfairness to third parties.) When a victim of
outrageous allegations, made under privilege in court in which he is
neither a party nor a witness, puts on public record immediately a short
and emphatic denial, he does not in our view commit contempt of court.
When Lord Goodman was mentioned in an unattractive light by a wit-

---

[47] *Hunt v. Clarke* (1889) 58 L.J.Q.B. 490.

ness in the Thorpe committal hearings, it is said that he went to the Attorney-General to demand redress, only to be advised that the best thing he could do was to stand on a soapbox in Trafalgar Square and proclaim his innocence. Limited protection against derogatory and irrelevant assertions can now be given by the criminal courts. These are discussed in Chapter 8.

Defendants' convictions, bad character or admissions

Publishing derogatory information about a defendant's character or previous convictions before the verdict runs a very high risk of being contempt. These will usually be kept from the jury so that they will not judge a defendant on his bad character in the past rather than on the evidence of his involvement in the offence with which he has been charged.

In 1997 the *Evening Standard* was fined £40,000 for publishing details of the previous convictions of prisoners accused of trying to escape from Whitemoor prison in the middle of their trial. The jury would, of course, have been told that the defendants were in jail, but they would not have known that some were convicted IRA terrorists. The trial had had to be aborted in consequence of the *Standard*'s article.[48]

The sport section of the *Sun* reported snooker player Ronnie O'Sullivan's determination to win the Master's title in celebration of his mother's release from prison after a 12-month prison sentence for VAT evasion. Unfortunately for the newspaper, Mrs O'Sullivan was then in the middle of a trial for dealing in obscene magazines. The jury, which should have been kept ignorant of her previous conviction, was discharged. The *Sun*'s publishers were fined £10,000 by the trial judge for an admitted contempt.[49]

In 1990 the Court of Appeal held that *Private Eye* had created a serious risk of prejudice to Sonia Sutcliffe's libel action against it by blackguarding her character.[50] The allegations were grave (providing her husband with false alibis for murder and defrauding the DHSS), the trial was scheduled to take place only three months later and the magazine's large circulation in London posed a serious risk that it would be read by a juror. Because it was intended to put pressure on her to settle, there was also "intentional contempt" (see p. 381).

Investigation of crime by newspapers can serve a valuable public interest and has been praised in the past by police and courts. However,

---

[48] [1998] E.M.L.R. 711.
[49] *The Times*, March 2, 1996.
[50] *Att.-Gen. v. Hislop* [1991] 1 Q.B. 514.

the different demands of newspapers and prosecutors can cause acute dilemmas.

After a *News of the World* reporter infiltrated a suspected gang of forgers, the paper told the police who provided the cash to purchase counterfeit money. The police wanted to widen the investigation, but the newspaper said that it intended to publish on the day after the counterfeit notes were bought. So the police made their arrests immediately. This meant that the defendants' proceedings were active and the subsequent story was held to be in contempt. The principal features which disturbed the court were the assumption of guilt (but since the reporter had been central to the "sting" operation it would have been difficult to write the story otherwise), frequent reference to previous convictions and bad character and the striking manner in which the story was written. Ironically, the fact that the reporter was likely to be a key prosecution witness told against the newspaper. The court thought this made it more likely that the article would be remembered by a juror who would also be likely to recall the aspects (notably the previous convictions) which were prejudicial. The publishers were fined £50,000. A second investigative piece ("New Terror Gang Takes on Triad Thugs") was found not to be contempt of proceedings against two men accused of running an extortion racket in Birmingham. Although the defendants were pictured and described as leaders of a notorious Vietnamese gang wanted for questioning over a series of violent incidents, it did not assume their guilt and did not attribute any previous convictions to the defendants.[51]

There is no mechanical rule that reference to a defendant's previous convictions will constitute contempt. The assumption is that juries will not hear about them in court and should not be told of inadmissible evidence by the press. If the Government carries out its threat to make previous convictions admissible in criminal trials, the media would have more latitude to report them, but probably only after a judge had ruled them admissible. The proper rule does not apply where the jury obviously knows of the conviction. In the Geoff Knights' case[52] Gillian Taylforth's boyfriend had been regularly in the news for the two previous years and only a month before the publications had been convicted of assaulting a police officer and fined £2,000. This very recent and extensive publicity (often referring to his previous convictions) coupled with the several months which were likely to elapse before the trial meant that articles after Knights' arrest which exaggerated the nature of the assault and referred to his previous convictions were not in contempt.

In 1992 Patrick Magee was arrested in connection with the murder of one

[51] *Att.-Gen. v. Morgan* [1998] E.M.L.R. 294.
[52] *Att.-Gen. v. MGN Ltd* [1997] 1 All E.R. 456.

police officer and the attempted murder of another. An early news broad-cast from ITN and the first editions of several newspapers referred to Magee's earlier escape from Belfast's Crumlin Road jail where he had been serving a life sentence for the murder of an SAS officer. The critical factors in the failure of the Attorney-General to secure contempt convictions were that the publishers swiftly eliminated the prejudicial material, the circulation of the offending copies was small (and the news bulletin was not likely to be remembered) and, most importantly, the trial did not start until nine months later.[53]

Similarly, while it is usually safer not to refer to other, unrelated charges which are outstanding against a defendant, there is no invariable rule that publication of such matters will constitute contempt.[54]

Even if the defendant has admitted his guilt to journalists it may be a mistake to assume that there is no risk of contempt—as the case of the cleaning lady and the fridge illustrates:[55]

In 1996 Mrs Gilluley, a home help for 82-year-old Mrs Burgess, was secretly videoed by Mrs Burgess' son apparently stealing his mother's pension from where it was kept—in the fridge. The *Manchester Evening News* confronted Mrs Gilluley. She broke down and declared "I won't be denying them. I don't know why I took it. I have just been ill. I wanted to see a psychologist." Mrs Gilluley also made admissions to the police in interview. Newspapers published the story after legal advice that there was no substantial risk of prejudice because the case against Mrs Gilluley was open and shut. The Divisional Court roundly criticised that approach. It must not be assumed that because someone "confessed" to a crime that they would plead guilty to it, or that they *were* guilty. However strong the evidence, an accused might contest the charge and, in this case, the act of taking the money from the fridge as shown in the video did not prove she had the necessary criminal intent to be guilty of theft. The admissions to the reporters had been made before she had taken legal advice and by publishing the video pictures, the newspaper was bringing to the attention of potential jurors material which might be held inadmissible. However, the newspapers were acquitted of contempt because many months were likely to elapse between publication and trial and hence there was a low risk that any potential juror would recall the story. The articles were striking but "many such stories are told nowadays and the memory of them rapidly fades".

The approach of the court in this case is in marked contrast to the restrictive attitude in *Att.-Gen. v. BBC and Hat Trick Productions Ltd.*[56]

---

[53] *Att.-Gen. v. ITN* [1995] 2 All E.R. 370.
[54] *Att.-Gen. v. Guardian Newspapers Ltd (No.3)* [1992] 1 W.L.R. 874.
[55] *Att.-Gen. v. Unger* [1998] E.M.L.R. 280
[56] [1997] E.M.L.R. 76, QBD.

Six months before the trial of Kevin and Ian Maxwell on fraud charges the programme *Have I Got News For You* asked contestants to pick the odd one out from Robert Maxwell, his two sons and Mirror Group pensioners. Angus Deayton said the correct answer was the pensioners ". . . from whose misfortunes the others have profited—no mentioning Maxwells, er, no names . . . the BBC are in fact cracking down on references to Ian and Kevin Maxwell just in case programme makers appear biased in their treatment of these two heartless scheming bastards." At the end of the programme, the following was included:

Ian Hislop: "You're not going to leave in that bit about the Maxwell brothers being heartless scheming bastards?"

Angus Deayton: "Well . . . ."

Hislop: "Nothing personal Angus, contempt of court has a statutory two-year imprisonment . . . T.V.'s Mr Wandsworth Prison . . . You will find a lot of inmates will fancy you in there, Angus . . . "

The court found that the programme was in contempt of court because of its popularity, the fact that it was repeated (despite the request of the Maxwells' solicitor not to do so) and because the speakers were well known. Each defendant was fined £10,000 for a "most serious contempt".

The court failed to appreciate the ephemeral nature of comedy: the show went out so long before the trial even started (and which then lasted nine months) that it could not sensibly have prejudiced the jury deliberations. The decision is a breach of Article 10 since freedom of expression includes, perhaps most valuably of all, the freedom to make jokes.

Defendant's photograph

Publishing defendants' photographs can be contempt in criminal cases where the correctness of identification is in issue. The danger is that eyewitnesses for the prosecution may then describe the person in the newspaper's picture, rather than the person they saw at the scene of the crime. In 1994 *The Sun* was fined £80,000 and its editor £20,000 for publishing the photograph of a defendant just before he was about to take part in an identification parade. The prosecution was aborted in consequence.[57] In 1976 the *Evening Standard* was fined £1,000 for a similar contempt on the eve of an identification parade of the young Peter Hain. It made no difference that the picture caption was "Hain, he's no bank robber".[58] It may be difficult for the media to know whether identity will be in issue. Defence solicitors may be willing to tell the press about their clients' defences, but they are under no obligation to assist the media.

---

[57] *The Independent*, July 6, 1994.
[58] *R. v. Evening Standard, ex p. Att.-Gen., The Times*, November 3, 1976.

The problem becomes acute when an arrest warrant has been issued for a suspect who is still at large. For example, photographs of Neville Heath, wanted for a sex murder, were not published after his first victim was discovered, for fear of contempt. If the press had published the photographs, he might have been arrested before he struck a second time.[59] In recognition of this problem, the Attorney-General has now said that pictures of wanted persons issued by the police can be published by the media without risk of contempt.[60] Since he has a monopoly on this type of prosecution for contempt, his assurance gives the media a practical immunity.

Witnesses

Many eyewitness accounts of crimes appear in the press without attracting contempt charges. It will be relatively rare for this to cause a "substantial risk of serious prejudice" and so satisfy the strict liability test. Since strict liability contempt can be committed only when a prosecution is under way, there is not even this risk if a suspect has not been arrested, charged or been made the subject of a warrant. However, any publication that seeks to deter or intimidate prospective witnesses will certainly be vulnerable to contempt proceedings. When a trade union journal severely criticised anyone who might give evidence against the union in a forthcoming case, this was held to be an illegal attempt at intimidation.[61] A specific offence of intimidating witnesses, potential witnesses or jurors was introduced in 1994 to supplement the contempt power.[62] It applies only to actual or potential criminal proceedings. There must have been an act which intimidated and was intended to intimidate a person knowing or believing that the other person was assisting in the investigation of an offence, or is a witness or potential witness or juror or potential juror with the intention of obstructing, perverting or interfering with the course of justice. It will not be contempt, however, to publish an advertisement for witnesses to come forward to assist a particular party, so long as the advertisement is worded neutrally and any reward is not extravagant.[63] It is also an offence under the Theft Act 1968, section 23 to advertise for the return of stolen goods and promise to ask no questions. Advertiser and publisher can be fined on level 3 (current maximum £1,000).

Payment to witnesses for their stories before they give evidence is

---

[59] Steve Chibnall, *Law and Order News,* Tavistock, 1977, p. 53.
[60] *Hansard,* H.C. Debs [1981] Vol. 1000, col. 34.
[61] *Hutchinson v. AEU, The Times,* August 25, 1932.
[62] Criminal Justice and Public Order Act 1994, s. 51.
[63] *Plating Co v. Farquharson* (1881) 17 Ch. D 49 at 55; *cf.* "Payment to Witnesses and Contempt of Court" [1975] Crim.L.R. 144.

usually undesirable and will attract judicial criticism, although curiously no contempt case has yet been brought to deter the practice. There is an obvious danger that bought witnesses will become sold on their stories. They are tempted to exaggerate evidence in order to increase its saleability, and they may become commited to inaccurate stories ghosted by reporters, and have a financial inducement to stick to them in the witness box. The worst example was the *Sunday Telegraph* arrangement to pay Peter Bessell an additional fee of £25,000 if his evidence secured the conviction of Jeremy Thorpe. This deal wholly discredited Bessell's evidence in the eyes of the jury.[64] The paper claimed that Bessell had already been committed to his story when he signed the contract, but there is no doubt that the "escalation clause" in the contract substantially prejudiced the prosecution case. Contracts with witnesses were made on a staggering scale in the trial of Rosemary West for murder. No less than 19 witnesses were alleged to have received money from or signed contracts with the media. One witness denied on oath that she had received payments from the press, but after Mirror Group Newspapers alerted the prosecution to the existence of an agreement, she accepted that she had been wrong. The trial judge warned the jury to keep these dealings in their minds when assessing witness's credibility. The jury nonetheless convicted and the Court of Appeal refused to quash the conviction.[65] The *News of the World* also included an escalation clause (£10,000 if acquittal, £25,000 if conviction) to the alleged victim of an indecent assault by the pop star Gary Glitter. The judge described the contract as "reprehensible" and to be deprecated, but not illegal.[66] Payments or other arrangements with witnesses could not, on their own, amount to strict liability contempt since this is confined to publications[67] but the arrangements might be a deliberate contempt if the necessary intention to prejudge the trial could be inferred. The Lord Chancellor's Department has produced a consultation paper on possible changes in the law concerning payment to witnesses.[68] The Government's intention to legislate was announced in 1998 but at the time of writing has not been implemented. At present, payments to witnesses are contrary to the Press Complaints Commission's declaration on "chequebook journalism" (see p. 699), although the widespread disregard for that declaration may cause the Attorney-General to take action for contempt in an appropriate case.

Not all payments to witnesses are objectionable. Experts who are

---

[64] See *New Statesman,* July 27, 1979.

[65] *R. v. West* [1996] 2 Cr. App. R. 374.

[66] The Press Complaints Commission's adjudication of December 5, 1999 in relation to this is on its website www.pcc.org.uk see further p. 699.

[67] Contempt of Court Act 1981, s. 2(1).

[68] October 1996.

due to give evidence, for instance, might be paid for summarising their conclusions on television. In the *Schering Chemicals* case the Court of Appeal said it was unlikely that their evidence would thereby be affected.[69]

The press has on many occasions aided the administration of justice by finding important witnesses. For instance *The Sunday Times* in 1976 discovered and interviewed a crucial witness who had set up drug deals on behalf of the police. The newspaper supplied a transcript of his evidence to the prosecution and defence: his allegations of police misconduct caused charges against 31 defendants arrested by the police team to be dropped.[70]

Sometimes witnesses have been jealously hidden from journalistic rivals. Again, this is not in itself contempt, though it may sow suspicion that the witness's evidence has been affected. The line is crossed if the witness's evidence is tampered with or the witness is concealed from the police or prosecuting authorities. In 1924 the *Evening Standard* was fined £1,000 for contempt when, amongst other things, it hid a key murder witness with the wife of a sub-editor.[71] When Monica Coghlan, the prostitute claiming to have had sex with Jeffrey Archer was being "minded" by the *News of the World,* she passed the time having sex with one her minders. This did not help her credibility or that of the tabloids when it was revealed at the libel trial.

Revealing a "payment into court"

"Payment into court" is a common tactical ploy by defendants in civil litigation. It is a formal offer to settle for the paid-in sum. If the offer is refused and less than that sum is eventually awarded, the claimants cannot recover their legal costs after the date of the payment in. Rules of court require such a payment to be kept secret, even from the trial judge.[72] A newspaper that disclosed the fact would run a serious risk of contempt.[73]

Television coverage of criminal trials

It is common for television to set up outside courts to cover the entries and exits of participants in notable trials. So long as there is no element of harassment, there can be no question of contempt (see p. 451) unless members of the jury are deliberately pictured or otherwise identified.

---

[69] *Schering Chemicals Ltd v. Falkman Ltd,* n.30 above.
[70] *R. v. Ameer and Lucas* [1977] Crim. I. R. 104.
[71] *R. v. Evening Standard ex p. DPP* (1924) 40 T.L.R. 833.
[72] Civil Procedure Rules, Pt 36, r. 19(2).
[73] *R. v. Wealdstone and Harrow News; Harley v. Sholl* [1925] W.N. 153.

The traditional concern to protect jurors from any kind of embarrassment or reprisal would incline any judge to rule that such media conduct would pose a serious threat to the administration of justice.

One difficulty that British justice has yet to confront stems from mass-media coverage of security arrangements, especially at trials of alleged terrorists. Television news eagerly shows the sharpshooters on the court roof, the police helicopters overhead and the sniffer dogs in the courtyard. There is no doubt that such reports conduce to an atmosphere in which the defendant's guilt as a terrorist comes to be generally assumed, and this factor may have played a part in the wrongful convictions of Irish defendants for the Guildford and Birmingham pub bombings. Highly prejudicial press and television reports of security arrangements have not in the past been prosecuted as amounting to a contempt. But where details are withheld from jurors, to avoid prejudice to the defendants, it will be difficult to resist rulings prohibiting the media from informing them of these arrangements, at least until the trial is over.

The "active" or *sub judice* period

The restrictions imposed by strict liability contempt do not apply from the moment that a crime is committed or a civil dispute flares up: legal proceedings must have been started and reached a particular stage at the time the story reaches the public. This section will examine these points at which a case becomes *sub judice* or, in the terminology of the 1981 Act, "active".[74] Unless a case is "active", there is no risk of committing strict liability contempt, but it is important to remember that "activity" is a necessary and not a sufficient condition. Stories can be written, even about active cases, as long as they do not then pose a substantial risk of serious prejudice.

Commencement of strict liability periods

Criminal proceedings become active as soon as the first formal step in launching a prosecution is taken. This may be an arrest by a police officer, or the charging of a person who has gone voluntarily to a police station or to court. The first step may alternatively be the issue of a warrant by a magistrate for a suspect's arrest or the issue of a summons ordering a person to appear at court on a specified day.[75] If one case involves several of these steps, it becomes active on the first.

Although these tests are more precise than the previous common law (by which the media could commit contempt if proceedings were

---

[74] Contempt of Court Act 1981, s. 2(3).
[75] Contempt of Court Act 1981, Sched. 1, para. 4.

"imminent"), they are still ambiguous. A man "helping the police with their inquiries" may or may not be arrested. An arrest warrant may or may not have been issued for a suspect. The media have no right to be told,[76] although they have a defence (see p. 374) if, after taking all reasonable care, they have no reason to suspect that one of the critical steps has been taken. If they know enough to realise that one of the steps might have been taken and they guess wrongly, they may be in contempt.

Press reporting is not frozen indefinitely if a suspect for whom an arrest warrant has been issued is not caught: 12 months after its issue the proceedings cease to be active and the media are then free to comment until the actual arrest.[77] Lord Lucan may be safely described as a murderer unless or until he resurfaces to stand trial.

Civil proceedings become active when a trial date is fixed or when the case is "set down for trial."[78] "Setting down" used to be a stage in High Court proceedings when a case entered the lists of those ready to be tried. The term is not used in the Civil Procedure Rules which now govern proceedings in both the High Court and county court and so the fixing of a date for the trial or hearing is the only practical determinant of when a civil case becomes active.

A party to civil proceedings may seek an order of the court on a procedural or interim matter before trial. These interlocutory applications are also shielded by contempt, although because the application will be heard by a legally qualified master or district judge the chance of it being prejudiced by press comment will in most cases be too remote. These applications are regarded as "active" from the time a date is fixed for the hearing until the hearing is completed.[79] When several applications are made, the case will resemble a restless poltergeist, passing through periods of activity and repose.

Journalists ought to be able to find out if a date has been fixed for a hearing by inquiring at the court where the case will be heard. The Attorney-General has instructed court officials to assist journalists.[80]

Termination of strict liability periods

Criminal proceedings are over if the jury returns a "not guilty" verdict, or if the prosecution drops the charges.[81] A guilty verdict is more com-

---

[76] *R. v. Secretary of State for the Home Department, ex p. Westminster Press Ltd* (1992) 4 Admin. L.R. 445.

[77] Contempt of Court Act 1981, Sched. 1, para. 11.

[78] *ibid.*, paras 12 and 13.

[79] *ibid.*

[80] This was said during the Committee stage of the Contempt of Court Bill: Standing Committee "A" May 12, 1981, col. 141.

[81] Contempt of Court Act 1981, Sched 1. para. 5.

plex. The proceedings continue to be active until the offender is sentenced. The courts have expressly disapproved of a premature press clamour that might give the appearance of affecting the sentence, although it is unlikely that contempt proceedings would be brought unless the publication amounts to a deliberate attempt to put pressure on a judge to hand down a particular sentence.

The period of activity continues if the court remands the defendant for a social inquiry report or if the case has been tried by magistrates who think their powers of sentence are insufficient and they decide to commit the defendant to the Crown Court for punishment. The case ceases to be active if sentence is formally deferred for a fixed period to allow the defendant a chance to show that he or she can make good.[82] If the jury disagrees, the proceedings remain active unless the prosecution indicates that it will not seek a new trial.[83] Since 1997 the possibility exists that a person who is acquitted may be re-tried for the same offence.[84] Ordinarily an acquittal is final, but if it is followed by a conviction of the defendant or some other person for an "administration of justice offence" (perjury, perverting the course of justice or intimidating witnesses or jurors) the judge at the second trial must consider whether there was a real possibility that the previous acquittal was tainted. If so, the second trial judge may issue a certificate. Thereafter, the original proceedings become active again for the purpose of strict liability contempt.[85] Before the defendant can be retried for the original offence, the prosecution has to obtain an order from the High Court quashing the original acquittal.[86] This may be many weeks after the certificate was issued because the order cannot be made if there is an appeal outstanding against the administration of justice offence. The High Court's decision (whether to make the order or not) must be sent to the Crown Court or courts concerned and they must display the notice in public for 28 days.[87]

Civil proceedings end when they are disposed of, discontinued or withdrawn.[88]

---

[82] *ibid.*, para. 6.
[83] *Att.-Gen. v. News Group Newspapers* (1982) 4 Cr. App. R. (S) 182.
[84] Criminal Procedure and Investigations Act 1996, s. 54.
[85] Contempt of Court Act 1981, Sched. 1 para. 4A. The Crown Court at which the administration of justice offence is tried and, if different, the Crown Court at which the original trial took place, must display a copy of the certificate in public for 28 days—The Crown Court (Criminal Procedure and Investigations Act 1996) (Tainted Acquittals) Rules 1997, S.I. 1997 No. 1054, r.7.
[86] Criminal Procedure and Investigations Act 1996, ss. 54 and 55.
[87] Tainted Acquittals Rules above, r.9.
[88] Contempt of Court Act 1981, Sched. 1, para. 12.

Appeals

Appeal proceedings are active from the time when they are launched by the lodging of a formal notice of appeal or application for leave.[89] The losing party's declaration of intent to appeal is not enough. There will often be a period, perhaps quite short, between the end of active trial proceedings and the commencement of active appeal proceedings during which the strict liability rule does not apply at all and comment is quite free. Even if appeal proceedings have become active, it is virtually inconceivable that appellate judges will be influenced by what appears in the media. When an appeal is disposed of, abandoned, discontinued or withdrawn, even this restraint is removed unless the case is remitted to the trial court or unless a new trial is ordered, in which case new proceedings are treated as active from the conclusion of the appellate proceedings.[90]

Defences

Public interest defence

An important defence is provided for the media by section 5 of the Contempt of Court Act. This is intended to ensure that public debate and criticism on matters of importance can continue, even though a side-effect of expounding the main theme is that ongoing proceedings might be prejudiced. The section reads:

> "A publication made as or as part of a discussion in good faith of public affairs or other matters of general public interest is not to be treated as contempt of court under the strict liability rule if the risk of impediment or prejudice is merely incidental to the discussion."

Section 5 was given a liberal interpretation by the House of Lords in the first test case:

> The Attorney-General accused the *Daily Mail* of prejudicing the trial of a doctor who was charged with allowing a Down's syndrome baby to die. The *Daily Mail* had published an article by Malcolm Muggeridge in support of a "Pro-Life" candidate in a contemporaneous by-election. He spoke disparagingly of what he described as the common practice of doctors deliberately failing to keep deformed children alive. The House of Lords said the defence was applicable. Even if the public understood the article as a reference to the trial, it was not contempt. Academics might

---

[89] *ibid.*, para. 15.
[90] *ibid.*, Sched. 1, para. 16.

enjoy abstract discussions, but the press was entitled to make great issues come alive by reference to concrete examples. "Gagging of bona fide discussion of controversial matters of general public interest merely because there are in existence contemporaneous legal proceedings in which some particular instance of those controversial matters may be in issue is what section 5 . . . was intended to prevent." The court also emphasised that protection was not lost merely because the article could have been written without the prejudicial material:

> "The test is not whether the article could have been written as effec-
> tively without the passage or some other phraseology might have been
> substituted for it that would have reduced the risk of prejudice to Dr
> Arthur's fair trial; it is whether the risk created by the words actually
> chosen by the author was merely incidental to the discussion which I
> take to mean no more than an incidental consequence of expounding
> the main theme".[91]

Sir John Junor was fined £1,000 and the *Sunday Express* £10,000 for a comment that prejudiced the same trial.[92] This piece directly criticised the doctor, on the basis of facts reported in the prosecution case that were subsequently proved incorrect. Section 5 was not applicable, because there was no discussion of wider issues. Neither writer nor newspaper tried to defend this blatant contempt, committed in mid-trial.

In 1989 the Divisional Court said that in deciding whether the risk of prejudice was incidental, it was necessary to look at the subject-matter of the discussion and see how closely it related to the particular legal proceedings.

> In the middle of a trial of a Reading landlord charged with conspiring to
> defraud the Department of Health and Social Security, TVS broadcast
> a programme called *The New Rachmans* about sham bed-and-breakfast
> accommodation in Reading. The court accepted that the programme
> attempted to analyse the cause of the new wave of Rachmanism in the
> South of England, but it focused on a small number of landlords in Read-
> ing. The programme included still photographs of two of the defendants,
> who were recognisable although their faces had been blacked out. The
> trial of the defendants was aborted at a cost of £215,000. The broadcaster
> and a newspaper that had previewed the programme under the headline
> "Reading's new wave of harassment . . . TV focus on bedsit barons" were
> found guilty of contempt.[93]

---

[91] *Att.-Gen. v. English*, n.27 above. See also the recommendation of the Phillimore Committee, para. 142, on which the s. was based, and the Australian decisions that spell out a similar defence: *Re "Truth & Sportsmen," ex p. Bread Manufactures* (1937) 37 S.R.N.S.W. 249; *Brych v. The Herald and Weekly Times* [1978] V.R. 727.

[92] *The Times*, December 19, 1981.

[93] *Att.-Gen. v. TVS Television; Att.-Gen. v. H.W. Southey & Sons Ltd, The Times*, July 7, 1989.

The defence is dependent on good faith. "Bad faith" means more than unreasonable or wrongheaded opinions. There must be an element of improper motive, such as a deliberate attempt to prejudice proceedings under cover of a public discussion. The burden of proving "bad faith", or of negating the defence generally, rests on the prosecution throughout[94]—another factor that makes the "public discussion" defence a broad shield for investigative reporting.

Section 5 does not afford protection only where the subject of general interest has already been under discussion before the proceedings commenced. It would apply in situations where the public interest has been generated by the proceedings themselves. Had the Muggeridge article not been tied to the platform of a by-election candidate, but rather had taken the form of a general discussion of the morality of euthanasia in relation to deformed babies, a topic given prominence by the trial, it should still have been protected by section 5.

> The sculptor Anthony Noel-Kelly made casts of parts of bodies which had been taken from the Royal College of Surgeons. He was on trial for complicity in their alleged theft when *The Observer* published a full-page critique of his work described as necrophilic art and displaying (but not in any sexual sense) a love of the dead as had the American mass murderer Jeffrey Dahmer. The paper was acquitted of seriously prejudicing the trial, but the court said it would have rejected the alternative argument that the paper was protected by section 5. It was prepared to accept that necrophilic art and Kelly's place in it were matters of public interest, but the reality was that the article about Kelly and his activities concerned matters of public interest because of (not independently of) the trial. Thus any prejudice was not "merely incidental" to the discussion.[95]

Some limits on section 5 are consonant with the requirements of the European Convention on Human Rights. In *Worm v. Austria*[96] the applicant had written a commentary about the ongoing prosecution of a former Vice-Chancellor of Austria for tax evasion. The court said that the existence of current court proceedings did not preclude media comment which could contribute to their publicity consistently with the fair trial guarantees in Article 6(1) as well as Article 10. Moreover, the media's right and duty to impart information and the public's right to receive it were all the greater where a public figure was involved. But public figures were entitled to a fair trial and the limits of permissible comment could not extend to statements which were likely to prejudice, whether intentionally or not, the chances of a person receiving a fair

---

[94] *Att.-Gen. v. English*, n.27 above.
[95] *Att.-Gen. v. Guardian Newspapers Ltd* [1999] E.M.L.R. 904.
[96] (1997) 25 E.H.R.R. 454

trial and especially when the tribunal includes lay persons who are more at risk of being influenced by the media.

Innocent distributors

Strict liability contempt is committed only by publishing an infringing story, but the definition of "publishing" is a wide one.[97] It applies to anyone in the chain of distribution from printer or importer to news vendor. However, distributors can usually rely on the defence that they did not know (having taken all reasonable care) that their wares contained a contempt and they had no reason to suspect that they were likely to do so.[98] To demonstrate this, distributors sometimes insist that magazines provide them with a lawyer's opinion that the publication is free of contempt. Even if the lawyer is wrong, the distributor will then have taken all reasonable care and can rely on the defence.

Innocent publishers

This defence is open to publishers and broadcasters, but it is much narrower. It helps only those who did not know and had no reason to suspect that the proceedings in question were active. Again all reasonable care must have been taken.[99] The burden lies on both distributor and publisher to show that the defence is established, although that burden may be satisfied on the balance of probabilities.[1] It is very important, therefore, that journalists should make contemporaneous notes of all their inquiries (e.g. to police or lawyers acting for the parties or at the court). These notes should be kept as evidence that the appropriate inquiries were made, and that nothing was said to alert the reporter to the fact that the case was "active".[2]

This defence does not help a paper that knew that the proceedings were active, but published by mistake a reference to the defendant's murky past.[3] Even if the paper takes ordinary precautions to eliminate prejudicial material, it is guilty of contempt. The requirement that the publisher had "no reason to suspect" that the proceedings were active narrows the defence still further. A journalist who knew that a man was helping the police with their inquiries would probably have reason to suspect that the man might be arrested before the paper was published, unless the police had said something to suggest otherwise.

---

[97] Contempt of Court Act 1981, s. 2(1).
[98] ibid., s. 3(2).
[99] ibid., s. 3(1).
[1] ibid., s. 3(3); R. v. Carr-Briant [1943] K. B. 607.
[2] e.g. Att.-Gen. v. News Group Newspapers Ltd, unreported, February 9, 1996—see The Yearbook of Media and Entertainment Law 1997/8, p. 323.
[3] R. v. Thomson Newspapers Ltd, ex p. Att.-Gen. [1968] 1 All E.R. 268.

If care has been taken to establish a sound vetting procedure, there can be no realistic danger of a prison sentence. When mistakes occur, as they inevitably do, even in well-regulated and "night-lawyered" newspaper offices, an apology to the court will normally mean a fine, and this will be visited upon the newspaper rather than the editor personally. Nonetheless, the contempt remains a criminal conviction. It would be fairer to allow publishers a simple and complete defence that the contempt was published despite all reasonable care.

Fair and accurate reports

No contempt is committed by contemporaneous publishing in good faith of a fair and accurate report of court proceedings, however prejudicial that report may be to a party involved in the case. The requirements of this defence are considered further at p. 458.

Gagging claims

A "gagging claim" is the device of attempting to suppress media criticism by issuing a writ for libel against one critic, and threatening contempt proceedings if the criticism, now the subject of litigation, is repeated. The courts have declined to allow their contempt jurisdiction to be exploited in this fashion by the likes of fascist leader Oswald Mosley and company fraudsman Dr Wallersteiner.[4] The interests of the administration of justice will prevail over freedom of speech only if the proposed publication would constitute "strict liability" contempt. As explained above, there will only be liability if the defence of public interest is not applicable and the publication would be likely to cause a substantial risk of serious prejudice.

The significance of the gagging claim is much reduced by the rule that strict liability for contempt does not begin with the issue of proceedings, but is only activated after a hearing date has been fixed. Nonetheless, the pertinent words of Lord Salmon may still need to be quoted to solicitors who try to bluff the media out of publishing criticisms of their clients with threats that the matter is "*sub judice*":

> "It is a widely held fallacy that the issue of a writ automatically stifles further comment. There is no authority that I know of to support the view that further comment would amount to contempt of court. Once a newspaper has justified, and there is some prima facie support for this justification, the plaintiff cannot obtain an interlocutory injunction to restrain the defendants from repeating

---

[4] *R. v. Fox, ex p. Mosley, The Guardian,* February 17, 1966; *Wallersteiner v. Moir* [1974] 3 All E.R. 217.

the matters complained of. In these circumstances it is obviously
wrong to suppose that they could be committing a contempt by
doing so. It seems to me equally obvious that no other newspaper
that repeats the same sort of criticism is committing a contempt of
court. They may be publishing a libel, and if they do so, and they
have no defence to it, they will have to pay whatever may be the
appropriate damages; but the writ does not, in my view, preclude
the publication of any further criticism; it merely puts the person
who makes the further criticism at risk of being sued for libel."[5]

DELIBERATE CONTEMPT

The 1981 Act is not an exhaustive treatment of the law of contempt.
It deals principally with strict liability contempt, which is committed
irrespective of the publisher's intentions, and it expressly preserves
other forms of contempt developed by the courts through their powers
at common law. The 1981 reforms have worked to restrict the ambit of
strict liability contempt, and in consequence the forces antagonistic to
media freedom (notably the British Government) have sought to exploit
the residual powers of the court to punish for "intentional" or "deliberate" contempt at common law.[6] The British Government was regrettably
successful during the *Spycatcher* saga, when the courts strove mightily
to staunch what judges perceived to be treasonable leaks from the security services by holding newspapers in contempt for breaching the spirit
of interim injunctions. The two other important areas of deliberate contempt relate to the creation of prejudice against a defendant before proceedings are "active", and the arcane crime of "scandalising the
courts". Deliberate contempt does not attract the public interest defence
in section 5 of the Act, although the requirement that the prosecution
must prove a specific intention to prejudice the administration of justice
offers some comfort to media defendants.[7] The offence carries no right
to trial by jury—a factor that undoubtedly secured convictions for the

---

[5] *Thomson v. Times Newspapers Ltd* [1969] 3 All E.R. 648 at 651.

[6] Contempt of Court Act 1981, s. 6(c).

[7] It may be that a form of public interest defence exists at common law, in so far as
the court may find that the public interest in freedom of expression outweighs, in
the instant case, the public interest in the administration of justice. This "balancing
act" has been adopted by the High Court of Australia: see *Hinch v. Att.-Gen. (Vic)*
(1987) 74 A.L.R. 353, and Sally Walker, *The Law of Journalism in Australia,* (Law
Book Co., 1989) pp. 70–5. It will be rare for a deliberate attempt to prejudice a
trial to escape a contempt finding on this test—although one example might be the
right of a defendant publicly to proclaim his innocence prior to his appearance in
court.

Government against newspapers that published Wright's memoirs, which it might not have obtained from a "gang of twelve".

Intentionally prejudicing potential criminal proceedings and civil jury trials

It is an offence at common law to publish material that is designed to prejudice criminal proceedings that are "imminent" although not yet under way. There is an important distinction between agitating for a prosecution to be brought against a particular individual, which is permissible, and deliberately poisoning the public perception of an individual whom you know is about to be prosecuted. This distinction was crucial to finding the *Sun* guilty of deliberate contempt in 1988 for viciously whipping up hostility to a doctor against whom it had already decided to bring a private prosecution:

> The editor of the *Sun* heard that the DPP had declined to prosecute a distinguished doctor over an allegation that he had raped a young child. He decided that the newspaper would pay for a private prosecution, to be brought by the child's mother, on the secret condition that the mother would provide interviews and pictures exclusively to the *Sun* and would not talk to any other media. The day after this deal was signed, the *Sun* published a vitriolic front-page character assassination of the unnamed doctor ("a beast and a swine"), declared him guilty of rape, and boasted that it was going to fund his prosecution. The next day, after a "dial-a-quote" M.P. had helpfully named the doctor under parliamentary privilege, the *Sun* continued its character-assassination, accusing the doctor of other sexual crimes and of permanently injuring his victim. Despite such blatant attempts to destroy the doctor's right to a fair trial, he was subsequently acquitted, unlike the *Sun,* which was convicted of criminal contempt and fined £75,000. The verdict itself cannot be questioned—the *Sun's* conduct would be regarded as wrong in any country that seriously endorses the principle that a defendant is entitled to a fair trial. The decision may be interpreted as turning upon the fact that the newspaper negotiated its agreement with the mother *before* it embarked upon the campaign to discredit the person whose prosecution it had undertaken to support. Had this course not been contemplated, and had the articles been designed instead to criticise the DPP (or even to put pressure on him to change his mind), this should not have been regarded as contemptuous.[8]

Thus, the *Sun* case does not prevent publishers or broadcasters trying to sting the authorities into bringing proceedings. Encouraging the initiation of a prosecution is not by itself prejudicial to the administration of justice. What made the *Sun* articles prejudicial was the newspaper's

---

[8] *Att.-Gen. v. News Group Newspapers plc* [1989] Q.B. 110.

intention to finance a private prosecution coupled with the article's assumption of guilt, the inflammatory language and the reference to allegations of similar but unrelated offences, which would (even if true) have been kept from a jury. Equally, it is not intentional contempt for defence campaigns to urge the police or the Attorney-General to abandon a prosecution. The decision to prosecute involves a consideration of the public interest, and defence committees are entitled to urge their view of what this entails. The same is true when the prosecution is brought by a private individual. The Attorney-General can always take over and stop a private prosecution, and a campaign pamphlet calling on him to do this would not be contempt. Any attempt to go further and to threaten prosecution witnesses with ostracism or calumny is much more dangerous and might well constitute contempt.

Although the House of Lords declined to hear an appeal by the *Sun,* some doubt about the correctness of the Divisional Court's decision that contempt could be committed by publications prior to arrest arises from the subsequent case of *Attorney-General v. Sport Newspapers Ltd:*

> A man with previous convictions for rape went "on the run" after a 15-year-old schoolgirl disappeared from her home. Police treated him as a suspect and notified all newspapers (through the Press Association) about his previous convictions, with a warning that nothing should be published about them lest this jeopardise his possible trial. It is no business of the police to tell newspapers what they may or may not print; it is their business to obtain arrest warrants for suspects, which in this case they failed to do until 10 days had elapsed and the *Sunday Sport* had treated its readers to a lurid account of the man's "sex monster" past, thanks no doubt to the police tip-off. The man was later caught and convicted of murder. The *Sport* could not be prosecuted for strict liability contempt, as the proceedings were not active at the time it published. The Divisional Court held that its editor had not been proved to have the necessary specific intention to prejudice a trial for the purposes of common law contempt, but the two judges were divided on the legal question of whether it was possible, at common law, to commit contempt in relation to proceedings that had not yet begun. Lord Justice Bingham, with some reluctance, held that the *Sun* case should be treated as correctly decided; Mr Justice Hodgson said that it was plainly wrong.

In the *Sport* case[9] Mr Justice Hodgson relied on previous authorities, both in Britain and Australia, to show that contempt could not be committed at common law in relation to proceedings that were not yet in existence, even if they were "imminent".[10] He justified this position

---

[9] *Re Sport* [1991] 1 W.L.R. 1194.
[10] See *Re Crown Bank, Re O'Mally* (1890) 44 Ch.D. 649; *Stirling v. Associated Newspapers Ltd* (1960) S.L.T. 5; *James v. Robinson* (1963) 109 C.L.R. 593.

with a number of powerful policy arguments anchored on the right of journalists to freedom of expression and the right of all individuals to fair trial only when alleged to have committed a crime. It was in the public interest that the media should be free to expose wrongdoers and demand that they should face trial. To render them liable for contempt at this stage would deter them from providing a useful public service. Moreover, it would extend a criminal offence for which defendants were deprived of their right to jury trial, a position that could be justified only by the need to give parties to active proceedings a swift and effective protection by High Court judges. Moreover, there was no safeguard against a private prosecution for intentional contempt brought by rich and powerful wrongdoers "exposed" in order to jolt the authorities into action: section 7 of the Contempt Act, which required the Attorney-General's consent to contempt proceedings, is limited to contempt under the strict liability rule. Despite the sex-crazed newspaper whose opportunistic conduct was the springboard for the judgment, and the obnoxious behaviour of the *Sun* in the case that preceded it, Mr Justice Hodgson's reasoning, both as to law and as to public policy, is to be preferred.

A further difference between strict liability contempt and the intentional variety is that distributors and importers are more vulnerable because they cannot in the latter case rely on the defence of innocent distribution (see p. 374). Moreover, the *Sun* case indicates that the prosecution must prove only a real risk of prejudice and need not satisfy the more exacting standard of showing that the article created a substantial risk of serious prejudice.

On the other hand, if the risk of prejudice is remote, there will be no contempt. Sir James Goldsmith failed in his contempt case against *Private Eye* for articles it published while his libel action was pending against the magazine. The articles were intended to persuade Goldsmith to drop his case and suggested he might have "nobbled" witnesses, but all this was unlikely to have any effect on the libel action's outcome.[11]

The court took more seriously a trade union paper's castigation of a member for taking his grievance to law, and its hint of the retribution he might face from his comrades.[12] Menacing a litigant with spiritual excommunication can also be contempt.[13] It is irrelevant that the black sheep would be expelled with full procedural regularity; the courts will punish threats, even threats of lawful acts, if they are intended as a deterrent, and have a real chance of success.[14]

---

[11] *R. v. Ingrams, ex p. Goldsmith* [1977] Crim. J.R. 240; see also *R. v. Duffy ex p. Nash* [1960] 2 Q.B. 188, 200.

[12] *Hutchinson v. ABU, The Times,* August 25, 1932.

[13] *Hillfinch Properties Ltd v. Newark Investment Ltd, The Times,* July 1, 1981.

[14] *ibid.*

A more difficult question is whether a modern-day thalidomide-style campaign would constitute contempt. The majority of the House of Lords found *The Sunday Times* guilty because the paper had prejudged the litigation between Distillers and the children. This constituted contempt irrespective of the paper's intention. That part of the decision was overturned by the 1981 Act. Two Law Lords, however, thought that, in addition, the newspaper was guilty of deliberate contempt because it was intentionally trying to pressurise Distillers into paying compensation. Theirs was a minority view. Lord Cross expressed a more liberal opinion:

> "To seek to dissuade a litigant from prosecuting or defending proceedings by threats of unlawful action, by abuse or by misrepresentation of the nature of the proceedings or the circumstances out of which they arose and such like is no doubt a contempt of court, but if the writer states the facts fairly and accurately and expresses his view in temperate language the fact that publication may bring pressure—possibly great pressure—to bear on the litigant should not make it a contempt of court."[15]

A majority of the judges would have allowed a *Venetian Times* to make a fair and temperate appeal to Shylock to abandon his legal right to a pound of Antonio's flesh, but they would doubtless have drawn the line at vituperative Jew-baiting from a *Rialto Gutter Press*. Of course, the wilder the language, the less likely it is to have any real impact, and for that reason even an intemperate appeal might not be guilty of contempt. Publishers may also take some comfort from the infrequency with which private litigants go to the expense of initiating contempt proceedings of this kind. In the course of the lengthy litigation over the alleged side-effects of the drug Opren the judge sounded a contempt warning over media campaigns to persuade the manufacturers, Eli Lilley, to pay generous compensation, but the issue was never tested by actual contempt proceedings.[16]

The intemperate nature of a *Private Eye* attack on Sonia Sutcliffe very nearly earned its editor, Ian Hislop, a prison sentence for intentional contempt in 1990:

> Three months before Sutcliffe's action against *Private Eye* (for alleging

---

[15] *Att.-Gen. v. Times Newspapers Ltd* [1974] A.C. 273 at 326 *per* Lord Cross. Lords Reid and Morris appear to agree, contrary to the less liberal view of Lords Diplock and Simon. In Australia this authority has been used to exculpate public statements calculated to bring pressure on a party to litigation, unless the expression is intemperate or full of factual errors. See *Commercial Bank of Australia v. Preston* [1981] 2 N.S.W. L.R. 554, *per* Hunt J.

[16] *Davies v. Eli Lilley and Co., The Independent,* July 23, 1987.

she had accepted money from a newspaper for telling of her marriage to the "Yorkshire Ripper") was fixed to be tried by a jury, Hislop threatened in print that if the action went ahead, she would be cross-examined about defrauding the DHSS and providing her husband with alibis for his murders which she knew to be false. Although Hislop believed these allegations at the time he published them, his intention in so doing was to deter her from proceeding with her case. His conviction turned on the fact that the articles went far beyond "fair and temperate criticism", and amounted to "plain abuse", over matters that had nothing to do with the issues in the libel action. The purpose of the articles was to place improper pressure on Sutcliffe to abandon her right as a litigant, and hence amounted to an interference with the administration of justice and an intentional contempt at common law. The court accepted that Hislop had no intention to prejudice the jury, so he was not guilty of common law contempt on this score, although the fact that the publication had objectively created a serious risk of prejudicing them meant that it was additionally a contempt under the strict liability rule. Hislop and his journal were fined £10,000 each.[17]

Of course, an essential ingredient of this type of contempt is "intent" to prejudice the proceedings. This is a difficult and confusing legal concept. It is not enough that the publisher simply intends to publish the newspaper or magazine. The law is concerned with the effect the contents are intended to have. "Intent" is not the same as "desire" or "motive". Nor, in this context, is it to be equated with recklessness.[18] But it may only be inferred if the publisher foresees prejudice as virtually certain and carries on regardless. The court can usually only infer such an intent from all the circumstances since there will rarely be direct evidence of a prejudicial intent.

The Independent, The Sunday Times and the London Daily News were found guilty of intentional contempt by publishing material from Peter Wright that other newspapers had been ordered to keep confidential. The judge rejected the argument that a person who knew of such an injunction and published anyway would necessarily be guilty of intentional contempt. These were matters from which intention could be inferred, but the court had to look at all the circumstances, including what legal advice was given, its basis and how it was understood. The editors did not desire to interfere in the administration of justice, but this did not negate their intent. Each paper was fined £50,000. The individual editors were not imprisoned since it was accepted that they believed on legal advice (albeit erroneously) that they were not committing contempt. The judge saw no point in fining the editors since they all had indemnities from their papers. The publishers' fines were quashed on appeal, on the grounds that it would

---

[17] Att.-Gen. v. Hislop [1991] 1 Q.B. 514.
[18] Att.-Gen. v. Newspaper Publishing plc [1988] Ch.33; Att.-Gen. v. News Group Newspapers Ltd [1989] Q.B. 110.

be wrong to punish editors in circumstances where the law was unsettled and their erroneous legal advice had coincided with the view taken by the judge who had decided a preliminary issue in their favour.[19]

The fullest discussion of the "intention" that has to be proved against a newspaper in order to obtain a conviction for deliberate contempt is found in the verdict against the *Sun* for prejudicing a prosecution that it had decided to fund. The court held that it was necessary for the Attorney-General to prove a specific intention to prejudice a fair trial; it was insufficient to show that the publication had been reckless or that the newspaper had some generalised intention to interfere with the course of justice. Newspaper editors, of course, will always deny criminal intentions, and the courts will not take them at their word; the issue will be decided by examining what they published and the circumstances surrounding publication, and asking whether they must have foreseen, for all practical purposes, that a real risk to the fairness of a trial would result. The editor of the *Sun* was held to have had the requisite intention, despite his disavowals, as he was plainly campaigning for the doctor's conviction in circumstances where that conviction would have proved financially beneficial to the newspaper: it would not only have recovered its legal costs, but it would have boosted its circulation on the back of the "world exclusive" for which it had bought up the alleged victim's mother.

Honest mistake is a complete defence to common law contempt. The banking correspondent of the *Daily Telegraph* was writing a story about Homes Assured Corporation PLC, some of whose directors were facing proceedings for disqualification. She visited the registry of the companies court and was told (correctly) that to inspect the file she would have to obtain the leave of the court. She was given the file to take to the registrar. While waiting forty minutes for her appointment, she openly made notes from the report of the official receiver, which was in the court file, and told the registrar she had done so. The registrar telephoned the city editor to complain, but the latter thought the problem was ethical rather than legal, and published two stories based on the report. The Chancery Division dismissed an application by the directors to commit the editor (Max Hastings) and his journalist for contempt. The essential vice of the offence lies in *knowingly* interfering with the administration of justice. The journalist had apparently never before inspected a court document and the court

---

[19] *Att.-Gen. v. Newspaper Publishing plc, The Independent*, May 9, 1989, Morritt J.; *The Independent*, February 28, 1990, CA. The decision was upheld on a different aspect, see *Att.-Gen. v. Times Newspapers Ltd* [1992] 1 A.C. 191, below p. 383. The Court of Appeal stressed that intention could be inferred from the circumstances only if the consequences were "virtually certain", "inevitable" or "overwhelmingly probable".

accepted that she did not know she was acting in breach of the rules. There had been no trickery or dishonesty.[20]

Campaigns over criminal proceedings raise different considerations. No decision to prosecute Dr Savundra had been made at the time of David Frost's televised interview in 1967 over his handling of the Fire and Auto Marine Insurance Company. At the time, the programme was criticised because Savundra's arrest was imminent.[21] Now "imminence" of an arrest is not enough; the proceedings would not be active and so there would be no risk of infringing the strict liability rule (see p. 368). However, part of the programme's apparent intention (like that of consumer programmes such as *Checkpoint*) was to sting the authorities into action. Even so, this is not intentional contempt, because encouraging the initiation of a prosecution is not prejudicial to the administration of justice.

Frustrating court orders against others

Court orders primarily affect another party to the lawsuit in which they are made. Ordinarily, basic fairness requires that before a person is ordered to do something by a court, he or she should have a chance to argue that the order should not be made. In addition, it is contempt for one person to aid or abet another to break a court order. However, during the *Spycatcher* saga the courts created a new inroad on the principle that court orders do not affect third parties:

> The Attorney-General obtained injunctions preventing *The Guardian* and *The Observer* from printing material derived from Peter Wright's memoirs. Subsequently *The Independent,* the *London Daily News,* the *London Evening Standard* and, later, *The Sunday Times* published various parts of Wright's allegations. These four newspapers had not obtained their information from the first two, and they certainly did not publish their stories as their agents. They were not parties to the proceedings in which the injunction was obtained. The House of Lords accepted that the newspapers could not break an injunction that was not addressed to them. However, it held that their publications could amount to deliberate contempt of court. It was contempt to destroy or seriously damage the subject-matter of an action if this impeded or prejudiced the administration of justice: the subject-matter of the first action was the allegedly confidential nature of the material in *Spycatcher,* which would be destroyed if someone else published it. The consequence of the publication was to nullify

---

[20] *Dobson v. Hastings* [1992] Ch. 394.
[21] *R. v. Savundranayagan and Walker* [1968] 1 W.L.R. 1761; see Frost's letter in reply to *The Times,* July 18, 1968. The Board of Trade had been investigating the companies but nothing had happened for months and there was no indication that it would.

the purpose of the trial by placing in the public domain information the Attorney-General contended was confidential and this amounted to interference with the course of justice in the confidentiality action.[22]

When the case was heard in full, the judge decided that the newspapers had been in contempt (see p. 381). It was immaterial that the Attorney-General's action had not in fact been prejudiced. It did not matter that the House of Lords subsequently found that the injunction was unjustified following the widespread circulation of the Wright material. In the contempt proceedings some of the newspapers argued that there could be no contempt because by the time they published, the American edition of *Spycatcher* had appeared and other papers had printed extracts. However, the judge said that each publication played its part in destroying the confidentiality; each newspaper committed contempt; and he drew no distinction in the penalties he imposed between the early and the late publishers.

This case shows just how far the law of contempt can be stretched, by judges overly supportive of Government and without a free speech guarantee to apply, when combined with the supple common law doctrine of breach of confidence. The subject-matter of the initial confidence action against *The Observer* was a report of Wright's allegations. This subject-matter was likened to an ice-cube: it would "evaporate" if exposed to the light of day by *The Independent* and *The Sunday Times*. There would be no point in the Attorney-General continuing his action against *The Observer* if Wright's revelations were published elsewhere. Since the contempt jurisdiction is a power deployed by the courts to prevent interference with the due administration of justice, the courts were entitled to punish the editors of *The Independent* and *The Sunday Times* by way of a criminal action for contempt of court on the ground that by publishing Wright's allegations they had destroyed the confidential nature of information that another court had injuncted *The Observer* from publishing pending the trial of the Government's claim to exclusive possession of this information. It was, said Lord Donaldson in the Court of Appeal, as if the Government and *The Observer* had commenced a legal action over the ownership of a racehorse, and the court had ordered the horse to be kept alive until the dispute over its possession could be resolved after a full trial. The editor of *The Independent* had shot the horse prior to that full trial, and thereby rendered the proceedings pointless. The Attorney-General, in his role as guardian of the administration of justice, was entitled to seek to commit *The Independent's* editor to prison for intentionally aborting legal proceedings in which, quite coincidentally, the Attorney-General happened to be a party.

---

[22] *Att.-Gen. v. Times Newspapers Ltd* [1992] 1 A.C. 191.

There can be no objection to the principle that courts should have power to protect judicial proceedings from third parties who deliberately set out to prejudice or subvert them, and the cases relied on by the House of Lords, which related to third parties who cut down trees or disposed of assets that were the subject of a court order, cannot be faulted. But they concerned property, not information. Where the argument in this case becomes metaphysical is in assimilating Wright's allegations (that MI5 plotted to assassinate Nasser, bug foreign embassies and destabilise the Wilson Government) to items of physical property like ice-cubes and racehorses. Information of this kind is not "subject-matter" that can be possessed exclusively by a department of State, any more than a conspiracy to murder is the exclusive property of the conspirators. The subject-matter of an action for breach of confidence is not the information itself, but the confidential relationship in the course of which it was acquired. In fact, *The Independent*'s publication did not abort the proceedings in the case against *The Observer,* which continued to trial and appeal, irrespective of the fact that over a million copies of *Spycatcher* had been published throughout the world and many copies had been imported into Britain. The ice-cube had by this stage been transformed into a flood of dirty water, but what was at stake in the litigation was the question of whether *The Observer* had become party to Wright's breach of his duty owed to the Crown by publishing his allegations. *The Independent* did not frustrate the administration of justice in that case by further publishing Wright's allegations, although by so doing it may well have become a party to his breach of confidence. *The Independent* should have been sued for breach of confidence, not prosecuted for the crime of contempt.

Nonetheless, the case stands for the proposition that it can be a crime for one newspaper to breach the spirit of an injunction imposed upon another, despite the fact that it has had no opportunity to present a case against the imposition of any restraint. It must go cap-in-hand to the court and ask for permission to publish. This was the course taken by Derbyshire Country Council which requested permission for its local library to stock a copy of *Spycatcher*.[23] Although numerous copies of the book had by this time been imported into the country, and were being sold by enthusiastic entrepreneurs at inflated prices, the High Court held that the book's availability in a public library would "constitute an interference with the due administration of justice" in the ongoing cases against *The Guardian* and *The Observer*. This decision shows just how far the contempt confidentiality doctrine was moving in the direction of prior restraint under pressure from the Thatcher Govern-

---

[23] *Att.-Gen. v. Observer Ltd; Re An Application by Derbyshire County Council* [1988] 1 All E.R. 385. The argument advanced in the text is developed in Geoffrey Robertson, *Freedom, the Individual and the Law* (Penguin, 1993).

ment during the *Spycatcher* saga. Many of the cases in this period do not show English judges at their independent best and can now be more politely distinguished as belonging to the era before the Human Rights Act.

The crime of intentional contempt is committed only by those who specifically intend to impede or prejudice the administration of justice, and even recklessness as to whether such prejudice may be caused is insufficient to ground a conviction.

> During the Ordtech (arms to Iraq) appeal the Crown had claimed public interest immunity from disclosure of certain documents. At a directions hearing the Court of Appeal ordered most of these to be produced to the defendants but restricted their use to the appeal and required their return at its conclusion. The Lord Chief Justice quoted extracts from some of the documents in his judgment after which he mentioned that the documents were to be returned to the Crown. *The Independent* had been passed a set of the documents by a confidential source (unconnected with the parties or their legal advisers). It tried unsuccessfully to find out precisely what the judge had ordered. Its report of the judgment included a picture of two of the documents mentioned in the judgment but revealing slightly more than the quotations given by the court. On an application to commit *The Independent*, its editor and the journalist for contempt the court accepted that the order was directed only at the parties and not at the press. A third party could be liable for intentional contempt but only if some significant and adverse effect on the administration of justice could be proved. The additional parts of the documents which *The Independent* had shown were trivial. The reproduction of these two documents themselves in the article did not constitute a significant interference with the administration of justice. The court was also influenced by the unavailing efforts made by the paper to find out the exact terms of the court's order which showed it did not have the requisite intention for common law contempt.[24]

Shortly after the Human Rights Act came into operation the publishers and editor of *Punch* were found guilty of this type of contempt in the High Court.[25] The magazine had published a column written by the ex-MI5 employee, David Shayler, which was contrary to the terms of an injunction which the Government had obtained against *The Mail on Sunday*. However, the Court of Appeal quashed this finding. It held that the defendants had been genuinely mistaken as to the ultimate purpose of the order which they thought was to restrain publication of material damaging to national security. This was understandable because of a proviso which allowed publication where the Attorney-General consented. The actual purpose was to prevent more Shayler

---

[24] *Att.-Gen. v. Newspaper Publishing plc* [1997] 1 W.L.R. 926, CA, Crim. Div.
[25] *Att.-Gen. v. Punch Ltd* (unreported) October 6, 2000, Silber J.

revelations, however innocuous, from entering the public domain for the first time. The defendants did not intend to frustrate this purpose and so were not guilty of contempt. But the Master of the Rolls did warn the media of another danger: independently of the *Spycatcher* type of contempt, those who aid and abet a person to breach an injunction which directly binds him it will themselves be guilty of contempt.[26]

The *Punch* case is a worthy attempt to circumvent some of the problems the courts created in their efforts to put the *Spycatcher* genie back in the bottle. It clarifies that a third party will not automatically breach a suppression order he knows about if he publishes material it might cover: he must knowingly defeat the purpose for which the order was made. The crucial offence is that of deliberately committing the potential wrong the interim injunction is designed to prevent, not (as Lord Donaldson argued in *Spycatcher*) that it would render the litigation pointless.

The Attorney-General failed in the *Punch* case because, despite cross-examination, he could not prove that the editor knew that publication would defeat the purpose underlying the injunction. The Attorney-General's claim that the proviso in the order required the editor to submit to him for vetting any material at all from Shayler (who had written about the pleasures of France, the country which had refused to extradite him), was rejected for the very good reason that "it submits the press to the ownership of the Attorney-General". The Court refused to countenance, on Article 10 grounds, a criminal offence which turned on the failure to submit what might be harmless material to the Attorney for censorship: this would have been a disproportionate restriction on freedom of expression and irreconcilable with section 12(3) of the Human Rights Act.

SCANDALISING THE COURT

"Scandalising the court" was a type of contempt invented in the eighteenth century to punish radical critics of the establishment, such as John Wilkes.[27] It has been defined as: "any act done or writing published

---

[26] *Att-Gen v. Punch Ltd* [2001] 2 W.L.R. 1713, CA.

[27] *R. v. Almon* (1765) Wilm. 243; 97 E.R. 94. This authority is distinctly shaky. It was an undelivered judgment of Justice Wilmott, published posthumously by his son, and uncritically accepted by Blackstone. It cites no authority for the proposition that judges have power to punish their press critics, and the better view is that it was wrongly decided; see Sir John Fox, *The History of Contempt of Court* (Oxford, 1927; reprinted Professional Books, 1972). In the context of eighteenth-century politics it was an attempt to protect Lord Mansfield from reasoned criticism of his oppressive judicial behaviour towards Wilkes and other critics of the Government;

calculated to bring a court or judge into contempt or to lower his authority".[28] Editorial barbs were thus equated with cat calls in court, both
being treated as affronts to judicial dignity. In Scotland the crime is
called "murmuring judges".

Despite its apparent breadth, scandalising the court should not prevent criticism of the judiciary even when expressed in strong terms.
"Justice is not a cloistered virtue" a senior Law Lord once said,[29] and
comment about the legal system in general or the handling of particular
cases once they are over sometimes deserves to be trenchant.

The Victorian press was outspoken in its condemnation of the bench.
Charles Dickens led a campaign of press criticism against one magistrate ("Mr Fang" in *Oliver Twist*) that resulted in his removal.[30] This
was not an isolated example. Press attacks on the judiciary were so
frequent that the Lord Chancellor retaliated by refusing to make editors
justices of the peace.[31] None of these papers was punished for scandalising the court, and by 1899 the Privy Council considered that the offence
was virtually a dead-letter in England.[32] However, it was revived the
following year when the *Birmingham Daily Argus* described Mr Justice
Darling, accurately enough, as an "impudent little man in horse-hair"
who was "a microcosm of conceit and empty-headedness". It was fined
for contempt. In the late 1920s the *New Statesman* was convicted of
scandalising the court for doubting whether birth control reformer Marie
Stopes would receive a fair trial from a Roman Catholic judge, and the
Daily Worker was fined for labelling a Tory judge "a bewigged puppet
exhibiting a strong class bias".[33] In retrospect, both comments had an
element of truth, and it is inconceivable that similar remarks would be
prosecuted today. Judges who have exhibited anti-women attitudes in
rape cases have been condemned by the press, while attacks on the
judges of the National Industrial Relations Court were made without
punishment. In 1992 *Legal Business* published the results of a survey
of the legal profession on High Court judges who were ranked in order
of the respect they commanded. Harman J., who came bottom of the

---

see D. Hay, "Contempt by Scandalising the Court: A Political History of the First
Five Hundred Years" (1987) 25 *Osgoode Hall Law Journal* 431.

[28] *Badry v. DPP of Mauritius* [1983] 2 A.C. 297 quoting *R. v. Gray* [1900] 2 Q.B. 36
at 40. The offence does not apply in respect of a defamatory attack on a judge in
his personal rather than his official capacity: *Re the Special Reference from the
Bahama Islands* [1893] A.C. 138.

[29] *Ambard v. Att.-Gen. for Trinidad and Tobago* [1936] A.C. 322 at 335 *per* Lord
Atkin.

[30] His real name was Allan Laing. See Marjorie Jones, *Justice and Journalism* (Barry
Rose, 1974) p. 27.

[31] (1883) *Justice of the Peace* 750; *cf.* Jones, n. 30 above, p. 43.

[32] *McLeod v. St Aubyn* [1899] A.C. 549.

[33] *R v. Gray,* n. 28 above; *R. v. Wilkinson, The Times,* July 16, 1930; *R. v. New
Statesman, ex p. DPP* (1928) 44 T.L.R. 301.

poll, attracted trenchant criticism that was repeated in the article. The judge continued on the bench but resigned in 1998 after he was castigated by the Court of Appeal for taking 20 months to deliver a judgment.[34] The modern attitude is exemplified in this 1968 case:

> Raymond Blackburn, the indomitable pursuer of pornography and gambling, tried to commit Quintin Hogg M.P. (later Lord Chancellor Hailsham) for contempt after he had written an article in *Punch* that was severely but inaccurately critical of the Court of Appeal. The Court of Appeal itself dismissed the application. Lord Denning said:
>
> > "It is the right of every man, in Parliament or out of it, in the Press or over the broadcast, to make fair comment, even outspoken comment on matters of public interest. Those who comment can deal faithfully with all that is done in a Court of Justice. They can say we are mistaken, and our decisions erroneous, whether they are subject to appeal or not."

Lord Salmon added: "No criticism of a judgment, however vigorous, can amount to contempt of court if it keeps within the limits of reasonable courtesy and of good faith".[35]

Scandalising the court is an anachronistic form of contempt. Lord Diplock has described it as "virtually obsolescent in the United Kingdom"[36] and it has not been used for 60 years.[37]

It is now inconceivable that action could be brought against publications that criticise the courts in moderate language, however much the criticism is misplaced. In 1987 the *Daily Mirror* published upside down photographs of the Law Lords who had injuncted *Spycatcher* under the banner headline "YOU FOOLS!" No prosecution was forthcoming. In 2000 a litigant disappointed in the result of his divorce case was charged

---

[34] *Legal Business*, May 1992; *Goose v. Wilson Sandford & Co., The Times*, February 19, 1998, CA.

[35] *R. v. Metropolitan Police Commissioner, ex p. Blackburn (No. 2)* [1968] 2 Q.B. 150.

[36] *Secretary of State for Defence v. Guardian Newspapers Ltd* [1985] A.C. 339, 347.

[37] It has, though, been dusted down and used in the Commonwealth (see Clive Walker's "Scandalising the Eighties" [1985] 101 L.Q.R. 359. A Canadian provincial minister was fined for describing a judge's verdict as "insane" and a "disgrace" (*R. v. Ouillet* (1977) 36 Crim. Reps. (Nova Scotia) 296). An Indian state premier was likewise punished for damning the judges as bourgeois and class-biased (*Nambooripad v. Mambiar* [1970] All India Reps 1318), and when a Trinidadian paper (*The Bomb*) published a thinly disguised "fictional" account of dishonesty and drunkenness in the local judiciary, its editor, Paddy Chokolingo, was imprisoned (*Chokolingo v. Att.-Gen. for Trinidad and Tobago* [1981] 1 All E.R. 244, PC). By contrast, an American judge who fined an attorney for a critical newspaper article was himself impeached and very nearly convicted by the U.S. Senate for encroaching on the writer's constitutional freedom of speech (Sir John Fox, *Contempt of Court*, p. 202 *et seq.*).

with "scandalising the court" by making hysterical claims in pamphlets about corrupt judges. *The Guardian* criticised the use of the charge as oppressive and the Attorney-General dropped it, a decision endorsed by Simon Brown L.J. on the ground that such insults are much better ignored.

The danger, of leaving such a crime on the books is well illustrated by recent contempt prosecutions in other countries that have inherited the common law, where robust condemnation of court decisions (Trinidad), suggestions that a decision was influenced by trade-union demonstrations (Australia) and minor inaccuracies in justifiable criticism of the conduct of proceedings against an opposition M.P. (Singapore) have all been treated as contempt. In certain Commonwealth countries there does exist an unhealthy relationship between the judges and the Government that appoints them and scandalising the court is a crime that has been invoked as an instrument of oppression, to silence honest criticism of biased judges.

In *Badry v. DPP of Mauritius*[38] the Privy Council urged ex-colonial courts to punish only "the most intolerable instances" of scandalisation, and held that the crime was not committed by asserting that a judge had made false statements and had not taken into account relevant evidence. Regrettably, however, it upheld the conviction of a political leader for a rabble-rousing speech accusing the Supreme Court of bias in favour of wealthy companies, because this was "clearly meant to shake public confidence in the administration of justice in Mauritius". Regrettably the Privy Council, which by 1999 was generally protective of free speech, delivered a judgment which suggested that "scandalising the court", whilst obsolete in Britain, might nonetheless be necessary in "small islands" like Mauritius. It did, however, emphasise the limitations of the offence. The court said:

> "it must be borne in mind that the offence is narrowly defined. It does not extend to comment on the conduct of a judge unrelated to his performance on the bench. It exists solely to protect the administration of justice rather than the feelings of judges. There must be a real risk of undermining public confidence in the administration of justice. The field of application of the offence is also narrowed by the need in a democratic society for public scrutiny of the conduct of judges, and for the right of citizens to comment on matters of public concern. There is available to a defendant a defence based on the right of "criticising, in good faith in private or public, the public act done in the seat of justice . . . ." The classic imputation of such an offence is the imputation of improper motives to a judge. But so far as *Ambard*'s case may suggest that

[38] [1983] 2 A.C. 297.

such conduct invariably be an offence their Lordships consider that such an absolute statement is not nowadays acceptable. For example, if a judge descends into the arena and embarks on extensive and plainly biased questioning of a defendant in a criminal trial, a criticism of bias may not be an offence."[39]

The Privy Council was endeavouring to re-phrase an unacceptably racist comment made by the court a century before, when it said that the crime might be necessary to support judicial authority in countries with "coloured populations"[40] but the new formula is unacceptably patronising and, in human rights terms, quite simply wrong. It is precisely in "small islands" like Singapore that the crime is used to suppress legitimate criticism of judges who decide in favour of the Government, and it is used to the same effect in other States (*e.g.* Malaysia). It is to be hoped that the Privy Council will in due course reconsider the dicta in *Ahnee* and rule that a criminal offence of criticising judges is incompatible with freedom of expression, whether in small islands like Mauritius or in small islands like Britain.

The history of contempt by scandalising the court, both in Britain and especially in the Commonwealth, argues strongly for its abolition. Its impact might be mitigated if it were held to contain a requirement of *mens rea*—an undecided issue, although the draft judgment in *Almon* is authority for intention as an ingredient of the offence.[41] The crime has no counterpart in American law, where similar offences have been declared unconstitutional,[42] and it is difficult to reconcile with Article 10 of the European Convention. The fullest forensic analysis of the concept is to be found in the Canadian case of *R. v. Kopyto*: the majority of the court held that the British law of contempt by "scandalisation" was incompatible with the "freedom of expression" guarantee in the Canadian Charter of Rights and Freedoms.[43]

It may be that the British press has itself to blame for Parliament's refusal to abolish this archaic head of contempt in the United Kingdom. During the 1981 reforms an amendment to this effect was rejected, after Lord Hailsham recalled a recent incident that had arisen after the Court of Appeal denied a divorce to a woman who claimed that her husband was unreasonable in having sex only once a week. A journalist from the Fleet Street gutter telephoned the wives of the three appellate judges to ask how often a week they regarded as reasonable. The offence of

---

[39] *Ahnee v. DPP of Mauritius* [1999] 2 A.C. 294, PC.
[40] *McLeod v. St. Aubyn* [1899] A.C. 549.
[41] *R. v. Almon*, n. 27 above.
[42] *Bridges v. California* 314 U.S. 252 (1941).
[43] *R. v. Kopyto* (1987) 47 D.I.R. (4th) 213.

scandalising the court, said the Lord Chancellor, was still required to deal with such conduct.

Section 8 of the Contempt of Court Act makes it an offence for a journalist "to obtain, disclose or solicit any particulars of statements made, opinions expressed, arguments advanced or votes cast by members of a jury in the course of their deliberations in any legal proceedings". This extension of the law came after the *New Statesman* was acquitted of contempt for publishing an interview with one of the jurors in the Thorpe trial, in which the juror revealed how the jury had reacted to certain witnesses and aspects of the evidence when considering its verdict. The public interest in publishing the interview was considerable: it revealed that the *Sunday Telegraph*'s deal with chief prosecution witness Peter Bessell (whereby he would receive £50,000 for his "exclusive" story if Thorpe were convicted, but only £25,000 were Thorpe acquitted) had irreparably damaged Bessell's credibility as a witness in the eyes of the jury.

It also suggested that the jury would have convicted the defendants had the DPP charged them with conspiracy to assault (rather than to murder) Norman Scott. The Attorney-General should have brought contempt proceedings against the *Sunday Telegraph* for prejudicing the Thorpe trial; instead, he brought them against the *New Statesman* for producing evidence that the *Sunday Telegraph* deal had prejudiced the case. The Divisional Court dismissed the charges, in a judgment that some lawyers feared might open the door to a new form of chequebook journalism: secrets of the Old Bailey jury rooms in notorious criminal trials.[44]

The Government's Contempt Bill was designed to stop this development, but it applied only to publications that named particular trials or jurors. If the *New Statesman* decision was to be cut back at all, these exceptions were sensible. They would have prevented vendettas by convicted defendants or their families without stifling all discussion of jury deliberations. Jury duty is a rare occasion when ordinary people take an active part in government. In can be a memorable experience. Others can benefit from their stories. In addition, like any aspect of government, it is an eminently appropriate subject for study and research. But the clause was amended so as to ban even anonymous accounts of unnamed trials. The change was made at the instigation of peers who feared that the jury system might not survive the full glare of publicity

---

[44] *Att.-Gen. v. New Statesman and Nation Publishing Co. Ltd* [1981] Q.B. 1.

if reporters were permitted to cross-examine jurors about the reasons behind their verdict. Lamentably, section 8 has worked to preclude any sensible or scientific research into the operation of the jury system: it notably frustrated the work of the Fraud Trials Committee (chaired by Lord Roskill), which could produce no hard evidence on the question of whether complex fraud cases were suitable for jury trial.[45] The first, and so far the only, reported contempt action under section 8 involving the press was taken against the *Daily Mail* for publishing an article based on interviews with several jurors in the Blue Arrow fraud case. The interviews had not been conducted by the paper or its journalist but by an independent American researcher who sold the transcripts to the reporter. The paper argued that no offence had been committed because only jurors could "disclose" what had taken place in the jury room. The House of Lords rejected the argument and ruled that "disclose" extended to a newspaper's publication (as long as the material was not already in the public domain). The paper was fined £30,000, the editor £20,000 and the journalist £10,000.[46]

The publishers' complaint to Strasbourg was declared inadmissible by the Commission[47] which said that the purposes of the prohibition on jury disclosures was to encourage frankness in exchanges in the jury room, and any possibility of intrusion on this privacy could undermine that confidence. But this is a weakly argued and fundamentally wrong Commission decision, which gives no satisfactory weight to freedom of expression and imputes to the section an intention that the Q.C. legislators who introduced it never had. They wanted to stop informed criticism of the jury system, which is precisely why the section is a breach of Article 10.

The section is ripe for amendment to permit research and voluntary post-trial disclosure, while specifically prohibiting unsought identification of jurors, and the soliciting or purchasing of their stories.[48]

Section 8 is not intended to hinder the working of the trial itself. The judge can ask the jury its verdict, and the jury can solicit help even if this hints at the way its members are thinking. The appearance of justice requires that these communications should be in open court,[49] and so they are freely reportable.

The media should not be frightened of making approaches to jurors for information after a trial is over. Section 8 prohibits the media only from intentionally soliciting information about the jury's *deliberations*

---

[45] Fraud Trials Committee Report (HMSO, 1986) para. 8.10.
[46] *Att.-Gen. v. Associated Newspapers Ltd* [1994] 2 A.C. 238.
[47] *Associated Newspapers Ltd v. U.K.* Application No. 24770/94, November 30, 1994.
[48] See the sensible recommendations of the NSW Law Reform Committee Report No. 48, *The Jury in a Criminal Trial,* 1986, Chap. 11.
[49] *R. v. Townsend* [1982] 1 All E.R. 509, CA; *R. v. Rose* [1982] A.C. 822.

in reaching their verdict. As the Attorney-General noted in the debate on the clause, it is not an offence to solicit or publish a juror's view of the desirability of the prosecution, of the quality of the advocates, of the sobriety of the judge or the attentiveness of the court usher.[50] Nor would it be contempt to interview trial jurors about their opinion on the length of the sentence. Shortly after the Act came into effect *The Sunday Times* published a story on the trial of the doctor charged with killing a Down's syndrome baby; the article included the opinion of a juror that the prosecution should never have been brought. The BBC has broadcast interviews with jurors complaining about coroners who tried to dictate their verdicts. In 1980 some of the jurors who had acquitted four anarchists on bomb conspiracy charges wrote to *The Guardian* in response to the trial judge's attack on their intelligence. Although this touched on what had taken place in the jury room, the Attorney-General has said that the offence would not prevent jurors in a comparable situation from publicly responding to judicial rebukes.[51] Section 8 does not apply at all to trials where the jury has been discharged prior to the stage at which it is asked to retire to consider its verdict. It follows that jurors may be interviewed without legal difficulty when cases are dismissed by the judge at "half-time" because of insufficient prosecution evidence. A prosecution under section 8 can only be brought by the Attorney-General.[52] Reporters need not hesitate to interview jurors, but they must remember to avoid any question designed to elicit an answer about what was said or done in the jury room.

DISOBEDIENCE TO COURT ORDERS

The risk of disobeying an order directed at the particular newspaper, broadcaster or journalist is in one sense obvious, but certain points are worth considering:

- there can only be contempt of this kind if the court has made an order rather than expressed a wish for the media not to publish material or behave in a particular way.[53]

- The court's order should be in clear terms: "If the court is to punish anyone for not carrying out its order, the order must in

---

[50] *Hansard,* H.C. Debs [1981] Vol. 9, col. 426.
[51] *ibid.,* col. 425.
[52] Contempt of Court Act 1981, section. 8(3), though proceedings can be brought on the motion of a court having jurisdiction to deal with it (*ibid.*).
[53] See *Att.-Gen. v. Leveller Magazine Ltd* [1978] 3 All E.R. 731.

unambiguous terms direct what is to be done".[54] Nonetheless, an order (or the construction which the court gives it) can be broken unintentionally.

The columnist Nigel Dempster was fined £10,000 and the publishers of the Daily Mail were fined £25,000 for a non-deliberate breach of an injunction not to repeat an allegation that Baron Bentinck (the claimant in a libel trial against the defendants) was mean. The judge said that if he had thought the breach was deliberate he would have jailed Dempster.[55]

● Ordinarily there must be proof that the defendant was given notice of the order. If it is prohibitory (*e.g.* an order not to publish something) the person concerned will have notice if he or she was present in court. Alternatively, notice can be given by fax or telephone or by other means such as receipt of a press agency copy.[56] If the order is mandatory (*e.g.* requiring disclosure of documents) a copy of the order must usually be served personally and it must include a notice expressly drawing attention to the consequences of disobedience.[57]

● Parliament has made breach of certain types of court orders (such as anonymity orders under the Children and Young Persons Act) summary offences which carry no risk of imprisonment and where the maximum fine is often less than for contempt. Prosecutors ought to consider using such offences rather than the blunderbuss of contempt although the courts have yet to rule on whether contempt proceedings could ever be appropriate where there exists the alternative of a statutory summary offence.[58]

● In contempt proceedings for breach of an order, it is not possible to argue that the court was wrong to make the order in the first place.

Channel 4 broadcast a programme by Box Productions called the "Committee". It alleged that there was a conspiracy of security service personnel and loyalist paramilitaries to murder republicans. The police were granted an order under the anti-terrorist legislation for the broadcasters

---

[54] *Iberian Trust Ltd v. Founders Trust and Investment Co. Ltd* [1932] 2 K.B. 87 at 95.
[55] *Media Lawyer,* Nov.–Dec., 1997, p. 5.
[56] Civil Procedure Rules, Sched. 1: RSC, O.45, r.7(6) and *Cleveland County Council v. W, The Independent,* May 5, 1988.
[57] *ibid.,* O. 45, r.7(2) and (4).
[58] See *R. v. Tyne Tees Television Ltd, The Times,* October 20, 1997, where a fine for contempt of £10,000, double the maximum for the statutory offence, was quashed on appeal.

to disclose their source (see p. 590). When they refused, the DPP took proceedings for contempt. The Divisional Court refused to reconsider the merit of the disclosure order and fined the broadcasters £75,000. This principle may now call for reconsideration. Orders imposed in breach of Convention rights from the outset would be unlawful by virtue of section 6(1) of the Human Rights Act and courts (which are "public authorities") are obliged to act compatibly with Convention rights.[59]

PROCEDURE AND PUNISHMENT

Contempt proceedings can be initiated by the judge or court that is affected. This is now rarely done except where there has been a disturbance in court or where the court's own order has been disobeyed. The more usual, and the proper, course is for the court to refer the matter to the Attorney-General.

If a judge does threaten reporters with immediate committal for contempt, they should obtain legal advice. When the lawyers come back before the judge, they should apply to have the matter referred to the Attorney-General: this is now accepted as the proper course, even for alleged misbehaviour by a journalist in the face of the court. Thus when *Observer* journalist Jack Lundin refused under oath to answer questions that would have revealed a source, the trial judge (Mr Justice Webster) agreed to refer the matter to the Attorney-General, so that it could be considered and dealt with in the calmer arena of the Divisional Court.[60] It is invidious for the judge immediately and personally concerned to double up as contempt prosecutor. It is also contrary to the principle, enshrined in Article 6 of the European Convention, that a judge must not act in his own cause.[61] After the Human Rights Act came into effect, the Court of Appeal rejected an argument that it was contrary to Article 6 for a judge to institute contempt proceedings of his own motion (although it was "regrettable" that the judge had then taken the alleged victim through her examination in chief).[62] This was not, however, a case of media contempt which rarely, if ever, will justify immediate action by the judge hearing the case which is alleged to have been prejudiced.

If the affected court accepts these arguments and does not mete out instant punishment of its own, contempt proceedings will be started by application to the Divisional Court of the Queen's Bench Division of

---

[59] *DPP v. Channel 4* [1993] 2 All E.R. 517, DC.

[60] *Att.-Gen. v. Lundin* (1982) 75 Cr. App. R. 90.

[61] Art. 6(1) of the European Convention on Human Rights, which requires that any punishment for a criminal offence be imposed by an impartial tribunal.

[62] *R. v. MacLeod, The Times*, December 20, 2000, CA.

the High Court.[63] This must also be the procedure if a publication is said to be in contempt of magistrates. They can punish only for contempts committed in or near their own courtroom and not those committed by the press or by broadcasters.[64] These have to be referred to the Divisional Court.

The Attorney-General's consent is essential where the contempt was unintentional but was in breach of the strict liability rule.[65] In all cases (even those brought by the Attorney), the court has to give its permission for contempt proceedings to begin.[66] This is considered on an application without notice and on hearing only the applicant's side. Sometimes the publisher is informed in advance, but this is not obligatory. The proper time for the Attorney-General to make his application is after the conclusion of the jury stage of the proceedings alleged to have been prejudiced. This will obviate any danger that publicity given to the contempt action will repeat the alleged prejudice, and will enable the Attorney-General to consider, with the benefit of hindsight, whether the risk of prejudice at the time of publication was real. Strictly speaking both the Attorney-General and the court ought to disregard subsequent events and in the case of the cleaning lady and the fridge (see above p. 363) the Attorney-General took contempt proceedings even though the defendant did in fact plead guilty and there was no jury to prejudice. But one of the reasons given for not prosecuting the coverage of the arrest of the "Yorkshire Ripper", Peter Sutcliffe, was his plea of guilty to manslaughter.[67] The real difference, perhaps, was that the police irresponsibly caused prejudicial publicity by their self-congratulatory press conference after Sutcliffe's arrest, whereas the Manchester police had acted reasonably and warned the *Manchester Evening News* against publishing its story.

All editors threatened by the Attorney-General with contempt proceedings, and their lawyers, should be aware of the "usual practice" of the Law Officers which emerged when the Taylor sisters attempted to obtain a court order that certain national newspapers should be prosecuted for prejudicing their trial.[68] The practice is to write to editors indicating in some detail the way in which their publication gave rise to a substantial risk of seriously prejudicing the course of justice and giving them the opportunity to make submissions (backed by counsel's opinion) arguing to the contrary. The preliminary decision is then recon-

---

[63] The procedure is set out in Civil Procedure Rules Sched. 1; RSC O. 52.

[64] Contempt of Court Act 1981, s. 12.

[65] *ibid.*, s. 7—unless, contrary to the principles in the text, the court acts on its own motion.

[66] CPR, Sched. 1; RSC, O. 52, r. 2.

[67] see Press Council Booklet No. 7, *Press Conduct in the Sutcliffe Case*, p. 75.

[68] *R. v. Solicitor-General, ex p. Taylor* (1996) 8 Admin. L.R. 206.

sidered with the help of "specialist counsel" and the counsel who prosecuted at the trial which was allegedly prejudiced. Having been described in court as the "usual practice", editors would have a legitimate expectation that it will be followed in the future and editors will have an opportunity to dissuade the Attorney from continuing with contempt proceedings.

Once the Divisional Court has given leave for the case to go ahead, the publisher will be served with a "claim form", accompanied by an affidavit setting out the applicant's case. In Divisional Court proceedings evidence is normally given on affidavit rather than orally, but publishers should scrutinise carefully the draft affidavits that their lawyers prepare because they might be cross-examined on them, and it is perjury to swear a false affidavit. Publishers can insist on having their say by giving oral evidence[69]; this gives them a day in court and may have publicity value, but it is unlikely to swing the judges in their favour. Applications to commit for contempt must be heard in open court except in certain cases to do with children (wardship, adoption, guardianship, maintenance, upbringing residence or contact), the mentally ill, secret processes, or where for reasons to do with national security or the administration of justice the court decides to sit in private. Before making a committal order in these cases the court must state in open court the name of the guilty person, in general terms the nature of the contempt, and the period of committal.[70] Contempt is the one serious criminal charge not decided by a jury. Although the Divisional Court is preferable from a publisher's point of view to the court that was allegedly prejudiced, it is still composed of judges who should be scrupulous to avoid any appearance of partiality as they weigh freedom of speech against the preservation of the administration of justice.

A publisher found guilty by the court can be fined an unlimited amount. Individuals who are convicted can in addition be sentenced to up to two years' imprisonment.[71] An appeal can be taken directly to the House of Lords, but the permission of either the Divisional Court or of the Lords themselves is necessary.[72]

If the application to commit is heard by a single judge of the High Court, the Crown Court or the county court, the appeal is made in the

---

[69] RSC, O. 52, r. 6(4).

[70] Contempt of Court Act 1981, s. 7.

[71] Contempt of Court Act 1981, s. 14(1). This is also the maximum that a county court can impose: County Courts (Penalties for Contempt) Act 1983. Other inferior courts, *e.g.* magistrates' courts, can imprison for only one month and/or impose a fine of up to £2,500. Contempt of Court Act 1981, s. 14(1). A person committed for contempt can apply at any time to the court for an earlier release (CPR, Sched. 1; RSC, O. 52, r.8(1)). Thus even dilatory contrition may result in a shorter sentence.

[72] Administration of Justice Act 1960, s. 13(2)(c).

first place to the Court of Appeal.[73] Where the High Court has made a committal order, exceptionally, it is not necessary to obtain permission before appealing to the Court of Appeal.[74] If that is unsuccessful, but a certificate is given that the case raises an issue of public importance, and either the Court of Appeal or the Lords consent, a further appeal can be made to the Lords.[75]

Pending an appeal to either the Court of Appeal or from the Court of Appeal to the House of Lords the Court of Appeal can grant bail to an appellant who is in custody.[76] An appeal court can give permission for fresh evidence to be produced if the interests of justice require it.[77] This means that the more stringent requirements for fresh evidence in civil appeals do not have to be satisfied.

Injunctions to prevent contempt

The courts have granted injunctions in the past to restrain an anticipated contempt of court. This was the course taken by the Attorney-General against *The Times* for its planned series on thalidomide and against the satirist Auberon Waugh's election address when he stood as the "Dog Lovers Party" candidate against Jeremy Thorpe, shortly to be tried for his alleged part in a botched attempt to kill a blackmailing ex-lover (the ex-lover's dog had been shot instead). It is still unclear whether the person affected can make the application without the backing of the Attorney-General when it is alleged that the publication would infringe the strict liability rule. The Court of Appeal in 1985 said that this was not necessary,[78] but the correctness of this view was challenged in another case in the House of Lords which chose to leave the matter open.[79] Allegations of intentional contempt are clearly not within section 7, but injuctions of this type should be narrowly confined[80] and the applicant must prove to the criminal standard beyond reasonable doubt that the publication will create a real risk of prejudice and that the defendants will publish their material with a specific intent of causing that risk. This is a considerably more onerous task than the courts used to require on an application for interlocutory injunctions,[81] but it is consistent with section 12(3) of the Human Rights Act.

---

[73] *ibid.* at s. 13(2)(b) and (bb).
[74] CPR, r.52.3(1)(a)(i).
[75] This was the course taken in *Home Office v. Harman* [1983] 1 A.C. 280
[76] CPR, Sched. 1; RSC, O. 109, r.4. The Divisional Court has a like power to grant bail pending appeal from it to the House of Lords: *ibid.*
[77] *Irtelli v. Squatriti* [1993] Q.B. 83.
[78] *Peacock v. LWT, The Times*, November 27, 1985.
[79] *Pickering v. Liverpool Daily Post and Echo Newspapers plc* [1991] 2 A.C. 370.
[80] *Taylor v. Topping, The Times*, February 15, 1990.
[81] *Coe v. Central TV plc* [1994] E.M.L.R. 433

CHAPTER 8

REPORTING THE COURTS

The most fundamental principle of justice is that it must be seen to be done. Lord Halsbury, in the great constitutional case of *Scott v. Scott,* proclaimed that "Every court in the land is open to every subject of the King".[1] The rule became established almost by historical accident from the fact that courts in the Middle Ages were badly conducted public meetings in which neighbours gathered to pass judgment on their district's notorious felons. The Star Chamber followed the practice and heard all its cases in public, in order that its vicious punishments would have a general deterrent effect. In time, jurists like Blackstone and Bentham elevated the practice into a fundamental precondition of justice. They acclaimed it on a number of grounds, principally as a safeguard against judicial error or misbehaviour. In Bentham's words, "Publicity is the very soul of justice. It is the keenest spur to exertion and the surest of all guards against improbity. It keeps the judge himself, while trying, under trial." Moreover, publicity deters perjury, in that witnesses are likely to come forward to confound lies when they learn that they are being told. Press reporting of court cases enhances public knowledge and appreciation of the workings of the law, it assists the deterrent function of criminal trials and it permits the revelation of matters of genuine public interest. On the other hand, of course, it can at times be shallow, sensational or just plain incompetent. Courts have some corrective powers and can usually protect parties from any prejudice. A more persuasive reason for restricting the right to report is the desire to protect witnesses against loss of face or loss of job, or even, where police informers are concerned, against possible loss of life. Does it really matter if a few cases go unreported so that prosecution witnesses are relieved from the anxiety of reading their names in newspapers? It does, for the reasons given by Blackstone and Bentham. Trials derive their legitimacy from being conducted in public; the judge presides as a surrogate for the people, who are entitled to see and approve the power exercised on their behalf. Those who assist the prosecution can and should be protected by other means. No matter how fair, justice must still be seen before it can be said to have been done.

---

[1] *Scott v. Scott* [1913] A.C. 417.

The open-justice principle is now firmly embedded, with the help of Blackstone and Bentham, in the constitutional jurisprudence of the United States and Canada. The Supreme Courts of both countries have endorsed Wigmore's reasoning as to the evidential consequences of the requirement for hearings in public:

> "Its operation in tending to *improve the quality of testimony* [our italics] is two-fold. Subjectively, it produces in the witness's mind a disinclination to falsify; first, by stimulating the instinctive responsibility to public opinion, symbolised in the audience, and ready to scorn a demonstrated liar; and next, by inducing the fear of exposure of subsequent falsities through disclosure by informed persons who may chance to be present or to hear of the testimony from others present. Objectively, it secures the presence of those who by possibility may be able to furnish testimony in chief or to contradict falsifiers and yet may not have been known beforehand to the parties to possess any information."[2]

The United States Supreme Court has gone further, by regarding openness as a defining characteristic of the integrity of a trial process,[3] while the Supreme Court of Canada has struck down legislation preventing the reporting of evidence in divorce cases as contrary to the guarantee of freedom of expression.[4] Justice Bertha Wilson concluded in that case:

> "In summary, the public interest in open trials and in the ability of the press to provide complete reports of what takes place in the courtroom is rooted in the need (1) to maintain an effective evidentiary process; (2) to ensure a judiciary and juries that behave fairly and that are sensitive to the values espoused by the society; (3) to promote a shared sense that our courts operate with integrity and dispense justice; and (4) to provide an ongoing opportunity for the community to learn how the justice system operates and how the law being applied daily in the courts affects them."[5]

In the United States and Canada the open justice rule is strictly enforced by reference to a "freedom of expression" guarantee. In Britain the courts pay lip-service to the rule, but enforce it, as we shall see, haphazardly and at times inconsistently. Ironically, this is one area where the European Convention has the potential to damage a United

---

[2] *Wigmore on Evidence*, para. 1834.
[3] *Richmond Newspapers v. Virginia* (1980) 448 U.S. 555.
[4] *Edmonton Journal v. Att.-Gen. for Alberta* (1989) 64 D.L.R. (4th) 577.
[5] *ibid.*

Kingdom free speech principle (see Chapter 1, p. 15). European countries have never been so wedded to open justice and the Convention treats it as a qualified right and gives it (in terms) to the parties (who frequently want a cover-up) and not to the press. Thus Article 6's guarantee is encrusted with exceptions. It says:

> "(1) In the determination of his civil rights and obligations or of any criminal charge, everyone is entitled to a fair and public hearing by an independent and impartial tribunal established by law. Judgment shall be pronounced publicly but the press and public may be excluded from all or part of the trial in the interests of morals, public order or national security in a democratic society, where the interests of juveniles or the protection of the private life of the parties so require, or to the extent strictly necessary in the opinion of the court in special circumstances where publicity would prejudice the interests of justice."

At least, the European Court of Human Rights has recognised that while the litigants can waive the right to a public hearing, they can only do so if court secrecy does not run counter to any important public interest.[6] It will also be important for courts to be reminded of section 11 of the Human Rights Act which strives to guard against any diminution of existing common law rights by adoption of the Convention.

For all the opportunities presented by the open justice principle, it must be said that the standard of legal journalism in Britain is not particularly high, certainly when compared to the United States. It may be that reporters, sitting snugly in their privileged "press bench", have come to regard themselves as part and parcel of the court process, rather than as "the eyes and ears of the public". It is often claimed on behalf of the media that it enjoys no special privileges over and above those enjoyed by ordinary citizens. In the case of court reporting, however, this is manifestly untrue. The media do enjoy special rights—to sit in the press bench and to be present on some of the occasions when the general public are excluded—and it is important for journalists to understand the reason why the courts recognise those privileges. In the words of the former Master of the Rolls, Lord Donaldson:

> "It is not because of any special wisdom, interest or status enjoyed by proprietors, editors or journalists. It is because the media are the eyes and ears of the general public. They act on behalf of the general public. Their right to know and their right to publish is

---

[6] *Hakansson v. Sweden* (1991) 13 E.H.R.R. 1, para. 66.

neither more nor less than that of the general public. Indeed it *is* that of the general public for whom they are trustees."[7]

If British journalists have been reluctant to probe the processes of justice, they are certainly concerned to report sensational stories that emerge in evidence in the course of legal proceedings. It has been thus for centuries; indeed, the first newspapers consisted of nothing but court reports. Daily "chapbooks" of Old Bailey trials were hawked in the streets of seventeenth-century London at one penny apiece, catering to the curious, the pitying, the righteous and the prurient, who will always be interested in the crimes and punishments of the court calendar.[8] Coverage of the latest excitement in a sensational criminal case will attract circulation, especially if the press report is spiced with some of the colour and drama of the trial. There is another great attraction to the modern newspaper in court reports: they are "privileged" against actions for libel. The courtroom is one of the few places where an English person can say "*J'accuse*" and have the accusation reported to the country. During the Helen Smith inquest, the nurse's father muttered an accusation that two named persons had killed her. Court reporters, who could not hear what he said from the press gallery, worked out his words from a specially amplified tape of the proceedings. Ron Smith's accusation was headlined in all the papers the following day, whereupon the coroner fined him for an "outburst" in court that he (the coroner) had not noticed at the time it was made.[9] The fact that the newspapers were reporting a statement in open court albeit made *sotto voce*, protected them from libel action. There may be doubts about the wisdom of a rule that gives parties to court proceedings the privilege of exploiting them to make defamatory statements that cannot be proved. Nonetheless, the probability that the privilege will be abused on occasions is the price that must be paid for allegiance to the open court principle.

There are always those who are willing to find the price of this principle too high. The case of *Home Office v. Harman,* in which solicitor and now solicitor-general Harriet Harman was held in contempt for showing documents to a journalist after they had been read in open court, is one example (see p. 478). The decision has been reversed by a change to the Rules of Court following a decision in her favour by the European Commission of Human Rights. The media must be prepared to fight all attacks on the open justice principle, wherever they

---

[7] *Att.-Gen. v. Guardian Newspapers Ltd (No. 2)* [1988] 3 All E.R. 595, 600, applied in *Re M* [1990] 1 All E.R. 205.

[8] Langbein, "The Criminal Trial Before Lawyers" (1978) 45 U. of Chicago L.R. 263, 267.

[9] See Geoffrey Robertson, *The Justice Game* (Vintage, 1999), Chap. 8.

occur. In 1982 lay justices in Surrey were prevailed upon to sentence a "supergrass" in secret: the local newspaper protested, and the behaviour of the justices was condemned by the Divisional Court.[10] That judgment had the result, of course, of publicising the very facts that the justices had sought to keep secret. The media have, in their ability to publicise, the best antidote against attempts to close the courtroom doors. Whenever there is secrecy, there will inevitably be some suspicion of impropriety. Those who seek to defy the open justice principle often find that machinations to this end prove counterproductive.

The open justice principle is based, however, on public interest considerations. It must give way when the public interest dictates a degree of privacy. The names of rape and blackmail victims, for example, are suppressed in the interests of mitigating their pain and encouraging other victims to come forward. Family disputes are heard in private when details might damage the children of a disrupted marriage. Postponement of publication of certain evidence in criminal trials is justified on occasions when it might cause irredeemable prejudice to other trials. These exceptions are reasonable, but the media must be on constant guard against allowing them to be extended or exploited to prevent genuine public interest revelations.

There are four categories of exception to the open justice principle:

- The most serious inroad is where journalists are neither admitted to the court nor able to report what happened. This will be the case where the court sits in private ("in chambers" was the previous term) or in secret ("*in camera*").

- There are occasions when press and public are banished, but an account gleaned from the participants *can* be published. An example of this is a hearing takes place before a judge "in chambers". It will be in private, but it is not generally contempt to report what took place.

- The press may be allowed access to the court, but be restricted in what it can report; *e.g.* when the press can attend and report the proceedings but without identifying certain participants such as rape victims or children.

- The press may be allowed to be present subject to a temporary ban on publication. Most committal proceedings (the preliminary inquiry by magistrates into whether there is enough evidence to justify a jury trial) are of this type. The 1981 Contempt

---

[10] *R. v. Reigate Justices, ex p. Argus Newspapers Ltd* (1983) 5 Cr. App. R. (S.) 181, DC.

of Court Act gives courts a power to make an order postponing
publication where this is necessary in the interest of justice.

These exceptions are all departures from the general norm of openness. In the great majority of court cases the press are free to attend and
report everything said in the course of the legal proceedings. The following sections of this chapter deal with cases in the first category,
enumerate the rules that restrict reporting in the other categories, look
at the means that the press can use to gather and record information
about legal proceedings, and examine in more detail the defences of
absolute and qualified privilege against claims for libel and slander that
court reports enjoy.

PUBLIC ACCESS TO THE COURTS

The general principle is that every court is open for citizens to see
justice being done. A court is not "open" if the judge takes deliberate
steps to keep the press at bay:

> A Government minister wanted to avoid the publicity of his divorce trial,
> so the judge obligingly agreed to hold the hearing in the court library.
> The only access was through a door marked "private". This was left ajar
> and the judge announced to the parties and their representatives before he
> started that the court was open. On appeal, the Privy Council said this
> was a sham and in reality the hearing had been in private. Because there
> was no jurisdiction at the time to hear such cases in secret, the proceedings
> were a nullity.[11]

English magistrates have not been averse to similar expedients, and
there are instances where they have heard cases earlier than normal or
at some unannounced venue.[12] When they are trying a criminal case,
they must now sit in open court and they must use their ordinary
courthouse or a formally designated substitute.[13] Whatever the intention,
there must be a real opportunity for a casual member of the public to
attend. Consequently an employment tribunal did not sit in public when
access was through a door which could only be opened with a key
code.[14] The Administrative Court has said that the test should be

---

[11] *McPherson v. McPherson* [1936] A.C. 177
[12] Marjorie Jones, *Justice and Journalism* (Barry Rose, 1974), pp. 28, 88–91.
[13] Magistrates' Courts Act 1980, ss. 121(3), (4), 147. Magistrates must also by statute
    sit in public when considering an application to deport a person to the Republic of
    Ireland to face criminal charges—see Backing of Warrants (Republic of Ireland)
    Act 1965, Sched. 2 para. 2.
[14] *Storer v. British Gas plc* [2000] 2 All E.R. 440, CA—see p. 499.

whether the arrangements as a whole sufficiently inhibit a member of the public from attending court as to make the hearing one in private.[15] In that case, district judge was held to have sat in public, though an usher had to be asked to gain access to the court. (Security was said to have required these measures.)

Whenever a magistrates' court deviates from the open justice principle it is subject to correction by the High Court, which has recognised that journalists and newspapers have a right to enforce the principle in the public interest. This right was most firmly established in a case brought by investigative reporter David Leigh:

> The magistrates of Felixstowe adopted a policy of refusing to allow the press and interested members of the public to know the names of individual J.P.s who tried particular cases. They feared that J.P.s would be exposed to nuisance calls and reprisals over unpopular decisions. The Divisional Court declared this policy unlawful and unconstitutional. It was an unwarranted obstruction of the fundamental right to know the identity of persons who sit in judgment ("There is no such person known to the law as the anonymous J.P."). The court described the court reporter as "the watchdog of justice", who plays an essential role in the administration of the law by noting any possible unfairness or impropriety on the part of the bench. The magistrate "will be more anxious to give a correct decision if he knows that his reasons must justify themselves at the bar of public opinion'.[16]

A Home Office circular recommends that the media should have copies of the court lists on the day of the hearings and, as a minimum, these should contain the defendant's name, address, age, profession (where known) and the alleged offence. Where provisional lists are prepared in advance, copies of these should be available to the media on request. Courts are, however, also strongly recommended to charge the full economic cost of this service.[17]

---

[15] *R. (on the application of Pelling) v. Bow County Court* [2001] U.K.H.R.R. 165, Admin. Court, application for permission to appeal dismissed January 22, 2001 [2001] E.W.C.A. Civ. 122.

[16] *R. v. Felixstowe JJ ex p. Leigh* [1987] 1 All E.R. 551, D.C. On the other hand, although the common practice is for jurors from the panel to be called to the jury box by name to be sworn, the court can permit them to remain anonymous if there are real fears of jury nobbling: *R. v. Comerford* [1998] 1 Cr. App. R. 235, CA.

[17] Home Office Circulars 80/1989. The staff of some magistrates' courts have been concerned that disclosing lists to the press would infringe the Data Protection Act 1998. However, following discussion between the Home Office, the Newspaper Society and the Information Commissioner (formerly the Data Protection Commissioner), the Commissioner has confirmed that courts can continue to provide lists, registers and other information in accordance with Circular 80/1989 and assist journalists with their inquiries to check accuracy and progress of cases without contravening the Data Protection Act: *Reporting Restrictions in the Magistrates'*

Usually a bench or table is set aside for the press close to the witness box and to counsel. Reporters may be exercising a public right, but they do so from a privileged position. Any attempt to commandeer the press bench, or to relegate reporters to barely audible positions at the back of the court, should be challenged. (see p. 18).

Exclusion in the public interest

What exceptional circumstances permit a court to sit in secret without rendering its proceedings a nullity? First, those circumstances in which Parliament, by express statutory enactment, has given permission to expel the public. The statutes containing such express powers are summarised below. Secondly, where for convenience of handling interim applications the case is heard by judges sitting in a private room, the public is effectively barred, although practice has shifted in recent years and judges are now encouraged to respond positively to press requests to be admitted. Generally there is nothing to stop the press from publishing accounts of what went on in chambers, if details can be discovered and the publication will not prejudice a future trial. But is there an inherent power in the court to exclude both press and public in the interests of justice?

In *Scott v. Scott*[18] the Law Lords were divided on the subject. Several said that a court had no power other than that given by statute. One thought that members of the public were only to be excluded if "administration of justice would be rendered impracticable by their presence". Viscount Haldane put the test thus: "To justify an order for a hearing *in camera* it must be shown that the paramount object of securing that justice is done would really be rendered doubtful of attainment if the order were not made."[19]

This rightly stresses the rigorousness of the test. Convenience is not enough: "It must be necessary to avoid the subordination of the ends of justice to the means."[20] There must also be material (though not necessarily formal evidence) on which the court can reasonably reach its conclusion.[21] This can be tendered or submitted in writing or agreed

---

Courts, Judicial Studies Board, Newspaper Society and Society of Editors (2001), p. 6.

[18] [1913] A.C. 417.

[19] *ibid.*, at 439, and see at 442, 446 and 448.

[20] Lord Devlin in *Re K* [1965] A.C. 201, 239 and see Lord Haldane in *Scott*, n. 18 above, at 438, Viscount Reading C.J. in *R. v. Lewes Prison (Governor), ex p. Doyle* [1917] 2 K.B. 254, 271 and *Att.-Gen. v. Leveller Magazine Ltd* [1979] A.C. 440 at 450, 464, 731 at 750, 761, *per* Lords Diplock and Edmund-Davies.

[21] *Att.-Gen. v. Leveller Magazine Ltd*, n. 20 above, at 471 *per* Lord Scarman.

in private,[22] but the decision whether the case should proceed in secret must normally be publicly announced.[23]

> An extreme example in 1983 concerned the New Cross Building Society's challenge to the legality of Government directions that it should cease taking money from the public. The Society claimed that the directions were invalid. It successfully persuaded the High Court that its reputation would be irreparably harmed if it had to contest the directions (which had not been announced) in public proceedings. There would be a run on its deposits if the public appreciated that there was even a chance that the directions might have to be implemented. An appeal to the Court of Appeal was also heard in secret. The secrecy of the court proceedings was lifted only when the Court of Appeal dismissed the Society's claim and upheld the validity of the directions.[24]

This approach was repeated in 1991 when the Court of Appeal agreed to hear some applications in respect of the Polly Peck collapse in private.[25] Lord Donaldson justified the secrecy on the grounds that banks, building societies and other financial institutions that depend on investor confidence might be irreparably damaged if the allegations against them in civil proceedings were made public at an early stage, and later proved false. This prospect is somewhat fanciful and, in any event, overlooks the interests of customers and investors who continue dealing with the bank in ignorance of allegations that are subsequently found to be true. There is no real distinction between private hearings for civil claims against banks and building societies, and private hearings for a restaurateur accused of violating health standards to avoid adverse publicity that will reduce custom (which the Divisional Court will not permit).[26]

The Haldane exception has much less force since the 1981 Contempt of Court Act introduced postponement orders. The court ought now to consider whether justice might not be sufficiently served by making a more limited order permitting the press to remain but postponing reporting until such time as it will do no harm to the interests of justice.[27]

In 1982 the Divisional Court issued a clear warning to magistrates and their clerks against excluding the press:

---

[22] *R. v. Tower Bridge Magistrates' Court ex p. Osborne* (1989) 88 Cr. App. R. 28, QBD.

[23] *R. v. Ealing Justices, ex p. Weaver* (1982) 74 Cr. App. R. 204.

[24] *R. v. Chief Registrar of Building Societies, ex p. New Cross Building Society* [1984] Q.B. 227.

[25] *Polly Peck International plc v. Nadir, The Times*, November 11, 1991, CA.

[26] *R. v. Dover Justices, ex p. Dover District Council* (1992) 156 J.P. 433, D.C.

[27] *Argus Newspapers*, n. 10 above.

A "supergrass" appeared before the Reigate justices on charges of burglary and theft. These offences had been committed after he had received a lenient sentence for informing, and after police had given him a new identity. The defence asked the justices to hear his mitigation in secret, and the bench succumbed when the prosecution supported the application. The defendant was given an inexplicably light sentence. There was a press outcry, and several newspapers ensured that the secrecy was counterproductive by identifying the defendant and giving details of his unrepentant criminal career. The Divisional Court, on an application by the *Surrey Mirror,* held that the justices had been wrongly advised: they were entitled to sit in secret only if proceedings in open court would "frustrate the process of justice". The question was whether secrecy was *strictly necessary,* rather than merely convenient or expedient.[28]

The warning was reiterated in 1988:

A woman motorist who had pleaded guilty to a charge of driving with excess alcohol persuaded a magistrates' court to hear her arguments in mitigation in secret. She was divorcing her husband. This had caused emotional problems and suicidal tendencies. She would not be capable of giving evidence of these matters unless the court sat in private. The prosecution did not oppose the application, which was allowed by the bench. Having heard the evidence in private, the court disqualified the defendant for only three (as opposed to the usual 12) months. A local journalist and his publishers applied for judicial review of the decision to sit in secret. The Divisional Court said that while magistrates did have jurisdiction to sit in secret, they should do so only if there were compelling reasons, the existence of which were likely to be rare. The order in the present case appeared wholly unsustainable and out of accord with principle. It was not surprising that in this case justice had neither been seen nor done.[29]

Regrettably, the court in the *Malvern Justices* case rejected a submission that magistrates, as creatures of statute, cannot sit in secret since they have no statutory power so to do. Such a ruling would have finally put an end to temptations dangled by skilled advocates before lay justices to protect their clients from the punishment of publicity, which is usually more severe than any financial penalty the court can impose. The worst recent development for the open justice principle is that advocates are permitted to make secrecy applications in secret, where they may advance reasons that would not stand up to public scrutiny.

This ruling, which has done more in practice to encourage breaches of the open justice principle than any other decision, comes as a result

---

[28] *ibid.* The background to this case is discussed by Ole Hansen in "Secret Justice: Questions Remain" [1983] LAG Bull. June, p. 6.

[29] *R. v. Malvern Justices, ex p. Evans* [1988] Q.B. 553, QBD. See also *R. v. Epping and Ongar Justices, ex p. Breach* [1986] Crim. L.R. 810.

of an entirely exceptional case in 1987, when a defendant's counsel found that he could not explain at committal proceedings why his client wanted her address kept from her husband (who was also charged) without revealing in open court sensitive matters relating to the evidence that would be called on her behalf at a subsequent trial.[30] This is a special situation, which may justify hearing in secret to avoid prejudice to a trial; what it did not justify was the Divisional Court's decision that magistrates should always sit in secret to hear applications that they should sit in secret or impose a reporting restriction. The consequence has been an increase in secret courts, as magistrates hear the applications behind closed doors and then, if the application is granted, keep the doors closed while they consider the merits of the case. The court reporters do not, at either stage, know what is going on. Lawyers, who will do everything ethically possible for their clients, have no hesitation in asking (in secret) for courts to cover up their clients' distress and humiliation by sitting in secret. In one case, counsel appearing for a reporter on *The Independent* asked that charges against her (of possessing a small amount of cocaine) should be heard in secret because of the "undue hardship" that publicity would bring. The magistrates rightly refused the application, perhaps having been influenced by the campaign against "secret courts" being run by *The Independent* at the time.

Committal proceedings

A criminal charge is either tried by magistrates[31] or by a judge and jury at a Crown Court. The latter is known as trial on indictment, the indictment being the formal accusation of the offence. Most indictments are preceded by committal proceedings. These are conducted by magistrates, who, when acting in this capacity, must sit in open court except where a statute provides to the contrary or where it "appears to them as respects the whole or any part of the committal proceedings that the ends of justice would not be served by their sitting in open court".[32] This will rarely, if ever, be the case, because if the normal reporting restrictions are not lifted, reports of the proceedings must be postponed until after the full trial; and if reporting restrictions are lifted, the magistrates have power to postpone reports of any evidence that may cause

---

[30] This appears, from the judgment, to have been the nature of the information in question: *R. v. Tower Bridge Magistrates' Court, ex p. Osborne* (1989) 88 Cr. App. R. 28.

[31] Magistrates are either "lay" (*i.e.* unpaid and not lawyers) or district judges (magistrates) who are professional lawyers and are paid. They were previously known as "stipendiaries" because they received a stipend.

[32] Magistrates' Courts Act 1980, s. 4(2).

serious prejudice to the trial (see p. 458). In consequence, committal proceedings are hardly ever reported other than in the barest of details.

Most committals are purely formal. The defence can submit that there is no case to answer, but the magistrates can no longer hear oral evidence.[33] They are confined to the documentary evidence put in by the prosecution. If the defence chooses not to make a submission, the magistrates need not even read the statements and the press in court will not know their contents except for the name and address of the maker which must be read out.[34]

Voluntary bills of indictment

Instead of asking magistrates to commit a defendant for trial, a prosecutor can apply to a High Court judge for a voluntary bill of indictment.[35] This is considered by the judge in private and neither the prosecution nor the defendant, let alone the press, has the right to be present.[36] It is an exceptional step, which may be justified where a magistrate has unreasonably refused to commit the defendant or where a suspect is caught shortly before any co-accused have been committed to stand trial.[37]

Official secrets

There is a presumption that prosecutions for breaches of the Official Secrets Acts are to be treated in the same way as any other prosecution and must be held in public. However, the Crown can apply for all or part of the public to be excluded during all or part of the evidence.[38] It must persuade the court that publication of the evidence would be prejudicial to national safety. It will be a rare judge who will deny the prosecution application, though secret hearings ought to be confined to the minimum. The restrictions can be applied to committal hearings, trial and appeal, but the sentence must be passed in public.[39] If the Crown (or defendant) in a criminal trial intends to ask the court to sit in secret for reasons of national security, it must give seven days' advance warning to the court, which must then prominently display a notice in the court stating that the application is to be made. The application must be

---

[33] See Magistrates' Courts Act 1980, s. 5A added by Criminal Procedure and Investigations Act 1996, s. 47 and Sched. 1, para. 3.

[34] Magistrates' Courts Rules 1981, S.I. 1981 No. 552, r. 70(6).

[35] Administration of Justice (Miscellaneous Provisions) Act 1933, s. 2(2).

[36] Indictments (Procedure) Rules 1971 (S.I. 1971 No. 2084) r. 10.

[37] *R. v. Raymond* [1981] Q.B. 910, CA.

[38] Official Secrets Act 1920, s. 8(4), extended to offences under the Official Secrets Act 1989 (except in relation to careless loss of documents, 1989 Act, s. 11(4)).

[39] Official Secrets Act 1920, s. 8(4).

made after the defendant has pleaded to the charge but before the jury is empanelled. If the court decides that it will sit in secret, it must adjourn for 24 hours to allow an appeal against this decision to be made to the Court of Appeal.[40] When these procedural rules are not observed the Court of Appeal is likely to quash a direction that the trial or any part of it be heard in private because the media (or any other interested person) will not have had even the limited opportunity which the Rules allow to challenge the order[41] In civil cases the court can hear technical information about defence contracts in secret if this is necessary or expedient in the public interest or in the interest of the parties to the proceedings.[42]

Private secrets

Some actions are brought to restrain the defendant from publishing or using information that the claimant alleges was acquired in confidence or over which the claimant has monopoly control. If these actions and those concerning secret inventions had to be held in public, their whole purpose would be frustrated. However, the court should agree to sit in secret only so far as is necessary and any part of the evidence that would not give away the secret should be heard in public in the normal way. In *Lion Laboratories v. Evans*[43] (the intoximeter case) the Court of Appeal declined to direct or request the press not to publish the confidential material set out in its judgment: appreciation of this material was necessary to enable the public to understand its decision.

In commercial cases applications are sometimes made for the court to sit in secret to prevent the disclosure of price-sensitive information. Even these should be considered critically and the courts should be wary of displacing the normal principle of open justice.

> When a company stopped paying its lawyers so that its application for the removal of a provisional liquidator had to be abandoned, the Vice-Chancellor dismissed the application in open court, even though all the argument had taken place in secret. He said that hearings in closed court "were contrary to the public interest and should only take place if it was clear that there was a contrary public interest which overrode the need for public justice". Once the application had been abandoned "the general public should be aware of what has been happening".[44]

---

[40] Crown Court Rules 1982, r. 24A.
[41] *Ex p. Guardian Newspapers* [1999] 1 All E.R. 65.
[42] Defence Contracts Act 1958, s. 4(3).
[43] *Lion Laboratories v. Evans* [1985] Q.B. 526 (see p. 240).
[44] *Re London and Norwich Investment Services Ltd* [1988] B.C.L.C. 226. See also *British and Commonwealth Holdings plc v. Quadrex Holdings Inc. The Independent,* December 13, 1988.

Similarly, the court refused to conduct the trials of Lloyds' cases in private. Instead, it used its powers to give directions to avoid unnecessary reference in open court to matters which could be commercially damaging, provided that the parties were not inhibited in developing their cases.[45]

Special measures for witnesses: private hearings

The Youth Justice and Criminal Evidence Act 1999 introduced a raft of measures to assist witnesses who were children, or disabled in some way or whose evidence might be prejudiced by fear or distress. Where the proceedings concern a sexual offence or it appears to the court that there are reasonable grounds for believing that anyone other than the accused has sought or will seek to intimidate the witness in connection with their testimony these "special measures" include excluding the public from the court.[45A] Unlike the position in youth courts (see p. 416) there is no right for all journalists to remain, but the order clearing the court must allow one representative of a news gathering or reporting organisation who has been nominated for the purpose by one or more of these organisations to stay in court. Where such an order looks likely, the journalists present will have to be ready to make a quick selection. No doubt it will be a condition of nomination that the representative shares his or her reporting with every other journalist who wants access to them. If no nomination is made, the judge can exclude all journalists. Even though the public and the rest of the press are excluded from court, the proceedings shall be treated as though they took place in public for the purposes of any privilege or exemption from liability in respect of fair, accurate and contemporaneous reports of legal proceedings held in public (*i.e.* essentially defamation and contempt).

Family cases

A court hearing wardship proceedings and applications under the Children Act 1989 is acting in a quasi-parental role. Full publicity is not appropriate and consequently these cases are usually (though not invariably) heard in private.[46] In 1997 the Court of Appeal confirmed that courts would only rarely exercise their discretion to hear Children

---

[45] *Hallam-Eames v. Merrett Syndicates Ltd, The Times,* June 16, 1995.

[45A] Youth Justice and Criminal Evidence Act 1999, s. 25. For other aspects of the "special measures" see p. 439.

[46] *Re F (A Minor: Publication of Information)* [1977] 1 All E.R. 114. For the High Court and County Court: Family Proceedings Rules 1991, r. 4.16(7). Magistrates' Courts can exclude the press if they consider it expedient in the interests of the child: Family Proceedings Courts (Children Act 1989) Rules 1991, r. 16(7).

Act cases in public.[47] Subsequently the European Court of Human Rights reviewed the issue. It said that it was not inconsistent with Article 6(1) to designate an entire class of cases as an exception to the general rule of open hearings where this was considered necessary on one of the grounds in Article 6(1) where private hearings are permitted. However, the need for such measures must always be subject to the Court's control.[48] Proceedings under the Child Abduction and Custody Act 1985 also take place in private.[49]

Adoption proceedings in the High Court may take place in chambers: in the county court they must do so.[50] Sometimes the court is asked to authorise the termination of life support services to a patient in a persistent vegetative state. These decisions, which are literally of life and death, arouse considerable public interest and for this reason the court is likely to sit in open court although the identity of the parties may be protected by anonymity orders.[51]

Parliament has given the courts power to sit in secret when hearing petitions for a declaration of marital status, the effectiveness of an overseas adoption, legitimacy or parentage.[52] The hearing will not automatically be in private. The courts must take into account the effect of publicity on the petitioner, including his or her health and occupation, and on third parties who might be affected by the revelation of family secrets. It must then weigh this against the traditional rule of public policy that justice should be administered openly.[53] If questions as to parentage are raised in other proceedings, they must be publicly resolved unless there is some other power to consider them in secret.[54]

Court rules now provide that evidence in divorce and nullity proceedings should normally be given in open court,[55] though in the common case where the divorce is undefended and the spouses have lived apart, the evidence will be heard in private and only the decision announced in open court.[56] Ancillary proceedings concerning such matters as maintenance and division of property are normally heard in chambers.[57] Matters concerning the financial support for children are also dealt with

---

[47] *P-B (A Minor) (Child Cases: Hearings in Open Court)* [1997] 1 All E.R. 58, CA.
[48] *B v. U.K., P v. U.K.* [2001] 2 F.C.R. 221.
[49] Family Proceedings Rules, r. 68.
[50] Adoption Act 1976, s. 64(a) and (b).
[51] *Re G (Adult Patient: Publicity)* [1995] 2 F.L.R. 528.
[52] Domestic and Appellate Proceedings (Restrictions of Publicity) Act 1968, s. 2; which reversed the decision of *B (P) v. Att.-Gen.* [1965] 3 All E.R. 253, and see Family Law Reform Act 1986, ss. 55–60 and Family Law Reform Act 1987, s. 22.
[53] *Barritt v. Att.-Gen.* [1971] 3 All E.R. 1183, Wrangham J.
[54] *Prior v. Prior* (1970) 114 S.J. 72, PDA Div, Latey J.
[55] Family Proceedings Rules 1991, r. 2.28(1).
[56] *ibid.*, r. 2.36(1) and (2).
[57] In Family Proceedings Rules 1991, r.2.66(2)—ancillary relief applications; r.3.9(1)—applications for an occupation order or non-molestation order.

by the Child Support Agency whose decisions may be appealed to the Child Support Appeal Tribunals (where hearing will normally be in private).[58] Further appeals on points of law to a Child Support Commissioner will however usually be in public.[59] Applications for injunctions (*e.g.* for occupation orders to oust one party from the shared home) are also normally made in chambers.[60] Further, where it is alleged that a marriage is a nullity because one spouse was unable to consummate it, evidence on the question of sexual capacity should be heard in secret unless the judge is persuaded that in the interests of justice it should be heard in open court.[61] As with Official Secrets, the press and the public should be excluded only while the sensitive evidence is being given.

The multiplicity of different rules regarding access to (and reporting of) family proceedings is bewildering. In 1993 the Lord Chancellor's Department produced a Consultation Paper on rationalising them,[62] but no codifying legislation has yet been proposed.

Magistrates must sit in private when sitting as a youth court, although representatives of news-gathering organisations are entitled to be present.[63] This duty overrides the provision in the Backing of Warrants (Republic of Ireland) Act 1965, Sched. 2 para. 2 that applications for deportation to the Republic to face criminal charges must be heard in open court.[64] The public, but not the press, can be kept out of an adult court while a child or young person gives evidence in relation of a sex offence.[65]

Although *Scott v. Scott* said that the indecency of evidence was no ground for closing the court at common law, magistrates have by statute the power to sit in private for this reason when hearing domestic proceedings.[66]

Outside these areas and wardship proceedings (see p.000) the general principle of open justice applies even in cases involving children. In October 1988 Mr Justice Boreham agreed to hear in chambers the settlement details of a medical negligence claim brought on behalf of a young child because the agreed damages were for a very large sum and the claimant's mother feared receipt of begging letters. The media protested. The judge recanted and apologised for exceeding his power.[67]

---

[58] The Child Support Appeal Tribunal (Procedure) Regulations 1992, reg. 17.
[59] The Child Support Commissioners (Procedure) Regulations 1992.
[60] *Practice Direction* [1974] 2 All E.R. 1119. Senior Registrar, Fam Div.
[61] Matrimonial Causes Act 1973, s. 48(2).
[62] *Review of Access to and Reporting of Family Proceedings.*
[63] Children and Young Persons Act 1933, s. 47, as amended by Youth Justice and Criminal Evidence Act 1999, Sched. 4, para. 2.
[64] *Re L* (1991) 155 J.P. 273.
[65] Children and Young Persons Act 1933, s. 37(1).
[66] Magistrates' Courts Act 1980, s. 69(4).
[67] *The Guardian*, October 10, 1988.

Appeals

An appeal court has a statutory power to sit in secret, if the trial court could do so. An application to adopt this procedure can itself be heard in the absence of the public. The decision on the merits of the appeal must be given in open court unless there are good and sufficient reasons for doing so privately.[68]

Although the Court of Appeal cannot sit in chambers,[69] it has the same common law power as other courts to exclude the public and proceed in secret. It is reluctant to do so. A rare example is when it is hearing an appeal concerning a private search warrant to detect pirated or bootlegged copies of tapes or films and a public hearing would give the defendant a chance to hide his stock.[70] Even here, it is questionable whether some lesser restriction might not sometimes be adequate. For instance, the Court of Appeal could follow Lord Justice Lawton's suggestions in *R. v. Waterfield* (see p. 17) and allow the press to remain to see the kind of evidence on which the court is prepared to make these awesome orders. An order postponing publication would prevent the defendant being given advance notice.[71] Nor will the court generally conceal the name of a party to an appeal. It refused the cloak of anonymity to a building society that was fighting a Government ban on the taking of further deposits.[72] Where a party to the appeal is under a disability—*e.g.* by being a mental patient—an order granting anonymity will often be made.

"In chambers" hearings

District judges in the county court and Masters in the Queen's Bench Division of the High Court hear pre-trial applications in chambers. In the Queen's Bench the more important applications (particularly injunctions) can be heard only by a judge, but each day a judge in chambers sits to consider these. The judge in chambers will also hear appeals from Masters. Despite its Dickensian image, the Chancery Division is more open. Pre-trial applications there are heard in open court. Many cases can be brought in either division and a desire for pre-trial privacy is often a motive for choosing the Queen's Bench. Judicial

---

[68] Domestic and Appellate Proceedings (Restrictions of Publicity) Act 1968, s. 1, based on a Report of the Law Commission Cmnd 3149 (1966).
[69] *Re Agricultural Industries* [1952] 1 All E.R. 1188 CA.
[70] *Practice Note (Anton Piller Orders: Appeals)* [1982] 3 All E.R. 924.
[71] A similar procedure was adopted in *EMI Records Ltd v. Kudhail, The Times,* June 28, where argument was heard in secret but judgment was given in open court subject to a 10-day postponement order. But see *Re Crook,* p.000.
[72] *R. v. Registrar of Building Societies, ex p. A Building Society* [1960] 1 W.L.R. 669.

impatience with this anomaly was forcibly expressed in 1997 by a Chancery judge[73] and by the Court of Appeal which said:

> "However, it remains a principle of the greatest importance that, unless there are compelling reasons for doing otherwise, which will not exist in the generality of case, there should be public access to hearings in chambers and information available as to what occurred at such hearings. The fact that the public do not have the same right to attend hearings in chambers as those in open court and there can be in addition practical difficulties in arranging physical access does not mean that such access as is practical should not be granted. Depending on the nature of the request reasonable arrangements will normally be able to be made by a judge (of course we use this term to include Masters) to ensure that the fact that the hearing takes place in chambers does not materially interfere with the right of the public, including the media, to know and observe what happens in chambers. Sometimes the solution may be to allow one representative of the press to attend. Another solution may be to give judgment in open court so that the judge is not only able to announce the order which he is making, but is also able to give an account of the proceedings in chambers. The decision as to what to do in any particular situation to provide information for the public will be for the discretion of the judge conducting the hearing. As long as he bears in mind the importance of the principle that justice should be administered in a manner which is as open as is practical in the particular circumstances, higher courts will not interfere with the judge's decision unless there is good reason for doing so."[74]

Since then, the Civil Procedure Rules have promulgated a common procedure for all Divisions of the High Court and the county court. They stipulate:

"39.2

    (1) The general rule is that a hearing is to be in public.

    (2) The requirement for a hearing to be in public does not require the court to make special arrangements for accommodating members of the public.

    (3) A hearing, or any part of it, may be in private if—

        (a) publicity would defeat the object of the hearing;

        (b) it involves matters relating to national security;

---

[73] *Forbes v. Smith* [1998] 1 All E.R. 973.
[74] *Hodgson v. Imperial Tobacco Ltd* [1998] 1 W.L.R. 1056, CA.

(c) it involves confidential information (including information relating to personal financial matters) and publicity
would damage that confidentiality;

(d) a private hearing is necessary to protect the interests of
any child or patient;

(e) it is a hearing of an application made without notice
and it would be unjust to any respondent for there to
be a public hearing;

(f) it involves uncontentious matters arising in the administration of trusts or in the administration of a deceased
person's estate; or

(g) the court considers this to be necessary, in the interests
of justice.

(4) The court may order that the identity of any party or witness
must not be disclosed if it considers non-disclosure necessary in order to protect the interests of that party or witness."

Practice Directions amplify the new rules. They emphasise that the
court must have regard to Article 6, but they nonetheless set out a long
list of matters which in the first instance are to be listed in private.
They include mortgagee and possession actions and landlord claims for
possession for non-payment of rent. Certain applications to do with
enforcement of judgments and assessment of legal aid costs will also
be listed for a private hearing. A hearing that involves the interests of
a child or patient may be in private and small claims may be heard in
private if the parties agree.[75]

If there is a sign on the door indicating that the hearing is in private,
the public will not be admitted. Where there is no sign, members of the
public will be admitted if there is room.[76] When high temperatures in
summer make the wearing of wigs and gowns intolerable in courtrooms
without air-conditioning, some judges will sit in the ordinary courtroom
"as though in chambers", but with no sign on the door the public are
free to enter. As if by silent revolution, at least in terms of dress, the
proceedings come to terms with the twenty-first century.

In the Crown Court there has been a welcome willingness to adjourn
police applications for special procedure material into open court.[77]
These are discretionary decisions and cannot generally be quashed on

---

[75] CPR, Pt 39—Practice Direction—Miscellaneous Provisions Relating to Hearings,
paras 1.1–1.7.

[76] ibid., para. 1.9 and 1.10.

[77] Chief Constable of Avon and Somerset v. Bristol United Press, Bristol Crown Court,
Stuart-Smith J., October 23, 1986; Re an Application under s. 9 of PACE 1984,
Central Criminal Court, Alliott J. The Independent, May 27, 1988.

judicial review.[78] Bail appeals from magistrates' courts to the Crown Court are heard in chambers unless a judge has directed otherwise,[79] although there is no obvious reason why the Crown Court could not (like magistrates) hear the application in public with a restriction on reporting until the conclusion of the proceedings.

On several occasions the Court of Appeal has reminded criminal courts of the importance of the public's right to know about sentencing. If, for instance, it is discovered that a sentence exceeds the court's powers or should for some reason be altered by the trial judge, the corrected sentence and the reason for it should be stated publicly.[80]

In the past small claims arbitrations in the county court have been held in chambers and the public have not been admitted. These hearings have become increasingly important as the number of claims automatically referred to arbitration has gone up. Under the Civil Procedure Rules, a "small claims hearing" will generally still take place in the judge's chambers. However, the general rule is that the hearing should be in public. The judge can decide to hold it in private if the parties agree or one of the grounds for holding a pre-trial application in private exists (see p. 419).[81] The Government would anyway have been required to change the procedure because the European Court of Human Rights has held that the former practice violated Article 6(1) and the right to a public hearing of civil disputes.[82] In practice, the arrangements in some courts will mean that journalists have to seek assistance from court staff in gaining physical access to the rooms where chambers' hearings are taking place.[83]

Secret and private hearings: contempts

It is a common but erroneous belief that the privacy of a chambers hearing means that it must also be kept secret. This is not necessarily so. The Administration of Justice Act 1960, section 12(1) says: "The publication of any information before the court sitting in private shall not of itself be contempt of court." In general, if reporters can persuade either of the parties to divulge details of the hearings in chambers, they can publish what they have been told without being in contempt. This is important, particularly in connection with pre-trial injunctions. Where, for instance, the claimant claims that the defendant intends to

---

[78] *R. v. Central Criminal Court, ex p. DPP The Independent,* March 31, 1988.
[79] *Practice Direction (Crown Court—Bail)* 77 Cr. App. R. 69, para. 4.
[80] *R. v. Balmer* March 7, 1994, CA, Crim. App. Office Index 1995 A–41; *R. v. Clue, The Times,* December 27, 1995, CA.
[81] CPR, PD 27, 4.1.
[82] *Scarth v. U.K.* [1999] E.H.R.L.R. 322.
[83] See *R. (on the Application of Pelling) v. Bow County Court* (above, p. 407).

publish a libel, break a confidence or call a strike, the hearing of an application for a pre-trial injunction may be more important than the ultimate trial of the action. There are rich pickings to be had in the Bear Garden (the ante-room to the judges' chambers in the High Court). The main handicap is that since the proceedings have not taken place in open court, the media cannot take shelter behind privilege if sued for defamation arising from a report of what happened in chambers. Similarly, if the press learns of details of a bail appeal, it must be careful about contempt: if the proceedings were not in open court, the press will not have the protection of section 4(1) of the Contempt Act (see p. 458). Yet in the absence of the public judges will sometimes incautiously reveal their prejudices. At one pre-trial review held in chambers a judge justified a jury vetting order so as to discover whether any jurors had been drawn from Kilburn "where there is a high content of Irish people and most of them go round to pubs collecting money for the IRA".[84] Publication of such comments may be embarrassing for the judge, but they could not be said to cause a substantial risk of serious prejudice to the proceedings.

The exceptions to the general rule, where publication of chambers hearings can constitute contempt, are reports of proceedings concerning:[85]

- the inherent jurisdiction of the court relating to children, applications under the Children Act 1989 or the maintenance or upbringing of children;

- Mental Health Act applications;

- national security;

- secret processes and inventions;

- "where the court (having the power to do so) expressly prohibits the publication of all information relating to the proceedings or of information of the description which is published".

This last provision does not give the court a free-standing power to impose restrictions, but is dependent on the court "having the power [from some other source] to do so." This was emphasised in a case in which a court was asked to put a ban on disclosure of any details of a hearing which had taken place in private. One of the litigants feared that word might reach the prosecuting authorities in his home country and stimulate them into investigating his affairs. The judge refused. He said that it was "not the function of the court to protect a litigant before

---

[84] Quoted in David Leigh, *Frontiers of Secrecy,* p. 70.
[85] Administration of Justice Act 1960, s. 12(2).

it from embarrassment and such risks."[86] This case was followed in
Clibbery v. Allan[87] where the judge was asked to prohibit further
reporting of a dispute over financial support between an unmarried and
childless couple. He refused after weighing the competing claim to freedom of expression under Article 10 of one litigant who wished to be
free to expose what she considered the bad behaviour of her ex-partner
and against the claim to privacy under Article 8 of her opponent who
wished to preserve the customary reserve of the Family Division.

Even in cases which do come within one of the categories listed
above, it is not contempt:

- to publish the text or summary of any order made by the court
  (unless it expressly prohibits this)[88];

- to publish material that came from one of these types of private
  proceedings if the publisher was ignorant of this fact[89];

- if the publication is made a sufficiently long time after the
  proceedings were held that the justification for privacy has
  passed[90];

- if the court gives permission for publication.[91];

It is not a defence for the publishers to say that they did not intend
to commit contempt, nor can they obtain an acquittal by pleading that
in the case of proceedings such as wardship, that are regularly held in
private, they did not know that the public had been excluded.[92]

Disorder in court

Courts have an inherent power to control their own proceedings. This
includes the power to limit numbers in the courtroom and to clear the
public entirely if disorder is threatened or actually occurs. However, as
with the other qualifications to the open justice principle, the court

---

[86] *Trustor AB v. Smallbone* [2000] 1 All E.R. 811, Ch D.
[87] [2001] 2 F.L.R. 819.
[88] *ibid.* and see *Forbes v. Smith* (above, n. 73) and *Hodgson v. Imperial Tobacco Ltd*
(above, n. 74). Even in cases concerning children it will be highly unusual for the
court to prevent publication of (at least) an anonymised summary of the order: *Re
G (Minors) (Celebrities: Publicity), The Times*, October 28, 1998, CA.
[89] *Re F* (above, n. 46). This case concerned reports to the court by the Official Solicitor
and a social worker. These should carry a warning that they must be kept confidential on penalty of proceedings for contempt. *Practice Direction (Divorce: Children:
Welfare Officer's Report)* [1982] 1 All E.R. 512.
[90] *Re F*, n. 46 above.
[91] *Re R (MJ) (Publication of Transcripts)* [1975] 2 All E.R. 749.
[92] *Re F*, n. 46 above.

should depart from it no more than is necessary, and it would be quite wrong to exclude journalists who are not joining in the disorder.

> Members of the Welsh Language Society appealed against their conviction for refusing to pay television licence fees, on the grounds that the court trying them had improperly excluded members of the public. These members of the public were, in fact, supporters of the defendants, who had begun to create a disturbance. The Divisional Court, rejecting the appeal, noted that a journalist from a local paper had been allowed to remain. The Lord Chief Justice said: "I find it difficult to imagine a case which can be said to be held publicly if the press have been actively excluded".[93]

REPORTING RESTRICTIONS

Attending court is merely the means to the end of publication. What takes place in open court "is necessarily and legitimately made public and being public property may be republished".[94] This section considers the exceptions to that general principle. Where reporters are admitted to court, when are they limited or prohibited from publishing what they hear? Where reporters are not allowed into court, when *can* they publish information from other sources?

Remands and committal hearings

Restrictions

Prior to 1967 committal hearings could be reported in full. It was the Moors Murder case that finally prompted the Government to act, and then more to spare the public a double dose of grisly details than to avoid prejudice to defendants.[95]

Reporting restrictions on committals are contained in the Magistrates' Courts Act 1980, section 8.[96] Unless the restrictions are lifted a report in print or in a programme service about committal proceedings in Great Britain can only refer to:

- the names of the examining justices and their court;
- the names and addresses and occupations of parties and witnesses, and the ages of the defendant and witnesses;

---

[93] *R. v. Denbigh Justices, ex p. Williams and Evans* [1974] 2 All E.R. 1052.
[94] *Richardson v. Wilson* (1879) 7 R. 237.
[95] Marjorie Jones, *Justice and Journalism*, pp. 109–15.
[96] These are now contained in s. 8 of the Magistrates' Courts Act 1980.

- the charges;
- the names of counsel and solicitors;
- the decision to commit or how the case was otherwise disposed of;
- the charges on which each defendant was committed;
- the date and place to which the hearing was adjourned;
- arrangements for bail;
- whether legal aid was granted or refused.

Consequently, for instance, the reasons given by the police for opposing bail or by magistrates for refusing it cannot be published.

These restrictions apply only temporarily. Full details of the committal can be reported after the trial.[97] But by then these are usually stale news and many editors consider it uneconomic to have a reporter in a court where proceedings cannot be promptly reported.[98]

All the details can be reported if the magistrates decide not to commit or if they exercise their right (with the defendant's consent) to change their role part way through the examination and try the case themselves. Where there are several defendants of whom some are committed for trial and some are dealt with by the magistrates, a reporter must take care to observe the restrictions in connection with those who are sent for trial.

Breach of these restrictions can lead to a maximum fine of £5,000 on the editor, publisher or proprietor of the paper. Other publishers are also liable and so are broadcasters: the BBC was the first to be prosecuted under the Act.[99] The Attorney-General must approve a prosecution, a safeguard intended to prevent proceedings for harmless or trivial breaches.[1] It did not stop prosecution of the *Eastbourne Herald,* which was fined £200 in 1973 for referring to the defendant as a "New Year's Day Bridegroom ... bespectacled and dark-suited" and for describing the charges he faced as "serious".[2] This decision is mistaken, and the newspaper could have succeeded on an appeal by arguing that these matters were not "part of the proceedings". Certainly the purpose behind the restrictions was not to silence such descriptions. The case was an aberration: minor violations that do not pose a risk of prejudice will not be prosecuted. A more serious breach was committed by the

---

[97] Magistrates' Courts Act 1980, s. 8(3).
[98] "Criminal Proceedings in English Magistrates' Courts and the Local Press", Stephen White (1977) *Justice of the Peace,* 457 and 472.
[99] Jones, *Justice and Journalism,* p. 120.
[1] Magistrates' Courts Act 1980, s. 8(6).
[2] *The Times,* June 12, 1973.

Gloucester Citizen when, in an article about Fred West's first appearance at the magistrate's court in 1994, it reported that he had already admitting killing his daughter. The paper's editor and publisher were each fined £4,500.[3]

Lifting the restrictions

A defendant has a right to have the restrictions lifted[4] and must be told of this at every hearing.[5] The right can be exercised at a first appearance, though no evidence is then called.[6] If the restrictions have been lifted at an earlier date, the clerk must announce this when the hearing is resumed.[7]

Until 1981, where there were a number of defendants, any one of them could apply for restrictions to be lifted. There was massive publicity after George Deakin, alone of the defendants, applied for restrictions to be lifted at the Minehead committal hearings relating to himself, Jeremy Thorpe and two others on charges of conspiracy to murder. The result was the Criminal Justice (Amendment) Act 1981. Since then, if any defendant objects to the application to lift reporting restrictions, the magistrates must refuse it if persuaded that retaining the restrictions is in the interests of justice.[8] The presumption is in favour of delayed reporting, and the High Court has said that only "powerful" arguments in favour of publicity will prevail. In a 1982 case a defendant's wish to publicise his allegations that police had reneged on a promise to drop charges against him was held not to be sufficient to override a co-defendant's objection to publicity.[9]

Magistrates who wrongly refuse an application to lift restrictions are acting beyond their powers. Newspapers, broadcasters, individual reporters and the National Union of Journalists (NUJ) could challenge such a refusal by applying to the Administrative Court within the High Court for a mandatory order to compel the magistrates to follow the law.[10] The court can act quickly. In one case the application was heard on one day's notice. The procedure is not an appeal. It must be shown that the justices were wrong in law: either by refusing to lift restrictions when the Act required them to do so or by exercising their discretion in an unreasonable way. In some cases, particularly for broadcasters, even this procedure may take too long. If they are sure that the restric-

---

[3] *Media Lawyer,* May 1996, p. 26.
[4] Magistrates' Courts Act 1980, s. 8(2).
[5] Magistrates' Courts Rules 1981 (S.I. 1981 No. 552) r. 5(1).
[6] *R. v. Bow St Magistrate ex p Kray (Reginald)* [1969] 1 Q.B. 473.
[7] Magistrates' Courts Rules 1981, r. 5(3).
[8] Magistrates' Courts Act 1981, s. 8(2A).
[9] *R. v. Leeds Justices ex p. Sykes* [1983] 1 All E.R. 460.
[10] *R. v. Horsham Justices ex p. Farquharson and Another* [1982] 2 All E.R. 269.

tions ought to have been lifted (*e.g.* because a lone defendant asked for them to be) and they broadcast a full account, they are most unlikely to be prosecuted for breach of a restriction order that was invalidly made or retained.

Transfers and preparatory hearings: fraud and other complex prosecutions

The length and complexity of some fraud trials has worried governments for many years. In 1986 the Roskill Committee recommended wide-ranging changes,[11] and the Criminal Justice Act 1987 made substantial procedural alterations in the way that major fraud prosecutions are conducted.

From the media's point of view the most important concern is the "preparatory hearing". In serious fraud cases the prosecution can now dispense with committal hearings by seeking a transfer order to an appropriate Crown Court. The Crown Court, in turn, can order a preparatory hearing. This can be used by the defence to argue that there is no case to answer. It can also be used by the judge as a pre-trial review. The judge can compel both prosecution *and defence* to set out their respective cases in considerable detail.

The preparatory hearing is treated as part of the trial[12] and the press and public have their common law right to attend, but reporting restrictions apply in the same way as to committal hearings.[13] They also apply to applications by the defence for the charges to be dismissed for failing to disclose a sufficient case. As with committal proceedings, a single defendant has the right to have these reporting restrictions lifted; where multiple defendants disagree, the court has a discretion to act in the interests of justice.[14] There is no discretion to lift the restriction partially.

If the restrictions are not lifted, the permitted details are virtually the same as those of a committal hearing. The principal difference is that "relevant business information" may also be published. This means, in brief, the name and address of any business that the accused was carrying on on his own account or in which he was a partner or of which he was a director.[15] The addresses can be those at the time of the events giving rise to the charges and those at the time of publication. These restrictions apply until either the charges are dismissed against all the

---

[11] *Fraud Trials Committee Report* (HMSO, 1986).
[12] Criminal Justice Act 1987, s. 8.
[13] *ibid.*, s. 11.
[14] *ibid.*, s. 11 (2)–(4) and see Henry J.'s ruling in *R. v. Saunders* [1990] Crim. L.R. 597.
[15] 1987 Act, s. 11(4).

defendants who make pre-trial applications or until the trial of the last of the defendants is concluded.[16]

Breach of the restrictions is an offence for which the editor, proprietor and publisher (or their equivalents in the case of a broadcast or cable programme) can be fined by a magistrates' court up to level 5, currently £5,000.[17] The Attorney-General's consent is needed for a prosecution.[18]

Transfers and preparatory hearings can also be ordered in other complex cases and will attract very similar reporting restrictions.[19] In all cases tried on indictment, judges have a further power to make binding pre-trial rulings on points of law or admissibility of evidence but these cannot be reported until the conclusion of the trial.[20] There are the same maximum penalties and need for the Attorney-General's consent as with serious fraud preparatory hearings.[21]

Other situations where there is no need for committal hearings and where the matter can be transferred straight to the Crown Court are charges involving sexual offences or offences of violence or cruelty against children[22] and charges which can only be tried on indictment in the Crown Court.[23] Similar reporting restrictions apply in these cases as well.

Children and the courts

Before criminal proceedings commence

Various restrictions are imposed on the identification of children involved in court proceedings. It used to be the case that the restrictions started only once proceedings had begun. In December 1997 William Straw, the 17-year-old son of the Home Secretary, was arrested for selling £10 worth of cannabis to a *"Mirror"* reporter. He was released without charge on police bail. When newspapers refused to give an undertaking not to name the boy, the Attorney-General applied for an injunction. This was granted (in plain breach of Article 10, which was

---

[16] Criminal Justice Act 1987, s. 11(5)–(7).

[17] *ibid.,* s. 11(12).

[18] *ibid.,* s. 11(13).

[19] Criminal Procedure and Investigations Act 1996, s. 37, but "business information" is not included in the permitted particulars: only the occupations of defendants and witnesses.

[20] Criminal Procedure and Investigations Act 1996, s. 41, although as with preparatory hearings the judge does have the power to allow reporting if it is in the interests of justice.

[21] *ibid.,* ss. 38 and 42.

[22] Criminal Justice Act 1991, s. 53 and Sched., 6 para. 6.

[23] Crime and Disorder Act 1998, Sched. 3, para. 3.

not at the time in domestic force) so as to preserve any future court's ability to retain his anonymity. However, the injunction did not apply in Scotland and after William's involvement had been widely publicised there, the English injunction was lifted.[24]

Parliament has since intervened to provide new controls on the reporting of children involved in a "criminal investigation".[25] There is a "criminal investigation" once the police or others charged with the investigation of offences are conducting an investigation with a view to ascertaining whether a person should be charged with an offence.[26] It is important to realise that an "investigation" can thus begin much earlier than the period when a criminal case becomes "active" for the purpose of strict liability contempt.[27]

At first, the new regime will protect only the alleged perpetrator of the offence. However, the Secretary of State will have power to extend the class of protected person to the alleged victim and possible witnesses.[28] Where the protections apply, nothing must be published (so long as the person concerned is under 18) which is likely to lead members of the public to identify him as a person involved in the offence. Identifying features include (but not exhaustively) the person's name, address, school, place of work or still or moving picture—but only if they would connect him with the offence.[29]

Once these provisions are in force they will apply automatically, but a criminal court (including a single justice of the peace) can dispense with them if satisfied that it is necessary in the interests of justice to do so. The decision by a magistrate to grant or refuse a dispensing order can be appealed to the Crown Court.[30]

Breach of the restrictions is a summary offence punishable with a fine up to the statutory maximum (currently £5,000). The editor, publisher and proprietor of a newspaper are liable, as are their equivalents in relation to a programme service. Prosecutions require the consent of the Attorney-General.[31] It is a defence to show that the defendant did not know and had no reason to suspect that the publication included the report or (alternatively) that a criminal investigation had begun.[32]

The media were very concerned that these restrictions would prevent the immediate reporting of tragedies involving children such as the mul-

---

[24] The events are reviewed in *Media Lawyer,* January 1998, pp. 5–9.
[25] Youth Justice and Criminal Evidence Act 1999, ss. 44, 49 and 50. The provisions had not been brought into force at the time of writing.
[26] *ibid.,* s. 44(13)(b).
[27] see p. 368.
[28] The 1999 Act, s. 44(4) and (5).
[29] *ibid.,* s. 44(2) and (6).
[30] *ibid.,* s. 44(7)–(11).
[31] *ibid.,* s. 49.
[32] *ibid.,* s. 50(1) and (2).

tiple murders at the school in Dunblane or the killing of Philip Lawrence, the headmaster, stabbed outside his school in West London. So a defence was added that permits the media to satisfy the court that the inclusion of the identifying material was in the public interest on the ground that the suppressive effect of this law would have imposed a substantial and unreasonable restriction on reporting.[33] It is important to remember, though, that even in these circumstances the defence does not permit the identification of the alleged perpetrator of any offence or an alleged witness to a sexual offence.[34]

Section 52 directs the court to have particular regard to various matters when considering the public interest. They include the interest in the open reporting of crime, the open reporting of matters relating to human health and safety, the prevention and exposure of miscarriages of justice, the welfare of any protected person, the views of a protected person who is 16 or 17, or the views of an appropriate person if the protected person is under 16.

Complex provisions are made for a curious defence of "consent" to media revelations.[35] This consent defence cannot be relied upon at all in connection with either an alleged victim or a witness who is under 16. But where consent can (potentially) be relied upon as a defence, it must be in writing and, if the protected person is under 16, must be given by an appropriate person *i.e.* a parent or guardian (unless the child is in the care of a local authority, in which case it must be an officer of the authority or a parent or guardian with whom the child is allowed to live). The "appropriate person" must have been given a written notice warning about the need to consider the welfare of the child. Furthermore, the consent can be withdrawn in writing although only if there is sufficient time to edit out the identifying material. The consent is nullified if it is shown that the "peace or comfort" of the child or appropriate person was interfered with in order to obtain the consent. It remains to be seen whether this thicket of provisions leaves a defence of any practical utility to the media.

The ITC's Code requires broadcasters to have "particular regard" to the potentially vulnerable position of child witnesses and victims before identifying them, and that "particular justification" is required before child suspects are named.[36] The Commission backed away from its position in April 2001 that there should be a blanket prohibition of any young person involved in an offence after considerable protest from the media.

---

[33] Youth Justice and Criminal Evidence Act 1999, s. 50(3).
[34] *ibid.*, s. 50(3)(b). The alleged victims of sexual offences have independent protection of their anonymity—see below p. 436.
[35] *ibid.*, s. 50(4)–(14).
[36] See para. 2.11.

Although the restrictions under section 44 come to an end if proceedings are commenced,[37] in cases involving children the media need to be alert to the possibility of further reporting restrictions.

Youth courts

The general public are refused entry to youth courts, but journalists can attend and can report the proceedings although they must not publish anything relating to a person under 18 if it is likely to lead members of the public to identify him as someone concerned in the proceedings. In particular, they must not reveal the name, address, school, workplace, or include any still or moving picture of the child if this would identify him as concerned in the proceedings.[38] It is the link between the court proceedings and the young person which is legally objectionable. Consequently background stories or interviews that do identify the young person can be published so long as all mention of the court case is scrupulously avoided. Conversely, feature articles can be written about the youth court, backed by anonymous examples. The same restrictions apply to appeals from youth courts and to proceedings for varying or revoking supervision orders and appeals from these proceedings.[39]

In three very different circumstances the court can give permission for a young person to be identified even though he is involved in youth court proceedings:

- Where identification is appropriate to avoid injustice to the child, such as to scotch local rumours that the child is a defendant when in reality he is a witness.

- To assist in the arrest of a child or young person who is unlawfully at large and who is charged with, or convicted of, a violent or sexual or particularly serious offence.[40]

- After conviction of the child or young person, the court considers that identification would be in the public interest.[41]

Government Guidelines on the use of these discretionary powers has been given in two publications: *Opening Up Youth Court Proceedings*[42]

---

[37] Youth Justice and Criminal Evidence Act 1999, s. 44(3).
[38] Children and Young Persons Act 1933, s. 49 as amended by Youth Justice and Criminal Evidence Act 1999, Sched. 2. Comparable restrictions apply to the broadcast media: Children and Young Persons Act 1933, s. 49(3).
[39] *ibid.*, s. 49(2).
[40] *ibid.*, s. 49(5)(b) and (6).
[41] s. 49(4A). The offence must have been committed after October 1, 1997—Crime (Sentences) Act 1997, s. 45(2).
[42] Published by the Home Office and Lord Chancellor's Department, June 1998.

and *The Changing Culture of the Youth Court: Good Practice Guide.*[43]

The Divisional Court has reviewed the principles to be applied by a youth court in deciding whether to lift restrictions under section 49(4A)[44]:

> The defendant who was 15 at the time of the offence to which he pleaded guilty had been arrested some 130 times over the previous four years. Having heard representations from a court reporter the magistrates decided to lift the reporting restrictions partially. The defendant could be named, but his address, school and photograph could not be published. He appealed by case stated to the Divisional Court. The Lord Chief Justice said that the magistrates were entitled to hear from the press. He referred to several international instruments which emphasised the importance to be placed on the welfare of the child even when a defendant in criminal proceedings. It was right for magistrates to be very cautious before lifting the restrictions. It would be wholly wrong to use publicity as a form of extra punishment and it would be very difficult to see any place for "naming and shaming". However, in this case the magistrates had approached the issue of "public interest" correctly and their decision was not unreasonable.

The Crime and Disorder Act 1998[45] introduced "anti-social behaviour orders" (ASBOs) which are made by magistrates in civil proceedings[46] and therefore the automatic restrictions in section 49 do not apply. However the courts still have the power to require anonymity in reports of the proceedings.[47] Local papers have had some success in persuading courts not to make section 39 orders in relation to such proceedings. They argue that ASBOs are much more likely to be effective if the local media can publicise not only that the fact the orders have been made but also the names of those who are bound by them. It is then more likely that any breaches of the orders will be reported. It is a criminal offence to breach an ASBO and therefore, in the case of young persons, breach proceedings are taken in youth courts. The Youth Court would be able to lift the restriction, but only if the conditions in section 49 are satisfied.

Other criminal courts

Apart from youth courts and subsequent appeals from them, there is no automatic restriction on the coverage of criminal proceedings where children are involved. However, there is a power to impose reporting

---

[43] Published by Home Office and Lord Chancellor's Department, March 2001.
[44] *McKerry v. Teesdale and Wear Valley JJ.* [2001] E.M.L.R. 127.
[45] s. 1(1).
[46] *R. (McCann) v. Crown Court at Manchester* [2001] 1 W.L.R. 340.
[47] Under Children and Young Persons Act 1933, s. 39—see below p. 432.

restrictions. Previously this was in the Children and Young Persons Act 1933, section 39, but once it is brought into effect, this power for criminal courts will be found in the Youth Justice and Criminal Evidence Act 1999, section 45. The court can direct that no matter relating to any person concerned in the proceedings shall (while he is under 18) be included in any publication if it is likely to lead members of the public to identify him as a person concerned in the proceedings. These matters include (but are not limited to) the person's name, address, school or workplace and any still or moving picture of him.[48]

A person is "concerned in the proceedings" if the proceedings are taken against or in respect of him or if he is a witness.[49] Under section 39 of the 1933 Act courts sometimes wrongly tried to prohibit the identification of a young murder victim. They are unable to do so. The victim of an offence may be a person "in respect of whom" the proceedings are taken,[50] but the interests which the legislation (both old and new) is designed to protect cannot survive the victim's death and anyway could not prevail over the public interest in unrestricted reporting of serious crime.

Under these powers courts cannot prevent the press from naming adults involved in the proceedings, unless to do so would indirectly disclose the child's identity. The standard direction under section 39 of the Children and Young Persons Act 1933 (CYPA) (and now section 45 of Youth Justice and Criminal Evidence Act 1999 (YJCEA) prohibits publication of information likely to lead to the identification of the child, but the court cannot go further and give the media directions as to what material it can or cannot publish to comply with this order.[51] This was established in the case of *Ex parte Godwin*:[52]

A trial involved serious allegations of child sex molestation against two members of a close and very orthodox Jewish community. The children were from the same community and the trial judge was persuaded by defence counsel to make a section 39 order prohibiting publication of the names and addresses of the defendants on the grounds that such details would allow the children to be identified. The Court of Appeal held that he had no power to do so. It was up to the media to decide how to comply with the standard order. If they misjudged it, they could be prosecuted, but they could not be subjected to additional prior restraint of the kind which the trial judge had imposed here. The judge could give "advice" to the media as to what might or might not breach the order, but unlike the order itself such advice would not be legally binding.

---

[48] Youth Justice and Criminal Evidence Act 1999, s. 45(3) and (8).
[49] *ibid.*, s. 45(7).
[50] *R (A Minor) (Wardship: Restrictions on Publication)* [1994] Fam. 254.
[51] Or at least not beyond the specific matters listed in s. 45(8)—see above note 000.
[52] [1992] Q.B. 190.

The court can vary the standard order under section 45 by making an "excepting direction" if it is satisfied that there would otherwise be a substantial and unreasonable restriction on the reporting of the proceedings and that it is in the public interest to remove or relax the restriction. The outcome of the proceedings is not, by itself, a sufficient reason for making an excepting directions.[53] Thus the fact that a young person has been convicted in an adult court is not, of itself, a sufficient reason for allowing the defendant to be named, although of course this can be taken into account. In deciding whether to make a section 45 order in the first place or an excepting direction, the court must have regard to the welfare of the young person concerned.

Cases under section 39 of the CYPA had emphasised that Parliament had clearly distinguished the different regime in the youth courts (where anonymity was the rule) and that in adult criminal courts (where it was necessary to obtain a specific order from the court curtailing the open justice principle).[54] Other decisions have stressed that the age of the child and potential damage of publicity must be given considerable weight.[55] The Administrative Court in 2000 reasserted the importance of the difference between youth courts where the presumption was in favour of anonymity and other courts where good reason had to be shown for imposing restrictions.[56]

In the notorious trial of the two 11-year-olds charged with the murder of Jamie Bulger, the judge imposed a section 39 order until conviction at which point he revoked the order and permitted them to be named. The public nature of their trial was part of the reason why the European Court of Human Rights upheld their complaints under Article 6.[57] The Lord Chief Justice in consequence issued a practice direction for the conduct of future trials involving children and young persons[58] which recognises that special measures must be taken to make the courtroom less intimidating in these circumstances. It does, however, tell judges that they should be mindful of the public's general right to be informed about the administration of justice in the Crown Court. If it is necessary to restrict reporters' access to the courtroom, arrangements should be made for the proceedings to be relayed audibly and if possible visually

---

[53] Youth Justice and Criminal Evidence Act 1999, s. 45(5). The statute gives guidance as to what is meant by the "public interest": see above p. 429.

[54] See for instance *R. v. Lee* [1993] 1 W.L.R. 103; *R. v. Central Criminal Court, ex p. S* [1999] 1 F.L.R. 480, QBD.

[55] *R. v. Inner London Crown Court ex p. B* [1996] C.O.D. 17, QBD; *R. v. Leicester Crown Court, ex p. S* [1993] 1 W.L.R. 111.

[56] *R. v. Central Criminal Court, ex p. W, B and C* [2001] 1 Cr. App. R. 7.

[57] *T v. U.K.; V v. U.K.* (2000) 7 B.H.R.C. 659.

[58] *Practice Direction (Crown Court: trial of children and young persons)* [2000] 1 Cr. App. R. 483.

to another room in the same court complex to which the media have free access.[59]

Other courts

The Children and Young Persons Act 1933, section 39 continues to apply in non-criminal courts.[60]

Notice of reporting restrictions concerning children

There should be no need for any notice of reporting restrictions in youth courts since these apply automatically, but where section 49 applies because an adult magistrates' court is being asked to vary or revoke a supervision order or on appeal from such an order, the court must draw specific attention to the application of the restrictions. If it does not, then they do not apply.[61]

Where other courts use their powers under section 39 (or section 45 of YJCEA), they should express their order in clear terms (identifying, in any cases of ambiguity, which children are protected), reduce the order to writing, advertise its existence in the daily cause list and make copies available to the press at the court office.[62]

Review of children reporting restrictions

Reporters Caroline Godwin and Tim Crook have taken the lead in objecting to court secrecy orders. Their example has been followed by an increasing number of journalists who have vigilantly objected to reporting restrictions. Making direct and informed representations to the judge who imposed the order can be a quick, cheap and effective means of resisting unwarranted intrusions on press freedom.

A court which has made a section 39 or section 45 order can always revoke it. A section 39 order can be varied and a section 45 order can be made subject to an "excepting direction". A sad example concerned a child who had judicially reviewed a health authority's refusal to fund necessary treatment. The child's identity was protected by a section 39 order but when the review failed, the father successfully applied for the order to be lifted so that a national newspaper could pay for the child's treatment privately in return for the family's exclusive story.[63]

---

[59] [2000] 1 Cr. Ap. R. 483, para. 15.
[60] It has been amended on several occasions, most recently by the Youth Justice and Criminal Evidence Act 1999, Sched. 2.
[61] Children and Young Persons Act 1933, s. 49(10).
[62] *Ex parte Crook* [1995] 1 W.L.R. 139.
[63] *R. v. Cambridge and Huntingdon Health Authority, ex p. B (No.2) The Times* October 27, 1995, CA.

A reporting restrictions order under section 45 or section 39 which is made by a magistrates' court can be judicially reviewed by the High Court. The order of a Crown Court imposing restrictions (or refusing to make an excepting direction) can be appealed to the Court of Appeal under section 159 of Criminal Justice Act 1988.[64] If there is an appeal in relation to the substantive criminal proceedings, an appellate court has power to make, revoke or vary an excepting direction.[65]

However, in the absence of a substantive appeal on some other ground (*e.g.* against conviction or sentence) a young person has no right to appeal to the Court of Appeal against the decision of the Crown Court to refuse to make a reporting restriction order or to include an excepting direction. The theory behind this different treatment is that the norm is open reporting and the media are entitled to appeal against orders which depart from that norm, whereas there needs to be no right of appeal against a decision upholding the norm of free reporting. However, the lack of a right of appeal has led many defendants to seek judicial review of the Crown Court's refusal to grant or continue anonymity. The obstacle in their way has been Supreme Court Act 1981, section 29(3) which allows the High Court to judicially review decisions of the Crown Court "other than its jurisdiction in matters relating to a trial on indictment". The Divisional Court has been incapable of giving a consistent answer to the question of whether an order under section 39 is a "matter relating to a trial on indictment" and so beyond judicial review.[66] The Youth Justice and Criminal Evidence Act 1999 gives no assistance, and the matter will only be resolved when an appeal eventually reaches the House of Lords. The Lords will probably decide, consistently with the purpose of section 29(3), which is to prevent diversionary appeal proceedings in the course of the trial[67] and which would delay the trial, that the section means there can be no review anonymity orders unless they are imposed after conviction.

Transfers to the Crown Court

Where a child has been the victim of, or witness to, a sexual offence or an offence involving violence or cruelty, the prosecution can sidestep the stage of committal proceedings by giving a notice of transfer to the Crown Court. The procedure is then similar to that in serious fraud cases

---

[64] See p. 433.
[65] s. 45(4) and (10).
[66] See most recently, *R. v. Winchester Crown Court, ex p. B* [2000] 1 Cr. App. R. 11, QBD, holding that there was no jurisdiction to judicially review such orders and *R. v. Harrow Crown Court, ex p. H & D* [2000] 1 Cr. App. R. 262, QBD, holding that there was, at least where the s. 39 order was lifted after conviction and sentence.
[67] *R. v. DPP, ex p. Kebilene* [2000] 2 A.C. 326.

(see above p. 426).[68] Again, like serious fraud cases, the defendant can apply to a Crown Court judge to have the charge dismissed. Reporting of these applications is confined to those details that are permitted in covering committals and similar applications in serious fraud cases.[69]

Procedure and penalty

Breach of any of these reporting restrictions is a summary offence. The maximum penalty is the statutory maximum fine (currently £5,000). The Attorney-General must approve the prosecution in most cases.[70]

Rape and sexual offences

In 1975 the Heilbron Report[71] recommended that rape complainants should be granted anonymity in an effort to improve the rate of reporting to the police. A study in the same year had shown that, despite ethical exhortations of the Press Council, in about half the press reports of rape prosecutions the victim was named and in about a third her address was given as well.[72]

The recommendation was adopted in the Sexual Offences (Amendment) Act 1976 and extended to a much wider range of offences in 1992 by the Sexual Offences (Amendment) Act 1992. For several years these two statutes operated in tandem, but by the Youth Justice and Criminal Evidence Act 1999[73] the 1976 provisions were merged into a re-vamped Sexual Offences Act 1992. As a result there is a common set of restrictions for rape and a wide range of other sexual offences.[74] The 1976 Act originally gave some protection to the identity of the *defendant* in rape cases, but these provisions were dropped in 1988 and defendants accused of rape or other sexual offences are now in no different position from other defendants except, of course, the report must not be written in such a way as to identify the complainant indirectly.

There are two levels of protection for complainants in sex offence cases. From the time that an allegation of an offence has been made, neither the name, address or a still or moving picture of the complainant

---

[68] Criminal Justice Act 1991, s. 53 and Sched. 6.

[69] *ibid.*, Sched. 6, para. 6.

[70] Youth Justice and Criminal Evidence Act 1999, s. 49; Criminal Justice Act 1991, Sched. 6 para. 6(10) and (11); Children and Young Persons Act 1933, s. 49(9)— the Att.-Gen.'s consent is not necessary under this provision.

[71] Advisory Group on the Law of Rape, Cmnd 6352 (1975).

[72] Keith Soothill and Anthea Jack "How Rape is Reported" *New Society*, June 19, 1975.

[73] Sched. 2, paras 6–14.

[74] See Sexual Offences (Amendment) Act 1992, s. 2.

can be published[75] during her lifetime if it is likely to lead members of the public to identify her as person against whom the offence is alleged to have been committed.[76] Once a person is accused of an offence[77] the degree of protection is increased. Thereafter and during the complainant's lifetime nothing may be published which would be likely to lead members of the public to identify the person concerned as the person against whom the offence is alleged to have been committed. This would include (but, as with the reporting restrictions concerning children, is not limited to), the complainant's name, address, school or educational establishment or place of work and any still or moving picture which in any of these cases would lead members of the public to identify her as the complainant.[78] Special rules apply in the case of incest or buggery and where the complainant is accused of a like offence.[79]

There are three important exceptions to the anonymity rule. First, the complainant may consent to being identified. Agreement must have been in writing and not obtained as a result of unreasonable interference with her peace or comfort and with the intention of obtaining her consent.[80] It may, and often will, be obtained by newspapers offering money for a story, which, for contempt reasons, will not be publishable until after the trial. Consent cannot be given by a victim who is under 16 at the time.[81] Secondly, the media are free to identify the complainant as a part of a report of criminal proceedings other than the trial or appeal of the person allegedly responsible.[82] This was apparently intended to cater for those rare cases where a complainant is herself (or himself) later charged with perjury.

Thirdly, the court itself can allow the complainant to be named. It may do so if this is necessary to persuade people who are protected defence witnesses to come forward.[83] The court can also lift the anonymity shield if it would impose a "substantial and unreasonable restriction on the reporting of the proceedings at trial and it is in the public interest to relax the restriction."[84] The defendant's acquittal or

---

[75] Most of the sex offences, including rape, can be committed against men or women.
[76] Sexual Offences (Amendment) Act 1992, s. 1(1).
[77] This is defined in *ibid.,* s. 6(3) as laying an information (which would precede a summons or arrest warrant), appearance in court charged with an offence, committal for trial or charged in a bill of indictment.
[78] *ibid.,* s. 1(1).
[79] *ibid.,* s. 3.
[80] *ibid.,* s. 5.
[81] *ibid.,* s. 5(3) added by Youth Justice and Criminal Evidence Act 1999, Sched. 2, para. 11.
[82] *ibid.,* s. 1(4).
[83] *ibid.,* s. 3(1).
[84] Sexual Offences (Amendment) Act 1992, s. 3(2).

some other outcome of the trial is not of itself a reason for relaxing
the anonymity rule[85] although a judge who takes a critical view of the
complainant's behaviour may be more inclined to let the public know
about it. As with other reporting restrictions it is now widely recognised
that courts ought to hear (or read) representations from or on behalf of
the media in support of lifting the suppression order.

Criminal charges for breach of these restrictions can only be brought
with the consent of the Attorney-General.[86] For the print media those
responsible are the proprietor, editor and publisher and, in the case of
the broadcast media, the company responsible for providing the programme service and the person with functions corresponding to the
editor of a newspaper.[87]

Reporting restrictions protecting witnesses in criminal proceedings

The Youth Justice and Criminal Evidence Act 1999 introduced a new
power to prohibit the identification of witnesses whose evidence (or
co-operation with a party in the case) was likely to be diminished
because of the witness's fear or distress at the prospect of being publicly
identified as a witness in the proceedings. Importantly, this power does
not extend to give anonymity to the defendant.[88] The Act lists matters
which must be taken into account in deciding eligibility. They include
the witness's age, social and cultural background, religious or political
opinions; and any behaviour towards the witness by the defendant, his
family or associates or any other person likely to be a defendant or
witness in the proceedings. The court must take into account the witness's own views (though these are likely to favour anonymity).[89]

Even if a witness is eligible for protection, the court must still exercise a judgment as to whether a reporting direction of this kind should
be made. It must consider whether it would be in the interests of justice
to do so and the public interest in avoiding the imposition of a substantial and unreasonable restriction on the reporting of the proceedings.[90]
Guidance on factors to weigh in the balance is given in the statute.[91]

A reporting direction directs that nothing relating to the witness is to

---

[85] *ibid.*, s. 3(3).
[86] *ibid.*, s. 5(4). The usual practice in contempt cases of inviting representations from
the prospective media defendant before a prosecution is brought (see p. 398) should
be followed here.
[87] *ibid.*, s. 5(1).
[88] Youth Justice and Criminal Evidence Act 1999, s. 46. The witness must be over
18. If under 18, the court has alternative powers (see p. 431).
[89] *ibid.*, s. 46(5).
[90] Youth Justice and Criminal Evidence Act 1999, s. 46(6).
[91] *ibid.*, s. 52—see above, p. 429.

be published in the witness's lifetime which would be likely to lead members of the public to identify him as being a witness in the proceedings. Specifically these matters include the witness's name, address, educational establishment, place of work or still or moving picture of the person concerned which would be likely to identify him as a witness in the proceedings. As with anonymity orders for children, the court can make an "excepting direction" if it would be in the interests of justice to do so or if the effect of the restrictions would otherwise be to impose a substantial and unreasonable restriction on the reporting of the proceedings.[92] The witness can consent to a publication which does name him, but the consent must be in writing[93] and must not be obtained by interfering with the peace or comfort of the witness.[94]

The reporting direction can be revoked and excepting directions can be made, varied or altered either by the same court or an appellate court. Again, as with children, an excepting direction cannot be made exclusively because of the outcome of the case.

The criminal courts have also been given powers by the Youth Justice and Criminal Evidence Act 1999 to take "special measures" to assist witnesses who are under 17, who suffer from a mental disorder, have impaired intelligence or a physical disability or disorder or whose evidence would be adversely affected by fear or distress.[95] "Special measures" include the use of screens in court so that the witness does not have to look at the defendant: allowing evidence to be given by live video link; removing wigs or gowns; hearings conducted informally out of the court room and replayed on video; the examination of witnesses through an intermediary and the giving of evidence in private (as to later see above p. 414).[96] In some cases the court can also give a direction restricting cross-examination by a defendant who is representing himself.

Reporting of a "special measures" direction or a direction limiting cross-examination and any legal argument about them is postponed until the relevant proceedings finish. The court can make an order lifting this restriction in whole or part, but must not do so over the objection of a defendant unless it is satisfied that this is in the interests of justice.[97]

Breach of such a reporting direction or reporting in breach of the restrictions on special measures or limitations on cross- examination is a summary offence. There is a defence that the beneficiary gave written

---

[92] *ibid.*, s. 46(9).
[93] *ibid.*, s. 50(7).
[94] *ibid.*, s. 50(8).
[95] Youth Justice and Criminal Evidence Act 1999, ss. 16 and 17.
[96] *ibid.*, ss. 19–30. Not all the special measures are available to all eligible persons.
[97] Youth Justice and Criminal Evidence Act 1999, s. 47. Even if an order is made lifting a restriction, the legal argument on the subject cannot be reported until the end of the case: *ibid.*, s. 47(4) and (5).

consent.[98] A defendant who has been convicted can be fined the statutory maximum (currently £5,000). A prosecution requires the consent of the Attorney-General.

Family cases

At one time the popular press thrived on divorce court scandals, and every salacious detail would be reported.[99] This practice has declined dramatically, in part because of the reporting restrictions and in part because it is no longer necessary to establish cruelty or adultery in order to obtain a divorce. Irretrievable breakdown is the sole ground, and this can be demonstrated merely by a period of separation. However, even where evidence of sensational adultery is given and discovered by journalists, they must be circumspect in their reports. Reports of proceedings for divorce, nullity, separation, financial provisions for a spouse or declarations of marital status, overseas adoption, legitimacy or parentage must be limited to the following[1]:

- names, addresses and occupations of parties and witnesses;
- a concise statement of the charges, defence and counter-charges in support of which evidence is given or (in the case of a declaration as to status), the declaration sought;
- submissions on points of law and rulings of the court;
- the judgment of the court and observations by the judge.

The charges and counter-charges may be the most interesting to a journalist, but they can be reported only if evidence is given in support of them. If the allegations are withdrawn, publication is prohibited.

In practice, the judgment of the court is usually very full and will review all evidence. Judicial comment of the sort: "the wife (of a merchant banker) was well-dressed, well-preserved, stupid in many ways but not uncultured" and the co-respondent (a window cleaner) was a "good physical specimen"[2] can be acidic and grossly unfair. Publication of such comments can be justified in the public interest on the grounds

---

[98] *ibid.*, s. 50(7).

[99] Jeremy Tunstall, *Journalists at Work* (Constable, 1971), p. 91.

[1] Judicial Proceedings (Regulation of Reports) Act 1926, s. 1(1)(b); Domestic and Appellate Proceedings (Restrictions of Publicity) Act 1968, s. 2(3); Matrimonial Causes Act 1973, s. 45; Family Law Reform Acts 1986 and 1987. But reporting of hearings to resolve financial matters between unmarried couples are not automatically restricted and in *Clibbery v. Allan* (2001) 2 F.L.R. 819 Form D (where no children were involved) Munby J. refused to impose a restriction.

[2] *Daily Express* January 25, 1969, quoted in Cretney, *Principles of Family Law*, (3rd ed., Sweet & Maxwell, 1979), p. 158.

that they say more about the judges than about the subjects of their comments. One High Court judge retired after a storm of protest over comments he made about the morality of Chelsea dustmen.

As with juvenile cases, the editor, proprietor and publisher are at risk rather than the journalist. "Publication" has been held by the High Court of Justiciary in Scotland to take place when the newspaper is printed and released for distribution.[3] It is thus used in a narrower sense than in the context of libel or obscenity. These differences can be of vital importance when a criminal court's jurisdiction depends on the place where the offence was committed or (as with summary offences) whether the proceedings were commenced in time. The Scottish case is one of very few prosecutions under the 1926 Act. The judge observed dryly, but illogically, that "the paucity of decisions is, presumably, a tribute to the effectiveness of the legislation". The maximum penalty is a fine at level 5, currently £5,000, and four months in prison. The Attorney-General's consent is necessary for any prosecution.[4]

This last safeguard is imperfect. While the persons affected by the report may not prosecute and cannot force the Attorney-General to prosecute, they may apply for a civil injunction to restrain its publication. Normally, the courts will not enjoin in advance the commission of a criminal offence.[5] They say that the proper course is to bring a prosecution after the event. However, where a person stands to suffer particular hardship, the position is different and in *Argyll v. Argyll* the court granted the Duchess an injunction to prevent the Duke reporting details of charges in their divorce proceedings that had not been backed by evidence.[6] The case is important because its rationale is capable of being applied to most, if not all, the restrictions on reporting examined in this section. An injunction should be refused if the threatened breach was trivial, but the publisher would be put to time and expense in opposing the action. This was the very vice against which the Attorney-General's veto was intended to guard, and the time and cost of High Court proceedings are much more serious than the cost of defending a prosecution in the magistrates' courts. But when this argument was put to Mr Justice Ungoed-Thomas in *Argyll v. Argyll,* he disregarded it. However, the difficulty of learning what a paper intends to publish in advance and the cost of obtaining an injunction have meant that there are few cases in this context where the *Argyll* precedent has been followed.

Applications without notice for an occupation order to oust one party from the family home are usually heard in private. However, when a power of arrest is attached to the injunction, this should be announced

---

[3] *Procurator Fiscal v. Scott* (September 7, 1999).
[4] Judicial Proceedings (Regulation of Reports) Act 1926, s. 1(3).
[5] *Gouriet v. Union of Post Office Workers* [1978] A.C. 435.
[6] [1967] Ch 302.

when the judge next sits in open court. A person who is arrested under this power has to be brought before a judge within 24 hours (excluding only Sundays, Good Friday and Christmas Day). If a regular court will not sit within that time, the arrested person can be taken before a judge elsewhere. In theory this will be a hearing in open court and there is a Practice Direction that no impediment should be put in the way of the press or any other member of the public who wishes to attend. In practice, of course, it will be rare for the press to learn that such a hearing is due to take place. If the person arrested is committed for contempt, there must be an announcement at the next regular sitting of the court. The name of the person committed, the period of the committal and the general nature of the contempt should be given.[7]

Children cases: automatic restrictions

The Children Act 1989 gives magistrates powers to The County Court and to The High Court. All of these courts can sit in private to exercise Children Act powers.[8] Whenever there are proceedings in any of these courts it is an offence to publish any material which is likely to identify a child as being involved in the proceedings or to publish the school or address as being that of a child involved in the proceedings.[9] The maximum penalty is a fine on level 4 (currently £2,500).

When family proceedings are taking place in the magistrates' court, the media are in any event limited to publishing the names, addresses and occupations of the parties and witnesses; the grounds of the application and a concise statement of the charges, defences, and counter-charges in support of which evidence had been given; submissions on any point of law and the court's decision; and the decision of the court and any observations made by the court in giving it.[10]

In adoption proceedings the restrictions go further: the parties must be anonymous, the charges cannot be summarised and nothing must be published that would identify the child; nor can the child's photograph be printed.[11] The maximum penalty is a fine at level 4 (currently £2,500) on the editor, proprietor, or publisher of a newspaper or periodical. Again the Attorney-General must consent. These restrictions also apply to the electronic media.

Neither press nor public usually has access to wardship hearings and

---

[7] *Practice Direction* [1998] 2 All E.R. 927–8.
[8] See above, p. 414.
[9] Children Act 1989, s. 97(2). In its original form this provision restricted reporting only of magistrates' courts, but it was significantly extended by the Access to Justice Act 1997, s. 72 to reports of High Court and county court proceedings as well.
[10] Magistrates' Courts Act 1980, s. 71—again the maximum fine is £2,500.
[11] Magistrates' Courts Act 1980, s. 71(2).

Children Act hearings and it may be contempt of court to publish any information relating to the proceedings. This was the position at common law[12] and it has been preserved by statute.[13] The Court of Appeal has said that "proceedings" include such matters as statements of evidence, reports, accounts of interviews and such like that are prepared for use in court once the wardship proceedings have been instituted.[14]

Similarly, where a local authority has intervened because of suspected abuse, the parents' version of how the child sustained injuries and their criticism of social workers involved in the case would be information relating to the proceedings. Information about the nature of the injuries (without mentioning their cause) would not be objectionable.[15]

This reporting restriction is paralleled by the imposition of a high degree of confidentiality on reports made by relatives, social workers and professionals that find their way into the court files. The confidentiality is given in order to encourage candour, and the reports will be protected from newspaper lawyers who seek to inspect them in order to defend libel actions.[16]

The ban does not mean that nothing can be published about a ward. The usual position is that it is not contempt under the 1960 Act to name a child as a ward of court or the subject of proceedings under the Children Act 1989, to publish the name, address or photograph of the child, or of the other parties to the proceedings, or to give the date, time or place of a hearing or explain the nature of the dispute or anything which has been seen or heard by a person behaving lawfully in a public place outside the court in which the hearing takes place.[17] However, the media needs to be careful of the overlapping restrictions that apply in this field and, as we have seen, the Children Act may impose an anonymity requirement which is of greater importance now that this restriction applies as well to Children Act proceedings in the High Court and County Court.

The press may also report the text or summary of the order unless there is a specific prohibition.[18] If publicity is likely to be damaging the usual practice is for the Official Solicitor to draft and the judge to approve a short statement giving the bare outcome of the proceedings.[19] The High Court has held that the fact that a child is a ward of court

---

[12] *Re F (a minor)* [1977] 1 All E.R. 114.
[13] Administration of Justice Act 1960, section. 12(1).
[14] Geoffrey Lane L.J. in *Re F,* n. 12 above, at 135.
[15] *Oxfordshire C.C. v. L and F* [1997] 1 F.L.R. 235.
[16] *Re X, Y and Z (Minors), The Times,* March 20, 1991, Waite J.
[17] See *X v. Dempster* [1999] 1 F.L.R. 894, 898–9.
[18] Administration of Justice Act 1960, s. 12(2).
[19] *Re G (Celebrities: Publicity)* [1999] 1 F.L.R. 409, CA.

does not, of itself, prevent the media from interviewing the child or broadcasting or publishing the interview.[20]

Even where information does relate to the proceedings, publication is not automatically contempt of court: it has to be shown that the publisher knew that the material related to the proceedings and that the proceedings were held in private.[21] The later condition gives scant protection: because Children Act proceedings are so commonly held in private, experienced editors will be assumed to know this fact. It is not a defence to a contempt charge that the material published was of public interest. However, this will be relevant to the penalty[22] and there would be no contempt at all if the court gave permission to publish. In one case it did so at the request of the local authority which considered that a fair and accurate report would be better than the inaccurate rumours being perpetuated by a man with whom the ward had become involved. The court agreed on condition that the parties remained anonymous.[23]

Family Division publicity injunctions

Where the information does not relate to court proceedings under the Children Act, wardship or the inherent jurisdiction of the courts over children, there is no automatic restriction on publicity. However, the courts have evolved a special jurisdiction to grant injunctions in cases involving children. The principles are:

Not only wards of court can be shielded

Although this power is associated with children who have been made wards of court, it is not limited to them. The court has an inherent jurisdiction (going back to medieval times) over all children and press injunctions can be granted even though the child is not a ward of court. This quasi-parental jurisdiction can also be exercised to protect others who are unable to take decisions for themselves (such as terminally ill patients).[24]

No injunction if harm to the child is tangential to publication

The jurisdiction to protect children from harm is not limitless: the courts will not prohibit a publication which does not directly concern the child,

---

[20] *Kelly v. BBC* [2001] 1 All E.R. 323.
[21] *Re F*, see above, n. 12.
[22] *Official Solicitor v. News Group Newspapers Ltd* [1994] 2 F.L.R. 174 where the publisher was fined £5,000 and the editor £1,000: the court said that the material taken went beyond what was necessary to tell the story that a nurse with Munchausen's Syndrome by Proxy was continuing to work in a hospital.
[23] *Re H (Publication of Judgment)* [1995] 2 F.L.R. 542.
[24] *Re C (A Minor)(Wardship: medical treatment)(No. 2)* [1990] Fam. 39.

even though it may be about the child's parent and be likely to upset the child. Thus in *Re X*[25] the Court of Appeal made ringing declarations in favour of freedom of speech. It refused to prevent publication of a book which made reference to the sexual behaviour of the deceased father of a ward of court despite evidence that this would psychologically damage the ward.

This principle was emphasised in a 1997 case concerning an unusual child support application.

> The BBC was making a programme about the Child Support Agency and featured a woman whose children had been born by AID from a donor who was not her husband. There were outstanding proceedings to decide whether her husband was nonetheless financially responsible for the children. The husband wished to prevent disclosure of the fact that he was infertile. The court decided that this probably was information which might be given to a court in private, but the purpose of section 12 was to protect children. This injunction would only be to protect the parent and so it was refused.[26]

The principle was applied in an important decision in 1994 concerning a Central Television programme on the work of the Obscene Publications Squad:

> The programme featured a man who had been convicted of indecency offences against young boys, which he had himself videoed. His ex-wife tried to prevent the programme from including his picture, for fear that her 5-year-old child would suffer serious distress as a result. The injunction was refused by the Court of Appeal, not after any balancing exercise between the rights of the child and freedom of expression, but because the court simply had no power to grant an injunction since the programme did not interfere with the effective working of the court's own jurisdiction in respect of children. Even if the programme would cause the child distress, this was not something that the court could prevent since it was in no way concerned with the care or upbringing of the child. In a strong judgment Lord Justice Hoffman forcefully reminded judges of the importance of respecting jurisdictional boundaries:
>
> > "It cannot be too strongly emphasised that outside the established exceptions (or any new ones which Parliament may enact in accordance with its obligations under the [European Human Rights] Convention) there is no question of balancing freedom of speech against other interests. It is a trump card which always wins."
>
> As for "balancing" different interests, he went on:

[25] [1975] Fam. 47—see p. 25 above.
[26] *M v. BBC* [1997] 1 F.L.R. 51.

"But a freedom which is restricted to what judges think to be responsible or in the public interest is no freedom. Freedom means the right to publish things which government and judges, however well motivated, think should not be published. It means the right to say things which "right thinking people" regard as dangerous or irresponsible. This freedom is subject only to clearly defined exceptions laid down by common law or statute."

The judges added that although Central had acted responsibly and humanely in taking steps to conceal the man's address and make sure not to refer to his wife and child, they were not legally obliged to take these steps.[27]

Lord Hoffman's views that there is an inevitable tendency for the Family Division judge at first instance to give too much weight to welfare and too little weight to freedom of speech has been acknowledged by the Court of Appeal. It observed that the tendency is reflected in the number of appeals in this field which succeed.[28]

The family court should also adopt a hands-off approach to the reporting of proceedings in other courts.[29] It should be for the judge conducting those other proceedings to decide whether to exercise any powers which he might have (e.g. under Children and Young Persons Act 1933, section 39 or the Youth Justice and Criminal Evidence Act 1999, section 45) to protect the child. The child's litigation friend would have standing to make an application in those other proceedings.[30]

In any balancing exercise, the interests of the child are important but not paramount

A second category of cases involve stories directed at the child or concerning its care or upbringing. The child killer Mary Bell was released on licence, having given birth to a child. The court refused an injunction to prevent these facts being given publicity, but it did prohibit the media from publishing the family's new name because of the harm to the child's upbringing if it had to suffer the resultant publicity.[31]

These types of injunctions may be justified even though the child will be oblivious to publicity. This was the case with the terminally ill Baby C, whom the court ruled should be allowed to die. Publicity would have impacted directly on the baby's carers, and indirectly this might have affected their treatment of her. The Court of Appeal imposed injunctions that not only preserved the child's anonymity, but also restrained dis-

---

[27] *R (Mrs) v. Central Television plc* [1994] Fam. 192, CA.
[28] *Re G (Celebrities: Publicity)* [1999] 1 F.L.R. 409, 418, CA.
[29] *R (Wardship: Restrictions on Publication)* [1994] Fam. 254, CA.
[30] *Ex p. Crook* [1995] 1 W.L.R. 139.
[31] *Re X (A Minor) (Wardship: Injunction)* [1984] 1 W.L.R. 1422. Fifteen years later the family was identified after Mary Bell told her story for a book.

closure of the hospital which was treating the child and the individuals responsible for the child's care. It also prohibited the solicitation of information relating to the child (unless it was already in the public domain) from the child's parents or staff at any hospital where she had been treated.[32]

In many of the cases where injunctions of this type have been sought, newspapers have wished to analyse and criticise the behaviour of local authorities in discharging their child protection functions. After the Cleveland affair, the courts have been more ready to accept the legitimacy of press investigations of this kind. At the same time, they have become more streetwise about tabloid entrapment techniques eliciting information from schoolchildren and unwary relatives and teachers. The result is often a limited restriction on publication which permits investigation and criticism of local authority actions, but without reference to details which might identify the children and with a specific ban on soliciting information from children, parents, teachers or carers. In Re W[33] the Court of Appeal distilled the following guidelines for balancing the interests of the child against the competing claims of freedom of speech:

● The Court attached great importance to safeguarding freedom of the press and to Article 10 of the European Convention.

● These freedoms were subject to exceptions, including restrictions imposed for the protection of children.

● In the balancing exercise the welfare of the child was *not* the paramount consideration.

● An important factor was the nature and extent of the public interest in the matter which it was sought to be publish.

● In almost every case the public interest would be satisfied without any identification of the child. However, the risk of some wider identification might have to be accepted on occasions if the story was to be told in a manner that would engage the interest of the general public. (In the particular case, the court refused to ban identification of the local authority because, although this might increase the risk of the child's identifica-

---

[32] *Re C (A Minor) (Wardship: Medical Treatment)(No. 2)* [1990] Fam. 39, CA. These restrictions will not automatically terminate with the patient's death although it would always be open to the media to return to court and argue that the balance of public interest had changed and some or all of the restrictions should be removed: *Re C (Adult Patient: Publicity)* [1996] 2 F.L.R. 251.

[33] [1992] 1 W.L.R. 100, see also *Re M (A Minor); Re N (A Minor)* [1990] Fam. 211, CA; *Re H-S (Minors) (Protection of Identity)* [1994] 1 W.L.R. 1141; and *In the Matter of X* October 13, 2000, Bracewell J.

tion, it was the authority's action which gave rise to the public interest.)

●   Any restraint was for the protection of the child and its carers. The restraint had to be in clear terms and no wider than necessary for that purpose. Save in exceptional circumstances, the child could not be protected from distress which might be caused by reading the publication.

Where the interests of the child are paramount

This position is exemplified by the unusual, indeed unique case of *Re Z*[34]:

> The father, a public figure, had notoriously abandoned his mistress after she had become pregnant. This child, whom he refused to meet, grew to teenage-hood with serious intellectual and physical handicaps. Such was the publicity given to these events that both father and mother, in the course of a maintenance dispute, applied for a wide-ranging injunction to protect the child from the media. Years later the mother appeared on a television programme and herself broke the injunction—in consequence, another injunction was imposed—this time, on her. Years passed, and the child progressed well, thanks to her mother's skills and devotion. Her devastating handicaps were particularly helped by a revolutionary new form of therapy she was undergoing in Israel, which was not available in Britain. *The Big Story* (Carlton) wanted to show, nationwide at prime time, how this therapy had benefited her. It would be a programme both inspirational and informative for parents with handicapped children, and so overwhelmingly for the public good. The viewing audience would have been large precisely because the parents were so well known. There was some evidence—and it was the mother's belief—that participating would do the child good, through increasing her self-esteem (although all the judges thought that the sensational nature of some of the ensuing press publicity, focusing on her father, would damage her). It would, of course, be mortifying for the father, who opposed (as, more authoritatively, did the Official Solicitor) the mother's efforts to untangle herself from the injunctions so the programme could be made.
>
> The Court of Appeal decided that she was still bound by them. The main (and probably determinative) ground was that injunctions already in place meant that the court was required to give preference to the interests of the child—as decided by judges who had never met her rather than by her devoted and intelligent mother. The interests of free speech were subsidiary. Overlooked in this approach, which gave more weight to speculative harm to the child than to the free speech rights of Carlton, not to mention the mother and the 14-year-old child, is that it never brought

---

[34] *Re Z (A Minor)(Freedom of publication)* [1997] Fam. 1, CA.

into the equation the rights of millions of viewers with handicapped children, who would have been informed and moved by the programme. On that calculus (given the uncertainty of any harm to the child) the moral balance came down heavily on the side of transmission: that the legal balance did not was probably because of the happenstance that injunctions against publicity were already in place. The courts have no right (even if they have the power) to stop Mrs Worthington from putting her daughter on the stage.

Hard cases make bad law, and this hard case was no exception. The court's decision was greeted with anger by some who knew the background, and very soon the father and mother, although covered by the court's anonymity orders, were named under privilege in Parliament.[35]

Mrs Worthington can at least put her daughter on the stage without seeking court approval. *Re Z* came about because the mother was already bound by injunctions that meant that the court had to consider a question about the upbringing of the child, which question required the child's interest to be paramount. That will not be the case where the press can publish what they wish without the child's own involvement or where the child is old enough to decide whether to assist the media or where the focus does not concern upbringing.[36]

A case which fell outside this third category concerned a 16-year-old who ran away from his grandmother's care to join a religious group. He was made a ward of court and the Family Division of the High Court ordered certain named individuals to hand the child over to the court's custody. The child contacted the BBC which recorded an interview with him and wished to broadcast it. Munby J. refused an injunction because the case was distinguishable from *Re Z*. The interests of the child were only paramount where he was the object of a process of upbringing. In this case the child was willingly co-operating with the interviewers—he was the subject of the activity in question not its object.[37] The judge also discharged an injunction that prevented the media from publishing comments by other members of the religious group on the subject of the child: although it was tempting to deprive them of the oxygen of publicity "the temptation must be sternly resisted" because it would deprive them of their right of free speech.

In the same case, Munby J. noted that *Re Z* was the only case which had thus far come within this third category.

The proliferation of child publicity orders can cause real difficulties

[35] *A and Byrne and Twenty-Twenty Television v. U.K.* (1998) 25 E.H.R.R. CD 159. Subsequently a complaint that this decision violated the rights of the mother and child to freedom from interference with family life and theirs and the TV company's freedom of expression was rejected by the European Commission of Human Rights.
[36] *e.g. Re W (Wardship: Discharge: Publicity)* [1995] 2 F.L.R. 466.
[37] *Kelly v. BBC* [2001] 1 All E.R. 323.

for the media. Where press injunctions are to be sought the case should be either brought in or transferred to the High Court.[38] The court should make quite clear that it is making an order rather than expressing a hope that publicity will be restrained. Similarly, the terms of the order should be as precise as possible.[39] Following the *Spycatcher* decisions (see p. 383) the party who sought the order, can extend its reach by giving notice to newspapers or broadcasters which might contemplate publicity. These orders are sometimes described as operating "*in rem*" or against the world, but that is not strictly accurate. A newspaper or broadcaster would only be in contempt if it knew of the order at the time of publication.[40] Wilful blindness is not a good defence. It is prudent for media organisations to establish a system for alerting their journalists to orders served on them.

Responsibility for reporting restriction offences

For the print media those responsible are the proprietor, editor and publisher. "Publisher" was given a wide interpretation in a 1998 case that upheld the conviction of the managing director of the publishing company on the grounds that he played a dominant role in the company and effectively controlled it.[41] This decision is difficult to square with the explicit provision in the same Act which makes directors and others liable for a company's crimes which were committed with their consent or connivance.[42] This managing director had no editorial input, had not read the article and did not suspect that it was going to be published. To say that he was nonetheless "in common sense terms" the publisher is to sweep aside the principle that companies have a legal personality distinct from their shareholders and officers.

A Scottish court had to consider a different aspect of publishing in connection with an Act prohibiting publication of evidence in divorce cases (see above p. 440). The charge had been brought in Paisley because that was where the divorce case had taken place and because the newspaper circulated there. The prosecution argued that the term "publish" should be treated as an activity that continued until the papers reached their ultimate readers. The paper (one of Express Newspapers titles) was printed and dispatched from London. The defendant argued that "publication" took place in London and the Scottish court had no

---

[38] *Re H-S Minors: Protection of Identity* [1994] 1 W.L.R. 1141.
[39] See, *e.g. Re L (A Minor) (Wardship: Freedom of Publication)* [1988] 1 All E.R. 418.
[40] See *Re L* above and *Cleveland County Council v. W, The Independent* April 29, May 4, 1988.
[41] *Brown v. DPP* (1998) 162 J.P. 333, QBD.
[42] Sexual Offences (Amendments) Act 1976, s. 5(4). Provisions like these are very common in statutes creating offences.

jurisdiction. The High Court of Justiciary ruled in the defendant's favour. It reasoned that the purpose of the legislation was to stop the offending material being put into the chain of distribution. This happened at the start of the chain of distribution and not at every stage thereafter. The court noted that the 1926 Act held responsible the proprietor, editor or publisher or printer but not a distributor, retailer or wholesaler. In this respect it contrasted with the Obscene Publications Act 1959 which did catch a wider category of people in the chain of selling obscene articles.[43] The 1933 Children and Young Persons Act, the Sexual Offences (Amendment) Act 1992 and the Youth Justice and Criminal Evidence Act 1999 cast their net in a similar way to the 1926 Act, though they are narrower because printers are not at risk.

This meaning of "publish" will determine not only the place of the alleged offence, but its timing. Most of the reporting offences are summary only offences. As such, they can (generally) only be prosecuted within six months. If the High Court's interpretation was followed in England, it would mean that the time for prosecution would not be extended if, for instance, a monthly magazine was sold in the shops or available for down-loading from the internet for some protracted period of time.[44]

Attorney-General's references to the Court of Appeal

A jury's verdict is final. However damning the evidence, a jury has an unreviewable power to return a verdict of not guilty. However, a legal ruling of the trial judge made before the acquittal can be referred by the Attorney-General to the Court of Appeal.[45] The court may decide the point of law in the Attorney-General's favour, but still cannot reverse the acquittal. To protect defendants, court rules require their identity to be kept secret unless they consent to be named.[46] These rules apply as well if there is a further appeal to the House of Lords.[47] In practice this means that the Court of Appeal or the House of Lords has to make an order prohibiting identification. If the restriction is broken, the publisher can be punished for contempt, but only if it knew of the order. A person who is identified in breach of an order does not have a right of action

---

[43] *Procurator Fiscal v. Scott* September 7, 1999, HCJ.
[44] See similarly *R v. Regan,* Southwark Crown Court, June 17, 1999 (unreported)—but see *The Yearbook of Copyright and Media Law 2000* (OUP, 2000), p. 436. This was a case under Representation of the People Act 1983, s. 106—see below, p. 540.
[45] Criminal Justice Act 1972, s. 36.
[46] Criminal Appeal (Reference of Points of Law) Rules 1973 (S.I. 1973 No. 1114), r.6.
[47] Criminal Appeal Act 1968, s. 35.

for damages.[48] The court in this case also emphasised that such orders were *not* intended to forestall any further journalistic investigation of the facts of the offence with a view to establishing whether the acquitted defendant was, in truth, guilty. If the paper got it wrong, his remedy was in libel. It is different where the Attorney-General refers to the Court of Appeal a sentence that he considers unduly lenient.[49] Here the court is not just concerned with the abstract question of whether the sentence was wrong in principle, but can increase or alter the sentence actually imposed. Consequently, there is no need for any special protection for the defendant and these references can be reported in the usual way.

Indecent evidence

An Act of 1926 prohibits publication in relation to any judicial proceedings of "any indecent matter or indecent medical, surgical or physiological details being matter or details the publication of which would be calculated to injure public morals".[50] The vulnerability of public morals must be judged by current standards,[51] which are permissive and the complete absence of recent prosecutions indicates that this section is now in practice a dead letter. The proceedings in both the *Lady Chatterley's Lover* and *Oz* magazine trials were published in book form and in television re-enactments without objection, despite the sexual explicitness and repetition of allegedly "obscene" passages.

The last edition of this work described the 1926 Act as a dead letter. However, in 1996, it was mysteriously invoked to stop the reporting of evidence in the Moynihan peerage case, a sordid scrap over who had the hereditary title to sit in the House of Lords—the Filipino child of the eldest Lord (a depraved brothel-owner) or his younger brother, the then Tory Minister for Sport. There was no rational reason for the order, which served only to cover up evidence which would have underlined the absurdity of giving parliamentary seats to hereditary peers.

SECRECY ORDERS

Section 11 orders

In certain circumstances the courts may invoke an inherent power to order that the names of witnesses should not be published. Blackmail

---

[48] *WB (An Individual) v. H. Bauer Publishing Ltd,* June 14, 2001, Eady J.
[49] Criminal Justice Act 1988, ss. 35 and 36.
[50] Judicial Proceedings (Regulation of Reports) Act 1926, s. 1(1)(a).
[51] *Knuller v. DPP* [1973] A.C. 435.

cases have provided one example.[52] The policy, as with rape cases, is to encourage victims to come forward to testify against their tormentors. Blackmail victims are rarely likely to testify unless assured that their guilty secrets will not leak out. The power is now formalised by section 11 of the Contempt Act, which provides:

> "In any case where a court (having power to do so) allows a name or other matter to be withheld from the public in proceedings before the court, the court may give such directions prohibiting the publication of that name or matter in connection with the proceedings as appear to the court to be necessary for the purpose for which it was so withheld."

Section 11 does not give courts a new power to take evidence in secret where one did not previously exist, but, where this is appropriate, it provides the means for punishing disclosure. In the absence of a statutory power this means that there must be some overwhelming reason in the interests of the administration of justice why the normal principle of open justice should be abrogated.

> The defendant to a minor road traffic offence was a former M.P. His home address was not given orally to the court because, he said, he feared further harassment from his ex-wife. The magistrates agreed and made an order under section 11 forbidding its publication. The Divisional Court held that while evidence could be communicated to the court in writing if the proper administration of justice demanded it, there were no good reasons in the present case. Many defendants would prefer that their identity was not revealed, "but section 11 was not enacted for the comfort and feelings of defendants". The order was quashed.[53]

---

[52] *R. v. Socialist Worker Printers & Publishers Ltd, ex p. Att.-Gen.* [1975] Q.B. 637.

[53] *R. v. Evesham Justices, ex p. McDonagh* [1988] 1 All E.R. 371, 384, QBD. It is a common failing of common law judges to supress names for reasons that appear reasonable, but that have nothing to do with the strict needs of the administration of justice. Powerful appellate rebukes of this behaviour are to be found in the Australian cases of *Raybos Australia Pty Ltd v. Jones* (1985) 2 N.S.W.L.R. 47 (reversing a suppression order on the name of a leading solicitor accused of conspiracy in a civil action, made because of damage to his professional reputation from possibly unfounded accusation) and *John Fairfax & Sons v. Police Tribunal of NSW* (1986) 5 N.S.W.L.R. 465 (reversing a suppression order on the name of a police informant, because it had already been mentioned in public and so the order could not have been necessary to secure justice in the particular proceedings). See also *R. v. Dover Justices, ex p. Dover District Council* (1992) 156 J.P. 433 where "exceptional circumstances" justifying restrictions on publicity did not include the fact that it might have dire economic consequences leading to the closure of the defendant's business. (The defendant was a restaurateur who failed to win approval for a ban on the reporting of proceedings brought against him by a council health department.)

The High Court in Northern Ireland similarly quashed a magistrate's order prohibiting publication of the name or address or the defendant or the charge against him in an indecent assault case.[54] The magistrate had been persuaded that there was a risk that the defendant would be attacked as had others facing similar types of allegations. The High Court said:

> "A possible attack upon the accused by ill-motivated persons cannot be regarded as a consequence of the publication of the proceedings of the court which should influence the court in its deliberations and the danger of its occurrence should not cause the court to depart from well-established principles."

If publication of the names or addresses of witnesses might lead to physical attack, the court may find a sufficient threat to the administration of justice to justify an order under section 11.[55] Even so, the claim for a suppression order should be reviewed critically. If the source of the threat already knows the witness's identity and address, there is no point in prohibiting publication. Physical threats of this type should also be distinguished from mere embarrassment:

> At a kidnapping trial an Old Bailey judge ordered that the identity of the main prosecution witness (the alleged victim) should not be publicised. She was a member of a wealthy and famous family. She was also undergoing treatment for heroin addiction and it was said that publicity would damage her recovery. The judge's section 11 order was challenged in the Divisional Court, which indicated that it would have quashed the order if it had jurisdiction to do so. There was a danger that the witness had been accorded special treatment because of her family connections. It was common for witnesses to be faced with embarrassment as a result of facts that were elicited in the course of proceedings or of allegations made without real substance. However, it was an essential part of British justice that cases should be tried in public and this consideration had to outweigh the individual interests of particular persons.[56]

A further reason for criticising the order of the judge in the *Belfast Telegraph* and *Crook* cases was that the person's name had been openly used in court. In a subsequent case in 1985 the Divisional Court confirmed that an order under section 11 cannot be made to prevent publica-

---

[54] *R. v. Newtonabbey Magistrates' Court, ex p. Belfast Telegraph Newspapers Ltd, The Times*, August 27, 1997; see though *Venables v. News Group Newspapers Ltd* above, p. 287.

[55] See, for instance *Appeal of East Anglian Daily Times Ltd* (unreported) June 11, 1992.

[56] *R. v. Central Criminal Court, ex p. Crook, The Times*, November 8, 1984; (1985) L.S. Gaz. 1408, QBD.

tion of a name (or other evidence) once it has already been spoken in proceedings before the court.[57] This rule can take by surprise judges who find it cumbersome to conceal the identities of witnesses from a public gallery which is often empty. Yet the principle is important. Although the press is segregated from the general public they are there as the eyes and ears of the public who cannot be present. Unless the legislation clearly says something different, if the public in court can hear evidence or names, the public outside court (through the medium of the press) should be free to do so as well.

This link between secrecy in court and out of court is broken by the Youth Justice and Criminal Evidence Act. Orders under section 46 (when in force) will allow a court to make an order conferring anonymity on witnesses who would be in fear or distress (see below).

If the prosecution or defence apply to a Crown Court for an order that all or part of a trial should be held in secret in order to protect the identity of a witness or any other person, advance notice must be given to allow an appeal against these restrictions on open justice to be taken to the Court of Appeal. The requirements are the same as where a court is invited to sit in secret for national security reasons (see p. 42).

It is increasingly common for civil courts to be asked to make section 11 orders. The common law test to be satisfied is the same: it must be shown that free reporting would frustrate or render impracticable the administration of justice.[58]

An application for judicial review of a housing authority's decision was brought by claimants who were HIV-positive. The court refused to allow them to be referred to by initials. They had not shown that publicity would impede justice and a general assertion that those with a similar condition might refrain from exercising legal remedies was not sufficient justification for the order.[59] In *R. v. Somerset Health Authority, ex p. S*[60] the court made an anonymity order for a claimant seeking review of a refusal to fund gender reassignment surgery but warned that more evidence would be needed at the substantive hearing to show that others would be dissuaded from seeking relief if publicity were given to their names. In *R. v. Huddersfield JJ., ex p. D*[61] a police informant was allowed to bring judicial review proceedings anonymously when

---

[57] *R. v. Arundel Justices, ex p. Westminster Press Ltd* [1985] 1 W.L.R. 708. Committal hearings are different "proceedings" to the trial for these purposes and so a Crown Court has power to make a s. 11 order prohibiting publication of names which were used openly before magistrates. However, this prior publicity is a factor which should disincline a judge to accede to a request for a s. 11 order: *Appeal of East Anglian Daily Times Ltd* (above, n. 55).

[58] *Att.-Gen. v. Leveller Magazine Ltd* [1979] A.C. 440.

[59] *R. v. Westminster City Council, ex p. Castelli* (1995) 7 Admin. L.R. 840.

[60] [1996] C.O.D. 244.

[61] [1997] C.O.D. 27.

he complained (successfully) of the magistrates' refusal to hear in private details of his assistance to the police.

A more difficult issue is whether the court should permit anonymity because publicity would cause significant harm to his or her mental health. The Court of Appeal made an order on these grounds when deciding whether a medical negligence claim for the loss of a penis should be tried by a jury or by a judge alone[62] but this point of law had nothing to do with the claimant's identity. More controversially a Divisional Court allowed an HIV claimant to remain anonymous after evidence that publicity would be extremely destructive psychologically, although it was not suggested that he would withdraw his claim if anonymity was refused.[63] The Divisional Court had previously allowed anonymity to a claimant who alleged she had been sexually abused by her step-father because of the psychiatric and psychological damage which public identification would cause.[64] However, a future applicant in the same position would have protection from identification under the Sexual Offences (Amendment) Act 1992 even without an order—see p. 436.

Anonymity will not be granted merely because publicity to the claim might damage the applicant's business. Thus a firm of solicitors who wished to challenge the Legal Aid Board's decision to remove their franchise for criminal legal aid was refused an anonymity order.[65] In this case the Court of Appeal made clear that it was insufficient to achieve an anonymity order that the claimant would otherwise not bring the case: there had to be some reasonable justification for that stance. The Court of Appeal has also warned that when both sides are agreed that information should be kept from the public the court should be most vigilant.[66]

The common law test rightly strives to confine the power to give anonymity. The Civil Procedure Rules, regrettably, are expansive: they say simply that "the court may order that the identity of any party or witness must not be disclosed if it considers non-disclosure necessary in order to protect the interests of that party or witness."[67] On their face these rules seem to be a dramatic and unprincipled erosion of open justice. It must be hoped that the courts will continue much as before by either exercising their discretion only in situations where justice would otherwise be rendered impracticable or by reading into the word "neces-

[62] *H. v. Ministry of Defence* [1991] 2 All E.R. 834.
[63] *Re D (Protection of Party Anonymity)* (1998) 1 C.C.L. Rep. 190.
[64] *R. v. Criminal Injuries Compensation Board, ex p. A* [1992] C.O.D. 379.
[65] *R. v. Legal Aid Board, ex p. Kaim Todner (A firm of solicitors)* [1999] Q.B. 966 where the Court of Appeal reviewed the applicable principles.
[66] *Ex p. P, The Times,* March 31, 1998, CA and *R. v. Legal Aid Board, ex p. Kaim Todner,* above.
[67] CPR, r.39.2.

sary" something more than an examination of what is required to protect the particular interests of the party or witness and instead only make
an order if those interests are so overwhelming that they should displace
the ordinary practice of open justice.

Before an editor or reporter can be held in contempt for disobedience
to a partial secrecy order, there must be a clear ruling expressed as a
formal order. So much is clear from *Attorney-General v. Leveller Magazine Ltd.*[68]

> During committal proceedings in the "ABC" Official Secrets case (see p.
> 557) the prosecution called an expert witness. The magistrates allowed
> his real name to be written down and shown to the parties, but said that
> he was to be referred to publicly as Colonel B, since the prosecution
> claimed that revelation of his true identity would prejudice national secur-
> ity. In the course of giving evidence, the Colonel provided information
> from which reporters in court, by subsequently consulting army publica-
> tions, deduced his name and position. The *Leveller* and other magazines
> gleefully published this discovery, and were prosecuted for contempt on
> the basis that they had flouted a court order. The House of Lords held
> that the press action was not contempt, for a number of reasons:
>
> ● It had not been shown to interfere with the administration of justice.
> ● The magistrates' action may well have amounted to an implied request
>   that the press should not publish the name, but before contempt could
>   be proved there had to be disobedience to a clear order by the court.
> ● The Colonel had effectively "blown his own cover" by his answers
>   to questions in open court.

As a result of section 11, any partial secrecy order should be in writing, state its precise scope, the time it should cease to have effect (if
appropriate) and the specific purpose of making the order. Courts must
normally give notice to the press that an order has been made and court
staff should be prepared to answer specific inquiries about orders.[69]

Postponement orders

Reports of evidence in a trial will not generally pose any risk at all
since they convey to the public at large only what has been presented
in open court. Consequently, they cannot be contempt of court.[70] Section
4(1) of the Contempt of Court Act 1981 formalises this position. It
gives an express right to publish in good faith a fair, accurate and con-

---

[68] *Att.-Gen. v. Leveller Magazine Ltd* [1979] A.C. 440.
[69] *Practice Direction: (Contempt of Court Act: Reports of Proceedings: Postponement
Orders)* [1983] 1 All E.R. 64 and see n. 81 below.
[70] *Buenos Aires Gas Co Ltd v. Wilde* (1880) 42 L.T. 657.

temporaneous report of public legal proceedings. A report is "accurate"
if its gist is correct even if not word perfect. Reports are contemporaneous if they are published as soon as practicable after a temporary legal
restriction on reporting ends.

Section 4(2) of the Act gives the court a power to make an order
postponing the publication of certain matters heard in open court:

> "In any such proceedings the court may where it appears to be
> necessary for avoiding a substantial risk of prejudice to the admin-
> istration of justice in those proceedings, or in any proceedings
> pending or imminent, order that the publication of any report of
> the proceedings, or any part of the proceedings, be postponed for
> such period as the court thinks necessary for that purpose."

Applications for orders under this section in criminal trials are usually
made in two situations. The first is where legal argument takes place in
the jury's absence so as to avoid any risk of prejudice. This purpose
would be frustrated if jurors could read an account of what was said in
the press the next day. Consistently with this purpose, orders made
under section 4(2) for this purpose ought to lapse once the jury has
returned its verdict.

Judges do not always remember to make section 4(2) orders to cover
discussions in the absence of the jury. If they do not then the media
ought to have a defence under section 4(1) to an allegation that a report
of the proceedings was a strict liability contempt. This was accepted in
the official secrets trial of Clive Ponting, where McCowan J. forgot to
make an order and *The Guardian* decided to report his comments about
Ponting's defence (the report did the defence no harm—Ponting was
acquitted). However, a guide to reporting restrictions in the Crown
Court published by the Society of Editors, the Newspaper Society and
the Judicial Studies Board[71] suggests that publication in these circumstances would be common law contempt because it would interfere with
the course of justice as a continuing process in criminal proceedings by
defeating the whole purpose of the jury withdrawing. However, this
type of publication is no more a general threat to the integrity of criminal justice than any other prejudicial publication. The issue remains
unresolved.[72]

Section 4(2) orders are unnecessary where statutory restrictions on
reporting will apply in any case, as with preparatory hearings and preliminary rulings.[73]

---

[71] August 2000.

[72] Of course a report of proceedings in the jury's absence would still have to be "fair"
and in "good faith" to attract the protection of s. 4(1)—see Miller *Contempt of
Court* (3rd ed., OUP, 2000) paras 10.96 and 10.108.

[73] see pp. 426.

The second type of situation where section 4(2) orders are often made is more controversial and much more common. Following a large police investigation there may be more charges and/or defendants than can be conveniently tried by one jury at a single trial. The prosecution will then elect, or the court will order, a series of trials. It is common for the defendants in the second or later trials to argue that reporting of the first or earlier trials would prejudice their cases. In considering such an application the judge should ask the following questions:

- *Are the proceedings which might be prejudiced the ones where reporting is to be restricted or some others "pending or imminent"?* Where a series of trials have been ordered they would all be pending. Less obviously, a future trial is "pending or imminent" at the time of committal proceedings even though none would take place if the magistrates were to rule that there was no case to answer.[74] Nonetheless magistrates should be wary of supplementing the reporting restrictions regime which applies in any event to committals by making an order under section 4(2). It will be rare that the remaining tests considered below will be satisfied.[75] A person whose acquittal of an offence is tainted by an "administration of justice offence" (perverting the course of justice, perjury or intimidation of witnesses or jurors) can be retried for the original offence. If a retrial is a potential possibility, it is to be treated as a pending or imminent proceeding so that a court dealing with the administration of justice offence can make a postponement order.[76] However, here as well, the court should only make a section 4(2) order if the remaining tests are satisfied.

- *If no order is made, will there be a substantial risk of prejudice?* Defendants who apply for postponement orders · often raise a fear of inflammatory and unfair reporting. This is not relevant because reporting which is prejudicial will in any case constitute contempt of court under the strict liability rule (see p. 352). If the prejudicial publicity is not a report of legal proceedings, or if the report is biased or otherwise unfair, the publisher will get no help from the defence in section 4(1) and an order under section 4(2) would be superfluous. Consequently, the court should focus its attention on the likely effect of reporting which does meet the criteria of the section 4(1)

---

[74] *R. v. Horsham JJ. ex p. Farquharson* [1982] Q.B. 762.
[75] *R. v. Beaconsfield JJ. ex p. Westminster Press* (1994) 158 J.P. 1055.
[76] Criminal Procedure and Investigations Act 1996, s. 57 adding s. 4(2A) to Contempt of Court Act 1981—see further on tainted acquittals p. 370.

defence, *i.e.* fair and accurate, in good faith, contemporaneous reporting of proceedings which took place in open court.[77]

It will be very unusual for reporting with these qualities to pose a *substantial* risk of prejudice. It is often said to be different if the trials have common defendants so that convictions in the first will be known by the jury in the second, or if there is a common prosecution witness whose standing in the eyes of a second jury may be enhanced if it knows that his evidence was believed by an earlier jury. Yet it is wrong to assume that substantial prejudice is likely in these situations. If there is an appreciable gap between the trials the jurors in the second trial may well not recall publicity surrounding the first. In any case, where the trial is lengthy (as each one in a series of trials often is), there is an acknowledged tendency for the jury to become more inward looking and to follow directions from the trial judge to disregard previous (or even contemporaneous) publicity.[78]

- *Is a restriction order necessary to avoid the risk of prejudice?* Necessity means more than convenience. No postponement order may be "necessary" if a substantial risk of prejudice can be avoided by other means. Delaying the start of the second trial or altering its venue may be feasible alternatives which would make a postponement of reporting of the first trial unnecessary. So, too, in *Central Television plc*[79] the Court of Appeal condemned a trial judge's order postponing television and radio reports of a case while the jury was sequestered in a hotel. The Court of Appeal did not accept that there was any risk of prejudice, but if there had been, it could have been avoided quite simply by directing that the jurors not have access to television and radio.

Yet even if the judge concludes that reporting would cause a substantial risk of prejudice which cannot be avoided by these other measures, it does *not* automatically follow that some kind of section 4(2) order must be made.[80] The court must go on to consider whether the public interest in free reporting outweighs the risk of prejudice in the particular case.

---

[77] *Scarsbrook v. H.M.A.*, September 7, 2000, High Court of Justiciary.
[78] See Lawton J. in *R. v. Kray*, 53 Cr. App. R. 412, 414, Sir John Donaldson M.R. in *Att.-Gen. v. News Group Newspapers Ltd* [1987] QB 1, 16, and Lord Taylor C.J. in *Ex parte Telegraph plc* (above) and see p. 355 as to the test for strict liability contempt.
[79] [1991] 1 W.L.R. 4.
[80] See for instance *R. v. Beck* (1992) 94 Cr. App. R. 376, 380; and *MGN v. Bank of America* [1995] 2 All ER 355, 368, Ch D.

Some courts analyse this as part of the "necessity" test[81] and recognise the affinity between "necessity" in this sense and the way that the expression is used in Article 10(2).[82] Others see it as the exercise of a separate discretion which the court has because the section 4(2) says an order "may" be made,[83] but all decisions are unanimous that such a balancing is essential. The common law principle of open justice is premised on the idea that absolutely free reporting is in the public interest. Where a case has acquired particular notoriety, where criminality of a particularly serious kind is alleged, where prominent people are involved or where for other reasons there is a heightened public interest in the media having freedom to report, judges ought to be even more reluctant to impose reporting restrictions. Especially in these cases the public interest is better served by fair and accurate reporting rather than inaccurate or misleading rumours which can proliferate when contemporaneous reporting is prevented.

It is no justification for a section 4(2) order that it will "merely" *postpone* rather than indefinitely prohibit reporting. Freedom of communication means the right to report news contemporaneously and no departure from that norm should be taken lightly. Besides, the practical reality is that a news organisation which cannot report a case contemporaneously is unlikely to assign journalists to it so that a temporary ban will, in practical terms, often be a permanent one.

- *If some order is to be made what is the minimum interference with the usual principle of free reporting?* The order can only be said to be "necessary" if it goes no further than is needed to prevent the risk of prejudice. Thus it may be that only reporting of certain parts of the evidence needs to be postponed, or it may be sufficient if the names of certain witnesses are not reported until the conclusion of the trial series. It is also important to remember that the section only empowers a court to order the postponement of "reports of the proceedings". Section 4(2) cannot, for instance, be used to prevent the broadcasting of a film of the defendant's arrest (these are not part of the proceedings),[84] a background article to the case

---

[81] *e.g. ex p. Telegraph plc* [1993] 1 W.L.R. 980, CA.

[82] *R. v. Sherwood, ex p. Telegraph Group, The Times,* June 12, 2001, CA.

[83] *e.g. MGN Pension Trustees v. Bank of America National Trust and Savings Association* (above).

[84] *R. v. Rhuddlan JJ., ex p. HTV Ltd* [1986] Crim. L.R. 329.

which is not a court report,[85] or the interviewing or filming of witnesses outside court. Of course, precisely because these are not court reports, journalists will not be protected by section 4(1) and independently of any order, they will have to be careful that such stories or investigations are not contempt of court.

In the Maxwell case, the judge rejected an argument that a fair trial was impossible because of extensive publicity. However, in his ruling he reminded the media of the strict liability rule and said that since the trial involved issues about the conduct of Robert Maxwell and his sons "I shall expect the media will forthwith desist from publication of matter that is derogatory either of these Defendants or of the late Robert Maxwell".[86] This was not, and could not be, an order, but it had some effect. A judge is in a powerful position to refer reports to the Attorney-General. Exhortations of this kind have to be considered seriously. However, because they are not orders, the ultimate issue for publishers remains whether any particular story will infringe the strict liability rule, not whether it will contravene the judge's wishes.

If the court does decide to make an order, a practice direction provides:

> "It is necessary to keep a permanent record of such orders for later reference. For this purpose all orders made under section 4(2) must be formulated in precise terms having regard to the decision of *R. v. Horsham Justices, ex p. Farquharson* [1982] 2 All E.R. 269; [1982] Q.B. 762, and orders under both sections must be committed to writing either by the judge personally or by the clerk of the court under the judge's directions. An order must state (a) its precise scope, (b) the time at which it shall cease to have effect, if appropriate, and (c) the specific purpose of making the order.
>
> Courts will normally give notice to the press in some form that an order has been made under either section of the 1981 Act and the court staff should be prepared to answer any enquiry about a specific case, but it is, and will remain, the responsibility of those reporting cases, and their editors, to ensure that no breach of any order occurs and the onus rests with them to make enquiry in any case of doubt".[87]

It is not sufficient, as used to be the practice at the Old Bailey until

---

[85] *Scarsbrook v. Her Majesty's Advocate*, September 7, 2000, High Court of Justiciary.
[86] See *Oxford Yearbook of Media and Entertainment Law* (1996), p. 356.
[87] *Practice Direction: (Contempt of Court Act: Reports of Proceedings: Postponement Orders)* [1983] 1 All E.R. 64.

1991, to rely on the shorthand writer's note of the order; the order itself must actually be put into writing.[88]

Derogatory assertions in mitigation

Courts were given new powers in 1997 to stop the reporting of derogatory assertions in pleas in mitigation or in sentence appeals.[89] "Derogatory" is not comprehensively defined but it includes allegations that the third party's conduct has been criminal, immoral or improper.[90] The court must have substantial grounds for believing that the assertion is false *or* irrelevant. Thus the reporting of a relevant allegation can be prevented merely because there are substantial grounds for believing that it is untrue.[91] There is an important safeguard in the further requirement that the assertion has not been made at the trial at which the defendant was convicted or during any other proceedings relating to the offence.[92] This will be no protection where the defendant has pleaded guilty and there has been no trial, but then, before an order is made, there must be some material on which the court could form the necessary judgment that there are substantial grounds for believing that the allegation is untrue or irrelevant.

The new power derives from a recommendation of the Runciman Commission on Criminal Justice which saw it as a "last resort" for use in "the extreme case of a defendant apparently using the opportunity of a speech in mitigation to do as much damage as possible to the reputation of the victim or a third party without risk of retaliation."[93] This recommendation was made and adopted without any evidence of the need for any such new power, which makes a serious inroad into the common law's "open justice" principle.

"Derogatory allegations" made in mitigation are occasionally very important—especially when they are made by counsel, who has a professional duty to ensure that they have some relevance. They can be accusations against more significant conspirators the police have not been smart enough to catch, or they might be allegations naming lawyers and accountants as professionals who have lent their services to frauds or criminal gangs. Sometimes they are newsworthy not because the allegation is true but because it is made by barristers and taken seriously by judges. In the 1970s, for example, barristers mitigating for

---

[88] *R. v. Nat West Investment Bank,* (unreported) January 11, 1991, (Central Criminal Court, McKinnon J.
[89] Criminal Procedure and Investigations Act 1996, ss. 58–61.
[90] *ibid.,* s. 58(4)(a).
[91] *ibid.,* s. 58(4)(b).
[92] *ibid.,* s. 58(5).
[93] Royal Commission on Criminal Justice (HMSO, 1993) Cm. 2263, para. 47.

rapists often said "she asked for it", and spouse-murders were reduced to manslaughter and then lightly punished because the wife was said by the defence counsel to be a nag or a feminist or promiscuous. These types of mitigation only stopped because they were widely reported, and widely and logically derided. It is wholly wrong that judges should have the power (whether or not they exercise it) to censor publication of what counsel or their clients say in open court.

The usual time for deciding whether to make an order will be after the court has determined sentence. The order must then be made as soon as reasonably practicable. The order continues in force for 12 months (unless it is previously revoked). But there will be few cases where the news value in a derogatory allegation is sufficient for editors to resurrect it for publication on its first anniversary. An interim order can be made where there is a real possibility of a final order being made. Although the power to make a final order is expressly not dependent on an interim order having first been made,[94] if the derogatory assertion has already received wide publicity, this would be a strong reason against making a final order.

Publication of the assertion in breach of the order is an offence punishable with a maximum fine of scale 5 (Currently £5,000).[95] There is a worrying uncertainty in the way in which the offence is drafted. The section appears to penalise publication of the assertion whether or not this is part of a report of the proceedings but this would be extraordinary. It is very difficult to see why a newspaper should be prevented from publishing a derogatory story (which it is prepared to defend in any libel proceedings) merely because the same allegation happened to have been made in a plea in mitigation by a defendant who had not done the same research or where the criminal court did not wish to be distracted by a lengthy examination of whether the allegations were true. Any such interpretation would clearly conflict with Article 10 of the European Human Rights Convention and section 3 of the Human Rights Act 1998 obliges the courts to adopt the "possible" alternative of reading down the offence so that it is confined to reports of the proceedings.

Challenging orders restricting reporting or access

Judges and magistrates have been tempted into making wide and unnecessary orders because frequently none of the parties before the court opposes them. It is usually defendants who make the application. The prosecution generally either supports it or stands aloof and indifferent.

---

[94] Criminal Procedure and Investigations Act 1996, s. 58(8)(d).
[95] *ibid.*, s. 60. Unusually for reporting offences, the Attorney-General's consent is not necessary.

The media interests who are affected and who do oppose them are not heard. Sometimes the media must go on the offensive to protect the public right to know.

How can such orders be challenged? There are four ways.

Application for revocation of order

The first is for the media representatives to ask the judge to revoke his or her order. It is unusual for outsiders like journalists to make applications to the trial court, but the media are so obviously affected by orders restricting publicity that it is manifestly fair that representations which they wish to make against proposed orders should be heard. The Divisional Court has expressly ruled that magistrates have this power[96] and the Divisional Court and Court of Appeal has encouraged Crown Courts to do the same, making (if really necessary) a temporary order until a suitable date can be arranged for hearing representations from the media.[97]

Publish and be damned

The second (and by far the most risky of the four) is to publish the report in defiance of the order. If the order is made without jurisdiction, it is most unlikely that contempt proceedings would be brought or, if they were, that they would result in any penalty. The risk is in gauging whether a court would subsequently agree that the order was not merely unwise but so badly wrong as to have been made without jurisdiction. This route remains a last option if the circumstances preclude any of the other methods of challenge and the order is blatantly erroneous.

Judicial review

The third way is for the journalist or the publisher to apply to the High Court for judicial review to quash the order. The procedure is the same as described for challenging the continuation of committal reporting restrictions (see p. 425). Again, the court will not come to its own view as to whether the order was right or wrong, but only whether it was lawfully made. This will include judging whether it was an order that any reasonable tribunal could have made. Any person with a "sufficient interest" in the decision to be challenged can apply for judicial review.[98] The media clearly have standing to contest the legality of orders

---

[96] *R. v. Clerkenwell JJ. ex p. Telegraph plc* [1993] Q.B. 462.
[97] *R. v. Beck* (1992) 94 Cr.App.R. 376 and *Att.-Gen. v. Guardian Newspapers Ltd (No. 3)* [1992] 1 W.L.R. 874.
[98] Supreme Court Act 1981, s. 31(3).

restricting reporting. However, defendants also have sufficient interest
to ask for a review of a refusal to impose reporting restrictions. They,
too, will fail unless they can show there was an error of law.[99] This
route is available if the order has been made by a magistrates' court or
by the Crown Court when it is hearing an appeal, a committal for sentence or a civil matter. However, nothing relating to a trial on indictment can be judicially reviewed (Supreme Court Act 1981, s. 29(1)). In
Crook (see p. 454) the Divisional Court found that because of this the
media were barred from using judicial review to challenge secrecy
orders erroneously made in the course of a Crown Court trial. This
unhappy position led the media to complain to the European Court of
Human Rights at Strasbourg, which, in turn, obliged the Government to
provide a statutory right to appeal (see below) but only to the Court of
Appeal and not further to the House of Lords.[1]

Appeal

The changes that the Government made to the law as a result of the
media's complaints to Strasbourg were incorporated in section 159 of
the Criminal Justice Act 1988. It allows an aggrieved person to appeal
against any of the following:

- partial secrecy (section 11) and postponement orders (section
  4(2)) made in relation to a trial on indictment (i.e., to a criminal
  trial at a Crown Court);

- any order restricting the access of the public to the whole or
  any part of a trial on indictment or any ancillary proceedings;

- any order restricting the publication of any report of the whole
  or any part of a trial on indictment or ancillary proceedings;

- a Crown court order restricting reporting of derogatory assertions.

Because openness and free reporting are the norm, a crown court
judge's *refusal* to restrict access or reporting is not amenable to the
special appeal under section 159.[2]

This new avenue of appeal extends beyond Contempt Act orders. It
would include, for instance, orders restricting the publication of the
identity of young witnesses or parties; orders under the Official Secrets
Act requiring part of the trial to be in secret; and orders under the

[99] *R. v. Clerkenwell JJ. ex p. Trachtenberg* [1993] C.O.D. 93.
[1] *Hodgson and Channel 4 v. U.K.* (1988) 56 D.R. 156.
[2] *R. v. S* [1995] 2 Cr. App. R. 347.

common law power to conduct part of the trial in the absence of the public where the administration of justice is said to demand it. Arguably, the public's access to part of the trial is also restricted if the court accepts evidence (*e.g.* a name or an address) in writing that is not read aloud.

There are, however, important limitations on this new route. It is not a *right* of appeal. Permission must first be obtained from the Court of Appeal. Because it applies only to criminal cases tried by juries, it is powerless to correct the decisions of magistrates or civil courts that, though wrong, are not so wrong as to be unreasonable or otherwise amenable to judicial review. It is also unusual in that the Court of Appeal has the last word. There is no further appeal to the House of Lords. The court can make "such order as to costs as it thinks fit"[3] but not for the costs to be paid out of central funds.[4] The possibility of asking for a costs order against the party who sought the restriction order is usually theoretical: defendants often have no money and the prosecution will usually confine itself to "assisting the court" in which case it is not usually ordered to pay costs unless it has improperly applied for an order that should not have been made.[5] Despite these qualifications, it is an important reform, which provides a long-needed avenue for curbing the proliferation of exclusion, secrecy and postponement orders in criminal cases.

Where the Crown Court has made an order restricting reporting, the application for leave to appeal must be made within fourteen days (although there is power to extend this). The application will need to set out the case fully because it can be determined without a hearing. If leave is granted the Court of Appeal can take evidence, but this will normally be in writing.[6] The court will not hesitate to quash an order even though its force has long since been spent. In *Re Central Television plc*[7] the order banning television and radio reports had applied for only one night, while the jury was at a hotel. Six months later, when the appeal was heard by the Court of Appeal, it ruled that section 159 could not provide an effective remedy unless it could be used to reverse spent orders, which might otherwise appear to have been made properly.

Appeals against a secret hearing on national security grounds or for the protection of a witness's identity are highly unsatisfactory. The rules allow only 24 hours for an application for leave to appeal (although a

---

[3] Criminal Justice Act 1988, s. 159(5)(c).
[4] *Holden and Co v. CPS (No. 2)* [1994] 1 A.C. 22.
[5] *Ex p. News Group Newspapers Ltd, The Times*, May 21, 1999.
[6] Criminal Appeal Rules, r.16A added by Criminal Appeal Amendment Rules 1989 (S.I. 1989 No. 1102).
[7] [1991] 1 W.L.R. 4.

precautionary notice can be set down in advance). In these cases both the leave application and the appeal itself are determined without a hearing.[8]

The Court of Appeal has held that these rules are within the intention of the 1988 Act. It noted that there was nothing to prevent an applicant putting written submissions before the court.[9] A written submission of this kind succeeded in 1998:[10]

> At an Old Bailey fraud trial the defendants wished to argue that the trial should be stayed as an abuse of process, but they wanted to make this argument in private on grounds of national security. Notably, the Crown was neutral on the application. Media representatives (and their lawyers) were excluded from court and the judge agreed that the "abuse" argument should be made in private. *The Observer*'s appeal against this ruling succeeded because proper notice had not been given, because it had not been told that the defendant's case also rested on danger to witnesses and because the judge had not insisted that the Crown express a view on the alleged threat to national security. The court gave strong support to the importance of trial judges having in mind the media's rights under Articles 6(1) and 10 of the European Convention.

There are many situations where public access is restricted to a trial or its ancilliary proceedings that are not covered by these regulations. There is, therefore, no prescribed time for appealing against such orders (although a long delay would make the Court of Appeal unwilling to allow the appeal). The press would have the usual right of an appellant to argue orally as to why permission should be granted and why the appeal itself should be allowed.

---

[8] *ibid.*, r.16B. A prosecutor or defendant who intends to apply for a secrecy order on grounds of national security or for the protection of a witness must give seven days' notice to the Crown Court before the start of the trial, and a copy of the notice should be displayed forthwith by court officials in a prominent place within the precincts of the court. This will give the press some advance notice that an application is to be made and an opportunity to prepare for any necessary appeal. The application will normally be considered after the defendant has made his plea but before the jury is sworn. If the application is successful, the trial must be adjourned for a minimum of 24 hours to allow for an appeal against the decision. The adjournment will continue until any appeal is disposed of (Crown Court Rules 1982, r.24A as added by S.I. 1989 No. 1103). A trial judge should not use the inherent power of the court to sit secret to circumvent a failure to comply with these provisions: *Re Godwin* [1991] Crim. L.R. 302. This procedure should be followed even if the application is to hear a pre-trial application (such as an application to stay the trial as an abuse of process) since the rule is to be read as covering all or part of the trial process. The notice outside court should be dated so that the media know how long they have to organise opposition: *Ex parte Guardian Newspapers Ltd* [1999] 1 All E.R. 65, CA.

[9] *Re Guardian Newspapers Ltd, The Times*, October 26, 1993.

[10] *Ex p. Guardian Newspapers Ltd* [1999] 1 All E.R. 65, CA.

The first case to be brought by the media under its new right to challenge Crown Court secrecy was an application by, appropriately enough, Tim Crook, the Old Bailey newshound whose case had been the genesis of the Strasbourg proceedings which had forced the government to concede a right of appeal.

The court formulated two important principles:

- A judge should adjourn into chambers only where he has a positive reason for believing that this is an appropriate course, and

- once in chambers he must resume sitting in open court "as soon as it emerges that the need to exclude the public is not plainly necessary".[11]

These rules do not go far enough to protect the open justice principle. The only exception allowed by *Scott v. Scott*—the rare occasion where justice cannot be done at all if it is done in public—needs further entrenchment, perhaps by a rule permitting the press to have access to the transcript of a chambers hearing at a future date to be determined by the judge. The decision of the Court of Appeal Civil Division in the tobacco litigation, urging courts when sitting in chambers to admit the press (see p. 418) is a very positive development which should spur the criminal courts to more openness.

GATHERING INFORMATION

There is more to a trial than meets the eye or catches the ear. What is said in open court is only the tip of an iceberg of investigation, documentation and analysis that goes into the preparation of a case for trial. If the accused pleads guilty, the prosecution counsel will provide a brief outline of the facts to help the judge decide on the appropriate sentence. In murder cases the judge has no discretion and must impose a life sentence, but the Lord Chief Justice has directed that a similar summary should nevertheless be given so that the public can know at least the outline of the offence.[12] This brief outline may give no more than a smattering of the hundreds of pages of witness statements and documentary exhibits. Even in a lengthy and contested trial there will be interesting material not put in evidence—because it is tangential to the charges or legally inadmissible. In civil cases judges may prefer to read important documents in their spare time rather than to have them tedi-

---

[11] *Re Crook's Appeal* (1991) 93 Cr. App. R.17, CA.
[12] *Practice Direction* (Plea of Guilty: Statement of Facts) [1968] 2 All E.R. 144.

ously read out, word for word. Journalists and authors covering a particular trial will naturally wish to have access to this class of material. In British law very little of it can be obtained by right.[13]

These limited rights stand in contrast to the position in the United States, where the media have the right to inspect the "court record", which includes all matters produced in evidence, and under the Freedom of Information Act all prosecution documents, even in spying cases, must eventually be disclosed. In a 1981 anti-corruption operation (known as Abscam) the FBI filmed leading politicians accepting bribes. The videotapes were the backbone of several prosecutions and the federal courts acknowledged that television stations had a right to transmit copies of the film.[14] The Supreme Court would similarly have allowed the Nixon tape recordings to be broadcast, but for a special statute dealing with presidential materials.[15] Although the American press has a privileged constitutional status, these cases did not depend on it. The courts looked back to the common law principle of open justice and saw the copying and supplying of all prosecution evidence to the media for publication as a natural and logical corollary.

Tape-recording

The right to attend court includes the right to take notes of what is said there.[16] This applies to the public as well as to the press, although court officials will sometimes (wrongfully) try to stop those in the public gallery from putting pen to paper.

The law has grudgingly recognised the invention of the tape recorder. The Contempt of Court Act 1981 bans the use of tape recorders unless the leave of the court has been obtained.[17] The judge has a discretion to give or withhold permission, but in the House of Lords debates the Lord Chancellor envisaged that it would normally be given and that regular court reporters would be given indefinite, if revocable, permission.[18] A Practice Direction for the High Court and Court of Appeal, and a Home Office circular for magistrates have given guidance on when permission

---

[13] *Gio Personal Investment Services Ltd v. Liverpool and London Steamship Protection and Indemnity Association Ltd, The Times*, January 13, 1999, CA.

[14] *National Broadcasting Company Inc. v. Meyers* 635 F2d 945 (1980).

[15] *U.S. v. Mitchell, Appeal of Warner Communications* 551 F2d 1252 (1976).

[16] This right has, for court reporters at least, accrued by custom: see *Re CNN's Application to the Harold Shipman Tribunal of Inquiry*, October 25, 2001, para. 61, *per* Smith J.

[17] 1981 Act, s. 9. See also Civil Procedure Rules Practice Direction to Part 39, para. 6.2.

[18] *Hansard*, HL, Vol. 416 col. 383.

should be granted.[19] Each lays down that there is no objection in principle to the use of tape recorders, and applications from the press and broadcasting institutions should be given sympathetic consideration.[20] The court must, however, take into account disturbance from noisy machines, and may attach conditions to its permission. In addition to the ordinary penalties for contempt a journalist or any other person who uses or intends to use a tape recorder that he or she has brought into court stands to forfeit the machine and any used tapes.[21] If journalists through oversight forget to ask for permission in advance, but are using their machines for the purpose which section 9 contemplated, magistrates or judges should consider giving retrospective leave. Magistrates have no inherent power to punish contempt of court and their statutory jurisdiction is limited to cases of wilful disturbance or interruption of the court's proceedings which may well be lacking in a case of simple oversight. In any case, before penalising reporters for contempt, the court should consider giving them an opportunity to seek legal advice and representation.[22]

Even where permission is granted, the tape cannot be broadcast. It is contempt of court subsequently to play the recording in the hearing of the public or a section of the public.[23] The Practice Direction recommends that a court giving permission should remind the user of this.

Transcripts and skeleton arguments

Whenever the High Court or Court of Appeal, crown court or county court is sitting, official shorthand writers will take a note of the proceedings.[24] They have a statutory right to use tape recorders, although the tapes are transcribed only on request.[25] The rules allow (but do not require) the sale of transcripts to people, including journalists, who are not parties to the action.[26] When shorthand writers have refused to pro-

---

[19] [1981] 3 All E.R. 848. and see Home Office Circular HO79/1981. The Lord Chancellor has extended it to county courts—*The Times*, December 9, 1981. See *Justice of the Peace*, September 12, 1981, p. 553.

[20] The circulars, but not the Practice Direction, speak of "accredited" representatives.

[21] Contempt of Court Act 1981, s. 9(3). This happened at Horseferry Road Magistrates' Court when a member of the public was spotted recording his wife's committal proceedings: *The Times*, December 4, 1981.

[22] *Re Patricia Hooker* [1993] C.O.D. 190.

[23] Contempt of Court Act 1981, s. 9(1). It would also be wrong to use the tape to coach waiting witnesses in what to say in order to be consistent.

[24] Civil Procedure Rules, Pt 39, Practice Direction, para. 6.1.

[25] Contempt of Court Act 1981, s. 9(4).

[26] Civil Procedure Rules, Pt 39, Practice Direction, paras 1.11 and 6.3. The position is different in family proceedings where non-parties require the leave of the court to obtain a transcript: Family Proceedings Rules, r.10.15(6).

vide transcripts, applications have been made to the Lord Chief Justice. No official shorthand note is kept of magistrates' courts.

The Court of Appeal and other courts ask lawyers to produce in advance outlines or "skeletons" of their arguments and legal submissions. The Court of Appeal has asked lawyers to produce an extra copy for the press (except when reporting is restricted)[27]. If the parties refuse to provide a copy of a skeleton argument or a written note of an opening speech reporters should apply to the judge. There should be a prima facie presumption in favour of ordering access.[28]

Court records

Claim forms

The Civil Procedure Rules (which came into force in April 1999) prescribe a common code for all civil proceedings. Writs, petitions, originating summonses and originating notices of motion are now legal history. All proceedings are commenced by issuing and serving a claim form (for some proceedings, such as judicial review, the court's permission is needed to start proceedings). Any person (on payment of the prescribed fee) can search for, inspect or copy a claim form which has been served (the restriction to "served" claims was a novelty that was introduced by the CPR), and any judgment or order given in public. The permission of the court is not needed. The court's permission is however, needed before a member of the public can inspect any other document on the court file.[29] But family proceedings are different and a non-party requires leave to inspect any document on the court file other than an order given in open court.[30] In children cases the rules arguably go further by stipulating that no document shall be disclosed other than to a limited category of persons without the leave of the judge.[31]

Other statements of case, affidavits and witness statements

The claim form will often have only an uninformative statement of the order that the claimant wants the court to make. More detail is set out in the "particulars of claim" which there is no automatic right to inspect.

---

[27] *Lombard North Central plc v. Pratt* (1989) 139 N.L.J. 1709, CA.

[28] *GIO Personal Investment Services Ltd v. Liverpool and London Steamship Protection and Indemnity Association Ltd* [1999] 1 W.L.R. 984, CA.

[29] CPR, r.5.4(2)(a) and (b). Until computer search facilities have been installed in county courts, these provisions do not apply to county court proceedings: CPR, Pt. 5 *Practice Directions—Court Documents,* para. 4.5.

[30] Family Proceedings Rules, r.10.20.

[31] Family Proceedings Rules, r.4.23(1).

However, sometimes this more detailed statement of the claimant's case is endorsed on the claim form itself and the right of inspection then extends to it. Should court officials refuse access, the right can be enforced by an application for judicial review to the Administrative Court.[32] In other cases the particulars of claim or the statements of case that follow it (usually a Defence and sometimes a Reply) are not automatically open to inspection by the public, nor are any of the other documents which may be on the court file such as affidavits or witness statements. There is no American-style right to inspect the court file. The court can grant leave to inspect,[33] but is likely to require particularly compelling reasons to do so.[34] The same restriction applies in Family Proceedings[35] although for 14 days after the pronouncement of a decree nisi on a "quickie" divorce, the public does have the right to inspect the evidence filed by the petitioner.[36]

Pre-trial publication of statements of case or affidavits or witness statements is not by itself a contempt of court.[37] Since almost all civil cases are tried by judge alone[38] it is extremely unlikely that he would be affected by publication of documents that he will anyway have to read at the trial.[39]

In extreme cases the Court can exercise its inherent power to restrict publicity or the use of affidavits or witness statements outside the litigation. However, there is a heavy onus on the party seeking the restriction to show that without it the documents would be improperly used.[40] Libel is a greater hazard. The privilege for reporting court proceedings will not attach to documents that have not been read in open court and a publisher must consider carefully whether they are defamatory and, if so, whether there is a defence to an action for libel.

Witness statements used at trial

A witness statement which was ordered to stand as the witness's evidence in chief should be open to inspection if access is requested during the trial. Any person can ask the court to direct suppression of the statement but this will only be done where it is in the interests of justice,

---

[32] *Ex p. Associated Newspapers* [1959] 3 All E.R. 878.
[33] Civil Procedure Rules, 5.4(2)(c); for previous rules see Rules of Supreme Court, Ord. 63, r.4(1)(c).
[34] Supreme Court Practice 1997, para. 63/4/1.
[35] Family Proceedings Rules, r.10.20(3).
[36] *ibid.*, and rr.2.36(4) and 2.24(3).
[37] *Re F (A Minor Publication of Information)* [1977] 1 All E.R. 114.
[38] There are important exceptions for most defamation cases and civil actions against the police.
[39] *Gaskell and Chambers v. Hudson and Dodsworth and Co* [1936] 2 K.B. 595.
[40] *Esterhuysen v. Lonhro plc, The Times,* May 29, 1989, CA.

or the public interest, or because the statement contains expert medical evidence or other confidential information (including information relating to personal financial matters), or affects the interests of any child or patient.[41]

Judgments and orders

When High Court judges give oral reasons for their decisions, the text is embargoed until the judge has finished speaking. The BBC was reproved in 1983 for quoting the advance text on its news bulletin before the judge had concluded.[42]

The Court of Appeal (Civil Division) and High Court judges often prepare written judgments in advance. These are passed to the lawyers a day or two before judgment is due to be given in open court, subject to a condition that their clients can only be told the result one hour before the hearing. In cases of particular interest, journalists who want copies should notify the clerk to the presiding Lord Justice in advance. They will then be provided with a copy when judgment is given in open court.[43] Copies can be obtained from the shorthand writers for a fee or, increasingly commonly, from one of the on-line electronic data bases. Transcripts of the Court of Appeal's decisions are also kept in the Supreme Court Library.

House of Lords judges give "speeches" rather than judgments although these are not actually read out. Printed copies are delivered to the parties and sold to the press as their Lordships go through the ritual motions of adopting the majority view. Within two hours the texts of the speeches ought to appear on Parliament's website.[44]

Where a hearing of the High Court, Court of Appeal or county court takes place in public, members of the public can obtain a transcript of any judgment given or a copy of any order made, subject to payment of the appropriate fee.[45] If the hearing was in private, a member of the public who was not a party to the proceedings must ask permission of the judge who gave the judgment or made the order.[46] Article 6 of the

---

[41] CPR, r.32.13. There is no automatic right to documents referred to in a witness statement or other documents referred to in open court, but applications can be made to the court for permission to inspect these and a rather more liberal approach now seems to be favoured: *FAI General Insurance Co Ltd v. Godfrey Merrett Robertson Ltd* [1999] C.L.C. 566, CA.

[42] *Att-Gen. v. Able* [1984] Q.B. 795.

[43] *Practice Statement (Supreme Court: Judgments)* [1998] 1 W.L.R. 825; *Practice Statement (Supreme Court Judgments (No.2)* [1999] 1 W.L.R. 1.

[44] See www.parliament.uk.

[45] CPR, Pt 39 *Practice Direction—Miscellaneous Provisions Relating to Hearings*, para. 1.11.

[46] *ibid.*, para. 1.12.

ECHR requires judgments on criminal charges or the determination of civil rights and obligations to be given publicly. There is no express qualification to this principle, but the European Court has held that decisions properly given in private can be withheld from public scrutiny if public access would frustrate the purpose of having the hearing in private.[47]

Insolvency proceedings

A record of steps taken and orders made in bankruptcy and winding-up proceedings is open to the public for inspection[48] although the Registrar of the Companies Court may refuse access if he "is not satisfied as to the propriety of the purpose for which inspection is required." Reporting should always be a legitimate purpose. If the Registrar does refuse permission there is a right to appeal forthwith and without notice to a judge.[49]

Electronic processing has made it feasible to copy the entire register of claims, but the Registrar has refused permission for access for this purpose on the ground that it would undermine the court's power to regulate the advertisement of proceedings. His decision was upheld by the judge and the Court of Appeal ruled that it had no jurisdiction to hear a further appeal, but one Appeal Court judge could see nothing wrong in the service which the appellant wished to provide.[50] A somewhat similar scheme in Spain met with a similar response from the Spanish Court. A complaint to the European Commission of Human Rights was dismissed as manifestly unfounded for the unsatisfactory reason that Article 10 gives no right to compel an unwilling person to supply information.[51] Where the information is of a public nature, the media should be entitled to access it and impart it to the public.

Obtaining access to court files by deceit or trickery is a punishable contempt.[52]

County court judgments

There is a privatised central register of county court money judgments.[53] Various classes of judgments are exempt from registration, notably judgments in family proceedings and orders made after a contested

---

[47] *B v. U.K., P v. U.K.* [2001] 2 F.C.R. 221.
[48] Insolvency Rules 1986, S.I. 1986 No. 1925, rr.7.27, 7.28.
[49] *ibid.*, r.7.28(2).
[50] *Ex parte Creditnet Ltd* [1996] 1 W.L.R. 1291, appealed dismissed *sub nom Re Austintel Ltd* [1997] 1 W.L.R. 616. CA.
[51] *Grupero Interpres SA v. Spain,* Application No. 32849/96 (1997) 89 D.R. 150.
[52] *Dobson v. Hastings* [1992] Ch. 394.
[53] County Courts Act 1984, sections. 73 and 73A.

hearing for payment of money other than by instalments where the creditor has not sought to enforce the judgment.[54] The current arrangements are for the Register to be kept by Registry Trust Ltd.[55] The register is open to public inspection[56] or RTL can be asked to conduct a search. Prescribed fees are payable.

Magistrates' courts

Magistrates are more secretive. The registers on which their clerks record the courts' decisions are not public documents and only the magistrates themselves have a right of access to them.[57] This secrecy is indefensible and the Home Secretary has encouraged all courts to provide their local newspapers with a copy of the court register when it is prepared.[58]

Freedom of Information Act

The Freedom of Information Act (FOIA) 2000 will make no difference to the rights of the public to have access to court records. Information is exempt information for the purposes of the 2000 Act if it is contained in document filed with or in the custody of the court for the purpose of proceedings in a particular cause or matter, or because it has been served on or by a public authority for the purpose of proceedings or it has been created by a court or a member of the court's administrative staff for the purposes of a particular cause or matter. There is no duty to confirm or deny the existence of any such information.[59]

Disclosed documents

Before trial

In the course of most civil litigation the parties must disclose to each other all the documents in their possession that are relevant to the case. The obligation is a broad one, and a document must be listed and produced however damning it is to the case of the party disclosing it. In a

---

[54] Register of County Court Judgments Regulations 1985, S.I. 1985 No. 1807, regs 4 and 5. In any case, the judgment debtor can ask for a note of satisfaction of judgment to be added to the register after payment has been made and, if this is done within a month of the judgment, the entry will be cancelled: reg. 8. Any entries still on the register after 6 years will be cancelled: reg. 9.

[55] At 173/175 Cleveland Street, London W1P 5 PE (tel. (020) 7380-0133).

[56] Register of County Court Judgments Regulations, reg. 10.

[57] Magistrates' Courts Rules 1981, r.66(12).

[58] Home Office Circular 80/1989.

[59] Freedom of Information Act 2000, s. 32—see p. 603 for further commentary on the FOIA.

very limited category of cases a party can plead privilege from discovery. It is not necessary, for instance, for parties to show to the other side correspondence with their lawyers. Public interest immunity can be claimed for government documents that are particularly sensitive. The fact that a document is confidential is not enough for it to be privileged, and some litigants settle their cases rather than show their most private papers to their opponents or have them read aloud in a public court.

Although this potential for publicity is inherent in disclosure, the law will normally protect the confidentiality of the documents unless and until they are used in court. The recipient of the documents impliedly undertakes to the court not to use them for any purpose other than one related to the litigation in question. But as with other confidential documents there may be an important reason for publicising their contents that outbalances the normal duty. In the course of the thalidomide litigation *The Sunday Times* bought some of the documents produced by Distillers on disclosure, which had also been given to a research chemist who had been retained as an expert witness for the injured children. The court enjoined the paper from making any further use of the documents. The paper's argument that the story was important was accepted, but the court did not agree that the public interest in publication was so great that the litigation confidence could be broken.[60] *The Sunday Times* could be restrained only because it *knew* that the documents had been produced on disclosure. If the paper had received them anonymously with no suggestion of their origin, its chance of defeating the injunction would have been much greater.

Again, English concepts of free expression lag behind those in the United States, where disclosed documents are considered part of the public record and are in the public domain from the time that they are produced. The courts can make "protective orders" restricting the use of documents, but this is recognised as an exceptional interference with the free speech of lawyer and litigant, and requires substantial justification.[61]

After trial

The extent to which disclosed documents may be shown to the media by an opposing party was the subject of a controversial decision in the case of *Home Office v. Harman.*[62]

Harriet Harman, then solicitor for the National Council for Civil Liberties,

---

[60] *Distillers Co (Biochemicals) Ltd v. Times Newspapers Ltd* [1975] 1 All E.R. 41.
[61] *Re Halkin* 598 F2d 176 (DC, CA, 1979).
[62] [1982] 1 All E.R. 532, HL.

conducted an action on behalf of a prisoner who alleged that his confinement in a "control unit" was illegal. The Home Office was forced to disclose embarrassing internal memoranda about the setting up of such units. These were read out in open court during the four-week trial. Journalist David Leigh approached her at the end of the trial and was shown copies of the disclosed documents, which he quoted in an article attacking the Home Office prison policy. The House of Lords narrowly decided, by 3 – 2, that Ms Harman's action was a contempt in that she, as a solicitor, was bound by the obligation to use disclosed documents only for the purposes of the litigation. Leigh could have sat through the trial and taken notes or purchased an expensive transcript, but he could not be assisted by direct access to the documents themselves. The impracticabilities of these alternatives for the working journalist were recognised in the minority opinion, which regarded the ruling as a breach of the freedom of communication guaranteed by the European Convention.

The European Commission on Human Rights found this a prima facie breach of Article 10. Had the Government chosen to take the case to the European Court, the response would have been similar to that in the *Weber* judgment in 1990. A campaigning environmentalist had been punished by the Swiss courts for disclosing details of judicial proceedings held in private, and the court found this to be a violation of Article 10—in part because the material was already public knowledge.[63] A friendly settlement of the *Harman* case was reached with the Government and Rules of Court now provide:

"(1) A party to whom a document has been disclosed may use the document only for the purpose of the proceedings in which it is disclosed, except where:

    (a) the document has been read to or by the court, or referred to, at a hearing which has been held in public;

    (b) the court gives permission; or

    (c) the party who disclosed the document and the person to whom the document belongs agree.

(2) The Court may make an order restricting or prohibiting the use of a document which has been disclosed, even where the document has been read to or by the court, or referred to, at a hearing which has been held in public."[64]

The undertaking ceases even if the document is not actually read aloud in court as long as it has been "read by the court, or referred to, in open court".[65]

---

[63] *Weber v. Switzerland* (1990) 12 E.H.R.R. 508.

[64] Civil Procedure Rules, Pt 31.22.

[65] *Derby and Co Ltd v. Weldon, The Times,* October 20, 1988, Ch D; some discovered documents that were included in affidavits were in turn, included in a bundle of

Some affidavits are covered by the *Harman* rule because they are the method by which a litigant is required to make discovery (discovery of assets or income is often ordered by affidavit). However, other affidavits and witness statements are not restricted and journalists should beware of unwarranted attempts to rely on *Harman* as an excuse for not allowing access to them. The filing of certain affidavits may be necessary for litigants to continue their fight, but *this* type of compulsion does not attract the *Harman* protection.[66] Similarly, the reports of potential expert witnesses that litigants exchange are *not* subject to the implied obligation since it is ultimately for the parties to decide whether or not to call experts. On the other hand, rules of court specifically restrict the use to which witness statements can be put.[67]

Documents in criminal proceedings

As part of the principle of fairness the common law developed rules requiring the prosecution to disclose to defendants all documents relevant to the offence or its investigation and the House of Lords held that that there was an equivalent to the *Harman* rule in criminal procedure.[68] The Criminal Procedure and Investigations Act 1996 has introduced a statutory code of disclosure obligations for both prosecutors and (in some circumstances) defendants. A defendant to whom documents are disclosed under these provisions cannot use them other than (broadly) for the purpose of the proceedings in which they were given until they have been used or the information in them has been communicated in open court. It is a statutory contempt to infringe these restrictions[69] although this offence would be committed by the party who leaked the documents rather than by the newspaper itself, unless it had incited or procured the leak.

The decision to publish other leaked documents may involve a nice balancing of political consequences. For example, on the morning before the trial of four anarchists opened in 1979, *The Guardian* published a confidential prosecution memorandum about potential jurors—a document prepared from police files for the purpose of "vetting" the

---

documents for the Court of Appeal. They were "referred to in open court". See also *SmithKlineBeecham Biologicials SA v. Connaught Laboratories* [1999] F.S.R. 284, CA.

[66] *Derby and Co Ltd v. Weldon* above at n. 65.

[67] Civil Procedure Rules, r.32.12; *Prudential Assurance Co Ltd v. Fountain Page Ltd* [1991] 1 W.L.R. 756. The same distinction between documents produced under compulsion and other documents applies also in the Family Division—*Clibbery v. Allan,* [2001] 2 F.L.R. 819, *per* Munby J.

[68] *Taylor v. Serious Fraud Office* [1999] 2 A.C. 177 overruling *Mahon v. Rahn* [1998] Q.B. 424, CA.

[69] 1996 Act, ss. 17 and 18

jury. It contained the gossip now routinely recorded on police files about citizens whose relations had been in trouble, who lived in squats and who had made complaints against the police. The trial judge angrily discharged the jury and urged the Attorney-General to prosecute the newspaper for contempt—presumably because its revelation that police had invaded their privacy might bias jurors against the prosecution. No action was taken, the Attorney perhaps concluding that the police action had been rather more upsetting than the newspaper's revelation of it.[70] Nor was action taken against London Weekend Television when one of its programmes revealed that the foreman of a "vetted" jury in the "ABC" Official Secrets case was an ex-member of the SAS (see p. 557), an outfit that the defendant journalists had regularly criticised. The trial was stopped as a result of this disclosure, but contempt proceedings, which might well have succeeded, would have been highly embarrassing to an Attorney-General already under attack for approving jury-vetting. These cases illustrate the extra-legal considerations that give the media a tenuous freedom to publish more than the strict letter of the law or rulings of the court would allow. If the documents prove hitherto unexposed official misconduct, the Attorney-General may consider that the public interest, well-served by publication, does not require prosecution.

Photographs and sketches

Other forms of recording apart from note taking and tape-recording are prohibited by section 41 of the Criminal Justice Act 1925. It is an offence to take any photograph or to make with a view to publication a sketch of any juror, witness, party or judge in the courtroom, the court building or its precincts. The offence can be committed even though the photographer or artist is standing outside and well clear of the court if the subject of the snap or sketch is entering or leaving the court. It is also an offence to publish such a photograph or sketch. The ban applies to civil and criminal proceedings.

The extent of this embargo has never been authoritatively decided. "Precinct" strictly means the space enclosed by the walls or outer boundary of a court building (*i.e.* the court yard) rather than public streets or highways surrounding court. No exception has ever been taken to television and stills photographers standing on the public footpath outside the Old Bailey or the High Court, although it is understandable that judges should be concerned about media circuses at the gates of criminal courts, which witnesses and jurors may find intimidating. The open justice principle would seem to imply the media's right to photo-

---

[70] David Leigh, *The Frontiers of Secrecy* (Junction Books, 1980), p. 171.

graph defendants and witnesses as they turn up for a public trial, although any attempts to photograph jurors would probably lead to a prosecution.

The above approach is supported by the Court of Appeal decision in *R. v. Runting*[71]:

> Runting was a photographer for the *Sun* newspaper. He was charged with contempt of court for his efforts to snap a camera-shy defendant, commencing as he emerged from court and continuing for some minutes as he made a dash for the nearest tube station, colliding with a lamppost in his flight. The Court of Appeal quashed Runting's conviction: although his behaviour caused inconvenience, it did not amount to "molestation" sufficient to form the basis of a contempt charge. The court warned photographers against hindering, jostling, "threatening with persistent following" and assaulting defendants and witnesses as they go to or from court. Significantly, however, it made no reference to section 41, and appeared to accept that photographing defendants as they emerged from court would be lawful in the absence of intimidating conduct.

If the sketch is a doodle made by someone in court but *not* with a view to publication, then a newspaper that obtains and publishes it would not commit the statutory offence. Commissioned sketches of courtroom incidents often appear in the press and on television. Those that are drawn from memory are unobjectionable. The Press Council recognised a long-standing tradition of such sketches being published.[72] Even drawings deliberately made in court for publication rarely attract a prosecution—perhaps because the sketches are flattering, perhaps because the maximum fine is only on scale 3, currently £1,000. In 1986 a solicitor's wife was fined £100 for photographing a judge in court.[73] Photography that disturbs the court's proceedings (*e.g.* by use of flash) might also be contempt of court, for which heavier penalties can be imposed.

Journalists will often seek help from the lawyers in court whose willingness to co-operate varies. Journalistic self-help is dangerous, though. The Court of Appeal has warned that the removal of photographs or other papers belonging to lawyers without their permission for the purpose of copying them could constitute contempt of court.[74]

---

[71] *R. v. Runting* (1989) 89 Cr. App. R. 243.
[72] Adjudication on complaints against *The Sunday Times* over publication of a sketch of the jury in the Thornton Heath murder case, *The Times*, December 13, 1982.
[73] *The Times*, July 15, 1986, cited by Miller, *Contempt of Court* (3rd ed., Oxford University Press, 2000), para.4. 102.
[74] *Re Paul Griffin, The Times*, November 6, 1996.

Television and the courts

Section 41 has also effectively precluded televising the courts. In 1977
the BBC wished to include footage of a consistory court (see p. 497)
sitting in a village church as part of a documentary on rural life. The
parties approved, as publicity for Church court proceedings had in the
past brought in sorely needed cash, but the judge ruled that section 41
prevented filming of the actual proceedings.[75] He referred to the "necessary privacy" of judicial proceedings, but this was at odds with the
principle of open justice, and the "pressures, embarrassment and discomfiture" that he wished to spare the participants are, in any event,
experienced by a witness over cross-examination.

These traditional arguments against televising the courts were convincingly refuted by the Report of the Royal Commission into arms ship-
ments to Colombian drug cartels.[76] This Commission was televised
throughout its sittings in Antigua, and extracts were screened in the
United Kingdom. The Royal Commissioner concluded that the public
and professional benefits of media coverage were "incalculable": it discouraged time-wasting and irrelevance and enabled the public to make
up its own mind about the testimony. The proceedings were in no way
disrupted by a single, discreetly placed television camera, and the witnesses were in no way disquieted. The report accepted that electronic
media coverage of criminal trials "requires careful and gradual introduction" but hoped that it would become routine for public inquiries
(which are beyond the scope of section 41—see p. 513). In 2001 Fiji's
Court of Appeal permitted the televising of the hearings in the case in
which it ruled that the military Government of the country was unlawful.

Dramatic reconstructions of courtroom dramas are unaffected by section 41. *The Trials of Oz* were relived in the West End by the Royal
Shakespeare Company after the verdict but before the appeal and the
BBC made a dramatised documentary of the *Gay News* trial, mainly
from court transcripts. When the director of *The Romans in Britain* was
charged with procuring an act of indecency (see p. 195), public read-
ings were given each evening of that day's proceedings at the Oxford
Playhouse. This neither offended section 41 nor (in the absence of prejudicial comment) could it constitute contempt.

Channel 4 has taken the lead in exploring the possibilities of contemporaneous television coverage of major trials. There are no difficulties

---

[75] *Re St Andrews* [1978] Fam. 121, Salisbury Consistory Court, Judge Ellison Chancellor.
[76] The report of the Royal Commissioner, Louis Blom-Cooper Q.C., is published by
Duckworth on behalf of the Government of Antigua and Barbuda, as *Guns for
Antigua,* 1990; see pp. 44–46.

in transmitting a "dramatic reconstruction" once the proceedings have concluded, and it is difficult to comprehend how jurors would be prejudiced by hearing evidence spoken by actors on television when they have already heard it delivered by witnesses in the courtroom, and can read it in summary form in the morning newspapers. Nonetheless, Channel 4 was not allowed by the Ponting trial judge to employ actors for their nightly *Court Report* of the trial—they had to be replaced by a panel of news-readers, whose presentation of the evidence the judge found unexceptional. Ironically, the very experienced producer of the programme had chosen to use actors precisely because they could be directed to avoid imparting emotion or conceivably prejudicial mannerisms to the script; news-readers were more liable to impart drama to the "parts" they were playing.

It is impossible to defend Britain's absolute prohibition on the broadcasting of legal proceedings. Many states in America permit both radio and television coverage of the courtroom. After initial doubts, there is now an acceptance that the result has been to make the judiciary better behaved, the advocates better prepared and the public better informed. The danger of distracting witnesses has not materialised. Two cases in the USA in particular energised public debate—the trials of O.J. Simpson for his wife's murder and the trial of Louise Woodward, a British nanny, for the killing of a baby in her care. Some commentators viewed the coverage with distaste. Others saw it as an exemplar of open justice in action and democratic access to trials which would in any event have been subject to enormous publicity.

The *Wall Street Journal* recently published a study of the effect on the U.S. justice system of televising the O.J. Simpson trial. It concluded that there were two:

(1) it caused an amazing drop in the number of people who wanted exemptions from jury service: citizens wished, much more than before, to play their part in justice;

(2) it caused those who did serve on juries to pay much less attention to lawyers and their arguments, and concentrate their deliberations on facts proved in evidence.

Is this bad for the administration of justice? Even if it may be thought unseemly to broadcast the highlights of notorious criminal trials, this objection does not apply to appeal hearings. In New Zealand these are routinely televised without any damage to the administration of justice. Until cameras are allowed in the courtroom, the media will have to make do with "dramatic reconstructions" of trials after they have taken place.

In principle, if every court in the land is open to every subject of the

King, does it not logically follow that subjects should be entitled, quite literally, to see justice done through the medium of television? The communications revolution can bring benefits to justice, and we are beginning to accept the advantages of videotaped testimony of child witnesses and the possibility of cross-examining overseas witnesses via satellite link-up. Appeal courts would be better able to evaluate the testimony of trial witnesses if they could see and hear it being delivered, and most barristers have had occasion to regret that they could not include in grounds of appeal against judges' summings-up some reference to prejudical tones of voice or body language, which are not apparent from a typed transcript.

The danger of course, is that witnesses may prove camera-shy and that television's coverage of the day's play in a sensational Old Bailey trial will feature heavily edited "highlights" chosen for entertainment value rather than as fair and accurate reporting. Nonetheless, the public is genuinely interested in significant court cases, and the arguments in favour of open justice apply with even greater force to aural or visual coverage. Present television news reporting, in 60-second "slots" with breathless presenters pictured outside court quoting snatches of evidence, sometimes over inaccurate "artists impressions" of the courtroom, is of minimal value. When Channel 4 launched its *Court Report* programme, on which news-readers read large slabs of the day's transcript in the Ponting trial for half an hour on every evening of the three-week trial, over 500,000 viewers watched every edition. There would seem to be little objection to radio coverage of important appellate proceedings, but the BBC has been refused permission to go even this far.

Section 41 and the statutory prohibition on televising the courts does not apply in Scotland. Experiments have been made in permitting television cameras, with the permission of both prosecution and defence, to film several trials, although the excerpts broadcast for a BBC documentary series had to be approved by the trial judge. The issue came to the fore in 2000 in connection with the trial of two Libyans for the Lockerbie bombings. Although the trial physically took place in the Netherlands, it was conducted by Scottish judges according to Scottish law. The BBC challenged in the Scottish High Court of Justiciary the refusal to allow them to televise the proceedings. The argument, based on Article 10 of the ECHR, failed because it was considered that broadcasting would prejudice the trial of the accused.[77] In a second round, the BBC sought access to an encrypted feed which was relayed from the courtroom to controlled sites around the world where the proceedings could be watched by the families of the dead. Again the challenge failed. The High Court of Justiciary referred to the *Leander* line of

---

[77] *BBC's Petition,* judgment of Lord MacFadyn, March 7, 2000 (HCJ).

Strasbourg cases that Article 10 could not be used to compel an unwilling person to supply information.[78]

Progress may lie in the art of the possible, namely by using section 3 of the Human Rights Act to re-interpret section 41 of the Criminal Justice Act 1925 "so far as is possible" consistently with Article 10 (if an English court was persuaded to view that guarantee more broadly than the High Court of Justiciary). Section 41—"no person shall take in court any photograph" says nothing about video-tape, and it is entirely possible to construe it as it was intended in 1925, as a rule against flash photography and box brownies. So the entire edifice on which the blanket ban on televising the courts is based might be pulled apart at the seams, by reference to the right to receive and impart public interest information about what goes on at the justice seat. That would enable courts to use their inherent powers to permit televising at least of sentence hearings and appeals.[79]

PROTECTION FROM LIBEL

One great attraction of court reporting is that it is virtually immune from actions for libel, whatever the gravity of the allegations bandied about in the courtroom and republished in the media. They do not have to be defended on grounds of justification or fair comment: they are privileged so long as the report is reasonably fair and accurate.

Absolute privilege

The privilege defence is discussed in Chapter 3. Absolute privilege is a complete defence, irrespective of the malice of the publisher of the account. The privilege goes back to the Law of Libel Amendment Act 1888, section 3, but this provision was repealed and replaced by the Defamation Act 1996, section 14. The 1888 Act protected a "fair and accurate report in any newspaper of proceedings publicly heard before any court exercising judicial authority" and which was published contemporaneously with the proceedings. The 1996 Act repeats the defence but with two principal extensions. Absolute privilege now applies also to contemporaneous reports of any tribunal or body in the United Kingdom which is exercising the judicial power of the State.[80] Other bodies whose proceedings may be contemporaneously reported with the protection of absolute privilege are: the European Court of Justice and any

---

[78] *BBC's Petition (No. 2),* April 20, 2000 (HCJ).
[79] see p. 529 for televising the Law Lords.
[80] See the discussion of this phrase at p. 515.

court attached thereto (*e.g.* the European Court of First Instance), the European Court of Human Rights and any international criminal tribunal established by the Security Council of the UN or by an international agreement to which the United Kingdom is a party, *e.g.* the Hague tribunal on war crimes in former Yugoslavia. Thus allegations made by lawyers, parties or witnesses in the trial of Slobodan Milosevic may be fully reported however defamatory they may be of the British politicians who dealt with him.

The second extension is that the 1996 Act is not confined to newspaper reports. This extension is less significant since earlier amendments to the 1888 Act had already given protection to radio, television and other programme services[81] but the 1996 Act now makes clear that incidental communications in the course of preparing a published court report can have absolute privilege and informal reports (*e.g.* on the internet) will have absolute privilege if they satisfy the other criteria.

To attract absolute or even qualified privilege, the report must be "fair and accurate". The privilege is not lost if the inaccuracy is minor—"trifling slips" are to be expected.[82] But major errors—such as reporting a contentious piece of evidence from a particular witness as though it were a proven fact, or recounting an incorrect charge or the wrong verdict—will lose the protection. Erroneous headlines composed by sub-editors who were not in court and have not understood the copy are a familiar danger. The proceedings must have been held in public, but the privilege applies whether or not both parties are present or whether an application (such as for a warrant or a summons) is made by one in the absence of the other.[83] Only words spoken in open court are covered by the privilege. Reporters taking their notes from a charge sheet, court list or other documents are at risk if magistrates deviate from the text.[84] It is partly to give the media the full protection of this privilege that the Home Office has told justices to be sure to identify defendants by reading aloud their names and addresses.[85]

The question of "fairness" is more difficult. The guiding principle is that reports should be impartial, carrying some account of both sides of the case. The exigencies of both the courts and newspapers make this a counsel of perfection. Trials can last for weeks or months, and often all the evidence given on a particular day will be in support of one side only. Additionally, the space available for court reports is limited. The

---

[81] See Broadcasting Act 1990, Sched. 20, para. 2.

[82] *Kimber v. Press Association* [1893] 1 Q.B. 65.

[83] *ibid.*

[84] *Furniss v. Cambridge Daily News Ltd* (1907) 23 T.L.R. 705, CA; *Harper v. Provincial Newspapers Ltd* (1937) S.L.T. 462.

[85] Home Office Circulars 78/1967: 50/1969, approved in *R. v. Evesham Justices, ex p. McDonagh,* [1988] 1 All E.R. 371, 384, QBD.

most workable test is whether the report, as published, gives a reasonable impression of the proceedings thus far. Concentration on one sensational aspect of a witness's evidence in chief, without reference to a significant retraction made under cross-examination, could amount to a serious misrepresentation of the proceedings. Reporters are present with their privileges in the courtroom as representatives of the public; if, by calculated selection or omission they give an impression of the proceedings that no fair-minded member of the public could have formed in their place, the report will lose both absolute and qualified privilege under the statute, and the qualified privilege that remains at common law will be open to challenge for malice.

The likelihood, of course, is that it will not be challenged; defendants cannot (generally) obtain legal aid for libel and will, in any event, be reluctant to revive matters that had led them into the dock in the first place. The best solution when court reporters err is for the lawyers involved in the case to mention the mistake in open court the following day. If there is no dispute about the error, the newspaper should be prepared effectively to correct it by reporting the fact that it was drawn to the court's attention. It should not be necessary to use the law of libel to obtain a correction of a matter of public record.

The most unfair aspect of contemporary court reporting is the tendency of reporters to attend the beginning of a trial in order to publish the prosecutor's opening statement, which puts the allegations at their most sensational. The reporters then disappear for several weeks while the allegations are painstakingly questioned and undermined. But the press returns, vulture-like, for the verdict. If there is an acquittal, a newspaper will sometimes not even bother to report it, or will mention the matter without giving it anything like the prominence accorded to the discredited opening statement. This is *not* fair reporting: the original report, at the time it was published, was fair and accurate, but failure to follow it up with a report of the acquittal could retrospectively entail loss of the privilege.[86]

An interesting question is raised by the not uncommon occurrence of "outbursts" in court—from the public gallery or from the defendant in the dock. Does a report of defamatory statements made by persons with no right to speak attract absolute privilege? Old cases suggested that they did not, but a more liberal view was taken in *Hope v. Leng Ltd*, when absolute privilege was accorded to the report of a shout of "It's all a pack of lies" from the well of the court during the claimant's evidence.[87] The decision could be artificially distinguished on the

---

[86] *Wright v. Outram* (1890) 17 R. 596 and *Turner v. Sullivan* (1862) 6 L.T. 130.

[87] (1907) 23 T.L.R. 243; *Farmer v. Hyde* [1937] 1 K.B. 728 concerned a heckler's interruption, but, fortunately for the paper, he began "May I make an application". He could not, but he was therefore treated as a party. Compare "Nothing short of

ground that the disruptor was a witness who had already given evidence and was then still technically under oath, but the court indicated its approval for a wider and more sensible view for the protection of court reporters. Outbursts in court are generally followed by admonitions from the judge; as a matter of common sense, they are part of the "proceedings" publicly heard before the court, and should therefore attract privilege.

The report must be published "contemporaneouly". This does not mean "immediately", but as soon as reasonably practicable, having regard to the schedules of the newspaper or the broadcasting organis-ation. A daily newspaper would be expected to carry the report on the following day; a fortnightly magazine would not lose the privilege if it published at the next reasonable opportunity, even though it was reporting matters said in court up to two weeks before. Summaries in Sunday newspapers of the events of the week in a long trial would be protected. At the end of a big trial, feature articles and programmes sometimes appear recapitulating parts of the evidence and, in the case of television, even re-enacting aspects of the trial. The protection is not limited to "day by day" proceedings and there seems no reason why it should not extend to cover such accounts of an entire trial, if they are reasonably fair and published as soon as practicable after the verdict. The protection of absolute privilege extends to reports published within a reasonable time of the conclusion of any period of postponement of reporting imposed by any statute or court order.[88]

Qualified privilege

At common law all fair and accurate court reports are protected by qualified privilege. This remains a safety net for coverage that falls outside the statutory protection of absolute privilege because, for example, it is not "contemporaneous". The privilege is "qualified" in the sense that it is lost if the court report is published "maliciously", *i.e.* for an improper motive such as to frighten off potential witnesses. Media court reports are unlikely to be deemed malicious, so the protec-tion is for practical purposes as effective as absolute privilege. To enjoy the qualified privilege, the report must still be fair and accurate, and the words must have been spoken in a public court. The criteria for fairness and accuracy are the same as with absolute privilege. The principle is that a reporter is "entitled to report on the proceedings or that part of it which he selects in a manner which fairly and faithfully gives an impression of the events reported and will convey to the reader what he

---

perjury" shouted from the gallery and held not privileged: *Lynam v. Gowring* (1880) 6 L.R. Ir. 259.
[88] Defamation Act 1996, s. 14(2).

himself would have appreciated had he been present during the proceedings".[89]

To attract qualified privilege the report need not be contemporaneous and is therefore of particular use to authors whose books about famous trials are published long after the case is over.

Reports of foreign court proceedings have qualified privilege at common law if the proceedings are of legitimate public interest in England,[90] but the significance of common law privilege in this respect has been largely overtaken by a statutory qualified privilege for fair and accurate reports of proceedings in public before any court anywhere in the world. It is still necessary to show that the matter is of public concern and the publication is for the public benefit[91] although these requirements will usually be satisfied in respect of newsworthy trials in other countries.

[89] *Cook v. Alexander* [1974] 1 Q.B. 279 at 290, *per* Buckley L.J.
[90] *Webb v. Times Publishing Co* [1960] 2 Q.B. 535.
[91] Defamation Act 1996, s. 15.

CHAPTER 9

REPORTING LESSER COURTS AND TRIBUNALS

There are about five hundred separate types of tribunal that have some of the features of a court, and that make decisions with some legal force and often considerable public interest. A few, such as courts martial and consistory (Church) courts, have powers to punish, and procedures similar to criminal trials. Professional disciplinary bodies cannot jail ethical transgressors, but may fine them or suspend them from practice. Immigration adjudicators affect the fate of families, employment tribunals decide the rights and wrongs of behaviour in the workplace and deal with allegations of racial and sexual discrimination, while a myriad of assessment bodies decide the level of rates and rents and pensions, and settle disputes over such disparate matters as mines and quarries, performing rights, plant varieties and value added tax (VAT). Public inquiries may fix the responsibility for a riot or the site of a new airport, while inquests at coroners' courts sometimes attract as much press attention as a sensational murder trial. The multiplicity of these potentially newsworthy tribunals, and the present uncertainty as to which of them are protected by the laws of contempt, justifies a treatment separate from that accorded to civil and criminal courts.

The bewildering array of tribunals has no simple explanation. In some cases, tradition has prevailed over consistency and even fairness; military courts, for example, have a criminal jurisdiction that inflicts upon members of the armed services an officer-class justice that may be very different from that received by civilians from a jury of their peers. Other tribunals have been established to facilitate the Welfare State, to provide a basis for decision-taking that is fair (in that it allows public arguments from both sides), yet more informal and expeditious than that available from the regular courts. Some tribunals, such as accident inquiries, adopt an inquisitorial model, in the sense that tribunal members themselves call witnesses, interrogate them, expound and test conflicting hypotheses, and then prepare a report examining the different causal theories and making recommendations to avoid similar accidents in the future. Other tribunals exist to make administrative decisions—whether a licence should be renewed, whether an income-tax assessment should be paid and so on. The "tribunal", with its quasi-legal procedures, its opportunities for both sides to state a case and to ask questions, is some concession to the concept of natural justice in public administration. Openness is a characteristic of natural justice, and tribunals and inquiries sometimes do provide important opportunities to scrutinise and oversee the activities of public servants.

"When is a court not a court?" may sound an absurd question, but upon the answer hinge consequences of great importance to the media. For example, magistrates normally sit as a court of law, protected against prior media coverage that might seriously prejudice their deliberations. But when they sit to decide whether to grant liquor licences or whether to withdraw gaming licences, they are in law meeting as administrators, and the law of contempt does not apply. The question of the application of contempt to various tribunals is important and difficult; it will be considered in this chapter after an outline of the characteristics of those lesser courts and tribunals that are most frequently in the news.

INQUESTS

Inquests can be particularly newsworthy events, as the cases of Helen Smith, the Gulf War friendly fire victims and the Hillsborough Football Stadium disaster demonstrate. It is easy to liken the attraction of reporters to inquests to the interest of the vulture in the dead body, but the public interest in picking at the circumstances in which a life has been lost is not unworthy or unimportant. Any society that values life must look closely at death. And when death comes unnaturally and unexpectedly—behind the closed doors of police cells or prisons, or in a foreign country, or through the oversight of employers or doctors or public officials—it deserves to be looked at very closely indeed. Some agency is needed that is sufficiently independent and impartial to satisfy the public conscience. Frequently, the only agency in England and Wales that attempts to fill this need is the coroner, and sometimes the coroner's jury, deliberating in a special procedure called an inquest.

In the Middle Ages the office of coroner was created because the king wanted a local official to keep a watchful eye on corrupt sheriffs and to preserve property rights that would accrue to the Royal Treasury on death. To assist him, in an age long before police forces and medical science, the coroner summoned a jury from the neighbourhood areas. The medieval coroner and his jury would squat around the body—often by a roadside or in a ditch—and look for tell-tale signs of disease or violence or suicide. Pooling their local knowledge, they would often come up with the name of a likely suspect, whom they would present for trial. Although these important functions were taken over by professionals—policemen and doctors and lawyers—the coroner survived, as a public official appointed by local councils to investigate unnatural deaths, receiving a fee for each body inspected. Unlike other local public officials, the coroner, owing to his origin as the king's man, could not effectively be disciplined or removed. In this century the coroners lost most of their powers of criminal inquiry; in cases of suspicious deaths they in effect unveil to the public the evidence upon which the police have failed to reach any conclusion.

The coroner's task is to determine exactly how the deceased met with death. When this does not become apparent from initial inquiries, they must hold an inquest: a formal investigation, clad in the trappings of a court, to which witnesses may be summoned and examined, ending with a "verdict", which is officially recorded. In certain limited cases the coroner is obliged to summon a jury: these are cases of deaths in prison, death by poison, deaths in police custody or from an injury caused by a police officer in the execution or purported execution of his duty, or deaths in circumstances "the continuance or possible recurrence of which is prejudicial to the health or safety of the public or any section of the public".[1] In 1980 the Court of Appeal compelled the Hammersmith coroner to sit with a jury for the inquest of Blair Peach, a New Zealand teacher who had been killed in the Southall disturbances. The family claimed he had died from a blow inflicted by an instrument wielded by an unidentifiable policeman from the Special Patrol Group. The court agreed that it would be prejudicial to public safety if the police were issued with dangerous weapons, or if senior officers turned a blind eye to their use.[2] Since 1983 any death resulting from injury caused by a police officer must be investigated by a jury.[3]

Inquests are unlike any other judicial proceedings. Coroners need not be lawyers; they may be doctors of at least five years' standing. Unlike lay justices, they do not have the assistance of a legally trained clerk. The closest equivalent at an inquest is a policeman, who acts as the "coroner's officer". This does not help to create an appearance of impartiality where the death is alleged to have been caused by the police. In addition, an inquest does not follow the usual adversarial pattern of most legal proceedings, where the truth is expected to emerge from the clash of opposing evidence and submissions. Instead, the coroner takes the initiative and leads the investigation. An inquest takes place after police investigations, which have been made available to the coroner. But the coroner is not obliged to show material collected by the police to representatives of the interested parties, and many coroners

---

[1] Coroners Act 1988, s. 8(3).

[2] *R. v. Hammersmith Coroner, ex p. Peach* [1980] All E.R. 7, CA. After protracted proceedings, the police made a payment of £75,000 (without admitting liability) to the family of Blair Peach.

[3] Administration of Justice Act 1982, s. 62.

refuse to give lawyers a sight of the evidence available to them.[4] This means that lawyers are sometimes unprepared for the evidence that the coroner decides to call. It means, too, that at inquests where police misconduct is alleged, the police lawyers will have exclusive access to statements taken by police officers, and so have an unfair advantage.

Coroners cannot behave like impartial judges. They receive and study the police evidence beforehand, usually discuss it privately with the police, and will in most cases have-formed a view before the inquest opens. There are coroners who behave like conjurors, putting witnesses into the witness box to make statements that the parties have been given no opportunity to check with other witnesses, or to rebut. The parties and their lawyers are present, as one judge put it, merely as "guests of the court"[5] and may not address the coroner or the jury on the facts. There are no final speeches. So the jury never hears the contentions of the parties about the cause of death put in a coherent form. This prevents a comprehensive account, a logical theory of the cause of death, from being presented by anyone other than the coroner. Where the evidence is complicated and confusing, the only coherent account that is ever given to the public is provided by the coroner in the summing up. This may be an unsatisfactory account. It may even be, as in the Helen Smith case, a preposterous account.[6] But there can be no alternative.

In cases where coroners sit with juries public esteem for the jury system in criminal courts invests the "verdict" with a degree of acceptability. But the role of the coroner's jury today is no more than symbolic. The final verdict is usually dictated by the coroner. All the coroner's jury can do is to announce one simple fact: how the deceased met with death. The law requires a narrow answer to a narrow question, but in some cases the public rightly expects much fuller answers to a whole range of questions. Coroners' juries cannot provide these answers—they are not even allowed by law to attempt them. But, as a result, the Government changed the law and inquest juries can no longer add recommendations for preventing similar deaths. The inadequacy of coroners and their procedures became a cause for which the relatives of the victims of the Thames pleasure boat, the *Marchioness,* fought long and hard and eventually won the right to an inquiry presided over by a High Court judge which exposed serious failings by the coroner. There is much to be said for a judicial inquiry instead of a coroner's inquest after all such catastrophes.

---

[4] See *The Death of Blair Peach: A Supplementary Report of the Unofficial Inquiry Chaired by Professor Michael Dummett,* NCCL, 1980; and Paul Foot (with Ron Smith), *The Helen Smith Story,* Fontana, 1983, p. 296.

[5] The "interested parties" who can be represented are now listed in the Coroners' Rules 1984 (S.I. 1984 No. 552).

[6] See Geoffrey Robertson, *The Justice Game* (Vintage, 1999), Chap. 8.

The inquest must be held in open court unless the coroner thinks that it is in the interest of national security to exclude the public.[7] In December 1983 the *Observer* successfully obtained an interim injunction to prevent a coroner holding in secret the inquest on a British businessman who had died in Moscow after expressing fears that his life might be threatened. The Government had denied that the man was a spy and the judge accepted that prima facie there was no reason why the death should not be publicly investigated. However, a coroner can, like a judge, permit a witness to give evidence from behind a screen if national security or the witness's own safety would be genuinely imperilled so that the administration of justice would be frustrated by the witness giving evidence in the ordinary way.[8]

The right for reporters to be present was not won without a struggle. Until 1951 coroners had an almost unfettered discretion to exclude the public and were often particularly tender to the relatives of suicides. Bertha Hall's death in 1887 was a not untypical suicide following an unwanted pregnancy. Atypically, the *East Anglian Daily Times* fought the coroner's ruling to sit in secret. After being physically ejected, its reporter persuaded the jury to go on strike and for 10 days they refused to sit without the press. During the First World War the Ministry of Munitions was eager that deaths of poison-gas workers should not be reported in such a way "as to affect the supply of labour to these processes".[9]

Documentary evidence will normally be read aloud and an interested party can usually insist that it is, although the coroner does have a discretion to direct that it should be tendered in writing.[10]

The law of contempt has been applied, without any sensible thought, to coroners' courts: their inquisitorial procedures do not, as a matter of principle, require or deserve the suppression of media comment. On the contrary, since the fundamental object of the inquiry is to establish the cause of death, any light that can be shed on this from any source, including the media, should be welcome. This principle was accepted at the Helen Smith inquest: a Thames Television *This Week* documentary, which was transmitted the week before the inquest opened, was re-screened for the benefit of the jury, because it featured interviews with vital witnesses who refused to come to Britain for the coroner's proceedings. The point that inquests are inquisitorial rather than adversarial was overlooked by the Court of Appeal in its haste to ban an LWT documentary about the death in police custody of a black "Hell's

---

[7] Coroners' Rules 1984 (S.I. 1984 No. 552) r.36(2), r.17.

[8] *R. v. H.M. Coroner for Newcastle upon Tyne, ex p. A* (1998) 162 J.P. 387.

[9] Rule 17 of the 1984 Rules overturns the discretion given by the common law in *Garnett v. Ferrand* (1827) 6 B. & C. 611. The examples in the text are taken from Public Record Office file, HO 45/23968.

[10] Coroners' Rules 1984, r.37.

Angel": it used as its pretext the concern that the coroner's jury might be prejudiced, although no jury had been sworn and the inquest stood adjourned indefinitely while police "investigations" proceeded.[11]

COURTS MARTIAL

Courts martial try offences against military, naval or air force law. Some of these correspond to civilian crimes, but others are of more questionable validity. The notoriously vague offence of "conduct prejudicial to good order and discipline" appears in all three codes, and can be used to punish behaviour that would be unexceptional from civilians. Insufficient media scrutiny is given to whether punishments are always justified by the exigencies of service life.

Courts martial are composed of officers with no particular legal training who pass judgement on "squaddies" accused of serious crimes like murder and rape and who have (like other citizens) a right to a jury of their peers. They are advised by an official misleadingly called a "judge advocate", who is neither a judge nor an advocate. Courts martial have extensive powers of punishment, and the "officer class" "justice" they dispense in the absence of jury trial deserves greater attention from the media.

The press, like the public, have a right of access. A court martial can sit in secret in the same circumstances as a civilian court (see p. 408) and, in addition, the public can be excluded if it appears that there might otherwise be a disclosure of information useful to an enemy.[12] At the end of the trial the court will be cleared while the officer-judges deliberate. They give their finding in public and then retire to consider the sentence. This is imposed in public. The United Kingdom's system of military justice has been found wanting in numerous ways in Strasbourg when measured against the fair trial requirements of Article 6 of the ECHR. In response to one of these criticisms the Armed Forces Discipline Act 2000 introduced a procedure for appeals from summary punishments imposed by commanding officers. These summary appeal courts will (presumptively) sit in open court[13] but can sit in private where the court considers this necessary in the interests of morals or public order, to safeguard the interests of persons under 18 or the private life of the appellant or where the interests of justice would be prejudiced by a public hearing.[14]

---

[11] *Peacock v. London Weekend Television* (1985) 150 J.P. 71.

[12] Naval Discipline Act 1957, s. 61(2); Army Act 1955, s. 94(2); Air Force Act 1955, s. 94(2).

[13] Armed Forces Discipline Act 2000, s. 19(3)—see "Stop Press" section for further details.

[14] See *e.g.* Summary Appeal Court (Army) Rules 2000, S.I. 2000 No. 2371, r.5. There are similar rules for the Navy and RAF.

CHURCH COURTS

Ecclesiastical courts have had a colourful history. Once, they dispensed soft justice to all who could claim "benefit of clergy", to escape death or prison sentences from the courts of the king. They decided questions of heresy, divorce, wills and defamation. Now they are limited to deciding disputes about Church property, and hearing charges of misconduct levelled against clergymen in their capacity as such.

Each diocese has a consistory court, and the Bishop's Chancellor—a senior lawyer—usually sits as judge. Clerical intermeddling is discouraged: when Bishop Mervyn Stockwood tried to adjudicate a dispute personally, he was roundly rebuked by his Chancellor, who suggested that the bill for unravelling the ensuing mess might be sent to His Grace.[15] The Chancellor sitting alone hears disputes about Church property, but in cases of clerical misconduct sits with a "jury" of four assessors. An appeal can be taken to the appropriate archbishop's court (the Arches Court of Canterbury and the Chancery Court of York) and then, ultimately, to the Privy Council, which advises the Queen, as formal head of the Anglican Church, on whether the appeal should be allowed. The general principle of openness applies to these courts. The High Court is reluctant to overturn an order to exclude the press and public if this was made "reasonably" to serve the ends of justice—e.g. to obtain evidence that would not be given at all if it had to be given in public. But there is no power to exclude because of the intimate or embarrassing nature of the evidence, or merely to deprive the tabloids of the opportunity to run stories about gay or adulterous vicars.[16]

There are proposals to replace consistory courts with new style tribunals for disciplining priests. These will sit in private although their judgments will be made public.

EMPLOYMENT TRIBUNALS

Employment tribunals (ET) consider a wide range of employment disputes. Claims of unfair dismissal, disputes over redundancy payments, and allegations of sex and race discrimination by employers are the most familiar issues, but employment tribunals can also decide whether an organisation is an independent trade union for collective bargaining, whether an employer has allowed adequate time off for trade union or public duties, and appeals against health and safety improvement orders.

---

[15] *Re St Mary's, Barnes* [1982] All E.R. 456.
[16] *R. v. Chancellor of the Chichester Consistory Court, ex p. News Group Newspapers,* *The Times,* July 15, 1991.

Each tribunal comprises a legally trained chairperson, a trade union representative and an employer's nominee. This mix is not intended to ensure that each side can depend on one vote, but rather to give the appearance of a balanced tribunal. Their affiliations are not publicly announced and it can sometimes be difficult to tell them apart. An appeal can be taken on a point of law to the Employment Appeal Tribunal (EAT), which is chaired by a High Court judge flanked again by two lay people.

Employment tribunals must sit in public unless a Government minister has directed a private hearing on grounds of national security or where the tribunal chooses to sit in private to hear evidence which the tribunal considers would be contrary to national security to hear in public, or where the evidence cannot be disclosed without breaching a statutory obligation, disclosing confidential information or substantially injuring the witness's business or place of employment (other than in the context of negotiations with employees).[17] Other substantial modifications are made to employment tribunal procedure in national security cases.[18] Similar provisions apply to the Employment Appeal Tribunal.[19] In national security cases the Tribunal can also take steps to keep secret all or part of the reasons for its decision.[20] The tribunal is under a duty to ensure that information is not disclosed contrary to the interests of national security.[21] Where an employment tribunal does conceal the identity of a witness or takes steps to keep secret all or part of the reasons for its decision, it is an offence to publish anything which is likely to lead to the identification of the witness or the secret part of the tribunal's reasons. The maximum penalty is a level 5 fine (currently £5,000) in the magistrates' court.[22]

The legislative requirement to sit in public is mandatory, an Employment Tribunal cannot sit "in chambers" (outside the provisions of the Rules) even though the Chairman is sitting alone.[23]

---

[17] Employment Tribunals Act 1996, ss. 10 and 10A (as substituted by the Employment Relations Act 1999, Sched. 8); Employment Tribunals (Constitution and Rules of Procedure) Regulations 2001, S.I. 2001 No. 1171, Sched. 1, r. 8.

[18] Employment Tribunals (Constitution and Rules of Procedure) Regulations 2001, reg. 6 and Sched. 2.

[19] Employment Appeal Tribunal Rules, S.I. 1993 No. 2854, r. 30. The substantial modifications for national security cases are made by the Employment Appeal Tribunal (Amendment) Rules 2001, (S.I. 2001 No. 1128).

[20] Employment Tribunals (Constitution and Rules of Procedure) Regulations 2001, S.I. 2001 No. 1171, r. 8(2)(c).

[21] *ibid.*, r.8(4).

[22] Employment Relations Act 1999, Sched. 8, para. 3, adding s. 10B to the Employment Relations Act 1996.

[23] *Storer v. British Gas plc* [2000] 2 All E.R. 440, CA, compare the similar but not identical facts in *R. (on the application of Pelling) v. Bow County Court* p. 407.

In this case, all the regular courtrooms were occupied and the chairman had used an office on a corridor which was separated from the public areas by a locked door which also bore a sign "Private No admittance to the public beyond this point". The EAT had overridden the objection on the ground that no member of the public had actually tried to enter the hearing. The Court of Appeal said that this was immaterial to the question of whether the hearing had taken place in public. It was a question of fact and degree in each case, but on these facts the hearing had not been in public, the employment tribunal chairman had thereby acted beyond his jurisdiction and his decision had to be quashed.

This approach accords with Article 6 of the ECHR which gives a right to a public hearing for the determination of civil rights or obligations. Strasbourg case law as to what is a "civil right or obligation" is unclear and not all rights, particularly not all challenges to the actions of public authorities, qualify. However, when civil rights or obligations are involved the right to a public hearing must be real and not illusory so that a hearing (for instance) of a serious criminal offence against a prisoner which was held in a closed prison did not satisfy the requirement.[24]

There is a Register of Employment Tribunal decisions which is open to public inspection.[25] The Register should include not only the Tribunal's bare decision but also its reasons (whether given in summary or extended form) unless the Tribunal has sat in private on a Minister's direction or unless it has heard evidence in private and the Tribunal has directed that its reasons should be omitted from the Register.[26]

The Register must also include particulars of employment tribunal applications. Approximately 100,000 applications are received each year and before 2000 it was the practice to respond to public inquiries with only the bare admission of the existence of the application. A charity, Public Concern at Work, wanted to investigate the use which was being made of new legislation to protect whistleblowers[27] and found that the bare information which was made available was useless. On judicial review, the High Court agreed. The publicly available information must include the names of applicant and respondent, the date the application was made and received, the relief which was sought and a summary of each of the grounds of claim sufficient to enable a member of the public exercising the right of inspection to understand the gist of the grounds. The obligation could be satisfied by placing a

---

[24] *Riepan v. Austria,* judgment of November 14, 2000.
[25] 2001 Regulations, reg. 12. The Register is kept at the Central Office of the Employment Tribunals: Employment Tribunals, Field Support Unit, 100 Southgate Street, Bury St Edmunds IP 332AQ.
[26] Employment Tribunals Procedure Rules, r. 12
[27] The Public Interest Disclosure Act 1998—see p. 268.

copy of the originating application itself or a precis on the register.[28] Subsequently the Procedural Rules were amended so as to specify more precisely what had to be entered in the Register. It must now contain "the type of claim brought in general terms without reference to its particulars".[29]

So far as the Employment Appeal Tribunal is concerned, any person may inspect (for free) and copy (for a charge) any notice of appeal, judgment or order. Other documents lodged with the Central Office of the EAT can be inspected and copied with the leave of the Tribunal.[30]

Where the case has involved allegations of a sexual offence the Register will not contain any matter which is likely to lead members of the public to identify any person affected by or making such an allegation.[31] The meaning of "sexual offence" is tied to the Sexual Offences (Amendment) Acts 1976 and 1992 (see p. 436).[32] One difference, though, is that names and other matter will be excluded from the Register if they identify a person *affected by* the allegation—not merely the person making the allegation as is the case under the 1976 and 1992 Acts. Although the registered decision will not contain the names of the alleged perpetrators, reporters who will have been free to attend the hearings will usually be able to establish their identity. The employment legislation does not make it an offence to reveal the details of promulgated decisions withheld from the Register and the 1976 and 1992 Acts would only penalise a publication which directly or indirectly identified the *victim* of the alleged offence.

Until the promulgation of its decision, an Employment Tribunal has a wider power—to make a "restricted reporting order". This is not confined to cases of alleged sexual offences but can be made whenever the application involves allegations of sexual misconduct.[33] This is defined as the commission of a sexual offence, sexual harassment or other adverse conduct (of whatever nature) related to sex (whether the relationship with sex lies in the character of the conduct or in its having reference to the sex or sexual orientation of the person at whom the conduct is directed).[34] On one reading "adverse conduct related to sex"

---

[28] *R. v. Secretary of Central Office of the Employment Tribunals (England and Wales), ex p. Public Concern at Work* [2000] I.R.L.R. 658.

[29] Employment Tribunals (Constitution and Rules of Procedure) Regulations 2001, S.I. 2001 No. 1171, reg.12 and Sched. 1, r.2.

[30] *Practice Direction (EAT: Procedure)* [1996] I.C.R. 422, para. 11. The Central Office of the EAT is at 58 Victoria Embankment, London EC4Y ODS.

[31] Employment Tribunal Procedure Rules above, r. 2(5); Employment Appeal Tribunal Rules, r. 23(2)

[32] Industrial Tribunals Act 1996, s. 11(6). As a result of the Youth Justice and Criminal Evidence Act 1999, the 1976 Act's anonymity protections are due to be amalgamated into the 1992 Act.

[33] Employment Tribunals Procedure Rules, r. 16(1).

[34] Employment Tribunals Act 1996, s. 11(6).

could embrace almost any allegation of sex discrimination, but the EAT has said that it should not be read so widely and that the alleged conduct requires some kind of moral obloquy.[35]

Parliament has recognised by granting this power that fear of publicity can be a powerful disincentive to bringing complaints of sexual harassment by employers.[36] However, as the Court of Appeal has said:[37]

> " . . . it is not to be exercised automatically at the request of one party, or even at the request of both parties. The industrial tribunal still has to consider whether it is in the public interest that the press should be deprived of the right to communicate information to the public if it becomes available. It is not a matter which is to be dealt with on the nod so to speak. *Scott v. Scott* establishes that, when both sides consent to an order prohibiting publication, that is exactly the moment when a court ought to examine with particular care whether, as a matter of discretion, such an order should be made."

Courts routinely repeat this pro-media rhetoric, but do nothing to discourage applications for suppression orders—*e.g.* by awarding indemnity (*i.e.* full) costs against wealthy parties who unsuccessfully try to gag the press. Employment tribunals provide many examples of a situation common to other tribunals, where the parties are either indifferent to publicity or positively wish to avoid it. The "media" for this purpose will very often be a local newspaper, unable to afford the costs needed to challenge a suppression order.

> There was scandal in the London Borough of Camden. The council's own solicitor (its deputy chief executive) was suing the council and its chief executive for sex discrimination and victimisation. One of many allegations was that the chief executive had failed to take any action when the solicitor complained that she had been sexually harassed by another council employee. Since ratepayers and council tax payers' money was being expended on the proceedings, the two local newspapers—*The Camden New Journal* and *The Hampstead and Highgate Express*—were properly anxious to report it. But Camden persuaded the tribunal chair that a restricted reporting order was necessary because the council and the chief executive were both "persons affected by" the allegation of sexual misconduct. The applicant did not support the application, but had no money or interest to oppose it. The local papers could not afford a court chal-

---

[35] *Chief Constable of West Yorkshire v. A* [2000] I.R.L.R. 465.
[36] *A v. B, ex p. News Group Newspapers Ltd* [1998] I.C.R. 55, 66, EAT. The same case is reported less coyly as *Chessington World of Adventures v. Reed, ex p. News Group Newspapers Ltd* in [1998] I.R.L.R. 56.
[37] *X v. Z Ltd* [1998] I.C.R. 43, 45–6.

lenge, and the evidence would have proceeded without being reported at all had *The Mail on Sunday* not applied for judicial review in the High Court, which struck the order down as "irrational and perverse". Keane J. said that a corporation could not sensibly be "a person affected by" allegations of sexual misconduct, and nor could the Chief Executive since he was only told about them later and had neither witnessed, perpetrated or been a victim of them. Parliament's purpose was to encourage victims—persons directly affected—to come forward, and no court should impose a restricted reporting order which was wider than necessary to achieve that purpose. Such a wide restriction on reporting as the tribunal had imposed was unsustainable, and the chief executive's preference to avoid any embarrassment was not a legitimate consideration, being "far outweighed by the public interest in contemporaneous reporting of the many other issues arising as between the chief executive and the deputy chief executive of a London Borough".[38]

Keane J.'s decision is important for media law generally in three respects:

(1) It acknowledges that the "public interest" served by media reporting is not confined to the legal points or the matters relevant to the judgment, but includes reporting of "the many other issues arising" in politically-charged tribunal proceedings.

(2) The judge held that "the importance of the public and contemporaneous reporting of court and tribunal hearings" was a principle of statutory interpretation which should be used to give a narrow construction to all statutes purporting to restrict coverage.

(3) He said that the European Convention adds nothing to the protection of court reporting, "given that the (open justice) principle . . . is so firmly embedded in the English common law". In the context of the Human Rights Act this is important because section 11 of the Act preserves existing common law rights.

A Tribunal when making an order must specify the persons who may not be identified.[39] It now seems settled that a corporation or other legal entity cannot be a "person . . . affected by the allegation".[40] The adverse effect of an allegation of sexual misconduct by its staff or officers on

---

[38] *R. v. London (North) Industrial Tribunal, ex p. Associated Newspapers Ltd* [1998] I.C.R. 1212, QBD.

[39] Employment Tribunal Procedure Rules, r. 15(5)(a).

[40] *Ex p. Associated Newspapers Ltd*, above n. 38 and *Leicester University v. A* [1999] I.C.R., EAT—not following *M v. Vincent* [1998] I.C.R. 73, EAT.

the trading reputation of a company is not enough to justify treating it as an affected person. However when a restricting reporting order is made nothing should be published which would be likely to lead members of the public to identify the individual concerned as being the person affected by or making the allegation of sexual misconduct. There may be cases where publishing the company's name would indirectly identify one of the individuals who had been given anonymity by the order, but there is still an important difference between this protection (which derives from anonymity given to someone else) and the direct prohibition of reporting of the company's name itself—this a tribunal cannot impose.[41]

A notice that a restricted reporting order has been made should be put on the notice board of the tribunal with any list of cases and on the door of the room where the proceedings are being heard.[42] Restricted reporting orders do not prohibit reporting indefinitely, but only until the tribunal's decision is promulgated (*i.e.* the date on the determination signifying when it was sent to the parties). Thereafter, the only restrictions on reporting are those which apply generally including the 1976 and 1992 Sexual Offences (Amendment) Acts—see above.

It is common practice for employment tribunals to decide questions of liability first and then, if the applicant is successful, to deal with remedies later. There has been a difference of view within the EAT as to whether the restricted reporting order comes to an end once the liability decision is promulgated or only after any issue as to remedies is concluded.[43]

It is an offence to publish identifying material in breach of a restricted reporting order or to include it in a programme service. The maximum penalty is a fine on scale 5 (currently £5,000).[44] Unusually for reporting offences, prosecution is not dependent on the consent of the Attorney-General.

Similar powers are given to Employment Tribunals to make restricted reporting orders in disability discrimination cases which are likely to include evidence of a personal nature, *i.e.* any evidence of a medical or other intimate nature which might reasonably be assumed to be likely to cause significant embarrassment to the complainant if reported.[45] Only the complainant can apply for an order (whereas any party to the

---

[41] See the similar distinction made by the court in *Ex p. Godwin* at p. 432.

[42] Employment Tribunal Procedure Rules, r. 16(5)(c).

[43] *Chessington World of Adventures v. Reed, ex p. News Group Newspapers* (above) said that it ended with the liability determination. *Chief Constable of West Yorkshire v. A* (above) said that the restriction on reporting would continue to cover the remedies proceedings.

[44] Employment Tribunals Act 1996, s. 11(1).

[45] Employment Tribunals Act 1996, s. 12 and Employment Tribunal Rules, r. 16(2) and (3).

proceedings can apply for a restriction order where there is an allegation of sexual misconduct—the Tribunal has power to make an order of its own motion in both cases). In disability cases the power is more broadly expressed because the focus is on the embarrassing character of the evidence rather than any allegation of misconduct.

> This difference was thrown into relief by *Chief Constable of West York-shire Police v. A*[46] where the applicant had undergone gender reassignment and wanted to join the police as a woman police constable. The police had refused her application as someone who had been born a man could not conduct searches of women so could not then be assigned to the full duties of a WPC. The EAT agreed that the Employment Tribunal Rules did not in these circumstances give a power to order anonymity. However, the applicant also relied on her right to equal treatment under the E.U.'s Equal Treatment Directive (ETD).[47] This included a right to an effective remedy (Article 6). The EAT found that without an anonymity order the applicant would not have an effective remedy and this justified the order.[48]

If Tribunals wish to protect the identity of people involved with allegations of sexual misconduct or disability discrimination, they must use restricted reporting orders. They cannot use their general power to control their own procedure to hear such applications in private or to make restricted reporting orders, even if they believe that the restricted reporting order will give inadequate protection.[49]

The EAT can make restricted reporting orders when it hears appeals against an ET's decision to make or refuse to make a restricted reporting order or when hearing an appeal on some other interlocutory matter.[50] On a further appeal to the Court of Appeal, the court will be likely to restrict reporting in a similar manner.[51]

The EAT is a superior court of record[52] and has the same rights, powers and privileges as the High Court.[53] It may be, therefore,[54] that it has the same inherent powers as the High Court to either exclude the public or restrict reporting when the stringent tests in *Scott* and *The Leveller* are satisfied (see p. 408).

---

[46] [2000] I.R.L.R. 465.

[47] 76/207/EC.

[48] The E.T.'s use of the order was not challenged on appeal and so the EAT did not need to rule on it, but it used Art. 6 of the ETD to justify itself making an anonymity order to cover the proceedings in the Appeal Tribunal.

[49] *R. v. Southampton Industrial Tribunal, ex p. INS News Group Ltd* [1995] I.R.L.R. 247; *Chief Constable of West Yorkshire Police v. A* (above).

[50] Employment Tribunals Act 1996, s. 31; Employment Appeal Tribunal Rules, s. 23.

[51] *X v. Z Ltd* [1998] I.C.R. 43, CA.

[52] Employment Tribunals Act, s. 20(3).

[53] *ibid.*, s. 29(2).

[54] See *Chessington World of Adventures v. Reed* (above).

Media opposition to a restricted reporting order can be made through representations to the Tribunal (if the Tribunal gives leave). Otherwise, publishers or journalists can apply for judicial review of an Employment Tribunal's order. Since 2000, the legality of the order would also have to be measured against the requirements of Article 10 of the Human Rights Convention and section 12 of the Human Rights Act.

Decisions of the EAT are not subject to judicial review.[55] One (rather clumsy) alternative is for the media group opposing reporting restrictions to apply to become a party to the appeal before the EAT. The EAT has a discretion but will be particularly willing to hear representations from the press when both the appellant and respondent to the appeal are content to have reporting restricted.[56]

IMMIGRATION APPEALS

Immigration adjudicators hear appeals against the Government's refusal to allow immigrants or visitors to enter or to stay in the country, and against deportation decisions. There is a further appeal (with leave) to the Immigration Appeal Tribunal (IAT).

Adjudicators and the IAT sit in public,[57] although they do have power to exclude all or any observers where they consider this necessary in the interests of morals, public order, national security, the interests of minors or when the private life of the parties so require or when publicity would prejudice the interests of justice. They may only exercise the power to the extent strictly necessary.[58] They must, however, sit in private where it is alleged that a passport or other document used to obtain entry has been forged and disclosure of the method of detection would be contrary to the public interest. In these cases even the appellant and his representatives are excluded from the hearing.[59]

Immigration appeals which have a national security dimension are not dealt with in the ordinary way but are heard by the Special Immigration Appeals Commission which sits in panels of three and is chaired by a High Court judge. When the Home Office presents its security sensitive material to the Commission, the appellant and his representatives are barred from the hearing (although a special advocate, appointed by the Attorney-General to represent the appellant's interests, is entitled

---

[55] Because, as a superior court of record, it is not subject to judicial review.
[56] *A v. B, ex p. News Group Newspapers Ltd* [1998] I.C.R. 55.
[57] Immigration and Asylum Appeals (Procedure) Rules 2000, S.I. 2000 No. 2333, r.40.
[58] *ibid.*, r.40(3).
[59] Immigration and Asylum Act 1999, Sched. 4, para. 6; Immigration and Asylum Appeals (Procedure) Rules (above), r.40(2).

to remain). From this part of the proceedings the public must be excluded.[60] From other parts of the proceedings the Commission can exclude the public for "any other good reason".[61] In the few appeals that it has heard so far, the Commission's general practice has been to sit in public for those sessions where the appellant is entitled to remain.

As a result of concern at the competency and integrity of some immigration "consultants" the Government introduced in 2001 a system of regulation by an Immigration Services Commissioner. Complaints against immigration advisers or representatives are taken to an Immigration Services Tribunal which sits in public unless the Tribunal directs otherwise.[62]

MENTAL HEALTH REVIEW TRIBUNALS

A matter of perennial interest to certain sections of the press is the danger to the public supposedly created by the release of once manic murderers. In law they are technically manslaughterers who are guilty on grounds of diminished responsibility and have been consigned to one of the four top-security mental hospitals. In many cases their mental illness will, in time, be cured or brought under control so that in fact their release will pose no danger to the public. But the horrendous nature of the original killing (the "index offence") is such that release is politically unpalatable to the Home Secretary and sensibly requires extreme caution. That decision is entrusted to a Mental Health Review Tribunal, a panel usually chaired by a circuit judge and comprising a consultant psychiatrist and a layperson. "Release" comes in stages—to a less secure mental hospital, and then, under restricted conditions, into the community. This last stage is not reached until after many years of psychiatric evaluation and screening, with every opportunity given to the Home Office to oppose it where any risk to the public is apprehended. There are rare cases of reoffending, attended with massive publicity that tends to obscure the fault that the overwhelming majority of releases that cause no problems. However, since reassertion of the original mental illness will pose a danger to life, there is a legitimate public interest in press coverage of Mental Health Review Tribunal decisions.

In the interests of the patient, however, very little coverage is permit-

---

[60] Special Immigration Appeals Commission (Procedure) Rules 1998, S.I. 1998 No. 1881, r.19(1).

[61] *ibid.*, r.19(2).

[62] Immigration Services Tribunal Rules 2000, S.I. 2000 No. 2739, r.20—complaints against lawyers are channelled to their professional disciplinary bodies, see below p. 509.

ted by law. The tribunal is a "court" for the purposes of the law of contempt, so that any prejudicial story about an imminent hearing that puts pressure on the tribunal members or upon expert witnesses may give rise to a prosecution.[63] The Mental Health Tribunal rules require that the tribunal shall sit in private, other than in the rare cases when the patient asks for a hearing in public and the tribunal is satisfied that this would not be contrary to the patient's best interests. The rules additionally and unnecessarily ban publication of information about tribunal proceedings, including the names of individuals who have been involved in them.[64]

In the important 1991 case of *Pickering v. Liverpool Daily Post and Echo Newspapers plc* the House of Lords interpreted narrowly the ban on publication of tribunal "proceedings" so as to permit the press to publish the fact that a particular patient had made an application for discharge, details of the date, time and place of the tribunal hearing, and the result. The ban was limited to reporting "the substance of the matters which the court has closed its doors to consider", such as evidence and expert reports, or the reasons for the decision and any condition imposed on the patient's release. Alongside this bare information, however, editors are free to republish lurid details of the applicant's original offences. The Law Lords, while conceding the great public concern about release of persons detained for horrifying acts of violence, warned editors against using this freedom to mount a "media campaign" of inflammatory articles against the discharge of an offender whose case is about to be considered by a tribunal. Such a campaign might well be a contempt.[65]

This is one of the few areas where some restriction on publicity is justified, in the interests both of the privacy of the patient and of protecting the tribunal system from a particularly violent form of pressure. The decision in *Pickering* that a tribunal was a "court" for the purposes of contempt overruled a previous High Court decision to the contrary, which had permitted hysterical press campaigns of vilification against certain patients and those psychiatrists who supported their release. The present restrictions seek to strike a balance: they do not preclude the press from describing an applicant's previous history or fears that may still be entertained about his or her stability, but require such stories to be moderate in tone and balanced in factual presentation. It will amount to a breach of confidence for the media to publish details of private psychiatric reports prepared for the purposes of a tribunal hearing; the High Court has held that the public interest defence will in such cases

---

[63] *Pickering v. Liverpool Daily Post and Echo Newspapers plc* [1991] 2 A.C. 238, CA overruling *Att.-Gen. v. Associated Newspapers plc* [1989] 1 All E.R. 604.
[64] Mental Health Review Tribunal Rules (S.I. 1983 No. 942), r.21.
[65] *Pickering v. Liverpool Daily Post and Echo Newspapers plc* [1991] 2 A.C. 238, H L.

be of no avail. However dangerous the patient may be depicted in the report, the public interest is satisfied if it is transmitted to the authorities, but not to the public at large.[66]

LICENSING

Some licences (*e.g.* for sex shops, dancing, cinemas and taxis) are granted by local authorities, but others (*e.g.* pubs, hotels, off-licences, betting shops) are considered by magistrates. J.P.s have this job because, before the establishment of a unified system of local councils, local administration was in their hands. The licensee must be a "fit and proper person", and the police or others can object and draw attention to the applicant's unsavoury past. The premises must also be suitable. Fire prevention and environmental officers are the most common objectors on this score, but local residents also have an opportunity to protest at the effect that the use would have on their neighbourhood. When exercising a licensing power, the justices are still acting in this administrative capacity—and here press reports are not constrained by contempt. The justices must hear the applications, and any objectors to them, in public.[67]

PLANNING INQUIRIES

Local authorities have a variety of powers to control development and land use in their areas. They can, for instance, refuse planning permission, make orders (enforcement notices) to stop or reverse unpermitted development, and compulsorily purchase land. They must also draw up long-term strategic plans for the development of their area. Objections to these actions are determined by the Secretary of State for the Environment, but in most cases an inspector will be appointed to hear both sides. In general, the inspector takes evidence and hears argument in public, and documentary evidence is open to inspection, although it can be kept private if the Secretary of State is satisfied that it relates to national security or if disclosure would jeopardise the security of any premises in a way that would be contrary to the national interest.[68]

For major planning inquiries a Department of Environment Code recommends that a register of participants be prepared, divided into

---

[66] Scott J. in *W v. Egdell* [1990] Ch. 359, CA.
[67] *Boulter v. Kent Justices* [1897] A.C. 556.
[68] Town and Country Planning Act 1992, s. 321.

those playing a major part in the proceedings, those wishing to give oral evidence but not otherwise play a major part in the proceedings, and those submitting written representations. The register should be publicly available. The Code also provides that outline statements and certain written submissions will be available to members of the public, who ought also to be able to attend pre-inquiry meetings and programme meetings.[69]

<h2 style="text-align:center">DISCIPLINARY HEARINGS</h2>

Disciplinary complaints against doctors are first considered in private by the Preliminary Proceedings Committee of the General Medical Council. If it finds a case to answer, the issue is tried by the Professional Conduct Committee. This committee sits in public, although it can exclude observers if it considers such an action is in the interests of justice, or desirable in regard to the nature of the case or the evidence. But while the committee has these powers to deliberate in private, it must give its decision in public.[70] Similar procedures apply to veterinary surgeons, opticians, nurses and pharmacists.[71]

Disciplinary proceedings against lawyers have become more open. The Bar Council's Disciplinary Tribunal must sit in public unless there has been a direction that it should sit in private and this direction has not been overruled by the Tribunal.[72] The Solicitors' Disciplinary Tribunal (SDT) also sits in public.[73] However, there is a lingering effect of a former preference for privacy in the arrangements for appeals from the SDT to the High Court: Rules of Court require that the appeal be listed without identifying the solicitor[74] and so every proposition of law in this jurisdiction is supported by a case with the same ubiquitous title: *Re A Solicitor*. This is an anomaly which the Court of Appeal has recommended should be changed. It will not permit it to be extended.[75]

---

[69] DOE 15/96, Annex 4.

[70] General Medical Council Preliminary Proceedings Committee and Professional Conduct Committee (Procedure) Rules 1988 (S.I. 1988 No. 2255), r.48.

[71] Veterinary Surgeons and Veterinary Practitioners (Disciplinary Committee) (Procedure and Evidence) Rules 1967 (S.I. 1967 No. 659), r.15(1). General Optical Council (Disciplinary Committee) (Procedure) Rules, Order of Council 1985 (S.I. 1985 No. 1580), r.11; Nurses, Midwives and Health Visitors (Professional Conduct) Rules 1993, S.I. 1993 No. 893, r.23. Pharmaceutical Society (Statutory Committee) Order of Council 1978 (S.I. 1978 No. 20), reg. 16.

[72] Bar Council Code of Conduct, Annexe K: Disciplinary Tribunals Regulations 2000, reg.12.

[73] Solicitors (Disciplinary Procedure) Rules 1994, S.I. 1994 No. 288, r.13.

[74] CPR Sched. 1, RSC, O.106, r.12(1).

[75] *R. v. Legal Aid Board, ex p. Kaim Todner* [1998] 3 All E.R. 541, 548, CA.

The move to greater openness is consistent with the common law's open justice principle. Article 6(1) of the European Human Rights Convention also guarantees litigants a "fair and *public* hearing" in the determination of their civil rights (with limited exceptions). Disciplinary proceedings by professional bodies are included in the concept of "civil rights".[76]

Disciplinary proceedings for police officers are automatically held in private,[77] and are vulnerable to challenge as contrary to Article 6(1).[78] It is likely that objections to secret hearing could be made not just by one of the parties to the disciplinary proceedings. Although one purpose of openness is to protect litigants against secret justice, another is to permit reporting so as to maintain public confidence in the courts.[79] The press are in the best position to defend this public interest and in a better position than the "defendant" who often has no desire for the details of his misconduct to receive any publicity.[80] Alternatively, this might be a situation where Article 10 does give a right of access to information.[81] At a time when the media demands openness for other tribunals, complaints against the press and broadcasters are swathed in secrecy. Typically and hypocritically, there are no demands by the press to attend PCC hearings or to televise the BSC.

PUBLIC INQUIRIES

A familiar Government response to a crisis is to appoint a committee or announce an inquiry. The openness of the inquiry will depend upon the particular power that is used to set it up. Royal Commissions and departmental or interdepartmental inquiries can be instructed to sit in public or in private; usually, they are allowed to exercise their discretion. Inquiries into police-related matters, such as the Scarman investi-

---

[76] *Le Compte v. Belgium,* [1981] 4 E.H.R.R. 1; *Diennet v. France* (1995) 21 E.H.R.R. 554

[77] The Police (Conduct) Regulations 1999, S.I. 1999 No. 730, r.2(6) and the Police (Conduct) (Senior Officers) Regulations, S.I. 1999 No. 731, r.15(1). The regulations now allow a complainant to be present when witnesses are being examined or cross-examined, but only after they have given their own evidence, subject to their good behaviour and liable to exclusion where the giving of evidence before them would harm the public interest.

[78] See *Diennet v. France* above.

[79] See *Diennet v. France,* above, at para. 33.

[80] *Hakansson v. Sweden* (1998) 13 E.H.R.R. 1 establishes that the Article 6 right to a public hearing can be waived but only if this does not conflict with some other important public interest.

[81] See Andrew Nicol, Gavin Millar and Andrew Sharland, *Media Law and Human Rights* (Blackstone, 2001), p. 131–2.

gations of the Brixton riots in 1981 and the Macpherson inquiry into the police response to the killing of Stephen Lawrence are usually held in public, but this is at the discretion of the Home Secretary, who sets up the inquiry.[82]

When formal gathering of evidence is necessary, a tribunal of inquiry may be appointed under the Tribunals of Inquiry Act 1921. Such a tribunal was set up under Sir Ronald Waterhouse to investigate abuse against children in local authority homes in North Wales and how the allegations were investigated. Another under Lord Cullen investigated the Dunblane massacre. Lord Saville is conducting the second Tribunal of Inquiry into the deaths on Bloody Sunday in 1972. The Tribunal's decisions that soldiers would not automatically be allowed to give evidence anonymously were quashed on two occasions because the Tribunal failed to give proper consideration to the right to life in Article 2 of the European Convention and the continuing threat of reprisals against the soldiers.[83]

Internal inquiries into transport accidents are usually private affairs, but greater publicity is given to an investigation by an outside appointee. Inquiries into sea deaths or casualties or disciplinary charges against merchant navy officers must generally be in public[84] and the inspector's report into an air accident or incident must be published.[85] The inquiries into the Southall and Ladbroke Grove rail accidents were held under the Heath and Safety at Work Act 1974. Inquiries of this type must be held in public unless the Government closes them on national security grounds or a public hearing would be likely to disclose a trade secret.[86]

An important precedent in favour of openness was set by the Divisional Court when it ruled in 2000 that the Secretary of State for Health had acted unlawfully by stipulating that the Inquiry to investigate the Dr Harold Shipman affair should hear evidence in private. Shipman had been convicted of murdering 15 of his elderly patients and was suspected of killing very many more. The case was of massive public interest and the families of the victims had pressed for a public inquiry. Their Article 10 rights to communicate freely the evidence which they gave to the Inquiry was a major factor in the court's reasoning.[87] After

---

[82] Police Act 1996, s. 49(2).
[83] See *R. v. Lord Saville, ex p. A* [2000] 1 W.L.R. 153, CA.
[84] Merchant Shipping (Section 52 Inquiries) Rules 1982, S.I. 1982 No. 1752, r.6(3) and The Merchant Shipping (Formal Investigations) Rules 1985, S.I. 1985 No. 1001, r.7(5).
[85] Civil Aviation (Air Accidents and Incidents) Regulations 1996, S.I. 1996 No. 2798, r.13, following the European Directive 94/66/EC.
[86] Health and Safety at Work Act 1974, s. 14(3) and Health and Safety Inquiries (Procedure) Regulations 1975 (S.I. 1975 No. 335), reg. 8(2) and (3).
[87] *R. v. Secretary of State for Health, ex p. Wagstaff* [2000] U.K.H.R.R. 875.

the court's decision, the Government announced that it would instead appoint a Tribunal of Inquiry chaired by Justice Janet Smith to sit in public. See "Stop Press" section for further details.

OTHER INQUIRIES

The pattern we have observed—namely a presumption of publicity coupled with a discretion to sit in private—is common to most other tribunals. The extent of the discretion varies widely. It may be dependent on proof of "exceptional reasons"[88-89] or where one party would be prejudiced by publicity[90] or the discretion may be limited to cases where disclosure would be "contrary to the public interest"[91] or where the tribunal is satisfied that by reason of disclosure of confidential matters or matters concerning national security it would be just and reasonable to hold the hearing in private.[92] All of these formulae require the tribunal to exercise some judgment which, if adverse to media rights, can be judicially reviewed. They mean that the presence of bureaucratic embarrassment is not enough to put the hearing into closed session. Much more objectionable are rules which require the hearing to take place in private unless both parties (as well as the tribunal) agree to allow the public to attend.[93] This is to turn the Article 6 presumption in favour of open hearings on its head and, when the right in issue is what Article 6 describes as a "civil" right, is ripe for challenge under the Human Rights Act.

Oral hearings by Social Security Appeals Tribunals are conducted in public unless the claimant requests a private hearing or the chairman believes that intimate personal or financial circumstances may have to be disclosed or considerations of public security are involved when the hearing must be in private.[94]

[88-89] Independent Schools Tribunals, which judge complaints by the Government against such schools, Independent School Tribunal Rules 1958 (S.I. 1958 No. 519), r.8; Agricultural Land Tribunals, which decide whether a farmer has acted fairly in evicting tenants from a tied house, Agricultural Land Tribunal (Rules) Order 1978 (S.I. 1978 No. 259), r.24

[90] e.g. appeals against valuations for council tax purposes: Council Tax (Alteration of Lists and Appeals) Regulations 1993, S.I. 1993 No. 290, r.25(3).

[91] e.g. The Gas (Underground Storage) (Inquiries Procedure) Rules 1966 (S.I. 1966 No. 1375), r.8(4).

[92] Lands Tribunal Rules 1996 (S.I. 1996 No. 1022), r.5.

[93] e.g. the procedure in national security appeals before the Data Protection Tribunal: Data Protection Tribunal (National Security Appeals) Rules 2000 (S.I. 2000 No. 206), r. 23.

[94] Social Security and Child Support (Decisions and Appeals) Regulations 1999 (S.I. 1999 No. 991), r.49(6).

TELEVISING TRIBUNALS

Royal Commissions and ordinary tribunals are not "courts" for the purposes of section 41 of the Criminal Justice Act 1925, which contains the only formal prohibition on televising proceedings (See p. 480). It follows that the tribunal will have a discretion to permit the electronic media to record and broadcast proceedings. Prior to permission to televise was never granted, but this is partly due to the fact that media interests never asked for such permission, at least with the determination to challenge any refusal by judicial review proceedings. The attitude towards televising courts has undergone a sea change in recent years: the Bar is now in favour, and the electronic media is beginning to televise some tribunal proceedings.

In the case of Royal Commissions and major public inquiries the argument for the right to broadcast proceedings is overwhelming. The very purpose of establishing a Tribunal of Inquiry is to restore public confidence by establishing the truth about allegations or events that have caused grave disquiet; and public confidence is best restored after the public have been able to see or hear for themselves the testimony and the procedures.[95] Since televising is the best evidence compared with a secondhand report in a newspaper, public understanding is likely to be enhanced. Since television reaches a larger audience than newspapers, it assists the Tribunal process: members of the public may come forward with evidence or ideas or ideas if they become aware of the Inquiry or its focus.

More generally, the public character of such an inquiry can best come from the broadcasting of its proceedings. This was the conclusion of Louis Blom-Cooper Q.C., who in 1990 opened to radio and television his Antiguan Royal Commission on the smuggling of arms to the Colombian drug cartels. His report concludes:

"My fears of physical obstruction were entirely misplaced: one single television camera behind Counsel, trained for the most part on the witness, soon went entirely unnoticed. No lights or other studio impedimenta were required. It was observed that some Counsel, who at first disdained microphones, very quickly and effortlessly learned to use them. The witnesses were in no way flustered or deterred, or for the most part even conscious of the recording. I am confident that they remained blissfully unaware

---

[95] Lord Salmon, *Tribunals of Inquiry,* 1967 Lionel Cohen Memorial Lecture, published by the Hebrew University, Jerusalem.

that their evidence was going to be relayed to the populace. If they were aware, they raised no objection and showed no sign of disquiet, let alone dissent. Several senior Counsel indicated to me that they felt an extremely beneficial discipline to ask relevant and comprehensible questions, and not to waste time. I felt, myself, the sense of Jeremy Bentham's argument in favour of open justice, namely, that "it keeps the judge, while trying, under trial". That the Commission proceeded as effectively and efficiently as it did, is, in my view, due in some measure to the fact that we could all be heard and seen . . . each evening on radio and television. The benefits of electronic media coverage, in terms of public understanding, were incalculable. It meant that citizens could receive accurate information about a great public scandal, and make up their own minds about the testimony. Although I accept that electronic media coverage of criminal trials requires a very careful and gradual introduction, I hope that it will come to be considered routine for public inquiries."[96]

Some progress has been made in this respect. The evidence given to the Southall Train crash was televised and in the Ladbroke Grove rail crash inquiry the opening and closing speeches were broadcast. In 2000 Lord Mackay of Clashfern, the former Lord Chancellor, permitted live television coverage of his Commission into the Administration of Justice in Trinidad: he pronounced his satisfaction that the public were able to see the evidence and cross-examination of politicians, judges and frustrated litigants. No legal challenge was ever mounted to the exclusion of their cameras from inquiries of such public importance as those into the Matrix Churchill "arms to Iraq" scandal, the Stephen Lawrence murder and the responsibility for BSE (bovine spongiform encaphalopathy). Instead of asserting the viewers' right to know what is going on at these inquiries, television companies settling instead for "dramatic reconstruction" which is nothing like the real thing. It took an American company—CNN— at the Harold Shipman Inquiry to assert the alternative and simple proposition that a public inquiry into a public scandal should actually be seen by the public—and on television.[97]

---

[96] Louis Blom-Cooper, *Guns for Antigua* (Duckworth, 1990), p. 46.
[97] See above, p. 512.

CONTEMPT

The 1981 Contempt of Court Act imposes strict liability in relation to stories that create a substantial risk of serious prejudice to active "legal proceedings".[98] "Legal proceedings", for the purposes of the Act, are proceedings that take place in a court, defined to include "any tribunal or body exercising the judicial power of the state".[99] Most of the lesser courts and tribunals discussed in this chapter have no power to take action of their own volition against the media, but the High Court has an overall supervisory power to punish contempt of "inferior courts".[1] The question thus becomes one of deciding whether a particular body is a court, albeit an "inferior" one. That question, an absolutely crucial one for the media, has no simple answer although guidance comes from general principles, applied on a case by case basis.

The general rule is that contempt covers all bodies that exercise the judicial power of the State. The meaning of this phrase was considered in the important 1980 case of *Attorney-General v. BBC*[2]:

> The BBC had made a programme that was extremely critical of the Exclusive Brethren. One branch of the sect had applied for rate relief to a local valuation court, and the case was to be heard a few days after the BBC proposed to transmit the film. The Attorney-General was granted an injunction to stop it, on the grounds that it would prejudice the Brethren's claim. The House of Lords held that the injunction was wrongly given: a local valuation court did not exercise the judicial power of the State, and hence could not be protected from contempt.

The judgments of the Law Lords will be sifted for dicta of help in deciding the issue in relation to other tribunals; their individual approaches to the question were as follows:

> Viscount Dilhorne drew a distinction between courts that discharge judicial functions and those that discharge administrative ones, and said that contempt did not apply in relation to the latter. He suggested, albeit in passing and inferentially, that immigration adjudicators, the Immigration Appeal Tribunal, the Lands Tribunal, pension appeal tribunals, the Transport Tribunal, the Commons Commissioners and the Performing Rights Tribunal were not to be regarded as courts that would put the media at risk of a contempt action.

---

[98] See further Lowe and Rawlings, "Tribunals and the Administration of Justice" [1982] *Public Law* 418.
[99] Contempt of Court Act 1981, s. 19.
[1] Civil Procedure Rules, Sched. 1; RSC, O.52, r.1(2)(a)(iii).
[2] [1980] 3 All E.R. 161, HL.

Lord Salmon adopted an approach particularly favourable to the media. He said:

> "Public policy requires that most of the principles relating to contempt of court which have for ages necessarily applied to the long-established inferior courts such as county courts, magistrates' courts, courts martial, coroners' courts and consistory courts shall not apply to valuation courts and the host of other modern tribunals which may be regarded as inferior courts; otherwise the scope of contempt of court would be unnecessarily extended and accordingly freedom of speech and freedom of the press would be unnecessarily contracted."

Lord Scarman accepted that courts martial and Church courts exercised, for historic reasons, the judicial power of the State and were protected in consequence. However, he took the view that legal policy was against protecting administrative courts and tribunals: if Parliament wanted to provide special protection, it must say so in the legislation establishing the body in question:

> "I would not think it desirable to extend the doctrine (of contempt) which is unknown, and not apparently needed, in most civilized legal systems, beyond its historical scope, namely the proceedings of courts of judicature. If we are to make the extension, we have to ask ourselves, if the United Kingdom is to comply with its international obligations, whether the extension is necessary in our democratic society. Is there a "pressing social need" for the extension?"

Lord Edmund-Davies and Lord Fraser were more circumspect, although the former echoed Lord Scarman's view that contempt protection to tribunals and other bodies ought to be given specifically by Parliament, and that the courts themselves should not extend contempt proceedings unless it is clear beyond doubt that the demands of justice make them essential".

The upshot of those judicial approaches is that contempt protection will not readily be extended, in the absence of statutory provision, to any "lesser" court or tribunal. It can be said with confidence that courts martial[3] and Church courts[4] are protected, although since the former are

---

[3] *The Daily Sketch and Graphic* was fined £500 for contempt because, at the time, the sentence could not be published at all until it was confirmed by the defendant's commanding officer. *R. v. Gunn, ex p. Att.-Gen. (No. 2), The Times,* November 14, 1953; [1954] Crim I.R. 53. This is no longer the case. Instead the 1981 Act provides that the proceedings are active until the completion of any review of a finding or sentence (Sched. 1, para. 8). This means that reporting and comment are permitted as long as they do not cause substantial risk of serious prejudice.

[4] Ecclesiastical Jurisdiction Measure 1963, s. 81(2) expressly gives the High Court power to punish contempt of Church courts. For a rare example, see *R. v. Daily Herald, ex p. Bishop of Norwich* [1932] 2 K.B. 402. The procedure is now modelled on that for Tribunals of Inquiry (see below p. 518): Care of Churches and Ecclesiastical Jurisdictional Measure 1991, s. 8 and Sched. 4, para. 11.

conducted by senior army officers and the latter by a distinguished judge or lawyer, the danger of a media story creating a serious risk of substantial prejudice is relatively small. Lord Salmon, in the passage quoted above, assumed that coroners' courts were protected and the Divisional Court has since confirmed that this is the case.[5] A coroners' court becomes "active" for the purpose of the strict liability rule as soon as the inquest is opened (which will usually be shortly after the death) even though the proceedings are then adjourned for a considerable time while the police carry out their investigations.[6] Employment tribunals are "courts"[7] and so are Mental Health Review Tribunals (see p. 507).

In all other cases the presumption must be that contempt does not apply. Planning inquiries make administrative rather than judicial decisions. Although professional bodies must act judicially, they do not wield the State's authority. The Court of Appeal in 1998 firmly applied the rule in *Att.-Gen. v. BBC* to quash an attempt by the General Medical Council (the doctors' disciplinary body) to claim that it was a court protected by the law of contempt from BBC criticism.[8] Similarly, arbitrators who are appointed to resolve a contractual dispute derive their authority from the private parties and not from the Government. Magistrates, as we have seen, act in an administrative capacity when sitting as licensing justices. A pet-shop owner once protested that his application to local magistrates for a licence was prejudiced by the BBC's *Checkpoint* programme. The Court of Appeal again ruled in favour of the BBC: the magistrates were acting administratively and the strict liability inhibition on comment did not apply.[9] For the same reason the media are free to comment on applications for liquor or gambling licences. On the eve of the sitting that was to decide whether the Playboy Club should retain its gaming licence, the BBC broadcast a documentary alleging that the club had consistently breached the Gaming Act. The programme was devastatingly prejudicial, pre-judging the issues that the magistrates would have to decide in the days that followed. It was not contempt, however, because a licensing body is not a court exercising the judicial power of the State.

Even if the body in question does exercise "the judicial power of the state", the High Court could penalise a newspaper or broadcaster only

[5] *R. v. West Yorkshire Coroner ex p. Smith* [1985] 1 All E.R. 100.
[6] *Peacock v. London Weekend Television* (1985) 150 J.P. 71.
[7] *Peach Grey and Co. (a firm) v. Sommers* [1995] I.C.R. 549, Q.B.D.
[8] *General Medical Council v. BBC* [1998] 1 W.L.R. 1573, CA.
[9] *Lewis v. BBC* [1979] Court of Appeal Transcript 193.

if the story satisfied the other requirements of contempt. In brief, the proceedings must have been active (*i.e.* the publication must have taken place before a hearing date was fixed, and before final disposal). The story must also pose a substantial risk of serious prejudice. None of the tribunals considered here (except on occasions the coroner's court) has a jury. Most are presided over or advised by persons with some legal experience. It will be rare for a story to create the necessary risk of prejudice to amount to contempt. And it must be remembered that even prejudicial material of this kind can be published if it is part of a discussion in good faith of public affairs and the risk of prejudice is only incidental (see further p. 371).

If the body is a "court", then reports of its proceedings have the same protection from contempt as other fair and accurate reports of legal proceedings. These cannot breach the strict liability rule unless the tribunal has made a postponement order (see p. 458). Lesser courts probably do not have power to make postponement orders or to ban publication of evidence that was not given publicly—the matter is undecided, although one appeal judge has said that if they do possess this power, they should hardly ever use it.[10]

Tribunals of Inquiry have special statutory powers. They can refer to the High Court any matter that would have been contempt if it had taken place in High Court proceedings.[11] The Vassal Tribunal into the activities of the Russian spy in the British Admiralty was a Tribunal of Inquiry, and it used this power to refer the cases of journalists who refused to reveal their sources. Three were jailed by the High Court for sticking to their professional ethics.[12] Following the flurry of interviews with witnesses to the Aberfan disaster, the Attorney-General warned the press of the danger of contempt, but it is highly unlikely that mere press comment would ever lead to contempt proceedings, especially after Lord Salmon's 1969 report, in which he discouraged the idea that such stories could influence a judge conducting an inquiry. He thought it important to preserve freedom of discussion, even if some witnesses might feel inhibited as a result.[13] There has been no case in which a newspaper has been punished for this type of contempt. The Contempt

---

[10] *R. v. Horsham Justices, ex p. Farquharson* [1982] 2 All E.R. 269, 284 *per* Lord Denning.

[11] Tribunals of Inquiry (Evidence) Act 1921, s. 1(2)(c).

[12] *Att.-Gen. v. Mulholland; v. Foster* [1963] 1 All E.R. 767, CA; *Att.-Gen. v. Clough* [1963] 1 Q.B. 773.

[13] Report of the Interdepartmental Committee on the Law of Contempt in Relation to Tribunals of Inquiry (1969) Cmnd. 4078, para. 26.

of Court Act assumes that the strict liability contempt may apply to Tribunals of Inquiry because it states that the proceedings are active from the time of the Tribunal's appointment[14] until its report is presented to Parliament. Given Lord Salmon's views however, this provision should in practice prove academic.

LIBEL

Media reports of proceedings and decisions of lesser courts and tribunals are protected from libel actions, but with varying degrees of efficacy. Reports about lesser courts that, nonetheless, exercise the judicial power of the State (*i.e.* those to which contempt law is applicable) will be fully protected by absolute privilege. Reports of proceedings in most other bodies will be protected by qualified privilege at common law, while in a few cases a special statutory privilege can be claimed only if the newspaper carrying the defamatory report has offered the victim a right of reply.

Absolute privilege

The best defence that a newspaper can have to a defamation action is that the report is absolutely privileged. This means that the person libelled has no claim, even if it can be shown that the paper acted maliciously in publishing its story (see p. 485). This defence, not surprisingly, is reserved to a narrow class of reports.[15] It applies only to reports of those bodies which are classified as "courts", *i.e.* they must exercise the judicial power of the State.[16] This is the same definition as is used in the Contempt of Court Act. Thus in those cases where the media are at risk of committing contempt under the strict liability rule, they at least have the benefit of absolute privilege against libel actions for reports of those proceedings. The further conditions are that the reports must be fair and accurate and contemporaneous and the proceedings must have been in public.

---

[14] This would be when both Houses of Parliament have passed the necessary resolution. "Time" was deliberately chosen over "date" to allow the media to comment on the morning prior to the establishment of the inquiry: Lord Hailsham on the Contempt of Court Bill, *Hansard* H.L. Debs Vol. 416, col. 390.

[15] Law of Libel Amendment Act 1888, s. 3.

[16] Defamation Act 1996, s. 14.

Qualified privilege

Qualified privilege is lost only if the publisher is malicious (see p. 488). There is a statutory qualified privilege defence in a variety of situations where publication is about a matter of public concern and is for the public benefit.[17] These situations include fair and accurate reports of public proceedings held before a court anywhere in the world. Thus this provision gives protection even if the report is not contemporaneous with the proceedings. Qualified privilege also attaches to fair and accurate reports of proceedings in public of a person appointed to hold a public inquiry by a government or legislature anywhere in the world or a fair and accurate copy of or extract from any register or other document which is required by law to be open to public inspection. A notice or advertisement published by or on the authority of a court or of a judge or officer of a court anywhere in the world also attracts qualified privilege as does a fair and accurate copy of or extract from matter published by or on the authority of a government or legislature anywhere in the world.

In all of these cases, the privilege is not contingent on offering a right of reply. A further and wider class of reports also attracts qualified privilege but not if the publisher refused or neglected to publish in a suitable manner a reasonable letter or statement by way of explanation or contradiction.[18] The burden is on the victim to propose the wordings: a newspaper is not obliged to compose its own correction if it received only a general demand for an apology.[19] A reply can also be rejected as being unreasonable if it is immoderate or if it attacks third parties (see p. 136).

The situations where qualified privilege comes subject to a right of reply include[20] reports of public proceedings before magistrates acting otherwise than as a court (*e.g.* as licensing justices), of a commission, tribunal, committee or person appointed for the purposes of any inquiry by any statutory provision, by the Queen, by a minister or a Northern Ireland Executive. The Act also gives qualified privilege to reports of private sports, trade and cultural associations when acting in a quasi-judicial capacity (*e.g.* disciplining their members) or deciding matters of general concern to the association. None of these reports attract qualified privilege unless they are fair and accurate, the matter is of public

---

[17] See Defamation Act 1996, s. 15 and Sched. 1, Pt. I.
[18] Defamation Act 1996, s. 15(2) and Sched. 1, Pt. II.
[19] *Khan v. Ahmed* [1957] 2 All E.R. 385.
[20] What follows is only a summary, the Act should be consulted for the details.

concern and publication is for the public benefit.[21] On the other hand, the report does not have to be contemporaneous. It does not have to be self-contained and, if fair and accurate, can be extremely brief.[22]

---

[21] Defamation Act 1996, s. 15(3). This issue is decided by the jury *Kingshott v. Associated Kent Newspapers Ltd* [1991] 1 Q.B. 880, CA, unless, as in *Tsikata* (below) the issue of whether the publication was privileged is tried as a preliminary issue, in which case the judge will decide.

[22] *Tsikata v. Newspaper Publishing plc* [1997] 1 All E.R. 655, CA, where the report was contained in two sentences.

CHAPTER 10

REPORTING PARLIAMENTS, ASSEMBLIES AND ELECTIONS

Parliament has a special importance to the media quite apart from its function as a forum for announcement and debate of Government policy. It shares with courts the privilege of being a place where allegations can be made, on any matter at all, and reported without risk. The privilege of free speech is guaranteed to all members of both Houses in the ninth article of the Bill of Rights of 1688, which declares:

> "That the freedom of speech and debates or proceedings in Parliament ought not to be impeached or questioned in any court or place out of Parliament."

The language of the Bill of Rights is unambiguous. Ever since the House of Lords reversed the conviction of Sir John Eliot and fellow M.P.s for seditious speeches made in Parliament, the principle has remained that no M.P. or peer may be brought before the civil or criminal courts for any utterance in parliamentary proceedings. With limited exceptions of largely theoretical interest, the media is entitled to a similar immunity in publishing these utterances. It follows that matters that cannot be mentioned in the media may, if ventilated in the course of a parliamentary question or debate, become public knowledge. There have been many occasions on which journalists have primed M.P.s to raise matters that could not otherwise be made public: the truth about Kim Philby, Sir Anthony Blunt and Colonel H. A. Johnstone ("Colonel B") were revealed by this device. Journalists who use an M.P. to raise a matter that cannot otherwise be put into print will lose exclusivity in the story (in the sense that other media will pick it up), but may be the first with the background detail that can be published in consequence. Parliamentary privilege can even trump a court injunction: in 1996 it was used by back-bench M.P. Brian Sedgemore to name the politically prominent father whose identity the courts had striven to protect in the *Re Z* case (see p. 448).

The extent to which parliamentary privilege may be used to avoid a court injunction was explored both in the courts and in Parliament when

Labour M.P.s booked a Committee Room in the House of Commons in order to show a private copy of the "Zircon" film in Duncan Campbell's *Secret Society* series, which was subject to an injunction on the grounds that its television transmission was not in the national interest:

> The Attorney-General asked a High Court judge to prohibit the screening within parliamentary precincts, arguing that this would amount to a contempt of court. Mr Justice Kennedy refused on the grounds that it was for Parliament to regulate its own proceedings. The Speaker of the House of Commons was reluctant to ban the screening; he did so only after being privately briefed by the Attorney-General that the screening would be "seriously harmful" to national security. The Committee of Privileges concluded that he had acted correctly in exercising his power of control over the Palace of Westminster. He was not interfering with Parliamentary privilege, since an M.P.'s private arrangement to show a film within the precincts of the House was not "a proceeding in Parliament". But the Committee reaffirmed the principle that there is nothing (other than their own judgment) to prevent M.P.s from divulging information that may damage national security in the course of parliamentary debates or committees. The Privileges Committee endorsed, as an absolute rule, the principle that any M.P. "must be free to make public, in the course of proceedings in Parliament, information which he believes should be published".[1]

The Bill of Rights does not protect M.P.s from the legal consequences of their statements outside the House and reports of such statements are vulnerable to actions for libel and contempt. (In 1986 Tam Dalyell M.P. was threatened with an action for contempt by the judge at the Ponting trial, who had read reports of his criticisms of the prosecution made outside Parliament while the proceedings were taking place.) Nor does the Bill of Rights safeguard M.P.s against discipline imposed by their colleagues for abuses of privilege. On numerous occasions M.P.s have been censured or admonished for breaches of the rules of the House, which oblige the Speaker to disallow questions and comment on a wide range of issues, including matters in current litigation in the courts. An M.P. who is determined to ventilate an issue of public importance can often "slip it past the Speaker" and consequently into print, at some risk of a retrospective reprimand. Questions of breach of parliamentary privilege by M.P.s or by the press are generally referred to the Privileges Committee, which reports back to the House.

Article 9 of the Bill of Rights has been interpreted in a succession of cases as meaning that proceedings in Parliament cannot be examined in

---

[1] First Report from the Committee of Privileges, *Speaker's order of 22 January 1987 on a matter of national security*, H.C. 365 (1986–87).

courts of law without the permission of the House itself. Thus the Church of Scientology, attempting to sue an M.P. for his criticism (made outside the House) of its methods, could not rebut his plea of "fair comment" with evidence of malice relating to what had taken place in Parliament.[2]

The rule in the Bill of Rights was underpinned by a constitutional convention that Parliament and the courts both respected each other's sphere of influence. Thus it also applied in the reverse situation from that in the *Church of Scientology* case—so that if a newspaper was sued by a parliamentarian it could not as part of its defence call into question anything which the claimant had said or done as part of Parliament's proceedings. The Privy Council (in an appeal from New Zealand) rejected the argument that by bringing the action the claimant had waived privilege.[3] The court said that the privilege belonged to Parliament (or the House to which the claimant belonged) and it was not for the individual member to waive it. At the same time the court recognised that there was scope for tremendous injustice if the claimant was awarded damages for a well-deserved attack on his reputation which the defendant was precluded from defending as true. The court resolved the quandary by ruling that if privilege seriously hampered the defendant in the conduct of its defence, the action would be stayed as an abuse of process. Famously, the libel action by Neil Hamilton M.P. against *The Guardian* over its articles alleging that he accepted "cash for questions" was stayed on these grounds in 1995.

The Defamation Bill then passing through Parliament was amended in direct response to this decision. Hamilton complained to the Prime Minister and the Lord Chancellor, who took uncalled-for pity on him and promoted an ill-thought out amendment, now section 13 of the Defamation Act 1996. It provides:

> "where the conduct of a person in or in relation to proceedings in Parliament is in issue in defamation proceedings, he may waive for the purpose of those proceedings, so far as concerns him, the protection of any enactment or rule of law which prevents proceedings in Parliament being impeached in any court or place out of Parliament".

This was a controversial measure which a Joint Committee of Privileges later recommended should be replaced by a system requiring the House as a whole to agree to the waiver of privilege.[4] It means that an

---

[2] *Church of Scientology of California v. Johnson-Smith* [1972] 1 All E.R. 294.
[3] *Prebble v. Television New Zealand* [1995] 1 A.C. 321.
[4] Report of Joint Committee of Privilege (1998–99) H.L. Paper 43–1, H.C. 214–1, pp. 23–29.

action for defamation brought by an M.P. need no longer be stayed if the M.P. waives his privilege and thus removes the inhibition on the media defendant probing his parliamentary behaviour as part of its defence. Neil Hamilton made use of the new right by waiving his privilege and reviving his action against *The Guardian*. His case collapsed on the eve of the trial when cabinet documents the newspaper obtained on discovery showed that he had told lies. After the Parliamentary Commissioner for Standards, Sir Gordon Downey, had produced a report that condemned Mr Hamilton over "compelling evidence" that he had received cash from Mohammed Al Fayed for asking questions in his interests in Parliament, he began yet another libel action this time against Al Fayed himself. Again he used his right to waive Parliamentary privilege. The defendant tried to have the action struck out on the argument that an individual M.P. could not waive the autonomous right of Parliament to investigate the conduct of its members. By the time the House of Lords finally rejected this,[5] the libel action had been heard and Mr Hamilton's claim had been rejected by the jury. Even so, section 13 had unfairly hampered Al Fayed's defence. What Downey found particularly "compelling" was that Hamilton's close M.P. colleague, Tim Smith, had been accused of receiving cash in the same way, for similar services: he had admitted the truth of the allegation. But because Smith refused to waive parliamentary privilege, the libel jury could not be told the details of the striking similarity. Section 13 causes obvious injustice to the media when it cannot tell the full truth about M.P.s, some of whom waive privilege and some of whom do not. In this situation, it may still be necessary for a court to consider whether there can be a fair trial or whether the proceedings have to be stopped.

The old rule that the House had to give its permission for *Hansard* to be referred to in court has long gone and *Hansard* can be quoted in relevant cases without leave.[6] Since the House of Lords abolished the rule that *Hansard* could not be consulted to determine the intention of Parliament in passing legislation,[7] references to *Hansard* in legal argument have become much more common.

THE PRIVILEGES FOR REPORTING PARLIAMENTARY DEBATES

In the course of his decision in *Attorney-General v. Times Newspapers,* Lord Denning stated: "Whatever comments are made in Parliament, they can be repeated in the newspapers without any fear of an action

---

[5] *Hamilton v. Al Fayed* [2000] 2 All E.R. 224.
[6] Resolution of Houses of Parliament, October 31, 1980.
[7] *Pepper v. Hart* [1993] A.C. 593.

for libel or proceedings for contempt of court."[8] This is a sound enough summary of the practical position, although it may not strictly accord with the law. In 1813 an M.P. was convicted of criminal libel contained in a copy of a speech delivered in the House that he afterwards circulated.[9] The authority of the case today is doubtful, although it was relied upon by the Director of Public Prosecutions in rather extraordinary circumstances in 1977:

> The controversial prosecution of journalists Duncan Campbell and Crispin Aubrey under the Official Secrets Act featured an expert witness from the Ministry of Defence, "Colonel B". The acronym was alleged by the Crown to be necessary in the interests of national security. The falsity of this claim was exposed by the *Leveller* and *Peace News,* which published the Colonel's true identity, which was discoverable from regimental magazines. The Attorney-General commenced proceedings against the newspapers for contempt of court (see p. 457). Before the case was heard, four sympathetic M.P.s contrived to mention the Colonel's real name—H. A. Johnstone—in the course of oral questions in the House. The DPP immediately issued a statement to press and broadcasting organisations advising them not to disclose the identity of Colonel B in their reports of the day's proceedings, on the grounds that it might amount to contempt of court. Almost every national newspaper ignored this advice, and radio and television news programmes broadcast the tape of the M.P.s asking their cover-blowing questions. There was an immediate constitutional rumpus, as the media invoked its privilege to publish proceedings in the House and some M.P.s demanded that the DPP be punished for contempt of Parliament. The Attorney-General, who was compromised in the whole affair, had the behaviour of the four M.P.s referred to the Committee of Privileges, but declined to test the position by prosecuting any media organisation for contempt of court.[10]

The "Colonel B" affair sheds little light on the technical question of whether the media can ever be liable for contempt or any other criminal offence by reporting words uttered, in breach of the rules of the House, by truculent M.P.s. It did, however, underline the practical impossibility of taking action, given the simultaneous broadcasting of parliamentary sessions. The DPP's advice was wrong in that no contempt could have been committed in any event, either in relation to the Divisional Court

---

[8] [1973] 1 All E.R. 815, 823, reversed on other grounds [1973] 3 All E.R. 54.
[9] *R. v. Creevey* (1813) 1 M. and S. 273; 105 E.R. 102.
[10] Second Report of the Committee of Privileges, H.C. 667 (1977–78). Three Australian High Court judges take the view that an accurate report of statements made in Parliament cannot amount to a contempt of court: see Mason C. J. and Gaudron *Hinch v. Att-Gen (Vic)* (1987) 74 A.L.R. 353 at 361–62 and 405 respectively; McHugh J.A. in *Att.-Gen. (N.S.W.) v. John Fairfax & Sons Ltd* (1986) 6 N.S.W.L.R. 695 at 714.

hearing or to the magistrates' court which made the original secrecy arrangement. For all practical purposes the media may rely upon their possession of a privilege to report all proceedings in Parliament without criminal consequences.

Reports of parliamentary proceedings that are fair and accurate and made in good faith enjoy qualified privilege from libel actions. This was established in the famous nineteenth-century case of *Wason v. Walter*:[11]

> *The Times* had printed extracts from a House of Lords debate, which included unflattering comments about the originator of an allegation that an eminent Law Lord had once lied to Parliament. The paper successfully defended a libel action. The court said that just as the public had an interest in learning about what took place in the courts, so it was entitled to know what was said in Parliament. Only malice or a distorted report would destroy the privilege.

In addition to this common law privilege, the Defamation Act 1996 gives a statutory qualified privilege for fair and accurate reports of proceedings in public of a legislature anywhere in the world.[12] The subject-matter has to be of public concern and publication for the public benefit[13] although this should not be a problem in the case of parliamentary reports. The question of whether privilege under the Act exists is for the jury rather than the judge[14] and in any event the publisher will usually be covered by the continuing common law privilege, which does not depend upon public concern or benefit.

Editorials or other comment based on the report of a parliamentary debate are also protected[15] and so too are "sketches" written to capture the spirit rather than the detail of a debate. These may be cryptic, amusing and highly selective, but so long as they give a fair and honest representation of what took place as it impressed the journalist, the defence can be invoked.[16] Reports of committee hearings are similarly protected.[18] Publication or inclusion in a programme service of a copy of or extract from a parliamentary report or paper is also protected by qualified privilege[19] which extends to a copy or extract of any matter published by or with the authority of any government or legislature anywhere in the world. Papers which the House orders to lie on the

---

[11] (1868) L.R. 4 Q.B. 74.
[12] Defamation Act 1996, Sched 1, para. 1.
[13] *ibid.*, s. 15(3).
[14] *Kingshott v. Associated Kent Newspapers Ltd* [1991] 1 Q.B. 880, CA.
[15] *Jason v. Walter* (1868) L.R. 4 Q.B. 74.
[16] *Cook v. Alexander* [1974] 1 Q.B. 279.
[18] *Gatley on Libel and Slander* (9th ed., Sweet & Maxwell, 1998), para. 14.89.
[19] See Defamation Act 1996, Sched., 1 para. 7.

table are included.[20] Statutory protection along these lines in relation to British Parliamentary papers has been available since the Parliamentary Papers Act 1840, section 3. Publishers may still need to dust down that provision if they publish summaries of Parliamentary reports rather than publish copies or extracts. Unlike the 1996 Act, the 1840 statute extends to reports of "abstracts" of the parliamentary papers.[21] Of great importance is a newspaper's right to make honest comment on apparently factual statements made in the debate that it has reported, even though these statements are later shown to be untrue.[22]

In 1989 the House of Commons finally allowed its proceedings to be televised—after a fashion. The rules devised by the Supervising Committee are calculated to avoid embarrassment when M.P.s misbehave. Whenever there is disorder, the cameras must switch immediately to the Speaker. No "reaction shots" or close-ups are allowed, and the public gallery and the press gallery must not be shown. It is difficult to disagree with Bernard Levin that these rules are "designed to make M.P.s look better behaved than they actually are" and to cocoon electors from the reality of "the jeering, the slapping of knees and pointing, the sniggering at an unintended *double entendre,* the late-dining drunks arriving and lurching towards the division lobbies, the barracking, the unwillingness to listen to speakers from the opposite side (or, frequently, from their own)". The rules were slightly relaxed by the Committee after the first six months of television had produced no obvious danger to the democratic process. BBC Parliament, a digital channel, has the coverage of the Commons, time-shifted coverage of the Lords and unedited footage of about 10 committees a week.

There is an officer of both Houses (the Supervisor of Parliamentary Broadcasting) who is responsible for ensuring that the arrangements authorised by each House are adhered to. A television signal is produced by an independent operator, the Parliamentary Broadcasting Unit Ltd (a company whose directors are members of both Houses) which then sells access to the feed to television companies. A similar arrangement exists for sound broadcasting. Archive tapes are kept for about two years.[23]

Broadcasting of the House of Lords' judicial proceedings requires the approval of the Law Lords.[24] Approval is occasionally given for the ritual giving of judgments to be broadcast but not, so far, the argument before the Law Lords.

---

[20] *Mangena v. Wright* [1909] 2 K.B. 958.
[21] On the other hand, unusually, the publisher has the burden of proving absence of malice.
[22] *Grech v. Odhams Press Ltd* [1958] 2 Q.B. 275.
[23] See Sir Thomas Erksine May, *Parliamentary Practice,* (22nd ed., Butterworths, 1997), pp. 229–230.
[24] H.L. Debs 1995–96, 5870, col.1374 and see Erskine May above, p. 230.

When the BBC approached the appellate committee of the House of Lords in 1996 asking to televise the hearing in *Thompson and Venables* (the Bulger appeal) it was told that legal discussion of House of Lords appeals could only be understood by lawyers who had read all the case papers; members of the public should not see appeals on television because they would not understand "the legal context", for example, "hypothetical questions will be asked which can easily be misunderstood as trivial or irrelevant".[25] But this approach is unacceptable in society committed to openness, especially when the House considers cases like *Pinochet*. The ritual giving of the decision looked, the first time, rather like a penalty shoot-out and on the occasion of the second decision the senior Law Lord read out a summary of their reasons which specially prepared for television, and which gently enhanced public understanding of a very long and complicated written judgment.

CONTEMPT OF PARLIAMENT

Each House of Parliament has the power to punish both members and outsiders for contempt.[26] The offence of Contempt of Parliament is defined by Erskine May as "any act or omission which impedes either House of Parliament in the performance of its functions or impedes any member or officer of such House in the discharge of his duty, or which has a tendency directly or indirectly to produce such a result." "Indirect tendencies" can include articles which "bring the House into odium, contempt or ridicule or lower its authority."[27] These definitions are vague in the extreme, and it is ironic that an institution whose function is to formulate rules of law with precision has been unable or unwilling to do the same for its own powers and privileges.

In modern practice, the power to punish for contempt may be justified in relation to M.P.s who take bribes or fail to declare interests, or in respect of outsiders who interrupt debates by throwing refuse from the public gallery. There is no justification for using it against hostile newspapers, and, despite some unedifying decisions in the 1950s, there is little danger that Parliament will run the risk of public obloquy by using it to stifle criticism. Its most relevant use is to reprimand the press for breaking embargoes on the publication of committee reports, or leaking evidence heard in secret. Thus Tam Dalyell M.P. was reprimanded by the House in 1967 for leaking to *The Observer* secret evidence given

---

[25] See Joshua Rozenberg, "The Pinochet Case and Cameras in Court" [1999] *Public Law* 178.
[26] See generally Erskine May, *Parliamentary Practice,* above, chaps 8 and 10.
[27] Erskine May, *Parliamentary Practice,* p. 120.

by the Porton Down Chemical Warfare Research Laboratory to a Commons Select Committee.[28] The publication of witnesses' submissions must officially await the authorisation of the committee,[29] although where evidence has been given in public, no complaint of privilege will be entertained on the ground that it was published before being reported to the House.[30] It is also a breach of the rules of the House to disclose or publish a committee's report before it is presented to the full House.[31] However, it is now unlikely that newspapers and their reporters will be made to suffer for publishing such leaks. In 1986 Parliament rejected a recommendation from the Committee of Privileges that *The Times* should suffer the loss of a lobby pass and its journalist should be suspended from the lobby for six months for publishing a draft report leaked from the Environment Committee.[32] The committee concerned is supposed to try and discover the source of the leak and assess whether it constitutes or is likely to constitute a substantial interference with its work. If it will, the committee reports to the House and the report is automatically referred to the Committee on Standards and Privileges.

Parliament's power to punish disrespectful publications is a parallel to the court's power to punish for scandalising the judiciary. British judges have deliberately played down this aspect of their power and not exercised it since 1931 (see p. 388), but the House of Commons has not been so self-restrained. At the time of the Suez invasion there was a flurry of allegations of contempt.[33] When, in 1975, the *Liverpool Free Press* was accused of contempt for an article that alleged double standards by an M.P., no action was taken. The M.P. was told to pursue his grievance in the courts.[34]

In 1978 the Commons resolved that its penal power should be used "sparingly" and

---

[28] H.C. 357 (1967–68). An appendix by the Clerk to the House gives further illustrations.

[29] See the House of Commons Resolution of April 21, 1837 and House of Commons Standing Order 135; May, *Parliamentary Practice*, pp. 119–120.

[30] House of Commons Standing Orders No. 35.

[31] May, *Parliamentary Practice*, p. 119.

[32] H.C. Debs 1 Vol. 98, col. 293, May 20, 1986 and see Environment Committee 2nd Special Report H.C. 211 (1985–6): Committee of Privileges 1st Report H.C. 376 (1985–86).

[33] *Sunday Graphic* H.C. 27 (1956–7); *Romford Recorder*. The *Evening News* was found in contempt for a cartoon on the same theme. H.C. 39 (1956–7); but Baroness Stocks was acquitted for remarks on *Any Answers*. 4th Report of the Committee of Privileges (1956–57), H.C. 74.

[34] H.C. 43 (1975–76). The article is reproduced in Brian Whitaker, *News Ltd*, p. 147. Compare the Committee's condemnation of a passage in *Travel Trade Gazette* accusing Gwyneth Dunwoody of attacking the Association of British Travel Agents for ulterior motives. No action was proposed because the editor apologised. H.C. 302 (1974–75).

"only when the House is satisfied that to exercise it is essential in order to provide reasonable protection for the House, its members or officers from such improper obstruction or attempt at or threat of obstruction as is causing or is likely to cause substantial interference with the performance of their respective functions."[35]

In future, it would take into account the mode and extent of the publication.[36] Although there is no formal defence of truth or fair comment to a charge of contempt,[37] the Commons decided to take into account the truth of, (or the publisher's reasonable belief in the truth of) the allegations if all reasonable care had been taken and if the publication was in the public interest and was published in a manner appropriate to the public interest. On the other hand, it rejected a proposal that contempt should be a procedure of last resort to be used only where the Member concerned has no legal remedy. It agreed that, as in the *Liverpool Free Press* case, this was a relevant consideration, but was not willing for it to be an inflexible bar. These changes are an improvement, and the number of complaints referred to the Privileges Committee has fallen sharply. It remains to be seen whether the change is permanent. In 1948 the Committee said that the contempt power should not be administered to discourage free expression of opinion however exaggerated or prejudiced.[38] Eight years later that opinion was ignored or bypassed in the petrol-rationing cases.[39] Old powers, like old habits, die hard and the Commons has a collective phobia of placing binding limits on its contempt power.

Contempt of Parliament has survived as an offence in modern times only because punishments have been mild. Although the House can banish culprits from the Palace of Westminster, and even imprison them, no one has been locked under Big Ben since the atheist M.P. Charles Bradlaugh in 1880. The Lords, but not the Commons, can impose a fine.[40] In 1975 the Committee of Privileges recommended that

---

[35] These and the following proposals were first made by the Committee of Privileges in 1967. H.C. 34 (1967–68). They were brushed off the shelf by a further report in 1977. H.C. (1976–77). They were adopted by the Commons on February 6, 1978. *Hansard,* Vol. 943, 5th Series, col. 1155–1198.

[36] Reports of an improper disclosure are now automatically referred to the Committee of Privileges to assess its significance and to try to discover its source (see Committee of 2nd Report H.C. 555 (1984–85)).

[37] This may be because the issue has never been squarely raised. Whether truth should be accepted as a defence is, according to the Clerk to the House, an ad hoc decision. See H.C. 302 (1974–75) Annex 1, para. 5 quoting H.C. 34 (1967–68) p. 5.

[38] Investigating a complaint in the *Daily Mail* that Labour M.P.s were Communist moles. H.C. 112 (1947–48).

[39] See above, n. 33.

[40] May, *Parliamentary Practice,* p. 138. The 1967 Committee proposed that a power to fine should be revived and when considering *The Economist's* leak of the wealth-

the editor and a journalist on *The Economist* be banished from the precincts of the House for six months for publishing a draft report on a proposed wealth tax, but on a free vote the House decided to take no action.[41] Indeed, few reprimands have been administered since the Second World War.[42] John Junor received one for his attack in the *Sunday Express* on M.P.s' special petrol allowances during the Suez crisis. His half-hearted apology and failure to check his facts caused the Committee to recommend the reprimand.[43] When Junor returned to the fray in 1983, claiming that M.P.s who suggested a pay-rise for themselves were hypocrites with "greedy snouts in the trough", Parliament's response was much more sophisticated: instead calling him to the Bar of the House for contempt, M.P.s enthusiastically tabled motions that allowed them to debate Junor's own salary—which they claimed was £100,000 a year—and to draw attention to the tax perks of egregious Fleet Street editors. The threat of sanctions for contempt need concern only lobby correspondents, who identify closely with the House. Others, at least those who are confident of the public interest in their story, should not be averse to the publicity that a reprimand would bring. However, M.P.s who are caught leaking can face suspension and, in one post-war case, expulsion.[44]

The objections to the offence of contempt of Parliament go beyond the vagueness of definition and the self-aggrandisement implicit in many of the cases. The procedure for "trial" breaches every important rule of natural justice, and shames a Commons proud of its historical opposition to the Star Chamber of the Stuart kings. The procedure begins, reasonably enough, with a private complaint by an M.P. to the Speaker. If the Speaker thinks there is a case to answer, he gives the M.P. leave to raise it as a matter of procedure over the day's business, and the House may, if impressed with it, pass a motion referring it to the Committee on Standards and Privileges, an 11-strong body dominated by lawyers and M.P.s, with the governing party in the majority.

There are no procedural safeguards. Accused persons may be condemned unheard, or summonsed for cross-examination without legal representation or notice of the charges, and without any right to challenge the evidence given against them or to call witnesses in rebuttal.

---

tax report in 1975, made it clear that it thought this an appropriate offence to fine. No action to implement these recommendations has been taken.

[41] H.C. 22 (1975–76).

[42] Hartley and Griffith, *Government and the Law,* p. 245. 1967 Report, para. 18.

[43] H.C. 74 (1956–57).

[44] Gary Allingham M.P., who alleged that M.P.s traded information for food and drink. The Committee of Privileges was particularly irked by his hypocrisy, since he had done precisely what he accused his colleagues of doing. It recommended a six-month suspension but the House went further and expelled him. H.C. 138 (1947–48).

The Committee sits in secret, and reports in due course to the Commons. The House decides whether and what punishment to inflict, after a further debate in which biased M.P.s vote entirely as judges in their own cause.

The procedures for dealing with contempt of Parliament are in blatant breach of at least three articles of the European Convention on Human Rights. Article 5 prohibits loss of liberty except by conviction for a clearly defined offence; Article 6 guarantees defendants a fair hearing by an independent and impartial tribunal, and specifically endorses the rights to present a defence, to legal representation, and to call and to cross-examine witnesses; and Article 10 upholds freedom of expression.[45] Despite the Human Rights Act, the United Kingdom courts would still not be able to investigate these issues because section 6(3) excludes Parliament (except the House of Lords in its judicial capacity) is excluded from the concept of "public authorities" which are required to abide by Convention rights.

At present, the very unfairness of the Committee's procedures can be a boon to those summonsed before it, in the sense that they can make great play of their role as victims. The contraventions of natural justice inherent in the Committee's traditional procedures are indefensible, and any journalist threatened by it should adopt the defiant stance of the "gang of four" M.P.s who were summonsed over their naming of "Colonel B".[46–47]

These procedural inadequacies are compounded by the extremely limited prospect of obtaining judicial review. The courts may decide whether or not a parliamentary privilege exists, but must not question the practical application of an undoubted privilege in any particular case. The resolution of the House and the Speaker's warrant will be treated as conclusive. The only exception is where the House of Commons exercises its power to imprison for contempt by issuing a warrant that specifies the conduct that is to be punished; in such cases the courts may decide whether the specified conduct is capable of amounting to a contempt—*i.e.* whether it could have a tendency to impede the performance of parliamentary functions.[48] But Parliament may readily exclude even this limited form of judicial review merely by issuing a general warrant.

---

[45] See for instance *Demicoli v. Malta* (1991) 14 E.H.R.R. 47.

[46–47] H.C. 669 (1977–78); H.C. 222 (1978–79).

[48] The most recent authority, which reviews all the eighteenth- and nineteenth-century English cases, is the Australian High Court in *R. v. Richards, ex p. Fitzpatrick and Browne* (1955) 92 C.L.R. 157, upholding the Federal Parliament's foolish decision to imprison two journalists for a defamatory article about an M.P.

MEMBERS' OF PARLIAMENT CONFLICTS OF INTEREST

Following the scandal involving the architect Poulson in 1974 and the growing suspicion that certain M.P.s had received benefits from him, the House of Commons resolved to take two steps to compel M.P.s to disclose their private financial interests. In any debates or committee hearings they were to announce any relevant financial interest.[49] This would be recorded in *Hansard*. The House also set up a register of M.P.s' interests.[50] Each M.P. is supposed to report any of the following interests:

- remunerated directorships, employment, offices, trades, professions or vocations;

- the names of clients when the interest referred to includes personal services by the Member that arise out of or are related in any manner to his membership of the House;

- financial sponsorship as a parliamentary candidate where this is known to contribute more than one quarter of their election expenses;

- financial sponsorship as an M.P., including a statement as to whether the M.P. is paid or receives any benefit or advantage, direct or indirect;

- Any gift to the M.P. or spouse where it is worth more than £125 or any material benefit (such as hospitality, tickets to sporting and cultural events, relief from indebtedness, loan concessions, provision of services, etc.), of a value greater than 0.5 per cent of the current parliamentary salary from any company, organisation or person within the United Kingdom which in any way relates to membership of the House (but not benefits available to all M.P.s or travel/subsistence costs for a conference or site visit within the United Kingdom).

- overseas visits relating to or arising out of membership of the House where all or part of the cost is not paid by public funds;

- any overseas gift to the M.P. or spouse of greater value than £125 or any material advantage of a value greater than 0.5 per cent of the current parliamentary salary from or on behalf of any investment, organisation or person which in any way relates to membership of the House;

---

[49] *Hansard* May 22, 1974.
[50] *Code of Conduct* together with the *Guide to the Rules Relating to the Conduct of Members* (1995–96) H.C. 688.

- land and property of substantial value or from which a substantial income is derived;

- interests in shareholdings held by the M.P., either personally, or with or on behalf of the M.P.'s spouse or dependent children, in any public or private company or other body which are:

  (a) greater than 1 per cent of the issued share capital of the company or body; or
  (b) less than 1 per cent of the issued share capital but more than £25,000 in nominal value.

  The nature of the company's business in each case should be registered;

- any relevant interest, not falling within one of the above categories, which nevertheless falls within the definition of the main purpose of the Register which is "to provide information of any pecuniary interest or other material benefit which a Member receives which might reasonably be thought by others to influence his or her actions, speeches, or votes in Parliament, or actions taken in his or her capacity as a Member of Parliament", or which the Member considers might be thought by others to influence his or her actions in a similar manner, even though the Member receives no financial benefit.

In addition, as a result of a resolution in 1995,[51] if M.P.s enter into agreements that involve the provision of services in their capacity as a Member, the agreements must be deposited with the Parliamentary Commissioner for Standards and must show into which of the prescribed bands any fees or benefits under the agreements come. The agreements can be inspected but for no good reason, cannot be copied.

The register is published at the beginning of each parliament and once a year thereafter. The register (together with more recent updates) can also be seen at the website.[52] The register and its updates can also be inspected at the House of Commons although the hours of access are limited.

Oversight of the register is one of the principal functions of the Parliamentary Commissioner for Standards. The office was established on the recommendation of the Nolan Committee[53] and its holder can only

---

[51] November 6, 1995.

[52] http://www.publications.parliament.uk/pa/cm200001/cmregmem/memi02.htm

[53] First Report of the Committee on Standards in Public Life (HMSO, 1995), Cm. 2850.

be removed by a resolution of the House of Commons (although reappointment at the end of her term is not secure). As well as maintaining the register of M.P.s' interests, the Commissioner also investigates complaints about the propriety of M.P.s' conduct. The present Commissioner, Elizabeth Filkin, has gained a reputation for persistence in her investigations of alleged improprieties and failures to abide by the registration obligations. For this reason several M.P.s opposed her re-appointment of a further term.

Although a judge in 1990 said that the Register of M.P.s' interests was, not a "proceeding in Parliament" for the purpose of the Bill of Rights,[54] the Privy Council has doubted whether this case was rightly decided[55] and a review by the Joint Committee of Privileges in 1999 expressly included such registers among the matters which ought to be protected by privilege.[56]

Parliament maintains other registers. Lobby journalists, journalists accredited to the Parliamentary press gallery or for Parliamentary broadcasting must register any employment or paid occupation for which their privileged access to Parliament is relevant. Similarly, people with passes as M.P.s' secretaries or research assistants and officers of All Party Committees and registered groups must also register their relevant occupations. These registers can be consulted by M.P.s in the House of Commons' Library, but for no good reason they are not open to the general public.[57]

GOVERNMENT OF SCOTLAND, WALES AND NORTHERN IRELAND

Devolution in Labour's first term of office took different forms in the three countries.

Scotland

The Scotland Act 1998 established the Scottish Parliament and the Scottish Administration. The Scottish Parliament has similarities to the Westminster Parliament although it has only one chamber. The Scotland Act requires the Standing Orders of the Scottish Parliament to oblige it to hold its proceedings in public, except in circumstances defined in the standing orders.[58] The Standing Orders require meetings of the Scottish

---

[54] *Rost v. Edwards* [1990] 2 All E.R. 641.
[55] *Prebble v. Television New Zealand Ltd* [1995] 1 A.C. 321.
[56] H.L. Paper 43, H.C. 214 (1998–99).
[57] See May, *Parliamentary Practice,* p. 928.
[58] Scotland Act 1998, Sched. 3, para. 3.

Parliament and any of its committees to take place in public.[59] The Standing Orders must also include provision for reporting the proceedings of the Parliament and for publishing the reports.[60] The Standing Orders also provide for the broadcasting of proceedings.[61]

Statements made in the Edinburgh Parliament are absolutely privileged and so are any publications which are made with its authority.[62] This will not extend to newspaper reports but under the Defamation Act 1996, fair and accurate reports of proceedings in public of a legislature anywhere in the world have qualified privilege.[63] Similarly a fair and accurate report in good faith of proceedings in the Scottish Parliament cannot be contempt under the strict liability rule.[64] The Parliament must establish a register of Members' interests which has to be open to public inspection.[65]

The legislative competence of the Scottish Parliament is carefully defined and many matters are reserved for action by the United Kingdom Parliament alone.[66] These include the BBC and the subject-matter of the Broadcasting Acts.[67] Other matters which are reserved include data protection,[68] election law,[69] the Video Recordings and Cinema Acts,[70] national security, anti-terrorism and the Official Secrets Acts,[71] copyright,[72] telecommunications and wireless telegraphy.[73] A general condition on the competence of the Parliament is that its acts must be compatible with rights under the European Convention on Human Rights.[74] A similar restriction is applied to the acts of the Scottish executive. Ultimately the Judicial Committee of the Privy Council (which is comprised mainly of the Law Lords) can rule on whether these restrictions have been broken.

Northern Ireland

The Northern Ireland Act 1998 was a product of the Good Friday Agreement and represents an intricate political compromise whose past has been shaky and whose future remains uncertain.

---

[59] Standing Orders of the Scottish Parliament, 15.1.
[60] *ibid.,* para. 4, see S.O. 16.3.
[61] See S.O. 16.4.
[62] *ibid.,* s. 41.
[63] Defamation Act 1996, Sched. 1, para. 1.
[64] Scotland Act 1998, s. 42.
[65] *ibid.,* s. 39.
[66] *ibid.,* s. 29 and Sched. 4 and 5.
[67] *ibid.,* Sched. 5, s. K1.
[68] *ibid.,* s. B2.
[69] *ibid.,* s. B3.
[70] *ibid.,* s. B5.
[71] *ibid.,* s. B8.
[72] *ibid.,* s. C4.
[73] *ibid.,* s. C10.
[74] *ibid.,* s. 29(2)(d).

It established the Northern Ireland Assembly which has many features in common with the Scottish Parliament. Thus the Assembly's Standing Orders must also make provision for the public to attend and for the publishing of reports of its proceedings.[75] Its Standing Orders must also include provision for a Register of Members' interests to which the public have a right of access.[76] There are very similar provisions for absolute privilege and a defence to the strict liability contempt rule for fair, accurate and good faith reports of the Assembly's proceedings.[77] Reports of its proceedings in the media would also attract qualified privilege under the Defamation Act 1996.

The Assembly's legislative competence, as in the case of the Scottish Parliament, is also defined. Matters reserved to the Westminster Parliament are listed.[78] Although the detail is different, there are broad similarities with the division of responsibility between Edinburgh and Westminster. The Freedom of Information Act 2000 extends to Northern Ireland and the Assembly is a public authority for the purposes of the Act.[79]

Wales

The Government of Wales Act 1998 set up a different model of devolution for Wales to that established in Scotland and Northern Ireland. The National Assembly for Wales was expected to take over most of the functions of the Secretary of State for Wales. It would be able to exercise ministerial functions, but would not have power to pass primary legislation.

However, as far as media law is concerned, there are common provisions. The proceedings of the Assembly itself must take place in public as must the meetings of its committees and sub-committees (except where Standing Orders allow otherwise).[80] The Assembly must arrange for reports of its proceedings to be published[81] and the officially authorised reports will have absolute privilege.[82] The Assembly is treated as a legislature for the purposes of the Defamation Act 1996[83]

---

[75] Northern Ireland Act 1998, Sched. 6, paras 2 and 3. See the Standing Orders of the Assembly, S.O.7.

[76] *ibid.*, s. 43. The Register is available on the Assembly's website.

[77] *ibid.*, s. 50.

[78] See Northern Ireland Act 1998, Sched. 3.

[79] Freedom of Information Act 2000, s. 88(2) and Sched. 1, para. 4.

[80] Government of Wales Act 1998, s. 70(1). The Standing Orders of the Assembly require plenary sessions to be in public—S.O. 6.1 and similarly committees must sit in public—S.O. 8.20, except in prescribed circumstances—S.O. 8.21.

[81] *ibid.*, s. 70(3).

[82] *ibid.*, s. 77(1).

[83] *ibid.*, s. 77(4)(a).

so that fair and accurate reports of its proceedings are protected by qualified privilege and a fair and accurate copy of or an extract from any matter published with its authority will also have qualified privilege. The limitation on privilege in the course of elections under Defamation Act 1952, section 10 (see p. 544) applies also to elections to the Assembly.[84] A fair and accurate and good faith report of the Assembly's proceedings cannot offend against the strict liability contempt rule.[85]

Whenever the Assembly publishes a document it must make a copy available for (free) public inspection. It must also have facilities for the public to take copies but it can charge for these.[86] The accounts of the Assembly are audited by the Auditor-General for Wales. The accounts, statements of account or report which he lays before the Assembly must be published as soon as reasonably practicable.[87] The Welsh Assembly is a public authority for the purposes of the Freedom of Information Act 2000.[88]

ELECTION REPORTING

Injunctions

Free speech is an essential part of the democratic process, but there must be some safeguard against its deliberate misuse to distort that process at election time.[89] Otherwise, an unscrupulous newspaper editor could influence the result by publishing a story, known to be false, about a party leader or candidate shortly before polling day. Publication could not be restrained by an injunction for libel if the editor stated he was prepared to defend it. A safeguard against such conduct is provided by section 106 of the Representation of the People Act 1983:

> "(1) Any person who ... (a) before or during an election, (b) for the purpose of affecting the return of any candidate at the election, makes or publishes any false statement of fact in relation to the personal conduct or character of the candidate shall be guilty of an illegal practice unless he can show that he has reasonable grounds for believing, and did believe

---

[84] *ibid.*, s. 77(5).
[85] *ibid.*, s. 78.
[86] *ibid.*, s. 119.
[87] *ibid.*, s. 103.
[88] Freedom of Information Act 2000, Sched. 1, para. 5.
[89] This s. refers to local as well as parliamentary elections. Except where indicated, the same rules apply also to elections for the European Parliament: European Parliamentary Elections Act 1978, s. 3 and Sched. 1, para. 2(3) and European Parliamentary Elections Regulations 1999, S.I. 1999 No. 1214.

the statement to be true and (2) may be restrained by interim or perpetual injunction by the High Court or the county court . . . from any repetition of that false statement or of a false statement of a similar character in relation to the candidate . . . prima facie proof of the falsity of the statement shall be sufficient . . . "

Since there can be no "candidates" before an election campaign begins, these injunctions can relate to publications only after the writ for the election has been issued or the other formal commencement of the campaign.[90]

This law requires only "prima facie evidence" of falsehood—an affidavit to that effect by the candidate (who is thereby lain open to a perjury charge if he or she has sworn falsely) might suffice. The false statement need not be defamatory, so long as it is calculated to influence the minds of electors. (It was once held that the false statement that a candidate had shot a fox would be sufficient in a country constituency— because the electors would be outraged that he had not done the gentlemanly thing and hunted it with dogs.)[91] The false statement must be about "personal character and conduct", not political performance or allegiance. To say, on the eve of an election, that the leader of the Labour Party is a Communist, would not merit an injunction[92] but to say that he was in the pay of the KGB most certainly would. Finally, the statement must be one of fact rather than opinion. The assertion of KGB paymastery is a statement of fact; the description "radical traitor" has been held to be a statement of opinion.[93] On the other hand a leaflet which said of Jack Straw that he "hates Muslims" was treated as a statement of fact. There was no qualification indicating an expression of opinion on the part of the writer and the court concluded that it would have been understood as a statement of fact. Since the court found that the fact was false and Mr Straw did not hate Muslims, section 106 was infringed.[94]

The candidate's affidavit of falsehood is not conclusively accepted. No injunction will be granted if the publisher can show reasonable grounds for believing that the story is true. By contrast with a defamation action, the burden is on the claimant to show that the statement is

---

[90] Parliamentary elections start with the dissolution of Parliament, the announcement by the Government that it intends to dissolve Parliament, or the issuance of a by-election writ. Local government elections run from five weeks before the date fixed for the poll or the publication of notice of the election: 1983 Act, s. 93(2).

[91] *Borough of Sunderland Case* (1896) 50 M. & H. at 62.

[92] *Burns v. Associated Newspapers Ltd* (1925) 42 T.L.R. 37.

[93] *Ellis v. National Union of Conservative and Constitutional Associations, Middleton and Southall* (1900) 44 S.J. 750 and see generally, *Gatley on Libel and Slander*, para. 25.22 *et seq.*

[94] *Pirbhai v. DPP* [1995] C.O.D. 259, QBD.

false. The section provides that prima facie proof of falsity is sufficient. But even if that threshold is crossed, the court still has a discretion and it would not be consistent with the Human Rights Act 1998, s. 12(3), if the judge were to grant the injunction even though evidence led by the defendant suggested that the claimant would not be likely to succeed at trial. However, again by contrast with defamation actions, the defendant would have to do more than assert that the story was true.

It is an offence knowingly to publish, in order to promote the election of one candidate, a false statement that a rival candidate has withdrawn.[95]

Advertisements

Newspapers can print election advertisements, but they must take care that these are authorised by the candidate or the election agent. Any other advertisement (by private supporters or well-wishers, for example) for the purpose of procuring a candidate's election is an offence.[96] The advertisement might praise the virtues of the favoured candidate or denounce the failings of the opposition: either way it must be authorised.[97] The same section also prohibits "otherwise presenting to the electors the candidate or his views or the extent or nature of his backing or disparaging another candidate".[98] There is a proviso which exempts expenses incurred by a person who was not acting in concert with others. Until 2001 the proviso was virtually meaningless because of a further condition that the expenses did not exceed £5. This changed as a result of *Bowman v. United Kingdom*[99]:

> Phylliss Bowman, director of the Society for the Protection of the Unborn Child, was prosecuted for offending against section 75(1)(c) when she circulated leaflets informing an electorate accurately of the candidates' views on abortion and experiments on human embryos. The prosecution of her was unsuccessful on technical grounds because it was brought out of time, but her complaint to the European Court of Human Rights was allowed to proceed nonetheless. The Court ruled that she was still a "victim" because the same law would stand in the way of similar activity at the next election and the fact that she had been prosecuted for the same action in the past showed that she was at continuing risk of prosecution

---

[95] 1983 Act, s. 106(5).

[96] Representation of the People Act 1983, s. 75(1)(b) and s. 75(5). There is an offence only if the paper intends to enhance a candidate's chances. If its motive is *only* to inform the public, it has a good defence: *Grieve v. Douglas-Home* 1965 S.L.T. 1861. But if one motive is to assist the candidate, then altruistic intentions are irrelevant: *DPP v. Luft* [1977] A.C. 962.

[97] *DPP v. Luft*, n. 96 above.

[98] Representation of the People Act 1983, s. 75(1)(c).

[99] (1998) 26 E.H.R.R. 1.

in the future. Her argument was that all pressure groups were inhibited from democratic campaigning by the ludicrous ceiling of £5: there was evidence that Friends of the Earth, Charter 88, anti-foxhunters and CND had all been stopped from providing information to electors about candidates' outlooks on single issues. The Court held that the restriction for independent third parties to £5 was disproportionate and therefore contrary to Article 10. The right of freedom of expression was particularly important at election times if the further Convention right in Article 3 of Protocol 1 (the right to free elections) was to be respected.

Obliged by the Bowman decision to change section 75, the Government did so by the Political Parties, Elections and Referendums Act 2000 ("PPERA"): £5 goes out and in its place comes "the permitted sum". In connection with a candidate at a parliamentary election the permitted sum is £500 and for local elections £50 plus 0.5p for every voter in the area.[1] It is highly questionable whether these sums are compatible with Article 10: a pressure group must be entitled to spend whatever amounts to the reasonable cost of printing a leaflet and distributing it throughout the electorate.

Until 2001 there was no restriction on expenditure which did not promote or disparage a particular candidate in a particular constituency. Thus a 1951 advertisement which damned the socialist programme of the post-war Labour Government was held to be merely propaganda which was unrelated to a particular candidate and so not an advertisement which had to be authorised by a candidate or his agent.[2] Now campaign expenditure[3] by or on behalf of a registered political party must be incurred by, or on the authority of, the treasurer, deputy treasurer or their written nominee[4] and is part of a new regime to cap the amount which parties can spend on their election campaigns. Expenditure by third parties on election material[5] is also controlled[6] but if the expenditure is in respect of a the publication of any matter relating to the election in a newspaper, a periodical, a BBC/S4C broadcast or a programme in a licensed programme service it is only controlled if it takes the form of an advertisement.[7]

In 1984 the Government legislated to restrict trade unions from spending money on political objects unless the expenditure came directly from contributions to a political fund by members who approved

---

[1] PPERA 2000, s. 131 amending s. 75 of the RPA 1983.
[2] *R. v. Tronoh Mines Ltd and Times Publishing Ltd* [1952] 1 All E.R. 697.
[3] Defined in PPERA 2000, s. 72 and Sched 8, Pt. 1—it includes "advertising of any nature".
[4] PPERA, s. 75.
[5] defined broadly in PPERA, s. 85.
[6] *ibid.*
[7] PPERA, s. 87.

of such expenditure. At the 1987 elections NALGO's literature condemning cuts in the Health Service was distributed in marginal constituencies with the object of discomforting Tory candidates: it was held
that this action was unlawful because the money for the leaflets did not
come from the political fund.[8]

Newspapers and periodicals are free to support or oppose individual
candidates in their news and editorial columns. Free publicity of this
sort is not included in computing the maximum election expenses that
a candidate can incur.[9] But newspapers must still be conscious of
defamation in deciding whether to publish election addresses. The
Defamation Act 1952 is unequivocal: an election address has no special
privilege.[10]

Broadcasting coverage of the campaign

The absence of privilege for election addresses, the possibility of an
injunction for a false statement about a candidate's character, and
the penalty for falsely announcing a candidate's withdrawal apply
equally to broadcasters. The rules about advertising are even more
strict. Political advertising is restricted on television and radio even
at election times.[11] In 1971 the European Commission of Human
Rights rejected a complaint that this prohibition was contrary to
Article 10 of the Convention finding that it was permitted by the
last sentence of Article 10(1) which permits Government licensing
of broadcasters.[12] But broadcasters are able to transmit statements by
or in support of candidates without committing an election offence.[13]
However, there are special controls to make sure that no individual
candidate gains an unfair advantage.

Codes

Until 2001 these controls were set out in the legislation. They operated
crudely. Thus it was unlawful during an election campaign to include a
programme about a constituency in which the candidate appeared on
film in a sound-bite unless the candidate gave his consent. This effectively gave candidates the power to control the editing of their contributions by threatening to withdraw their consent if they did not like what

---

[8] *Paul v. NALGO* [1987] I.R.L.R. 413.
[9] 1983 Act, s. 75(1)(c)(i).
[10] 1952 Act, s. 10.
[11] Broadcasting Act 1990, ss. 8 and 92—and see p. 828.
[12] *X and the Association of Z v. U.K.*, App. No. 4515/70, July 11, 1971.
[13] Representation of the People Act 1983, s. 75(1)(c)(ii).

they saw. Worse, all the candidates in the constituency had to consent to the programme. So this power of veto operated undemocratically. The PPERA 2000 has re-written the previous provision (section 93 of the Representation of the People Act 1983). The broadcasting regulators (the ITC, the BBC, the Radio Authority and S4C) are each required to draw up their own codes of practice with respect to the participation of candidates at a parliamentary or local government election in items about the constituency during the election period. In drawing up their codes the broadcasting authorities must have regard to the views of the Electoral Commission. The codes of the ITC, BBC and Radio Authority can be found on their websites[14] and S4C's can be obtained from its office.[15] Once their Codes are adopted the BBC and S4C must observe them and the ITC and Radio Authority must each do all it can to secure that their Codes are observed.

Balance

The Independent Television Commission is under a duty to do all it can to ensure that "due impartiality is preserved on the part of persons providing the service as respects matters of political . . . controversy or relating to current public policy".[16] By self-denying assurances, the BBC accepts similar standards.[17]

Balance can be achieved through a series of programmes,[18] but at election time broadcasters are super-sensitive to charges of bias. In the run-up to the 1987 elections the BBC turned down a play that depicted Mrs Thatcher behaving heroically and compassionately during the Falklands War. In February 1974 *The Perils of Pendragon*, a comedy programme, was rescheduled because of its unflattering portrayal of a Communist. In 1964 the BBC agreed to move *Steptoe and Son* from peak time on polling day at the request of Harold Wilson, who feared it would keep Labour voters at home. The BBC declined his further suggestion to "replace it with Greek drama, preferably in the original".

---

[14] www.itc.org.uk; www.bbc.co.uk; www.radioauthority.org.uk.
[15] Tel.: 029-2074-7444.
[16] Broadcasting Act 1990, s. 6(1).
[17] See clause 5(1)(c) of the Agreement of January 25, 1996 between BBC and the Heritage Secretary. In *Lynch v. BBC* [1983] 6 Northern Ireland Judgments Bulletin, Hutton J. had found that the BBC was not under any legal duty to comply with what was then only an undertaking to observe impartiality in a letter from Lord Normanbrook, chairman of the BBC's governors. However, since then the Licence and Agreement has been amended to incorporate an impartiality obligation. The courts have indicated that the obligation can be enforced by judicial review—see *R. v. BBC and ITC, ex p. Referendum Party* [1997] E.M.L.R. 605, and Chap. 16— Broadcasting Law.
[18] Broadcasting Act 1990, s. 6(2).

Party political broadcasts

A limited number of party political broadcasts are allowed each year on all channels, determined by the Party Political Broadcast Committee, comprising representatives from the BBC and ITC together with the major parties, chaired by the Lord President of the Privy Council. Airtime is parcelled out according to seats held in Parliament and performance at recent polls, although no definitive formula has been adopted. Party political broadcasts during election periods have become an influential part of the democratic process. In 1987 Hugh (*Chariots of Fire*) Hudson produced a remarkable propaganda film that boosted Neil Kinnock's personal rating by 16 per cent overnight, while the Tories counter-attacked with a theme tune specially composed by Andrew (*Evita*) Lloyd-Webber. These broadcasts, too, are allocated by the Party Political Broadcast Committee: by tradition, the Opposition has the penultimate broadcast and the Government has the very last one before the election. These arrangements have worked satisfactorily for the major parties (and especially the Lib. Dems, whose appeal to broadcasting executives is always much higher than it is to the electorate) decision in 1974 to give one propaganda slot to every party fielding more than 50 candidates led to an inevitably controversial broadcast by the National Front.

At the time of the 1997 General Election, the Referendum Party challenged these criteria on the basis that they discriminated against new parties, such as the Referendum Party, which was fielding in almost every constituency. It had been allocated one five-minute broadcast whereas the Conservative and Labour parties had five 10-minute slots and the Liberal Democrats had four 10-minute programmes. The application failed. The court said that the broadcasters' judgment could not be castigated as irrational.[19]

The court showed a similar deference to the judgment of the BBC when faced with a challenge from the Pro-Life Alliance, whose party political broadcast had been rejected as unacceptable on taste and decency grounds. The programme had included shots of aborted foetuses, many of which were multilated. The court held that there was not even an arguable ground of challenge on irrationality or unlawful curtailment of Article 10 rights—the rights of others (which could be a legitimate aim of restricting freedom of expression) included the right not to be subjected to unduly offensive material.[20]

Party propaganda is not welcomed by viewers even at election time. In 1984, when the SDP/Liberal Alliance felt that it was losing out in news coverage, it complained to the Broadcasting Complaints Commis-

---

[19] *R. v. BBC and ITC, ex p. Referendum Party* [1997] E.M.L.R. 605.
[20] *R. v. BBC, ex p. Pro-Life Alliance Party* [1997] C.O.D. 457.

sion (the predecessor of the Broadcasting Standard Commission) that it was being denied, as a matter of policy, a coverage in which viewers might perceive it as an alternative Opposition. The courts upheld the Commission's refusal to adjudicate the question, on the ground that it raised issues of policy that were for the broadcasting authorities to determine.[21]

The European Commission of Human Rights has similarly been unwilling to question the judgment of broadcasters at election times. In *Huggett v. United Kingdom*[22] the applicant was an independent candidate at the elections for the European Parliament in 1994. He was not allowed an election broadcast because it was the broadcasters' policy to reserve these to parties which had candidates in at least 12.5 per cent of the seats. The Commission said that the threshold was needed to ensure that limited airtime was given only to political opinions which were likely to be of general interest and command some public support. A complaint about inadequate access to broadcasting by the Austrian Freedom Party was rejected in *Haider v. Austria*.[23] Jorge Haider also claimed that the hostile manner in which he had been interviewed violated his rights under the Convention. But, as the Commission said, "with regard to interviews of politicians, it is in the interests of freedom of political debate that the interviewing journalist may also express critical and provocative points of view and not merely give neutral cues for the statements of interviewed persons, since the latter can reply immediately."

Section 36 of the 1990 Broadcasting Act empowers the Independent Television Commission to require licence holders to carry party political broadcasts on Channel 3 (ITV), Channel 4 and Channel 5, and permits the ITC itself to determine which political parties shall be allowed such broadcasts, how often and for how long. The Radio Authority is given similar powers.[24] Before making rules for these purposes the ITC and Radio Authority must have regard to the views of the Electoral Commission (a body charged with supervising many aspects of election law by the PPERA). In determining their policies regarding party political broadcasts the BBC and S4C must do the same.[25] Broadcasters can in any case only allow registered parties to make party political broadcasts[26] and during referendum campaigns only organisations which have been formally designated by the Electoral Commission.[27] The cosy

---

[21] *R. v. BCC. ex p Owen* [1985] 2 All E.R. 522, and see *Wilson v. IBA* (No. 2) (1988) S.L.T. 276; *James Marshall v. BBC* [1979] 1 W.L.R. 1071.

[22] App. No. 24744/94 (1995) 82 D.R. 98.

[23] App. No. 25060/94 (1995) 83 D.R. 66.

[24] Broadcasting Act 1990, s. 107.

[25] PPERA, s. 11.

[26] *ibid.*, s. 37.

[27] *ibid.*, s. 127.

arrangements between the broadcasters and the major political parties can come unstuck if their deal contravenes the due impartiality requirements of the Broadcasting Act. In 1979 the IBA was injuncted from showing a set of four party political broadcasts, agreed with the major parties, three of which favoured a "yes" vote for the form of Scottish devolution offered by the referendum. The court held that the statutory duty on the IBA to maintain a proper balance required approximately equal time for each case.[28] That duty has not been imposed on the ITC, but if the situation were to recur, a similar result might be achieved by reference to the due impartiality duty.

Much less satisfactory has been the broadcasting authorities' craven acceptance of the right of parties to dictate the choice of spokespeople. Election discussion programmes have become a cosy dialogue between chosen broadcasters and chosen politicians, with none of the fire traditionally associated with the hustings. Questions at carefully arranged press conferences and studio discussions are predictable and deferential—professional broadcasters were put to shame in the 1983 elections, when the only person to subject the Prime Minister to searching questions about the sinking of the *Belgrano,* the Argentinian warship, was a housewife who took part in a phone-in programme. In the 1987 elections the Labour Party was allowed to keep its left-wing candidates well away from the television screen; while much was heard about Ken Livingstone from other parties, he was never permitted to speak for himself to national audiences. At the general election in 2001 controversial minister Keith Vaz, suffered a similar fate, and he was quietly dropped after the election.

Ministerial broadcasts

The BBC accepts a special duty to permit ministerial broadcasts on matters of national importance, which may range from a declaration of war to emergency arrangements for coping with a drought. So long as there is general consensus on the subject-matter of the broadcast, no right of reply will be given to the Opposition. Where there is, however, an element of partisan controversy in a ministerial broadcast, the Opposition must be given equal time to broadcast a reply.[29] When Mr Tony Benn sought to make a ministerial broadcast in 1975 on the Petroleum and Submarine Protection Act, the BBC detected political controversy in his script and informed him that the Opposition would be

---

[28] *Wilson v. IBA* (1979) S.L.T. 279.
[29] See the "Aide-Memoire" of April 3, 1969, between the BBC and the Conservative and Labour parties.

entitled to put its point of view. He cancelled the broadcast rather than allow his opponents free air-time. Section 10 of the Broadcasting Act places a statutory duty on the ITC to comply with a notice from a minister of the Crown requiring it to direct licence holders to publish an official announcement, "with or without visual images". Licence holders will be contractually bound to comply with such a direction, but they may reveal the direction's existence to their viewers.

Foreign radio and television stations must not be exploited by interested parties to influence British elections, but otherwise their programmes can be broadcast by arrangement with the BBC or ITC.[30]

Access to meetings

At election times schools and public meeting rooms have to be made available to candidates so that they can promote their campaigns.[31] Consistent with this objective, a candidate can book one of these venues only for a *public* meeting. A popular or controversial candidate may not be able to accommodate every member of the public who would like to be admitted, but, as in other contexts, it is difficult to see how a meeting could be correctly described as "public" if the press were actively excluded. Journalists who are ordered to leave election meetings by organisers unhappy with press coverage should insist on their right to remain. If forcibly ejected, they could obtain damages for assault.

Access to election registers and candidates' returns

The lists of electors are public documents, which the media are free to inspect and copy. Reporters have this access not just at election times but during normal business hours. One copy of the register is kept at the electoral officer's office (normally the town hall) and usually at public libraries as well.[32]

Within 35 days of the announcement of the result, the election agents for all the candidates must file a return with the electoral officer detailing the candidates' expenses. The electoral officer has 10 further days to advertise in two newspapers that circulate in the constituency giving notice of where and when the returns can be inspected. The

---

[30] Representation of the People Act, s. 92.
[31] *ibid.*, s. 95 (parliamentary elections), s. 96 (local government elections).
[32] Representation of the People Regulations 2001, S.I. 2001 No. 341, reg. 43 (right to inspect); reg. 7 (right to copy). Currently, copies of the register can be purchased in data or printed form: *ibid.*, reg. 48. The powers in Representation of the People Act 1983, Sched. 2, paras 10–11 (as substituted by Representation of People Act 2000, s. 9) to allow voters to opt out of having their names and addresses included in an edited version of the register which would be the only version available for sale have not yet been implemented.

returns and accompanying documents can be inspected and copied there (usually at the town hall) by any member of the public for two years after the election.[33] A fee of £5 can be charged for the inspection and 20p per page for copies.[34]

Exit polls

The Representation of the People Act 2000 introduced a prohibition on the publication of exit polls before the official polls close.[35] The prohibition relates to any statement regarding the way in which voters have voted at a parliamentary or local government election where that statement is or might reasonably be taken to be based on information given by voters after they have voted. Forecasts of the result which are also based (or might reasonably be seen to be based) on such information are also prohibited. Publication in breach is a summary offence with a maximum penalty of a fine on level 5 (currently £5,000).

This is an unnecessary restraint on free speech, apparently passed because political spin doctors feared that party supporters would not bother to vote if early exit polls showed that their party was well in the lead. But it is more likely that exit polls would spur the citizens' interest and encourage them to go out and vote—a matter of public benefit given the appallingly low turnout at the 2001 general election. A Canadian ban on opinion polls in the three days prior to federal elections was held by the Supreme Court to be an unconstitutional restriction on freedom of speech.[35A]

REGISTERED POLITICAL PARTIES

Until 1998 legislation barely recognised the existence of political parties. There were two particular pressures which brought about change. On the one hand there was the exponential growth in the money which parties were putting into election campaigns and which the Government wished to bring under control. On the other was the use by some fringe parties of names which were confusingly similar to established parties (e.g. the Literal Democrat who stood against a Liberal Democrat). Both

---

[33] Representation of the People Act 1983, ss. 81, 88 and 89. Parish Council returns are kept for only one year: *ibid.,* s. 90(1)(b) and Sched. 4, para. 8(1); as are returns of European Parliamentary elections: European Parliamentary Elections Regulations 1999, S.I. 1999 No. 1214: Sched. 1.

[34] Representation of the People Regulations 2001, S.I. 2001 No. 341, reg. 10.

[35] Representation of People Act 2000, Sched. 6, para. 6 adding s. 66A to Representation of the People Act 1983.

[35A] *Thompson Newspapers Co. Ltd. v. Att.-Gen.* (1998) 5 B.H.R.C. 567, Can. S.C.

pressures led the Government to introduce a system of registration of political parties and the regime is now set out in PPERA 2000.[36] Registration is necessary if candidates are to stand in an election on behalf of a political party.[37] Various other benefits accorded to political parties in an election (such as party political broadcasts) depend on the party being registered (see above p. 548) and Electoral Commission has power to make grants for policy development[38] but only to registered political parties.

The Electoral Commission is responsible for the register. An application can be rejected if the proposed name is the same as an existing registered party or would be confusingly similar; if it contains more than six words, is obscene or offensive; if it includes words whose publication would be an offence; if it includes any script other than roman; or if it includes any prescribed words. If two or more simultaneous applicants want to use the same name, the Commission has to consider by reference to the history of each party which has the better claim.[39]

Registered political parties are subject to disclosure obligations. Most notably, the Commission has to maintain a register of recordable donations to registered parties.[40] The provisions as to what donations have to be recorded are complex[41] but broadly they include donations over £5,000. Parties have to make reports of donations to the Commission regularly—ordinarily each quarter, but weekly during a general election. There are also registers of "recognised third parties" (a scheme intended to give greater transparency to individuals and bodies who are providing support for particular parties)[42] and of bodies intending to campaign in relation to a referendum.[43] All of these registers (as well as the register of political parties itself) are open to public inspection and, for a charge, may be copied.[44]

The Commission will also receive and must make available for inspection the annual accounts of each registered party,[45] a return from

---

[36] Ironically, after the PPERA the courts found another way of stopping the use of party names which would confuse voters—the law of passing off: *Burge v. Haycock* (unreported) May 31, 2001, CA.

[37] PPERA, s. 22.

[38] *ibid.*, s. 12.

[39] *ibid.*, s. 28 and Registration of Political Parties (Prohibited Words) Order 2001, S.I. 2001 No. 82.

[40] PPERA, s. 69.

[41] *ibid.*, ss. 62–68 and Sched. 6.

[42] *ibid.*, ss. 85–89.

[43] *ibid.*, ss. 105–107.

[44] *ibid.*, s. 149.

[45] *ibid.*, ss. 46 and 149.

each party showing its election campaign expenditure,[46] and expenditure by recognised third parties,[47] and a return showing expenditure on a referendum campaign.[48]

[46] PPERA, ss. 84 and 149—the Commission will keep these returns for two years
[47] *ibid.*, ss. 100 and 149.
[48] *ibid.*, ss. 124 and 149.

CHAPTER 11

REPORTING WHITEHALL

"It is an official secret if it is in an official file".
Sir Martin Furnival-Jones, Head of MI5,
evidence to Franks Committee on Official Secrets.[1]

Secrecy, said Richard Crossman, is the British disease. Government administrators catch it from the Official Secrets Act and supporting legislation. It is aggravated by bureaucratic rules and arrangements that conspire to place the United Kingdom toward the bottom in the league table of openness in Western democratic government. Against those who would hide their publicly paid behaviour from the public eye, the professional journalist can have only one response: to press on investigating and publishing, irrespective of the law. Most of the secrecy rules described in this chapter deserve to be broken, and many are, in fact, broken by the media regularly and without repercussions. The Human Rights Act 1998 and (when it is brought into operation) the Freedom of Information Act do provide opportunities to roll back secrecy, but require media organisations to take legal action to challenge official decisions against disclosure.

"Whitehall" stands for the executive and military branch of central government. The Palace of Whitehall was the home of the first civil servants, who served the despotic Stuart kings. They now serve a democratic government, and justify the secrecy of their service by reference to an outdated theory that "ministerial accountability" requires information requested by representatives of the public to be forthcoming only from, or with the approval of, ministers responsible for Whitehall departments. In practice, however, ministerial involvement in departmental decisions occurs only at levels of high policy, and executive errors must be of the magnitude of the failure to foresee the invasion of the Falkland Islands before a minister will resign a portfolio. The truth is that ministers neither control nor are answerable for thousands of decisions made by middle-ranking departmental officers—decisions

---

[1] *Report of the Departmental Committee on the Reform of s. 2 of the Official Secrets Act 1911,* Cmnd 5104, Vol. III, p. 249.

that may vitally affect individuals and communities. If executive accountability is ever to be made a reality in Britain, the Freedom of Information Act must be interpreted to permit the inspection of information accumulated and acted upon by administrators. Such legislation has become a defining characteristic of democratic government in other Western countries, where evidence has accumulated that public participation in government leads to better government.

None of the justifications for our present level of secrecy is convincing. National security might be threatened by the revelation of a limited class of information to foreign powers, but too often this danger is used as a pretext for the Government to withhold embarrassing information from its own citizens. The Government does gather many intimate details about individuals that it ought to keep confidential, but privacy as a rationale for secrecy is less persuasive when it concerns the social impact of corporate policies, and still less when it concerns policy discussions within Government. The argument that civil servants would be less frank if their advice were shortly to be made public is a canard; the evidence from other countries suggests that the advice would be better considered and better expressed. Even if some information is no longer written down and, instead, communicated orally, this cannot be routine in bureaucracies the size of Whitehall. The great attraction for blanket secrecy laws within the civil service seems to be that it fosters a sense of self-importance. Mandarins with a high security clearance have a status derived more from the exclusivity of their access to information than from its intrinsic significance. Even junior civil servants, according to a former head of MI5, approved the discredited and now abolished "section 2" of the Official Secrets Act 1911,

> " . . . they find a kind of pride in being subjected to the criminal law in this way . . . the fact that they . . . are picked out as being people who are doing work so dangerous if you like that it brings them within the scope of the criminal law if they talk about it, has a very powerful effect on their minds . . . it is not that they are deterred by the fear of prosecution, but in a sense it is a spur to their intent."[2]

A vast quantity of information does, of course, pour out of Whitehall in the form of press releases from the press officers now attached to all departments. Even Army officers are taught how to give interviews, and the media give ample space for these official hand-outs. The difficulty is to extract information that is not "authorised" or "vetted"; the civil servant who speaks out of turn in some cases faces the vague threat of prosecution, but more often the immediate danger of disciplinary sanc-

---

[2] Evidence to the Franks Committee, n. 1 above, Vol. III, p. 261.

tion by way of transfer, demotion or dismissal. Britain does now have some protection for "whistleblowers", the Public Interest Disclosure Act (see p. 268), but it is a cautious piece of legislation whose impact is likely to be very limited. However, for all the difficulties posed by secrecy laws and conventions, the Government is reluctant to court media unpopularity by prosecuting journalists over revelations of genuine public interest. Thus in 2000, the Government declined to prosecute *The Mail on Sunday*'s editor and journalists over their dealings with David Shayler who was paid £40,000 after his revelation that MI5 had kept secret files on such youthful "subversives" as Jack Straw, Peter Mandelson, Harriet Harman and Patricia Hewitt. It dropped Official Secret Act charges made against Tony Geraghty over his book, *The Irish War,* after constant media criticism of the Attorney-General for pursuing the case (see the "Stop Press" section for further details). This chapter will seek to give the Official Secrets Acts and other secrecy conventions a realistic appraisal. It will explain how valuable source material can be obtained through public records legislation and by invoking policy directives, which can help journalists to negotiate the disclosure of more recent public documents.

The Official Secrets Acts

The Official Secrets Act 1911 was rushed on to the statute books at a time of national panic, as German "gunboat diplomacy" at Agadir coincided with sensationalised newspaper stories about German spies photographing the fortifications at Dover harbour.[3] It completed its entire parliamentary progress in one day, hailed by all parties as an urgently necessary measure to protect the nation's secrets from enemy agents. No M.P. spoke on section 2 of the Act, which had been carefully drafted within Whitehall some time before with the purpose of stopping leakage of official information to the press.[4] The press was soon to suffer: the very first prosecution brought under the new Act was to punish a war office clerk for supplying information to the *Military Mail* that cast his superiors in a poor light.[5]

Section 2 managed, by tortuous drafting, to create more than 2,000 different offences in a few statutory paragraphs. These could be roughly divided into two groups: those most likely to be committed by inside

---

[3] Franks Report, n. 1 above, Vol. I, App. III.
[4] K. G. Robertson, *Public Secrets: A Study of the Development of Government Secrecy,* Macmillan, 1982, p. 63.
[5] Franks Report, n. 1 above, Vol. I, App. III. See also Jonathan Aitken, *Officially Secret* (Weidenfeld & Nicolson, 1971).

sources (*i.e.* by communicating official information to an unauthorised person) and those that directly affected journalists who received or retained official information without authorisation. The more serious section 1, which has a maximum penalty of 14 years' imprisonment, is aimed at spies and saboteurs, although the Government has once, in the "ABC" case (see p. 556), tried to extend it to journalists. Finally, the Act gave the police extraordinary powers to arrest, seize documents and to question suspects, including journalists. The 1989 Act, which replaced section 2 with narrower (and hence more formidable) offences, has not often been invoked. More than any other piece of legislation, its use is circumscribed by political considerations.

The Attorney-General in the past had to approve every prosecution under the Act (the exception under the Official Secrets Act 1989 is considered below), and take into account the degree of culpability, the damage to the public interest that resulted from the disclosure, and the effect that a prosecution would have on the public interest.[6] A number of top-level spies have gone unprosecuted since the Second World War because it has been deemed inexpedient to expose to the public (and to Britain's allies) the extent of Soviet penetration even with the protection possible through secret hearings. At the other extreme, Attorneys-General have been reluctant to prosecute newspapers for routine breaches. The appearance of secret Whitehall documents in the press is usually followed by a "leak inquiry", conducted by Scotland Yard, with the object of discovering the civil servant responsible. So long as journalists decline to answer questions or supply leaked copies of documents that might incriminate their source, these inquiries are usually fruitless.

The Attorney-General, as a party politician, will be disinclined to use oppressive and discredited legislation against the press. However, he may come under heavy pressure from the military and security establishment, unswayed by any concern for civil liberties and perhaps anxious to impress American "cousins" with their resolve to protect Allied secrets. Insecure Labour law officers, desirous of proving themselves "responsible" in such matters, twice succumbed to this pressure. The first occasion, in 1970, had the result of discrediting section 2 of the Act:

> Jonathan Aitken, then a young journalist and parliamentary candidate, came by a secret Army document about the state of the Biafran war that contained information at variance with Prime Ministerial statements to

---

[6] 1911 Act, s. 8. The criteria in the text were given by the Attorney-General in evidence to the Franks Committee, n. 1 above, Vol. II, p. 7. Any function of the Attorney-General can instead be exercised by the Solicitor-General (Law Officers Act 1997, s. 1), but the Solicitor-General is also a party politician.

Parliament (such a document would be covered by the 1989 Act because it revealed Army logistics and deployment). He was given it by a general, who had received the report from a colonel attached to the British Embassy in Nigeria. Aitken, to the general's embarrassment, arranged for it to be published in the *Daily Telegraph.* The Attorney-General authorised a section 2 prosecution of the colonel, Aitken, and the editor of the *Daily Telegraph,* with the general cutting a sorry figure as chief prosecution witness. Various technical defences were canvassed, based on the prosecution's difficulty in proving that original disclosure by the colonel to the general, his former commanding officer, was "unauthorised". Both journalist and editor additionally claimed that they had a moral duty to make the information public in order to rectify false statements in Parliament. The defence claimed the case was a "political prosecution", initiated by a petulant Labour Government, and the trial judge in a sympathetic summing up told the jury that it was high time that section 2 was "pensioned off". All defendants were acquitted.[7]

The outcry provoked by the prosecution led to the establishment of a committee headed by Lord Franks to examine section 2 of the Official Secrets Act. It condemned the width and uncertainty of the section, and urged its replacement by a law narrowly defining the categories of information that deserved protection.[8] The Government, in 1976, accepted that mere receipt of secret information by the press should not amount to an offence.[9] Reform of the Act was put in abeyance, however, by the extraordinary security service vendetta against journalist Duncan Campbell:

Campbell was a young freelance journalist specialising in defence and working mainly for small-circulation magazines. In company with Crispin Aubrey, a news reporter from *Time Out,* he interviewed a disaffected ex-soldier, John Berry, who 10 years before had worked at a signals intercept base in Cyprus. He had written to the magazine volunteering to reveal security "scandals", although the information he could give the journalists added little to what Campbell had already collected, from published sources about British Signals Intelligence operations. The three men were arrested, and Campbell's entire home library was removed in a pantechnicon to Scotland Yard. The "ABC" case, which then commenced its passage, had side consequences already noted. The prosecution, for the first time, used section 1 charges against journalists.

The result was that Campbell alone was charged, under section 1, with collecting information of use to an enemy relating to a number of defence installations. The case on this count collapsed after two weeks of evidence demonstrating that Campbell's information and photographs had come

---

[7] *R. v. Aitken and Others,* and see also Aitken, *Officially Secret.*

[8] Franks Committee Report, n. 1 above.

[9] *Hansard,* November 22, 1976 [*Hansard*] H.C. Debs Vol. 919, col. 1878 *et seq.*

from published sources—in some cases, Ministry of Defence press hand-outs. The incompetence of the security services, which had instructed the Attorney-General that Campbell's information was top secret, was, in effect, conceded by the Crown prosecutor when withdrawing this ill-conceived charge.

The two journalists were charged under section 1 with obtaining information of use to an enemy (Berry's account of his time in Cyprus) for a purpose prejudicial to the security of the State. The "purpose prejudicial" was alleged to be their intention to publish it in *Time Out*. These charges were withdrawn at the insistence of the judge, Mr Justice Mars-Jones, who described them as "oppressive". Although the wide wording of section 1 of the Act was not necessarily confined to spies and saboteurs, he said that its harsh provisions (including a reversal of the burden of proof and facilitation of guilt by association) made it undesirable for use against persons not alleged to be in league with a foreign power.

Section 2 charges were brought home against each defendant. Berry was found to be in breach of the Act by passing information to the journalists, and they were found guilty of receiving this information. Berry received a six-month suspended sentence; both journalists were given conditional discharges.[10]

The effective collapse of the "ABC" prosecution may make future Attorneys reluctant to use section 1 against investigative journalism. The Attorney-General of the time, Sam Silkin Q.C., defended his decision to prosecute on the grounds that he had been misled by the Ministry of Defence and the security service as to the sensitivity of the information in Campbell's possession.[11] Colonel B was less impressive under skilled cross-examination than he had been in the Attorney's chambers. The case had the additional importance of undermining the seriousness of section 2 by the lightness of the sentences visited upon the journalist offenders.

The 1989 Act offered the media a Faustian bargain: it lifted the possibility of prosecution for much routine information within Whitehall (revelation of which would never in practice have been prosecuted under the old section 2) while it made much easier the prosecution of revelations about intelligence work, defence and foreign affairs. In these cases it replaced a blunderbuss with an armalite rifle, designed to hit defendants who repeat the conduct of the likes of Aitken, Campbell and Clive Ponting. The Government firmly resisted a public interest defence, which might have protected the media and their sources in relation to leaks that demonstrate discreditable conduct within the defence and intelligence establishment.

---

[10] Andrew Nicol, "Official Secrets and Jury Vetting" [1979] Crim L.R. 284. Geoffrey Robertson, *The Justice Game*, Chap. 5 "Ferrets and Skunks? The ABC trial" (Vintage, 1999).
[11] Crispin Aubrey, *Who's Watching You?* (Penguin, 1981).

The 1989 Act offences fall broadly into those that are most likely to be committed by "insiders" and those designed with "outsiders", such as the press, in mind. We start with the former because they introduce categories and classifications that span both groups.

Offences by "insiders"

These are subdivided into four groups.

Security and intelligence

This group is further subdivided into members of the security or intelligence services and those who work closely with them, and other Crown servants or government contractors who learn of information concerning security and intelligence in the course of their work.

Persons who are or have been members of the security and intelligence services commit an offence if they disclose any information, document or other article relating to security or intelligence that they have acquired in the course of their intelligence work.[12] There is no stipulation that the information must be secret, and the courts would probably follow their stance under the old section 2[13] and find the offence was committed even though the information was not secret in any meaningful sense.

Significantly, under this, offence the Crown does not have to prove any damage or harm. The trial judge in the *David Shayler* case held that this remained the position even after the Human Rights Act (see the "Stop Press" section for further details). These severe obligations of secrecy can be extended by written notice to others who, though not actually members of the secret services, work closely with them.[14]

For Crown servants and government contractors who are not members of the secret services and who are not made honorary members by notification there is a narrower offence of making a *damaging* disclosure of information relating to security or intelligence.[15] "Damage" here means damage to the work of, or any part of, the security and intelligence services.[16] It is not apparently sufficient if work in support of the security services is harmed. Although there may, of course, be a knock-on effect, it is harm to the secret services themselves that must be shown. Here and throughout the Act it is enough if damage would

---

[12] Official Secrets Act 1989, s. 1(1) "security or intelligence includes work in support of the security services"; s. 1(8).
[13] *R. v. Crisp and Homewood* (1919) 83 I.P. 121; *R. v. Galvin* [1987] 2 All E.R. 851.
[14] Official Secrets Act 1989, s. 1(1)(b) and s. 1(6).
[15] *ibid.*, s. 1(3).
[16] *ibid.*, s. 1(4)(a).

be "likely to occur" as a result of the disclosure. In the present context alone the definition is wider. The prosecution does not have to prove that the particular information would be likely to cause harm. It may merely show that it is of a class that might have this effect.

"Crown servants" are the principle group of "insiders". They include civil servants, the armed forces, and the police (and their civilian assistants).[17] The employees of certain privatised corporations and regulatory bodies have been brought within the definition of Crown servant by ministerial "prescription" permitted by the Act—without parliamentary debate or public notice.[18] In 1990 the Government moved by "prescription" to button the lips of all employees of British Nuclear Fuels, the Atomic Energy Authority and Urenco (Capenhurst) Ltd, together with all persons employed by the Parliamentary Commission for Administration (the Ombudsman), the Auditor General and the Health Service Commissioner—posts that are ostensibly independent of Government.[19] The failure of the Ombudsman to object to the extension of this draconian Act to his staff is a disturbing reflection on his ability to judge where the public interest lies, namely in permitting the public reasonable scrutiny of bodies supposed to act in their interest. Local government employees are not and never have been Crown servants. The 1911 Act expressly applied to colonial governments; the 1989 Act does not, but the Government can extend its reach to the Channel Islands, the Isle of Man or any colony by statutory instruments.[20] The Act also reserves the power to add other groups to the definition of "Crown servant" by ministerial order with only the minimal protection that a draft of the order must be approved by each House of Parliament.

The definition disingenuously includes ministers and members of the Scottish Executive and junior Scottish ministers.[21] They are undoubtedly Crown servants, but despite the ministerial "briefings" that

---

[17] Official Secrets Act 1989, s. 12. Employees of a county council seconded exclusively to police stations were "in employment under a person who holds office under Her Majesty" for the purposes of the 1911 Act: *Loat v. Andrews* [1985] I.C.R. 679 and they would no doubt be "employed . . . for the purposes of any police force" under the present law. The Government has asserted that the decision of the Home Secretary to issue a written notice would be judicially reviewable: see H.C. Debs, Vol. 145, col. 148 (January 26, 1989). As British judges tend to be overimpressed whenever the Government ministers defend their action with the magic words "national security", this is unlikely to offer much comfort to individuals deprived of their freedom of expression by receipt of a notice. See *R. v. Secretary of State for the Home Department, ex p. Cheblak* [1991] 2 All E.R. 319.

[18] *ibid.*, s. 12(f) and (g).

[19] Official Secrets Act 1989 (Prescription) Order 1990 (S.I. 1990 No. 200) as amended by S.I. 1993 No. 847.

[20] Official Secrets Act 1989, s. 15(3).

[21] Official Secrets Act 1989, s. 12(1)(a) as amended by the Scotland Act 1998, Sched. 8, para. 26.

are the bread and butter of political reporting, no minister has ever been prosecuted under the Official Secrets Act. This is excused by the "fig-leaf" theory that ministers are able to authorise themselves to make disclosures. The naked truth is that prosecutions must be approved by the Attorney-General, who in the recent past has always been a member of the same political party as the blabbermouth minister. Resignation is the most severe penalty that has been imposed on ministers who have been indiscreet. J.H. Thomas was not prosecuted for leaking budget secrets in 1936, as the Attorney-General said he had been drunk at the time.[22] George Lansbury passed a Cabinet paper to his son in 1934; the son was prosecuted, the minister was not. The Attorney-General took civil action (see p. 234) against Richard Crossman's publishers over his Cabinet memoirs but conceded that there was no criminal liability.[23] Leon Brittan was not prosecuted for authorising the leak of legal advice to the Government over the Westland affair, and Cecil Parkinson survived allegations that he had whispered Falklands War secrets to his mistress during moments of non-connubial bliss.

"Government contractor" means companies and their employees who provide goods or services for a minister, the civil service, the armed forces or a police force, the Scottish administration or the National Assembly for Wales. Additionally, it applies to contractors with governments of other States or international organisations.[24]

Defence

Crown servants and government contractors commit an offence if they disclose information that they have acquired in their jobs and that concerns defence.[25] Damage must be proved by the prosecution. In this context "damage" means damage to the capability of any part of the armed forces, loss of life or injury to its members or serious damage to its equipment or installations. It can also mean jeopardy to, or serious obstruction of, British interests abroad or danger to the safety of British citizens abroad.

International relations

This, again, is a category that applies to Crown servants and government contractors. It concerns information relating to international relations[26]

[22] *Hansard,* June 10, 1936, col. 206.
[23] See Hugo Young, *The Crossman Affair* (Hamish Hamilton and Jonathan Cape, 1976), p. 33.
[24] Official Secrets Act 1989, s. 12(2). It also applies to contracts that the Secretary of State certifies are for the purposes of implementing the contracts referred to in the text.
[25] *ibid.,* s. 2, defence is comprehensively defined in s. 2(4).
[26] Official Secrets Act 1989, s. 3.

or confidential information that has been obtained from another State or an international organization.[27] The information of either type must be acquired in the course of the defendant's job.

Damage has to be shown by the prosecution. As with defence matters, this can be jeopardy to, or serious obstruction of, British interests abroad or danger to the safety of British citizens abroad. If the information was derived from another State or an international organisation, the prosecution can rely on the fact that it was confidential or on its nature or contents to establish that its disclosure would be likely to cause damage. The jury is nonetheless entitled to find that no damage would be likely to result from disclosure since the section provides only that these elements *may* be sufficient to establish harm.[28]

Crime

This category is loosely described as information concerning crime,[29] but it is really far broader. It concerns information the disclosure of which would be likely to result in the commission of an offence, facilitate the escape of a detained person, or impede the prevention or detection of offences or the apprehension or prosecution of suspects. There is no further requirement that the prosecution must show that the information is likely to cause damage. The Government argued that the categories of information are, by definition, likely to cause harm.

This dubious argument does not apply to a subcategory that rides on the back of "crime". It is an offence to disclose any information obtained from mail or telephone intercepts under a ministerial Regulation of Investigatory Powers Act (RIPA) warrant or information obtained by the security services under warrant. This prohibition extends to information obtained by reason of the intercept or secret service interference or any document or article used for or obtained by the intercept or interference.[30]

Authority and mistake

None of the insider offences are committed unless the disclosure was unauthorised. For Crown servants and "honorary" members of the security services that means a disclosure that is not in accordance with their official duty. In Clive Ponting's prosecution the trial judge ruled that it was for the Government of the day to decide what was the duty

---

[27] "International relations" means the relations between states and/or with international organisation, *ibid.*, s. 3(5).
[28] *ibid.*, s. 3(3).
[29] *ibid.*, s. 4.
[30] *ibid.*, s. 4(3).

of civil servants.[31] However, the judge could not direct the jury to convict, and Ponting's acquittal showed that the jury took a more robust view of where his duty lay. "Authorised" means, in the case of a government contractor, disclosure to a Crown servant or in accordance with a Crown servant's directions.[32]

The prerequisite of authorisation provides some prospect of a defence for the media: in the *Aitken* case it was argued that if original disclosure by the ex-colonel was "authorised", the subsequent chain of disclosure could not be in breach of the Act. The section 2 case of *R. v. Galvin*[33] is also of assistance:

> The Court of Appeal quashed an Official Secrets Act conviction on the ground that the issue of "authorisation" had not been left to the jury. The document concerned was an MOD manual that had been classified as "restricted" and had been obtained by the defendant by subterfuge. Nonetheless, it emerged at the trial that the manual had, in fact, been circulated to some outside bodies by the MOD, without specific restrictions on its further use. It was open to the jury to find, on this evidence, that the MOD had "impliedly authorised" circulation of the information, notwithstanding the "restricted" classification stamp on the copy obtained by the defendant.

None of the offences is committed if the defendant can persuade the jury that he did not know or have reason to believe that the information concerned security, defence, international relations or the categories of crime. In cases where the prosecution must prove damage it is similarly open to the defendant to prove that he did not know or have reason to believe that the disclosure would or might have the damaging effect.[34]

Retention of documents and careless loss

Crown servants and honorary members of the security services who have in their possession documents or articles that it would be an offence for them to disclose commit an offence if they retain the document or article contrary to their official duty. They have a defence if they believed they were acting in accordance with their duty and no reasonable cause to believe otherwise.[35]

Government contractors commit a similar offence if they fail to

---

[31] *R. v. Ponting* [1985] Crim. I.R. 318, scc also Clive Ponting, *The Right to Know*, 1985.
[32] Official Secrets Act 1989, s. 7.
[33] [1987] 2 All E.R. 851.
[34] Official Secrets Act 1989, ss. 1(5), 2(3), 3(4), 4(4), 4(5).
[35] *ibid.*, s. 8(1)(a), 8(2).

comply with an official direction for the return or disposal of the document or article.[36]

Both Crown servants and government contractors can be guilty of failing to take reasonable care to prevent the unauthorised disclosure of such documents or articles.[37] A Foreign Office civil servant was fined £300 under the predecessor to this provision for carelessly leaving secret diplomatic cables on a tube train. Extracts from the cables were later published in the London magazine *City Limits*. No action was taken against the magazine.[38]

The effect of the Human Rights Act

Article 10 applies to "everyone" and the European Court of Human Rights has held that "everyone" includes civil servants,[39] members of the armed forces,[40] and even those working on secret military projects.[41] Any restriction on freedom of speech must be justified by the three tests: Was the restriction prescribed by law? Was it imposed for a legitimate aim? Was it necessary in a democratic society?

The "law" must have sufficient accessibility and have an application which is reasonably predictable, but those are requirements which the Official Secrets Acts would pass. Their aims, the protection of national security and prevention of crime, would also be "legitimate" in terms of Article 10(2), although where the connection with national security (as in the *Spycatcher* case after publication throughout the world) is attenuated, the real purpose of the measure may deserve closer examination.[42] As so often with Article 10 questions, the critical issue is whether the restriction is "necessary in a democratic society". In cases concerning security measures the European Court has allowed Member States a substantial "margin of appreciation", recognising the difficult judgments which have to be made.[43] Although even here, the Court has refused to find that it was necessary for courts to try to ban publication of material which was already in the public domain.[44] The Court has

---

[36] Official Secrets Act 1989, s. 8(1)(b).

[37] *ibid.*, s. 8(1).

[38] *Observer*, December 5, 1982.

[39] *e.g. Ahmed v.* (1998) 29 E.H.R.R. 1.

[40] *Engle v. Netherlands* (1976) 1 E.H.R.R. 647.

[41] *Hadjianastassiou v. Greece* (1992) 16 E.H.R.R. 219.

[42] In *Rotaru v. Romania*, judgment of May 4, 2000, seven of the judges said that they found it hard to see how the suppression of data collected on a student going back 50 years and which was demonstrably false could be said to be justified on the grounds of national security. The case concerned Article 8, but the analysis of "legitimate aim" would have common features with Article 10.

[43] See *e.g. Leander v. Sweden* (1987) 9 E.H.R.R. 433; *Hadjianastassiou v. Greece* (1992) 16 E.H.R.R. 219.

[44] *Guardian and Observer v. U.K.* (1991) 14 E.H.R.R. 153.

found a violation of Article 10 on this basis even where the material had previously been made public by the person who was the object of the measures which gave rise to the Article 10 challenge.[45]

In the course of defending charges under the 1989 Act, section 1 and section 4 (disclosure of information from intercepts) the ex-MI5 officer, David Shayler, has argued that the absence of any public interest defence on the face of these provisions of the Act conflicts with Article 10. He has submitted that it cannot be necessary in a democratic society to punish ex-members of the security services for disclosing information even where (for the sake of argument) the information concerned dangerous and illegal activities of those services. The argument was rejected by the trial judge, Moses J. and the Court of Appeal[46] on the basis that an officer who learnt of such activities could, compatibly with the 1989 Act, disclose the information to his superiors, a staff councillor or, with the permission of his management, to the Commissioner or Tribunal which has power to review the activities of the security services.[47] If the management refused permission to approach the Commissioner or Tribunal, the officer could, according to the judges, have sought judicial review.

Offences by "outsiders"

These are the offences of most direct relevance to the media.

Disclosure of leaked or confidential information

The 1989 Act replaces section 2 of the 1911 Act with what will in time become known as section 5,[48] although the latter's notoriety will depend on a number of unresolved questions of interpretation. Broadly, section 5 makes it a specific offence for journalists and editors to publish information that they know is protected by the Act, although the prosecution must additionally prove that they had reason to believe that the publication would be damaging to the security services or to the interests of the United Kingdom. If charged under section 5, editors can at least testify as to their state of mind in deciding to publish, and will

---

[45] *Vereinging Weekblad Bluf! v. Netherlands* (1995) 20 E.H.R.R. 189, and see similarly *Weber v. Switzerland* (1990) 12 E.H.R.R. 508.

[46] *R. v. Shayler*, judgment of September 28, 2001, CA.

[47] The events in the *Shayler* case preceded amalgamation of review functions into the Regulation of Investigatory Powers Tribunal—see p. 275. Members of MI5, MI6 and GCHQ cannot take advantage of the Public Interest (Disclosure) Act 1998 (see p. 268) because they are excluded from its provisions by Employment Relations Act 1999, Sched. 8, para. 1.

[48] Official Secrets Act 1989, s. 5.

be entitled to an acquittal if the jury accepts that there was no rational basis for thinking that the disclosure would damage British interests.

The new offence is complex. It involves looking at the type of information concerned and the outsider's knowledge that it is of this type (we shall assume that the outsider is a journalist). It turns also on the character of further disclosure that takes place and the journalist's awareness that it has this character. Each ingredient needs more consideration.

Type of information. The information must be protected against disclosure by an insider, *i.e.* it must relate to security or intelligence, defence or international relations or to crime.[49] The information must also have originated from a Crown servant or government contractor. It is arguable that in this context an offence is committed by an outsider only if the source is a Crown servant at the time of the leak and that the offence does not extend to disclosures by former servants of the Crown. This confusion over whether section 5 extends to publication of the memoirs of *former* employees was exposed (and confounded) by the decision of the House of Lords in *Lord Advocate v. Scotsman Publications*[50] (the "Cavendish Diaries" case):

> The Law Lords lifted a breach of confidence injunction on newspaper publication of Cavendish's memoirs of life in the secret services after the war because no danger to national security could be apprehended by publication. Two judges considered whether the publication would amount to a breach of section 5. Lord Templeman considered that the newspaper would fall within the provisions of the section by publishing, notwithstanding that Cavendish was a former Crown servant and section 5 in terms refers only to revelations by "Crown servants". Lord Jauncy, however, stated that this interpretation "may well be unjustified having regard to the obscurity of the language". Both Law Lords agreed that a newspaper editor could, in any event, be found guilty only if the disclosure of the information was, in fact, damaging to national security.

On principle, Lord Jauncy's approach is preferable: criminal statutes should be narrowly construed, and Parliament has only itself to blame if the words "Crown servants" are defined to exclude persons who are not Crown servants by the time the offence was allegedly committed. It must not be assumed, however, that this interpretation will be finally adopted by the courts. Section 5(3) refers to documents "protected from disclosure by sections 1 to 3 above" and these sections protect against

---

[49] Official Secrets Act 1989, s. 5(1)(a).
[50] [1989] 2 All E.R. 852 at 860 and 864.

disclosures by "retired Crown servants"—a reference that the courts could seize upon to interpret "Crown servants" in section 5(1) to include "former Crown servants".

In addition, the information must have been disclosed without authority (either to the journalist or to someone else), or entrusted in confidence to the journalist or passed in breach of confidence to the journalist or someone else.[51] If the information was leaked by a government contractor or a confidee of a Crown servant or government contractor, there is a further restriction. That disclosure must have been made by a British citizen or taken place in the United Kingdom, the Channel Islands, the Isle of Man or a colony.[52]

Journalist's knowledge of the type of information. The prosecution has to prove that the journalist knew or had reasonable cause to believe that the information was protected against disclosure and that it has reached him by one of the routes described above.[53]

Type of further disclosure. There is an offence only if the further disclosure is without lawful authority (see p. 563). More significantly, if the information relates to security, intelligence, defence or international relations, the prosecutions must show that its further disclosure by the journalist will be damaging. The definitions of damage are the same as those for insider offences (see above pp. 560–562).[54] The Government refused to concede a specific public interest defence or a defence that the disclosed material had already been published before. This obduracy was unfortunate and unnecessary: juries have been loathe to convict when disclosures were made on public interest grounds (*e.g.* Clive Ponting and Jonathan Aitken) and the "damage" requirement is not a perfect substitute for a public interest defence. Prosecutors will no doubt argue that the statute requires only some harm and, once this is proved, it is not for juries to balance the harm against an alleged benefit from disclosure. In any case, damage does not have to be shown where the information relates to crime. Nonetheless, the fact that the material has been published already or that it is in the public interest that it should be made known would be powerful arguments against there being any harm where damage does have to be proved. Damage, of course, would have to be real damage to the efficacy or operations of the service rather than embarrassment flowing from the disclosure of improper behaviour.

---

[51] Official Secrets Act 1989, s. 5(1)(d).
[52] *ibid.,* s. 5(4).
[53] *ibid.,* s. 5(2).
[54] *ibid.,* s. 5(3).

Journalist's knowledge of character of further disclosure. The journalist must know or have reasonable cause to believe that his further disclosure would be damaging.[55] The insider offences include something similar as a defence but the burden of proof is then on the Crown servant. Here, knowledge by a media defendant that the further disclosure would be likely to be damaging must be proved by the prosecution beyond reasonable doubt.

Media complicity with an "insiders" offence

There is no doubt that section 5 offers the media a considerable advance on the abolished section 2: the drafting is clumsy and obscure, and the questions of "damage" and knowledge may be developed by way of defence before the jury. The real danger, largely ignored both by Parliament and the press in the debates over section 5, is that it will not be used at all. Instead, the publishers of information from future Wrights and Massiters could simply be charged with offences of incitement, conspiracy, or aiding and abetting a breach of the strict liability section 1 of the 1989 Act. This danger will be particularly present if payment is made for the information, or if the information is published by agreement with the errant insider. The confusion over whether section 5 applies to publication of disclosures by former Crown servants could be side-stepped by charging the media in such cases with the crime of complicity in an offence against section 1, which applies to former Crown servants as well as those presently serving the state (see the "Stop Press" section for further details).

Whether such draconian action would be taken will depend, as ever, upon political considerations. In 1990 the Government admitted to having misled Parliament when denying allegations by Colin Wallace about disinformation exercises by the security services in Northern Ireland in the early 1970s. Wallace was not prosecuted under the 1989 Act. By the autumn of 2001 no journalist had been prosecuted to trial under the 1989 Act. Tony Geraghty did face charges under section 5 in connection with his book *The Irish War* which was published in 1998, but these were dropped. The case against his alleged source, Nigel Wylde, was also dropped before trial. Other newspaper sources have been successfully prosecuted. In 1999, for instance, a Royal Navy petty officer was jailed for 12 months for leaking details about a feared Iraqi biological weapons attack on Britain to the *Sun*. He said he had been under tremendous financial pressure and the newspaper had paid him £10,000.[56]

---

[55] Official Secrets Act 1989, s. 5(3)(b).
[56] *Media Lawyer* May/June, 1999, p. 26

Disclosure of information from spying

A simple offence is created by the 1989 Act of disclosing without lawful authority any information, document or article that the defendant knows or has reasonable cause to believe has come into his possession as a result of a breach of section 1 of the 1911 Act.[57] Section 1 principally concerns spying (see p. 570) and it will be rare for journalists to come into the possession of such information.

Information from abroad

A separate offence is created by the 1989 Act for the unauthorised disclosure of information that has come from another State or international organisation.[58] This offence also needs to be broken down.

Type of information. This offence concerns only information relating to security, intelligence, defence or international relations which has been passed by the United Kingdom in confidence to another State or international organisation. It must have come into the journalist's possession without the authority of that State or organisation.[59]

Journalist's knowledge. The journalist must know or have reasonable cause to believe that the information is of the type described above.[60]

Type of disclosure. There is no offence if the journalist's disclosure is made with lawful authority.[61] It is not a defence, as such, that the material has been previously published abroad unless it was published with the authority of the State or organisation concerned.[62] However, the prosecution must show that the publication by the journalist is damaging,[63] and if it has been previously published (even without authority), this will be virtually impossible to do.

Journalist's knowledge of the consequences of further disclosure. The prosecution must again show that the journalist knew or had reasonable cause to believe that the further disclosure would be damaging.[64]

Retention and careless loss. A person given a document or other

---

[57] Official Secrets Act 1989, s. 5(6).
[58] *ibid.*, s. 6.
[59] *ibid.*, s. 6(1)(a).
[60] *ibid.*, s. 6(2).
[61] *ibid.*, s. 6(3).
[62] *ibid.*
[63] *ibid.*, s. 6(2), "damage" has the same meaning as under the insider offences.
[64] *ibid.*

article in confidence by a Crown servant or government contractor is guilty of an offence if he or she fails to take reasonable care[65] to prevent its unauthorized disclosure.[66] It is also an offence to fail to comply with an official direction for the return or disposal of a document or article whose disclosure would be an offence under either sections 5 or 6. There is an offence only if the journalist (or other outsider) is in possession of the document or article at the time its return is demanded. This simply adds to the incentive to dispose of leaked documents before their return is demanded: parting with possession is itself a disclosure (see section 13(1)) and so care would have to be taken in deciding whether disposal would be an offence.

These offences are triable only by magistrates, who can impose a fine on scale 5 (currently £5,000) or sentence to prison for up to three months. The price for being categorised as relatively minor offences is that there is no right to trial by jury. This is worrying, since juries in the past have played an important role in keeping the widely drawn Official Secrets Acts within some reasonable limits.

Codes, Keys and other access information

This offence concerns information that is or has been in the possession of a Crown servant or government contractor and can be used to obtain access to any information, document or article that is protected against disclosure by the Act. It is an offence for anyone (whether insider or outsider) to disclose this type of information where the circumstances are such that it would be reasonable to expect it to be used for such a purpose without authority.[67]

1911 Act, section 1: "penalties for spying"

Headed "penalties for spying", this section is generally used against enemy agents. It carries a maximum penalty of 14 years, which has often been invoked for serious espionage: George Blake was sentenced to 42 years imprisonment for three offences.[68] The section makes it an offence:

"if any person for any purpose prejudicial to the safety or interest of the State—

(a) approaches, inspects, passes over or is in the neighbourhood

---

[65] Official Secrets Act 1989, s. 8(4) and (5).
[66] *ibid.*, s. 8(4)(b).
[67] *ibid.*, s. 8(6).
[68] *R. v. Blake* [1961] 3 All E.R. 125.

of, or enters any prohibited place within the meaning of this
Act; or

(b) makes any sketch, plan, model, or note which is calculated
to be or might be or is intended to be directly or indirectly
useful to an enemy; or

(c) obtains, collects, records or publishes, or communicates to
any other person any secret official code word, or password
or any sketch, plan, model, article or note or other document
or information which is calculated to be or might be or is
intended to be directly or indirectly useful to the enemy."

The actions by themselves may be quite trivial—approaching a prohibited place, such as a nuclear power station (see below), or sketching
a map that could be useful to a potential enemy. War need not have
been declared: *potential* enemies are included, although it is agents of
enemy governments who are targeted—spies for terrorist groups have
not been prosecuted under this section.[69] Where the information concerns prohibited places, it is up to defendants to show that their possession of it is not for a disloyal purpose. In addition, contrary to the
normal evidential rule against guilt by association, the prosecution can
give evidence of the defendants' characters and associations to show
that their purpose was prejudicial.[70]

In 1920 the Attorney-General told the House of Commons that the
opening words of the section, "for any purpose prejudicial to the safety
or interests of the State", meant that the section was aimed at spies in
the employ of foreign powers.[71] This assurance that section 1 was so
limited was repeated by another Attorney-General in 1949. But in 1964
the House of Lords extended it to peaceful protest by upholding the
conviction of anti-nuclear demonstrators who "sabotaged" at a
V-bomber base by sitting down on the runways. The CND protesters
wished to argue that their purpose was to preserve the safety of the
State by removing nuclear weaponry, but the courts held that it was for
the Government to decide the State's best interests.[72] In 1977, section 1
charges were brought against journalists Duncan Campbell and Crispin
Aubrey in the "ABC" case (see p. 557), but were withdrawn after the
judge described them as oppressive.

The media should have nothing to fear from section 1. Their right to
report and to comment upon issues of national security may boost the
propaganda claims of foreign governments, but it is none the less exer-

---

[69] *R. v. Parrott* (1913) 8 Cr. App. Rep. 186.
[70] Official Secrets Act 1911, s. 1(2).
[71] House of Commons, June 24, 1948, col. 1711. See B.D. Thompson, "The Committee of 100 and the Official Secrets Act 1911" [1963] Public Law 201.
[72] *Chandler v. DPP* [1964] A.C. 763.

cised for a legitimate purpose, and not "for a purpose prejudicial to the safety and interests of the State". The security services, however, believe that journalism that exposes their activities amounts to "espionage by inadvertence",[73] and it was upon this theory that the deportation of the American writer Mark Hosenball was based. Indeed, Hosenball was evicted because he had the misfortune to put his name to an article about signals intelligence written largely by Duncan Campbell.[74] Section 1 may be wide enough in its literal language to be applied to the press by a determined Government; whether it will be so applied again will depend on the media's willingness to protest (see the "Stop Press" section for further details).

Police powers and compulsory questioning

Search and arrest

The Official Secrets Act gives the police special powers to investigate suspected offences. If they can convince a magistrate that they have reasonable grounds for believing that a crime under the Act has been or is about to be committed, they can obtain a warrant to search for and seize potential evidence.[75] Such warrants have been issued on two occasions to search Duncan Campbell's home. On the first occasion, in 1977, the police seized his entire library of files, including press cuttings, telephone directories, personal letters, and a collection of novels.[76] On the second occasion, in 1984, the police haul of suspicious items included his copies of photographs that had been produced by the prosecution for the "ABC" trial. Following the 1989 Act the warrant cannot authorise seizure of items subject to legal privilege.[77] A magistrate cannot grant a warrant to seize excluded material or special procedure material (see p. 270 for the meanings of these terms). The police can, however, apply to a circuit judge for an order that the possessor of this type of material hand it over to them.[78] Normally, these orders can be made only after the judge has heard both sides, but if the material is

---

[73] Head of MI5 to Franks Committee, n. 1 above, Vol. III, pp. 243–6.

[74] Leigh, *Frontiers of Secrecy*, p. 231. No official explanation was given for Hosenball's deportation other than it was conducive to the public good: see *R. v. Secretary of State for Home Affairs, ex p. Hosenball* [1977] 3 All E.R. 452.

[75] Official Secrets Act 1911, ss. 1(2), 9(1).

[76] Including *For Whom the Bell Tolls*. Aubrey, *Who's Watching You?* (Penguin, 1977), p. 24. Robertson, *The Justice Game*, Chap. 4.

[77] Police and Criminal Evidence Act 1984, s. 9(2) and Official Secrets Act 1989, s. 11(3).

[78] Police and Criminal Evidence Act 1984, s. 9(1) and Sched. 1, para. 3(b). *R. (Bright) v. Central Criminal Court* [2001] 1 W.L.R. 662.

subject to a restriction on disclosure, the police can apply secretly and without notice to the possessor.[79] The police relied on these provisions to obtain search warrants for the *New Statesman*'s offices (which they occupied for four days) after the magazine had published Duncan Campbell's article on the Zircon spy satellite affair. No prosecution followed. The Scottish police relied on an Official Secrets Act warrant to seize from the Glasgow offices of BBC Scotland not only the Zircon film that Campbell had made but also all the other programmes in his *Secret Society* series.[80] In an emergency where the interests of the State seem to the police to require immediate action, a magistrate may be dispensed with, and a police superintendent can sign the warrant.[81] No warrant at all is necessary to arrest a person who is reasonably suspected of having committed (or being about to commit) an offence under the Acts.[82]

Police questioning

Those suspected of section 1 offences can be deprived of their right to stay silent under police questioning. The Home Secretary can order an investigation (in an emergency the chief of police's authorisation will suffice) and it is a criminal offence to refuse to answer the inquisitor's questions.[83] The staff of the *Daily Telegraph* were compulsorily questioned in the 1930s after the paper leaked the Government's plans to arrest Mahatma Gandhi, and the interrogation stopped only when the proprietor let it be known that the Home Secretary himself was the correspondent's source.[84] A journalist on the *Daily Despatch* was convicted under this section in 1938 for refusing to name a policeman who had given him a police circular about a wanted fraudsman.[85] This use of compulsory questioning to trace the source of embarrassing leaks caused a public outcry and in 1939 Parliament amended the Act so that this power can now be used only where there is a suspected breach of

---

[79] Police and Criminal Evidence Act 1984, Sched. 1, paras 12 and 14(c)(i) and s. 11(2)(b).

[80] See Peter Thornton, *The Civil Liberties of the Zircon Affair* (NCCL, 1987). The Police and Criminal Evidence Act 1984, with its restrictions on the seizure of excluded and special procedure material, does not apply in Scotland.

[81] Official Secrets Act 1911, s. 9(2).

[82] *ibid.*, s. 6. Offences under the 1911, 1920 and 1989 Official Secrets Acts (except for retention or loss of documents) are arrestable offences for the Police and Criminal Evidence Act 1984, see 1984 Act, s. 24(2)(a) and 1989 Act, s. 11(1).

[83] Official Secrets Act 1920, s. 6. But journalists can insist on their reasonable expenses for attending and can refuse to answer questioning from an officer junior to an Inspector.

[84] Aitken, *Officially Secret*, p. 79.

[85] *Lewis v. Cattle* [1938] 2 All E.R. 368.

section 1 of the 1911 Act.[86] Even in this context, it is difficult to see
how answers obtained under such compulsion could be used against the
person questioned. To do so would be a clear violation of Article 6.[87]

Judicial questioning

Journalists may also be questioned in court or before a Tribunal of
Inquiry about their sources. The Contempt of Court Act 1981 imposes
a limited ban on such interrogation but it expressly exempts questions
that are necessary in the interests of national security.[88] Three journalists
were sent to prison in 1963 for refusing to disclose the source of their
published stories about the Admiralty spy Vassall to a Tribunal of
Inquiry investigating the security implications of his treachery.[89]

Proceedings

With one exception, any prosecution under the Official Secrets Acts
must be approved by the Attorney-General. The exception is where the
information relates to crime in which case the approval of the Director
of Public Prosecutions is sufficient.[90] At a time when meanings of sections of the 1989 Act are still untested by litigation, journalists who
come to be arrested under the Act or become the subject of police
suspicions will doubtless wish to dissuade the Attorney-General from
approving a test case prosecution. Their submissions to the law officers
may find support in the comforting words of the Government's White
Paper *Reform of Section 2 of the Official Secrets Act 1911,* which was
issued in 1988. Designed to mollify the media, it is full of promises
that "responsible media reporting would not be affected by the Government's proposals" and that criminal offences would not be committed
by making "disclosures which are not likely to harm the public interest"[91] (see the "Stop Press" section for further details).

All the offences can be tried by a jury at the defendant's election
except charges of retention or careless loss of documents. The maximum penalty for these offences is a fine on scale 5 or three months'
imprisonment.

For other offences under the 1989 Act, the maximum penalty is two

---

[86] Official Secrets Act 1920, s. 6 (as substituted by Official Secrets Act 1939, s.1).

[87] *Saunders v. U.K.* (1997) 23 E.H.R.R. 313; *Brown v. Procurator Fiscal
(Dunfermiline)* [2001] 2 W.L.R. 817.

[88] Contempt of Court Act 1981, s. 10. See p. 260.

[89] *Att.-Gen. v. Mulholland and Foster* [1963] 1 All E.R. 767; *Att.-Gen. v. Clough*
[1963] 1 Q.B. 773.

[90] Official Secrets Act 1911 s. 8; 1989 Act, s. 9.

[91] Cm. 408 (1988) paras 77 and 78.

years' imprisonment[92]; magistrates can impose the statutory maximum fine (now £5,000) and a six-month term of imprisonment.

Nuclear secrets

Nuclear secrets are protected by an adjunct to the Official Secrets Acts. Although employees of the Atomic Energy Authority are no longer deemed to be Crown servants, the Government has designated five properties owned by the Atomic Energy Authority (AEA)/British Nuclear Fuels (BNF) as "prohibited places" for the purpose of section 1 of the 1911 Official Secrets Act.[93] Disclosure of information about atomic energy processes or plant can additionally be prosecuted under the Atomic Energy Act 1946. There is no requirement that the information must be secret, but the Secretary of State should not give his consent to a prosecution if the information is not important to defence.[94]

Other statutes

The Atomic Energy Act is but one example of the dozens of statutes that prohibit civil servants from disclosing specific types of information received by the Government. The Franks Committee found 66 that had been passed between 1911 and 1971. By 1987 the Home Secretary admitted that the list had grown to 137 statutory provisions. A few, like the Atomic Energy Act or the Army Act 1955, deal with security matters. The Rehabilitation of Offenders Act 1974 is intended to protect personal privacy, and several are concerned with secret trade processes. These are not objectionable. Much more questionable is the political deal that is often struck with a regulated industry: government regulators may compel the provision of information on condition that it must be kept secure by special provisions to punish leaks. The reform of section 2 was incomplete because it did not revise these secrecy clauses at the same time. At present, they operate to prevent the disclosure of information of importance to public health and safety.[95] However, industry cannot stop a government department that wishes to publicise

---

[92] Official Secrets Act 1989, s. 10(1).
[93] Atomic Energy Act 1954, s. 6(3); Atomic Energy Act 1965, Sched. 1, para. 3. British Nuclear Fuels' sites at Sellafield and Capenhurst and Urenco's site at Capenhurst, the Atomic Energy Authority's sites at Harwell and Windscale are prohibited places: The Official Secrets (Prohibited Places) Order 1994, S.I. 1994 No. 968.
[94] Atomic Energy Act 1946, s. 11.
[95] James Michael, *The Politics of Secrecy* (NCCL, 1979), pp. 10–11.

the information. The High Court refused an injunction to a trader with a bad consumer record who had been compelled to give an assurance of improvement to the Director-General of Fair Trading and who wanted to stop the Director-General announcing the assurance in his customary press release. Lord Justice Donaldson said the Director-General was entitled to "bark as well as bite" and that publicity was one way of seeing that the trader lived up to his promises.[96]

Radio eavesdropping and telephone tapping

Air may be free but ether is not. Unauthorised eavesdropping on radio messages is an offence, and so is disclosure of any information thus acquired.[97] The penalty is a fine of up to £5,000.[98] There is little likelihood of prosecution of journalists, although the risk increases in the case of systematic monitoring of radio traffic or if a journalist incorporates the information into a story that makes clear that it was obtained in a prohibited way.[99] *Sunday Times* reporters discovered a plot against the Seychelles Government with the help of a transmitter bug placed (by others) in a London hotel room. When they voluntarily handed over their material to the police to help them prosecute the conspirators, they were threatened with a prosecution for illegal eavesdropping.[1] It did not, of course, materialise.

Unauthorised interception of the post or a public (and, in certain circumstances, a private) telecommunications system is also an offence. The penalty can be a fine of the statutory maximum in a magistrates' court (currently £5,000) or an unlimited fine and up to two years' imprisonment in the Crown Court.[2] The DPP must approve any prosecution.

Authorised telephone tapping and mail interceptions are conducted at the request of the police and security service officials who should obtain a warrant from the Home Secretary authorising the intercept for a particular period of time. Under the Regulation of Investigatory Powers Act 2000 (RIPA) intercept warrants may be issued in the interests of national security, for the purpose of preventing or detecting serious crime, or for the purpose of safeguarding the economic well-being of the United Kingdom. The Home Secretary ought to consider whether

---

[96] *S. H. Taylor and Co v. Director-General of the Office of Fair Trading,* July 4, 1980, unreported, but see *The Times,* July 5, 1980 and R. G. Lawson, "Fair Trading Act 1973—A Review" (1981) N.L.J. 1179.

[97] Wireless Telegraphy Act 1949, s. 5(b)(i).

[98] *ibid.,* s. 14(1c).

[99] The purpose of the eavesdropping is immaterial. *Paul v. Ministry of Posts and Telecommunications* [1973] R.T.R. 245.

[1] *The Guardian,* November 24, 1982.

[2] Regulation of Investigatory Powers Act 2000, s. 1.

the information could reasonably be obtained by other means and whether the conduct is proportionate to what is sought to be achieved.[3]

The Government's objective (the Labour Government as much as its Conservative predecessor) is to remove these surveillance operations almost entirely from public view. Under the 2000 Act nothing can be said in or for the purpose of legal proceedings which suggests that there has been an interception or discloses its content.[4] Under sections 4 and 5 of the Official Secrets Act 1989, the leaking or publishing of any details about official intercepts is an offence. The 2000 Act established a Tribunal to consider complaints (including human rights complaints) about the interception of communications and various other activities of the intelligence and security services.[5] Essentially, the Tribunal's function is to assess the legality of the challenged action. This involves considering in most cases whether it was rational (or, in human rights matters, proportionate) rather than whether the Tribunal would also have agreed that the action was right.[6] The Tribunal's procedure is carefully structured so as to give nothing away to complaints. Any oral hearing which it does hold must take place in private.[7] Its predecessors, such as the Security Services Tribunal, never found occasion to uphold a complaint. The 2000 Act also established a "judicial monitor", the Intelligence Services Commissioner (bringing into one post the jobs which had formerly been given to the Security Services Commissioner and the Intelligence Services Commissioner). The reports of the previous commissioners were bland and uninformative, disclosing only rare occasions where clerical errors have led to taps being placed on the wrong phone. These arrangements offer little protection to the public and almost total protection to Government eavesdroppers against any media investigation of their work.

DA-NOTICES

D-notices (now called Defence Advisory or "DA" notices) are the responsibility of the Defence Press and Broadcasting Advisory Committee, which consists of representatives of the armed forces, senior civil servants and various press and broadcasting institutions. The Committee's stated purpose is to advise editors and publishers of categories of

---

[3] RIPA 2000, s. 5.
[4] *ibid.*, ss. 17 and 18.
[5] *ibid.*, s. 65.
[6] *ibid.*, s. 67.
[7] The Investigatory Powers Tribunal Rules 2000, S.I. 2000 No. 2665, r.9(6).

information the secrecy of which is alleged to be essential for national security.[8] The Committee was established in 1912, shrouded in secrecy: for 40 years its existence was not publicly known.[9]

The Committee currently issues five general notices of guidance. They concern military operations and capabilities; nuclear and non-nuclear weapons and equipment; ciphers and secure communications; sensitive information and home addresses; United Kingdom security and intelligence services and special forces. In addition, "Private and Confidential Notices" can be sent giving warning that specific stories would threaten national security. The Secretary of the Committee, who has always been a high-ranking officer from the armed forces, is available for advice and consultation on short notice. No part of this system has any legal force. Stories are regularly printed in breach of the contemporary notices without attracting proceedings. In 1967, for example, Chapman Pincher revealed MI5's practice of monitoring all overseas cables. The Wilson Government claimed the story contravened a D-notice, but no action was taken.[10] Conversely, an editor who assiduously follows the Committee's advice is not guaranteed immunity from prosecution under the Official Secrets Acts. The editor of the *Sunday Telegraph* faced charges along with Jonathan Aitken for receiving the Biafran War report, although the secretary of the D-notice Committee had told him that its publication would create no danger to national security.[11-13]

The D-notice Committee is not to be trusted. In 1985 it asked a publisher for an advance copy of a book by Jock Kane about defective security in signals intelligence. The näive publisher, thinking that the Committee would offer helpful "guidance", received instead an expensive injunction, which has meant that the book can never be published. The Committee had sent the advance copy directly to the Treasury Solicitor. A few weeks before the 1991 Gulf War commenced, a careless RAF officer had a briefcase with secret documents and a lap-top computer containing details of the deployment of British forces in the Gulf stolen from his car. The Government was forced to admit the theft of the briefcase (which was soon found with contents intact), but issued a D-notice on any mention of the missing computer. All editors of all national newspapers and all broadcasters complied for a week, enabling the minister and Ministry of Defence to issue incorrect statements sug-

[8] House of Commons Defence Committee 3rd Report, 1979–80; *The D-Notice System* H.C. 773, 640 i-v.
[9] D.G.T. Williams, *Not in the Public Interest* (Hutchinson, 1965), p. 85.
[10] See Chapman Pincher, *Inside Story;* Hedley and Aynsley, *The D-Notice Affair;* Lord Radcliffe, E. Shinwell and S. Lloyd *"Report of the Committee of Privy Councillors Appointed to Inquire into "D" Notice Matters"* Cmnd. 3309, HMSO (1967).
[11-13] Aitken, *Officially Secret.*

gesting that all the "lost" information had been recovered. The true story was published by an Irish newspaper, but the D-notice was not lifted until the *Sun* (of all newspapers) indicated its intention to publish the truth.[14] It is astonishing that certain editors try to give credence to this discredited Committee by remaining members of it (see "Stop Press" section for further details).

MINISTERIAL AND CIVIL SERVANT MEMOIRS

Ministers

There is little danger of ministers being prosecuted for breaches of the Official Secrets Act even after they have left office. In 1975 the Attorney-General used the civil law of confidence to try to ban the Crossman diaries. The court found the secrets too old to require suppression, but in principle the court accepted that Cabinet confidences could be protected by injunction if they still affected national security.[15] In Australia a High Court judge refused to injunct as a breach of confidence a book that reprinted diplomatic cables between Canberra and Djakarta, because the Government failed to show that the public interest required restrictions on material that might cause diplomatic embarrassment and political criticism.[16] Democracy entails a measure of acceptance of such consequences as incidents of government.

After the Crossman diaries affair, the Government adopted new guidelines proposed by Lord Radcliffe.[17] The Secretary of the Cabinet continues to act as censor of the first draft, but on national security matters and foreign relations the author can now appeal to the Prime Minister, whose decision is final. Publication in defiance of a rejected appeal could be injuncted on grounds of national security. The embargo on confidential material that does not threaten security is lifted automatically after 15 years. This is a conventional period, not a legal limitation. A minister can choose to ignore the advice of the Secretary of the Cabinet, and publish at an earlier time.[18] Hugh Jenkins refused to delete from his book *The Culture Gap* references to civil servants who had

---

[14] See James Dalrymple, *The Sunday Times,* January 6, 1991.
[15] *Att.-Gen. v. Jonathan Cape Ltd* [1975] 3 All E.R. 484.
[16] *Commonwealth of Australia v. John Fairfax & Sons* (1981) 32 A.L.R. 485.
[17] *Report of Committee of Privy Councillors on Ministerial Memoirs,* Cmnd. 6386 (1976).
[18] At least in relation to matters not affecting national security or foreign affairs. The guidelines require notice to be given to the Secretary of the Cabinet. This presumably is so that further pressure can be put on the minister, and so that the Government has the opportunity to seek an injunction.

advised him when he was Arts Minister. The book was published shortly after he left office, when most of the civil servants were still in place.[19] Although the Radcliffe guidelines are worded in legalistic terms, they remain no more than guidelines. If a minister defies them, a prosecution will be successful only if a breach of the Official Secrets Act can be established; and a civil injunction will depend on whether the liberal public interest test of the Crossman diaries case is satisfied (see "Stop Press" section for further details).

Civil servants

Civil servants' memoirs have occasionally been targets of the Official Secrets Act. In 1926 the Governor of Pentonville prison was fined for publishing his life story in the *Evening News*,[20] and the biography of Pierrepoint, the public hangman, was held up for many years by threats of an Official Secrets Act prosecution.[21] On taking up their employment, civil servants are required to sign a promise to submit any publications for prior written approval. As the head of the Home Office acknowledged to the Franks Committee, this gives the misleading impression that failure to comply is automatically an offence under the Acts.[22] This overstates the risk of prosecution, since sufficient authorisation can be given in other ways under the Acts, although a publisher would have to consider the possibility of an injunction for breach of confidence or for breach of the official's contractual obligation. With the abolition of the old section 2, prosecution is not a realistic prospect so long as members avoid discussion of defence and intelligence issues.

The rules relating to memoirs have been discredited by the inconsistencies in their application. Memoirs by senior civil servants, which show Whitehall in a favourable light, never encounter difficulty. Both Sir Robert Mark, the former Metropolitan Commissioner of Police, and Sir Norman Skelhorn, the former Director of Public Prosecutions, published memoirs within a few years of leaving office. The Government's reluctance to use the law means that a determined civil servant has little to fear, and the publishers of Leslie Chapman's *Your Disobedient Servant* went ahead without receiving the retribution that had been threatened for his revelations of waste and inefficiency in Whitehall. There was both public and official displeasure expressed when Ronald

---

[19] *The Guardian,* September 19, 1978. See Michael Supperstone, *Brownlie's Law Relating to Public Order and National Security* (2nd ed. Butterworths, 1981), p. 266.

[20] *The Times,* December 16, 1926.

[21] Franks Report, n. 1 above, Vol. I, App. II, p. 116.

[22] Sir Philip Allen in oral evidence to the Franks Committee, n. 1 above, Vol. III, p. 13.

Gregory, the Chief Constable responsible for the inept hunt for the "Yorkshire Ripper", cashed in by selling his story to a newspaper shortly after his retirement. A breach of confidence action might well have succeeded against both policeman and newspaper, but the possibility was not mentioned by the Home Secretary when he deplored the incident in Parliament. However, such an action has been brought against a former police officer who used material taken from Myra Hindley's statements to police in his autobiography.

In 1991 the political motive behind Cabinet Office vetting of civil service and ministerial memoirs (and the willingness of their publishers to collaborate) was hilariously exposed through a mistake made by HarperCollins, publishers of *Kill the Messenger*, the "authorised" autobiography of Thatcher press secretary Bernard Ingham. They sent to *The Sunday Times* (which had bought serialisation rights) a copy of the book proofs *before* it had been submitted for Cabinet Office vetting, and a comparison with the final version allowed the newspaper to deduce which passages had been censored. The Cabinet Secretary, Sir Robin Butler, had not wielded the blue pencil on the basis of national security or justifiable confidentiality, but only to delete or dilute criticisms of still-serving ministers (particularly Michael Heseltine) that might be politically embarrassing to the Government (see the "Stop Press" section for further details).

PUBLIC RECORDS

Most public records are transferred after 30 years to the Public Record Office at Kew, as a result of the Public Records Acts of 1958 and 1967.[23] Kew holds the records for England and Wales[24] and the United Kingdom. Separate national record offices exist for Scotland and Northern Ireland. Although primarily of interest to historians, some journalists have used this right of access to explore the early careers of today's prominent politicians, as well as reviewing old controversies in the light of newly released material. The Government has the power to "weed out" and withhold records that it thinks should be kept secret for a longer time. The main categories are:

---

[23] The 1967 Act reduced the presumptive period from 50 years. Technically, the Acts apply only to England; in practice, the Scottish Office follows the same procedure; Paul Gordon, "Public Records in Scotland", Journal of the Law Society of Scotland, January 1981. The Office has a website at www.pro.gov.uk

[24] There is power under the Government of Wales Act 1998, ss. 116 and 117 to transfer Welsh public records to Wales.

- distressing or embarrassing personal details about living persons or their immediate descendants;

- information received by the Government in confidence;

- some papers on Ireland; and

- "certain exceptionally sensitive papers which affect the security of the State".[25]

The weeders are super-sensitive to national security and until 1998 they extended the embargo on a document if it so much as mentioned MI5 or MI6.[26] The period of "extended closure" may be 50 years or longer. Records "relating to the private affairs of the Royal Family" are routinely closed for 100 years. The "secret" files at the PRO take up about 4,500 feet of shelf space.

As long ago as 1981 a departmental committee recommended more liberal access. It criticised the practice whereby the Lord Chancellor can order an entire *class* of documents to be kept secret for a century without considering the specific documents that make up that class. It proposed that more files should be released before the 30-year embargo is up, that "embarrassment" should no longer be a ground for suppression, that the power to keep files secret forever should be abolished, and that there should be a right to appeal from secrecy orders. The Government rejected the report.[27]

The notion of "embarrassment to descendants" is sometimes manipulated to cover "embarrassment to the descendants of civil servants". Closure for a century of files relating to official treatment of suffragettes, prisoners and mental patients prior to the First World War cannot conceivably be justified on privacy grounds. Records of field executions in the First World War were withheld for 70 years, ostensibly to avoid embarrassment to relatives of the long-dead soldiers, but when those documents were finally released, it became clear that the secrecy had been used to avoid exposing the arbitrariness and brutality of justice in the trenches. Quite apart from the absurdity of sealing files about arrangements for police dental treatment during the Second World War, a good deal of information of historical significance in relation to British foreign policy is suppressed, together with material of contemporary importance about the investigation of war crimes.

The Freedom of Information Act 2000 has made modest adjustments

---

[25] Lord Gardiner, The Lord Chancellor, *Hansard* [1967] Vol. 282, 5th Ser., col. 1657–58. Certain Commonwealth documents are also restricted.

[26] Michael, *The Politics of Secrecy*, p. 185.

[27] *Modern Public Records*, 1981, Cmnd. 8024; White Paper Response (1982) Cmnd. 8531; see *State Secrecy and Public Records*, State Research Bulletin, 1982, No. 30, p. 128; Chapter by M. Roper in Chapman and Hunt (eds) *Open Government*, 1987.

to extend the release of historical documents. It sets maximum periods beyond which certain exemptions from the Act's disclosure obligations cannot be claimed. Thus, for instance, after 30 years an FOIA application cannot be denied on grounds of prejudice to economic interests of the United Kingdom, that the information was obtained with a view to prosecution (except informers' details), court records, audit functions, ministerial correspondence, conduct prejudicial to public affairs, communications with the Royal Family, legal professional privilege or commercial interests. After 60 years the exemption concerning conferment of honours falls away and various other exemptions disappear after 100 years,[28] but no formal end point is created for intelligence or security matters.

EUROPEAN UNION

Rights of access to documents

Beginning with the Maastricht Treaty, the E.U. has recognised that it, too, needs to pay some regard to the principle of freedom of information. In response the Council of Ministers[29] and the Commission[30] produced Codes both of which begin with a declaration of principle that the public should have a right of access to their respective documents.[31]

Inevitably this is followed by exceptions. They fall into two categories. The first category is mandatory (*i.e.* the Council or Commission must deny access). This applies where disclosure could undermine the protection of the public interest (public security, international relations, monetary stability, court proceedings, inspections and investigations), the protection of the individual and of privacy, the protection of commercial and industrial secrecy, the protection of the Community's financial interests, the protection of confidentiality as requested by the natural or legal persons that supplied the information or as required by the legislation of the Member State that supplied the information.[32] The second exception is discretionary and allows the Council or Commission to refuse access "to protect the confidentiality of [the Council's or Commission's] proceedings."[33]

While these exceptions are lengthy and ultra-cautious, the European

---

[28] Freedom of Information Act 2000, s. 63.
[29] Council Decision 93/731 on public access to Council documents.
[30] 94/90 on public access to Commission documents.
[31] The Commission has published a booklet *Access to Commission Documents* which is available on the Europa website—http://www.europa.eu.int.
[32] See Art. 4(1) of the Council Decision.
[33] *ibid.*, Art. 4(2).

Court of First Instance which hears challenges to refusals of access has established some principles limiting their effect.[34] Thus the Council and Commission are not allowed to apply the discretionary exception in a blanket manner. A standard form response that the documents "contain confidential information relating to the position taken by the members of the Council during its deliberations" was struck down as a result of a challenge by *The Guardian*'s John Carvel.[35] The same case by case analysis is required when the first exception is invoked. The Commission or the Council must consider "in the case of each document to which access is sought, whether in the light of the information available to [it], disclosure is in fact likely to undermine one of the facets of the public interest protected by the first category of exceptions".[36] The Council or Commission must also identify which particular mandatory ground it relies on and its decision will be annulled if it does not.[37] The reasons for refusal must show that it has carried out a concrete assessment of the documents in question. If the applicant for disclosure has put forward reasons why the grounds for refusal do not apply, the Council or Commission must engage with them and explain why those factors are not such as to warrant a change of position.[38] Furthermore, the principle of proportionality applies, so that if (without excessive work) the Council or Commission can identify parts of the requested documents which could be disclosed without harming the interests in the exception, then it should do so.[39] Access to EU documents is a general right and it is not necessary for an inquirer to demonstrate any "need to know".[40] As the Court said in 1998 "The objective of decision 93/731 is to give effect to the principle of the largest possible access for citizens to information with a view to strengthening the democratic character of the institutions and the trust of the public in the administration."[41]

The Amsterdam Treaty included in the Treaty of Union a right of access to the documents of the European Parliament, Council and Commission subject to limitations to be set by the Council and Parliament

---

[34] The CFI's decision can be appealed to the European Court of Justice, but the ECJ has shown a similar willingness to confine the exceptions, see *e.g.* Cases C-174/98 & C-189/98 *Van der Wal v. Commission,* January 11, 2000.

[35] Case T-194/94 *Carvel v. E.U. Council* [1995] E.C.R. II-2765.

[36] Case T-188/98 *Kuijer v. E.U. Council* [2000] 2 C.M.L.R. 400; Case T-174/95 Svenska *Journalistforbundet v. E.U. Council* [1998] E.C.R. II-2289.

[37] Case T-105/95 *World-wide Fund for Nature v. Commission* [1997] E.C.R. II-313.

[38] *Kuijer v. E.U. Council* (above).

[39] *Kuijer v. E.U. Council* (above).

[40] Case T-124/96 *Interporc v. E.C. Commission* [1998] 2 C.M.L.R. 82; *Svenska Journalistforbundet v. E.U. Council* (above).

[41] This is an adaptation of the words of the Declaration No. 17 to the Maastricht Treaty which provided the genesis for the Commission and Council's Codes.

acting together.[42] A Declaration attached to the Amsterdam Treaty, however, said that the limitations to be enacted will allow a Member State to request the Commission or the Council not to communicate to third parties a document originating from that State without its prior agreement. Ironically, the only post-Amsterdam amendment which has so far been made to the Council Decision 93/731 has been to *strengthen* the secrecy provisions for documents coming from the General Secretariat of the Common Foreign and Security Policy Committee and which are marked "Top Secret".[43]

Restrictions on disclosures by staff

Eurocrats are not servants of the Crown and, generally, leaks from Brussels are not punishable under the Official Secrets Acts. However, as with British civil servants, their conditions of employment require them to preserve the confidentiality of any document or information "not already made public". They must exercise "the greatest discretion with regard to facts and information coming into their knowledge in the course of or in connection with the performance of (their) duties". Like servants of the British Government the restrictions continue after they have left their office or job. Staff regulations also prohibit them from "alone or together with others publishing or causing to be published without the permission of the appointing authorities, any matter dealing with the work of the communities". However "permission shall be refused only where the proposed publication is liable to prejudice the interests of the Community".[44]

Breach of these provisions can lay employees open to disciplinary action, and journalists still need to take care to preserve the anonymity of such sources. Leaking cannot, however, lead to a criminal prosecution of an employee or journalist. The only exception concerns EURATOM (European Atomic Energy Community). Employees and officials of EURATOM and even those who in their "dealings in any capacity (official or unofficial) with any EURATOM institution or installation or with any EURATOM joint enterprise" acquire "classified information" commit an offence if they communicate it to any unauthorised person or make any public disclosure of it.[45]

The European Council of Ministers and the European Commission both sit in private. There is no public right of access to their meetings. The European Court of Justice and the European Court of First Instance

---

[42] Treaty Establishing the European Community, Art. 255 (ex-Art. 191a).
[43] Council Decision 2000/527 of August 14, 2000.
[44] EEC Reg. 31 and Euratom, Reg. 11, both of December 18, 1961.
[45] European Communities Act 1972, s. 11(2)—"classified information" is defined in Arts 24–7 of the Euratom Treaty.

sit in public for the oral part of their procedure. By English standards, these hearings are very brief. Most of the argument is presented in written form. At least in the Court of First Instance, there is no right for the public to have access to the court file. When an organisation of Swedish journalists published an edited version of the European Council of Minister's defence to their complaint about the withholding of access to Council documents, the Court rebuked the organisation for abusing its procedures. Although the complaint was successful, the Court ordered the Council to pay only two-thirds of the journalists' costs because of this abuse.[46]

REPORTING NORTHERN IRELAND

Information of use to terrorists

Journalists reporting or investigating matters in Northern Ireland need to be aware that the anti-terrorism legislation may impact upon them. Section 103 of the Terrorism Act 2000 prohibits collecting, recording, publishing or attempting to elicit any information (including taking photographs) concerning the army, police, judges, court officials or prison officers that is likely to be of use to terrorists.[47] It is also an offence to collect or record any information that is likely to be useful to terrorists in carrying out an act of violence, or to possess any record or document containing any of these types of information.[48] Like the Official Secrets Act 1911, section 1, the provisions' overt purpose is to punish espionage, although the section is broad enough to cover normal journalistic activities. The Act does allow a defence of reasonable excuse or lawful authority[49] and "reasonable excuse" should include collecting information for the purposes of legitimate journalism, but the burden of proof is placed on the defendant. A journalist working on a story, e.g. about Army behaviour would have a "reasonable excuse" to collect information of the sort described in the Act, unless there was evidence that his ulterior motive was to assist terrorists' intelligence by, for instance, passing the information to them privately. The consent of the DPP of Northern Ireland is necessary for a prosecution under section 103.[50]

---

[46] Svenska Journalistforbundet v. E.U. Council (above).
[47] This offence applies only in Northern Ireland: Terrorism Act 2000, s. 130(3)(b).
[48] ibid, s. 58. This offence applies throughout the U.K.
[49] ibid, s. 58(3), s. 103(5).
[50] ibid, s. 117.

Reporting demonstrations

In Northern Ireland it is an offence knowingly to take part in an unlawful procession.[51] In 1987 the Northern Ireland Court of Appeal held that a reporter who had been simply covering the procession for his newspaper had been properly acquitted of a charge under this provision. It required something more than physical presence, and the reporter did not attend to share in, or experience, the objectives of the marchers.[52] This decision will be a useful guide to the position on the mainland, where reporters may also wish to report demonstrations that have been prohibited.[53]

Prevention of terrorism in Northern Ireland

The Police and Army in Northern Ireland have a power to question compulsorily any person regarding any recent explosion or other incident endangering life or concerning any person killed or injured in such an incident or explosion. It is an offence to refuse to answer their questions or to fail to do so to the best of one's knowledge and ability.[54]

The police also have wide powers under the Terrorism Act 2000. While the origins of these powers lay in Northern Ireland, they now have a much broader reach and they are discussed in the next section.

Until 2001 there was a positive duty to tell the police of any information that might have been of material assistance in preventing an act of terrorism or in apprehending, prosecuting or convicting someone suspected of terrorism.[55] However, when the Terrorism Act 2000 came into force, this offence was repealed.[56] The potential impact for such offences while they continued (and if they should ever be revived) was shown in 1980 when the BBC was threatened with prosecution when it filmed a Provisional IRA roadblock at Carrickmore. Similar threats were made against the media in 1988 unless it handed over photographs and film of a Republican funeral at which two British army corporals were murdered. The media complied. In 1971 Bernard Falk was committed for four days to prison for refusing to identify a source who claimed to be a member of the IRA.[57] Although the former Prevention of Terrorism Act has been repealed, journalists who are contemplating interviewing members of the Real IRA or any other proscribed organis-

---

[51] Public Order (Northern Ireland) Order 1981 (S.I. 1981 No. 609), art. 3.
[52] *McKeown v. McDermott* [1987] 7 N.I.L.B. 93, CA.
[53] Under Public Order Act 1986, s. 13.
[54] Terrorism Act 2000, s. 89.
[55] Prevention of Terrorism (Temporary Provisions) Act 1989, s. 18.
[56] Terrorism Act 2000 (Commencement No. 3) Order 2001, S.I. 2001 No. 421.
[57] *The Times*, May 5, 1971, and Miller, *Contempt of Court* (3rd ed., 2000), para. 4.56.

ation will have to take care of the restrictions which have been erected by the 2000 Act.[58]

Broadcasting censorship

Television coverage of the province can be directly censored. But even before the broadcasting bans of 1988, broadcasters were censoring themselves. The IBA banned a number of programmes outright, including a *This Week* report on Amnesty International's findings about ill-treatment of suspects. Sometimes it required cuts in emotive scenes—a hunger striker in an open coffin, or flowers on a terrorist's grave. It postponed other programmes, so that some of their topicality was then lost, or pushed them into late night slots, although in 1988 it withstood Government pressure and permitted transmission of *Death on the Rock*.[59] The IBA was, and the ITC can be, susceptible to official pressure because of the statutory duty to avoid a programme that "offends against good taste or decency or is likely to encourage or incite to crime or to lead to disorder or to be offensive to public feeling".[60] The BBC Board of Governors has voluntarily accepted the same obligations, although its work on Northern Ireland has been marginally more robust.[61] In 1972 it refused to buckle under a Government request to stop *A Question of Ulster,* a live debate chaired by Lord Devlin, but its resolve has been weakened, partly as a result of Government appointments to the Board, and in 1987 the governors banned the *Real Lives* programme about two factional leaders in the province.

There are other, non-legal pressures that can be used by officials to influence media reporting of Northern Ireland. These range from "buttering-up" journalists with generous hospitality at Army units, to freezing out hostile critics from regular briefings.[62] There have been disturbing examples of "black propaganda", and Colin Wallace has convincingly confessed to planting false stories in the media (especially through the foreign press) in his role as a Government press officer in Northern Ireland. *The Sunday Times* has claimed that the Army has set off explosions that were then falsely attributed to the IRA.[63]

---

[58] See below "Other anti-terrorism measures", p. 589.
[59] "Banned Censored and Delayed" by Paul Madden in *The British Media and Ireland*. The Campaign for Free Speech in Ireland. Alex Schmid and Jenny de Graff, *Violence as Communication: Insurgent Terrorism and the News Media* (Sage, 1982) pp. 158–62.
[60] Broadcasting Act 1990, s. 6(1).
[61] See Philip Schlesinger, *Putting Reality Together* (Constable, 1978), p. 214.
[62] Steve Chibnall, *Law and Order News* (Tavistock, 1977), pp. 178–82.
[63] March 13, 1977.

OTHER ANTI-TERRORISM MEASURES

Proscribed organisations

The idea of banning organisations engaged in terrorism is not new but in recent times it has, until 2000, been confined to various groups in Northern Ireland. The Terrorism Act 2000 took away this limitation. The "traditional" proscribed organisations (such as the IRA and the Loyalist Volunteer Force) are still banned,[64] but the Home Secretary is given power to supplement the list by regulation to add any organisation which he believes is concerned in terrorism. The first regulations were issued in 2001[65] and included, as well as Al Q'aida, the Tamil Tigers who are fighting what is effectively a civil war in Sri Lanka and the Kurdish organisation, the PKK. The Act established a mechanism for appeals against a banning order to the Proscribed Organisations Appeal Commission.[66] However, as long as an organisation is proscribed it is an offence to belong to it[67] or to invite support for it.[68] Elaborate provisions are made to stem the funding of such organisations.[69]

It is also an offence to address a meeting if the purpose of the address is to encourage support for the organisation.[70] There is a further offence of arranging, managing or assisting in arranging or managing a meeting which the person concerned knows is to support or further the activities of a proscribed organisation. It may be unusual for any of these to impinge on the media, but a yet further offence is arranging a meeting which the person concerned knows is to be addressed by a person who belongs to a banned organisation.[71] This may be problematic for journalists wishing to interview members of proscribed organisations because a "meeting" is defined as a meeting of three or more persons whether or not the public are admitted.[72] It seems bizarre that a journalist would not be at risk under this provision if he arranged a one-to-one interview with a member of such an organisation, but would be if the meeting was filmed by a cameraman. If a prosecution were to take place in such a situation there may be scope for persuading a court to "read down" the offence in line with the court's obligation under section 3 of the

---

[64] Terrorism Act 2000, Sched. 2 lists these and various other Irish groups.
[65] Terrorism Act (Proscribed Organisations) Amendment Order 2001, S.I. 2001 No. 1261.
[66] Terrorism Act 2000, Sched. 3.
[67] Terrorism Act 2000, s. 11.
[68] *ibid.*, s. 12(1), other than by providing money or property.
[69] *ibid.*, Pt III.
[70] *ibid.*, s. 12(3).
[71] *ibid.*, s. 12(2)(c).
[72] *ibid.*, s. 12(5)(a).

Human Rights Act to interpret legislation as far as possible compatibly with Convention rights.

Payment for any interviews with members of a proscribed organisation might be held to infringe the prohibition on providing money or other property for the purposes of terrorism.[73] The purposes of terrorism are not limited to acts of violence, but include action taken for the benefit of a proscribed organisation.[74]

Terrorist investigations

The police are given wide powers when they are conducting a "terrorist investigation". Although this term obviously includes investigating actual acts of terrorism, its statutory meaning is far wider. Thus it embraces an act which appears to have been done for the "purposes of terrorism", an investigation of the resources of a proscribed organisation and an investigation into the possibility of making an order proscribing a new organisation.[75]

The police conducting a terrorist investigation can obtain a search warrant from a magistrate and, in some circumstances, from a senior police officer but neither ought to give permission if the object of the search is "special procedure material" under the Police and Criminal Evidence Act 1984 (see p. 271).[76] This term includes material held for the purposes of journalism.

If the police do wish to obtain journalisatic material, they ought to apply to a Circuit judge.[77] The procedure is modelled on that under the Police and Criminal Evidence Act (PACE) 1984 in ordinary criminal investigations. Thus the judge must be satisfied that there are reasonable grounds for believing that the material is likely to be of substantial value whether by itself or together with other material, to a terrorist investigation.[78] In 1994 Channel 4 and an independent production company persuaded a judge that the police could not satisfy this condition. They had filmed an interview with a Sinn Fein member about the problems of republicans who were suffering from domestic violence but who did not trust the RUC. The interviewee implied that after a number of warnings, a message would be passed to an armed republican group which would impose summary punishment. The police wanted to see the out-takes of the interview to see if there was any hint of the inter-

---

[73] Terrorism Act 2000, s. 15(4).
[74] ibid., s. 1(5).
[75] ibid., s. 32.
[76] Terrorism Act 2000, Sched. 5, para. 1(5)(b)—magistrates' warrants; para. 3(6)(b)—police officer authorisation.
[77] ibid., Sched. 5, paras 4–9.
[78] ibid., Sched. 5, para. 6(2).

viewee's contact in the terrorist groups. However, the court was persuaded that if there had been, the programme would have shown it. Besides, the interviewee was sufficiently astute to be guarded in what she said. She was well known to the police in Northern Ireland who could easily have interviewed her directly in the interval of several months before the application had been made to the court.

The second condition that must be satisfied is that there are reasonable grounds for believing that it is in the public interest that the material should be produced having regard to the benefit likely to accrue to the terrorist investigation if the material is obtained and to the circumstances under which the person concerned has any of the material in his custody or power.[79] The second condition is particularly important. Production orders under PACE cannot usually extend to material which journalists hold in confidence.[80] There is no similar limitation under the Terrorism Act powers. Thus an application may relate to confidential material (including material which would identify sources). Although that is not in itself a bar to a Terrorism Act production order, it requires special consideration. To be compatible with Article 10 of the European Convention on Human Rights there must be some overwhelming need for disclosure before journalists can be forced to reveal their sources.[81]

Even if these two conditions are fulfilled, the court has a discretion as to whether a production order should be made. The comments which the court has made in the context of PACE production orders in cases such as *Bright*[82] are applicable and no less important in this context. Indeed, although an application under PACE, *Bright* concerned the activities of the ex-MI5 officer, David Shayler. The judge said:

> "Inconvenient or embarrassing revelations, whether for the security services or for authorities should not be suppressed. Legal proceedings, directed towards the seizure of the working papers of individual journalists, or the premises of the newspaper or television programme publishing his or her report, or the threat of such proceedings tends to inhibit discussion. When a genuine investigation into possible corrupt or reprehensible activities by a public authority is being investigated by the media, compelling evidence would normally be needed to demonstrate that the public interest will be served by such proceedings. Otherwise, to the public's disadvantage, legitimate inquiry and discussion and 'the safety valve of effective journalism' would be discouraged, perhaps stifled."

---

[79] Terrorism Act 2000, Sched. 5, para. 6(3).
[80] See p. 270. The position is different if before PACE the police would have had a power of search, *e.g.* under the Official Secrets Acts.
[81] See p. 253.
[82] See *R. v. Central Criminal Court, ex p. Bright,* above p. 272.

A second important difference from PACE is that a Terrorism Act production order is made in the first place without notice to the respondent. If the order is made it requires production within a specified time. There is a procedure for applying for the order to be set aside or varied, but it means that the media respondent must move swiftly and an effective objection might depend on the police or the court agreeing that the order should be suspended until the contested hearing takes place. This would be a sensible course if the contest is to have any point, but it may still be the subject of argument.

As with the PACE model, the circuit judge can issue a warrant for a search if it is not appropriate to go through the production order procedure because it is not practicable to communicate with any person entitled to produce the material or the terrorist investigation might be seriously prejudiced if immediate access is not given.[83] In cases of great emergency and where immediate action is necessary, a search order can be given by a Superintendent of police or above. A report must be made on any use of this power to the Home Secretary.[84]

OTHER POLITICAL OFFENCES

Treason

In the heat of the Falklands War circulation campaign the *Sun* accused *The Guardian* and the *Daily Mirror* of treason.[85] The allegation was nonsense. As the Commons Defence Committee said,[86] in a democracy the interests of the Government are not synonymous with the national interest, and differences of view as to the value of a Government aim or the cost of achieving it were quite legitimate. The incident echoed the allegation by Edward Hulton, proprietor of *Picture Post,* that a pho-

---

[83] Terrorism Act 2000, Sched. 5, paras 11 and 12.

[84] *ibid.*, Sched. 5, para. 15.

[85] "Dare Call it Treason", May 7, 1982. See Robert Harris, *Gotcha: The Media, the Government and the Falkland Crisis* (Faber, 1983); pp. 38–53. *The Guardian*'s cartoon of a shipwrecked sailor on a raft with the caption "The price of sovereignty has been increased—official" mirrored the cartoon by Zec that the *Daily Mirror* had published in 1942 over the caption "The price of petrol has been increased by one penny—official" and which together with the consistent criticisms of the Government by the paper very nearly caused the Government to ban the paper. Neil Stammers, *Civil Liberties in Britain during World War Two* (Croom Helm, 1983), pp. 147–51. In the war on the Taliban in 2001, the *Daily Telegraph* contented itself with describing journalists opposed to the war, mainly on *The Guardian*, as "useful idiots".

[86] Report of the Defence Committee, *The Handling of the Press and Public Information during the Falklands Conflict,* H.C. 17 (1982–83), para. 35.

tograph showing the brutality of South Koreans, which the magazine's editor proposed to publish, would give "aid and comfort" to the North Korean enemy. The editor refused to withdraw it and was dismissed as a result.[87] Treason can be committed by adhering to the Crown's enemies or by giving them aid or comfort, but the prosecution must show that the defendants intended to aid or comfort an enemy contrary to their duty of loyalty.[88] There has not been a treason trial since 1946, when William Joyce ("Lord Haw-Haw") was convicted for making Nazi propaganda broadcasts. Joyce was executed for his offence, but capital punishment for treason was abolished in 1998.[89]

Treason Felony

The Treason Felony Act 1848, section 3 makes it a felony (amongst many other things) to "compass, imagine, invent devise or intend to deprive or depose . . . the Queen". In 2001 *The Guardian* ran a campaign for the (non-violent) replacement of the monarchy with a republican form of government. It unsuccessfully sought an assurance from the Attorney-General that it would not in consequence be prosecuted under the 1848 Act. It challenged the Attorney's decision under the Human Rights Act on the grounds that the existence of the legislation and the refusal of the Attorney to give his assurance amounted to an interference with its freedom of expression contrary to Article 10. The Administrative Court said that proceedings of this kind would have to be brought as a judicial review, and permission to do so would be refused because it thought that *The Guardian* had not been a "victim" of any interference with its Convention right as a result of the refusal to give an assurance.[90] It is bizarre that Labour law officers should wish to uphold a law so obviously incompatible with the European Convention and which was last used in 1848 to send several Irish editors and journalists to Botany Bay.

Sedition

Sedition is still defined in the terms of a nineteenth-century jurist as:

> ". . . any act done, or words spoken or written and published which (i) has or have a seditious tendency and (ii) is done or are spoken

---

[87] Phillip Knightley, *The First Casualty: The War Correspondent as Hero, Propagandist and Myth Maker* (rev. ed, Quartet, 1982), p. 330.
[88] Supperstone, *Brownlie's Law*, pp. 230–4.
[89] Crime and Disorder Act 1998, s. 36.
[90] *Rusbridger and Toynbee v. Att.-Gen.* June 22, 2001 (appeal pending at time of writing).

or written and spoken with a seditious intent. A person may be said to have a seditious intention if he has any of the following intentions, and acts or words may be said to have a seditious tendency if they have any of the following tendencies: an intention to bring into hatred or contempt, or to excite disaffection against the person of, Her Majesty, her heirs or successors, or the government and constitution of the United Kingdom, as by law established, or either House of Parliament, or the administration of justice, or to excite Her Majesty's subjects to attempt, otherwise than by lawful means, the alteration of any matter in Church or State by law established or to raise discontent or disaffection among Her Majesty's subjects, or to promote feelings of ill-will and hostility between different classes of subjects."[91]

This definition is frighteningly broad and the crime has been used in the past to suppress radical political views.[92] Even in the twentieth century it was used against an Indian nationalist and against Communist organisers.[93] However, the post-war tendency has been to narrow the offence considerably. First, it has been stressed that political speech, even revolutionary speech, should not be punished as sedition unless it is meant to excite people to "tumult and disorder".[94] Incitement to violence alone is insufficient: it must be "violence or defiance for the purpose of disturbing constitutional authority".[95] Secondly, on one line of authority, it is not enough that "tumult and disorder" were likely to follow unless the publisher did actually intend these consequences.[96] There has been no prosecution for sedition since 1947, and the offence now serves no purpose in the criminal law. In terms of Article 10, it is hard to see how it is necessary in a democratic society or proportionate to any legitimate aim. The deliberate provocation of public violence or disorder is amply covered by offences contained in the 1986 Public Order Act.

In 1990 the Divisional Court decisively rejected an attempt to bring sedition charges against the author and publisher of *The Satanic Verses*.

---

[91] Stephen, *Digest of the Criminal Law* (9th ed.) Art. 114.
[92] *e.g.* against John Wilkes for his satires in 1764 in *The North Britain* and Tom Paine for *The Rights of Man*.
[93] *R. v. Aldred* (1909) 22 Cox C.C. 1; Wal Hannington, *Never on Our Knees*, 1967, pp. 188–93.
[94] *R. v. Caunt* (1948) L.Q.R. 203, see also defendant's account, *An Editor on Trial*, privately published, 1947; *Boucher v. R.* [1951] 2 D.L.R. 369.
[95] *Boucher v. R*, n.94 above, and see *R. v. Burns* (1886) 16 Cox 355.
[96] *R. v. Caunt*, n.94 above. A different view was taken in *R. v. Aldred* (above). In *R. v. Lemon* [1979] A.C. 617 the House of Lords decided by 3–2 that intention of this kind was not relevant for blasphemous libel, but several of the speeches favour the view that a specific intent is required for the crime of sedition.

It stressed that the gist of the crime was an attack against the State, and that the prosecution must prove that the speech or writing incites readers to violence against democratic institutions.[97]

Incitement to mutiny and disaffection

The Incitement to Mutiny Act 1797 was passed in a panic after naval mutinies at the Spithead and Nore. It covered:

"any person who shall maliciously and advisedly endeavour to seduce any person or persons serving in H.M.'s forces by sea or land from his or their duty and allegiance to His Majesty or to incite or stir up any person to commit any act of mutiny or make or endeavour to make any mutinous assembly or to commit any traitorous or mutinous practice whatsoever."

A critical word in this definition is the "and" between duty and allegiance. Tempting soldiers from their *duty* was not an offence if it did not also encourage them to be disloyal. This link was broken in the Incitement to Disaffection Act 1934, which created an offence in almost identical terms except that "or" was substituted for "and".

The 1934 Act also added draconian subsidiary offences. Possession of any document became an offence if its dissemination to the forces would be punishable,[98] and a High Court judge can issue a search warrant to the police to look for material that might infringe the Act.[99] The Incitement Acts were also used against radicals. The editors and printers of *The Syndicalist* were convicted in 1912 for publishing a letter calling on soldiers not to fire on workers. In 1925 twelve Communist leaders were convicted for a similar offence.[1]

In addition to these statutes, the services' legislation makes it an offence to obstruct or interfere with the forces in the execution of their duty or to procure or persuade a member of the forces to desert or go absent without leave.[2] A comparable offence of doing any act "calculated to cause disaffection among members of any police force" or "doing any act calculated to induce any member of the police force to withhold his services" was created after the police strike in 1919.[3]

---

[97] *R. v. Bow Street Magistrates' Court, ex p. Choudhury* [1991] 1 All E.R. 306.

[98] Incitement to Disaffection Act 1934, s. 2(1).

[99] Incitement to Disaffection Act 1934, s. 2(2).

[1] Tom Young, *Incitement to Disaffection* (Cobden Trust, 1976), pp. 15–18, 45–7.

[2] Army Act 1955, s. 193 (obstruction), s. 97 (persuading desertion); Air Force Act 1955, s. 193; Naval Discipline Act 1957, s. 94 is on similar lines.

[3] See now Police Act 1996, s. 91 and Ministry of Defence Police Act 1987, s. 6 and Police Act 1997, ss. 43 and 87 which create similar offences for the Ministry of Defence Police, NCIS and the National Crime Squad respectively.

The Aliens Restriction (Amendment) Act 1919 was passed at the same time to stem what was then perceived as foreign Communist agitation. It is an offence for an alien to attempt or do any act calculated or likely to cause sedition or disaffection amongst forces of the Crown or the Crown's allies or the civilian population. It is also an offence for an alien to promote industrial unrest in any industry in which he has not been bona fide engaged for at least two years immediately preceding in the United Kingdom.[4]

This discrimination against aliens will be difficult to attack under the European Convention on Human Rights. Article 16 provides "Nothing in Articles 10, 11 and 14 shall be regarded as preventing the High Contracting Parties from imposing restrictions on the political activity of aliens." This provision has rarely been relied upon[5] and is looking increasingly anachronistic. As long ago as 1977 the Parliamentary Assembly called for it to be abolished.[6] However, it was one of the Convention provisions which was incorporated into United Kingdom law by the Human Rights Act.

Incitement to Disaffection charges were last brought in the mid-1970s against the British Withdrawal from Ireland Campaign. Pat Arrowsmith was convicted under the Incitement to Disaffection Act 1934 for distributing to soldiers a leaflet called *Some Information for Discontented Soldiers,* which called on them to leave the Army rather than serve in Northern Ireland.[7] She failed to persuade the jury that the leaflet was to inform rather than incite. Her sentence of eighteen months' imprisonment was reduced on appeal to nine months. Ms Arrowsmith complained to the European Commission that the conviction violated her right to freedom of thought, conscience and religion under Article 9(1) of the Convention. The Commission accepted that pacifism was a protected "belief", but held the complaint inadmissible because the distribution of the leaflets was not a means of "practising" the belief: the leaflet expressed a nationalist rather than pacifist philosophy.[8] The prosecution did not stop distribution of the leaflet and in 1974 a further 14 were prosecuted under the 1934 Act. On all the contested charges the defendants were acquitted by the jury. As a result, pending prosecutions

---

[4] Aliens Restriction (Amendment) Act 1919, s. 3.

[5] In the case of *Piermont v. France* (1995) 20 E.H.R.R. 301, France argued that measures taken against the German applicant in French Pacific territories could not be criticised under the Convention because of Article 16, but the Court held that her status as a Member of the European Parliament meant that the provision could not be invoked against her application.

[6] Recommendation 799 (1977), January 25, 1977.

[7] *R. v. Arrowsmith* [1975] QB 678.

[8] *Arrowsmith v. United Kingdom,* Application No. 7050/75, 19 Decisions and Reports 5. Her complaint under Art. 10 was also dismissed.

against other distributors of the leaflet were dropped.[9] Incitement to disaffection charges have not been used since the Old Bailey acquittals in 1975, and the then Attorney-General, Sam Silkin, expressed regret that this much-publicised case was ever brought.

Reform

The 14 acquittals under the Incitement to Disaffection Act increased the demand for the repeal of anti-free speech laws that had been hastily passed, were broad in the extreme and would lie dormant for many years until being revived to deal with a political crisis. The Law Commission has since recommended that treason should be limited in peacetime to attempting to overthrow the Government by armed means, and that sedition should be abolished, as should incitement to mutiny and aliens legislation. It thought that the Incitement to Disaffection Act should be confined to seduction of the forces away from their allegiance as opposed to their duty.[10]

WAR REPORTING

Protection of war correspondents

Journalists who cover armed conflicts will generally be under the protection of the force to which they are accredited. In the case of British forces, the Ministry of Defence will insist that they sign an accreditation document, which includes undertakings to comply with military censorship and to seek permission before interviewing soldiers and filing a wide range of stories. Correspondents will have no alternative but to sign this document, but it is not legally binding and the only sanction for disobedience to its onerous terms will be loss of accreditation, which will normally mean expulsion from the war zone. The accredited correspondent will be assigned an officer rank, which will give entitlement to drink in the officers' mess and to be given priority in an evacuation of the wounded.

Over and above the dangers of injury and death common to all who work in war zones, correspondents are at special risk of being arrested and punished for spying on the forces whose activities they are attempting to report, and of being treated by opposing forces as if they were combatants. The international covenants that seek to regulate gov-

---

[9] Young, *Incitement to Disaffection*, pp. 85–94.
[10] *Codification of the Criminal Law: Treason, Sedition and Allied Offence,* Working Paper No. 72, 1977.

ernments in their conduct of hostilities have attempted to give journalists some protection against these dangers.

Article 13 of the Hague Convention 1907 provides that war correspondents who follow an army without directly belonging to it should, if they fall into the hands of opposing forces, be treated as prisoners of war and receive minimum standards of humane treatment.[11]

The Geneva Conventions of 1949 make similar but more detailed provision for captured war correspondents. If wounded or sick, they are to have the same rights to humane treatment as wounded or sick prisoners of war, including the right to receive assistance from international relief agencies.[12]

The protection afforded by the Hague and Geneva Conventions is contingent upon captured correspondents possessing authorisation from the armed forces they are accompanying, attesting to their status. These conventions do not give any special protection to journalists; they simply accord them (along with other non-combatant camp followers) the same basic right as captured members of armed forces.

The only provision in international law that relates specifically to journalists engaged in dangerous missions in areas of international armed conflict is Article 79 of the first Protocol to the Geneva Conventions 1977.[13] It provides that:

> "Journalists engaged in dangerous professional missions in areas of armed conflict shall be considered as civilians . . . (and) shall be protected as such under the Conventions and this Protocol, provided they take no action adversely affecting their status as civilians . . . ".

Under Article 79, journalists are entitled to immunity from military discipline and must not be made the specific objects of an attack or the victims of reprisals by any party to the conflict. They should not be manipulated or exploited by the opposing forces. Their entitlement to civilian status is jeopardized by an "action adversely affecting" it; carrying a gun or rendering special assistance to the armed forces might deprive them of their protection. The rights guaranteed by Article 79

---

[11] Hague Convention IV Respecting Laws and Customs of War on Land Annexed Regulations 1907, Art 13. For the texts of these and the following conventions, see Roberts, *Documents on the Laws of War* (OUP, 2000).

[12] Geneva Convention for the Amelioration of the Wounded and Sick in Armed Forces in the Field 1949, Art 13; Geneva Convention for the Amelioration of the Condition of Wounded, Sick and Shipwrecked Members of Armed Forces at Sea 1949, Art. 13; Geneva Convention Relative to the Treatment of Prisoners of War 1949, Art. 4A.

[13] Protocol Additional to the Geneva Conventions 1949 and Relating to the Protection of Victims of International Conflicts 1977.

do not detract from the general entitlement of accredited war correspondents to be treated as prisoners of war if captured by hostile forces.
Article 79 also entitles a journalist to obtain an identity card attesting
to his status from "the Government of the State of which the journalist
is a national or in whose territory he resides or in which the news
medium employing him is located".

International law has no direct sanction to punish breaches of these
rules, other than condemnation at the bar of international public opinion.
This can, of itself, be a deterrent to combatants, who are usually mindful
of the importance of favourable publicity. Even the Taliban, at the
height of their demonisation, treated fairly and returned a *Daily Express*
correspondent who had blundered into its clutches in 2001. Domestic
journalists suffer death or disappearance in some countries with a
frequency that is hardly noticed in the West. In 2000, 24 journalists
were killed.[14] The following year, Martin O'Hagan, a veteran reporter
on sectarian violence, was killed in Northern Ireland by loyalist paramilitaries.

International law is not oblivious to the harm which inflammatory
propaganda can cause. The International Covenant for Civil and Political Rights provides that:

"(1) Any propaganda for war shall be prohibited by law.
(2) Any advocacy of national, racial or religious hatred that con-
     stitutes incitement to discrimination, hostility or violence
     shall be prohibited by law."

Military censorship

There is ample evidence that "the first casualty when war comes is
truth".[15] The reason for the phenomenon is sometimes the cynical
opportunism of journalists confronted with chaos and news blackouts,
as definitively portrayed in Evelyn Waugh's novel *Scoop*. Frequently,
it stems from the acceptance of propaganda claims by rival forces, or
the censorship controls instigated in war zones. More subtle pressures
of patriotism are involved in coverage of British forces in action. In
British military engagements that fall short of declared war, there will
be few specifically legal inhibitions on reporting, but heavy censorship
will be applied by the military authorities through the control of access
to information and their ability to command avenues of communication.

There is an abiding belief in Allied military circles that America lost
the Vietnam War by its failure to control correspondents and television

[14] See the web site of the Committee for the Protection of Journalists http://
www.cpj.org
[15] Senator Hiram Johnson 1917; see Knightley, *The First Casualty*.

news teams. This article of simplistic faith has bred suspicion and hostility towards the media, evidenced by the treatment of reporters during the Falklands and Grenada invasions. The British Navy originally decided to exclude journalists entirely from the Falklands task force: political pressure produced a limited number of places, but only for "acceptable" newsmen from British organisations. A two-tier level of censorship was imposed: dispatches were censored at source and were then routed via the Ministry of Defence in London, where they were often further censored or delayed. The movement of journalists on the ground was strictly controlled by military authorities, and each group was allocated a "minder"—civil servants from the MOD with a concern, which was often greater than that of military commanders, to suppress potentially embarrassing information. The authorities refused to set up facilities for television coverage. Some of the correspondents later admitted to self-censorship of stories that would have depicted British troops in a poor light, and confessed to overcredulous acceptance of official claims. In London, information was withheld until it was politically acceptable to release it, and on several occasions the media were encouraged to publish false information in the hope that it would mislead Argentinian monitors. The effects of these measures of news management were not necessarily helpful to the British cause: there was concern that Britain had "lost the information war" by its censorship, which had the inevitable effect of leaving a gap that was filled by Argentinian propaganda claims. In the parliamentary post-mortem that followed, military and MOD authorities were prepared to concede that some of the restrictions had been overzealous.[16] None the less, draft regulations for war correspondents issued by the MOD in 1983 were found to be restrictive to the point of unworkability.[17]

Following the Falklands conflict, a committee set up by the Ministry of Defence under the chairmanship of General Sir Hugh Beach made recommendations on how censorship in future conflicts should be managed.[18] For major conventional wars, they broadly endorsed the system used in the Second World War of "voluntary" censorship reinforced by emergency regulations making it an offence to disclose information useful to an enemy and by a government power to suppress publications that systematically fermented opposition to the war. They did propose, however, that once information had been made public overseas, there should be no restriction on its dissemination in the United Kingdom.

---

[16] Defence Committee Report, n. 86 above.

[17] "Defence Ministry Reporting Rules lead to Press Freedom Fears", *The Guardian*, October 24, 1983, and "Letter of Law for War Reporters", *The Guardian*, October 27, 1983.

[18] *The Protection of Military Information*, Report of the Study Group on Censorship chaired by General Sir Hugh Beach (HMSO, 1983), Cmnd. 9112; for the Government response, see Cmnd. 9499.

The Gulf War presented different problems of news management for the British Government. In conjunction with United States authorities, it hit upon the idea of "pools" of accredited reporters who would be attached to major force deployments, receiving protection and information in return for submitting every report to military censorship. Although in theory a "pool" means that reports of journalists travelling with military units are available to all media, in practice it came to denote a privileged group who were permitted to witness events at the front and to receive official co-operation in return for submitting to military censorship.[19] The British "pool" reporters were duly spoon-fed information by military authorities, which they had little alternative but to publish, as MOD rules prevented them from publishing virtually anything else without authorisation.

These rules, and the discipline of the "pool", ensured that news from the Allied side of the conflict was controlled and sanitised. Journalists who refused to accept military supervision were refused access to the front and opportunities to go on special assignments; some had equipment confiscated while others were threatened with deportation from Saudi Arabia. Still photographs were carefully vetted, and the Saudi authorities allowed visas for only three British photographers, from pro-war popular newspapers. The Allied command was anxious to prevent the Western media from showing images of carnage of a sort that affected public morale during the Vietnam War; it could not, however, prevent Western correspondents from accepting invitations to return to Baghdad, where Iraqi authorities were anxious for them to depict civilian casualties, but without permitting them to report damage to military targets or to civilian morale.

The most absurd casualties of the war were scheduled films and songs and comedies, which were banned from television and radio for the duration of the Gulf conflict. Media executives determined to help the war effort by removing all jokes about Hitler (*Allo! Allo!*), the American military (*M.A.S.H.*) and English soldiers (the BBC solemnly replaced *Carry on up the Khyber* with *Carry on Cowboy*). Even Channel 4 cancelled a programme that showed American bombing of Vietnam, while the BBC warned its radio stations against playing no less than 67 popular songs, ranging from "Light my Fire" and "Killing Me Softly" to "Everybody Wants to Rule the World". These ludicrous decisions showed that for broadcasting executives, the first casualty of war is the right of viewers and listeners to be treated as intelligent adults. This was again proved during the bombing of Afghanistan, when the first record banning was a satirical calypso "Hey Mr Taliban".

UN enforcement actions since the Gulf War have had fewer reporting

---

[19] See Robert Fisk, "Free to Report What we're Told", *The Independent*, February 6, 1991; *The Gulf War and Censorship,* Art. 19, February 1991.

problems since the military and the Government have been anxious to obtain publicity for their role in "peace offensives" in places like Sierra Leone and East Timor. But a measure of censorship affected coverage of the NATO bombing of Serbia in 1999, especially after some media criticism of the bombing of a television propaganda station in Belgrade. The BBC correspondent there, John Simpson, was criticised from Downing Street for pro-Serb bias, but his commentaries told it like it there was no attempt by government to silence him or censor pictures of bombed bridges or buildings.

"Open Government is a contradiction in terms. You can be open, or you can have government." Sir Humphrey Appleby, the quintessential mandarin from *Yes Minister*, epitomises Whitehall's 30 years of opposition to demands for freedom of information. Freedom of information (FOI) laws first emerged in Scandinavia and the U.S. in the 1960s and were soon successfully translated to advanced westernized democracies like Canada, New Zealand and Australia. In 1974 Freedom of Information was a Labour election promise, on which it quickly reneged ("Only two or three of your constituents would be interested" quipped the Home Secretary sarcastically in answer to an indignant back-bencher). The Conservative Government was implacably opposed to the notion that the public should have a legal right of access to public records before at least 30 years had elapsed (the minimum time laid down by the Public Records Act for disclosure of government information). Its opposition was two-fold: FOI would undermine ministers' traditional accountability to Parliament, and would deter civil servants from writing honest and candid reports. Both excuses were exploded by the Matrix Churchill scandal in 1992, when Whitehall documents extracted over ministerial objections at the trial of men accused of exporting arms to Iraq exposed a conspiracy amongst Thatcher ministers to deceive Parliament about their Government's secret approval of these exports. Civil servants had advised and helped to promote the deception of Parliament and the public. The Labour Party proclaimed Freedom of Information, a means of ensuring transparency in government, as a safeguard against ministerial irresponsibility towards Parliament and as a deterrent to civil servants tempted to advise ministers to act dishonestly.[20]

"Freedom of information is for opposition", said New Labour's first Home Secretary, Jack Straw: his draft legislation was dubbed "The

---

[20] See Charter 88 Pamphlet (1993) and the Scott Report.

Restraint of Information Bill" when it was eventually tabled, since it contained numerous exceptions from disclosure and stringently protected the very class of information—policy advice to ministers—that had exposed the "Arms to Iraq" scandal. However, it had been preceded by a White Paper in which the Prime Minister had described as his key pledge "giving people in the U.K. the legal right to know",[21] and the absolute exemptions were whittled down in the course of the Bill's parliamentary passage. Whether any significant information will be divulged remains to be seen, and will remain for some time to be seen: the Government has indicated that the Act will not come into force until 2005. Much will depend on the determination of journalists and their media employers to pursue tenaciously claims under the Act to the Appeal Tribunal and/or the courts, and upon the willingness of the "Information Commissioner" to construe all the exemptions narrowly, so as to infuse freedom of information practice with the spirit of transparency. The message of the Scott Report into the "Arms to Iraq" affair was that, *pace* Sir Humphrey, open government would mean better government, but this benefit can only accrue if the media and its lawyers surmount all the obstacles that the new law strews in their path before they get their hands on documents which a Government department objects to producing. These exemptions will be used as pretexts to conceal the real reason for suppression, namely political embarrassment (or, in Whitehall-speak, "presentational difficulties"). Whether the Act works will depend on the independence and robustness of the Information Commissioner and the Appeal Tribunal.[22]

The Freedom of Information Act begins with a flourish, by vouchsafing to citizens a brand new, legal right of access to information held by public authorities:

"1(i) Any person making a request for information to a public authority is entitled

(a) to be informed in writing by the public authority whether it holds information of the description specified in the request, and

(b) if that is the case, to have that information communicated to him."

So far so good—and "public authority" is very widely defined to include not only Government departments, the Houses of Parliament and the armed forces, but local authorities and their committees,

[21] *Your Right to Know*, Cmnd. 3818 (1997).
[22] For an analysis of the Act see John Wadham, Jonathan Griffiths, Bethan Rigby, *Freedom of Information Act 2000* (Blackstone, 2001).

National Health Service authorities, schools, police authorities, and a vast range of quangos and committees (including the Arts Council, the Broadcasting Standards Commission, the Commission for Racial Equality, the Committee on Standards in Public life, the Criminal Cases Review Committee, the Gaming Board, the GMC, the Parole Board, the Police Complaints Authority, the Political Honours Scrutiny Committee and so on).[23] The Independent Television Commission is deemed a "public body", and so too are the BBC and Channel 4, although only "in respect of information held for purposes other than those of journalism, art or literature"—an exemption which protects broadcasters from having to divulge their programme research. Notable absentees from the list are the Press Council, ASA, ICSTIS and the BBFC, although they might in time be added by the Home Secretary because they "exercise functions of a public nature".[24] Publicly owned companies are made subject to the Act, but regrettably privatised utilities are excluded, despite the importance of monitoring the conduct of quasi-monopolies in providing services of major public importance.

The threshold duty on an authority in respect of an information request is to "confirm or deny" that it possesses the sought-after document. If anyone destroys or defaces the document with the intention of preventing its disclosure, a criminal offence is committed (section 77) although punishable merely by a fine. Any information supplied by third parties which is published as a result of an FOI request has statutory qualified privilege from libel action (section 79). Requests must be in writing and must "describe the information requested"—the first obstacle for a seeker after truth who suspects that information exists but who cannot describe its origin and provenance with any specificity. Even if this hurdle is overcome, however, there are certain categories of information in respect of the existence of which the public body is relieved of the duty "to confirm or deny" —

- Information which is accessible by other means (*e.g.* if it has already been published or is available at HMSO).[25]

- Information supplied "directly or indirectly" by the security service, SIS, GCHQ, or special forces or security tribunals, or even which "relates to" these bodies.[26] A certificate signed by a Government minister, to the effect that information falls into this category is "conclusive evidence" that it does.

---

[23] FOI Act 2000, s. 3 and see Sched. 1, which lists several hundred committees which are deemed "public bodies" for the purposes of the Act.
[24] FOI Act 2000, s. 5.
[25] *ibid.*, s. 21.
[26] *ibid.*, s. 23

- Information filed with a court or served on a public authority in respect of court proceedings.[27]

- Information covered by parliamentary privilege.[28]

- Personal information which has been collected on the applicant or personal information the revelation of the existence of which would breach the Data Protection Act.[29]

- Information the revelation of the very existence of which would constitute an actionable breach of confidence.[30]

- Information the very existence of which is prohibited from revelation by any law or E.C. obligation or which would be punishable as a contempt of court.[31]

These "absolute exceptions" are unnecessarily broad, and will give Government department a ready-made excuse to avoid the threshold duty "to confirm or deny" that it has collected information that an applicant suspects it to possess. Indeed, unless the courts are prepared to read down these "absolute exceptions" they provide an easy means for hostile bureaucrats to sabotage the spirit of the Act—for example, by claiming that revelation of the existence of embarrassing information would be an "actionable" breach of confidence—even though any such "action" would be unlikely to succeed. Even if such an excuse were rejected after judicial review, its advancement would delay the release of the information and force the applicant to bring expensive legal proceedings in order to refute it. The principal object of the "absolute exemption" device is to avoid the embarrassment which was visited upon the CIA and FBI when American radicals used FOI legislation to prove that they had been spied upon for political purposes. (In the 1970s MI5 similarly targeted such youthful idealists as Peter Mandelson, Jack Straw, Harriet Harman and Patricia Hewitt.) English victims of improper surveillance will not be permitted to obtain access to their security service files by the "absolute exemption" device of placing them in a class of document in respect of which all Government departments are relieved of the duty of admitting whether or not they exist.[32] These absolute exemptions may also be open to challenge under the European Convention when the information concerns the private life of the inquirer. Although the Strasbourg court has allowed States a wide margin of appreciation to determine their own national security needs,

---

[27] FOI Act 2000, s. 32
[28] *ibid.*, s. 34.
[29] *ibid.*, s. 40.
[30] *ibid.*, s. 41(1).
[31] *ibid.*, s. 44.
[32] *ibid.*, s. 24.

the storing of data on a person's private life is a form of interference
which must be justified as "necessary in a democratic society" under
Article 8(2) of the Convention.[33]

Even when Whitehall cannot bring its objection to disclosure within
a particular head of absolute exemption, it may nonetheless refuse to
confirm or deny if,

> "in all the circumstances of the case, the public interest in main-
> taining the exclusion of the duty to confirm or deny outweighs the
> public interest in disclosing whether the public authority holds the
> information".

This formula calls for the balancing of the two public interests in the
light of the circumstances of the actual request. It makes the highly
questionable, if not oxymoronic and undemocratic, assumption that
there is a public interest in public ignorance (an assumption made
instinctively in Whitehall, which until 1989 refused to confirm or deny
the existence of MI5). It is regrettable that the FOI Act should so cent-
rally embody this assumption, which can have no validity save in
respect of ongoing criminal or terrorist investigations.

A public authority which cannot reject or stall a request by claiming
exemption from its duty to confirm or deny must respond promptly, and
no later than 20 days (*i.e.* four working weeks) after receiving the
request. This period may be extended if the authority asks for a fee for
obtaining and copying the information—its response may be delayed
until the fee is paid.[34] There is no duty to respond if the request is
vexatious or unnecessarily onerous, although under section 16 every
public authority has a duty to advise and assist applicants to make
effective requests, and a duty under section 19 to adopt a scheme by
which information generated within the department and available under
FOI will either be published or at least be identifiable by potential
applicants. These duties, as with others imposed by the Act, are supervised by the "Information Commissioner"—the new name for the Data
Protection Commissioner, an office previously established under the
Data Protection Act.

An authority which decides to refuse a request must notify the applicant of its reasons, which must relate to an exemption category defined
by the Act. The absolute exemptions have been outlined above; the
main exemptions from disclosure for documents which can be confirmed to exist are that they contain information:

- which will be published in due course;[35]

---

[33] See, *e.g. Leander v. Sweden* (1987) 9 E.H.R.R. 433.
[34] FOI Act 2000, s. 10.
[35] *ibid.*, s. 21.

- the suppression of which "is required for the purpose of safeguarding national security", and the minister may sign a certificate which is "conclusive evidence" of that fact;[36]

- likely to prejudice the defence of the United Kingdom or its colonies, or the capability of the United Kingdom's armed forces or its allies;[37]

- likely to prejudice foreign relations (or relations with international organisations) or the United Kingdom's foreign interests, or else the information has been supplied in confidence by another State or by an international organisation;[38]

- likely to prejudice the economic or financial interests of the United Kingdom;[39]

- likely to prejudice the protection or detection of crime, the apprehension or prosecution of offenders, the administration of justice, tax collection, immigration control, or other legal process brought to safeguard an important public interest;[40]

- which, other than statistical information, relates to the formulation of government policy, ministerial communications or the operation of ministerial private offices;[41]

- which would, in the reasonable opinion of the minister, be likely to prejudice the convention of collective ministerial responsibility or to inhibit the free and frank provision of advice or exchange of views or otherwise prejudice the effective conduct of public affairs;[42]

- relating to communications with the monarch or "with other members of the Royal Family or with the Royal Household" or about "the conferring by the Crown of any honour or dignity";[43]

- likely to endanger the physical or mental health, or the safety, of any individual;[44]

---

[36] FOI Act 2000, s. 24 (see the "Stop Press" section for further details).
[37] *ibid.*, s. 26.
[38] *ibid.*, s. 27.
[39] *ibid.*, s. 29.
[40] *ibid.*, s. 31.
[41] *ibid.*, s. 35.
[42] *ibid.*, s. 36.
[43] *ibid.*, s. 37.
[44] *ibid.*, s. 38.

- covered by legal professional privilege;[45]
- about trade secrets.[46]

These "non absolute" exemptions protect almost all Whitehall information of any interest or significance which is not already covered by the overlapping "absolute exemptions". Sir Humphrey's triumph is, by section 36, complete: government must not be open if it "would be likely to prejudice . . . the free and frank exchange of views for the purposes of deliberation . . . [or] the maintenance of the convention of collective responsibility of ministers of the Crown"—the very basis upon which the Government attempted to suppress evidence of ministerial and Whitehall complicity in the supply of arms to Iraq at the Matrix-Churchill trial. If these exemptions are rigidly enforced, the prospect of using FOI to extract any politically embarrassing information is minimal—unless the embarrassment is hidden in statistical tables, the only class of information that the Act actually declares to be "free". The only provision which prevents the Act from being described as fraudulent is section 2(2), which requires suppression of all information subject to an absolute exemption but which permits suppression of information subject to non-absolute exemption:

"if or to the extent that . . .

   b) in all the circumstances of the case, the public interest in
      maintaining the exemption outweighs the public interest in
      disclosing the information".

This is the "window of opportunity" for media applicants in search of internal information to monitor or critically assess Government performance. It posits a hypothetical public interest in maintaining the category of documents as exempt from disclosure, but permits this consideration to be "outweighed" by the general public interest in disclosure, as fortified by the circumstances of the particular case. (Presumably, an application by an investigative journalist for information to support reasonably held suspicion of official misconduct will (or should) have a greater tendency to outweigh any public interest in concealment than an application by a busybody in search of scandal or a corporation in search of commercial advantage). For this all-important balancing exercise there is no "burden of proof" to be borne by the applicant, but nor is there any presumption in favour of freedom of information. The public authority must make a judgment as to where the public interest lies.

---

[45] FOI Act 2000, s. 42.
[46] *ibid.*, s. 43.

Appeal

When a public authority decides in favour of concealment, the applicant may complain to the Information Commissioner.[47] She will decide the complaint on its merits, and issue a "decision notice" which either side may take on appeal to the Information Tribunal (formerly the Data Protection Tribunal) comprising lawyers appointed by the Lord Chancellor's Department.[48] The tribunal will adopt an adversarial procedure, hear both sides and may quash the Commissioner's decision and substitute its own, based on a fresh evaluation of the evidence. Either side may appeal a Tribunal decision to the High Court, although only in so far as it involves a point of law.

These provisions make it possible to overrule concealment decisions made by officials in departments which may have a motive to cover-up. The independent Commissioner investigates the complaint and makes the first adjudicative decision, which can be subjected by either party to a full Tribunal appeal with judicial review of legal error by the High Court. But the system only operates independently when it suits the Government. It has taken the extraordinary liberty, by section 53 of the Act, of giving itself absolute power to nullify the Commissioner's decision in favour of disclosure, and to by-pass the appeal process entirely. This "Government knows best" power relates to decisions concerning either exempt or absolutely exempt information, and it may be exercised (through issuing a certificate) by the Law Officers or a relevant cabinet minister. The only "safeguard" is that a ministerial decision to abort the appeal process must be reported to Parliament, although in a Parliament where the Government has a large majority this is not much of a safeguard. Section 53 has the effect of empowering the Executive to suspend the FOI Act in any particular case, denying applicants an independent and impartial tribunal (or indeed, any tribunal at all) for determining their civil rights. It is a power of political override, any exercise of which will amount to a blatant breach of Article 6 of the European Convention in those cases where a right of access to information is a "civil right".

---

[47] FOI Act 2000, s. 50
[48] ibid., s. 57–8.

CHAPTER 12

REPORTING LOCAL GOVERNMENT

"Elected Members and officials must deliberately establish and maintain working relationships with those responsible for news-papers, broadcasting and television to seek their help in keeping open the two-way communication between the public and local government."

Royal Commission on Local Government, 1969[1]

Local papers and most local councils have not been slow to respond to this plea from the Royal Commission responsible for the present pattern of local government. Local council reporters have "established and maintained" a relationship with council contacts who can provide a quick quote to flesh out a dry committee minute or tip the journalist off to agenda items that will spark rhetorical flourishes or have local public interest. Reporting set-piece council debates is safe from a libel action: newspapers can carry, under the shield of qualified privilege, the insults and allegations that rival politicians trade in the public chamber. But these "working relationships" rarely work to uncover incompetence in local government, let alone the sort of corruption spread by the Poulson gang. This type of investigation ruffles the feathers of regular contacts and jeopardises reporters' access to information needed for more mundane work.[2] To the shame of the hundreds of reporters covering local government in the North-East, the corruption that riddled that area in the 1960s was discovered and disclosed by lawyers acting for Poulson's creditors. The media saw and heard no evil; certainly they spoke none through the decade in which local authority contracts were awarded by bribery and improper influence.

The media cannot blame the secrecy laws for their failure; on the contrary, the law provides rights of access to a wide range of council

---

[1] Redcliffe-Maud Report on Local Government Reform, Cmnd. 4040 (1969). para. 319.

[2] See further Dave Murphy, "The Silent Watchdog: the Press in Local Politics" and "Control without Censorship" in James Curran (ed.), *The British Press: A Manifesto* (Macmillan, 1978).

papers. Council electors, including locally based reporters, have rights of inspection that, compared with access to Whitehall, are quite remarkable. This chapter will examine:

- the rights of admission to meetings of councils and other local bodies;
- rights to inspect documents;
- the special rules of libel concerning reports of and by local authorities.

RIGHTS OF ADMISSION

Council meetings

Before statute intervened, the courts gave no help to newspapers wishing to report local council meetings. Councillors, like members of a private club, could eject those of whom they disapproved, and a reporter or editor whose stories caused umbrage could be barred from future meetings without legal redress.[3] The courts were out of tune with the times. In 1908 Parliament gave reporters a statutory right to attend council meetings.[4] This was extended in 1960 to the public generally by a statute known after one of its sponsors as the Thatcher Act.[5] Further extensions were made in 1972 and again in 1985.

Consequently, there is no longer a single regime for all public bodies. Journalists will deal most frequently with *principal councils*. These are county, district and London borough councils and also the Common Council of the City of London, a joint authority, a statutory joint committee, a police authority, the Metropolitan Police Authority, a combined fire authority, and (for most purposes) the Joint Consultative Committees set up for liaison between the National Health Service and local councils and the Community Health Councils (CHCs), which are Health Service user groups.[6] In Wales counties and county boroughs

---

[3] *Tenby Corp. v. Mason* [1908] 2 Ch. 457.
[4] Admission of Press to Meetings Act 1908.
[5] Public Bodies (Admission to Meetings) Act 1960. Mrs Thatcher introduced its second reading with her maiden speech. B. E. M. Cotter, "The Admission of Press and Public to Meetings of Local Authorities" (1974) 138 L.G.R. 174 and 202 has a good description of the Act's legislative history.
[6] Local Government Act 1972, ss. 270(1) and 100J as added by the Local Government (Access to Information) Act 1985; Health Service Joint Consultative Committees (Access to Information) Act 1986, Community Health Councils (Access to Information) Act 1988.

are principal councils. The Greater London Assembly is also a principal council.[7] The duties of all these bodies to admit the public and to allow inspection of their documents are set out in the Local Government Act 1972.[8]

The Thatcher Act still determines the obligations of parish and community councils, the Council of the Isles of Scilly, joint boards or committees of any of these authorities or one of these authorities and a principal council, parish meetings of rural parishes, the Land Authority of Wales, Health Authorities, and special Health Authorities (if the order setting them up directs so), NHS trusts, and bodies (other than principal councils) that can set a rate.[9]

Although these lists may seem extensive, there are significant omissions. Decisions regarding the Metropolitan Police are not taken in public: the London police are under the control of the Home Secretary rather than any local authority or joint committee.[10] The Tory Government's penchant for protecting private business is reflected in the secrecy with which Urban Development Corporations, Enterprise Zone Authorities and Housing Action Trusts can take their decisions. This is an approach continued by New Labour whose Regional Development Agencies are also outside the "open government" regime of local authorities. Privatised bodies (such as the water companies) and their regulators (such as the Environment Agency) similarly have no obligation to admit the public to their meetings.

Committees, sub-committees and caucuses

The Thatcher Act requirements apply only to full meetings of the council or body concerned or committees of the whole organisation.[11] Parish and community councils must admit the public to their committee meetings (even if not all councillors are members).[12] The obligations of principal councils to open their doors is much more extensive. Committee and sub-committee meetings must be open to the public except for the limited purposes discussed below.[13] This applies to the committees that a local authority must establish by statute—education, police, local fisheries (where relevant), children, regional planning, social services,

---

[7] Greater London Authority Act 1999, s. 58(1).
[8] For a useful discussion of rights of access to meetings and documents see Tim Harrison, *Access to Information in Local Government* (Sweet & Maxwell, 1988) and Patrick Birkenshaw, *Government and Information* (Butterworths, 1990), Chap. 4.
[9] Public Bodies (Admission to Meetings) Act 1960, Sched.
[10] Police Act 1996, s. 101(1).
[11] *ibid.*, s. 2(1).
[12] Local Government Act 1972, ss. 100 and 270(1).
[13] *ibid.*, ss. 100A, 100E; Community Health Councils (Access to Information) Act 1988, s. 1.

superannuation—as well as to committees that an authority sets up voluntarily.[14]

However, in many authorities policy is really made at caucus meetings of the majority party, where there is absolutely no right of access. The line is a fine one. There is no automatic legal obstacle to committees composed of just one party, and councils are free to have a "working party" composed of members of just the ruling party,[15] but if these were to be set up, operate and report back in a way that was indistinguishable from a committee or sub-committee, they could not escape the duty to allow the public to be present.[16]

Executive government

Regulation of local government has been in a state of almost perpetual motion. Most significantly in 2000 the government introduced a new regime requiring most local councils to separate their executive functions into one of three basic models: a directly elected mayor plus two or more councillors appointed by the mayor; a council leader ("the executive leader") selected by the council itself and two or more councillors chosen either by the executive leader or the council; or a directly elected mayor and an officer of the council ("council manager").[17] Whichever model is chosen, the council must establish an oversight and scrutiny committee which does not include members of the executive and which can review and scrutinise decisions or actions of the executive. The scrutiny and oversight committee is a committee for the purpose of the provisions of the 1972 Act which allow public admission and public access to documents.[18]

Local authorities have to consult on which option to adopt and, if they wish to choose the option of an elected mayor plus cabinet executive or mayor and council manager, they must hold a local referendum. The legislation allows for petitions by local voters for holding a referendum on the adoption of a particular type of executive government. The local council may have strong views on referenda of these kind, but they are constrained in what they can say in the 28 days preceding the poll. They cannot publish information about the question or arguments on either side except in answer to a specific request, or information relating to

---

[14] See Local Government Act 1972, ss. 101(9) and 102.

[15] R. v. Eden District Council, ex p. Moffat, The Independent, December 16, 1988, CA.

[16] See R. v. Sheffield City Council, ex p. Chadwick (1986) 84 L.G.R. 563, London Borough of Southwark v. Peters [1972] L.G.R. 41. The subjective intention of the council in setting the body up is likely to be critical: R. v. Warwickshire District Council, ex p. Bailey [1991] C.O.D. 284.

[17] Local Government Act 2000, s. 13.

[18] ibid., s. 21.

the holding of the poll—or in the spirit of "right of reply"—to refute or correct any inaccuracy in material published by a person other than the authority.[19] Once the choice is settled, the local authority must publicise the arrangements and allow inspection of its details at their principal office.[20] A local authority "constitution" consisting of information prescribed by the Secretary of State, the authority's standing orders and its code of conduct must be made available at its principal office at all reasonable hours. Copies must be supplied although a reasonable fee can then be charged.[21]

Part of the purpose of the changes in the 2000 Act was to take some decision-making away from the traditional structure of local authority committees. In some cases, these decisions can be taken by individual members of the executive where the idea of a "meeting" simply does not apply. In other cases, the decisions can be or must be taken by the executive as a group. Even here, though, the legislation envisages that generally speaking the decisions can be taken at a meeting which is either held in public or in private, the choice being made by the executive itself.[22] The government, though, has prescribed that certain decisions must be taken at a public meeting of the executive.[23]

As a result, in general, meetings of the authority's executive or its committees at which "key decisions" are to be taken must be in held in public.[24] A decision is "key" if it will have a significant effect on the authority's budget or a significant effect on two or more wards or electoral divisions in the authority's area.[25] The "two or more wards" test prompted considerable criticism in Parliament. Government guidance urges local authorities (unless it is impracticable) to treat, as if they were "key", decisions which are likely to have a significant impact on communities in any one ward or electoral division. It gives the example of a school closure whose impact may be confined to one ward but would still be very significant for that ward.[26]

There are exceptions where even key decisions do not have to be made in public. These are confidential matters that broadly correspond to the exceptions to the requirement that meetings of the council itself

---

[19] Local Authorities (Conduct of Referendums) (England) Regulations 2001, S.I. 2001 No. 1298, reg.5.

[20] Local Government Act 2000, s. 29.

[21] *ibid.*, s. 37.

[22] *ibid.*, s. 22(1) and (2).

[23] Local Authorities (Executive Arrangements) (Access to Information) (England) Regulations 2000, S.I. 2000 No. 3272.

[24] *ibid.*, reg.7.

[25] *ibid.*, reg.8.

[26] The guidance is available on the website of the Department of Environment. Transport and the Regions: www.detr.gov.uk

must be in public.[27] An additional category of unnecessarily confidential information is the advice of political advisers or assistant.[28]

The intention is that local authorities will produce a forward plan for four months which will be then updated on a monthly basis.[29] The plan should identify the subject-matter of the decision, the precise person or body who will take the decision, the date on which the decision is to be made, the principal groups who are to be consulted and how consultation will take place, how other representations can be made and a list of documents submitted to the decision maker for consideration, but it will not include any exempt or confidential information.[30] Forward plans must be made publicly available and the authority must publish in a local newspaper details of where and when inspection can take place.[31] Key decisions can be taken outside the scheme of the forward plan, but only where their inclusion in the plan would be impracticable and where (generally) three clear days' public notice has been given.[32] These requirements can only be circumvented in cases of special urgency and where the chairman of the oversight and scrutiny committee has agreed that the decision cannot reasonably be deferred.[33]

"Secrecy motions" and other limitations on access

The right of admission is not absolute. The public must be admitted to committees only "so far as is practicable",[34] but the courts have insisted that a committee must not deliberately choose to meet in a room that is too small for the expected audience.[35] Although there is power to clear the public gallery to prevent or suppress disorder,[36] the members of the press are unlikely to be part of any disturbance and so they should be allowed to stay when the protesters are swept out. The principle is the same as that which applies to disruptions in court (see p. 422).

Until the Local Government (Access to Information) Act 1985 councils and their committees had a general power under the Thatcher Act

---

[27] Local Authorities (Executive Arrangements) (Access to Information) (England) Regulations 2000, reg. 21, and see below p. 617.

[28] *ibid.*, reg. 21(4).

[29] *ibid.*, reg. 13.

[30] *ibid.*, reg. 14.

[31] *ibid.*, reg. 12.

[32] *ibid.*, reg. 15.

[33] *ibid.*, reg. 16—there are more detailed provisions for situations where there is no such chairman.

[34] Local Government Act 1972, s. 100(1).

[35] *R. v. Liverpool City Council, ex p. Liverpool Taxi Fleet Operators Association* [1975] 1 All E.R. 379—see below p. 618.

[36] Local Government Act 1972, s. 100A(8); Public Bodies (Admission to Meetings) Act 1960, s. 1(8). See also *R. v. Brent Health Authority, ex p. Francis* [1985] 1 All E.R. 74.

to exclude the public when publicity would have been prejudicial to the public interest by reason of the confidential nature of the business to be transacted or for other special reasons stated in the resolution.[37] This still applies to those bodies governed by the Thatcher Act (see p. 613). But the overfrequent use of this power by the larger councils and the reluctance of the courts to interfere prompted Parliament in the 1985 Act to specify more precisely when the public could be excluded from principal councils, their committees and sub-committees.

The council, committee or sub-committee *must* sit in secret if there would otherwise be disclosed information that it has received from a government department in confidence or information which cannot be disclosed because of a statutory duty or court order.[38]

The council or committee *can* choose to debate "exempt information" in secret session. The price of greater constraint on the ability of local authorities to sit in private session is that this term has a very cumbersome definition. In summary, the categories of exempt information are[39]:

- information relating to council employees, occupants of council accommodation, or recipients of council services or financial assistance; past, present and prospective persons in these categories are included but only if the information relates to an individual of this description in that capacity;

- information relating to adoption, care, fostering or education of any particular child;

- information relating to the financial or business affairs of any particular person (other than the authority), but not if the information has to be registered under the Companies Acts or similar legislation;

- the amount to be spent by the authority under a contract for the acquisition of property or the supply of goods and services, but only if this would give an advantage to a contractor or prospective contractor;

- proposed or actual terms of a contract under negotiation by the authority for acquisition or disposal of property, goods or services if publication of these would prejudice the authority;

- the identity of the authority as a tenderer for a contract for goods or services;

---

[37] Public Bodies (Admission to Meetings) Act 1960, s. 1(2).
[38] Local Government Act 1972, s. 100A(2) and (3).
[39] *ibid.*, Sched. 12A.

- information relating to consultations or negotiations over a labour relations matter the disclosure of which would prejudice the authority in those or other labour negotiations or consultations;

- instructions to, and advice from, a barrister, and information obtained or action to be taken in connection with legal proceedings or the determination of any matter affecting the authority;

- information showing that the authority intends to give a notice, make an order or issue a direction to a person who might then be given an opportunity to defeat the purpose of the notice, order or direction;

- action in connection with the prevention, investigation or prosecution of crime;

- the identity of a person giving information about a criminal offence, a breach of statutory duty, a breach of planning control or a nuisance;

- in relation to Joint Consultative Committees and CHCs, information relating to the physical or mental health of any person or information relating to anyone who is, was or has applied to provide services as a doctor, dentist, ophthalmist or pharmacist or their employee.[40]

The Secretary of State for the Environment can add to this list of exempt information.

The authority can exclude the public only if its secrecy resolution states the category of exempt information that will be discussed.[41] Under the Thatcher Act the courts have held that a failure to spell out the reasons for exclusion does not invalidate the resolution.[42] The legislation for principal councils is differently worded,[43] and an authority would probably be acting beyond its powers if it did not conform to these requirements.

A committee of Liverpool City Council was considering a plan to increase the number of taxi licences. The committee room had 55 seats, 22 of which were occupied by councillors, and 17 by officers. The matter had aroused local interest, and many taxi drivers and others wanted to attend and to make representations to the committee. The committee ruled that

---

[40] Health Service Joint Consultative Committees (Access to Information) Act 1986, s. 2(4); Community Health Councils (Access to Information) Act 1988, s. 2(6).
[41] Local Government Act 1972, s. 100A(5).
[42] R. v. Liverpool City Council, n.35 above.
[43] See Local Government Act 1972, s. 100A(4) and (5).

while the press could stay, the rest of the public should be excluded. The special reasons were, first, the lack of space and the impracticability of allowing in only some of the public and, secondly, a preference for hearing representations individually in the absence of other members of the public who generally wished to make submissions. The Divisional Court agreed that these reasons were adequate because the committee had not deliberately chosen a room that was too small, the press had been allowed to stay, and on the special facts of the case it was reasonable to exclude the public who were also potential "witnesses" before the committee.[44]

The case is important because of the court's emphasis on the presence of the press, and for its indication that deliberate attempts to avoid publicity by a council can be challenged in court on grounds of bad faith.

The secrecy motion is sometimes passed to cover up a council's blunders or to hide an official's embarrassment rather than in the public interest. In one case the public were excluded while the council debated the reasons for the failure of a redevelopment project. Through the gaps in the door frame reporters overheard that the development company had run short of funds and was threatening to abandon the project unless the council increased its subsidies.[45]

If a secrecy motion is proposed, journalists should ask the chair to follow the *Liverpool City Council* case and allow the press to stay. If this request is refused and there is no valid justification for the secrecy motion, the decision could be challenged by applying to the High Court to quash the secrecy order and any decision of the meeting taken after discussion behind closed doors. Journalists should in such cases ask the chair either to adjourn consideration of the matter until the challenge is heard by the court or to tape-record the deliberations so that the press can at least hear the tape if the court rules in its favour.

Agendas

Councils and other local government bodies whose meetings are public must give three clear days' notice of all such meetings.[46] Newspapers

---

[44] *R. v. Liverpool City Council*, n. 35 above.
[45] Dave Murphy *The Silent Watchdog*, p. 25.
[46] Public Bodies (Admission to Meetings) Act 1960, s. 1(4)(a). Local Government Act 1972; s. 100A(6)(a). Seven clear days' notice must be given in the case of the Service Authority of National Crime Squad (Local Government Act 1972, s. 100J(3A)). "Clear days" means excluding the day on which the notice is given and the day on which the meeting is held—*R. v. Swansea City Council, ex p. Elitestone Ltd* (1993) 66 P. & C. R. 422; unless the meeting is convened on shorter notice, when notice to the public must be given at the same time.

and news agencies have the right to be sent copies of the agendas and any statements which indicate the nature of the agenda items. They should also be sent copies of every report for the meeting unless the responsible official believes it is likely to be discussed at a closed session. If the officials think fit, the media should also be sent copies of any other documents supplied to members of the authority in connection with an agenda item. For these services the media can be charged only postage or other necessary costs for transmission.[47] Alternatively, copies of the agenda and reports can be inspected at the authority's offices in the three days before the meeting. The press may still find it worth making an expedition to the authority's offices, because officials of principal councils must prepare a list of the background papers for each report that is required to be publicly available. Any document that discloses facts or matters on which the report was based and which was relied upon to a material extent in preparing the report must be included on the list. Considerable judgment is left to the officers concerned, but in extreme cases the courts would review the decision. The list and at least one copy of each paper (unless it contains exempt or confidential information) must be open to public inspection, although, unusually, authorities can impose a reasonable charge for this right of inspection.[48] The media might argue that these additional documents should be sent to them with their agendas, but councils, who can charge only postage, might baulk at the cost of copying. Documents inspected at the Town Hall can be copied there, but a charge can be made for this. A reasonable number of agendas and the officers reports should also be available for the public at the meeting itself.[49] Since the 1985 Act all these provisions apply as well to meetings of committees and subcommittees of principal councils.[50]

We have seen that council executives must prepare a forward plan which is updated monthly. This will show when key decisions are expected to be made. In certain circumstances key decisions can be taken outside the forward plan but must still be made at a public meeting of the executive (except where the secrecy requirements are satisfied). The publicity which must be given to agendas and reports to be considered at public meetings of the executive broadly follow the

---

[47] Local Government Act 1972, s. 100B(7). A "newspaper" is defined as including a news agency that systematically carries on the business of selling and supplying reports or information to newspapers, and any organisation that is systematically engaged in collecting news for sound or television broadcasts or any other programme service: *ibid.*, s. 100K. See also Public Bodies (Admission to Meetings) Act 1960, s. 1(4)(b) and s. 1(7).

[48] Local Government Act 1972, ss. 100D and 100H.

[49] *ibid.*, s. 100B(1)–(6).

[50] *ibid.*, s. 100E.

requirements for meetings of the council and its committees.[51] Here, too, newspapers[52] can require the local authority to send a copy of the agenda and reports to be considered, such further statements or particulars, if any, as are necessary to indicate the nature of the items contained in the agenda and, if the proper officer thinks fit in the case of any item, a copy of any other document supplied to members of the executive in connection with the item. They must pay any necessary charge for transmission.[53]

Reporting

Accredited representatives of the press must at open meetings be given reasonable facilities for taking notes and for telephoning reports, unless the building in which the meeting is held does not have a telephone or does not belong to the local authority.[54] "Reasonable facilities" mean chairs and a table conveniently placed to hear and see what is going on.[55] There is no right to take photographs of the meeting, to use any means to enable persons not present to see or hear the proceedings, or to make an oral report of the proceedings as they take place.[56] The authority can thus prohibit tape-recording of the proceedings for the purpose of public broadcasting, but it is doubtful whether it can ban reporters from tape-recording for their own use as an aide-memoire.[57] It is important to note that these restrictions are discretionary; they do not prevent a local council from granting permission to film or record if it wishes. Meetings of local authorities and their committees can be broadcast on radio and television without conflicting with any of the statutory duties imposed on political broadcasts.[58]

---

[51] The Local Authorities (Executive Arrangements) (Access to Information) (England) Regulations 2000, S.I. 2000 No. 3272, regs. 10 and 11.

[52] A term defined to include news agencies and "any organisation which is systematically engaged in collecting news for (i) sound or television broadcasts or (ii) for inclusion in . . . any programme service"—*ibid.,* reg. 2.

[53] *ibid.,* reg.11(7).

[54] Public Bodies (Admission to Meetings) Act 1960, s. 1(4)(d), Local Government Act 1972, s. 100A(6).

[55] Ministry of Local Government Circular 21/61, App. 1, para. 8.

[56] Public Bodies (Admission to Meetings) Act 1960, s. 1(7) and Local Government Act 1972, s. 100A(7).

[57] This Interpretation of Public Bodies (Admission to Meetings) Act 1960, s. 1(7) and Local Government Act 1972, s. 100A(7) would be in line with modern views of tape recorders in courts: see p. 470.

[58] This was the position under Broadcasting Act 1981, s. 7(b) and is unlikely to be different under the ITC's Code.

Accounts and supporting documents

Local government has a prototype freedom of information law that is buried in an obscure section of the Audit Commission Act 1998. Section 15 gives "to any person interested" (including reporters) the right to inspect a local authority's accounts, and "all books, deeds, contracts, bills, vouchers and receipts relating to them".[59]

This enormous volume of documentation is a resource under-used by the media. It can provide fascinating stories—as a local paper in Bedfordshire discovered when through this route it obtained details of firearm purchases by its police force.[60] Contracts and other documents directly related to expenditure can be inspected even though they are described as confidential.[61] Similarly, the local authority cannot fob off inquirers with an extract from the accounts showing only gross payments.[62]

This window on a local authority's affairs is open only for the 15 full working days prior to the annual audit.[63] An advertisement giving 14 days' notice of this crucial period must be published in one or more local newspapers.[64] At other times of the year a local elector can demand to see the statement of account,[65] orders for the payment of money by the authority[66] and a breakdown of allowances and expenses paid to councillors.[67] These accounts will not be as detailed as the pre-audit material and a council can fulfil its duty by making a computer printout available.[68] If it chooses to do this, electors will see only the amount of councillors' expenses and not the fuller details on the claim forms themselves.[69]

---

[59] As well as local authorities, the right applies to a wide range of other public bodies. They include police and fire authorities, the Service Authority for the National Crime Squad, the Broads Authority and health service bodies: see Audit Commission Act 1998, Sched. 2.

[60] *U.K. Press Gazette*, November 6 and 20, 1995.

[61] *London Borough of Hillingdon v. Paullsson* [1977] J.P.L. 518. Personal information about staff in connection with their employment is excepted: Audit Commission Act 1998, s. 15(3)–(5).

[62] *Oliver v. Northampton Borough Council* (1986) 151 J.P. 44.

[63] Accounts and Audit Regulations 1996, S.I. 1996 No. 590 reg.12.

[64] *ibid.*, reg.11.

[65] Audit Commission Act 1998, s. 14.

[66] Local Government Act 1972, s. 228(2).

[67] Local Authorities (Members' Allowances) Regulations 1991, S.I. 1991 No. 351, reg. 26. Each year the authority must also publish the total sums paid to each member as a basic allowance, special responsibility allowance and attendance allowance: reg. 26A.

[68] *Buckingham v. Shackleton* [1981] 79 L.G.R. 484.

[69] *Brookman v. Green* [1984] L.G.R. 228.

Journalists who are not trained accountants will find it hard to make sense of the pile of paperwork available under these provisions. However, the courts have said that people who are local electors would be entitled to take accountants with them, even though the accountants came from outside the authority's area.[70] It is not necessary to identify the particular document required. It is possible to ask for an entire class of documents, and a request for "all orders for payment" could be refused only if the class turned out to be unmanageably large.[71] A reporter, like other members of the public, also has a right to make copies of documents.[72] Inspection is free, but copies may be charged for at a reasonable rate. It is a criminal offence to refuse a proper demand for a copy or to obstruct a person entitled to inspect one of these documents. The maximum fine is £1,000.[72A] In 1996 Haringey Council was fined £650 and ordered to pay costs of £2,000 for obstructing a local resident who wanted to exercise these rights.[73]

Audit

One purpose of allowing inspection of an authority's books just prior to the audit is to allow local electors to question the auditor about the accounts.[74] These can be taken in public, but there is a discretion to hear them in private.[75] The Audit Commission's code reminds auditors that there is no statutory requirement to have an oral hearing. They have to decide whether justice and fairness would be served by a hearing and, if so, whether the hearing should be in public. If surprise allegations are made at a hearing the auditor should adjourn to allow written representations.[76]

The Conservative Government's philosophy of requiring local authorities to put certain services out to tender ("compulsory competitive tendering") was changed by the Labour Government in 1999. Most local authorities are given the new sobriquet of "best value authorities". They must each prepare plans for continually improving their services "having regard to a combination of economy, efficiency and effect-

---

[70] R. v. Glamorganshire County Council, ex Collier [1936] 2 All E.R. 168; R. v. Bedwellty UDC Price [1934] 1 K.B. 333.

[71] Evans v. Lloyd [1962] 2 QB 471.

[72] Audit Commission Act 1998, ss. 14 and 15.

[72A] Audit Commission Act 1998, s. 14(3).

[73] Hampstead and Highgate Express, September 13, 1996.

[74] Audit Commission Act 1998, s. 16. But inspection is not confined to those who wish to challenge the accounts: Stirrat v. Edinburgh City Council, 1998 s. C.L.R. 971, OH, interpreting Local Government (Scotland) Act 1973, s. 101(1).

[75] R. v. Farmer, ex p Hargrave [1981] 79 L.G.R. 676.

[76] Code of Audit Practice for Local Authorities and the NHS in England and Wales (Audit Commission, 1995) paras 103–15.

iveness".[77] Plans are audited each year and the auditor's report must be published by the authority.[78]

The auditor's report on any objections to the accounts and on the accounts generally must be sent to newspapers, news agencies, and television and radio stations that receive local authority agendas.[79] Those not on the mailing list will be notified by advertisement in a local paper that the report is available.[80] It can then be inspected as of right by any local elector, who may also purchase copies of all or part of it.[81]

If the auditors come across a matter of particular concern during the course of their investigation, they can make an immediate report, rather than waiting for months until they conclude their final report.[82] These "immediate reports" must be made publicly available by the council concerned, which must also advertise their existence in the local press. It is a summary offence to obstruct a person trying to exercise his or her rights under the new provision.[83]

When an auditor's report is received by the local authority it must meet to consider the report and any recommendations which it includes. The meeting must be within four months of the report being received unless the auditor grants an extension.[84] It must be advertised in the local press at least seven clear days in advance and after the meeting of the authority a notice (approved by the auditor) setting out its decisions in consequence of the report must be published.[85]

Minutes, reports and records of decisions

For parish and community councils, only the minutes of the authority itself and its committees need to be made public.[86] For principal councils, the obligation extends to committee and sub-committee minutes. For six years the authority must keep copies of the minutes, the agenda and any report for an item that was considered in public. If the public was actually excluded because exempt information was under discussion, the minutes of that part of the meeting will be sealed. If this means that it is impossible to understand the proceedings, council officials should prepare a summary to give a fair and coherent record without

---

[77] Local Government Act 1999, s. 3.
[78] *ibid.*, s. 9.
[79] Audit Commission Act 1998, s. 10(5)(a).
[80] Accounts and Audit Regulations, 1996 regs. 14 and 16.
[81] Audit Commission Act 1998, s. 10(5)(b).
[82] *ibid.*, s. 8.
[83] *ibid.*, s. 13(2).
[84] *ibid.*, s. 11.
[85] *ibid.*, s. 12.
[86] Local Government Act 1972, s. 228(1).

disclosing exempt information.[87] Background papers that are open to public inspection must be kept for four years.[88] During these periods agendas, minutes and reports can be inspected without charge, but the authority can impose a reasonable fee for inspecting background reports and for copying.[89] Copying can be refused if this would infringe copyright in the document, but not if the only copyright is owned by the authority itself.[90] Obstructing access to such documents without a reasonable excuse is a criminal offence, although the maximum fine is only level 1 on the standard scale (currently £200).

Key decisions apart, the executives of councils are free to decide to hold their meetings in private. To this extent, the 2000 Act represents a regressive step in relation to open government. However, although decisions can be taken in private, a written record must be made "as soon as reasonably practicable" of the decision, the reasons for it, details of any alternative options considered and rejected, any conflicts of interest declared and any dispensation by the local authority's standards committee.[91] These records are open for public inspection together with any report considered at the meeting or by the individual decision-maker and a newspaper can require the authority to send it copies of these documents (on paying a reasonable copying and transmission charge).[92] The local authority must also make available for public inspection a list of background papers to a report considered at a public meeting of the executive and at least one copy of each document listed.[93] As with the 1972 Act, unusually *this* right of inspection can be subject to payment of a reasonable fee.

Wherever documents have to be made available to the public, copies can be made or requested on payment of a reasonable fee,[94] but this does not permit the making of a copy which would infringe someone's copyright (unless the owner of the copyright is the local authority). By making documents available to the public under these arrangements, the authority will "publish" them for the purposes of the law of defamation, but a special qualified privileged is granted so that there will be no liability in the absence of malice.[95] Records of executive decisions taken

---

[87] Local Government Act 1972, s. 100C; three years in the case of CHCs, Community Health Councils (Access to Information) Act 1988, s. 1(1)(c).

[88] Local Government Act 1972, s. 100D(2); four years in the case of CHCs, Community Health Councils (Access to Information) Act 1988, s. 1(1)(c).

[89] Local Government Act 1972, s. 100H(1) and (2).

[90] *ibid.*, s. 100H(3).

[91] The Local Authorities (Executive Arrangements) (Access to Information) (England) Regulations 2000, S.I. 2000 No. 3272, reg. 3 and 4.

[92] *ibid.*, reg. 5.

[93] *ibid.*, reg. 6.

[94] *ibid.*, reg. 22(2).

[95] The Local Authorities (Executive Arrangements) (Access to Information) (England), reg. 22(4).

in private and reports considered at the time have to be kept for public inspection for six years from the date of the decision. Background papers must be kept for four years.[96] The regulations make it a criminal offence for a person with custody of a document which must be made available to the public if without reasonable excuse he intentionally obstructs a right of access or refuses to supply a copy. The maximum penalty is a fine not exceeding level 1 which is currently the modest sum of £200.[97]

Local authorities must maintain registers of councillors showing their membership of committees and subcommittees and principal councils must have list of officers to whom powers have been delegated.[98] The register and a list must be open to public inspection. Councils should also maintain for the public a written summary of rights to attend meetings and inspect documents.[99]

Councillors' conflicts of interest

The law in this area was substantially revised and extended by the Local Government Act 2000. This established a multi-layered structure of regulation and adjudication. In the first place the Secretary of State can lay down general standards to be observed. These[1] build on principles set out by the Nolan Committee on Standards in Public Life in Local Government. The Government's principles include "Accountability: Members should be accountable to the public for their actions and in the manner in which they carry out their responsibilities, and should co-operate fully and honestly with any scrutiny appropriate to their particular office" and "Openness: Members should be as open as possible about their actions and those of their authority, and should be prepared to give reasons for their actions".[2]

The Government can then also establish a model code of conduct for local authority members and co-opted members. This can include some

---

[96] The Local Authorities (Executive Arrangements) (Access to Information) (England), reg. 22(5) and (6).

[97] *ibid.*, reg. 23.

[98] Unless this is for a period less than six months: Local Government Act 1972, s. 100G added by the Local Government (Access to Information) Act 1985.

[99] See above and Local Government Inspection of Documents (Summary of Rights) Order (S.I. 1986 No. 854). The register must also list the names and addresses of other members of the committee or sub-committee who are not councillors (Local Government Act 1972, s. 100G(17) (c)). Joint Consultative Committees and CHCs must prepare comparable registers and summaries of rights of access: Health Services Joint Consultative Committees (Access to Information) Act 1986, s. 3; Community Health Councils (Access to Information) Act 1988, s. 2.

[1] The Relevant Authorities (General Principles) Order 2001, S.I. 2001 No. 1401.

[2] *ibid.*, Sched., paras 4 and 5.

provisions which are mandatory and others which are optional.[3] Local authorities must adopt their own code of conduct shortly after the Government has promulgated the model code and the authorities' codes must include the mandatory parts of the model.[4] Councillors and co-opted members must give a written undertaking to abide by their authority's Code.[5]

Each authority must set up a standards committee with the function of advising the authority on its Code and monitoring its operation.[6] But enforcement is not left to the authorities themselves. The 2000 Act also established a Standards Board which is empowered to appoint ethical standards officers who will investigate allegations that a member or co-opted member has failed to comply with the authority's Code. If the complaint is not dismissed or not worthy of further action, the ESO can refer it to the monitoring officer of the authority for it to take action, or it can be referred to the Adjudication Panel for a decision.[7] The Adjudication Panel can ultimately decide that the member or co-opted member must be suspended (for up to a year) or disqualified (for up to five years).[8]

The 2000 Act also requires each local authority to have a register of interests of members and co-opted members. The Secretary of State's model code must include in its mandatory provisions requirements to register specified financial and other interests, to declare the interest before taking part in any business related to that interest and to make provision for preventing or restricting the participation of any member or co-opted member in relation to such business. The ban is not complete because the Government can prescribe circumstances in which the authority's standards committee can grant dispensations from these provisions. The register must be open to the public and as soon as practicable after the register has been established its existence and where it can be inspected must be advertised in a local paper.[9]

In addition to a Code for members and co-opted members, the Government can issue a Code for local authority officers. The contracts of employment of officers are then deemed to incorporate the Code.[10]

---

[3] Local Government Act 2000, s. 50.
[4] *ibid.*, s. 51.
[5] *ibid.*, s. 52.
[6] *ibid.*, ss. 53–56.
[7] *ibid.*, s. 59.
[8] *ibid.*, s. 79.
[9] *ibid.*, s. 81.
[10] *ibid.*, s. 82.

Rates and council tax

Local taxes are essentially of two kinds: the council tax imposed on domestic properties and a "non-domestic" rate on business premises.

The business rate is fixed nationally, but it is applied to the value of each premises. Lists of valuations will normally be held by the valuation officer, the billing authority and, nationally, by the Department of the Environment. The current lists and those in force in the previous five years are open to (free) inspection and copying (for a reasonable charge). The same rights apply to proposals to alter the lists or notices of appeal against proposals.[11] Disputes about valuations are heard by Valuation Tribunals. These sit in public (unless the tribunal orders otherwise) having been satisfied that a party's interests would be prejudiced by a public hearing.[12] The decisions on appeals are kept for six years and are open to inspection.[13] There is a further right of appeal to the Lands Tribunal which sits in public unless, because of confidential or national security considerations, it is just and reasonable to exclude the public.[14]

Council tax rates are set by local authorities (within constraints set by central government). Domestic properties also have to be valued, but they are grouped in bands. The valuation lists (kept usually by the billing authority) will show into which band each property comes. There are rights to inspect and copy these valuation lists, to attend appeals heard by valuation tribunals and to access the tribunal's decisions, all of which parallel the arrangements for business properties.[15]

Planning

Planning applications are kept on a register that is open to public inspection.[16] If development is carried on without planning permission, the local authority can issue an enforcement notice requiring the owner to restore the land to its previous use or condition, or a breach of condition

---

[11] Local Government Finance Act 1988, Sched. 9, paras 8 and 9.
[12] Non-Domestic Rating (Alteration of Lists and Appeals) Regulations 1993, S.I. 1993 No. 291, reg. 40(3).
[13] *ibid.,* reg. 46(4) and (5).
[14] Lands Tribunal Rules 1996, S.I. 1996 No. 1022, reg. 5.
[15] See Local Government Finance Act 1992, ss. 28 and 29 and Council Tax (Alteration of Lists and Appeals) Regulations 1993, S.I. 1993 No. 290, regs 25(3) and 31.
[16] Town and Country Planning Act 1990, s. 69. It is divided into those that are pending and those that have been finally disposed of: Town and Country Planning (General Development Procedure) Order 1995, S.I. 1995 No. 419, Art. 25. The register also says what action has been taken on the application.

notice if the terms on which permission was granted have not been followed. The owner can appeal and cannot be compelled to obey the enforcement notice unless the local authority also issues a "stop notice". These are not made automatically, because the authority must pay compensation if it loses the appeal. There are public registers of enforcement, breach of condition and stop notices.[17] Applications for certain other kinds of local authority licences (ranging from sex shops to zoos) must also be made available to the public.[18]

In addition to actions affecting individual properties, local authorities are required to plan strategically. Their plans in draft and as actually adopted, together with supporting documents, must be open to public inspection.[19] Similarly the public are entitled to see the council resolution setting up Housing Improvement Areas and the authority's registers of listed buildings and of tree preservation notices.[20]

Local ombudsmen

Just as a Parliamentary Commissioner for Administration, or ombudsman, has been established to hear complaints of poor administration in central government, so a number of local Commissioners of Administration exist to hear complaints of maladministration against local authorities. The complaint must relate to the procedure of decision-making rather than its merits, and in order to succeed will generally have to reveal bias, neglect, inattention, delay, incompetence, ineptitude, perversity, turpitude or arbitrariness. Complaints are normally made through a local councillor, but unlike the parliamentary ombudsman, the local commissioners can receive complaints directly from the public.[21] The local ombudsman reports back to the authority concerned, which will then normally have to give the public a chance to inspect the report for a three-week period that has been advertised by at least one week's advance notice in the local press. Inspection of the ombuds-

---

[17] Town and Country Planning Act 1990, s. 188, and General Development (Procedure) Order 1988, Art. 26.

[18] Sex shops: Local Government (Miscellaneous Provisions) Act 1982, Sched 3, para. 10 (7)–(13); Zoos: Zoo Licensing Act 1981, s. 2(3). The Food Safety Act 1990, allows the Government to require a similar system of registering food premises.

[19] Town and Country Planning (Development Plan) Regulations 1991, S.I. 1991 No. 2794, regs 26–28.

[20] Inner Urban Areas Act 1978, Sched, para. 1(3)(a) (housing improvement areas); Town and Country Planning Act 1990, s. 214 (tree preservation); Planning (Listed Buildings and Conservation Areas) Act 1990, s. 2 (listed buildings).

[21] Local Government Act 1974, ss. 23–34.

man's report is free of charge. It can be copied, and it is an offence to obstruct anyone exercising these rights to inspect or copy.[22]

Local parliamentary bills

Certain documents have to be deposited with the local authority under the Standing Orders of each House of Parliament. These are mainly private bills that are sponsored by, or affect, the locality.[23] The detailed plans that must accompany them may be of particular interest in the case of controversial construction projects. These documents are also open to inspection and copying, although the council can charge for viewing them: 10p for the first half hour and 10p per hour thereafter.[24]

Environmental controls

Responsibility for controlling pollution rests with local authorities and the Environment Agency. Traditionally, council officials have preserved the secrecy of the information that they have been given by local industries on the pretext that their co-operation was essential and depended on confidentiality. Environmentalists suspected that the real fears were of greater public pressure for higher standards, and of criticism at the inefficiency of the means of control.[25]

Slowly Parliament has demanded more publicity. The impetus has principally come from the E.U. whose directives have demanded more openness.[26] Thus, for instance, there are now extensive disclosure requirements in relation to waste management by the Environment Agency (as the regulator) and local authorities (as waste collection authorities).[27] The Environment Secretary can direct that certain

---

[22] *ibid.*, s. 30. Apart from naming the authority, the report will usually keep others involved anonymous, but if the maladministration involved a member of the authority acting in breach of the National Code of Local Government Conduct he or she should be named unless the Ombudsman considers that it would be unjust to do so: s. 30(3A).

[23] Standing Orders of the House of Commons (Private Business) H.C. 416 (1980) Orders 27–47.

[24] Local Government Act 1972, ss. 225 and 228(5).

[25] See Maurice Frankel, "The Environment" in Rosemary Delbridge and Martin Smith (eds), *Consuming Secrets* (National Consumer Council and Burnet Books, 1982), pp. 93–126.

[26] See, *e.g.* Council Directive, June 7, 1990, 90/313/EEC, O.J. No. L 158, 23.6.90, p. 56. The directive's reference to "information relating to the environment is to be given a broad interpretation"—Case C-321/96 *Mecklenburg v. Kreis Pinneberg Der Landral* [1999] All E.R. (EC) 166.

[27] Environmental Protection Act 1990, s. 64 and Waste Management Licensing Regulations 1994, S.I. 1994 No. 1056, regs 10 and 11.

information be excluded on grounds of national security.[28] Information can also be excluded on grounds of preserving confidential business information: commercial needs are often pitched against the demands for transparency. Detailed procedures have been put in place to allow confidentiality claims to be made and adjudicated upon by the authority maintaining the register on appeal and by the Secretary of State.[29] Registers with exclusions on a similar model are required for local authorities and the Environment Agency in their roles as regulators of air and other environmental pollution;[30] genetically modified organisms;[31] contaminated land[32] and for local authorities in connection with hazardous substances.[33]

In addition, local authorities which have declared noise abatement zones must keep a public record of the noise levels there.[34]

Housing

Public housing authorities must publish details of their arrangements on matters of housing management, policies on allocation of council housing and on transfers. These are open to inspection and copying—the latter for a reasonable fee—although the authority must provide a free copy of a summary of its allocation priorities to anyone who asks for it.[35] If a local authority has established a register of houses in multiple occupation, this must be open to public inspection.[36] Local rent officers must maintain a register of the rents that they have registered in their area for tenants who are "protected" under the Rent Act 1977.[37]

Education and social services

Local education authorities (LEAs) must publish their arrangements and policies for admission of pupils to their schools. LEAs must also spell out their means for enabling parents to express their preference for schools and the mechanism for appealing refusals.[38] The authority's pol-

---

[28] Environmental Protection Act 1990, s. 65.
[29] Environmental Protection Act 1990, s. 66.
[30] *ibid.,* ss. 20–22.
[31] *ibid.,* ss. 122–123.
[32] *ibid.,* ss. 78R–78T.
[33] See Planning (Hazardous Substances) Act 1990, s. 28.
[34] Control of Pollution Act 1974, s. 64.
[35] Housing Act 1985, s. 106; Housing Act 1996, s. 168.
[36] Housing Act 1985, s. 349(3).
[37] Rent Act 1997, s. 66. Rent assessment panels can fix rents for "restricted contracts" and "assured tenancies". There are public registers of these decisions: Rent Act 1977, s. 79; Housing Act 1988, s. 42 and Assured Tenancies and Agricultural Occupancies (Rent Information) Order, S.I. 1988 No. 2199.
[38] Education Act 1996, s. 414.

icies on school transport, provision of milk and meals and school clothing, and provision for children with special education needs must be
published. The devolvement of managerial powers to individual schools
has led to them being obliged to disclose their policies including admission criteria and a summary of results in national assessments.[39] School
governors have a discretion to hold their meetings in public, and, in
general, the minutes of their meetings must be open to inspection.[40] A
school's curriculum policies must likewise be publicly available.[41]

Authorities with social service departments must make known their
services for the blind, deaf, handicapped and disabled. They must keep
public registers of homes for the old, disabled, drink or drug depend-
ants, or the mentally ill.[42] Local authorities must publish information
about the services that they provide for children in need, day-care facilities, and accommodation for children.[43]

Annual reports

The Local Government Planning and Land Act 1980 introduced mandatory disclosure requirements, which were consistently with the Conservative Government's concern to compare and cut back public
spending. Local authorities (including fire authorities and police
committees) must produce an annual report that contains the information required by the Environment Minister's Code of Practice.[44] The
code, published in 1981, requires authorities to publish statistics com-
paring their expenditure for each service with the average for authorities
of the same class.[45] Comparisons must be made between projected and
actual expenditures, and capital expenditure must also be noted. Rate
and other income must be given, as well as statistics for major services.
The authority's workforce must be tabulated by staff category. The
Government has also recommended that local authorities (like
companies) should disclose policies for hiring staff who are disabled.[46]
The code says that the reports should be made available to the press

---

[39] Education (School Information) Regulations 1998 (S.I. 1998 No. 2526).
[40] Education (School Government) Regulations 1989 (S.I. 1989 No. 1503) regs 21 and
     24.
[41] Education (Schools Curriculum and Related Information) Regulations 1989 (S.I.
     1989 No. 954).
[42] Chronically Sick and Disabled Persons Act 1970, s. 1(2)(a); Registered Homes Act
     1984, s. 7.
[43] Children Act 1989, ss. 17, 18, 20 and 24 and Sched. 2, para. 1.
[44] Local Government Planning and Land Act 1980, s. 2.
[45] *Local Authority Annual Reports* (HMSO, 1981); Dept of Environment Circular
     3/81.
[46] Clive Walker "Public Rights to Information in Central and Local Government"
     (1982) Local Government Review 931, 932.

and to members of the public.[47] More details about the authority's man-power are required by a separate code.[48] The press must be notified of the annual report, and it must be made available at the council's offices and public libraries.[49] The Audit Commission can also require local authorities to make comparative information available. It must be published in a local paper and kept for inspection and copying by local electors.[50]

Land ownership

Central government has the power to require local authorities to maintain registers of publicly owned unused land. In the early 1990s such registers had to be kept, but the obligation was scrapped in 1996.[51] The power is based on the fallacious assumption that only publicly-owned land is left unproductive. Derelict land is often in private ownership, but there is no power to compile open lists of the speculative holdings of development companies.

There is a register of land titles covering most of the country and it is open to public inspection.[52] The public can inspect and copy (subject to prescribed charges) entries on the register and documents (other than leases or charges) that are referred to in the register and that are in the registrar's custody. Regulations may prescribe that certain other documents in the registrar's possession may be inspected as of right; any others will be available only at his discretion.

Leaks

Since local authority officials do not "hold office under the Crown" they are not bound by the Official Secrets Acts and it is not a crime for them or for elected councillors to show secret documents to the press, unless the information has been entrusted in confidence to them by a person who is a Crown servant. However, local government officials show no greater readiness to leak secrets than their Whitehall counterparts. In part this is because officials face dismissal under the National Joint Council's Conditions of Service if they communicate to the public

---

[47] *Local Authority Annual Reports,* n. 45 above, para. 1.8.
[48] Local Government (Publication of Staffing Information) (England) Code 1995, DOE Circular 14/95 Annex.
[49] *Local Authority Annual Reports,* n. 45 above, para. 1.8.
[50] Audit Commission Act 1998, ss. 44–47. The "local paper" can be a free sheet but only if it is published independently of the authority and distributed to all dwellings in the area: *ibid.,* s. 45(4).
[51] DOE Circular 3/96.
[52] Land Registration Act 1925, s. 112, and see Land Registration (Open Register) Rules 1992, s. 1. 1992 No. 122.

the proceedings of any meeting or the contents of any document relating to the authority, unless required by law or unless they are expressly authorised to do so. There is also considerable social pressure not to undermine colleagues.[53] Councillors caught leaking can be disciplined by their party or struck from circulation lists for receiving sensitive documents.[54] But journalists may at least reassure their sources in local government that they are in no danger of prosecution, unless the information has been supplied as a result of a bribe.

Libel

One of the inducements for the media to cover the formal proceedings of local authorities is the special protection against libel actions that is given to such reports. The Defamation Act 1996 confers qualified privilege on:

- fair and accurate reports of any open meeting of the authority, one of its committees or sub-committees[55];

- fair and accurate reports of a public hearing by any person appointed by the authority to hold an inquiry under any statutory provision[56];

- fair and accurate reports of any public hearing of a commission, tribunal, committee or person appointed to hold an inquiry under any statutory provision by the Crown, a Minister or a Northern Ireland department or a tribunal, board, committee or body constituted by or exercising functions under any other statutory provision[57];

- fair and accurate copy or extract from a notice or other matter issued for the information of the public by any authority performing governmental functions in any Member State[58];

---

[53] Sisella Bok, "Whistleblowing and Professional Responsibilities" in Daniel Callahan and Sisella Bok (eds), *Ethics Teaching in Higher Education* (Plenum, New York, 1980).

[54] For a thoughtful analysis of what makes documents politically sensitive see A. T. J. Maslen, "Secrecy, Public Information and Local Government" (1979) 5 Local Govt Studies 47.

[55] Defamation Act 1996, Sched. 1, paras 11(1)(a) and (2).

[56] *ibid.*, para. 11(1)d).

[57] *ibid.*, paras 11(1)(c) and (e).

[58] *ibid.*, para. 9(1). After concern expressed by the media, the Act expressly states that "governmental functions" include police functions, *ibid.*, para. 9(2).

● fair and accurate copy of or extract from any register or other document which is required by law to be open to public inspection.[59]

These are defences of qualified privilege[60] which means that they do not apply if the publisher is malicious (see p. 126). Unlike their equivalents under the 1952 Act, they can be invoked by anyone—not just newspapers or broadcasters. The material covered in the story is not protected unless it is of public concern and its publication for the public benefit.[61] Of the categories listed in the last paragraph, the first four are dependent on the publisher or broadcaster providing a right of reply (see p. 136).

In the past, stories in greater depth had also to contend with the hazard of a libel writ from the council itself.[62] That is not so now. The House of Lords has held that an organ of local government is unable to sue for defamation.[63] It reversed the old rule because of the chilling effect on freedom of expression. The right of individual councillors who are defamed to sue for libel remains although this possibility may have an equally chilling effect especially if the council underwrites their legal costs. A council itself can still sue for malicious falsehood but this will be less of a threat to the media. Not only does the council have to prove falsity and malice, but it must also show that the publication caused financial loss (or in certain circumstances was likely to cause this kind of loss).

LOCAL AUTHORITY SPONSORED PUBLICATIONS

The 1980s were marked by a breakdown of consensus on the role of local authorities. Local council publications and advertisements defending their role and articulating policies that were an anathema to Whitehall incurred the Government's wrath. As a result of court action and legislation, authorities are considerably circumscribed in their ability to publish or promote controversial matters.

In 1985, the Greater London Council was enjoined from continuing

---

[59] *ibid.,* para. 5. The prior "publication" (in the defamation law sense) by the authority to inspecting members of the public is also covered by qualified privilege; Local Government Act 1972, s. 100H(5) and (6); Public Bodies (Admission to Meetings) Act 1960, s. 1(5).

[60] Defamation Act 1996, s. 15.

[61] s. 15(3)—these are questions for the jury—*Kingshott v. Associated Kent Newspapers* [1991] 1 Q.B. 880, CA.

[62] *Bognor Regis UDC v. Campion* [1972] Q.B. 169.

[63] *Derbyshire County Council v. Times Newspapers Ltd* [1993] A.C. 534.

its anti-abolition advertising campaign because its objective of persuading people to its point of view could not be justified under a statutory power of publishing information on matters related to local government.[64]

An inquiry under David Widdicombe Q.C. recommended further restrictions and these were adopted in two stages in 1986 and 1988.[65] Their net effect is that local authorities are prohibited from publishing, whether directly or through others, material that appears to be designed to affect public support for a political party. The general power that local authorities have of providing information is restricted to information about services provided by the authority, central government, charities or voluntary organisations or to the functions of the authority. The Government can issue Codes of Guidance on local authorities' publicity, to which they must have regard. By contrast, central government retains a wide discretion over its publicity. As the court said when asked to declare that a 1989 leaflet about the poll tax was unlawful, it will interfere only in the most extreme cases where it could be shown that a government department had misstated the law or if a publication was manifestly inaccurate or misleading.[66]

Clause 28

The 1988 Bill also contained the notorious "clause 28". This prohibits a local authority from intentionally promoting homosexuality or publishing material with the intention of promoting homosexuality. It is also prohibited from promoting the teaching in any maintained school of the acceptability of homosexuality as a pretended family relationship. None of the prohibitions apply to anything done for the purpose of treating or preventing the spread of disease.[67] The provision aroused anger at the State's censure of a matter that was essentially one for individual choice, and fear that it would lead to an intensification of discrimination against gay men and lesbian women. The Government insisted that this was not its intention and that local authorities would not be debarred from publishing material to do with homosexuality.

It is doubtful whether section 28 has the consequences that its sponsors desired or its opponents fear. It applies only to local authorities, *i.e.* bodies that have no direct responsibility for, or control over, what

---

[64] *R. v. GLC, ex p. Westminister City Council, The Times,* January 22, 1985 see also *R. v. ILEA, ex p. Westminister City Council* [1986] 1 W.L.R. 28.

[65] Local Government Act 1986, ss. 2–6; Local Government Act 1988, s. 27.

[66] *R. v. Secretary of State, ex p. London Borough of Greenwich, The Independent* May 17, 1989.

[67] Local Government Act 1986, s. 2A added by the Local Government Act 1988, s. 28.

is taught in schools. As a result of the 1986 Education Act, the conduct of maintained schools is under the direction of the governing body and it is the ultimate responsibility of the head teacher to determine and organise the secular curriculum within the framework of the national curriculum. Thus section 28 does not permit teachers to be dismissed for discussing homosexuality sensibly and truthfully. Even where local authorities have an advisory role, section 28 must be read subject to the Education Act, whereby the need "to encourage pupils to have due regard to moral considerations" permits the teaching of tolerance in order to counter pupils' ignorance or hatred of homosexuals.

A local authority does not infringe section 28 unless, at the time it decides to grant funds to a homosexual group, it either desires or is well aware of the fact that its action will "promote homosexuality", *i.e.* result in an increase in the number of homosexuals. It follows that there is nothing to stop a local authority from funding gay youth groups or counselling services where the intention is not to "promote" homosexuality but rather to assist homosexuals to cope with an existing orientation. There is a crucial distinction between promoting homosexuality and promoting tolerance towards homosexuals. In 2000 the provision was amended to make clear that it did not prevent the head teacher or governing body of a maintained school from taking steps to prevent any form of bullying.[68] Nonetheless, section 28 had a chilling effect on a few local authorities, who used it as an excuse for not providing to homosexuals services similar to those provided for other disadvantaged groups. A council that is panicked into misusing section 28 as an excuse for prejudice and discrimination in the provision of services will be open to challenge in the courts. In 2001 the government tried to repeal section 28: it narrowly failed in the House of Lords. The cull of hereditary peers and new appointment arrangements for peers may see its abolition during Labour's second term.

[68] Local Government Act 1986, s. 2A(2)(b) added by the Local Government Act 2000, s. 104.

CHAPTER 13

Reporting Business

Investigative business journalism has an honourable history. The term "muckraker" was first applied by President Theodore Roosevelt to American newspapermen who reported the web of monopolistic practices and price fixing that characterised the heyday of free enterprise. The cabal that operated the meat industry had a particular disregard both for hygiene and for the stomachs of its customers. Upton Sinclair's novel *The Jungle,* set in the meat-packing factories of Chicago, gave a realistic and awesome account. Tinned beef took on a sinister meaning, meat sales dropped by half, and legislation followed as a direct result.[1] Although the United States and Britain now have a wide range of regulatory agencies, they are often stung into effective action only by pressure from the media. Even where no formal action is taken, a press campaign can damage a product's reputation and devastate its sales. Publicity is a potent weapon against businesses that sell to the public, but care must be taken to reserve its use for deserving targets: ruining a business runs the risk of heavier damages than ruining an individual's reputation.

This type of business reporting focuses on production and on dealings with consumers. The financial journalists who write for the business pages will usually be more interested in the efficiency and profitability of companies. Stories of dishonesty and other shady dealings are a speciality of *Private Eye,* whose record for accuracy, in this regard at least, is uncanny. There have been outstanding investigations into the ownership and control of businesses, and the conflict between private advantage and public interest. Investigations of defence contractors and other government suppliers will, of course, have to find their way around the Official Secrets Acts. But the abject failure of British journalism to expose the rottenness of Lloyd's of London or the commercial chicanery of Robert Maxwell until after his death in 1991—failure both of skill in investigation and in courage in the face of libel actions—serves

---

[1] Sinclair intended his novel as an appeal to socialism. He said ruefully: "I aimed at the public's heart and by accident hit it in the stomach". See Robert Downs, *The Jungle* (New American Library, 1960), p. 349.

as a reminder of the blandness and inadequacy of much business coverage.[2]

The non-legal pressures of low budgets, and tedious and often unre-
warding research are common to all investigative reporters. Business
stories have the added hurdle of incurring advertisers' displeasure.
Wales Gas in 1979 withdrew all its advertising from the *North Wales
Western News* because of a critical story about its liquid petroleum gas
depot in Llandudno.[3] W. D. & H. O. Wills cancelled a £500,000 advertising order with *The Sunday Times* when one of its brands was named
as the favourite smoke of a heart transplant patient. In the middle of the
article was an advertisement for the same brand.[4] Pressure from advertisers is usually more subtle: they help to set the newspapers' agenda.[5]
Space given to financial news has expanded dramatically since the war,
in direct correlation with financial advertising, but the stress on company gossip, Stock Exchange activity and tipster articles reflects the
predominance of advertisements for company results, recruitment and
unit trusts.[6] From time to time there are calls for public libraries not to
stock publications in response to their content or the conduct of their
publishers. During the Wapping dispute many local authorities banned
Murdoch papers from their libraries—the High Court ruled that this was
an abuse of power and quashed the decisions.[7]

This chapter will describe the ways in which the law can help
reporters by requiring that certain information is made available to them
and will give a brief outline of the legal structures that a business
reporter will have to understand before advantage can be taken of the
facilities for corporate investigation.

COMPANIES

A beginner's lexicon

The most important form of commercial organisation today is the registered company. It has its own identity, or legal personality, which is

---

[2] Tom Bower, *Maxwell—The Final Verdict* (Harper Collins, 1995).
[3] *Daily Telegraph,* April 19, 1979. See Hartley & Griffith, *Government and the Law*
(2nd ed, Weidenfeld & Nicolson, 1981), p. 281.
[4] *New Statesman,* February 27, 1981.
[5] James Curran, "Advertising and the Press" in James Curran (ed.), *The British Press:
A Manifesto* (Macmillan, 1978), p. 238. Compare Harold Eley's advice to advertisers in 1932, in *Advertising Media,* Butterworths. The Government used its advertising expenditure to influence papers in the early nineteenth century. *The Times* was
particularly vulnerable. (Aspinall, *Politics and the Press 1780–1850,* chap. V).
[6] Curran, *The British Press,* p. 240.
[7] *R. v. Ealing Borough Council, ex p. Times Newspapers Ltd* (1987) 85 L.G.R. 316,
QBD.

distinct from those who contribute its capital or manage its affairs. It can own property, make contracts, and start and defend lawsuits.

Its capital is usually a mixture of long-term loans provided under a formal written agreement called a debenture (by creditors who are thus known as debenture holders) and equity capital. The equity is divided into shares and is held by shareholders, who are also referred to as the members of the company. Loans can be repaid, and commonly bear a fixed rate of interest, although shareholders can be paid a dividend only if the company makes a profit. Preference shares are a hybrid. The holders are members of the company and can take a dividend only if there is a profit. Their payments take priority over those to ordinary shareholders, but their voting rights are usually restricted. The ratio of loan to equity capital is known as the company's gearing and is an important factor in assessing its economic viability.

Most companies are formed by registration with the Companies' Registrar, more commonly referred to as "Companies House". This is an agency within the Department of Trade and Industry (DTI),[8] which exercises supervision over companies (see p. 662 for its powers of investigation). Two documents make up the constitution of a company. Its Memorandum of Association specifies its name, initial shareholders, whether its registered office (the company's formal address) is in England and Wales or Scotland, and its objects. The latter are generally drawn so as to give the company the greatest possible latitude and will not pinpoint what the company actually does. The Articles of Association are like the rules of a club, specifying the respective powers of the shareholders, the board of directors and the managing director. They also regulate the summoning and procedure of meetings of the shareholders and the board. If the rights of shareholders are not uniform, the Articles will also prescribe the rights of each class of shares. To restrict ownership of the shares to a select group, the Articles may also prohibit transfer without the board's consent and confer a right of pre-emption, giving the other shareholders a right of first refusal if one of them wishes to sell out.

Companies can be either private or public. The principal requirement for a public company (signified by "plc" after its name) is that its nominal share capital must be at least £50,000; the main advantage is that it can then raise capital by selling shares to the public at large.[9] Most, but not all, public companies will have a listing or quotation on the Stock Exchange. This makes trading in its shares much easier and consequently increases their value. The Stock Exchange expects a greater degree of frankness from its listed companies, and reporters can

---

[8] For more information, see its website: www.companies-house.gov.uk
[9] Companies Act 1980, s. 4.

gain access to important company documents as a result of its quasi-legal requirements.

When a company wishes to raise equity capital, it announces an issue of new shares. A public company will almost always enlist the services of a financial institution for this purpose. It must produce a prospectus disclosing information required by law and, in the case of quoted companies, by the Stock Exchange. This can offer a valuable window on the company's past record and dealings.

Some offerings of new shares are limited to existing members (rights issue), and some of these are given free (bonus issue), in which case they simply fragment the existing shares into smaller units. Shares are usually issued as "fully paid up", which means that once the company has received the initial price, it has no further claim on the shareholders. In those rare cases where shares are not fully paid, the company can make a "call" for the balance. A nominal value is attached to each share. Shares are issued at par if this is also their actual selling price, or at a premium if they are above par; they cannot be issued at a discount. A company cannot generally buy or finance the purchase of its own shares, although this prohibition was relaxed in 1981.

The directors of a company are fiduciaries, which means they owe a duty of trust to the company and must not allow themselves to get in a position where their personal interest conflicts with the company's—or at least not without making full disclosure to the board or its members. Although the most powerful members will have representatives on the board, they cannot ignore the interests of the minority. The court, for instance, prevented Lord and Lady Kagan, the majority shareholders, from compelling Kagan Textiles Ltd to accept the blame for fraudulent trading in indigo dye with which Lord Kagan was also charged. This would have been a fraud on the minority shareholders. Directors also have a legal duty to take account of their employees' interests.

The most attractive feature of a company for an investor is the limited liability that it usually enjoys. However small the company—even if it is run by only one person—creditors cannot normally sue the shareholders or the management if the company has insufficient assets to pay its debts. Institutional lenders, like banks and finance houses, that are not satisfied with the creditworthiness of the company will bind the principal shareholders through a guarantee. William Stern a 1970s property tycoon, for instance, guaranteed his companies' debts and so became personally liable when they could not pay. He could not pay either, and his bankruptcy in 1978 (discharged in 1985) was the largest there had then been. Major lenders, in particular those lending long-term capital, will also condition their co-operation on the provision of security. This usually is a mortgage on the business's fixed assets, such as land and machinery, and a floating charge on the circulating assets (those that are bought and sold, accounts receivable, etc.). The lender then has a right to claim this property to satisfy the debt, although other unsecured creditors may be left with only pennies in the pound. Debentures almost invariably include both types of security.

Ownership and control

Registers of share and debenture holders

At first blush it seems an easy matter to find out who owns a company. Every member's shareholding is registered and the register is a public document.[10] If the shares are divided into classes, the register will show to which class each shareholder belongs.[11] If a company has more than 50 members, it must also maintain an index of them. This must be kept at the same place as the register.[12] If a company has issued debentures and maintains a register of debenture-holders, this must also be open for public inspection.[13] The shares may be registered in the name of another company. If this is registered in the United Kingdom, the procedure can be repeated. If it is incorporated in other countries with similar disclosure requirements, the chase can be pursued, albeit more expensively. But if it is the creature of tax havens such as Belize or the Cayman Islands, the scent will be lost. As well as charging very little tax, these countries allow investors to preserve a veil of secrecy around their holdings by laws that have virtually no disclosure requirements.

Real ownership

Frequently, the registered shareholder is only a nominee for some other person who is really or beneficially entitled to the shares. Many banks have companies holding shares for their clients that include the word "nominee" in their name. It will then be apparent from the register of such companies that someone else is beneficially entitled to the shares. This will not always be the case with other nominees. A shareholder has generally no obligation to tell the company that it is acting as a nominee.

Automatic registration

Parliament has created exceptions to this principle. Public companies must be notified if anyone has a beneficial interest in 3 per cent[14] of their shares that carry unrestricted voting rights. This obligation arises

---

[10] Companies Act 1985, s. 356.
[11] *ibid.*, s. 352.
[12] *ibid.*, s. 354.
[13] *ibid.*, s. 190–1.
[14] Companies Act 1989, s. 134(2).

when the member knows or learns that the holding has reached the required percentage.[15] It was the failure of a NatWest subsidiary to report that its holding in Blue Arrow had crossed the 5 per cent threshold that led in 1989 to a highly critical report by Department of Trade and Industry inspectors and the resignation of the bank's chairman. The requirement does not extend to debentures (which have no voting rights). A person has an interest if the shares are held by his or her family or a company that they control, or if they have an option over them.[16] Agreements amongst shareholders to accumulate a 3 per cent holding between them must also be notified.[17] This was in response to preparations for the "dawn raid" on Consolidated Gold Fields, when a group of investors each accumulated just under the declarable percentage of shares before making a sudden bid for control of the company. The 3 per cent threshold applies to material interests in shares. If this is not crossed, but the total value of shares in which a person has an interest (whether material or not) is 10 per cent or more, a similar duty to notify applies.[18]

When the shareholding reaches the notification mark, the company must be told the names in which the shares are registered, the size of the interest and any dealings in the shares.[19] It must maintain a register of the information it receives; this must be indexed and open to public inspection for at least two hours a day. Inspection is free. Copies can be charged for but must be provided within 10 days.[20]

Investigations by the company

The above transactions must be reported automatically to the company. In addition, the company can act on its own initiative to identify its real shareholders and others with interests in the shares.[21] These powers apply to all public companies. The inquiries can relate to shareholders over the previous three years. They can be asked about agreements to buy up shares or to vote in concert. Where shares are held in a United Kingdom company through a United Kingdom nominee holder, the

---

[15] Companies Act 1985, ss. 198–210. This applies not just to those companies with a Stock Exchange listing. The shareholder's brokers cannot maintain a discreet silence about their clients' acquisitions and dispositions. They are under a duty to inform them of these (s. 210).

[16] *ibid.*, s. 203 (families); s. 208 (options).

[17] *ibid.*, ss. 204–5.

[18] Disclosure of Interests in Shares (Amendment) Regulations 1993, S.I. 1993 No. 1819.

[19] *ibid.*, s. 202. The company must be told within two days.

[20] *ibid.*, s. 211 (register), s. 219 (inspection). There is an exemption for companies carrying on business, or with subsidiaries, overseas where disclosure would be harmful to business, s. 211(9).

[21] *ibid.*, s. 212.

company's right to discover the beneficial owners of its shares under this provision applies even though the beneficiary has no other connection with the United Kingdom.[22] A holder of shares who is obliged to provide this information cannot avoid his duty to answer by undertaking to sell the shares.[23] If the directors are reluctant to delve into these secrets, they can be compelled to do so by the holders of one-tenth of the voting capital.[24] These requests and their answers (so far as they relate to present interests in shares) must be recorded in a separate part of the 3 per cent register, and must be kept for six years.[25] Some company secretaries have been reluctant to let journalists see this part of the register, but it is clear that the Act requires it to be public and it is clear, too, that this obligation exists whether or not the true owners are shown to have a holding of 3 per cent.

Although the initiative rests with a company to demand disclosure of this kind, the information obtained may have a spill-over effect. Institutional nominees often use the same account number for all the shares bought by them for a particular client. Sometimes the entry on the register will include this number, and so might appear as "X Bank Nominees Acc No 12345". Once one company investigation has identified the owner of an account number, it would not be surprising if the same code in other company registers concealed the same owner. An index of such nominees has been published.[26]

The obligation to require nominees to disclose the names of their clients is principally intended to avoid surprise changes of control. For journalists, however, these registers present a wider opportunity. Owners of shares cannot maintain complete secrecy about their investments, and those who receive a share of the profits from companies that have been the target of widespread public criticism may deserve to find some of that criticism turned in their direction.

Major shareholdings by companies

Sometimes, further clues as to a company's ownership can be traced in the accounts of other companies. Companies are required to note holdings that amount to one-tenth or more of the voting or total capital in another company.[27] Banking and insurance[28] are excepted. One further

---

[22] *Re FH Lloyd Holdings plc* [1985] B.C.L.C. 293.
[23] *Re Geers Gross* [1987] 1 W.L.R. 1649.
[24] Companies Act 1985, s. 214.
[25] *ibid.*, s. 213 (register); s. 217 (six years).
[26] Richard Bellfield and Christopher Hird, *The Index of Nominees and their Beneficial Owners* (9th ed., Fulcrum Research edited by Richard Davies, 2000).
[27] Companies Act 1985, Sched. 5, paras 7–13.
[28] *ibid.*, s. 257; until the Companies Act 1989, the exemption applied to shipping companies as well.

defect in these provisions for the investigator is that they apply only to shares held at the end of the accounting company's financial year. If a company wished, it could "board out" its holdings by lodging them with someone else for the critical few days and lawfully omit any reference to them. A second drawback is that as part of the accounting requirements, the directors can leave out this information if it would be excessive and the ownership of the shares did not materially affect the company's financial position.[29]

Directors' dealings

Shareholdings in their companies

It is accepted that directors will want some stake in the enterprise they manage, but the dangers of this are recognised and their dealings are circumscribed. They cannot, for instance, agree to buy or sell their company's shares for delivery on a future date, and they are restricted in their use of inside information for their own advantage.[30] In addition, directors must make public their holdings in the shares and debentures of the company or its associated companies. They cannot avoid this duty by farming out their shares to spouses or children, or by trying to hide behind a trustee or nominee owner of the shares because these holdings must also be reported. Nor can they evade the restrictions by taking shares in a parent, subsidiary or sibling company.[31] Any change in their holding must be reported. Most importantly, directors must disclose the price at which their shares or debentures were bought or sold.[32] This registered information must also be indexed and remain open to public inspection.[33]

Contracts of service

Shareholders are also entitled to see copies of a director's contract of service with the company.[34] In the case of companies quoted on the Stock Exchange the public are entitled to see these in two circumstances. The listing agreement, which every quoted company makes with the Stock Exchange, obliges it to make service contracts available "to any person" at its registered office and for at least 15 minutes before

---

[29] Companies Act 1985, Sched. 5, para. 11.

[30] *ibid.,* ss. 323 and 327.

[31] *ibid.,* s. 324 and Sched. 13.

[32] *ibid.,* Sched. 13, para. 17(2).

[33] *ibid.,* s. 325 and Sched. 13, Pt IV. The directors' report will also include details of shareholdings by board members at the year's end, *ibid.,* Sched. 7, para. 2.

[34] *ibid.,* s. 318; unless the contract has less than 12 months to run or the company can terminate the contract within 12 months without paying compensation.

the AGM.[35] The company must disclose full particulars of remuneration including salary and other benefits, commission or profit sharing, any provision for early retirement and any other arrangements necessary to establish the company's possible liability on early retirement of a director. One intention behind these requirements is that those planning a takeover or a coup within the company can assess how much compensation directors will have to be paid for the premature termination of their contracts. However, the contracts can make interesting reading to those sharpening pens rather than long knives (one service contract, for instance, revealed that a director was required to take his wife with him whenever he made an overseas visit). The chairman's earnings must be stated in the annual accounts.[36]

Interests in company contracts

Other contracts or arrangements with the company in which a director has a material interest must be disclosed in the company's annual accounts. In particular, the accounts must disclose any loan, guarantee or credit transaction that a company has made for the benefit of a director or officer.[37] The circumstances in which the company is permitted to enter into these types of transactions are, in any event, narrowly defined.[38] They do include the giving of financial assistance to allow a director to buy a house. One company put up about £140,000 for a £200,000 house. No doubt to maximise the tax advantage, director and company owned the house together. The company would enjoy a share of the capital gain in the house and the director was to pay £23 per week for the privilege of living in a mansion. Since directors must disclose their home addresses, an enterprising journalist was able to publish details of the company's generosity alongside a photograph of the residence in question.[39]

Directors' organisations have lobbied hard for removal of the need to disclose home addresses and have cited the harassment and intimidation at the homes of directors of some companies (such as those involved with experiments on animals). The Government responded by including section 45 in the Criminal Justice and Police Act 2001—a

---

[35] Listing Rules of the London Stock Exchange (last updated December 1997) 16.9–16.11.

[36] Companies Act 1985, Sched. 5, para. 24(2). The earnings of the highest paid director must also be stated if this was more than the chairman's: para. 25(3)–(5). There are exemptions where the board as a whole did not earn more than £60,000 (unless a holding or subsidiary company) or where the chairman/director's job was mainly overseas.

[37] *ibid.*, ss. 232, 233.

[38] *ibid.*, s. 330.

[39] *New Statesman*, July 24, 1981.

provision for the Secretary of State to make a "confidentiality order". Before doing so he must be satisfied that if the director's usual residential address was open to public inspection there would be a serious risk that he or a person who lives with him would be subjected to violence or intimidation.[40]

Other directorships

The interlocking interests of directors with other companies cannot be so easily traced. However, the company must record present directorships of its board members in the other corporations and any past directorships over the previous five years. The register is also publicly available.[41] Details of changes should also be included in the company's annual return.

Economic performance

Accounts to be published

Since one of the principal aims of the disclosure requirements is to permit investors and creditors to judge the economic performance of a company, it may not seem surprising that the law lays great emphasis on company accounts, the overriding requirement of which is that they should give a true and fair view of the company's financial state of affairs and profit and loss in the relevant financial year.[42] However, it has been a hard-fought battle; it was only in 1967 that private as well as public companies were required to prepare accounts, and only in 1976 that these had to be made public.[43]

Since then, there has been serious back-sliding. "Small" companies (which must now have at least two of the following: a balance sheet total of less than £1.4 million; turnover of less than £2.8 million; fewer than 50 employees) need not prepare a profit and loss account and only a perfunctory balance sheet is required. They have no duty to submit a directors' report. "Medium" size companies (with two of the following: balance sheet total less than £5.6 million; turnover less than £1.2 million; fewer than 250 employees) have to provide the normal directors'

---

[40] Criminal Justice and Police Act 2001, s. 45 adding s. 723B to Companies Act 1985.
[41] Companies Act 1985, s. 289.
[42] *ibid.*, s. 226(2).
[43] Companies Act 1976, s. 1. Companies without limited liability could still keep their accounts to themselves, a qualification that spawned new interest in what hitherto had been an historical curiosity. Following the Companies Act 1989, s. 7, the conditions on which the exemptions are dependent are more restrictive: see s. 254 of Companies Act 1985.

report and balance sheet, but are allowed to submit a modified profit and loss account and need not give a breakdown of turnover.[44] "Small" and "medium" sized groups of companies have similar relief from the duty to provide group accounts.[45] In 1999 it was estimated that about 90 per cent of all registered companies qualified as "small".[46] Investors, creditors and journalists will all be the worse off, particularly as information about a private company that is not required to be disclosed by law will generally be protected from disclosure by the courts on grounds of confidence.

Banking and insurance companies are also exempt from particularising their accounts, but they are subjected to much more rigorous scrutiny by the Department of Trade and Industry.[47] When they are quoted companies they also have to comply with the listing requirements of the Stock Exchange, which requires disclosure in line with accounting standards.

Auditors

The accounts that a company prepares must be professionally audited. The auditor's report must be sent with the accounts to the Companies Registry, where it is open to inspection.[48] However, even this requirement is qualified. Small companies no longer have to have their accounts audited,[49] nor do small groups.[50] Auditors are in a difficult position. They are hired by the directors, but their responsibilities are

---

[44] Companies Act 1985, s. 247, Sched. 8 (duties), s. 248 (definitions). The amounts have been increased from time to time.

[45] Companies Act 1985, s. 249. The exemption applies if either the parent company meets the requirements for individual companies or if the group as a whole satisfies two or more of the following (small first, medium in brackets): aggregate turnover: £2.8 million net or £3.6 million gross (£11.2 million net or £13.44 million gross); aggregate balance sheet total: £1.4 million net or £1.68 million gross (£5.6 million net or £6.72 million gross); employees 50 (250). A group cannot be exempt if it includes a bank insurance company or an authorised person under the Financial Services Act 1986.

[46] *Companies in 1998–99* (HMSO, 1999) Cmnd. 9794, para. 8.5.

[47] Companies Act 1985, ss. 255, 255A and Sched. 9.

[48] *ibid.*, auditor's report: s. 235 (as amended by the Companies Act 1989, s. 9); duty to send to registrar: ss. 239 and 242 (as amended by the Companies Act 1989, s. 11); inspection: s. 709. For a good account of the auditor's role see Leonard Leigh, *The Control of Commercial Fraud* (Heinemann, 1982), pp. 208–18.

[49] Companies Act 1985, s. 249A. For these purposes a company not only has to be "small" for the purposes of the accounting exemption (see above) but its turnover must be not more than £1 million and its balance sheet total not more than £1.4 million.

[50] *ibid.*, s. 249B. For these pruposes collective turnover must be less than £1 million net (or £1.2 million gross) and balance sheet total of not more than £1.4 million net (£1.68 million gross).

to the investors, creditors and the public at large. Qualifying the accounts may make the auditors unpopular with the board. Consequently, they can be sacked only by the shareholders and they have a statutory right to put their case to a shareholders' meeting.[51] The auditors are precluded from slipping out quietly to avoid an impending disaster: on resigning they must certify that their departure has nothing to do with the state of the company's affairs, or, alternatively, they must explain in full the circumstances that have impelled them to leave.[52] Some solve the dilemma of effectively serving both board and shareholders by adding an inscrutable or unfathomable qualification to the accounts. Others simply ignore the requirements. A study in 1999 reported that of 766 resignation letters to publicly-listed companies between 1988–92, only 19 contained any matters relevant to shareholders or creditors even though in 108 cases resignation followed qualified audited reports.[53]

Even if all auditors were honest and efficient, there are practical limits on the checks that can be run. In a large company the auditors can at best run only sample spot checks on stock values and other realities behind the figures presented to them by the company. There have been a number of scandals where grave irregularities have not been spotted by auditors. Ironically, the growing practice among auditors of over-cautiously qualifying the accounts may diminish the impact of any warning they mean to deliver.

Directors' report

Attached to the accounts must also be a report by the directors.[54] This report must give a "fair review of the business of the company and its subsidiaries during the financial year", particulars of any important events affecting the business during the year and an indication of likely future developments.[55] These obligations tend to produce bland reports. The Stock Exchange regulations require a much more detailed report from quoted companies.[56] This frequently takes the form of a chairperson's statement, which is published in the financial press.

More concretely, the report must note significant changes in the values of the company's fixed assets, record any interests held by directors in the company's shares at the end of the financial year, and

---

[51] Companies Act 1985, ss. 386 and 387.
[52] *ibid.*, s. 390; the resignation statement must be sent to the Registry where it can be inspected, *ibid.*, s. 709.
[53] *Palmer's Company Law,* para. 9.514.
[54] Companies Act 1985, s. 237.
[55] *ibid.*, and Sched. 7.
[56] Stock Exchange Admission of Securities to Listing, s. 5.

report details of any shares in the company that the company itself owns.

Political pressure has achieved an odd assortment of additional disclosure obligations. The most interesting is the requirement to disclose political donations over £200, which was re-vamped in 2000.[57] The identity of the donee and the total amount of the contributions must be disclosed where the beneficiary is a registered political party or other E.U. political organisation.[58] The company must also disclose the total amount of "E.U. political expenditure".[59] Contributions to non-E.U. political parties must also be disclosed.

The 2000 Act additionally requires a company to have advance approval of the members in general meeting before making donations to E.U. political organisations or before incurring E.U. political expenditure. In both cases the company's resolution must specify the maximum amount of donations or expenditure. Groups of shareholders are given new rights to take legal action if these requirements are infringed.[60]

The company's annual report must also disclose the total amount donated for charitable purposes if this exceeds £200.[61] Additionally, the directors' report must note any research or development activities, and information specified by regulations concerning health and safety at work. If the company employs over 250 people, the report must give an account of the company's policies for hiring disabled people and for consulting employees.[62]

Public share issue

In addition to these regular reports, a company must expose its financial performance to further scrutiny if it intends to issue shares for public sale. Requirements are imposed by law[63] and by the Financial Services

---

[57] Political Parties, Elections and Referendums Act 2000, ss. 140 substituting paras 3–4 in Companies Act 1985, Sched. 7.

[58] Defined in Companies Act 1985, s. 347A(6) and (7) as essentially political parties in a Member State other than the U.K. or organisations (whether or not in the U.K.) intended to affect public support for a political party or independent candidates or to influence voters in a national or regional referendum in a Member State.

[59] Defined in Companies Act 1985, s. 347A(5) in terms which embrace political advertising, promotional or publicity material in support of any E.U. political organisation.

[60] See Companies Act 1985, Part XA.

[61] Companies Act 1985, Sched. 7, para. 5 as substituted by Political Parties, Elections and Referendums Act 2000, s. 140.

[62] Companies Act 1985, Sched. 7. There are no regulations yet concerning health and safety at work.

[63] Principally the Financial Services and Markets Act 2000, Pt VI for listed securities and Public Offers of Securities Regulations 1995, S.I. 1995 No. 1537, for unlisted securities.

Authority. The Authority will in due course make its own Listing Rules but in the meantime the London Stock Exchange's requirements in *The Yellow Book* (*The Admission of Securities to Listing*) impose parallel requirements. The details are complex but their net effect is that the company must issue a public document setting out in considerable detail its past performance and expectations.

Penalties for non-compliance

Non-compliance has proved an endemic problem. The introduction of standard civil penalties (effectively fines) for companies who fail to submit accounts on time has helped.[64] By 1999 it was estimated that 95.4 per cent of companies were up to date. But even so, in the year to March 1999 over 100,000 were fined for late filing. A company may fail to comply with its duty because it is inefficient or because it does have something to hide. If reporters ask company secretaries for copies of the documents that should have been filed and they refuse to co-operate, this can safely be mentioned in the story. It will not improve confidence in the company's management.

Inspecting public documents

Not all the public documents and registers can be consulted in the same place. Some are kept at the Companies Registry—known also as Companies House—with branches in London and Cardiff. Some are kept at the particular company's registered office or at a more convenient nominated address.[65] Most of the large public companies nominate a bank to maintain their public documents. This address, or the address of the registered office, will appear in a statement that is lodged with the Registrar prior to the company's formation. The company can change its registered office but must notify the Registrar within 14 days.[66]

- *At the registered office:* registers and indices of shareholdings[67]; debenture holders[68]; directors' shareholdings[69]; 3-per-cent shareholders[70]; directors' contracts[71] (when available).

---

[64] Companies Act 1985, s. 242A.
[65] *ibid.*, s. 353.
[66] *ibid.*, s. 287.
[67] *ibid.*, ss. 352, 353.
[68] *ibid.*, ss. 190, 191.
[69] *ibid.*, Sched. 13, para. 25.
[70] *ibid.*, s. 211(8)
[71] Listing Rules of the London Stock Exchange—see above.

- *At Companies House:* annual accounts, reports of auditors and directors,[72] annual return of changes in shareholdings,[73] Memorandum and Articles of Association.[74]

- *At both:* list of directors (including other directorships) and company secretary; register of charges.[75]

- *At the Company's AGM:* any person attending the AGM is entitled to inspect the register of directors' interests.[76]

Companies House keeps records going back five years on microfiche. There are four parts: general (Memorandum and Articles of Association, list of directors and secretary); annual return (accounts, reports, changes in shareholding); mortgage documents; register of charges. Mortgages are not just of interest to cautious moneylenders. It was by inspecting this section of the fiche for Times Newspapers Ltd that *Sunday Times* journalists discovered in 1982 that Rupert Murdoch had transferred the title of the papers to another of his companies and away from TNL (where it could not have been sold without the approval of a board of directors independent of Murdoch). The ensuing outcry forced Murdoch to transfer the titles back.[77]

Records over five years old must be consulted at Cardiff. Journalists offered illegible copies have a right to see the originals unless they are over 10 years old, in which case the documents will probably have been destroyed.[78]

A journalist, like other members of the public[79] can be charged a fee for inspecting these documents. The fees are now set by regulations which currently allow a charge of £2.50.[80] Companies House charges £5 for inspection of a basic set of microfiches.[81]

The right to inspect includes the right in all cases (except directors' contracts) to have copies made. A company can charge for this at the rate of £2.50 for the first 100 entries, £20 for the next 1,000 and £15 for every subsequent 1,000. These charges apply to registers and reports. Copies of other documents are assessed at 10p per 100 words.[82]

---

[72] Companies Act 1985, ss. 239, 241.
[73] *ibid.*, s. 363.
[74] *ibid.*, ss. 10, 18.
[75] *ibid.*, s. 288 (directors and company secretary), s. 401 (charges).
[76] *ibid.*, Sched. 13, para. 29.
[77] *New Statesman,* February 18, 1982.
[78] Companies Act 1985, ss. 709, 715.
[79] Though not members of the company who can inspect without charge.
[80] Companies (Inspection and Copying of Registers, Indices and Documents) Regulations 1991, S.I. 1991 No. 1998.
[81] Companies (Fees) Regulations 1991, S.I. 1991 No. 1206, as amended.
[82] Companies (Inspection and Copying of Registers, Indices and Documents) Regulations (above).

Journalists can economise by asking for a copy of only a part of the register or document that is needed. However the regulations do say that companies cannot be required to make available details of members or debenture holders sorted by geographical location of their addresses, their nationality, whether the holdings are of a certain size, whether they are natural or legal persons (such as companies) or their gender.[83] Journalists can avoid any charge for copying by making their own notes or transcriptions and the regulations specifically allow for this.[84] Copies of those documents which are kept at Companies House can be obtained by personal attendance (charge £5.00) or requests can be made online (£8.00) or copies can be posted (also £8.00).[85]

Meetings

Most Annual General Meetings of the shareholders of public companies are formal occasions. The institutional investors, who tend to be the predominant shareholders, generally prefer to exercise their influence behind the scenes. In the absence of a crisis, items on the agenda are passed "on the nod" and the running of the company is left to the directors. Nevertheless, the law gives important residual powers to other shareholders, including a right, which cannot be taken away from them, to dismiss the directors.[86] If the company has been performing poorly or if a takeover is in the air, the shareholders' meetings may be the place for tough questioning. In addition, public interest groups have sometimes purchased a single share in a company in order to attend a shareholders' meeting and to challenge the board about the social consequences of its policies.

Journalists have no right to attend a general meeting, although they are frequently invited. If the press and public are excluded, reporters may gain admission by buying a share in the company or persuading an existing shareholder to allow them to attend as a proxy.

If there is a crisis and the exchanges become heated, there is more likely to be a newsworthy story. The risk of a writ for defamation is minimal because in the case of the general meeting of a public company the press and broadcast media have a statutory qualified privilege.[87] The statutory privilege was widened in 1996 so that it now extends to the publication of fair and accurate extracts from any document circulated

---

[83] Companies (Inspection and Copying of Registers, Indices and Documents) Regulations 1991, S.I. 1999 No. 1998, reg. 4(3).

[84] *ibid.*, reg. 3(2)(b)—although the journalist would need to be ready to be self-sufficient—a company cannot be required to provide facilities for this form of note taking—*ibid.*, reg. 3(3).

[85] Companies (Fees) Regulations 1991 as amended.

[86] Companies Act 1985, s. 303.

[87] Defamation Act 1996, s. 15 and Sched. 1, para. 13(1).

to members of a United Kingdom public company by or with the authority of the board, by the auditors or by any member in pursuance of a member exercising a statutory right.[88] In addition, there is the same privilege for a fair and accurate extract from any document circulated to members of a United Kingdom public company which relates to the appointment, resignation, retirement or dismissal of directors of the company.[89] The "United Kingdom" does not normally include the Channel Islands or the Isle of Man, but in this context the same privilege extends to reports of the equivalent meetings and documents of public companies established either in these territories or in other Member States.[90] The privilege is destroyed by malice, or by a refusal of the publisher or broadcaster to print a reasonable letter or statement by way of explanation or contradiction if required by the person defamed (see p. 136).

The privilege does not apply to private companies' meetings.

If for some reason the defence of privilege failed, the publisher or broadcaster could always fall back on the general defences of truth or fair comment. "Fair comment" can be made only if the matter is of public interest. The affairs of the public company would certainly be of public interest. So, too, would those of a private company if they concerned the reliability of, or deficiencies in, its public documents or the social impact of the company's policies.

Takeovers

Takeover battles present another opportunity for journalists to find out more about the internal workings of quoted companies. A great deal of financial and other information about both predator and prey must be disclosed. It has already been noted that directors' service contracts are publicly available during this period. The rules are primarily intended to ensure that all the participants have common access to certain basic information, and the role of the press in disseminating this information is acknowledged. Thus a company can hold meetings with selected shareholders to explain the terms of an offer only if the press is invited.[91]

These obligations are contained in the Stock Exchange Regulations and the City Code on Takeovers and Mergers. Particularly in the case of the City Code, the sanctions for breach lack sufficient bite to deter some financiers from conducting secretive and shady manoeuvres. The

---

[88] Defamation Act 1996, Sched. 1, para. 13(2).
[89] *ibid.*, para. 13(3).
[90] *ibid.*, para. 13(5).
[91] City Code on Takeovers and Mergers. The 6th edition was published on July 12, 2000, with subsequent amendments.

abolition of exchange control has allowed greater access to markets by overseas enterprises, which have even less to fear from the wrath of the City's institutions.[92] Like the Press Complaints Commission, the Stock Exchange and the Takeover Panel lack the power to compel attendance of witnesses, the production of books or the giving of evidence. Their private and confidential investigations of suspected rule violations depend entirely on voluntary co-operation.[93]

The Code discourages participants in a takeover bid from appearing on television programmes. The excuse is that the subtleties of the bid will be lost in a simplified discussion although the result is to confine knowledge to city insiders and to minimise critical media coverage. The Code recommends that interviews should be given only if they are recorded and then only on condition that there is no editing and that a transcript is provided before the broadcast. A panel discussion between offeror and offeree or between competing bodies sends shivers down the City Panel's spine: it deprecates anything resembling gladiatorial combat.[94] These views do not reflect any legal requirement, but they may explain why participants in a merger battle are reluctant to put their case to a television test. This attitude is antediluvian and diminishes the legitimate role that the broadcast media should play in exploring the public interest consequences of takeover. A spate of knocking-copy advertisements in 1985 led the panel to prohibit all advertisements in connection with a takeover offer unless they fell within narrowly drawn exemptions.[95]

PRESS MONOPOLIES

Over the last 40 years the process of concentration of newspaper ownership in Britain has developed alarmingly, to the extent that Britain has one of the most concentrated newspaper ownership arrangements in the Western World. The danger of such monopolistic tendencies was identified by the first Royal Commission on the Press in the following terms:

> "The monopolist, by its selection of the news and the manner in which it reports it, and by its commentary on public affairs, is in a position to determine what people shall read about the events

---

[92] Leigh, *Commercial Fraud,* p. 192. Even criminal penalties are difficult to apply to foreign companies.
[93] *ibid.,* p. 93.
[94] City Code, Rule 19.6.
[95] *ibid.,* Rule 19.4.

and issues of the day, and to exert a strong influence on their opinions. Even if this position is not consciously abused, a paper without competitors may fall below the standards of accuracy and efficiency which competition enforces."[96]

In 1965 the Government gave additional powers to the Board of Trade (subsequently, to the Secretary of State for Trade) to refer proposed newspaper mergers to the Competition Commission (formerly the Monopolies Commission). The procedure is set out in sections 57–62 of the Fair Trading Act 1973. The minister is, in certain circumstances, required to refer newspaper sales or mergers to the Competition Commission. The Commission must report back to the minister within three months on:

"whether the transfer in question may be expected to operate against the public interest, taking into account all matters which appear in the circumstances to be relevant and, in particular, the need for accurate presentation of news and free expression of opinion."[97]

Transfers of newspapers to proprietors whose existing press interests (together with the acquired newspaper) have a circulation in excess of 500,000 copies per day are unlawful without the consent of the Secretary of State. Normally, the Secretary of State must refer the proposal to the Competition Commission, but he need not do so if the newspaper concerned has a circulation of less than 50,000 copies.[98] The Secretary of State must give his consent without a report from the Commission and without conditions if satisfied that the newspaper to be acquired is "not economic as a going concern" and is not going to continue as a separate title.[99]

The Monopolies Commission was involved in an important test case by the 1966 application to sell *The Times* to the Thomson Organisation. In spite of being the owner of two television companies, 33 newspapers (including *The Sunday Times*), 62 magazines and numerous other interests in publishing, Lord Thomson's purchase of *The Times* from Lord Astor met with the Commission's approval. Dealing with the question of concentration of ownership, the Commission admitted in its report to Parliament that Thomson's takeover of *The Times* would be a continuation of the movement towards concentration in the ownership of the press, which must ultimately tend to stifle the expression of variety of opinion. The

---

[96] Royal Commission on the Press, Cmnd. 7700 (1949) para. 274.
[97] Fair Trading Act 1973, s. 59(3).
[98] *ibid.*, s. 58(4).
[99] *ibid.*, s. 58(3)(b).

report went on, however, to say that the Commission did "not consider that the proposed transfer would lead to an undue concentration of newspaper power". It was equally tolerant when laying down the conditions that were to be attached to any transfer of ownership of *The Times*. Although recognising that a proposal to put four "national figures" on the main board of Times Newspapers Ltd would be merely "window dressing"—"no more than a declaration of good intent by the Thomson Organisation designed to reassure the public"—the Commission agreed to the proposal on the grounds that it could devise nothing better.[1]

In 1981 Times Newspapers was sold to Rupert Murdoch, thereby concentrating a large amount of national newspaper power in one controversial pair of hands. Ownership of *The Sun* and *The Times* gave Murdoch a 30 per cent share of daily newspaper readership, while *The Sunday Times* and the *News of the World* added up to a 36 per cent share of Sunday readership. The ethical record of Murdoch's British papers was questionable, and his reputation in Australia and America for interfering with editorial independence and exploiting his papers for political purposes raised serious doubts about whether the takeover could serve the public interest. All these matters could, and should, have been investigated by the Commission, on a reference from the Secretary of State for Trade, John Biffen.

The exemption where the minister is satisfied that the newspaper to be purchased is "not economic as a going concern" may have been an accurate description of *The Times,* but it was not of *The Sunday Times.* The journalists of *The Sunday Times* were advised by Queen's Counsel that there was a compelling case for obliging the minister to refer the sale to the Commission. Proceedings were started but were dropped two days before the case was due to be heard—largely through the journalists' concern at the risk of legal costs should it be fought through all appellate stages.[2]

In March 1981, a few weeks after *The Times* takeover, Atlantic Richfield, the American oil company that had owned the *Observer* since 1976, announced that it was selling the paper to Mr "Tiny" Rowland of Lonrho. Once again, efforts were made by the parties to avoid any detailed examination of the nature of the takeover. Although its tendency to concentrate ownership was much less dramatic than Rupert Murdoch's acquisition of Times Newspapers, Mr Biffen this time agreed to refer the matter to the Monopolies and Mergers Commission. The Commission recommended that the transfer be allowed provided,

---

[1] The Monopolies Commission: *The Times Newspaper and the Sunday Times Newspaper,* (1966) House of Commons Paper No. 273, especially paras 162–3, 176.

[2] The sorry story is told in some detail by Harold Evans, *Good Times, Bad Times,* (Weidenfeld & Nicolson, 1983), Chap. 7, "Biffin's Missing Millions". See also William Shawcross, *Murdoch* (Chatto, 1992) pp. 231–235.

amongst other things, that "independent directors" were appointed by Lonrho. It accepted that:

" . . . the proposed transfer involving a major provincial publisher acquiring a national title does represent yet another move in the continuing growth of concentration of ownership of provincial and national newspapers, which was seriously increased by the recent acquisition of *The Times* and *Sunday Times* by companies controlled by Mr Rupert Murdoch."[3]

The refusal by the Government to refer the takeover of Times Newspapers to the Monopolies and Mergers Commission illustrates the inadequacy of the referral procedure embodied in the Fair Trading Act as a method of scrutinising concentrations of ownership. Biffen's refusal to refer was plainly unlawful, but when the journalists dropped their case, there was nobody prepared to ask the courts to enforce the law. The Attorney-General, as guardian of the public interest, refused a request to guard it against dereliction by his fellow minister. If the Commission is to properly oversee monopolistic tendencies in the press, a number of amendments to the Fair Trading Act would be required.

At present the law allows the Secretary of State to give unconditional consent to a transfer without reference to the Competition Commission if satisfied that the newspaper to be sold is "not economic as a going concern". The very fact that the Government could decide, in 1981, that *The Sunday Times* fell into this category, on the basis of highly questionable projections of future income supplied by parties to the sale who were eager to avoid a referral, shows how easily the requirements may be side-stepped. Where the intention is to keep the newspaper alive as a separate publication (a fact that would normally indicate that it was a viable economic proposition), the minister may consent if "the case is one of urgency".[4] Again, in the *Sunday Times* case, that urgency was dictated by the timetable devised by the parties to the transaction. In cases where the intention is to close the newspaper, or to absorb it under a rival title, the minister has no alternative but to give unconditional consent to the sale.[5] Such transactions can sometimes be avoided by arrangements that still give the selling proprietor a reasonable recompense.

If the Competition Commission is to have effective control over concentrations of ownership in the newspaper industry, all such loopholes in the Fair Trading Act will need to be closed. Whether the paper is

---

[3] *The Observer and George Outram & Co Ltd,* House of Commons Paper No. 378, Chap. 8, para. 33.
[4] Fair Trading Act 1973, s. 58(3)(a).
[5] *ibid.*, s. 58(3)(b).

"economic as a going concern" would then be one of the factors the
Commission could take into account in deciding whether to recommend
the transfer, after its own independent assessment of the viability of the
newspaper's future and after considering any alternative offers that
would preserve publication or avoid further concentration of ownership.

The public interest test that the Commission has applied in its reports
on newspaper transfers since 1965 is also unsatisfactory. Under the Fair
Trading Act it is required to report on "whether the transfer in question
may be expected to operate against the public interest".[6] The burden of
proving this speculation falls upon opponents of the transfers. As the
third Royal Commission on the Press pointed out: "In individual cases
it is almost impossible to establish this to the Commission's satisfaction
and in none of the cases so far referred has it been established".[7] That
Royal Commission recommended that the Monopolies and Mergers
Commission should reverse its onus of proof: it should withhold
approval unless positively satisfied that the merger would *not* operate
against the public interest. This is the test applied in other restrictive
trade practices legislation, and the Royal Commission believed it would
"provide a more satisfactory basis for judgment by the Commission".

One important aspect in a newspaper transfer is, as all Royal Commissions have recognised, the danger of creating an imbalance in the
political affiliations of the press. Newspapers have, as the Press Council
has continually held, a right to be politically partisan; but it must surely
be against the public interest if press outlets in a particular area, or in
the nation as a whole, come to favour overwhelmingly one particular
side of the political spectrum as a result of monopolistic tendencies.
However, when this question was raised by some objectors to the
Lonrho takeover of the *Observer* (*i.e.* the danger that a politically neutral newspaper might, by the decision of its new proprietor, join the
ranks of papers supporting the Conservative Party), the Commission
declared it inadmissible. "It would be a serious development of our role
for us to take such a point into account" was its reason for refusing to
examine the proposed proprietor's political plans for the newspaper.[8]
While the Commission's reluctance to examine proprietorial politics is
understandable, the Fair Trading Act requires it to take into account
"all matters which appear in the circumstances to be relevant" to the
question of whether the transfer would operate against the public interest. This does not call for an evaluation of the merits of political policies, but an assessment of the consequences of the transaction on the
availability to the public of a reasonable variety of editorial opinion. It

---

[6] Fair Trading Act 1973, s. 59(3).
[7] Royal Commission on the Press, Cmnd. 6810 (1977) Chap. 14, para. 28.
[8] *The Observer and George Outram*, Chap. 8, para. 28–9.

is a serious mistake for the Commission to interpret the Act so as to disallow consideration of this important dimension.

Some indication of a willingness to reach a judgment on this type of issue was shown by its 1999 report into the proposed acquisition of Mirror Group by Trinity plc and Regional Independent Media Holdings. The Commission considered whether this would affect the *Mirror*'s "left of centre political stance" but decided that it would not. It was concerned that the sale of one of the Mirror Group's Northern Ireland titles (*News Letter*) would lead to a loss of a "distinctive voice representing Unionist opinion" and if this happened "it would threaten the adequate representation in the press of the range of political opinion in Northern Ireland". The Commission proposed that Trinity be required to give an undertaking to sell on some of the Northern Ireland titles including *News Letter*.[9]

In making its judgment about the public interest the Commission must have particular regard to the "need for accurate presentation of news and free expression of opinion".[10] In 1990 it ruled against the acquisition of a controlling interest in the *Bristol Evening Post* and the *Western Daily Press* by David Sullivan (the proprietor of the *Daily Sport* and a string of pornographic publications). It thought Mr Sullivan "could be expected to influence editorial policy and the character and content of these papers and that this would harm both the accurate presentation of news and the free expression of opinion. We also consider that the acquisition could harm the standing of the papers in their community and that there could be some adverse effects on circulation."[11] In 2000 Richard Desmond, another publisher with a swag of pornographic titles, was not prevented from acquiring Express Newspapers.

Adverse judgments by the Commission in relation to newspaper mergers are rare. Of the 19 reports since 1990 only three have detected a damaging effect on the public interest.

In cases of newspaper merger referrals the Competition Commission must report within three months, and must include in that report "a survey of the general position" with respect to the transfer, "and of developments which have led to that position".[12] It may recommend that the Government attach conditions to the transfer that would minimise dangers to the public interest. These statutory duties call for

[9] Report of a merger situation—Trinity plc/Mirror Group plc/Regional Independent Media Holdings Ltd, July 23, 1999 —available on the Commission's website at www.competition-commission.org.uk

[10] Fair Trading Act 1973, s. 59(3).

[11] Commission's Report on the Proposed Transfer of a Controlling Interest to David Sullivan in *Bristol Evening Post* plc, May 31, 1990.

[12] Fair Trading Act 1973, s. 61(1)(b).

considerable investigation and knowledge of the industry, and up to three additional members may be appointed by the Government to assist the Commission in such referrals.[13] However, this power of ad hoc appointment is no substitute for the Commission being placed in a position to judge, from its own monitoring work, what the impact of a particular sale is likely to be. This could be achieved if the Commission were given a permanent responsibility to monitor, and from time to time to report publicly on developments that tend towards greater concentration of press holdings.

BROADCASTING AND PRESS CONGLOMERATES

New and complicated restrictions were introduced in the Broadcasting Act 1990 to limit the ownership of multiple television and radio licenses and also to restrict the extent to which a person or a company with interests in one medium can branch out into other media. The provisions are of Byzantine complexity: they have been amended by regulation, superseded by further legislation, and affected by Directives from the E.C.[14] There is little alternative but to consult an up-to-date version of Schedule 2 of the Broadcasting Act 1990. The Broadcasting White Paper promised a liberalisation of the rules, but broadcasting was not mentioned in the 2001 Queen's Speech as a subject for immediate legislation.

DTI INVESTIGATIONS

The Department of Trade and Industry has wide powers to investigate the affairs of a company. It may appoint an inspector to carry out a formal investigation if it believes that the company is untruthful, fraudulent or unfairly prejudicial to part of its members, or if it has failed to disclose information that its members could reasonably expect.[15] Either in conjunction with a formal investigation or independently, the Department can call for the production of specified documents.[16] It can also crack the codes of nominees and investigate the true ownership and

---

[13] Fair Trading Act 1973, Sched. 3, para. 22.
[14] See particularly Broadcasting Act 1996 and the Television Broadcasting Regulations 1998, S.I. 1998 No. 3196, which implement the Directives 89/552/EEC and 97/36/EEC.
[15] Companies Act 1985, s. 432.
[16] *ibid.*, s. 447.

control of the company.[17] It was an impending investigation of this kind that pushed the shareholders into their dawn raid on Consolidated Gold Fields.

A formal investigation is normally conducted by two specially appointed inspectors, a senior barrister and a chartered accountant. Its proceedings are inquisitorial, although cross-examination is sometimes allowed. They have been held in private since 1932, as the result of an unsatisfactory House of Lords decision.[18] The secrecy of investigations is now additionally buttressed by provisions against revealing documents compulsorily disclosed by the company in response to an order of the DTI, and by a maximum penalty of two years' imprisonment.[19] The offence covers revelations of any oral explanations of the disclosed material but not, apparently, answers given to the inspector's general inquiries on other matters unrelated to the company's documents, nor does the offence cover disclosure of information given by those outside the company.[20] Although the inspectors question witnesses in private, it does not follow that they can insist on a witness giving an undertaking to keep quiet about what he was asked or said in reply. The material which the inspectors put to the witness may be confidential (in which case notifying the witness of this will itself impose a duty on him to respect the confidence), but the inspectors cannot insist on creating an obligation of confidence which would not otherwise arise.[21]

The inspectors report to the Secretary of State, who may send a copy of the report to the company itself.[22] The minister can also make the report publicly available.[23] This is always done when external inspectors are appointed, although only after any criminal proceedings have finished. Lonrho unsuccessfully challenged the refusal of the DTI in 1989 to publish its report on the takeover of Harrods by the Al Fayed brothers. The minister said that criminal proceedings were still under consid-

---

[17] Companies Act, s. 442 and see s. 444 (power to obtain information as to those interested in shares) and s. 446 (investigation of share dealings).

[18] *Hearts of Oak Assurance Co Ltd v. Att.-Gen.* [1932] A.C. 392. Until this case, investigations were held in public as a matter of course. The Attorney-General's defence of the practice was halfhearted in the House of Lords, but it is still surprising that the Lords left the inspector no discretion to take evidence in public. As a dissenting judge said in the Court of Appeal, the inspector might reasonably believe that witnesses would be less likely to lie in public and that an open airing of the accusations would prevent inflated rumours of more serious wrongdoing [1931] 2 Ch. 370, 396 *per* Lawrence L.J.

[19] Companies Act 1985, s. 449.

[20] *ibid.*, s. 447(5)(a) unless the outsider was in possession of the compulsorily acquired documents.

[21] *Re An Inquiry into Mirror Group Newspapers plc* [2000] Ch. 194.

[22] *ibid.*, s. 437(3)(a).

[23] *ibid.*, s. 437(3)(c), although the Department can appoint inspectors on the basis that their reports will not be published. See Companies Act 1985, s. 432(2A).

eration, and the courts refused to overturn his view that publication might prejudice any future prosecution.[24] Where outside inspectors have not been used, but the Department has called for documents, the results of the investigation are not generally released unless they disclose material of importance that the Department wishes to publicise.[25] The inspectors' reports usually reveal more incompetence than dishonesty, but their reprimands can be severe,[26] and their descriptions (*e.g.* "an epidemic loss of money" or "for this managing director truth was a moving target") acidic. In other respects, however, the DTI lives down to its nickname ("The Department of Timidity and Inaction"). It has failed to move against well-connected city operators involved in share manipulation. Its abject failure to cope with the Lloyd's scandal has become legendary. Its investigation into Jeffrey Archer was inconclusive and, because the Government refused to publish it, its thoroughness could not be assessed by the media.

The DTI can similarly appoint inspectors to investigate suspected insider dealing.[27] It was in the context of such an investigation that the *Independent* journalist, Jeremy Warner, refused to disclose his source of information and was punished for contempt of court (see p. 256).

(see p. 256)

OTHER BUSINESSES

The need to structure a capital base and the attraction of limited liability lead most sizeable businesses to opt for corporate form. This is just as well for reporters, because there is a dearth of disclosure obligations on the principal alternatives: partnership, unincorporated associations (such as clubs) and sole trading. Unless they acquire charitable status or a licence to lend money or one of the other privileges considered below, such businesses have virtually no legal disclosure obligations and the investigator will be dependent on volunteered information or leaks.

Partnerships

Partnerships must reveal the names of their members. This obligation was first imposed in 1916, not to forestall fraudsters but to prevent entrepreneurs of German origin trading under the guise of an Anglicised

---

[24] *R. v. Secretary of State for Trade and Industry, ex p. Lonhro plc* [1989] 1 W.L.R. 525, HL.
[25] Leigh, *Commercial Fraud,* pp. 168, 176.
[26] *ibid.*, pp. 172–4.
[27] Financial Services Act 1986, s. 177.

name. The partnership must keep a list of its partners' names at its principal place of business and allow inspection there.[28]

Limited liability partnerships

The impetus for a new form of business organisation came from professional partnerships (particularly accountants) that were concerned at the level of damages (and costs) which they might face in negligence actions and which might exceed their professional indemnity insurance cover. The Limited Liability Partnerships Act 2000 allows a hybrid between a company and a partnership. Like a company it has its own legal existence and its liability can be limited. However, like a partnership, the members are entitled (broadly speaking) to structure the rights and responsibilities between themselves as they wish.

The disclosure requirements are very similar to those of companies. Thus the incorporation document (which will list the partners names and addresses) must be sent to the Companies Registry[29] and changes must be notified.[30] Limited Liability Partnerships will be identifiable by the new abbreviation "llp". Audited accounts must be supplied to the Registry each year in much the same way as companies are required to do.[31]

Co-ops and housing associations

Co-ops and housing associations are normally set up either as companies or as friendly societies and are registered under the Industrial and Provident Societies Act 1978. Like companies, they must make an annual return, which must include accounts and an auditor's report.[32] The balance sheet and auditor's report have to be displayed in a conspicuous place at the registered office.[33] Not-for-profit providers of housing can be registered as a "social landlord" with the Housing Corporation. The register is open for inspection at the Corporation's head office.[34]

Building societies

Building societies come under the jurisdiction of the Building Societies Commission. They, too, must submit accounts, though in much more

---

[28] Business Names Act 1985, s. 4.
[29] Limited Liability Partnerships Act 2000, ss. 2 and 3.
[30] ibid., s. 9.
[31] Limited Liability Partnership Regulations 2001, S.I. 2001 No. 1090, reg. 3.
[32] Industrial and Provident Societies Act 1965, s. 39.
[33] ibid., s. 40.
[34] Housing Act 1996, s. 1. The head office is at 149 Tottenham Court Road, London W1T 7BN.

detail.[35] Since 1986 these have been similar to the requirements for companies and banks. As with companies, the purpose of disclosure is principally to reassure creditors and depositors. This overlooks the social role of building societies as the main supplier of loans for private homes. If a society refuses to lend in a particular area ("red-lining"), it can have a devastating effect on property values. The societies may fear that the neighbourhood is in decline and a risky place to invest but, if the area is starved of home loans, this becomes a self-fulfilling prophecy. It is impossible to tell from an annual report whether a society is red-lining, since it is not obliged to say anything about the location of properties on which loans have been made. Building societies, like companies, must disclose any loan made to directors, managers, etc. Only members and depositors are entitled to a copy of the report, but since a journalist could easily open an account, it is normally given out on request without this formality.[36] Building societies must belong to an ombudsman scheme for dealing with complaints. The body administering the scheme must be permitted to publish the whole or any part of an ombudsman's determination.[37]

SPECIAL PRIVILEGES

Charities

Charities do not pay income tax, capital gains or capital transfer tax (unless they engage in trade). They pay no more than half the rates of a comparable occupier and they are entitled to miscellaneous reliefs from VAT, Stamp Duty and National Insurance. It is also easier for them to raise money because they may recover from the Inland Revenue the income tax paid by the donor on a gift. Donations to charities are free of capital transfer tax and capital gains tax. These are significant State subsidies, but there is a paucity of public information about the objects of such largesse.

To secure these advantages, it is in practice necessary for a charity to register with the Charity Commissioners. They will scrutinise its purposes to see if they conform to the legal definition of a charity. This has been developed by the courts by reference to an ancient statute of 1601. Broadly, there are four categories: religious, educational, those for the relief of poverty and those for other purposes beneficial to the

---

[35] Building Societies Act 1986, s. 73 and the regulations made under it.
[36] *ibid.*, s. 81.
[37] *ibid.*, Sched. 12, para. 10.

community. An organisation may run a business and still be a charity if its ultimate object comes within one of these categories.

Some charities will be companies and must therefore comply with the ordinary disclosure requirements, but a reporter investigating those that are unincorporated can look only to the Charities Act 1993. The charity must lodge its trust deed or the instrument specifying its objects for public inspection.[38] This will be drafted more precisely than the objects clause of an ordinary company's Memorandum of Association because the Charity Commissioners will withhold their blessing unless every purpose comes within the charitable definition. Nevertheless, within these limits it will still be drawn so as to give the organisation the maximum latitude and may therefore be a poor guide as to what the charity actually does.

Charities must prepare annual accounts, although where the income does not exceed £100,000 these are in a simplified form.[39] If the charity's income in the current year (and each of the two preceding years) exceeds £250,000 the accounts must be audited.[40] If the income is less than this, but more than £10,000 the accounts must be reviewed by an independent person who must produce a report.[41]

An annual report must be sent to the Charity Commissioners and must include the accounts and the report of an auditor or independent person. If the charity has an income of less than £100,000 it must give a brief summary of the main activities and achievements during the year. If the income is over £100,000 the annual report must review all the activities and achievements including material transactions, significant developments and achievements, any significant change in activities, any important events affecting those activities since the end of the year and any likely future developments. The report will also include basic information such as the names of the trustees and the charity's principal address. However, the Commissioners can dispense with these requirements if disclosure of them would expose the trustee or anyone at the charity's office to personal danger.[42] The charity must keep the reports for six years.

The public has a right to inspect the annual reports at the Commissioners' offices[43] and to have copies made.[44] A member of the public can also require the organisation to provide a copy of the most recent

---

[38] Charities Act 1993, s. 5.3(8).
[39] Charities Act 1993, s. 42.
[40] ibid., s. 45.
[41] ibid., s. 43.
[42] Charities (Accounts and Reports) Regulations 1995, S.I. 1995 No. 2724, reg. 10.
[43] Charities Act 1993, s. 47(1).
[44] ibid s. 84.

accounts.[45] Some charities, generally large public institutions, are exempt from these provisions.[46]

In certain circumstances the Commissioners have powers to establish alternative schemes for the administration of a charity, and to appoint or remove trustees, or officers or managers of a charitable trust, but they must give advance public notice.[47]

The media have, with a few exceptions, signally failed to alert the public to scandals in charity administration that stem from outdated legal definitions and absence of expert public oversight. There are 140,000 registered charities, with assets of about £5 billion accumulated with the help of tax privileges. Many "charities" have nothing to do with the relief of poverty or oppression. Some of the wealthiest—private schools and private medical funds, for example—cater mainly to the wealthy. Thanks to the idiosyncrasies of interpretation of the 1601 statute embodying the social values of the Elizabethan age, some charities-in-law are positively uncharitable. The *Daily Mail* exposed how the "Moonies" spent tax subsidies on brainwashing converts and breaking up families. Others are simply eccentric: *e.g.* the Relaxation League, the Fun Palace Trust, the Cat Protection League, the Fund for Polishing Regimental Silver, the Friends of Locomotives of the Great Western Railway. On the other hand, any organisation that seeks to change the law—even in order to relieve poverty and oppression—is debarred from registration as a charity. In 1981 it was decided in the High Court that Amnesty International could not obtain tax privileges as a charity because it sought actively to change the laws of fascist and Communist countries.[48] The anomalies stemming from the legal definition of charity are endless: anti-social or downright silly organisations are allowed tax advantages denied to important and humane causes. There have been proposals to rationalise the law, but to no avail. The importance of the Charity Commissioners, and the lack of power to scrutinise the activities of those businesses that batten on to compassionate instincts by raising money for charities that see very little of it at the end of the day, make the entire field a fertile one for exposure journalism.

Investment business

The Financial Services Act 1986 revamped the legislative scheme of investor protection. Anyone engaged in investment business must be

---

[45] Charities Act 1993, s. 47(2).

[46] *ibid.*, Sched. 2.

[47] *ibid.*, s. 20.

[48] *McGovern v. Att.-Gen.* [1981] 3 All E.R. 493. See p. 828 for the difficulties which Amnesty experienced for similar reasons in trying to have its advertisements broadcast.

authorised by the Securities and Investment Board (SIB) directly, by a self-regulating organisation that has been recognised by the SIB, or by a recognised professional body. The SIB keeps a register of authorised persons, self-regulating organisations and recognised professional bodies.[49] This is open to public inspection without charge.[50] There is a further part of the register that contains details of people whom the SIB has decided are not fit and proper persons to be employed in connection with investment business.[51] The public does have a right to ascertain whether a named individual is included in this part of the register and, if so, to inspect his or her entry. A more general search of this part can be conducted only if there is good reason for seeking the information. The SIB can also restrict its subsequent use.[52] It was suggested during the Bill's parliamentary passage that a bona fide investigative journalist would have a good reason to inspect.[53]

The definition of "investment business" includes giving investment advice[54] and could therefore have embraced much financial journalism. However, the Act exempts advice given in a newspaper, journal, magazine or other periodical publication if the principal purpose of the publication taken as a whole and including any advertisements contained in it is not to lead people to put money into any particular investment.[55] The mainstream press therefore will not need authorisation. If a journal is concerned as to whether it comes within the exemption, it can apply for a certificate from the SIB.[56] A similar exemption has been added for broadcast or cable programmes and teletext transmission.[57]

The 1986 Act will be replaced by the Financial Services and Markets Act 2000. The self-regulating organisations will be superseded by a single and statutory Financial Services Authority (FSA). The FSA's powers are far greater than those which could be deployed under the 1986 scheme and the legislation was the subject of bitter debate as to whether there was adequate protection for the basic rights of those who would be regulated. These include investment advisers although journalists again have an exemption on virtually the same terms as under the previous regime.[58] On the application of a media proprietor, the FSA

---

[49] Financial Services Act 1986, s. 102.

[50] *ibid.*, s. 103.

[51] *ibid.*, s. 59.

[52] *ibid.*, s. 103(2)–(4).

[53] House of Commons Standing Committee E. col. 484.

[54] Financial Services Act 1986, Sched. 1, para. 15.

[55] *ibid.*, para. 25(1).

[56] *ibid.*, para. 25(2).

[57] *ibid.*, para. 25A added by Financial Services Act 1986 (Restriction of Scope) Order 1988 (S.I. 1988 No. 318).

[58] The Financial Services and Markets Act 2000 (Regulated Activities) Order 2001, S.I. 2001 No. 544, Art. 54.

can provide a conclusive certificate that a publication or service is exempt.[59] The FSA has very broad powers so the role of the new appeals body, the Financial Services and Markets Tribunal, will be particularly important. By summer 2001 no rules of procedure had been published, but they should certainly make provision for the hearings to be in public (see the "Stop Press" section for further details).

Financial journalists who predict the stock market performance of particular companies have a serious conflict of interest if they or persons close to them stand to gain by the market reaction to their story. Some newspapers for this reason debar financial journalists from having their own portfolio, while the Press Council has issued some nebulous rules that do not really come to grips with the ethical problems (see p. 705). The temptation to profit personally from foreknowledge of press stories was highlighted by the prosecution in New York of Foster Winans, a journalist who arranged for others to trade in shares about to be "tipped" by his influential column in the *Wall Street Journal*. In Britain a journalist who entered into similar arrangements could be prosecuted under the Theft Act for dishonestly obtaining a pecuniary advantage for himself or another. A dishonest arrangement with company "insiders" to affect share prices through the leakage and publication of price-sensitive information would amount to a conspiracy to contravene the Financial Services Act 1986 or its 2000 equivalent. The share-tipping scandal at the *Daily Mirror* in 2000 is dealt with at p. 705. The police did nothing and the DTI did very little. The PCC made great play of adopting an amendment to its Code.

Consumer credit

Almost all business dealings with consumers involving credit must now be licensed.[60] About 100,000 licences are involved. Initially, these are issued almost automatically by the Office of Fair Trading. The register of licences is open for public inspection and includes particulars of applications and licences, and notes whether a licence has ever been suspended or refused.[61] Rogue motor dealers constitute the largest group to have licences refused or revoked, and not merely for mishandling the credit side of their business. Alteration of odometers (mileage recorders) or consistently selling unroadworthy vehicles will justify barring a dealer from further credit transactions. The register is also one of the

---

[59] The Financial Services and Markets Act 2000 (Regulated Activities) Order 2001, Art. 54(3).
[60] Consumer Credit Act 1974 Part III.
[61] OFT-Consumer Credit General Notice No. 5, January 16, 1976. It is open between 10 a.m. and 4 p.m. at Government Buildings, Bromyard Avenue, Acton, West London.

few public documents that must disclose the officers of *unincorporated* associations. The system has been in operation since 1976 and is a useful source of information about shady characters on the way up again as time passes and memories of crooked consumer scandals begin to fade.

Other registers

There are numerous other public registers. By law the General Medical Council must publish an annual list of doctors.[62] The clerk to most magistrates' courts will also be the clerk to the licensing justices and will keep a register of everyone entitled to sell alcoholic drinks. This will also show the owner of the premises and any conviction of the licensee in his trade or for bribery or treating at an election.[63] The performance of television and radio companies can be measured against their ambitions by inspecting that part of its application that sets out its programming policy.[64]

INSOLVENCY

The insolvency procedures (winding up for companies, bankruptcy for individuals, receivership where the debts are backed by security) are intended to gather in what assets can be traced and to distribute them to the creditors according to set rules of priority.

The whole of insolvency law was reformed in the 1980s. One aim was to harmonise the codes of procedure for individuals and companies. This has largely been achieved but the two regimes continue their separate existence.

A company in financial difficulties has a wide range of options. Normally, the first step is for the major creditors to appoint a receiver who, at least temporarily, will take over the running of the business. The outgoing directors or others responsible for the company must prepare a statement of its affairs.[65] A copy is filed with the court. The court file is not a public document. It can be consulted as of right only by those immediately connected with the insolvency proceedings. There is a discretionary power to allow any person to inspect the file; conversely, the

---

[62] Medical Act 1983, s. 54, and, for dentists, see Dentists Act 1984, s. 22.

[63] Licensing Act 1964, ss. 30–34; Representation of the People Act 1983, s. 168(7).

[64] Broadcasting Act 1990, s. 15(6) requires the Commission to publish in such manner as they consider appropriate a Channel 3 applicant's programming proposals and to invite representations.

[65] Insolvency Act 1986, s. 47.

court can prohibit inspection.[66] The receiver will prepare a report on the company's predicament, which he must make available to all the creditors.[67] He also has to send a copy of the report to the Registrar of Companies, where it can be inspected.[68]

If the company's disease is terminal, it is wound up, or "liquidated". This may be done with the company's acquiescence (a "voluntary winding up" may be convenient as part of a corporate restructuring for a company that is healthy and solvent). Alternatively, a company may be wound up on its creditors' insistence. The process begins with the presentation of a petition to the court. The petition must then be advertised in the *London Gazette*. The court can exempt a petitioner from this requirement and will ban the advertising of a petition if it is considered an abuse of process.[69] The petition is heard in open court.[70] Following a winding-up order, a statement of affairs by the directors must be produced to the Official Receiver.[71] This will be filed in court and (except in voluntary liquidations) is open to inspection by those immediately concerned in the winding-up, although the court does have power to restrict access to all or part of the statement.[72]

The Official Receiver can apply to the court for the public examination of any officer of the company.[73] This power was widened following the strong recommendation of the Cork Committee, whose proposals led to the transformation of insolvency law.[74] Public examination is no longer dependent on a prior report by the Official Receiver suggesting fraud.

Directors who are found in the course of winding up to have been involved in fraudulent trading may be disqualified from being a director or from promoting, forming or managing a company for a specified period.[75] Similiar orders can be made against a director who commits a number of Company Act offences, including persistent default in sending accounts, returns or reports to the Registry.[76] This was intended to reduce the shamefully high incidence of noncompliance with these obligations. Even in the absence of a specific offence, a disqualification

---

[66] Insolvency Rules, rr. 3.5, 7.31 It is a contempt of court to inspect the file without permission: *Dobson v. Hastings* [1992] Ch. 394.

[67] Insolvency Act 1986, s. 48.

[68] Companies Act 1985, s. 709.

[69] Insolvency Rules 1986, r. 4.11.

[70] *Practice Direction (No. 3 of 1986)* [1987] 1 W.L.R. 53.

[71] Insolvency Act 1986, s. 131.

[72] Insolvency Rules 1986, r. 4.35.

[73] Insolvency Act 1986, s. 133. There is an alternative power to summon under s. 236. This examination is not expressly required to be in public and therefore a registrar must, and a judge can, conduct it in chambers, Insolvency Rules, r. 7.6.

[74] Review Committee on Insolvency Law and Practice (Cmnd. 8558), Chap. 12.

[75] Company Directors Disqualification Act 1986, ss. 1 and 4.

[76] *ibid.*, ss. 2, 3 and 5.

order can be made if the company is involvent and the director is considered to be unfit to manage a company.[77] The director must be given an opportunity to be heard at a public hearing before the court.[78] The Secretary of State can now accept an undertaking from the director (for instance, not to act as a company director for a specified period) instead of seeking a court order.[79] There is a register of disqualification orders and undertakings that is kept by the DTI and Companies House and which is open to public inspection.[80]

Bankruptcy proceedings follow a similar pattern to winding-up. They also begin with a petition to the court, which again, may be made by either the debtor or one of the creditors. Prior to the 1986 Act it was the norm for bankruptcies to be examined in public. A public examination now will take place only if the Official Receiver applies to the court for one.[81]

If the debtor is adjudged bankrupt, he or she will be disqualified from acting as a director,[82] unable to obtain most credit and barred from holding certain public offices. Bankruptcy decisions are advertised in the *London Gazette* and in local papers.[83] The individual insolvency register, maintained by the Insolvency Service, has details of bankruptcy orders and individual voluntary arrangements.[84] The bankruptcy now comes to an end automatically after three years (two if the speedier "summary administration" method is used) for first-time bankrupts. Others still have to apply to the court to be discharged.

---

[77] *ibid.*, s. 6.
[78] Insolvent Companies (Disqualification of Unfit Directors) Proceedings Rules 1987 (S.I. 1987 No. 2023).
[79] Insolvency Act 2000, s. 6 adding s. 1A to the Company Directors Disqualification Act 1986.
[80] Company Directors Disqualification Act 1986, s. 18.
[81] Insolvency Act 1986, s. 290; again, there is an alternative power to examine the debot in privated, s. 366.
[82] Company Directors Disqualification Act 1986, s. 11.
[83] Insolvency Rules 1986 (S.I. No. 1925) r.6.34(2). The court has the power to suspend this obligation, r.6.34(3).
[84] Search requests can be sent to the Insolvency Service, Bankruptcy Public Search Room, 2nd Floor, West Wing, 45–46 Stephenson Street, Birmingham B2 4UP.

CHAPTER 14

MEDIA SELF-REGULATION

Notwithstanding the large and increasing number of legal restraints on the media, it still has power to damage reputations by falsehoods, invade privacy and conduct partisan campaigns. The unavailability of legal aid effectively deters all but the intrepid or wealthy from taking action for libel, and there is as yet no direct protection for privacy in British law. Blatant examples of unfair and unethical media behaviour towards individuals and organisations have led to demands for more statutory controls, which media industries have sought to avoid by trumpeting the virtues of "self-regulation". They have established tribunals that affect to regulate media ethics through adjudicating complaints by members of the public who claim to have been unfairly treated by journalists and editors. Complaints about newspapers and journals may be made to the Press Complaints Commission (PCC), a private body funded by newspaper proprietors. It has no legal powers, but its adjudications will be published by the paper complained against, albeit usually in small print and without much prominence. Allegations about false or offensive telephone services may be made to ICSTIS, an adjudicative body set up by British Telecom. The Advertising Standards Authority (ASA) is the body that will hear complaints that advertisements are not "legal, decent, honest and truthful". Although a private company funded by the advertising industry, it derives a powerful sanction from the preparedness of newspapers and journals to withhold space for advertisements that are in breach of its code.

Journalists should recognise the political purpose behind these organisations.[1] They are public relations operations, funded by media industries to give the impression to Parliament that the press, the telephone service providers and the advertising industry really can put their houses in ethical order without the need for legislation. Press proprietors are prepared to invest over £1 million per year in the PCC because its existence offers a form of insurance against new laws to safeguard personal privacy, prohibit chequebook journalism and to guarantee a right of reply. The advertising industry funds the ASA, to a tune of more

---

[1] See G. Robertson, *People Against the Press* (Quartet Books, 1983).

than £3 million annually, to avoid exposure to laws against deceit and indecency. Both organisations have performed imperfectly from the public point of view, but owe their continued industry support to that mixture of fear, prudence and masochism identified by Hilaire Belloc:

> "Always keep a-hold on nurse
> For fear of finding something worse."

Whether "something worse"—*i.e.* a statute rather than a self-help arrangement—would be worse for the public, as well as for the newspaper and advertising industry, remains debatable. The PCC has failed to demonstrate many virtues in self-regulation: it has designed an ethical code which it declines to monitor, and its decisions are accorded a degree of cynicism, bordering on contempt, by editors—especially when they relate to coverage of the Royal Family, which the PCC spends a lot of its time trying to protect, often from its own media gaffes. Although tabloid editors give lip-service to PCC guidelines on privacy, chequebook journalism and race reporting, they are often prepared to break them in the interests of increasing circulation. One of the serious consequences for journalistic standards is the way newspapers, out of self-interest, contrive to pretend that PCC rulings are both effective and newsworthy, and never tell their readers that the organisation is something of a confidence trick.

Nonetheless, the PCC and the ASA are significant organisations, with a potential for good and a capacity to inhibit genuine investigative reporting and the amount of information available to the public. A code of practice promulgated by an authoritative organisation can be of great assistance to journalists in resisting editorial pressures to behave unethically in the quest for circulation-building stories of prurient, rather than public, interest. Some of the journalists who were held to have "ferociously and callously harassed" relatives of a "Yorkshire Ripper" victim evinced a sense of shame, but excused themselves on the ground that they were only obeying editorial instructions.[2] A code of conduct should assist journalists to develop the moral muscle to resist unethical orders to invade privacy and sensationalise private grief, especially if the code has been incorporated in their contract of employment. The ASA code has practical force because media outlets will not accept advertisements ruled to be in breach of it, and the PCC code, which has no practical force at all, may develop a legal impact through the operation of section 12(4) of the Human Rights Act, which requires courts to pay attention to "any relevant privacy code" in deciding whether to impose prior restraint. The assumption is that courts will be more likely to injunct if the alleged breach of confidence also involves a breach of

---

[2] Press Council, *Press Conduct in the Sutcliffe Case,* 1983, Chap. 18.

the code—which will be interpreted by judges, not the more media-friendly PCC. The danger is that privacy codes which are too widely or loosely drawn, or which go beyond what the law requires (*e.g.* the amendments made to the PCC code in the wake of Diana's death) will prove counterproductive in the courts, and may become trip-wires for important investigative journalism based (like much of that genre) on confidential leaks from "insiders".

THE PRESS COMPLAINTS COMMISSION

From Press Council to PCC

The idea that disputes over the content of newspapers might be resolved by some independent but non-legal body developed first in Sweden, where publishers and journalists established a Press Fair Practices Board in 1916. In due course, all major Swedish newspapers bound themselves by contract to accept the rulings of a press ombudsman—a judge who rules on complaints from the public, orders newspapers to print retractions of false statements, and fines them for proven deviations from a code of conduct drawn up by the country's Press Council.[3] In Britain the idea of a Press Council was first mooted by the National Union of Journalists (NUJ) after the lifting of wartime censorship in 1945. The union was alarmed at the concentration of ownership in the provincial press, the suppression or distortion of news for politically partisan or commercial reasons, and the proprietorial pressures imposed upon editors and journalists. There were debates in Parliament, and journalist-M.P.s like Michael Foot claimed that some editors were merely "stooges, cyphers and sycophants". The First Royal Commission on the Press reported in 1949, and suggested that the industry should establish "a General Council of the Press", which, "by censuring undesirable types of journalistic conduct and by all other possible means, would build up a code of conduct in accordance with the highest professional standards".[4] The next four years were spent in desultory and unenthusiastic discussions amongst proprietors, until a private member's bill was introduced in Parliament to set up a statutory council. This prospect brought a speedy end to discussions, and a General Coun-

---

[3] Lennart Groll, *Freedom and Self-Discipline of the Swedish Press,* Swedish Institute, 1980; Lennart Groll and Geoffrey Robertson, "Legal Constraints on the Press: Swedish and British Viewpoints" in *Freedom and the Press* (Department of Visual Communication, Goldsmith's College, 1979).

[4] Royal Commission on the Press, Cmnd. 7700 (1949), para. 650.

cil of the Press commenced operations in 1953.[5] It had no lay membership, and its first chairman was the then proprietor of *The Times.*

The first decade of the Council's operations was unimpressive. Its
rulings were oversensitive to Government and to royalty—its first
declaration was that a *Daily Mirror* readership poll on the question of
whether Princess Margaret should be allowed to marry Group Captain
Townsend was "contrary to the best traditions of British journalism".[6]
Its poor performance was subjected to scathing criticism by the second
Royal Commission on the Press, reporting in 1962, which urged the
Government to set up a proper disciplinary body with statutory powers
if the Council failed to reform itself immediately.[7] The renewed threat
of legislation made newspaper proprietors jump to attention: they supplied the Council with increased finance, appointed a retired Law Lord,
Lord Devlin, as chairperson, and changed the constitution so that 20 per
cent of members were drawn from outside the media. Under Devlin's
leadership, the Council began to display a more impressive tone and
authority. It began to reprimand press misconduct in positive terms, and
evinced a powerful concern for press freedoms. However, its higher
profile on press freedom issues caused it to be perceived publicly as a
champion of the press rather than a watchdog for the public.[8]

The first detailed study of the Press Council's work was conducted
by the third Royal Commission of the Press, chaired by Lord Mac-
Gregor.[9] It found evidence of "flagrant breaches of acceptable standards" and "inexcusable intrusions into privacy". "We feel strongly", it
stated, "that the Press Council should have more power over the press
. . . There is a pressing call to enhance the standing of the Press Council
in the eyes of the public and potential complainants."[10] It called upon
the newspaper proprietors who fund and effectively control the Council
to ensure that it had sufficient funds to advertise its services and to
monitor press performance. Complaints upheld by the Council should
be published on the front page of the offending newspaper, and a written
code of conduct for journalists should be produced. The Council should
give more support to an effective right to reply, condemn journalistic
misbehaviour in a more forthright way and take a stronger line on inac-

---

[5] The Press Council Bill had its second reading in November 1952. It was moved by
C. J. Simmons M.P., who reminded the House that "nearly three-and-a-half years
after [the Royal Commission Report] we are still awaiting its formation by the Press
of their own volition". See generally H. Phillip Levy, *The Press Council*, Macmillan, 1967, Chaps 1 and 2.
[6] "A Royal Romance: Princess Margaret and Group Captain Townsend", *Daily
Mirror* February 21, 1954 (Press Council).
[7] Royal Commission on the Press, Cmnd. 1811 (1962), para. 325.
[8] Report of the Committee on Privacy, Cmnd. 5012 (1972), para. 189.
[9] Royal Commission on the Press, Cmnd. 6810 (1977), chap. 20, para. 15.
[10] *ibid.*, para. 48.

curacy and bias. The Council responded to these criticisms by increasing its lay membership to half but in other respects it failed to improve its image. A study of its work published in 1983 revealed that even successful complainants were overwhelmingly critical of the services it offered.[11] Its adjudication procedures were obstacle courses and its delays in judgment ensured that any redress it provided was usually ineffectual. Its principles were confused and inconsistent, rulings were not respected and it did not work to improve the ethical standards of the British press.

A new chairperson, Louis Blom-Cooper Q.C., instituted a thoroughgoing review of the Council's role and function but its basic problem remained: its failure to make its Declarations of Principle stick in the absence of any effective sanction. Editors at every level defied and derided it: the *Daily Telegraph* publicly refused to abide by its ethical convention on race reporting while the *Sun* took a malicious delight in vilifying individuals who "successfully" complained about it to the Council. It was no longer serving as an insurance policy against new press laws, and in 1989 support from M.P.s from all parties threatened to advance the passage of a private member's bill to establish a statutory body to enforce a right of reply. The progress of this bill was halted only when the Government set up a committee chaired by David Calcutt Q.C. to respond to press intrusions and privacy.

Calcutt correctly identified the Council's central problem in terms of its contradictory claims both to safeguard press freedom and to condemn press malpractice.[12] It was this latter function that should be performed by a Press Complaints Commission, an expert body with sufficient funding to adjudicate speedily and effectively complaints by members of the public about breaches of an expanded code of practice. The Calcutt Committee was profoundly unimpressed by the cynical attitudes displayed towards the Council in the past by editors and proprietors, and it evinced no great confidence that its proposed Press Complaints Commission would be allowed to work effectively if it remained a voluntary body. So it drew up plans for a statutory complaints tribunal which would wait notionally in the wings, to be wheeled out if there was a "less than overwhelming rate of compliance" with the new Commission's adjudications.

The Calcutt "fallback" recommendation for a statutory tribunal served to concentrate the minds of newspaper proprietors. The newspaper industry, through the Newspaper Publishers' Association (representing the owners of national newspapers) and the Newspaper Society (representing owners of provincial newspapers), acted

---

[11] Robertson, *People Against the Press,* Chap. 3.
[12] *Report of the Committee on Privacy and Related Matters* (HMSO, 1990), Cmnd. 1102.

speedily to establish a Press Complaints Commission, which commenced operations in January 1991. The new body abandoned the Press Council's contentious efforts to defend press freedom and combat media monopolies; it existed solely to adjudicate complaints that editors of newspapers had infringed the published code of conduct.

The early days of the PCC were underwhelming: Calcutt, invited to report again for the Government in January 1993, recommended jettisoning voluntary self-regulation in favour of his statutory Press Complaints Tribunal with its power to injunct impending privacy breaches and to fine reckless journalists.[13] John Major's government dared not antagonise the media, especially after its exposure of David Mellor (the minister who had accused editors of "drinking in the last chance saloon") who was bugged whilst having exhaustive sexual intercourse with a "resting" actress. Despite further demands in 1993 for statutory controls by the Lord Chancellor's Department[14] and the National Heritage Select Committee,[15] and a private member's bill which failed only on its third reading, the Conservative Government compromised: afraid of alienating newspapers before a general election, it gave "self-regulation" its approval, subject to "strengthening the system still further"[sic].[16] The Labour Government in its first term was just as emollient, legislating section 12(4) of the Human Rights Act on the assumption that the PCC's "relevant privacy code" would be a suitable subject for judicial notice. By dint of immediate condemnations of gross invasions of royal privacy and decisions favourable to important politicians, the PCC has kept its head, although in a shape which may not be much in the interest of either the press or the public. Its 10th anniversary party, in January 2001, featured Princes Charles and William—chaperoned by Lord Wakeham, who introduced them to their tabloid tormentors with the discreet aplomb of a high-class madam. The party symbolised the inter-dependence between celebrity and paparazzi, which like that between thief and receiver, makes the relationship profitable for both unless disturbed by the law.

Is the PCC reviewable?

The history sketched out above provides a clear answer: the PCC is exercising a recognised public adjudicative function, as a government-brokered alternative either to a Calcutt-devised complaints tribunal (which exists for broadcasters: see Chapter 16, the BSC) or to a privacy

---

[13] Sir David Calcutt, Review of Press Self-Regulation, Cm. 2135 (1993).
[14] The Lord Chancellor's Department has forcefully recommended legislating a new tort of infringement of privacy: Consultation Paper, July 1993.
[15] Report on Privacy and Media Intrusion 1992–3, H.C. 294–1.
[16] Cm. 2918 (July 1995).

law introduced by Act of Parliament.[16] The reasoning which has led the courts to declare the ASA reviewable applies by close analogy to the PCC: it is a body "clearly exercising a public function which, if the ASA did not exist, would no doubt be exercised by (a statutory office)".[17] Why in its first decade no-one—except for Moors Murderer Ian Brady and T.V. newsreader Anna Ford—has attempted to review the PCC is probably because nobody has regarded its decisions as important enough to quash. But the advent of the Human Rights Act, with its reference to "a privacy code", may lead to more reviews of PCC decisions and judicial insistence that the Commission comply with the requirements of the Convention, as a step towards a system of judge-made privacy law.

> The Sun ran a story about Moors Murderer Ian Brady receiving inappropriate hospital treatment, which it illustrated with an indistinct photograph, unobjectionable other than that it had been taken through a telephoto lens while he was in the hospital. This was technically a breach of the PCC privacy code (no pictures on private property without consent unless in the public interest) but the Commission made no finding because any breach would not warrant censure since the article itself had been in the public interest, and the picture had been obtained without intrusion or harassment. Brady sought judicial review, but the courts could see no basis for interfering with this decision: any breach which may have occurred was not serious and the PCC was entitled to decide that The Sun was not deserving of censure. The court "assumed" that the PCC was a body amenable to judicial review.[18]

It would be sensible in future cases for the PCC to concede review-ability, because this would have the practical and tactical advantage of making the PCC a more impressive alternative to privacy law—a public tribunal subject to court supervision, as distinct from a private industry committee. In the Brady case Lord Woolf made clear that any exercise of jurisdiction over the PCC "would be reserved for cases where it would clearly be desirable for this court to intervene". The courts will not trip the PCC up on technicalities, but only when it makes a fundamental error of interpretation. (If, for example, the PCC had decided that Brady's crimes were so horrendous that he had forfeited all right to privacy, that decision would have been so plainly wrong it would have been quashed.) Unsatisfied complainants will have to show an irrational interpretation of the code or a decision flatly inconsistent with other precedents or else a serious misunderstanding of the facts before

[16] Cm. 2918 (July 1995).
[17] R. v. ASA, ex p. The Insurance Service [1990] 2 Admin. L.R. 77, per Glidewell L.J.
[18] R. v. PCC, ex p. Stewart-Brady [1997] E.M.L.R. 185; followed by Silber J. in R. v. PCC ex p. Anna Ford (unreported), July 29, 2001.

judicial review is likely to succeed. It may be, however, that judicial review proceedings could successfully attack some of the unfair aspects of the PCC's procedures—its refusal to give complainants a hearing or an opportunity to cross-examine editors, for example, or infringements of the Article 6 rule requiring tribunal members to be independent and impartial (the Chairman, who is lavishly paid by the very newspapers complained about, may be vulnerable on this score, as may editor-members who decide cases involving their rivals).

The Complaints Procedure

The PCC operates from a small building inherited from the Press Council at 1 Salisbury Square, just off a Fleet Street where national newspapers are no longer situated. It has a small staff and a full time Director, Guy Black, serving on a 16-person Complaints Committee which has been chaired since 1995 by Lord Wakeham. Seven of the Committee are newspaper and magazine editors. The full time Director is also a commissioner along with the chairman and eight other worthy citizens: five are peers; there is a knight, a Bishop ("formerly clerk of the closet to the Queen") and a former director of the Royal Hospitals. The Royal connection is appropriate, since the PCC spends a good deal of its time upholding complaints made by Buckingham Palace. These public members, wholly unrepresentative of the general population, are chosen by an appointments committee cosily chaired by Lord Wakeham. The PCC has an all-press committee responsible for its ethical code: its membership includes editors whose ethics are constantly called into question. The operation costs about £1.3 million a year, funded by a levy on newspaper and magazine publishers. Their contributions are not "generous" (as the PCC Annual Review for the year 2000 states no less than three times): the amount is much less than the funding of the ASA or even of ICSTIS, and it is paid out of self-interest—*i.e.* to finance a body which they hope will help them to stave off further legal regulation.

The PCC receives several thousand complaints each year, yet it actually adjudicates only 50 to 60 cases. It claims that it "resolves" the complains that it does not adjudicate, but in 2000, one-third of these complaints were "outside its remit" while others were "made by third parties" a class of complaint which for no good reason the PCC does not accept, however grievous the breach complained about. Many complaints are settled by an editorial offer of a reply or a correction, but in the year 2000, 2,225 complaints were received and merely 57 were adjudicated, of which only 24 were upheld. About 60 per cent of all complaints concern inaccuracies, with privacy infringements featuring in 15 per cent. Adjudications are short for the benefit of the paper that must publish them with "due prominence" (which generally means under a banner headline if it is cleared, but in small print on an inside page if it is criticised). Successful complainants have no right to an apology, let alone to costs or expenses or compensation—their "victory" is especially hollow in privacy cases, when the adjudication can provide an occasion for re-publicising the breach (a reason why so many victims of privacy invasions do not complain or take their case to court). The PCC has refused to adopt one of Calcutt's main recommendations, namely that it should monitor the media for breaches of its code. It has no evidence to support its regular claim that press ethics are improving.

The PCC has no "hotline" procedure for intervening between the time of code-breach (*e.g.* by invasion of privacy) and the time of publication. This fact alone ensures that the code is not enforced when it really matters, *i.e.* to prevent invasions of privacy which have no public interest justification. There is one exception, in that the PCC is always at the beck and call of Buckingham Palace. This was demonstrated in 2001 when the Countess of Wessex was caught, by a *News of the World* undercover operation, promoting her P.R. company on the back of her royal connection. When the Queen's private secretary learnt of the problem, three days before publication, he summonsed Lord Wakeham and Guy Black, who came running to advise the Royal Family on how to minimise their embarrassment. They had to deny media suggestions that it was their advice that led the Countess to give a disastrous interview to *News of the World* ("SOPHIE: My Edward is NOT gay").[19]

The Commission adjudicates complaints by reference to its 16-clause Code of Practice. It meets for half a day each month to consider rulings drawn up by the chairperson and the staff, which are subsequently issued in the form of a quarterly bulletin. It refuses oral hearings and decides each case upon written submissions. Its adjudications will be sent, as a matter of courtesy, to parties shortly before publication of its quarterly bulletin, although it will not entertain any protest prior to publication. It will not consider any complaint about press conduct falling outside its written code. A particular problem is encountered in relation to complaints from individuals who might also have a legal remedy against the newspaper by suing for libel. The Press Council practice—severely criticised by Calcutt—was to extract a "legal waiver" from such individuals as a quid pro quo for the newspaper's agreement to co-operate with the Council and to publish its adjudication. This waiver was effective to bar any subsequent libel action, but only if it was expressly made and signed—a complaint to the Council did not of itself operate as an implied waiver.[20] As Calcutt pointed out, it is plainly wrong in principle that a complainant should be obliged to surrender a legal right to damages before obtaining an adjudication as to whether an ethical standard has been breached. The PCC has in theory

[19] See "A Right Royal Farce", *The Observer*, April 8, 2001, p. 13.
[20] *Franks v. Westminster Press Ltd, The Times*, April 4, 1990.

abandoned the waiver, although it exercises a discretion to postpone any adjudication if it relates to a matter that is or may be the subject of litigation.

Any member of the public, or any organisation, may complain to the Commission about a breach of the Code of Practice by an editor of a newspaper or magazine. The complaint will be accepted against an editor, even if it relates to conduct by a journalist or a freelance. Complaints are forwarded to that editor, who is required to contact the complainant direct and reach an amicable settlement. If this is not achieved within a short time-frame, the editor will be required to provide a written response, which will be sent to the complainant with an invitation to comment. This process will continue until the issues are clear and each party has had an opportunity to deal with the other's contentions in writing. There will be no contested hearing and no opportunity for parties to cross-examine or to discover the other side's documents.

The PCC staff, in consultation with the chairman, produce a draft adjudication which is despatched to Council members who will communicate their agreement. Draft adjudications that evoke disagreement are debated and finalised at the monthly Commission meeting. The Commission's adjudications are published in a bulletin issued every three months. The defending editor is under no duty to publish favourable adjudications, although these are generally reported, often as triumphs for free speech or in ways that belittle unsuccessful complainants. However, the Code preamble insists that "Any publication which is criticised by the PCC must print the adjudication in full and with due prominence". The PCC does not indicate what prominence is "due" and does not monitor compliance. A typical example is the privacy complaint upheld on behalf of *Coronation Street* actress Jacqueline Pirie, whose private life was splashed, without a shred of public interest, over the *News of the World* in January 2000. The PCC adjudication criticising the newspaper was published three months later, in small print and surrounded by advertisements, on page 40 of the offending paper.[21] It is difficult to understand how this could amount to a prominence that was "due", either to the victim or proportionately to the publicity given to the original story.

The Code of Practice

The PCC Code has emerged from a number of sources. Much of the language is adapted from the Calcutt Committee's draft, in turn influenced by a series of Press Council "Declarations of Principle" issued over the 36 years of its operation, developed and refined at times by

---

[21] *News of the World,* April 9, 2000, p. 40.

major adjudications or reports. The PCC pays some attention to these precedents but it claims that the Code derives its influence from the fact that it is regularly reviewed by a group of senior editors on its Code Committee. The Code provisions are:

"1. Accuracy

(i) Newspapers and periodicals must take care not to publish inaccurate, misleading or distorted material, including pictures.
(ii) Whenever it is recognised that a significant inaccuracy, misleading statement or distorted report has been published, it must be corrected promptly and with due prominence.
(iii) An apology must be published whenever appropriate.
(iv) Newspapers, whilst free to be partisan, must distinguish clearly between comment, conjecture and fact.
(v) A newspaper or periodical must report fairly and accurately the outcome of an action for defamation to which it has been a party".

These are "motherhood" provisions which need little elucidation. Most complaints are about inaccuracies, which are easily put right by prompt and prominent corrections. There is no definition of "due prominence": the PCC should insist upon a correction being carried on the same (or a similarly prominent) page to that on which the offending article was originally published. The PCC does not have the investigative or forensic resources to decide whether a story is false, and should not be regarded as a tribunal for establishing the truth. It will depend on the newspaper to admit error, or else insist that the complainant establish falsity by producing documentary evidence. Otherwise, it maintains that "it is not the Commission's job to establish the facts of the matter when two parties dispute the accuracy of an article but to consider, under the Code, whether sufficient care has been taken by a newspaper not to publish inaccurate material".[22] This is *not* a rule against inaccuracy, but a rule that newspapers should think twice before publishing allegations they cannot prove. Journalists accused of "inventing" quotations will be expected to have kept their notebooks, but the PCC never insists that they be submitted to an ESDA test. Editors cannot rely on having given the complainant an opportunity to correct the story unless that has been a real and considered opportun-

---

[22] *Macleod v. Sunday Mail,* Report No. 52, January 24, 2001.

ity,[23] and in the case of some stories (such as sexual gossip) editors cannot rely on a refusal to comment as corroboration.[24]

The PCC will, however, conduct its own investigation into a complaint if the complainant is sufficiently important. When the Prime Minister and his wife alleged that *The Mail on Sunday* had breached the Code by a story about their daughter whom it alleged had jumped the queue to attend a new school, the PCC took pains to establish the facts. There had in fact been no preferential treatment for the Prime Minister's daughter, although some parents honestly believed the contrary: the paper should not have published their speculation in a manner which suggested it was well-founded.[25] This ruling was a valuable exercise in fact-finding which served to put the record straight: it is not a service vouchsafed to many others who complain of inaccuracy. But when complaints are made by Buckingham Palace, the PCC loyally accepts Queen's evidence:

> The Queen complained that her wealth had been greatly exaggerated by *Business Age* magazine, which had placed her at the top of its "RICH 500". The magazine explained that it had included not only her racehorses and shareholdings, worth £158 million, but some art treasures, jewellery and palaces which brought her assets up to £2.2 billion. The magazine added, truthfully, that its estimate of what she owned in her own right "was a matter of legal argument" and that "royal retainers are willing to go to remarkable lengths to minimise estimates of the monarch's personal wealth". The lengths included a letter to the PCC by her Press Secretary, who complained that the Queen's personal income was "a private matter" and in any event it did not exceed £100 million: the magazine had failed to check with the Palace before publication. The magazine defended its estimate at length and requested an oral hearing to present expert legal and accounting evidence and to question the royal estimates. This was refused: the PCC, in a decision conspicuous for its unfairness and partiality, found the magazine in breach of the Code because it had not reported sufficiently the basis for its valuation, and had "presented speculation as established fact". This was manifestly wrong, since the journal had made plain to readers that its valuation was open to legal dispute—a dispute which the PCC royally refused to entertain.[26]

The rule that newspapers must report the outcome of defamation actions to which they are a party is an unnecessary fetter both on editorial discretion and a newspaper's legal tactics in libel actions. When a

---

[23] See *Bernie Grant M.P. v. The Times* PCC Report No. 2, 1991, p. 24 (message left on victim's answering machine inviting him to call the newspaper was not a sufficient check for accuracy).

[24] *Calthorpe v. Sunday Express,* PCC Report No. 50, July 27, 2000.

[25] *Blair v. The Mail on Sunday,* PCC Report No. 47, October 27, 1999.

[26] *The Queen v. Business Age* (1998) PCC Report No. 34, pp. 5–8.

paper settles, as many do, for "commercial" reasons (*i.e.* merely to avoid legal costs) there is no reason why they should report the outcome unless this is made a term of the settlement.[27]

2. Opportunity to Reply

"A fair opportunity to reply to inaccuracies must be given to individuals or organisations when reasonably called for."

This is not the fabled "right of reply" but a mere opportunity, couched in vague and question-begging language and unacceptably limited to replies to factual inaccuracies. It is regrettable that the newspaper industry should fudge a principle of basic fairness, noncompliance with which has been a major issue of public dissatisfaction with the British press. Rule 2 marks a retreat from the Press Council's principle that a right of reasonable reply should be provided to any "attack" on an individual or organisation, and from the draft Calcutt code, which called for "a proportional and reasonable right to reply to *criticisms or alleged inaccuracies*" [our italics]. Rule 2 permits the editor to be the judge of what amounts to an "inaccuracy", and implies that it may be reasonable to refuse an opportunity to put right a published misstatement of fact. Editors should always offer to publish letters from persons severely criticised by way of comment or conjecture, or by factual statements that cannot be verified but that the complainant alleges to be untrue. That said, there are genuine difficulties in deciding whether a published reply is "reasonably called for". Press Council precedents have held that no right of reply arises where the attack is contained in a news report of a speech by a third party, or where the person seeking to reply has threatened or commenced a libel action against the newspaper, or where the reply submitted is overlong or contains defamatory attacks on the newspaper's employees, or where an opportunity to reply has already been afforded in the original story.[28]

3. Privacy

"Everyone is entitled to respect for his or her private and family life, home, health and correspondence. A publication will be expected to justify intrusions into any individual's private life without consent."

This key provision, given legal import in breach of confidence cases

---

[27] See *Givenchy SA v. Time Out,* Report No. 46, July 28, 1999, where the PCC acknowledges the inappropriateness of the rule by declining to censure *Time Out.*

[28] See Robertson, *People Against the Press,* pp. 79–88 (above, n. 1).

by Section 12(4) of the Human Rights Act, begins with a statement of the right to privacy guaranteed by Article 8(1) of the ECHR. Any intrusion must be "justified"—but on what basis? The PCC adopts a different standard to the Convention, which requires any infringement to be (i) in accordance with law, (ii) pursuant to a legitimate aim and (iii) necessary and proportionate to the interests of public safety, health or morality, the prevention of crime, or the rights of others in a democratic society. Under the Code, editors have an easier task: their infringements may be justified "in the public interest", defined (for the purposes of this and other sections of the Code) as *including* (*i.e.* not limited to):

(i)   detecting or exposing crime or a serious misdemeanour;

(ii) protecting public health and safety;

(iii) preventing the public from being misled by some statement or action of an individual or organisation.

The infringement of a child's privacy calls for an *exceptional public interest* justification.

The Code formulation of the privacy principle and the public interest defence (together with its associated rules relating to harassment, intrusion into grief and shock, hospitals and listening devices) are likely to feature in any common law development of privacy, whether as a free-standing tort or through the doctrine of breach of confidence. It was because Earl and Countess Spencer had failed to sue tabloid newspapers for breach of confidence that the European Commission of Human Rights rejected their complaint that the United Kingdom insufficiently protected privacy:

In 1995, the *News of the World* published a front page article, "DI'S SISTER IN BOOZE AND BULIMIA CLINIC", which contained details of family problems and illnesses illustrated with a telephoto picture of the applicant captioned "SO THIN: Victoria walks in the clinic grounds this week". The applicants complained to the PCC, which judged that the paper had breached section 3 (ii) of the Code (see below). The newspaper apologised (but only to the Countess) and published the adjudication. Nonetheless, the applicants complained to Strasbourg that they could not obtain any "effective remedy" in the United Kingdom. The European Commission noted that although newspapers were bound to print adjudications with due prominence "the PCC has no legal power to prevent publication of material, to enforce its ruling or to grant any legal remedy against the newspaper in favour of the victim". For those reasons the PCC could not be considered an "effective remedy", and the United Kingdom Government did not even attempt to argue that it was. The Spencers were wrong-suited, however, because they had failed to go to court to obtain one available remedy, namely an injunction and damages under the developing civil law of breach of confidence.[29]

Although the PCC claims in its advertising material that it offers an "effective remedy" for breaches of privacy, the *Spencer* case shows that neither the Government nor Strasbourg consider that this claim is true.

It is noteworthy that the code is confined to an individual's private life and offers no protection to individuals in their business capacity or to any public or private company, unless subject to unjustifiable subterfuge or harassment. The justification for invasion of privacy must be based on specific public interest: it cannot be contended that press revelation of adultery or homosexuality or run-of-the-mill heterosexual behaviour qualifies, unless the victims are hypocrites. There is an unsatisfactory lack of clarity in the phrase "serious misdemeanour": it did not appear in the Calcutt draft, but was inserted by newspaper interests as something that might, in addition to "crime", be properly exposed through invasion of privacy. The excuse of "preventing the public from being misled by some statement or action of that individual" permits the press to invade the privacy of public figures who have acted contrary to their professed beliefs, so stories about adulterous vicars, politicians, and the like are justified under this exception.

The PCC has consistently condemned "kiss and tell" (more accurately, "kiss and sell") stories about celebrities and soap stars which are a staple of the British tabloids. These breach Rule 3 of the Code because they reveal intimate personal details (what the "star" is like in bed) without any trace of public interest. Granada Television regularly takes up cudgels on behalf of *Coronation Street* actresses whose sexual performances are luridly related by well-paid former boyfriends: editors offer humbug defences (they were upholding the ex-lover's "right" to free speech; for actors, all publicity is good publicity) which are routinely held to fall short of any "public interest" defence.[30] The editors are usually censured, and continue to publish similar stories about other celebrities, most of whom are advised that it is pointless to complain to the PCC. The proven inability of the PCC to stamp out this genre of privacy invasion gives the lie to its claim that its Code is honoured by British editors (other than in the breach rather than the observance).

Determinations under section 3(1) of the Code will depend on the circumstances of the particular case. The PCC is at heart a public relations operation, and in the hysterical aftermath of Diana's death (in a

---

[29] *Earl and Countess Spencer v. U.K.* Application No. 28851/95, [1998] E.M.L.R. CD 105; and see *Spencers v. News of the World,* PCC Report No. 29, (1995), p. 60.

[30] See *Pirie* case, above, and *Granada TV and Taylor v. Sunday Sport,* PCC Report No. 51, October 25, 2000, Case 1.

car crash at first wrongly attributed to menacing paparazzi) some ill-considered amendments were made to the Code to assuage public anger:

> "3(ii) The use of long lens photography to take pictures of people in private places without their consent is unacceptable.
>
> **Note:** Private places are public or private property where there is a reasonable expectation of privacy."

What constitutes "a reasonable expectation of privacy" has been the subject of a number of conflicting decisions, some plainly influenced by the status of the complainant. What principle, for example, underlies the following two rulings?

- Prince William was photographed hiking on a public trail and fording a river at a public crossing, during his "gap year" in Chile. The pictures were published as part of a hagiography in *OK!* magazine. Buckingham Palace complained, and the PCC decided the Code was breached because "Prince William was on a trip to a place where he had a reasonable expectation of privacy". It additionally condemned *OK!* for "making the Prince's life more uncomfortable" and for "harassment"— although there was not the slightest evidence that the photographer had come near the Prince. But when the Palace calls, the PCC jumps, even to conclusions: "William was not in a place where photographers would normally have been and must, therefore, have been followed by foreign paparazzi".[31]

- Moors Murderer Ian Brady was photographed in the grounds of a hospital. He was in a police van, about to be driven to another hospital (the curtains had been "left open"—doubtless by pre-arrangement—so a picture could be taken). The PCC ruled that since "the picture was taken in an area of the hospital grounds which was open to the public" the complaint failed.[32]

The true distinction between these two decisions is not that between the wilderness of South America and the confines of an English mental hospital, it is between a much-loved Prince and a much-loathed child murderer. What weighs with the PCC is the nature of the person rather than the nature of the place. Thus the Aga Khan, a royal and a spiritual leader of millions, had a "reasonable expectation of privacy" whilst

---

[31] *HRH Prince William v. OK! Magazine* PCC Report No. 52, January 24, 2001, Decision No. 3.

[32] *Stewart-Brady v. Liverpool Echo and The Mirror,* PCC Report No. 49, April 26, 2000, Case No. 10.

sunbathing on his luxury yacht at the height of a Mediterranean summer (No "Highness" can be expected to go below decks)[33] but Anna Ford, a mere BBC newsreader, had no such expectation when she and her companion were targeted by telephoto lens whilst sunbathing on their private hotel beach in Majorca.[34] Ms Ford could hardly have expected to be stalked by two paparazzi or that their sneak pictures would appear in colour in a national newspaper, prompting poison pen letters. When Ms Ford becomes Dame or Baroness, doubtless the PCC will uphold her complaints as it does for knighted pop stars: Sir Elton John's privacy was invaded by pictures of guests "relaxing" at his home in the South of France, even though the pictures were taken from a public footpath,[35] and Sir Paul McCartney was unaccountably held to have suffered a loss of privacy by being pictured in *Hello!* walking with his children by the banks of the Seine and eating lunch outside a café. (The publication of a further photograph, as he lit a candle inside Notre Dame Cathedral, was rightly found to be "deeply intrusive".)[36] What the PCC is attempting to do by this anti-paparazzi rule is to enforce a prohibition which goes far beyond any present legal requirement. It does so inconsistently. In our view, privacy can reasonably be expected in cemeteries, churches and changing rooms, but not whilst fording rivers or sitting in street-cafés or lounging in hotel lobbies.

Occasionally the PCC suggests that the *tone* of the picture might be relevant, although as a matter of logic the existence of a breach cannot depend on whether the result is unflattering (in law, this would go to damages, not liability). Sometimes a "public interest" defence is applied by association with the text (the Brady picture illustrated an article which *was* in the public interest, concerning his suicide attempt). Although the inside of a public servant's office is protected, there is no reasonable expectation of privacy in a private club for sado-masochists—or anywhere else that undercover *News of the World* reporters might wish to frequent.[37-38] (See the "Stop Press" section for further details.)

4. Harassment

"(i) Journalists and photographers must neither obtain nor seek

---

[33] *His Highness the Aga Khan v. Daily Mail,* PCC Report No. 46, p. 10.

[34] *Anna Ford v. Daily Mail and OK!,* PCC Report No. 52, January 24, 2001, Case No. 5. The High Court declined Ms Ford leave to review the decision: *R. v. PCC ex p. Anna Ford,* July 29, 2001, unreported.

[35] *Elton John v. Daily Star,* PCC Report No. 45, April 28, 1999, p. 7.

[36] *Sir Paul McCartney v. Hello,* PCC Report No. 43, November 4, 1998, p. 12.

[37-38] *Desyre Foundation v. News of the World,* PCC Report No. 48, January 26, 2000, p. 11.

to obtain information or pictures through intimidation, harassment or persistent pursuit.

(ii) They must not . . . persist in telephoning, questioning, pursuing or photographing individuals after having been asked to desist; must not remain on their property after having been asked to leave and must not follow them.

(iii) Editors must ensure that those working for them comply with these requirements and must not publish material from other sources which does not meet these requirements."

These post-Diana amendments are directed at foreign and freelance paparazzi, whose activities they have not in any way curbed. Editors are repeatedly ticked off for purchasing snatched or long-lens photographs, but the menace of snappers in hot pursuit has only been stopped effectively in California (by a criminal law which has put several British photographers in jail) and in New York, where a tort action for damages brought by Jacqueline Onassis was held compatible with the First Amendment. The PCC Code fails to draw a sensible line between public figures who genuinely wish to protect their privacy and those who wish to protect it only after they have exhausted the prospect of favourable publicity. The advent of celebrities—Diana herself was one—who invade their own (or their husband's) privacy and complained if they dislike the results (or were found out) make such distinctions important. One particularly unpleasant form of indirect harassment, namely the publication of addresses of a person against whom readers might seek reprisals, has not been consistently censured. The *Evening Standard* was condemned as irresponsible for publishing the address of a well-known Englishman's holiday home in Wales in an article about burning down such houses.[39] But the *New Nation* was not censured when it published the addresses of the suspects for the Stephen Lawrence murder, in a column suggesting that readers might like to visit them "to enhance their facial features".[40] Is the inconsistency explained by the fact that the Lawrence suspects are violent racists, while the English country gentleman was a former chairman of the Press Council?

5. Intrusion into grief or shock

"In cases involving grief or shock, enquiries must be carried out and approaches made with sympathy and discretion. Publication must be handled sensitively at such times, but this should not be interpreted as restricting the right to report judicial proceedings."

[39] *Sir Louis Blom-Cooper v. The Evening Standard*, PCC Report No. 7, (1992).
[40] *Norris et al v. New Nation*, PCC Report No. 45, April 28, 1999, pp. 16–17.

Clause 5 waters down a key clause in the Calcutt draft, which expressed the view that the press should not intrude unsolicited into personal grief or shock, especially after accidents and tragedies, unless justified by exposure of crime or anti-social behaviour or to protect public health and safety. Quite plainly, the press is not, as an industry, prepared to hold its hand on these occasions, save to offer "sympathy and discretion" to the newly breaved it continues to besiege in efforts to obtain tear-jerking "human interest" stories. This is an area where the Press Council was notably ineffective in curbing media misbehaviour. Professor Harry Bedson's suicide was partly attributed by the Coroner to press harassment after an outbreak of smallpox in his Birmingham University Department. The Council declared that people under stress as a result of breavement or involvement in a public crisis should not be put under pressure by the press.[41] In 1981 it upheld a complaint that a newspaper harassed the family of a child heart-transplant donor, and directed newspapers to co-operate in arrangements to relieve the effect of cumulative inquiries on people suffering severe personal grief. In 1983 it was driven to conclude that both Peter Sutcliffe's wife and the relatives of his victims were harassed by the media "ferociously and callously".[42] Yet in 1989 it had once again to condemn many newspapers for callous and intrusive behaviour in reporting the Hillsborough tragedy. The PCC, "enforcing" the weasel words of Clause 5, has had no more success in mitigating the distress press inquiries cause after major tragedies. Calcutt's recommendation was that editors should be held responsible for unjustifiable decisions to dispatch reporters in the first place; clause 5 is drafted in a way that assumes they will dispatch reporters, and will attract only vicarious criticism if the reporters they dispatch act insensitively.

The PCC has repeatedly defended the right of journalists to "doorstep" families in crisis, especially when their children are missing, presumed dead. Censure is reserved for those occasions when an "insensitive" reporter actually breaks news of the death to family and friends,[43] or harasses them for interviews.[44] A more difficult problem is encountered over editorial decisions to publish close-up pictures of victims of rail and car crashes: here the complaints of shocked relatives tend to be brushed aside on the ground that the Code does not cover tasteless or offensive photographs, although this will not have been the point of the complaint.[45] A public interest defence will normally succeed where the

[41] Press Council, *People Under Pressure*, 1980.
[42] Press Council, *Press Conduct in the Sutcliffe Case*, Chap. 18, para. 22.
[43] As in *Mckeown v. Evening Chronicle*, PCC Report No. 40, January 28, 1998.
[44] *Ajayi v. New Nation*, PCC Report No. 52, January 24, 2001, Case 7.
[45] See *Telford v. Lancaster Guardian*, PCC Report No. 50, July 26, 2000, Case 7; *Salisbury v. Lancaster Evening Post*, PCC Report No. 51, October 25, 2000, Case 7.

photograph makes a political point, *e.g.* about the inadequacies of the NHS, even though it identifies the sick or dying and invades the privacy of hospital patients.[46] One newspaper avoided censure for publishing pictures of a mentally ill man jumping off a railway bridge situated directly opposite the editor's office, from where the photographs were taken. This had been a tragic but public news event, gathering a crowd and lasting several hours, and the distress to the suicide's family was not covered by Clause 5 of the Code. The PCC does occasionally invoke this clause to criticise newspapers for publishing detailed evidence from inquests into suicides, although such criticism is contrary to the wording of the clause and is more appropriately directed to a law which unnecessarily requires coroners to examine all suicide cases in detail and in public.

6. Hospitals

> "(i) Journalists or photographers making enquiries at hospitals or similar institutions must identify themselves to a responsible executive and obtain permission before entering non-public areas.
>
> (ii) The restrictions on intruding into privacy are particularly relevant to enquires about individuals in hospitals or similar institutions."

Unless, that is, the inquiries are into a Moors murderer, or any other "psycho" (in tabloid speak), in which case the PCC will readily find a public interest excuse (*e.g.* to question the appropriateness of his treatment or the possibility of his public release).[47] The ease with which hospitals may be infiltrated came to public attention during the last days of television personality Russell Harty, when reporters in white coats and wearing stethoscopes obtained access to his medical notes and the occupants of other beds in his terminal ward were besieged with bouquets of flowers in which requests for an update on his condition were hidden.[48] Clause 9 was adopted following the outrageous behaviour of a *Sunday Sport* journalist and photographer who sneaked into actor Gorden Kaye's hospital room to "interview" him as he was coming round from brain surgery—behaviour which led the Court of Appeal to call for a statutory privacy law (see pp. 282).

---

[46] *Harrison v. Daily Mail*, PCC Report No. 46, July 28, 1999, pp. 15.

[47] See *Brown v. The Sun*, PCC Report No. 47, October 27, 1999, pp. 20.

[48] The bouquet delivered to the bedside with a calling card message to contact a reporter remains a common subterfuge: see *Taylor v. Sunday Mercury*, PCC Report No. 49, April, 26, 2000, Case 13.

7. Listening Devices

"Journalists must not obtain or publish material obtained by using clandestine listening devices or by intercepting private telephone conversations."

Some journalists routinely tape telephone conversations, but this practice has brought no criticism from the PCC. The rule in terms prohibits the publication of intercepts obtained by eavesdroppers, although some of the biggest newspaper scoops—"Camillagate", "Squidgygate", etc.—were obtained through interception of mobile telephone calls. The press can always claim a public interest, even in royal adultery, and since intercepts are likely to be truthful the victims rarely if ever complain to the PCC for fear of re-living their embarrassment. Secret recordings of David Mellor M.P.'s adulterous exertions with an actress were not only published (in the public interest of revealing how his ministerial energy was being sapped) but also played to telephone callers, until ICSTIS threatened to close down the line, in the interest of public decency (broadly defined).

8. Misrepresentation

"(i) Journalists must not generally obtain information or pictures through misrepresentation or subterfuge.
(ii) Documents or photographs should be removed only with the consent of the owner.
(iii) Subterfuge can be justified only in the public interest and only when material cannot be obtained by any other means."

Journalists who remove documents or photographs without the consent of the owner run the risk of conviction for theft, unless they can prove an intention to return them. Subterfuge is a common and sometimes necessary technique, but provokes few complaints. When one of the social workers criticised for over-zealousness in the Cleveland child abuse inquiry set up a practice to counsel adult victims, a *Daily Mail* reporter pretended to be such a victim in order to gather information about her methods. This subterfuge was approved by the PCC in the interests of "protecting public health", although the paper had no evidence (and failed to obtain any) that the counselling service was unprofessional.[49] On this basis, journalists could use subterfuge to test the advice of any professional person, whether or not it was controversial. The distinguished psychiatrist Dr Pamela Connelly has found undercover tabloid reporters in her Los Angeles consulting rooms, com-

---

[49] *Sue Richardson v. Mail on Sunday*, PCC Report No. 2 (1991) p. 15.

plaining (perhaps accurately) of their own sexual dysfunction, in the hope of writing about their treatment at the hands of the wife of Billy Connolly. The PCC has failed to make clear that this kind of behaviour is unacceptable.

Subterfuge is, in fact, becoming an increasingly productive tabloid technique. In 2001 the PCC somewhat unnecessarily censured *News of the World* when two of its journalists "crashed" a party for the cast of *Emmerdale* at a private hotel, carrying covert video equipment, even though the journalists left before they were spotted and no story was published. But no censure—only news attention and increased circulation—followed when a reporter dressed as an Arab engaged in an expensive charade to hoodwink Sophie Rhys-Jones and her business partner into offering her royal connections for the promise of large sums of money. Whether this was really in the public interest the PCC declined to investigate: it had in any event been hopelessly compromised by Lord Wakeham's attempts to assist the palace before the story was published (see earlier, p. 683).

9. Children

> "(i) Young people should be free to complete their time at school without unnecessary intrusion.
>
> (ii) Journalists must not interview or photograph children under the age of 16 on subjects involving the welfare of the child or of any other child, in the absence or without the consent of a parent or other adult who is responsible for the child.
>
> (iii) Pupils must not be approached or photographed while at school without the permission of the school authorities.
>
> (iv) There must be no payment to minors for material involving the welfare of children nor payment to parents or guardians for material about their children or wards unless it is demonstrably in the child's interest."

Although this section of the code notionally applies to infants, the PCC sensibly permits stories which relate more to the public life of the infant's parents (such as the prime ministerial adviser who left his eight-month-old baby in the care of an attendant at the Groucho Club[50]). It censored the *Daily Sport* for publishing a photograph of the Prime Minister's son kissing a dance partner at a private ball, although what was really objectionable was the dishonest caption ("Horny Blair") rather than the photo, which was not in fact a breach of clause 6(ii) since dancing is hardly "a subject involving the welfare of the child".[51]

---

[50] *Holm v. Mail on Sunday*, PCC Report No. 51, October 25, 2000, Case 3.
[51] *Blair v. Daily Sport*, PCC Report No. 79, April 26, 2000, Case 1.

Interestingly, the photographs in this case were hawked around national newspapers before they found a buyer in the *Daily Sport*: an indication that the mainstream press will sometimes exercise a restraint over and above code requirements, at least towards the children of famous people they like (or, alternatively, fear). However, when the PCC condemned *The People* for publishing a covert picture of the Duke of York's baby daughter frolicking naked in the garden, the paper republished the picture alongside a picture of the naked Duke of York, and invited readers to participate in a telephone poll over whether either or both pictures were offensive.[52]

A major part of the PCC's work involves protection of the Royal princes. This is the only subject on which it is prepared to monitor press coverage: its Annual Review has a special section entitled *The Royal Princes* (more recently *Prince William—Life after School*) and it has from time to time, unbidden, issued long statements instructing the media on how to behave ("editors should continue to err on the side of caution . . . it is far better that matters proceed by agreement and consent between editors and the Palace"[53]). Complaints by Buckingham Palace are immediately taken up with editors and with their proprietors, and are quickly resolved to the Palace's satisfaction. Lord Wakeham acts, in effect, as the royal press agent, brokering photo opportunities (*e.g.* William's "coming out" at the PCC's 10th anniversary party) and mediating between tabloid editors and the Palace to ensure a coverage which burnishes their image and partly satisfies the demand for royal gossip. He takes great pride in the fact that "no unauthorised picture of the Royal princes in school time has appeared in a British publication since 1995 (when Prince William started at Eton)—although they regularly do so in foreign newspapers and magazines".[54]

10. Crime Reporting

Three clauses of the code seek to constrain the reporting of court cases, in the interests of children (clause 7), friends and relatives of defendants (clause 10) and victims of sexual assault (clause 12). These clauses are well intentioned, although they enjoin editors to show more restraint than is required by an exceedingly complex and comprehensive law governing court reporting (see Chapter 8). The word "incest" may not be used if a parent is identified as the offender, for example. In such cases the main problem is "jigsaw identification", where the anonymous child will be readily identified if the defendant's name and the relationship is given or bracketed with the word "incest". The present

---

[52] PCC Report No. 1 (1991), p. 16.
[53] Statement on Reporting the Royal Princes, PCC Report No. 46, July 28, 1999.
[54] PCC Annual Review 1998, p. 12.

convention—to give the defendant's name but omit reference to "incest"—is a sensible compromise which gives correct priority to naming the defendant, at the cost of some obfuscation about the crime. The effect of compliance with clause 7 may be to protect, undeservedly, adult offenders who are related to the child, and whose name might have to be suppressed in order to avoid the child's identification. In such cases, at least if the law permits, the code may be breached on public interest grounds, although it emphasises that:

> "In cases involving children editors must demonstrate an exceptional public interest to override the normally paramount interests of the child."

The laws which restrict court reporting are elaborate and under constant review (*i.e.* extension) by Parliament: the PCC should be cautious about censuring editors for publications which the law allows, although in the rare cases of sexual assault where it is possible to publish identifying material, clause 12 of the Code requires "adequate justification" for so doing. This ethical sensitivity harks back to a notorious case in 1986 when the *Sun* published, over three full columns on its front page, a picture of the victim of a rape at an Ealing vicarage, taken as she was leaving her church the following Sunday. The victim's family told the Press Council that the thin black line masking her eyes still left no doubt of her identity and the *Sun*'s coverage had been deeply distressing. The Council condemned the newspaper for taking and publishing the photograph: "Both were insensitive and wholly unwarranted intrusions into privacy at a time of deep distress for the subject and neither served any public interest." The *Sun* showed no remorse. Its managing editor told the Council, with more than the usual display of humbug, that the newspaper had a duty to present rape as sordid crime and the picture was published to highlight the victim's "ordinary, girl-next-door qualities".[55] Public outrage at the newspaper's conduct produced a law that now prohibits the media from publishing any picture of an alleged rape victim from the moment a complaint has been made, and this prohibition lasts for her lifetime—even if the complaint is not pursued or the man complained against is acquitted.[56]

Chequebook journalism

Press payments to criminals, their associates and their relatives have long been a feature of the coverage of sensational trials. In the days

---

[55] Press Council, *The Press and the People*, 1987, p. 241.
[56] Criminal Justice Act 1988, s. 158, supplemented by the Sexual Offences Amendment Act 1992 and now consolidated in the Sexual Offences Act 2000. See p. 436.

before legal aid was routinely granted to defendants charged with murder, newspapers hired fashionable Q.C.s to defend accused persons facing the death sentence, in return for "exclusives" from them and their about-to-be-bereaved families. The practice of paying "blood money" in any form for such stories was widely condemned in the aftermath of the "Yorkshire Ripper" prosecution, and the Press Council forbade the practice in a detailed declaration after its inquiries revealed a host of unedifying offers of money by editors of national newspapers to friends and relatives of Peter Sutcliffe. Many years later, the same vice of payments to witnesses threatened to undermine the prosecution case against Rosemary West, who collaborated with her husband in committing perverted murders. In 1979, Liberal leader Jeremy Thorpe was acquitted of conspiracy to murder because of the behaviour of *The Sunday Telegraph* in suborning the main witness with a payment of £25,000 and a promise of a further post-trial payment of £25,000 if his evidence secured Thorpe's conviction. Twenty years later, the *News of the World* bore a heavy responsibility for the acquittal of Gary Glitter on indecent assault charges by a similar "jackpot on conviction" contract. The trial judge told the jury:

> "Here is a witness who first made public her allegations of sex abuse in return for the payment of £10,000 and who stands to make another £25,000 if you convict the defendant on any of the charges. That is a clearly reprehensible state of affairs. It is not illegal, but it is greatly to be deprecated".[57]

Had such conditional offers been outlawed after the *Thorpe* trial, the *News of the World* editor might have been jailed rather than slapped on the wrist by the PCC for breach of clause 16.

"16: Payment for Articles

Payment or offers of payment for stories or information must not be made directly or through agents to witnesses or potential witnesses in current criminal proceedings except where the material concerned ought to be published in the public interest and there is an overriding need to make or promise to make a payment for this to be done."

This falls far short of the prohibition on conditional payments which will, eventually, have to be imposed either by statute or by extending the crime of contempt. Otherwise, the code does not dissuade newspa-

---

[57] Butterfield J, November 1999. See *Taylor v. News of the World* PCC Report No. 48, January 26, 2000, Case 1.

pers from making arrangements to interview witnesses after the conclusion of the trial, so long as payment is discussed at that later stage.
The reference to "witnesses or potential witnessess" causes practical
difficulties, because it is impossible to foretell, in the days after arrest,
how the prosecution and defence cases are likely to develop. In the
Sutcliffe case the Press Council rejected the excuse that police had
informed editors that Sutcliffe had confessed and that there was unlikely
to be a contested trial: it pointed out that experienced editors should be
aware that defendants frequently repudiate confessions made in police
custody. Clause 16(1) does not make what should in practice be a crucial distinction between a witness to disputed facts (whose testimony
must be kept free from any influence) and a witness to matters of formal
record or to character. The interests of justice served by a rule against
paying witnesses do not apply with very great force to witnesses of the
latter kind.

The Code does not apply to witnesses who are on the run, or whom
journalists discover themselves. One of the most notable pieces of
recent investigative journalism was the tracing and interviewing of a
potential witness in a drugs trial by David May of *The Sunday Times*,
which led to the exposure of police corruption and the abandonment of
the prosecution.[58] Such "exceptional circumstances" may justify payments to witnesses for their time or their future protection, although
they should never be made conditional on the story standing up in court.
If a paper pays a witness for an interview it cannot publish (for contempt reasons) until after the trial, but the witness's credibility is
destroyed at the trial, then it must accept the fact that its story is worth-
less. With witnesses, a "success fee" should never be contemplated.

In its report on press conduct in the "Yorkshire Ripper" case the
Press Council inveighed against payments of "blood money" to criminals and associates: "the practice is particularly abhorrent where the
crime is one of violence and payment involves callous disregard for the
feelings of the families".[59] This declaration was issued in the context
of public outrage over the behaviour of the press in offering enormous
sums of money to Mrs Sonia Sutcliffe (who refused them) for no other
reason than that she was the wife of a notorious mass murderer. The
Press Council prohibition is now embodied in Clause 16 (ii) of the PCC
code:

> "(ii) payment or offers of payment for stories, pictures or
>   information, must not be made directly or through agents to
>   convicted or confessed criminals or to their associates—
>   who may include family, friends and colleagues—except

---

[58] See *R. v. Ameer and Lucas* [1977] Crim.L.R. 104.
[59] Press Council, *Press Conduct in the Sutcliffe Case*, Chap. 15, paras 5–10.

where the material concerned ought to be published in the public interest and payment is necessary for this to be done."

The PCC is much more relaxed about "blood money" payments than the Press Council, which applied a more stringent test of an overriding public interest:

In 1987 the *News of the World* was censured for blood-money payments to girlfriends of major criminals. The newspaper accepted that it had made payments (although it refused to say how much it paid) to the girlfriend of convicted murderer Jeremy Bamford in return for the right to publish a prurient "world exclusive" about their sex lives. Although the girlfriend had been innocent—she had informed on and given evidence against him—the story was nonetheless "sold on the back of crime" and had no public interest justification. Another payment, to an Irish barmaid who had been innocently duped by terrorist Nizar Hindawi into carrying a bomb on board an Israeli airliner, elicited a story that was plainly of public interest, but the Council nonetheless held that this was insufficiently "overriding" to justify the payment. It is difficult to see how this woman (who had testified against Hindawi) could meaningfully be regarded as his "associate"— she was intended to be amongst his many victims when the jumbo jet exploded over London. Her story was of enormous public interest, and had been sold to newspapers in many other countries: a strict compliance with the Council's declaration would have denied the British public an insight into a dastardly crime that would have caused many British casualties.[60]

The PCC has censured papers which pay murderers' girlfriends for "exclusives" on their sex lives: the "public interest" is not engaged and such brazenness only exacerbates the grief of relatives.[61] It condemned an interview in *Hello!* conducted from prison with fraudsman Darius Guppy which glorified his crimes,[62] and it condemned *The Daily Telegraph* for paying Jonathan Aitken's daughter for a soppy mitigation of his perjury ("My Father is Paying Too Heavy A Price").[63] Inconsistently, however, it declined to censure *The Sunday Times* for paying to serialise Aitken's *mea culpa, Pride and Perjury*.[64] In a confused adjudication, it said it was "necessary" to pay the publishers for serialisation rights (but that payment would obviously benefit Aitken, the convicted criminal). It said the extracts were in the public interest because Aitken had held high ministerial office and "the articles went some way to

[60] Press Council, *The Press and the People*, p. 210.
[61] See *Collier v.Sunday Sport*, PCC Report No. 51, October 25, 2000, Case 5.
[62] *Huins v. Hello!*, PCC Report, August–September 1993.
[63] *Barlow v. Daily Telegraph*, PCC Report No. 47, October 27, 1999, p. 10.
[64] *Bradley v. The Sunday Times*, PCC Report No. 50, July 26, 2000, Case 6.

explaining for the first time why he had embarked on the strategy which in the end exposed his lies". Darius Guppy did the same explaining to *Hello!*—had he held ministerial office, doubtless the magazine would have been exculpated.

The PCC ruling in Aitken deprives clause 16 (ii) of much significance in respect to payments to celebrated convicts, or those whose convictions are in any doubt. The "public interest" is invariably engaged, so the PCC thinks, by protestations of innocence or by any "revelation of new material". Thus Deborah Parry and Lucille MacLaughlan,[65] convicted of killing a fellow nurse in Saudi Arabia, and nanny Louise Woodward,[66] convicted of manslaughter in Boston, were permitted to profit from complaining about justice in other countries. Had all papers abided by the letter of clause 16 (ii), these defendants would doubtless have told their stories, free of charge, at a press conference: money was not "necessary" to elicit their eager self-justifications. The PCC pretends ignorance of the obvious—these payments are not made to obtain information, but to ensure exclusivity.

When the PCC rightly rejected some complaints against *The Times* for serialising *Crimes Unheard*, Gita Sereny's important book about child-killer Mary Bell, it noted in passing how other newspapers had searched for and harassed Mary Bell and her daughter, forcing the mother to admit her previous identity to her child. Did the PCC censure any newspapers for this inhumane conduct? Of course not: "no complaint of harassment was received—without which it was impossible for the Commission formally to investigate".[67]

An absolute rule against press payments to criminals and associates would deter criminals from revealing incriminating associations with powerful people. In such cases shady characters with a public interest story to tell are often in genuine need of some remuneration for telling it. If they are prepared to go public with revelations about policemen or employers or persons in authority, they need financial protection against reprisals. The real question is whether the importance of the story and the exigencies of its author justify the size of the payment, rather than whether payment should be made at all. So long as newspapers continue to refuse to divulge the size of their payments to informants, the PCC will be unable to decide this question. It should be noted that criminals who are paid money in return for recounting details of an offence for which they have yet to be convicted may have the payment seized, on the theory that it is part of the profit they have made from the offence. Section 71 of the Criminal Justice Act 1988 gives the sentencing court

[65] PCC Report No. 43 (1998) pp. 5–9.
[66] *Bright v. Daily Mail*, PCC Report No. 44, January 27, 1999, pp. 12–17.
[67] Report No. 43, (1999) p. 9.

wide powers to confiscate property obtained "in connection with" an offence, and the High Court may make charging orders to secure the position until the verdict. These powers were used against Michael Randle and Pat Pottle, authors of *The Blake Escape: How We Freed George Blake and Why*, when a High Court judge directed that their homes be charged to the Crown for an amount equivalent to the royalties they had earned on their book. They argued that the royalties had been earned by recounting an experience rather than in connection with a crime committed 25 years before, but the order was allowed to stand until it was discharged on their acquittal.[68] Where an advance and royalties were due to George Blake from the publisher of his own book, however, the courts decided it should be held in trust for the Government, on account of the traitor's breach of the confidence he owed to MI6.

In 2001 *The Sun* indirectly made large payments to Ronald Biggs and another "great" train robber as part of its operation to return him from Brazil to spend his dying days at the taxpayer's expense in a British prison. The PCC fell for the *Sun*'s defence—derided by its rivals—that those payments to criminals were necessary in the public interest,[69] although they were more in the interests of Biggs. The story they elicited about his farewell to his grandchildren—"Ronnie sobs as tot gets a final cuddle"—may have interested the Brazilian public, but left British readers unamused (*The Sun* dropped in circulation). Nonetheless the message was clear: the PCC will decline to take a view about the public interest which conflicts with that of a powerful newspaper, unless the newspaper's view is unarguably wrong.

The Code has no provision relating to payments to non-criminal informants, jilted lovers and other familiar sources of kiss-and-tell stories. There is often no public interest justification for such tales, and on occasion the tabloid press has paid large sums of money to drug addicts and prostitutes in order to tell them. It is ironic that the people who would be prosecuted for the serious crime of blackmail if they threatened their victim with public exposure unless they were paid a sum of money can now obtain that sum quite legally by taking their story direct to a newspaper. It has been suggested that newspapers that purchase sensational stories of this sort should be required to disclose the amount of the payment on publication: this would serve to alert their readers to the possibility that the sensation in the story may be related to the sensation of receiving a large amount of money for telling it.

---

[68] *Re Randle and Pottle, The Independent*, March 26, 1991, Webster J.
[69] See "Sun cleared over Biggs", *The Guardian*, July 4, 2001, p. 6.

"13. Discrimination

(i) The press must avoid prejudicial or pejorative reference to a person's race, colour, religion, sex or sexual orientation or to any physical or mental illness or disability.

(ii) It must avoid publishing details of a person's race, colour, religion, sexual orientation, physical or mental illness or disability unless these are directly relevant to the story."

These simple provisions are difficult to apply in practice. In 1987 the editor of the *Daily Telegraph,* Max Hastings, announced his newspaper's intention to defy Press Council censure for describing convicted criminals as "black", however irrelevant this was to their offence, on the grounds that he could communicate the same information by publishing their photograph.[70] However, editors have over the years become more sensitive to allegations about racist reporting.

The rule that the press should avoid pejorative or prejudicial language in relation to classes of citizens who often suffer from discrimination has had some effect in moderating press polemics, especially against sexual minorities. There is a valuable role a voluntary standards body can play, in discouraging the use of "socially unacceptable language" that denigrates groups on the basis of race or gender or sexual preference, by marking public distaste for language that stigmatises whole classes of citizens. In 1991 the PCC censured the *Daily Star* for encouraging the persecution of homosexuals in a lead story about "Poofters on Parade" in the army, which attacked gay rights groups as "preachers of the filth'".[71] The editor of the *Star,* a homophobe named Brian Hitchen, continued the vilification (which was based on falsely stated facts) in his own column, but that was not censured—he was an editor member of the PCC at the time.

The PCC has shrunk from trying to abate the jingoistic fervour whipped up by tabloids before Euro-finals, although this has been said to encourage football hooliganism. In 1996 it declined to censure violently anti-German headlines, of the "Let's Blitz Fritz" and "Bring on the Krauts" variety, on the specious reasoning that clause 13 prohibits racist treatment of individuals but not of national groups.[72] In 1998 it repeated that "nationalist fervour and jingoism" was inevitable before international sporting events. Thus it found emotionally acceptable the *Daily Star*'s proposition that "as we proved at Agincourt and Waterloo, a good kicking on their gallic derrières is the only language the greedy frogs understand".[73]

---

[70] Press Council, *The Press and the People,* p. 146.
[71] PCC Report No. 2, n.16 above, p. 9.
[72] PCC Report No. 35 (1996), pp. 22–24.
[73] *Waller v. Daily Star,* PCC Report No. 42, July 29, 1998, p. 9.

Financial journalism

The Press Council, in an effort to ward off requirements for financial journalists to register as "professional advisers" like other share tipsters, produced a code on this subject, beginning with the platitude "They should not do a deal of which they would be ashamed if their readers knew." Clause 14 spells out three basic rules:

> "14 Financial journalism
>
> (i) Even where the law does not prohibit it, journalists must not use for their own profit financial information they receive in advance of its general publication, nor should they pass such information to others.
>
> (ii) They must not write about shares or securities in whose performance they know that they or their close families have a significant financial interest, without disclosing the interest to the editor or financial editor.
>
> (iii) They must not buy or sell, either directly or through nominees or agents, shares or securities about which they have written recently or about which they intend to write in the near future."

These rules, in fact, reflect the law relating to "insider dealings", which financial journalists should always bear in mind (see p. 670). Some newspapers insist on a much more rigid code, which requires that their financial journalists should not own shares or securities at all. Other newspapers, however, have connived for many years at share dealing by their tipsters, who sometimes tip off their editors. An insider-dealing scandal engulfed *The Daily Mirror* in 2000 when it emerged that the writers of its "City Slicker" column had been dealing extensively in the shares they tipped: they were dismissed for gross misconduct by the management. But they claimed to have passed on advance information about their next "tip of the day" to both the editor and the deputy editor, who were proved to have dealt at the time in these very shares, although they denied the allegations that they had done so as a result of a tip. The PCC tried to restore public confidence with an "investigation": a pathetic affair in which it made no attempt to cross-examine the editor over his dealings in shares, or to discover whether the journalist's allegations were true or false. ("The Commission does not find it necessary to choose between the conflicting versions.") The PCC condemned the two journalists (who had admitted misbehaviour and been dismissed) and made no finding against the editor other than that he had "failed to take sufficient care" to supervise them.[74] The

---

[74] PCC Report No. 50, July 26, 2000, pp. 5–11 (*The Mirror*).

scandal—and the PCC's inability to a proper inquiry—led to a proposal by the Government early in 2001 to bring business and city journalists within the statutory regulation of the Financial Services Authority.

Confidential sources

Clause 15 of the Code of Practice reads simply: "Journalists have a moral obligation to protect confidential sources of information." Journalists do not, however, have any legal obligation to protect their sources: on the contrary, they will sometimes have a legal obligation to betray their source (see p. 260). Although the Code is binding only on editors, this provision may be useful to journalists who seek editorial support to defy court orders requiring disclosure. An editor who disciplined or dismissed a journalist for refusing to disclose a source, even in disobedience to a court order, would thus be deserving of PCC censure.

Does the PCC work?

The PCC is a public relations exercise. It was established by newspaper interests as a means of convincing politicians and opinion formers that self-regulation can guarantee privacy and rights of reply better than statutory provisions. The Press Council, established to serve the same purpose, was abandoned when it lost public confidence and had its pretensions to both discipline and defend the press derided by Calcutt. If the PCC suffers the same fate, the statutory tribunal recommended by Calcutt waits in the Westminster wings, as does the draft statute prepared by the Law Commission to enable victims of media infringement of privacy to recover damages. It has been the danger apprehended from these developments which spurred proprietors and editors to co-operate with the PCC through its first decade, obeying its dictates over coverage of the Royal princes and publishing its adjudications without complaint (although also without prominence). The Code continues to be breached as often as ever, but few victims complain (since they can achieve nothing) and the PCC does not accept complaints from unaffected parties or do any monitoring itself (except to keep an eye on coverage of the Royal Family). With the PCC as its fig leaf, the newspaper industry has used its considerable political clout to scupper efforts under both Tory and Labour Governments to introduce privacy laws: political leaders, desperate for tabloid support, praise "self-regulation" because that is a pre-condition for obtaining it. The wild card in this arrangement is the judiciary, armed with new powers under the Human Rights Act 1998. Unafraid of tabloid pressure, some judges are minded to develop a tort of privacy, or to extend breach of confidence to the same effect, and they may do so by using the PCC code provisions as the test (since they are drafted by editors, the press can hardly object if the courts take them seriously). Editors would then have fashioned a noose for their own necks, with (for example) the code prohibition on photographing people in places where they have "a reasonable expectation of privacy" being used as a basis not for another meaningless adjudication, but for an award of damages against the photographer and the newspaper, and an injunction on further publication.

The PCC was modelled on the Advertising Standards Authority, which had achieved considerable success in persuading Parliament that self-regulation worked better (and more cheaply) than statutory regulation of advertising content. However, the analogy falters:

- The ASA works because its rulings are backed by a severe sanction (advertisements held to breach of code will not be published again). The PCC has no sanction; it does not offer to compensate any victim, or require a censured editor to publish its censure with any degree of prominence, or to refrain from repeating the breach.

- The PCC has not solved the intractable problem that tabloids are entertainment-based and will continue to publish circulation-boosting stories irrespective of adverse adjudications. Calcutt recognised that the improbability of all sections of the print media following PCC adjudications was the factor that would be most likely to fuel demands for statutory regulation.

- The PCC's refusal to monitor compliance with its code or even responses to its own adjudications is a fatal mistake. The ASA is the more respected precisely because it engages in monitoring and may act against breaches without the need to await a complaint from an interested member of the public. As Calcutt recognised, a monitoring exercise is essential to any code that purports to regulate intrusions into privacy, as victims (other than of notorious infringements) will be reluctant to give the matter further publicity by making a complaint.

- The PCC will face problems over its procedures in the event that it becomes judicially reviewable. Its evident desire to exclude lawyers and to operate informally, with nudges and winks transmitted along a network of editors, is not calculated to satisfy complainants or (inevitably) their legal advisers. Unsuccessful complainants feel that they have not been given a fair hearing when they are given no hearing at all, especially when disputed issues of fact are decided against them on the strength of written communications with newspaper representatives.

A more serious problem once the PCC is perceived by the courts as having quasi-judicial status is the bias which might be apprehended from its membership. Its part-time chairman receives a large salary (reported to be £150,000 a year for working one day a week), paid for by a levy on the companies which own the newspapers complained against. His presence on an adjudicative panel might on this basis be challenged.

The PCC does valuable but unpublicised work in mediating between "non-celebrity" complainants and newspapers, obtaining acknowledgments of error, corrections and apologies which provide some satisfaction to falsely maligned individuals. They could for the most part obtain this redress by contacting the editor (but they lack confidence) or having a lawyer contact the editor (but they lack money to retain one). The PCC serves a valuable function as an informal conciliator, leaning on newspapers to admit mistakes or oversights, and there is no reason why this service should not continue irrespective of whether a privacy law becomes available for victims of more serious intrusions. Regrettably, the PCC devotes much of its "annual review" to shrill propagandistic claims of the kind:

> "the application and observance of the Code are part of the culture of every news room and every editorial office . . . (the PCC) has clearly raised standards of reporting . . . most activities which brought newspapers and magazines into disrepute in the 1980s have long since vanished—and the PCC continues to ratchet up standards on the back of adjudications".[75]

On the contrary, privacy invasions of the 1980s have continued, and a vicious new development—the newspaper as vigilante, encouraging the lynch mob to visit alleged paedophiles at their published addresses and whipping up hatred against the youths who killed Jamie Bulger (putting their security at risk when they are released) makes it arguable that British press ethics are at their lowest ebb. There is no evidence that the PCC's self-regulation has been any more successful than the Press Council's. The only difference is that while the Press Council decisions—and the Press Council—were often vigorously condemned by the press itself, Lord Wakeham has succeeded in persuading proprietors and editors that it is in their interests to support—*i.e.* not to criticise—the PCC. There is a queasy irony here for a British press which trumpets its commitment to free speech, because this wider public interest aspect of the PCC's relationship with the industry it affects to regulate has gone unremarked. That the PCC gets a "good press" is unsurprising, but an example of media hypocrisy nonetheless. Do editors and journalists, so quick to find fault with the performance

---

[75] PCC Annual Review 2000.

of other public bodies, turn a blind eye to PCC failings because they have an economic and political interest in fostering a public perception of its success? The fact is that national newspapers report adjudications as if they were as meaningful as court cases, and have never published a serious critical analysis of the organisation. After *The Sun* enraged public feeling (as whipped up by *The Mirror* and other competitors) by publishing an old photo of Sophie Rhys-Jones, bare at one breast, before her marriage to Edward Windsor, the PCC issued an immediate and overblown condemnation: "The decision to publish these pictures was reprehensible and such a mistake must not happen again". This was repeated as "news" by all newspapers, under portentous headlines ("Lord Wakeham's Statement") which presented it as a ruling which was bound to deter further privacy invasions.[76] Only *The Guardian* permitted itself a touch of editorial candour over this "smack on the wrist", and hinted at the truth: "The only time the PCC jumps is when Royalty complains".

The PCC has so far failed to raise the tone or the profile of debate over media ethics, although it has encouraged the development of procedures within newspaper offices (including the appointment of ombudsmen and "readers' representatives") that enable complaints to be answered quickly. Its adjudications are short and usually oversimple, reflecting only on editors, who do not appear discomforted by its statements that they have breached a code of practice. One fateful decision made in its first year was to take the *Sunday Sport* seriously and to treat it as a newspaper. The PCC embarked upon a solemn investigation into a front-page story entitled "THIS NUN IS ABOUT TO BE EATEN. She's soaked in sauce, barbecued then carved up like a chicken . . . turn to pages 15, 16 and 17 if you dare." The editor of the *Sport* relished the complaint, describing his article as "pioneering investigative journalism at its best", which he was proud to have published. He dared the PCC to condemn him for exposing necrophilia in a Buddhist monastery in Thailand, "a country regularly visited by British tourists". The PCC rose to the bait, describing the story as "an extreme breach of the spirit of the Code of Practice" although it was outside its letter, since the Code does not purport to regulate matters of taste.[77] *Private Eye* is the only print journal which refuses to recognise the PCC, on the basis (says Ian Hislop) that certain editor-members of the

---

[76] Even a respected commentator like Roy Greenslade could proclaim, nonsensically, that this adjudication left *The Sun* editor "bleeding . . . the wounds might well prove fatal": "Bring Me Your Woes", *The Guardian,* June 7, 1999. However, there are occasional signs that a columnist realises that the emperor has no clothes: see Catherine Bennett, "The Waste of Space that is Lord Wakeham", *The Guardian G2,* July 5, 2001.

[77] PCC Report, No. 2, July—September 1991, p. 23.

Commission are themselves so morally questionable that no ethical judgment they make deserves to be recognised.

NUJ CODE OF CONDUCT

The National Union of Journalists has a code with which all members are expected to comply. The code itself is impressive, although attempts to enforce it have been less so. No journalist has been expelled for breach of the code, and disciplinary hearings tend to be unsatisfactory for all concerned in that victims of unethical behaviour can only complain to the NUJ branch of which the offending journalist is a member. If any branch member is impressed by the complaint, he or she could formally begin disciplinary proceedings on behalf of the victim. This procedure is not satisfactory: it relies upon journalists to take up cudgels against their colleagues, and provides no assurance that the complaint will be dealt with either independently or impartially.

THE ADVERTISING STANDARDS AUTHORITY

In 1962 the advertising industry was threatened with statutory regulation by the Moloney Committee on Consumer Protection, so it turned to the then credible Press Council as a self-regulatory model which seemed to satisfy politicians and public alike. The Advertising Standards Authority (ASA) was established, with its guiding mission to ensure that advertisements are "legal, decent, honest and truthful" by ordering their removal from newspapers if they infringe the Advertising Code. Ironically, the Press Council was in due course condemned as a confidence trick which failed to inspire confidence, while the ASA went from strength to strength, becoming in turn the "code adjudicator" model chosen in 1991 for the PCC. Given the general acceptability of some restrictions on commercial speech, the ASA has not suffered very much public criticism. This is because (unlike the PCC) it has real power, derived from its agreement with newspapers and journals that they will not carry any advertisement it judges to have breached the Code, and from its power to refer persistent code-breakers to the Director-General of Fair Trading who has a statutory duty to obtain injunctions against false advertising. Even so, there are signs that the self-regulatory system for advertising does not fully satisfy the public interest: since the ASA can threaten no criminal sanctions, deceitful advertisers will "get away with it" for weeks or months until a complaint is upheld, and will not suffer a fine or any other sanction. The large and increasing number of justified complaints may itself be an indication that self-regulation has failed to deter. There is also evidence that the cosy, industry-friendly arrangement, with its *grundnorm* that "NO ADVERTISEMENT SHOULD BRING ADVERTISING INTO DISREPUTE"[78] can operate to curb the free speech rights of protest groups who choose to advertise in order to make political points.

The Advertising Code, with its spin-off codes dealing with sales promotions, cigarettes, children, etc., is devised and amended by representatives of the commercial and professional bodies which comprise the advertising industry, sitting as the Committee of Advertising Practice (CAP). There is no lay participation: this trade body puts the sanctions in place and fosters awareness of the Code and the ASA procedure. The ASA purports to act as a tribunal at arm's length from the industry, although the fact that it shares a secretariat with CAP belies this outward impression. Both bodies are funded by a levy on advertising and marketing revenues, raised by the Advertising Standards Board of Finance (another industry body) in the amount that is judged necessary to keep the system operating with sufficient success to stave off statutory regulation. The ASA itself has been set up as a limited company, with a council of 12 part-time members, a majority of whom work outside advertising. Its adjudicatory powers apply to all advertisements placed in newspapers and magazines or shown in cinemas or on video trailers; to posters displayed in public; to circulars, mail-shots and to advertisements sent as fax transmissions or e-mail. It refuses, however, to regulate classified ads (on grounds of privacy), flyposting (on grounds of impossibility), or drug promotions to the medical profession (on grounds of lack of expertise). Television and radio commercials are left to the specialist authorities (see Chapter 16) while ICSTIS deals with premium rate telephone calls.

The ASA's remit covers some 30 million advertisements placed in the press each year, 100,000 posters on paid hoardings and four million mail shots. These elicit on average 12,000 complaints from members of the public, mainly directed to false claims made for the likes of slimming treatments, insurance and rare salesmanship, and about 20 per cent concerning matters of taste and decency. The Code provisions are expressed in general terms, and the main provisions are:

Truthfulness

No advertisement should mislead, or exploit the credulity or inexperience of consumers. Obvious exaggerations are permitted, but whenever objective claims are made for a product the advertiser must be in a position to confirm them with documentary proof. Ads must not show

---

[78] Advertising Code (1999), Principle 2:4.

or encourage unsafe practices—speeding cars are a particular target. So are "get rich quick" schemes: as the Authority notes in its 1999 report, "if something seems too good to be true, it probably is". Truth must be trimmed in the interests of social responsibility, so there are limits to portraying the pleasures of alcohol: drinking may be shown as sociable or thirst-quenching, but not as an indulgence or a solitary pastime for young people. Smoking has a special code negotiated between the tobacco industry and the DTI: advertisements must never incite people to start smoking, or admit that the experience might be pleasurable or indulged in by fashionable or wealthy people, or associated with "social, sexual, romantic or business success".

Decency

"Advertisements should contain nothing that is likely to cause serious or widespread offence", especially offence on grounds of "race, religion, sex, sexual orientation or disability". (The code says nothing about discrimination on the grounds of age, which is endemic in advertising.) Advertisements may be distasteful—up to a point—and offensive to some people: the "widespread" nature of the offence is not judged by the number of complaints alone. In 1998, for example, the advertisement which topped the complaint poll featured a cow which craved to be made into a burger if it could be washed down by a particular drink (the ASA correctly concluded that the majority of viewers would not be seriously offended). In December 2000 it ordered the removal of "porno-chic" posters advertising Opium perfume which featured Sophie Dahl naked, open legged and open mouthed—the subject of 700 complaints. Many decency complaints are from organisations representing Muslims, but the Authority tends to be more respectful to religious sensibilities over advertisements which exploit the Christian message: a *Sunday Times* promotion featuring a half-naked model on the cross (a "heavenly body"—geddit), and an advert for jeans worn by the Virgin Mary were condemned as likely to give serious offence. The question is whether religion "is seen to be mocked or treated disrespectfully"—a picture of a Bishop puffing on a joint whilst wearing the advertiser's brand of watch was judged unacceptably mocking rather than amusing.[79] Such complaints spring from a sensitive minority, so the ASA asks "whether it so deeply offends that minority that it would be reasonable for their interests to prevail against the rights of the advertiser to free expression; and whether the unoffended majority should be prevented from seeing the advertisement".[80] This test, of course, will depend upon the respect that the ASA committee has for

---

[79] Advertising Standards Authority Annual Review (1998), p. 10.
[80] ASA Annual Review (1999), p. 5.

the offended minority: it has shown great respect for mainstream churches, racial equality groups and the monarchy, but rather less for animal lovers and feminists.

The ASA has often been robust in rejecting complaints about sexual innuendo, notably the poster with a laid-back model advertising Gossard "translucent" lingerie ("Who said that a woman can't get pleasure from something soft") and the Wonderbra advertisement with the talking breasts ("Hello boys. We've been apart for too long").[81] Sexist sniggering is fine, but the ASA draws the line at mockery directed to male sex organs, whether featured in advertisements for underpants ("The Loin King") or for club 18–30 (bulging boxer shorts with the tag "Girls—can we interest you in a package holiday?").[82] The ASA correctly applies a narrower test of decency to public posters which gratuitously confront passers-by and motorists, than to advertisements which are run in specialist journals or for target audiences. Context and circumstances can make all the difference: in an interactive news magazine, salacious copy about oral sex is acceptable.[83] "Grave or widespread offence" is usually predictable, and national sensibilities rule out some advertising—especially featuring naked children—that is acceptable on the Continent. In 1991 the Italian clothing chain, Benetton, caused grave and widespread offence by plastering a colour picture of a new-born baby on British billboards: offence was caused not because the picture was indecent, but because it was exploitative. The public is quick to protest when black humour is put to commercial use: 2,000 complaints were received about a billboard advertisement for *Today* newspaper that showed Mrs Thatcher, Mr Kinnock and Mr Owen each hanging from a noose, above the caption: "Would Britain be better off with a hung Parliament?"

Crude language gives widespread and understandable offence on posters and in newspapers and magazines for general readership: the ASA report "Delete Expletives" summarised its surveys showing that 86 per cent disapprove of four-letter words in public advertisements to which children may be exposed. Inconsistently and inappropriately, however, the Authority approved use of the slogan "FCUK" to promote a French clothing chain, perhaps reasoning that some public irritation was better than giving the company valuable publicity through news coverage of a ban. This purpose was stymied by the broadcasting regulators who turned down the television campaign: the ASA's permissiveness only made the T.V. censorship more newsworthy. The "FCUK" affair showed both the absurdity of having too many regulators, and

---

[81] ASA Annual Report (1995), p. 21.
[82] *ibid.*, p. 21.
[83] See, *e.g.* the rejection of a complaint against Dennis Publishing Ltd in ASA Monthly Report, June 14, 1997.

how advertising agencies may outsmart them by capitalising on their inconsistencies. A news story about a decision to suppress an advert for a particular product is usually more valuable (because it is more widely and alertly read) than the advertisement which has been suppressed.

Privacy

The Code insists that *advertisers should not unfairly portray people in an adverse or offensive way*, and should obtain prior written permission before identifying individuals. The ASA, like the PCC, appoints itself as protector of the institution of monarchy—the code has specific provisions prohibiting any mention of members of the Royal Family (although the use of the "by Royal Appointment" warrant is the most misleading advertisement of all) or the use of royal arms or emblems. It banned an advertisement for a newspaper featuring a mock-up of a photo of Princess Diana kissing Paul Gascoigne, captioned "Who knows what the future holds?".[84] (the Palace complained, not Paul Gascoigne), but refused to condemn a sniggering invasion of Peter Mandelson's privacy in an advertisement in *The Times* for a football match. ("A humorous and entertaining play on words linking the match to speculation about Mandelson's sexuality".[85]) The ASA is quick to ban advertisements which offend royalty and corporations which place advertisements (see the *Tesco* adjudication below) but offers little protection to public figures who are made the butt of puerile jokes by copy writers.

Party Political Advertising

The ASA has finally decided to opt out of this controversial area, having been widely criticised for its ban on the Conservative poster prior to the 1997 election which depicted Tony Blair with demonic red eyes.[86] The ASA condemned the fact that it showed the Labour leader as "sinister and dishonest", an adjudication which gave the Saatchi advertisement massive free publicity. Quite aside from this counter-productive consequence, the ban was wrong in principle: at election time, it is crucial for voters to judge the morality of political parties by the nature of the messages they send (the "demon eyes" propaganda was valuable to show the electorate the depths to which Tories would sink in negative campaigning).

---

[84] ASA Monthly Report No. 59, 1995.
[85] ASA Monthly Report (April 1999).
[86] ASA Monthly Report No. 65, 1997.

Pressure Group Advertising

The voluntary system is geared to commercial advertising, where free speech can readily be subordinated to countervailing values of protecting consumers and avoiding gratuitous public offence.[87] There is much to be said for removing political campaigning advertisements from its remit, so long as these are readily identifiable. Why should the 13 members of the ASA Council, all chosen by its chairman (usually himself a superannuated middle-of-the-road politician) presume to judge the honesty and accuracy of pressure group causes? Much time was spent by the ASA during 1998–2000 in resolving claims and counter-claims about hunting made by the Countryside Alliance and the RSPCA: advertisements from both groups were criticised for exaggeration and inadequate documentary support.[88] The International Fund for Animal Welfare is another campaigning organisation which has had its free speech curbed for questionable reasons: an advertisement in the *Financial Times* calling upon the chairman of Tesco's to ban the sale of Canadian salmon in protest against the Canadian Government's approval of seal-killing was condemned, on the bizarre ground that *Financial Times'* readers might think (from a photo of a sealer clubbing a baby seal) that the chairman of Tesco's was the man on the ice-floe with the raised club.[89] This adjudication survived a judicial review, on the grounds that the ASA could rationally make it, but shows how the system works to insulate business leaders from personal confrontation over their corporate ethics.

It is in this respect that the European Court will come to the advertisers' aid. It has ruled that Article 10 applies to commercial speech, but will only be accorded full weight when there is a public interest component. This test will be met when advertisements are banned for their message rather than for the way in which it is expressed:

> The Swiss meat industry had been heavily promoting beef in television commercials, so an animal rights group made a counter-commercial featuring nervous pigs and the message "eat less meat, for the sake of your health, the animals and the environment!" The commercial broadcaster refused, pursuant to a law which forbade political advertising. The European Court found a breach of Article 10 precisely because of the political content of the message, which gave it more protection than enjoyed by

---

[87] Commercial speech is nonetheless protected in principle by Art. 10: the ECHR is unlikely to intervene if the advert has no public interest dimension, but where it conveys significant information to the public the court has held that it should not be shackled by professional rules (*e.g.* lawyer's advertising) or bans imposed for partisan reasons—see n.90, below.

[88] ASA Annual Report 1998, p. 8.

[89] ASA adjudication, January 24, 1996.

the usual commercial inviting viewers to purchase goods and services. The Court was also influenced by the fact that the advertiser was not a wealthy political party or other group which could endanger the broadcaster's independence. It noted that the prohibition applied only to television and not to other media, and drew the conclusion that it could not therefore be a necessary response to a pressing social need.[90]

Competition

The ASA Code provides that *"Advertisers should not unfairly attack or discredit other businesses or their products"*. British advertising is remarkable for the absence of mildly aggressive comparisons, let alone cut-and-thrust competition, and the ASA's role in reducing this necessary aspect of a free market is deserving of severe criticism. It took a Directive from the European Union to make clear that comparative advertising (*i.e.* advertisements identifying rival products) is permissible in the interests of competition and public information, on condition that it is not misleading and genuinely compares like with like.[91]

Procedure and Review

Complaints by members of the public must be directed to the ASA Council, which may additionally consider advertisements referred by its Secretariat, which monitors publications (somewhat diffidently) for breaches of the code. The Council has 13 members, all selected by the Chairman who since January 2001 has been Lord Borrie, formerly Director-General of the Office of Fair Trading. He and his predecessors' choice of colleagues has produced upper middle class worthies who are wholly unrepresentative of the working classes or indeed of the consumers on whose behalf they act. There are several professors and top public servants, the inevitable Church of England clergyman, some successful businessmen and a private school headmistress, sitting with representatives of the advertising industry. Complaints about advertisements by rival agencies or producers are discouraged (so much for competition) and neither complainant nor advertiser is ever vouchsafed an oral hearing or an opportunity to confront or cross-examine. The ASA's procedure is speedy: once complaints are taken seriously, advertisers must respond promptly. In cases of urgency, where an ongoing campaign has provoked outrage or claims of deceit, a response may be required within 24 hours. In such emergencies an immediate adjudica-

---

[90] *VGT Verein Gegen Tierfabriken v. Switzerland* 10 B.H.R.C. 473.
[91] Directive 97/55/EC on comparative advertising, implemented by the Control of Misleading Advertisements (Amendment) Regulations 2000, S.I. 2000 No. 94.

tion can be made or "interim measures" imposed by the Secretariat (such as asking for the advertisement to be withdrawn pending a full ASA decision). Such cases are rare: normally the acceptability of an ad campaign is decided at the Council's monthly meeting, by which time any damage will have been done. Adjudications are short, prepared by the Secretariat and in most cases agreed by the Council at its monthly meeting. There is no appeal from a Council decision, although complainant and advertiser can ask for the adjudication to be "reviewed" if there is fresh evidence or irrationality: since the Council chairman and the chair of its funding body comprise two of the three members of the appeal panel, this procedure is biased from the outset. It cannot in any event reverse a Council decision, but merely "review" the matter by sending it back for further consideration, which hardly makes the exercise worthwhile.

The ASA is subject to judicial review. In an important precedent for the supervision of all such voluntary bodies, the Divisional Court ruled that it served a public law function which would otherwise have to be exercised by a statutory body—doubtless by the Director-General of Fair Trading.[92] Like the Takeover Panel, the ASA exercises power *de facto* by interpreting and applying a written ethical code, enforced through effective sanctions.[93] In this first case, the court quashed an adjudication reached without giving the advertiser a fair opportunity to respond. In later cases, however, the Court has been more prepared to defer to the experience and expertise of the ASA, declining to interfere with decisions like *IFAW v. Tesco*,[93A] which may be unreasonable but are not irrational. The ASA will not be stopped from publishing a decision, however, even if leave for judicial review has been granted:

A football pools company was informed that the ASA had decided its advertisement was in breach of the code, and the adjudication would be published in the next monthly bulletin. It immediately obtained leave to move for judicial review, and then sought to injunct publication of the adjudication until the court case had been decided. Laws J. held that the "general principle of our law" that expression will not be restrained "save on pressing grounds", applied to the expression of a public body as much as an individual: potential damage to Vernons from publication did not provide a sufficiently pressing reason to suppress the ASA's opinion of the advertisement.[94] This case is additionally important because it turns on a common law right rather than Article 10. The ASA, as a "public authority" for the purposes of the Human Rights Act will not be a "victim" for the purpose of enjoying an Article 10 right, and will have

[92] *R. v. ASA, ex p. The Insurance Service plc* [1990] 2 Admin. L.R. 77.
[93] *R. v. Panel on Take overs and Mergers, ex p. Datafin* [1987] Q.B. 815.
[93A] *R. v. ASA, ex p. International Fund for Animal Rights*, July 7, 1997, *per* Dyson J.
[94] *R. v. ASA, ex p. Vernons* [1992] W.L.R. 1289.

to rely on the common law principle adumbrated in this and other cases.

The same approach has been evident in other cases that have come before the courts on judicial review applications. Minor procedural irregularities will not invalidate a decision which does not appear irrational.[95] Although the ASA is now bound to render decisions which conform with Article 10 of the ECHR, once a court is satisfied that the Authority could reasonably conclude that an advertisement in a national newspaper caused "serious and widespread offence", it would logically follow that there was a "pressing social need" to censor it.[96]

Advertisers up before the ASA cannot be condemned on vague or novel grounds: restriction must be "prescribed by law". There is one High Court decision that the ASA codes are sufficiently precise and accessible to satisfy this test.[97]

Sanctions

The ASA has a graduated range of sanctions. They are not calculated to deter incorrigibly deceitful advertisers, for whom there is no fine or prison sentence, but they can stop a deceptive or offensive promotional campaign in its tracks. That sanction is available not by law or contract but simply through media industry co-operation. When asked by the ASA to withdraw an advert, most agencies do comply: they know that newspapers and journals will simply not publish advertisements which the ASA has declared to be a breach of the code. A recalcitrant advertising agency or its client may be denied industry services or further newspaper space. The Authority naively asserts that the prospect of adverse publicity from its rulings may prove a deterrent, but for companies like Benetton (a regular offender) all publicity is good publicity. Ironically for a body dedicated to proclaiming the virtues of self-regulation, its one real sanction derives from legislation.

In 1988 the Director-General of Fair Trading was given statutory powers to deal with false advertisements, as a result of implementation of the European Community's Directive on Misleading Advertising. These powers will be used only as a last resort, if the ASA's voluntary self-regulation system fails, as it did with the advent of the *Sunday Sport:*

---

[95] *R. v. ASA, ex p. DSG Retail Ltd,* Popplewell J. December 4, 1996.

[96] *R. v. ASA, ex p. City Trading* [1997] C.O.D. 202. The decision was delivered before the Human Rights Act, and its factual basis—that it was not unreasonable to find that advertisements in the *Daily Mirror* for a "sex education video" would cause widespread offence—may be doubted. So too may the logic of always inferring a "pressing social need" from "widespread offence", although the existence of such offence would give prima facie support to a ban.

[97] *R. v. ASA, ex p. Matthias Rath BV, The Times,* January 10, 2001.

The ASA upheld complaints against advertisements for a new slimming aid, but the distributors continued to run advertisements in the *Sunday Sport*. The ASA, powerless to prohibit their continuing publication, referred the matter to the Director-General, who was granted an injunction against the distributors preventing them from publishing the same or any similar advertisement.[98]

The ASA is extremely reluctant to make such references—10 only in the decade since the power was provided. The reason may be that it thinks a reference implies that self-regulation has failed, and a body which perceives itself as an advocate for self-regulation does not wish to give that impression. What the ASA has yet to understand is that its brand of "self-regulation" only works *because* it is underpinned by this statutory power: there should be no inhibition against invoking it. The ASA has avoided much of the criticism levelled at the PCC because its budget is three times larger, its remit less controversial and its preparedness to monitor its Code, rather than ignore the most blatant breaches if the victim does not complain, is reassuring. Nonetheless, closer scrutiny of its "monitoring" exercises suggests they are amateurish, and used for dubious public relations claims that "98 per cent of advertisements are ethical". The Council members lack the class and ethnic composition that would be required of a statutory body, and there is always a question of whether a group of "chairman's friends", funded by the industry it purports to judge, can ever be truly impartial. The ASA has a somewhat sinister provision hidden in its rules which permits its joint secretariat to send cases straight to CAP for an advisory opinion, which the ASA must take into account—thereby giving the commercial advertisers a privileged standing in such adjudications and undermining the ASA's integrity.[99] The most insightful attack on its mere "veneer of independence" was made by Professor Ross Cranston in his days as a consumer law expert:[1] his few years as Solicitor-General, were not marked by any Government scepticism over the apparent capacity of the advertising industry to regulate its own behaviour.

Trade Descriptions Act

Editors should be aware of the potential criminal liability they may incur under the Trade Descriptions Act if they falsely market their own publications:

---

[98] *Director-General of Fair Trading v. Tobyward* [1989] 2 All E.R. 266.
[99] CAP: The British Codes of Advertising and Sales Promotion, para. 68.34.
[1] Ross Cranston, *Consumers and the Law* (2nd ed., 1984) p. 48.

Woman magazine appeared with a cover announcement "Exclusive! At last, the real Anne Diamond". Instead of an interview with the popular television presenter, however, the feature to which the cover referred comprised headless pictures of eight women (one of whom was Ms Diamond) together with a "character analysis" of their clothing. The publishers, IPC Magazines, were fined £600 with £400 costs for applying a false and misleading trade description to the contents of their product.

The crime of applying a false description to a book or magazine is, under the Trade Descriptions Act, a strict liability offence committed if a cover is in fact misleading, even if the publisher had no intention to trick potential readers. In 1991 HarperCollins suffered embarrassment and a fine of £6,250 (and an order to pay £4,150 prosecution costs) for some sharp practice exposed at Stratford-upon-Avon by local trading standards officers:

> Alastair Maclean was a popular and prolific author, who bequeathed his publishers a number of "outlines" for future stories. HarperCollins hired an unknown, never-before-published author, who just happened to be named Alastair MacNeill, to write books based on these story-lines after Maclean's death. The first, *Nightwatch,* was published with a cover description: "ALASTAIR MACLEAN'S *Nightwatch*" and the name Alastair MacNeill in small print at the bottom. The court had no hesitation in finding that the use of the apostrophe could mislead customers into thinking that the book had been written by the famous novelist, a misrepresentation compounded by the similarity of his name with that of the real author.

Newspapers from time to time suffer reprisals from advertisers as a result of editorials or investigative journalism that is critical of the advertiser's product or personnel. The reprisal usually takes the form of withdrawal of future advertising. The ASA will be of no assistance in cases where the petulant advertiser is a private organisation, but the case of *R. v. Derbyshire County Council, ex p Times Supplements Ltd* demonstrates how judicial review may be used to provide redress against local authorities (or government departments) that cancel advertisements for political reasons:

> Derbyshire County Council regularly advertised teaching positions in the *Times Education Supplement,* which is owned by Rupert Murdoch. Another Murdoch paper, *The Sunday Times,* published a series of attacks on the Labour-controlled council and its leader, David Bookbinder. The Labour group on the council vindictively decided to end all advertising in Murdoch publications, and used its majority on the council's education committee to switch the advertising of teaching posts (worth some £60,000 per year) from the *TES* to *The Guardian.* The Divisional Court quashed this decision as a result of evidence that demonstrated that it had

been made solely because of the Labour group's vendetta against the Murdoch press, and not for any bona fide reason related to education or to the council's operations; "It was thus an abuse of power contrary to the public good".[2]

Icstis

The privatising of British Telecom led to a mushrooming of "live conversation" and "adult entertainment" services available to telephone inquirers at a premium rate (*i.e.* charged at the rate for dialing the Irish Republic). B.T. and its service providers were criticised in the press and in Parliament, and fearing legislation, looked to the ASA and the Press Council as a model for the self-regulatory alternative. Their services were made subject to codes of practice drawn up and monitored by the Independent Committee for the Supervision of Standards of Telephone Information Services (ICSTIS), comprising 10 members appointed by British Telecom and currently chaired by Peter North Q.C. ICSTIS derives its power from clauses in the contracts between service providers and Telecom, which entitles the latter to act on an ICSTIS recommendation to close any service that is found to have breached the relevant code. Complaints may be made, sensibly enough, by telephone, by calling freephone 0800 500212.

There are 615 million calls made to premium rate services each year, lasting two minutes each on average (since many are for aural sex services, the shortness of this time period may reflect of a national inability to maintain an erotic conversation, or an erection). The revenue generated is £290 million, of which £1.62 million supports the 30-strong ICSTIS Secretariat, handling 6,000 public complaints each year and monitoring telephone chat lines. Most complaints concern deceitful promotions or misleading information; those who dial for "adult entertainment" are reluctant to complain if these self-described "wank lines" do not live up to their own descriptions. A number of cases which attract the severest sanctions each year are really examples of serious fraud— *e.g.* mailshots which threaten legal action unless a premium rate number is dialled, or which encourage calls and faxes to premium rate lines by falsely promising incredibly cheap travel or that all charges will be donated to a non-existent charity. It would be a more effective deterrent if organisers of these scams faced criminal prosecutions rather than small ICSTIS fines.[3] The Code requires service providers to publicise clearly the "charge per minute" in all advertisements and promotions.

---

[2] (1991) 3 Admin. L. Rep. 241.
[3] See ICSTIS Activity Report, 1999, Case studies 1 and 4.

It has familiar provisions prohibiting incitement to unlawful conduct or content which features violence, sadism or cruelty, and services must not invade privacy or promote racial disharmony or prostitution or "cause grave or widespread offence".[4] The Code adopts ASA provisions against misleading and inaccurate material, and against unprofessional advice, and has stringent rules against exploiting the credulity of children (all services for children must automatically terminate after £3.00 has been expended). ICSTIS has developed some better procedures and sanctions than the PCC and ASA: it has an emergency procedure that operates (by telephone, of course) to provide an interim remedy in a matter of hours, and in difficult or important cases a service provider can obtain an oral hearing. The fairness of the whole procedure was enhanced in 2001 when the organisation set up an independent appeals tribunal, chaired by a retired circuit judge.

The range of sanctions available to ICSTIS, and its preparedness to use them, marks it out as the most effective of the self-regulatory bodies. Unlike either the PCC or the ASA, it considers a punishment which fits not only the crime but also the offender's previous record. Under section 5.7.2 of the code it may then impose the following penalties:

(a) require the breach to be remedied;

(b) demand an assurance about future behaviour;

(c) require future services or promotional material to be submitted to ICSTIS for approval;

(d) bar access to the offending telephone numbers for a defined period, by arrangement with the network operator;

(e) prohibit the operator from providing a premium rate service for a defined period, or impose a permanent ban;

(f) impose a fine;

(g) in the case of damage caused by virtual chat services, require the payment of reasonable claims for compensation.

These powers, enforceable through contracts with Telecom and the network operators, are similar to those which would be made available to any statutory regulator. ICSTIS has not hesitated to use its power to fine, and occasionally to close down lines and ban operators, for serious or repeated breach. In 1999, it approved compensation payments totalling £35,000, imposed a total of £140,000 in fines on 94 service providers, and barred two individuals from the premium rate industry per-

---

[4] See ICSTIS Code, Section 3.2 (Decency).

manently. As the newcomer in the field of voluntary regulation, it leads where the PCC and the ASA dare not follow, and in the Government White Paper on broadcasting ICSTIS was held up as the preferred model for the new all-purpose regulator (OFCOM).

The code for live telephone services is considerably more detailed than that for recorded messages, and is regularly monitored. It requires service providers themselves to monitor their services continually, to record all conversations and to retain the recordings for a six-month period in the event that these are required by ICSTIS. They are under a duty to use "all reasonable endeavours" not to allow talk that might encourage criminal offences, drug-taking or racial disharmony, or that might cause grave offence by reference to sex or violence or by use of foul language. They must operate procedures to ensure that persons under 18 do not use the service, and to warn callers both of the charges they are running up and of the fact that their conversations are being recorded. Under British Telecom, telephone talk is neither cheap nor free, although it has established a compensation fund to help pay the telephone bills of subscribers whose children or guests have incurred heavy premium rate charges without authorisation.

In 1991 ICSTIS promulgated new rules purporting to restrict the manner in which sex line services are advertised, banning such advertisements entirely from free or unsolicited publications and requiring that all ads in publications not normally carried on the "top shelf" of newsagents "must not contain pictures or words of a sexually suggestive nature which are unacceptably offensive". The rules are an unreasonable restraint on trade, since it must be for newspapers and free sheets to decide for themselves whether to carry lawful advertisements. The providers of adult entertainment services, supported by those newspapers that carry their advertisements (the *Sport, Mirror* and *Star*), challenged the new rules on the basis that what is "unacceptably offensive" is unacceptably subjective and unpredictable. A confused majority judgment finally admitted: "There is a subjective element to our approach and we regard it as unavoidable." ICSTIS then moved on to rule that an advertisement for "Unzip my suspenders" was not acceptable, but "Dial-a-Bonk" was. A dissenting opinion by the chairman found this "an untenable approach for a body such as ICSTIS which operates in an area of public administration".[5] Nonetheless, in 1999 it embarked upon an investigation which uncovered 60 services which had breached its rules about advertising offensively in generally available, "non-top shelf" publications. It imposed fines of up to £5,000 in 23 cases, and banned access for up to 30 weeks in 21 cases.

Consistently with its commitment to procedural fairness, ICSTIS

---

[5] ICSTIS adjudication in respect of advertisements in the *Mirror*, *Star* and *Sport*, August 28, 1991.

does not shrink from the rigours of judicial oversight. In the only case which has so far been brought, *R. v. ICSTIS, ex p. Firstcall,* it accepted that as a "public body" it was amenable to judicial review, a contention a strong Divisional Court saw no reason to doubt.[6] Firstcall tried to stop an adjudication of a complaint against it from proceeding, on the ground that its particular contract with BT excluded ICSTIS jurisdiction. But the court ruled that a public law body could not be fettered by any clause in a contract to which it was not a party. Only in exceptional circumstances would the court injunct such a body from proceeding: the appropriate course was to receive the adjudication before deciding whether to challenge it.

ICSTIS has been pro-active in dealing with complaints against companies exploiting new forms of electronic communications by (for example) sending unsolicited faxes and emails which invite recipients to dial premium rate numbers for misinformation. Most of its decided cases involve minor forms of customer deceit, although it has occasionally adopted an unnecessarily censorious position—fining one communications company for causing "widespread offence" by conducting a fax poll on railway safety too soon after a train disaster.[7] Television regulators may reasonably require some sensitivity in scheduling after a major incident (violent movies were replaced in the days following the Hungerford and Dunblane shootings) but retrospective fines on service providers merely for expressing or soliciting public opinion breaches Article 10 of the ECHR. ICSTIS has adapted its Code to cover internet and interactive services which use premium rate as a payment mechanism, and its remit has been extended to advertising on the internet for premium rate services which can be accessed via modems.

The internet

Regulation of the internet is, for techno-libertarians, a contradiction in terms. But those who place obscenities and defamations on their websites are open to criminal and civil actions as much as any offline publisher, and there are special amendments (described in Chapter 4) extending the provisions of the Child Protection Act (1978) to those who operate and frequent child pornography sites. Although the U.S. Supreme Court gave paedophile sites the benefit of First Amendment freedom in *ACLU v. Reno,*[8] no such largesse is extended by Article 10(2) of the ECHR: any infringements relating to child pornography will be upheld as necessary "for the prevention of crime". Internet

---

[6] [1993] C.O.D. 325, Sir Thomas Bingham M.R., Kennedy and Evans L.JJ.
[7] *Crosby Communication Case,* ICSTIS adjudication February 19, 2001. The company was fined £300.
[8] *ACLU v. Reno* 521 U.S. 844 (1997).

service providers are well aware that their commercial interest in avoiding statutory regulation is served by the public and political perception that they do their best to exclude such perverted material: for this reason the Internet Service Providers Association (ISPA) and the London Internet Exchange (LINX), in co-operation with the DTI and the Home Office, have established a self-regulatory body called the Internet Watch Federation. As its name implies, it monitors the net and encourages users to contact its website (www.iwf.org.uk) and send an email (to report@iwf.org.uk) if they encounter anything of interest to paedophiles. Although principally funded by the United Kingdom industry, it does, unusually for a self-regulator, receive public finance for its "complaints hotline" from the European Union, as part of its Safer Internet Action Plan.[9] The IWF investigates but does not adjudicate—its role is limited to passing evidence to the police. It makes a threshold judgment on whether material emanating from a suspect site is indecent (the test under the Protection of Children Act). In 2001 it was condemned by that guardian of popular morals, *The News of the World,* for doing nothing to stop the Saatchi gallery photographs from appearing on websites scoured by paedophiles.[10] In this respect the IWF was correct (the photos were not "indecent") and the newspaper was partly to blame: it had provoked the misguided police action in the first place, thus giving the pictures international notoriety. After five years' operation, IWF claimed "We have been responsible for the removal of some 26,000 images of child pornography from U.K. servers". But such claims create expectations which the organisation (in reality, the police) cannot fulfil; it is "toothless" in the sense that it has no more teeth than any other non-statutory busybody.

Cybersquatting

Under the impetus of the U.S. Government and the World International Property Organisation a global regulator was set up in 1998 with a special role in resolving the problem of "cybersquatting". ICANN—the Internet Corporation for Assigned Names and Numbers—issues directives to .com and .net and .org domains to transfer or cancel names after adjudications of what are essentially "passing off" disputes, over domain names that are confusingly similar or identical to the complainant's own name or trade mark. The issue, decided by a panel of ICANN adjudicators, is whether the name has been registered for genuine and

---

[9] For European Commission thinking on internet regulation, see DG XIII "Communication of Illegal and Harmful Content on the Internet" (Com. (96) 487) and DGX "Protection of Minors and Human Dignity in Audiovisual and Information Services" (Com. (96) 483).

[10] *News of the World,* March 18, 2001.

fair use or with intent to mislead, exploit, or interfere with the complainant's legal rights (its rules and decisions may be accessed at www.icann.org).

> In *Jeanette Winterson v. Mark Hogarth,* the English author complained that Hogarth's registration of jeannettewinterson.com was an infringement of her "work"—*i.e.* the recognition that attached to her own name, a right which the English law against "passing off" would entitle her to protect. The panel had no difficulty in concluding that Hogarth had acted in bad faith (despite his claimed ignorance of English law) because he had no pre-existing goodwill in the work and had registered it with the intention of auctioning it off to the highest bidder.[11] In *Billy Connolly v. Stewart,* the comedian wrested the name www.billyconnolly.com from a pedigree dog of the same name, whose owner had registered the site to advertise its stud services. The ICANN panel rejected the argument that the website was named after the dog: the registration had been in bad faith as a pretext for trading in domain names.

The ICANN complaint procedure is not cheap—fees for a panel adjudication are of the order of £1,000—but are much less than a contested court action. The procedure does not involve any legal waiver—unsuccessful complainants are not debarred from commencing actions for trademark infringement or passing off. The service is proving helpful in reducing confusion and exploitation: it dealt promptly with 3,900 cases in its first 18 months, deciding 75 per cent in favour of complainants. It has been accused of favouring "big business" at the expense of freedom of expression by ordering transfers of "dotsuck" sites (created in the name of public figures or corporations in order to criticise them— *e.g.* under kissingersucks.net). Dotsuck.uk sites are permitted by Nominet, the body responsible for administering .uk domain names. It proposes to set up a similar arbitration system to which registrants will be obliged by their contract to submit (see www.nic.uk). The regulation of this global technology is in its infancy, and several dozen repressive States have passed laws to control internet access.[12] In Britain, the Government has announced a preference for applying existing laws: in 2000, the Official Secrets Act empowered police to shut down a local website on which renegade MI6 agent Richard Tomlinson had posted the names of 100 of his former colleagues.

---

[11] Case No. D2000-0235, May 22, 2000.
[12] See: *Censor Dot Gov: The Internet and Press Freedom* (Freedom House, 2000).

CHAPTER 15

CENSORSHIP OF FILMS AND VIDEO

"Before the children's greedy eyes with heartless indiscrimination are presented, night after night . . . terrific massacres, horrible catastrophes, motor car smashes, public hangings, lynchings. All who care for the moral well-being and education of the child will set their faces like flint against this new form of excitement."[1]

"We can't have freedom for adults in this country, because we can't trust adults to protect children."[2]

The most obvious shift in the British approach to censorship of the visual media has been away from the courts and towards quasi-statutory regulation. The jury—the traditional body for deciding issues of freedom of expression—is no longer trusted to make the detailed judgments required before films and videos are regarded as fit for public exhibition and sale. In practice (although not in theory—films and videos may still be prosecuted for obscenity) the jury's function has been taken over by an institution of State-approved censors, which calls itself the British Board of Film Classification (BBFC). The term "classification" is a euphemism—although much of the Board's task involves classification of films and videos as suitable for particular age-groups, the "cuts" it requires for this certification are in practice censorship directives. In some cases it refuses certification altogether for adult viewing; such a refusal will amount to a legal ban (in the case of a video) or a powerful extra-legal deterrent (in the case of a feature film for cinema release). This distinction arises from the Board's history as a private body set up by the film industry; it retains this advisory capacity in relation to the cinema, but has been given statutory powers by Parliament to decide whether video-cassettes are "suitable for viewing in the home". Its operations additionally have a determinative influence on the feature films that are shown on television: the licensing bodies for that medium insist that films possess a BBFC certificate before they can be screened.

---

[1] "Cinematography and the Child"—editorial in *The Times* demanding exclusion of children from all cinemas, April 12, 1913.

[2] James Ferman, Chief Censor, on *Right to Reply* (Channel 4, 1993).

Film censorship is the most complicated and controversial area of legal and extra-legal regulation. Movies that are exhibited in cinemas or viewed in the home on video-cassettes are subject to the Obscene Publications Act, and may be prosecuted on the grounds that they would tend to deprave and corrupt a significant proportion of likely viewers. Additionally, they may be prosecuted at common law for blasphemy or sedition. Cinema films, however, are subject to special pre-censorship arrangements: a classification system operated by the BBFC that is in theory voluntary but, in practice, a requirement insisted upon by local councils, which license cinemas. These councils may themselves prohibit films that have BBFC approval or, indeed, permit the screening of films that have been refused certification. In the case of video-cassettes, BBFC certification is required by law before they can be sold to particular age groups, and must be withheld from movies that are deemed "unsuitable for viewing in the home", however unexceptionable they may be for screening to adults in licensed cinemas. Neither theatre promoters nor book publishers suffer institutional censorship imposed by bureaucracies or local councillors, and the standards of acceptability endorsed by these bodies are such that cinema censorship is more pervasive, and more arbitrary, than the limitations imposed on other forms of artistic expression.

The reasons for additional layers of censorship in relation to films are partly historic (in so far as cinemas required local authority licences for reasons of health and safety), partly practical (distributors and exhibitors of film have preferred the security of BBFC censorship to protect their profits and their persons from the vagaries of obscenity prosecutions) and partly philosophical. As the Williams Committee put the latter argument, film is a "uniquely powerful medium ... the close-up, fast cutting, the sophistication of modern make-up and special effects techniques, the heightening effect of sound effects and music, all combine on the large screen to produce an impact which no other medium can create". What is left of the insubstantial pageant once the credits have faded and the bus ride home has been taken is a matter of inconclusive evidence, but "it seems entirely sensible to be cautious".[3]

In the case of home video, caution is regarded as even more sensible in light of the ability of viewers—especially youngsters—to use the technology to dilate repeatedly upon particular scenes. The BBFC explains that it is much stricter with scenes depicting sexual violence on video than on film, "since the fact that a scene might be searched out and repeated endlessly out of context in the privacy of one's home could condition some viewers to find the behaviour sexually exciting,

---

[3] *Obscenity and Film Censorship: Committee Report* (the Williams Committee), (HMSO, 1979), Cmnd. 7772.

not just on film, but in real life."[4] In 1984 this concern led Parliament, after a frenetic campaign about the dangers of "video-nasties", to designate the BBFC as the body empowered to decide which films were appropriate for home viewing on video-cassette. As a result, this small private body, established and funded by the film industry, has become a bureaucratic apparatus recognised by law, exercising a determinative control over the contents of publicly available films and videos. Its certificate, while not a guarantee of immunity from prosecution under the Obscene Publications Act, has in practice become just that, and the prospect of proceedings against those who purvey films and cassettes protected by its classification must be regarded as remote. In 1985 the Government undertook that in order to avoid "local variations in prosecution policy" and to ensure that "any prosecution should be undertaken only after the most careful consideration of the case", the police would seek the advice of the DPP before prosecuting for obscenity in relation to any work certified by the BBFC.[5] This cosy arrangement has had the effect desired both by the cinema and video industries and by the law enforcement authorities: no prosecution has since been mounted against a BBFC-certified film or video work. The price to the film-loving public has been a lot of cuts, and occasional outright suppression, imposed by a Government-approved censorship body.

FILM CENSORSHIP

History

The BBFC began as a voluntary body, established by the film industry in 1912 in an effort to provide some uniform guidance to local authorities empowered to license premises for the screening of particular films. The 1909 Cinematograph Act gave local authorities power to impose conditions on film exhibitions in order to protect the public against fire hazards, but they soon began to use them to quench the flames of celluloid passion. The first banned film—a newsreel of an American prize fight—earned a disapproval "not unconnected with the fact that it showed a negro defeating a white man".[6] The film industry took fright

---

[4] BBFC Annual Report (1986).

[5] ibid.

[6] See Neville March Hunnings, *Film Censors and the Law*, Allen & Unwin 1967, p. 50. Until 1932 the annual reports of the BBFC listed the reasons for which cuts had been requested or films refused a certificate. They included "abdominal contortions in dancing" (1925), "equivocal situation between white girls and men of other races" (1926), "British possessions represented as lawless sinks of iniquity" (1928), "police firing on defenceless populace" (*ibid.*), "themes likely to wound

at the prospect that distribution might be subjected to the whims of different local councils, and a consensus emerged that "it would be far better for the trade to censor its own productions than to see all films at the mercy of an arbitrary authority".[7]

In 1912 the Cinematographic Exhibitors' Association announced the formation of the British Board of Film Censors, whose duty "would be to induce confidence in the minds of the licensing authorities, and of those who have in their charge the moral welfare of the community generally".[8] In 1924 the BBFC received its judicial imprimatur in the case of *Mills v. London County Council* when the Divisional Court upheld the validity of a condition that "no cinematograph film . . . which has not been passed for . . . exhibition by the BBFC shall be exhibited without the express consent of the council". So long as a council reserved the right to review BBFC decisions, it was entitled to make the grant of a cinema licence contingent upon the screening of certified films.[9] The position was approved by the Court of Appeal in 1976. Lord Denning said:

> "I do not think the county councils can delegate the whole of their responsibilities to the board, but they can treat the board as an advisory body whose views they can accept or reject; provided that the final decision—aye or nay—rests with the county council".[10]

The cutting-room counsels of the BBFC avowedly err on the side of caution, in an effort to protect the established film industry from criticism as well as from prosecution. Although the BBFC is (save for its role in approving video-cassettes) an unofficial body, unrecognised by statute and financed through fees imposed upon every film submitted for censorship, it exercises a persuasive and in most cases determinative influence over the grant of local authority licences. "I freely admit that this is a curious arrangement" conceded the Home Secretary, Mr Herbert Morrison, in 1952, "but the British have a very great habit of making curious arrangements work very well, and this works. Frankly, I do not wish to be the Minister who has to answer questions in the

---

the just sensibilities of friendly nations" (*ibid.*). The practice was ended because "for some unaccountable reason critics have seized upon isolated sentences and by taking them out of context have placed mischievous constructions upon them" (1932). The Reports are gathered in PRO file, H045/24024.

[7] *ibid.*, p. 51.

[8] *ibid.*, p. 54.

[9] *Mills v. London County Council* [1925] 1 K.B. 213.

[10] *R. v. GLC. ex p Blackburn* [1976] 1 W.I.R. 550, *per* Lord Denning, at pp. 554–555.

House as to whether particular films should or should not be censored".[11]

Section 3 of the 1952 Cinematograph Act (now section 1(3) of the 1985 Cinemas Act) imposed a duty on licensing authorities to place restrictions on the admission of children to cinemas that show works "designated, by the licensing authority or such other body as may be specified in the licence, as works unsuitable for children". The reference to "such other body" was the first parliamentary acknowledgment of the BBFC, and the 1952 Act established its position, if not as a censorship body, at least as an authorised classification tribunal for films unsuitable for young people, and its classification decisions have for this purpose won considerable approval. The present classification, endorsed by all local councils and by the Home Office, is:

U Universal: suitable for all.
PG Parental guidance: some scenes may be unsuitable for young children.
12 Suitable only for persons of 12 years and over.
15 Suitable only for persons of 15 years and over.
18 Suitable only for persons of 18 years and over.
18R Suitable only for restricted distribution through licensed sex shops to which no one under 18 is admitted.

The 12 category was adopted in 1989, so that the Board could stop children under 12 from seeing films such as *Batman, Crocodile Dundee* and *Gremlins,* which it was reluctant to confine to the 15 category, but believed (without good reason) would be damaging to pre-teenagers. (Anomalously, the 12 category does not apply to video.) The Board has become quite obsessive about its arbitrary age-limits (it insisted on 25 cuts to *Indiana Jones and the Temple of Doom* before it agreed to a PG certificate) and film exhibitors invariably buckle under its rulings in order to obtain the extra profits that derive from teenage admission fees. They will happily cut scenes from major motion pictures in order to achieve a 15 rating, and will in many cases agree to cut further scenes in order to obtain a 12 rating. The result is that adults in Britain are obliged to see cut versions of major films that are screened unexpurgated in America and in other countries in Europe. The film industry has traditionally preferred the pursuit of profit to the principle of artistic freedom, and rarely appeals against the Board's decisions. Film makers may be able to assert their "moral right" under the Copyright Act against exhibitors who agree to multilate their work (see p. 332) although most production contracts require that this right be waived.

[11] (1952) 385 H.C. Debs 504.

The BBFC has effectively become the authorised censor for feature films in cinemas and on television, and for those marketed on video-cassettes. Its position derives, not from the law, but from various "understandings" it has reached with prosecuting authorities, local councils and the Home Office. The basis for the "understanding" was frankly expressed by the DPP to the Parliamentary Select Committee on obscenity in 1957:

> "If I wished to prosecute a film—and it has been suggested on two occasions to me that certain films that had passed the British Board of Film Censors were obscene—my answer would be, as it was in those two cases, I shall have to put the British Board of Film Censors in the dock because they have aided and abetted the com-mission of that particular offence. So it inhibits me to that extent. As long as I rely on the judgment of the British Board of Film Censors as to the suitability, under the various categories, of films for public showing, which I do, I do not prosecute".[12]

In fact, the DPP was wrong in law—the BBFC certification of a movie is, technically, no more than its expression of opinion, upon which local councils place reliance when they exercise their responsibil-ity for licensing an exhibition. So there is no danger of Mr Whittam-Smith, the current BBFC President, ending up in the dock as an "aider and abetter". But there is now no real danger of anyone ending up in the dock over the screening of a certified film or the age-appropriate sale of a certified video. The DPP has never prosecuted over a cinema screening of a certified film. There were two private prosecutions back in the mid-70s, both of which came to grief. The case against *Last Tango in Paris* collapsed on technical grounds,[13] and an Old Bailey jury acquitted the exhibitors of *The Language of Love* of the common law offence of outraging public decency. Common law offences may no longer be charged, and private prosecutions no longer threaten, thanks to the 1977 reforms which brought cinema screenings within the Obscene Publications Act and required all prosecutions to be brought by or with the consent of the DPP. (See earlier p. 187) It is virtually inconceivable that he would prosecute exhibitors of a certified film for obscenity, unless perhaps in respect of an "18" screening which they permitted large numbers of children to attend. So far as videos are concerned, prosecutions were brought in the early 80s against "video nasties" like *The Evil Dead* and *The Burning,* which had been certified "18" for cinema release. The resultant chaos and confusion produced the 1984 Video Recordings Act, which required all video cassettes

---

[12] See John Trevelyan, *What the Censor Saw* (Michael Joseph), 1973), p. 141.
[13] *Att.-Gena.'s Reference No. 2 of 1975* [1976] 2 All E.R. 753.

dealing with sex and violence to be separately certified by the BBFC as suitable for viewing in the home. The 1985 "understanding" (see above) requiring police to obtain DPP consent before prosecuting a certified video for obscenity has ensured that no such prosecutions have been brought.

Local council licensing

The Cinemas Act 1985 consolidates all the previous provisions, dating from 1909, relating to the licensing of cinemas. Subject to certain exemptions for casual or non-profit making enterprises, it is an offence, punishable by the somewhat extravagant maximum fine of £20,000, to use unlicensed premises for film exhibitions. Local councils may attach conditions to licences, and these normally require that all films shown carry a BBFC classification certificate and that admission be refused to persons outside the certified class. Failure to comply with such conditions is also an offence. On the basis of *Mills v. London County Council* (see p. 730) local authorities must retain a supervisory function over and above the BBFC, and some exercise this power to prohibit particular films that have been granted certification. Thus controversial releases may be banned in some districts and licensed in others, sometimes only a short bus ride away. Monty Python's *The Life of Brian* was banned entirely in many jurisdictions, and given a more restricted classification in others.

Local film censorship is usually delegated to magistrates or entrusted to standing committees: some councils rely upon their Fire Brigade Committees to extinguish any flames of passion that may have escaped the BBFC hose, while one Cornish borough solemnly bans films despite the fact that there are no cinemas within its jurisdiction. This kind of censorship, duplicating the BBFC and the obscenity law, was regarded by the Williams Committee as a waste of public time and money, but the licensing provisions were re-enacted in 1982 and consolidated in the Cinemas Act of 1985. In addition, local councils have powers over "sex cinemas", provided by the Local Government (Miscellaneous Provisions) Act of 1982. Although there are few enforcement actions, cinemas do their best to impose age restrictions, even on children accompanied by parents. So when Princess Diana took an underage princeling to *The Devil's Own* it was the cinema, not the mother, which was threatened with prosecution.

Most local authorities adopt "model licensing conditions" drafted by the Home Office, of the kind:

> (a) no film, other than a current newsreel, shall be exhibited unless it has received a certificate of the British Board of Film Classi-

fication or is the subject of the licensing authority's permission;

(b) no young people shall be admitted to any exhibition of a film classified by the Board as unsuitable for them, unless with the local authority's permission;

(c) no film shall be exhibited if the licensing authority gives notice in writing prohibiting its exhibition on the ground that it would offend against good taste or decency or would be likely to encourage or incite to crime or to lead to disorder or to be offensive to public feeling;

(d) the nature of the certificate given to any film shall be indicated in any advertising for the film, at the cinema entrance (together with an explanation of its effect), and on the screen immediately before the film is shown;

(e) displays outside the cinema shall not depict any scene or incident not in the film as approved.

These conditions import the legal requirements that the local authority should retain the ultimate discretion rather than delegate it entirely to the BBFC. Condition (a) allows a liberal authority to permit screening of a film that the BBFC has refused to certify, and condition (c) enables a repressive authority to refuse permission to the exhibition of a certified film. (The grounds in condition (c) are precisely those which section 6 of the Broadcasting Act (1990) applies to television and radio programmes).

Certain classes of film exhibition are exempted from licensing requirements by sections 5–7 of the 1985 Act. These include occasional exhibitions, children's film clubs, screenings by educational and religious institutions and organisations certified as non-profit making. The sections are carefully drafted to prevent profit making cinema clubs from obtaining an exempt status, as many did through a loophole in the 1952 Act. This loophole had fostered the device of the "sex cinema club" as a means of escaping local authority licensing requirements. Now, any screening that is "promoted for private gain" is likely to be caught. Those that are not, but that nonetheless feature sexually explicit films (e.g. demonstration of films that are for sale in sex shops) will probably be caught by the provisions of the 1982 Local Government (Miscellaneous Provisions) Act, which applies to "sex cinemas" that do not require licences under the 1985 Cinemas Act. Section 3(1) of Schedule 3 to the Local Government Act permits local authority control of any premises used to exhibit films "relating to sexual activity or acts of force or restraint which are associated with sexual activity or ... genital organs or urinary or excretory functions".

The effect of these statutes is to bring almost every commercial film exhibition within local authority licensing powers, with the concomitant requirement for BBFC classifications. This requirement is spelled out by Section 1(3) of the 1985 legislation, which imposes a duty on licensing authorities to "impose conditions or restrictions prohibiting the admission of children to film exhibitions involving the showing of works designated, by the authority or by *such other body* [our italics] as may be specified in the licence, as works unsuitable for children". "Such other body" is a reference to the BBFC, and although local councils sometimes disagree with its decisions to grant or withhold certification for adult viewing, its age group classification decisions are rarely interfered with.

The practical result of this array of legislation is a censorship system that pivots upon cutting and classification directives by the BBFC, enforced through threats of prosecution of cinemas if they do not police the age restriction placed by the BBFC on film certificates. It is a pervasive system which indirectly affects all cinema attendees—and there were 143 million attendances at British cinemas in the year 2000. The most serious victims of film censorship are (a) persons under 18, who are denied the right to see films that the BBFC consider unsuitable for their age group, and (b) parents, who are denied the right to take their children to films they believe are suitable for them. Most civilised societies with pre-censorship systems for movies adopt age classifications that are advisory, or permit children to attend any film if accompanied by a parent or guardian. The United Kingdom system of censorship interferes both with the right to receive information and with the right of parents to determine family life: it is ripe for challenge under the ECHR.

THE ADVENT OF VIDEO

The home video market in Britain has been a remarkable success: by the year 2000, 85 per cent of all homes in the United Kingdom had at least one video recorder, whilst one in four children aged 12 to 15 could boast of a video player in their bedroom. But like all new communications technology, its advent provoked moral panic. The earliest scare came when the first court to confront this new technology decided that video cassettes fell outside the Obscene Publications Act—they had not, after all, been envisaged when that legislation was formulated in 1959. Before pornographers had much time to dance in the streets, the Court of Appeal was urgently reconvened in the middle of a summer vacation to rule, on an Attorney-General's reference, that video cassettes did comprise "matter to be looked at" within the scope of the 1959 act.[14] In subsequent prosecutions video cassettes were treated like books: the question was whether their contents, taken as a whole, would tend to corrupt those likely to see them. In determining their potential audience, the jury could consider the fact that they were for screening in the home, and decide whether children were likely to obtain access to them as a result. But fears of this novel technology—its fascination for children, its ability to freeze-frame and to replay favourite episodes, its mushroom growth—were soon exploited in a manic press campaign against "video-nasties".

By 1983 there was an early video vogue for run-of-the-mill horror movies: to capitalise on it, distributors promoted films that explicitly depicted violence and brutality. The label "video-nasty" was used indiscriminately by the press, but it reflected the prevailing fear that meretricious movies that dwelt on rape and mayhem would affect the minds of young children permitted to watch them by negligent parents. The Obscene Publications Act was a suitable tool for prosecution of such films where there was any prospect that a significant number of children might view them, and in 1983 a jury convicted the distributors of *Nightmares in a Damaged Brain* on account of its detailed depictions of sex and violence. But the campaigners—led by the Festival of Light and the *Daily Mail*—saw the opportunity to erect a new censorship apparatus that went far beyond the scope of the Obscene Publications Act. With a remarkable talent for passing off propaganda as scientifically valid research, they convinced politicians and newspapers of the accuracy of such claims as "37 per cent of children under 7 have seen a 'video-nasty'" and that "the nasty video has replaced the conjurer at children's birthday parties".[15] "Scientific" research purported to show that very young children in working class homes up and down the country were watching sadistic sex while their single parents were down at the pub. Sensationalised research claims, timed to coincide with important stages of the Video Recordings Bill, created a mild form of hysteria among politicians of all parties and the bill was rushed through with only two Tory M.P.s and one Labour peer dissenting. Subsequently, the much-publicised "research" was largely discredited, but it had served the purpose for which it was apparently designed: the transformation of the BBFC, from a small body voluntarily cutting cinema films to a bureaucracy with statutory power to pre-censor all videos containing scenes of sex or violence.

The climate engendered by the campaign against video-nasties in the

---

[14] *Att.-Gen.'s Reference No. 5 of 1980* [1980] 3 All E.R. 816.
[15] See the chapters by Graham Murdock and Brian Bown in Martin Baker (ed.), *The Video Nasties* (Pluto Press, 1984), and Michael Tracey, "Casting Cold Water on the Ketchup", *The Times*, February 25, 1984.

early 1980s affected police forces throughout the country, who raided video shops and prosecuted owners for X-certified horror movies perceived as "nasties". There was a two-year period of utter confusion, as some juries acquitted and others convicted the same film, and a few video traders went to prison for stocking films that had been seen by thousands when on previous cinema relase. Under heavy pressure from organisations representing the retail trade, the Attorncy-General finally issued a "list" of some 60 film titles that the DPP regarded obscene because of depictions of violence. Retailers who wished to avoid police seizures could collect a copy of the list from their local police station and remove any offending titles. The "DPP's list" was the first modern example of an "Index" in Britian; video traders greeted it with relief, although many of the films on the list had been acquitted by juries while others, such as *The Evil Dead* and *Andy Warhol's Frankenstein,* had received critical acclaim. Some of the "nastiest" films (even *I Spit on Your Grave,* the most frequently condemned film of this genre) have been intelligently defended as containing a moral message or as depicting brutalities such as rape in order to condemn them or their perpetrators.[16]

In 1984 the DPP's guidelines for deciding whether a particular video or film is obscene were tabled in Parliament:

> "The basic factor is the tendency to deprave and corrupt those who are, having regard to all the circumstances, likely to see it. The DPP therefore has to consider who is likely to view videos taken into the home. While this is ultimately for the court to decide in each particular case, the DPP considers that, in many cases, a significant number of the viewers will be children or young people."

In applying this basic factor, the film is considered as a whole. A work is likely to be regarded as obscene if it portrays violence to such a degree and so explicitly that its appeal can only be to those who are disposed to derive positive enjoyment from seeing such violence. Other factors may include:

- violence perpetrated by children;
- self-mutilation;
- violent abuse of women and children;
- cannibalism;
- use of vicious weapons (*e.g.* broken bottle);

---

[16] Baker, *Video Nasties,* Chaps 3 and 7. See also David Edgar, "Presumption of Innocence", *New Statesman,* October 5, 1984.

- use of everyday implements (*e.g.* screwdriver, shears, electric drill);

- violence in a sexual context.

These factors are not exhaustive. Style can also be important: "The more convincing the depictions of violence, the more harmful it is likely to be".[17]

These "guidelines" were inherently confusing: how could the DPP tell whether a significant number of viewers would be children? Did "harm" in the case of a child mean the engendering of fear or shock, or some deeper trauma, or a tendency to emulate the violent behaviour? If the basis for the prosecution was that the video's appeal was to those who found "positive enjoyment" in seeing violence, did this not apply to audiences for James Bond, Rambo and war films? The "guidelines" offered insufficient guidance to nervous retailers and distributors, whose desire for immunity from prosecution chimed with the tabloid demand for a censorship body: the Government obliged, in the Video Recordings Act, by giving the BBFC statutory powers to pre-censor video cassettes.

The Video Recordings Act 1984

The scheme of this Act is to require all video-cassettes (and any "other device capable of storing data electronically") destined for public availability and dealing in any respect with sex or violence to be submitted to a designated authority (at present and for the foreseeable future, the BBFC) for classification generally as suitable for circulation and particularly as suitable for various age-groups. The Act applies to every "video work", defined as

"any series of visual images

(a) produced electronically by the use of information contained on any disc or magnetic tape, and

(b) shown as a moving picture."

The only categories of video work (including both cassettes and discs) that are exempt from the need to be classified are those that, "taken as a whole", are:

(a) designed to inform, educate or instruct;

(b) concerned with sport, religion or music; or

[17] Statement by the Attorney General, House of Commons, June 23, 1984.

(c) video games.[18]

However, a video work in the above categories loses its prima facie exemption if "to any significant extent" it depicts:

(a) human sexual activity or acts of force or restraint associated with such activity;

(b) mutilation or torture of, or other acts of gross violence towards, humans or animals;

(c) human genital organs or human urinary or excretory functions, or is designed to any significant extent to stimulate or encourage anything falling within paragraph (a); or in the case of anything falling within paragraph (b), is designed to any extent to do so.[19]

The only case to offer any elucidation of these provisions suggests that the courts will give them the broadest possible interpretation, notwithstanding that they carry criminal penalties (and should, on principle, be narrowly construed). In *Kent Trading Standards Department Multi-Media Marketing* an operation called *The Interactive Girls Club* was prosecuted for producing discs of computer games which rewarded their winner with a few second's glimpse of naked women in provocative poses.[20] The Divisional Court ruled that the brevity of the display did not prevent the image from "being shown as a moving picture" so as to satisfy the definition of a "video work". Nor could it claim exemption as a "video game", because although the erotic tease was a "reward" for successful completion of an exempt game it was a severable and distinct clip designed to follow, rather than be part of, the game itself. *The Interactive Girls Club* decision went on to consider in depth the nature of interactive girls who might win exemption from the Act:

A bench of world-weary lay justices had been left unaroused by the clips of interactive women pulling at their panties, bending over naked to reveal pubic hair, and stroking their breasts: these images did not depict "human sexual activity" (which the justices took to involve "at least masturbation") or "human genital organs" (which they thought meant sight of a labia minora): the scenes were so mild that the magistrates found "it would strain credulity to assert (they) could either stimulate or encourage sexual activity". The Divisional Court judges, however, were

---

[18] Video Recordings Act 1984, s. 2(11).

[19] *ibid.,* s. 2(2).

[20] *Meechie (for Kent County Council Trading Standards Department) v. Multi-Media Marketing (trading as Interactive Girls Club)* (1995) 94 L.G.R. 474.

set a lower stimulation threshold: they had no hesitation in defining "sexual activity" to include a stroke of the breast or a touch of the crotch. Having engaged in an exercise that can only be described as pubic hair-splitting, Lord Justice Simon Browne concluded that "none of this material is in any real sense offensive", but that was a consideration which affected penalty, not exemption from classification. The mildest forms of video strip-tease will, in consequence, require submission to the BBFC.

The maximum fine for offering to supply a non-exempt video-cassette without a classification certificate is an extravagant £20,000; the cost of an application to the BBFC for a certificate will be over £1,000, depending on the length of the video (the BBFC charges about £10.00 per minute). It follows that most distributors will prefer to err on the safe side and submit videos for classification if there is any legal doubt about whether they are exempt. It is, however, a defence to the criminal charges of supply and possession for supply of non-exempt and non-classified videos created by sections 9 and 10 of the Act to prove that the accused reasonably believed he was dealing with an exempted work even if he was not. It would be "reasonable" for a distributor to act on a legal opinion that a work was exempt, even if a court subsequently construing section 2 of the Act were to hold that the opinion was mistaken.

The Video Recordings Act does not affect merely the handful of films that could be deemed video-nasties: it is a measure ultimately imposing liability to censorship and classification on the vast majority of cinematic works transferred to video-cassette or disc. The fact that the work has been made by, or shown on, television is irrelevant: the Minister of State for Home Affairs took pleasure in announcing that BBC programmes like *The History Man, Tinker, Tailor, Soldier, Spy* and *The Borgias* would require classification before they could be sold to the public on video-cassettes.[21] There is no requirement that films containing scenes of torture, mutilation or other acts of gross violence need to do so in any sexual context, and it was clearly envisaged by the Act's sponsors that videos of current affairs programmes showing the Falklands War, for example, or scenes of football hooliganism or a nuclear holocaust or acts of terrorism would require certification. So, too, do sex education videos or any video made by a counselling group about "human sexual activity", unless it were for the purpose of medical training or not distributed as part of a business.

Section 2 of the Act bristles with problems of interpretation. To claim

---

[21] Mr David Mellor, December 14 1983, Standing Committee on Video Recordings Bill (fourth sitting).

an exempt status for a video work it is necessary to establish first that "taken as a whole" it is designed to inform or is concerned with sport, religion, music, etc. If this question is resolved in favour of exemption, that status is nonetheless lost if human sexual activity, etc., is depicted "to any significant extent". It is not clear whether "significance" is judged in terms of time taken in the film, or importance to plot, or relates to the extent of the depictions. "Human sexual activity" means more than statuesque nudity, but might (on the authority of the *Interactive Girls Club* case) include simulated orgy scenes in the brothels of *The Rake's Progress* or the gondolas of *The Tales of Hoffman*. Nor is it clear whether the "acts of force or restraint" have to be associated with sexual activity in the film in question or merely in general estimation. "Acts of gross violence towards humans and animals" would seem to catch news films of bombings and battles and bullfights. How a court would decide whether films designed to inform about the dangers of sexually transmitted diseases depict human sexual activity to any significant extent, or (if they do not) nonetheless stimulate or encourage it to any significant extent by promoting the use of prophylactics, remains to be seen. The section is so badly drafted that courts should give defendants who can bring their work within section 2(1) the benefit of any doubt as to whether section 2(2) in fact operates to remove the exemption.

If the video is not exempted from classification requirements, the offences of supplying, offering to supply and possessing for the purpose of supply will not be committed where the supply concerned is exempt, or the supplier reasonably believes it to be exempt. The main situations in which non-exempt videos may be supplied without classification certificates are:

- where the video is given away free, and without a business purpose (section 3(2));

- where the video is supplied to people within the industry, (section 3(4)) or for television use (section 3(8)) or to the BBFC (section 3(9));

- where the video is made at some special occasion (*e.g.* a celebration or a conference) and is provided to those who took part in it or to their friends and associates, so long as it does not "to any significant extent" depict or simulate "human sexual activity" or the other matters set out in paragraph 2(2) (section 3(5));

- where the video is dispatched for export to a country outside the United Kingdom (section 3(4)(iii)).

The Censorship Test

Section 4 of the Act contains its main censorship implication: the Secretary of State is to designate "an authority (the first and only authority to be designated was the BBFC) to determine whether works are suitable for classification "having special regard to the likelihood of (certified) video works being viewed in the home". This test applies to every video submitted for classification, even those that are to be restricted for sale only in licensed sex shops. In one sense it serves to emphasise the "target audience" test in the Obscene Publications Act, whereby the court must consider the effect of the work on the potential audience, including persons who would view it in the home. Section 4 requires "special regard" to be accorded to this fact, and was designed to underline the greater potential for harm by the technological capacity to freeze-frame and replay scenes of sex or violence. The Act does not, as some mistakenly assume, lay down that videos must be "suitable for viewing in the home" in the sense of being appropriate for family viewing: that would be to negate the whole system of age-classification and point of sale restriction. The video must be "suitable for classification" in a particular category, having special regard to the impact it will have upon persons in that age-group and below through the devices available for home viewing.

Some M.P.s in 1984 wanted Parliament to insist that all videos must be suitable for children: this illiberal urge was rejected, and the classification system imposed by the Act assumes a degree of parental responsibility. However, these video-hostile legislators, usually led by David (now Lord) Alton and whipped up by the *Daily Mail,* made regular demands for more pervasive censorship: in 1994 the Government purported to make concessions to this lobby by spelling out the subject-matter which should make a video more difficult to certify, or more likely to be classified as fit for older age brackets. By a new section 4A of the Act,[22] "suitability" for a certificate (or a certificate in a particular age bracket) which depends upon various relevant factors, is henceforth to be decided by the BBFC after giving

> "special regard (among the other relevant factors) to any harm that may be caused to potential viewers or, through their behaviour, to society by the manner in which the work deals with—
>
> (a) criminal behaviour;
> (b) illegal drugs;
> (c) violent behaviour or incidents;

---

[22] Section 4A is inserted into the 1984 Video Recordings Act by s. 90 of the Criminal Justice and Public Order Act 1994.

> (d) horrific behaviour or incidents; or
> (e) human sexual activity . . .

and any behaviour or activity referred to in subsections (a)–(e) above shall be taken to include behaviour or activity likely to stimulate or encourage it."

These subjects are precisely those likely to provoke prosecutions under the Obscene Publications Act, and to which the BBFC had always given special regard. Spelling them out in a statute seemed little more than a sop to the Alton lobby. However, a certain sting was added by a definition of the "potential viewer" whose proneness to harm was a key consideration:

> " 'potential viewer' means any person (including a child or young person) who is likely to view the video work in question if a classification certificate or a classification certificate of a particular description were issued".

This poses an interesting question: if a child is not "likely" to view a particular video work (*e.g.* because it has been classified 18R or because it is too sophisticated to appeal to children) but it is perfectly *possible* that a few children will get to see it (because it has been "left around the house" or because they are precocious) then children as a class cease to be "potential viewers" for the purposes of the test, and any harm which may be done to these "unlikely" (but possible) viewers must be disregarded. This approach—which seems to follow from the statutory wording—boils down to the Obscene Publications Act test which requires harm to a significant number of likely viewers. Although section 4A highlights subjects to which "special regard" must be paid, the Home Office minister said when introducing the amendment that "It is very important to bear it in mind that those statutory criteria are not intended to be exhaustive and the amendment states only that the Board is to consider them".[23] Earl Ferrers, Government spokesman in the House of Lords, said when introducing section 4A that:

> "It leaves the BBFC with discretion to decide what to do once it has considered a work on the basis of the criteria . . . If it concludes, for example, that the work will set a bad example to very young children, it need not ban the video altogether but it can place it in an age-restricted category. There may be some works which the Board believes would have such a devastating effect on individuals or on society if they were released that there should be a

---

[23] Speech of Mr Norman Baker, House of Commons, October 1994.

possibility of their being refused a video classification altogether, and the clause leaves the board free to do that".[24]

The question must first be whether the video is likely to appeal to children and be seen by a significant number of them. If the answer is "yes", then the second question is whether the video will harm those children or cause them to behave in a way that harms society because of the video's treatment of crime, drugs, sex or violence. If the answer again is "yes", then the factor of risk to children must be given special weight (along with other relevant factors) in determining whether the video should be certified at all, or else given a high age-restriction. This three-stage approach was approved by the Divisional Court in 2000[25]; it permits the Board to ignore the danger to children where the risk that a significant number will see it is remote, and to consider instead the danger of adult viewers being morally corrupted or being persuaded to emulate anti-social acts.

18R: From *Makin' Whoopee* to *Horny Catbabe*

Section 7 of the Video Recordings Act 1984 (VRA) requires video works to be certified either as suitable for general viewing (*i.e.* U or PG) or as suitable only for viewing by and supply to persons who have attained a particular age (12, 15 or 18) or else certified as 18R, a category which must carry "a statement that no video recording containing that work is to be supplied other than in a licensed sex shop". Councils which grant sex shop licences do so sparingly—in 2001 there were only about 90 such "adults only" outlets in England. The Home Office, under both Michael Howard and Jack Straw, had always insisted that videos which featured real (rather than simulated) copulation should not be certified at all, even in the 18R category. This rule, and the paucity of sex shop outlets, meant that distributors of sex films would pay the BBFC to cut their films to an "18" standard—a sleazy and time-consuming exercise, which made the Board's examiners complicit in producing soft-core pornography and denied adults in the United Kingdom the right to watch "medium core" pornography on video. James Ferman pointed out that "the resulting regime is stricter than that of any of our continental partners in the E.C.".[26] In 1997, he decided to certify as 18R some porn videos of a kind which juries were acquitting in section 2 prosecutions under the Obscene Publications Act.

This sensible approach allowed adults who chose to enter sex shops

---

[24] Statement of Earl Ferrers, House of Lords, June 1994.
[25] *R. v. Video Appeals Committee, ex p. BBFC* [2000] E.M.L.R. 850 at para. 12 (Hooper J.).
[26] BBFC Annual Report for 1990 (BBFC, 1991) para. 34.

to obtain "straight up and down the wicket" pornography. Their new freedom infuriated the Home Secretary: Jack Straw brought intense and effective pressure on the BBFC to revert to its ban on "real sex", which the Home Office claimed would be condemned as obscene by magistrates' courts (this might be true, but since magistrates are unrepresentative of the robust individuals who sit on juries, the Home Office point was misleading). The consequent BBFC policy back-flip in the course of 1997 was challenged by the distributors of *Makin' Whoopee,* an unpretentious porn video denied 18R because it featured a few bouts of penetrative sex. The Video Appeals Committee demonstrated its independence—both from the BBFC and the Home Office—by upholding the appeal on the ground that juries would be unlikely to convict pictures of straightforward sexual intercourse. Applying contemporary standards, the VAC decided that *Makin' Whoopee* would not corrupt a significant number of its potential viewers—a class from which children could be excluded by its 18R sale to adults in licensed outlets.[27]

The Home Secretary was mightily displeased, and the incoming BBFC Director (Robin Duvall) and President (Andreas Whittam-Smith), anxious lest their new jobs would entail non-stop pornographic viewing, challenged the *Makin' Whoopee* decision by refusing an 18R certificate to a similar porno movie called *Horny Catbabe*—unless it were edited to remove "all shots of penetration by penis, hand or dildo as well as all shots of a penis being masturbated or taken into a woman's mouth". But the VAC stood its ground: *Horny Catbabe,* it decided, must be classified 18R. Its 33-page reasoning, however, was convoluted, inconsistent and obscure. It agreed that the video lacked all artistic merit: it was a cheap and trashy product containing no more than an inter-linked series of explicit sex scenes. But the VAC went on to apply, not so much the words of section 4A, but the gloss provided by Earl Ferrers in the House of Lords, suggesting that the BBFC could only refuse classification of the video if it would have a "devastating effect on individuals or society"—*Horny Catbabe* and other ideologically vapid porn movies were not in that class. The VAC did consider the effect on children: it noted recent research that 50 per cent of girls have intercourse by the age of 17[28] and inferred from this—illogically—that they (and their under-18 partners) "would not be harmed by watching videos such as these". The VAC declined to hazard any guess as to the number of child viewers or the prospect of a significant portion of them suffering harm. It found that the BBFC guidelines banning penet-

---

[27] Video Appeals Committee, Appeal No. 0014 of 1998, *Makin' Whoopee.* The VAC specifically rejected the approach in *R. v. Reiter* [1954] Q.B. 16 and agreed to look at material which had recently been acquitted in order better to appreciate current standards: transcript, p. 5.

[28] K. Wellings *et al*, *Sexual Behaviour in Britain* (Penguin, 1994).

rative (but not masturbatory) sex to have little relevance to what might be damaging to children ("Is an erect penis in the hands of a woman masturbating a man likely to be less upsetting than an erect penis entering a woman's vagina?") and allowed the appeal, noting merely that "we might have taken a different view if there was evidence that the effects were affecting more than a small minority of children or were devastating if this did happen".[29]

The confusions and illogicalities in this reasoning led the BBFC to take the extraordinary step of judicially reviewing its own Appeals Committee. The case, *R. v. Video Appeals Committee of the BBFC, ex p. BBFC*, was decided by Hooper J. in May 2000[30]:

> The BBFC argued that the VAC should have applied the principle of "better safe than sorry", since it had no evidence of how many children would be affected, or how seriously, it should have refused to certify at 18R until the risk could be properly assessed and found acceptable. (This approach is plainly inconsistent with Article 10 of the European Convention, which puts the burden of proof on the would-be censor). Hooper J. rejected it: he interpreted section 4A as requiring the BBFC (and, on appeal, the VAC) to ask:
>
> (1) Was a child *likely* to view the video if it was classified?
> (2) Might such "potential viewers" be harmed, or might harm be caused to society through their behaviour resulting from the manner in which the video dealt with human sexuality?
>
> When both questions were answered in the affirmative, then this factor— the risk of harm to children—had to be given special (but not definitive) weight in the "balancing act" over whether to classify the video. The VAC had answered both questions affirmatively, but had decided the risk of harm was fairly insignificant so the case for banning the work had not been made out—an approach that was appropriate.

In other words, although section 4A requires complicated findings to be factored into a balancing act, if the censor fails to establish that a significant number of likely viewers will be harmed, an 18R certificate should (at very least) be granted, irrespective of pornographic content. The Divisional Court in *Horny Catbabe* applied the familiar presumption that the courts will not second-guess any censorship decision made by a body of experts. Hooper J. tried to make the decision more comprehensible by pointing out the appropriate test and finding some indications that the VAC had applied it. But what the VAC was really doing was applying a proportionality test: there was no evidence of harm, since children were unlikely to get their hands on 18R videos (although

---

[29] Video Appeals Committee, *Horny Catbabe et al*, August 16, 1999.
[30] *R. v. VAC, ex parte BBFC* [2000] E.M.L.R. 850.

a few would): in the absence of such evidence, it would be disproportionate to deny to adults their right to dilate over pornography.

Neither the BBFC nor the Home Office appealed the Divisional Court decision: the BBFC surrendered and issued new 18R guidelines. This category, the guidelines assert, exists "primarily for explicit videos of consenting sex between adults" including (without distinction between heterosexual and homosexual activity) scenes which feature "aroused genitalia, masturbation, oral-genital contact including kissing, licking and sucking, penetration by finger, penis, tongue, vibrator or dildo, group sexual activity, ejaculation and semen". However, the guidelines exclude any video with contents which breach the criminal law, or are likely to encourage interest in paedophilia or incest, non-consensual sex, infliction of pain or involuntary humiliation, or which depict methods of restraint (*e.g.* ball-gags), penetration by dangerous objects or "degrading and dehumanising activity" (defined to include "bestiality, necrophilia, defecation, urolagnia").[31] Good clean pornography, however, shall henceforth receive the Board's 18R imprimatur.

Video Games

The market for video games, played on cheap play-stations or expensive personal computers, has rocketed in recent years: there are 120 British companies involved in designing and manufacturing software and distributing these playthings, represented by a trade association, ELSPA (European Leisure Software Publishers Association). They participate in a system of voluntary self-regulation operated by the Video Standards Council which has hired a senior Scotland Yard officer to police the age ratings (12, 15 and 18) it agrees with manufacturers. Video games played in amusement arcades are not "exhibitions of moving pictures" for the purposes of the Cinematograph Act 1909, so they do not require licensing by local authorities.[32] Video and computer games are exempted from BBFC classification under section 2 of the VRA unless "to any significant extent" they "depict" human sexual activity, or acts of gross violence towards humans and animals, or are likely to encourage such behaviour. A vogue in the nineties, for games which involve the elimination—usually, the obliteration—of animated or digitised cartoon figures, raised the difficult legal question of whether such humanoid characters (robots, dragons, zombies and dinosaurs, etc.) counted as "human" or "animal", or indeed whether enjoyment derived from blasting them to smithereens was likely to encourage violent behaviour in real life. The better view is that games which involve battles between non-realistic cartoon characters do not require classification,

---

[31] BBFC Classification Guidelines (September 2000) pp. 18–19.
[32] *BACTA v. Westminster City Council* [1988] 1 All E.R. 816.

unless players are meant to take pleasure in acts of torture or mutilation. Similarly, if the game called for player involvement in the sexual activity of animated characters, it might "stimulate or encourage sexual activity" and so require classification. Manufacturers submit their games to the Video Standards Council for voluntary age-classification: if the VSC considers that the game is non-exempt, or if M.P.s and the press begin to pontificate against its dangers to youth, submission to the BBFC for age certification will be the safest course.

The benchmark for video games was set by the Video Appeals Committee in 1997 in the *CARMAGEDDON Case.*[33] This computer product of British creative technology and black humour sold in hundreds of thousands in 57 countries, but was banned by the BBFC after press attacks which accused it of encouraging road rage ("Ban Killer Car Game: M.P.s Enraged by Sick Computer Game"). The game, playable only on P.C.s costing upwards of £1,200, offered harmless dodgem-car style fun to experienced players in the driving seat who ran over mad digitised cows and a poisonous tube of blobs ("sprites") which squealed when hit and splattered green "blood" on the windshield. It had been given a "15" certificate by Tribunals in Australia and New Zealand but in Britain, James Ferman refused to countenance "a game which gives the player permission to carry out atrocious acts of carnage in this safety-contained world of the PC screen . . . well heeled, laddish young men will take great delight in the game's savage delinquency . . . parents from poorer families often buy expensive games for their offspring . . . it positively encourages the players to commit acts of gross violence against defenceless targets who cannot fight back (children, old people, the infirm) . . . the lethal weapon is one that many of us wield every day, the motor car, and the death toll caused by cars is a major problem in every advanced nation". To deconstruct this hyperbole, the *CARME-GEDDON* manufacturers arranged for the five members of the VAC actually to play the game—an experience a majority of them seemed to enjoy—and commissioned research which demonstrated that the PC game market was an adult one (mid-20 to early 30s); that players understood the macabre humour and would never permit themselves in real life to mow down pedestrians in the manner in which they despatched the mad cows and evil pixels of the *CARMAGEDDON* demolition derby.[34]

The VAC, by a majority, upheld the SCI appeal and classified *CAR-MEGGEDON* as "18". Its reasoning was:

---

[33] *Carmageddon Case: Appeal of Sales Curve International,* VAC, November 20, 1997, (App. IV, BBFC Report 1997–99).

[34] Guy Cumberbatch, Samantha Woods and Sally Gauntlett, *BBFC Classification of Carmegeddon,* June 1997.

(i) the BBFC bore the burden of proving harm to potential viewers, and had adduced no real evidence to this effect;

(ii) there had been over 300,000 sales already in other countries, without reports of "copycat" effects;

(iii) Because the game was only playable on an expensive PC it was unlikely that teenagers would play, adults being much less likely to permit their children to access their PCs than their video recorder.

(iv) There was an important distinction between a video or film, and a game. The latter was much less likely to have an imitative effect.

(v) VAC members when playing the game did not experience a "delinquent feeling" when hitting a cow or a pedestrian "sprite". The game was fast and furious, and players had to concentrate on scoring points rather than engaging in violence. The fantasy of playing it on a virtual motorway was clearly distinguishable from driving in real time.

The VAC verdict was notable for standing against the political hysteria and approving technologically clever, tongue-in-cheek entertainment. It was a narrow victory—the VAC split 3 – 2, and would probably have decided in favour of a ban if the game had been for play stations costing £35 rather than for PCs costing £1,500. The burden of proof borne by the censor had been an important consideration: the BBFC relied on hyperbole while SCI commissioned and called evidence to refute its speculative fears. The game was undoubtedly in bad taste, even though its animated pedestrians had transmogrified (on counsel's advice) into green blobs by the time it was submitted for classification. Whether it actually required classification was not decided (although the VAC thought it did); its manufacturers preferred to fight their battle with the BBFC in the Video Appeals Committee rather than as a defendant charged with the criminal offence of supplying an uncertified video work.

Offences

It is, incredibly, quite a serious offence to supply an uncertified video cassette: the punishment is a fine without limit or imprisonment for up to two years. There is no excuse for this severity, which is out of all proportion to punishment which befits a labelling mistake: originally the courts had no power to imprison, but the Government in 1994 increased the penalties as a sop to David Alton's lobby.[35] Even the offence of supplying a certified video in breach of its age restriction (*e.g.* selling a "15" video to a 14-year-old) can result in a fine of £5,000 and up to six months in prison, although at least it is a defence that the supplier did not believe the purchaser to be below the appropriate age. In 1993 the law was amended to provide a defence of due diligence, if all reasonable precautions are taken and all due diligence was exercised to avoid the commission of an offence.[36]

The issues for the court will generally be straightforward and uncluttered by any need for aesthetic judgment, unless a defendant pleads "due diligence", that he or she had reason to believe the work was exempted from classification under section 2. Magistrates may issue warrants for search and seizure if satisfied that there are reasonable grounds for suspecting offences, and police may arrest persons suspected of offences under the Act if they refuse to give their names and addresses. The court may, as an additional punishment, order the videos to which the offence relates to be forfeited—an action more likely to be taken where they are unclassified than where they have merely been mislabelled or sold to under-age persons. There is a special provision (section 21(2)) whereby the court cannot order forfeiture without giving an opportunity to any person other than the defendant who claims ownership of the videos to show cause why such an order should not be made. In accord with section 71 of the Criminal Justice Act 1988, the court can additionally confiscate any profits made from the offence. The police are not primarily responsible for enforcing the Act; this task falls on trading standards officers.

Packaging rules

The Act and the regulations made pursuant to it lay down detailed requirements for packaging and labelling videos with the appropriate classification symbol. Regrettably, there is no duty to mark a video as an exempt work, although failure to do so will be likely to cause confusion among retailers.

The overall purpose of the regulations is to ensure that no prospective purchaser or borrower is misled as to the suitability for various age-groups of the work or works contained in the recording. It follows from this purpose that where a recording contains a number of separate works (*e.g.* a feature film and trailers for other feature films), the recording must bear the classification of the work that is least suitable for viewing in the home. This purpose is achieved in terms by section 2(5) of the

---

[35] Criminal Justice and Public Order Act 1994, s. 88.
[36] Video Recordings Act 1993, amending the 1984 legislation by adding the due diligence defence as s. 14A.

Video Recordings (Labelling) Regulations 1985, which provides "where a video recording contains more than one video work in respect of which classification certificates which are not equally restrictive have been issued, the video recording shall be taken to contain only the most restrictively classified video work of these works". Thus, if a feature film classified as 15 is combined with a trailer classified as 18, the cassette package should be labelled 18, the category of the cassette being in such cases determined by the category of the trailer.

The BBFC 2000: Classification Guidelines

The BBFC classifies films on behalf of local authorities which license cinemas, and classifies videos, DVDs and computer games under the Video Recordings Act. In September 2000, the post-Ferman regime issued their detailed guidelines for the various classification categories, as a general gesture towards transparency and out of concern that the Human Rights Act would require more clarity in classification rules (else a ban could not be said to be "prescribed by law"). The categories are the same for movies and for videos, although the BBFC warn that the latter may be stricter because of "the increased possibility of under-age viewing . . . and of works being replayed or viewed out of context". The classification categories are:

U: Universal

Must be suitable for children of all ages, "set within a positive moral framework". No sex (other than "kissing" and references to "making love"); no drugs; no realistic weapons; only very mild bad language and fleeting violence; any element of threat or horror should have a "reassuring outcome" (*i.e.* good must triumph over evil).

PG: Parental Guidance

Must not disturb children as young as eight. Crime and domestic violence may feature, but must never be condoned. No references to drugs, or to sex (other than by implication); only "mild" bad language and "moderate" violence if justified by its setting as a vehicle for comedy or fantasy or a re-enactment of history. No glamorisation of weaponry or elucidation of fighting techniques.

12: Age Restriction

Nudity must be "brief and discreet"; bad language ("*e.g.* fuck") rare and "justified by context"; but sexual references "may reflect the familiarity of most adolescents today with sex education through school". Violence must not be depicted in any detail (no focus on injuries or blood and gore) and imitable combat or suicide techniques must be avoided. Horror, however, is permissible. There may be at least a whiff of cannabis, if justified by context, but the film "should indicate the dangers" (but what are these? The danger of dropping out, or of being caught?).

15: Age Restriction

Strong language may be used frequently, but not aggressively or sexistly ("*cunt* is only rarely acceptable"). Nudity is unconstrained "in a non-sexual context" and sex may be portrayed although not in detail and if casual "should be handled responsibly". Hard drugs may be shown but not if their use is encouraged; violence and horror must not dwell on pain or injury; dangerous combat techniques (ear claps, head butts, rabbit punches) are forbidden, and scenes of sexual violence must be brief and discreet.

18: Age Restriction

The BBFC says that it respects the right of adults to choose their own entertainment, and will impose no restraints at this level on violence, bad language, nudity or horror. However it may cut or ban any film or video with a "detailed portrayal of violent or dangerous acts likely to promote the activity . . . instructive detail of illegal drug use . . . more explicit images of sexual activity, unless justified by context."[37]

These guidelines, issued in September 2000, were a welcome replacement for the more subjective standards imposed on the medium by the BBFC's former director, James Ferman, who retired in 1999 after 23 years as chief censor. Nonetheless, 90 years of film, and later video, censorship has operated with some consistent assumptions (about "copycat" effects and the impressionability of children) and some consistent targets. Towards the end of his reign, Ferman talked in semi-mystical terms about taking into account "the moral position of the film-maker towards his own material" which he tried to establish by asking:

- Is the sympathy of the film maker on the side of the victim or the aggressor?

- Is the process of the violence indulged in for its own sake, rather than to tell us anything significant about the motives or state of mind of the persons involved?

---

[37] BBFC Classification Guidelines, September 2000, pp. 12–17.

- Does the camerawork or editing belie the ostensible moral stance of the film by seeking to enlist or encourage our vicarious enjoyment of the atrocities portrayed?

But, like Miss Prism's view of fiction, the BBFC's definition of a good uncut video feature or film is one in which the good ended happily and the bad unhappily. Ferman's questions, like the DPP's guidelines, serve to give some rational justification for cuts that are made because the violence is of a kind that turns the examiner's stomach. Thus films that glorify wars and mercenary operations have been passed without deletions; those that depict extremes of violence have always been censored, however "moral" the context. The advent of the BBFC "Guidelines 2000", under the Whittam-Smith/Duvall regime, presages more sensible and predictable censorship directed to scenes identified as taboo—a rejection of Ferman's more moralistic mission to improve films by "trimming" them to send out more acceptable messages.

WHAT WILL BE CENSORED?

Cruelty to animals

This is a peculiarly British concern, and the only subject which is specifically banned by a law passed in 1937 after the release of Errol Flynn's *The Charge of the Light Brigade*—a movie in the making of which horses suffered almost as severely as those in the original charge. The Cinematograph Films (Animals) Act of 1937 prohibits the exhibition of "any scene . . . organised or directed in such a way as to involve the cruel infliction of pain or terror on any animal or the cruel goading of any animal to fury". The BBFC tends to cut such scenes automatically, without asking whether the director both intended and caused the cruelty, which should be the legal test. It has ordered cuts in many films featuring bullfights and in westerns where horses are brought down by a tripping device—although a double standard applies here since it has never prohibited British films featuring fox-hunting. It may be doubted whether its cuts help animal welfare abroad: they certainly eliminate part of the real world where cock-fighting, bullfights, battery farming and experiments with rodents and beagles are undoubtedly a part of life which film makers should be entitled to depict. Many of the BBFC cuts are silly: a sex scene was removed from John Waters cult movie *Pink Flamingos* not because of the sex but because the copulating couple squashed a squawking chicken[38]; *The Blood of Fu Man Chu* lost a scene

---

[38] BBFC Annual Report 1997/8, p. 30.

where rubble fell on a snake[39] and in 1997 the BBFC solemnly announced that it had censored a scene of "an iguana smoking a cigarette".[40] Ferman's concern for the emotions of movie characters extended to rodents: he cut a scene in which a rat was dunked in liquid oxygen (an experiment that did not cause it any physical injury) because "for the rat, it was a traumatic return to the condition of the womb".[41] In 2001 the BBFC showed greater sense when it rejected the RSPCA's demand that it censor the Oscar-nominated film *Amores Perros* to remove a key scene of a dog fight in a gambling den.[42] This time, the Board made inquiries of the director to satisfy itself that no cruelty was intended or suffered by the animals. The RSPCA keeps an over-wary eye on film and video companies: in 1994 it prosecuted CIC Video for cruelty to the pet snakes it had distributed to video stores as a gimmick advertising *The Serpent and the Rainbow*. After a two-week hearing the Croydon magistrates dismissed the charges: the video company had taken expert advice on snake-care, and reptiles did not deserve quite the same consideration as lovable household pets.

Drug-taking

Scenes depicting the administration of hard drugs, or glamorising or trivialising the consequences of drug-taking in any way, are censored. There are exceptions made for quality films: Woody Allen was allowed to attempt the inhalation of cocaine for comic effect in *Annie Hall,* and *Christianne F* was permitted to shoot up heroin, albeit in shadow and with three minutes of close-ups deleted, because the overall message of the film was aversive. However, the comic cocaine-sniffing scene in *Crocodile Dundee* was excised before the film was granted a 15 certificate for video release. In Warhol's *Trash,* and later in *Pulp Fiction* and *Trainspotting*, heroin-injecting scenes were cut to remove what the BBFC called the "seductive imitability" of "the sight of a needle puncturing the skin" which apparently holds "a masochistic fascination for some addicts".[43] Assumptions of this kind are blandly made by the BBFC to justify censorship without any evidential or expert support: for almost all viewers, injection scenes are aversive. The Board is on firmer ground in cutting episodes which depict the preparation of dangerous mixtures of cocaine and opium. In 1999 the BBFC took a sensible view in certifying films which depicted ecstasy and heroin-taking honestly and responsibly, without glamorisation, but its more relaxed

[39] BBFC Annual Report 1999, p. 25.
[40] BBFC Annual Report 1996/7, p. 17.
[41] BBFC Annual Report 1989, p. 12.
[42] " 'Cruel' Dog Film to be Shown in Britain" *The Guardian,* March 1, 2001.
[43] BBFC Annual Report; 1995 (p. 18), 1996–7 (p. 16).

approach to depictions of soft drugs did not prevent an absurd interference with a five-minute short made by pro-marijuana campaigner Howard Marks. It insisted on adding, after the credits, for the sake of zombies in the cinema, that "smoking cannabis is a criminal offence".[44]

Criminal techniques

Techniques for picking locks, stealing cars or making Molotov cocktails have always been censored, especially from videos (where replays may help to instruct). Combat techniques are "trimmed" where the BBFC fears a danger of imitation—as in neck chops, ear claps and head butts. There has been great concern about the importation of oriental fighting methods—scenes with rice-flails were "banned absolutely", even when they are wielded by teenage mutant Ninja turtles. Particular attention is paid to deleting scenes where everyday instruments such as cigarette lighters and garden tools are used to inflict violence, because the BBFC really believes that viewers might not think of such uses without seeing cinematic examples. It has been particularly concerned to eliminate pictures of crossbows—"restricted by law but too photogenic for film-makers to resist". Crossbows were difficult for armies to resist, too, in many historic battles that film makers may now wish to re-enact. Kung Fu kicks and metal throwing-objects were excised from the 12-rated *Tomorrow Never Dies*.

BBFC reports have consistently inveighed against Bruce Lee style martial techniques in oriental and Asian films, sometimes in terms that appear almost to discriminate on grounds of race. In 1999 the Board admitted its approach was out of date—today's teenagers are far more taken with digitally-enhanced special effects—and out of line with what is permitted on television. A new approach would "treat all weapons equally" (*i.e.* would no longer dwell on the race of the characters who use them) and concentrate on the extent to which they were glamorised.[45] Suicide techniques remain a particular and justified concern, at least for child viewers: one of the most popular "12" films of 2000, *The Mummy,* lost 14 seconds from a sequence involving hanging.

Children

The Protection of Children Act 1978 makes it an offence to have persons under 16 participate in "indecent" scenes in films, or to distribute or advertise movies containing such sequences. The BBFC applies a strict interpretation of this measure to all films submitted, and will require evidence of age if a teenager performs in an "indecent" scene.

---

[44] BBFC Annual Report 1999, p. 25.
[45] BBFC Report 1999, p. 24.

After the Act was introduced, the BBFC recalled the film *Taxi Driver* and required a cut in one suggestive sequence involving the 12-year-old Jodie Foster. Films that show violence against children will also be carefully vetted—not for "indecency" but for any action that may attract emulation.

The Board spends much of its time deleting expletives on behalf of children, whom it believes should never hear them until they turn 12, and then only on very rare occasions until they turn 15 (BBFC film examiners call themselves "The British Board of Fuck Counters"[46].) In 1999 Disney's *Pocahontas II* suffered the excision of three "bloodys", and a drama documentary about the history of lunar exploration lost historical accuracy (but gained a PG certificate) by bleeping "coarse language" from actual astronautical conversations.[47]

Children of all ages are the real victims of obsessive BBFC censorship decisions taken ostensibly in their interests, but without much expert insight into what might cause them harm. They will always be permitted nightmares over the wicked witch in *Snow White* and the death of Bambi's mother: why deny them until the age of 12 the enjoyable fantasy exploits of James Bond or the moral missions of *The Phantom*? If they can cope with Uncle Scar killing the king, his brother, in *The Lion King,* why deny them various video versions of *Hamlet*? Most parents would be thrilled if their 14-year-old children took an interest in *Shakespeare in Love* (15) or if their 16-year-olds wanted to see *The End of the Affair* (18): who knows?—the effect might be to make them read Shakespeare and Graham Greene. The BBFC is consistently irresponsible in placing movies like these out of teenage reach— doubly so since the rights they deny are additionally those of parents who should be entitled to decide the films they wish to accompany their children to the local cinema to view.

By insisting upon cuts to films before certifying them for the category which will attract the largest audience—15—the BBFC ensures that profit-driven distributors who aim for that category have no alternative but to accept severe censorship. Indeed, most films are already cut for "15" by the producers and distributors before they are submitted to the Board. The result is that many British films do not appear, on screen, as good as they should or could be: after censorship for a "15" audience, they will have been shorn of the bite and adult wit which might have made them a critical success or less of a critical failure.

Concern about children—particularly schoolgirls—is taken to such extremes that in 1990 the BBFC actually drew up "rules to cover the use of schoolgirl attire in sex videos". The film it looked at most often and most nervously was Adrian Lynne's remake of *Lolita,* featuring a

[46] Maggie Mills "Sinful Days in Soho", *Sunday Times,* November 1, 1998.
[47] BBFC Annual Report 1999, p. 26.

remarkable performance by Jeremy Irons. A 14-year-old actress played Lolita as a naughty schoolgirl (a 19-year-old "body double" was used for her sex scenes) rather than as the subject of paedophile attraction. The film was to this extent a distortion of the book, but nonetheless a powerful study of the desolation and self-destruction involved in forbidden obsessions. The BBFC refused to certify the film for a year, until its new President (Andreas Whittam-Smith) took expert psychiatric and legal advice and granted an "18" certificate. His openness disarmed even the *Daily Mail,* and the film's eventual release was uneventful.

Violence

The BBFC distinguishes between violence "of a relatively conventional and undisturbing nature" in war films and westerns, and scenes that "might lead to highly disturbing imagery being planted in vulnerable minds". This test is particularly applied to videos, where executions and death agonies are cut before they are classified "18". Over half the running time of the cuts made by the BBFC in recent years has involved scenes of violence. The Board seeks to distinguish between "video-nasties" and "conventional thriller or fantasy horror videos". On the basis of the approach adopted by the Williams Committee the test is whether "highly explicit depictions of mutilation, savagery, menace and humiliation are presented for entertainment in a way that emphasises the pleasures of sadism".

These platitudes offer ample scope for busy, nit-picking censorship. The fate of *Rambo III* may serve as an example. It was screened uncut to adults (and even teenagers) in America and many European countries. The BBFC, however, insisted on many cuts before it could be screened (for adults only) in the cinema or sold as an "18" video. It was feared that Rambo's weapon-wielding would "encourage anti-social violence on the streets of Britain", notwithstanding that the film was set in Afghanistan and most of Rambo's military arsenal was unavailable at corner stores. The Board required cuts "in bloodshed and in glamorisation of military weaponry", finding it particularly objectionable that Rambo "killed, on the battlefield though never at home, with a deadly efficiency which seemed increasingly out of place in a world struggling towards new, more reasonable means of settling international disputes".[48] These sentiments are all very fine, if very dated, after September 11, 2001, but was it ever any business of the BBFC to promote international harmony? The notion that *Rambo III* would provoke fighting in the streets if shown uncensored to British adults is comical. All that the Board achieved by its fussy "topping and tailing" of violent

---

[48] BBFC, Annual Report for 1988, para.2.

scenes was the sanitisation of violence—and sanitised violence is more attractive than the real thing.

The BBFC's emasculation of *Rambo* appears absurd beside the scenes of massive violence that are family television news viewing from Rwanda and Jerusalem but the Board has always been prone to make political judgments about the kind of violence it cuts, and confessed as much when it censored the James Bond film, *Licence to Kill,* before it could be certified "15". Bond films had not previously been expurgated, but the Board admitted that "the key to this change was the [film maker's] decision to present Bond not as an urbane British intelligence man, but as an embittered vigilante seeking personal revenge . . . "[49] It cut scenes of a woman being whipped and a man being fed to sharks that would, no doubt, have been perfectly acceptable had the urbane 007 loyally taken these actions in the service of British intelligence. The Board has behaved bizarrely in respect of other James Bond films. James Ferman boasted that Britain was the only country in the world to impose cuts on *Tomorrow Never Dies* (for a "12" certificate): the BBFC insisted on advising the producers throughout the making of the movie, and even censored its music ("a loud and aggressive soundtrack had to be toned down in Britain to retain the '12'").[50] James Bond films are appreciated by everyone as fantasy, and most 10-year-old boys watch the videos irrespective of age categories. This fussy censorship excluded them from family movie matinees, not only of Bond films but of *Titanic, Independence Day* and *Star Trek,* which were also unjustifiably certified as "12" rather than "PG".

The Whittam-Smith/Duvall regime has not shaken off the Ferman approach: in 1999 it banned *Bare Fist—The Sport that Wouldn't Die* an argument for the legalisation of bare-knuckle fighting. This suppression of opinion was a clear breach of the Human Rights Act's freedom of expression guarantee.[51] The BBFC attitude to violence has reacted to publicity following notorious crimes, ever since some teenage murders were blamed on Stanley Kubrick's film *Clockwork Orange* in the early 70s. The Williams Committee refuted the claim that *Clockwork Orange* had inspired "copycat" killings, but Kubrick personally took the film out of circulation and the video version was not placed on the market (certificate "18") until after his death in 2000. *Natural Born Killers* has been another victim of industry self-censorship: although the BBFC gave an "18" certificate to Oliver Stone's film (once it was satisfied of the falsity of allegations that it had incited murders in America) and was prepared to give a similar certification to the video, Warner Brothers took fright after the massacre of schoolchildren at Dunblane and

[49] BBFC, Annual Report for 1989, para. 20.
[50] *ibid.*, pp. 8 and 21.
[51] BBFC Annual Report 1999, p. 21.

have refused to distribute the video in the United Kingdom.[52] The trial judge in the *Bulger* case blamed horror videos for the shocking delinquency of the 10-year-old murderers: his comments inflamed the parliamentary debate over the VRA amendments in 1993 and 1994. The consequent Home Office research which concluded that "the police reports did not support the theory that those crimes had been influenced by exposure either to any particular video, or videos in general" was given little or no publicity.[53]

One superstition which was finally laid to rest by the new BBFC regime was that *The Exorcist* maintained a unique power to endanger youth and terrify young adults. This early 70s horror film was a classic of the genre, but notwithstanding its religious message (it was banned as Catholic propaganda by the Marxist Government of Tunisia) James Ferman stubbornly refused to give it a video certification. His continuing belief in its danger only enhanced its reputation: in 1999 it returned as a box office cinema success, trading on the BBFC ban which was lifted by Robin Duvall. There have been no reported incidents of demonic possession as a result. Where "video-nasties" are concerned, time is the great healer: most of those which appeared on the "DPP's list" in 1983 as fit for obscenity prosecution have been quietly certified "18", including *Driller Killer* and *Zombie Flesh Eaters*.

Sexual violence

The BBFC is the strictest censorship board in the world in deleting scenes of violence against women, especially in a sexual context.[54] Scenes of torture, threats with weapons, sexual taunting and forcible stripping have been deleted, because of "the danger in eroticising such material for the pleasures of a male audience". Scenes of forcible sex "must not be trivialised or endorsed by the context in which they are presented". Scenes of sexual violence leading to rape are usually reduced, and often excised completely. Standards are noticeably stricter for video than for film: scenes that are "trimmed" on an "18" film may be cut entirely on an "18" video, to remove even the *idea* of the particular form of aggression.

The BBFC's explanation in its 1985 report still reflects its thinking:

---

[52] Warner Home Video actually invited the BBFC to review its "18" classification after Dunblane, in the hope that its own (in fact, Oliver Stone's) movie would be banned. The Board refused to be party to this corporate cowardice, although it pointed out that the company was under no compulsion to release the title: Annual Report 1995–6, p. 5; 1996–7, App. V.

[53] "Sex, Lies and Censors", James Ferman, *The Independent on Sunday*, February 21, 1999, p. 29.

[54] BBFC, *Guide to the Video Recordings Act 1984*.

"We are very careful with rape scenes, even those which in the cinema were found justifiable by context. On video, with its technological capacity for selective or repeated viewings, such scenes could lend themselves to viewing out of context, perhaps repeatedly by persons whose fantasy life might incline them to act out such images of forcible sex because of the extent to which they have found them arousing in private. The same is true of sadistic material, even where the point of view of the film as a whole is a critical one. We realise the importance here of balancing freedom against responsibility, but the issues must be faced.

The Board in this respect abandons the "taken as a whole" test in the Obscene Publications Act, and goes back to the "purple passages" approach that applied to books prior to 1959. This may mean that even films of great merit will be cut for video release because of the danger apprehended from a few viewers obsessing over replayed scenes of sex or violence. The BBFC has always applied a more liberal test to films of recognised social or cinematic merit, by analogy with the "public-good" provisions of the Obscene Publications Act, although the same largesse is not shown to video works. In 1991 the Board finally brought itself, after 13 years, to give an "18" certificate for film screening to Oshima's *Empire of the Senses,* a work of recognised cinematic merit, but it has not approved this film for video distribution. *Straw Dogs,* with its notorious rape scene, is still refused BBFC certification for video sale. The Board concluded, as recently as 1999, that the rape scene "was filmed in a manner which could arouse some viewers and that the victim's enthusiastic reaction dangerously endorsed the male myth that women enjoy being raped".[55]

In that year, however, it did breach a traditional taboo certifying for "18" cinema release one much-publicised French film which depicted actual rather than simulated sex. *Romance* was a portentous exercise in Gallic existentialism, but it featured the acting equipment of Rocky Siffredi, hitherto seen exclusively in banned hard-core movies. The Board interpreted the film as "a frank exploration of female sexuality" and passed it as politically correct, including a rape scene which "although brutal and shocking, was filmed in a manner which avoided offering sexual thrills". Adult cinema audiences were vouchsafed the sight of a well-read penis, fully and frequently engorged, and the protests—even from the *Daily Mail*—were muted. Not so the hysteria which had greeted the release of the more interesting and less explicit David Cronenberg film *Crash,* which disturbed the popular press through its ironic association of sexual excitement with car crashes. The Board valiantly maintained its position that the film was unlikely to

---

[55] BBFC Annual Report 1999, p. 30.

encourage deviancy; but opposition diminished only after groups representing disabled people claimed that the film supported their right to sexual feelings. In all these cases, the BBFC has in effect applied the "public good" defence which would ensure a jury acquittal in the event of an obscenity prosecution. In 2001 the Board broke another taboo by permitting scenes of real, raw sex between reputable British actors: Mark Rylance (in his time, a fine RSC Hamlet) was fellated by actress Kerry Fox in the film *Intimacy,* which was granted an "18" certificate. The BBFC was under the impression that it was a good film (on the illogical ground that it was based on a book by Hanif Kureishi) although audiences did not flock to see it. Criticism of the BBFC decision to grant a certificate was limited, but could well increase if less "artistic" and more popular hard-core pornography is certified "18".

Blasphemy

This can become a serious problem for a censorship body as craving of public support as the BBFC. It risks condemnation from fundamentalist Christian groups if it gives "approval" to films that distort the Bible story, but its application of a controversial and discriminatory law earns it the contempt of the creative community it also purports to serve. The Board launched a massive public relations exercise in support of *The Last Temptation of Christ* (a Hollywood epic that featured Christ fantasising on the cross about married life with Mary Magdalene), yet it banned a 20-minute British video about the *Visions of Ecstasy* of Saint Teresa. *The Last Temptation* was more explicit than *Visions,* but was also a much more substantial work of cinematic art. *Visions* was banned by the BBFC on the grounds that it was likely to be convicted of blasphemy by a jury, although this was entirely a matter of speculation. The DPP would certainly not have prosecuted in the wake of the Salman Rushdie affair (which discredited the blasphemy laws in the eyes of all but fundamentalists and the BBFC). It follows that the exercise of asking "what would a jury do in the event of a hypothetical prosecution?" was unreal, since no prosecution would ever have eventuated. Although the BBFC is required by the Home Secretary's letter which designates it as the classifying authority under the VRA to avoid certifying works which infringe the criminal law, the determination of what does infringe will depend, first, on the DPP's prosecuting policy and, secondly, upon the verdict of a jury. In the case of anachronistic common law offences like blasphemy, sedition and criminal libel, the Board should realise that prosecutions are unlikely to be brought and even more unlikely to succeed, and should refrain from using the existence of such laws as an excuse for refusing classification. (This point was sensibly made by a unanimous VAC when it overturned a ban on *International Guerrillas* which the Board claimed was a criminal libel on Salman Rushdie.) Should the law of blasphemy or criminal libel ever be invoked, the case should actually be decided by a jury, and not by a film censor (or appeals committee) guessing at what a jury might decide.

The Video Appeals Committee

Section 4 of the Video Recordings Act requires the BBFC to establish a system of appeal "by any person against a determination that a video work submitted by him" for certification has been either refused or placed in the wrong age category. This statutory language ensures that only persons who submit videos for classification can activate the appeals procedure, thereby excluding pressure groups and busybodies, but also shutting out producers and directors who may be aggrieved by cuts consented to by the distributors who have submitted their work for classification. The appeals procedure is available only in relation to videos—it is quite anomalous that there should be no provision for appeal by film exhibitors.

The appellate panel is selected by the BBFC itself, but has demonstrated a robust independence. The present members represent a reasonable mix of perspectives, but difficult decisions will hinge on whether the more conservative or more liberal members dominate the five-person appeal panel selected for the particular case. This factor was highlighted in the *Visions of Ecstasy* appeal, when the distinguished novelist Fay Weldon, a member of the Committee who had not been invited to sit on the judging panel, turned up nonetheless to give evidence in favour of the video. The Committee voted 3–2 in favour of the ban—a verdict that would have gone the other way had Ms Weldon (and perhaps other "uninvited" liberal members such as Professors Richard Hoggart and Laurie Taylor) been asked to sit in judgment. If the BBFC is serious about the "representativeness" of its Appeals Committee, it should invite the whole panel to sit on such controversial appeals.

The Appeals Committee permits legal representation and sits in public: there is no reason why it should not permit its proceedings to be televised. It gives a reasoned judgment, upholding the BBFC decision or indicating how it should be varied. Appeal fees will be reimbursed to successful appellants, but there is no provision for awarding them their legal costs, a deterrent to distributors who can usually obtain the classification category they want simply by making the cuts rather than by appealing them. The Appeals Committee will reconsider the matter afresh, and can substitute its own view of the case rather than merely deciding whether the Board's decision was reasonable. It is a measure of how cosy the relationship has become between the BBFC and the video distributors that an average of only one appeal a year is taken to the Committee, despite the numerous films that suffer cuts and, in a few cases, outright refusals. The Committee has not, in consequence, been able to afford much guidance for film censorship policy. Its first decision was that a video "consisting largely of women's nude mud wrestling taking place before a mixed audience in a pub in Devon" was "suitable for viewing in the home" by adults.

The Appeals Committee's first real test came with *Visions of Ecstasy,* the video that the BBFC had rejected for certification on the grounds of blasphemy. The Committee accepted the Board's submission that it was under a duty to reject any video that infringed the criminal law, but was divided on the question of whether a jury was likely to convict the makers of *Visions of Ecstasy* for blasphemy. The majority took a remarkably literal-minded approach to the video, finding it significant that the actress was younger than the historical personage (St. Teresa did not experience her mystical visions until middle age) and demanding historical evidence to support the film maker's imaginative interpretation of a sixteenth-century nun's mystical trance. The Appeals Committee majority judgment did not even mention the expert evidence that was adduced to show that the film was a legitimate artistic exploration of its theme. Three members of the Committee decided that a jury would be likely to convict; while two members decided that a jury would be unlikely to convict.[56] The decision to uphold the ban on this basis is manifestly illogical: if the Appeals Committee was split, the assumption must be that a jury would also be divided. PEN, an organisation representing the country's most distinguished authors and playwrights, condemned the ban as "a serious betrayal of cultural freedom in the United Kingdom".

The Appeals Committee unanimously adopted a more robust attitude to its next major test case, when it reversed the Board's decision to refuse a certificate to *International Guerillas,* a James Bond-style epic of the Pakistani cinema that portrayed Salman Rushdie as a mass murderer and torturer. The Board, relying on the *Visions of Ecstasy* principle that it was entitled to reject a work that a jury would be likely to convict of a criminal offence, rationalised its ban on the basis that the film amounted to a criminal libel on Rushdie. It argued, in its usual pseudo-sociological jargon, that the film "had the emotional weight and symbolic authority that makes the polarisation of good and evil a source of moral support and reaffirmation of communal identity". The Appeals Committee, however, was more inclined to agree with Rushdie himself, who described the film as a piece of trash. It decided the film had as much "emotional weight and symbolic authority" as an old cowboy-and-Indian movie, and that not even the most gullible viewer of such

[56] *Visions of Ecstasy* Appeal No. 0006, December 23, 1989. See BBFC, Report for 1989 pp. 17–20.

escapist entertainment would take it seriously. On this occasion it took into account both the unlikelihood that criminal libel proceedings would, in fact, be instituted (a point the *Visions of Ecstasy* majority had ignored) as well as the improbability of a jury convicting.[57] It may be hoped that this decision will discourage the Board from dredging up arcane criminal laws as an excuse to ban videos. It is noteworthy that the film (pirate video copies of which had been selling for £100 while the ban was in force) was not a commercial success after the appeal, and cinema showings in cities with large Muslim populations were so poorly attended that the legitimate video version was never released.

The VAC has had a determinative influence on liberalising censorship policy in the 18R category, by its decisions permitting video sales in sex shops of *Makin' Whoopee* and *Horny Catbabe* (see above p. 744). After these decisions were upheld by the High Court, the Home Secretary peevishly proposed that members of the Appeals Committee should be appointed by the Lord Chancellor, rather than by the BBFC itself.[58] This suggestion was dressed up in the language of openness and accountability, but was evidently designed to produce a bench of Government placemen ("senior lawyers who may be specialists in child welfare") rendering appeal judgments more to the liking of the leader-writers of the *Daily Mail*.[59] The plan is to replace independent spirits who are moderately distinguished and culturally aware with more strait-laced legal careerists who may know or care little about cinema and video. This would have the result of making VAC decisions more conservative and legalistic, which would only invite more challenges in the courts. To head this off, the BBFC should reform its procedures for VAC appointments by advertising the positions and establishing an independent appointments board to screen and select suitable candidates.

IN THE REALM OF THE CENSORS

Film censorship has continued, as it began, as a device to protect the profits of distributors and exhibitors. They finance it through the fees they pay (over £1,000) for a certification which will persuade local authorities to grant exhibition licences, and will dissuade the DPP from bringing prosecutions, and generally for a respected organisation that can reassure the public (if not the *Daily Mail*) that any risks to children

---

[57] BBFC Report for 1990, VAC judgment.
[58] Consultation Paper on the Regulation of R18 videos, Option 3 (Home Office, 2000).
[59] David Pannick Q.C. "Horny Catbabe Fails to Save Straw's Blushes" *The Times*, September 19, 2000.

have been removed. This system denies parents the right to decide what films their children may watch, and imposes cuts (in some cases, bans) on videos which would not suffer the same degree of censorship anywhere else in the advanced world. This price the industry is certainly prepared to pay, since it protects them from the vagaries of prosecution. But it is a remarkable tribute to the power of film censorship (or to the power of film) that British liberal intelligentsia and media, so hostile to other infringements of free speech, never seriously challenge it. Yet the BBFC censorship apparatus is perceived as an anomaly in Europe, where erotic and violent movies appear in cinemas and video shops and even on late-night television without any of the fuss that attends them here. Even countries which use the BBFC as a model, like Australia and New Zealand, make its age classification advisory only, so that children can see any films on general release if accompanied by an adult. It should be recognised that however sensible the censor, the BBFC system will have the following results:

(1) Intelligent adult viewers choose to enjoy film and video: their viewing rights will be restricted by the mere possibility of damage to a few deranged minds, or by the prospect that children will view.

(2) The BBFC may diminish the degree of explicit sex and violence, but not the number of videos dealing with these themes or the prominence given to them. Distributors always discern the level of "acceptable" sex and "acceptable" violence, and their films are full of it. The process of "sanitising" or "trimming" violence does not necessarily make it less acceptable.

(3) The BBFC tries to hush up the high level of its classification fees (the subject is not mentioned at all in its recent reports). Some films of real worth are not distributed in the United Kingdom because the profits from art house audiences do not justify the high classification fee (which currently ranges between £10 and £12 for every minute of the work's length). A charity rate of about £4 per minute is available to charities and student film makers, but this is entirely in the Board's discretion.

(4) The system as constituted breaches the rule against double jeopardy, at least for video distributors, because it keeps alive the power of police, DPP and private prosecutors to proceed under the Obscene Publications Act, notwithstanding that their works have undergone the certification process.

(5) The age classifications are arbitrary. (Why not a "10", a "14" and "16"? or just two: "13" and "18"?). It is well known that

children mature at different ages: classification denies many teenagers access to cinema films they would harmlessly enjoy, perhaps hindering their development of a lifetime love of films.

(6) The system denies parents one of the rights of family life, namely to bring their children up as they, and not the chief censor, believe appropriate. Why deny to responsible parents the right to take their 11-year-old to *Titanic* or their 14-year-old to *The Full Monty* or *Billy Elliott*? In this respect Britain is out of step with all other progressive countries, which make ratings advisory so as to encourage parents to share cinema experiences with their children.

(7) Age classification of videos can be counter-productive, serving to incite children (particularly young boys) to obtain and watch "15" and "18" videos as an act of defiance, or to tempt them to savour "forbidden fruit".

(8) The certification system can actually damage the quality of films, especially British-made films. As the industry catch-phrase goes, "the higher the certification, the lower the return". Distributors want "12" or at least "15" to maximise profit from general release movies, and will cut relentlessly (usually before the movie is even submitted) in order to obtain it. What will be lost at this level is not sex and violence as such, but witty word-play and rudery about those aspects of sex and violence which censors believe should be kept from 14-year-old schoolgirls. There are a number of British film failures in recent years whose most redeeming aspects lie on the BBFC cutting room floor.[60]

The Video Recordings Act transformed the BBFC from a family-size firm of 12 to a bureaucracy of 60. What it cuts from film and video can be seen on the world wide web, and sometimes on satellite television. The technological revolution may bring further changes: in December 2000 a Government Green Paper canvassed the idea of a new censorship body—OFCOM—which could regulate video, as well as television, radio and the internet (and it makes no sense to designate a new body to censor video unless it is given a statutory remit to classify cinema films as well). The human rights culture, if it catches on, will require changes to the Cinema Act so that parents can take their children to whatever film they consider suitable. Censors of the future will have a more limited and more automatic function, "applying guidelines" rather

---

[60] Some examples of clumsy censorship which damaged British films or reduced the audience for them are provided by Tom Dewe Matthews, *Censored: The Story of Film Censorship in Britain* (Chatto, 1994) Chap. 15.

than pondering, like James Ferman, about questions of moral philosophy. They will also have a more limited tenure. Ferman's 23-year reign was accounted a considerable success in its first decade, but the longer it lasted the more he lost the respect of some examiners ("Ferman loved to fiddle, snip and trim, like an enthusiastic barber" said one,[61] while another claimed to have watched him change over time into "a control freak who would sit in his office alone, late into the night, obsessively watching videos"[62]). Andreas Whittam-Smith and Robin Duvall, the President and Director who took office in 1998, affect a more open and consistent regime with a "lighter touch". Their decisions to cut and to classify are more transparent, but may be no less controversial. When the outcry over the Saatchi gallery pictures erupted in 2001, Whittam-Smith was the only significant figure in the cultural community in favour of their removal from exhibition: in two years the job had transformed a respected liberal into a censor.

[61] Ros Hodgkiss, *The Guardian* (*G2* interview), November 20, 1998.
[62] Maggie Mills, "Sinful Days in Soho", *The Sunday Times*, November 1, 1998.

CHAPTER 16

BROADCASTING LAW

"We want to ensure the widest possible access to a choice of diverse communications services of the highest quality . . . And we want to make sure that the right balance is struck between freedom of speech and basic standards of decency and quality . . . We seek to combine a lighter touch in many aspects with tough protection of the genuine public interest in others . . . we will create a new regulator, an Office of Communications (OFCOM) with the expertise and the vision to understand the converging communications landscape and to act according to a clear set of principles. OFCOM . . . will regulate TV and radio by means of a new framework which will allow flexibility for industry whilst fully meeting the expectations of viewers and listeners maintaining high levels of quality and diversity".

Stephen Byers and Chris Smith, Introduction to White Paper, *A New Future for Communications.*[1]

THE AGE OF CONVERGENCE

With these familiar platitudes, the Government launched in December 2000 its plans for the future regulation of broadcasting in what is commonly called the age of multi-media "convergence"—the buzzword used to describe the exponential expansion of networks previously limited in the amount or kind of information they were capable of delivering. Broadcasting, first by radio then by television, was a method of communicating facts and opinion to the general public which called forth excessive regulation in the interests of good taste and good politics. Telecommunications, on the other hand, developed without much restraint other than by "common carrier" duties implied by the general law: even privatisation led only to anti-competitive practices being mon-

---

[1] Introduction to White Paper, issued December 16, 2000 (by DTI and the Department of Culture, Media and Sport), accessible at www.communicationswhitepaper.gov.uk

itored by OFTEL (the office of telecommunications). The computing
industry, which seemed at first to have no need either for freedom of
expression or censorship, was subject like any other industry to the
general law. But the advent in the late 1990s of digital technology
brought these three industries together through a shared method of
transmission: the information and opinions broadcast on television
could now be received on the computer screen and through the telephone. This "converging" of the means of transmission calls into question the continuing relevance of the overlapping censorship bodies
erected to control the content of radio and television alone, and poses
the question of whether and to what extent their assumptions, contained
in codes and precedents, should apply to an age when everything is
available on the internet. The Government's solution—one big regulator, in the form of OFCOM—promises the virtues of simplicity and
consistency, subject to Orwellian fears of big brotherhood.

Broadcasting law in this transitional stage can only be understood in
terms of the technological and political assumptions at the time the
relevant statutes were passed. It may be divided roughly as follows:

(i) The Voice of Britain. Until 1954, the BBC had a monopoly of
public broadcasting. Its remit, developed famously by Lord Reith, was
to unite the nation and to give the people what a political and cultural
elite thought was good for them. The Government had power to take
over broadcasts in an emergency, but effectively controlled the Corporation's policy by appointing the Board members and the Director General. Internal rules about taste and impartiality were so strict there was
no call to subject the Corporation to statutory duties or to obscentity
law.

(ii) The advent of commercial broadcasting. Inauguration of commercial television in 1954 was deemed to require the creation of a tough
regulatory body, the Independent Broadcasting Authority (IBA) with
statutory duties to ensure that political coverage was balanced and that
programmes did not overreach the boundaries of good taste. When the
60s began to swing in BBC studios (notably with the first satire programme *That Was the Week That Was*) the Corporation was required
by the satirised Government to bind itself to accept identical obligations
to avoid transmission of material which could cause public or political
offence. The IBA and the BBC came under ferocioius attack in the
late 60s and throughout the 70s by the National Viewers and Listeners
Association (brainchild of Colchester housewife and moral rearmament
campaigner, Mrs Mary Whitehouse) to which they both responded by
developing regimes of institutional censorship, through internal codes
and "guidelines". Mrs Whitehouse and other vigilantes took the IBA to

court in the mid-1970s in judicial review proceedings which were ultimately unsuccessful but unnerved the broadcaster nonetheless. When commercial radio was introduced in the early 70s, the IBA subjected it to "guidelines" similar to those which constrained television.

(iii) The Thatcher Years. The Thatcher Government had a turbulent and truculent relationship with broadcasters, particularly over their IRA coverage ("oxygen for terrorists"). Its thinking was schizophrenic nonetheless: it sought to encourage greater commercial freedom, through cable and later satellite services, but to regulate sex with Whitehousian vigour and to curb "unbalanced" political reporting. In 1980 it established the *Broadcasting Complaints Commission*, to condemn "unfair treatment" by television and radio programmes. This was followed by the Video Recordings Act of 1984, which designated the BBFC as the statutory regulator for this industry, and in the same year it set up the Cable Authority with statutory powers to oversee the contents of cable television. In 1988 it established the *Broadcasting Standards Council*, under William Rees-Mogg, to monitor sex and violence. However, the Government's commitment to free-market philosophy so that developments of fibre-optic cable systems and direct broadcast satellites could provide a multiplicity of channel choice was reflected in the recommendations of the 1986 Peacock Committee,[2] which became the basis for the new "semi-deregulated" framework of the 1990 Act.

(iv) The Broadcasting Act 1990. This was, and remains, the centrepiece of radio and television legislation. It replaced the IBA with two bodies, the *Independent Television Commission* (ITC) and the *Radio Authority*, both with a mandate for "lighter touch" regulation. Essentially, this meant an end to the IBA practice (required by the decision in *McWhirter*'s case) of previewing controversial programmes: pre-censorship was superseded by a new set of ITC reprisal powers ranging from warnings to fines to the ultimate sanction, loss of licence. The Act occupied a great deal of parliamentary time, emerging as a massive statute with 204 sections and 22 schedules. Much of the political debate focused on the requirement of a new "due impartiality" code which Mrs Thatcher insisted on including, in the hope of deterring programmes like *Death on the Rock* which had provoked a major conflict with the Government by voicing allegations about the SAS "execution" of three IRA members in Gibraltar (deterrence was more effectively achieved by the subsequent ITC decision to deny a franchise to Thames television, which had made the programme). Opposition spokesman Roy Hattersley volubly promised to repeal the requirement

---

[2] Report of the Committee on Financing the BBC (chaired by Professor Alan Peacock) Cm. 9824 (1986).

for a "due impartiality" code when Labour came into office: needless to say, this promise was not honoured.[3] The 1990 Act ushered in a decade in which freedom of expression was bounded not by precise laws but by imprecise codes, drafted and interpreted by Government appointees on a number of bodies whose jurisdiction overlapped and whose decisions could not be appealed or attacked on their merits: judicial review was sometimes sought, but would usually result in judicial deference to the assumed "expertise" of the members of the body in question, although most of these political appointees were not "experts" in any meaningful sense. Thus programme-makers had to comply with codes promulgated by the ITC, the BBC and the Radio Authority, the Broadcasting Standards Council and the Broadcasting Complaints Commission, all dealing with the same subject-matter but with slightly different emphasis: they were exposed to a "triple jeopardy" in that complainants who did not at first succeed (*i.e.* with the BBC or ITC) could try and try again (by complaining to the BCC or BSC, and in the event of failure by attempting judicial review). In 1996 a supplementary Broadcasting Act, necessary to provide for digital television, saved some public time and money by amalgamating the Complaints Commission and the Standards Council into a new regulatory body, the *Broadcasting Standards Commission* (BSC), but otherwise left the 1990 framework unchanged.

(v) The 2000 White Paper. The Labour Government produced a White Paper at the end of its first term, proposing to amalgamate all censorship bodies (which it euphemistically calls "negative content regulators") into something called OFCOM. This new body would assume the regulatory role of the ITC, OFTEL, the Radio Authority and BSC, together with that of ICSTIS, and of the BBFC in respect of video. It would also advise the Home Secretary on whether and when to exercise his power under section 177 of the 1990 Act to proscribe a foreign satellite service. Otherwise, the White Paper is deliberately vague about OFCOM and its powers: it would "end the double jeopardy of the current system" and its objectives would be:

● protecting the interests of consumers;

● maintaining high quality of content, a wide range of programming, and plurality of public expression;

● protecting the interests of citizens by maintaining accepted community standards in content, balancing freedom of speech against the need to protect against potentially offensive or

---

[3] See *Hansard*, House of Commons, October 25, 1990, Vol. 178, No. 162, col. 1512.

harmful material, and ensuring appropriate protection of fairness and privacy.[4]

These are traditional regulatory objects, although it shall also give weight to: "the special needs of people with disabilities and of the elderly, of those on low income and if persons living in rural areas." These are more novel, and mark the increasing awareness of and need to combat discrimination on ground of disability (physical and mental) and the emergence of "country" as distinct from "town" as a special constituency. The special needs of the poor ("those on low income" and presumably, those on no income at all) have not previously featured as a focus for regulatory activity: will *The Big Issue* receive favourable consideration if it applies for a television licence? OFCOM will have the enforcement powers available to the ITC and OFTEL, and a proper appeals process is promised, *i.e.* an appellate body which can consider the factual merits of the case rather than pick over errors of law and procedure on judicial review.[5] The Office of Communications Bill, introduced in Parliament in October 2001 to establish OFCOM, provides that its "initial functions" shall include liaising and co-operating with the existing regulators in respects of the government's future proposals for the regulation of communications, without foreshadowing what form these will take.

The threshold question, of course, is why broadcasting should be accorded a different legal regime to that governing the publication of books and newspapers. Initially, the justification was technological: "spectrum scarcity"—the limit to the number of terrestrial frequencies—required close control in the public interest to ensure they were put to the best use. Hence duties to demonstrate "good taste" and "due impartiality" were imposed on a television service which supplied only four channels to the entire nation. But re-imposing them in identical terms, with additional tiers of codes and regulators, on services carrying numerous channels to audiences who pay for the pleasure of viewing them, was the response of parliament (or at least of the Thatcher Government).

The irony that in 1990 "deregulation" meant *more* regulation is a tribute to the perceived power of television to influence as well as to reflect ideas and social behaviour. The tabloid newspapers, which most people read, require no statutory controls, although their impact on moral standards must be much greater than late night television programmes which play to self-selecting audiences. Much of the debate over the Act was concerned with the problem of maintaining "quality" in the market place, an objective that requires a licensing body to evaluate the prospective programme performance of applicants rather than

---

[4] n. 1 above, p. 79 (para. 8.5.1).
[5] *ibid.*, para. 8.9.1, p. 81.

concentrating on the highest bidder. The regulation of programme content by codes and disciplinary bodies in the interests of good taste and good politics does not involve a judgment on their quality but on their potential to shock and disturb. In its first report the Broadcasting Standards Council described television as "a guest in the home", whose conduct might acceptably become "more relaxed and informal" as the evening wears on.[6] The paternalistic notion that television existed on sufferance, and owed a duty to behave itself according to social norms expected of Lord Rees-Mogg's dinner guests, infused the debates over the 1990 Act: that it lingers was demonstrated a decade later when his successor at the BSC, Lord Richard Home, was forced to resign when adultery and a penchant for soft-core porn disqualified him from the role of chaperone.

By the turn of the twenty-first century almost everyone, everywhere in the United Kingdom, could receive terrestrial television (99.4 per cent of the population, although some—doubtless to their relief—could not receive Channel 5). There were 250 commercial channels available, which together with the BBC pumped out 40,000 hours of viewing every week. Over 25 per cent of United Kingdom homes had gone digital, two-thirds of all households had more than one television, there were 30 million people with mobile phones, while PCs and laptops were being acquired at such a rate that official statistics could not keep count. About 4 per cent of all consumer spending was on television and telecommunications, industries which were growing considerably faster than the rest of the economy. "In other words" (those of the 2000 White Paper) "the era when the extent of broadcasting was determined by spectrum scarcity is drawing to a close".[7] With the switch to digital, every home will have access to dozens of channels. On the internet, citizens "would be able to order the programme they want from any provider, anywhere in the world". Rather than interpret these figures as pointers to the futility of regulation, the Government used them to argue for the importance of regulation as a guarantee for the continuance of public service broadcasting, which still retains its hold on the United Kingdom public (the BBC and Channel 4 command 60 per cent of viewing time). The White Paper asserts that OFCOM will be necessary to maintain original and high quality programming, maintaining standards (and peak slots) in news and current affairs, and ensuring diversity in broadcast opinion.

This argument, which assumes that statutory duties and programme codes and disciplinary bodies all work to improve quality and creativity in programme-making, is at best unproven, at worst naïve. The laws of defamation and indecency and confidence and copyright are onerous

---

[6] Broadcasting Standards Council, *Annual Report 1988-89,* p. 29.
[7] White Paper, para. 5.2.4, p. 48.

enough, without a further layer of ethical prescripts to which compliance is required by a contract of employment. The White Paper never asks why "public service broadcasting" these days so notably fails to expose public scandal or malfeasance: since the 1990 Act, almost all the most important exercises in investigative journalism have been books and newspapers. This sombre fact is not accounted for by the inherent limitations of television, a picture-driven and necessarily simplistic medium, because in previous times programmes like *This Week* and *World in Action* and *Panorama* competed with the press for the best investigative journalism. Today BBC and ITV "news" is more often a beat-up of what is in the newspapers, or what is covered at greater length by CNN or Sky. To what extent have the layers of regulation imposed by programme codes, over and above the general law, led to punch-pulling and nervousness about serious current affairs or documentary investigation? Even late-night discussion programmes can be suffocated by the imperative of avoiding offence. For example, in the 2001 debate over the Saatchi Gallery photographs, *The Guardian* published them, uncensored and in full colour, but the BBC refused to focus its cameras on them, even at 11.30 p.m. on BBC2.[8] The result was cowardly television, compared with honest coverage in a newspaper not shackled by rules and codes and programme controllers and standards commissions. If OFCOM is to work in the interests of public service broadcasting, it should leave regulation of programme content to the general law and to the courts.

THE FREEDOM TO BROADCAST

The Human Rights Act 1998 incorporates Article 10 of the European Convention on Human Rights, which begins "Everyone has the right to freedom of expression . . . " but ends "This Article shall not prevent states from requiring the licensing of broadcasting, television or cinema enterprises".

This proviso permits the establishment of licensing systems, but it does not underwrite specific licensing refusals made by regulatory bodies. The European Court emphasised the importance of this distinction in two cases decided in 1990.

> *Groppera Radio v. Switzerland*[9]: The Swiss government prohibited a Swiss company from retransmitting the pop music programmes of an Italian radio station that did not use transmitters approved by international

---

[8] *Newsnight Extra*, Friday March 9, 2001.
[9] (1990) 12 E.H.R.R. 524.

communications conventions. The company claimed that this ban on retransmission amounted to a breach of its Article 10 rights to impart information freely and regardless of frontiers. The court held:

- Popular music and commercials could properly be regarded as "information" and "ideas", so that the ban was prima facie an interference with Article 10 rights.
- The provision in Article 10 permitting states to licence broadcasting was of very limited scope and did not amount to an exception to the basic right guaranteed by Article 10. It permitted states to control the organisation and technology of broadcasting within their territories, but the licensing measures themselves had to be justified as necessary in a democratic society on the grounds set out in Article 10(2).
- That said, the ban was justifiable under Article 10(2) because it had the legitimate aim of preventing the evasion of international law and protecting the rights of others. The ban was not directed at the content of the programmes and had not been applied by use of disproportionate measures (such as jamming transmissions).

Autronic AG v. Switzerland[10]: The Swiss government this time failed to convince the court that its concern for international telecommunications law was justified. It had stopped a company specialising in home electronics from demonstrating how its dish aerial equipment could receive Soviet television programmes picked up from a Soviet telecommunications satellite, on the grounds that international law required the consent of the broadcasting state for such interceptions.

The court held that the freedom of expression guarantee in Article 10 was given to corporations as well as to individuals, and applied to restrictions on the means of transmission and reception as well as to restrictions on the content of programmes. It emphasised that interference had to be convincingly established as "necessary in a democratic society", and was not persuaded that international law required that every interception from a satellite transmission should have the consent of authorities of the country in which the station transmitting to the satellite was situated. It followed that the restriction could not be justified by the exceptions to Article 10(2), and that the Swiss authorities had breached the Convention.

These decisions establish that the broadcasting proviso in Article 10(1) does not itself justify a licence refusal, which must (like any other interference) always be justified as necessary in a democracy for one of the objectives excepted by Article 10(2). This is because broadcasting stations, like newspapers and internet websites, are vehicles for communicating information and ideas, and the right of free expression includes a presumptive right to operate this means of communication. Any licensing system hinders ("interferes with") the freedom of expres-

---

[10] (1990) 12 E.H.R.R. 485.

sion both of those refused licenses as well as members of the public whose right to receive information from a plurality of broadcast sources is curtailed.[11] In a series of important decisions against Austria, the European Court of Human Rights used the principle of pluralism to ring the death-knell of the national broadcasting monopolies which prevailed at the time the Convention was drafted. The State has a duty to guarantee pluralism in broadcasting, and this is violated if it fails to provide a system under which citizens can apply for licences and have their applications fairly determined according to relevant public interest criteria:

> In *Lentia v. Austria*[12] the ECtHR declared that a State broadcasting monopoly was a breach of Article 10, notwithstanding the licensing proviso. Although public monopolies might contribute to quality and balance of programming, a prohibition on *any* competition was impossible to reconcile with the duty of a democratic State to guarantee pluralism. No longer could justification be found in spectrum scarcity or in the small size of the market: freedom of enterprise was a necessary concomitant of freedom of speech (in this case, Austria's defence was weakened by the Government's obvious desire to be sole beneficiary of advertising revenue: it did not take the point that the complainant was a company founded by Jorge Haider, seeking a licence to promulgate racism.)

Austria was reluctant to bring its law into conformity with the Convention: it delayed, then permitted only two private licences, through a law which turned out to be unconstitutional. The Eurocourt held that the Convention breach continued, for as long as private licences were effectively suspended.[13] It has subsequently reaffirmed the importance of access to the airwaves: the State must prove convincingly the need for any interference.[14] Its case will be convincing where a licence refusal—or even a ban on any particular licence application—serves the overall objective of pluralism.

> In *United Christian Broadcasters v. United Kingdom*[15] a religious organisation complained of the Broadcasting Act ban on religious or political bodies applying for national radio licences. The United Kingdom justified this infringement by virtue of the limited availability of national licences, given the Government's decentralising policy of reserving most available frequencies for local radio. This policy in itself encouraged diversity (religious bodies could apply for local licences) and the ban on sectional

---

[11] See *Red Lion Broadcasting v. FCC* (1969) 395 U.S. 367 at 386 *et seq.*
[12] *Informationsverein Lentia v. Austria* (1993) 17 E.H.R.R. 93.
[13] *Radio ABC v. Austria* (1998) 25 E.H.R.R. 185.
[14] *Tele 1 Privatfernsehgesellschaft MBH v. Austria,* Application No. 32240/96, September 21, 2000.
[15] *UCB v. U.K.,* Application No. 4482/98, November 7, 2000.

interests applying for any of the four national licences protected "the
rights of others" (*i.e.* of the national listening audience) to have music
and talk of widespread interest rather than a station devoted to partisan
religion or politics.

These Article 10 principles have been considerably extended by the
Privy Council to strike down biased decisions by Government licensors
in several Caribbean countries with constitutional free speech guarantees. The question always is whether the licence refusal has been fair
in procedure and reasonable in practice, in the context of any local
technical or public policy constraints. There must be a clear and non-
discriminatory procedure for licence applications and a reasonable and
rational criteria for awarding them. Everyone has a presumptive constitutional right to a licence: the notion that its bestowal is an Executive
privilege was roundly condemned in *Observer Publications Ltd v. Mat-
thew and Att.-Gen. of Antigua*[16]:

> The applicant, a newspaper critical of the island's Government, applied
> for a licence to run an FM station: under the law, grant of such licences
> was in the discretion of the Cabinet. After a year-and-a-half of procras-
> tination, the telecommunications officer was directed by the Cabinet to
> refuse it. The only other licensed broadcaster in Antigua, apart from the
> Government-controlled radio and television station were a commercial
> radio station (owned by the Prime Minister, his two brothers and his
> mother) and a cable television station owned by one of the Prime Minis-
> ter's brothers. The Antiguan courts denied relief on the grounds that no
> one had a "right" to a broadcasting licence and the cabinet's unreasoned
> refusal had to be presumed constitutional. The Privy Council, however,
> held that it *was* unconstitutional to refuse a broadcasting licence without
> any stated grounds, or on grounds inconsistent with the exceptions defined
> by the Constitution as limiting free speech. Freedom of expression prin-
> ciples must, the Court held, be implied in the discretions granted to regu-
> lators by telecommunications legislation, and it added (significantly) that
> "the approach will be much the same in the United Kingdom under sec-
> tion 3 of the Human Rights Act 1998". The Government had claimed to
> have a policy against granting further licences until the legislation was
> re-vamped, "but a policy motivated by a desire to suppress or limit criti-
> cism of the Government of the day is never acceptable in a democratic
> society".

Notwithstanding its genesis in small island nepotism, the *Observer
Publications Ltd* case is an example of a court *implying* free speech
guarantees in licensing laws which make no mention of them, by reference to the Constitutional guarantees (or, in the United Kingdom, to the

---

[16] *Observer Publications Ltd v. Campbell "Mickey" Matthews; the Commissioner of
Police and the Att.-Gen. of Antigua* (2001) 10 B.H.R.C. 252.

1998 Act). European case law (notably *Lentia*) establishes that a refusal of a radio or television licence is an infringement of the freedom to disseminate ideas and information. Such a refusal "may nevertheless be upheld . . . to the extent that the law in question makes provision that is reasonably required for a certain range of purposes. The onus upon those supporting the restriction is to show that it was reasonably required. If the latter onus is discharged, the burden shifts to the complainant to show that the provision or the thing done is not reasonably justified in a democratic society."[17]

The importance of "constitutionalising" broadcasting law is that all licensing decisions, and decisions by the ITC over whether to fine broadcasters for code breaches, and even (arguably) decisions by the BSC that codes have been breached, must now be justified by reference to the "democratic necessity" principle. One intriguing application of the principle by the Privy Council resulted in the award of damages to Mr John Benjamin, the presenter and originator of a popular talk back programme on the Government-run Radio Anguilla. Benjamin's programme was cancelled by the minister after (and because) it attacked the Government's plans for a national lottery. The Privy Council held that a breach of the free speech guarantee had occurred, although the programme's closure was not a breach of contract and the claimant may not have had any general right to broadcast[18]: in the particular circumstances, the minister clearly intended to hinder free speech by cancelling the programme as a reprisal for its criticism of his Government. This was the relevant motive, and there was no excuse of falling ratings or jaded audiences or of the programme having run its allotted course. The Government's motive was to stop the expression of hostile views, and its arbitrary and capricious withdrawal of the platform it had made available for free expression entitled the presenter to damages.[19]

Benjamin is a remarkable case, which applies the historic decision in *Olivier v. Buttigieg*[20] (when the Privy Council used Malta's free speech clause to strike down a ban on bringing anti-Catholic newspapers into government offices) to decisions to interfere with programmes. It offers programme makers and journalists the prospect of legal redress when they suffer reprisals for genuine exercises in free speech. The European Court of Human Rights has similarly held that Member States have a duty to protect television journalists from reprisals for speaking out

---

[17] (2001) 10 B.H.R.C. 252, transcript pp. 12 *per* Lord Cooke of Thorndon. See also *Cable & Wireless (Dominica) Ltd v. Marpin Telecoms* (2000) 9 B.H.R.C. 486.

[18] See *X & Z v. U.K.* (1971) 38 C.D. 86; but compare *Fernando v. Sri Lanka Broadcasting* (1986) 1 B.H.R.C. 104 and *Haider v. Austria* (1995) 83 D.R. 66.

[19] *Benjamin v. Minister for Broadcasting and Att.Gen. of Anguilla* (2001) 10 B.H.R.C. 237.

[20] *Olivier v. Buttigieg* [1967] 1 A.C. 115.

against management policies.[21] What was particularly noteworthy about
Benjamin is the way the Court brushed aside as irrelevant the fact that
cancellation of the programme was a form of settlement with the company which ran the lottery and which had threatened to sue for defamation. The principle could also apply to protect a journalist victimised
by a private employer. Although Benjamin's talk-back programme was
suspended by order of the minister, the Privy Council rationale would
apply to a decision by the BBC Board of Governors (who are Government appointees) should they cancel a programme for political rather
then professional reasons.

The European Court of Human Rights has extended the protection
offered by Article 10 to a radio presenter who commented on a newspaper article written by another journalist on a subject of public interest.
Although the article defamed public officials (who had in consequence
sued the presenter) the latter was entitled to disseminate it—so long as
he did not adopt the libels—in order to provide information to the
public.[22] *Benjamin* and *Thoma* and *Fuentes Bobo* are straws in the constitutional wind which may be made into bricks for the foundation of a
wider principle that will prohibit punitive reprisals for programme content if they cannot be justified either by reference to the excepted values
in Article 10(2) or by reference to accepted professional or commercial
broadcasting criteria. The distinctions made in *Benjamin* mark the
beginning of what will become a crucial juristic exercise for the legal
protection of broadcasters: the identification and stigmatisation of an
act of impermissible *censorship,* as opposed to an action justifiably
taken because of mediocre performance, genuine policy changes, dimin-
ishing audiences and the like.

There were no claims about denial of free speech rights made by
disappointed applicants in 1991, when the ITC first issued television
licences under the 1990 Broadcasting Act. No Human Rights Act was
in force, and the House of Lords in the case of *Brind* had diminished the
significance of Article 10 for British law.[23] Several television company
applicants were refused judicial review on the grounds that they had
failed to act promptly, so the rights of shareholders in rival companies
which had won franchises would be affected if attempts were made
three months later to overturn the award.[24] Judicial Review is a discretionary remedy, and courts are traditionally reluctant to entertain belated
applications from bad losers—although this concern for the smoothness
of share trading sits uneasily with their duty to remedy injustice. The
market should be capable of digesting the fact that ITC decisions are

[21] *Fuentes Bobo v. Spain,* E.C.H.R., February 29, 2000.
[22] *Thoma v. Luxembourg* (No. 38432/97) March 29, 2001.
[23] *R. v. Secretary of State for Home Dept, ex p. Brind* [1991] 1 A.C. 696.
[24] *R. v. ITC, ex p. TV Northern Ireland, The Times,* December 30, 1991.

open to a challenge that may be mounted within three months (the outside time for a challenge, although the overarching requirement is to apply promptly. The court can decide, as it did in this case, that a challenge was not made "promptly" even though it was well within three months of the decision). One challenge—by Television South West—did reach the House of Lords, but the court did little more than rubber-stamp the ITC decision to reject the application because of doubts whether TSW, although the highest bidder, could maintain the service through the 10-year licence period. The court emphasised that it was not empowered to act as an appeal body or to substitute its own views for that reached by the ITC experts—it confined its role to ensuring that the Commission had considered the evidence carefully and fairly, and had not abused its powers.[25] This is an excessively narrow approach to the review function, requiring an applicant to prove the decision irrational or the procedure improper, but it means that applicants have in reality but one bite at the broadcasting cherry. There is a view that human rights law requires the availability of a proper appeal on the merits of decisions of such importance, although the 2000 White Paper did not foreshadow any Government intention to provide one.

LAWS AND STATUTORY DUTIES

The general law

It is difficult to understand why the general law relating to taste and decency (obscenity, outraging public decency, blasphemy and race hate offences) should apply to a medium which is so heavily censored by regulators and adjudicative bodies. A programme maker stands in triple jeopardy on matters of taste: he may (1) be prosecuted for outraging public decency or publishing obscenity or (2) be found by the ITC or the BBC to be in breach of its codes, or (3) condemned by the Broadcasting Standards Commission for a breach of *its* code. In reality, of course, the codes and their regulators are so suffocating that nothing has ever been broadcast that could seriously be suggested as a candidate for prosecution. Nonetheless, Mrs Thatcher's tribute to Mrs Whitehouse in the 1990 Broadcasting Act was to apply the Obscene Publications Act to radio and television.[26] This means that persons responsible for a transmission deemed to be likely "to deprave and corrupt" a significant proportion of its likely audience are, on conviction by a jury, liable for

---

[25] *R. v. ITC, ex p. TSW Broadcasting Ltd The Times*, March 30, 1992. See also *R. v. ITC, ex p. Virgin & Others, The Times*, February 17, 1996.
[26] Broadcasting Act 1990, s. 162 and Sched. 15.

up to three years' imprisonment. Broadcasting had been specifically exempted from the Act when it was passed in 1959, and it is unlikely that any programme transmitted in the succeeding 30 years would have been found obscene by a jury. However, clean-up campaigners convinced the Government that broadcasters should be subject, like other publishers, to the criminal law of the land, in addition to their liability to fines and loss of licence if they breach the statutory prohibitions against transmitting offensive material (see below). The 1990 law also removed the broadcast media's exemption from prosecution for incitement to racial hatred.

The general law of obscenity, explained in Chapter 4, applies to television and sound broadcasting in much the same way as it applies to books and films, with a public good defence which can be advanced by expert witnesses. No prosecution, however, may be brought other than with the consent of the DPP, and none has been brought. There is a special provision in the Act that enables a magistrate to require the BBC or the ITC or the Radio Authority to supply a visual or sound recording relating to a programme that police have "reasonable grounds for suspecting" has constituted an offence.[27] The power extends only to material that has already been broadcast; it does not enable police to obtain advance copies of programmes expected to be controversial. It is unlikely, given the stringent duties not to cause public offence, that programme makers will be prosecuted; if they are, much will depend on the transmission time of the programme and whether children are likely to comprise "a significant proportion" of viewers. There is a useful defence for presenters and contributors, who may not be convicted unless they had reason to suspect beforehand that the programme would contain material justifying a conviction.[28] A particular danger, that the DPP may choose forfeiture proceedings decided by magistrates rather than a jury trial, was avoided by a Government promise that prosecuting authorities would not favour forfeiture proceedings.[29]

The statutory duties

The duties imposed by statute on independent television, and later annexed to the licence of the BBC and echoed in the laws relating to independent radio and to cable television, were formulated in 1954. They reflect the exaggerated fears of that period about the advent of commercial television. In an atmosphere where Lord Reith could solemnly liken commercial television to the black death, it was understand-

---

[27] Broadcasting Act 1990, s. 167.
[28] *ibid.*, Sched. 15(5)(1).
[29] House of Commons, Standing Committee F on Broadcasting Bill, Official Report Col. 1190 (David Mellor).

able that ITV should be placed under the close scrutiny of a licensing body, required to ensure:

"(a) that nothing is included in the programmes which offends against good taste or decency or is likely to encourage or incite to crime or to lead to disorder or to be offensive to public feeling;

(b) that any news given (in whatever form) in its programmes is presented with due accuracy and impartiality;

(c) that due impartiality is preserved on the part of persons providing the programmes as respects matters of political or industrial controversy or relating to current public policy."

This was the IBA's duty under section 4 of the 1981 Broadcasting Act, and it is a duty that has been inherited by the ITC and by the Radio Authority under section 6 of the 1990 Broadcasting Act.

In 1964 the BBC Board of Governors undertook to comply with the same standard:

"The Board accept that so far as possible the programmes for which they are responsible should not offend against good taste or decency, or be likely to encourage crime or disorder, or be offensive to public feeling. In judging what is suitable for inclusion in programmes, they will pay special regard to the need to ensure that broadcasts designed to stimulate thought do not so far depart from their intention as to give general offence."[30]

This undertaking is now annexed to the BBC's licence, although (unlike the statutory duties on the ITC) it may be more difficult to enforce against the Corporation.[31] The extent of the BBC's invulnerability to judicial review proceedings is open to question: since the undertaking echoes government policy and would otherwise have statutory backing, the better view is that an egregious misapplication of or departure from it would be susceptible to judicial review.[32] In any event the BBC as a public body is subject to claims under the Human Rights Act, so it is possible that potential victims will seek to persuade courts to injunct programmes that will breach codes, *e.g.* on privacy to which the court must pay attention.

The ITC's duties to secure "due impartiality" go beyond a general

---

[30] Letter from Lord Normanbrook (Chairman, BBC) to Postmaster-General, June 19, 1964. The undertaking was reaffirmed when the BBC licence was renewed in 1969, 1981 and (more forcefully) in 1996 and the contents of the letter are noted in the prescribing memorandum under Clause 13(4) of the BBC Licence and Agreement.

[31] *Lynch v. BBC* (1983) 6 Northern Ireland Judgments Bulletin, *per* Hutton J. *McAliskey v. BBC* [1980] N.I. 44.

[32] See Buckley J. in *R. v. BBC, ex p. McAliskey* [1994] C.O.D. 1498.

supervision of programme output. They are specifically charged to draw
up a code "giving guidance as to the rules to be observed" and must
"do all that they can to secure that the provisions of the code are
observed" (section 6(3)). This duty is somewhat complicated by controversial subsections inserted in section 6 after pressure from Tory peers
who expressed grave dissatisfaction at the way in which they alleged the
IBA had watered down the "due impartiality" duty under the previous
legislation. Section 6(5) requires that the code shall in particular have
rules that reflect the need to preserve due impartiality on "major matters" of political or industrial controversy or relating to current public
policy. This confusing subsection leaves open the possibility of a legal
challenge to the ITC code on the basis that it does not take sufficient
account of the need to ensure due impartiality in minor or routine (as
distinct from major) matters of controversy. The Government, however,
appeared to think that it would eliminate the need to offer another view
in response to every contentious comment:

> "The purpose of the wording . . . is to make it clear that we do not
> expect impartiality to be achieved over every nuance of a matter
> of political or industrial controversy . . . we would expect that treat-
> ment of the Gulf issue, for example, should be handled in an impar-
> tial way. But that does not mean that every statement or sentiment
> expressed about the Gulf should receive some kind of equal and
> opposite rejoinder."[33]

On this footing section 6(5) may eventually be interpreted as no more
than an indication that the ITC should concentrate its code (and its
enforcement of that code) on the need for impartiality in the case of
matters that are "major" both because of their prominence and because
of the important consequences of any decision that must be made over
them; issues that could affect electoral votes or be the cause of a crippling strike are obviously matters that require a stricter "balance" in
current affairs programmes than new policy ideas or familiar debates
about manners and morals. This is the approach in fact taken by the
ITC code on impartiality, which indicates that "major matters" relates
to political or industrial issues of national importance "such as a
nationwide strike or significant legislation passing through Parliament"
or for licensees serving a regional audience, issues of comparable
importance within their region. On such questions, licensees must
"ensure that justice is done to the full range of significant views and
perspectives". This approach is supported by the concluding words of
section 6(6), which require the rules to "indicate that due impartiality
does not require absolute neutrality on every issue or detachment from

---

[33] Government spokesperson (Earl Ferrers), House of Lords, October 22, 1990.

fundamental democratic principles". This permits broadcasters to bias their programmes in favour of life, liberty and the pursuit of happiness; even if (say) the resurgence of racism becomes a "major matter" of political controversy, impartiality will not be "due" to the racist side of the argument.

The "Series Qualification" provides that in applying the "due impartiality" requirement "a series of programmes may be considered as a whole". But section 6(5) requires that the ITC shall make specific rules as to what actually constitutes a "series"; what time–limit shall be imposed before a "balancing" programme is transmitted (section 6(6)(c)); and as to the publicity that should be given to the balancing programme so as to ensure that it reaches a similar audience (section 6(6)(d)). These subsections are designed to concentrate the minds of the ITC and its licensees, and to send a clear signal that any current affairs or feature programme that presents a controversial viewpoint should not be made (or, if made, should not be transmitted) unless plans for a balancing programme are under way. But it is nonsensical to expect a current affairs team that has come to a particular conclusion about a subject of political controversy to make another programme supportive of a conclusion they do not believe to be justified by the evidence. The answer to this dilemma is to confine the "series" qualification to "personal view" programmes that have been labelled as such, and to argue that a due degree of impartiality has been provided within the give and take of the current affairs feature, even if its treatment of the evidence (necessarily, a fair treatment) has favoured a particular side of the controversy. Whether this approach will be sufficient to satisfy the courts remains to be seen.

Enforcement against the ITC

The statutory duties may be enforced by the Attorney-General, as guardian of the public interest, although no case has occurred in which he has been minded to bring an action in the High Court to force the ITC to take action against any programmer or broadcaster. However, the courts permitted private citizens to bring actions against the IBA (which unlike the ITC was responsible as publisher for all commercial television and radio programmes) on the somewhat tenuous basis that, as licence holders, they may be directly affected by screenings in breach of a statutory duty.

The first case, *Attorney-General, ex rel. McWhirter v. IBA*,[34] concerned a documentary about the life and work of Andy Warhol.

Although senior IBA staff had ordered a number of deletions from the

---

[34] [1973] 1 Q.B. 629.

programme, it had not been personally vetted by the 18 members of the authority at the time its scheduled transmission was injuncted by the court on the strength of sensational newspaper publicity. Subsequently, it was viewed and approved by all IBA members and the court declined to hold that their decision was unreasonable, although it sternly reminded them of their duty to ensure that "nothing" is included in any programme that offends good taste. "These words", Lord Denning emphasised, "show that the programme is to be judged, not as a whole, but in its several parts, piece by piece", although the court did concede that each "piece" could be judged according to the purpose and character of the whole programme. It stressed the personal duty laid on each member by the legislation—a duty that could not be delegated, at least in controversial cases, to members of the IBA staff.

The *McWhirter* case was overlooked by the IBA when it approved transmission of the controversial film *Scum* without referring this decision for Board approval:

Scum was the film of a play that had previously been banned by the BBC because of its explicit scenes of violence in a borstal. The Director-General of the IBA and his staff approved it for transmission on Channel 4 at 11 p.m. with a warning about the violent scenes. They did not, however, refer it to the IBA Board for its approval prior to transmission. The High Court declined to hold that *Scum* was so offensive to public feeling that no reasonable licensing body could allow it to be shown, but it declared, in reliance on *McWhirter,* that the failure to refer the matter to the Board for approval was unlawful. The Court of Appeal, however, took a much more relaxed view of the IBA's approach to its statutory duties. It was entitled to rely on its experienced staff and the system it had established (involving monitoring, audience reaction studies and continuous discussions) to provide sufficient compliance with the statutory duty. The Court of Appeal warned potential applicants for judicial review that the mere fact that one blatantly offensive programme might slip through the IBA's safety-net would not mean that it was in breach of its duty—any such finding would require evidence that the Authority was not maintaining a satisfactory system of safeguards.[35]

Both *McWhirter* and *Whitehouse* emphasise the difficulty of challenging a regulatory body's decision on its merits: once the body has approved a transmission (whether before or after it has taken place) the courts will be hard put to stigmatise the decision as irrational or perverse. Moreover, the approach in *Whitehouse* takes a much more permissive attitude towards the IBA's procedures for complying with the statutory duties, which Lord Donaldson M.R. described as being:

---

[35] *R. v. IBA, ex p. Whitehouse, The Times,* April 4, 1985, CA.

"none of them precise. All require value judgments . . . Parliament was creating what might be described qualitatively as a "best endeavours" obligation and was leaving it to the members [of the IBA] to adopt methods of working, or a system, which in their opinion, was best adapted to securing the requirements set out in the section."

In effect, the courts should intervene only when convinced that the system adopted by the regulatory body was so bizarre that no reasonable person could believe it would assist in maintaining programme standards at the general level required by the Act. The Court of Appeal's description of the statutory duties of the IBA also puts paid to fears that members of the ITC could properly be joined in any prosecution of a television company or programme contractor for assisting breaches of criminal law. A general supervisory duty cannot carry personal liability for aiding and abetting a programme transmitted in breach of the law unless there is both knowledge of the illegal content of the programme and a positive encouragement to transmit it. In exceptional cases these elements may be present, but normally the regulatory body can safely leave such questions to the television companies and their legal advisers. The duty detected in *McWhirter* to preview a programme known to be controversial cannot apply to the ITC.

The IBA's duty, under the 1981 Act, was "to satisfy themselves that, so far as possible, programmes broadcast by the Authority comply . . . [with the statutory duties]". Under the 1990 Act, however, the ITC does not itself broadcast programmes—it merely licenses television stations to do so, and enforces the terms of its licence agreements by penalising them if they fail to observe the statutory duties, which are amongst the terms of the licence. Under section 6 of the 1990 Act, "The Commission shall do all that they can to secure that every licensed service, complies with [the statutory duties] . . . ". This is a somewhat weaker "best endeavours" clause, and it follows from *Whitehouse* that the ITC will be amenable to judicial review only if it were to turn a blind eye to programmes from a television station that persistently caused widespread public offence. After *Whitehouse* it is difficult to imagine the courts interfering with the ITC's interpretation of its statutory duties, although they might intervene if the ITC imposed a disproportionate or unjustified punishment (such as a massive fine or revocation of licence) for a trivial breach or failed to produce a code on impartiality that satisfied the requirements of the Broadcasting Act.

The ITC must interpret its duties in respect of programme standards in the context of other general duties imposed upon it by the statute. Thus, it has a duty to provide the public with programmes of "high quality" and "wide range" that are "calculated to appeal to a variety of tastes and interests". It must additionally encourage "innovation and experimentation" on Channel 4, and see to it that programmes on this channel "contain a suitable proportion of matter calculated to appeal to tastes and interests not generally catered for" by other commercial channels. It follows that the Commission may permit greater latitude in taste and potential offensiveness to programmes of obvious merit or those directed at particular minorities, or those that are screened on Channel 4. The ITC's basic duty to provide the public with programmes of diversity and quality is set out in section 2 of the Act, which is headed "Function of Commission". It requires the Commission to discharge its functions "in the manner which *they consider* [our italics] is best calculated to ensure" programmes that, "taken as a whole", are of high quality and wide appeal to a variety of tastes and interests. It follows that any legal challenge to the ITC must confront the plain parliamentary intention to make the Commission the judge of what will best serve the public interest, and it will be difficult to convince a court that the ITC has acted perversely in any decision taken against broadcasters in relation to programme content.

THE BROADCASTING STANDARDS COMMISSION

This body came into existence as a result of the 1996 Broadcasting Act, which amalgamated the Broadcasting Complaints Commission (created by the 1981 Act to adjudicate complaints about unfair treatment and unwarranted infringement of privacy) and the Broadcasting Standards Council (given statutory powers in the 1990 Act to draw up and to enforce codes relating to sex and violence). The object was to save administrative costs and to avoid public confusion between the two bodies. The BSC is a body corporate whose members, appointed by the Government, must not "be concerned with, or have an interest in" the preparation or provision of radio or television programmes—a restriction which deprives it of any current broadcasters.[36] Section 107 requires the BSC to draw up codes *which will help avoid*:

    (a) unjust or unfair treatment in programmes,

    (b) unwarranted infringement of privacy in, or in connection with the obtaining of material included in, such programmes.

    Under section 108, it shall further draw up codes *giving guidance as to*:

---

[36] Broadcasting Act 1996, s. 106 and Sched. 3(3)(1).

(a) practices to be followed in connection with the portrayal of violence,

(b) practices to be followed in connection with the portrayal of sexual conduct,

(c) standards of taste and decency for such programmes generally.

The BBC, and broadcasters holding licences awarded by the ITC and the Radio Authority, must reflect the BSC rules in their own codes—the cause of the "double jeopardy" of which the 2000 White Paper complains. The BSC has a statutory duty to consider and adjudicate complaints relating to "fairness" (*i.e.* the section 107 issues) and "standards" (the section 108 issues) by applying its own code provisions. *Standards complaints* may be made by anybody (or by any busybody) so long as they are lodged within two months of the offending television programme or three weeks from the date of radio transmission. *Fairness complaints,* on the other hand, need merely be made "within a reasonable time" after the programme (or any repeat thereof) and may even be made from the grave (by family member or executors) within five years of death. However, fairness complaints can only be made by "persons affected" by the allegedly unfair treatment, or (in the case of children or incapacitated persons) by family members or closely connected bodies, who have (in the case of fairness complaints but not privacy complaints) "a sufficiently direct interest in the subject-matter of that treatment" (section 111). A "person affected" for the purposes of a complaint about unfair treatment means either a participant in a programme who was given the treatment or else a person who had "a direct interest in the subject-matter of that treatment". A person affected for the purposes of a privacy complaint is simply "a person whose privacy was infringed" (section 130).

The jurisdictional remit of the BSC to consider fairness and privacy complaints is in similar statutory terms to that of its predecessor, the BCC, a body which was the subject of a number of legal challenges. The court held that it had no power to entertain a complaint from a person who was not mentioned in the programme and had no direct interest in the subject-matter of the allegedly unfair treatment. Hence it quashed a BCC decision that a researcher had been treated unfairly by a programme which failed to mention her work, because there was no power to entertain her complaint: she had no "direct interest" in the subject-matter which *was* broadcast, however much interest she had in her unused contribution.[37] An important limitation on the rights of pressure groups to harass programme makers came when the BCC was stopped from entertaining a complaint against *Panorama* by the

---

[37] *R. v. BCC, ex p. BBC* [1994] E.M.L.R. 497 (Laws J.).

National Council for One-Parent Families, which claimed that all single parents had been traduced by comments about "Babies on Benefit". The Council did not have authority to represent any of the single parents who actually featured on the programme, and the court found that its interest in complaining on behalf of over one million unidentified individuals was palpably "indirect". The court applied Article 10, noting the serious consequences for free speech if broadcasters were to be forced to defend themselves whenever they made a programme which upset a pressure group.[38] The court doubted the correctness of an earlier ruling which had permitted a parish council to complain about a programme alleging racism in its parish.[39]

Whether treatment is unjust or unfair depends upon the programme as broadcast, but invasion of privacy by programme makers "in connection with the obtaining of material included in such programmes" may not be apparent from the programme itself. The BSC is therefore entitled to hear a privacy complaint about research which may not feature in the final edit, as long as there is "some nexus or connection between the material actually broadcast and the (act alleged to be an unwarranted infringement)".[40] If the programme so much as mentions the complainant, any privacy invasion to which its researchers have subjected him may be investigated by the BSC. Illogically, however, when that invasion is so gross or so embarrassing that the programme itself is not transmitted, the BSC has no power to receive a complaint. This follows from section 107(5), which confines its jurisdiction to programmes which are "broadcast by the BBC" or "included in a licensed service". Furthermore, since these phrases are in the past tense, a victim of a privacy breach cannot launch a pre-emptive strike by complaining to the BCC and seeking a hearing before the programme is edited or transmitted:

> The Barclay brothers, reclusive newspaper proprietors, owned a Channel Island on which they were building a castle. John Sweeney, reporter for a BBC programme *The Spin,* was denied permission to land, so he hired a boat and had himself pictured trespassing on their property. The Barclays complained immediately, some weeks before the programme was broadcast. Sedley J. held, with marked reluctance, that thanks to the wording of section 107(5) "the Commission is without adjudicative power. It cannot therefore entertain an anticipatory complaint, even where, once the programme is broadcast, the complaint is bound to succeed". Succeed the Barclay brothers did, after *The Spin* was broadcast, because the Commission ruled that Sweeney and his producers had no evidence of misconduct

---

[38] *R. v. BCC, ex p. BBC* [1995] 3 E.M.L.R. 241, Brooke J.
[39] *R. v. BCC, ex p. Channel 4, The Times,* January 4, 1995.
[40] *R. v. BCC, ex p. Lloyd* [1993] E.M.L.R. 419.

by the Barclays or suspicious behaviour on their private island which could justify the trespass.[41]

The decision on the merits of the Barclay brothers' complaint turned, as so many privacy invasions will, on the question of whether an otherwise minor infringement was "warranted"—*i.e.* whether the journalist had any real reason to suspect that his invasive conduct would produce solid evidence of wrongdoing or was otherwise justifiable. A *fortiori* more serious infringements, by bugging or secret filming, will require even greater justification before it can be "warranted". On this distinction the BSC condemned a *Watchdog* programme for secretly filming at a Dixons store in the hope of obtaining hard evidence that the company was selling, as new, some second-hand appliances. Since Dixons had been convicted twice before of this offence there was at least suspicion, but no more, that it might not have learnt its lesson. The Court of Appeal upheld the BSC finding of breach, rejecting two perfectly good arguments, namely that privacy is an inherent right of the human personality which cannot sensibly attach to trading corporations, and that the surreptitiousness of the method of breach (secret filming) does not itself bestow privacy on a transaction (sales to customers over a store counter) which is conducted openly and without any desire for seclusion.[42] On both these scores the Court of Appeal was mistaken, although its approach was attributable to its sense of the BSC as a light-weight source of opinion on ethics rather than as a serious enforcement body. (Thus the court made clear that its ruling might not apply to privacy decisions in other contexts.) Lord Woolf's comment that "what constitutes an infringement of privacy . . . is very much a matter of personal judgment . . . not an area in which the courts are well equipped to adjudicate"[43] did not seem to be shared by his Court of Appeal brethren in *Michael Douglas v. Hello!*.[44] Judges are better equipped than anyone else (and certainly better equipped than peers, ministers of religion and retired broadcasters who people the BSC) to decide what amounts to a breach of privacy. The Chief Justice's remarks should be read as no more than a restatement of the traditional "hands off" approach by the courts to merits decisions made by "expert" statutory bodies.

---

[41] *R. v. BCC, ex p. Barclay, The Times* October 11, 1996, (Sedley J.).

[42] *R. v. Broadcasting Standards Commission, ex p BBC* [2000] 3 All E.R. 989. To refute the second argument, the court sought support in its earlier decision that re-publication of an old conviction *could* amount to an infringement of privacy, although the fact was in the public domain. But this is a different issue, because digging up an old conviction can be "unwarranted" and contrary to the spirit of the Rehabilitation of Offenders Act. See *R. v. Broadcasting Complaints Commission, ex p. Granada Television Ltd* [1995] E.M.L.R. 163, CA.

[43] [2000] 3 All E.R. 989 at 994 G–H.

[44] *Douglas v. Hello!* [2001] E.M.L.R. 199, see p. 238.

The BSC is given a wide statutory discretion to refuse to entertain complaints which are frivolous or the subject of ongoing court proceedings or which it decides are "inappropriate" because the complainant has an available legal remedy, or for any other reason.[45] But the courts will not interfere with a BSC decision to entertain a complaint which could give rise to a libel action unless it is demonstrably unreasonable,[46] *e.g.* if the same issues that the BSC has to decide will also arise for jury decision at a trial.[47] The complaints body is not empowered to make policy rulings, so it was inappropriate to hear a complaint by David Owen M.P. that broadcasters were not giving his party (*i.e.* himself) news coverage commensurate with its electoral support. His "complaint" was not seeking a condemnation of any particular programme so much as a change in editorial policy, a matter beyond the competence of the BCC.[48]

Procedure

Once a complaint is accepted, the BSC must send a copy to the broadcasting body responsible for the programme, which is under a duty to provide a written response and, if requested, to provide the BSC with a copy of the programme, a transcript and any relevant correspondence.[49] For this purpose, broadcasting bodies are under a duty to retain copies of all broadcast programmes for 90 days (in the case of television) and 42 days (radio).[50] The BSC has a discretion to decide complaints without a hearing, although hearings are normally vouchsafed if there is a conflict of evidence or an important principle is at stake. (A refusal to hold a hearing in defiance of natural justice principles could be overturned by the court.) Regrettably, the statute requires that "fairness complaints" be heard in private, although the BSC has power to open hearings of "standards complaints" if it thinks fit.[51] This breach of the open justice principle is inexcusable (other than for invasion of privacy complaints): the BSC is a quasi-judicial tribunal and requires the discipline of open (preferably televised) hearings to enable the public to judge its work. The Annan Committee, which first recommended a BSC-type body, regarded public hearings as providing an important remedy for

---

[45] Broadcasting Act 1996, s. 114(2).
[46] *R. v. Broadcasting Complaints Commission, ex p. BBC* (1989) 128 S.J. 384; *The Times,* May 17, 1989.
[47] *R. v. Broadcasting Complaints Commission, ex p. Thames Television, The Times,* October 8, 1982.
[48] *R. v. Broadcasting Complaints Commission, ex p. Owen* [1985] Q.B. 1153.
[49] See ss. 1150–116 of the Broadcasting Act 1996.
[50] *ibid.,* s. 117.
[51] *ibid.,* s. 115(2); s. 116(1).

media misrepresentation.[52] In "standards cases" a private hearing is otiose, given that the BSC's purported objective is to promote public debate and public involvement with media standards. Although responsibility for this breach of the open justice principle belongs to parliament, the BSC is content with its "hole in the corner" position and so, it must be said, are the broadcasters who appear before it, reluctant to have their dirty linen washed in public. At a time when other professionals—lawyers, doctors, dentists—accept that their disciplinary proceedings *must* be open to the public, it is wrong that broadcasters should escape the very publicity on which, in all other respects, they thrive.

That said, the BSC procedures are not always fair to them. The power to deny a hearing could be used unjustly, especially to programme makers who may not be notified of the complaint or may be inadequately represented by a broadcasting body that answers it, lukewarmly. It must always be remembered that such bodies—the BBC, ITC and corporate licence holders—may have a different agenda to the programme makers who are frequently independent producers. The latter should approach the BSC directly and insist on their right to make separate submissions and to attend any hearing—a court would then strike down any BSC decision taken without considering their representations. The BSC, if it does order a hearing, has a statutory duty to give an opportunity to attend to any person "responsible for the making or provision of the programme".[53]

Although the BSC cannot award compensation to a successful complainant, it does have power to pay travelling expenses and subsistence.[54] This is not confined to complainants—broadcasters should demand recompense as well if they have attended hearings, and travelling expenses for witnesses brought (if necessary from overseas) to refute baseless complaints.

Publication of adjudications

The BSC has only one sanction, namely publication of its adjudications. These all appear in digest form in its monthly bulletin, but cases where broadcasters are found at fault may require a wider dissemination to counter the original mischief. So section 119 provides the BSC with power to direct a broadcasting body to publish an approved summary of the complaint and its findings, in such manner as the BSC determines. This permits a direction specifying that the findings must be reported as the first item on the next news programme, although the BSC has not given such a direction and its decisions are rarely treated as "news"

---

[52] Report of the Committee on the Future of Broadcasting, 1977 Cmnd. 6753, Chap. 6.
[53] Broadcasting Act 1996, s. 115(2)(d); s. 116(2)(d).
[54] *ibid.*, s. 118.

by broadcasters although they are occasionally covered by the press. Normally, the BSC directs that a 200-word summary of its findings should be broadcast during a later edition of the programme complained against, certainly in cases where the complaint is upheld. It may also direct a broadcasting body it found at fault to take out a paid advertisement in newspapers to bring the decision to the public attention. All ITC and Radio Authority licences have conditions which require the licence holder to behave as the authority thinks necessary to comply with directions given to that body by the BSC.[55] The BBC, ITC and Radio Authority have a duty to publicise the existence and role of the BSC,[56] which may further be gleaned from its website: www.bsc.org.uk.

Adjudications

The BSC has promulgated a code which is more elaborate than that of the PCC, although less detailed than the ITC code and the BBC's "Producer's Guidelines". The only statutory guidance defines "unjust or unfair treatment" as "treatment which is unjust or unfair because of the way in which material in the programme has been selected or arranged"[57]—*i.e.* because of the way in which the programme had been edited. Complaints will be upheld if contributions (especially by experts) are distorted or slanted in the editing, or if contributors are misled as to the nature of the programme or not given advance notice of areas of questioning, or if undertakings about anonymity or confidentiality are not kept. News and documentary programmes will be expected to correct any erroneous statements promptly, and to provide an effective "right of reply" to any person who is made the subject of an attack. This is an important principle: the BSC serves as the means by which Article 8 of the European Convention on Transfrontier Television is effectuated. It provides:

> "every natural or legal person, regardless of nationality or place of residence, shall have the opportunity to exercise a right of reply or to seek other comparable legal or administrative remedies relating to programmes transmitted or retransmitted within its jurisdiction ... In particular, it shall ensure that timing and other arrangements for the exercise of the right of reply are such that this right can be effectively exercised."[58]

The prospect of complaining to the BSC satisfies the Convention

---

[55] Broadcasting Act 1996, s. 119(7).
[56] *ibid.*, s. 124(1).
[57] *ibid.*, s. 130.
[58] See also Art. 23 of the 1989 EEC Directive on Broadcasting.

because its remedy for unfair treatment is to provide a right of reply by directing a broadcast correction or ordering a summary of its decision to be published in newspapers or magazines which those who heard the original attack would be likely to read. This is fine in theory, but the effectiveness of the remedy is undermined by the unnecessary and inexcusable delays which have always attended BSC adjudications; in 2000, the 21 complaints upheld by the BSC took from six to 15 months, with an average of 10 months.[59] The most serious complaints—against *Panorama, Channel 4 News* and *The Cook Report*—all took 14 to 15 months, and after this lapse of time a decision, however well publicised, could not have provided any real satisfaction to the successful complainants. As a quick and effective remedy for unfairness, the BSC is, on this important score, an abject failure.

BSC adjudications are always short—the average is 200 words—a practice which suits the media (since any "summaries" they are directed to broadcast take up little airtime) but does not assist the development of coherent case law. Many fairness decisions are unexceptional, but some are over-pernickety or excessively generous to unprepossessing complainants. From its early days as the BCC, this body has had a charitable instinct to "give something" to complainants, by upholding one or two minor grievances against public interest programmes which expose them as crooks or charlatans. These complainants—often corporations—are then able to claim they have "won", and to exploit this "victory" to tarnish the original programme. The BSC has made the same mistake, and has failed to develop the rule (reflected in libel law) that a programme which is substantially fair and accurate should not be made the subject of a "complaint upheld" finding for minor errors.

There is a sense in which broadcasters are always "unfair" to those they interview—in fading light, or under harsh studio light, and with the invariable pressure of editing for a short sharp slot. The BCC in its first rulings accepted that "fairness" had to be considered in relation to the programme as a whole rather than individual elements[60] and that current affairs programmes should be hard hitting with interviewers who played "devil's advocate".[61] These decisions should be taken further, by applying what lawyers would term the *de minimis* principle, *i.e.* that occasional lapses of objectivity do not justify condemnation of a programme which on the whole serves the public interest. The BSC should be more astute to reject complainants who, for example, try to salvage their reputations after a poor performance by claiming the interviewer was unfair. It must preserve the broadcaster's right to sim-

[59] Details supplied by BSC website, January 3, 2001.
[60] *National Anti-Fluoridation Campaign v. Medical Express,* BCC Report 1981–82, p. 7.
[61] *Life v. Nationwide,* BCC adjudication, August 25, 1982.

plify complicated issues, reserving its censure for programmes that are over-simplistic at the complainant's expense.

There is little point in analysing BSC "fairness" decisions, since they turn on particular facts rather than on principles. Many are unexceptional: in February 2001, for example, *Panorama* was censured for distorting facts about Great Ormond Street Hospital's treatment of children with chronic fatigue syndrome, Channel 4 was upbraided for a programme about the sex slave trade which had failed to honour promises of anonymity for interviewed sex slaves, and Channel 4 News was taken to task for putting questions without notice to a doctor which he could not answer because of patient confidentiality.[62] Other decisions have been more questionable, as when it upheld a complaint against the *Cook Report* for putting robust questions to a doctor permitted to practise after a conviction for serious crime,[63] and when it censured a programme for unfairness to the family of a dead man by voicing very reasonable suspicions that he had been murdered in the course of warfare between rival criminal groups.[64] In such cases the BSC is substituting its own editorial judgment for that of the programme makers, and it is by no means clear that the Commission's judgment is preferable. It fails to apply the correct test, used in determining civil liability for negligence in respect of other professionals, namely whether the impugned programme was made so carelessly or so unreasonably that no competent broadcaster could make it.

Most of the Commission's decisions on privacy, like the *Dixons* and *Barclay Brothers* cases, turn on whether the infringement was warranted by public interest considerations—*i.e.* by having reason to believe that the infringement would expose misconduct. It has delivered some controversial rulings about the use of news footage of accident victims, in one case censuring a road safety programme for re-broadcasting pictures of an injured driver receiving roadside medical treatment, although it might be thought that the overriding importance of the message warranted that particular infringement.[65] The logic of many privacy decisions is impossible to judge, since it merely announces that a privacy complaint against a particular programme has been upheld—full stop. This is asinine; it preserves the privacy of the complainant but provides no guidance for broadcasters or anyone else. It is perfectly possible, as the courts have found in confidentiality cases, to set out the basic facts and applicable principles in a decision, without publicly identifying the complainant.

---

[62] BSC Bulletin No. 40, February 28, 2001.
[63] *Doctors from Hell,* BSC Bulletin No. 38, December 21, 2000.
[64] *Godfathers* (Meridian), BSC Bulletin No. 37, November 30, 2000.
[65] *Motorway* (ITV), BSC Bulletin No. 36, October 26, 2000.

Standards complaints

The BSC upholds numerous complaints against broadcasters for breaches of what it assumes to be current standards of decency, in respect to the depiction of sex and violence and the use of bad language. Many relate to scheduling decisions, especially if adult themes have been allowed to intrude before the magic "watershed" hour of 9 p.m., when children are presumed (optimistically) to be in bed. Broadcasters will sometimes admit to errors of taste, especially those that creep into live or unrehearsed programmes. But the BSC has erred from the outset in its obsession for political correctness and its profound lack of any sense of humour. It routinely condemns Channel 4 and BBC 2 for satire and "alternative" comedy (a genre which its members do not seem to understand) and in so far as its decisions influence broadcasting executives (the BBC claims to take it seriously) it may well have discouraged the development of innovative programmes. Here is a flavour of some recent decisions: it is sobering to think that the *Goon Show* or *Monty Python* might never have been broadcast had the BSC been in existence.

- *Loose Ends,* Ned Sherrin's long running Saturday morning "live" show, condemned for "vulgarity . . . likely to have exceeded the expectations of the audience" (which would doubtless have been delighted—only one listener complained).[66]

- *Freak Out,* Channel 4's "ground breaking new show with a satirical edge" featured an American TV celebrity, "Hank the angry dwarf". The BSC decided, after only one viewer complained, that Hank had been "exploited" by the feature, the whole point of which was to show how disabled people were challenging traditional perceptions of disability.[67] (Will the BBC ever risk BSC condemnation by replaying the Peter Cook/Dudley Moore sketch about Mr Spiggot, the one-legged actor auditioning to play Tarzan?)

- *The 11 O'clock Show.* This topical satire programme was written and performed "live" after 11 p.m. It commented on issues such as school bullying and care in the community. The Commission declared itself "troubled by the selection of some subjects for satire . . . particularly involving vulnerable

[66] BSC Adjudication March 27, 1996, p. 6.
[67] *Freak Out,* Channel 4, CN 2156/BSC Bulletin 38, December 21, 2000.

groups".[68] This is a censor speaking: no subject is beyond
satire, the only question should be whether the satire succeeds. The BSC view that "vulnerable groups" (and particularly the pressure groups that claim to represent them) are
taboo is to uphold political correctness at the expense of the
Article 10 guarantee of freedom of expression. Similarly,
another adjudication condemned the same show for "offensive remarks" about the Irish and the Scots (two viewers
complained) although in another case Anne Robinson's more
severe remarks about the Welsh were let pass, despite a
record 427 complaints. In a bizarre finding, the BSC said
that Welsh "achievements, both historical and current, gave
it a strength and resilience not available to other more vulnerable groups"—thereby making an offensive racist
reflection on the vulnerability (through lack of achievement?)
of the Scots and the Irish.

- *Rory Bremner—Who Else?* Condemned for an amusing and
topical sketch, broadcast by Channel 4 at 10.45 p.m., sending
up the award of the Booker Prize to an author (James Kelner)
who obsessively used the word "fuck" (so, of course, did the
sketch).[69]

- *Week Ending,* Radio 4's satire programme, made an ironical
Christmas comment on the barbaric treatment of pregnant
women at Holloway during a time when the nation was
celebrating the nativity. The BSC, apparently ignorant of the
purpose of satire, upheld a complaint (by one listener)
because it was "rather insensitive" to "lampoon the nativity
so near to such an important date in the Christian religious
calendar".[70]

- *Pay and Display* (ITV), a popular comedy, condemned because
two viewers had complained about the use of the phrase "sympathy shag" in a laugh-line at 9 p.m.[71]

- *South Park.* The point of this critically acclaimed and
extremely popular U.S. comedy consistently eludes the BSC.

---

[68] See BSC Report No. 35, CN 4342.3, October 4, 2000, p. 7; BSC Report No. 30,
March 30, 2000, p. 5 (CN 3764.2).
[69] Adjudication No. CN 3150.7, 1995.
[70] Adjudication No. CN 4825.9, April 24, 1996.
[71] BSC Bulletin 38, December 21, 2000.

Although transmitted at 10 p.m., it has been condemned as "going beyond acceptable boundaries for this time of night" and its Christmas record could not be played on FM music stations at Christmas because it might "give offence to Christians".[72]

- *The Awful Truth,* a powerful factual comedy from America broadcast by Channel 4 at one o'clock in the morning satirised the pro-gun lobby, inter-cutting footage from real tragedies caused by gunmen. Incredibly, and at the behest of one viewer, the BSC found that this necessary and valuable element of this highly moral programme "took the item beyond acceptable limits" at 1 a.m. (would the BSC prefer viewers to switch to all the "acceptable" pornography around at that hour?).[73–74]

- *Juice FM.* On a show aimed at Liverpool youth culture, a presenter described Cliff Richard as "crap" and a single listener actually lodged a complaint which the BSC then solemnly upheld. The comment was "gratuitously offensive and had gone beyond acceptable limits for broadcast".[75]

There are dozens of similar examples. They demonstrate an urgent need to appoint a comedian to the Commission, whose present numbers are obviously lacking in any sense of humour (or in the case about Cliff Richard, any sense of music). Some decisions about violence have been equally inane. The award-winning documentary *Culloden,* depicting the bloodiest battle ever fought on British soil, was condemned for (wait for it) "excessive violence",[76] whilst a Granada programme about the falling safety standards in air travel was censured for showing an aircraft in flames—because there *had* been an aircrash two weeks before transmission (a fact which should have made the programme more topical).[77] This latter decision was part of a continuing dialogue with television schedulers, who are themselves alert to questions of inappropriate transmissions after a public tragedy, and it is sometimes doubtful

---

[72] *South Park* (Channel 4) CN 5235.2; *Robin Banks* (XFM) CN 3940, BSC Bulletin No. 30, March 30, 2000, p. 3.
[73] *The Awful Truth,* (Channel 4) CN 3938; March 30, 2000.
[75] *ibid,* p. 6.
[76] BSC Adjudication CN 5350, August 29, 1996. One viewer complained.
[77] BSC Bulletin No. 38, December 21, 2000, p. 5.

whether the BSC's hindsight is preferable. For example, it condemned BBC 2 for scheduling several episodes of the surreal costume drama *Gormenghast* before the watershed, lest it disturb younger viewers,[78-79] Most parents (there were only seven complaints) would be delighted if their children chose to watch *Gormenghast*—they might be encouraged to read the novel. On this, as on so much else, the public service broadcasters (BBC and Channel 4) are more in touch with their viewers than the BSC which purports to represent them.

The BSC upholds many complaints about crude language, although not all its decisions pay proper respect to the context (See the "Stop Press" section for further details). A late night tribute to John Lennon, screened by Channel 4 on what would have been his sixtieth birthday, was preceded by a clear warning about "strong language" in a rare and important interview. Two viewers complained, whereupon the BSC decided that strong language "was gratuitous in a programme otherwise dedicated to music".[80] (It was dedicated to John Lennon.) An important ITV exposure of aggressive telephone sales techniques bleeped out most of the bad language used by these unsavoury "Salesmen from Hell", but left in their use of the word "wanker"—a word the BSC claims (surprisingly) is rated "strong" and so inappropriate for audience ears until well after 9 p.m.[81] This foolish decision would mean that public affairs programmes which expose offensive people should either clean them up (and so understate the extent of their offensiveness) or move out of prime time. The BSC's obsession with political correctness is evident in its continual censure of talkback programmes, even when the talk is true. It condemned *Straight Talk* on BBC News 24 over a contributor's description of killings in Sierra Leone as "a bunch of savages killing another bunch of savages",[82] although anyone conversant with the killings in that country could not dispute the accuracy of that description as applied to Foday Sankoh and his followers. Where crimes against humanity are concerned, the BSC does not understand the importance of calling a savage a savage, whether he (or she) is black or white.

What emerges from analysis of the upheld complaints is that the BSC continually errs, as a matter of law, in discharging its statutory duty. Its remit under the 1996 Act is to draw up and enforce through complaints adjudications a code "giving guidance (to broadcasters) as to practices to be followed in connection with the portrayal of violence . . . sexual conduct, and standards of taste and decency for such programmes gener-

---

[78] *Gormenghast* (BBC 2) CN 4195.3, BSC Bulletin 34, July 27, 2000; CN 4232.5, BSC Bulletin 36, p. 6.

[80] *John Lennon Night: Shine On,* CN 5446.5.

[81] *Salesmen From Hell* (ITV) CN 4760.2, BSC Bulletin 34, July 27, 2000, p. 5.

[82] *Straight Talk* (BBC News 24), CN 4816, BSC Bulletin 35, October 4, 2000.

ally".[83] But the code, the taste and decency standards and any adjudication thereon must be related to the core duty imposed on broadcasters by section 6 of the 1990 Broadcasting Act, namely to avoid programmes "offensive to public feeling". (The BBC undertaking is to eschew programmes which "give general offence".) What the BSC is doing, time and again, is censuring programmes without the slightest evidence of general or widespread public offence. Most of the complaints upheld are made by a single viewer (perhaps an easily offended monitor for Mediawatch, a reincarnation of Mary Whitehouse's National Viewers and Listeners Association). It cannot be said that *South Park* or Ned Sherrin or Rory Bremner or any of the comedy and satire programmes it censures are offensive to public feeling generally, when the only objection comes from one shocked or possibly deranged (the BSC never check) member of the public. The BSC in such cases applies an idiosyncratic standard, not shared by ordinary viewers, who either enjoy the anarchy of alternative comedy or are perfectly happy for those who do to watch it in late night slots.

The fact that the BSC has not been challenged in court over its "standards" adjudications may reflect legal advice that courts will generally defer to "experts" on questions of standards, or the fact that nobody takes BSC adjudications very seriously. The BBC affects to do so, however, whilst ITC licence holders must avoid having too many previous convictions from the BSC on their record when their franchise comes up for renewal. To the extent that this is a factor in commissioning programmes or editing them, the BSC is damaging to innovation and experiment in broadcasting, and especially to alternative comedy.

In respect of sex, the BSC has been locked in a long battle with Channel 5 over its ingenious attempts to pass off pornography as public interest television—generally by showing it in programmes which purport to "discuss whether pornography is by its nature exploitative". This was the broadcaster's defence of its *Sex and Shopping* series which the BSC found "unacceptably explicit", although it congratulated the Channel on developing into a fine art the pixellation techniques which distort obscene images.[84] Although the BSC has been forced to concede that research shows most viewers to be relaxed about late night sex romps, it still drew the line at "a continuing process by Channel 5 of seeking to extend the boundaries of acceptability with regard to the depiction of sex on free to air television".[85] This is hardly surprising, since terrestrial television now competes in most homes with cable or satellite channels and encrypted services offering porn of soft or medium core. The BSC has failed to explain why it imposes a more

---

[83] Broadcasting Act 1996, s. 108(1).
[84] *Sex and Shopping* (Channel 5) CN 4250 BSC Bulletin 34, July 27, 2000.
[85] *X Certificate* (Channel 5) CN 4672, BSC Bulletin No. 38, December 21, 2000.

stringent standard on "free to air" channels. Channel 5's Chief Executive, David Elstein, likened this to the 1961 decision to prosecute the
paperback edition of *Lady Chatterley's Lover* after taking no action
against the more expensive hardback. "The BSC is anachronistic and
patronising in seeking to challenge the right of free-to-air viewers to
watch what would be perfectly acceptable on pay TV . . . it is simply
seeking to assert its own aesthetic judgment over the clearly stated preferences of Channel 5 viewers".[86] Both protagonists in this debate met
sticky ends: the preferences of the BSC Chairman for adultery and pornographic "spanking" magazines were revealed by the *News of the
World* whereupon he felt obliged to resign, and Channel 5 dispensed
with the service of Mr Elstein, whom it regarded as too high-brow to
satisfy the clearly stated preferences of its viewers.

The BSC will in due course be subsumed by OFCOM: it will be
remembered not for sophisticated judgments on taste and decency but
for promoting the arcane art of "pixellating" the act of sexual intercourse.

THE CODES OF PRACTICE

The relationship between the BSC, on the one hand, and the ITC and
the Radio Authority, on the other, is jurisprudentially curious. The ITC
has a general duty to secure the exclusion from licensed services of any
offence to standards of taste and decency (Broadcasting Act 1990, s.
6(1)) and a specific duty to draw up a code giving guidance as to the
rules to be observed with respect to depicition of violence (s. 7). The
Radio Authority has parallel duties (ss. 91-2). These bodies, together
with the BBC (which has no statutory duty to impose codes, but has
done so for many years in its Producer's Guidelines) are amenable to
the jurisdiction of the BSC in relation to public complaints about their
services, and are required (by section 108(2) of the 1996 Broadcasting
Act) to reflect in their codes "the general effect" of codes drawn up by
the BSC in relation to the portrayal of violence and sexual conduct, and
standards of taste and decency. They are required to cooperate with the
BSC in its adjudication of complaints, and to publish its verdicts, but
the statute is silent about what (if anything) should follow a breach of
the BSC code. Amongst the proliferating codes, it is not uncommon
that a programme breaches a BSC rule but not an ITC/BBC/Radio
Authority rule, or vice versa. Indeed on several occasions broadcasting
authorities have supported programmes that have been subsequently
condemned by the BSC; in so far as this condemnation involves a ques-

---

[86] "Channel 5 Defence of Erotic Fiction", letter to *The Times,* January 26, 2000.

tion of principle extrapolated from the BSC code, it would appear that section 108(2) requires the broadcasting authority to reflect the "general effect" of the BSC principle when next reviewing its own code. The Codes themselves are endlessly overlapping. The BSC is the shortest, and its somewhat pious generalities are duly echoed in the ITC Code and the BBC Producers Guidelines. The ITC condescends to somewhat greater detail, and is astute to place responsibility for compliance on its licensees. The BBC guidelines are almost of book length, and particularly detailed about relationships with politicians (as a result of regular complaints by their parties). The Guidelines do provide examples of politically correct BBC usage (*e.g.* "There is no place in factual programmes for our use of words like "dyke" . . . when contributors use them they should be challenged wherever possible").[87] The following section of this book highlights only the most significant common provisions.

The Watershed

The BSC code begins its section on scheduling with a curious echo of the Rees-Mogg philosophy of television as a "guest in the home", supplemented by a touch of Rousseau:

> "There is an implied contract between the viewer, the listener and the broadcaster about the terms of admission to the home. The most frequent reason for viewers or listeners finding a particular item offensive is that it flouts their expectation of that contract . . .".

This explains the frequent basis of upholding complaints as "exceeding the expectations of the audience", but it is an arcane and unrealistic way of judging a breach of what should be objective standards. Nonetheless, a fundamental term of this contract is deemed to be "the watershed hour"—9 p.m.—by which time children are optimistically assumed to be both in bed and too tired to operate the remote control switch for the television set often located in their bedroom. The BSC paternalistically insists that the purpose of the watershed policy is to alert parents to their responsibility to exercise caution in permitting their children to watch television after this time, to which it might be objected, first, that parents should exercise such caution at all times, secondly, that it is wrong to confine challenging and important programmes to the late evening ghetto (when many adults are too tired to view them) and, thirdly, that parents who responsibly decide that their sons and daughters would benefit from watching such programmes

---

[87] Producers Guidelines, 29/04/99, Rule 7.3.

should not have to keep them up late in order for them to do so. However, "the watershed" has become a scheduling shibboleth, slavishly
endorsed by the ITC and the BBC. So pervasive is the fear of giving
offence before the witching hour of 9 p.m. that when Ken Starr's interrogation of President Clinton began at 3 p.m. United Kingdom time,
neither the BBC nor the ITC companies dared to put it out live, and
only permitted edited extracts late at night. The ITC went so far as to
advise CNN and Sky that they should operate a censorship mechanism
so as to remove "indecent" questions and answers: Sky duly operated
a delay system, although CNN, transmitting to the rest of Europe, sensibly declined to tamper with the Presidential cross-examination.

The watershed begins at 9 p.m. and ends at 5.30 a.m. The BSC code
warns that it should not signal "an abrupt change from family viewing
to adult programming. It is not a waterfall, but a signal to parents that
they should exercise increasing control over their children's viewing
after this time . . . Broadcasters should provide sufficient information to
assist . . . and further bear in mind that children tend to stay up later
than usual on Friday and Saturday nights . . . ". The watershed applies
to cable and licensed satellite services, although specially encrypted
services can begin their soft porn and violence at 8 p.m., and unleash
"material of a more adult nature" after 10 p.m. Radio has no watershed,
and can run provocative items at any hour, although special caution
must be used at breakfast time.

The ITC code has special watershed rules for movies, adopting their
BBFC classification:

   (a) no "12" movie can begin before 8 p.m.;

   (b) no "15" movie can begin before 9 p.m.;

   (c) no "18" movie should begin before 10 p.m.;

   (d) no "R18" or any movie refused classification can be screened
       at any time.

The BBC loyally accepts the watershed, with the grudging note that
"it is not a simple question of dividing the output into "bland" and
"adult" fare"—although it often is. "Seventy per cent of homes do not
contain children and many viewers expect a full range of subject matter
throughout the day". Nonetheless, the watershed is now "a widely
understood convention", albeit one which cannot sensibly apply to
worldwide television, transmitting to different time zones.

Television's statutory duties in respect of standards (they are not relevant to fairness or privacy) must always be judged against watershed
considerations. They are as follows:

"Offending against good taste or decency"

Some assistance may be derived from the definition of "indecency" in the criminal law (see p. 198). The concept relates to what is likely to shock, disgust or revolt ordinary people. It must, however, be remembered that there is a distinction between what shocks and disgusts in real life, and what is likely to have that effect when shown as part of a television programme. The context is all-important, and much material will lose its capacity to turn the stomach if it is incorporated in a programme for the bona fide purpose of illuminating discussion.

The subjects that the BSC finds the most tasteless are:

Bad language

The BSC at first regarded "bastard" as "a word whose repeated use generally appears to arouse deep resentment in a majority of people" until it realised that the word was a term of affection in Australian soaps. Words and phrases with sexual origins should be used only with the greatest discretion: "The abusive use of any of the synonyms for the genital organs, especially the female organs, or of "fuck" and its derivatives should be permitted only after reference to the most senior levels of management."[88] So said the BSC in its first code, although this advice was dropped from the 1998 edition apparently because the advice itself contained the word "fuck". The ITC Programme Code requires any use of bad language to be defensible in terms of context and authenticity, while "the most offensive language should not be used before 9 p.m."

Sex

"*Broadcasters must ensure that actual sexual intercourse is not transmitted,*" says paragraph 5 of the BSC code. This applies only to humans—actual sexual intercourse between animals, birds and particularly insects is permissible (and probably mandatory in any programme made by David Attenborough). The BSC concedes for the first time in its 1998 revised code that audiences have become more liberal and relaxed about portrayals of sex, and encrypted and pay-per-view services may offer explicit sexual content, subject of course to the law of obscenity. "Observe the watershed, avoid exploitation and have an editorial rationale" is the general advice of its code. "Representation of sexual intercourse should be reserved until after 9 p.m. Exceptions to this rule may be allowed in the case of nature films, programmes with a serious educational purpose, or where representation is non-graphic."

---

[88] Code of Practice (1989 ed.), p. 43.

Race, religion and disabilities

Racial stereotyping and derogatory racial references should be avoided unless warranted by the context. Religious sensitivities must be borne in mind, and the use of "Christ" and even "God" as an expletive is actively discouraged. Care should be taken in the depiction of people with disabilities, especially to avoid any hint of exploitation in charitable appeals. The ITC Programme Code requires the avoidance of "patronising expressions" such as "handicapped" and "crippled with", while disabled persons must always "use" rather than "be confined to" a wheelchair. The Code urges avoidance of jokes that play upon exploitation or humiliation, and extends this consideration to other minorities, homosexuals and members of minority religious faiths.

The BSC code reminds broadcasters that over six million people— one in 10—have a physical disability or mental health problem, and warns against the twin evils of prejudicing and patronising. Words like "loony", "nutter" and "schizo" should not be used (but since they are, in real life, is this ban not itself patronising?). It is wrong (in fact, as well as in tact) to suggest that persons suffering from schizophrenia are always or mainly dangerous.

The BBC Producers' Guidelines are most detailed, and (alone among the codes) evince concern for discrimination against women, who form the majority (51.6 per cent) of the population. Sexist words like "policeman", "newsmen", and even "manning" must be replaced by "police officers", "journalists", and "staffing". Words like "spastic", "retarded", or "defective" must not be used, while "deaf and dumb" is "hardly ever acceptable". Pejorative words like "queer", "fairy", "poof" (and, of course, "dyke") have no place in factual programmes, although may still feature in the vocabulary of low-life characters in BBC drama. There are 12 million people over 60 (an age which most BBC senior executives are rapidly approaching) and "many will have vigorous and fulfilling lives", so a "rocking chair" image and ageist references are inappropriate.

The BBC guidelines gamely make the case for alternative comedy which "challenges popular notions of taste and decency . . . and is an important part of the BBC's output (although) it may be distasteful to some viewers and listeners" (and if just one of them lodges a complaint, the BSC will probably uphold it). That this form of comedy does not feature much in the BBC's output these days (Channel 4 has picked up the baton) may be a result of the kind of BSC decisions derided above.

"Likely to encourage crime or lead to disorder"

The evidence that portrayal of criminal conduct on television programmes has a "copycat" effect is not conclusive. However, the codes urge caution: programmers should not glamorise the criminal or condone his actions, and defendants should not be presented as heroic figures or the stuff of legends. Relations and associates of criminals should not be paid for retelling their stories unless there is an "overriding public interest". The ITC and BBC codes provide detailed guidelines for treatment of crime and anti-social behaviour. The following subjects are discussed, amongst others.

Interviews with criminals

There always needs to be careful consideration of whether or not such an interview, and any payment for it, is justified in the public interest.

Interviews with people who use or advocate violence or other criminal measures

Any plans for a programme item that explores and exposes the views of people who within the British Isles use or advocate violence or other criminal measures for the achievement of political ends must be referred to the licensee's chief executive before any arrangements for filming or videotaping are made. A producer should therefore not plan to interview members of proscribed organisations without previous discussion with his or her company's top management.

Hijacking and kidnapping reports

It is unacceptable to broadcast any information, whether derived from monitoring of communications or from any other source, that could endanger lives or prejudice the success of attempts to deal with hijacking or kidnapping.

Demonstration of criminal techniques

In programmes dealing with criminal activities, whether in fictional or documentary form, there may be conflict between the demands of accurate realism and the risk of unintentionally assisting the criminally inclined. Careful thought should be given, and, where appropriate, advice taken from the police before items are included that give detailed information about criminal methods and techniques.

Presence of television cameras at demonstrations and scenes of public disturbance

Every effort must be made to place what is being seen and heard in context, so that viewers can properly evaluate the significance of activities that may have been "set up" to attract television coverage. Incidents known to be "manufactured" for the cameras should either be excluded or revealed for what they are.

The test of whether a programme or sequence is "likely to encourage or incite to crime or to lead to disorder" needs little analysis. Anything that "incites" *a fortiori* "encourages". The "disorder" referred to must have an element of lawlessness. It is not enough that a programme would lead viewers to take to the streets in protest meetings or demonstrations: that is their lawful right. Nor is it enough to fear that such demonstrations might occasion a "degree" of disorder by virtue of their size or the angry feelings of their participants. In the context in which it is used in section 6 of the 1990 Broadcasting Act, the "disorder" to be guarded against seems to be civil lawlessness and mob violence. Thus, a film about a protest movement would not be objectionable if viewers swelled protest rallies, but only if it led them to go further and to join sorties involving civil trespass on, or criminal damage to, the property of others.

There is no guidance in the statute as to how many persons must be encouraged to criminal acts or disorder. There must be the danger of a general encouragement to reasonable viewers before this prohibition should be invoked. In construing similar legislative language in the Obscene Publications Act (a tendency to deprave and corrupt likely viewers) the Court of Appeal interpolated "a significant number" of likely viewers.[89] This would be a useful gloss on the section 4(1) duty. "Significant", of course, may mean much less than "substantial", but it is nonetheless a yardstick that excludes reactions from any "lunatic fringe" of viewers. On this basis, the test is whether, on the balance of probabilities, the programme or sequence in question is likely to encourage a numerically significant number of persons who would view it at the hour of transmission to engage in criminal or lawless conduct.

Quite apart from the codes, journalists should be aware of criminal law provisions that affect the interviewing of criminals on the run. A prison escapee must not be given any assistance designed to hinder his recapture,[90] while a person known to be guilty of an "arrestable" (*i.e.* moderately serious) offence must not have his arrest or prosecution impeded.[91] Except in the case of persons believed to be involved in

---

[89] *R. v. Calder & Boyars* [1969] 1 Q.B. 151.
[90] Criminal Justice Act 1961, s. 22.
[91] Criminal Law Act 1967, s. 4(1).

terrorism,[92] there is no positive duty to provide information or assistance to the police, but any payment of money, provision of a "safe house" or assistance with travel outside the jurisdiction may amount to an offence. It is alo an offence to use a wireless receiver to intercept police messages, or to publish information about messages intercepted without authorisation.[93]

Violence

The most intractable problem in television scheduling is the possible impact on children of realistic violence. Although research is inconclusive, there is some evidence that brutality associated with screen heroes may encourage youthful emulation, and that constant exposure to television violence may weaken moral inhibitions against resorting to force as a means of problem solution.[94] The codes outlaw "gratuitous" violence and close-up details of assaults and murders, and discourage the depiction of torture techniques capable of easy imitation. They accept the desirability of avoiding scenes that might cause viewers unnecessary anxiety or disturbance, a prospect thought more likely if violence occurs in realistic contemporary settings than in historical contexts or stylised settings. Concern about the largely uncontrolled and unpredictable effects of television violence is understandable in relation to glamorised popular serials and movies, but it has less relevance to contemporary features and current affairs coverage, which may serve to arouse compassion for the injured and anger against the injurer. Nonetheless, broadcasters are warned about using CCTV coverage and are told to avoid close-ups of death and injuries and asked not to show hangings and executions until after the watershed. The BSC is concerned about the possibility that regular exposure to acts of violence (whether real or fictional) may "desensitise" the audience and make it apathetic towards cruelty and brutality and is worried about the "copycat" effect. Although neither proposition can be conclusively established, its code strives to minimise the dangers.

Reportage

There should be no concentration or "lingering" on the casualties of war or crime. Only in the rarest circumstances should broadcasting dwell on the moments of death. There should be no description of

---

[92] See the Terrorism Act 2000, s. 19.
[93] Wireless Telegraphy Act 1949, s. 5.
[94] Professor J. D. Halloran, "Research Findings on Broadcasting", Annan Report, (HMSO, 1977) Cmnd. 6753, App. F. See also *Violence and the Media*, BBC Publications, 1988.

methods of suicide especially if there is a novel technique which could
be copy-catted. Even historic footage of death or disaster must be used
with caution.

Drama

The question is always whether the violence is "legitimate" or "gratuitous". Context is crucial, and the audience's ability to appreciate the
conditions within which the drama is being played out is a key factor.
There is more anxiety about violence depicted in the home and other
familiar situations than violence in Rwanda or the Wild West or in
conventional spy thrillers or car-chase films ("less realistic, therefore
less disturbing"). In drama produced for children, violence must not be
initiated by heroes, nor should villains go unpunished.

Warnings

All codes require clear warnings, prior to the screening of violent programmes, that viewers may find some scenes disturbing. The ITC sensibly rejects the "sanitisation" approach adopted by the BBFC, pointing
out that it may be just as dangerous to conceal or minimise the consequences of violent behavior as to show them in gruesome detail. It
warns against depiction in "family viewing" time of dangerous behaviour easily imitated by children, while ingenious or unfamiliar methods
of inflicting pain or injury, "which are capable of easy imitation",
should not be included in dramatic works.

Drink and drugs

Programmes must not encourage smoking—*e.g.* by associating it with
sophistication, and drinking must not be portrayed glamorously, and
nothing should be done to promote the taking of drugs and solvents.
All health advice, the ITC warns, must be professional: astrologers,
palmists and tarot cards must not be consulted.

Privacy

The media must take particular care not to take advantage of people at
a time when they are in deep shock, *e.g.* in the aftermath of a disaster
or at funeral services. The BSC's generalised remarks on the subject of
privacy are not as helpful as the ITC's Programme Code, which deals
with common problems confronting broadcasters. The ITC rules may
be summarised as follows:

● Invasion of privacy must always have a public-interest justification—for example, the exposure of crime, protection of public health and safety, or exposure of hypocrisy and incompetence in public office.

- Particular care must be taken against intruding upon situations of bereavement and personal distress. Sensationalism must be avoided, so too must "insensitive" questions.

- When recording the words spoken or action taken by individuals in public places, these must be sufficiently in the public domain to justify their being communicated to a radio or television audience without express permission. This applies in particular to use of CCTV footage.

- Specific consent should generally be sought for filming in hospitals, factories, schools and other "closed" institutions. Inmates whose appearance is not "incidental" should also be asked to give consent.

- When by reason of handicap or infirmity a person is not in a position either to give or to withhold agreement, permission to use the material should be sought from the next of kin or from the person responsible for the individual's care.

- Interviews or conservations conducted by telephone should not normally be recorded for inclusion in a programme unless the interviewer has identified himself and the general purpose of the programme, and the interviewee has consented. The "rare exception" may be approved by the licensee's senior management if it involves the investigation of criminal or disreputable behaviour.

- The use of hidden cameras and microphones to record individuals secretly is acceptable only where such evidence is essential to establish the credibility and authority of the story, and where the story itself is clearly of public interest.

- Any interviewing of children requires care. Children should not be interrogated to elicit views on private family matters. Sexual offences against children must not be reported (even if the law permits) so as to identify a living victim under 16.

"Due accuracy and impartiality"

Section 6 of the 1990 Broadcasting Act requires the ITC to ensure that news is presented with "due accuracy and impartiality" and that "due impartiality is preserved" on the part of the programme providers "as respects matters of political or industrial controversy or relating to current public policy". It was this provision that sparked the most serious attacks on broadcasters during the passage of the legislation. Many Tory peers and M.P.s were convinced that the statutory duty was regularly breached by anti-Government elements in broadcasting organisations, and had to be strengthened by statutory provision for immediate rights of reply, discussion programmes and counterbalancing documentaries transmitted within a short time of any "partial" programme, and by giving the BSC the power to condemn any lapse from strict objectivity. During the passage of the legislation the Government strengthened the due impartiality duty by requiring the ITC to promulgate and enforce a code on the subject, although it did not specify the rules that this code should contain. The ITC Programme Code contains special provisions for achieving due impartiality. These provisions are enforced, like the rest of the Code, by a contractual commitment made by licensees to abide by them, on pain of suffering a range of sanctions that the ITC is empowered to impose.

The term "due" is significant in the phrase "due impartiality": "it should be interpreted as meaning adequate or appropriate to the nature of the subject and the type of programme . . . it does not mean that "balance" is required in any simple mathematical sense or that equal time must be given to each opposing point of view, nor does it require absolute neutrality on every issue".[95] This permits one-sided programmes if the side taken is generally acceptable. Thus the ITC will not be required to secure impartiality on matters such as drug-trafficking, cruelty, racial intolerance or other subjects on which "right-thinking people" are largely unanimous. The BBC, too, claims that there can be no duty to balance the claims of "basic moral values", defined by Sir Hugh Greene as "truthfulness, justice, freedom, compassion and tolerance". As the Home Office minister explained during the debates over the due impartiality provision in the Bill:

> "Due impartiality means that there may be higher considerations which need occasionally to override the requirement of absolute impartiality. Broadcasters should not expect to be impartial between truth and untruth, justice and injustice, compassion and cruelty, tolerance and intolerance, or even right and wrong. How can one be impartial on such matters? Broadcasters should not be obliged to be morally neutral as well as politically neutral."[96]

This approach is emphasised by the injunction in section 6(6) that the ITC rules "shall, in particular, indicate that due impartiality does not require absolute neutrality on every issue or detachment from funda-

---

[95] ITC Programme Code, s. 3.2(1).
[96] *Hansard* (House of Lords) July 1, 1990, col.366.

mental democratic principles". One of the most fundamental democratic principles is freedom of expression, and the ITC code emphasises that "licensees may make programmes about any issues they choose", subject only to the obligation of fairness and respect for the truth.

The due impartiality duty is subject to the important caveat that "in applying the subsection . . . a series of programmes may be considered as a whole".[97] The ITC Code defines a "series" very broadly, as more than one programme clearly linked to others that share the same title or deal with the same issues. The Code introduces the concept of "impartiality over time", whereby a licensee may be able to demonstrate that opposing views have been sufficiently aired in the course of frequent attention to a controversial issue. The Act (section 6 (1)(c)) requires due impartiality on "matters of political or industrial controversy or relating to current policy", although the rules of the code need provide only for impartiality on "major matters" of controversy on current policy (section 6(5)(a)). This is an important qualification to an otherwise general duty: the code does not bite on every controversial issue, but is directed to "political or industrial issues of national importance, such as a nationwide strike or significant legislation currently passing through Parliament."[98]

"Personal view" programmes

An important exception to the due impartiality requirement is the "personal view" programme, which must be clearly labelled as expressing the personal opinion of its presenter. These may take the form of a series, in which a broad range of personal views and perspectives are expressed (not necessarily on the same subject) or by balancing a particular personal view programme with a right-to-reply programme or a studio discussion. This permits committed, partial and provocative views to be aired, although the ITC insists that licensees ensure that statements of fact are accurate and that opinions expressed, however exaggerated, do not rest upon false evidence.

The ITC code makes special reference to the attainment of "due impartiality" in the following contexts.

Drama and drama documentary

The measure of impartiality "due" from plays and films that deal with matters of political and industrial controversy is not the same as must

---

[97] Broadcasting Act 1990, s. 6(2). The code is drawn up in accordance with s. 6(3) and published under s. 6(7). The references in this book are to the revised code published in autumn 1998.
[98] ITC Programme Code, s. 3(4).

be expected from current affairs programmes. "Drama documentaries", however, are more problematic, and any reconstruction of actual and recent events "must not be allowed to distort the known facts". The evidence upon which dramatic reconstructions are based "should be tested with the same rigour required of a factual programme". Where dramas and documentaries point to a conclusion about current controversies, due impartiality should be secured by providing an opportunity for the airing of conflicting views, *e.g.* in a subsequent studio discussion programme.

Factual programmes

Due impartiality is secured by "the fair representation of the main differing views on the matter". This does not mean that balance is required in a simple mathematical sense, or by giving equal time to each conflicting view, but rather that the programme taken as a whole should avoid giving a biased treatment to any one point of view.

Interviews

Where interviews are conducted on issues that fall within the due impartiality provisions, they must not be edited to distort or misrepresent the known views of the interviewee. The interviewee must not be taken by surprise in relation to the format of the programme or the use of his or her contribution. The Code provides little assistance in the common situation where spokespersons for one side of an issue decline to accept an invitation to debate it. The ITC says that this "need not prevent the programme from going ahead", although often it does because "an impartial account of the subject under discussion" must still be given. Discussion of controversial issues is frequently handicapped—especially on BBC programmes—when the progenitor of the controversy (often a Government minister) refuses an invitation to appear. Both the ITC Code and the BBC guidelines dodge this issue, and the guidelines even insist on "fairness to the absentee . . . it is rarely acceptable to exclude the missing view altogether"[99]—failing to understand that it is much less acceptable to cancel a debate because one side is too cowardly to turn up.

The rigorous "due prominence" rules were imposed by the Thatcher Government, determined to harass broadcasters it perceived as politically hostile because of "unsupportive" coverage of the miners' strike, the bombing of Libya and "Death on the Rock". The mentality of politicians in the pre-internet 1980s was to assume that news coverage by the four terrestrial television channels would continue to dominate the

---

[99] Chap. 3, section 3 ("Refusals to take part").

way in which public opinion was shaped. Most M.P.s who contributed to the Broadcasting Act debate had no idea that a decade hence, most households would have a 60 channel choice, and that opinion-formers would log on rather than switch on. Television's contribution to public affairs since the 1990 Act has been lacklustre in terms of exposure journalism and agenda-setting (other than by visualisation of disasters, such as wars, rail crashes and the foot and mouth epidemic). Its executives are cautious and conventional: they have done nothing to lobby for television coverage of courts or inquiries, they have not insisted on protecting viewers from that mind-numbing propaganda, the "party political broadcast", and they have continually displayed the most abject obeisance to the military. Both the BBC and the ITC collaborate in the discredited "DA Notice" system—the BBC by appointing a senior official to the Defence, Press and Broadcasting Advisory Committee and the ITC by requiring every licensee to appoint a liaison officer with that dubious body.[1] The BBC Producers' Guidelines go so far as to invest DA notices with bogus importance: although a notice has no legal force, "a broadcast which ignores it might weaken our defence if we were prosecuted".[2] (This is nonsense: since a DA notice is merely opinion, it is inadmissible in evidence for the prosecution). The question needs to be asked whether the "due impartiality" duties continue to be relevant and sensible for mainstream television, and whether in fact they restrain this medium from serving the public interest by covering controversial issues in the way open to press broadcasting and the World Wide Web. The ITC accepts that the "due impartiality" rules are inappropriate for local radio and television services: it has opted[3] to relax them by a requirement that "undue prominence" must not be given to one side or participant in political or industrial controversies. This is a sensible and fair test, which allows the media much more freedom to cover controversies without descending into propaganda: it should replace the outdated "due impartiality" requirement across the board.

ENFORCING THE CODES

The ITC

Both the BBC and the licensed companies supervised by the ITC and the Radio Authority will be subject to rulings by the BSC. The ITC and

---

[1] ITC Code, s. 6(3).
[2] BBC Producers Guidelines, Chap. 15, para. 8.2. The Guidelines may be found on the BBC website: www.bbc.co.uk.
[3] Pursuant to its powers under s. 47(4) of the Broadcasting Act.

the Radio Authority are, in addition, expected to monitor and enforce compliance with their own codes. It is the responsibility of the licensed companies to decide whether to transmit programmes that may be accused of breaching code provisions. Although the ITC is prepared to give general guidelines on the interpretation of its code, and will monitor the programmes by licensees, it does not preview programmes or approve specific script proposals.[4] The code is enforced by a set of potential sanctions, ranging from a rebuke to a revocation of the licence in the case of a persistent offender. The financial penalties include a power to fine a licensee a maximum of 3 per cent of its advertising revenue for a first offence and 5 per cent of advertising revenue for further offences—a formula which allows the ITC to impose penalties of millions of pounds. Television companies prefer to err on the safe side rather than to put their profits at risk of sanctions of this magnitude.

ITC discipline has been rare but severe. Its first financial penalty (on Granada, in 1994) was £500,000; in 1998 it punished Central Television, for the crime of deceiving its viewers, by imposing the whopping fine of £2 million. Interestingly, Central did not seek judicial review of this decision, which concerned a public affairs programme called *The Connection* which pretended to have infiltrated and exposed a gang bringing large amounts of drugs into the United Kingdom via a new route. Most of the evidence was faked, and the ITC explained that "the size of the financial penalty reflects the scale of the programme's ambition and the consequent degree of deception of viewers". This was hardly fair on Central, other than as a warning to investigate more carefully the bona fides of independent programme makers bearing sensational stories. The ITC has no power to get at independent producers other than through punishing the licensees who have engaged them. In 1999 the ITC deployed for the first time its powers under section 45A and revoked a licence—for the satellite channel Med TV, broadcast across Europe predominantly to and for Kurds. It had been warned and fined on previous occasions for lapses in "due impartiality" (*i.e.* for slanting its news coverage against Turkey) but the arrest and trial of PKK leader Ocelan caused the channel to throw "due impartiality" to the winds. And why not, if freedom of expression includes the right to broadcast in a cause which has some support in international law (*i.e.* the right of Kurds to self determination)? This liberal position (taken by other European countries, to which Med TV relocated) can only be resisted on the basis that any British broadcasting licence, even for a service provided to ethnic minorities in other countries, must nonetheless carry the ITC stamp of "due impartiality". Since this is the stance

---

[4] See the Broadcasting Act 1990, s. 11(2). The licensee must retain a recording of every one of its programmes for up to three months and produce it at the ITC's request.

of the Broadcasting Act, the ITC was justified (Med TV did not waste money on judicial review). However, the decision had disquieting features. It came after constant pressure from the Turkish Government, but there were virtually no complaints from the British public. The ITC condemned its coverage of PKK rallies on political grounds ("the PKK is engaged in a guerrilla war with the Turkish authorities") so the licence revocation operated as political censorship, shutting up dissidents. But in truth Med TV was a victim not of the ITC but of the "due impartiality" rule: whether the decision is acceptable depends on whether the rule itself is acceptable (or whether its extension to such satellite licences is appropriate).

The BBC

The BBC is established by Royal Charter, last renewed (for 10 years) in 1996, pursuant to an agreement with the Government (represented by the Secretary of State for Culture, Media and Sport). This agreement recites in clause 2.1 that:

> "The Corporation shall be independent in all matters concerning the content of its programmes and the times at which they are broadcast or transmitted and in the management of its affairs".

That said, the Corporation is subject to indirect pressures which ensure a degree of deference to the Crown, the framework of government and the party politicians who occupy the high offices of State. The Chairman, Vice Chairman and board of BBC Governors are all appointed by the Government of the day, and the Corporation is dependent on the Government for fixing the licence fee that provides its funding. The power of patronage has an editorial influence, evidenced through the programmes that the BBC never makes (exposure of political corruption; challenges to official secrecy; attacks on British foreign policy) rather than those it does. The licensed bumptiousness practised by BBC interviewers on *Today* and *Newsnight* presents a public face of independence, at least towards individual Government ministers, but towards British institutions the BBC is invariably uncritical. Towards the monarchy, it is obsequious.

The comfortable, conservative ethos in which BBC policy is made was long thought to be unchallengeable through the courts. The BBC, creature of Royal Charter, was above the law, its undertakings the promises of gentlemen, unlike the statutory duties imposed in identical language on the players of commercial television by the Broadcasting Act.[5] However, this immunity is no longer sustainable. The BBC performs

---

[5] See *Lynch v. BBC* [1983] N.I. 193.

public functions of democratic importance, and the fact that its power derives from the Royal Prerogative does not exclude its discretionary decisions from judicial review.[6] The courts are coming to recognise a variety of areas in which BBC decisions can be reviewed,[7] especially if they have constitutional significance, such as the allocation of party political broadcasts in the run up to the elections. However, the significance of the courts as a means of challenging the broadcasting/political establishment is limited both by the absence of a constitution and the deference that judges are prone to show to Government-appointed "experts". This was illustrated in 1997 by the rejection of the Referendum Party challenge to the broadcasters' bias towards the main parties in allocation of party political broadcasts. These valuable propaganda slots were allocated mainly on the basis of past electoral support, something that a new party could not, by definition, show. The Referendum Party, fielding candidates in almost all constituencies, argued that the allocation principle was discriminatory and undemocratic but the judges said that "fairness" in this context was a matter for the broadcasters, whose decision could not be disturbed unless irrational or made without considering the Referendum Party's complaints.[8] American and Canadian courts have taken a more principled approach on similar issues, and the Human Rights Act now provides a direct method of challenging the decisions of the BBC as a "public body": the judges may (or may not) superimpose objective standards of fairness. In matters of taste and decency, however, judicial review will be on strict "*Wednesbury* reasonableness" lines, and courts will rarely if ever interfere with BBC judgments. In 1997, a BBC decision to obscure images of an aborted foetus in a Pro-Life Alliance Party political broadcast was held to be within its "margin of discretionary judgment".[9]

There is a curious anomaly in the fact that the BBC is now a "public body" for the purposes of the Human Rights Act (HRA). This means that it may be sued by "victims" of any decision to censor programmes or punish employees for speaking out, but may not be able itself to rely on Article 10 since a public body (as an arm of the State) cannot itself be a "victim": Article 34 permits only non-government bodies to complain to Strasbourg, and the HRA incorporated the Article 34 test for victimhood. It would be extraordinary and wrong to deny Article 10 remedies to the BBC (and to Channel 4) because they are "public

---

[6] Any more than the decisions of universities made under the perogative: *Thomas v. University of Bradford* [1987] A.C. 795; *R. v. TakeOver Panel, ex p. Datafin* [1987] 1 Q.B. 815, especially 849 D–E.

[7] *R. v. BCC, ex p. Owen* [1985] 1 O.B. 1153, at 1172H *per* May J; *R. v. BBC, ex p. McAliskey* [1994] C.O.D. 498; *Houston v. BBC* [1995] S.C. 433.

[8] *R. v. BBC and ITC, ex p. Referendum Party* [1997] E.M.L.R. 605.

[9] *R. v. BBC, ex p. the Pro-Life Alliance Party*, March 24, 1997, Dyson J.

authorities"—they are in fact at arms length from government in terms of their programme making powers. The question has been noted, but not resolved.[10]

The BBC has undertaken to comply in general terms with the statutory duties placed upon independent television. This undertaking is given a prominent status by being annexed to the Corporation's licence agreement and it is possible to argue that the undertaking is an "implied term" of the licence, so that the High Court may supervise the BBC's compliance. The BBC is in any event a "public body" for the purposes of the 1998 Human Rights Act, and may thus be sued by persons claiming it has infringed rights to life or privacy, or indeed (by acts of internal censorship) the viewers' and listeners' rights to free speech. Normal BBC censorship operates by a process of "reference up" the Corporation hierarchy. Any producer who foresees possible offence must alert middle management, which must pass borderline cases to departmental heads, who may in turn consult the Managing Director or even the Director-General. The classic definition of "reference up" still holds good:

> "The elimination or alteration of material considered unsuitable for public broadcasting is an integral part of the whole system of editorial control . . . reference is obligatory in matters of serious dispute or matters of doubt, and the wrath of the corporation in its varied manifestations is particularly reserved for those who fail 'to refer' ".[11]

Programme rules

The rules for journalists working in the BBC are set out in the Producers Guidelines, a very detailed code which emphasises the importance of "referring up" difficult ethical or legal questions. These Guidelines mirror the provisions in the ITC Code although they give many more examples and nuances: it is the most comprehensive and "politically correct" of all the codes, and the most cautious—there is a danger that it will become the "counsel of perfection" when journalistic standards are considered in the courts. It should therefore be seen for what it is: a carefully crafted defence of public service broadcasting forged against those twin terrors, Mrs Whitehouse and Mrs Thatcher, by reference to lofty Reithian values (generally denoted by the use of the Royal "we").

[10] See *BBC v. U.K.*, App. No. 25798/94, January 18, 1996; *BBC Scotland v. U.K.*, App. No. 34324/96, (1997) 25 E.H.R.R. CD 179.
[11] "Control over the Subject-Matter of Programmes on BBC Television": Appendix 2 to *Report of Joint Committee on Censorship of the Theatre*, H.C. 255 (1967).

There are plenty of banal and pompous generalities, of the kind "BBC journalists will not go on what are known as fishing expeditions" (but why not—in case they land a big fish?) although some of the detail in the small print is sensible and streetwise.

Government controls

In extreme circumstances the Government does have certain direct legal powers over radio and television. In the case of the BBC, these are contained in the Licence Agreement that forms part of the Corporation's charter. Section 19 enables the Home Secretary, when in his opinion there is an emergency and it is "expedient" so to act, to send troops in to "take possession of the BBC in the name and on behalf of Her Majesty". This clause was framed during the General Strike, when Winston Churchill and other members of the Government wanted to commandeer the Corporation. It has never been used for that purpose, although Sir Anthony Eden contemplated invoking it for Government propaganda during the Suez crisis, and during the Falklands recapture it provided the legal basis for the Government's use of BBC transmitters on Ascension Island to beam propaganda broadcasts at Argentina.

A more dangerous power is contained in section 13(4) of the Licence Agreement, which gives the Home Secretary the right to prohibit the BBC from transmitting any item or programme, at any time. The power is not limited, like section 19, to periods of emergency. The only safeguard against political censorship is that the BBC "may" (not "must") tell the public that it has received a section 13(4) order from the Home Secretary. This safeguard was invoked in 1972 by the Director-General, Lord Hill, when the Home Secretary Reginald Maudling threatened a section 13(4) order to stop transmission of a debate about Government actions in Ulster. Lord Hill called his bluff by threatening to make public the reason why the programme could not be shown. A less courageous Director-General could simply cancel the programme without revealing the existence of a Government order. A parallel power in section 10(3) of the 1990 Broadcasting Act entitles the Home Secretary to order ITC licensees to "refrain from broadcasting any matter or classes of matter" on commercial television. The exercise of these powers cannot be successfully challenged in the courts unless it can be shown that the Home Secretary has acted unreasonably or perversely.

These powers were invoked in 1988 for the purpose of direct political censorship when the BBC and the IBA (the predecessor of the ITC) were ordered not to transmit any interviews with representatives of Sinn Fein, the Ulster Defence Association, the IRA or certain other extremist groups, or to broadcast any statement that incited support for such groups. The ban was a plain infringement on the right to receive and impart information: it prevented representatives of lawful political organisations (Sinn Fein had an M.P. as well as dozens of local councillors) from stating their case on matters that had no connection with terrorism, and it denied to the public the opportunity to hear those who support violent action being questioned and exposed. The Thatcher Government believed that terrorists survived by "the oxygen of publicity", but television confrontations generally demonstrate the moral unattractiveness of those who believe that the end justifies the means. The ban prevented the re-screening of history programmes with interviews with IRA veterans. The BBC and the IBA meekly complied with the ban, which the House of Lords refused to strike down when it was challenged by John Pilger and other broadcasters.[12]

The Government has reserved to itself the more benign power of listing events of national interest that must not be monopolised by "pay-as-you-view" channels.[13] There is no bar on pay-as-you-view screenings that take place at least 48 hours after the event. Although sporting events such as the Olympic Games, cricket test matches played in England, the Wimbledon finals and the Grand National are the primary candidates for protection, "national interest" is defined to include English, Scottish, Welsh and Northern Irish interests, and the list is not confined to major sporting fixtures: any attempts to purchase exclusive rights to King Charles's coronation would certainly provoke Government intervention.

The Government has also reserved a specific power to order any broadcasting body to "carry out any function" required to enable the United Kingdom to live up to its international obligations.[14] This power is necessary to implement directives emanating from Europe, but it could be interpreted more widely to direct broadcasters to transmit announcements regarded by Government as necessary to comply with UN and NATO commitments, or international treaties.

ITC licences

The ITC has a general duty to ensure that a wide range of television programme services is available throughout the United Kingdom, and "to ensure fair and effective competition in the provision of such services".[115] To this end, it must allocate licences for Channel 3 (the 16 ITV stations) and Channel 5 (local television stations) to the highest

---

[12] *R. v. Secretary of State for the Home Department, ex p. Brind* [1991] 1 A.C. 696. The European Commission regarded the consequent complaint as inadmissible: *Brind v. U.K.* (1994) 18 E.H.R.R. CD 76.
[13] See Broadcasting Act 1996, sections. 98–104. (See the "Stop Press" section for further details).
[14] Broadcasting Act 1990, s. 188.
[15] *ibid.*, s. 2(2).

cash bidder, subject to an exception that permits it to award a licence to a lower-bidding applicant whose proposed quality of service is exceptionally high, or at least substantially higher than the service proposed by the applicant who has put in the highest bid.[16] Every successful applicant must meet a "quality threshold", judged by a proposed programme schedule that gives sufficient time to high quality national and international news and current affiars, and other high quality feature programmes. The programme schedule must offer an appeal to "a wide variety of tastes and interests", include a sufficient number of religious and children's programmes, and ensure that at least 25 per cent of its programmes are made by independent producers and that a "proper proportion" is of European origin.[17]

The IBA awarded franchises in darkest secrecy, so that public scrutiny and feedback on its performance was minimal. Section 15(6) of the 1990 Broadcasting Act marks an important gain for journalists: it requires the ITC to publish, as soon as reasonably practicable after the closing date for applications, details of the bidders and their proposals and "such other information connected with the application as the Commission considers appropriate". It must also issue a notice inviting public comment on the published applications. The only situation in which the Government may directly influence a licence award occurs if the ITC has grounds for suspecting that an applicant's funds may derive from a source that raises public interest concerns, in which case it must refer this application to the Home Secretary, who may veto it if the source of funds "is such that it would not be in the public interest for the licence to be so awarded".[18] If the funds were coming from criminal sources or from unfriendly foreign countries, or from persons who would otherwise be disqualified or judged unfit to hold a licence, the Home Secretary would presumably be justified in exercising this veto.

Licences are to be awarded for a period of 10 years, and may be revoked if there is a change of ownership of the applicant that has not met with the prior approval of the ITC.[19] The ITC shall refuse to give its approval in these circumstances if the suggested new owner would be prejudicial to the programme schedule submitted by the original applicant, or if it considers the change "inappropriate". The ITC must not, however, revoke the licence without giving the holder a reasonable opportunity to make representations as to why the change should be permitted. In their consideration of licence applications, and in dealings with licences, the ITC and the Radio Authority are subject to judicial

---

[16] Broadcasting Act 1990, s. 17(3)and (4).
[17] *ibid.*, s. 16.
[18] *ibid.*, s. 17(5) and (6).
[19] *ibid.*, s. 20(1).

review if they act unfairly. The courts will not superimpose a judicial view of the merits of a decision, but will supervise the procedural steps and ensure that the ITC applies a correct interpretation of the Act.

Licence holders have the ITC's statutory duties incorporated as terms of their contract. Channel 3 licences must in addition contain undertakings to maintain high-quality news and current affairs programmes at peak times, ensure that "sufficient" time is dedicated to religious and children's programmes, maintain a proper proportion of programmes originating from Europe (*i.e.* at least 50 per cent, including from the United Kingdom, under the Convention on Transfrontier Television) and to fill at least 25 per cent of their air-time with the work of independent producers. Some of these conditions are not applicable to Channel 5 licences, although these at least require high-quality news services at peak periods. Channel 4 is licensed as a separate corporation, with the duty to maintain a "distinctive character" by encouraging innovation and experiment and appealing to tastes and interests not catered for by Channel 3. It is, most importantly, specifically enjoined to provide the "public service" trifecta of "information, education and entertainment".[20] There are further provisions for licensing of cable delivery services, satellite television, local delivery services and teletext, and the Broadcasting Act of 1996 makes extensive provision for digital and interactive services and multiplex licences. The general principles of ITC licensing apply, although the details and the differences are beyond the scope of this book.

"Fit and proper person"

Section 3(3) of the 1990 Act provides that the ITC "shall not grant a licence to any person unless they are satisfied that he is a fit and proper person to hold it", and enjoins it to revoke the licence if the holder ceases to merit this description. This statutory wording suggests that the ITC must make a judgment not on the licensee's character as such, but on his fitness to hold a licence: it follows that an old criminal conviction may be overlooked, and that stewardship and quality achieved in other media enterprises should be taken into account.

An ITC determination that an applicant or existing holder is not a fit and proper person is subject to judicial review, and the English courts would be likely to adopt the approach to this question taken by the High Court of Australia in 1990 in the case of *The Australian Broadcasting Tribunal v. Alan Bond*. That tribunal, like the ITC, is charged to revoke a licence if no longer satisfied that a particular person is fit and proper to hold it. Bond effectively controlled the company that held the licence for a television network, and had demonstrated both unfitness and

---

[20] Broadcasting Act 1990, s. 25.

impropriety by threatening a business opponent with unfavourable coverage on one of his network's current-affairs programmes; by paying a bribe, dressed up as an extravagant settlement for a libel action brought against his television company by the corrupt premier of Queensland; and by failing to make full and frank disclosure of the circumstances of the libel payment to the tribunal at an earlier inquiry. The High Court held that these matters were capable of supporting the tribunal's decision to revoke the licence, and that although the actual licence holder was a company (which was not corporately involved in the improper behaviour), the tribunal was justified in "lifting the corporate veil" and inputing unfitness as a result of the character and conduct of a person closely associated with it. Chief Justice Mason remarked:

> "Commercial broadcasting is a very important medium in the communication of information and ideas. Moreover, a commercial broadcasting licence is a valuable privilege which confers on the licensee the capacity to influence public opinion and public values. For this reason, if for no other, a licensee has a responsibility to exercise the power conferred by the licence with a due regard to proper standards of conduct and a responsibility not to abuse the privilege which it enjoys. Possession of a licence or the exercise of the privilege which it confers has been described as 'in the nature of a public trust for the benefit of all members of our society . . .'. A licensee which lacks a proper appreciation of these responsibilities or does not discharge them is not, or may be adjudged not to be, a fit and proper person."[21]

The Court accepted that the test involved an assessment of the conduct, character (as an indication of future conduct) and reputation (as an indication of public perception as to future conduct) of the applicant or licensee. The tribunal was entitled to find a licensee unfit if satisfied that the community could not have confidence that he would not abuse the potential for influence provided by a broadcasting licence. Bond's exploitation of his company's licence for political dealings designed to promote his other business interests "did not exhibit an appreciation of the proper relationship between those with control of media interests and governments". Although the same comment may be made of other "larger than life" media moguls like Rupert Murdoch or the late Robert Maxwell, a court will require more than evidence of interventionist tendencies to uphold an "unfitness" finding against a would-be proprietor. Although the ITC has not as yet made such a finding, it has warned that applicants who collude to defeat the objects of the "cash bid"

---

[21] (1990) 64 A.L.J.R. 462, at 474.

requirement will be deemed "unfit".[22] In 1998 the Radio Authority had no difficulty in ruling that Owen Oyston was an improper person to hold a radio licence after his conviction and imprisonment for rape, but they minimised his discomfort by permitting him to transfer his majority holdings in four radio stations to what it described as "independent" trusts.[23]

Penalties

The ITC is given a range of statutory powers to enforce licence conditions.[24] If satisfied that a breach has occurred, it may order the licence holder to:

● broadcast a correction or apology;

● refrain from re-broadcasting an offending programme;

● pay a fine up to a maximum amount calculated by reference to advertsing revenue, the ceiling being raised in the case of a second offence;

● accept a reduction of the 10-year licence period by up to two years; or

● rectify a failure within a specified time, or else to suffer revocation of the licence.

The last three penalties are draconian: the maximum level of the financial penalties for most licence holders will be several million pounds (as Central discovered when fined £2 million over *The Connection*) as would the cost of losing one or two years of licensed operation (at least, if the licence were not renewed). The safeguard, in every case, is merely that the licence holder must be given "a reasonable opportunity to make representations" before notice of the punishment is served. This would be unfair if the licence holder's representations were to be directed to a decision the ITC has already taken, rather than to the question of whether it ought to take such a decision in the first place.

The ITC's power to revoke a Channel 3 or 5 licence is subject to more stringent procedural safeguards. It must first permit the licensee to make representations about the matters that may end its broadcasts, and then (if dissatisfied) serve a notice indicating the respect in which

---

[22] ITC Annual Report 1995, p. 22.
[23] *Radio Authority Agrees to Transfer of Control of Licenses Held by Owen Oyston*, Press Release 9, April 1998.
[24] Broadcasting Act 1990, ss. 40–42.

the licensee is breaking the licence agreement or failing to comply with
an ITC directive, and specifying a time period within which the licensee
must remedy its behaviour, and any specific steps it must take to do so.
If the licensee fails to meet these requirements, the ITC may revoke the
licence if satisfied that it is in the public interest to do so. It may revoke
a licence without going through these procedures (other than to give an
opportunity for an explanation) if satisfied that the licensee provided
materially false information in its application or deliberately misled the
ITC in the course of the application process. It must conform, overall,
with Article 6 of the Convention by acting as an independent and impartial tribunal.

The ITC must correlate its corrective and punitive powers with the
much less severe powers of the BSC to oblige licence holders to publish
adverse adjudications. The licence holder is in a position of double
jeopardy, in that a BSC decision that it has breached a canon of good
taste will also amount to a finding that it has breached a condition of
its licence, and render it liable to an ITC penalty—unless the ITC inter-
prets the canon differently to the BSC. In practice, the ITC supports the
BSC code but regards the publication of its adverse adjudications as a
sufficient penalty for it to refrain from exercising its own punitive
powers. The ITC's exercise of its punishment powers will be subject to
judicial review on grounds that it has acted irrationally or disproportion-
ately or has not properly appreciated the evidence, and the Court would
certainly intervene if it relied on a BSC adjudication as a warrant for a
fine or revocation without exercising its independent judgment on the
offence.

Editorialising

The BBC licence and its prescribing memoranda requires the Corporation "to refrain from expressing its own opinion on current affairs or
matters of public policy". The BBC values its reputation for impartiality
and insists that all programme intentions be clearly labelled. Specialist
correspondents may indulge in personal "explanations and assessments", and although journalists on current affairs programmes must
normally observe strict objectivity, the BBC recognises that "a journalist or broadcaster can rise to a stature where he not only has the right
but is expected to express judgment of his own".

The ITC has a duty to ensure that its licensees do not exploit their
privilege to broadcast their own views on politically controversial matters, other than on questions relating directly to broadcasting policy.
This means that if directors or executives of a licence holder do hold
forth on contentious subjects, it must be made clear that they are
speaking in a personal capacity. The ban on editorialising is limited to
"matters of political or industrial controversy or (which) relate to cur-

rent public policy"—which is not wide enough to cover the case of a licensee who manipulates his programmes so as to promote his non-broadcast business interests. Behaviour of this kind should be regarded by the ITC as evidence that he is not a "fit and proper person" to hold a licence.

Religion

An important change effected by the 1990 Broadcasting Act is to provide much greater freedom of evangelical broadcasting. There is no bar to religious groups obtaining licences to run cable or satellite channels or local radio stations, although the ITC will doubtless disqualify cults or religious extremists if it considers them "inappropriate". Having obtained a licence, religious groups will be permitted to editorialise by propagating their faith, so long as they do not exploit the susceptibilities of the audience or abuse the religious beliefs of others. Advertising by religious organisations is now permitted on mainstream channels, subject to a strict code, which excludes advertisements that play on fear, exploit categories of vulnerable viewers (such as the elderly or bereaved) or proselytize doctrine or denigrate other faiths or philosophies of life. No advertisement may include an appeal for funds (although special dispensation may be given to religious charities that assist humane causes). The object is to avoid the hell-fire preaching, mass emotional appeal and dubious fund-raising motives that characterise American tele-evangelism.

In respect to mainstream television the ITC has a statutory duty to secure that licensees display "due responsibility" by ensuring that religious programmes do not involve "improper exploitation" of audience susceptibilities or "abusive treatment" of other religions. Its Programme Code contains detailed rules for achieving due responsibility, requiring that programmes must clearly identify all religious bodies featured, and should generally reflect the worship and thought of orthodox (mainly, though not exclusively, Christian) religious traditions in the United Kingdom. Programmes must not be designed to recruit viewers into any particular faith, to prey on fears or make claims that living persons have "special powers or abilities".

Advertising

Fears of advertising excesses were responsible for the original prohibition on bad taste and offensiveness in commercial broadcasting. In 1987 the advent of AIDS made the IBA finally relent in its total ban on condom advertisements, although it rejected most that were submitted. Any trace of humour, any attempt to put information about condoms across in ways that might actually appeal to a youthful audience, was rejected as being "in poor taste". The ITC has proved more understanding, but is overseen by the BSC, whose remit to monitor "good taste and decency" applies both to programmes and to advertisements.

Section 8(2) of the 1990 Broadcasting Act sets out the three basic rules for advertising on commercial television:

- there must be no advertising by bodies whose objects are "wholly or mainly of a political nature" or are "directed towards any political end";

- there must be no "unreasonable discrimination" in acceptance of advertisements, either for or against a particular advertiser;

- programmes must not, without ITC approval, be sponsored by companies whose products or services cannot be advertised under the ITC code.

The prohibition on advertising of a "political" nature has caused some confusion. In the 1997 case about Amnesty International, the Court of Appeal accepted that section 92 imposed a restriction on freedom of communication and that consequently its ambiguous terms had to be narrowly construed. The ban on advertisements by bodies whose objects were "wholly or mainly" political should only apply to bodies whose objects are "primarily", *i.e.* more than 75 per cent, political. However, the court approved a broad definition of a "political" object, to include campaigns to change existing law or government policy (even foreign government policy) and even if the change was urged to conform with international human rights standards.[25] This result is, by free speech standards, absurd (Amnesty was for some time banned from advertising its campaign against unlawful torture in Iraq) and requires reconsideration under the interpretation provisions of the Human Rights Act. "Political" should be interpreted to mean "party political", or else (consistently with section 6 of the 1990 Act) to refer to issues of current political or industrial controversy in Britain rather than abroad.

The prohibition on "unreasonable discrimination" is valuable, and can be asserted against ITC attempts to ban advertising by newspapers catering for minorities. The ITC must specifically approve any sponsorship of a programme by the manufacturer of products that its code deems unacceptable for direct advertisement; these include all tobacco products, guns and pornography. The ITC additionally regards as unacceptable all advertisements for gaming and betting services, private

---

[25] *R. v. Radio Authority, ex p. Bull* [1998] Q.B. 294. The Court of Appeal judgment drew attention to inadequacies in the decision of the Radio Authority, which subsequently reversed its stance and allowed Amnesty to advertise. See below p. 835.

detective agencies and commercial services offering advice on personal or consumer problems (other than firms of solicitors).

Section 9 of the Act imposes a duty on the ITC to draw up a code relating to advertising standards, which it is empowered to enforce by giving directives to licensees in respect either of general classes of advertisements that should not be accepted or of particular unacceptable examples. Its directives also indicate the maximum amount of television time to be given to advertisements in each hourly period, and the spacing of such advertising breaks. Currently, the total amount of advertising on Channels 3 to 5 must not exceed an average of seven minutes per hour, and must not exceed an average of seven-and-a-half minutes in peak hours (7 a.m.–9 a.m.; 6 p.m.–11 p.m.). Both the ITC and the Radio Authority have promulgated detailed codes on advertising, sponsorship and "product placement", which are enforced by warnings and fines. (In 1994 Granada was fined £500,000 for repeated breaches of the sponsorship code on its breakfast programme.) The Authorities conduct investigations themselves, which may be triggered by public complaints or by their own monitoring. Comparatively few complaints are upheld, since television advertisements are previewed and pre-vetted for compliance with the ITC codes by the Broadcasting Advertising Clearing Centre (BACC). Nonetheless, it is still possible to overlook the peculiar sensitivities of the British public. A BACC approved advertisement for Levi jeans which poked fun at a hamster that died of treadmill boredom produced a wholly unanticipated deluge of complaints from hamster-loving households. The ITC ruled that it must never be screened again before the watershed.[26]

The BACC is funded by the broadcasters and employs 20 executives to preview and pre-vet scripts for all television advertisements. Its decisions usually err on the side of caution, and it has been condemned for censoring innovation and creativity in the medium. It certainly lacks a sense of humour: it cut a scene of a herd of cows because they were "too menacing" for a jokey milk commercial, and rejected a scene for a drink advertisement showing men running after a donkey "because of the sexual overtones"[27] (sic). A commercial for cough sweets showing a model trying to catch a cold as an excuse for buying them was deemed irresponsible because it "encouraged the public to get ill"—crediting the viewing public with a remarkably high level of cretinism. The BACC and the ITC must now take on board the ECHR decision in VGT Verein Gegen Tierfabriken v. Switzerland[28] which extended Article 10 protection to "political" advertisements, in that case by an animal rights group which showed cows and pigs being menaced rather than being

---

[26] ITC, Television Advertising Complaints Report, August 1998, p. 19.
[27] See Belinda Archer, "Drop the Sexy Donkey", Guardian G2, March 12, 2001.
[28] (2001) 10 B.H.R.C. 473.

menacing. Although the case turned partly on the fact that this was an "infovertisement" rather than an incitement to product purchase, the court made clear that it would be difficult to establish an Article 10 "pressing social need" to ban an advertisement on television which could be featured without ASA restraint in the press. The ASA displays give considerable latitude to humour, and the BACC should do likewise.

Under the Control of Misleading Advertisement Regulations (1988) the ITC has a duty to investigate complaints about misleading advertisements, and it will regard a factual claim as inaccurate (and hence a breach of its rule against misleading advertising) unless adequate evidence to support it can be furnished by the advertiser. In drafting and revising its codes and in issuing directives, the ITC must take account of the United Kingdom's international obligations, and its code incorporates most of the relevant provisions of the European Convention on Transfrontier Television.

The European Conventions

The international obligations that have become increasingly important for the British media stem from Europe, where broadcasting signals and satellite transmissions cannot distinguish between jumbled national borders. British law must accommodate legal instruments produced by the pan-European organisations—the broader Council of Europe (guarantor of the ECHR) and the economic and political Union of the European Community. Their respective instruments are: the 1989 European Convention on Transfrontier Television, adopted by the Committee of Ministers of the Council of Europe, and the E.C. Directive on Television without Frontiers (the Television Directive).

The Convention begins by endorsing the guarantee of freedom of expression in Article 10 of the European Convention on Human Rights as an "essential condition of a democratic society", and aims to "enhance Europe's heritage and develop audio-visual creation . . . through efforts to increase the production and circulation of high quality programmes". It applies to all broadcasting formats, whether cable, terrestrial transmitter or satellite, which can be received (directly or indirectly) in another country that is party to the Convention. The duties upon nations that are parties to the Convention include adherence to Article 10, and ensuring that its laws restrain broadcasters within its jurisdiction from transmitting pornography or incitements to violence or racial hatred, and that they afford a "right of reply". Parties must ensure that coverage of events of "high public interest" across Europe is not restricted by exclusive rights deals so as to deprive a large part of the public in another European country from watching them on television. Broadcasting organisations in each country must reserve at least

50 per cent of transmission time (excluding that taken up by news, sport and advertising) for programmes of European origin.

These Convention objectives are secured in Britain by appropriate provisions in the 1990 legislation. In relation to television advertising, the ITC reflects them in its code of practice and enforces them through its power to issue directives. Article 11 of the Convention requires all advertisements to be fair and honest and to have regard to the special susceptibilities of children. The amount of advertising shall not exceed 15 per cent of the daily transmission time, or take up more than 12 minutes in any one hour (Article 12). Article 14 causes great anguish to British advertisers and money-minded programme executives: it strikes a notable blow for artistic creativity by providing that advertisements may not be inserted so as to damage "the integrity and value of the programme". To this end, advertisements must be transmitted only during natural breaks in sports programmes; films and documentaries must be interrupted only once every 45 minutes, and other programmes must last at least 20 minutes before an advertising break; religious services must not be interrupted at all, and nor should news and current affairs and religious and children's programmes that last less than 30 minutes.

The Convention requires bans on tobacco products and on prescription medicines (Article 15). The rules relating to alcohol advertisements are particularly strict: drinking must not be associated with "physical performance" or driving or the resolution of personal conflicts. Abstinence or moderation must not be presented in a negative light.

The Convention is astute to prevent advertisers and sponsors from influencing, whether overtly or covertly, the content of programmes or their impact on viewers. Advertisements must be plainly distinguishable as such and there must be no "product placement" (the frequent device of being paid to use an advertiser's product as a prop in drama programmes). News and current affairs presenters must not lend their names or their faces to product promotions (Article 13). Sponsored programmes must be clearly identified as such, the sponsor must not be permitted to influence editorial or scheduling judgments (Article 17), and these programmes shall not promote products or services of the sponsor or anyone else (Article 17). There shall be no sponsorship of news and current affairs programmes (in Britain, the weather is not regarded as "news") and no programme may be sponsored by the manufacturers of tobacco products, alcoholic drinks or prescription medicines.

The E.C. Treaty, for all its concerns with free movement of goods and services between members of the Common Market, originally had no specific provision about broadcasting although the European Court of Justice soon defined "services" to include television signals and advertisements.[29] "Culture" was first mentioned in the Maastricht Treaty (1993) and the Treaty of Amsterdam (1999) amended the E.C. Treaty so that Article 151 now requires contributions to "the flowering of the cultures of the Member States" and supplementary joint action in the area of "artistic and literary creation, including in the audiovisual sector". The *Television Without Frontiers Directive* aims to provide an "internal market" for broadcasting by removing barriers to transmissions across the borders of Member States. Unlike the Television Convention, the Directive is directly enforceable throughout the E.C., and one of its first impacts was to strike down the British rule that permitted the jurisdiction of local courts over all broadcasts emanating from the United Kingdom. The ECJ ruled that the correct test for deciding which country had jurisdiction over a European broadcast was to determine where the broadcaster was "established"—a criterion "referring to the place in which a broadcaster has the centre of its activities, in particular the place where decisions concerning programme policy are taken and the programmes are finally put together".[30] Thus the humourless television regulators of Belgium could not prohibit their local cable operators from re-transmitting Cartoon Network, a satellite service provided by a broadcaster based in the United Kingdom. The Belgians claimed they were protecting "European Content" because the cartoons came from America, but the "choice of forum" rule pivots on the seat of the broadcaster, not the place of origin of the material in broadcasts.[31]

The Television Directive (Article 2A) permits the United Kingdom to take unilateral action to restrict broadcasts from other Member States only in respect of "programmes which might seriously impair the physical, mental or moral development of minors", in particular programmes that involve pornography or gratuitous violence (subject to whether they can be encoded, or transmitted at hours when minors are asleep) and programmes inciting racial, sexual, religious or ethnic hatred.[32] The United Kingdom has utilised Article 2A in attempts to "proscribe" pornographic satellite services received from Denmark (under section 177 of the 1990 Act, such proscription makes it an offence for anyone in Britain to assist, sell or advertise the service). One such proscription order (against *Red Hot Dutch*) was challenged, although the broadcaster went out of business before the issues identified by the Divisional Court could be decided by the European Court of Justice.[33] The issues were

---

[29] *Italy v. Saachi* [1974] E.C.R. 409.

[30] *Commission of the European Communities v. U.K.* [1996] E.C.R.I.–4025 at 4077–8, and see *VT4 Ltd v. Vlaamese Gemeenschap* [1997] I-3143; Television Directive, Arts 2(3) and (4).

[31] *Paul Denoit Case* [1997] 3 C.M.L.R. 943.

[32] Television Directive, Arts 22 and 23.

[33] *R. v. Secretary of State for the National Heritage, ex p. Continental Television BV* [1993] 2 C.M.L.R. 333.

whether the Television Directive permits the Government to issue a proscription (a) against foreign satellite services received in, rather than transmitted within, the United Kingdom, and (b) in respect of broadcasts which because they are encoded or transmitted in the early hours, are unlikely to attract child viewers. The Television Directive also contains controversial Articles (4 and 6) imposing obligations to increase European content, emanating largely from chauvinistic French concerns about the threat of "cultural imperialism" from the popular American programmes (the alternative—of requiring measures to improve the comprehensibility of French culture—was not considered). These ill-begotten quota provisions have not been rigidly enforced, because they probably breach Article 10 of the ECHR, and possibly the General Agreement on Tariffs and Trade (GATT). Less controversial is Article 23, which requires that any person "damaged by an assertion of incorrect facts in a television programme must have a right of reply or equivalent remedies . . . transmitted within a reasonable time". The United Kingdom claims that its Article 23 obligations are fulfilled by the corrective powers of the BSC, in cases of unfair treatment (see earlier, p. 794).

Advertisers, although restricted in some circumstances by the Convention, do have redress under European law against any EEC member country that tries to discriminate against advertisements broadcast from other member countries. In other words, any legal restrictions on advertising must apply irrespective of the nationality of the advertiser or the country from which the broadcast has originated.[34] In *Bond van Adverteers v. The Netherlands* the European Court held that a prohibition on advertising broadcasts from other countries directed at citizens of the receiving country was an unlawful restriction on the freedom to provide services and was contrary to Article 59 of the EEC treaty.[35]

> The Dutch Government's objective in banning all broadcast advertising directed at its citizens from cable stations in other countries was to ensure that a public foundation in Holland received all the revenue from advertising directed at its nationals. This economic objective was not a satisfactory "public policy" exemption from compliance with Article 59. It might reasonably require foreign broadcasters directing their promotions to Dutch citizens to comply with local laws relating to the duration of advertisements or banning the touting of certain products, but it could not erect a barrier against all foreign-originated advertising in the economic interests of its own broadcasters.

---

[34] *Procureur du Roi v. Debauve* (1980) E.C.R. 833.
[35] Case No. 352/85. Judgment, April 16, 1988.

The Radio Authority

The Radio Authority has duties and powers for sound broadcasting which mirror the ITC's duties and powers in relation to television. It must do all it can to ensure a diversity of national services, at least one devoted predominantly to the spoken word and one broadcasting "music other than pop music", together with a range and diversity of local services.[36] Licences are to be granted for eight years to "fit and proper" people (persons convicted for radio piracy offences in the preceding five years are excluded from this category), and the statutory duties relating to good programme taste and the provision of accurate and impartial news are repeated.[37] Some latitude, however, is provided for partial opinions in current political and industrial controversy—the Radio Authority's duty is merely to ensure that such opinions are not given "undue prominence" and are not presented as editorial.[38] Local radio stations can thus allow organisations in the area to present programmes that explain their own partisan views.[39] Government may issue directives banning particular broadcasts, on the same basis as it may suppress certain television broadcasts. The Radio Authority has parallel enforcement powers to the ITC. Thus it can fine national broadcasters up to 3 per cent of their advertising and sponsorship revenue for a first offence and up to 5 per cent for subsequent offences. For local licence holders the maximum fine is £50,000.[40] Although not of the same magnitude as some of the ITC's fines, the Radio Authority's penalties can still be substantial. In 2000, it fined Virgin Radio £75,000 for remarks by Chris Evans supporting Ken Livingstone in the London Mayoral election. This was not the first time that Virgin Radio had been fined for a Chris Evans programme. The previous year it had been fined £10,000 when Evans gave out the telephone number of a photographer who had allegedly been involved in a scuffle with Oasis's Liam Gallagher. Evans told his listeners to hound the photographer "until he goes toes up".[41]

The Radio Authority has drawn up detailed codes pursuant to its statutory duties as regulator of the airwaves. These reflect the code promulgated by the BSC (which adjudicates complaints about radio programmes as well as television) and reprise the ITC code, with special concern for talkback and other phone-in programmes and the conduct and use of telephone interviews. It also promulgates an advertising and

---

[36] Broadcasting Act 1990, s. 85.
[37] ibid., ss. 86–9.
[38] ibid., s. 90.
[39] ibid., s. 94.
[40] Broadcasting Act 1990, s. 110.
[41] Media Lawyer, May/June 1999, p. 27.

sponsorship code, relentlessly sexist in its obsession with "sanitary protection products", pregnancy testing kits and family planning services which "may be unsuitable for children and those listening to religious programmes". It betrays a greater concern for advertisers than for listeners in its demands for sensitive scheduling (*e.g.* "a commercial for an airline should be immediately withdrawn if a neighbouring news bulletin features details of a plane crash")[42]—heavy-handed paternalistic regulation of this kind is not part of the Radio Authority's business. The High Court is so reluctant to intervene that it is questionable whether judicial review offers the citizen any real remedy against abuse of power by these government-appointed regulators. Reasonably enough, judges respect the Radio Authority's factual evaluations in determining whether to grant or revoke licences[43] and were prepared to expose the Radio Authority's errors in deciding to ban an advertisement for Amnesty International. This decision should have been quashed because it impacted on free speech, but the Court declined to interfere with "a regulatory body consisting of lay members which is intended to take a broad approach to its task". (The Radio Authority was, however, sufficiently chastened by the judgment to reconsider, and permit Amnesty to advertise.) The Broadcasting Act did not place a duty on the Authority to get things right, merely "to do its best . . . if the Authority did go wrong . . . it was not because of want of trying".[44] It is precisely because "lay bodies" with broad mandates do tend to "go wrong" by honest but unprincipled exercise of their powers that courts should put them right whenever their decisions deny freedom of speech.

It is an offence under section 1 of the Wireless Telegraphy Act of 1949 to make wireless transmissions without a licence,[45] and under the Broadcasting Act it is an offence to run a radio service that is not licensed by the Radio Authority. The 1990 legislation contains stringent powers to eradicate radio pirates, both on the high seas and on the high streets.[46] It is an offence not merely to produce an illegal broadcast, but to own or assist in the control of premises or to supply apparatus used in unlicensed broadcasts. Every conceivable act of assistance is caught by these provisions, and offences may be committed by delivering a "lecture, address or sermon" on a pirate radio station or by publishing any details of unlicensed broadcasts. Any "vehicle, vessel or aircraft, or any structure or other object or any apparatus" used in connection

---

[42] Radio Authority, Advertising and Sponsorship Code, s. A12, Practice Note.
[43] See, for example, *R. v. Radio Authority, ex p. Guardian Media Group* [1995] 2 All E.R. 139; *Re Trax FM Ltd* (March 21, 1996) Lexis.
[44] *R. v. Radio Authority, ex p. Bull* [1997] 2 All E.R. 561 at 573 (*per* Lord Woolf M.R.; see the critique by Stevens and Feldman, *Public Law* (Winter 1997) p. 615.
[45] The offence is one of strict liability: *R. v. Blake* [1997] 1 Cr.App.R. 209.
[46] *ibid.*, ss. 168–74.

with the commission of an offence may be forfeited to the Crown, and inspectors may use reasonable force in the course of their investigations. These provisions are remarkably savage and something of a tribute to the tenacity and popularity of backstreet ratio stations. The provision that makes it an offence to publish "details of any unauthorised broadcasts" may well be a breach of the "freedom of expression" guarantee in Article 10 of the European Human Rights Convention, certainly if it is used against publishers of articles or programmes that discuss the social phenomenon of pirate radio.

The popularity of pirate radio ships on the high seas during the 1960s was an important factor in breaking down the BBC's rigid monopoly of the airwaves. In retrospect, the salvos fired by Mr Wedgwood Benn against Radio Caroline appear comical, and many of the original pirates (such as John Peel) are now household names on licensed stations. Nonetheless, the fears that gripped the governments of Europe at the threat to their nationalised broadcasting arrangements produced an early treaty obliging firm action against unauthorised broadcasters, and its terms are embodied in the Marine Broadcasting (Offences) Act of 1967.[47] This Act (the terms of which are revised and extended by Schedule 16 of the 1990 Broadcasting Act) makes it an offence to broadcast from a ship or aircraft within the jurisdiction of the United Kingdom, and an offence for any British citizen to broadcast on or above the high seas. It is an offence to facilitate pirate broadcasts capable of being received in Britain that emanate from beyond territorial waters, and "facilitation" is widely defined to include provisioning of the radio ship, advertising on the pirate station or publishing any details of its programmes.[48] For many years the London listings magazine *Time Out* published a column giving programme details for Radio Laser, Radio Caroline and other pirate stations within and without the jurisdiction; a prosecution against it under the 1967 Act failed on a technicality, but the column has not reappeared. In 1990 the Court of Appeal upheld the conviction of a number of British subjects for a conspiracy made in the United Kingdom to breach the 1967 Act by procuring the unlicensed broadcasts of Radio Laser, notwithstanding that these emanated from a Panamanian ship, moored outside territorial waters and manned by Americans.[49]

---

[47] European Agreement for the Prevention of Broadcasts transmitted from Stations Outside National Territories (Strasbourg, January 22, 1965) ratified by the United Kingdom Government in 1967.

[48] Lord Wilberforce has severely criticised the extra-territorial impact of these provisions: *Hansard* (House of Lords) July 26, 1990, cols 1657–1660.

[49] *R. v. Murray & Ors., The Times*, March 22, 1990.

Satellite Broadcasting

The era of satellite broadcasting was ushered in by the launch of Sky television in 1988. The ITC is responsible, under the 1990 Act, for granting licences for satellite television services. Since the British take sex a good deal more seriously than other European nationalities, considerable ingenuity has been expended to find ways of stopping the pornography that is offered in many continental countries from infiltrating via satellite. Domestic satellite operators are subject to the Obscene Publication Act and the "good taste and decency" terms of their licences, but material that originates abroad and is transmitted by companies resident outside the jurisdiction cannot be so readily controlled. If pornography originates from a broadcaster established in an E.C. country, the British Government may be able to require action to be taken under the Television Directive (see the *Red Hot Dutch* case, above) but courts may disagree on the definition of the "pornography" that is discouraged by that instrument.

There is no entirely satisfactory solution to the prospect of pornography from outer space. The broadcasts might be jammed, but the technology is not precise and other channels would suffer interference. Detector vans could be programmed to detect whether television sets inside households are switched to a particular satellite channel, but it is not yet an offence merely to view obscenity. The Government has chosen to rely upon powers provided to the Home Secretary to proscribe a foreign satellite service that repeatedly offends against good taste and decency.[50] A "proscribed" satellite service shall be treated, in law, in the same way as a pirate radio ship: it will be a criminal offence (punishable by up to two years' imprisonment) to supply programmes or equipment to it, or to advertise upon it, or to publish any details of its programmes.[51] These somewhat ludicrous provisions are to be triggered by a report from the ITC that the satellite service is "unacceptable" because it repeatedly offends public feeling or incites crime or broadcasts indecent material. Although these powers stem from an obsessive concern with pornography, a Home Secretary might also be moved to proscribe a channel for political reasons—e.g. if it were a Taleban propaganda station or a channel that gave air-time to spokespersons from terrorist groups banned from appearing on British television.

Satellite transmissions create complex problems for defamation law. If a cable system picks up the satellite signals and relays them to its subscribers, then the cable operator will be responsible for the libels so transmitted. If the programme originates from England, then

---

[50] Broadcasting Act 1990, s. 177.

[51] *ibid.*, s. 178.

the person sending the libel up to the satellite for retransmission will also be liable. There may be a difficulty, however, if the programme originates abroad and is sent up to the satellite from a foreign country, by whose law it is not defamatory. For example, the American law of defamation puts the burden of proving falsity on the claimant and provides a "public figure" defence—anything said about someone in the public eye will not be actionable unless spoken with malice. So under American law a libel action bound to fail will often succeed under English law. Such circumstances provide a strong incentive for wealthy and powerful public figures to go forum-shopping in London's High Court.

The general rule is that, so long as a tort is committed in England, English law principles will apply. For libel, so long as there is an act of publication in England, only defences known to English law will apply. It has been held that so far as broadcasts are concerned the tort is committed where the broadcast is received, rather than where it is transmitted.[52] Any broadcast received in England is "published" in England, and English libel law would apply. If the principle is applied to satellite transmissions, there would be no question of applying foreign law. The only problem for a claimant in England trying to sue a foreign defendant in respect of a transmission originating abroad would be in obtaining permission to serve the defendant with a writ out of the jurisdiction. Permission is always at the discretion of the court, and whether an action can be begun will depend on the facts of the case (see Chapter 3, p. 100). But if the rule for broadcasts is not followed for satellites (because of the lack of control over the area over which signals can be picked up, and the presumption against applying English rules extraterritorially), then there will be no publication in England—the tort will be committed abroad only, where the signals are transmitted to the satellite. In this case, to sustain an action in England for a tort committed abroad, the tort must be actionable by English law and by the law of the place where the actions took place (*i.e.* where the signals originated). Only if actionable by both systems of law would a claimant succeed in bringing an action.[53]

These problems have been compounded by the advent of the internet. Can libel actions be brought wherever defamatory material is downloaded, (*i.e.* in any jurisdiction in the world) or only in the place where the web server is established? The parallel with television is not precise, because of the technical distinctions between broadcast transmission, beamed directly to a country, and "request" messages

---

[52] *Jenner v. Sea Oil* [1952] D.L.R. 526; *Gorton v. ABC* [1974] 22 F.L.R. 181; *Whitlam Victoria Broadcasting* [1979] 37 F.L.R. 15.
[53] *Chaplin v. Boys* [1971] A.C. 356.

sent through cyberspace to a website "server" in another country. When the man at the modem in jurisdiction A sends a "request" message to a server in jurisdiction B, it is rather like sending a servant across state lines to buy a book and then bring it back—an action which could not involve the seller in publishing the libel in jurisdiction A. It will be important for internet freedom in the long term to confine libel actions to the place the website is established (as long as this is not adventitious or a "defamation free zone") so as to protect internet publishers and providers from being dragged into jurisdictions which have harsh (sometimes criminal) laws of defamation and sedition.

Many international treaties and conventions proclaim the principle of a free flow of information. However, this principle is generally subject to reservations of national sovereignty, based on the assumption that every state has an exclusive right to regulate its own broadcasting system to prevent transmission of unacceptable programme material and propaganda. Thus, the Soviet Union has in the past insisted that the overriding consideration must be the right of states to pursue political and social development free from outside interference. Some Third World countries argue that the free flow of information principle is contingent upon equal access to the source, and fear cultural domination of developing nations by superpower satellites. The United States and the United Kingdom, the two most constant champions of the free flow principle, are the two leading exporters of television programmes. The European Court of Human Rights in the *Autronic* case firmly rejected the notion that states were entitled to control the reception of television programmes uplinked from their cities or transmitted by their satellites (see p. 776), and its championship of the right to impart and receive information across national frontiers will prevail in the broadcasting laws of Europe, West and East.

Article 1 of the Outer Space Treaty of 1966 establishes the general principle that "outer space . . . shall be free for exploration and use by all states without discrimination of any kind". The United Nations General Assembly set up the Committee on the Peaceful Uses of Outer Space (COPUOS), but its deliberations on satellite broadcasting have been marked by disputes over the need for "prior consent" by the receiving state, with a majority of the group taking the position that prior consent was necessary. The group has defined unacceptable programme material to include incitements to war, racial hatred or enmity between people; or programmes aimed at undermining the foundations of a local culture. If any such material is aimed specifically at a foreign state without its express consent, the transmission would be illegal. The fundamental fear is of overspill propaganda. The only way to combat this is by international agreement, but neither the United States nor the United Kingdom is convinced of the danger of overspill, and the rift between the advanced and the developing countries has precluded any worthwhile international agreement.

The conference that settled the law of the sea continued for nine years before agreement was reached; a satisfactory agreement over the law of outer space may take even longer. Work on the law of cyberspace is only just beginning.

TABLE OF CASES

All references are to page numbers

TABLE OF STATUTES

All references are to page numbers—references in bold are where that legislation appears in full

TABLE OF STATUTORY INSTRUMENTS

All references are to page numbers—references in bold are where that legislation appears in full

TABLE OF EUROPEAN CONVENTION ON HUMAN RIGHTS

All references are to page numbers

INDEX

All references are to page numbers